THE OXFORD HANDBOOK OF
AESTHETICS

THE OXFORD HANDBOOK OF

AESTHETICS

Edited by

JERROLD LEVINSON

OXFORD

UNIVERSITY PRESS

OXFORD

UNIVERSITY PRESS

Great Clarendon Street, Oxford OX2 6DP

Oxford University Press is a department of the University of Oxford.
It furthers the University's objective of excellence in research, scholarship,
and education by publishing worldwide in

Oxford New York

Auckland Bangkok Buenos Aires Cape Town Chennai
Dar es Salaam Delhi Hong Kong Istanbul Karachi Kolkata
Kuala Lumpur Madrid Melbourne Mexico City Mumbai Nairobi
São Paulo Shanghai Taipei Tokyo Toronto

Oxford is a registered trade mark of Oxford University Press
in the UK and in certain other countries

Published in the United States
by Oxford University Press Inc., New York

British Library Cataloguing in Publication Data

Data available

Library of Congress Cataloging in Publication Data
The Oxford handbook of aestehtics / edited by Jerrold Levinson.
p. cm.
Includes bibliographical references and index.
1. Aesthetics–Handbooks, manuals etc. 1. Levinson, Jerrold.
BH56 .O94 2003   111'.85–dc21   2002038148
ISBN 0-19-825025-8
1 3 5 7 9 10 8 6 4 2

Typeset by
Newgen Imaging Systems (P) Ltd., Chennai, India
Printed in Great Britain
on acid-free paper by
Butler & Tanner Ltd., Frome, Somerset

PREFACE

....

The aim of this Handbook is to present the state of the art in philosophical aesthetics as it is practised in the English-speaking world. Handbook in hand, a reader with a general philosophical background should be in a position to follow and, if so inclined, enter into debates on questions in aesthetics as they are currently being conducted in books, journals, and conferences across the United States, the United Kingdom, Canada, Australia, New Zealand, Scandinavia, and other centres of anglophone thought.[1]

The *Handbook* includes forty-six systematic chapters on virtually all the major issues in philosophical aesthetics that are active topics of discussion and research. In addition to these systematic chapters on specific topics, there are two chapters, at the beginning of the *Handbook*, which serve as a kind of introduction to the subject as a whole. One is a general overview of the field of philosophical aesthetics, in two parts: the first is a quick sketch of the lay of the land, and the second an account of the development of five central problems over the past fifty years. The other chapter is an extensive survey of recent work in the history of modern aesthetics, or aesthetic thought from the seventeenth to the mid-twentieth centuries.

The systematic contributions are of three kinds, and constitute the bulk of the *Handbook*. Part I comprises chapters dealing with general problems in aesthetics, such as expression, fiction, or aesthetic experience, considered apart from any particular artform. The second part contains chapters on problems in aesthetics as they arise in connection with particular artforms, such as music, film, or dance. Chapters in Part III address relations between aesthetics and other fields of inquiry, or explore viewpoints and concerns complementary to those prominent in mainstream analytic aesthetics.

The relatively large number of contributions in the *Handbook* is justified by the diversity, complexity, and vigour of the field of aesthetics as it currently exists. If aesthetics fifty years ago was something of a backwater in philosophy, it is no longer, and the interactions in both directions between aesthetics and other branches of philosophy—in particular, metaphysics, ethics, philosophy of mind, philosophy of language, and political philosophy—only continue to grow.

---

[1] This is not to deny the existence of work in a similar vein in certain non-anglophone countries, such as France, Italy, Spain, and Germany; but in general what is done under the rubric of 'aesthetics' in those places is of a rather different nature.

The chapters in the *Handbook* vary in size, from about 4,500 words for chapters of fairly narrow scope (e.g. 'Metaphor', 'Environmental Aesthetics') to about 12,000 words for those of broader scope (e.g. 'Music', 'Definition of Art'), with an average length of about 8,500 words.[2] In addition, all chapters include ample and up-to-date bibliographies.[3]

The orientation of the *Handbook* is clearly Anglo-American, with the methodology of analytic philosophy largely, though not everywhere, in evidence. That said, contributors have been encouraged to acknowledge and, where appropriate, comment on perspectives on the problem under discussion deriving from other philosophical and critical traditions. Though most contributors are based in the USA or the UK, some are based in Canada, Scandinavia, and Australasia.

Handbook authors are all well-known aestheticians, visible in the field and credible on the topics being surveyed through having contributed importantly to existing debate on them. Assignment of specific subjects to specific contributors was made on the basis not only of contributors' authoritativeness on and appropriateness to a given topic, but also on their earlier efforts for related ventures, some attempt having been made to avoid the duplicating of chapters written for other reference works.

A distinctive feature of the *Handbook* is that a number of contributors are responsible for two chapters rather than the more usual one. The result is arguably more unity of style and coverage, and a closer interrelating of the concerns of certain pairs of chapters. At the end of every chapter is a list of cross-references to other chapters in the *Handbook* treating of related matters.

The *Handbook* is explicitly targeted at scholars in aesthetics, that is graduate students, professors, and researchers in departments of philosophy. However, the *Handbook* should also prove useful to serious critics, theorists, and historians of the arts concerned to keep abreast of current directions in philosophical aesthetics, as well as to the philosophically informed general reader with a theoretical interest in the arts.

A few words are in order on how the *Oxford Handbook of Aesthetics* distinguishes itself from two recent and recommendable reference works of roughly similar aim. The *Handbook* differs from the *Routledge Companion to Aesthetics* (London 2001) in at least three respects. First, contributions that follow are geared, for the most

---

[2] The *Handbook*, it will be noted, rather unusually contains *two* chapters devoted to the issue of aesthetic realism. This is because one of the two, originally commissioned under a different rubric, turned out ultimately to be about aesthetic realism as well. However, given the importance and complexity of the issue—whether there are aesthetic properties, whether aesthetic judgements have truth values, whether aesthetic descriptions are objective—the duplication is not to be regretted, especially as the two articles end up on different sides of the issue, with Aesthetic Realism 1 ultimately embracing aesthetic realism, and Aesthetic Realism 2 ultimately rejecting it.

[3] The bibliographies are, however, almost entirely restricted to items in English, notice being taken of only a few items in other languages.

part, to graduate rather than undergraduate students; second, the chapters are significantly longer, and contain more extensive bibliographies; third, there are more systematic contributions in the *Handbook*, made possible by the decision to forgo chapters on individual historical figures or movements. The *Handbook* also distinguishes itself from the *Encyclopedia of Aesthetics* (New York, 1998) in being a one-volume rather than a four-volume affair, and in virtue of its more uniformly analytic orientation and more exclusively philosophical focus.

It has naturally not proved possible, for reasons of space, to include in the *Handbook* chapters on quite *all* the topics of interest in contemporary aesthetics, for instance, taste, genius, criticism, formalism, and so on. However, readers will find that a number of these nominally missing topics are in fact discussed, at least in passing, in one or more of the chapters in the *Handbook*. The following should serve as a guide to some of these hidden topics:

Aesthetic judgement: *see* chapters on Aesthetic Realism 1, Aesthetic Realism 2, Aesthetic Experience, Value in Art, Beauty.
Aesthetic pleasure: *see* Aesthetic Experience, Value in Art.
Aesthetic property: *see* Aesthetic Realism 1, Aesthetic Realism 2.
Art and society: *see* Aesthetics and Cultural Studies, Aesthetics of Popular Art, Art and Politics, Feminist Aesthetics.
Autonomy: *see* Aesthetics of the Avant-Garde, Art and Politics.
Censorship: *see* Art and Politics.
Comedy: *see* Humour.
Craft: *see* Aesthetics of the Everyday, Definition of Art.
Criticism: *see* Aesthetic Realism 1, Aesthetic Realism 2, Interpretation in Art, Literature.
Depiction: *see* Representation in Art.
Erotic art: *see* Art and Morality, Feminist Aesthetics.
Forgery: *see* Authenticity in Art.
Formalism: *see* Aesthetic Experience, Beauty, Feminist Art, Value in Art.
Genius: *see* Creativity in Art.
Genre: *see* Interpretation in Art, Literature, Medium in Art.
Imagination: *see* Aesthetics and Cognitive Science, Fiction.
Improvisation: *see* Creativity in Art, Music.
Opera: *see* Music, Theatre.
Originality: *see* Authenticity in Art, Creativity in Art.
Performance: *see* Creativity in Art, Dance, Music, Theatre, Ontology of Art.
Pictorial realism: *see* Representation in Art.
Pragmatism: *see* Aesthetics of the Everyday, Aesthetics and Postmodernism.
Skill: *see* Creativity in Art, Medium in Art.
Sublime: *see* History of Modern Aesthetics.
Taste: *see* Aesthetic Experience, Beauty.

Many thanks to Peter Momtchiloff at Oxford University Press for having entrusted me with this *Handbook*, for his editorial advice and assistance during the four or so years from inception to completion, and for his confidence in my ability to bring the project to fruition. Thanks to Andrew Kania for his excellent work on the index. Finally, sincere thanks to the thirty-seven authors whose contributions to the *Handbook* essentially make it what it is: a guide to the best research in philosophical aesthetics for the foreseeable future.

J.L.

College Park, Maryland
February 2002

Contents

PART III AESTHETIC ISSUES OF SPECIFIC ARTFORMS

PART IV FURTHER DIRECTIONS IN AESTHETICS

CONTRIBUTORS

Philip Alperson, Department of Philosophy, Temple University, Philadelphia: 'Creativity in Art' (Chapter 13).

John W. Bender, Department of Philosophy, Ohio University, Athens: 'Aesthetic Realism 2' (Chapter 4).

Malcolm Budd, Department of Philosophy, University College London: 'Aesthetics of Nature' (Chapter 6).

Noël Carroll, Department of Philosophy, University of Wisconsin–Madison: 'Dance' (Chapter 33); 'Humour' (Chapter 19).

Ted Cohen, Department of Philosophy, University of Chicago: 'Metaphor' (Chapter 20).

Gregory Currie, Department of Philosophy, University of Nottingham, England: 'Aesthetics and Cognitive Science' (Chapter 42); 'Interpretation in Art' (Chapter 16).

David Davies, Department of Philosophy, McGill University, Montreal: 'Medium in Art' (Chapter 9).

Stephen Davies, Department of Philosophy, University of Auckland, New Zealand: 'Ontology of Art' (Chapter 8); 'Music' (Chapter 28).

Mary Devereaux, Department of Philosophy, University of California, San Diego: 'Feminist Aesthetics' (Chapter 38).

Denis Dutton, Department of Philosophy, University of Canterbury, New Zealand: 'Authenticity in Art' (Chapter 14); 'Aesthetics and Evolutionary Psychology' (Chapter 41).

Richard Eldridge, Department of Philosophy, Swarthmore College, Pennsylvania: 'Aesthetics and Ethics' (Chapter 43).

Susan Feagin, Department of Philosophy, University of Missouri, Kansas City: 'Painting' (Chapter 29).

John A. Fisher, Department of Philosophy, University of Colorado at Boulder: 'Environmental Aesthetics' (Chapter 39).

Berys Gaut, Department of Moral Philosophy, University of St Andrews, Scotland: 'Art and Knowledge' (Chapter 25); 'Film' (Chapter 37).

Lydia Goehr, Department of Philosophy, Columbia University, New York City: 'Art and Politics' (Chapter 27).

Alan H. Goldman, Department of Philosophy, College of William and Mary, Williamsburg, Virgina: 'Representation in Art' (Chapter 10).

Gordon Graham, Department of Philosophy, University of Aberdeen, Scotland: 'Architecture' (Chapter 31).

Paul Guyer, Department of Philosophy, University of Pennsylvania, Philadelphia: 'History of Modern Aesthetics' (Chapter 2).

Kathleen Higgins, Department of Philosophy, University of Texas at Austin: 'Comparative Aesthetics' (Chapter 40).

Robert Hopkins, Department of Philosophy, University of Sheffield, England: 'Sculpture' (Chapter 32).

Gregg Horowitz, Department of Philosophy, Vanderbilt University, Nashville, Tennessee: 'Aesthetics of the Avant-Garde' (Chapter 45).

Gary Iseminger, Department of Philosophy, Carleton College, Northfield, Minnesota: 'Aesthetic Experience' (Chapter 5).

Matthew Kieran, Department of Philosophy, University of Leeds, England: 'Art and Morality' (Chapter 26).

Deborah Knight, Department of Philosophy, Queen's University, Kingston, Ontario: 'Aesthetics and Cultural Studies' (Chapter 48).

Peter Lamarque, Department of Philosophy, University of York, England: 'Fiction' (Chapter 21).

Jerrold Levinson, Department of Philosophy, University of Maryland, College Park: 'Philosophical Aesthetics: An Overview' (Chapter 1).

Paisley Livingston, Department of Philosophy, Education and Rhetoric, University of Copenhagen, Denmark: 'Intention in Art' (Chapter 15); 'Literature' (Chapter 30).

Alex Neill, Department of Philosophy, University of Southampton, England: 'Art and Emotion' (Chapter 24); 'Poetry' (Chapter 35).

David Novitz, Department of Philosophy and Religious Studies, University of Canterbury, New Zealand: 'Aesthetics of Popular Art' (Chapter 44).

Aaron Ridley, Department of Philosophy, University of Southampton, England: 'Expression in Art' (Chapter 11); 'Tragedy' (Chapter 23).

Stephanie Ross, Department of Philosophy, University of Missouri, St Louis: 'Style in Art' (Chapter 12).

Crispin Sartwell, Department of Humanities, Maryland Institute of Art, Baltimore: 'Aesthetics of the Everyday' (Chapter 46).

Richard Shusterman, Department of Philosophy, Temple University, Philadelphia: 'Aesthetics and Postmodernism' (Chapter 47).

Robert Stecker, Department of Philosophy, Central Michigan University, Mount Pleasant: 'Definition of Art' (Chapter 7); 'Interpretation in Art' (Chapter 16).

Nigel Warburton, Department of Philosophy, Open University, Milton Keynes, England: 'Photography' (Chapter 36).

George M. Wilson, Department of Philosophy, University of California, Davis: 'Narrative' (Chapter 22).

Paul Woodruff, Department of Philosophy, University of Texas at Austin: 'Theatre' (Chapter 34).

Nick Zangwill, Department of Philosophy, University of Glasgow, Scotland: 'Aesthetic Realism 1' (Chapter 3); 'Beauty' (Chapter 18).

PART I

BACKGROUND

CHAPTER 1

....

PHILOSOPHICAL AESTHETICS: AN OVERVIEW

....

JERROLD LEVINSON

1. THE DOMAIN OF AESTHETICS

....

1.1 Introduction

AESTHETICS is the branch of philosophy devoted to conceptual and theoretical inquiry into art and aesthetic experience. In this chapter I offer first an outline of the structure of philosophical aesthetics as a whole, and then a selective sketch of the development of Anglo-American aesthetics over the past fifty years, focusing on five central topics: the concept of the aesthetic, the definition of art, the ontology of art, representation in art, and expression in art. These topics are, of course, also addressed at greater length in corresponding chapters elsewhere in this volume.

One may usefully think of the field of philosophical aesthetics as having three foci, through each of which it might be adequately conceived. One focus involves a certain kind of *practice* or *activity* or *object*—the practice of art, or the activities of making and appreciating art, or those manifold objects that are works of art. A second focus involves a certain kind of *property, feature,* or *aspect* of things—namely, one that is *aesthetic,* such as beauty or grace or dynamism. And a third focus involves a certain kind of *attitude, perception,* or *experience*—one that, once again, could be labelled *aesthetic.*

Not surprisingly, there are intimate relations among these three conceptions. For example, art might be conceived as a practice in which persons aim to make objects that possess valuable aesthetic properties, or that are apt to give subjects valuable aesthetic experiences. Or aesthetic properties might be conceived as those prominently possessed by works of art, or those on which aesthetic experience is centrally directed. Or aesthetic experience might be conceived as the sort of experience that figures centrally in the appreciation of works of art or the aesthetic properties of things, whether natural or man-made.

The question of which of these three foci is the most fundamental, and in particular whether it is the idea of *art* or the idea of the *aesthetic* that is conceptually prior, has been much debated (Scruton 1974; Wollheim 1980/1968; Danto 1981). In any event, the three conceptions can claim to be naturally related in that art, in its creative and receptive dimensions, plausibly provides the richest and most varied arena for the manifesting of aesthetic properties and the having of aesthetic experiences. There is also no denying that contemporary analytic aesthetics is in very large measure the philosophy of art, even if the analysis of aesthetic phenomena outside of or apart from art is by no means neglected.

What might seem to be major concerns of aesthetics that do not immediately fall under one or another of the three conceptions are, first, the aesthetics of nature; second, the theory of criticism; and third, the nature of craft. But on closer inspection, the first of these can be seen to fall comfortably under the second or third conception noted above, and the second and third of these, under the first conception noted above.

The aesthetics of nature can be understood to concern itself either with certain distinctive properties of natural phenomena that can be classified as aesthetic, e.g. beauty, sublimity, grandeur, or profusion, or with certain kinds of experience distinctively provoked by nature, or certain kinds of attitudes appropriately brought to nature. The theory of criticism can be understood as a study of part of the practice of art: that part concerned with the reception of artworks, including their description, interpretation, and evaluation. And craft can be readily conceived as art-related or quasi-artistic activity.

1.2 Three Foci of Aesthetics

Let us now return to the three foci indicated above, which we may simply label *art*, *aesthetic property*, and *aesthetic experience*. Although, as we have seen, these foci can be put into relation with one another and interdefined in various ways, without some independent anchoring of each it is not clear that more than relative illumination of the aesthetic sphere has been achieved. It is useful at this point to sketch some traditional and current conceptions of the basic content of those three foci. What, in short, is art, or counts as an aesthetic feature, or constitutes an aesthetic experience?

Art

One conception of art sees it as specially concerned with perceptible *form*, with the exploration and contemplation of such form for its own sake. This view has roots in the work of the eighteenth-century German philosopher Immanuel Kant, who thought that the beauty of objects, artworks and natural phenomena alike, consisted in their ability to stimulate the free play of the cognitive faculties in virtue of their pure forms, both spatial and temporal, and without the mediation of concepts. The early twentieth-century English theorists Clive Bell and Roger Fry took a similar line, holding that spatial form was the only relevant aspect of visual art taken as art, and that possessing 'significant form', in Bell's famous phrase, was the necessary and sufficient condition of something's being art at all.

Another conception of art of long standing sees it as essentially a vehicle of *expression* or of *communication*, especially of states of mind or non-propositional contents. The early twentieth-century Italian philosopher Benedetto Croce located the essence of art in the expression of emotion, underlining the indissociability, amounting even to identity, of content and vehicle in such cases. The English philosopher R. G. Collingwood developed this line further, stressing the way in which the making of works of art was at the same time a way for the artist to articulate or make clear the exact nature of his or her emotional condition. The Russian novelist Leo Tolstoy advanced a view of art that identified it with emotional communication from one person to another by indirect means, that is, a structure of signs in an external medium.

A third conception of art sees it as tied to the *mimesis, imitation*, or *representation* of the external world, perhaps in distinctive ways or by distinctive means. This conception of art has very deep roots, and can be located, though with some anachronism, in the earliest works in the canon of aesthetics, the *Republic* of Plato and the *Poetics* of Aristotle. The view, modified so as to allow for representation of matters beyond the visible, finds expression in the aesthetic theories of Lessing, Hegel, and Schopenhauer, among later thinkers. Modern discussions of art as representation, or, more broadly, as semiotic or symbolic in nature, include Langer (1953), Goodman (1976/1968), Danto (1981), and Walton (1990).

Other important conceptions of art regard it as an activity aimed explicitly at the creation of beautiful objects, including faithful representations of natural and human beauty; as an arena for the exhibition of skill, particularly skill in the fashioning or manipulating of objects that is capable of exciting admiration (Sparshott 1982); as a development of play, stressing play's structured and serious aspects (Gadamer 1986); or as the sphere of experience as such, in which the interplay of active/creative and passive/receptive phases in engagement with the external world is made a focus of attention and dwelt on for its own sake (Dewey 1934).

Some more recent conceptions of art view it as the production of objects intended or designed to afford aesthetic experience (Beardsley 1981); as the investing of objects with aboutness or meaning in the context of a specific cultural framework, the artworld (Danto 1981); as a particular social institution, identified by its constituent rules and roles (Dickie 1997; Davies 1991); or as activity only historically identifiable as art through a connection to earlier activities or objects whose art status is assumed (Wollheim 1980/1968; Levinson 1990*a*, 1993; Carroll 2001).

Aesthetic Property

Aesthetics conceived as the study of aesthetic properties evidently requires some conception of when a property is an aesthetic one. It is widely agreed that aesthetic properties are perceptual or observable properties, directly experienced properties, and properties relevant to the aesthetic value of the objects that possess them; but beyond that the demarcation of the class of aesthetic properties is subject to dispute. Some of the earmarks of aesthetic property status that have been proposed are: having gestalt character; requiring taste for discernment; having an evaluative aspect; affording pleasure or displeasure in mere contemplation; being non-condition-governed; being emergent on lower-level perceptual properties; requiring imagination for attribution; requiring metaphorical thought for attribution; being notably a focus of aesthetic experience; being notably present in works of art. (In the last two cases, obviously, the demarcation of aesthetic property is thrown back on that of either aesthetic experience or art.)

Despite debate over the status of the above marks, there is substantial convergence in intuitions as to what perceivable properties of things *are* aesthetic, as this open-ended list suggests—beauty, ugliness, sublimity, grace, elegance, delicacy, harmony, balance, unity, power, drive, elan, ebullience, wittiness, vehemence, garishness, gaudiness, acerbity, anguish, sadness, tranquillity, cheerfulness, crudity, serenity, wiriness, comicality, flamboyance, languor, melancholy, sentimentality—bearing in mind, of course, that many of the properties on this list are aesthetic properties only when the terms designating them are understood figuratively. Finally, though the class of aesthetic properties and that of expressive properties are not coincident, it is evident that expressive properties, which arguably attach only to works of art and not to natural objects, constitute a significant subset of aesthetic properties (see Goodman 1976/1968; Tormey 1971; Scruton 1974; Beardsley 1982; Levinson 1990*a*; Sibley 2001).

Aesthetic Experience

Aesthetics conceived as the study of certain distinctive experiences or states of mind, whether attitudes, perceptions, emotions, or acts of attention, similarly requires some conception of when a state of mind or mental activity is an aesthetic one. Among the marks that have been proposed as distinguishing aesthetic states of mind from others are: disinterestedness, or detachment from desires, needs and practical concerns; non-instrumentality, or being undertaken or sustained for their own sake; contemplative or absorbed character, with consequent effacement of the subject; focus on an object's form; focus on the relation between an object's form and its content or character; focus on the aesthetic features of an object; and figuring centrally in the appreciation of works of art. (Once again, in the last two cases the demarcation of aesthetic experience is thrown back on that of either aesthetic property or art.) Whether these criteria, either individually or in some combination, manage adequately to mark out the boundaries of aesthetic experience as a distinctive state of mind remains a matter of ongoing controversy. (For scepticism, see Carroll 2001.)

1.3 Problems and Issues in Aesthetics

As is evident from the preceding, among the problems of aesthetics are the interrelated characterizations of the nature of art, the nature of aesthetic properties, and the nature of aesthetic experience. But those broad problems radiate out into many more specific ones, including those making essential reference to particular artforms or aesthetic phenomena.

From a concern with the definition of art as such, one moves naturally to a concern with the ontology of art, with the process of artistic creation, with the demands of artistic appreciation, with the concept of form in art, with the role of media in art, with the analysis of representation and expression in art, with the nature of artistic style, with the matter of authenticity in art, and with the principles of artistic interpretation and evaluation. It is unsurprising, in light of most of these concerns, that the philosophy of art is sometimes conceived of as *metacriticism*, or the theory of art criticism (Beardsley 1981).

It is necessary to at least touch on some of the problems falling under the concerns just enumerated. The *ontology of art* centres on the question of exactly what sort of object a work of art is, and how this might vary from artform to artform. Philosophers have asked whether the work of art is physical or mental, abstract or concrete, singular or multiple, created or discovered, notationally definable or only culturally specifiable, and have queried what its authenticity consists in (Collingwood 1938; Goodman 1976/1968; Wollheim 1980/1968; Wolterstorff 1980; Currie 1989; Levinson 1990, 1996d). Interest in creativity in art revolves around the question of whether there are any sustainable generalizations regarding it, and on the question of the relevance of knowledge of the creative process, and of the historical context of creation more generally, to appreciation of works of art (Wollheim 1980/1968; Beardsley 1982; Currie 1989; Walton 1990; Levinson 1990a, 1996d). Issues about artistic form include those having to do with the defensibilty of formalism as a theory of art, about the different kinds of form manifested in different artforms, and about the relation of form to content and of form to medium (see Kivy 1990; Budd 1995; Carroll 1999).

Among the modes of meaning that artworks exhibit, the most important are *representation* and *expression*. (Goodman 1976/1968, however, argues for *exemplification* as an equally important mode.) Theorists have offered accounts of representation, usually with special reference to pictorial representation or depiction, in terms of resemblance between object and representation, perceptual illusion (Gombrich 1960), symbolic conventions (Goodman 1976/1968), seeing-in (Wollheim 1980/1968, 1987), world-projection (Wolterstorff 1980), make-believe (Walton 1990), recognitional capacities (Schier 1986), resemblance between visual experience of object and representation (Peacocke 1987; Hopkins 1998), and information content (Lopes 1996). Theorists have offered accounts of artistic expression, usually with special attention to the expression of emotion, in terms of personal expression by the artist, induced empathy with the artist, metaphorical exemplification (Goodman 1976), correspondence (Wollheim 1987), evocation (Matravers 1998), imaginative projection (Scruton 1997), expressive appearance (Kivy 1989; Davies 1994), and imagined personal expression (Levinson 1996b).

Concerning artistic style, attention has focused on the distinction between individual and period style, on the psychological reality of style, on the interplay between style and representational objective, and on the role that cognizance of style plays in aesthetic appreciation (Gombrich 1960; Wollheim 1987; Lang 1987). Concerning the interpretation of art, attention has focused on the relevance of artists' intentions, on the diversity of interpretive aims, on the debate between critical monism and critical pluralism, on the similarities and differences between critical and performative interpretation, and on the relationship between interpretation and the maximizing of value (Currie 1990; Davies 1991; Budd 1995; Goldman 1995; Levinson 1996d; Stecker 1997). Finally, as regards the *evaluation of art*, attention has carried to the question of its objectivity or subjectivity, to the relation between artistic value and pleasurability, to the relation between the value of art as a whole and the value of individual works of art, to the existence of general criteria of value across artforms, and to the relevance of a work's historical impact, ethical import, emotional power, and cognitive reward to its evaluation as art (Beardsley 1982; Goodman 1976/1968; Goldman 1995; Budd 1995; Stecker 1997; Levinson 1998b).

In addition to the foregoing, there are problems revolving around a number of concepts relevant to the understanding of many if not all works of art, and which cut across artforms—concepts such as those of *intention, fiction, metaphor, narrative, tragedy, genius*, and *performance*. Next, there are a set of issues that concern the relationships between art and other domains or aspects of human life. Probably the most important are those that can be encapsulated under the rubrics *art and emotion, art and knowledge, art and morality*, and *art and politics*. For example, there is the issue of how we can sensibly have emotions for characters whom we know to be fictional; the issue of whether art can be a vehicle of knowledge and of what kind; the issue of whether art can contribute to moral education; and the issue of whether art is rightly subject to censorship or other forms of societal control. There are, of course, also problems specific to individual artforms, such as painting, poetry, or photography. For example, there are the issues of whether film is an inherently realistic medium; of whether poetry can be usefully paraphrased; of whether the basic form of music is local or global; of whether painting is essentially two-dimensional; of whether narration operates similarly in literature and film; and of whether music or words should dominate in a hybrid artform such as opera.

A concern with the nature of aesthetic properties leads naturally to concerns with *realism* about such properties, with the *supervenience* relation between aesthetic properties and the properties on which they appear to depend, with the range of aesthetic properties to be found in the natural world, with the special status of *beauty* among aesthetic properties, with the difference between the beautiful and the *sublime*, with the degree of *subjectivity* or *objectivity* of judgements of beauty, with the relations between *artistic beauty*, *natural beauty*, and *human beauty*, and with the relationship between the aesthetic properties of artworks and what may be called their *artistic* properties, e.g. originality or seminality or revolutionariness, which, although appreciatively relevant, are not directly perceivable in works in the manner of aesthetic properties (Levinson 1990*a*; Goldman 1995; Sibley 2001). Finally, a concern with the nature of aesthetic experience opens up into discussions of the nature of various *mental states*—e.g. perceptions, imaginings, reasonings, feelings, memories, moods—that figure in response to art or nature, and so into discussions on the bearing of cognitive science on the analysis of such experience.

2. Five Problems in Analytic Aesthetics

2.1 The Concept of the Aesthetic

The term 'aesthetic' in something like its modern sense dates to Alexander Baumgarten, a German eighteenth-century philosopher, who defined aesthetics as 'the science of how things are cognized by means of the senses' (1735). In modern thought, however, 'aesthetic' clearly has a more specific meaning than that of having to do with sensory perception in general. The British eighteenth-century taste theorists, notably Shaftesbury, Hutcheson, and Burke, helped to shape this more specific meaning by emphasizing a mode of sensory perception not centrally driven by personal desires or concerns, and characterized by an absorption in the object for its own sake. This line of thinking culminated in the Kantian conception of aesthetic perception as *disinterested* perception, or perception of something without regard for its real existence or connection to one's interests, but just for the appearances it affords, and the Schopenhauerian conception of aesthetic perception as *objective* perception, or perception of something in abstraction from its relation to one's will, and thus merely for the type it instantiates. Two twentieth-century conceptions in the same vein are Edward Bullough's account of aesthetic perception as involving psyhcic *distancing* of the perceived object, or a disengagement of the practical self in relation to it, and Clive Bell's account of aesthetic perception as focused exclusively on *form*, or the arrangement of elements in a sensuous medium, independent of all knowledge of the world.

The idea of the aesthetic as marking a distinctively disinterested, objective, distanced, and form-focused manner of perceiving still has currency, but it has detractors as well, including some who are wary of the element of disinterestedness on political grounds, and some who are sceptical of there being any such distinctive manner of perceiving at all. In addition, the qualifier 'aesthetic' is sometimes thought to apply more fundamentally to attitudes or experiences or pleasures or judgements or evaluations or properties, than to modes of perception. In what follows I review some modern attempts to capture the essence of the aesthetic, sometimes in relation to one, sometimes in relation to another, of these substantives to which the qualifier 'aesthetic' can be attached.

Discussion of the idea of the aesthetic in analytic aesthetics begins with Urmson (1957). While denying that there were any specially aesthetic properties or emotions, Urmson proposed that an evaluation could be considered aesthetic if based primarily on how an object looks or sounds or presents itself to the senses, rather than on how it is actually is, a conception of the aesthetic that does not significantly depart from the Kantian idea of aesthetic judgement as concerned exclusively with appearances. Also in a Kantian vein is the proposal of Stolnitz (1960), that aesthetic attention be understood as attention that is disinterested, discriminating, sympathetic, and intransitive—that is, not aiming beyond the object but instead terminating on it.

The key notion in attempts to theorize the aesthetic by Beardsley, beginning in 1958 and continuing into the 1980s, is that of *aesthetic experience*. Beardsley (1981) characterizes such experience as involving firmly fixed attention, relative freedom from outside concerns, affect without practical import, exercise of powers of discovery, and integration of the self. Such experiences have value in virtue of sharing the unity, intensity, and complexity of the objects—notably artworks—on which they are directed, and such objects have aesthetic value precisely in so far as they have the potential to afford such experiences.

Dickie (1964, 1965) represent powerful attacks on traditional conceptions of the aesthetic attitude and aesthetic experience such as those that Stolnitz, Beardsley, and others had proposed. Dickie (1964) makes a strong case that the aesthetic attitude as traditionally conceived is a 'myth', that there is nothing more to it than simple attention. In particular, Dickie tries to show that the putative differentiae of aesthetic perception, such as disinterestedness and distancing, concern only the motivation and not the nature of the perception involved, and that the differences between one case of perception and another can be accounted for entirely in terms of objects and degrees of attention. Dickie (1965) charges that Beardsley's suggestion according to which valuable features of perceptual objects, such as unity, intensity, and complexity, are standardly paralleled in the experiences had of such objects, giving them a corresponding aesthetic character, is in effect a category mistake. Experiences do not admit of features of that sort, Dickie claims, and Beardsley has simply confused 'the experience of completeness' with 'the completeness of an experience'. The debate between Beardsley and Dickie is pursued in Beardsley (1969), Dickie (1974), and Beardsley (1982).

Despite Dickie's attacks, accounts of what is distinctive about the aesthetic attitude and aesthetic experience continued to be elaborated, often with an emphasis on cognitive elements therein. For instance, Scruton (1979) insists that aesthetic experience is necessarily permeated by imaginative thought, that such experience always involves conceptions of objects or their features under certain descriptions. An object not consciously conceived in one fashion or another cannot, for Scruton, be an object in which one is finding aesthetic, as opposed to merely sensual, satisfaction. And Levinson (1996c) proposes an account of aesthetic pleasure in which the cognitive is similarly central: pleasure in an object is aesthetic, says Levinson, when it is grounded in a perception of and reflection on the object's individual character and content, both for themselves and in relation to the structural base on which they rest. In that light, the core of specifically aesthetic appreciation of an object, whether the product of art or nature, might be said to be a focus on the relation between its perceivable form and its resultant character and content. (For recent turns in the debate over distinctive aesthetic states of mind, see Carroll 2001 and Goldman 2001.)

Analytic philosophers have also tried to elucidate the concept of the aesthetic by focusing on what counts as an aesthetic *property*, sometimes going on to explicate other uses of aesthetic in relation to that, for example construing aesthetic perception or experience precisely as perception or experience of aesthetic properties.

Work on aesthetic properties in analytic aesthetics begins with Sibley's seminal paper of 1959, 'Aesthetic Concepts', which was followed by several other essays of importance (see Sibley 2001). In Sibley's view, the distinctive feature of aesthetic concepts is their *non-condition-governedness*, or non-rule-governedness: that an aesthetic term is true of some object cannot be justifiably inferred from any description of the object in non-aesthetic terms. The non-condition-governedness of aesthetic concepts does not, however, prevent aesthetic properties from being dependent on and determined by non-aesthetic properties; the relation between those sets of properties, however, remains broadly causal rather than conceptual. Sibley also claimed that a special capacity—*taste*—was required to perceive aesthetic properties, and so to apply aesthetic concepts correctly. Sibley's analysis was challenged by Cohen (1973), which questioned whether any principled distinction could even be drawn between aesthetic and non-aesthetic properties, and by Kivy (1973), which attempted to show that at least some aesthetic concepts were indeed condition-governed. Many writers, even those who acknowledge aesthetic properties as a distinct class and non-condition-governedness and supervenience as marks thereof, balk at the idea of a special faculty of taste being needed to discern them. The problem of the demarcation of aesthetic properties from non-aesthetic properties, exacerbated by Cohen's critique, has generated a fair amount of discussion. It is widely agreed that aesthetic properties are perceptual properties, dependent on lower-level perceptual properties, directly experienced rather than inferred, and linked in some way to the aesthetic value of the objects possessing them. In addition, most would follow Sibley in finding aesthetic properties to be non-condition-governed. But beyond that, matters are open to dispute. Some of the further marks of aesthetic property status that have been proposed are: having regional character (Beardsley 1973); being value-tending or value-contributing (Beardsley 1973); being implicitly evaluative (Goldman 1995); being evaluatively relevant (Levinson 1990b); being the subject of terminal attributions (Kivy 1975); and requiring imaginative or metaphorical thought for their attribution (Scruton 1974; Gaut 1997). Despite debate over these marks, there is substantial intuitive convergence as to what perceivable properties of things are aesthetic, as noted earlier.

Mention must also be made here of Goodman (1968), a rather different approach to theorizing the aesthetic, which offers five symptoms, not of aesthetic property-hood, but of *aesthetic functioning* on the part of a symbol system: syntactic density; semantic density; relative repleteness; exemplificationality; and complex reference. On such a multi-dimensional conception, aestheticness obviously becomes very much a matter of degree.

Walton (1970), in a highly influential paper, follows Beardsley and Sibley in taking aesthetic properties to be perceptual, gestalt-like, non-rule-governed, and dependent on an object's lower-level perceptual properties. But Walton insists, developing a suggestion in Gombrich (1963), that aesthetic properties depend as well on the perceptually distinguishable *artistic categories*—for instance, ones of style or genre or medium—under which works of art can be seen to fall. The consequence is that a work's aesthetic complexion is not a function of its lower-level or structural perceptual features alone, and that its aesthetic appreciation must thus involve bringing the right categories into play in one's experience of the work. Rightness of category, in turn, is partly a matter of the surrounding *art-historical context,* including factors such as the artist's intention, the artist's oeuvre as a whole, the artistic traditions in which the artist worked, or the artistic problems to which the artist appears to be responding. (For related discussion see Wollheim 1980/1968; Levinson 1996d.)

The question of whether aesthetic attributions are objective or subjective, and, relatedly, whether it is realism or anti-realism about aesthetic properties that is justified, have been importantly addressed in recent literature (see Scruton 1974; Budd 1995; Goldman 1995; Bender 1996). Two further issues concerning the aesthetic much discussed at present are, first, that of the relation of the aesthetic to the *artistic,* and whether this is a relation of inclusion, exclusion, or partial overlap (see Goldman 1995; Stecker 1997; Levinson 1998b); and second, that of the relation of the aesthetic to the *moral* or *ethical* and, once again, whether this is a relation of inclusion, exclusion, or partial overlap (see Levinson 1998*a*).

2.2 The Definition of Art

Discussion in analytic aesthetics of the problem of defining art begins in scepticism, scepticism rooted in the anti-essentialism of Wittgenstein. Weitz's (1956) 'The Role of Theory in Aesthetics' has proved seminal. (But see also, in a similar vein, Ziff 1953.) Weitz argued convincingly that earlier modern theories of art, such as those of Tolstoy, Bell, and Collingwood, were in effect disguised recommendations in favour of particular kinds of art, or briefs for what good art consisted in, and not really accounts of the phenomenon of art with any claim to descriptive adequacy. But that, said Weitz, was as it should be, for two reasons: first, the evaluative component of ascriptions of arthood is central and ineliminable, and second, the concept of art is inherently open, and so always resists circumscription in terms of necessary and sufficient conditions of application. Thus, according to Weitz, there is no stateable essence of arthood, and all the things called art exhibit at best only a 'family resemblance' to one another.

Two of Weitz's arguments for the conclusion that the concept of art is inherently open and so resistant to definition were that the creativity that is inseparable from the idea of art necessarily dooms to failure any attempt to close the concept of art in terms of determinate conditions; and that the boundaries between the sub-categories of art (e.g. poem, painting, opera) are constantly in flux, and so the same must be true of the broader category of art itself, which it would thus be futile to attempt to define. But neither of those arguments is compelling. With respect to the first, the fact that creativity must be allowed to characterize the in principle ever changing objects of art in no way entails that creativity must therefore characterize the concept of art itself in such manner as to forestall the possibility of definition. With respect to the second, the fact that boundaries between genres of art may be fluid or permeable in no way entails that the concept of art encompassing them all must therefore have a constantly changing outline, if only because the domain of art is broader than, and not equivalent to the union of, all existing artistic genres. (For further criticisms, see Carroll 1999.)

Later writers, notably Dickie, have also challenged the first of Weitz's conclusions—that art is an eliminably evaluative concept—by making a case for a classificatory or descriptive concept of art, one with respect to which the idea of bad or even worthless art is not an oxymoron. But a prior response to Weitz was Mandelbaum (1965), which importantly suggested that the reason Weitz failed to discern any properties common to all and only artworks was that he had focused on exhibited and intrinsic properties (such as beauty or form or material), rather than on non-exhibited and relational properties, for example intentional and causal ones, such as connect works to their contexts or their creators. Mandelbaum also underlined, ironically, that a characterization of artworks as displaying 'family resemblances' at least suggested underlying unifying links of a genetic or historical sort.

In the wake of the exchange between Weitz and Mandelbaum on art's definability emerged institutional theories of arthood, which proposed that a non-manifest relation to a social framework was what made something an artwork, not its manifest or observable properties. According to Danto's celebrated 1964 essay, 'The Artworld', directly inspired by the Dadaist ready-mades of Duchamp and the Pop Art simulacra of Warhol, an artwork is an object that bears an appropriate relation to a background framework of critical theory—what Danto dubbed 'the artworld'. This account was later elaborated at length in Danto (1981), where emphasis is put on artworks acquiring aboutness and meaning in virtue of their relations to the artworld that surrounds them. According to Dickie (1969), developed further in Dickie (1974), an artwork is an artefact offered as a candidate for appreciation by someone acting on behalf of the artworld, the social structure invoked by Danto, and alternatively dubbed 'the republic of art' in Diffey (1969). According to Binkley (1977), in the most minimal of institutional theories, an artwork is merely something indexed in accord with artworld practices of indexing, i.e. indicating or identifying, objects. Finally, Dickie (1997, first published 1984), a revamped version of Dickie (1974), holds that an artwork is an artefact of a kind created to be presented to an artworld public. It is evident in all such definitions that a great weight is implicitly placed on the artworld as an institution identifiable apart from identification of objects that are artworks in relation to it, lest vicious circularity result. Some institutional theorists, however, do not regard such circularity as fatal, taking it instead to be an inevitable reflection of the 'inflected' nature of art (Dickie 1997). Mention should also be made here of more traditional attempts to define art relationally, by appeal to aesthetic projection rather than institutional connection, as for example in Beardsley (1981), which takes an artwork to be something created or intended to afford aesthetic experience.

Another sort of relational definition of art, the historical definition of art, prompted by some brief remarks in Wollheim (1980/1968), first appeared in Levinson (1979). (See Levinson 1993 for further development.) On that account, an artwork is roughly anything intended for regard or treatment in the way some past artworks were correctly regarded or treated. Like institutional definitions of art, Levinson's intentional–historical definition does not locate arthood in any intrinsic properties of the object; but, unlike institutional definitions, it holds as crucial not the connection of an object to the social framework of the artworld, but rather the connection an object bears to the preceding concrete history of art taken as a datum—a connection intentionally established, in one way or another, by the would-be artmaker. By in effect characterizing the present *intension* of 'art' only in terms of the past *extension* of 'art', the charge of circularity is circumvented, since the meaning of 'art' is not presupposed in the course of defining 'art'. (See

Carney 1994 for replies to problems raised by this style of definition generally.) If the historical definition of art is on the right track, then the domain of art might be said to have a roughly *recursive* structure, but the historical definition is not as such a strictly recursive one. (For criticism of the historical definition, see Carroll 1994, 1999, 2000; Stecker 1997; Davies 1997; and Currie 2000; for responses to some of those criticisms, see Levinson 2002.)

In the same spirit as the historical definition, though explicitly renouncing its definitional ambition, is Noel Carroll's *narrative* theory of arthood (see Carroll 2001), which principally aims to explain how we *identify* objects as artworks. Arthood, for Carroll, resides in connections to the past, ones that can be exhibited in a coherent and convincing narrative showing how a candidate object is related, either by repetition, amplification, or repudiation, to artworks that preceded it. If such a narrative is constructible, the candidate object is an artwork, or has a claim to art status; if not, then not. Note that, so elucidated, the *narrative* theory of art might be more accurately labelled the *narrativizability* theory of art.

A useful higher-order classification of theories of art is provided in Davies (1991), which also reviews and criticizes a number of contemporary accounts. Davies divides theories of art into *functional* ones, which see art as definable in terms of some essential function that its objects fulfil or are intended to fulfil (examples of which would be Beardsley's aesthetic definition or the traditional definition of art as representation), and *procedural* ones, which see art as definable in terms of the performance or occurrence of certain procedures internal to a social practice (examples of which would be the institutional definitions of Dickie, Diffey, and Binkley). Unfortunately, not all current theories fit under one or the other of these headings, notably historical and narrative theories. In addition, some current theories, of hybrid character, incorporate procedural, functional, *and* historical considerations (Stecker 1995). Finally, reminiscent of Weitz's 'family resemblance' view of art is the *cluster concept* account of art, a view that is also difficult to classify as either procedural or functional. According to that account, though the concept of art resists classical definition, there are, none the less, a variety of conditions that are yet conjunctively sufficient and disjunctively necessary for arthood (Gaut 2000).

2.3 The Ontology of Art

The ontology of art is concerned with the question of what kinds of entities artworks are; what the identity and individuation conditions of such entities are; whether the metaphysical status of artworks is uniform or diverse across artforms; what work authenticity amounts to in different artforms; and whether a reductive or eliminativist position regarding artworks can be justified. Philosophers have asked whether works of art are physical or mental, abstract or concrete, singular or multiple, created or discovered. Perhaps the most fundamental distinction in the metaphysics of artworks is that between artforms where the work of art appears to be a concrete particular—a unique spatio-temporally circumscribable object or event—as in painting, drawing, carved sculpture, and improvised music, and artforms where the work appears to be rather an abstract entity—a type, kind, universal, pattern, or structure—as in etching, engraving, cast sculpture, composed music, poetry, and film. Philosophers have also queried the status of forgeries, reproductions, copies, versions, translations, transcriptions, and adaptations of works of art, and the extent to which interpretation is involved in producing instances of works in the performing arts.

The agenda of ontology of art in analytic aesthetics was largely set by three works: Goodman (1976/1968), Wollheim (1980/1968), and Wolterstorff (1975) (see also Wolterstorff 1980). Goodman introduced the distinctions of *singular v. multiple* artforms, *one-stage v. two-stage* artforms, *autographic* (or forgeable) *v. allographic* (or non-forgeable) artforms, and the idea of a work-defining *notation*, applicable in at least certain arts. (For discussion, see Levinson 1990*a*.) Goodman's moderate nominalist conception of a musical work, in particular, is that it is a class of performances compliant with a score, scores being complex symbols in a notation. Wollheim argued against identifying all artworks with physical objects, and against the opposite conception of artworks, perhaps attributable to Croce, Collingwood, and Sartre, according to which works of art are mental entities. Wollheim also introduced the idea of musical and literary artworks as *types*, rather than classes, and analysed the way in which properties of an artwork type are transmitted to or inherited by its *tokens*. Wolterstorff proposed that musical and literary works were types of a special sort, which he called *norm kinds*, meaning that they, like biological kinds, could have correct and incorrect, or properly formed and improperly formed, instances (for example peformances containing wrong notes).

In addition to those seminal writings, we may note Margolis (1974, 1977), which suggest conceiving of artworks as *abstract particulars*, ones culturally emergent and embodied in concrete objects, and the related conception of artworks in Danto (1981) as creatures of theory distinct from the 'mere' objects that incarnate them, thus allowing for distinct works that stand in a relation of *perceptual indiscernibility* to one another. Though the proposals of Margolis and Danto strive explicitly to be adequate to works of avant-garde visual art of the late twentieth century (pop art, ready-mades, minimal art, and conceptual art), their validity is presumably not restricted to avant-garde modes of artmaking. An important suggestion regarding avant-garde musical works, but perhaps applicable to traditional ones as well, can be found in Tormey (1974), construing them as akin to *recipes* or prescriptions, not for sounds as such, but rather for actions to be undertaken by performers.

More recent accounts of the ontology of art are those of Currie and Levinson, which emphasize the importance to the identity of a work of the historical context in which the work arises, and stress, *pace* Goodman, the insufficiency of a work's observable structure alone to fix that identity, even in artforms where notation plays a crucial role (Currie 1989; Levinson 1980, 1996*d*). Currie views artworks as *action types*, where the action in question is the complex sequence of steps by which the artist, with certain objectives in mind and working in a given creative context, arrives at a given manifest object: that which we ordinarily, though mistakenly, identify as the artwork itself. Currie believes that all artworks are types, even those that, like paintings and drawings, are ostensibly unique particulars (see also Zemach 1986). Levinson, on the other hand, insists on the traditional distinction between particular (singular) and type (multiple) arts; but like Currie he eschews a structuralist view of artwork types for a historicist one. According to Levinson, a musical or literary work is an *indicated structure*, a species of *initiated type*: roughly, a tonal or verbal structure-as-indicated-by-X-in-art-historical-context-C. On that conception, musical works are both creatable and entities in which creator and context figure essentially.

Four very recent studies may be mentioned which go in the same historicist and contextual direction as Levinson and Currie: D. Davies (1999), S. Davies (2001), Howell 2002*a,b*). These studies also effectively underline how only a pluralist ontology of works of art can be adequate to the great diversity of existing artworks, art-forms, and art traditions—from high art to folk art, primitive art to technological art, and western art to non-western art in all its manifestations. Apart from their all being artefacts, artworks are very many kinds of things, and are thus not all encompassable within a single metaphysical category. (For objections to historicist-contextualist proposals, see Dodd 2000 and Predelli 2001.)

2.4 Representation in Art

The topic of representation in analytic aesthetics has for the most part been pursued with reference to *pictorial representation* (or *depiction*). Work was prompted most significantly by the 1960 publication of *Art and Illusion*, a landmark book by art historian Ernst Gombrich. Gombrich famously argued against 'the innocent eye' model of picture perception, and for a view that acknowledged the history of pictorial representation, which Gombrich conceptualized as a progressive march towards ever more realistic, illusion-sustaining images, arrived at through a protracted process of 'making and matching'. This was followed in 1968 by Goodman's *Languages of Art* (Goodman 1976), which, while accepting Gombrich's thesis of the historicity of representation, rejected his emphasis on illusion, arguing that pictorial representation was entirely a matter of denotation, conventionally established, and had nothing to do with illusion or its psychological cousin, perceived resemblance.

Subsequent theorists have offered accounts of depiction, and of our responses to such depictions, in terms of seeing-in (Wollheim 1980/1968, 1987), world-projection (Wolterstorff 1980), make-believe (Walton 1990), recognitional capacities (Schier 1986), resemblance between visual experience of object and representation

(Peacocke 1987; Budd 1993; Hopkins 1998), and information content (Lopes 1996). I next sketch the two currently most influential accounts: Wollheim's 'seeing-in' theory (Wollheim 1987) and Walton's 'make-believe' theory (Walton 1990).

Wollheim's theory is a development of Wittgenstein's idea of aspect perception, or perceiving one thing as another, e.g. a gnarled tree as an old woman. But instead of seeing-as, Wollheim proposes a variant notion, seeing-in, as the core of pictorial perception. Seeing-in differs from seeing-as in at least two ways: first, the former applies to the parts of a picture, the latter only to the picture as a whole; and second, the former involves awareness of the picture's surface simultaneously with awareness of the picture's depicted content. (Wollheim calls this feature of seeing-in 'twofoldness'.) Seeing-in is thus for Wollheim a primitive visual capacity, at first exercised on natural phenomena, e.g. stained rock faces, and later harnessed for deliberate image making, explicitly aimed at such seeing-in. So for Wollheim a picture is essentially an arrangement of marks intended for seeing-in which in fact supports such seeing-in. A large part of the aesthetic interest in pictures is tied to the basic twofoldness of seeing-in, wherein we necessarily appreciate what is depicted, in a fictive three-dimensional space, in relation to the real two-dimensional pattern of marks that underlies it.

Walton's theory understands pictures as props in visual games of make-believe, where making believe is in turn understood as an activity of guided imagining. Confronted with a picture, we are prompted to imagine that we are seeing such and such an object *by* the configuration of marks that constitutes the picture, and we imagine precisely *of* our seeing those marks that it is a seeing of the object the picture depicts. Pictures generate fictional worlds ('work-worlds'), whose content is given by what it is correct to imagine seeing in them, itself determined by implicit rules and conventions of the game in question. In addition, in imagining the content of pictures in virtue of visually interacting with them, fictional worlds specific to the viewer ('game-worlds') are also generated, albeit passingly.

Whether Wollheim's and Walton's proposals are ultimately reconcilable is an open question. For Walton, Wollheim's seeing-in is to be analysed without remainder in terms of imagined seeing; whereas for Wollheim, seeing-in is an activity prior to and more fundamental than imagined seeing, however important such seeing is in later phases of pictorial appreciation. (For further discussion see Levinson 1996a, Lopes 1996, and van Gerwen 2001.)

The cognitive turn in the theory of pictorial representation, already evident in the writings of Gombrich, Goodman, Wollheim, and Walton, is more pronounced still in Schier (1986), which appeals directly to facts about ordinary visual processing in support of a theory of pictures. Schier proposes that a representation is pictorial just in so far as it recruits the visual recognitional capacities that subjects already possess for familiar objects, so that a picture represents an object O if it triggers, in subjects who view it, the same capacities for recognition that would be triggered by the sight of O in the world. Schier underlines that pictorial competence, unlike language learning, is characterized by *natural generativity*, whereby, once a subject can decipher a few pictures of a given sort, he can generally decipher any number of such pictures, however novel their content.

A more recent study, Lopes (1996), maintains that the key to pictorial representation is the furnishing of similar visual information by picture and object. Lopes proposes an *aspect-recognition* theory of depiction, according to which successful pictures embody aspectual information sufficient to trigger recognition of their objects in suitable perceivers, which aspectual information is non-conceptual in form. Lopes's most interesting idea, a development of Gombrich (1960), is that the heart of depiction as a mode of representation is its inevitable *selectivity*, so that, no matter what style of depiction is involved, a picture, unlike a description, is explicitly noncommittal about certain represented properties of its object, precisely in virtue of being explicitly committal about others.

2.5 Expression in Art

That artworks express states of mind, or are expressive of such states, is a commonplace of criticism, and such expression or expressiveness is usually thought of as a primary locus of art's interest. Expression is generally regarded as a distinct mode of artistic meaning, differing from representation in its logical features, mode of operation, and range of objects (e.g. abstract conditions *v.* concrete particulars). Analytic theorists have offered accounts of artistic expression in terms of personal expression, empathy, metaphorical exemplification (Goodman 1976/1968), correspondence (Wollheim 1987), imaginative projection (Scruton 1997), evocation (Ridley 1995; Matravers 1998), expressive appearance (Kivy 1989; Davies 1994), warranting of inference to state of mind (Vermazen 1986), and ready perceivability as personal expression (Levinson 1996*b*). Most recent theories of expression in art have centred on the problem as it presents itself in relation to *music*, and with the expression of *emotion* as the central case. The relation between expression in art and expression in its primary, i.e. behavioural, sense is often a main focus of attention.

For Goodman (1976/1968), expression in art is just a matter of an artwork exemplifying, or drawing attention to, some property it metaphorically possesses, in the context of its general symbolic functioning. Tormey (1971) proposes that artistic expression is a matter of an artwork's possessing expressive properties, properties designated by terms which in their primary use designate intentional states of persons, and that such expressive properties (for instance cheerfulness or anguish) are ambiguously constituted by the non-expressive structural features (such as rhythms and timbres) underlying them. Wollheim (1987), which focuses on painting rather than music, suggests that expressiveness is a matter of intuitive correspondence or fit between the appearances that works of art or natural objects present and feeling states of the subject, which are then projected on to those works or objects in complex ways (see also Wollheim 1993). Davies (1994) offers a theory of expressiveness in terms of emotion-characteristics-in-appearance, which are grounded in resemblances between musical patterns and human emotional behaviour and countenance, and explores the variety of responses, mirroring or reactive, that listeners have to such perceived expressiveness (see also Kivy 1989). Levinson (1996*b*) following Vermazen (1986), suggests that musical expressiveness consists in the hearability of music as the personal expression of inner states by an indefinite agent or persona, and explores the complicated interplay between imagination, arousal, and projection that the perception of such expressiveness involves (see also Robinson 1994; Ridley 1995). Scruton (1997) locates the perception of musical expressiveness in the listener's ability to inhabit from the inside the gestures that music in its movement appears to embody, and thus adequately to imagine the inner states corresponding to such gestures. Finally, Matravers (1998) gives a sophisticated defence of the arousalist position on musical expression, which takes a musical work's expressiveness to consist in its disposition or power to evoke parallel or related emotions in audiences.

Whether or not the evocation of emotion by music is rightly tied conceptually to musical expressiveness, the character and variety of emotional responses to music has been extensively discussed by analytic aestheticians. It has been asked whether such responses are fully fledged emotions or just moods or feelings, with no or minimal cognitive content; whether imagination or make-believe is involved in the generation of such responses; whether such responses have objects, and if so what those objects are; whether such responses constitute part of musical understanding; and whether such responses are a sign of musical value (see Levinson 1990*a*, 1996*d*). Of particular interest has been the musical 'paradox of negative emotion', which is related to the classic 'paradox of tragedy' (see Carroll 1990; Lamarque 1996; Levinson 1997). The problem is to explain how negatively emotional music can have such a powerful appeal for us if, as seems to be the case, it has a strong tendency to evoke corresponding negative emotions in listeners (see Levinson 1982; Davies 1994; Ridley 1995; Matravers 1998; Kivy 2001).

BIBLIOGRAPHY

General

Beardsley, M. (1969). 'Aesthetic Experience Regained', *Journal of Aesthetics and Art Criticism* 28: 3–11.
—— (1973). 'What Is An Aesthetic Quality?' *Theoria* 39: 50–70.
—— (1981/1958). *Aesthetics: Problems in the Philosophy of Criticism*. Indianapolis, Ind.: Hackett (first published 1958).
—— (1982). *The Aesthetic Point of View*. Ithaca, NY: Cornell University Press.
Bell, C. (1914). *Art*. London: Chatto & Windus.
Bender, J. (1996). 'Realism, Supervenience, and Irresolvable Aesthetic Disputes', *Journal of Aesthetics and Art Criticism* 54: 371–81.

Binkley, T. (1977). 'Piece: Contra Aesthetics', *Journal of Aesthetics and Art Criticism* 35: 265–77.

Budd, M. (1993). 'How Pictures Look', in D. Knowles and J. Skorupski (eds.), *Virtue and Taste*. Oxford: Blackwell.

——(1995). *Values of Art*. London: Penguin.

Carney, J. (1994). 'Defining Art Externally', *British Journal of Aesthetics* 34: 114–23.

Carroll, N. (1990). *The Philosophy of Horror*. New York: Routledge.

——(1994). 'Identifying Art', in R. Yanal (ed.), *Institutions of Art*. University Park, Pa.: Penn State University Press.

——(1999). *The Philosophy of Art*. London: Routledge.

——ed. (2000). *Theories of Art Today*. Madison, Wis.: University of Wisconsin Press.

——(2001). *Beyond Aesthetics*. Cambridge: Cambridge University Press.

Cohen, T. (1973). 'Aesthetic/Non-Aesthetic and the Concept of Taste', *Theoria* 39: 113–52.

Collingwood, R. G. (1938). *The Principles of Art*. Oxford: Oxford University Press.

Currie, G. (1989). *An Ontology of Art*. London: Macmillan.

——(1990). *The Nature of Fiction*. Cambridge: Cambridge University Press.

——(1995). *Image and Mind*. Cambridge: Cambridge University Press.

——(2000). 'A Note on *Art* and Historical Concepts', *British Journal of Aesthetics* 40: 186–90.

Danto, A. (1964). 'The Artworld', *Journal of Philosophy* 61: 571–84.

——(1981). *The Transfiguration of the Commonplace*. Cambridge, Mass.: Harvard University Press.

Davies, D. (1999). 'Artistic Intentions and the Ontology of Art', *British Journal of Aesthetics* 39: 148–62.

Davies, S. (1991). *The Definition of Art*. Ithaca, NY: Cornell University Press.

——(1994). *Musical Meaning and Expression*. Ithaca, NY: Cornell University Press.

——(1997). 'First Art and Art's Definition', *Southern Journal of Philosophy* 35: 19–34.

——(2001). *Musical Works and Performances*. Oxford: Clarendon Press.

Dewey, J. (1934). *Art as Experience*. New York: G. P. Putnam.

Dickie, G. (1964). 'The Myth of the Aesthetic Attitude', *American Philosophical Quarterly* 1: 55–65.

——(1965). 'Beardsley's Phantom Aesthetic Experience', *Journal of Philosophy* 62: 129–36.

——(1969). 'Defining Art', *American Philosophical Quarterly* 6: 253–6.

——(1974). *Art and the Aesthetic*, Ithaca, NY: Cornell University Press.

——(1997/1984). *The Art Circle*. Chicago: Chicago Spectrum Press (first published 1984).

Diffey, T. (1969). 'The Republic of Art', *British Journal of Aesthetics* 9: 145–56.

Dodd, J. (2000). 'Musical Works as Eternal Types', *British Journal of Aesthetics* 40: 424–40.

Gadamer, H. (1986). *The Relevance of the Beautiful and Other Essays*, trans. N. Walker. Cambridge: Cambridge University Press.

Gaut, B. (1997). 'Metaphor and the Understanding of Art', *Proceedings of the Aristotelian Society*, n.s. 97: 223–41.

——(2000). ' "Art" as a Cluster Concept', in N. Carroll (ed.), *Theories of Art Today*.

Goehr, L. (1994). *The Imaginary Museum of Musical Works*, Oxford: Clarendon Press.

Goldman, A. (1995). *Aesthetic Value*. Boulder, CO: Westview Press.

——(2001), 'The Aesthetic', in B. Gaut and D. Lopes (eds.), *Routledge Companion to Aesthetics*. London: Routledge.

Gombrich, E. (1960). *Art and Illusion*. Princeton: Princeton University Press.

——(1963). 'Expression and Communication', in his *Meditations on a Hobby Horse and Other Essays*. London: Phaidon.

Goodman, N. (1976/1968). *Languages of Art*, 2nd edn. Indianapolis: Hackett (first published 1968).

—— (1984). *Of Mind and Other Matters*. Indianapolis: Hackett.

Hopkins, R. (1998). *Picture, Image and Experience*. Cambridge: Cambridge University Press.

Howell, R. (2002a). 'Ontology and the Nature of the Literary Work', *Journal of Aesthetics and Art Criticism* 60: 67–79.

—— (2002b). 'Types, Indicated and Initiated', *British Journal of Aesthetics* 42: 105–27.

Kivy, P. (1973). *Speaking of Art*. The Hague: Martinus Nijhoff.

—— (1975). 'What Makes "Aesthetic" Terms Aesthetic?' *Philosophy and Phenomenological Research* 35: 197–211.

—— (1989). *Sound Sentiment*. Philadelphia: Temple University Press.

—— (1990). *Music Alone*. Ithaca, NY: Cornell University Press.

—— (2001). *New Essays on Musical Understanding*. Oxford: Clarendon Press.

Lamarque, P. (1996). *Fictional Points of View*. Ithaca, NY: Cornell University Press.

Lang, B. (ed.) (1987). *The Concept of Style*, 2nd edn. Ithaca, NY: Cornell University Press.

Langer, S. (1953). *Feeling and Form*. New York: Scribner's.

Levinson, J. (1979). 'Defining Art Historically', *British Journal of Aesthetics* 19: 232–50.

—— (1980). 'What a Musical Work Is', *Journal of Philosophy* 77: 5–28.

—— (1982) 'Music and Negative Emotion', *Pacific Philosophical Quarterly* 63: 327–46.

—— (1990a). *Music, Art, and Metaphysics*. Ithaca, NY: Cornell University Press.

—— (1990b). 'Aesthetic Supervenience', in Levinson (1990a).

—— (1993). 'Extending Art Historically', *Journal of Aesthetics and Art Criticism* 51: 411–23.

—— (1996a). 'Making Believe', in Levinson (1996d).

—— (1996b). 'Musical Expressiveness', in Levinson (1996d).

—— (1996c). 'What is Aesthetic Pleasure?' in Levinson (1996d).

—— (1996d). *The Pleasures of Aesthetics*. Ithaca, NY: Cornell University Press.

—— (1997). 'Emotion in Response to Art: A Survey of the Terrain', in M. Hjort and S. Laver (eds.), *Emotion and the Arts*. Oxford: Oxford University Press.

—— ed. (1998a). *Aesthetics and Ethics*. Cambridge: Cambridge University Press.

—— (1998b). 'Evaluating Music', in P. Alperson, ed., *Musical Worlds*. University Park, Pa.: Penn State University Press.

—— (2002). 'The Irreducible Historicality of the Concept of Art', *British Journal of Aesthetics* 42: 367–79.

Lopes, D. (1996). *Understanding Pictures*. Oxford: Clarendon Press.

Mandelbaum, M. (1965). 'Family Resemblances and Generalizations Concerning the Arts', *American Philosophical Quarterly* 2: 219–28.

Margolis, J. (1974). 'Works of Art as Physically Embodied and Culturally Emergent Entities', *British Journal of Aesthetics* 14: 187–96.

—— (1977). 'The Ontological Peculiarity of Works of Art', *Journal of Aesthetics and Art Criticism* 36: 45–50.

Matravers, M. (1998). *Art and Emotion*. Oxford: Clarendon Press.

Peacocke, C. (1987). 'Depiction', *Philosophical Review* 96: 383–410.

Pouivet, R. (1999). *L'ontologie de l'oeuvre d'art*. Nîmes: Jacqueline Chambon.

Predelli, S. (2001). 'Musical Ontology and the Argument from Creation', *British Journal of Aesthetics* 41: 279–92.

Ridley, A. (1995). *Music, Value, and the Passions*. Ithaca, NY: Cornell University Press.

Robinson, J. (1994). 'The Expression and Arousal of Emotion in Music', *Journal of Aesthetics and Art Criticism* 52: 13–22.

Schier, F. (1986). *Deeper into Pictures*. Cambridge: Cambridge University Press.

Scruton, R. (1974). *Art and Imagination*. London: Methuen.

——(1979). *The Aesthetics of Architecture*. Princeton: Princeton University Press.

——(1997). *The Aesthetics of Music*. Oxford: Clarendon Press.

Sibley, F. (1959). 'Aesthetic Concepts', *Philosophical Review* 68: 421–50.

——(2001). *Approach to Aesthetics*. Oxford: Clarendon Press.

Sparshott, F. (1982). *Theory of the Arts*. Princeton: Princeton University Press.

Stecker, R. (1997). *ArtWorks: Definition, Meaning, Value*. University Park, Pa.: Penn State University Press.

Tormey, A. (1971). *The Concept of Expression*. Princeton: Princeton University Press.

——(1974). 'Indeterminacy and Identity in Art', *Monist* 58: 203–15.

Urmson, J. (1957). 'What Makes a Situation Aesthetic?' *Proceedings of the Aristotelian Society*, Suppl., 31: 75–92.

van Gerwen, R. (ed.) (2001). *Richard Wollheim on the Art of Painting*. Cambridge: Cambridge University Press.

Vermazen, B. (1986). 'Expression as Expression', *Pacific Philosophical Quarterly* 67: 196–224.

Walton, K. (1970). 'Categories of Art', *Philosophical Review* 79: 334–67.

——(1990). *Mimesis as Make-Believe*. Cambridge, Mass.: Harvard University Press.

Weitz, M. (1956). 'The Role of Theory in Aesthetics', *Journal of Aesthetics and Art Criticism* 15: 27–35.

Wollheim, R. (1980/1968). *Art and its Objects*. 2nd edn. Cambridge: Cambridge University Press (first published 1968).

——(1987). *Painting as an Art*. Princeton: Princeton University Press.

——(1993). 'Correspondence, Projective Properties, and Expression in the Arts', in *The Mind and its Depths* (Cambridge, Mass.: Harvard University Press).

Wolterstorff, N. (1975). 'Towards an Ontology of Art Works', *Nous* 9: 115–42.

——(1980). *Worlds and Works of Art*. Oxford: Clarendon Press.

Zemach, E. (1986). 'No Identification Without Evaluation', *British Journal of Aesthetics* 26: 239–51.

Ziff, P. (1953). 'The Task of Defining a Work of Art', *Philosophical Review* 62: 58–78.

Introductions to Aesthetics

Carroll, N. (1999). *The Philosophy of Art: A Contemporary Introduction*. London: Routledge.

Cometti, J. P., Morizot, J., and Pouivet, R. (2000). *Questions d'esthétique*, Paris: Presses Universitaires de France.

Dickie, G. (1997). *Introduction to Aesthetics*. Oxford: Oxford University Press.

Fisher, J. A. (1991). *Reflecting on Art*. Mountain View, Calif.: Mayfield.

Graham, G. (2000). *Philosophy of the Arts*, 2nd edn. London: Routledge.

Hanfling, O. (ed.) (1992). *Philosophical Aesthetics*. Oxford: Blackwell.

Hospers, J. (1982). *Understanding the Arts*. Englewood Cliffs, NJ: Prentice-Hall.

Lyas, C. (1997). *Aesthetics*. London: UCL Press.

Sharpe, R. A. (1991). *Contemporary Aesthetics*. Brighton: Harvester Press.

Townsend, D. (1997). *An Introduction to Aesthetics*. Oxford: Blackwell.

Reference Works in Aesthetics

Cooper, D. (ed.) (1992). *A Companion to Aesthetics*. Oxford: Blackwell.

Craig, E. (ed.) (1998). *Routledge Encyclopedia of Philosophy*, 9 vols. London: Routledge (contains over forty substantial articles on aesthetics).

Gardiner, S. (1995). 'Aesthetics', in A. C. Grayling (ed.), *Philosophy: A Guide through the Subject*. Oxford: Oxford University Press.

Gaut, B. and Lopes, D. (eds.) (2001). *Routledge Companion to Aesthetics*. London: Routledge.

Kelly, M. (ed.) (1998). *Encyclopedia of Aesthetics*, 4 vols. New York: Oxford University Press.

Levinson, J. (2002). 'Aesthetics', in *Macmillan Encyclopedia of Cognitive Science*. London: Nature Publishing Group.

Scruton, R. (1995). 'Aesthetics', in *The New Encyclopaedia Britannica*. Chicago: Encyclopaedia Britannica.

Turner, J. (ed.) (1996). *The Dictionary of Art*, 25 vols. London: Macmillan (contains over thirty substantial articles on aesthetics).

CHAPTER 2

HISTORY OF MODERN AESTHETICS

PAUL GUYER

PHILOSOPHERS have at least intermittently debated the nature and importance of both beauty and art—two distinct, although in most periods overlapping, subjects—since Plato called for the expulsion of the poets from his ideal republic and argued that the products of painters were at a further remove from the Forms than those of carpenters and bridlemakers. But the academic discipline now called 'aesthetics' was not baptized until 1735, when the twenty-one-year-old Alexander Gottlieb Baumgarten, in his dissertation 'Philosophical Meditations on some matters pertaining to Poetry', introduced the term to designate 'the science for directing the inferior faculty of cognition or the science of how something is to be sensitively cognized'; and, although the new discipline had not actually waited for this baptism before getting to work, it had not preceded Baumgarten's work by more than a couple of decades, having actually begun, if not with the Earl of Shaftesbury's *Characteristics* of 1711, then certainly with Joseph Addison's essays on 'The Pleasures of the Imagination' in the *Spectator* in June and July 1712, Jean-Baptiste Du Bos's *Critical Reflections on Poetry, Painting, and Music* of 1719, and Francis Hutcheson's treatise 'Concerning Beauty, Order, Harmony, Design', the first part of his *Inquiry into the Original of our Ideas of Beauty and Virtue* of 1725.

Yet the term 'aesthetics' did not acquire the predominant sense it has had throughout the twentieth century—as the designation for philosophy of art rather than the study of beauty and other qualities that may be found in nature or art—until the posthumous publication in 1835 of Georg Wilhelm Friedrich Hegel's lectures on the fine arts, which he had given in Berlin from 1819 to 1829, under the title of 'Aesthetics: Lectures on Fine Art'. Not surprisingly, then, although Plato (see especially Janaway 1995 and Nehamas 1999, chapters 12 and 13) and Aristotle (see Halliwell 1986; Belfiore 1992; and the essays collected in Rorty 1992; on both Plato and Aristotle, see Schaper 1968 and Nussbaum 1986) have continued to be intensively studied, most recent work on the history of aesthetics has focused on the period beginning in the eighteenth century. Two obvious questions for such work surely ought to be, first, why topics that had previously been discussed in poetics and literary criticism and the theory of painting and architecture suddenly became central to mainstream philosophy at the beginning of the eighteenth century, and, second, why the new discipline of aesthetics, which during the eighteenth century gave such prominence to the description and analysis of the experience of the beauty and sublimity of nature, suddenly became virtually restricted in the nineteenth century to the philosophy of art.

The first part of this chapter will review a number of recent general approaches to the history of modern aesthetics. We will see that some of the most prominent work on the history of the subject by philosophers working within the paradigm of analytical aesthetics has not had much to say about these historical questions, but instead has taken both the very existence of the field of aesthetics and its post-eighteenth-century identification with the philosophy of art pretty much for granted; such work has generally used interpretations of historical figures, especially from the eighteenth century, to support or criticize positions in contemporary aesthetics. Perhaps work in the history of philosophy is often a foil for contemporary debates; but this work on the history of aesthetics has arguably discussed an unduly restricted range of the issues about both nature and art that animated eighteenth-century thinkers, reflecting an equally restricted conception of contemporary aesthetic theory. We will have to turn to works from outside the analytical tradition to find a broader conception of the projects of modern aesthetics and, at least by implication, a broader conception of the possibilities for contemporary aesthetics. In these works we will find greater awareness of the need for an historical explanation of the sudden prominence of aesthetics in eighteenth-century philosophy, as well as its restriction to philosophy of art in the nineteenth century. But in the end, these narratives too suffer from an undue constriction of their subjects. The most prominent histories of aesthetics of the last decade, whether written by Britons or Europeans, have in fact been strikingly Eurocentric in their focus, and have neglected some of the most important themes and figures in British and American aesthetics from the eighteenth to the twentieth centuries. In reviewing these works, therefore, I will also draw some attention to themes and figures that have not recently received adequate coverage.

Following this survey, the second part of the chapter will be a bibliographical essay listing some of the most important recent work on the major movements and individual figures in aesthetics from the beginning of the eighteenth century to the middle of the twentieth.

1. General Approaches to the History of Modern Aesthetics

1.1 Analytical Aesthetics and the History of Modern Aesthetics

Within that sphere of Anglo-American academic aesthetics dominated by the paradigm of analytical philosophy, the most distinctive historiographical theses have been those put forward, first, in papers published by Jerome Stolnitz in the 1960s and 1970s (Stolnitz 1961a,b, 1978) and, second, in those developed by George Dickie (1996), in an historical book that aims to provide foundations for a theoretical position developed over a long career in contemporary aesthetics. Both of these authors have appealed to eighteenth-century aesthetics in defence of what they take to be the proper approach to contemporary aesthetics. In an important paper, Noël Carroll (1991) has argued against the constraint of contemporary practice in aesthetics by what he takes to be the eighteenth-century identification of beauty as the primary goal of art; this argument is representative of much recent thinking on the relation between art and beauty, so we will pause over this work as well. (Carroll's paper is now reprinted, with a number of related pieces, in Carroll 2001.)

Stolnitz argued that, beginning with the publication in 1711 of the *Characteristics of Men, Manners, Opinions, Times* by Anthony Ashley Cooper, third Earl of Shaftesbury, which touched upon the nature of beauty at various places, but most importantly in the third of its three major essays, 'The Moralists: A Philosophical Rhapsody' (see Shaftesbury 1999: especially 273–88 and 316–32), British aesthetics in particular was founded on the principle of the disinterestedness of aesthetic experience. Further, Stolnitz argued that the British philosophers understood disinterestedness as a distinctive way of approaching an object, by means of what would be called the 'aesthetic attitude' in twentieth-century philosophy, beginning with Edward Bullough's famous paper of 1912, ' "Psychical Distance" as a Factor in Art and an Aesthetic Principle' (Bullough 1957: 91–130), and culminating in Stolnitz's own paper (1960). In approaching an object from the aesthetic attitude, Stolnitz held, 'we do not look at the object out of concern for any ulterior purpose which it may serve'; in this frame of mind, 'there is no purpose governing the experience other than the purpose of just having the experience' (Stolnitz 1960: 35). Stolnitz in turn interpreted 'having the experience' as a special mode of perception, in which the sensory capacities, typically restricted to the eye and the ear, freed from the pressure of practical concerns or even theoretical inquiry, can simply play over the perceivable form and matter of external objects and enjoy the impressions thereby received. Thus, on Stolnitz's account of Shaftesbury,

disregard for possession or use is only an inference from or a specification of the broader proposition that the aesthetic spectator does not relate the object to any purposes that outrun the act of perception itself...the aesthetic interest is in perception alone and...it terminates upon the object itself.... the aesthetic interest is indifferent to the causal and other relationships which the object has to things beyond itself. (Stolnitz 1961a: 134)

Stolnitz then maintained that both the concept of disinterestedness and this interpretation of it as a distinctive mode of purely perceptual engagement with an object remained characteristic of subsequent British writers, including Joseph Addison (whose essays on 'The Pleasures of the Imagination' appeared only one year after Shaftesbury's *Characteristics*), Francis Hutcheson, Edmund Burke, Alexander Gerard, and Archibald Alison (Stolnitz 1961a: 134–41), Schopenhauer (at least in part) (Stolnitz 1978: 419–21), and twentieth-century writers (now largely neglected) such as David Prall, C. J. Ducasse, and DeWitt Parker (Stolnitz, 1961a: 141). Moreover, Stolnitz clearly believed that, in introducing this conception of disinterestedness, Shaftesbury had properly introduced the foundational concept for modern aesthetics, and thus that aesthetic experience is properly interpreted simply as disinterested perception and the enjoyment of it. Stolnitz's account constitutes a highly debatable interpretation both of Shaftesbury himself and of many of his successors: while Hutcheson clearly argued that aesthetic response is sensory rather than rational, Shaftesbury hardly drew a line between the senses and higher cognitive powers such as reason; and later writers such as Burke and Alison intimately connected our response to both the beautiful and the sublime to our deepest drives and emotions as well as to mere perception. Dickie (1996) makes this point about Alison, although as we will see he disapproves of Alison for precisely this reason. Stolnitz's thesis also neglects the centrality of the analysis of artistic creativity, under the guise of the concept of genius, in eighteenth-century aesthetics.

In his initial response to Stolnitz, however, Dickie criticized him for a different reason. Dickie argued that Stolnitz neglected the major difference between what he called the 'taste' theorists of the eighteenth century and the 'attitude' theorists of the nineteenth and twentieth centuries: while Stolnitz conceived of the kind of disengagement with other concerns that can be called disinterestedness as facilitating the possibility of pleasure in perception itself that could be stimulated by any object approached in the proper frame of mind, in his view eighteenth-century thinkers by no means foresaw such a generalized potential for pleasure in disinterested perception, but instead assumed that the pleasures of taste would be triggered only by certain specially suited properties in objects (Dickie 1974: chapter 2, e.g. 58; see also Rind 2002). Dickie argued in the 1960s and 1970s against the idea of the aesthetic attitude itself, holding it to be a vacuous concept, meaning nothing more than that we should attend to a work of art in whatever way is appropriate to appreciate it, and insisted that no informative theoretical constraints can be placed on such appreciation. He thus rejected the idea that aesthetic experience can be reduced to the enjoyment of disinterested perception, or to anything else similarly specific. This is why he resorted to his famous 'institutional analysis', defining a work of art as anything put forth by a member of the art world as a candidate for appreciation, where all the work is to be done by the concept of the art world and no restriction is implied by the concept of appreciation (Dickie 1974: chapter 1). As we will see below, however, in Dickie (1996) he would praise the other side of the 'taste theory' of the eighteenth century, that is, the project of specifying a range of properties in the objects of taste that can induce aesthetic responses and judgements of taste.

Noël Carroll (1991) agrees with Dickie's critique of Stolnitz that the eighteenth-century theorists had not only a theory of the aesthetic attitude, but also a theory of beauty as the characteristic object of this aesthetic attitude; however, he then argues that recent analytical philosophy of art has been fundamentally disserved by the supposition that the primary purpose of art is to produce beautiful objects and thereby to induce the response to beauty. Carroll thus rejects what he takes to be the eighteenth-century invention of the 'aesthetic theory of art', as contrasted to a theory of art on which it could have purposes other than that of producing a response to beauty. The main figures in Carroll's narrative are Hutcheson, Kant, the early twentieth-century British critic Clive Bell, and the mid-twentieth-century American philosopher Monroe Beardsley. Carroll considers Hutcheson's theory, that the experience of beauty is an immediate sensory response to uniformity amidst variety, and Kant's theory, focused on 'free beauty', that ' "x is beautiful" is an authentic judgement of taste (or an aesthetic judgement) if and only if it is a judgement that is (1) subjective, (2) disinterested, (3) universal, (4) necessary, and (5) singular, concerning (6) the contemplative pleasure that everyone ought to derive from (7) cognitive and imaginative free play in relation to (8) forms of finality' (Carroll 1991: 316–17). Carroll argues that these theories, although perhaps not actually intended by their authors as comprehensive theories of art (Carroll 1991: 318), nevertheless seduced twentieth-century writers such as Bell into supposing that art is properly concerned only to produce objects which by means of their formal properties will in turn induce a distinctive response, detached from all other human concerns, such as Hutcheson's immediate sensation of unity amidst variety, or Kant's free play of the cognitive faculties in response to forms of finality. In Bell's case, the end of art is a distinctive 'aesthetic emotion' in response to 'significant form', 'a rapturous emotion...independent of concerns of practical utility, and cognitive import' (Carroll 1991: 319), the whole point of which is indeed precisely to liberate us from our ordinary concerns with purpose and utility—here Carroll rightly observes that 'Bell's theory recalls Schopenhauer's insofar as the very point of art seems to be identified with bringing about a divorce from everything else' (Carroll 1991: 321). In Beardsley's case, the point of art is to produce objects of perceptual or 'phenomenal' experience that will induce 'aesthetic experience', characterized by 'object directedness; felt freedom (a sense of release from antecedent concerns); detached affect (emotional distance); active discovery (a sense of intelligibility); and wholeness (contentment, and a freedom from distracting and disruptive impulses)' (Carroll 1991: 324). In Carroll's view, however, such theories lead to an implausible restriction on the objects of art, excluding from the domain of art properly so called all work, especially avant-garde art, that does not strive for beauty at all, and to a restriction on both artist and audience that excludes concerns with 'knowledge, morality, politics, and so on' that are in fact not 'anomalous given the range of preoccupations found in traditional art' (Carroll 1991: 327). In other words, the aesthetic theory of art that according to Carroll can be traced back to Hutcheson and Kant not only lacks an adequate theoretical justification for restricting the concern of art proper to beauty and a special detached pleasure in it, but also is false to the real history of art, which manifestly displays the expression of a far wider range of human concerns. By implication, of course, Stolnitz's revival of the conception of the 'aesthetic attitude' that he found in the eighteenth century is a fundamental mistake for contemporary aesthetics.

Carroll acknowledges that neither Hutcheson nor Kant may actually have intended a purely 'aesthetic theory of art'. This should certainly be underlined: although Hutcheson did think that the objects of all aesthetic experiences could be subsumed under the abstract idea of 'uniformity amidst variety', he also classifed mimesis or representation as itself a form of uniformity amidst variety, and clearly allowed that art could aim at producing an essentially cognitive response to mimesis as well as a purely sensory response to form (Carroll 1991: 315); and Kant, as Carroll notes but hardly stresses, in fact emphasized the presence of 'aesthetic ideas in art' (Carroll 1991: 318), which means that for Kant art paradigmatically has moral content, and our response to art is thus by no means a simple harmony between imagination and understanding, but rather a much more complicated play among imagination, understanding, and reason. Further, to ascribe the 'aesthetic theory of art' to the eighteenth century omits the eighteenth-century fascination with the sublime, with tragedy, and with art as the expression of the strongest human emotions, so prominent in writers such as Burke, Mendelssohn, and Alison. Moreover, it is also misleading to suggest that the 'aesthetic theory of art' has been the predominant tendency of modern aesthetics, or even just of Anglo-American aesthetics. Of course, there is a line of aesthetic thought leading not so much from Kant as from Schopenhauer, through literary figures such as Théophile Gauthier, Gustave Flaubert, Charles Baudelaire, and Walter Pater, to art critics like Clive Bell, and finally to several analytical aestheticians such as Stolnitz and Beardsley (for brief surveys of this movement, see Sartwell 1998 and Guyer, forthcoming), but such a view of art on the part of both theorists and practitioners has been intermittent and never uncontested. For every Schopenhauer, Pater, or Bell, there has been a Friedrich Schiller, John Ruskin, William Morris, or John Dewey, arguing that aesthetic experience is distinctive in its freedom from our most immediate obsessions with purpose and utility, but that the freedom it thereby allows us is not a freedom for the simple contemplation of beauty with no further concerns or implications, but rather a freedom to develop our imaginative and cognitive capacities, to gain knowledge of ourselves and others, and to imagine new ways of life, a freedom that is valued not simply for its own sake but also because of the benefits the development of these capacities can bring to the rest of our lives. (See the treatments of both Kant and Schiller in Savile 1987 and Guyer 1993*a*.) Apart from a narrow school of analytical aesthetics in the 1950s and the 1960s, it has probably been the tradition of Schiller and Dewey rather than that of Schopenhauer and Bell that has been the dominant influence throughout nineteenth- and twentieth-century aesthetics, even academic aesthetics.

More like Stolnitz than like Carroll, Dickie demonstrates in his 1996 book *The Century of Taste* a remarkably narrow conception not only of the historical tendencies of aesthetics but also of the prospects for contemporary aesthetic theory. Although Dickie subtitles his book *The Philosophical Odyssey of Taste in the Eighteenth Century*, he discusses in any detail only five authors, namely Hutcheson, Alexander Gerard, Archibald Alison, Kant, and Hume—and in that order, so that his account can culminate in praise of Hume. He thus leaves out, among many others, Du Bos and all other French writers, Joseph Addison, Edmund Burke, Lord Kames, and Adam Smith among other Britons, and Moses Mendelssohn and Friedrich Schiller along with a host of other Germans. And even in the writers he does discuss, Dickie's choice of issues is limited. Thus, he omits any treatment not only of the sublime, a central topic for a wide range of eighteenth-century figures, but also of genius, in spite of its obvious importance to both Gerard and Kant, who are central to Dickie's narrative. Dickie thus omits virtually all discussion of eighteenth-century views about the relations between aesthetic experience on the one hand and human morality and creativity on the other. This is because he wants to focus on what he calls 'taste theory', which concerns only the specification of the proper objects of judgements of taste and the character of the response to them—a subject that need not reach the specific issues of the nature of art, its typical subject matter, or the conditions for its creation. Moreover, Dickie's celebration of eighteenth-century 'taste theory' is ultimately misleading, because he criticizes all of his chosen authors, except for Hume, both for placing too much theoretical restriction on the objects of taste, and—especially—for venturing any informative hypotheses about the nature of aesthetic response at all. In the end, Dickie praises Hume for reducing aesthetic theory to an open-ended enumeration of beauty-making characteristics, while rejecting, in line with his famous scepticism about causation, any hypotheses about the mechanisms by means of which various beauty-making characteristics might cause the pleasure that we take in them. Dickie's historiography is thus in service of a conception of aesthetics diametrically opposed to that of Stolnitz, but equally narrow: instead of theorizing the aesthetic attitude, aesthetic theory for Dickie can ultimately do nothing more than prescribe due attention to the open-ended list of objects that might be offered by representatives of the art world as candidates for our appreciation, whatever their properties and whatever the nature of our appreciation of them might be.

Hutcheson, of course, argued that our response to beauty is always an immediate response of an essentially sensory nature to the perception of unity amidst variety among the properties of objects, ascribing this response to an 'internal sense' dependent upon, but not identical to, any of the five external senses; and Dickie criticizes him for failing to prove both that our response to beauty is always of the same essentially sensory character and that it is always unity amidst variety that induces this response (Dickie 1996: 25). Dickie is surely right on the first point, a point also argued by Peter Kivy (see Kivy 1976a: chapters II and III). But he does not do justice to the variety of beauty-making characteristics that Hutcheson actually subsumes under his abstract idea of unity amidst variety. Dickie makes little of Hutcheson's idea of the beauty of theorems, which certainly involves what the Germans of the time called the 'higher cognitive powers' in the activities of the 'internal sense'; and, while he does recognize that Hutcheson includes representation or mimesis as a form of unity amidst variety, under the rubric of 'relative beauty', he does not note that Hutcheson also includes correspondence between intention and outcome as another form of relative beauty, thereby allowing room for the appreciation of the artistry manifest in an artefact, as well as for the particular beauty-making characteristics that such artistry may have produced, and thus opening the door for subsequent theories of genius as well as beauty. This is a first example of Dickie's simplification of the actual complexity of eighteenth-century aesthetic theories. (For a more balanced view of Hutcheson, see Korsmeyer 1979a,b.)

Dickie credits Gerard for introducing the idea of the 'coalescence of ideas'—really, multiple pleasures—in our response to objects of taste in Gerard's 1759 *Essay on Taste*. (He fails to notice Mendelssohn's at least as important idea of 'mixed sentiments' in his writings beginning in 1755; see Mendelssohn 1997: e.g. 72–5, 131–8.) Dickie praises Gerard for expanding the list of beauty-making characteristics; but then, although he had criticized Hutcheson for restricting aesthetic response to sense, he criticizes Gerard for expanding the list of cognitive capacities too far beyond sense and thereby allowing too much room for relativism in judgements of taste (Dickie 1996: 41, 47–8). One would have thought that the Dickie who would place no restrictions on what the art world can offer as candidates for our appreciation would have welcomed Gerard's more catholic conception of the faculties involved in aesthetic response, while having no special reason to object to a dose of relativism.

Turning to Alison, Dickie criticizes him for identifying aesthetic response exclusively with 'coalescence', that is, for holding that what we respond to in matters of taste is never the purely physical properties of objects of perception but rather always the human emotions, thus qualities of mind, that we connect with strictly perceivable properties by 'trains of association' (a thought that is of course not new in Alison, but rather is revived from Shaftesbury—see Shaftesbury 1999: 322–4). Dickie is right that Alison fails to prove that all forms of beauty reduce to this association (Dickie 1996: 71–3); Alison surely went overboard in holding that all the pleasures of form and matter offered by works of both nature and art are pleasures of emotional association. But Dickie goes too far when he insists that Alison's view of the necessity of emotional association for the enjoyment of objects of taste is 'massively wrongheaded and a dead end from which nothing can be salvaged' (p. 75): this just rejects without argument the fundamental project of properly characterizing the undeniable role of emotions in our responses to art that has animated aesthetics from the time of Du Bos and Burke to that of Tolstoy and Collingwood, to recent writers such as Richard Wollheim, Kendall Walton, and Stanley Cavell, and that continues to be a central focus of aesthetic theory. Further, Dickie's insistence that Alison's emphasis on the trains of association started by an object of taste can only lead to distraction from, rather than due attention to, the proper object of taste (p. 74) is simplistic: surely many works of art, such as the tone poems of Liszt or Strauss, are meant at least in part precisely to trigger such trains of association; and the possibility of tension between attention to a work of art and the trains of association it may stimulate should not be dismissed as a sign of theoretical error, but rather should be celebrated as a genuine recognition of the complex phenomenology of aesthetic experience and one of the reasons why we seek such experience.

Dickie's interpretation of Kant is also controversial. Dickie correctly insists on the teleological character of Kant's aesthetics, but he misunderstands what that is. In Dickie's view, Kant presented the argument of the *Critique of the Power of Judgement* backwards: on his account, Kant thinks that all beauty consists in the distinctive appearance of a special kind of purposive design found in natural organisms, so he should have placed the 'Critique of Teleological Judgement' before the 'Critique of Aesthetic Judgement'. Of course, Dickie also thinks that the reduction of beauty to such an alleged appearance of organic purposiveness is utterly implausible. In fact, he fails to understand that Kant's conception of a beautiful object as one that induces a free play of the cognitive powers of imagination and understanding (or of a sublime object as one that ultimately induces a harmony between imagination and reason) is a conception of the subjective purposiveness of such an object, that is, a conception of it as answering to our own aims in cognition, although in a distinctive way—not a conception of a special appearance of organic design, which Kant never posits. In fact, Kant's argument for the necessity of a concept of purposiveness in our comprehension of organisms is founded on the centrality of purposiveness in our self-understanding: it is a regulative rather than a constitutive transference of our own intentionality, and indeed artistry, in order to make sense of certain puzzling phenomena in nature (see especially Kant 2000: §65). In other words, Kant's teleological conception of nature is based on his conception of the subjective purposiveness of our own cognitive constitution and the intentional purposiveness of human artistic production; for Kant, we have to understand certain phenomena in nature on the analogy with our own art, but we do not understand beauty in either nature or art on the basis of a prior conception of organic function, let alone its supposed distinctive appearance (see Guyer 1997).

Finally, Dickie praises Hume for claiming that 'in criticism we can discover a number of objects of taste, which he calls "beauties" and "blemishes", that function as reasons to support evaluations concerning the beauty and ugliness of works of art' (Dickie 1996: 127), and for simply tabulating these beauties and blemishes in open-ended lists (pp. 128–9), rather than attempting any theoretical explanation of them by means of some single model for the causation of aesthetic response. But this approach to Hume's aesthetics stakes everything on his apparent assumptions in the famous but late essay 'Of the Standard of Taste', and neglects his reduction of the vast majority of cases of beauty to actual or apparent utility enjoyed by means of sympathy or other mechanisms of the imagination in *A Treatise of Human Nature* (see Hume 2000: 235–6, 368–9). There may be tension between Hume's account of beauty in the *Treatise* and his assumptions in 'Of the Standard of Taste', but by simply omitting any discussion of these tensions, Dickie misses, just as he does by so radically misunderstanding and thereby rejecting Kant's conception of the subjective purposiveness of aesthetic response, an opportunity to discuss one of the most fundamental issues of eighteenth-century aesthetics, which is nothing less than the question of how to understand the complex relationship between the inescapably teleological character of human thought and the distinctive freedom of aesthetic response from at least immediate and superficial concerns with use and possession. This problem was crucial for British writers from Shaftesbury to Hume and Burke and for German writers from Leibniz and Wolff to Mendelssohn and Kant; but, by choosing what is actually the least theoretical of Hume's approaches to aesthetics as his paradigm of a proper theory of taste, Dickie simply sweeps it under the rug.

These works by Stolnitz, Carroll, and Dickie focus narrowly on the perception of beauty as a basically formal property of objects, neglecting such central eighteenth-century questions as the relation between beauty and utility; the relation between aesthetic experience and human emotion, manifest in such typical topics as the sublime and the paradox of tragedy, and central to the work of figures such as Du Bos, Burke, and Mendelssohn; and the nature of artistic creativity, a vital concern for writers such as Gerard, Kant, and Schiller. Even on the topic of beauty, these three authors exaggerate the prevalence of a purely perceptual model of aesthetic response in the eighteenth century. Shaftesbury started eighteenth-century aesthetic thought with the recognition that there is a vital difference between the pleasures associated with the use or consumption of an object, which are dependent upon the possession of it, and the enjoyment of its beauty or other of what we now call its aesthetic qualities (Shaftesbury 1999: 318–19). But he did not think either that this condition of disinterestedness is equivalent to bare perception of an object, or that our appreciation of the beauty of an object terminates in bare perception of it. On the contrary, for Shaftesbury abstraction from possible grounds for personal interest in the possession of an object opens the way for an appreciation of beauty as both an analogue and an example of the inherent order of the cosmos, an order that is appreciated by reason as much as by mere perception. In Shaftesbury's unorthodox but still deeply religious philosophy, our appreciation of that cosmic order ultimately leads to admiration for the formative power that is the source of all beautiful forms, whether directly, in the case of natural beauties, or indirectly, in the case of man-made beauties (Shaftesbury 1999: 322–3).

Following Shaftesbury rather than Hutcheson, almost all thinkers in the eighteenth century recognized the complex rather than simple nature of aesthetic response, the interplay between perception and the higher cognitive capacities of understanding and reason in aesthetic experience, and the variety of both aesthetic experiences and aesthetic objects. Even Hume, who seems to advocate a purely perceptual conception of aesthetic response in such popular essays as 'The Sceptic' and 'Of the Standard of Taste', where he pretends that we can say nothing more about beauty than that 'Some particular forms or qualities, from the original structure of the internal fabric are calculated to please, and others to displease' (Hume 1963: 238), in fact suggested in the *Treatise of Human Nature* a complicated theory of beauty, in which such purely perceptual beauty is the minority case, the majority of experiences of beauty instead involving the response of the imagination, through sympathy, generalization, and the association of ideas, to real or apparent utility (Hume 2000: 235–6, 368–9; see also Korsmeyer 1976; Guyer 1993*b*; Gracyk 1994; and Townsend 2001: chapter 3). And Kant, although he certainly insisted on both the disinterestedness of aesthetic judgement (Kant 2000: §2) and on perceptual form as the proper objects of 'pure' judgements of taste (§14), nevertheless held that our pleasure in even those simplest cases of beauty is due to a free play between the imagination and understanding (§§9, 35), while our more complex pleasure in the sublime is due to a disharmony between imagination and understanding accompanied by an awareness of harmony between imagination and reason (§§23–9), and our pleasure in art involves an equally complex interplay between ideas of reason and material of the imagination (§49). In short, the dominant aesthetic theories of the eighteenth century were complex rather than reductive, recognizing that our pleasures in the beautiful, the sublime, and more are independent of self-regarding interest but are nevertheless intimately involved with the deepest and most general aspects of human psychology (see Townsend 1987 and Guyer 1993*a*: chapters 2–3).

These works also fail to address our opening question, concerning just why aesthetics became such a vital part of eighteenth-century philosophy at all. I now turn to several recent works which at least broach the latter question, and which carry the discussion on into the nineteenth and twentieth centuries.

1.2 Post-Analytical Histories of Modern Aesthetics

The British literary critic Terry Eagleton and the French philosophers Luc Ferry and Jean-Marie Schaeffer have all recently published histories of modern aesthetics which take the reader from the eighteenth to the twentieth century. These authors see aesthetic theories as reflecting larger philosophical and ideological agendas and as having been brought to prominence beginning in the eighteenth century because of these larger agendas. Eagleton sees the project of modern aesthetics as having been inspired by a naïve conception of the potential of aesthetic experience for a programme of moral and political improvement led by the bourgeoisie that emerged during the eighteenth century, but as a project that collapsed because of the inadequacy of the bourgeoisie as an instrument of widespread improvement of that sort. Ferry similarly associates the rise of aesthetics with an Enlightenment conception of the possibility of individual development and self-expression within a liberal political framework that was initially the property of the bourgeoisie, but he has a more optimistic assessment of the potential contribution of art and aesthetic experience to conditions in which democracy can flourish beyond the confines of a single socioeconomic class. For all their differences, both of these works are striking in their omission of central thinkers concerned with the relation between aesthetic experience and political freedom, such as John Ruskin in the nineteenth century and John Dewey and R. G. Collingwood in the twentieth. Schaeffer, for his part, argues that the impulse to speculative metaphysics from Hegel to Heidegger has distorted Kant's original sense of the freedom of artistic creation from undue restriction by theoretical and moral agendas, and finds some twentieth-century avant-garde artists to have remained closer than twentieth-century aestheticians to the Kantian sense of the freedom of artistic creation from dominance by metaphysics itself. But he too has a monolithic and Eurocentric view of the history of philosophical aesthetics from Schlegel to Heidegger, and fails to note how the conception of the freedom of artistic creation from dominance by the agenda of speculative metaphysics that can be found—although perhaps only partially—in Kant and Schiller remained alive in many corners of academic aesthetics throughout the nineteenth and twentieth centuries, in all sorts of figures, from Hermann Lotze and George Santayana to Dewey and Collingwood and even to George Dickie and Arthur Danto. Ironically, perhaps even Danto's insistence on the 'death of art', because of its alleged identification with philosophy, should be understood as a plea for the freedom of contemporary art from domination by a single philosophical programme (see Danto 1997).

Eagleton's (1990) book *The Ideology of the Aesthetic* is the most comprehensive but also the most dispiriting of these three works. In his view, aesthetic theory began in self-delusion and has ended in despair: the eighteenth-century's optimistic appeal to the aesthetic as an instrument of both personal liberation and social progress was at best a delusion about the nature of emerging capitalist society and at worst a hypocritical attempt to serve capitalist society, while twentieth-century theories of art, whether Freudian, Marxist, or postmodernist, have basically been expressions of the alienation and powerlessness of modern humans in the face of the apparently equal devils of fascism and capitalism. In Eagleton's gloomy story, only the young Marx succeeded in envisioning an 'aesthetic interfusion of form and content' as a possibility for a genuinely 'emancipated society' (Eagleton 1990: 210), but Marx's vision was not realized even by would-be heirs in the twentieth century such as Benjamin and Adorno, who ultimately saw art merely as an expression of alienation rather than an instrument with which to resist it.

Eagleton considers a range of figures from the eighteenth century to the twentieth, some of whom have been influential on contemporary Anglo-American aesthetics, and others of whom have been more influential in broader debates about the nature of modern society and culture. Among eighteenth-century figures, Eagleton discusses at lesser or greater length Baumgarten, Shaftesbury, Hume, Burke, Rousseau, Kant, and Schiller; in the nineteenth century, Fichte, Schelling, Hegel, Kierkegaard, Schopenhauer, Marx, and Nietzsche; in the twentieth century, Freud, Heidegger, Marxists including Lukács, Benjamin, and Adorno, and postmodernists such as Foucault. Here only some highlights of Eagleton's narrative can be mentioned. Eagleton argues that with Baumgarten 'Aesthetics is born as a discourse of the body' (1990: 13), meaning by this that the discipline of aesthetics arose because of the need to recognize the importance of perception, sensation, and emotion in addition to more abstract reasoning in the panoply of human capacities. But he characteristically concludes that Baumgarten's 'innovative gesture' succeeded only in opening up 'the whole terrain of sensation...to...the colonization of reason' (p. 15); that is, the new recognition of art's potential appeal to the affective side of human nature only afforded new instruments for the reason employed by the dominant economic and political forces of emerging bourgeois society to exercise control over individuals. Similarly, Rousseau envisioned autonomous individuals who through self-legislation could retain their 'unique individuality, but now in the form of a disinterested commitment to a common well-being', a 'fusion of general and particular, in which one shares in the whole at no risk to one's unique specificity', and which 'resembles the very form of the aesthetic artefact'. However, while the 'enheartening expression of this doctrine, politically speaking, would be: "what appears as my subordination to others is in fact self-determination"; the more cynical view would run: "my subordination to others is so effective that it appears to me in the mystified guise of governing myself"' (p. 25). This jaundiced view sums up Eagleton's history of modern aesthetic theory: the possibility of individually autonomous yet socially harmonious self-creation that is supposed to be both realized in and symbolized by artistic production and aesthetic experience is either a feeble and doomed cry against the powers that be, or is actually perverted into one more instrument of social control by those powers.

There are further key claims of Eagleton's story. 'Against a social philosophy founded upon egoism and appetite', he is prepared to admit, 'Kant speaks up for a generous vision of a community of ends, finding in the direction and autonomy of the aesthetic a prototype of human possibility equally at odds with feudal absolutism and possessive individualism', that is, early capitalism (p. 100). But Eagleton endorses without reservation Hegel's criticism that Kant's moral and political principles are too abstract for anyone to use in the actual creation of freer individuals and better societies, although Hegel's critique of Kant has been seriously questioned by contemporary moral philosophers such as John Rawls and scholars such as Allen Wood. Eagleton then turns around and argues that, although Hegel proposed replacing Kant's abstract principles of morality and justice with real social institutions such as the family, civil society, and historically situated polities, the Hegelian dialectic was not up to the 'patient probings of dialectical reason' that are necessary to transform these institutions themselves, 'given the strata of false consciousness which intervene between empirical consciousness and the whole' in them (p. 151).

Nor does Schopenhauer's version of aesthetic disinterestedness help: it has 'little in common with an Arnoldian large-mindedness, impartially weighing competing interests with an eye to the affirmative whole; on the contrary it demands nothing less than a complete self-abandonment, a kind of serene self-immolation on the subject's part' (p. 163). But then Eagleton includes no extended discussion of Arnold, Ruskin, or William Morris, let alone Dewey or Collingwood, so their claims for the contribution of aesthetic experience and artistic creation to a genuine large-mindedness go unexamined or, what is worse, are rejected without argument. The young Marx, Eagleton maintains, 'is in entire agreement with the Earl of Shaftesbury—an unlikely candidate, otherwise, for his approval—that human powers and human society are an absolute end in themselves', 'the single most creative aspect of the aesthetic tradition' (p. 226). Here Eagleton misses an opportunity to mention John Stuart Mill, whose defence of individuality against Victorian conformism in the third chapter of *On Liberty* is based precisely on this idea, as it were an English idea that has returned to him by a way of a detour through Wilhelm von Humboldt.

What Eagleton does argue is that, unlike Hegel, Marx recognizes that a transformation of the conditions of labour, including such a practical and obvious change as the shortening of the work-day, will be necessary to allow an equitable realization of this ideal. Yet Eagleton seems to think that the failure of Marx's bold hope that 'History would be transformed by its most contaminated products, by those bearing the most livid marks of its brutality' (p. 230), that is the proletariat, needs no explanation or even explicit assertion. In any case, the history of aesthetic theory after Marx, even Marxist aesthetic theory, is for Eagleton nothing but a succession of counsels of despair. Nietzsche sees art as opening up 'fresh possibilities of experiment and adventure' in human life, but for him 'the release of individual human powers from the fetters of social uniformity' can be realized only in the 'disdainful isolation' of the *Übermensch* (pp. 238, 245). For Freud, art is 'no privileged realm, but is continuous with the libidinal processes that go to make up daily life', and on Eagleton's assessment of Freud there seems to be no possibility that the achievement of self-knowledge through therapy will allow us to gain control over, and thus genuine satisfaction of, those libidinal processes: instead, 'The humanist dream of fullness is itself a libidinal fantasy, as indeed is the whole of traditional aesthetics' (pp. 262–3). Here the work of a modern Freudian such as Richard Wollheim remains unexamined. Heidegger's conception of *Dasein* is an 'unholy alliance', Eagleton continues, 'at once a remorseless assault on the philosophy of the autonomous subject…and at the same time the latest in a long series of privileged, aestheticized, quasi-transcendental "subjects" jealously protecting their integrity and autonomy from the taint of the quotidian' (p. 297). That Heidegger's philosophy is an assault upon genuine autonomy seems indisputable, but that Heidegger, instead of Dewey or Collingwood, should be chosen as the representative aesthetician of the mid-twentieth century reflects a narrow conception of twentieth-century philosophy, to say the least.

Among the Marxists, Eagleton avers, Georg Lukács foolishly imagined that bourgeois art forms could readily be enrolled in the ranks of revolution, while Walter Benjamin and especially Theodor Adorno more honestly but also hopelessly recognized that 'art can only be authentic if it silently acknowledges how deeply it is compromised by what it opposes; but to press this logic too far is precisely to undermine its authenticity' (p. 349); art cannot successfully achieve autonomy for itself, and show the way for the achievement of autonomy in the broader spheres of economy and morality, because there really is no chance for the latter. Again, the underlying assumption that in the modern world the project of establishing conditions for the genuine realization of autonomy is not just difficult but a pipedream is not defended. Most recently, postmodernism is by no means a response 'to a system which has eased up, disarticulated, pluralized its operations, but to precisely the opposite: to a power-structure which, being in a sense more "total" than ever, is capable for the moment of disarming and demoralizing many of its antagonists. In such a situation, it is sometimes comforting and convenient to imagine that there is not after all, as Foucault might have said, anything "total" to be broken' (p. 381).

Of course, one must remember that Eagleton's book was written prior to the genuine expansion of democracy in many countries in Europe and South America as well as several in Africa and Asia during the 1990s, and thus prior to the evidence that the work of an artist such as Vaclav Havel could actually help people imagine the possibility of democracy. But in any case, it is clear that Eagleton falls short of actually demonstrating that the project of enlisting art in the cause of human liberation is a hopeless liberal self-delusion. Undoubtedly, someone like Schiller had excessive expectations for the liberating power of aesthetic education; but Eagleton's pessimism seems as naïve as Schiller's optimism, a bitter response to inflated expectations rather than a judicious assessment of the more modest but genuine contributions that engagement with art can make to personal and political liberation.

That twentieth-century history showed that the realization of moral, political, economic, and even aesthetic autonomy in a wide percentage of the human population would be more difficult than the Enlightenment imagined can hardly be denied. But the pessimism of Eagleton's view both of aesthetics and of modern history more generally is unwarranted. A more optimistic interpretation of several of the figures discussed by Eagleton is offered by Luc Ferry in his book *Homo aestheticus: The Invention of Taste in the Democratic Age*, which originally appeared in the same year as Eagleton's polemic. The central figure of Ferry's account of the centrality of aesthetics in the development of modern philosophy as a whole is Nietzsche, who recognizes that 'in a universe that is now wholly perspectival, in a world once again become infinite in that it offers the possibility of an infinity of interpretations, only art presents itself authentically as what it is: an evaluation that makes no pretence of truth' (Ferry 1993: 186). But for Ferry this is not a counsel of despair, and to give up all pretence to truth is not, it turns out, for art to give up all claim to truth. What art represents better than anything else is the impossibility of a single systematic and comprehensive theory of the world that must be accepted by every individual, and, instead, the reality of the multiplicity of viewpoints that must be accepted in an age of genuinely democratic individualism, not just because of the inevitable differences among the preferences of persons, but also because of the irremediably complex nature of the rest of reality as well. However, Ferry argues, this has been better recognized not by aesthetic theory in the twentieth century, but rather by successful avant-garde movements in twentieth-century art itself.

Ferry begins his work with a survey of eighteenth-century figures, focusing on Du Bos in France, Hume in Britain, and Baumgarten in Germany. His argument here is that these figures recognized, contrary to Leibniz, that an appeal to God could no longer be relied upon to guarantee the possibility of harmonious bonds among discrete individuals, and instead turned to something within human experience that could 'ground objectivity on subjectivity, transcendence on immanence', or both recognize differences among persons and establish common ground between them—namely, 'the beautiful ... which at the same time brings us together the most easily yet most mysteriously' (Ferry 1993: 25). This line of thought culminated in Kant's conception of the judgement of taste as the product of the reflecting power of judgement using indeterminate rather than determinate concepts, which showed 'how to think aesthetic intersubjectivity without grounding it either on a dogmatic reason or on a psycho-physiological structure' (pp. 85–6). However, such a foundation for the possibility of intersubjective agreement in something so subjective as our sentiments and preferences comes under criticism by Hegel, who is not prepared to surrender the promise of Leibnizian rationalism.

Ferry argues correctly against those who would see Hegel as an avatar of a genuinely modern historicism, in which what can be perceived as truth and can be represented as such in art is entirely open to ever-changing historical forces. Instead, Ferry argues, 'The Hegelian project is not at all one of opening philosophy up to history, but of absorbing historicity back into the concept', a project that is 'a direct descendent of Leibniz's' (p. 147; see also pp. 128–9). Within aesthetic theory, what this means is basically that what Hegel called classical art was not merely a historical phase within the development of art that could be replaced by others equally appropriate to their historical circumstances: rather, classical art embodied the essence of art, and thus, when the continued creation of classical art was no longer an historical possibility, it was art itself that had to be superseded by religion and then philosophy. 'With the introduction of historicity into truth, Hegel intended to reestablish the primacy of the divine and the intelligible' that had been rejected by eighteenth-century thinkers from Du Bos to Kant. 'The aesthetic sphere, born out of the legitimation of the sensible, must thereby be reintegrated into the whole of the system. The philosophy of art must thus embrace its object the better to kill it' (p. 129). On this account, Hegel is not simply reporting the death of art, but rather is ordering its assassination in the name of a revived rationalism.

Ferry, however, unlike Arthur Danto (see Danto 1997), is not tempted to accept Hegel's thesis of the death of art as an historical inevitability. He treats Hegel as only a detour on the way from the eighteenth century to Nietzsche, whose understanding of art as a model of the inexhaustibility of valid perspectives upon a complex and changing reality, and perhaps even as a source of such perspectives, is in turn the foundation for a lively tradition of avant-garde art in the twentieth century. The heart of Ferry's approach is the idea that 'Nietzsche's philosophy takes the form of a monadology with neither subject nor system', by which he means that according to Nietzsche individuals do not have fixed and determinate natures, but are free to create themselves as they create works of art—indeed, at least in part through their creation of works of art. The 'multiplicity of points of views' that results from individual creation and self-creation is itself a genuine, indeed is the only genuine expression of the nature of reality (Ferry 1993: pp. 167–8). 'The truth' is precisely the multiplicity of truths, and art expresses this better than anything else. 'Neither one of these two terms, objectivity and subjectivity, exists, … there are only interpretations without interpretans or interpretandum, … and this is what justifies the foremost position art should have as the finally adequate expression of the essence of what is, of life or the will to power' (p. 180). This insight, in turn, paves the way for avant-garde art in the twentieth-century—not all avant-garde art, to be sure, since some of it is just classicism in a new disguise, that is, a pretence to have discovered the new but still uniquely right way to view reality—but rather that kind of avant-garde art which recognizes that reality itself is 'chaotic and "different"' and thus can be represented only by art that is itself in incessant revolution (p. 232). Ferry concludes by drawing an ethical lesson from this history: 'the history of aesthetics teaches us—and I believe the lesson is also valid for ethics—that the withdrawal of a shared world is not synonymous with decadence' (p. 259). Rather, he argues, the Nietzschean vision shows the possibility of 'a return of the principle of excellence within the democratic universe' (p. 260), although spelling out just what that means is a task left to political philosophy (about which Ferry has written extensively; see Ferry 1990; Ferry and Renaut 1992).

Another recent French work that looks to the history of modern philosophy to argue for the possibility of continued artistic creativity in a democratic society is

Jean-Marie Schaeffer's *Art of the Modern Age* (Schaeffer 2000). However, Schaeffer argues that, while Kant had already begun to provide room for this possibility, the whole subsequent history of aesthetic theory, not only Hegel but even Nietzsche, places a metaphysical burden upon art that constrains it as a venue for the full expression of creativity and the realization of pleasure of which modern human beings are capable. Schaeffer makes his own position clear at the outset: 'the essentialist quest makes no sense: art is not an object endowed with an internal essence; like every intentional object it is (becomes) what people makes of it—and they make the most diverse things of it' (Schaeffer 2000: 6). But his fundamental antipathy to what he characterizes as the 'speculative theory of Art', whose chief proponents have been the Romantics Novalis and Friedrich Schlegel, Hegel, Schopenhauer, Nietzsche, and Heidegger, does not prevent him from giving detailed and lucid accounts of the views of these figures. His accounts of the complex structure of Hegel's system of aesthetics and of the development of Nietzsche's view of art through three main stages are particularly valuable.

Schaeffer's exposition of Kant begins by stressing the free play of imagination and understanding in the experience of beauty, thus the role for indeterminate concepts only in our response to and judgement of beauty. He then stresses the tension this causes in Kant's thought about art, which is clearly a product of intentional human activity on the one hand, thus imbued with determinate concepts of the ends to be achieved by such activity, yet must be free of constraint by determinate concepts on the other. Schaeffer argues that Kant attempts to resolve this tension through his theory of genius, but that he ends up allowing an unresolved conflict between genius and taste within his conception of artistic production, thereby reproducing rather than resolving the tension (Schaeffer 2000: 40–9); here, however, one might reply that this tension is not so much a theoretical failure as an accurate reflection of the real challenge of achieving a balance between originality and public accessibility in artistic innovation. Schaeffer believes that Kant is more successful in analysing the complex relationship between the aesthetic and the moral, in which works of art can symbolize specific moral ideas without sacrificing the indeterminacy that is essential to the free play of imagination and understanding, while that free play itself, or 'the disinterested pleasure that finality without representation of a specific end elicits', whether induced by a work of art or nature, can serve as a symbol of morality in general, thus constituting 'a symbol of the pleasure that a direct contemplation of the good would provide, if such a direct contemplation were possible' (p. 53). Yet, in the rejection of the Enlightenment that quickly followed its Kantian apotheosis (p. 70), Kant's complex analysis of the delicate relations between the aesthetic and the moral is transformed into the 'sacralization of art' that is at the heart of the 'speculative theory of Art': Kant's thesis that both works of art and aesthetic experience itself can symbolize the morally good is transformed into the thesis that art and only art offers speculative access to the Absolute, or the true nature of reality (p. 53). The imposition of this metaphysical mission on art constrains the possibilities for human creativity in a way that Kant, in spite of his thesis that all art expresses aesthetic, and through them rational, ideas, never intended.

Schaeffer sees the Romantics as rejecting Kant's complex theory of human thought and action and refusing to accept Kant's denial of theoretical rather than only practical insight into the ultimate nature of reality, and then assigning art privileged access to the ultimate reality they imagine we can apprehend.

Romanticism seeks to short-circuit the third *Critique* by reducing the beautiful to the True and by identifying aesthetic experience with the presentative determination of an ontological content. At the same time, we no longer encounter artistic works but only manifestations of Art: if Art reveals Being, then artistic works reveal Art and are to be deciphered as such, that is, as so many empirical realizations of the same ideal essence. (Schaeffer 2000: 71)

Hegel agrees with the Romantics in understanding art as a mode of access to a metaphysical absolute, thus sharing their rejection of Kant's view that it is only as an autonomous venue for the creation of pleasure that aesthetic experience can even symbolize something essential about morality; but he does not see art as the most privileged mode of access to the Absolute, arguing rather that it must be—and indeed has been—superseded first by religion and then by philosophy. Hegel 'retains the heart of the romantic revolution, namely the establishment of Art as ontological knowledge, and hence the definition of artistic practices as having a speculative function', but places art 'lower than philosophy' (Schaeffer 2000: 137). Hegel's subordination of the epistemological role of art to those of religion and philosophy goes hand in hand with a sophisticated analysis of the historical development of the epistemic potential of art and an analysis of the epistemological capabilities of different forms of art: 'Hegel's profound originality resides in the fact that he is the first theorist of art who tries seriously to associate a historical hermeneutics with a semiotic analysis of the arts' (p. 138). These intersecting axes of analysis allow Hegel to develop a far more detailed system of the arts than those of such predecessors as Novalis, Schegel, or F. W. J. Schelling, which Schaeffer describes in useful detail; yet Hegel's preconceptions about the epistemological and metaphysical functions of art still constrain his assessments of the comparative value of the various media of art (p. 174) and of the possibilities for creativity and invention within these various media. Schaeffer thus provides a more complex appraisal of Hegel's contribution to the history of aesthetics than does Ferry, although in the end his appraisal is still negative.

For all his contempt of Hegel, Schopenhauer too saw art as a privileged mode of access to ultimate reality, although of course his conception of reality itself was quite different from that of the absolute idealists: the absolute is not any form of rationality that we can embrace with satisfaction, but an irrational striving that we must learn to renounce. Schaeffer argues that there is tension between Schopenhauer's theory of the Platonic Ideas as the essences captured by the different arts and his 'fundamentally empiricist' theory of knowledge (Schaeffer 2000: 192), which is certainly open to discussion (see Janaway in Jacquette 1996). More convincingly, Schaeffer stresses that in Schopenhauer, as in Hegel, the experience of art does not realize our ultimate attitude to reality: for Schopenhauer as well as Hegel, art must be superseded by philosophy, although for Schopenhauer what philosophy ultimately teaches is resignation in the face of the irrationality of reality rather than reconciliation with its rationality (p. 203).

Schaeffer follows his account of Schopenhauer with an even more illuminating account of Nietzsche. The essence of this account is a tripartite chronology, according to which the Schopenhauerian image of an ecstatic access to Dionysian reality in *The Birth of Tragedy* is superseded first by a genealogical or 'positivist' critique of the pretensions of art, along with those of morality, religion, and philosophy, inaugurated by *Human, All Too Human*, that is in turn superseded by a 'reinterpretation of the question of art within the framework of the theory of the will to power and the eternal return in *Thus Spake Zarathustra*' and other late writings (Schaeffer 2000: 210). The essence of this late view is the recognition that what are, at the second stage of Nietzsche's thought, debunked as mere errors are in fact 'the type of error without which a certain species of living beings cannot live', or are creative assertions of the will to life and power rather than denials of it (p. 231). And the arts epitomize this transformation of error into a new kind of truth: 'the arts, beyond their function as a stimulus to life, paradoxically recover a kind of cognitive bearing: if being is always something created, if the world is a projection or effectuation of the will to power, then the arts, in so far as they present themselves overtly as creations, are the most transparent mode of the projective activity' (p. 233). So in the late Nietzsche the arts regain the potential for genuine creativity that Kant struggled to grant them, although they still carry a heavy philosophical burden, having to reveal 'the structure of the world as a fiction' (p. 234). Here is a contrast with Ferry's Nietzsche, where the arts more simply get to exploit the freedom that this metaphysical fact allows them.

Before the arts can be liberated from a philosophical burden, they must survive their enslavement by Heidegger, who returns to the territory of early Romanticism by enlisting poetry in the service of a philosophy that is supposed to open itself to a Being deeper than anything that can be grasped by mere science and technology. In his final chapter, however, Schaeffer provides a hopeful account of modern art and aesthetic theory as escaping from the constraining influence of the speculative theory of art in general and from the baneful influence of Heidegger in particular. Invoking C. L. Stevenson, in at least one appeal to American philosophy of a sort that is all too rare in these works, Schaeffer argues that we can now see that the speculative theory of art was a persuasive definition, which attempted to restrict the meaning of the term 'art' by endowing it with a laudatory function and shrinking its denotation only to those works showing themselves to be in conformity with this evaluative definition (Schaeffer 2000: 285). Building upon Kant's sense of freedom in artistic creation, however, Schaeffer hopes that we can now see that giving up the speculative theory of art and its essentialist assumptions 'would allow us a more diversified and more fecund perspective on works' of art; it would allow us 'to reinsert art in the highest meaning of the term into the broader field of which it constitutes the richest form', and thus to see that 'the work of art is a product of human creative behaviour, but it is not the only one, nor is it hermetically sealed off from other human works'; and finally, it would allow us to admit the legitimacy of pleasure in our experience of art, to escape from the 'exacerbated Puritanism' of the 'sacralization of the work of art' that 'has led us to cut the work of art off from the gratification it provides' (p. 274).

Schaeffer seems right to argue that the work of creating genuine room for artistic creativity in an age of democratic liberalism was not achieved by the speculative theory of art but remains to be done, although with renewed inspiration from Kant. And one can only hope that his optimism about the future of both art and aesthetic theory is better founded than Eagleton's despair. However, although Schaeffer does briefly mention George Santayana and Nelson Goodman, as well as referring to Arthur Danto in several footnotes, even his optimistic appraisal of the prospects for contemporary art as well as aesthetic theory is unnecessarily hampered by his failure to consider the great figures of twentieth-century Anglo-American aesthetics such as Dewey and Collingwood, and their nineteenth-century predecessors Arnold, Ruskin, and Morris. Ruskin's argument that art can be an expression of human freedom, in his famous chapter on the Gothic in *The Stones of Venice*, which could itself be seen as making more concrete Schiller's conception in his *Kallias* letters of beauty as the image of freedom (see Ellis 1976), and perhaps even more importantly the insight of both Ruskin and Morris that art can introduce elements of both freedom and pleasure into modern life without themselves being expected to bear all the burden of introducing justice into the modern economy and polity, deserve more of a hearing than they get in any of these works. Dewey's argument, also inspired by Schiller, that in aesthetic experience we learn a kind of creativity that we can carry over to the rest of our life, would provide valuable support for Schaeffer's hopeful attempts to overthrow the burdens of the speculative theory of art. And Collingwood's argument, not in the scorned Part I of *The Principles of Art*, where his case against the use of art as 'magic' or propaganda appears to collapse into an extreme form of the doctrine of art for art's sake, but rather in its neglected Part III, where he shows that art provides a valuable vehicle of knowledge, not metaphysical knowledge of some supposed ultimate reality, but self-knowledge of our own emotions, would be a valuable addition to Dewey. An understanding of our own emotions, while hardly a sufficient condition for moral and political progress, is certainly a necessary condition, and that is what Collingwood was attempting to argue, with the spectacle of European fascism and its use of artistic media for the manipulation of human emotions before his eyes. More recently, Richard Wollheim and Stanley Cavell have explored art as a means for self-knowledge, where that is understood primarily psychoanalytically in Wollheim and more broadly in Cavell.

The Eurocentrism common to the works of Eagleton, Ferry, and Schaeffer is as serious a shortcoming in them as is the focus on just a narrow part of eighteenth-century British aesthetics in the work of Stolnitz, Dickie, and Carroll. A history of modern aesthetics that gives proper weight to the enduring contributions of both Dewey and Collingwood—although certainly Dewey if not Collingwood receives some detailed discussion in an older history such as Beardsley (1965)—and then carries the story on to the recent work of figures such as Goodman, Cavell, Wollheim, and Danto, thus remains to be written.

2. Bibliographical Essay

The following survey concentrates on literature published since about 1970 on the major movements and figures in aesthetics from the beginning of the eighteenth to the middle of the twentieth centuries. It is for the most part confined to monographs and essay collections rather than the vast journal literature, although it includes references to articles cited above and a few others. With several exceptions, it is restricted to work in English. Works cited in Section I but not mentioned below are also included in the bibliography that follows.

Several works including surveys of eighteenth-century aesthetics that have not been discussed above but are worth attention are Caygill (1989), Norton (1995), and Mortensen (1997). A number of critical articles on eighteenth-century aesthetics can be found in Mattick (1993). Two major works in contemporary aesthetic theory that are deeply informed by the modern history of aesthetics, and have especially valuable discussions of Hume and Kant, are Savile (1982) and Mothersill (1984); see also Sparshott (1982) and Budd (1995). An idiosyncratic work on the theory of beauty that is deeply informed about the history of aesthetics, ancient and medieval as well as modern, and that also includes an extended argument for the distinction between the theory of beauty and the theory of art, is Kirwan (1999). The only recent extended survey of thought about the sublime is the vastly well informed Saint Girons (1993), but see also several chapters in Crowther (1993); an anthology of eighteenth-century British sources on the sublime is Ashfield and de Bolla (1996). A neglected work on the treatment of the imagination in authors including Hume, Kant, Schelling, and Coleridge is Warnock (1976). A recent introductory work on aesthetics that is historically well informed is Cothey (1990). A general survey of art theory from antiquity to the present, concentrating more on artists and art criticis than on philosophers, is Barasch (1985, 1990, 1998).

The most important works on Shaftesbury remain Stolnitz (1961*a*,*b*), Townsend (1982, 1987), and Kivy (1976*a*: chapter 1); see also Mortensen (1997: chapter 12), and Caygill (1989: chapter 2). The new edition of the *Characteristics* edited by Lawrence E. Klein (Shaftesbury 1999) includes a helpful guide to work on Shaftesbury's moral philosophy and work on him by literary scholars.

The major work on Hutcheson's aesthetics remains Kivy (1976*a*); for his more recent view of Hutcheson, see Kivy (1995). In addition to Dickie (1996), Korsmeyer (1976, 1979*a*,*b*), and Townsend (1987, 1991), see also Michael (1984), Caygill (1989: chapter 2), Matthews (1998), and Mortensen (1997: chapter 14).

The literature on Hume is extensive. An important study of the historical sources as well as philosophical character of Hume's aesthetics is Jones (1982); a systematic survey of Hume's aesthetics including an extensive bibliography is von der Lühe (1996). Most recently, Townsend (2001) offers a detailed treatment of the historical background to Hume's aesthetics as well as a systematic analysis. Current discussion of 'Of the Standard of Taste' begins with Kivy (1967) and Osborne (1967). Subsequent contributions to this discussion, in addition to the chapters in Kivy (1976*a*), Mothersill (1984) and Dickie (1996), include Korsmeyer (1976, 1995); Wieand (1983); Carroll (1984), Kivy (1989); Mothersill (1989); Shusterman (1989), also reprinted in Mattick (1993); Guyer (1993*b*); Savile (1993: chapter 4); Cohen (1994); Gracyk (1994); Shelley (1998); and Levinson (2002). For a treatment of Hume's concept of imagination in the context of his aesthetics, see Warnock (1976: part II).

Philosophers have done little with Burke. In addition to treatments in Caygill (1989) and Saint Girons (1993), see the literary theorists Weiskel (1976) and Ferguson (1992). Adam Smith, who is largely neglected in general histories of his aesthetics, is touched upon in Caygill (1989); two works devoted primarily to his moral and political philosophy, Fleischacker (1999) and Griswold (1999), do include some discussion of his theory of aesthetic judgement. Thomas Reid's aesthetics have been discussed in Kivy (1976*b*), Gracyk (1987), and Nauckhoff (1994). Alexander Gerard's theory of genius is discussed in Kivy (2001).

Literature in English on German aesthetics before Kant remains limited. Monographs on Baumgarten are available only in German; see especially Franke (1972) and Solms (1990). For briefer treatments in English, however, see Gregor (1983) and the extended discussion in Caygill (1989: especially 148–71). Moses Mendelssohn's work has become available in English in Daniel Dahlstrom's edition of Mendelssohn (1997). For discussion of Mendelssohn, see Guyer (1993*a*: chapter 4). Baumgarten, his disciple Georg Friedrich Meier, and Mendelssohn are also discussed in a work focusing primarily on Mendelssohn's friend and collaborator Gotthold Ephraim Lessing in Wellbery (1984); on Lessing, see also Wellbery (1984), which includes chapters on Wolff, Baumgarten, and Mendelssohn as well as a detailed study of Lessing's *Laocoön*, and Savile (1987: chapters 1–3). A discussion of Lessing in the context of theories of the depiction of the body by contemporaries including Winckelmann, Herder, and Goethe is Richter (1992). The anti-rationalist Johann Herder is also discussed in Solms (1990), and has received book-length treatment in English in Norton (1991). A detailed study of German theories of artistic genius from the eighteenth to the twentieth centuries is Schmidt (1985).

There has been an enormous amount of publication on Kant's aesthetics, and with one exception the following list will be confined to monographs. Contemporary discussions of Kant's aesthetics begin with Crawford (1974), Guyer (1997; first published 1979) and Schaper (1979). The most recent monograph on Kant's theory of taste is Allison (2001). Guyer (1993a) places Kant's aesthetics in historical context, discussing his relation to British aesthetics, Mendelssohn, Karl Philipp Moritz, Schiller, and Hegel, and also discusses topics omitted from Guyer (1997) such as the sublime and in general the relation of Kant's aesthetics to his moral theory. Guyer (1997) adds a chapter on Kant's conception of the fine arts to its original 1979 edition. A controversial interpretation of Kant's theory of art is Kemal (1986); Pillow (2000) argues that it is Kant's analysis of the sublime rather than of the beautiful that grounds his theory of art. Other work on the relation between Kant's aesthetics and his moral philosophy include the essay by Cohen in Cohen and Guyer (1982), Rogerson (1986), and especially the judicious treatment in Savile (1987); for further work by Savile on Kant and art, see Savile (1993). See also Recki (2001). Kant's theory of genius is treated in Kivy (2001). An extended treatment of Kant on the sublime is Crowther (1989); an important critique of Kant's treatment of the sublime is Budd (1998); and samples of French 'deconstructive' and 'postmodernist' interpretations of Kant are Derrida (1987) and Lyotard (1994), which also focuses on the sublime. In addition to Warnock (1976), a more recent attempt to interpret Kant's aesthetics in light of his general conception of the imagination is Gibbons (1994); another recent work that situates Kant's aesthetics in his general theory of the mind is Matthews (1997). A hermeneutical approach to Kant's aesthetics is offered in Makkreel (1990). A brief introduction to Kant's aesthetics by a distinguished German scholar is in Henrich (1992). See also Wieland (2002). A controversial interpretation of the development of Kant's aesthetics is Zammito (1992), now supplemented by Zammito (2001); a better account of this topic is Dumouchel (1999). Extensive bibliographies of work on Kant's aesthetics can be found in Cohen and Guyer (1982) (along with important articles by Guyer, Aquila, Savile, and Crawford); Meerbote and Hudson (1991); and Parrett (1998), which is a vast anthology of articles in several languages, including valuable papers by Crowther, Guyer, Kemal, Kneller, Ameriks, Allison, Makkreel, and others.

A general treatment of Schiller's philosophical works, including his aesthetics, is Miller (1972). Schiller's 1793 *Kallias* letters, his first treatment of beauty, have been studied in Ellis (1976); a detailed study of the 1795 *Letters on the Aesthetic Education of Mankind* is Murray (1994). Other work on Schiller's aesthetics includes Podro (1972), which also discusses Kant, Herbart, and Schopenhauer; Schaper (1979: chapter 5); Henrich in Cohen and Guyer (1982); Savile (1987); Chytry (1989: chapter 3);

Sychrava (1989); Norton (1995: chapter 6); and Martin (1996). Both Herder and Schiller are discussed by Dahlstrom in Ameriks (2000).

German idealism has been the object of intensive study in recent years. There are surveys of the aesthetic theories of the German Romantics and absolute idealists by Charles Larmore and Andrew Bowie in Ameriks (2000) and Larmore (1996); a far more detailed study, beginning with Baumgarten and Kant and continuing through the high Romantics such as Solger and Tieck, is Frank (1989). See also Beiser (2002) and Richards (2002). The major event for the study of F. W. J. Schelling's aesthetics in English has been the translation of his lectures on *The Philosophy of Fine Art* in Schelling (1989); these reveal Schelling to have provided an interesting alternative to Hegel's historical determinism and 'death of art' thesis. For commentary, see Bowie (1990: chapter 4; 1993: chapter 3). The hermeneutical theory of Friedrich Schleimacher has also been made available to English readers by a new translation, Schleiermacher (1998); for commentary, see Bowie (1997: chapter 5). Hegel has certainly received the most attention, however. A new translation of Hegel's lectures on the fine arts was published in Hegel (1975). A reliable overview of Hegel's aesthetics is provided by Robert Wicks in Beiser (1993), and a more detailed study, focusing on Hegel's treatments of the visual arts and literature, is Bungay (1984). A more speculative interpretation of Hegel's philosophy as a whole from the point of view of his aesthetics is offered in Desmond (1986). For an extended contrast between Kant and Hegel, see Pillow (2000). Wyss (1999) analyses Hegel's influence on later speculative theories of art history; for the influence of Hegel on more traditional art historians, see Podro (1982). Arthur Danto has appealed to Hegel for support of his own theory of the end of the project of modern painting throughout Danto (1997). A variety of new essays on Hegel's aesthetics can be found in Maker (2000).

Schopenhauer's thesis that aesthetic experience offers an escape from the frustrations of desire as well as from the tension between that thesis and his equally well-known thesis that music—in his view the highest form of art—offers direct access to the will that lies beneath appearance, are both central to his philosophy; thus, the analysis of his aesthetic theory is prominent in all surveys of Schopenhauer's philosophy. For an overview, see Young (1987) and Levinson (1998). A recent collection devoted especially to Schopenhauer's aesthetics is Jacquette (1996), which includes essays touching on those themes by Christopher Janaway, John Atwell, and Paul Guyer, as well as related essays by Julian Young and Cheryl Foster, who also writes on Schopenhauer's aesthetics in Janaway (1999). That volume also includes Martha Nussbaum's treatment of the relation between Schopenhauer and Nietzsche's views in *The Birth of Tragedy*, a theme also studied by Ivan Soll in Janaway (1998). The topic of art is equally central to the thought of Nietzsche, in both his youthful work, *The Birth of Tragedy* (1872) and his later works, especially *Human, All Too Human* (1878) and *The Gay Science* (1882). Young (1992) offers a survey and critique of the treatment of art in all of Nietzsche's major works. Raymond Geuss's introduction to Nietzsche (1999) is a useful short survey of *The Birth of Tragedy*, while Silk and

Stern (1981) is an exhaustive work, including treatments of the book's relation to more orthodox classical philology and to earlier German aesthetic theory as well as a treatment of its reception. Staten (1990) is an important study of Nietzsche's psychology of morality that makes extensive use of *The Birth of Tragedy*, and also includes a critical analysis of leading 'deconstructive' readings of the work by Paul de Man and Philippe Lacoue-Labarthe. The primary exemplar of the 'deconstructive' approach to Nietzsche, however, is Derrida (1979). The major work on Nietzsche's later philosophy of art is Nehamas (1985), which explores Nietzsche's use of the idea of artistic creation as an image for self-fashioning in general; see also Nehamas (1998: chapter 5). On Nietzsche's relation to more recent conceptions of 'modernity' in art, see the essay by Nehamas in Magnus and Higgins (1996) as well as Rampley (2000). Nietzsche's relation to Schiller rather than Schopenhauer is studied in Martin (1996). Finally, Kemal *et al.* (1998) offers essays on a variety of themes in Nietzsche's treatment of art, including useful essays by Randall Havas, Aaron Ridley, Henry Staten, and Salim Kemal Another major figure from the end of the nineteenth century is, of course, Tolstoy; his aesthetic theory receives book-length treatment in Diffey (1985) and a briefer treatment in Lyas (1997) and Graham (2000); Lyas's introductory work also includes an interesting discussion of Bendedetto Croce, whose work in aesthetics, very influential in the first decades of the twentieth century, has lately been neglected. Lyas has also produced a new translation of the systematic portion of Croce's chief work in aesthetics in Croce (1992), although for a translation of Croce's history of aesthetics one must still go to Croce (1922).

Marxist aesthetics, especially in the twentieth rather than nineteenth century, is a broad subject. Surveys include Arvon (1973) and Jameson (1971). A study of Marx's own scattered remarks on the visual arts is M. Rose (1984). Marcuse (1978) and Bourdieu (1984) are both recent works in a strongly Marxist vein, in addition to the work of Eagleton discussed above. Most recently, the work of the unorthodox Marxists or 'critical theorists' Theodore Adorno and Walter Benjamin have received the most attention. For Adorno, see G. Rose (1978), Jameson (1990), Zuidevaart (1991), Bernstein (1992, 2001), Nicholson (1997), and the collection of essays Huhn and Zuidevaart (1997). For Benjamin, see Wolin (1982), Buck-Morss (1989), and Caygill (1998). Both figures are also discussed in Bowie (1997).

The vast work of John Ruskin had an enormous influence on many areas of both artistic practice and theory in the nineteenth and earlier twentieth century, including philosophical aesthetics, in writers from Bernard Bosanquet to R. G. Collingwood, but has been little studied by philosophers in recent years. For a general survey of his life and works, see Hilton (1985, 2000); for a study of his aesthetic theory in particular, see Landow (1971). Collingwood's philosophy of art has also not received as much attention recently as it deserves. Apart from the brief general introduction (Johnson 1998) and the even briefer introduction to Collingwood's aesthetics (Ridley 1999), which does contain a good list of recent journal articles, one must still turn to the older Donagan (1962) and the collection Krausz (1972), which contains a particularly useful survey of Collingwood's philosophy of art by Peter Jones. The aesthetics of John Dewey has recently been receiving more attention than that of Collingwood, including monographs by Alexander (1987), Shusterman (1991), and Jackson (1998), as well as the collection of essays edited by Seiple and Haskins (1998).

'Analytical' aesthetics since the 1950s has yet to receive a full-dress history, but see Lüdeking (1988) for a start. The single largest influence on analytical aesthetics has been the work of Ludwig Wittgenstein, primarily his general work (Wittgenstein 1953) rather than the two slender volumes containing some explicit remarks on art and the aesthetic (Wittgenstein 1967, 1980). (However, the suggestion in Wittgenstein 1967 that the term 'beauty' is just a provocation for discussion rather than a genuine predicate has been influential.) Wittgenstein's critique of philosophical theory itself was the source of doubts about the very possibility of aesthetic theory in the 1950s and 1960s; see especially the paper by Kennick in Barrett (1965). Wittgenstein's idea that concepts convey family resemblances rather than determinate necessary and sufficient conditions was the source for the attack upon the possibility of a traditional definition of art beginning with Mandelbaum (1965); for a survey of this movement, see Davies (1991). This aspect of Wittgenstein's work was also the source for Frank Sibley's approach to aesthetic concepts; see Sibley's paper in Barrett (1965) and Sibley (2001); for a collection of papers on Sibley's work, see Brady and Levinson (2001). Wittgenstein's attack upon traditional conceptions of introspective access to mental phenomena lies behind Dickie's attack upon the concept of aesthetic experience and his use of the externally accessible 'artworld' instead in his definition of art; see Dickie (1974). Wittgenstein's attack upon the separation of perception and interpretation, exemplified in his conception of 'seeing as', influenced the work of Richard Wollheim, particularly Wollheim (1980, 1987), and Roger Scruton, particularly Scruton (1974, 1979); see also van Gerwen (2001). Finally, Wittgenstein's rejection of the idea of privileged self-knowledge was influential on the work of Stanley Cavell, especially Cavell (1969, 1979). For general works on Wittgenstein and aesthetics, see Hagberg (1994, 1995), Cometti (1996), Allen and Turvey (2001), and Lewis (2002).

Among subsequent influential analytical aestheticians, Nelson Goodman's work, especially Goodman (1968), was the focus of a special issue of *Theoria* in 1973; Goodman's subsequent work in aesthetics is represented in Goodman (1972, 1978, 1984). George Dickie's work is the focus of the essays in Yanal (1994). Arthur Danto's work, especially Danto (1981, 1986), is addressed by the essays in Rollins (1993).

Martin Heidegger has certainly been as influential on aesthetic thought in the second half of the twentieth century as Wittgenstein, although not as influential on the way aesthetics has been practised in American and British philosophy departments. Heidegger's most famous work in aesthetics was his essay, originally written in the 1930s although not published until the 1950s, 'On the Origin of the

Work of Art'; a translation is in Heidegger (1971). Heidegger's thesis here, that works of art put us in touch with 'Being' in a way that ordinary concepts do not, is reminiscent of Schopenhauer's view that music directly expresses the nature of the will as the basis of all appearance. Heidegger's writings on the German poet Friedrich Hölderlin have also been influential, for instance on the literary critic Paul de Man: see de Man (1983). For commentary on Heidegger, see Kockelmans (1985), Harries and Jamme (1994), and Young (2001). Among those influenced by Heidegger are Hans-Georg Gadamer, in Gadamer (1975, 1986), and Jacques Derrida, in Derrida (1979). For an alternative to Heidegger's approach to Hölderlin, see Henrich (1997).

BIBLIOGRAPHY

Alexander, T. M. (1987). *John Dewey's Theory of Art, Experience, and Nature: The Horizons of Feeling.* Albany, NY: State University of New York Press.

Allen, R. and Turvey, M. (eds.) (2001). *Wittgenstein, Theory, and the Arts.* London and New York: Routledge.

Allison, H. E. (2001). *Kant's Theory of Taste.* Cambridge: Cambridge University Press.

Ameriks, K. (2000). *The Cambridge Companion to German Idealism.* Cambridge: Cambridge University Press.

Arvon, H. (1973). *Marxist Aesthetics,* trans. H. Lane. Ithaca, NY: Cornell University Press.

Ashfield, A. and de Bolla, P. (eds.) (1996). *The Sublime: A Reader in Eighteenth-Century Aesthetic Theory.* Cambridge: Cambridge University Press.

Barasch, M. (1985). *Theories of Art from Plato to Winckelmann.* New York: New York University Press.

—— (1990). *Modern Theories of Art, 1: From Winckelmann to Baudelaire.* New York: New York University Press.

—— (1998). *Modern Theories of Art, 2: From Impressionism to Kandinsky.* New York: New York University Press.

Barrett, C. (ed.) (1965). *Collected Papers on Aesthetics.* Oxford: Basil Blackwell.

Beardsley, M. C. (1965). *Aesthetics from Classical Greece to the Present: A Short History.* University, Ala.: University of Alabama Press.

Beiser, F. C. (1993). *The Cambridge Companion to Hegel.* Cambridge: Cambridge University Press.

—— (2002). *German Idealism: The Struggle against Subjectivism 1781–1801.* Cambridge, Mass.: Harvard University Press.

Belfiore, E. S. (1992). *Tragic Pleasures: Aristotle on Plot and Emotion.* Princeton: Princeton University Press.

Bernstein, J. M. (1992). *The Fate of Art: Aesthetic Alienation from Kant to Derrida and Adorno.* University Park, Pa.: Pennsylvania State University Press.

—— (2001). *Adorno: Disenchantment and Ethics.* Cambridge: Cambridge University Press.

Bourdieu, P. (1984). *Distinction: A Social Critique of the Judgment of Taste.* Cambridge, Mass.: Harvard University Press.

Bowie, A. (1990). *Aesthetics and Subjectivity from Kant to Nietzsche.* Manchester: Manchester University Press.

—— (1993). *Schelling and Modern European Philosophy: An Introduction.* London and New York: Routledge.

—— (1997). *From Romanticism to Critical Theory: The Philosophy of German Literary Theory*. London and New York: Routledge.

Brady, E. and Levinson, J. (eds.) (2001). *Aesthetic Concepts: Essays after Sibley*. Oxford: Clarendon Press.

Buck-Morss, S. (1989). *The Dialectics of Seeing: Walter Benjamin and the Arcades Project*. Cambridge, Mass.: MIT Press.

Budd, M. (1995). *Values of Art: Pictures, Poetry and Music*. London: Allen Lane/The Penguin Press.

—— (1998). 'Delight in the Natural World: Kant on the Aesthetic Appreciation of Nature'. *British Journal of Aesthetics* 38: 1–18, 117–26, 233–50.

—— (2001). 'The Pure Judgement of Taste as an Aesthetic Reflective Judgment'. *British Journal of Aesthetics* 41: 247–60.

Bullough, E. (1957). *Aesthetics: Lectures and Essays*, ed. E. M. Wilkinson. Stanford, Calif.: Stanford University Press.

Bungay, S. (1984). *Beauty and Truth: A Study of Hegel's Aesthetics*. Oxford: Clarendon Press.

Carroll, N. (1984). 'Hume's Standard of Taste'. *Journal of Aesthetics and Art Criticism* 43: 181–94.

—— (1991). 'Beauty and the Genealogy of Art Theory'. *Philosophical Forum* 22: 307–34.

—— (2001). *Beyond Aesthetics: Philosophical Essays*. Cambridge: Cambridge University Press.

Cavell, S. (1969). *Must We Mean What We Say?* New York: Scribners.

—— (1979). *The Claim of Reason*. New York: Oxford University Press.

Caygill, H. (1989). *Art of Judgement*. Oxford: Blackwell.

—— (1998). *Walter Benjamin: The Colour of Experience*. London: Routledge.

Chytry, J. (1989). *The Aesthetic State: A Quest in Modern German Thought*. Berkeley and Los Angeles: University of California Press.

Cohen, T. (1994). 'Partial Enchantments of the Quixote Story in Hume's Essay on Taste'. In R. J. Yanal (ed.), *Institutions of Art*. University Park, Pa.: Pennsylvania State University Press, pp. 145–56.

—— (2002). 'Three Problems in Kant's Aesthetics'. *British Journal of Aesthetics* 42: 1–12.

—— and Guyer, P. (eds.) (1982). *Essays in Kant's Aesthetics*. Chicago: University of Chicago Press.

Cometti, J.-P. (1996). *Philosopher avec Wittgenstein*. Paris: Presses Universitaires de France.

Cooper, A. A. *see* Shaftesbury.

Cothey, A. L. (1990). *The Nature of Art*. London and New York: Routledge.

Crawford, D. W. (1974). *Kant's Aesthetic Theory*. Madison, Wis.: University of Wisconsin Press.

Croce, B. (1922). *Aesthetic as Science of Expression and General Linguistic*, trans. D. Ainslie. London: Macmillan.

—— (1992). *The Aesthetic as the Science of Expression and of the Linguistic in General*, trans. C. Lyas. Cambridge: Cambridge University Press.

Crowther, P. (1989). *The Kantian Sublime: From Morality to Art*. Oxford: Clarendon Press.

—— (1993). *Critical Aesthetics and Postmodernism*. Oxford: Clarendon Press.

Danto, A. (1981). *The Transfiguration of the Commonplace*. Cambridge, Mass.: Harvard University Press.

—— (1986). *The Philosophical Disenfranchisement of Art*. New York: Columbia University Press.

Danto, A. (1997). *After the End of Art: Contemporary Art and the Pale of History.* Princeton: Princeton University Press.

Davies, S. (1991). *Definitions of Art.* Ithaca, NY: Cornell University Press.

de Man, P. (1983). *Blindness and Insight.* Minneapolis: University of Minnesota Press.

Derrida, J. (1979). *Spurs: Nietzsche's Styles,* trans. B. Harlow. Chicago: University of Chicago Press.

—— (1987). *The Truth in Painting,* trans. G. Bennington and I. McLeod. Chicago: University of Chicago Press.

Desmond, W. (1996). *Art and the Absolute: A Study of Hegel's Aesthetics.* Albany, NY: State University of New York Press.

Dickie, G. (1974). *Art and the Aesthetic: An Institutional Analysis.* Ithaca, NY: Cornell University Press.

—— (1996). *The Century of Taste: The Philosophical Odyssey of Taste in the Eighteenth Century.* New York: Oxford University Press.

Diffey, T. J. (1986). *Tolstoy's 'What is Art?'.* London: Croom Helm.

Donagan, A. (1962). *The Later Philosophy of R. G. Collingwood.* Oxford: Clarendon Press.

Dumouchel, D. (1999). *Kant et la Genèse de la Subjectivite esthétique.* Paris: Vrin.

Eagleton, T. (1990). *The Ideology of the Aesthetic.* Oxford: Blackwell.

Ellis, J. M. (1976). *Schiller's 'Kalliasbriefe' and the Study of his Aesthetic Theory.* The Hague: Mouton.

Ferguson, F. (1992). *Solitude and the Sublime: Romanticism and the Aesthetics of Individuation.* London and New York: Routledge.

Ferry, L. (1990). *Rights: The New Quarrel between the Ancients and the Moderns,* trans. F. Philip. Chicago: University of Chicago Press.

—— (1993). *Homo aestheticus: The Invention of Taste in the Democratic Age,* trans. R. de Loaiza. Chicago: University of Chicago Press (translation of *Homo Aestheticus: L'invention du goût à l'âge démocratique.* Paris: Editions Grasset & Fasquelle, 1990).

—— and Renaut, A. (1992). *From the Rights of Man to the Republican Idea.* Chicago: University of Chicago Press.

Fleischacker, S. (1999). *A Third Concept of Liberty: Judgment and Freedom in Kant and Adam Smith.* Princeton: Princeton University Press.

Frank, M. (1989). *Einführung in die frühromantische Ästhetik: Vorlesungen.* Frankfurt am Main: Suhrkamp.

Franke, U. (1972). *Kunst al Erkenntnis: Die Rolle der Sinnlichkeit in der Ästhetik Alexander Gottlieb Baumgartens.* Studia Leibnitiana, Supplementa, Band 9. Wiesbaden: Steiner.

Gadamer, H.-G. (1975). *Truth and Method,* trans. G. Barden and J. Cumming. New York: Seabury Press.

—— (1986). *The Relevance of the Beautiful and Other Essays,* trans. N. Walker, ed. R. Bernasconi. Cambridge: Cambridge University Press.

Gibbons, S. (1994). *Kant's Theory of Imagination: Bridging Gaps in Judgement and Experience.* Oxford: Clarendon Press.

Goodman, N. (1968). *The Languages of Art.* Indianapolis, Ind.: Bobbs-Merrill.

—— (1972). *Problems and Projects.* Indianapolis, Ind.: Bobbs-Merrill.

—— (1978). *Ways of Worldmaking.* Indianapolis, Ind.: Hackett.

—— (1984). *Of Mind and Other Matters.* Cambridge, Mass.: Harvard University Press.

Gracyk, T. (1987). 'The Failure of Thomas Reid's Aesthetics'. *Monist* 70: 465–82.

—— (1994). 'Rethinking Hume's Standard of Taste'. *Journal of Aesthetics and Art Criticism* 52: 168–82.

Graham, G. (2000). *Philosophy of the Arts*, 2nd edn. New York: Routledge.

Gregor, M. J. (1983). 'Baumgarten's *Aesthetica*'. *Review of Metaphysics* 37: 357–85.

Griswold, C. L., Jr (1999). *Adam Smith and the Virtues of Enlightenment.* Cambridge: Cambridge University Press.

Guyer, P. (1993*a*). *Kant and the Experience of Freedom.* Cambridge: Cambridge University Press.

—— (1993*b*). 'The Standard of Taste and the Most Ardent Desire of Society', in T. Cohen, P. Guyer, and H. Putnam (eds.), *Pursuits of Reason: Essays in Honor of Stanley Cavell.* Lubbock, Tex.: Texas Tech University Press, pp. 37–66.

—— (1997/ 1979). *Kant and the Claims of Taste*, 2nd edn. Cambridge: Cambridge University Press (first published 1979).

—— (forthcoming). 'Form and Feeling: Art at the Turn of the Century', in T. Baldwin (ed.), *Cambridge History of Philosophy, 1870–1945.* Cambridge: Cambridge University Press.

Hagberg, G. (1994). *Meaning and Interpretation: Wittgenstein, Henry James and Literary Knowledge.* Ithaca, NY: Cornell University Press.

—— (1995). *Art as Language: Wittgenstein, Meaning, and Literary Theory.* Ithaca, NY: Cornell University Press.

Halliwell, S. (1986). *Aristotle's Poetics.* Chapel Hill, NC: University of North Carolina Press.

Harries, K. and Jamme, C. (eds.) (1994). *Martin Heidegger: Politics, Art, and Technology.* New York: Holmers & Meier.

Hegel, G. W. F. (1975). *Aesthetics: Lectures on Fine Art*, 2 vols., trans. T. M. Knox. Oxford: Clarendon Press.

Heidegger, M. (1971). *Poetry, Language, Thought*, trans. A. Hofstadter. New York: Harper & Row.

Henrich, D. (1992). *Aesthetic Judgement and the Moral Image of the World: Studies in Kant.* Stanford, Calif.: Stanford University Press.

—— (1997). *The Course of Remembrance and Other Essays on Hölderlin*, trans. E. Förster. Stanford, Calif.: Stanford University Press.

Hilton, T. (1985). *John Ruskin: The Early Years.* New Haven: Yale University Press.

—— (2000). *John Ruskin: The Later Years.* New Haven: Yale University Press.

Huhn, T. and Zuidevaart, L. (eds.) (1997). *The Semblance of Subjectivity: Essays in Adorno's Aesthetic Theory.* Cambridge, Mass.: MIT Press.

Hume, D. (1963). *Essays Moral, Political, and Literary.* Oxford: Oxford University Press.

—— (2000). *A Treatise of Human Nature*, ed. D. Fate Norton and M. J. Norton. Oxford: Oxford University Press.

Hutcheson, F. (1738). *An Inquiry into the Original of our Ideas of Beauty and Virtue*, 4th edn. London: D. Midwinter.

Jackson, P. W. (1998). *John Dewey and the Lessons of Art.* New Haven: Yale University Press.

Jacquette, D. (ed.) (1996). *Schopenhauer, Philosophy, and the Arts.* Cambridge: Cambridge University Press.

Jameson, F. (1971). *Marxism and Form: Twentieth Century Dialectical Theories of Literature.* Princeton: Princeton University Press.

—— (1990). *Late Marxism: Adorno, or, the Persistence of the Dialectic.* London and New York: Verso Press.

Janaway, C. (1995). *Images of Excellence: Plato's Critique of the Arts.* Oxford: Clarendon Press.

Janaway, C. (ed.) (1998). *Willing and Nothingness: Schopenhauer as Nietzsche's Educator*. Oxford: Clarendon Press.

—— (ed.) (1999). *The Cambridge Companion to Schopenhauer*. Cambridge: Cambridge University Press.

Johnson, P. (1998). *R. G. Collingwood: An Introduction*. Bristol: Thoemmes Press.

Jones, P. (1982). *Hume's Sentiments: Their Ciceronian and French Context*. Edinburgh: Edinburgh University Press.

Kant, I. (2000). *Critique of the Power of Judgement*, ed. P. Guyer, trans. P. Guyer and E. Matthews. Cambridge: Cambridge University Press.

Kemal, S. (1986). *Kant and Fine Art: An Essay on Kant and the Philosophy of Fine Art and Culture*. Oxford: Clarendon Press.

—— Del Caro, A., Conway, D., and Gaskell, I. (eds.) (1998). *Nietzsche, Philosophy, and the Arts*. Cambridge: Cambridge University Press.

Kirwan, J. (1999). *Beauty*. Manchester: Manchester University Press.

Kivy, P. (1967). 'Hume's Standard of Taste: Breaking the Circle'. *British Journal of Aesthetics* 7: 57–66.

—— (1976a). *The Seventh Sense: A Study of Francis Hutcheson's Aesthetics and its Influence in Eighteenth-Century Britain*. New York: Burt Franklin.

—— (1976b). 'The Logic of Taste: Reid and the Second Fifty Years'. In S. F. Barker and T. L. Beauchamp (eds.), *Thomas Reid: Critical Interpretations*. Philadelphia: Temple University Press, pp. 118–32.

—— (1989). 'Recent Scholarship and the British Tradition: A Logic of Taste—The First Fifty Years'. In G. Dickie, R. Sclafani, and R. Roblin (eds.), *Aesthetics: A Critical Anthology*. New York: St Martin's Press.

—— (1995). 'The "Sense" of Beauty and the "Sense" of Art: Hutcheson's Place in the History and Practice of Aesthetics'. *Journal of Aesthetics and Art Criticism* 29: 349–57.

—— (2001). *The Possessor and the Possessed: Handel, Mozart, Beethoven, and the Idea of Musical Genius*. New Haven: Yale University Press.

Kockelmans, J. (1985). *Heidegger on Art and Art Works*. Dordrecht: Kluwer.

Korsmeyer, C. W. (1976). 'Hume and the Foundations of Taste'. *Journal of Aesthetics and Art Criticism* 35: 201–15.

—— (1979a) 'Relativism and Hutcheson's Aesthetic Theory'. *Journal of the History of Ideas* 36: 319–30.

—— (1979b). 'The Two Beauties: A Perspective on Hutcheson's Aesthetics'. *Journal of Aesthetics and Art Criticism* 38: 145–51.

—— (1995). 'Gendered Concepts and Hume's Standard of Taste'. In P. Z. Brand and C. Korsmeyer (eds.), *Feminism and Tradition in Aesthetics*. University Park, Penna: Pennsylvania State University Press.

Krausz, M. (ed.) (1972). *Critical Essays on the Philosophy of R. G. Collingwood*. Oxford: Clarendon Press.

Landow, G. P. (1971). *The Aesthetic and Critical Theories of John Ruskin*. Princeton: Princeton University Press.

Larmore, C. (1996). *The Romantic Legacy*. New York: Columbia University Press.

Levinson, J. (1998). 'Schopenhauer, Arthur'. In M. Kelly (ed.), *Encyclopedia of Aesthetics*, vol. 4. Oxford: Oxford University Press, pp. 245–50.

—— (2002). 'Hume's Standard of Taste: The Real Problem', *Journal of Aesthetics and Art Criticism* 59: 227–38.

Lewis, P. (ed.) (2002). *Wittgenstein, Philosophy, and the Arts*. Aldershot: Ashgate.

Lüdeking, K. (1988). *Analytische Philosophie der Kunst*. Frankfurt am Main: Athenäum.

Lyas, C. (1997). *Aesthetics: An Introduction*. Montreal and Kingston: McGill-Queen's University Press.

Lyotard, J.-F. (1994). *Lessons on the Analytic of the Sublime*, trans. E. Rottenberg. Stanford, Calif.: Stanford University Press.

Magnus, B. and Higgins, K. M. (eds.) (1996). *The Cambridge Companion to Nietzsche*. Cambridge: Cambridge University Press.

Maker, W. (ed.) (2000). *Hegel and Aesthetics*. Albany, NY: State University of New York Press.

Makkreel, R. A. (1990). *Imagination and Interpretation in Kant: The Hermeneutical Import of the Critique of Judgment*. Chicago: University of Chicago Press.

Mandelbaum, M. (1965). 'Family Resemblances and Generalizations concerning the Arts', *American Philosophical Quarterly* 2: 219–28.

Marcuse, H. (1978). *The Aesthetic Dimension: Towards a Critique of Marxist Aesthetics*. Boston: Beacon Press.

Martin, N. (1996). *Nietzsche and Schiller: Untimely Aesthetics*. Oxford: Clarendon Press.

Matthews, P. M. (1997). *The Significance of Beauty: Kant on Feeling and the System of the Mind*. Dordrecht: Kluwer Academic.

—— (1998). 'Hutcheson on the Idea of Beauty'. *Journal of the History of Philosophy* 36: 233–60.

Mattick, P. (ed.) (1993). *Eighteenth-Century Aesthetics and the Reconstitution of Art*. Cambridge: Cambridge University Press.

Meerbote, R. and Hudson, H. (eds.) (1991). *Kant's Aesthetics*. North American Kant Society Studies in Philosophy, vol. 1. Atascadero, Calif.: Ridgeview.

Mendelssohn, M. (1997). *Philosophical Writings*, ed. D. O. Dahlstrom. Cambridge: Cambridge University Press.

Michael, E. (1984). 'Francis Hutcheson on Aesthetic Perception and Aesthetic Pleasure'. *British Journal of Aesthetics* 24: 241–55.

Miller, R. D. (1972). *Schiller and the Ideal of Freedom: A Study of Schiller's Philosophical Works with Chapters on Kant*. Oxford: Clarendon Press.

Mortensen, P. (1997). *Art in the Social Order: The Making of the Modern Conception of Art*. Albany, NY: State University of New York Press.

Mothersill, M. (1984). *Beauty Restored*. Oxford: Clarendon Press.

—— (1989). 'Hume and the Paradox of Taste'. In G. Dickie, R. Sclafani, and R. Roblin (eds.), *Aesthetics: A Critical Anthology*, 2nd edn. New York: St Martin's Press, pp. 269–86.

Murray, P. T. (1994). *The Development of German Aesthetic Theory from Kant to Schiller: A Philosophical Commentary on Schiller's Aesthetic Education of Man*. Lewiston, NY: Edwin Mellen Press.

Nauckhoff, J. (1994). 'Objectivity and Expression in Thomas Reid's Aesthetics', *Journal of Aesthetics and Art Criticism* 52: 183–91.

Nehamas, A. (1985). *Nietzsche: Life as Literature*. Cambridge, Mass.: Harvard University Press.

—— (1998). *The Art of Living: Socratic Reflections from Plato to Foucault*. Berkeley and Los Angeles: University of California Press.

—— (1999). *Virtues of Authenticity: Essays on Plato and Socrates*. Princeton: Princeton University Press.

Nicholson, S. W. (1997). *Exact Imagination, Late Work: On Adorno's Aesthetics*. Cambridge, Mass.: MIT Press.

Nietzsche, F. (1996). *Human, All Too Human*, trans. R. J. Hollingdale. Cambridge: Cambridge University Press.

—— (1999). *The Birth of Tragedy*, trans. R. Spiers. Cambridge: Cambridge University Press.

—— (2002). *The Gay Science*, trans. J. Nauckhoff. Cambridge: Cambridge University Press.

Norton, R. E. (1991). *Herder's Aesthetics and the European Enlightenment*. Ithaca, NY: Cornell University Press.

—— (1995). *The Beautiful Soul: Aesthetic Morality in the Eighteenth Century*. Ithaca, NY: Cornell University Press.

Nussbaum, M. (1986). *The Fragility of Goodness: Luck and Ethics in Greek Tragedy and Philosophy*. Cambridge: Cambridge University Press.

Osborne, H. (1967). 'Hume's Standard and the Diversity of Aesthetic Taste'. *British Journal of Aesthetics* 7: 50–6.

Parret, H. (ed.) (1998). *Kants Ästhetik–Kant's Aesthetics–L'esthétique de Kant*. Berlin and New York: de Gruyter.

Pillow, K. (2000). *Sublime Understanding: Aesthetic Reflection in Kant and Hegel*. Cambridge, Mass.: MIT Press.

Podro, M. (1972). *The Manifold in Perception: Theories of Art from Kant to Hildebrand*. Oxford: Clarendon Press.

—— (1982). *The Critical Historians of Art*. New Haven: Yale University Press.

Rampley, M. (2000). *Nietzsche, Aesthetics and Modernity*. Cambridge: Cambridge University Press.

Recki, B. (2001). *Ästhetik der Sitten: Die Affinität von ästhetischem Gefühl und praktischer Vernunft bei Kant*. Frankfurt am Main: Vittorio Klostermann.

Richards, R. J. (2002). *The Romantic Conception of Life: Science and Philosophy in the Age of Goethe*. Chicago: University of Chicago Press.

Richter, S. (1992). *Lessing's Body and the Aesthetics of Pain*. Detroit: Wayne State University Press.

Ridley, A. (1999). *Collingwood*. London: Routledge.

Rind, M. (2002). 'The Concept of Disinterestedness in Eighteenth-century British Aesthetics'. *Journal of the History of Philosophy* 40: 67–87.

Rogerson, K. F. (1986). *Kant's Aesthetics: The Roles of Form and Expression*. Lanham, Md: University Press of America.

Rollins, M. (ed.) (1993). *Danto and his Critics*. Oxford: Blackwell.

Rorty, A. O. (1992). *Essays on Aristotle's Poetics*. Princeton: Princeton University Press.

Rose, G. (1978). *The Melancholy Science: An Introduction to the Thought of Theodore W. Adorno*. New York: Columbia University Press.

Rose, M. A. (1984). *Marx's Lost Aesthetic: Karl Marx and the Visual Arts*. Cambridge: Cambridge University Press.

Saint Girons, B. (1993). *Fiat lux: une philosophie du sublime*. Paris: Quai Voltaire.

Sartwell, C. (1998). 'Art for Art's Sake'. In M. Kelly (ed.), *Encyclopedia of Aesthetics*. Vol. 1. Oxford: Oxford University Press, pp. 118–21.

Savile, A. (1982). *The Test of Time: An Essay in Philosophical Aesthetics*. Oxford: Clarendon Press.

—— (1987). *Aesthetic Reconstructions: The Seminal Writings of Lessing, Kant and Schiller*. Aristotelian Society Series, vol. 8. Oxford: Blackwell.

—— (1993). *Kantian Aesthetics Pursued*. Edinburgh: Edinburgh University Press.

Schaeffer, J.-M. (2000). *Art of the Modern Age: Philosophy of Art from Kant to Heidegger*, trans. S. Rendall. Princeton: Princeton University Press (translation of *L'Art de l'âge moderne: l'Esthetique et la philosophie de l'art du XVIIIe siècle à nous jours l'homme*. Paris: Gallimard).

Schaper, E. (1968). *Prelude to Aesthetics*. London: George Allen & Unwin.

—— (1979). *Studies in Kant's Aesthetics*. Edinburgh: Edinburgh University Press.

Schelling, F. W. J. (1989). *The Philosophy of Fine Art*, trans. D. W. Stott. Minneapolis: University of Minnesota Press.

Schleiermacher, F. (1998). *Hermeneutics and Criticism, and Other Writings*, trans. A. Bowie. Cambridge: Cambridge University Press.

Schmidt, J. (1985). *Die Geschichte des Genie-Gedankens in der deutschen Literatur, Philosophie und Politik 1750–1945*, 2 vols. Darmstadt: Wissenschaftliche Buchgesellschaft.

Schopenhauer, A. (1958). *The World as Will and Representation*, 2 vols., trans. E. F. J. Payne. Indian Hills, Colo.: Falcon's Wing Press; reprinted 1966, New York: Dover.

Scruton, R. (1974). *Art and Imagination*. London: Methuen.

—— (1979). *The Aesthetics of Architecture*. Princeton: Princeton University Press.

Seiple, D. and Haskins, C. (eds.) (1998). *Democracy and the Aesthetics of Intelligence: Essays in Deweyan Pragmatism*. Albany, NY: State University of New York Press.

Shaftesbury (A. A. Cooper), Earl of (1999). *Characteristics of Men, Manners, Opinions, Times*, ed. L. E. Klein. Cambridge: Cambridge University Press (first published 1711).

Shelley, J. (1998). 'Hume and the Nature of Taste'. *Journal of Aesthetics and Art Criticism* 56: 29–38.

Shusterman, R. (1989). 'Of the Scandal of Taste: Social Privilege as Nature in the Aesthetic Theories of Hume and Kant'. *Philosophical Forum* 20: 211–29; reprinted in Mattick (1993).

—— (1991). *Pragmatist Aesthetics: Living Beauty, Rethinking Art*. Oxford: Blackwell.

Sibley, F. (2001). *Approach to Aesthetics: Collected Papers on Philosophical Aesthetics*, ed. J. Benson, B. Redfern, and J. Cox. Oxford: Clarendon Press.

Solms, F. (1990). *Disciplina aesthetica: Zur Frühgeschichte der ästhetischen Theorie bei Baumgarten und Herder*. Stuttgart: Klett-Cotta.

Sparshott, F. (1982). *The Theory of the Arts*. Princeton: Princeton University Press.

Staten, H. (1990), *Nietzsche's Voice*. Ithaca, NY: Cornell University Press.

Stolnitz, J. (1960). *Aesthetics and Philosophy of Art Criticism*. Boston: Houghton Mifflin.

—— (1961a). 'On the Origins of "Aesthetic Disinterest"'. *Journal of Aesthetics and Art Criticism* 20: 131–43.

—— (1961b). 'On the Significance of Lord Shaftesbury in Modern Aesthetic Theory'. *Philosophical Quarterly* 11: 97–113.

—— (1978). 'The "Aesthetic Attitude" in the Rise of Modern Aesthetics'. *Journal of Aesthetics and Art Criticism* 36: 409–23.

Sychrava, J. (1989). *Schiller to Derrida: Idealism in Aesthetics*. Cambridge: Cambridge University Press.

Townsend, D. (1982). 'Shaftesbury's Aesthetic Theory'. *Journal of Aesthetics and Art Criticism* 41: 205–13.

—— (1987). 'From Shaftesbury to Kant: The Development of the Concept of Aesthetic Experience'. *Journal of the History of Ideas* 48: 287–305; reprinted in P. Kivy (ed.), *Essays on the History of Aesthetics*, Library of the History of Ideas, vol. 5. Rochester: University of Rochester Press, 1992.

—— (1991). 'Lockean Aesthetics'. *Journal of Aesthetics and Art Criticism* 49: 349–61.

—— (2001). *Hume's Aesthetic Theory: Taste and Sentiment*. London and New York: Routledge.

van Gerwen, R. (ed.) (2001). *Richard Wollheim on the Art of Painting: Art as Representation and Expression*. Cambridge: Cambridge University Press.

von der Lühe, A. (1996). *David Humes ästhetische Kritik*. Hamburg: Felix Meiner.

Warnock, M. (1976). *Imagination*. Berkeley and Los Angeles: University of California Press.

Weiskel, T. (1976). *The Romantic Sublime: Studies in the Structure and Psychology of Transcendence*. Baltimore: Johns Hopkins University Press.

Wellbery, D. E. (1984). *Lessing's Laocoon: Semiotics and Aesthetics in the Age of Reason*. Cambridge: Cambridge University Press.

Wieand, J. (1983). 'Hume's Two Standards of Taste'. *Philosophical Quarterly* 34: 129–42.

Wieland, W. (2002). *Urteil und Gefühl: Kants Theorie der Unrkeilskraft*. Göttingen: Vandenboeck & Ruprecht.

Wittgenstein, L. (1953/1968). *Philosophical Investigations*, trans. G. E. M. Anscombe. London: Macmillan (3rd edn. 1968).

——(1967). *Lectures and Conversations on Aesthetics, Psychology and Religious Belief*, ed. C. Barrett. Berkeley and Los Angeles: University of California Press.

——(1980). *Culture and Value*, trans. P. Winch. Chicago: University of Chicago Press.

Wolin, R. (1982). *Walter Benjamin: An Aesthetic of Redemption*. New York: Columbia University Press.

Wollheim, R. (1980). *Art and Its Objects*, 2nd edn. Cambridge: Cambridge University Press.

——(1987). *Painting as an Art*. Princeton: Princeton University Press.

Wyss, B. (1999). *Hegel's Art History and the Critique of Modernity*, trans. C. D. Saltzwedel. Cambridge: Cambridge University Press.

Yanal, R. J. (ed.) (1994). *Institutions of Art: Reconsiderations of George Dickie's Philosophy*. University Park, Pa.: Pennsylvania State University Press.

Young, J. (1987). *Willing and Unwilling: A Study in the Philosophy of Arthur Schopenhauer*. Dordrecht: Kluwer.

——(1992). *Nietzsche's Philosophy of Art*. Cambridge: Cambridge University Press.

——(2001). *Heidegger's Philosophy of Art*. Cambridge: Cambridge University Press.

Zammito, J. H. (1992). *The Genesis of Kant's Critique of Judgment*. Chicago: University of Chicago Press.

——(2001). *Kant, Herder, and the Birth of Anthropology*. Chicago: University of Chicago Press.

Zuidevaart, L. (1991). *Adorno's Aesthetic Theory: The Redemption of Illusion*. Cambridge, Mass.: MIT Press.

PART II

GENERAL ISSUES
IN AESTHETICS

CHAPTER 3

AESTHETIC REALISM 1

NICK ZANGWILL

IN this chapter I shall consider the nature of our aesthetic thought and experience. I will not tackle head-on the issue of whether or not we should think that reality includes mind-independent aesthetic properties and thus mind-independent aesthetic states of affairs in which objects or events possess mind-independent aesthetic properties. However, thinking about the nature of our aesthetic thought and experience unavoidably involves us in thinking about the metaphysics that we are committed to in our aesthetic thought and experience. The issue is whether or not aesthetic thought and experience is 'realist', in the sense that we represent aesthetic properties and states of affairs in such thoughts and experiences. If so, 'common sense' or 'folk aesthetics' has metaphysically dirty hands, though whether or not this common-sense metaphysics is true is another matter. In contrast with realists, there are 'non-realists', who deny that ordinary aesthetic thought and experience have such metaphysical commitments.

1. AESTHETIC REALISM

Let us first focus on the realist view of aesthetic thought and experience. We can reasonably neutrally say that the judgement of taste, that is, the judgement of beauty or aesthetic merit, is based on a particular sort of pleasure: aesthetic pleasure. The question is: what makes a pleasure an *aesthetic* pleasure?

It might be suggested that what is distinctive of a realist view of aesthetic pleasure is that such pleasure has a distinctively aesthetic *content*. But I think that we need to be careful here. The realist will say that, in aesthetic pleasure, we represent objects or events as possessing aesthetic properties. And the realist will also say that, unlike judgements about the niceness and nastiness of food, aesthetic judgements are based on a pleasure, the content of which is ineliminably aesthetic, in the sense that its content deploys distinctively aesthetic concepts. This enables the realist to capture two very important contrasts, which we find in the first 'moment' of Kant's *Critique of Judgment* (Kant 1928). First, aesthetic pleasure is unlike what we might think of as sensuous pleasure, which has no content at all—for example the pleasure I feel on taking a warm bath on a cold night. (See Korsmeyer 1999 for an interesting discussion of this traditional low assessment of bodily pleasures in aesthetics.) Second, aesthetic pleasures are unlike 'interested' pleasures, which have non-aesthetic content—for example pleasure in winning a lottery or pleasure in the morally good. The appeal to aesthetic content thus succeeds in distinguishing aesthetic pleasure from pleasure that has no content at all and from pleasure that has non-aesthetic contents. However, although it is true that the realist must say *at least* that, it may not be something that is *distinctive* of the realist approach. This is because we have not yet given a realist account of the nature of aesthetic contents and concepts. We should not assume without argument that the existence of aesthetic contents and concepts implies a realist account of aesthetic pleasure. For it may be that a non-realist can construct aesthetic contents and concepts without realistic representational content. (Compare Simon Blackburn's quasi-realist project in moral philosophy: Blackburn 1984, 1993, 1998.) A non-realist who *constructs* aesthetic contents and concepts could also capture the contrast between aesthetic pleasure and non-intentional pleasure (sensuous pleasure), and between aesthetic pleasure and pleasure that has non-aesthetic contents (such as prudential and moral pleasure). So appealing to aesthetic contents and concepts may not suffice to characterize aesthetic realism.

How then should we characterize aesthetic realism? Widening the focus from aesthetic pleasure to aesthetic experience more generally, a realist might say that aesthetic experience is experience that is endowed with *aesthetic representational content*. This means that our aesthetic experience represents aesthetic states of affairs, situations, or facts. This, in turn, means that in aesthetic experience the world is represented as possessing genuine aesthetic properties. Such experiences ground or rationally cause our aesthetic judgements, which also have such realistic representational content. For example, on a realist view of music, the content of our experience of music is the representation of a musical state of affairs. This means that we represent sounds as having certain musical properties, such as passion, poignancy, anger, elegance, beauty, and so on. So the realist has an easy answer to the question of what it is to appreciate or understand music. It is, first, to *experience* sounds as possessing the aesthetic properties that they do in fact possess, and second, to *judge* that the sounds possess those properties. If for example the melody is passionate, then we appreciate and understand it if and only if we experience it as passionate and because of this come to judge that it is passionate.

I am inclined to stipulate that a realist thinks that the aesthetic properties we represent are *mind-independent*, although I don't think that much hangs on this stipulation. The simplest mind-dependent view would say that the aesthetic properties of things depend on our actual reactions to them. More complex mind-dependent views would say that the aesthetic properties of things depend on our *disposition* to react to them or on their *disposition* to cause us to react to them. Such dispositional views are often compared to 'secondary quality' views of colours. However, the discussion of dispositional theories can be rather messy, both in moral philosophy and in aesthetics. Such views are sometimes compatible with realism. For example, perhaps that in virtue of which an object has a disposition to produce an effect on people is a mind-independent moral or aesthetic property. Or perhaps that in the object in virtue of which it *warrants* the response we are disposed to have is a mind-independent moral or aesthetic property. And some 'rigidified' versions of such views are not committed to the mind-dependence conditional that, if we had different reactions to things, then the things would have different aesthetic properties (Vallentyne 1996). We should thus be wary of classifying dispositional views as realistic or non-realistic. What we can say is that there are broadly three views of aesthetic experience: we represent aesthetic properties and they are mind-independent; we represent aesthetic properties and they are mind-dependent; and we do not represent aesthetic properties. It doesn't much matter if we label some mind-dependent view 'realist' or 'non-realist'.

Philosophers often cast the realism issue in moral philosophy in terms of an opposition between 'cognitivism' and 'non-cognitivism'. I think that this is a mistake and that it confuses the issue, which is about the contents of both beliefs and desires. I have been careful to cast the issue about aesthetic thought as one about *representational content*. I did not say that it is the type of *propositional attitude* that marks the crucial difference between realist and non-realist conceptions of our thought. It is thus easy to see that it would be a mistake to think that the experiential nature of aesthetics, which virtually everyone agrees on, favours a non-realist view of aesthetic judgements and experience. This is because everything depends on what we say about the content of aesthetic experience in general, and of aesthetic pleasure in particular. There can be competing realist and non-realist conceptions of aesthetic experience. This is one reason why it is a mistake to see the realism/non-realism debate as a matter of cognitivism versus non-cognitivism. For pleasure is a non-cognitive state. Yet there can be realistic and non-realistic conceptions of both cognitive and non-cognitive states. (Some philosophers appeal to something they call 'non-conceptual content', which they think can be found in aesthetic experiences (DeBellis 1995). Unfortunately, the notion of non-conceptual content has never been satisfactorily explained; and, in so far as it is intelligible, an aesthetic realist has special reasons to be suspicious of using it to understand aesthetic experience. Of course, we may not have *words* for all our aesthetic concepts, just as we don't have words for all our colour concepts. But for a realist, veridical aesthetic experience deploys aesthetic concepts that pick out mind-independent aesthetic properties (Zangwill 2001: chapter 10).)

An objection to aesthetic realism would be this: if aesthetic judgement is a realistic affair, why is it necessary that it be based on feeling or response? Compare a realist theory of moral judgements. On such a theory it is plausible that we can and do have moral beliefs that are not grounded on moral experience. It is not plausible that we have moral experiential states that ground moral judgements—although of course moral emotions may flow in the wake of a moral judgement. For the moral realist, any moral feelings are rationally caused by our moral beliefs, not vice versa. Here belief is primary and feeling derivative or consequential; but in aesthetics, matters are the other way round.

I don't think that this argument is very persuasive because it may be that this asymmetry in the direction of rational causation is one thing that distinguishes morality from aesthetics. And anyway, we can see that in general there is nothing suspect about a range of judgements that are grounded on experiences, since we make judgements about the external world on the basis of perceptual experience. Perceptual experience is experience with representational content, and our beliefs about physical reality are grounded in or rationally caused by such experiences. A realist view of aesthetics would be analogous in that we judge on the basis of experience. Of course, in both cases we do not advance from experience to judgement in any simple manner. In both cases, there is an element of holism affecting the passage. Other judgements are brought to bear. I would quickly add that there are many disanalogies between aesthetic experience and judgement and perceptual experience and judgement. The dialectical point is just that there is nothing in general inimical to realism about judgements that are grounded on experiences.

2. THE PROBLEM FOR NON-REALISM

Aesthetic non-realism comes in varieties. In his seminal paper 'Understanding Music', Scruton locates what is essential to our understanding of music in the representational properties of experience (Scruton 1983; see also Scruton 1997). But he is no realist, because he thinks that these contents are ordinary non-musical ones that are not 'asserted' or genuinely held to be true. So, for example, we describe or think of sounds in terms of *height, weight, motion* or *emotion,* but none of these literally apply to sounds. Scruton claims that in judgements about music, the very same concepts are applied as in non-aesthetic judgements; only they are not used to ascribe properties, as they are when normally employed. This is what he calls 'metaphorical transference'. For at least a significant range of cases, Scruton denies that there is an autonomous sphere of distinctively aesthetic concepts. So aesthetic 'judgements' are not really judgements at all, since they are said to be the deliberate non-assertion of propositions that, if asserted, would assert ordinary non-aesthetic facts, although usually false ones.

One of the ways that philosophy has improved in the last generation has been the realization that no metaphysically interesting theory can be cast merely in terms of linguistic force or the pragmatics of language. For example, a distinction on the linguistic level between 'stating' and 'evincing' needs to be *explained* by drawing some distinction at the level of thought. Considerations of linguistic force can only be the beginning of theory, not the end. I described Scruton's theory in terms of the linguistic act of 'assertion'. But this may be inessential, because Scruton has a lot to say about the mental states in question. For Scruton this kind of aesthetic thought about music is said to be closely related to mental states such as *pretending* or *imagining* that p, when we know all along that p is false; or it is like what happens when we see 'aspects' in things, for example when we see something *as* an X. Scruton's theory hinges on these kinds of mental states. I suspect that ultimately he thinks that this kind of aesthetic judgement about music is expressive of such experiences. It should not go unremarked that this kind of account is rather problematic for predicates such as 'beautiful' or 'graceful', which have no serious non-aesthetic use, and is more appropriate to predicates like 'delicate' or 'passionate', which do have a serious non-aesthetic use. This is a problem for Scruton, for if he gives some *other* account of aesthetic judgements of beauty and gracefulness he will have a fractured theory. He will not have a theory of what makes *all* aesthetic judgements aesthetic.

Scruton's aspectualist view has its intellectual roots in Kant's appeal to the harmonious free play of the cognitive faculties of the imagination and understanding (Kant 1928, § 9 onwards). Scruton's non-realist view contrasts with a view that has its roots more in Hume's sentimentalism. On such a view, aesthetic judgements are a matter of having or expressing aesthetic *attitudes* or *sentiments*—perhaps we *like* some things and *dislike* others. This view will have an advantage over Scruton's aspect theory account in that it will have an easier time with notions that lack any non-aesthetic application. (In fact, this *is* something like the account that Scruton himself gives of these notions in chapter 10 of *Art and Imagination*: Scruton 1974.) On the other hand, this view will find it harder than Scruton's to explain what is going on in metaphorical descriptions of music.

I shall focus on what I think is the fundamental problem for both Scruton's aspectualism and Hume's sentimentalism. We must take realism very seriously because of the *normativity* that attaches to aesthetic judgements; for normativity encourages realism and discourages non-realism. The first defining features of aesthetic judgements is their experientiality—the fact that they are grounded in a subjective response. The second defining feature of aesthetic judgements is their normativity—the fact that such judgements can be better or worse. There are some judgements that we ought to make and some that we ought not to make. It is not the case that 'anything goes'. This thought plays a pivotal role in both Hume's and Kant's aesthetics. Ordinary aesthetic judgements have a certain normative aspiration. And the deep Hume/Kant question is: how is this aspiration possible? The answer seems to be that it is possible only if our aesthetic judgements and experiences have realistic representational content. Only then can we understand how they can succeed and fail.

I mentioned earlier that some philosophers are attracted to the idea that aesthetic properties are mind-dependent—that they are some kind of relation between objects and human responses. However, the trouble with such views, in those forms that do not collapse into realism, is that the variety of our actual and possible responses makes the normative aspiration impossible. Perhaps I respond one way and you respond another to the same thing. Or perhaps I am disposed to respond one way and you are disposed to respond another way. Then, on both the simple and the dispositional mind-dependent theories, we can both be right. But we will have lost the ordinary idea of correctness. This means that such accounts cannot be correct as 'folk aesthetics', that is, as an account of our actual aesthetic thought. Hence, mind-dependent accounts do no better than sentimentalist or aspectualist theories at respecting the normative aspiration of aesthetic judgements.

Alan Goldman and John Bender have argued that differences in taste are irreconcilable, and they think that this favours non-realism (Goldman 1995; Bender 1996). Well, it may be true that people who make very different aesthetic judgements cannot be brought to agree. (The same is true of moral judgements.) Some people just cannot be persuaded; they cannot be forced, willy-nilly, to see the error of their ways. But they may be wrong nonetheless. It is hardly an objection to *realism* that it opens up a gap between our judgements and the truth. This is just part of a realist view (see Nagel 1987). So the Goldman/Bender objection is question-begging. We should also note that their arguments presuppose an answer to the problem I have been exploring here—of explaining the claim to correctness that is implicit in ordinary aesthetic judgements, since they begin from the phenomenon of disagreement in judgement. But such disagreement makes sense only if both sides in the disagreement think of themselves as holding the correct judgement and of the others as holding an incorrect judgement.

The crucial two-word question upon which everything devolves is: whence normativity? Realism has an easy answer, for the vices and virtues of judgements and experiences consist in their corresponding or failing to correspond to the facts or states of affairs that the judgements and experiences purport to represent. All sorts of non-realism, on the other hand, have a serious problem. The realist explanation is not available, and it is difficult to see any other. If understanding music is merely a matter of hearing aspects, as Scruton says, then why isn't any aspect-experience as good as any other? If people have different aesthetic responses when listening to the same sounds, then what can the Humean point to as that which validates one response and invalidates another? Why aren't all responses on a par? This is deeply problematic for anyone who wants to avoid the incredible conclusion that all of our aesthetic thought and experience is a vast mistake.

3. Hume's Attempted Solution

Hume was very aware of the normative problem for non-realism. He set about the task of fixing the problem in his essay 'Of the Standard of Taste' (Hume 1985).

Hume points out that we think that not all judgements of taste are correct (Hume 1985: 230–1). We can get things wrong. Not all judgements are equally appropriate. Hume's problem is to explain this normativity given his sentimentalist framework. On a cognitivist view, by contrast, according to which we cognize a genuine quality of beauty in things, normativity would be easily explained. We get it wrong if the world is not like that. But if aesthetic judgements are simply expressive of felt pleasures or displeasures, why should any judgement not be as good as any other? This is the problem that Hume sets himself.

Hume has some extremely clever suggestions as to how the non-realist can construct normativity. His underlying idea is that the idea of correctness in judgement is subordinate to that of an *excellent* critic, so that the correct judgement is that which an excellent critic would make. Given this underlying idea, Hume goes on to characterize virtues and vices in sensibilities in a way that, at least on the face of it, does not refer to whether or not such sensibilities produce the correct judgements.

Hume seeks to use the figure of the excellent critic to explain the normative aspirations of our judgements of taste. So we need to consider how convincing Hume's various suggestions are concerning what makes for an excellent critic. Here is the passage in which he sums up his various suggestions after having described each one in detail:

When the critic has no delicacy, he judges without any distinction, and is only affected by the grosser and more palpable qualities of the object: The finer touches pass unnoticed and disregarded. Where he is not aided by practice, his verdict is attended with confusion and hesitation. Where no comparison has been employed, the most frivolous beauties, such as rather merit the name of defects, are the objects of his admiration. Where he lies under the influence of prejudice, all his natural sentiments are perverted. Where good sense is wanting, he is not qualified to discern the beauties of design and reasoning which are the highest and most excellent.

Under some or other of these imperfections, the generality of men labor; and hence a true judge is observed, even during the most polished ages, to be so rare a character: Strong sense, united to delicate sentiment, improved by practice, perfected by comparison, and cleared of all prejudice, can alone entitle critics to this admirable character; and the joint verdict of such, wherever they are to be found, is the true standard of taste and beauty. (Hume 1985: 241)

Let us separate out the five marks of an excellent critic that are offered in this passage. (*a*) There is the 'delicacy' of taste, which Hume has earlier illustrated with the wine-tasting example from Don Quixote (Hume 1985: 234–7). Our experience, and the judgement we base upon it, can be more or less fine-grained in discrimination. (*b*) We need practice in judgement. It is good to have a well exercised sensibility (see also Hume 1985: 237–8). (*c*) A broad experience is important, for it gives us the scope to make useful comparisons. Inexperience leads to crude and naive judgement (see also Hume 1985: 238). (*d*) Prejudice should be avoided. We must remove obstructions to true appreciation, such as any jealousy or affection we might feel for the author; and we must not blindly follow fashion (see also Hume 1985: 239–40). (*e*) We need what Hume calls 'good sense', which is the operation of our normal cognitive faculties. We need good sense for many purposes: to keep our prejudices in check; to understand and compare the parts of a work; to assess a work in respect of its purposes; to understand and assess the plot and characters of a work of literature, and, more generally, to understand the representational features of works of art (Hume 1985: 240–1). (*f*) In addition, Hume mentions in passing another possible source of defective judgement, which does not seem to fit into any of the previous five categories:

A perfect serenity of mind, a recollection of thought, a due attention to the object; if any of these be wanting, our experiment will be fallacious, and we will be unable to judge of the catholic and universal beauty. (Hume 1985: 232–3)

That is, we must be in the right mood and paying attention.

These six features are supposed to tell us what an excellent critic would be like. The figure of the excellent critic is Hume's solution to the normative problem for non-realism, since a judgement is correct if it is one that would be made by the excellent critic.

4. ASSESSMENT OF HUME'S SOLUTION

This is an interesting proposal. But does it work? I will cast doubt on Hume's account of the excellent critic by employing the device of appealing to a comparison of judgements of beauty and ugliness with judgements of niceness and nastiness as applied to food and drink. The latter contrast with judgements of beauty and ugliness in an important respect. Like judgements of beauty and ugliness, judgements of niceness and nastiness are based on the sentiments of pleasure and displeasure. But they lack the normative aspirations of judgements of beauty and ugliness. (Kant makes a similar contrast when he says that judgements of the niceness of Canary wine lack 'universal voice': Kant 1928: §§ 1–5.) As far as judgements of niceness and nastiness are concerned, anything goes. If you do not like smoked salmon, you are not lacking in judgement in the way that you are if you do not appreciate the beauty of the Alhambra. To think that there is an equality of niceness between smoked salmon and baked beans is not like thinking that there is 'an equality of genius between OGILBY and MILTON, or BUNYAN and ADDISON' (Hume 1985: 230–1). People might sometimes say that others are wrong to like certain food or drink, but, in contrast with the aesthetic case, this is not something that they insist on for long when faced with those with radically different likes and dislikes. The normative claim of aesthetic judgements has a certain *robustness* in the face of radically different judgements.

The six sources of failings in a critic's reactions to which Hume appeals divide into internal and external sources. I shall begin with internal sources.

The first of these sources is the delicacy of taste, or what has been called 'fineness of discrimination'. It is not too difficult to show that this is not successful by itself. Hume hopes that the appeal to delicacy or fineness of discrimination will give him a way of assessing aesthetic sensibilities as better or worse, in the same way that it apparently gives us a way of assessing our sensory capacities. Hume again draws attention to the analogy of aesthetic judgements with our judgements about secondary qualities, such as colour. But, although there are certainly *some* minimal normative constraints in our secondary quality thought, it is doubtful whether they are as robust as those operating in our aesthetic judgements. And delicacy or fineness of discrimination illustrates this. Fineness of discrimination can certainly provide normativity to some extent. We need our sensory experiences in order to get around in the physical world. Fine-grained experiences are good for this, since the more finely we discriminate among secondary qualities, the finer, subtler, and more accurate will be our judgements of physical qualities. So we will be more successful in practical terms; we will do better at evading hungry bears, or at detecting whether there is metal or leather in a hogshead of wine. In this respect, and to this extent, we can certainly assess sensory capacities as better or worse. However, as Michael Tanner and Colin McGinn pointed out, this does not generate the kind of robust normative claim that we need in aesthetics or morality (Tanner 1968; McGinn 1982). Consider those who have an inverted spectrum, or Martians who see green where we see red. They make judgements of secondary qualities that are as fine-grained as those made by someone with a normal spectrum. But since each is equally fine-grained, there are no grounds for preferring one above the other on the score of fine-grainedness. Each sensory capacity is equally good for evading hungry bears. But we must be able to rank one above the other if there is to be even a remotely plausible analogy with aesthetics or morality, because, where two sets of aesthetic or moral judgements collide like this, we need to be able to say that they cannot both be right. The normativity we seek in aesthetics or morality requires at least that. So fine-grainedness, by itself, cannot give us the robust kind of normativity that we require in aesthetics or morality. Fineness of discrimination may be a virtue in a sensibility, but it is not a sufficient basis from which to construct the idea of correctness that Hume requires, since it fails to adjudicate between radically divergent and yet equally delicate sensibilities.

Hume's second internal source is practice in judgement. He writes:

When [the critic] is not aided by practice, his verdict is attended with confusion and hesitation. (Hume 1985: 241)

Can this help? It seems not. I might be well practised in judging the exquisite culinary delights of smoked salmon. But we do not expect my judgements about this subject to improve, in the sense that there is an increase in the frequency with which my judgements are correct. What needs explaining is why we might expect this in the aesthetic case, but not for judgements about the niceness of smoked salmon. On a cognitivist view, according to which we are sensitive to independently existing aesthetic qualities, we could understand why practice would improve judgement. For it would improve our sensitivity to the independently existing aesthetic qualities. But it is difficult to see *why* being well exercised should be a virtue in a Humean sensibility. The appeal to practice in judgement cannot, by itself, bear much weight.

For the same reason, Hume's idea that we need a broad range of experience is probably true, but it is not clear how it is relevant. We do indeed need access to an adequate and varied basis on which to make aesthetic judgements. But why should that mean that our reactions improve with time? Hume makes the point that judgements of beauty are comparative (Hume 1985: 238–9), and that inferior objects can arouse inappropriate reactions if we are not acquainted with superior ones. This is all true. But it *assumes* that wider experience leads to more appropriate judgements of relative value: it does not explain it. So it does not help to *construct* normativity. The problem is to explain why a broad experience makes us judge better.

Hume's most interesting idea, I think, is his appeal to prejudice. This is an 'external' rather than an 'internal' failing in a sensibility. We must abstract from, or take account of, the character and opinions of the author and intended audience. And the critic's personal connection with the author—such as friendship or enmity—should be discounted. The idea comes close to Kant's more complex idea of disinterestedness. Hume writes:

When any work is addressed to the public, I must…consider myself as a man in general, [and] forget, if possible, my individual being and peculiar circumstances. (Hume 1985: 239)

However, surely prejudice is only a matter of the warping or 'perverting' (Hume 1935: 239) of the taste function from outside; it does not concern what can go wrong with the taste function itself. How can the invasion of alien impurities suffice to account for aesthetic error? To be sure, such invasion is a part of aesthetic life, and it is something a cognitivist also needs to note. But does Hume think that if our judgements were pure and uncorrupted, correct judgements would always be forthcoming, given that our sensibilities were well exercised, broadly experienced and finely discriminating? Surely, uncorrupted but healthy sensibilities might still produce incorrect judgements. Furthermore, one can also be prejudiced in one's judgements about niceness and nastiness. One might be put off certain food and drink because of the way certain people talk about it in an irritating holier-than-thou manner. And a meat pie might not taste quite the same when one finds out that it is made from one's pet dog. (Recall the ill-fated kings whom the ancient dramatists portray discovering that they are eating their own children.) There is *a* sense in which one ought to taste the food for what it is. One ought to be unprejudiced in one's culinary judgements. Still, such judgements lack the robust normativity we seek. So the appeal to prejudice alone cannot do the work Hume requires.

One external source of error might be thought to lie in our ordinary cognitive understanding of the thing to which we respond with pleasure or displeasure. This is part of the idea of Hume's appeal to the 'good sense' that is involved in understanding works of art. Now, our aesthetic sensibility is the function from non-aesthetic input—whether physical, sensory or semantic—to sentiments, and then from these sentiments to judgements. So, although we need our cognitive faculties, as Hume rightly points out, a critique of our ordinary cognitive faculties cannot do justice to our intuitive idea of aesthetic fallibility; for perfect knowledge of the physical, sensory, or semantic properties about which we make judgements is compatible with widely divergent sentimental responses to the same cognitive input. So appealing to the 'good sense' that is involved in understanding works of art seems ineffective by itself.

Lastly, another external source of error is Hume's idea that we must be in the right mood if we are to judge of beauty and deformity. However, this is also necessary for fully appreciating the deliciousness of smoked salmon. We enjoy it more when we are relaxed and paying attention, rather than when we are preoccupied with something else. But such judgements of niceness and nastiness lack the normativity that is characteristic of aesthetic judgements.

The trouble, in short, is that all of the virtues and vices that Hume cites apply equally to our capacity to experience pleasure in food and drink. As far as food and drink goes, we can be more or less finely discriminating, more or less well practised, more or less widely experienced, more or less prejudiced, and more or less possessed of good sense, and in better or worse moods. The virtues and vices of a sensibility that Hume specifies could have been those of a connoisseur of food and drink. So it seems dubious whether any of these virtues can do the job of explaining normativity in the case of the sensibility whose products are judgements of beauty and ugliness. For judgements of the niceness and nastiness of food and drink do not make the same claim to correctness as do judgements of beauty and ugliness. (Maybe they make some such claim, but certainly nothing as robust as those that judgements of beauty and ugliness make.) Hume's virtues and vices are consistent with a range of judgements that do not have the normative aspirations of judgements of beauty and ugliness. Therefore, these virtues and vices do not suffice to construct that normativity in the case of judgements of beauty and ugliness. The comparison with judgements of niceness and nastiness serves to remind us of exactly how much still needs to be achieved for judgements of beauty and ugliness. Hume's appeal to the figure of the excellent critic is subtle and imaginative, but it cannot do the job that Hume wants. So Hume fails to rescue normativity for the non-realist.

5. Non-Humean Attempts to Capture Normativity for the Non-realist

In moral philosophy, Simon Blackburn has attempted to defend a Humean sentimentalist view. And he is inspired by the overall strategy adopted in Hume's essay on taste. But Blackburn has proposed certain subtle ideas that are not to be found in Hume (Blackburn 1984, 1993, 1998). Maybe these can help us in aesthetics.

One of Blackburn's suggestions is that normativity might be captured for a Humean view by appealing to the possibility that we may take a moral attitude to our moral sensibilities. So our moral sensibilities can be assessed, and can be found wanting, from the perspective of our own moral attitudes. But this idea cannot be transposed to aesthetics, for it does not seem likely that we could find some aesthetic sensibilities more pleasing than others, or that we could perceive aspects in them. Psychological states are not the right sort of thing themselves to be the object of aesthetic experiences or aspect experiences. So we cannot critically turn our aesthetic reactions on themselves. By contrast, there is nothing straightforwardly incoherent about morally disapproving of a moral sensibility.

Another of Blackburn's ideas is that the idea of moral mind-independence is itself a moral principle. But the idea that the principle of aesthetic normativity—that there are correct and incorrect aesthetic judgements and attitudes—could itself be read as an aesthetic commitment is bizarre. We might be aesthetically moved to find deer dainty or aardvarks ugly. But we surely cannot be aesthetically moved by the idea that whether deer are dainty or aardvarks ugly does not depend on what I think. And in endorsing such negated counterfactuals, we are surely not expressing our delight in sensibilities that do not infer a thing's aesthetic qualities from beliefs about their own attitudes. For, again, mental states are the wrong kind of things to be the object of aesthetic appreciation or gestalt experiences. Of course, those mental states might be realized in brain states, which have aesthetic properties. But those brain states are probably similar—aesthetically—to those of someone with the opposite mental states.

A third idea in Blackburn is that moral judgements have normative aspirations because only if they do will it serve our 'needs and purposes'. How might this fare when transposed to aesthetics? Might a certain kind of aesthetic sensibility aid some project quite distinct from our aesthetic lives? The idea would be that we have normative aspirations in our aesthetic thought because such thought serves certain needs and purposes. So the assessment of our aesthetic lives would take place from a perspective outside of it. This would avoid the problem besetting the other two techniques, since they sought a justification from within aesthetic thought.

We should not rule out this idea at the outset because of Kant's idea that aesthetic pleasure is 'disinterested'—that is, very roughly, the idea that our pleasure in a thing is not based on an awareness of the thing's relationship to our desires, purposes, and needs. Disinterestedness is a feature of aesthetic thought that all sides should agree on, for it is arguably implied by the normative claim of aesthetic judgements; for, if aesthetic pleasure or the judgement on which it is grounded were based on a desire or need, then, as Kant says, it would be 'very partial' (Kant 1928: 43). Aesthetic correctness would become relative to whether a person happened to possess some desire, and with that the normative aspiration would be lost. The non-realist hopes to appeal to our needs and purposes in order to explain why it is *worthwhile* for us to engage in a form of thought that involves disinterested pleasure. The hope is to explain the exist-ence, possibility and legitimacy of judgements based on disinterested pleasure.

However, what is obscure is exactly what might be the needs or purposes that our aesthetic life allegedly serves. We need to know more about these needs and purposes before we can think about using them to explain aesthetic normativity. Compare humour. A comedian may have a purpose in thinking in terms of humour. He wants to evoke laughter. Nevertheless, we do not think that our judgements of humour are correct and those of others incorrect, not at least in the same robust way that we think that aesthetic judgements can be correct or incorrect. Judgements of humour are like judgements of the niceness and nastiness of food in their lack of robust normative aspirations. Humour may also have a psychological function, in the sense in which children's imaginative play is often said to have a function. Humour is also important to us because a person's sense of humour tells us a great deal about their personality and values. But for all that, we do not take humour seriously, in the sense of operating with a robust notion of correctness and incorrectness for judgements of humourousness.

One suggestion might be that, just as it is often said that moralizing makes things go well in our day-to-day affairs, because we cooperate, so aestheticizing helps things to go well in our leisure hours. Poetry may give more pleasure than pushpin, and Shakespeare's poetry more than that of an inferior poet. However, this appeal to hedonism is too crude. For the inferior poet may in fact give more pleasure than Shakespeare. Aesthetic normativity concerns what pleasures we *ought* to have. So quantitative hedonistic purposes cannot help us here.

We are, then, short of an account of the needs and purposes that aestheticizing allegedly serves. Perhaps this is what we should have expected all along, since surely we can take our aesthetic thought and its normativity seriously only if we think of it as an end in itself. But an interesting variant of this idea would be that the external source to which our aesthetic sensibilities are compared is morality itself. Maybe the underlying needs and purposes of aesthetic thought are *moral* needs and purposes. The idea would be that some aesthetic sensibilities, or particular aesthetic reactions, are morally preferable to others (see e.g. Scruton 1974: final chapter; Elliot 1968). This may fare better than taking the external source to be ordinary needs and purposes, which rendered the normative claim problematic. The normativity of aesthetics would derive from an external source, and would be secure provided that there are correct and incorrect moral judgements about the value of aesthetic experiences or sensibilities. We could then bracket off the aspirations of moral judgement for separate treatment. This would be to rest the legitimacy of one faculty on the legitimacy of another, on which we assume we can rely. If by some means it can be shown that moral judgements make legitimate claim to correctness, then maybe there can be moral assessment of aesthetic sensibilities. This certainly seems a coherent idea. Surely G. E. Moore was right to think that aesthetic experience is morally valuable (Moore 1903: final chapter), although this is a first-order moral view, and one it is possible to reject. But if aesthetic experience is in general morally good, then it seems likely that different aesthetic sensibilities can differ in respect of how much moral value they possess. And if that is so, then maybe we can say that some aesthetic judgements are better than others.

While attractive, this idea is not as straightforward as it initially appears. There are two main difficulties. First, we are in danger of eliminating the aesthetic in favour of the moral, rather than accounting for the aesthetic in terms of the moral. It may be true that the quality of life of someone who gains pleasure from the inferior poet differs significantly from that of someone who appreciates Shakespeare. But if we want to use that to explain why we ought to judge that Shakespeare is better than the inferior poet, then it seems that we will have explained the 'ought' that our judgements of taste carry with them as a disguised moral obligation to have a certain experience in so far as this is possible. This seems unsatisfactory, because we will not have demonstrated the distinctively *aesthetic* normativity of judgements of taste. The danger remains even if we widen the theory so that it is our *capacity* to have a range of experiences that is morally evaluated. It is plausible that at some point moral and aesthetic value must be brought together; however, to try to do so too crudely may not bring them together but rather may eliminate one in favour of the other.

The second problem with the moral approach is more decisive. It is not obvious why we would think that aesthetic experience is morally valuable unless we already credited it with normative aspirations. The moral value of our aesthetic thought would be mysterious without the normativity that inheres in it. Aesthetic experience is morally valuable not just because of the pleasure it involves, but because of the specific *nature* of that pleasure. But the most important peculiarity of aesthetic pleasure is that it licenses judgements that lay claim to *correctness*. After all, it is common to object to simple hedonistic forms of utilitarianism that they are implausibly indiscriminate about the intentional objects of the pleasures to which they appeal. Surely sadistic pleasures are not good just in so far as they are pleasures. The contents of pleasures matters morally. Similarly, if aesthetic pleasures are to matter morally, it cannot be just because they are pleasures, but because of the specific sort of pleasures they are. As we have seen, normativity is essential to aesthetic pleasure. Thus, we can make sense of the moral value of aesthetic pleasure only if we *assume* this normativity. So we cannot use morality to explain normativity in aesthetics.

The problem is that it is very difficult to understand exactly why aesthetic experience might be thought to be morally valuable. We need more of an idea of the *way* that our aesthetic sensibility is morally significant. Compare humour. Humour is enormously important—but it is morally important for that of which it is symptomatic. A sense of humour reveals that which is of central moral importance—a person's character and values, yet, for all that, our thought about humour does not have robust normative aspirations. Aesthetics must be important in a different way from humour if the appeal to morality is to help. Once we look at the details, the non-realist strategy of appealing to the moral assessment of our aesthetic reactions is less helpful than it initially appears. We remain short of a non-realist account of the source of aesthetic normativity.

Another possible external source of aesthetic normativity would be our ordinary cognition of the world. Just as we tried to show how some aesthetic reactions might be better than others from the point of view of morality, so perhaps it could be argued that some aesthetic reactions might be better than others from the point of view of knowledge; this was Kant's own solution to the normative problem. Kant has much to teach us about the deep psychology of the judgement of taste (Kant 1928). There is much in what he says about disinterestedness, and about many other matters. However, Kant also has a positive account of aesthetic judgements. Like Hume's account, Kant's is non-realist. And like Hume's account, Kant's involves a projective element. (Kant writes: 'We speak of beauty as if it were a property of things': Kant 1928: 52.) Kant's view, however, is not sentimentalist, since for Kant pleasure in the beautiful is, or is intimately bound up with, the *free play* of our cognitive faculties (Kant 1928: §§ 35–9). The cognitive faculties are normally deployed in the acquisition of *knowledge*. But in the judgement of taste, they are, as it were, on holiday, not engaged in their regular business. Presumably our cognitive faculties include many things besides knowledge or belief. For example, entertaining thoughts is cognitive, but it is not a matter of knowledge or belief. And imagination is similar. However, I am sceptical about whether this account has the resources to provide for the 'universal validity' of judgements of taste. For why should this free play of the cognitive faculties be constrained to play freely in one way rather than another? In my view, there is nothing in the *Critique of Judgment* to answer this fundamental question. And if so, Kant's view is in the same boat as Hume's: namely, it is a view that eschews realism, but fails to be able to capture the normative aspirations of aesthetic judgements. Only full-blooded realism, it seems, can do justice to them.

6. THE DIALECTICAL SITUATION

Hume puts the overriding difficulty for non-realism nicely when he says that he seeks to provide his sentimentalist non-realist with a way of avoiding the conclusion that

A thousand different sentiments, excited by the same object, are all right: Because no sentiment represents what is really in the object. (Hume 1985: 230)

For the realist, by contrast, accounting for normativity is as easy as falling off a log. The source of normativity lies in conformity to aesthetic fact. Competing aesthetic judgements and experiences match or fail to match aesthetic reality; and this is what makes one judgement better, or more correct, than another. In Hume's language, aesthetic judgements 'represent what is really in the object'. The realist has an easy explanation of the robust normative nature of aesthetic truth. The non-realist, by contrast, has a severe problem; for, if making aesthetic judgements is just a matter of having attitudes or aspect experiences, then why isn't any attitude or aspect experience as good as any other?

Both realism and non-realism are on a par as far as the experiential aspect of aesthetics is concerned. But when it comes to explaining the normativity of aesthetic judgements, the realist is ahead. Realism and non-realism are equal as far as the first defining feature of aesthetic judgements goes, but they are not equal as regards the second. Thus, overall, realism better explains the nature of our aesthetic thought.

I have not considered the credentials of realism in great depth. Perhaps realism is objectionable on metaphysical or epistemological grounds. But, however things may be with realism, things are not well with non-realism. The net result of our investigation here is that a realist view of aesthetic judgement is on balance more attractive than a non-realist view when it comes to explaining normativity. For, by contrast with the realist, the non-realist lacks an adequate account of the normative aspirations of our aesthetic judgements. This mode of argument is inductive. We have looked at only a few non-realist strategies. Perhaps there are others that can do better. The strategies we have looked at do not deliver what they promise; and if we cannot think of any alternative strategies, the prospects for non-realism look gloomy. However, in spite of what I have argued, perhaps normativity can after all be constructed on a non-realist basis. If so, there could be an answer to the

Hume/Kant question of how a judgement of taste is possible, that is, of how judgement is possible which has subjective grounds and normative aspirations. However, until the non-realist comes up with something, realists have reason to feel confident. It is clear where the onus of proof lies.

I conclude that folk aesthetics is thus realist. Whether or not the tacit folk metaphysical commitment to aesthetic facts or states of affairs is justified is another matter, but our aesthetic judgements presuppose that metaphysics. What is not an option is holding some non-realist view, be it Humean, Kantian, or dispositional, while thinking we can unproblematically retain our ordinary practice of making aesthetic judgements.

See also: Aesthetic Realism 2; Beauty; Aesthetic Experience; Value in Art.

BIBLIOGRAPHY

Bender, J. (1996). 'Realism, Supervenience, and Irresoluble Aesthetic Disputes'. *Journal of Aesthetics and Art Criticism* 54: 371–81.
Blackburn, S. (1984). *Spreading the Word*. Oxford: Oxford University Press.
—— (1993). *Essays in Quasi-realism*. Oxford: Oxford University Press.
—— (1998). *Ruling Passions*. Oxford: Oxford University Press.
DeBellis, M. (1995). *Music and Conceptualization*. Cambridge: Cambridge University Press.
Elliot, R. K. (1968). 'The Unity of Kant's Critique of Aesthetic Judgment'. *British Journal of Aesthetics* 8: 244–49.
Goldman, A. (1995). *Aesthetic Value*. Boulder, Colo.: Westview Press.
Hume, D. (1985). 'Of the Standard of Taste', in *Essays: Moral, Political and Literary*, ed. E. Miller. Indianapolis: Liberty.
Kant, I. (1928). *Critique of Judgment*, trans. J. C. Meredith. Oxford: Oxford University Press.
Korsmeyer, C. (1999). *Making Sense of Taste*. Ithaca, NY: Cornell University Press.
McGinn, C. (1982). *The Subjective View*. Oxford: Clarendon.
Moore, G. E. (1903). *Principia Ethica*. Cambridge: Cambridge University Press.
Nagel, T. (1987). *The View from Nowhere*. Oxford: Oxford University Press.
Scruton, R. (1974). *Art and Imagination*. London: Methuen.
—— (1983). 'Understanding Music', in *The Aesthetic Understanding*. London: Methuen.
—— (1997). *The Aesthetics of Music*. Oxford: Oxford University Press.
Tanner, M. (1968). 'Objectivity in Aesthetics'. *Aristotelian Society Supplementary Volume* 42: 55–72.
Vallentyne, P. (1996). 'Response-Dependence, Rigidification, and Objectivity'. *Erkenntnis* 44: 101–12.
Zangwill, N. (2001). *The Metaphysics of Beauty*. Ithaca, NY: Cornell University Press.

CHAPTER 4

....

AESTHETIC REALISM 2

....

JOHN W. BENDER

1. INTRODUCTORY CAUTION

....

THERE is a contemporary debate over aesthetic property realism as robust as that in ethical theory over the status of moral properties. This may seem peculiar. What *worse* candidate could there be for a 'real' property? Many aesthetic properties have, or are claimed to have, higher-order features that problematize a realistic attitude towards them.

Aesthetic properties, or at least many of them, are: (*a*) not purely descriptive, (*b*) metaphorical, (*c*) partly evaluative, (*d*) often abstract, (*e*) allegedly 'cultural', (*f*) seemingly about subjective and sometimes affective reactions, (*g*) dispositional, (*h*) relative to our canons of taste, (*i*) rhetorical in their function, and (*j*) in no obvious or rule-governed way susceptible to verification. What more daunting, seemingly hopeless task to set an ontologist than to argue realism for a class of properties with such features! Any one of these characteristics, it might be suggested, should weaken the knees of the staunchest realist.

Perhaps understandably, the aesthetic discussion, driven more by certain epistemological concerns, shies away from the most fundamental ontological questions, such as 'Can we be realists about abstract properties; about metaphorical properties; about "secondary" properties?' Thus, to a large extent these very basic issues remain unresolved, and their resolution may have an impact on the particular debate over aesthetic property realism. Perhaps it is felt that, since there is nothing parochially aesthetic about these ultimate questions, they remain in the metaphysician's, not the aesthetician's, province. But this discussion of aesthetic realism begins with the caution that the relevance of the sidelined basic ontological issues should not be wholly ignored.

2. AESTHETIC AND NON-AESTHETIC

Aesthetic property realism would seem to be committed to at least some version of the following two claims: (*a*) there is a distinctive category of predications or attributions used in describing art works and other objects of our aesthetic attention; and (*b*) it is correct to construe these attributions as asserting that certain aesthetic properties exist and are objectively true of art works and other objects.

Although anti-realist challenges have focused mainly on deconstructing (*b*), there has also been considerable scepticism over (*a*), i.e. over the very concept of aesthetic properties. The distinction between the aesthetic and the non-aesthetic is one of those distinctions that has strong intuitive credibility but yields grudgingly to philosophical analysis. Ted Cohen (1973) has argued that the distinction does nothing, and that for every purportedly aesthetic term it is possible to find applications that require no particularly aesthetic aptitude. According to Roger Scruton, the failure of the theory of aesthetic perception (and therefore the failure of aesthetic realism) can be traced to that theory's 'creating too sharp a divorce between the aesthetic and non-aesthetic use of terms' (Scruton 1982: 41). Marcia Eaton (1994) has recently denied any ontological distinction between aesthetic and non-aesthetic properties, claiming that any physical property (e.g. being yellow) can also be an aesthetic property, provided only that it is an intrinsic property of an object (i.e. is verifiable by direct inspection of the object) and is culturally identified as a property worthy of attention. It will be prudent, then, to attempt to characterize the category 'aesthetic property' before progressing to the debate over realism.

Notice first that the putative category is a very mixed bag, and this may well be the source of scepticism about the aesthetic. Even if we start with our perhaps ill-justified conviction that we have a reasonably clear grasp of what is *not* aesthetic, viz. purely descriptive attributions of formal or structural features that can be perceived or comprehended and agreed to by normal percipients confronting a given artwork, the *complementary* category remains extremely diverse.

Goran Hermeren (1988*a*,*b*) has done aestheticians the service of organizing aesthetic attributions into five types. He distinguishes: emotion qualities ('sad'), behaviour qualities ('restrained'), Gestalt qualities ('unified'), taste qualities ('garish', 'beautiful'), and reaction qualities ('moving'). Alan Goldman goes further and offers eight categories (Goldman 1995: chapter 2; 1992): pure value properties ('beautiful'), emotion properties ('sad'), formal properties ('balanced'), behavioural properties ('daring'), evocative properties ('stirring'), representational properties ('realistic'), second-order perceptual properties ('vivid'), and historically related properties ('original'). Do these various properties have a common characteristic or a shared function in virtue of which aesthetic properties constitute a kind?

Frank Sibley (1959) suggested that more than common perceptual ability is involved in the attribution of these properties, and that an exercise of *taste* is essential in every case. But this answer is vulnerable to a charge of circularity, since taste seems to be nothing but a sensitivity to the aesthetic properties of an object. Monroe Beardsley (1973) proposed that aesthetic qualities are 'regional qualities' (features of complexes or regions of an artwork that emerge from more basic qualities of its parts) and may all be 'human qualities', i.e. qualities similar to those true of persons, including their intentional states, demeanour, and behaviour. But it is unclear that all formal and second-order perceptual qualities are grounded in an analogy to human qualities.

Perhaps more promising is another of Beardsley's proposals, which has received support from a number of other writers (Zangwill 1995; Goldman 1995). Beardsley (1973) suggests that all aesthetic qualities are intimately connected to normative critical judgements. More precisely, most aesthetic qualities are 'value-grounding qualities', qualities that can be cited independently as reasons supporting a critical evaluation. (Some aesthetic predicates may be purely value-*designating* rather than value-grounding, Beardsley admits.) Hence we might say that aesthetic attributions function either to offer critical evaluations of an artwork or to offer the reasons supporting those evaluations. Alan Goldman states this position succinctly: 'we may accept as our basic criterion for identifying aesthetic properties that they are those that ground or instantiate in their relations to us or other properties those values of artworks that make them worth contemplating' (Goldman 1995: 21).

This view defines aesthetic properties in terms of aesthetic value, and there may be doubts about whether this gets things backwards. An account of aesthetic value cannot, then, assume that we know which properties are aesthetic. Nevertheless, this position has merit. We value art because it is the source of rewarding experiences of a perceptual, cognitive, and/or affective nature. Art works engage our senses, imagination, thoughts, reactions and emotions; and they do this, to a large extent, through various broadly semantic or symbolic functions including referring, representing, depicting, exemplifying properties, expressing emotions, embodying or constituting metaphors, symbolizing objects or states of affairs, and so forth. For the most part, these functions are the result of complex relations that obtain among the more basic structural, compositional, and perceptual features of the work.

The symbolic functions performed by artworks and the manner in which the works execute these functions are often deemed valuable by us because they engage us in the experiential ways already mentioned. Any attribution that attempts to capture the value-making 'content' of a work, or that expresses the manner in which the work *is* valuable as a result of its content, is an aesthetic attribution. Hence Beardsley and Goldman are right that aesthetic attributions either ascribe aesthetic value to a work or can be considered as independently comprising a reason that grounds such an evaluation. But, given what has just been offered about the way art functions, it should perhaps be added that any attribution expressing the broadly interpretative or metaphorical content of a work—content of a sort that is potentially value-making—should be considered an aesthetic attribution. Roughly, then, aesthetic properties are the properties referred to in the metaphorical, interpretative, expressive, and evaluatively-laden attributions we make to art. The question now is, what it means to say that they are real properties.

3. REALISM OR OBJECTIVE TRUTH?

The hard-boiled metaphysician would surely require any realism about aesthetic properties to imply an *existential commitment* to those properties. In other words, to be an aesthetic realist, one must acknowledge properties such as elegance, complexity, vividity, and irony as real features of objects, and as items in one's ontology over which one is not hesitant to quantify. Yet, the properties that bring out the realist in most philosophers are *physical* properties, such as having a certain mass or freezing point, being negatively charged, or having a certain genetic fingerprint. Probably no one believes that aesthetic properties are in every respect on a par with such fundamental physical properties.

Moreover, we have already acknowledged that at least many aesthetic properties are evaluative in nature. It has also been suggested that for the most part they have a relational character: they are expressing something about the way humans respond to the objects said to possess the property. In this, aesthetic properties appear similar to classic 'secondary properties' such as being of a certain colour. But do values or colours really exist in the world? If this question presupposes that aesthetic or sensory properties, to be real, must be true of objects independently of how humans react or respond to them, then in one sense it is an illegitimate one, since implicitly denying the very nature of aesthetic and sensory phenomena. Yet if all we are talking about are human reactions, it might be replied, then aesthetic attributions are just subjective and do not actually ascribe real properties to objects.

We are at the point where greater philosophical sophistication is required. There can be objective facts of the matter regarding humans' responses to certain objects, and consequently there can be real, if relational, properties ascribable to those objects. This is the reason why many philosophers and most of the general population have no qualms with colour-property realism, for example. Something can be really blue even if it appears grey to you because it is true that normal human percipients in common lighting conditions will see the object as blue. And even though many are persuaded by often-rehearsed philosophical claims, such as that the world is a world of facts, that there is a 'fact/value distinction', and that values are not part of the world but are our projections on to it, nevertheless, there are just as many who are prepared to say that it is *just true* that the Holocaust was evil, and that helping those in need is objectively right.

So it is at least coherent to suggest that aesthetic properties are real, provided their relational nature is kept clearly in mind. Aesthetic properties are not mind-independent properties of the physical world in the sense that they are true of objects no matter what *anyone* thinks or how *anyone* reacts, but they may be true of those objects independently of how any *particular* person might respond to them. So in this sense they are not just subjective reactions.

The idea that property realism is bound up with being able meaningfully to distinguish the truth about a work's properties from how that work might appear to or might be thought of by a given percipient has become a central point in the formulation of the realism/anti-realism debate. And in aesthetics, as elsewhere in philosophy, after the 'linguistic turn' this idea has been refashioned as the claim that to be realistic about aesthetic properties is to accept that attributions of aesthetic predicates have objective truth-conditions. Here is Michael Dummett on realism and anti-realism in general:

[T]he preferred characterization of a dispute between realists and anti-realists is one which represents it as relating to a class of *statements*, e.g., statements about the physical world, statements about mental states, statements in the past tense, statements in the future tense, etc. This class I shall term ... 'the disputed class.' Realism I characterize as the belief that statements of the disputed class possess an objective truth-value, independently of our means of knowing: they are true or false in virtue of a reality existing independently of us. (Dummett 1978: 146)

And here is Alan Goldman on aesthetic realism in particular:

A property is real in the relevant sense if the truth of its ascription is independent of the subject's evidence and system of beliefs. It is possible for one to make an error about the presence of a real property despite its appearing to be present and despite one's belief in its presence cohering with other beliefs. If aesthetic qualities are real properties of objects, then there must be some distinction between how they appear and how they are. (Goldman 1995: 26–7)

The substance of the realism debate turns, then, on whether aesthetic attributions have objective truth-conditions, and whether, correlatively, the aesthetic facts about a given object are distinct from the ways that object might seem or appear to a given individual. This is, indeed, a substantive debate. However, what is not often noticed in this discussion is that affirmation of objective truth-conditions is a necessary but *not* a sufficient condition for accepting realism. To see this, consider that a property *nominalist* grants that aesthetic predications have objective truth-conditions. Aesthetic attributions could be construed substitutionally rather than objectually and still be considered objective. This point is important because it highlights the fact that the realist/anti-realist debate as it is usually conducted is somewhat truncated, ignoring certain areas of potential difficulty for the realist. For example, there may be serious problems with *individuating* aesthetic properties, or with conceiving them as *types*. Is the poignancy of a Debussy prelude *the same property* as the poignancy of a Brahms sonata? Or are these attributions implicitly indexical in ways that may be troublesome for the realist? Only recently have these issues begun to be discussed in depth (Vaida 1998; see also Walton 1970). These questions would be missed if our attention were focused solely on the nature of the truth-conditions for aesthetic attributions.

4. Worries over Truth-Conditions

It could be argued that aesthetic attributions simply lack sufficiently robust truth-conditions to be genuine assertions. There is room to wonder, for example, exactly what is being asserted when the wine before you is said to be 'vivacious' or 'aristocratic', and just how this could be established. If realism is tied to aesthetic attributions' having clear assertoric force, there may be grounds for doubt.

Crispin Wright has suggested that genuine assertions are statements that must have truth-conditions of a kind such that:

one who is sincerely unwilling to assent to such a statement when, by ordinary criteria, those conditions obtain, can make himself intelligible to us only by betraying a misunderstanding or some sort of misapprehension, or by professing some sort of sceptical attitude. (Wright 1980: 463)

That is to say, the truth-conditions of genuine assertions are such that, if one believes that those conditions are satisfied, then one cannot deny the assertion without calling into question whether one really understands what is being asserted. 'Strict' truth-conditions, on this view, are conditions that, when believed, allow no room for reasonably demurring from the assertion they characterize.

The argument here against aesthetic realism can be seen as analogous to Moore's 'open question' argument regarding moral properties. Just as no naturalistic conditions are 'strict' enough to close the question of whether an object meeting those conditions also possesses a certain moral property, so too it might be argued that no set of truth-conditions believed to be true by someone closes the question of whether that person might reasonably, and with understanding, deny that the object satisfying the conditions possesses a certain aesthetic property (Sibley 1959).

Challenging the assertoric nature of aesthetic attributions in this way, however, is radically verificationist. A very wide range of apparent assertions will fail these strictures. For instance, could it not be an objective fact that a certain economy is presently 'sluggish' even though someone, because of certain ideological proclivities, reasonably demurs as a result of overestimating some positive economic factors? And yet, the attribution of sluggishness to the economy is at best a 'quasi-assertion' on the view being discussed. If aesthetic attributions can keep this kind of company, that may be realism enough for the aesthetic realist. Hence it is not clear that a serious challenge to realism can be mounted on the basis of worries about the lack of strictness of aesthetic predications' truth-conditions.

But there is a related and detailed position, which has been offered by Roger Scruton, that may be more threatening to aesthetic realism. Scuton begins with the observation that at least many aesthetic descriptions involve predicates used in an extended sense. Calling a musical piece 'sad' clearly is not literally describing it with this predicate: rather, in calling it 'sad' we are saying that a certain experience or response is appropriate to the music. In fact, aesthetic descriptions do not so much *assert* that a certain state of mind is justified, he says, as give direct *expression* to that state of mind itself (Scruton 1982, p. 48). Aesthetic descriptions may therefore lack truth-conditions in the strong sense, and admit only of acceptance conditions that, if they involve reference to responses of a non-doxastic nature, differ from the acceptance conditions of pure descriptions, statable in terms of beliefs. This explains what Scruton takes as a fundamental symptom of aesthetic descriptions, viz. that one must directly experience the object in order to truly know that such an attribution is appropriate: one cannot know this via indirect testimony, as is possible in the case of 'pure' descriptions.

certain aesthetic descriptions are non-descriptive in that they express not beliefs but rather 'aesthetic experiences'. To understand such an aesthetic description involves realizing that one can assert it or assent to it sincerely only if one has had a certain 'experience,' just as one can assert or assent to a normal description only if one has the appropriate belief....

The affective theory of aesthetic description argues that the acceptance condition of an aesthetic description may not be a belief but may rather be some other mental state.... To agree to an aesthetic description is to 'see its point', and this 'seeing the point' is to be elucidated in terms of some response or experience.... Hence aesthetic descriptions need not have truth conditions in the strong sense, and to justify them may be to justify an experience and not a belief. (Scruton 1982: 49–52)

The idea here is that aesthetic attributions can function to express an appropriate non-doxastic response to an artwork without implicating a realist interpretation of these attributions as property ascriptions equipped with knowable truth-conditions. One is not seeing how the work *is* as much as one is seeing the work *under a certain aspect*, and responding appropriately.

Scruton's view appears a deep and powerful alternative to aesthetic property realism. But the argument rests on several points that a realist might not find persuasive. The position begins from the 'observation' that in aesthetics one must see for oneself; that there is no possibility of indirect knowledge of the truth or warrantedness of aesthetic predications. In contrast, objective property ascriptions can be known by testimony from reliable others. Now it may be true that aesthetic descriptions lack much of their point in the absence of first-hand experience of the object, and that coming to 'see' a work as sad, taut, or muscular is more important to aesthetic appreciation than merely coming to believe that the work has these properties. Nonetheless, it is doubtful than one *cannot* come to warrantedly believe and to know that an object has a certain aesthetic property by being told this by a qualified person one knows to have tastes similar to one's own, and with whom one almost always agrees aesthetically.

Surely, one comes to know that the third movement of Beethoven's E-flat string quartet, Op. 74, 'The Harp', has a powerful forward thrust when told this by someone whose musical ear one knows and trusts. Practically speaking, how could he go wrong about this? Admittedly, this indirect transmission of aesthetic knowledge may break down at very precise levels of description: one might only be able to come to know that this new bottle of Bordeaux has a 'level of breeding beyond even that of the 1986 Chateau Mouton-Rothschild', by making the comparison first-hand. But this may indicate not that there is no warranted aesthetic communication, but only that the concept of same or shared taste does not guarantee agreement on every judgement, no matter how detailed or precious.

Scruton's focus, clearly, is on the *assertability* conditions for aesthetic ascriptions, and his pivotal claim is that these conditions refer to affective states rather than belief states. We have already seen that it is unclear that aesthetic ascriptions are never warranted on the basis of beliefs alone, even when their etiology is testimonial and indirect rather than perceptually based. But perhaps a deeper response to Scruton comes from noticing that there is little reason to think that any condition that refers to a non-doxastic mental state is immediately disqualified as a realistic *truth*-condition for an aesthetic ascription. In other words, nothing Scruton argues about assertability conditions establishes that realistic truth-conditions for aesthetic attributions cannot make reference to certain affective reactions or experiences. The fact that the occurrence of such reactions might be less than strictly verifiable counts against realism only if we accept a strict verifiability theory of truth-conditions, and this is not mandatory for the realist.

So, although Scruton's affective theory may well be an interesting and possible way to couch anti-realism, there is nothing yet imposing such a view upon us.

5. Two Models for Realism

Philip Pettit (1983) has attempted to show that two problematic features of aesthetic characterizations are in fact consistent with a qualified sort of realism.

The first of these features, familiar from the preceding discussion, is the essentially perceptual nature of aesthetic characterizations: why it is that in order justifiedly to claim to know that an aesthetic characterization is true, one must have direct perceptual access to the object. Ordinary secondary properties can be known via testimony. If the realist model for aesthetic properties is roughly the model of secondary properties, then aesthetic properties seem to be diverging from it in an epistemically important way. Can the realist explain this?

The second feature is aesthetic characterizations' perceptual elusiveness. By this, Pettit means that no amount of perceptual experience guarantees sincere assent to the aesthetic characterizations true of the object perceived. One might look and look and yet never see a painting's elegance or poignancy. Real properties, it might be thought, do not exhibit this mysterious power to evade indefinitely.

Of course, Scruton's affective theory has little trouble explaining either of these features: the assertability conditions for aesthetic attributions make reference to certain non-cognitive experiences one can have only in response to the actual work, but whose occurrence is not guaranteed by perceptual scrutiny of the work. Pettit's intent is to look for a conditional of the form 'X is sad if and only if X is such that it looks sad under circumstance C', in which the details of 'circumstance C' explain why aesthetic descriptions are both essentially perceptual and perceptually elusive, and yet stay close in spirit to a realist analysis of secondary properties.

The simple version of Pettit's suggestion is this: to see the sadness of an artwork requires that the object is *properly positioned* for/by the viewer. Proper positioning for colour perception involves standard conditions of presentation, and some knowledge in the perceiver of what the relevant contrast classes are. But this requires only normal information and memory. Properly positioning an artwork so as to see its sadness, on the other hand, requires imagination to place it in relation to a certain appropriate reference class:

The hypothesis put forward is that every picture on which an aesthetic characterisation is fixed is seen against the background of a certain class of discernible variations.... The variations are made into a reference class for the picture; they are used to determine what we have called its positioning.... According to the hypothesis, X is sad if and only if X such that it looks sad under standard presentation and under suitable positioning. The positioning of the work is determined by the reference class against the background of which it is viewed. The class is assumed to be available only on the basis of imagination, not by the introduction of normalized examples. (Pettit 1983: 32–3)

The need for proper positioning of this sort is meant to explain both the essentially perceptual and perceptually elusive nature of aesthetic characterizations. One must have perceptual access to the object to begin the imaginative process of positioning. Yet we have no independent way, as we do when determining if an object is standardly presented, of being sure that an object is suitably positioned for a person.

The concept of proper positioning brings with it the possibility of alternative and deviant positionings, which can seem fatal for realism. First, if art works appear to have different aesthetic properties when positioned in different ways, then at best the truth of aesthetic ascriptions is relative to the reference class in which one positions the work (see Walton 1970). Even worse, if for any work and any aesthetic property one can find some positioning, regardless of how deviant, from which the work appears to have that property, realism becomes negligible, being nothing more than the *ad hoc* privileging of one subjective positioning over another. At the very least, 'suitable positioning' seems to have introduced a normative element into the description of the imaginative and perceptual process supposedly involved in 'seeing the sadness'.

Pettit recognizes that, unless we acknowledge that 'suitable' positioning incorporates certain normative constraints, aesthetic realism must be abandoned. He defends by introducing two types of constraint. Positioning regarding one aesthetic property of a work will be constrained by the positioning required for the other aesthetic properties it possesses. Each must allow for seeing the object as a coherent unity. These are holistic constraints. In addition, humanistic constraints on positioning arise from the demand to see the art work as an intelligible production of a human being about whose cognitive and psychological constitution we are willing to make at least very basic assumptions.

We are left, then, with the following schema: 'X is A if and only if (1) it is such that it looks A under standard presentation and under suitable positioning and (2) it is such that the positioning found suitable, assuming there is one, is allowed by the appropriate constraints' (Pettit 1983: 37).

It would be incorrect to argue that, by introducing normative considerations into the schema, this view effectively undermines realism by turning a work's aesthetic properties into *evaluative* properties. It does not follow from the fact that the responses referred to are normatively characterized that the aesthetic property attributed to the work must be seen as itself evaluative rather than descriptive.

Consider a relational property, such as *being the ball of preference of all of golf's great players*, where 'great player' is defined as 'player winning more than four major championships'. It can be a purely descriptive—and real—fact that a certain brand of golf ball is preferred among a group of golfers that satisfies some normative standard; the introduction of evaluative considerations in specifying the reference class need not turn the property had by the ball into an evaluative feature of it, whose realistic status might thereby be called into question. The ball may be preferred because of its good properties, but a fact about good players' choices is not in itself an evaluative attribution to their chosen object.

There are, though, more substantial worries about Pettit's defence of realism. First, notice that it is not the realist aspects of his schema that provide the answer to the two supposed obstacles to realism, viz. aesthetic attributions' essential perceptual nature and their perceptual elusiveness. Rather, these problems are addressed by the ascription to the viewer of a non-doxastic mental process—the perception of the aesthetic object and the imaginative positioning of it within a reference class. In essence, this does not differ from Scruton's anti-realist suggestion that non-cognitive mental states or experiences explain the same two features of aesthetic attributions, yet do so without engaging us in the project of providing truth-conditions for such predications. Therefore, Pettit has at most shown that these two alleged characteristics of aesthetic attributions do not block a realist interpretation, but he has provided no reason to *prefer* it to the affective theory or to other anti-realist views. Moreover, we have already found reason to question whether aesthetic attributions are in fact essentially perceptual.

Even more troublesome is whether Pettit's realism is 'realism enough'. The relativization of aesthetic attributions to specific reference classes or 'positionings' may, as suggested earlier, entail an indefensible privileging of the 'suitable' over the 'deviant' ones. How are we to defend the idea that a painting is 'really' tragic rather than merely expressive of personal depression, if both positionings are coherent and reasonable, given humanistic and holistic constraints? The worry, of course, is that no plausible and non-*ad hoc* list of constraints will eliminate the bulk of apparently reasonable aesthetic disagreements. This point will be further elaborated as we consider the work of Alan Goldman.

Like many analytic aestheticians, Goldman is deeply interested in the nature of the link between the perception of non-aesthetic and non-evaluative aesthetic properties, on the one hand, and the ascription of evaluative aesthetic properties on the other. Clarifying the nature of this connection seems crucial to understanding how a work's non-aesthetic and non-evaluative properties can plausibly be cited as reasons for ascribing given evaluative properties to the work.

Goldman's most recent view (1995: 14) denies that the link between a work's objective properties and its evaluative aesthetic properties is logically a reductive link (involving necessary and sufficient conditions), conceptual (involving meaning relations), a criterial one (involving non-inductive relations short of entailment), or one of supervenience (the idea that necessarily a change in a work's evaluative properties requires a change in some of its objective properties.) The link, Goldman suggests, is simply inductive or causal: in making evaluative judgements, critics are implying that others with similar tastes will react to the same objective properties in the same ways, if free of shortcomings of attention, interest, experience, or sensitivity:

...aesthetic judgments ascribing [evaluative] properties are justified by appeal to non-evaluative base properties on which evaluative aesthetic properties depend. The dependence relation is...causal.... [A]scriptions of aesthetic properties are true, relative to certain tastes, when base properties of artworks cause certain responses in critics with ideal characteristics. Such judgements are justified when we are justified in ascribing these causal relations. (Goldman 1995: 44)

Goldman is less than perfectly clear as to the nature of the response evoked in an ideal critic by a work truly characterized by an evaluative aesthetic property, A. But the basic idea seems to be that, if a percipient with certain tastes claims that an object x has A, then this claim is true just in case x would cause ideally positioned critics of similar taste to assent to x's being A, to believe that x is A, to see x as being A, to experience x as being A, to feel pleasure or displeasure at x's being A, in virtue of x's more basic, non-evaluative properties (1995: 22–3). The model on which this analysis is based is the 'ideal observer' theory of moral predications: an act is morally right or praiseworthy just in case the ideally knowledgeable and morally sensitive observer would respond positively to the act (Firth 1952).

One might think that an ideal observer analysis could save realism even though the reference class whose responses are relevant to the truth of an aesthetic predication is normatively characterized, because there might nevertheless be an objective fact of the matter as to what those responses are. Interestingly, the fundamental logical structure of this view hardly diverges from that of Pettit's brand of realism, which could be schematized as follows:

Object O has aesthetic property P = there is a certain group of percipients in which O causes a certain experiential response of kind R (O's seeming P), as a result of these percipients engaging in certain imaginative/psychological processes ('positioning') satisfying certain relevant normative constraints.

Compare the 'Humean structure' that Goldman provides for the ideal viewer analysis of aesthetic attributions:

Object O has aesthetic property P = O is such as to elicit response of kind R in ideal viewers of kind V in virtue of its more basic properties B. (Goldman 1995: 21)

An account having this form, despite its evaluative elements and its reference to viewer responses, could then satisfy the basic constraints on realism, because the facts about the nature of the responses of ideal viewers are seemingly independent of the beliefs of actual viewers about them, and a distinction is maintained between how objects appear to certain viewers and how they really are.

But this realism founders when we ask the question, 'What happens if ideal viewers disagree in their responses?' Contradiction is what follows for the realist, for the analysis would entail ascribing incompatible properties to the same work—the realist's worst nightmare.

6. Goldman's Anti-realism and Beyond

Goldman's central tenet is that aesthetic judgements are seriously relative to tastes, so that even ideally situated viewers with divergent tastes will fail to share aesthetic judgements (1995: 36–9). His account agrees with the realist that the truth of aesthetic judgements is not solely a matter of how objects appear to given viewers; but he emphasizes that:

the truth of such judgments is not independent of ways they appear to ideal critics, of all evaluative responses to them, or of other aesthetic judgments and beliefs that constitute different tastes. . . . There is a distinction possible between aesthetic properties and how they appear to us but not between how they are and how they appear to ideal critics of different tastes. (Goldman 1995: 38–9)

So aesthetic property-judgements are relative to tastes yet still vulnerable to error, since one may be wrong in claiming that ideal critics who share one's tastes will respond in a certain fashion.

Goldman characterizes this view as anti-realist on the grounds that disagreements among ideal critics will result in the ascription of incompatible properties to the same work of art (1995: 29). Although disagreement among actual viewers is compatible with a realist view, since some viewers may be inexperienced, inattentive, or biased in certain ways, the existence of persistent disputes among ideal critics whose tastes differ is sufficient to enjoin anti-realism.

But the argument for anti-realism may be even stronger than Goldman allows. There is a question whether references to 'same' or 'different' tastes can be non-vacuously elaborated. It seems manifest that individuals with the same taste can nonetheless faultlessly disagree over the aesthetic properties of a certain work. If so, sameness of taste cannot guarantee aesthetic agreement. To deny this would reduce the condition of shared taste to the claim that those who agree that object x has property A agree that x is A. But if critics of similar taste can disagree, even if they are similarly experienced, attentive, perceptive, and sensitive, then the rock bottom obstacle to aesthetic realism is not that well-positioned percipients may disagree about an object's aesthetic properties because they have different tastes, but rather, that any irresolvable dispute among well situated and experienced critics, regardless of shared or disparate tastes, is enough to raise the anti-realist flag.

A further alteration of Goldman's theory may take us even closer to the truth. His theory is, on the one hand, a *causal* theory: base properties of an object cause certain aesthetic judgements in a defined group of viewers. On the other hand, it is a type of ideal observer theory: the defined group is ideally situated to make its judgement. The ideal viewer, being omniscient about the relevant historical relations a work may have to others, cannot, he says, tire of viewing some work, therefore changing his evaluation of it. The ideal critic would know from the beginning how well a work would withstand repeated viewings (1995: 42). It follows, then, that no actual viewer could be an ideal critic, since anyone might tire of even the most spectacular works. But if the ideal viewer is a non-realizable abstraction, does it make sense to talk of real causal relations between aesthetic objects and ideal viewers?

It is unclear that inflecting the view into the subjunctive would solve the real problem; for, were we to refer to the reactions an ideal viewer *would* have to aesthetic objects, we would arrive at an analysis formally similar to the so-called 'epistemic' conception of truth. Roughly, that conception has it that 'X is P' is true if and only if epistemically ideally situated observers would believe that x is P. But it has been forcefully argued that this view is ultimately parasitic upon a presupposed, pre-theoretic, and undefended realistic conception of truth (Williams 1996: chapter 6). An anti-realism regarding aesthetic properties that was similarly and implicitly dependent upon property realism would not be sustainable.

It seems, then, that we must limit the notion of an 'ideal' observer to something like an 'appropriately knowledgeable, sensitive, attentive observer', a characterization that can be instantiated by real viewers. If we add this revision to the earlier claim that similar tastes do not guarantee sameness of aesthetic judgement, it becomes extremely difficult to see how one might deflect the conclusion that there are irresolvable disputes in aesthetic attributions even among equally informed and well situated critics or experts. The problem of such irresolvable disputes is the true nemesis of aesthetic realism.

7. Aesthetic Properties as Essentially Phenomenal

In several essays Jerrold Levinson has attempted to save realism from the problem of irresolvable disputes by distinguishing firmly between aesthetic properties themselves and evaluatively laden descriptions of the aesthetic object (Levinson 1990, 1994, 2001). In this way, it becomes possible to see most disputes as deriving from differences in viewers' tastes, sensibilities, or attitudes of approval and disapproval, while none the less insisting that underlying such differences in evaluative descriptions there are *shared* phenomenal, perceptual, or experiential impressions that are caused in normal, appropriately backgrounded viewers by the particular array of non-aesthetic, formal, structural features that a given art work presents (Levinson 1994: 353). Aesthetic properties, on this view, can be realistically conceived, much like secondary properties, as dispositions of an object to afford such distinctive phenomenal impressions or effects. One can register the particular exuberant quality of the finale of Tchaikovsky's Symphony No. 4, Levinson says, independently of whether one is put off by that quality and hence describes it as 'bombastic', or is attracted to it and hence describes it as 'exciting':

... there is an aesthetic quality that I ascribe mentally to the music, a quality not reducible to the particular timbres, rhythms, harmonies, and loudnesses on which it is based, and one I can hear as what it is regardless of my current attitude towards it ... (Levinson 1994: 353).

There are difficulties with this phenomenally based aesthetic realism, however. First, it requires us to be able to distinguish not only aesthetic from non-aesthetic terms, but also evaluatively neutral from evaluatively laden aesthetic terms. The view then seems to postulate that different cognitive processes are involved in the use of these two types of aesthetic term, with only the evaluative terms engaging the viewer's 'tastes' or 'preferences'. But, in fact, evaluatively laden aesthetic terms and those that are more or less evaluatively neutral are commonly used in a continuous fashion that gives no evidence of involving different processes depending on the instance. Consider the following continuum of terms for the intensity of emotional expressiveness: Cold—Restrained—Expressive—Emotional—Sentimental—Maudlin. There is no reason to think that a viewer is employing his taste any less when he chooses one of the neutral middle terms as the most appropriate than when he selects one of the more evaluatively laden terms at the extremes of the continuum (Bender 1996).

A second and deeper point is that it is by no means obvious that judges who disagree about a work's aesthetic properties are, in fact, afforded the same phenomenal impression of the work. If the same wine tastes searingly acidic to one taster but refreshing and zingy to another, do they nonetheless share some common phenomenal impression of the wine's acid level? What is shared, of course, is an awareness of the particular *non-aesthetic* properties of the wine that cause *different* reactions and certainly cause different aesthetic judgements. To claim that something more is shared, something phenomenal and in principle individuable, seems implausible.

It is worth noting, furthermore, that disagreements over which aesthetic description of an object is best can, at least in some cases, indicate a possible difference in the degree of sensitivity each viewer has to certain properties. Might not one person truly be more sensitive to so-called 'gaudy' colours than another, who finds them only 'bright'? If so, we would not find shared phenomenal impressions underlying these disagreements, but precisely the contrary.

8. TRANSCENDENTAL ARGUMENTS
FOR REALISM

Eddy Zemach (1991, 1997) has argued for aesthetic realism in a rather different way. At least some aesthetic properties must be real, according to Zemach, and massive error about our aesthetic predications impossible (*à la* Davidson), because aesthetic terms would otherwise lack meaning. The meanings of at least some such predicates must be learned by ostension; we must be able to 'see' that some things have an aesthetic property, A, if 'A' is to have a stable and public meaning (Zemach 1991; 1997: chapters 2 and 3). There must (echoing Wittgenstein) be agreement on at least paradigm or central cases. Hence at least some aesthetic properties are observable, and therefore real. Disagreements are about difficult new and marginal cases and are to be explained by identifying the observation conditions that are *standard* for the various properties really possessed by art, and by determining that at least one disputant is not in these standard observation conditions.

Three criticisms can be offered of this 'paradigm case' argument for realism. First, if correct, it is difficult to see how the argument would not be a defence of realism for *any type* of purported property, no matter how abstract or otherwise problematic. Hence the argument proves too much. Second, it is unclear how the semantic assumption that aesthetic terms have shared or public meaningfulness establishes a metaphysical conclusion about the status of aesthetic properties. It does not follow from the fact that aesthetic predicates are meaningful that there must be a common core of cases in which everyone can observe that an object has a certain aesthetic property, or that all instances of disagreement are over borderline cases. Might not the stability and intersubjectivity of objects' non-aesthetic properties be sufficient to determine that a certain constellation of aesthetic predicates can reasonably be applied while other predicates are deemed inappropriate, without having a fixed core of cases about which we all aesthetically agree? Could the intelligibility of aesthetic predicates be explained in this way without the need for paradigm cases whose aesthetic properties are real?

Lastly, it is an implication of Zemach's argument that all cases of aesthetic disagreement are traceable to non-standard conditions, and this seems implausible. Even if we allow certain skills to count as part of the standard conditions for observing a given artwork (as Zemach suggests) what one person identifies as a 'moving, romantic view of nature' is another's 'wide-eyed sentimentality'. Conditions can be as standard as you wish, and yet the music of Delius can seem uplifting and releasing one day and precious and uncontrolled another. Must one's skills, abilities, or conditions have been in flux for this change of reaction to occur? It seems not.

Zemach offers a second argument, which might be called 'the argument from scientific realism', to the effect that any realist about theoretical properties of our best science must, under pain of contradiction, also be an aesthetic realist (Zemach 1991; 1997: 64–7).

Zemach's zeal for realism derives from his view that aesthetic properties are irreducible to physicalistic ones, and perform ineliminable explanatory work regarding our experiences. To experience x as F is to be acquainted with F. One cannot relinquish phenomenal and aesthetic properties for scientific and physicalistic ones because science is based on experience. Adjudication of true theories essentially involves making aesthetic judgements about those theories—judgements of beauty, simplicity, unity, coherence, and so forth. Any scientific realist, Zemach argues, must be an aesthetic realist, roughly because beauty is truth-tropic. If theory T is true, then it is beautiful. If an aesthetic theory, AT, implies that T is beautiful, then AT is true. AT's basic predicates denote features of the world. So aesthetic properties are real.

Of course, the second premiss of this argument is false if taken to mean that AT in its entirety is true: a theory false in the main might yet have the right result about T. But more generally, the argument must be flawed, as can be seen by analogy. Compare it with the following dubious argument that any moral realist must be a theist. If T is the correct theory about what actions are right, then T accords with God's commands. Therefore the theistic theory, TT, that says that T captures what God commands, is true. So the basic predicates of T must then refer to something in the world. Hence, the property of being consistent with God's commands is a real property.

Furthermore, it is unclear that simplicity, coherence, and unity have univocal meanings when applied to scientific theories and to aesthetic objects, as they must be for the argument to succeed. Consider the simplicity of design that characterizes Shaker furniture. This visual simplicity is very likely the result of quite complex and subtle formal relationships between the parts of furniture, suggesting that 'theoretical simplicity' and 'aesthetic simplicity' are quite different matters. Similar remarks could be made about 'elegance', 'powerfulness', 'coherence,' and other properties. And even if some aesthetic properties do apply univocally to art works and scientific theories, this is a very small subset of the properties coming under the rubric, 'aesthetic'. Hence the argument from scientific realism does not support aesthetic realism as a general metaphysical position.

9. CONCLUDING SUGGESTIONS

A compelling argument for aesthetic realism has not been forthcoming. Anti-realism appears to be the consequence of the fact that there are unresolvable aesthetic disputes even between appropriately positioned and backgrounded experts. But if aesthetic attributions are not predications of real properties to objects, then how are we to conceive them? Is there an anti-realist model that may be offered to illuminate their status?

Perhaps such a model can be found in the judgements commonly made of other people's actions, demeanour, bearing, and motivations. These are judgements about which individuals obviously and vehemently disagree, and yet it is an area in which 'property talk' easily gets a foothold. Furthermore, although such personal attributions express our reactions to the individual being characterized, we nonetheless admit that reasons supporting those reactions can be demanded, and a distinction can be drawn between justified and unjustified attributions. In the face of disagreements with a third party, we also commonly retreat to a more subjective assertion that the individual strikes *us* a certain way, much as we do with aesthetic attributions. And as with aesthetic properties, personality characteristics might seem (whether correctly or not) to be 'supervenient' upon, or 'emergent' from, more basic features of the person's actions and comportment.

As obvious and real as personality features seem to be, disagreement over them is, at every turn, possible, and due at least in part to the differences in the 'taste' of those who interact with the person being characterized. The same basic behaviours stand to be 'interpreted' differently by people with different 'tastes' in personality types. The same conversation, for example, may be taken by one as evidence of a person's boorishness and by another as symptomatic of his or her dogged intelligence. We may be wholly convinced that ours is the right or true 'take' on a given personality, but when confronted with another reasonable interpretation, we must be satisfied with the realization that, justified as it may be, our view may not be the unique 'fact of the matter.'

See also: Aesthetic Realism 1; Beauty; Aesthetic Experience; Value in Art.

BIBLIOGRAPHY

Beardsley, M. (1963). 'The Discrimination of Aesthetic Enjoyment'. *British Journal of Aesthetics* 3: 291–300; reprinted in Wreen and Callen (1982).

—— (1973). 'What Is An Aesthetic Property'? *Theoria* 39: 50–70; reprinted in Wreen and Callen (1982).

Bender, J. (1996). 'Realism, Supervenience, and Irresolvable Aesthetic Disputes'. *Journal of Aesthetics and Art Criticism* 54: 371–81.

—— (2000). Review of Eddy Zemach, *Real Beauty*. *Philosophy and Phenomenological Research* 60: 714–17.

—— (2001). 'Sensibility, Sensitivity, and Aesthetic Realism'. *Journal of Aesthetics and Art Criticism* 59: 73–83.

Brady, E. and Levinson, J. (eds.) (2000). *Aesthetic Concepts: Essays after Sibley*. Oxford: Oxford University Press.

Cohen, T. (1973). 'Aesthetic/Non-aesthetic and the Concept of Taste'. *Theoria* 39: 113–52.

Currie, G. (1990). 'Supervenience, Essentialism and Aesthetic Properties'. *Philosophical Studies* 58: 243–57.

Dummett, M. (1978). *Truth and Other Enigmas*. Cambridge, Mass.: Harvard University Press.

Eaton, M. (1994). 'The Intrinsic, Non-Supervenient Nature of Aesthetic Properties'. *Journal of Aesthetics and Art Criticism* 52: 383–97.

Firth, R. (1952). 'Ethical Absolutism and the Ideal Observer'. *Philosophy and Phenomenological Research* 12: 317–45.

Goldman, A. (1992). 'Aesthetic Properties', in D. Cooper (ed.), *A Companion to Aesthetics*. Oxford: Blackwell Publishers.

—— (1995). *Aesthetic Value*. Boulder, Colo.: Westview Press.

Hermeren, G. (1988a). 'The Variety of Aesthetic Qualities', in Mitias (1988, pp. 11–23).

—— (1988b). *Aesthetic Qualities*. Lund, Sweden: Lund University Press.

Levinson, J. (1990). 'Aesthetic Supervenience', reprinted in his *Music, Art, and Metaphysics*. Ithaca, NY: Cornell University Press, pp. 134–58.

—— (1994). 'Being Realistic about Aesthetic Properties'. *Journal of Aesthetics and Art Criticism* 52: 351–4.

Levinson, J. (2001). 'Aesthetic Properties, Evaluative Force, and Differences of Sensibility', in E. Brady and J. Levinson (eds.), *Aesthetic Concepts: Essays after Sibley*. Oxford: Clarendon Press.

Mitias, M. (ed.) (1988). *Aesthetic Quality and Aesthetic Experience*. Amsterdam: Rodolpi B.V., pp. 11–23.

Pettit, P. (1983). 'Aesthetic Realism', in Shaper (1983).

Putnam, H. (1981). *Reason, Truth and History*. Cambridge: Cambridge University Press.

Scruton, R. (1982). *Art and Imagination: A Study in the Philosophy of Mind*. London: Routledge & Kegan Paul.

Shaper, E. (ed.) (1983). *Pleasure, Preference and Value*. Cambridge: Cambridge University Press.

Sibley, F. (1959). 'Aesthetic Concepts'. *Philosophical Review* 68: 421–50.

——(1965). 'Aesthetic and Non-aesthetic'. *Philosophical Review* 74: 135–59.

——(1983). 'General Criteria and Reasons in Aesthetics', in J. Fisher (ed.), *Essays on Aesthetics: Perspectives on the Work of Monroe Beardsley*. Phildelphia: Temple University Press, pp. 3–20.

Tormey, A. (1973). 'Critical Judgments'. *Theoria* 39: 35–49.

Vaida, I. (1998). 'The Quest for Objectivity: Secondary Qualities and Aesthetic Qualities'. *Journal of Aesthetics and Art Criticism* 56: 283–97.

Walton, K. (1970). 'Categories of Art'. *Philosophical Review* 79: 334–67.

Williams, M. (1996). *Unreasonable Doubts*. Princeton: Princeton University Press.

Wreen, M. and Callen, D. (eds.) (1982). *The Aesthetic Point of View: Selected Essays of Monroe Beardsley*. Ithaca, NY: Cornell University Press.

Wright, C. (1980). *Wittgenstein on the Foundations of Mathematics*. London: Duckworth.

Zangwill, N. (1995). 'The Beautiful, the Dainty and the Dumpy'. *British Journal of Aesthetics* 35: 317–29.

Zemach, E. (1991). 'Real Beauty'. *Midwest Studies in Philosophy* 16: 249–65.

——(1997). *Real Beauty*. University Park, Pa.: Pennsylvania State University Press.

CHAPTER 5

AESTHETIC EXPERIENCE

GARY ISEMINGER

1. THE AESTHETIC STATE OF MIND

THERE is a long history of discussions of the aesthetic and of art in which the fundamental concepts are psychological, in the sense of being or including concepts of states of mind. Examples include Aristotle's discussion of the tragic emotions of pity and fear, Aquinas's account of beauty in terms of delight in contemplation, and Kant's discussion of the disinterested pleasure characteristic of awareness of the beautiful. In addition to aesthetic emotion, aesthetic contemplation, and aesthetic pleasure, such concepts have included aesthetic perception, the aesthetic attitude, and aesthetic appreciation.

This chapter surveys attempts by aestheticians writing in the Anglo-American analytic tradition during the last half of the twentieth century to clarify, defend, and use the idea of a distinctively aesthetic state of mind. Their ambitions typically include most or all of the following: (i) giving an account of what distinguishes the aesthetic state of mind from other states of mind that are like it in some ways, such as sensual pleasure or drug-induced experience, or from those connected with other realms of human concern, such as the religious, the cognitive, the practical, and the moral; (ii) giving that account in a way that appeals neither to any prior idea of the aesthetic nor to the concept of art; (iii) explaining related ideas of the distinctively aesthetic, e.g. the ideas of aesthetic properties, qualities, aspects, or concepts, of the aesthetic object, of the aesthetic judgement, and of aesthetic value, in terms of the idea of the distinctively aesthetic state of mind; and (iv) defending some more or less close connection between the realm of the aesthetic thereby explained and the realm of art, while recognizing that the aesthetic state of mind may appropriately be directed towards or grounded in non-art (e.g. nature) as well.

2. TWO CONCEPTS OF EXPERIENCE

The concept of *aesthetic experience* has sometimes been taken as the generic idea of a distinctively aesthetic state of mind, covering any or all of the more specific states mentioned above. Experience in general, however, is typically conceived of in more determinate ways than merely as an otherwise unspecified state of mind. Two different, more specific, concepts of experience are that of experience as something characterized primarily by 'what it is like' to undergo it, and that of experience as involving direct or non-inferential knowledge: the first may be called a *phenomenological* concept of experience, the second an *epistemic* one. The former is invoked when we wonder what the experience of bats is like; the latter, when we claim that hearing rather than seeing is the primary mode of experience whereby bats know their location relative to neighbouring objects.

A phenomenological conception of *aesthetic* experience, accordingly, is a conception of what it is like to have an aesthetic experience. Versions of the idea of an introspectively identifiable and phenomenologically distinctive aesthetic experience appear in some of the canonical works of such early twentieth-century Anglo-American aestheticians as Clive Bell, Edward Bullough, and John Dewey. (Not surprisingly, twentieth-century continental phenomenologists such as Roman Ingarden and Mikel Dufrenne also develop and defend related ideas.)

An epistemic conception of aesthetic experience, on the other hand, is a conception of a non-inferential way of coming to know something—comparable, say, to seeing that something is a chair—which deserves to be thought of as aesthetic. Monroe Beardsley, one of the founders of the Anglo-American aesthetic tradition of the latter half of the twentieth-century, began by defending a phenomenological idea of aesthetic experience. Under persistent pressure from George Dickie, another influential and important early aesthetician in this tradition, however, his views gradually evolved in the direction of an epistemic notion. Most recent attempts to defend the notion of aesthetic experience within this tradition, while not in general incompatible with the idea of a phenomenologically distinctive aesthetic experience, see it in fundamentally epistemic terms. This chapter traces the evolution from Beardsley's early phenomenological account and Dickie's critique to current epistemic accounts and continuing critiques of the whole idea of an aesthetic state of mind.

3. THE BEARDSLEY–DICKIE DEBATE

Monroe Beardsley (1958), although influenced by contemporary linguistic philosophies to identify aesthetics with the study of the principles involved in 'clarifying and confirming critical statements', was also influenced by Dewey's account of the 'consummatory' experience he identified with the aesthetic. Beardsley's account, and the subsequent exchanges between him and George Dickie, were seminal for later Anglo-American discussions of aesthetic experience.

Beardsley (1958) eschews any definition of art, but works rather from a disjunctive account of the notion of what he calls an aesthetic object. Contrary to appearances, this appeal to the idea of the aesthetic object does not really involve abandoning the idea of the aesthetic experience as basic in the aesthetic realm. Beardsley says: 'We can...group together disjunctively the class of musical compositions, visual designs, literary works, and all other separately defined classes of objects, and give the name "aesthetic object" to them all...' (p. 64), and this sounds more like an account of the work of art than a first move in an account of the aesthetic. If such a disjunctive account suggests anti-essentialist scruples about defining art of the sort that were just then beginning to be expressed, it is also the case that such scruples were being expressed about the concept of the aesthetic in general and about aesthetic experience in particular. For Beardsley, nevertheless, such a rough indication of the extension of the class of aesthetic objects (works of art) is sufficient to motivate the search for the characteristically aesthetic experience in the form of the question whether there are certain features of experience that are peculiarly characteristic of our intercourse with such objects.

Introspection, checkable by each enquirer, yields the result that these experiences do indeed have something distinctive in common. They are complex, intense, and unified (this latter in two different ways, as coherent and complete). Experiences similar in some ways, for example watching an athletic contest or appreciating a mathematical proof, have some but not all of the relevant features. The degree of complexity, intensity, and unity (in sum, the magnitude) of the aesthetic experience, though directly related to the complexity, intensity, and unity of the aesthetic object on which it is directed, is not reducible to them: it is a feature of the experience itself. The aesthetic value of aesthetic objects (works of art), then, lies in their capacity to produce experiences of this kind, and these experiences are in turn valuable in various ways for those who have them—for example in integrating the self, refining perception and discrimination, and developing imagination and sympathy.

Dickie (1965) criticizes Beardsley's transfer of terms such as complexity, intensity, and unity from the objects of aesthetic experience to the experience itself, concentrating especially on the coherence and completeness that on Beardsley's view constitute the unity of the aesthetic experience. Dickie grants that aesthetic objects (works of art) can be coherent and complete, for example, and that we can experience their coherence and completeness; but he insists that it is simply a mistaken vestige of idealism that leads us to take an experience *of* certain properties as an experience of *having* those properties. We confuse an experience of completeness with the completeness of an experience. In a context where the very idea of an aesthetic experience is that of an experience that is phenomenologically identifiable as unified, then the upshot is that there are no such things as aesthetic experiences, so that any account of the aesthetic value of objects based on their capacity to produce such experiences is radically ill founded. (Some philosophers might find the idea that works of art objectively have properties like unity more dubious than the idea that an experience can be unified; others, who might grant that both experiences and their objects can have properties such as unity, intensity, and complexity, might think it too good to be true that these properties 'line up' in such a way that the objects of unified, intense, and complex experiences are, as Beardsley maintains, themselves unified, intense, and complex.)

Beardsley (1969), replying to Dickie, defends the completeness of the experience in addition to that of the object experienced, claiming, as against Dickie, that the experience of a complete aesthetic object is only part of a complete experience—a fulfilment of an expectation, for example—and that such an experience, even though extended in time, *becomes* phenomenologically complete in itself when the expectation is fulfilled.

In Beardsley (1969) there is also a somewhat different and more formal account of what an aesthetic experience is:

A person is having an aesthetic experience during a particular stretch of time if and only if the greater part of his mental activity during that time is united and made pleasurable by being tied to the form and qualities of a sensuously presented or imaginatively intended object on which his primary attention in concentrated. (Beardsley 1969: 5)

The concept of unity—the Deweyan idea of *an* experience *par excellence*—remains prominent, but the concepts of intensity and complexity fade into the background. The concept of pleasure, mentioned only incidentally in Beardsley (1958), becomes an essential feature of the aesthetic experience, and the experience is essentially and not merely contingently tied to the 'form and qualities of a sensuously presented or imaginatively intended object'. Notice, too, that neither an antecedent conception of the aesthetic nor the concept of a work of art is invoked in this characterization.

This account seems to be edging towards the border between the phenomenological and the epistemic notions of experience. The essential inclusion of the tie to the presented or intended object and its form and qualities suggests that the experience *is* a kind of cognition. On the other hand, Beardsley is clear that the object and qualities in question need be only *phenomenally* objective—that is to say that, like colours but unlike pains, for instance, they *present* themselves to us *as* qualities of something other than ourselves—but they need not be properties of actual objects distinct from ourselves. By the same token, it seems that, even though there might be only some aspects of the experience—its being unified and pleasurable for example—concerning which one can sensibly ask what it is *like* to have an experience of that sort, the aesthetic experience as described, unlike seeing or knowing of a genuinely epistemic kind, *is* plausibly entirely accessible introspectively.

Responding to Beardsley (1969), Dickie (1974) concedes that experiences as well as their objects can be unified, interpreting this as the claim that 'affects' (feelings, emotions, expectations, satisfactions) can be related to one another in such a way as to constitute a complete and coherent experience. He objects, however, that, even granting this much to Beardsley, Beardsley's revised account of aesthetic experience invoking this experiential unity is too narrow in at least two ways. First, Dickie argues, there are undoubted aesthetic experiences that arouse none of the affects mentioned above, for instance the experience of certain kinds of abstract paintings. (Dickie cites no specific examples, but perhaps has in mind works like some of those by Kenneth Noland or Sol LeWitt.) Further, where affects are aroused, as by watching a decent production of *Hamlet*, there is no reason to suppose that those affects must be unified. Dickie concludes that aesthetic experiences 'do not have any affective features which are peculiarly characteristic and which distinguish them from other experiences', and that such experiences can be distinguished from others, if at all, only by their being derived from what is antecedently characterizable as an aesthetic object.

To these arguments, Beardsley (1982) replies that the elements whose connections with one another might make a passage of experience coherent (and thus unified) comprise not only feelings but also thoughts, so that aesthetic experiences might still be unified even if they do not include feelings. He claims further that Dickie's examples of allegedly affectless aesthetic experiences are plausible only if one confuses feelings with 'full-fledged' emotions (presumably involving conceptual as well as affective elements); the absence of emotion from a passage of experience by no means implies the absence of feeling.

Beardsley (1982) thus continues to defend the existence of something like the Deweyan idea of *an* aesthetic experience, involving an overarching unity in some stretch of one's mental life. Significantly, however, he concedes that 'only a very limited account of our aesthetic life' can be given in terms of experiences of this sort. He therefore introduces 'a broader concept of the aesthetic in experience, while reserving the term "aesthetic experience," as a count noun, for rather special occasions'.

He suggests that his introduction of the concept of pleasure in Beardsley (1969) was a first move in this direction, presumably because pleasure is more common than Deweyan consummatory experiences, but he now finds it 'threateningly reductionistic' to take pleasure as definitive of the aesthetic, even as he concedes that his original Deweyan view erred in the opposite direction.

He also backs away from any claim of jointly sufficient and separately necessary conditions for this broader notion of the aesthetic in experience, instead proposing five 'criteria', concerning which he claims that the first is necessary and that it and any three of the other four are sufficient. The first criterion is *object directedness*, 'a willingly accepted guidance over the succession of one's mental states by phenomenally objective properties'; the others are *felt freedom*, 'a sense of release from the dominance of some antecedent concerns about past and future', *detached affect*, 'a sense that objects on which interest is concentrated are set a little at a distance emotionally', *active discovery*, 'a sense of actively exercising constructive powers of the mind', and *wholeness*, 'a sense of integration as a person...and a corresponding contentment'.

In this account, then, although anti-essentialist scruples once again come to the fore, now concerning aesthetic experience rather than art, and although there is only a faint echo of the Deweyan idea of unity, now conceived of as the 'wholeness' of the self rather than as the coherence and completeness of one of its experiences, Beardsley still claims to distinguish an aesthetic state of mind and to do so without appeal to any prior idea of the aesthetic or the artistic.

The other ambitions mentioned at the beginning of this chapter are still intact in Beardsley (1982), in which he proposes to define the aesthetic point of view in terms of aesthetic value:

To adopt the aesthetic point of view with regard to *X* is to take an interest in whatever aesthetic value *X* may possess (p. 19)

and to define aesthetic value in terms of aesthetic gratification (where 'aesthetic gratification' is a variation on 'aesthetic experience'):

The aesthetic value of *X* is the value that *X* possesses in virtue of its capacity to provide aesthetic gratification *when correctly perceived*. [emphasis in the original]. (p. 26)

The move outside the circle of aesthetic notions is made in the claim that

Gratification is aesthetic when it is obtained primarily from attention to the formal unity and/or the regional qualities of a complex whole, and when its magnitude is a function of the degree of formal unity and/or the intensity of regional quality. (p. 22)

In making this move, Beardsley notes that he here distinguishes aesthetic gratification from other kinds of gratification solely in terms of what it is gratification *in*.

Concerning the relationship between aesthetic states of mind and non-art items, Beardsley says hardly anything, but there seems to be no reason to suppose that nature cannot provide aesthetic gratification as he describes it, and he does give at least one example of the aesthetic point of view being adopted towards a natural scene.

Regarding the relation of the aesthetic state of mind to art, he overcomes anti-essentialist scruples about art long enough to hazard a disjunctive *definition* of a work of art as fundamentally something intended to produce that state of mind:

An artwork is *either* an arrangement of conditions intended to be capable of affording an experience with marked aesthetic character *or* (incidentally) an arrangement belonging to a class or type of such arrangements. (p. 299)

The virtual abandonment of anything like the Deweyan conception of *an* experience as a condition of the aesthetic, however, makes the resulting view look even less phenomenological than its immediate predecessor. By the same token, the suggestion that aesthetic experience is in fact not just aesthetic gratification, but aesthetic gratification afforded by the *correct* perception of an object, evidently entails that it is no longer possible to determine introspectively that one's experience is aesthetic, for one cannot in general determine introspectively that one's perception of an object is correct. For the same reason, the appeal to correct perception is a major step in the direction of an overtly epistemic way of thinking about aesthetic experience.

Though phenomenologists writing in English continue to defend phenomenological accounts of the aesthetic experience (see e.g. Mitias 1988), most recent Anglo-American philosophers sympathetic to any project involving the four aims mentioned at the beginning of this chapter have assumed or tried to defend epistemic accounts of experiencing aesthetically.

4. Problems for Theories of the Aesthetic State of Mind

The objections by Dickie to Beardsley just discussed concentrate on the very intelligibility of Beardsley's attempts to delineate the aesthetic in psychological terms more than on their extensional adequacy, and the criticisms of the latter kind that Dickie offers are also pyschological in the sense that they claim that Beardsley's view is too narrow in placing unwarranted pyschological limitations on aesthetic experience (for instance, that it must involve affect).

A more common way of arguing that a conception of aesthetic experience is too narrow is to claim that it results in an excessively formalistic view of what matters about works of art, and thus of what the appreciator must notice in order to experience them correctly and what the critic should consider in interpreting and evaluating them.

The basis for this sort of objection is not only a claimed close connection between art and the aesthetic (e.g. the claim that aesthetic qualities *are* the qualities a critic or appreciator of art must grasp in order to understand and evaluate a work), but also the assumption of a connection between aesthetic experience and some other area of the realm of the aesthetic (e.g. the assumption that aesthetic qualities can be explained as the appropriate objects of aesthetic experience).

This objection often begins by appealing to another psychological notion of the aesthetic, the notion of the *aesthetic attitude*, a state of mind variously described as distanced, detached, or disinterested. (Dickie 1974 subjects various versions of this view to criticisms similar to the ones he brings against Beardsley's account of the aesthetic experience, though Bearsdsley himself does not appeal to the notion of the aesthetic attitude.) The idea of the aesthetic attitude is often taken to be logically prior to that of the aesthetic experience—an aesthetic experience is what one has if, under the right circumstances, one takes the aesthetic attitude. The crucial thing about this attitude is that in it one *ignores or suppresses* some occurrent state or states of mind, for example the desire that a concert one is attending be financially successful and the thought that the hall is barely half full, in the interests of making room for another, say, the enjoyment of the concert.

Given this picture of different states of mind competing for mental space, and the obvious fact that *some* states of mind can effectively preclude anything that could be called an aesthetic experience (as preoccupation with a concert's finances can prevent one from enjoying it), there is a strong temptation to try to make the mind safe for aesthetic experience, so to speak, by lengthening the list of states of mind to be ignored or suppressed in the aesthetic attitude, consequently shortening the list of states of mind compatible with aesthetic experience, and, correlatively, the list of properties appropriate as the object of such experience, and thus relevant for the interpretation, appreciation, and evaluation of works of art. The question is where to draw the line, but the extreme to which this process tends is a view of aesthetic experience as resolutely segregated from historical or contextual knowledge or moral, religious, and political beliefs, and a view of qualities of form and design of works of art as exhibited in their mere appearances as their only aesthetically relevant properties. (Beardsley's list of the properties that afford aesthetic gratification, quoted above, goes some distance in the direction of this extreme but does not reach all the way to it, given its inclusion of 'regional qualities', among which Beardsley numbers features such as garishness and gracefulness.)

Another problem for accounts of aesthetic experience in general has been that they are in danger of being too broad, seeming to encompass experiences that are not aesthetic, for instance sexual experiences and drug experiences. The view that such experiences are not aesthetic seems to depend on the very plausible assumption that sexual partners and pills are not works of art, as well as the more contentious assumption that the connection between art and the aesthetic is such that granting that experiences like these *are* aesthetic would imply that they were (or at least had some claim to being considered to be) works of art.

Finally, to the extent that these accounts are genuinely psychological (as opposed to, say, to being sociological, historical, or anthropological), they seem to presuppose that aesthetic experience is in some sense generically *human*, not restricted to any one historical period, social class, or culture. In consequence, their defenders must have some reply to theorists who suggest that the very idea of the aesthetic as it is understood by contemporary philosophers is a creation of the eighteenth-century European bourgeois Enlightenment (see e.g. Eagleton 1990) and to anthropologists who find it highly problematic that people in non-Western or pre-literate or pre-historic societies have anything like the same kind of experience that we contemporary Westerners characteristically have when we attend to works of art.

Recent epistemic accounts of aesthetic experience, then, have generally not only been constructed with most or all of the four ambitions listed at the beginning of this chapter in mind: they must also have been designed to confront charges of psychological myth-making, of excessive formalism about art, of a failure adequately to distinguish aesthetic experience from its near neighbours, and of the dubious attribution of a characteristically modern Western experience to pre-modern and/or non-Western people.

5. Four Recent Epistemic Accounts of the Aesthetic State of Mind

Prominent recent epistemic accounts of aesthetic experience include those offered by Malcolm Budd, Jerrold Levinson, Kendall Walton, and Roger Scruton.

In Budd (1995) the discussion of aesthetic experience is part of an account of value in works of art. Budd's central claim is that the 'artistic value' of a work of art consists in the 'intrinsic value of the experience the work offers', where the experience the work offers is taken to be an experience in which the work is understood and its qualities directly grasped.

A notable feature of this claim is that the notion of the aesthetic does not appear in it. Budd does not call the experience the work offers an aesthetic experience; in fact, he rarely uses the term 'aesthetic'. At one point he does say that a work's *artistic* (not aesthetic) value depends on its *aesthetic* (not artistic) qualities, so it would perhaps be possible to construct on the basis of this and his central claim an account of the aesthetic experience as the experience of what the work offers, and to conjecture that substituting 'aesthetic' for 'artistic' in the phrase 'artistic value' would not be seriously misleading in this context. To do this would shift the explanatory burden to the notion of aesthetic qualities—or else run the danger of making *any* quality of a work of art that can be experienced with understanding relevant to its artistic value. Unless something like this is done, however, it is not at all clear that the experience in question, explained as it is in terms of the understanding of works of art and yielding a criterion of value for works of art, could be afforded, for example, by nature.

On the other hand, Budd might well view the whole enterprise of carving out a realm of the aesthetic—the whole apparatus of aesthetic experience, aesthetic objects, aesthetic qualities, aesthetic value, and their ilk—as fundamentally misguided. What would remain is an epistemic state of mind that is especially appropriate to works of art, that is indeed intitially identified by its relation to artworks. Budd plausibly claims that his view is free of such psychological myths as a specific aesthetic emotion or a 'disconnected' attitude appropriate to art, and there seems no reason to suppose that one must be literate or Western or have a particular—indeed, any—concept of the aesthetic to value intrinsically the experience that something affords.

Budd's view, moreover, is far from narrowly formalistic, for he insists that an understanding of a work's message and its history is essential to 'the experience it affords'. Nor is there any danger that this state of mind, defined in Budd's way, will be confused with, for example, drug experiences. But neither is it clear how he would deal with the intuition that appropriate experiences of nature and of works of art have something in common that distinguishes them from drug experiences. Finally, read this way, the whole account is hostage to a prior understanding of the concept of art. Budd's view may perhaps best be taken as an attempt to capture the idea that what matters most about works of art is the experience they afford, *without* appealing to the idea of a specifically aesthetic experience (or the idea of an aesthetic anything else).

Levinson (1996) provides an account of aesthetic pleasure based, at least implicitly, on an account of what it is to experience something aesthetically:

Pleasure in an object is aesthetic when it derives from apprehension of and reflection on the object's individual character and content, both for itself and in relation to the structural base on which it rests. (Levinson 1996: 6)

Levinson immediately infers something tantamount to the claim that apprehending and reflecting on something in the specified way is *appreciating* it aesthetically, from which it seems to follow straightforwardly that *experiencing* something aesthetically is apprehending and reflecting on its individual character and content, both for itself and in relation to the structural base on which it rests.

This account resembles Beardsley's account of aesthetic gratification, in that it distinguishes aesthetic pleasure (or appreciation or experience) from other kinds in terms of its intentional object. In Beardsley's case it was not entirely clear whether the object in question was merely phenomenal. In Levinson's it seems clear that it is not, which suggests that in some sense what is aesthetic about the state of mind is no longer its mental aspect. In one way, at least, the basic idea of the aesthetic here seems to be the idea of the properties and relations apprehended, which might as well be dubbed aesthetic properties.

It may be, therefore, that Levinson no longer wholeheartedly shares the ambition of distinguishing an aesthetic state of mind. He is thus perhaps relatively unlikely to be suspected of psychological myth-making; in general, too, there seems no reason to suppose that prior to the eighteenth-century invention of the aesthetic, or in pre-literate or pre-historic societies, people were unable to 'apprehend and reflect on' something's 'individual character and content'. (Anthropological evidence that they do or did is presented in Maquet (1986), and relevant philosophical support is supplied in Davies (1999) and Dutton (1999), albeit in a context in which the main question is whether other cultures have art, rather than whether people in those cultures have aesthetic experience.)

Levinson clearly does aim to explain the aesthetic as independent of art, and he views nature as experienceable aesthetically in the same sense as art is. A start is made towards articulating connections between aesthetic pleasure and other parts of the realm of the aesthetic. The concept of aesthetic pleasure articulated here clearly does not apply to the pleasures of sex or drugs. Finally, the idea of what is to be 'apprehended and reflected on' in aesthetic appreciation is explicitly designed to be 'art-appropriate' in including matters of content and the way in which content is expressed that go well beyond the narrowly formal.

Walton (1993) discusses aesthetic pleasure in the course of developing a theory of aesthetic value, a theory initially focused squarely on the value of works of art. To gain the benefits of a work's value is to appreciate it, which is more than enjoying it:

'Aesthetic' pleasures include the pleasure of finding something valuable, of admiring it. One *appreciates* the work. One does not merely enjoy it; one takes pleasure or delight in judging it to be good. (Walton 1993: 504)

This account of aesthetic pleasure as pleasure taken in *noting* something's value is modified by requiring that the pleasure in question must not be merely self-congratulatory but must be pleasure in the *thing's* 'getting... [one] to admire it', and it must be pleasure that is *appropriate*, in some sense that includes but is evidently not limited to *moral* appropriateness.

This account of the complex and self-referential aesthetic state of mind is clearly an epistemic one. Though it is explicitly tailored to the experience of works of art, it is not clear on that account that one could not get aesthetic pleasure from a work *without* appropriately experiencing *it*, for example by hearing it, if it is a piece of music, so long as one *knew* that, for example, it was elegantly economical in expressing what it does. Couldn't one come to know this, for instance, by examining the score and the text, and thus come to enjoy admiring the piece?

There seems, though, to be nothing psychologically dubious or peculiarly modern and Western about the state of mind described, and the account speaks to the problem of distinguishing aesthetic pleasure from the merely sensual or drug-induced, while somewhat warily admitting some perhaps not obviously aesthetic pleasures into the club, such as pleasure in a hoe that is marvellously suited to its task. At the same time, the view, insisting as it does on the aesthetic relevance of a work's message and morality, is not formalistic.

Various other aesthetic notions, chiefly aesthetic value (the capacity to elicit aesthetic pleasure in appreciators), are explicated by Walton in terms of the aesthetic state of mind, while none of the terms used in explicating it ('appreciate', 'enjoy', 'admire', 'find value in') makes appeal to any prior notion of the aesthetic or the artistic.

Given that the account is explicitly framed to deal with the evaluation of works of art, or at least of artefacts in general, and given Walton's claim that 'admiration is paradigmatically, if not essentially, an attitude we have in part towards people', the idea that nature can be the object of the aesthetic state of mind seems initially problematic for his view. The solution, which Walton suggests accounts for both similarities and differences between the appreciation of art and the appreciation of nature, is to claim that it is possible to replace *admiring* with a related attitude, such as *being in awe of* or *wondering at*, in *taking pleasure in admiring something*, without the resulting state of mind ceasing to be aesthetic.

The most striking feature of the concept of aesthetic experience defended in Scruton (1974) is the role the concept of imagination plays in it. Scruton insists that, for example, the sadness in a piece of music is not a genuine property of it, and that the judgement that a piece is sad is, therefore, *not* cognitive in the sense of having a truth value. Sadness is rather an 'aspect' of a piece, and our making the judgement that a piece is sad involves *imagining* that it is—entertaining but not asserting the thought that it is sad in the way that people are.

Aesthetic appreciation is then, roughly, the appropriate enjoyment of an object for its own sake. The force of the phrase 'enjoyment of an object for its own sake' is to restrict appreciation pretty much to direct experience of something, for example hearing a piece of music—neither free-floating fantasies nor purely intellectual cognitions generally qualify. Being thus restricted to 'an object for its own sake', it is natural, if not logically necessary, that we enrich our experience of it by exercising our imagination, 'thinking of, and attending to, a present object (by thinking of it, or perceiving it, in terms of something absent)', and the thoughts and feelings thus aroused by the object become 'part of the experience . . . itself, transform[ing] it without diverting it from its original object'.

Despite Scruton's explicit denial that aesthetic experience is cognitive in the sense of putting us in contact with properties of its objects, imaginative thinking, as an ingredient in aesthetic experience, must remain *grounded in* and *appropriate to* the object. To have an aesthetic experience of a piece of music as sad, for example, it must be appropriate to experience the piece in a way consonant with the thought of it as a sad person. This is sufficient, on Scruton's view, to make aesthetic appreciation an activity that is subject to rational evaluation, and seems to be enough to make the view an epistemic one in the broad sense that in it aesthetic experience is conceived of as subject to epistemic standards.

Scruton speaks of 'the aesthetic attitude' as essentially aiming at aesthetic appreciation as just characterized. But this is not a psychological myth of the sort critiqued by Dickie, nor does it or the aesthetic appreciation aimed at seem restricted to modern, literate, Western societies. Further, although imagination is not, for Scruton, definitive of the aesthetic, it is intimately enough associated with it to make it important that the concept of imagination be respectable; and Scruton certainly shows that it is an idea with wide application, and not just one conjured up for immediate theoretical purposes. Again, the object-directed and normative aspects of the aesthetic experience serve to distinguish it from such things as drug experiences, and the incorporation of thought into the imaginative experience that so naturally enriches it both distinguishes aesthetic experience from sexual experience and allows aesthetic appreciation to extend beyond the narrowly formal.

Scruton, in contrast to Budd, shows no reluctance to invoke a wide variety of aesthetic notions—aesthetic aspects, aesthetic properties, aesthetic perception, the aesthetic object, aesthetic judgement—some of which he criticizes but others of which he uses relatively uncritically. Although he does not go far in relating them systematically, nothing but a lack of interest appears to stand in the way of his doing so.

Finally, it is for Scruton an important fact, but only a contingent one, that 'the principal objects of aesthetic interest are works of art'. That this fact is contingent is shown by our clear ability to take an aesthetic attitude, incorporating imaginative thought, towards nature. On Scruton's view, however, the discernment of expressive and representational features of objects, central to our aesthetic experience of them, typically depends on an understanding of those objects *as* works of art, which is not required for our appreciation of natural beauty:

The thoughts and feelings involved in aesthetic interest can acquire a full elaboration only if the aesthetic object possesses just those features that are characteristic of art. (Scruton 1974: 163)

Most epistemic accounts of aesthetic experience seem to assume a realistic account of the properties that are the objects of that experience. In something like the same way that non-realistic accounts of truth can sustain a distinction between knowledge and belief even in the absence of a commitment to real properties of objects, however, Scruton's non-realistic account of aesthetic aspects can support a genuinely epistemic account of aesthetic experience, with the further advantage that a non-realistic account of aesthetic features seems more initially plausible than non-realism about properties generally.

6. Two Critiques of Recent Theories of Aesthetic Experience

Richard Shusterman (1997) and Noël Carroll (2000), both of whom associate the recent revival of interest in the concept of aesthetic experience among philosophers with a reaction within the general culture to what Shusterman calls 'the anaesthetic thrust of [the twentieth] . . . century's artistic avant-garde', criticize the results of this revival in different ways.

Shusterman identifies four central features of the 'tradition of aesthetic experience':

First, aesthetic experience is essentially valuable and enjoyable; call this its evaluative dimension. Second, it is something vividly felt and subjectively savored, affectively absorbing us and focusing our attention on its immediate presence and thus standing out from the ordinary flow of routine experience; call this its phenomenological dimension. Third, it is meaningful experience, not mere sensation; call this its semantic dimension.... Fourth, it is a distinctive experience closely identified with the distinction of fine art and representing art's essential aim; call this the demarcational–definitional dimension. (Shusterman 1997: 30)

While situating his own work in both the analytic and Deweyan traditions, Shusterman usefully summarizes critiques of aesthetic experience by twentieth-century continental writers (e.g. Adorno, Benjamin, Heidegger, Gadamer, Bourdieu) as focusing on a conception of aesthetic experience 'narrowly identified with fine art's purely autonomous reception' and requiring 'mere phenomeno-logical immediacy to achieve its full meaning', and he argues convincingly that such a faulty conception is not a necessary consequence of the four central features of the tradition he has identified.

Shusterman argues, however, that the Anglo-American critique and development of the concept of aesthetic since Dewey, beginning with Dickie's critique of Beardsley, has unfortunately slighted the evaluational dimension, promoted the semantic at the expense of the phenomenological, and emphasized the demarcational–definitional, in contrast to a Deweyan 'transformational' conception, which would aim to 'revise or enlarge the aesthetic field', rather than merely to 'define, delimit, and explain the aesthetic status quo'.

Shusterman does not discuss any of the epistemic accounts mentioned above, but not only do they appear to be fully capable of answering the Continental cri-tique as he describes it, but also they challenge in various ways his narrative of the trend in recent Anglo-American aesthetics and point in some of the same direc-tions he favours. For one thing, although none emphasizes—and some deny—a distinctive phenomenology of aesthetic experience, the example of Beardsley suggests that this denial is not entailed by epistemic accounts. The distinction between phenomenological and epistemic accounts need not be an exclusive one, and epistemic accounts are not prevented from conceiving aesthetic experience as 'vividly felt and subjectively savored'. Again, the value and enjoyability of aesthetic experience is a major theme in epistemic accounts, though Shusterman says more than they tend to say in defending that value against the anaestheticization not only of aesthetic theory, but of recent art.

On the other hand, the connection that epistemic accounts propose between aes-thetic experience and art, though typically intimate, need not be a defining one. Moreover, even if it is, it typically does not 'delimit' the aesthetic experience in the sense of restricting it to art; nor does it necessarily promote the 'aesthetic status quo' in the sense that it is inimical to the idea that aesthetic experience may be afforded by novel and unexpected objects. It is not clear, therefore, that epistemic accounts are necessarily wrong to decline to follow Shusterman all the way back to Dewey.

If Shusterman seeks to recover a concept of aesthetic experience that began to erode with Dickie's critique of Beardsley, Carroll aims to reinforce and amplify that critique. On his view, the most that can be said about the aesthetic experience of an artwork is that it

involves design appreciation and/or the detection of aesthetic and expressive properties and/or attention to the ways in which the formal, aesthetic, and expressive properties of the artwork are contrived. (Carroll 2000: 207)

Such a 'deflationary, content-orientated, enumerative' approach is foreshadowed in the previously discussed writings of both Budd (1995) and Levinson (1996), following Beardsley (1982); but in Carroll's paper it more clearly emerges from a thoroughgoing critique of more ambitious views. (Note, too, that Carroll explicitly limits his discussion to the aesthetic experience of artworks, thus deliberately bypassing the question whether there is some aesthetic state of mind common to our intercourse with artworks and with nature, a policy perhaps in keeping with his deflationary conclusion.)

Carroll argues that the 'essentialist' aim of discovering some 'common thread' that runs through experiences of the sorts of properties just enumerated is a failure, in particular, that what he takes to be the central thesis of those who defend more substantive accounts of the aesthetic state of mind—the thesis that an essential feature of aesthetic experience is that it is valued for its own sake—cannot be sustained. (Like Shusterman, Carroll does not discuss any of the epistemic accounts mentioned above, but the idea of intrinsic value has been seen to be particularly prominent in Budd 1995.)

In defending this position, Carroll first points out that there is a long history of instrumental defences of aesthetic experience, and that in fact people who value the experience of the mentioned properties of artworks frequently insist that they value such experiences instrumentally, for the various goods such as insight, self-improvement, and the like that they allegedly provide. (Recall claims of this sort, mentioned above, in Beardsley 1958.) As an objection to the idea of intrinsic valuing, this observation seems to depend at least in part on supposing that, if one values something intrinsically, then one cannot *also* value it instrumentally. Such a view could perhaps be reasonably attributed to those who think of the aesthetic state of mind as largely excluding other states of mind (those, for example, who defend certain conceptions of the 'distanced' aesthetic attitude); but the defenders of the aesthetic state of mind as in part constituted by intrinsic valuing are not necessarily to be found among them—at least, not in virtue of their commitment to that view of the aesthetic state of mind.

Even if this point is waived and it is supposed, as seems plausible, that nothing logically prevents someone from simultaneously valuing an experience both intrinsically and instrumentally, this fact makes the attribution of intrinsic valuings of such experiences in particular cases problematic in the face of what Carroll sees as the general adequacy of instrumental valuings to explain people's motivations in seeking out such experiences, for such attributions would then come to depend on dubious intuitions about what people *would* have done had they *not* valued such experiences instrumentally. Valuing intrinsically, then, at least as applied to aesthetic experience, threatens to dissolve into another psychological myth.

Even if we suppose that the idea of valuing an experience intrinsically is not in itself suspect, however, Carroll insists that the view that

aesthetic experience is necessarily a matter of experience valued for its own sake... seems wildly implausible. (Carroll 2000: 204)

He asks us to imagine two people in 'precisely the same type-identical computational state relevant to understanding and processing' a painting, one of whom values that understanding and processing intrinsically but not instrumentally, the other of whom values it instrumentally but not intrinsically. (We may imagine that the latter is, say, an evolutionary psychologist who espouses a theory according to which experience of a painting is never in fact valued intrinsically but is seen as worth having only because it provides benefits such as enhancing the viewer's discriminatory powers.) One's experience has been motivated by a belief different from the other's, but it seems 'perfectly arbitrary and completely unsatisfactory' to maintain, as one who takes a finding of intrinsic value to be logically necessary for the having of an aesthetic experience must, that '[one] ... is undergoing an aesthetic experience, but [the other] ... is not' (and indeed cannot, so long as he persists in holding a theory incompatible with his intrinsically valuing such experience).

The defender of intrinsic valuing as essential to aesthetic experience may reply, first, that the alleged incapacity of the evolutionary psychologist to have an aesthetic experience on the view in question seems no more necessary than, say, the alleged inability of a sceptic to know anything, or of an eliminative materialist to hold any beliefs at all. That a theory entails that a certain state of mind is impossible does not itself entail that a holder of that theory cannot *be* in that state.

On the other hand, the 'mental processing' that is 'type-identical' between Carroll's two imagined viewers certainly exemplifies the kind of state that epistemic accounts of the aesthetic state of mind emphasize, and it perhaps deserves to be called an aesthetic *experience* in the epistemic sense of 'experience' if anything does. But it seems to be open to the defender of the idea of a distinctively aesthetic state of mind to regard that state as complex in something like the way that, on the account in Walton (1993), aesthetic pleasure, i.e. pleasure in judging something to be good, is. Just as that state, according to Walton, is compounded out of taking pleasure and finding value, the aesthetic state of mind, on the view to which Carroll objects, may be compounded, in a different way, out of finding value and experiencing in an epistemic sense. Whether such an account could evade Carroll's objections and at the same time fulfil most or all of the four ambitions mentioned at the beginning of this chapter remains to be seen. (For an attempt to characterize an aesthetic state of mind—specifically, aesthetic appreciation, in something like this way—see Iseminger 1981; for a development of this characterization specifically in the service of an aesthetic account of the nature of art, see Anderson 1999.)

7. CONCLUSION

In general, epistemic accounts of the aesthetic state of mind need not depend on psychologically mythical states of mind (at least, not on mythical states of mind that are peculiarly aesthetic), nor on states of mind unavailable to members of pre-literate, pre-historic, or non-Western societies. They are capable of answering the most obvious objections to the effect that they lead to excessive formalism about art and that they are unable to distinguish the aesthetic state of mind from those associated with drug experiences or sensual pleasures. They can be characterized without appeal to the concept of art or to prior concepts of the aesthetic. They are consistent with, but do not entail, the view that aesthetic experience has a distinctive phenomenology. Where a defender of such an account aims to use it to articulate such related notions as aesthetic value, an epistemic idea of aesthetic experience appears to enter into relations appropriate for such articulation, though it may be that in pursuing this aim some other idea of the aesthetic, such as aesthetic properties, ultimately emerges as basic. Epistemic accounts of aesthetic experience seem able to explain the close connection between art and the aesthetic while still allowing for the aesthetic experience of nature. If one is inclined to believe that there is an aesthetic state of mind and that it is worthwhile to be in it, it seems reasonable to continue to pursue most or all of the four aims mentioned at the beginning of this chapter in the course of trying to make precise an idea of the aesthetic state of mind that incorporates an epistemic conception of aesthetic experience.

See also: Aesthetic Realism 1; Aesthetic Realism 2; Beauty; Aesthetics of Nature; Value in Art; Aesthetics and Cognitive Science.

BIBLIOGRAPHY

Anderson, J. (1999). 'Aesthetic Concepts of Art', in N. Carroll (ed.), *Theories of Art*. Madison, Wis.: University of Wisconsin Press, pp. 65–92.

Beardsley, M. (1958). *Aesthetics: Problems in the Philosophy of Criticism*. New York: Harcourt Brace.

—— (1969). 'Aesthetic Experience Regained'. *Journal of Aesthetics and Art Criticism* 28: 3–11.

—— (1982). *The Aesthetic Point of View*. Ithaca, NY: Cornell University Press.

Budd, M. (1995). *Values of Art*. London. Penguin Books.

Bullough, E. (1912). 'Psychical Distance as a Factor in Art and as an Aesthetic Principle', *British Journal of Psychology* 5: 87–98.

Carroll, N. (2000). 'Art and the Domain of the Aesthetic'. *British Journal of Aesthetics* 40: 191–208.

—— (2002). 'Aesthetic Experience Revisited'. *British Journal of Aesthetics* 42: 145–68.

Davies, S. (1999). 'Non-Western Art and Art's Definition', in N. Carroll (ed.), *Theories of Art*. Madison, Wis.: University of Wisconsin Press, pp. 199–216.

Dewey, J. (1934). *Art as Experience*. New York: Putnam.

Dickie, G. (1965). 'Beardsley's Phantom Aesthetic Experience'. *Journal of Philosophy* 62: 129–36.

—— (1974). *Art and the Aesthetic: An Institutional Analysis*. Ithaca, NY: Cornell University Press.

Diffey, T. J. (1990). 'Schopenhauer's Account of Aesthetic Experience'. *British Journal of Aesthetics* 30: 132–42.

Dutton, D. (1999). ' "But They Don't Have Our Concept of Art" ', in N. Carroll (ed.), *Theories of Art*. Madison, Wis.: University of Wisconsin Press, pp. 217–38.

Eagleton, T. (1990). *The Ideology of the Aesthetic*. Oxford: Basil Blackwell.

Genette, G. (1999). *The Aesthetic Relation*, trans. G. M. Goshgarian. Ithaca, NY: Cornell University Press.

Iseminger, G. (1981). 'Aesthetic Appreciation'. *Journal of Aesthetics and Art Criticism* 41: 389–97.

Levinson, J. (1996). *The Pleasures of Aesthetics*. Ithaca, NY: Cornell University Press.

Maquet, J. (1986). *The Aesthetic Experience*. New Haven: Yale University Press.

Mitias, M. (1988). *The Possibility of Aesthetic Experience*. Dordrecht: Martinus Nijhoff.

Nehamas, A. (1998). 'Richard Shusterman on Pleasure and Aesthetic Experience'. *Journal of Aesthetics and Art Criticism* 56: 49–51.

Petts, J. (2000). 'Aesthetic Experience and the Revelation of Value'. *Journal of Aesthetics and Art Criticism* 58: 61–71.

Rosebury, B. (2000). 'The Historical Contingency of Aesthetic Experience'. *British Journal of Aesthetics* 40: 73–88.

Scruton, R. (1974). *Art and Imagination*. London: Methuen.

Shusterman, R. (1997). 'The End of Aesthetic Experience'. *Journal of Aesthetics and Art Criticism* 55: 29–41.

Stolnitz, J. (1961). 'On the Origins of "Aesthetic Disinterestedness" '. *Journal of Aesthetics and Art Criticism* 20: 131–44.

Walton, K. (1993). 'How Marvelous! Toward a Theory of Aesthetic Value'. *Journal of Aesthetics and Art Criticism* 51: 499–510.

CHAPTER 6

AESTHETICS OF NATURE

MALCOLM BUDD

THE long period of stagnation into which the aesthetics of nature fell after Hegel's relegation of natural beauty to a status inferior to the beauty of art was ended by Ronald Hepburn's ground-breaking paper (1966). In this essay, which offers a diagnosis of the causes of philosophy's neglect of the aesthetics of nature, Hepburn describes a number of kinds of aesthetic experience of nature that exhibit a variety of features distinguishing the aesthetic experience of nature from that of art and endowing it with values different from those characteristic of the arts, thus making plain the harmful consequences of the neglect of natural beauty. The subtlety of Hepburn's thought precludes simple summary, and I will do no more than enumerate a few of his themes that have been taken up and developed in the now flourishing literature on the aesthetics of nature (although not always with the nuanced treatment accorded them by Hepburn).

First, there is the idea that, through being both in and a part of nature, our aesthetic involvement with nature is typically both as actors and spectators. Second, there is the idea that, in contrast to what is typical of works of art, natural things are not set apart from their environment as objects of aesthetic interest: they are 'frameless'. Third, there is the idea that the aesthetic experience of nature should not be restricted to the contemplation of uninterpreted shapes, colours, patterns, and movements. Finally, there is the idea that the imaginative realization of the forces or processes that are responsible for a natural thing's appearance or are active in a natural phenomenon is a principal activity in the aesthetic experience of nature.

1. An Aesthetics of Engagement

Arnold Berleant (1993) stresses the first two of these ideas in the course of proposing what he calls an 'aesthetics of engagement' for the aesthetic appreciation of nature (something he recommends as a model for the appreciation of art also), which represents the aesthetic subject as being an active participant in a condition of perceptual immersion in the natural world, with a sense of continuity of the subject's self with the forms and processes of nature, in place of traditional aesthetics, which is an aesthetics of disinterested contemplation, the subject being an observer distanced from a clearly circumscribed object of aesthetic interest. But an aesthetics of engagement is not a sound development from these two ideas and it suffers from three principal defects. First, as Hepburn (1998) has insisted, being essentially *in*, not over-against, the landscape does not prevent our aesthetic experience from being contemplative, which often it properly is. Second, the principal conception of the notion of disinterestedness in traditional aesthetics is Kant's, according to which a positive affective response to an item is disinterested only if it is not, or is not just, pleasure in the satisfaction of a desire that the world should be a certain way, a way indicated by one's perception. And disinterestedness of response in this sense is not only compatible with the various aspects of engagement that Berleant articulates which are aesthetic, but is a condition that, it seems, any satisfactory understanding of the notion of an aesthetic response must satisfy. Third, Berleant's rejection of both contemplation and disinterestedness, coupled with a failure to replace them with alternatives that are viable components of specifically aesthetic experience or appreciation, disqualifies his aesthetics of engagement with nature from being acceptable either as an account of nature appreciation or as a conception of aesthetic experience of nature.

2. Environmental Formalism

One version of the view, rejected by Hepburn, that aesthetic appreciation consists in the aesthetic appreciation of uninterpreted items—items considered independently of the kinds they exemplify—is formalism. Environmental formalism is formalism about the aesthetic appreciation and evaluation of the natural environment. Allen Carlson (1979b) has developed an argument against environmental formalism built on the first two of Hepburn's ideas listed above. Formalism maintains that (i) aesthetic appreciation should be directed towards those aspects that constitute the form of the object, and (ii) the aesthetic value of an object is entirely determined by its formal qualities. The perceived form of an object consists of 'shapes, patterns, and designs'.

Formal qualities are 'qualities of such forms, such as their being unified or chaotic, balanced or unbalanced, harmonious or confused'. So formal qualities are qualities that objects or combinations of objects have in virtue of their shapes, patterns, and designs. But these arise from (consist of) the relations among the sensory qualities of objects—qualities of textures, colours and lines. So in a wider sense the perceived form of an object consists of textures, colours, lines, shapes, patterns, and designs.

It is this wider notion of perceived form that figures in Carlson's understanding of the doctrine of formalism. Accordingly, environmental formalism holds that, in the aesthetic appreciation of the natural environment, one must abstract from the nature of the items that compose the environment—land, water, vegetation, or hills, valleys, rivers, trees, and so on—and focus solely on the environment's perceived form, its lines, colours, and textures and the relations in which they stand to one another; and that a portion of nature is aesthetically appealing in so far as its perceived form is unified, is balanced, possesses unity in variety or whatever, and is aesthetically unappealing in so far as it is disharmonious or lacks integration.

The essence of Carlson's argument against environmental formalism is this. A crucial difference between traditional art objects and the natural environment is that, whereas works of art are 'framed or delimited in some formal way', the natural environment is not. And this entails a difference between the formal qualities of (traditional) works of art and those of the natural environment. For the formal qualities of a work of art 'are in large part determined by the frame': they 'are (or are not) unified or balanced within their frames and in relation to their frames'. Hence a work's formal qualities, the recognition of which must underpin a correct evaluation of the work, 'are an important determinate aspect of the work itself' and so can be easily appreciated. But it is only a framed view of the natural environment, not the environment itself, that possesses formal qualities: any part of the environment can be seen from indefinitely many different positions and framed in indefinitely many different ways, and whatever formal qualities it is seen to possess will be relative to the frame and the position of the observer, appearing unified or balanced from one position as framed in a certain manner, chaotic or unbalanced from a different position or when framed differently.

Now the conclusion that the natural environment does not itself possess formal qualities, but only appears to possess formal qualities when framed from particular positions, does not seem to make much, if any, dent in the doctrine of environmental formalism. For the formalist can concede the relativity of formal qualities to frames and points of view, and so the necessity of framing to aesthetic appreciation, and yet still maintain that the aesthetic appreciation of the natural environment consists in the appreciation of formal qualities—the different formal qualities presented by the environment as variously framed from whatever points of view an observer chooses.

The conclusion that Carlson favours is the stronger claim: that the natural environment as such does not possess formal qualities, by which he means that, *when appreciated aesthetically in the appropriate mode*, it is *not possible* to see it as having any formal qualities. His argument runs as follows. The appropriate mode of appreciation of the natural environment is 'the active, involved appreciation of one who is in the environment, being a part of and reacting to it'. But:

In framing a section of the environment, one must become a static observer who is separate from that section and who views it from a specific external point. But one cannot be engaged in the appropriate active, involved appreciation while maintaining the static, external point of view required by framing. In short, one cannot both be in the environment which one appreciates and frame that environment; if one appreciates the environment by being in it, it is not a framed environment which one appreciates. (Carlson 1979*b*: 109–10)

But this argument is not compelling. Even if the appropriate mode of aesthetic appreciation of the natural environment is of the active, involved kind, this should not be understood to imply that one must never become a static observer on pain of forfeiting one's right to be thought of as engaged in the aesthetic appreciation of the environment. There is nothing amiss in being a static observer of an ever changing skyscape, and choosing a spot to stop at and contemplate a scene from is a proper part of the aesthetic appreciation of the natural environment, not something inconsistent with it. So Carlson has not established that the natural environment cannot be appreciated and valued aesthetically in terms of its formal qualities just because the appropriate mode of aesthetic appreciation precludes this.

Nevertheless, environmental formalism's insistence that the aesthetic appreciation of the natural environment must not be directed at items in the environment conceptualized as what they are (clouds, trees, valleys, and so on) is certainly unwarranted, being a product of a conception of aesthetic appreciation that, without adequate justification, restricts aesthetic experience to the experience of items in abstraction from the kinds they exemplify, a conception no better suited to the aesthetic appreciation of the natural environment than to that of art.

3. Nature's Expressive Qualities

The alternative that Carlson (1979*b*) proposes to environmental formalism is that the natural environment must be appreciated and valued aesthetically in terms of its various non-formal aesthetic qualities, such as expressive qualities (serenity, majesty, sombreness) and qualities like gracefulness, delicacy, and garishness. One weakness with this proposal is the unclarity of the range and nature of expressive qualities. If austerity is severe simplicity, serenity tranquillity (calmness, lack of disturbance), ominousness the property of being threatening, and majesty the property of being grand (imposing), then (i) a desert landscape is *literally* austere (severely simple), a quiet meadow serene (lacking in disturbances), the sky before a storm ominous (indicative of an approaching threat), and a mountain range majestic (imposing in virtue of being formidable, and so inspiring fear, respect, or awe); and (ii) no specifically aesthetic sensibility is needed to detect the austerity, serenity, ominousness, and majesty (so that, on one understanding of the aesthetic, they are not *aesthetic* qualities). But if this is typical of so-called expressive qualities, expressive qualities will be limited to those qualities that items literally possess, a non-standard use of the notion and one that, it seems, Carlson himself (1976) does not embrace. And this suggests either that the kind of understanding proposed above, of austerity, serenity, ominousness, and majesty, is mistaken—'majestic' could of course be understood to import the ideas of dignity and nobility, properties that a mountain range does not literally possess—or that Carlson's notion of expressive qualities accommodates qualities of heterogeneous kinds. It is regrettable that, although in recent years a considerable body of work has been produced on expression in art, no satisfactory account has been given of the experience of nature as the bearer of expressive properties (despite the notable attempt of Wollheim 1991).

But the uncertain character of expressive qualities does not itself weaken the force of two arguments that Carlson has developed in which expressive qualities figure, one being directed specifically against environmental formalism, the other not.

The argument directed specifically against environmental formalism (Carlson 1977) maintains that formalism cannot explain the loss of aesthetic value to the natural environment caused by various intrusions into it by humanity, such as the construction of a power line that passes through it. For from a formalist point of view a power line might not only be aesthetically attractive in itself but, taken together with its environment, constitute an aesthetically attractive formal design, even, perhaps, helping to frame or balance a view of the landscape. So what does explain the loss of aesthetic value? Carlson's answer is: 'the non-formal aesthetic qualities of the natural environment which are affected by the actual presence of the power line and/or by its own non-formal aesthetic qualities':

For example, the relevant natural environment may have certain expressive qualities due to its apparent or actual remoteness, but the expression of these qualities may be inhibited by the presence of the power line, or the power line may itself have certain expressive qualities which, unlike its formal qualities, do not 'fit' with the expressive qualities of the natural environment. (Carlson 1997: 159)

(The idea is that the expressive qualities of the power line, perhaps aggression and power, might be incongruous with the expressive qualities of the natural environment, perhaps tranquillity.)

Carlson's other argument (1976) is a defence of the view (the 'eyesore argument') that one good reason why the natural environment should be cleaned of the human detritus that clutters it is that (i) the refuse is not aesthetically pleasing, and (ii) an aesthetically pleasing environment is preferable to one that is not. The objection that

Carlson wishes to counter is that there is a cheap alternative to removing the refuse: if the refuse is initially found aesthetically displeasing, one can develop one's *camp sensibility* such that it becomes aesthetically pleasing. He meets this objection in two ways. The first concedes that the camp alternative to cleaning up the environment works fine against the eyesore argument in the sense in which something can be aesthetically pleasing in virtue of its colours, shapes, textures, patterns (the 'thin sense'), but not in the sense in which something can be aesthetically pleasing in virtue of these *and* its expressive qualities (the 'thick sense'). (Carlson considers roadside clutter to be unsightly primarily because of its [negative] expressive qualities.) For (i) the expressive qualities of litter are such qualities as waste, disregard, and carelessness; and (ii) although camp sensibility can make us more aware of such qualities, most of us are unable to enjoy aesthetically the expression of such qualities.

Furthermore, if we are unable to find an object aesthetically pleasing in the thick sense because of the negative nature of its expressive qualities, this often makes it difficult or impossible to aesthetically enjoy the object in the thin sense. Hence if camp sensibility makes us more aware of an item's negative expressive qualities, it will render us unable to enjoy it aesthetically at all. Accordingly, an object with such negative expressive qualities cannot be aesthetically enjoyed by adopting camp sensibility. But, since this argument depends on two empirical claims that might be contested, Carlson offers the following sketch of an alternative line of argument—a moral/aesthetic argument. To enjoy aesthetically the expressive qualities of refuse would be to condone the values and attitudes that are responsible for it and in virtue of which it possesses those expressive qualities, since aesthetic enjoyment of something counts against wishing to eliminate it. But these values and attitudes—waste, disregard, carelessness—are morally unacceptable, and condoning the morally unacceptable is itself morally unacceptable. Accordingly, even if it is possible to enjoy litter aesthetically (in the thick sense), morally we should not.

Carlson (1977), and to some extent Carlson (1976), has been critically examined by Yuriko Saito (1984). But her focus shifts away from aesthetically unfortunate intrusions of humanity into nature to the destruction of nature; and the dilemma she ends by confronting Carlson with is ineffective against a position that does not conceive of the aesthetic as a realm impermeable by ethical considerations—a position embraced by Carlson (1986).

4. The Aesthetic Appreciation of Nature as Nature

Given that the aesthetic appreciation of nature should not be thought of as the aesthetic appreciation of (arrays of) uninterpreted particulars, how should it be understood? A surprisingly popular conception, one that aligns the aesthetic appreciation of nature with the appreciation of art extremely closely, represents the aesthetic appreciation of nature as consisting in nature's being regarded as if it were art. But it is clear that any version of the view that the aesthetic appreciation of nature involves regarding nature as if it were art will suffer from two defects. First, it will be unable to provide a successful argument that takes us from the undeniable fact that it is possible to regard a natural object as if it were a work of art to the conclusion that this is how we must or should regard natural objects when we experience them aesthetically. Second, it will be untrue to the phenomenology of the aesthetic experience of nature—at least, to the character of my own and many others' experience (Budd 2000).

The rejection of this conception of the aesthetic appreciation of nature raises the question of what the correct alternative is. The obvious alternative is that the aesthetic appreciation of nature should be thought of as the aesthetic appreciation of nature *as* nature—more particularly, the aesthetic appreciation of a natural item *as the natural item it is* (Budd 1996). (Compare artistic appreciation, which is the appreciation of art *as* art, so that, accordingly, the artistic appreciation of a particular work of art is the appreciation of it *as the work of art it is*, which involves experiencing it under the concept of the kind of work it is, as a painting rather than a colour photograph, for example.)

5. CATEGORIES OF NATURE AND OBJECTIVITY

Carlson (1981) both argues for this conception of the aesthetic appreciation of nature and uses it to counter the view that, whereas aesthetic judgements about works of art—judgements about the aesthetic properties of works of art—aspire to and are capable of being objectively true, aesthetic judgements about nature are condemned to relativity. In other words, the view is that, whereas a work of art really does possess certain aesthetic properties, so that it is straightforwardly true that it is exuberant, serene, or full of a sense of mystery, for example, natural items can properly be thought of as possessing certain aesthetic properties only relative to whatever the way may be in which someone happens to perceive them. His argument turns on ideas expressed by Kendall Walton.

Walton (1970) has shown, with respect to works of art, that (i) what aesthetic properties an item *appears* to possess—what aesthetic properties we perceive or experience the item as possessing—is a function of the category or categories under which it is experienced (i.e. what sort of thing it is perceived as being); and (ii) what aesthetic properties an item *really* possesses is determined by the right categories to experience the item as falling under—it really possesses those aesthetic properties it appears to possess when perceived (by a duly sensitive person, under the appropriate conditions, and so on) in the *right* categories to experience the item as belonging to, that is in its *correct* categories. The aesthetic significance of the categories under which a work is perceived is due to the fact that various non-aesthetic perceptual features are what Walton calls 'standard', 'variable', or 'contra-standard' with respect to a ('perceptually distinguishable') category, and the perceived aesthetic character of a work is a function of which of its non-aesthetic perceptual features are standard, variable, or contra-standard for one who perceives the work under that category. (A category is perceptually distinguishable only if, in order to determine perceptually whether something belongs in it, it is never necessary to decide this partly or wholly on the basis of non-perceptual considerations.)

The question is whether Walton's two theses transfer to nature, as Carlson argues they do. The essence of Carlson's argument is this: The psychological thesis does. That is, it is at least sometimes true that what aesthetic properties a natural item appears to possess are a function of the category under which it is experienced. For consider, first, the aesthetic appreciation of a natural *object*—an animal of a certain species, say. If we have some knowledge of what is standard for animals of that species—their adult size, for example—this knowledge will affect the aesthetic properties an animal of that kind, perceived as such, appears to us to possess if, for example, it falls far short of, or is considerably greater than, that standard size. Thus, Shetland ponies are perceived as charming and/or cute and Clydesdale horses are perceived as majestic and/or lumbering when perceived as belonging to, and judged with respect to, the category of horses. Consider, second, the aesthetic appreciation of the natural environment. Here is an example of Hepburn's:

Suppose I am walking over a wide expanse of sand and mud. The quality of the scene is perhaps that of wild, glad emptiness. But suppose I bring to bear upon the scene my knowledge that this is a tidal basin, the tide being out. The realization is not aesthetically irrelevant. I see myself now as walking on what is for half the day sea-bed. The wild glad emptiness may be tempered by a disturbing weirdness. (Hepburn 1966)

(Note that the aesthetic properties a natural item is experienced as possessing might well *not* change if the item is experienced first under one natural category— say, a category it does not in fact belong to—and then under another—one it does belong to: the apparent aesthetic properties of a heavenly body that I have landed on, considering it to be a planet, need not be vulnerable to the later realization that it is, not a planet, but a moon.)

What about the philosophical thesis? Are there, from the aesthetic point of view, correct and incorrect categories in which nature can be perceived, or should the correctness or otherwise of aesthetic judgements about nature (unlike those about art) be understood as *relative* to whatever category someone happens to perceive something natural as falling under? If there are such categories, then the 'category-relative inter-pretation' of aesthetic judgements about nature—the interpretation of them as impli-citly containing a reference to some particular category or set of categories, so that apparently opposed judgements about the aesthetic properties of a natural item are compatible—is mistaken. Carlson's answer is that there are correct categories, both for natural objects and for the natural environment. These are the categories, established by natural history and natural science, that the natural item falls under: the correct categories are the categories that natural items actually belong to.

The main difficulty that needs to be overcome if the philosophical thesis is to be transferred successfully to nature is the establishment of the correct categories (if there are such) in which nature can be perceived, which means *which* of those con-cepts of nature a natural item falls under—for it falls under many—it should be perceived under *from the aesthetic point of view*, where this means that perception under these concepts discloses the aesthetic properties it really possesses and thereby makes possible a proper assessment of its aesthetic value. For example, the reason, in the case of art, for prioritizing a more specific category to which an item belongs over a less specific category to which it belongs—for identifying the more specific category as the correct category to perceive the item under from the aes-thetic point of view—where the artist intended it to be perceived not just under the more general category but under the more specific category as well, is lacking in the case of nature. On the other hand, a reason would need to be provided for prior-itizing a less specific category—for insisting that a Shetland pony or a Clydesdale should be perceived not under the category Shetland pony or Clydesdale, but under the category horse. In the absence of such reasons, neither a more specific nor a more general category can be deemed the correct category, in which case a nat-ural item cannot be deemed to possess a particular set of aesthetic properties, but will possess contrasting sets for at least some of the categories of which it is a mem-ber. But in any case, there are important disanalogies between art and nature which render the application of the philosophical thesis to nature problematic, and which are relevant to an assessment of the doctrine of positive aesthetics with respect to nature (see Section 8 below).

6. Positive Aesthetics

Positive aesthetics with respect to nature maintains that, from the aesthetic point of view, nature is unlike art in that negative aesthetic evaluative judgements are out of place—out of place because pristine nature is essentially aesthetically good, that is always has a positive aesthetic value. Two linked questions immediately arise: 'What exactly is the force of this doctrine?' and 'Is there any good reason to embrace it?' Clearly, the acceptability of the doctrine depends on what form it takes, and it can assume many different forms in accordance with the answers it gives to three kinds of question: (i) of scope (what elements or aspects or divisions of nature it applies to); (ii) of strength (whether, e.g. it disallows the attribution of negative aesthetic qualities to nature, or disallows comparative judgements about natural items that assign a higher aesthetic value to one item than to another); and (iii) of modal status (Godlovitch 1998a,b; Budd 2000).

It would be a very small step from the proposition that no natural item, or combination of items, possesses negative aesthetic qualities to the conclusion that every natural item, or array of such items, has a positive overall aesthetic value—a step vanishingly small, given the kind of freedom that characterizes the aesthetic appreciation of nature (see Section 8). For this freedom guarantees that any natural item will offer *something* of positive aesthetic value, something that is aesthetically rewarding, even if the rewards are very small. But, while it is clear that nature is immune to many of the defects to which works of art are liable—nature cannot be trite, sentimental, badly drawn, crude, insipid, derivative, or a mere pastiche, for example—the premiss is questionable, holding true for, at most, items that are not, or do not contain, forms of life. A negative aesthetic quality is a quality that, considered in itself, makes a negative contribution to an item's aesthetic value and so constitutes an aesthetic defect in the item. For a work of art to possess a negative aesthetic quality in the relevant sense, it must be defective *as a work of art*. Likewise, for a natural item to possess a negative aesthetic quality, it must be defective *as a product of nature*. But this means that it must be defective as an instance of the kind of natural thing it is. And this is possible only for forms of life: a cloud, a sea, a boulder, cannot be a defective cloud, sea, or boulder, for the kinds of things they are— clouds, seas, boulders—lack natural functions that particular instances of them might not be well suited to perform. Perhaps one species of organism can properly be thought of as being defective in comparison with another such species. But however that might be, a member of a species can be a defective instance of that species, for example malformed, or unable to function in one or more ways normal for the species, perhaps disabling it from flourishing in the manner characteristic of the species; and only living things can be in an unhealthy state, be ill, decline, and die.

If the possibility that nothing in nature, or nothing within the scope of the doctrine of positive aesthetics, can possess negative aesthetic qualities, qualities that, unless outweighed, would endow their subject with a negative aesthetic value overall, is left aside, then arguments for a positive aesthetics of nature—arguments that do not rest on that assumption—do not appear compelling. Allen Carlson (1984) has demolished three arguments that might be offered in support of the doctrine, but has provided two of his own, one (Carlson 1984) based on the claim that positive aesthetic considerations partly determine the categories that are created by science to render the natural world intelligible, the other (Carlson 1993) maintaining that the appreciation of nature must be understood as a form of so-called 'order appreciation', which implies that the appreciation of nature consists in the *selection* of objects of appreciation in the natural world and focuses on the *order* (the natural order) imposed on them by the forces of nature, the selection, 'which makes the natural order visible and intelligible', being governed by the story given by natural science.

It is unclear exactly which version of positive aesthetics with respect to nature these arguments are intended to establish. But it is clear that they certainly fail to establish the most ambitious version of positive aesthetics: that *each individual* natural item, *at each moment of its existence* (or, slightly weaker, *considered throughout its duration*), has a roughly equal positive overall aesthetic value; and there are reasons for believing that it is *not possible* to show that the superstrong version of positive aesthetics is correct (Budd 2000). To change the scope of the doctrine of positive aesthetics from *individuals* to *kinds* would effect no alteration in the doctrine unless sense can be given to the idea of a kind possessing a positive aesthetic value that does not reduce to the idea that each instance of the kind has that value. But even if this is possible—perhaps it would be possible to invoke the idea of a *normal* instance of the kind—the doctrine would still be hazardous. One reason is the diversity of categories of nature, introducing different principles of identity and individuation for the items that belong to them, and recording such different phenomena as mere visual appearances, items defined as what they are by the use made of them, by what has brought them about, or by their relation to other natural items—think for instance of the categories of cloud, tributary, seashell, gust of wind, stamen, sky, forest, egg, flash flood, geyser, cave, stalactite, lodge or nest, eye of storm, swamp, herd, school, or swarm, bone, snakeskin, dune or wave, nut, eclipse, fossil, aurora. Given this diversity, given that nature was *not* perfectly designed for aesthetic contemplation or appreciation by human beings, and on the assumption that natural things *are* possible subjects of negative aesthetic qualities, it would be remarkable if everything in nature, no matter how nature is cut at the joints, were to have a roughly equal positive overall aesthetic value.

7. MODELS OF NATURE APPRECIATION

Carlson has suggested that a model of the aesthetic appreciation of nature, and in particular of the natural environment, that will indicate *what* is to be aesthetically appreciated and *how* it is to be aesthetically appreciated—something we have a good grasp of in the case of works of art—is needed. In the case of art, we know what to appreciate in that we can distinguish a work and its parts from anything else and its aesthetically relevant aspects from those that are not aesthetically relevant; and we know how to appreciate in that we know what actions to perform in order to appreciate the work. But what about nature and the natural environment? This is problematic in the case of nature because of a vital difference between art and nature. Our knowledge of what and how to appreciate in the case of art stems from the fact that works of art are our own creations. But nature is not our creation. Carlson's (1979a) proposed solution to this problem is his natural environment model.

The leading idea of the natural environment model is that, to appreciate nature aesthetically for what it is and for the qualities it has, the fact that the natural environment is (a) natural, and (b) an environment must play a central role. Now an environment is our surroundings, the setting within which we exist, which we normally experience through all our senses, although usually only as background. To appreciate it aesthetically, we must (using all our senses) foreground it—that (in outline) is *how* to appreciate an environment aesthetically. But the natural environment is natural, not a work of art, and as such has no boundaries or foci of aesthetic significance. So *what* is to be aesthetically appreciated in the natural environment? The answer is that the considerable common-sense/scientific knowledge of nature that we possess, which transforms our experience from what would otherwise be meaningless, indeterminate, and confused to being meaningful, determinate, and harmonious, provides 'the appropriate foci of aesthetic significance and the boundaries of the setting'. Accordingly, 'to aesthetically appreciate nature we must have knowledge of the different environments of nature and of the systems and elements within those environments'. And, because there are different natural environments, *how* to aesthetically appreciate the natural environment varies from environment to environment:

we must survey a prairie environment, looking at the subtle contours of the land, feeling the wind blowing across the open space, and smelling the mix of prairie grasses and flowers. But...in a dense forest environment...we must examine and scrutinize, inspecting the detail of the forest floor, listening carefully for the sounds of birds and smelling carefully for the scent of spruce and pine. (Carlson 1979a: 273–4)

Furthermore, a requirement of the natural environment model—one that Carlson uses against the so-called object model—is that the appreciation of a natural item, whether or not it is still in its environment of creation, must involve the consideration of it as located in its environment of creation and shaped by the forces at work in that environment (on pain of misrepresenting the item's expressive properties).

There are many problems with the natural environment model. I will highlight two problems of scope that afflict it. First, there is the question of the intended scope of the model. Although focused on the appreciation of the natural environment, it appears to be offered as the correct model not just for the appreciation of the natural environment, but for the aesthetic appreciation of nature. But this would be to identify the aesthetic appreciation of nature with the aesthetic appreciation of the natural environment, and would rule out the possibility of aesthetically appreciating a natural object (as natural) that is not in its natural environment of creation, unless in appreciating it it is considered (in imagination) in relation to its place and history in its former context. But trees planted in towns, for example, can be aesthetically appreciated as being natural objects, even though they are located in and have grown up in a non-natural or partly non-natural environment, and have spent their early weeks in pots in a greenhouse, as can—to take the most obvious case—the flowers in one's garden. In any case, Carlson's natural environment model seems skewed to the appreciation of inanimate objects, or of living natural objects that lack the power of locomotion. Creatures capable of movement have no natural position in their environment of creation and need not, and often do not, remain in it—as with birds, who emerge from their eggs and leave their nests (in one sense their environments of creation) and move around in the atmosphere and on the surface of the earth.

The second problem of scope concerns not the scope of the model, but the scope of the knowledge relevant to the aesthetic appreciation of nature. Carlson's thesis is that common-sense/natural scientific knowledge of nature is essential to the aesthetic appreciation of nature. But how much knowledge about a natural item is relevant? If not all, what makes a piece of knowledge relevant to the item's aesthetic appreciation? For instance, what knowledge of the sun and its relation to the earth (the sun's great or exact distance from the earth) is relevant to the appreciation of a sunset, and in virtue of what is this knowledge relevant? On the one hand, it is clear that not everything that is true of a natural item needs to be understood in order to appreciate it aesthetically as the natural item it is. A flower is the sexual organ of a plant. But to judge a flower to be a beautiful flower it is not necessary to know its function as the sexual organ of a plant, let alone to appreciate it with respect to how well it performs that natural function. On the other hand, it is clear that scientific knowledge can enhance the aesthetic appreciation of nature (Budd 1996). The effectiveness of Carlson's claim that knowledge of what is standard for natural things of a certain kind will affect the aesthetic properties an item of that kind appears to possess can be conceded. But this does not go far enough. All it shows is the aesthetic relevance of a certain sort of category of nature that an item is perceived as instantiating: it does not engage with the issue of what the distinction is between relevant and irrelevant knowledge of nature. Carlson appears not to recognize this lacuna in his position.

As an illustration of this deficiency in Carlson's account, Robert Stecker (1997) has responded in the following way to Carlson's use of Hepburn's example of a tidal basin, the wide expanse of sand and mud which appears to have different aesthetic qualities depending on whether it is perceived as just a beach or as a tidal basin. The shore of a tidal basin can be appreciated in three ways, none of which is mal-founded: as beach, as sea-bed, as sometimes beach–sometimes sea-bed. And although the last is more 'complete' than the first two, since it comprehends each of them, there is no good reason to prefer the more complete conception, which might, but well might not, enhance one's appreciation. Furthermore,

The more complete conception can still be supplemented indefinitely with knowledge of the physics of tides, the ecosystems of the basin, and additional facts from biology, chemistry and geology . . . Nature does not guide us in selecting among this possible information, since encompassing all these facts, it is indifferent about which we mine in pursuit of aesthetic enjoyment. (Stecker 1997: 398)

For Carlson, the aesthetic qualities that an item actually possesses are those that it appears to possess (to the right perceiver, under the right conditions) when it is perceived in its correct category. The correct category in which to perceive the expanse of sand and mud is the category of tidal basin; accordingly, the quality of the expanse of sand and mud is not just that of wild, glad emptiness, but of wild, glad emptiness tempered by a disturbing weirdness (Carlson 1984). Note that, although the expanse of sand and mud appears to have different qualities when perceived in the categories *beach* and *tidal basin*, the categories are not incompatible: each of them is *a* correct category—the category *only a beach, never a sea-bed* would be an incorrect category—and the qualities are related in the following way. The second is the first with an additional feature, a qualifying characteristic. Accordingly, in itself the example is relatively unproblematic for Carlson: what would be deeply problematic would be a case in which the qualities the item appears to possess when perceived in two correct categories are incompatible. Nevertheless, Carlson shows no awareness of the fact that both beach and tidal basin are correct categories and appears to select as the correct category the more encompassing one, simply because it is more encompassing.

Stecker draws the conclusion that 'it is not clear that knowledge of nature can perform the same function as that of art', namely that of delimiting aesthetically relevant knowledge. But the notion of delimiting aesthetically relevant knowledge of nature is ambiguous, and there are two questions that must be distinguished. (I focus on natural *objects*.) On the one hand, there is an issue about what *can* properly figure in the aesthetic appreciation of a particular natural object: are there facts about a natural object that are irrelevant to its aesthetic appreciation (as natural), i.e. that could not constitute part of its aesthetic appeal or inform its aesthetic appreciation? On the other, there is an issue about what *must* figure in that appreciation if the appreciation is not to be defective, imperfect, shallow, or in some other way inadequate: is there a set of facts about a natural object, each of which is essential to its (full) aesthetic appreciation, no fact outside the set being relevant? Stecker's conclusion gives a negative answer to the second question. But this does not imply a negative answer to the first. In fact, the first should receive a positive answer, although it is not easy to explain why various kinds of fact are disqualified from figuring in the aesthetic appreciation of a natural item (Hepburn 1996; Budd 1996).

Noël Carroll (1993) has advanced an arousal model, not as a replacement for the natural environment model, but as 'a co-existing model' (each of these models applying to some, but not all, of those responses to the natural world that constitute aesthetic appreciation of it, the two models sometimes overlapping). Carroll's model is simply that of being emotionally moved by nature, of emotions being appropriately aroused by nature, not all such emotions being rooted in a cognitive component containing a scientific category as part of its content. For example,

we may find ourselves standing under a thundering waterfall and be excited by its grandeur; or standing barefooted amidst a silent arbor, softly carpeted with layers of decaying leaves, a sense of repose and homeyness may be aroused in us. (Carroll 1993: 245)

When we are overwhelmed and excited by the grandeur of the towering cascade of water, we focus on certain aspects of the natural expanse—'the palpable force of the cascade, its height, the volume of water, the way it alters the surrounding atmosphere, etc.'—a focusing that does not require any special scientific, or even common-sense, ecological knowledge. And being exhilarated by grandeur is an appropriate response to what is grand. Hence there is a form of aesthetic appreciation of nature (as nature) that does not conform to the natural environment model. (Note that Carroll understands Carlson's natural environment model to require *systematic knowledge of natural processes*, so that the common-sense knowledge that is involved in the aesthetic appreciation of the waterfall—that what is falling down is water, for example—is not common-sense knowledge of nature of the kind the natural environment model demands.) Moreover, so Carroll argues, this mode of aesthetic appreciation of nature is such that (*a*) it can yield the conclusion that aesthetic judgements about nature can be objectively correct—a conclusion that Carlson appears to believe can be yielded only by the natural environment model—because aesthetic judgements based on or expressive of emotional responses to *appropriate* natural objects possess objectivity; and (*b*) there is no good reason to accept that it must be a less deep appreciation of nature than one informed by natural history, if depth of response is a matter of intensity and 'thoroughgoingness' of involvement.

Carroll neglects to specify that, for an emotion appropriately aroused by nature to constitute aesthetic appreciation of nature, the emotional response must be an *aesthetic* response, and not every emotional response to nature is an aesthetic response, let alone an aesthetic response to nature as nature; moreover, not only does he not provide an account of what makes a response an aesthetic response, but some of his examples of emotional responses to nature are definitely not aesthetic responses. However, these defects are easily rectified.

Carlson (1995) does not press this point and adopts a different tack: prescinding from the question of what constitutes an aesthetic response to an item, he focuses on the notion of *appreciation*. (Carlson's 1995 account of appreciation is contested by Godlovitch 1997. Carlson 1997 effectively counters Godlovitch's critique.) Since the appreciation of an item requires some information about it (sizing it up), correct or appropriate appreciation of an item requires knowledge of that item. It follows that, if a certain piece, or number of pieces, of knowledge is required for appropriate appreciation of nature, then an emotional response not based on the required knowledge is not an appreciative response. It is clear that the arousal model does not exclude whatever knowledge is required for appropriate appreciation of nature from being the basis of an emotional reaction to nature that constitutes aesthetic appreciation of nature. The question, therefore, is whether it incorrectly deems cases of emotional response to nature that are not based on the required knowledge as instances of appropriate appreciation of nature. This depends on what knowledge is required for aesthetic appreciation of nature. The natural environment model maintains that the required knowledge is 'that which is provided by the natural sciences and their commonsense predecessors and analogues', whereas the arousal model rejects such knowledge as being required for appropriate appreciation of nature.

Carlson here makes two moves. The first exploits a feature of one of Carroll's examples in an attempt to show that the arousal model *collapses into* the natural environment model. The example is one of being moved by the grandeur of a blue whale, 'its size, its force, the amount of water it displaces'. But knowledge of the amount of water a blue whale displaces—by which it is clear that Carroll means not exactly how much water, but only that the amount is large—is, 'if not exactly straightforwardly scientific, at least the product of the commonsense predecessors or analogues of science'; so that appreciation of the whale, grounded partly in the amount of water it displaces, is based on knowledge of the kind required by the natural environment model, 'even though that knowledge comes from the commonsense end of the spectrum ranging from science to its commonsense analogues'. Similarly, Carlson is inclined to regard the knowledge that what, in Carroll's waterfall example, is cascading down is water as the product of the common-sense predecessors and analogues of natural science. And, although he is prepared to concede that perhaps this is not 'systematic knowledge of nature's working', this is, for him, a negligible concession. For Carlson concludes that instances of appreciation of nature in accordance with the arousal model that are based on knowledge only of this kind are at best minimal, so that, as far as the knowledge element of appropriate appreciation of nature is concerned, there is no significant difference between the arousal and natural environment models, the first focusing on the most minimal, the second on the fuller and richer levels of such appreciation.

It will be clear that Carlson's response runs up against the problematic issue of the extent of aesthetically relevant knowledge of nature. And, since not every kind of appreciation is *aesthetic* appreciation, a response based on a deeper, as opposed to a shallower, appreciation (in the sense of understanding) of the nature of a natural item is not automatically indicative of a deeper, as opposed to a shallower, *aesthetic* response to that item, one that is the manifestation of a fuller and richer appreciation of that item *from the aesthetic point of view*. Without an account of what it is for appreciation to be specifically aesthetic, and a principled distinction between knowledge that is relevant and knowledge that is not relevant to the aesthetic appreciation of a natural thing, Carlson cannot press home his critique of the arousal model.

8. Objectivity, Positive Aesthetics, and Models of Nature Appreciation

I can now make good my claim (in Section 5) about the existence and significance of disanalogies between art and nature with respect to the constraints imposed on appropriate appreciation by the relevant categories to which the items belong, and to indicate the consequences this has for the idea of a natural item's aesthetic properties and value and so for the viability of the transference to nature of Walton's philosophical thesis, for the doctrine of positive aesthetics with respect to nature, and for the idea that a model of the aesthetic appreciation of nature is needed.

The various art forms are sometimes divided into those for which the members are immutable types (such as composed music) and those for which the members are spatio-temporal individuals (such as paintings). But some philosophers reject the distinction, maintaining that all works of art are types. Whichever position is to be preferred, individual natural items differ from works of art in ways that have far-reaching consequences for the aesthetic properties they can properly be deemed to possess, considered as the things they are, and for their overall aesthetic value as such natural things.

First, lacking the immutability of types, they are subject to change, and the changes they undergo will result in the possession of different aesthetic properties at different times; and, unlike what is characteristic of works of art that are mutable spatio-temporal individuals (if any are), they lack an optimal condition, according to their creator's intention, in which their aesthetic properties are manifest.

Second, the relation between the category of art that a work belongs to and the appropriate artistic appreciation of that work is very different from the relation between the category of nature that an item belongs to and the appropriate aesthetic appreciation of that item (as the natural item it is). For, whereas a work's artistic category (i) is definitive of the mode of perception required for the appreciation of the work, if there is a single mode, or of the various modes, if more than one is necessary, or of the order in which the work's contents should be assimilated, if no particular mode or set of modes is necessary, but only one capable of processing information in the right manner, as with the novel; (ii) deems certain modes of perception and engagement with the work inappropriate; and (iii) indicates how the appropriate mode or modes of perception should be employed, i.e. at what it should (or should not) be directed and under what conditions, a natural thing's category of nature does none of these things. Accordingly, not only do a natural item's aesthetic properties change over time as it undergoes change, without any set constituting *the* aesthetic properties of the item *qua* the natural item it is, but its appearance is affected by climatic conditions, the observer's point of view, season, time of day, sense modality, power of magnification or amplification, and so on, none of these being optimal or mandatory, so that the range of its aesthetic properties is typically open-ended in a manner uncharacteristic of works of art.

It follows that the aesthetic appreciation of nature is endowed with a freedom denied to the appreciation of art, which renders the search for a model of the aesthetic appreciation of nature, in particular the natural environment, that will indicate what is to be appreciated and how it is to be appreciated—something we have a good grasp of in the case of works of art—a chimerical quest. Now, either the truth-value of a judgement about the aesthetic properties and value of a natural item is understood (as usually it is) in a relative manner—as relative to a particular stage in the item's natural history, a perceptual mode, a level and manner of observation, and a perceptual aspect—or it is not. If it is not, then in general there is no such thing as the appropriate aesthetic appreciation of nature, if by this is meant 'that appreciation of an object which reveals what aesthetic qualities and value it has' (Carlson 1984), and the idea of a natural item's aesthetic value, considered as the natural thing it is, is ill-defined, in particular often being plagued by irresoluble uncertainty as to the relevance or irrelevance of one or another aspect of the world in which the thing is involved to its own aesthetic value. (The artistic value of works of art that diverge from what is, or has been, characteristic of art is, to the extent that there is such a divergence, subject to the indefiniteness that characterizes the aesthetic value of nature.) Accordingly, through its uncritical use of the notion of a natural item's aesthetic value, the doctrine of a positive aesthetics of nature, advanced in a version that does not disallow the possession of negative aesthetic qualities by natural items, and understood as a thesis about instances of kinds of natural thing, must have an uncertain status.

See also: Beauty; Aesthetic Experience; Environmental Aesthetics.

BIBLIOGRAPHY

Berleant, A. (1993). 'The Aesthetics of Art and Nature', in S. Kemal and I. Gaskell (eds.), *Landscape, Natural Beauty and the Arts*. Cambridge: Cambridge University Press, pp. 228–43.

Budd, M. (1996). 'The Aesthetic Appreciation of Nature'. *British Journal of Aesthetics* 36: 207–22.

—— (2000). 'The Aesthetics of Nature'. *Proceedings of the Aristotelian Society*, 100: 137–57.

Carlson, A. (1976). 'Environmental Aesthetics and the Dilemma of Aesthetic Education'. *Journal of Aesthetic Education* 10: 69–82.

—— (1977). 'On the Possibility of Quantifying Scenic Beauty'. *Landscape Planning* 4: 131–72.

——(1979a). 'Appreciation and the Natural Environment'. *Journal of Aesthetics and Art Criticism* 37: 267–75.

——(1979b). 'Formal Qualities in the Natural Environment'. *Journal of Aesthetic Education* 13: 99–114.

——(1981). 'Nature, Aesthetic Judgement, and Objectivity'. *Journal of Aesthetics and Art Criticism* 40: 15–27.

——(1984). 'Nature and Positive Aesthetics'. *Environmental Ethics* 6: 5–34.

——(1986). 'Saito on the Correct Aesthetic Appreciation of Nature'. *Journal of Aesthetic Education* 20: 85–93.

——(1993). 'Appreciating Art and Appreciating Nature', in S. Kemal and I. Gaskell (eds.), *Landscape, Natural Beauty and the Arts*. Cambridge: Cambridge University Press, pp. 199–227.

——(1995). 'Nature, Aesthetic Appreciation, and Knowledge'. *Journal of Aesthetics and Art Criticism* 53: 393–400.

——(1997). 'Appreciating Godlovitch'. *Journal of Aesthetics and Art Criticism* 55: 55–7.

Carroll, N. (1993). 'On Being Moved by Nature: Between Religion and Natural History', in S. Kemal and I. Gaskell (eds.), *Landscape, Natural Beauty and the Arts*. Cambridge: Cambridge University Press, pp. 244–66.

Eaton, M. (1998). 'Fact and Fiction in the Aesthetic Appreciation of Nature'. *Journal of Aesthetics and Art Criticism* 56: 149–56.

Godlovitch, S. (1997). 'Carlson on Appreciation'. *Journal of Aesthetics and Art Criticism* 55: 53–5.

——(1998a). 'Valuing Nature and the Autonomy of Natural Aesthetics'. *British Journal of Aesthetics* 38: 180–97.

——(1998b). 'Evaluating Nature Aesthetically'. *Journal of Aesthetics and Art Criticism* 56: 113–25.

Hepburn, R. (1966). 'Contemporary Aesthetics and the Neglect of Natural Beauty', in B. Williams and A. Montefiori (eds.), *British Analytical Philosophy*. London: Routledge & Kegan Paul, pp. 285–310.

——(1996). 'Data and Theory in Aesthetics: Philosophical Understanding and Misunderstanding', in A. O'Hear (ed.), *Verstehen and Humane Understanding*. Cambridge: Cambridge University Press, pp. 235–52.

——(1998). 'Nature Humanised: Nature Respected'. *Environmental Values* 5: 267–79.

Matthews, P. (2001). 'Aesthetic Appreciation of Art and Nature'. *British Journal of Aesthetics* 41: 395–410.

——(2002). 'Scientific Knowledge and the Aesthetic Appreciation of Nature'. *Journal of Aesthetics and Art Criticism* 60: 37–48.

Saito, Y. (1984). 'Is there a Correct Aesthetic Appreciation of Nature?' *Journal of Aesthetic Education* 18: 35–46.

Stecker, R. (1997). 'The Correct and the Appropriate in the Appreciation of Nature'. *British Journal of Aesthetics* 37: 393–402.

Walton, K. (1970). 'Categories of Art'. *Philosophical Review* 79: 334–67.

Wollheim, R. (1991). 'Correspondence, Projective Properties, and Expression in the Arts', in I. Gaskell and S. Kemal (eds.), *The Language of Art History*. Cambridge: Cambridge University Press, pp. 51–66.

Zangwill, N. (2001). 'Formal Natural Beauty'. *Proceedings of the Aristotelian Society* 101: 209–24.

CHAPTER 7

DEFINITION
OF ART

ROBERT STECKER

'ART' is most often used to refer to a set of forms, practices or institutions. However, when we ask: 'Is that art?' we are usually asking whether an individual item is a work of art. The project of defining art most commonly consists in the attempt to find necessary conditions and sufficient conditions for the truth of the statement that an item is an *artwork*. That is, the goal is normally to find a principle for classifying all artworks together while distinguishing them from all non-artworks. Sometimes the goal is set higher. Some look for a 'real' definition: that is, one in terms of necessary conditions that are *jointly* sufficient for being an artwork. Sometimes the aim is to identify a metaphysical *essence* that all artworks have in common.

A definition of art should be distinguished from a philosophical theory of art, which is invariably a broader project with vaguer boundaries. Such a theory may touch on many issues other that the issue of definition, or may even studiously avoid that issue in favour of others. A theory of art will typically concern itself centrally with questions of value, for example whether there is some unique value that only artworks offer. In any case, it will attempt to identify the valuable properties of art that are responsible for its great importance in most, if not all, cultures. It may give attention to cognitive issues, such as what one must know to understand an artwork, and what it is for an interpretation of a work to be good, acceptable, or true. A theory of art may be interested in other sorts of responses or attitudes to artworks, such as emotional responses. It may focus on the fictionality characteristic of so many works of art, or on their formal, representational, or expressive properties. It may deal with the social, historical, institutional, or intentional characteristics of art. A theory of art will address several of these issues, display the connections among them, and sometimes, but only sometimes, attempt to formulate a definition either of art or of artistic value, or both on the basis of some of these other artistic properties.

This chapter will survey the main trends that mark the history of the project of defining art in the twentieth century before discussing the most important efforts in the past thirty years.

1. HISTORICAL BACKGROUND

Even before turning to the twentieth century, something should be said about the historical roots of the attempt to define art. It is sometimes supposed that the earliest definitions of art are to be found in the writings of ancient philosophers such as Plato and Aristotle. In fact, one will not find, in these writers, a definition of art, in the sense of an item belonging to the fine arts or of art in its current sense, if that departs from the concept of the fine arts. It is now widely accepted that the former concept was not fully in place until some time in the eighteenth century, and hence it seems implausible that the ancients would think in terms of, or try to define, art in that sense. What is true is that they wrote about such things as poetry, painting, music, and architecture, which came to be classified as fine arts, and saw some common threads among them. Plato was very interested in the fact that poetry, like painting, was a representation or imitation of various objects and features of the world, including human beings and their actions, and that it had a powerful effect on the emotions. Aristotle also emphasized the idea of poetry as imitation and characterized other arts, such as music, in those terms.

This way of thinking of the arts wielded enormous influence in the Renaissance and Enlightenment, and so when the concept of the fine arts solidified the first definitions of art were cast in terms of representation, by such important figures as Hutcheson, Batteux, and Kant. It is not necessary to set out the exact content of all of these definitions here, since in the later period in which we are interested they were superseded by other approaches. Of those earlier definitions, Kant's is the one that has had truly lasting influence. Fine art, according to Kant, is one of two 'aesthetic arts', i.e. arts of representation where 'the feeling of pleasure is what is immediately in view'. The end of *agreeable art* is pleasurable sensation. The pleasure afforded by the representations of *fine art*, in contrast, is 'one of reflection', which is to say that it arises from the exercise of our imaginative and cognitive powers. Fine art is 'a mode of representation which is intrinsically final . . . and has the effect of advancing the culture of the mental powers in the interest of social communication' (Kant 1952: 165–6). There are elements in this conception that survive even after the idea that the essence of art is representation is abandoned.

One is a series of contrasts between (fine) art, properly understood, and entertainment (agreeable art). Art makes more demands on the intellect but offers deeper satisfactions. Art is 'intrinsically final', i.e. appreciated for its own sake. Art has some essential connection with communication.

The struggle to replace the mimetic paradigm takes place in the nineteenth century. This occurs on many fronts, just as did the formation of the concept of the fine arts a century earlier. Artistic movements such as romanticism, impressionism, and art-for-art's-sake challenge ideals associated with mimeticism and direct attention to other aspects of art, such as the expression of the artist and the experience of the audience. Debates among critics in response to these movements raise questions about the boundaries of art. The invention of photography challenges the mimetic ideal in painting, at least if that is regarded as the increasingly accurate, life-like representation of what we see. The increasing prestige of purely instrumental music provides at least one clear example of non-representational art. For some, such music provides a new paradigm captured by Walter Pater's claim that all the arts aspire to the condition of music. In response to all this, new definitions of art appear, especially expression theories, formalist theories, and aesthetic theories.

What all these theories have in common with each other, as with mimeticism, is that they each identify a single valuable property or function of art, and assert that it is this property that qualifies something as art. Call these *simple functionalist theories*. Such theories dominate the attempt to define art right through the middle of the twentieth century. Although they now no longer dominate, they are still regularly put forward. Those cited at the end of the last paragraph have been the most important and influential examples of this type of theory. Each deserves attention in some detail.

2. Art as Expression

The ostensible difference between expression and representation is that, while the latter looks outward and attempts to re-present nature, society, and human form and action, the former looks inward in an attempt to convey moods, emotions, or attitudes. We seem to find instances of expressive art where representation is de-emphasized or absent. It is very common to think of instrumental music, or at least many pieces of music, in these terms. As the visual arts moved towards greater abstraction, they too often seem to de-emphasize, or abandon representation for the sake of expression. One can even extend this to literature, which pursued expressivist goals from the advent of romantic poetry through the invention of 'stream of consciousness' and other techniques to express interiority. So it might seem that one could find art without representation but not without expression. This might encourage the further thought, independently encouraged by various romantic and expressivist movements in the nineteenth and twentieth centuries, that, even when expression and representation co-occur, the real business of art is expression.

Space permits the examination of only one specific proposal to define art in terms of expression. The definition comes from Collingwood's *Principles of Art* (1938). Collingwood defines art primarily as an activity: that of clarifying an emotion, by which he means identifying the emotion one is feeling not merely as a general type, such as anger or remorse, but with as much particularity as possible. Collingwood does not deny that one can rephrase this definition in terms of a work of art rather than an activity, but he believes that the work exists primarily in the minds of artist and audience, rather than in one of the more usual artistic media. However, he seems to think of the job of the medium as enabling the communication of the emotion to the audience who then have the same clarified emotion in their minds, which is to say, for Collingwood, the work of art itself.

The definition has well known problems. First, even if expressiveness, in some sense, is a widespread phenomenon in the arts, it is far too narrowly circumscribed by Collingwood. He prescribes a certain process by which a work of art must come about, whereas it is in fact a contingent matter whether works are created in the way he recognizes. Not unexpectedly, the definition rules out many items normally accepted as art works, including some of the greatest in the Western tradition, such as the plays of Shakespeare, which by Collingwood's lights are entertainment rather than art. The definition assumes that the emotion expressed in a work is always the artist's emotion, but it is not at all clear why a work cannot express, or be expressive of, an emotion not felt by the artist when creating the work. In recent years, the idea that art expresses an actual person's emotion has given way to the idea that art is expressive of emotion in virtue of possessing expressive properties, such as the property of being sad, joyful, or anxious, however such properties are analysed. Such properties can be perceived in the work, and their presence in a work does not require any specific process of creation.

Traditional expression theories like Collingwood's have been widely rejected, even if some still believe they point towards one of the central functions of art. However, the idea that art is expression, qualified by a number of additional conditions, lives on in work of Arthur Danto. Though properly regarded as an expression theory of art, I would claim that Danto's version of this theory arises within a sufficiently different intellectual and artistic context as to be best treated at a later stage of this discussion. So, putting it on hold for now, we turn to other simple functionalist conceptions of art.

3. FORMALISM

Developing alongside expression theories of art were formalist theories. If one stops thinking that art is all about representation, a natural further thought, if one is thinking in simple functionalist terms, is that what art is all about is form rather than representational content. This thought gained support from various developments in the arts during the time of high modernism, a long, exciting period roughly between 1880 and 1960. Though many artforms contain modernist masterpieces, the work of painters were the paradigm and inspiration for many of the most influential formalist theories. Cézanne in particular was the darling of the early formalists Clive Bell (1914) and Roger Fry (1920). Cézanne's paintings contain perfectly traditional representational subjects—landscape, portraiture, still life—but his innovations could be seen as formal, with virtually no concern, furthermore, to express anything inner other than Cézanne's eye making features of visual reality salient. These innovations involved the use of an wide-ranging palette, a handling of line, and an interest in the three-dimensional geometry of his subjects, which give his figures a 'solidity' not found in his impressionist predecessors, while at the same time 'flattening' the planes of the pictorial surface. Taking such formal features as the *raison d'être* for these paintings became the typical formalist strategy for understanding the increasingly abstract works of twentieth-century modernism, as well as for reconceiving the history of art. Like the other simple functionalist theories under discussion here, formalism is not just an attempt to define art. It is a philosophical theory of art in the sense indicated above. It also attempts to identify the value of art, and what needs to be understood in order to appreciate an artwork.

A formalist attempt to define art faces several initial tasks. They all have to do with figuring out how to deploy the notion of form in a definition. One can't just say: art is form or art is what has form, because everything has form in some sense. The first task is thus to identify a relevant sense of 'form' or, in other words, to identify which properties give a work *form*. Second, if objects other than artworks can have form in the relevant sense, one has to find something special about the way artworks possess such form.

The best known and most explicit formalist definition of art is Clive Bell's. According to Bell, art is what has significant form. Significant form is form that imbues what possesses it with a special sort of value that consists in the affect produced in those who perceive it. Bell calls the affect 'the aesthetic emotion', though, as Carol Gould (1994) has pointed out, this is probably a misnomer since what he has in mind is more likely a positive, pleasurable reaction to a perceptual experience. So Bell performs the second task mentioned above by claiming that what is special about form in art is that it is valuable in a special way.

However, until Bell dispatches the first of the tasks mentioned above, i.e. until we know what he means by form, his claims about significant form are unilluminating. Unfortunately, regarding this task, Bell is remarkably cavalier. Being concerned primarily with the visual arts, he sometimes suggests that the building blocks of form are line and colour combined in a certain way. But this is not adequate to his examples, which include: St Sophia, the windows at Chartres, Mexican sculpture, a Persian bowl, Chinese carpets, and the masterpieces of Poussin. Perhaps even three-dimensional works such as buildings, bowls, and sculptures in some

abstract sense are 'built' out of line and colour. A more straightforward way to item-
ize the formal properties of a bowl would be colour, three-dimensional shape, and
the patterns, if any, that mark its surfaces. Notice that any three-dimensional object
has formal properties so characterized, and those that have significant form are
a subclass of those that have form. Essentially the same is true in the cases of buildings and sculptures, though these are typically far more complex in having many
parts or sub-forms that interact with each other and with a wider environment. But
a similar complexity can be found in many three-dimensional objects, both manu-
factured and natural.

In the case of pictures in general, and paintings in particular, which is the sort of
visual art in which Bell was most interested, speaking of form as arising from line
and colour is, if anything, more unilluminating because all sorts of its properties,
including the representational properties so arise. Further, it gives no indication of
the complexity of the concept as it applies to a two-dimensional medium capable
of depicting three dimensions. The fact is that the form of a painting includes, but
is hardly confined to, the two-dimensional array of lines and colour patches that
mark its surface. As Malcom Budd (1995) has pointed out in one of the most sensitive treatments of the topic, it also includes the way objects, abstractly conceived,
are laid out in the represented three-dimensional space of the work and the interaction of these two- and three-dimensional aspects.

If we can pin down the sense of form as it applies across the various art media,
can we then go on to assert that something is an artwork just in case it has significant form? Bell's definition hinges on his ability to identify not just form, but
significant form, and many have questioned whether he is able to do this in a non-
circular fashion. His most explicit attempts on this score are plainly circular or
empty, involving the interdefinition of two technical terms, significant form being
what and only what produces the aesthetic emotion, and the aesthetic emotion
being what is produced by and only by significant form. Others (Gould 1994),
however, have claimed that a substantive understanding of when form is significant can be recovered from formalist descriptions of artworks purportedly in possession of it.

Even if Bell can successfully identify significant form, his definition is not satisfactory. It misfires in a number of respects that are typical of the simple functionalist approach. First, it rules out the possibility of bad art, since significant form is
always something to be valued highly. Perhaps there can be degrees of it, but it is
not something that can occur to a very small degree unless one can say that a work
has negligible significant form. Second, it displays the common vice of picking out
one important property for which we value art, while ignoring others at the cost of
excluding not just bad works but many great works. Thus, someone who defines art
as significant form has little use for artists like Breughel whose paintings, many of
which teem with vast numbers of tiny human figures, give a rich sense of many
aspects of human life but lack art's defining feature as Bell would understand it.

Perhaps there is a better way to deploy the notion of form or formal value in a definition of art. This is a possibility that, whatever its merits, has gone largely unexplored. Instead, those who remained attached to the simple functionalist model turned to an alternative approach using a more flexible concept, that of the aesthetic. So, rather than exploring hypothetical formalisms, we turn to this new approach.

4. Aesthetic Definitions

The concept of the aesthetic is both ambiguous and contested, but there are other chapters in this volume devoted to the explication of those issues, and so little will be said about them here. For our purposes, we can stipulate that the aesthetic refers in the first instance to intrinsically valuable experience that results from close attention to the sensuous features of an object or to an imaginary world it projects. Aesthetic properties of objects are those that have inherent value in virtue of the aesthetic experience they afford. Aesthetic interest is an interest in such experiences and properties. Aesthetic definitions—attempts to define art in terms of such experiences, properties, or interest—have been, with only a few exceptions, the definitions of choice among those pursuing the simple functionalist project during the last thirty years. The brief exposition above of definitions of art in terms of representational, expressive, and formal value suggests why this is the case. Each of the previous attempts to define art do so by picking out a valuable feature of art and claiming that all and only things that have that feature are artworks. One of the objections to each of the definitions was that they excluded some works of art, even some possessing considerable value, but not in virtue of the feature preferred by the definition. Hence such definitions are not extensionally adequate.

By contrast, aesthetic definitions seem, at first glance, to be free of this problem. Form and representation can both afford intrinsically valuable experience, and, typically, such experience does not exclude one aspect in favour of the other. The same is true for the experience afforded by the expressive properties of works. All such experience can be regarded under the umbrella of aesthetic experience.

Aesthetic definitions of art are numerous and new ones are constantly on offer. I mention here a few of the better known or better constructed definitions.

- An artwork is something produced with the intention of giving it the capacity to satisfy aesthetic interest (Beardsley 1983).
- A work of art is an artefact which under standard conditions provides its percipient with aesthetic experience (Schlesinger 1979).
- An 'artwork' is any creative arrangement of one or more media whose principal function is to communicate a significant aesthetic object (Lind 1992).

Despite the fact that the notion of the aesthetic better serves the simple functionalist than the notions of representation, expression, or form, such definitions are still are far from satisfactory. To bring this out, consider two basic requirements on the definition of any kind (class, property, concept) K: (i) that it provide necessary conditions for belonging to (being, falling under) K, and (ii) that they provide sufficient conditions for belonging to (being, falling under) K. To be an artwork, is it necessary that it provide aesthetic experience or even that it be made with the intention that it satisfy an interest in such experience? Many have thought not. Those who deny it are impressed with art movements like Dadaism, conceptual art, and performance art. These movements are concerned, in one way or another, with conveying ideas seemingly stripped of aesthetic interest. Dadaist works, such as Duchamp's readymades, appear to be precisely aimed at questioning the necessary connection between art and the aesthetic by selecting objects with little or no aesthetic interest, such as urinals, snow shovels, and bottle racks. Some instances of performance art appear to be based on the premiss that political ideas can be conveyed more effectively without the veneer of aesthetic interest. Conceptual works seem to forgo or sideline sensory embodiment entirely.

Defenders of aesthetic definitions take two approaches to replying to this objection. Some (Beardsley 1983) attempt to deny that the apparent counter-examples are artworks, but this seems to be a losing battle as the number of ostensible counter-examples increase and gain critical and popular acceptance as artworks. What has recently come to be the more common tack in replying to the objection is to claim that the apparent counter-examples do have aesthetic properties (Lind 1992). The readymades, for example, have such properties on more than one level. Simply regarded as objects, they have features that to a greater or lesser degree reward contemplation. As artworks, they powerfully express Duchamp's ironic posture towards art.

Can we deploy the notion of the aesthetic to provide a sufficient condition for being an artwork? As the previous paragraph already begins to suggest, any object has the potential to be of aesthetic interest, and so providing aesthetic experience is hardly unique to art. Beardsley's definition rules out natural objects, since they are not made with the requisite intention, but it seems to rule in many artefacts that are not artworks, but are made with aesthetically pleasing features.

There are three ways in which a defender of aesthetic definitions of art might try to cope with the pervasiveness of the aesthetic outside of art *per se*. One way is to redefine what counts as art as any artefact with aesthetic interest. (Zangwill 2000 suggests this approach.) The problem with this move is that it just changes the subject from an attempt to figure out why we classify objects as art to a mere stipulation that something is art if it is an aesthetic object. A definition that includes doughnut boxes, ceiling fans, and toasters, even when not put forward as readymades, is simply not a definition of art in a sense others have attempted to capture. Second, one can attempt to rule out non-art artefacts by claiming that artworks have a 'significant' aesthetic interest that distinguishes them from the 'mere' aesthetic interest possessed by other artefacts (see Lind 1992). But this line is equally unlikely to succeed. The more one requires such 'significance', the less likely it is that all artworks will possess it, for we have seen that many recent works are not concerned primarily with creating a rich aesthetic experience. The last strategy is to claim that, despite intuitions to the contrary, aesthetic experience is something that is either uniquely or primarily provided by art. This strategy faces the daunting task of specifying an experience common to all artworks, and one that art uniquely or primarily provides, but without making essential reference to the concept of art. Though some, such as Beardsley (1969), have attempted such a specification, the consensus is that no proposal has been successful.

5. Anti-Essentialism

Although aesthetic definitions of art continue to have adherents, the dominant trend within this topic since the 1950s has been to reject simple functionalism in all of its forms. This rejection began with the more sweeping thought that the attempt to define art is misguided because necessary and sufficient conditions do not exist capable of supporting a real definition of art. The most influential proponents of this anti-essentialism were Morris Weitz (1956) and Paul Ziff (1953). Guided by Wittgenstein's philosophy of language, they claimed that it was atypical for ordinary language empirical concepts to operate on the basis of such conditions. Rather, as Weitz put it, most such concepts were 'open-textured', meaning that the criteria by which we apply the concept do not determine its application in every possible situation. While the concept of art is by no means unique in being open-textured for Weitz and Ziff, the concept still stands apart from many other empirical concepts in one respect. For many empirical concepts, open texture merely creates a theoretical possibility that situations may arise in which criteria no longer guide us, and a new decision is needed whether the concept applies. Weitz and Ziff conceived of art as requiring such decisions on a regular basis as new art movements continually create novel works. This novelty provides a constant source of counter-examples to simple functionalist definitions.

Instead of being classified by necessary and sufficient conditions, claimed Weitz and Ziff, works are classified as art in virtue of 'family resemblances', or sets of similarities based on multiple paradigms. So one work is art in virtue of one set of similarities to other works, while another is art in virtue of a different set of similarities. An alternative approach, also Wittgensteinian in spirit, is that art is a cluster concept (see Gaut 2000). This means that we can discern several different sets of properties the possession of any of which suffices for an object to achieve art status, but no one of which is by itself necessary for such status.

Each of these suggestions, while proposing that the concept of art is best captured by something other than a definition, in fact lays the ground for new approaches to defining art. The family resemblance view claims that the concept of art is formed by a network of similarities. But which ones accomplish this? If none are specified then the view is empty, since everything bears a similarity to everything else. In fact, Ziff suggested that the relevant domain of similarities will be social or functional in nature, though, in the case of the latter, not in the way simple functionalists had hoped for. As for the cluster concept view, if the set of conditions sufficient for being an artwork are finite and enumerable, it is already equivalent to a definition of art, viz. a disjunctive definition.

While attempting to demonstrate that art cannot be defined, anti-essentialism actually resulted in a whole new crop of definitions, most of which look completely different from their simple functionalist predecessors and rivals.

6. Danto and Dickie

In a highly influential article, Maurice Mandelbaum (1965) was among the first to point out that the appeal to family resemblance does not preclude, but rather invites, definition. It may be true that when we look at the resembling features within a literal family, we may find no one *exhibited* likeness that they all have in common. However, Mandelbaum observes, family resemblance is no more satisfactorily explicated in terms of an open-ended set of similarities differentially shared among the family's members; for people outside the family may also possess the exhibited features without these thereby bearing a *family* resemblance to the original set of people. Rather, what is needed to capture the idea of family resemblance is a *non-exhibited* relation, namely that of resemblance among those *with a common ancestry*. Without proposing a specific definition, Mandelbaum suggested that in attempting to define art we may fill in the gap left to us by the family resemblance view by appealing to some non-exhibited relational property—perhaps one involving intention, use, or origin.

Among the first to explore the possibility of defining art in these terms, and certainly the most influential proponents of this approach, were Arthur Danto and George Dickie. In part because both cast their thought about art in terms of 'the artworld', in part because Danto was not explicit about his proposed definition, for some time it was thought that they were advancing similar definitions of art. However, it is now understood that each was developing quite different theories, Danto's being historical and functional and Dickie's, radically afunctional and institutional.

In some early papers, Danto (1964, 1973) outlines desiderata to which a definition of art must conform without yet setting forth a definition that satisfactorily meets the desiderata. The first point, illustrated by the readymades as well as by such works as Warhol's Brillo Boxes, is that art and non-art can be perceptually indistinguishable and so cannot be marked off from each other by 'exhibited' properties. (A corollary to this is that one artwork cannot always be distinguished from another by appeal to exhibited properties.) Second, an artwork always exists in an art historical context, and this is a crucial condition for it to be art. Art historical context relates a given work to the history of art. It also provides 'an atmosphere of artistic theory', art being 'the kind of thing that depends for its existence on theories' (Danto 1981: 135). Third, 'Nothing is an artwork without an interpretation which constitutes it as such' (p. 135). Every work of art is about something, but, equally, invariably expresses an attitude of the artist towards the work's subject or 'way of seeing' the same. An interpretation, then, tells us what the work is about and how it is seen by its maker; further, it expresses the artist's intention on this score.

Danto's most important work in the philosophy of art, and his most sustained attempt to discern the essence of art, is his book *The Transfiguration of the Commonplace* (1981), in which he elaborates on the considerations stated above and adds others. However, it was left to commentators to fashion an explicitly stated definition of art from this material. The best statement, and one endorsed by Danto, is provided by Noël Carroll (1993: 80) as follows. X is a work of art if and only if (*a*) X has a subject (*b*) about which X projects an attitude or point of view (*c*) by means of rhetorical (usually metaphorical) ellipsis (*d*), which ellipsis requires audience participation to fill in what is missing (interpretation) (*e*), where both the work and the interpretation require an art-historical context.

To a considerable extent, this definition follows the pattern of traditional simple functionalist definitions of art. Basically, conditions (*a*) and (*b*) give to art the function of projecting a point of view or attitude of the artist about a subject, and this puts it in the broad class of attempts to define art in terms of expression. That this function is accomplished in a special way (*c*), and requires a certain response from the audience (*d*), are not uncommon features of expression theories. If anything sets Danto's definition apart from other simple functionalist proposals, it is the final condition, (*e*), which requires that a work and its interpretation stand in a historical relation to other artworks.

It is this last feature that has made Danto's definition influential, but it is not clear that it helps very much to save it from the fate of other simple functionalist definitions. Many believe that there are works of art that fail to meet all of the first four conditions. For example, aren't many works of music, architecture, or ceramics, and even some abstract or decorative works, which are arguably not *about* anything, nevertheless instances of works of art?

George Dickie's artworld is different from Danto's. Rather than consisting in historically related works, styles, and theories, it is an institution. In attempting to define art in terms of an institution, Dickie abandons the attempt to offer a definition not only in terms of exhibited features, but in terms of functions of any sort. Dickie originally conceived of this institution as one that exists to confer an official status, even if it does so through informal procedures. Increasingly, however, he came to view it differently, as one geared to the production of a class of artefacts and to their presentation to a public.

As might be guessed from his changing understanding of the institution of art, Dickie has proposed two distinct institutional definitions of art, the second being based on his own rejection of the first. Both, however, have received a great deal of attention and exercised considerable influence, so each deserves some discussion here. The first definition goes as follows:

Something is a work of art if and only if (1) it is an artifact, and (2) a set of aspects of which has had conferred upon it the status of candidate for appreciation by some person or persons acting on behalf of the Artworld. (Dickie 1974: 34)

Notice that the status conferred that makes some artefact an artwork is the status not of being art (at least, not straightforwardly that), but of being a candidate for appreciation, and this status is conferred on a set of aspects of the item rather than on the item itself. Dickie's definition itself does not tell us who in the artworld typically confers status. One might think it would be people like critics, art gallery owners, or museum directors, because they are the ones who select and make salient to a broader public aspects of a work for appreciation. However, Dickie's commentary on the definition makes clear that he thinks artists are the exclusive agents of status conferral. Since conferring would seem to be an action, one might wonder what an artist does to bring it about. It can't just be making something with properties capable of being considered for appreciation. Stephen Davies (1991: 85) has suggested that conferral consists in someone *with the appropriate authority* making, or putting forward, such an object.

For many, the crucial idea that makes this definition of art institutional is that being an artwork consists of possessing a status conferred on it by someone with the authority to do so. However, this is precisely the idea that Dickie eventually rejected. Rightly or wrongly, he came to view status conferral as implying a formal process, but felt that no such process need occur—nor, typically, does it occur—in bringing artworks into existence.

Dickie's second definition of art is part of a set of five definitions that present the 'leanest possible description of the essential framework of art':

1. An artist is a person who participates with understanding in making a work of art.
2. A work of art is an artifact of a kind created to be presented to an artworld public.
3. A public is a set of persons whose members are prepared in some degree to understand an object that is presented to them.
4. The artworld is the totality of all artworld systems.
5. An artworld system is a framework for the presentation of a work of art by an artist to an artworld public. (Dickie 1984: 80–1)

The basic idea here is that the status of being art is not something that is conferred by some agent's authority, but instead derives from a work being properly situated in a system of relations. Pre-eminent in this system is the relation of the work to the artist and to an artworld public. It is the work's being created by the artist against the 'background of the artworld' (Dickie 1984: 12) that establishes it as an artefact of a kind created to be presented to an artworld public, i.e. an artwork.

If we abstract from the particulars of Dickie's two definitions, one can discern a common strategy that gives rise to a set of common problems for his approach. In both definitions, Dickie set out a structure that is shared with other institutions or practices beyond the 'artworld'. Conferral of status occurs in many settings, and even the conferral of the status of candidate of appreciation frequently occurs outside the artworld (whether or not it occurs within it). For example, an 'official' tourist brochure issued by a tourism board confers the status of candidate for appreciation on some particular place. So does official recognition that a building is 'historical'. (Remember that Dickie self-consciously refuses to say what kind of appreciation is conferred by agents of the artworld.) Even advertising might be thought to confer such status, as is certainly its aim.

How does Dickie's first definition distinguish between these conferrals of candidacy for appreciation from art-making conferrals? Only by referring to the artworld, i.e. gesturing towards artforms and their making, distribution, and presentation, without explaining what marks these off from other status-conferring practices. Similarly, regarding the second definition, there are many artefact production and presentations systems outside the artworld. Wherever a product is produced for consumers, there is such a system. How does Dickie distinguish artworld systems from other artefact presentation systems? He does so only by naming the artworld systems 'artworld systems', i.e. by gesturing towards the relevant systems without explaining what marks them off.

This strategy gives rise to the problems of circularity and incompleteness (see Walton 1977; Levinson 1987; Davies 1991; Stecker 1986, 1997). Dickie acknowledges that his definitions are circular, but denies that this is a problem. It is clearly a problem, however, when a definition is insufficiently informative to mark off the extension of what it is attempting to define. Because Dickie's definitions simply gesture towards the artworld without marking it off from similar systems, it is incomplete for lack of informativeness. Dickie (1989) replies that it is ultimately arbitrary whether or not a system is part of the artworld, but such a claim seems to be an admission that the definition cannot be completed.

7. HISTORICAL APPROACHES AND THE REVIVAL OF FUNCTIONALISM

Others have proposed that the situation is not as hopeless as Dickie (inadvertently) suggests. Kendall Walton (1977) was among the first to suggest that the artworld systems that Dickie gestures towards might be defined historically. Walton's suggestion is that the artworld consists of a limited number of proto-systems plus other systems that develop historically from these in a certain manner (1977: 98). Dickie (1984: 76) has pointed out that this leaves unsettled the issue of why the proto-systems belong to the artworld in the first place, and has expressed the belief that no real explanation is possible. This assessment may again be over-hasty. One possible place to look for the set of original proto-systems would be the formation of the system of the fine arts in the eighteenth century, with poetry, painting, sculpture, architecture, and music (possibly confined to vocal music) being the paradigmatic proto-artforms. Surely, there is an explanation of why these forms comprised an important category at this time. This explanation might refer to a common functional property, or, it might itself be historical. A residual problem with this approach is whether it accounts for all items classified as artworks. The view appears to imply that to be art it is necessary and sufficient that it belong to an artform or art system, and not everyone would accept both parts of that claim (Levinson 1979; Stecker 1997). The view, even rehabilitated along quasi-historical lines, may also fail to account for artworks and artforms from non-western and earlier western cultures that are conceptually but not historically linked in the right way to the eighteenth-century prototypes.

Stephen Davies is the most important defender of the institutional approach since Dickie. Davies does not actually offer a definition of art, but sketches lines along which it should develop. First, it should reinstate the idea that the artworld is structured according to roles defined by the authority they give to those who occupy them. Art status is conferred on works by artists in virtue of the authority of the role they occupy. Second, artworld institutions should be understood historically. Davies's discussions of the historical roots of art has come to focus more on individual artworks than on artworld systems. Consider very early artworks. Did such works exist in an institutional setting? If so, what gave rise to these institutions? Surely, it was even earlier works around which the institutions grew. Davies initially attempted to give an institutional analysis to cases like this as well as cases of isolated artists whose work is disconnected from art institutions as we know them (Davies 1991). His current view, however, is that the earliest art, the prototypes from which art and its institutions arose, are to be understood functionally. Such items are art because their aesthetic value is essential to their function. However, once art institutions become established, art can develop in ways that no longer require an aesthetic—or any other—function (Davies 1997, 2000).

In addition to attempts to historicize the institutional approach to defining art, a number of philosophers have explored other forms of historical definition. Jerrold Levinson has proposed that an historical relation holding among the intentions of artists and prior artworks is definitive of art (Levinson 1979, 1989, 1993); James Carney claims that the relation is one holding among historically evolving styles (1991, 1994); while Noël Carroll, though not offering a definition, has put forward the suggestion that art is identified by historical narratives which link later works to earlier ones (Carroll 1994). Robert Stecker asserts that art is defined in terms of historically evolving functions (1997).

Levinson's proposal is one of the best worked out and most carefully defended. It is that 'an artwork is a thing that has been seriously intended for regard-as-a-work-of-art, i.e., regard in any way pre-existing artworks are or were correctly regarded' (Levinson 1989: 21).

One wants to know more about what it is to intend a thing for regard-as-a-work-of-art, and why this core aspect of Levinson's definition does not make it as tightly circular as Dickie's. It turns out there can be two relevant types of intention. On the 'intrinsic' type, one intends a work for a complex of regards for features found in earlier artworks without having any specific artwork, genre, movement, or tradition in mind. One might intend it for regard for its form, expressiveness, verisimilitude, and so on. Alternatively, there is the 'relational' type of intention, in which one intends an object for regard as some particular artwork, genre, etc. is or was correctly regarded. When one fills in these possible regards, in theory, one eliminates the expression 'as-a-work-of-art', which is the basis of Levinson's defence against the charge of circularity.

As with some other historical accounts (such as Carney's and Carroll's), Levinson's main idea is that something is a work of art because of a relation it bears to earlier artworks, which are in turn art because of a relation they bear to still earlier works, and so on. Once this is clear, it becomes obvious that, as one moves back along the relational chain, one will come across artworks for which there are none earlier. These earliest artworks have come to be called 'first art'. We need a separate account of what makes first artworks art, and a reason for thinking that this separate account won't serve to explain why all artworks are art, obviating the need for a historical approach. Davies now gives an essentially functional account of first art in his historicized institutional approach (1997, 2000), and would claim that this won't explain why all artworks are art because, within an art institution, objects can acquire art status while lacking the original function of art.

Levinson prefers to avoid this straightforwardly functionalist approach to first art. For him, what makes something first art is that it is 'the ultimate causal source and intentional reference of later activities we take as paradigmatically art'. Furthermore, first art aims at 'many of the same effects and values, that later, paradigmatic art has enshrined' (Levinson 1993: 421). These remarks come close to a functional approach similar to that of Davies, but substitute causal and intentional relations to functions for direct reference to the functions themselves.

There are a number of objections to Levinson's definition. Against taking it as a sufficient condition for being art, various examples have been offered where the requisite intention is purportedly present, but the item in question is arguably not an artwork. In 1915, Duchamp attempted to transform the Woolworth Building into a readymade. He was not successful, but not for lack of an appropriate intention (Carney 1994). A forger of a Rembrandt self-portrait may intend that his work be regarded in many ways as the original is correctly regarded, without thereby creating another artwork (Sartwell 1990: 157). There are also objections questioning whether the definition provides a necessary condition for being art. There can be objects that achieve functional success as art, in that they reward a complex set of intrinsic regards, but lack the required intention. They may spring from an artistic intention based on a misunderstanding of earlier works, or from a utilitarian intention that adventitiously results in an object with artistically valuable properties. For example, one might set out just to make a vessel that holds water and end up with a remarkably beautiful pot.

Levinson has replies to all of these counter-examples (see Levinson 1990, 1993). Duchamp failed because he lacked the relevant 'proprietary right' to the building. The forger does not create an artwork because, though he intends the forgery to receive many of the regards correctly directed to the Rembrandt, they are not correctly directly to his own painting. Levinson seems to admit that there can be art that lacks the intentions he ordinarily requires for arthood, but holds that this points to further, less central, senses of art. All these replies, as well as the above remarks on first art, add new conditions to, and hence considerably complicate, Levinson's original definition. Sometimes, too many qualifications can kill a proposal. In this case, though, the patient is arguably still alive and attempting to recuperate.

Still, at a number of junctures it appears that Levinson might have achieved a simpler definition by appealing directly to functions or regards rather than intentions. Robert Stecker (1997) formulates a definition of art that appeals more directly to an historically evolving set of functions, without completely dispensing with a reference to artistic intentions. (For another such attempt, see Graves 1998.) Stecker does not define art explicitly in terms of an historical relation linking the art of one time with the art of an earlier time. Rather, his definition proceeds by reference to time-relative artforms and functions. At any given time, art has a finite set of functions that range from genre-specific values to those widespread representational, expressive, formal, and aesthetic values enshrined in the simple functional definitions considered earlier. The functions of art at a given time are to be identified through an understanding of the artforms central to that time. However, that does not mean that items that don't belong to a central artform are never art. According to Stecker, almost anything can be art, but artefacts outside the central artforms have to meet a higher standard. This motivates a disjunctive definition of art: an item is an artwork at time t, where t is not earlier than the time at which the item is made, if and only if (a) it is in one of the central artforms at t and is made with the intention of fulfilling a function that art has at t, or (b) it is an artefact that achieves excellence in achieving such a function.

With this definition too there are various problems. The appearance of circularity is handled in much the same way as with Levinson's definition: by eliminating reference to art by enumerating central forms and functions. However, this requires that Stecker provide some account of these items. What makes something a central artform? How are genuine functions of art distinguished from accidental functions (e.g. using sculptures as a doorstops or paintings for insulation) and extrinsic functions (e.g. using art an investment)? Further, not every function is appropriate to every candidate artwork, so functions have to be coordinated with their appropriate forms. Finally, there are things that appear to fulfil functions of art to a high degree, but no one would call them artworks. Suppose there were a pill that induced a fine aesthetic experience. The pill is not a work of art even though it appears to fulfil a function of art with excellence. (For replies to these and other objections see Stecker 1997: 51–65.)

Views like those of Davies, Levinson, and Stecker suggest that a consensus is developing about how art should be defined (see Stecker 2000; Matravers 2000). Though each at first appears to represent a different approach (institutional, intentional, functional), the similarities among these views are more striking than the differences. All accept Danto's view that art must be defined historically; and all, in the end, are committed to a definition that consists of a disjunction of sufficient conditions rather than a set of necessary conditions that are jointly sufficient (so-called real definitions). Further, unlike simple functionalist definitions, these definitions do not form the kernel of a larger, normatively aimed theory of art, but are compatible with many different theories. In particular, these definitions, like Dickie's definitions, distinguish an understanding of what art is from a conception of the value of art. In fact, the disjunctive character of recent definitions suggests not only that there is no one value or function essential to art, but that there is no essence of art at all.

Whatever the extent of this consensus, it excludes two parties to the debate. One comprises those who are still interested in pursuing a simple functionalist definition, typically in terms of aesthetic experience or properties (see Anderson 2000; Zangwill 2000). The other comprises those who are sceptical of the possibility of any definition of art (Tilghman 1984; Novitz 1996).

It is an interesting question just where future work in this area should direct its efforts (see Stecker 2000). On one side of the issue, those in the sceptical camp might do more to develop their arguments. On the other side of the issue, instead of developing more proposals of the sort we have just been considering, it would be worthwhile for the non-sceptical to step back to ask more basic questions. What is it that we are trying to define? Is it the concept of art, the property of being art, or a classificatory (or possibly evaluative) social practice, or something else? Suppose we say we are trying to define a concept. There is an interesting general literature on this question (Peacocke 1992; Fodor 1998) which it might be useful to bring to the issue of defining art. What should we hope to achieve with such a definition? The traditional goal was to identify the essence of art. If we follow recent definitions in abandoning that goal, what are we doing instead—describing or idealizing, for instance? Should we even continue to assume that we are looking for a single correct definition, or should we now accept the possibility that there can be several equally useful definitions of art, several equally good solutions to the same problem—or perhaps several problems calling for different solutions?

See also: Value in Art; Ontology of Art; Aesthetics of Popular Art; Aesthetic Experience.

BIBLIOGRAPHY

Anderson, J. (2000). 'Aesthetic Concepts of Art', in N. Carroll (ed.), *Theories of Art Today*. Madison: University of Wisconsin Press, pp. 65–92.

Beardsley, M. (1969). 'Aesthetic Experience Regained'. *Journal of Aesthetics and Art Criticism* 28: 2–11.

——(1983). 'An Aesthetic Definition of Art', in H. Curtler (ed.), *What is Art?* New York: Haven Publications, 15–29.

Bell, C. (1914). *Art*. London: Chatto & Windus. Reprint New York: Capricorn Books, 1958.

Budd, M. (1995). *Values of Art: Pictures, Poetry, and Music*. London: The Penguin Press.

Carney, J. (1991). 'The Style Theory of Art'. *Pacific Philosophical Quarterly* 72: 273–89.

——(1994). 'Defining Art Externally'. *British Journal of Aesthetics* 34: 114–23.

Carroll, N. (1993). 'Essence, Expression, and History: Arthur Danto's Philosophy of Art', in M. Rollins (ed.), *Danto and his Critics*. Oxford: Basil Blackwell, pp. 79–106.

——(1994). 'Identifying Art', in R. Yanal (ed.), *Institutions of Art*. University Park, Pa.: Pennsylvania State University Press, pp. 3–38.

——(ed.) (2000). *Theories of Art Today*. Madison: University of Wisconsin Press.

Collingwood. R. G. (1938). *Principles of Art*. Oxford: Oxford University Press.

Currie, G. (1993). 'Aliens Too'. *Analysis* 53: 116–18.

——(2000). 'A Note on Art and Historical Concepts'. *British Journal of Aesthetics* 40: 186–90.

Danto, A. (1964). 'The Artworld'. *Journal of Philosophy* 61: 571–84.

——(1973). 'Artworks and Real Things'. *Theoria* 39: 1–17.

——(1981). *The Transfiguration of the Commonplace*. Cambridge, Mass.: Harvard University Press.

Davies, S. (1991). *Definitions of Art*. Ithaca, NY: Cornell University Press.

——(1997). 'First Art and Art's Definition'. *Southern Journal of Philosophy* 35: 19–34.

——(2000). 'Non-Western Art and Art's Definition', in N. Carroll (ed.), *Theories of Art Today*. Madison: University of Wisconsin Press, pp. 199–216.

Dickie, G. (1974). *Art and the Aesthetic: an Institutional Analysis*. Ithaca, NY: Cornell University Press.

——(1984). *The Art Circle*. New York: Haven Publications.

——(1989). 'Reply to Stecker', in G. Dickie, R. Sclafani, and R. Roblin (eds.), *Aesthetics: a Critical Anthology*, 2nd edn. New York: St Martin's Press.

Fodor, J. (1998). *Concepts: Where Cognitive Science Went Wrong*. Oxford: Oxford University Press.

Fry, R. (1920). *Vision and Design*. London: Chatto & Windus. Reprint New York: Dover, 1998.

Gaut, B. (2000). ' "Art" as a Cluster Concept', in N. Carroll (ed.), *Theories of Art Today*. Madison: University of Wisconsin Press, 25–44.

Gould, C. (1994). 'Clive Bell on Aesthetic Experience and Aesthetic Truth'. *British Journal of Aesthetics* 34: 124–33.

Graves, L. (1998). 'Transgressive Traditions and Art Definitions'. *Journal of Aesthetics and Art Criticism* 56: 39–48.

Kant, I. (1952). *The Critique of Judgement*, transl. J. C. Meredith. Oxford: Oxford University Press.

Levinson, J. (1979). 'Defining Art Historically'. *British Journal of Aesthetics* 19: 232–50.

—— (1987). Review of *The Art Circle*. *Philosophical Review* 96: 141–6.

—— (1989). 'Refining Art Historically'. *Journal of Aesthetics and Art Criticism* 47: 21–33.

—— (1990). 'A Refiner's Fire'. *Journal of Aesthetics and Art Criticism* 48: 231–5.

—— (1993). 'Extending Art Historically'. *Journal of Aesthetics and Art Criticism* 51: 411–24.

Lind, R. (1992). 'The Aesthetic Essence of Art'. *Journal of Aesthetics and Art Criticism* 50: 117–29.

Mandelbaum, M. (1965). 'Family Resemblances and Generalization Concerning the Arts'. *American Philosophical Quarterly* 2: 219–28.

Matravers, D. (2000). 'The Institutional Theory: a Protean Creature'. *British Journal of Aesthetics* 40: 242–50.

Novitz, D. (1996). 'Disputes about Art'. *Journal of Aesthetics and Art Criticism* 54: 153–63.

Peacocke, C. (1992). *A Study of Concepts*. Cambridge, Mass.: MIT Press.

Sartwell, C. (1990). 'A Counter-Example to Levinson's Historical Theory of Art'. *Journal of Aesthetics and Art Criticism* 48: 157–8.

Schlesinger, G. (1979). 'Aesthetic Experience and the Definition of Art'. *British Journal of Aesthetics* 19: 167–76.

Stecker, R. (1986). 'The End of an Institutional Definition of Art'. *British Journal of Aesthetics* 26: 124–32.

—— (1996). 'Alien Objections to Historical Definitions of Art'. *British Journal of Aesthetics* 36: 305–8.

—— (1997). *Artworks: Definition, Meaning, Value*. University Park, Pa.: Pennsylvania State University Press.

—— (2000). 'Is it Reasonable to Attempt to Define Art?' in N. Carroll (ed.), *Theories of Art Today*. Madison: University of Wisconsin Press, 45–64.

Tilghman, B. (1984). *But Is It Art?* Oxford: Blackwell.

Walton, K. (1977). Review of *Art and the Aesthetic: An Institutional Analysis*. *Philosophical Review* 86: 97–101.

Weitz, M. (1956). 'The Role of Theory in Aesthetics'. *Journal of Aesthetics and Art Criticism* 15: 27–35.

Zangwill, N. (2000). 'Aesthetic Functionalism', in E. Brady and J. Levinson (eds.), *Aesthetic Concepts: Essays after Sibley*. Oxford: Oxford University Press.

—— (2002). 'Are There Counterexamples to Aesthetic Theories of Art?'. *Journal of Aesthetics and Art Criticism* 60: 111–18.

Ziff, P. (1953). 'The Task of Defining a Work of Art'. *Philosophical Review* 62: 466–80.

CHAPTER 8

ONTOLOGY OF ART

STEPHEN DAVIES

1. INTRODUCTION

ONTOLOGY is the study of the kinds of things there are in the world. The ontology of art considers the matter, form, and mode in which art exists. Works of art are social constructs in the sense that they are not natural kinds but human creations. The way we categorize them depends on our interests, and to that extent ontology is not easily separated from sociology and ideology. Nevertheless, some classifications and interests are likely to be more revealing of why and how art is created and appreciated. It is these that our ontology should reflect.

There are a number of traditional classifications of the arts, for instance in terms of their media (stone, words, sounds, paint, etc.), their species (sculpture, literature, music, drama, ballet, etc.), or their styles or contents (tragedy, comedy, surrealism, impressionism, etc.). The ontology of works of art does not map neatly on to these classifications, however. In the plastic arts, a wide variety of media and structures are used. In music and drama, not all works are for performance; for instance, tape compositions and theatrical films are not. Not all works of a kind are organized at the same levels, and higher levels cannot generally be analysed in terms of lower ones. Not all literary works are reducible to word sequences, and not all share a given set of narrative elements or persona (Howell 2002*a*). Similarly, not all musical works are reducible to note sequences and not all contain tonally structured melodies (Davies 2001).

In the following, I distinguish singular from multiple works of art and, within the latter, performance art from other varieties. These ontological divisions, I maintain, are fundamental to the ways we conceive and describe art.

It might be thought I have already begged an important question by confining my attention to *works* of art, since art might exist in the absence of works. It might be said that the product of free musical improvisation is singular and therefore not a musical work, since musical works are always potentially repeatable and thereby multiple. An opponent of this suggestion could argue that improvisations are potentially repeatable (Carroll 1998), or he might contend that they are works, even if they are singular (Alperson 1984; Kivy 1993). Let us, for the sake of simplicity, concede the point: the products of art can be ontologically singular, whether or not they are also works. Nevertheless, in what follows I concentrate on the ontology of works of art, because most artforms generate products that can properly be seen as works, so long as we do not adopt an ideologically loaded notion of 'work of art'.

2. Singular and Multiple Works of Art

Oil paintings, such as Leonardo's *Mona Lisa*, and hewn statues, such as Michelangelo's *David*, are singular works of art. These particular pieces result from the artist's working directly on the materials of which they are comprised, but this is not necessary. Polaroids, which produce a picture directly, rather than a photographic negative, result in singular pieces. The same is true of those woodblocks and lino-cuts for which the method of production involves the alteration of the original template at each new stage of the printing process.

Typical examples of multiple works of art include cast bronzes, such as del Verrochio's *Equestrian Monument of Colleoni*, photographs produced from negatives, such as Adams's 'Moon and Half Dome', novels such as Austen's *Persuasion*, operas, such as Verdi's *Aïda*, poems, such as Shelley's *Ozymandias*, ballets, such as Delibes's *Coppelia*, plays, such as Shakespeare's *Hamlet*, woodblock prints, such as Dürer's 'Apocalypse' series, musical works, such as Beethoven's Fifth Symphony, and films, such as Welles's *Citizen Kane*. As this list indicates, multiple works of art are of many sorts. They can usefully be subdivided into those that are for performance and those that are not: operas fall into the former camp and novels into the latter. Alternatively, they can be separated by whether they are conveyed and specified via instances that have the status of exemplars or by sets of instructions that prescribe how to make an instance; poems typically fall into the former category and plays into the latter.

2.1 Singular Works of Art

Though it is widely accepted, the distinction I have just drawn has been challenged by Currie (1988) and Zemach (1992), who argue that, in principle, all works of art are multiple. Imagine a machine such that, if we placed the *Mona Lisa* in it and pushed the button, we would retrieve two objects that are the same down to the molecular level. If there were no way of identifying one as the original and the other as the copy, should we not accept that all singular works are multiple in principle?

One answer would insist that the identity of a work of art depends not just on its appearance but also on its causal provenance. Currie accepts the point, but argues that what is needed for aesthetic identification and appreciation is not information regarding the origin of the copy, but knowledge of the original's causal origin coupled with a guarantee that the copy is qualitatively identical at the physical level. If we know that the *Mona Lisa* was painted on canvas in about 1504, we do not need to know if the 'painting' before us is the original or a perfect replica before we can appreciate it; and, in appreciating it, it is Leonardo's work, not something else, we comprehend.

Levinson (1996) objects that this underplays the way contact with the original brushstrokes puts one in closer touch with the artist's creativity, which is something we value. Another critic, Carroll (1998), observes that, over time, the original and the replica would come to differ, and therefore, could not be identical. That point is not decisive, however, because it applies equally to a work, such as a print, with multiple instances; that the individual prints age in their own ways does not mean that they are not instances of the same work. And Carroll's objection is not strengthened by noting that the artist might intend that the identity of the work evolves through time. Such an intention can be realized in the ageing of works with multiple instances.

There is every reason, however, to maintain the distinction between multiple and singular works, because it reflects real differences in the way we identify and evaluate works of art. If a supercopier were invented tomorrow, it would likely affect the way we would approach tomorrow's art, but it is not apparent that we would revise retrospectively the ontological descriptions we offer of works created prior to its invention. We may accept that a supercopy of the *Mona Lisa* is an invaluable substitute for people who do not live near the Louvre, without also conceding that the supercopy is an *instance* of the work that Leonardo created. One might learn a great deal about the appearance of a work from something that looks like it, but similarity in appearance does not entail that the two are instances of the same thing (Shields 1995).

2.2 Differences between Singular and Multiple Works of Art

The distinction between singular and multiple works of art is not simple or straightforward. For a few kinds of art, it is not obvious if their products are mainly multiple or singular. Take buildings. The architect produces plans from which builders work. On the face of it, these plans can be executed more than once. Many houses in a subdivision might be based on a single design. So, we might think of architects' plans as being like musical scores and of architectural works as multiple. The issue is not so clear, however, when we focus on buildings that deserve the status of art, like the Taj Mahal. Many of these are singular, and this does not seem to be solely because the plans have not yet been followed for a second or third time. Instead, it reflects the practice of designing art buildings for specific sites or milieux. If buildings are site-specific, they must be singular, unless sites themselves can be designed and constructed. Now, some kinds of site are multiple and can be duplicated, but others are not, especially when they include distinctive natural or social environments, or are rich in historical significance and associations. For these, architects' plans are more like sketches and notations made by a sculptor for his assistants than like a musical score. A reasonable, though messy, conclusion might accept that, among art buildings, some are singular and others are multiple, with no stark division marking the boundary between the two (Davies 1994).

Also, the distinction between multiple and singular works need not be apparent in a work's number, despite the terminology of 'singular' and 'multiple'. A multiple piece might have only one instance, in fact. (Moreover, the creation of others might now be impossible, as when the moulds for a bronze happen to be destroyed after only one statue has been cast.) And while a singular work, to exist, can have one and only one instance, it could have many copies, including ones that are perceptually indistinguishable from it. The image of the *Mona Lisa* is the most reproduced icon in art's history, and the statue that stands in Piazza della Signoria is a copy of Michelangelo's *David*, which is housed in the Accademia.

As just hinted, one key difference between singular and multiple works lies in the distinction between something's being a copy of a distinct work and its being an instance of the same work. That difference is not a matter of accuracy of reproduction. Prints from a single woodblock might be differently coloured, yet all count as instances of the same work, while no other physical painting could be the actual *Mona Lisa*, even if it were an accurate duplicate. If I copy out Austen's *Persuasion*, I produce another instance of her novel, even if my calligraphy is unlike hers, but I cannot make another instance of a painting by Rembrandt, no matter how faithfully I duplicate the material and appearance of the original.

On what does the difference between a thing's being a copy and its being an instance depend? One possibility notes that there is likely to be a difference in the intentions of the artists of singular and multiple pieces, and in those of their copiers. The person who copies a singular work aims typically to acquire the relevant skills by emulating their achievement, or intends to create a forgery that might be passed off as the original, but in neither case sees herself as creating a further instance of the same work as that incarnated in the original. By contrast, a person who produces an instance of a multiple work by following the methods or instructions prescribed by its artist does not expect to generate a new and different work. The artist who creates a potentially multiple work intends it to have various instances and, where the work is for performance, expects these to differ in the interpretations they offer. Only where there is a limit to the number of legitimate instances a multiple work can possess, as when the run of a lithograph is specified and individual instances are marked as the nth in a series of, say, thirty prints, is there doubt about whether following the artist's instructions or duplicating her method results in a new instance. Differences in intentions, even if they are important, are not sufficient to establish the distinction between singular and multiple works. No dramatist, simply by willing it, could make his play a singular work if it were scripted in the orthodox way, though he might be effective in preventing performances beyond the first. It is crucial to appreciate the social arrangements and conventions on which intentions of the kind discussed above depend, not only for their efficacy, but also for their intelligibility. It is only within the context of an art practice and tradition that artists can formulate the sorts of intentions that establish, for example, whether a given product is a singular piece or, instead, is an exemplar that provides the model for further work instances.

By way of illustration, compare freely improvised music and poetry. Earlier I allowed that a freely improvised musical performance might be singular, but I am less inclined to think the same of an improvised poem. What makes the difference has more to do with the artistic practices and norms that poetry presupposes than with the maker's intentions. Musical extemporization, which takes its point from the challenges posed by creating music in real time, has a long pedigree. Rhyming for the sake of rhyming, within fixed time limits, could have been similar, but has not developed that way in our literary culture. Moreover, even long poems are easier to remember and record after the event than are extended jazz improvisations. For these reasons, an improvised poem might best be seen as an exemplar of a multiple work, even if it does not receive subsequent instances.

2.3 Three Kinds of Multiplicity in Works of Art

Works of art allowing for multiple instances are created and communicated in three, rather different, ways. In the first, an instance with the status of an exemplar is produced. For example, a novelist produces a manuscript that is both an instance of her novel and a model with the normative function of setting the standard that other instances of her novel must emulate. Not every feature of the model is exemplary. A facsimile copy reproduces the appearance of the manuscript, but a faithful copy of the novel might have font, point size, and even spellings that differ from the original. What is crucial to the novel's identity? At first blush, one might say that it is the specified word sequence. Howell (2002a; see also Ingarden 1973) argues that ballads, folk tales, and the like cannot always be equated with word sequences, plots, or character lists, and the same is likely to be true of some avant-garde or inter-active novels. Just what is crucial to a story's or novel's identity is likely to be settled by reference to its genre and the literary practices, conventions, and histories on which it draws.

In oral musical traditions, works are also created and transmitted through per-formances with the status of exemplars. Again, not all the features of the model are work-constitutive. The person who would be guided by the model faces the task of sorting work features from features distinctive solely of the given interpretation. This must be done in light of a conception of the nature of the work in question, and that conception is guided not only by the verbal instructions issued by the composer, where available, but also by the conventions and practices already estab-lished for works in the relevant genre. When works are complex or are preserved over many years within an oral tradition, it can be anticipated that a spread of vari-ants will be tolerated as authentic. This is often the case, but it is also true that these musical practices are capable of preserving pieces that are precise and rigid, as is evident in the church chant traditions. I observed earlier that singular works must have one and only one instance. Multiple works specified through an exemplar must also have at least one instance, though they may have many more.

The second way of creating and propagating a multiple work of art is through creating and issuing what I call an 'encoding'. A typical example of an encoding is a photographic negative, or a suitably marked silkscreen, or a cast for a bronze statue, or, for a purely electronic musical work, a magnetic tape or digital computer file. Instances of the work are generated through a decoding, which involves submitting the encoding to an appropriate device or process. In some cases, as when bronzes are cast or prints are taken from copper engravings, skilled labour may be involved, but the decoding process is often mechanical. The decoding of a purely electronic musical piece is automatic, provided one has the relevant equipment in good working order and an undamaged encoding. What counts as 'relevant equipment', 'good working order', and 'undamaged encoding' depends on norms set within the indus-try or artform practice (Fisher 1998). For instance, the sound systems used to play back the tape of an electronic musical piece are likely to vary, with the result that the decodings will not all sound exactly the same. These various soundings count as faithful instances of the piece, however, if the differences in sound systems fall within limits set formally by relevant organizations or informally through accept-ance within listening practice.

Motion pictures provide an instructive example. One might think that the mas-ter print of a film is to be described as an exemplar that instances the work it is of, as well as providing the standard for faithful copies, which should resemble it in its appearance, frame by frame. Yet, if an instance of the film is, instead, what one sees when the film is screened in the appropriate fashion—to wit, a series of two-dimensional moving images—the master print would better be described as an encoding, not as an exemplar. One cannot see the film by looking directly at the master print or its clones. We tend to talk of audiotapes, CDs, negatives, and photographic films as if they are the works they encode, but this mode of speaking involves a misleading ellipsis. In fact, the works in question are instanced not by those artefacts but by the result obtained by decoding them with an appropriate output device (Fisher 1998).

Many modern artforms rely on 'mass technologies' for the duplication of instances specified via exemplars, or for encoding, cloning, and decoding works. Carroll (1998) calls works of art that can be delivered simultaneously to many people and different sites of reception 'mass art'. Many artforms are of this mass kind—motion pictures, television drama, novels. Carroll believes that works of mass art have a distinctive ontology. They are multiple-instance or type works of art whose token reception-instances are generated by templates, or by relays of templates that are themselves tokens. If 'templates' are equivalent to exemplars or encodings, the first part of Carroll's account is like my own. I disagree, however, with the qualification he introduces at the close. The template of a novel, as an exemplar, is a token instance of the work the novelist creates. The same is not true, though, of works specified via encodings. The celluloid print that is the template for a motion picture is not itself a token of the work. The work is instanced only when the template is decoded, by being screened with appropriate devices. Similarly, the template for a digital musical work is a string of os and 1s, for a printed photograph is a negative, and for a bronze statue is a cast—and none of these is a token of the work it specifies.

Another to consider the impact of technology on art is Benjamin (1968). He describes works of art as cultic objects surrounded with an aura of mystery, part of which derives from their rarity and inaccessibility to ordinary art patrons. Mechanical reproductions demystify art, he suggests, by making proxies available to all. It seems to me that Benjamin's remarks, if true, apply mainly to singular works. Admittedly, the appeal of multiple works can pall when our environment is over-saturated with their instantiations (Brown 2000); but in general, the status or power of multiple works is not undermined by the wider availability of their instances made possible by technology. Recordings and videos of works such as Beethoven's or Shakespeare's have not cheapened them. Moreover, new kinds of multiple works of art, such as movies and TV shows, have been developed in conjunction with, and to take advantage of, the technologies of mass dissemination. Finally, multiple works conveyed by encodings need have no instances at all. If the encoding has never been decoded, the work has no instances.

The third way of creating and propagating a multiple work of art is through writing and issuing a set of instructions for the production of its instances addressed to their performers or executants. Musical works specified by scores and plays indicated by scripts are in this category. Pieces specified via notated instructions are often much 'thinner' in properties than are the performances that instance them faithfully (Davies 1991). In other words, many of the features of any instance belong to it and the interpretation it embodies, without being work-identifying. As a result, performances of pieces specified by such notations can differ considerably while remaining equally and ideally faithful to the works they are of.

As regards notation, it is important to distinguish indefiniteness from incompleteness. A notation's instructions may be indefinite about many details that will have to be determinate in the work's instances, but this does not mean the notation is incomplete, so long as the work itself is indefinite in the ways indicated (Davies 2001). For example, many details of props, sets, and costumes are not specified in play scripts, but that does not mean those scripts, or the works they encode, are incomplete. Instead, such matters are not work-determinative, but belong to the interpretative freedom enjoyed by the performer. Similarly, an eighteenth-century musical score with a figured bass outlines a chord structure but leaves the player to determine the details of its realization. Such scores are not incomplete: rather, the works they specify are indeterminate in the relevant respect, with the result that many different realizations of the bass and middle parts are consistent with the work's faithful presentation. There are likely to be stylistic constraints on what is apt, but, within those, the performer is free to exercise her judgement and taste.

Multiple works indicated via instructions need have no instances at all. If the work indicated by the musical score or play script has never been performed, it has no instances.

Reading a work-determinative notation is not always straightforward or mechanical. Work-determinative notations may not be transparent as to the works they specify. Often, they do not include some work-constitutive elements because it can be assumed that readers familiar with the appropriate performance practices will know to realize them. Also, they may record non-compulsory wishes or interpretative preferences alongside work-determinative instructions. Again, the distinction between these will be apparent only to the person who knows what is licensed by the relevant performance practices. Accordingly, work notations need to be read in terms of the appropriate notational and performance conventions. Because these can alter over time, as is shown clearly by the case of musical notations, the conventions in terms of which the notation is to be read are those shared by the artist with those he was addressing—in other words, of the period of the work's specification.

Goodman (1968) attempts to outline the condition that must be satisfied by a notation before it can specify works unambiguously. In particular, he rules out the use of vague indicators that might share compliants. For Goodman, if *forte* and *mezzo-forte*, or *presto* and *prestissimo*, determine overlapping classes of compliants, those notational characters cannot play a work-defining role within a notation. Similarly, if individual notes are work-constitutive, *tr* (meaning 'trill') cannot be notational because the number of notes needed to comply with the instruction is ambiguous. Goodman tries to pack all the specificity of the work into the notation required to indicate it, with the result that the notational system he describes does not correspond to that actually used. He ignores the context provided by the musical genre and practice to which the work in question belonged, and thereby fails to appreciate how these could play a crucial role in disambiguating notations that, on his view, could not be work-identifying. In general, Goodman is mistaken in trying to characterize notations as closed systems specifiable without reference to the social context of their use, because no notation can specify within itself all the conventions or rules in terms of which it is to be interpreted.

2.4 Faithfulness in Renditions of Multiple Works

To be ideally faithful to it, the instances of a multiple work must exemplify it by realizing all of its work-constitutive features. In the first instance, a complete and unambiguous encoding, exemplar, or set of instructions must be authorized in some public fashion. An encoding is acknowledged as a master from which sub-sequent copies are to be cloned, the work is published or commercially issued, the artist signs and dates the manuscript, or whatever.

Complete and unambiguous work specifications or exemplars are not always available, however. Perhaps the artist did not finish the work (for instance Schubert's Eighth Symphony in B minor), or the text or instructions have become hopelessly corrupted (as with Marlowe's *Massacre at Paris*). The interesting cases are those in which it is the artist himself who undermines the definitive specification of his work. Different, incompatible encodings, exemplars, or sets of instructions are offered for a given piece by the work's author, with none established as authoritative.

The appearance of ambiguity can sometimes be misleading. This can easily occur where the artist interprets and performs, as well as creates, the work. For instance, performer composers often annotated their own works with embellishments or additions not found in the printed edition. Where these indicate their interpretative preferences or choices, rather than work-determinative instructions, they do not imply ambiguity in the work's identity. In other cases, though, the ambiguity is deliberate and unquestionable. For instance, Bruckner constantly revised and altered his symphonies after their publication. Some analysts interpret related cases as showing that the 'work concept' was not established in the minds of such authors (Kallberg 1996). An alternative explanation simply regards such artists as psychologically incapable of leaving their finished works alone.

Anyway, ambiguity and incompleteness need not be totally subversive of work identity. We can play what we have of the unfinished final fugue of Bach's Art of the Fugue, and we can indicate which version (that of 1889, say) of Bruckner's Eighth Symphony we are playing. Some works exist in several versions, such as Shakespeare's *Othello*, but these versions have enough in common to preserve a robust sense of the piece's identity.

Supposing one has a more or less complete and sufficiently unambiguous, appropriately authorized, exemplar, encoding, or set of work-determinative instructions, what more is required for the generation of an ideally faithful instance of the work? The simplest case is that of encodings that can be decoded mechanically. Provided the required machinery meets the appropriate standards, is in good working order, and is operated correctly, the instance that results should be ideally faithful. The same applies to works presented via exemplars, such as novels, which have work-definitive properties that can be mechanically produced. The situation is subtler where the work presented via an exemplar is for performance. Potential performers must have sufficient acquaintance with the style, genre, and tradition to know what in the exemplar is work-constitutive and what not. There can often be uncertainty about such matters, but there is no reason to think that oral traditions must always be unreliable. Indeed, the gamelan traditions of Indonesia provide compelling evidence to the contrary, for, within them, complex works are sustained over many decades or longer while being varied and interpreted. In some ways, the situation of a work communicated through written instructions is clearer, since those instructions concern the work and what they do not cover is left up to the performer. But the correct interpretation of the written instructions does require a familiarity both with the convention of the notation and with the performance practice that is assumed as its background. Even when they are correctly interpreted, the execution of instructions for making an instance of a given work might require considerable artistic talent. A mastery of the specified instruments and playing styles is required of the musician, and the actor must be able to act. Where the required skills or instruments are lost, the work can no longer be instanced accurately. One cannot perform a fully faithful version of an opera calling for a castrato when none is available.

I have been writing of what is required in producing an instance that is faithful in that it displays all features constitutive of the work it is of. How should we describe the case in which some but not all of those features are reproduced? Most people would accept that, so long as the work remains recognizable in the rendition, one gets an imperfect instance of it. In other words, a work can be instanced more or less accurately. One has seen the movie *Casablanca*, say, even if the print is somewhat scratched and a few of the words are obliterated by static. In that case, the notions of 'instance', 'rendition', and 'performance' are normative.

Goodman (1968) does not share this view. For a musical work in which each note is work-identifying, he thinks that any wrong note disqualifies a performance from instancing the work. A less stringent standard would entail the identity of disparate pieces, since one could get from one to the other by a series of innocuous note changes. Once again, Goodman is forced to an extreme position as a result of ignoring the social conditions in terms of which musical scores are followed, not merely matched. One reason for regarding an imperfect performance as of a musical work is that it (*a*) is intended to be of the given piece and (*b*) preserves intact a causal chain linking it via scores or exemplars to the composer's creation of the given piece. Moreover, Goodman fails to notice that higher musical structures, such as melodies, are not always reducible to the note sequences that constitute them. If the identity of a melody is not destroyed by some wrong notes, that melody still can contribute to making the instance in which it occurs one that is of the work.

If a performer systematically disregards an artist's exemplars or instructions, what she produces will not be an instance of that artist's piece. But suppose that, for the sake of creating an original and interesting interpretation, the performer departs intentionally from reproducing crucial features of the model, or from following some of the work-determinative instructions. In other words, suppose she trades authenticity off against some other performance value, but not to an extent that undermines her claim to be instancing the work in hand. Is this proper? Proponents of the 'authentic performance movement' prominent in the performance of pre-twentieth century music would argue that it is not.

The answer depends on what one takes the point of work instancing to be. I have so far assumed that we are interested in performances not only for their unique features but also for the access they provide to, and the way they reflect on, the works they are of. Where this is the overriding goal, the pursuit of faithfulness could not be merely one among a range of valued but competing interpretative options. It must be a primary value, if not the only value, in instancing works. Where works are such that it is the care their creators put into their details that distinguishes the good from the poor ones, the decision to perform them inevitably carries with it a commitment to be faithful where one can be. Any other approach calls into question a concern with works as the creations of their artists. This is not to deny that, in the performing arts, we can be just as interested in what the performer contributes and in her interpretative insight. The point is that in works for performance, the performer's great freedom is consistent with her commitment to faithfulness, because such pieces underdetermine much that belongs to their accurate renditions.

There is another side to the coin, though. For genres in which works are less complex and challenging, our interest in a rendition might pay little regard to the piece's authorship. We might be more concerned with the performance than with the work it is of. This is the case, I think, with pop songs, if they are construed as melodies with accompanying chords. Moreover, instances may be generated under many constraints and serve many purposes. In acquainting school groups with classic plays, it might be more appropriate to make drastic cuts and to use fewer actors than the fullest authenticity would tolerate. And when it comes to amateur productions undertaken for fun, it would be silly to complain that the battle scenes are under-populated and the swordsmanship unconvincing.

2.5 Works for Performance versus Ones that Are Not

A different way of cataloguing works with multiple instances divides them into those that are for performance and those that are not. (On the nature of performance, see

Thom 1993 and Godlovitch 1998.) This distinction maps neatly on to that between multiple works conveyed via instructions, like play scripts or musical scores addressed to performers, and multiple works specified by encodings, like photographic negatives or magnetic tape. The former are always for performance, whereas the latter never are. The distinction does cut across the other category of multiple works, however. Some multiple works specified by exemplars are for performance, such as most ballets, and others, such as novels, are not.

The notion of works for performance is familiar. Most music and drama is of this kind. I say 'most' because, even in earlier times, this was not true of all cases. Musical pieces created for mechanical organs and music boxes are not for performance.

A work for performance might incorporate films, musical tapes, and the like, which are replayed as a performer executes instructions issued by the artist for instancing her piece. The performer's part might be insignificant within the whole. However small that part is, its existence makes the work one for performance. Such a piece is for mixed media and performer and comes with prescriptions addressed to the work's potential performers, as well as with film and tape that is to be played back in the manner specified.

The status of some artforms may be unclear. If poetry is to be declaimed, then it is a performance art, but if it is for silent reading it is not. That would be no problem if, within the genus, different kinds of poetry came marked as of one kind or the other: sagas for performance and metaphysical poems for reading, say. The problem, if that is what it is, arises because most poems could be treated in either fashion. (If a poem is set to music, though, it does become part of a hybrid that is for performance. One such piece is Walton's *Façade*, which sets poems by Edith Sitwell.)

Some multiple works are not for performance. When a print is run off a woodblock or a statue is cast in bronze, we would not normally say that the print or statue is performed. The point is not that these processes are mechanical, whereas acting requires artistic talent; it might, in fact, require a great deal of skill to print a photograph from a negative, set up and use a silk screen, or work with molten alloys. What is the difference, then, between merely creating another instance of a work and performing a work?

Photographic prints, cast statues, and screen prints exist in time. They are created at a particular time and destroyed at another. Yet temporality is not part of their identity *qua* work-instances, because the works they are of do not require in their instances a more or less given duration. It is only works that do require this that can be performed. (The duration of a work for performance sometimes is variable, but only within limits.) Performances are events that take place in continuous chunks of real time, where the duration (and separation) of those chunks is a function of the identity of the piece the performance is of (see Levinson and Alperson 1991). This helps explain why one's reading a novel is not a performance of the work. The novel is temporal to the extent that narrative order is essential to its identity, but the reader is free to backtrack or skip on as she chooses. Moreover, there is no rule central to the book's identity that governs the pace at which it is to be read, the number of reading episodes needed, or the length of the gaps between them.

The point just made does not explain why we do not regard the screening of a movie, or the playing of a CD of a purely electronic musical piece, as a performance of the work. The screening or replaying lasts as long as, and corresponds temporally with, the instancing of the work, and tinkering and adjustments might be made to the output devices throughout, but movies are for screening and CDs are for playback, not for performance. We might sometimes call such events 'performances', but it would be odd to regard them as performances of the works they instance (Carroll 1998). While a performance of a work inevitably presents that work via an interpretation, the playback of a film or music track does not involve its interpretation. In some respects, making a movie is like performing a play: acting is involved in both. For the movie, though, acting contributes to its creation, but not, as in the case of play, to the delivery of an already completed piece. The shooting script of a movie provides instructions for the creation of the work, not for its post-completion performance. The same applies to purely electronic musical works issued on tape or disk. They are for playback, not performance, even if musicians sing and play in the usual fashion while contributing the raw material from which the work is fashioned. Neither drama nor music is exclusively a performance art.

A live performance of a play or musical piece might be recorded and subsequently released on video or disc. The result would be a copy or representation of the performance. Performances, like singular works, can be copied, and they remain singular events when this is done. The difference between the video of a play performance and a movie, or between a CD of a live musical performance and a purely electronic piece that is not for performance, is not in the product but lies in the relation between what is encoded and the work in question. The master print of a movie encodes the work, not a performance of it.

Gracyk (1996) has argued that rock music, construed broadly, is ontologically analogous to motion pictures. The work is the totality of what is encoded on discs accurately cloned from the master. As such, it is for playback, not performance. This explains why lip-synching is acceptable in rock as it is not in classical music intended for live performance. When rock performers do play live, their efforts are measured against what is on their recording, whereas in classical music we test what is on the recording against an ideal of live performance. Musical playings of familiar kinds go into making rock recordings, but they contribute to the work's composition. And electronic interventions that are antithetical to live performance—multi-tracking and complex collaging—become central.

I am not convinced that rock music has removed itself so far from the performance tradition. It could be that rock songs are conceived for studio performance, not live performance. They are of a kind in which the 'performance' concerns the electronic sculpting of sound and aims at effects relying on the paraphernalia of the studio. A given piece can be performed again (or 'covered'), but to be faithful to the original it must also set out to create an electronic soundscape unlike that of the live environment (Davies 2001).

How can we choose between the idea that rock works are not for performance and the suggestion that they are for a distinctive kind of performance that finds its home in the recording studio? The relevant indicator is the way in which we identify and count 'rock works'. If Gracyk's view is correct, covers must be new, but related, works, distinct from the original. According to the alternative view, they are new performances of the work first performed on the original disc. To be performances of the same song, they need not emulate the original in all its detail, though this is a common approach to 'best hits' covers. Rather, they simply need to follow the melody, words, and harmony, if only as points of departure, and subject these to electronic filling-out.

2.6 The Relation between Multiple Works and their Instances

What is the relation between a multiple work and its instances? This has been described by philosophers as that of a class to its members (Goodman 1968), a type to its tokens (Wollheim 1980; Margolis 1980; Zemach 1992; Dipert 1993), a kind to its instances (Wolterstorff 1980), and a pattern to its realization (Walton 1988; Bender 1993).

The first suggestion is counterintuitive. On this view, all unperformed works are the same, since they share the null set as the class of their members. Also, it follows that Shakespeare's *Hamlet* is now much bigger than it was in 1620, because it has had more performances since then; or, if one considers the class of performances over all time, it follows that *Hamlet*, the play, has exactly (say) 1,234,567 constituents.

It has been argued that, because classes are generally unlike their members, they provide an inappropriate model for the relation between a work of art and its instances. The type/token relation—if you answer 'two' when asked how many letters there are in the word 'noon', you are counting letter types, not letter tokens—is regarded as more apt in this respect. When we think of 'the US dollar' we are liable to picture something that looks like an actual US dollar bill. An alternative to regarding works as types argues that, instead of sharing actual properties, it is predicates that are shared between a work and its instances. Just as it is true that the grizzly bear growls and is brown only if something cannot be a properly formed instance of a grizzly without being brown and growling, so Beethoven's Fifth Symphony is noisy and triumphant at its close only because accurate performances of the work must display these features. On this last view, multiple works of art are kinds.

Wolterstorff (1980), who defended the idea that works of art are kinds, observed that, like natural kinds, they are normative rather than merely descriptive. They permit of more or less well-formed instances. As noted above, a performance might still be of a given play though some of its lines are misspoken or forgotten. Goodman rejects the suggestion that instances could be less than ideally faithful to the works they are of, but this is not strictly required by his view. Classes, types, or patterns, no less than kinds, could be normative.

2.7 Multiple Works as Fictions

What manner of things are multiple works? Whether they are classes, types, or kinds, multiple works of art are abstract entities. We cannot examine them directly. We learn about them via our acquaintance with their concrete instances or, where they have them, with the instructions issued to their potential executants. According to one view, our talk of works is fictional, for there is nothing over and above their instances.

The position maintaining that, not only do we learn about multiple works from their instances or specifications, but also our referring to such works picks out nothing beyond their instances or specifications, is most forcefully presented by Rudner (1950). He holds that, if 'Beethoven's Fifth Symphony' is a referring expression, its referents are past, present, or future performances, or copies of the score. And if it makes sense to say the work is witty or sad, this is because these predicates apply to parts of its performances. To characterize the work of art as abstract, Rudner thinks, is to deny that it can be experienced, which runs contrary to aesthetic theory and intuition.

Rudner's ontology is called into question whenever a particular instance fails to display properties we wish to attribute to the work it is of. Unless all performances of Beethoven's Fifth Symphony end triumphantly, Rudner's position entails that the work is not triumphant. But it is not difficult to amend the theory to avoid this objection. It could be maintained that 'the work is so-and-so' is equivalent to holding that most of its instances are so-and-so, or that all its well-formed instances are so-and-so.

Still, it does seem obvious that works of art have properties other than those of all, or even most, of their correct instances. For example, the piece can be created in France, performed simultaneously in Germany and Greece, and be the last of its artist's juvenilia, with none of these things being true of all or most of its well-formed performances. Moreover, a conception of the work has a role in determining what is to count as a well-formed instance, especially where the work is presented and transmitted via an exemplar. Without a notion of the work as distinct from its exemplar, we could not judge if renditions based on, but differing in some details from, its exemplar were well-formed instances of the piece. Anyway, the idea that the work exists as a convenient fiction is not more intuitively appealing than the suggestion that it is abstract. As indicated above, holding that Beethoven's Fifth Symphony is abstract does not entail that the work cannot be noisy and triumphant at its close. Instead, it requires that these descriptions of the work are true if those properties are prescribed for its well formed instances.

3. WORKS OF ART AS UNIVERSALS

An alternative position holds that works of art are universals, not fictions. This theory can be illustrated by drawing an analogy with colours. We know what red or redness is by abstracting a universal form from the particulars in which it is instanced. When we come to recognize the nature of a work of art, we do so by a similar process. The work of art must be a universal, a form underlying the concrete particular or particulars that embody it.

This position appears to face a serious difficulty: in the standard, Platonic view, universals exist eternally, yet a work of art is created at one time and may be obliterated at a later one. Michelangelo's large cast bronze portrait of Julius II was destroyed by the Bolognese some four years after its completion in 1508. Some theorists, such as Currie (1988) and Kivy (1993), are prepared to bite this bullet. Works of art, they maintain, are discovered, not created. To make the suggestion more plausible, it is argued that the possibility of something's being discovered can be as historically conditioned as is the notion of creation. Some discoveries become possible only under very particular social circumstances, and only by a person with distinctive characteristics. One way of arguing both that works of art are created and that they participate in an eternal form is by considering them as norm classes, types, or tokens. There is a descriptive universal—for instance, a set of rhythmically articulated pitch and timbre relationships corresponding to the one indicated by Beethoven for his Fifth Symphony—that exists eternally and might be instanced at any time. Beethoven selected this universal form and created his symphony by making that form normative for the work. In other words, the artist prescribes the realization of that universal, thereby creating his work. To instance his work, it is not sufficient that the descriptive universal is realized. As well, it must be realized as a result of following the artist's prescriptions. (Whether this last argument concedes enough to those who hold that works of art are created is debatable, though; see Levinson 1990 and Fisher 1991.)

If proponents of the view just described continue to maintain that works of art are universals, they are liable to lean towards a more Aristotelian characterization of universals, according to which they may be created and destroyed, and they are present in their instances, rather than existing in a parallel but abstract realm.

Universals are contrasted with particulars. It could be argued that singular works of art—that is, ones that necessarily possess one and only one instance—are particulars.

This is not an attractive alternative, however. As particulars, either works of art are abstract or they are concrete. Claims for the existence of abstract particulars are regarded as unacceptably contentious within metaphysics in general (but see Campbell 1990). Meanwhile, the second option has its own difficulties. As I explain further in the next section, the identity of the work of art transcends that of the material stuff from which it is constituted, yet there are no other concrete particulars with which it can be plausibly identified. And for multiple works of art, the possibility of their having numerous instances is at odds with their being particulars. They are individuals, certainly, just as shapes and colours are, but are not thereby particulars.

4. IDEALISM AND SUPERVENIENCE IN REGARD TO WORKS OF ART

In addition to being abstract, works of art have been described as existing in the realm of the mental (Croce 1909; Collingwood 1938). The work is in the mind of its creator. This view might seem most plausible when applied to pieces conveyed by instructions or encodings, since these need not have any actual realizations to exist, but the theory is applied more widely, including to singular works like oil paintings. In these cases, the material object produced by the artist is regarded as an external representative of the true work, which is mental. To appreciate the artist's work, her audience must produce in themselves a mental experience that matches hers. The material representation of the work, its outward manifestation, serves as a prop in this process.

This view has counterintuitive consequences, for example that we do not have direct acquaintance with Leonardo's work of art when we stand in front of the *Mona Lisa*, and that the *Mona Lisa* no longer exists. It must regard the work's content as largely independent of the physical medium in which the artist works, whereas many artistic properties seem to rely on, or otherwise derive from, the manner in which the piece's material is treated (Wollheim 1980; Ingarden 1989). Accordingly, it cannot account readily for the differences between painting in oils and watercolours, or between sculpting in ice and marble.

Yet, if works of art are not purely mental, neither are they reducible to the physical stuff of which they are comprised. As Genette (1997) puts it, they are immanent in material things that they transcend. If Michelangelo's *David* were turned to marble dust, the work would be destroyed but the matter constituting it would not be. A wax statue might be melted down and the wax recast as something else. Moreover, works of art display many properties that are not possessed also by the materials of which they are comprised, and vice versa. A painting might show depth of perspective and power, though these are not features of its paint-daubed canvas. A copy of Tolstoy's *War and Peace* has a certain weight, but the novel does not. When works are presented via instructions, there may be little in common between the two. The score of Beethoven's Fifth is not loud in parts, and *Hamlet* is not more expensive now than formerly, even if these observations apply to the musical score and the play's script (Ingarden 1973, 1989).

Even if a work's aesthetic properties are not reducible to those of its material substrate or to those of the physical item in which it is encoded or in which instructions for its realization are recorded, still there is an ontological dependence of the former on the latter. No work of art can be created without either receiving a public exemplification or being correlated with a public item or event. A poem, to be established as a re-identifiable individual work, must be recited or written down. To exist as such, a play created for live performance must be publicly exemplified or must have its work-determinative instructions publicly embodied. Conceptual works rely for their existence on titles, specifications, or instructions. Moreover, the piece's artistic features depend directly or indirectly on properties of the stuff in which it or its instructions are embodied. If the word sequence in the novel or play script had been different, it is likely the work's aesthetic properties would have been affected. If the artist had chosen paint of a lighter hue, the scene would not have been so sombre.

To use a technical term, one can say that the existence and aesthetic features of works of art supervene on the materials constituting them, or their exemplars, or their encodings, or the instructions by which they are specified. This is not to say that philosophers of art agree on the analysis of supervenience, or on its usefulness in aesthetics.

According to eighteenth- and nineteenth-century theory, a piece's aesthetic properties depend entirely on its content, form, and medium. Two items that are qualitatively identical in their perceptible properties must possess the same aesthetic features. Matters external to the item's boundaries are irrelevant to its aesthetic character. In some versions of this theory, the perceiver needs also to put aside her knowledge of all the relations the item bears to things outside itself in order to appreciate fully its aesthetic character. It is a consequence of this position that a forgery or copy is no less aesthetically valuable than is the original, provided the two look exactly the same. On this view, the supervenience relation comes to this: there cannot be a change in the aesthetic character of a work without there being some change that affects its appearance or the appearance of its instances. If the work is singular, there will be a systematic relation between its appearance and the disposition of the materials that constitute it. If the piece is multiple, there will be a systematic relation between the appearance of its instances and the disposition of the materials that constitute them. In all cases, changes in the piece's aesthetic features must be traceable to changes in the substance in which it or its instances inhere.

5. CONTEXTUALISM AND ONTOLOGY

The above view, which might be qualified as 'formalist-empiricist', has been criticized by advocates of what might be called 'contextualism'. Contextualists maintain that various features of the art-historical and social context within which the work was created contribute to its identity. For instance, a property common to all the members of a genre carries less significance than one that is variable from member to member, which means that one can evaluate the significance of a given property only by seeing the work in relation to the art historical or intentional context that settles its genre membership (Walton 1970). In consequence, two otherwise identical items might have different aesthetic properties if the contexts of their creation differ. It follows that, when a forgery is first identified as such, it is appropriate to re-evaluate it. Because the forgery's context of creation is different from what was supposed, its aesthetic properties are likely to have been misperceived. For example, forgeries that are copies misrepresent the artistic achievement they involve (Dutton 1983).

A variety of contextualism is foreshadowed by Borges (1970). In his fictional story, 'Pierre Ménard, Author of the Quixote', Ménard, a contemporary French writer, authors a text that is word for word identical with (part of) Cervantes's *Don Quixote*. Ménard's work is very different from Cervantes's. For example, the former deliberately adopts an antique form of a foreign language, whereas the latter writes in the vernacular and avoids archaisms; the former rejects contemporary approaches to the novel in favour of a return to the picaresque form, whereas the latter forges his own style largely in the absence of models. Borges suggests that Ménard's work contains allusions to psychoanalysis and to pragmatism that are absent from Cervantes's. As a result, it is 'almost infinitely richer' (see Morizot 1999 for elaboration).

Philosophers have taken up and developed the thesis hinted at in Borges's fiction. In particular, Danto (1964, 1981) has argued that perceptually indistinguishable works of art might differ in their subject matter and aesthetic value, and that a work of art might possess very different properties from a 'mere real thing' with which it is perceptually identical. Contextualist ontologies have been developed also in Currie (1988) and Levinson (1990).

According to contextualism, the work's identifying properties depend on, among other things, the context in which the piece is created. Which aspects of the context are relevant? The most obvious are its art-historical location, function, style, and genre, along with wider cultural or technological factors that impinge directly on these.

Levinson (1990) goes further in holding that the artist's identity is crucial to the work's identity. In other words, two antecedently artistically distinct authors living at the same time and place must create different novels if they work independently, even if their texts are identical. Levinson recommends this position as giving an intuitive account of how, for music, performances are assigned to works, and as avoiding paradoxes generated by the fact that the respective pieces later acquire different properties as their creators' careers take separate paths. It might be no less intuitive, however, to maintain that a piece authored in fact by Schubert could have been written by one of his contemporaries (Currie 1988). And the air of paradox might be dispelled by recalling that different people with contrasting careers have sometimes independently invented or discovered the same, single thing (Davies 2001). (But see Levinson 1996 for responses.)

5.1 Works of Art as Action Types

In contrast with idealism, which regards the work as mental, I have suggested that the work is an abstract individual that either supervenes on a singular material object or event, or is specified via an object or event that provides instructions for the creation of its instances. On either view, the work is an object or event; but there is another possibility. Currie (1988) has argued that works of art are actions. The work is a structure created in a certain way, which he calls the 'artist's heuristic path'. Pieces discovered via different heuristic paths differ in their identities, even if they share the same structure. And if the same heuristic path is followed in arriving at different structures, again the pieces differ. Currie adopts his position as the best way of acknowledging the kind of contextualism that has been discussed here. Works are more than structures, since different pieces could share the same structure. Rather, they are to be identified with the action type through which they are discovered, since that takes account not only of what was done but also of how it was done. In other words, the canvas of the *Mona Lisa* is merely the structure, and not an instance of the work. The work is a type that received one instance via Leonardo's actions. Any act of discovering the given structure via the given heuristic path would produce an instance of the work. And this is why Currie insists that all works of art are multiple. Why does Currie regard the work as an action type rather than as a historically contextualized individual that is indicated or instanced in objects such as painted canvases or play scripts? He does so because he insists that, in appreciating a work of art, we are appreciating its artist's achievement. But the conclusion follows only if that is all there is to appreciate, which seems implausible (Shields 1995). As Levinson (1996) puts it, we appreciate the thing made as well as the making of it. Currie's position has counterintuitive corollaries. All works are multiple, though most will have only one instance; they are discovered, not created; we could directly encounter an instance of the work only if we were present at its discovery; when we regard the *Mona Lisa* or hear Beethoven's Fifth Symphony, we gain acquaintance only with the work's pattern. We can concede many of the contextualist observations that Currie makes, while avoiding these unattractive corollaries, by accepting both that the work is an indicated structure embodied or instanced in actual objects and that an appreciation of its nature involves awareness of the artist's achievement (Levinson 1996).

5.2 Works of Art as Culturally Emergent

A more radical contextualism than those so far considered is propounded by Margolis (1999). He believes that the identity of the work is 'culturally emergent', and in an open-ended way. The work's identity remains wedded to its context and thereby changes as that context evolves through time. Rather than being fixed at the outset, the identity of the work is re-constituted through the unfolding process of its subsequent reception and interpretation, yielding what Margolis calls the 'unicity' of the work.

The claim is not that the work lacks an identity until it is interpreted. Rather, it is that interpretations modify without destroying an identity that persists through time. To avoid the suggestion that interpretations are true, in which case they must identify properties the work already possesses, Margolis claims they are subject to a multivalent logic, being assessed for plausibility rather than truth.

Its interpretation inevitably confers on the work at least one property it did not have previously: that of having been interpreted thus-and-so. Moreover, there can be no denying that the significance and history of a work is conditioned by its interpretation and reception. The issue is whether these amount to changes in the work's identity.

Margolis's account supposes that the object of interest exists always in the present. We talk of it as its creator's work for ease of reference, but the accident of its origin is incidental, since the object of our concern has already transcended those circumstances. Is this a plausible sociology of our relation to works of art? I doubt it. Art involves achievement and, often, great skill. We cannot be indifferent to its location in art history, for with no sense of that we cannot comprehend the contribution it makes. I allow that Margolis's account reflects some current ('postmodern', perhaps) approaches to works of art, but these approaches are far from the paradigm that gives life to our current concept. If they became the norm, it might be more accurate to say that the concept of art had changed out of recognition than to insist that individual works of art possess an identity that constantly is in flux.

This brings us to a new possibility, one that concerns itself not with the historicity of art but with the historicity of the concept of the work of art. That concept has a history, of course, and it has been suggested that, for the case of music, the notion did not apply prior to the nineteenth century (Goehr 1992). Goehr reaches this conclusion by identifying as central to the work concept notions and values that did not emerge clearly in earlier periods. For example, she thinks that the concept was not regulative until composers produced texts specifying every note to be played.

A preferable alternative would have it that musical works became thicker with constitutive properties over several centuries of Western music, not that the work concept came into existence only at the close of this process. In this view, works, thought of as entities that invite and can be re-identified in more than one performance, pre-existed the nineteenth century, though composers often produced given works in several versions and left much to the performer. Why is this alternative preferable? Because it makes more sense of the continuities binding the history of Western music into a single narrative. Goehr's position identifies a radical break in the historical thread; a new and unprecedented kind of musical entity, the work, emerged and dominated from the nineteenth century on. Yet, while there were differences between the early nineteenth century and what went before, as there had been previously when prevailing stylistic and other musical paradigms altered, there is no reason to take the exaggerated claims the Romantics made for their own originality at face value. More explanatory ground is gained by seeing those local changes as part of a pattern towards the 'thickening' of works that began four centuries earlier and continued to the mid-twentieth century (Davies 2001).

5.3 Autographic versus Allographic Art

The contextualisms discussed above are antithetical to the major ontological division proposed for art by Goodman (1968; see also Genette 1997). A work is autographic if even the most exact duplication of it does not count as genuine. This might seem to suggest that autographic works of art correspond to those I previously described as singular. Though all singular works are autographic, Goodman regards some multiple ones—namely those that are printed from etchings, or cast from moulds, and the like—as autographic also. If one of these is copied, rather than being run off the specified plate, it is not genuine. By contrast, an *allographic* work of art is defined by its 'spelling' or sequence, so that anything reproducing that sequence thereby qualifies as an instance of the work. Necessarily, allographic works of art are multiple. Goodman's examples are of musical pieces and novels. In other words, its history of production is crucial to the identity and genuineness of an autographic work of art, but is irrelevant for an allographic work of art, where only 'sameness of spelling' matters.

Why does Goodman adopt a classification that cuts across the singular/multiple categorization in this way? He does so because his concern lies with the difference between works that are notational and those that are not. Allographic pieces are of the former kind and autographic ones are of the latter. I have already discussed and criticized Goodman's account of notations, arguing that he cannot, as he hopes, prevent the context of their specification and use from affecting their semantic content and, thereby, the works they specify. Those points already suggest that Goodman's distinction is vulnerable to contextualist objections, which I now develop further.

A first criticism observes that Goodman's distinction is meant to be exhaustive. He himself later admitted that it could not cover some of John Cage's non-notational music, and Brown (1996) has argued that improvised music—and hence jazz—cannot be accommodated by Goodman's categories. A yet more damaging objection denies that notational works are allographic. The identity of novels and musical works indicated by texts or scores depends on more than their word or note sequence, as was argued in defending contextualism. Rather than generating another instance of Cervantes's novel, Ménard creates a new one, though it has the same word sequence as Cervantes's. If novels or musical works could have been created by only one person, they would turn out to be autographic, not allographic (Levinson 1990). Alternatively, if we allow that the work's identity depends only on the art-historical context of its creation, the work will be neither allographic (since pieces with the same 'spelling' created independently in a different art historical setting will be different) nor autographic (since different people sharing the same art-historical location but working independently would not create different works if they specified lexically identical works). Either way, the distinction as it was described by Goodman fails.

6. HYBRID ARTFORMS

So far I have tended to concentrate on the arts in their 'pure' forms—painting, prints, sculpture, literature, drama, music. It is significant, though, that some artforms and artkinds are essentially hybrid in nature (Levinson 1990). Opera, for example, combines music and drama, ballet melds music with dance, and concrete poetry joins pictorial representation with poetry. The ontology of hybrids is likely to vary with the nature of the mix, as is evident when ballet is considered.

Stravinsky's *Rite of Spring* has been danced with many choreographies other than the one devised by Nijinsky for its first production. In this and many other cases, the music appears to be more important than the dance in determining the ballet's identity. There are notations for dance movements, e.g. Labanotation, so it is not the lack of a written record that explains why the music is dominant. Also, works for performance can be promulgated by means of exemplars, and first productions can be taken as such. Petipa's choreographies of Tchaikovsky's ballets have remained in the repertory. Nevertheless, a majority of ballets are identified with their music.

The suggestion that the music is more important than the dance to the identity of a ballet, though, is surely odd. Our predominant interest in ballet is not the music. Ballets are created by choreographers at least as much by composers. Moreover, some ballets appropriate established instrumental works for their music. George Balanchine's Concerto Barocco cannot derive its identity primarily from its music, which is Bach's Concerto for Two Violins in D minor. Some cases that make the dance primary are by Twyla Tharp—her *The Bix Pieces* is created and rehearsed to music by Haydn but performed to pieces by Bix Beiderbecke—and Merce Cunningham who, working with John Cage, created pieces the music of which was random, or was generated by the dancers' movements triggering electronic devices.

The identities of some ballets might depend as much on dance notations as on music ones. In some cases, a single ballet might have an open-ended set of choreographies. In others, a ballet indicated mainly by an established choreography might be combined with an open-ended set of musical accompaniments. In many cases, a production instances a ballet as a result of being intended to do so and by falling within an historically continuous tradition that can be traced back to the original production.

Ballet is not unusual among the hybrid arts for displaying a range of not clearly differentiated ontological types. And even among non-hybrid artforms, most are ontologically various.

See also: Music; Dance; Medium in Art; Authenticity in Art; Interpretation in Art; Aesthetic Realism 1; Aesthetic Realism 2.

BIBLIOGRAPHY

Alperson, P. (1984). 'On Musical Improvisation'. *Journal of Aesthetics and Art Criticism* 43: 17–30.

Bender, J. W. (1993). 'Music And Metaphysics: Types and Patterns, Performances and Works', in J. W. Bender and H. Gene Blocker (eds.), *Contemporary Philosophy of Art: Readings in Analytic Aesthetics*. Englewood Cliffs, NJ: Prentice-Hall, pp. 354–65.

Benjamin, W. (1968). 'The Work of Art in the Age of Mechanical Reproduction', in H. Arendt (ed.), *Illuminations: Essays and Reflections*, trans. H. Zohn. New York: Harcourt Brace & World, pp. 253–64.

Borges, J. L. (1970). 'Pierre Ménard, Author of the Quixote', in *Labyrinths*, trans. J. E. Irby. London: Penguin Books, pp. 62–71.

Brown, L. B. (1996). 'Musical Works, Improvisation, and the Principle of Continuity'. *Journal of Aesthetics and Art Criticism* 54: 353–69.

—— (2000). 'Phonography, Repetition and Spontaneity'. *Philosophy and Literature* 24: 111–25.

Campbell, K. (1990). *Abstract Particulars*. Oxford: Blackwell.

Carroll, N. (1998). *A Philosophy of Mass Art*. New York: Oxford University Press.

Collingwood, R. G. (1938). *The Principles of Art*. London: Oxford University Press.

Croce, B. (1909). *Aesthetics*, trans. D. Ainslie. London: Vision Press/Peter Owen.

Currie, G. (1988). *An Ontology of Art*. London: Macmillan.

—— (1991). 'Work and Text'. *Mind* 100: 325–40.

Danto, A. C. (1964). 'The Artworld'. *Journal of Philosophy* 61: 571–84.

—— (1981). *The Transfiguration of the Commonplace*. Cambridge, Mass.: Harvard University Press.

Davies, S. (1991). 'The Ontology of Musical Works and the Authenticity of their Performances'. *Noûs* 25: 21–41.

—— (1994). 'Is Architecture Art?' in M. H. Mitias (ed.), *Philosophy and Architecture*. Amsterdam: Rodopi, pp. 31–47.

—— (2001). *Musical Works and Performances: A Philosophical Exploration*. Oxford: Oxford University Press.

Dipert, R. (1993). *Artefacts, Art Works, and Agency*. Philadelphia: Temple University Press.

Dodd, J. (2000). 'Musical Works as Eternal Types'. *British Journal of Aesthetics* 40: 424–40.

Dutton, D. (ed.) (1983). *The Forger's Art*. Berkeley: University of California Press.

Edlund, B. (1996). 'On Scores and Works of Music: Interpretation and Identity'. *British Journal of Aesthetics* 36: 367–80.

Fisher, J. A. (1991). 'Discovery, Creation, and Musical Works'. *Journal of Aesthetics and Art Criticism* 49: 129–36.

—— (1998). 'Rock 'n' Recording: The Ontological Complexity of Rock Music', in P. Alperson (ed.), *Musical Worlds: New Directions in the Philosophy of Music*. University Park, Pa.: Pennsylvania State University Press, pp. 109–23.

Genette, G. (1997). *The Work of Art: Immanence and Transcendence*, trans. G. M. Goshgarian. Ithaca, NY: Cornell University Press.

Godlovitch, S. (1998). *Musical Performance: A Philosophical Study*. London: Routledge.

Goehr, L. (1992). *The Imaginary Museum of Musical Works: An Essay in the Philosophy of Music*. Oxford: Clarendon Press.

Goodman, N. (1968). *Languages of Art*. New York: Bobbs-Merrill.

Gracyk, T. A. (1996). *Rhythm and Noise: An Aesthetics of Rock Music*. Durham, NC: Duke University Press.

Howell, R. (2002*a*). 'Ontology and the Nature of the Literary Work'. *Journal of Aesthetics and Art Criticism* 60: 67–79.

—— (2002*b*). 'Types, Indicated and Initiated'. *British Journal of Aesthetics* 42: 105–27.

Ingarden, R. (1973). *The Literary Work of Art*, trans. G. G. Grabowicz. Evanston, Ill.: Northwestern University Press.

—— (1989). *Ontology of the Work of Art*, trans. R. Meyer with J. T. Goldthwait. Athens, Ohio: Ohio University Press.

Janaway, C. (1999). 'What a Musical Forgery Isn't'. *British Journal of Aesthetics* 39: 62–71.

Kallberg, Jeffrey (1996). *Chopin at the Boundaries: Sex, History, and Musical Genre*. Cambridge, Mass.: Harvard University Press.

Kivy, P. (1993). *The Fine Art of Repetition: Essays in the Philosophy of Music*. New York: Cambridge University Press.

Levinson, J. (1990). *Music, Art, and Metaphysics*. Ithaca, NY: Cornell University Press.

—— (1996). *The Pleasures of Aesthetics*. Ithaca, NY: Cornell University Press.

—— and Alperson, P. (1991). 'What is a Temporal Art?' *Midwest Studies in Philosophy* 16: 439–50.

Margolis, J. (1980). *Art and Philosophy*. Atlantic Highlands, NJ: Humanities Press.

—— (1999). *What, After All, Is a Work of Art?* University Park, Penna: Pennsylvania State University Press.

Morizot, J. (1999). *Sur le problème de Borges*. Paris: Éditions Kimé.

Pouivet, R. (1999). *L'Ontologie de l'oeuvre d'art*. Paris: Éditions Jacqueline Chambon.

Predelli, S. (2001). 'Musical Ontology and the Argument from Creation'. *British Journal of Aesthetics* 41: 279–92.

Rudner, R. (1950). 'The Ontological Status of the Esthetic Object'. *Philosophy and Phenomenological Research* 10: 380–88.

Sagoff, M. (1978). 'On Restoring and Reproducing Art'. *Journal of Philosophy* 75: 453–70.

Schwartz, R. (1993). 'Works, Works Better'. *Erkenntnis* 38: 103–14.

Shields, C. (1995). 'Critical Notice of Currie's An Ontology of Art'. *Australasian Journal of Philosophy* 73: 293–300.

Thom, P. (1993). *For an Audience: A Philosophy of the Performing Arts.* Philadelphia: Temple University Press.

Walton, K. L. (1970). 'Categories of Art'. *Philosophical Review* 79: 334–67.

—— (1988). 'The Presentation and Portrayal of Sound Patterns', in J. Dancy, J. M. E. Moravcsik, and C. C. W. Taylor (eds.), *Human Agency: Language, Duty and Value.* Stanford, Calif.: Stanford University Press, pp. 237–57.

Wollheim, R. (1980). *Art and Its Objects.* Cambridge: Cambridge University Press.

Wolterstorff, N. (1980). *Works and Worlds of Art.* Oxford: Clarendon Press.

Zemach, E. M. (1992). *Types: Essays in Metaphysics.* Leiden: E. J. Brill.

CHAPTER 9

MEDIUM IN ART

DAVID DAVIES

In its most general sense, a medium is a *means* of transmitting some matter or content from a source to a site of reception. The function of a medium, so construed, is *mediation*. Natural media such as air and water mediate the transmission of sounds. An art medium, then, is presumably something that mediates the transmission of the content of an artwork to a receiver. Art media, so conceived, have been characterized in a number of different ways: as material or physical kinds (e.g. oil paint, bronze, stone, bodily movements); as ranges of sensible determinables realizable in material or physical kinds (e.g. pitch, tone, texture, colour); as ways of purposively realizing specific values of such determinables (e.g. brushstrokes, gestures), or as systems of signs ('languages' in a more or less strict sense). A less common view, which I shall not further examine, takes the *artist* to be a medium which serves as a conduit for a content, much as a spiritualistic medium is supposed to be a conduit: this view, presented by Plato in the *Ion*, is echoed in the German Romanticist conception of the artist as a being of unusual sensitivity through whom language itself (Novalis) or the infinite (F. Schlegel) speaks.

Given such a broadly 'instrumental' conception of an art medium, philosophical interest will focus upon how, and how well, this mediating function is performed, and what significance it has for our understanding of what artworks are and what their appreciation involves. We will want to determine, for example, whether there are significant differences between art media as to the kinds of content they can mediate, and whether the same content can be differently mediated in different arts. Relatedly, we will ask whether there can be art without a medium of some sort, whether being in a particular medium is a constitutive property of an artwork in that medium, and to what extent knowledge of a work's medium is necessary for its proper appreciation.

There are, as we shall see, good reasons to conclude that art media, instrumentally conceived, make an ineliminable contribution to both the being and the being appreciated of artworks. This conclusion is open to two sorts of challenge, however. First, it might be argued that art media, as mediators of art content, contribute nothing essential to the existence or appreciation of works. Second, it might be argued that art media, while essential to the existence and appreciation of works, are not rightly conceived in instrumental terms.

Challenges of the first kind are grounded in conceptions of the artwork that see the latter as standing in a merely contingent relation to an artist's working of a medium. One such conception is the view usually associated with Croce (1922) and Collingwood (1938), according to which a work is the product of an act of expression that takes place in the mind of its creator and is only contingently externalized in an intersubjectively accessible medium of some kind. Artistic expression, as an internal process, is quite distinct from the exercise of *craft* involved in working an external medium to achieve a given effect. Something like Collingwood's distinction between art and craft has been endorsed by 'conceptual' artists such as Sol LeWitt (1967), who maintain that the 'art' in their works lies in an act of conception, and that the manipulation of an external medium is merely a matter of 'execution', which can be delegated to those having the relevant skills or 'crafts'. On such a view, working in a publicly accessible medium is not, or need not be, essential to the existence of the artwork, but serves only to make the work available to others.

Critics of this view (e.g. Wollheim 1980: 36–43) argue that it fails to take account of the manner in which the artist's *conceptual* activity proceeds by reference to the public medium in which she works—the medium *in terms of which* she thinks as an artist—and also of the ways in which the *recalcitrance* of the medium in which an artist works enters crucially into the creative process, and into the sorts of qualities we attend to and value in appreciating works. It is even arguable that it is because of their resistance to manipulation that certain materials are selected as vehicles for artistic expression. While some have tried to meet the first objection by positing a 'conceived medium' in terms of which an artist thinks (see Hospers 1956), this fails to address the second objection, and thus still entails a radically revisionist view of our critical discourse about works.

The significance of art media, instrumentally conceived, can also be questioned if one thinks of the object of appreciative and critical attention as an 'aesthetic object' whose constitutive properties are those elicited in a receiver in a direct experiential encounter with something created by an artist. Monroe Beardsley, the foremost modern defender of such a view, maintains that the notion of an artistic medium is 'almost useless for serious and careful criticism' in the arts (1958: 82). First, he claims, the term is used in many different ways, and this may lead to imprecision and confusion. More significantly, even if talk of media in the arts can be rendered more precise, such talk will serve no useful purpose in our critical discourse about artworks. For, to the extent that we take the medium to be the *physical basis* of the work—for example canvas and oil paint—it is not part of the aesthetic object; and, to the extent that we identify the medium with some set of perceptible qualities, such as the flatness or transparency of the coloured array, there is no principled way of distinguishing those statements about an aesthetic object that concern its medium from those that do not.

A full response to Beardsley's charge would require answers to more basic questions on the ontology and epistemology of art. But the direction such a response might take is clear if we avail ourselves of a distinction between what Joseph Margolis (1980: 41–2) terms the 'physical medium' and the 'artistic medium' of a work. In the case of paintings, for example, the physical medium consists of pigments (oils, tempera, water colours) applied to a surface (wood, canvas, glass), while the artistic medium is 'a purposeful system of brushstrokes'. Similarly, in talking about dance, the physical medium of bodily movements is to be distinguished from the artistic medium of articulated steps. While the artistic medium may be physically embodied, we must think of the work as made up not of physical elements as such but of elements like dance steps or brush-strokes that are 'informed by the purposiveness of the entire work' (cf. Levinson 1984: sect. I). Arthur Danto (1981: 159) similarly insists that we cannot identify the medium of a painting with the physical material of which it is composed, given the ways in which we talk about artworks. The artist characteristically works *in* a particular artistic medium when *working* a physical medium. To think of a painting as in an artistic medium is to relate its perceptible properties to the agency of a maker whose purposeful composition in that medium is the source of those properties.

To the extent that our engagement with something as an artwork requires that its 'manifest' properties be so conceived, we have an answer to Beardsley's second and more serious charge. A work's artistic medium is not to be identified with its physical medium, but neither is it inextricably entangled with its aesthetic object in Beardsley's sense. Rather, it is that to which such an aesthetic object must be related in order for our appreciation to be artistic and not merely aesthetic in a narrow sense. Beardsley, who steadfastly denies that the intentionality of the artist has a legitimate place in our critical engagement with works, rejects this defence of the notion of medium on the grounds that it builds an ineliminable appeal to artistic intention into the very fabric of our talk of (artistic) media (1958: 493–4). Resolution of this debate depends once more upon how we answer deeper questions, relating now to the place of artistic intentions in the being, and the being appreciated, of works.

We have critically examined two ways in which one might try to minimize the significance of the notion of medium for the philosophy of art. There is a contrary tendency, however, evident in much recent theorizing about art, which may err in the opposite direction, in according overriding significance to the medium, seeing the latter as the primary engine of artistic activity and as containing within itself the principal criteria for evaluating the fruits of that activity. At its extreme, this tendency issues in the doctrine of 'medium purity', and amounts to the rejection of the 'instrumental' conception of the medium. The arguments for medium purity have their roots in the instrumental conception, however, in the kinds of considerations adduced by Lessing in the *Laocoön*, in his famous discussion of the limits of the verbal and visual arts (Lessing 1957). Lessing appeals to a salient difference between the media employed in poetry and in the fine arts to explain why a given event might be represented differently by a poet and a sculptor. Both painting and poetry, as imitative arts, aim at eliciting aesthetic experience in receivers through their representational content. But painting 'employs wholly different signs or means of imitation from poetry—the one using forms and colours in space, the other articulate signs in time'. As a result, poetry and painting are naturally suited to represent different subjects: 'succession in time is the province of the poet, co-existence in space that of the artist'. This has implications for the way in which a given event should be represented in the two arts, however, given the common purpose of eliciting aesthetic experience. For a picture or a sculpture can elicit such experience directly, whereas the poet must employ indirect means, appealing through her words to our imaginative capacities. Our responses to visual presentations, in being direct, are also much more powerful, and the representation in a visual work of certain kinds of events will hinder or prevent an aesthetic appreciation of the work.

This argument assumes an instrumental conception of art media, and draws its conclusions from further premises concerning the particular ulterior purposes served by such media and the ways in which those purposes are best served. In these respects, the arguments presented by Rudolph Arnheim (1938) against the combining of sound and image in the 'talking film' are an extension of Lessing's reasoning. Arnheim, like Lessing, takes art media to be means for achieving the ulterior purpose proper to the arts. In Arnheim's opinion, this purpose is *expression*, and a medium mediates such expression to the extent that its manipulation by an artist involves creative *choices* from which the receiver is able to infer what the artist's representation expresses about its subject. Film, for Arnheim, is a suitable medium for art because many dimensions of choice confront the film-maker in the presentation of her subject, permitting the viewer to infer expressive intentions from the resulting images.

Arnheim begins by setting out some general conditions that must be met if the combining of different media in a single work is to be an artistic success. First, we require an overall unity at the level of expression, to which the different media must make distinct contributions. Second, the combining of media is artistically justified only if it permits the production of works expressively richer than would be possible in a single medium. Finally, in any successful artistic composite, one medium will always be dominant. In bringing these conditions to bear on talking pictures, however, Arnheim also appeals to a principle of *medium-differentiation*, whereby successful composite artforms must differ in their dominant medium. He maintains that the moving image, and not language, must be the dominant medium in talking pictures, given the role that the latter medium plays in theatre. The combining of the moving image and sound in the talking film is an artistic failure, then, because dialogue does not permit the realization of significant expressive values in film that are not already available in literature, and may even lessen the expressive power of the moving image.

The doctrine of 'medium purity' endorses a principle of medium differentiation while apparently repudiating the instrumental conception of the medium that Lessing and Arnheim share. Morris Weitz characterizes the doctrine as follows: 'Each art...has a specific function, which gives it its uniqueness; and this function is determined by the nature of the medium' (1950: 120). This thesis underlies the formalism of Clive Bell (1914), who, in defending post-impressionist painting, rejects the pursuit of representational ends in art. In an extended critical discussion of the doctrine, Weitz illustrates how influential this view had become in artistic practice by mid-century. The doctrine achieves its purest formulation, however, in the art theory of the following twenty years, and in particular in the writings of Clement Greenberg. Greenberg (1961) saw modernism in the arts as part of a broader tendency to employ 'the characteristic methods of a discipline to criticize the discipline itself, not in order to subvert it, but to entrench it more firmly in its area of competence'. The aim of modernism in the arts is to employ the medium of a given artform in such a self-critical manner, in order to clarify the 'essential norms or conventions' to which something must conform if it is to be received as a work of that kind. These norms and conventions, according to Greenberg, relate to 'the effects peculiar and exclusive' to an artform, where these, in turn, are determined by the distinctive features of its medium. In the case of painting, the norms pertain to the flatness of the picture plane, its finish, the texture of the paint, and the contrast of colours. More generally, modernism aims to 'purify' the different arts, and to ensure their autonomy, by 'eliminat[ing] from the effects of each art any and every effect that might conceivably be borrowed from or by the medium of any other art'.

As Noël Carroll (1986) points out, the doctrine of medium purity is a form of essentialism, holding that each artform has a specific nature determined by its medium. It is a restricted form of essentialism in also subscribing to the principle of medium differentiation, which requires that the nature of an artform be determined by what is *uniquely* possible in a given medium. Critics of the doctrine ask what argument could be offered for such a restrictive view (see e.g. Carroll 1988). We should of course grant, with Weitz, that artists who have subscribed, implicitly or explicity, to the doctrine of medium purity have produced some of the more important works of the last century. But this demonstrates only that there are important artistic values to be realized by purist art, not that these are the only, or even the most important, artistic values worth pursuing.

Indeed, there is something deeply paradoxical about the doctrine of medium purity taken as a general theoretical pronouncement in the axiology of art. For, so taken, the doctrine can be read as a repudiation of the instrumental conception of the medium, putting in its place the idea that a medium should be celebrated *for its own sake*, or for its *intrinsic* values. But what is essential to something's being a medium, rather than a mere kind of stuff, is just that it serves some *extrinsic or ulterior* purpose. If a medium is intrinisically a means of transmitting or communicating something, then to appreciate the medium *for its own sake* in appreciating a work is to attend not simply to *what* is communicated but to *the manner in which* that thing is communicated. Appreciation, so construed, exhibits what Wollheim terms 'twofoldness', requiring that we attend both to the content of a work and to the way in which that content is articulated in the medium (1980: 213ff; see also Budd 1995; Eldridge 1985).

The purist might argue that she in fact is preserving the instrumental conception of the medium, her claim being that the values properly pursued in a given artform are those that maximize the *expressive* potentials of the medium. But a physical medium can be ascribed an expressive potential only in so far as it is seen as the embodiment of an artistic medium in the sense distinguished above, and thus as subject to the purposive manipulations of an expressing agent. It is systems of brushstrokes or other artistic media realizable in the physical media of painting that have certain expressive potentials, for example. But once we focus on the *use* of a physical medium, given its intrinsic qualities, as an artistic medium, there is no basis for the restrictive claims of the purist. We can grant that the artist should strive to utilize as effectively as possible the expressive possibilities of her medium without subscribing to the 'purist' thesis that the expressive content of the work as a whole must be dictated *solely* by the medium, or to the principle of medium differentiation, which restricts legitimate expression in a medium to that which is possible *only* in that medium.

The preceding reflections suggest that medium matters in art, but that its significance is to be elucidated in broadly instrumental terms. We may now return to the issues raised earlier concerning the bearing of the notion of art medium on questions on the ontology and epistemology of art. Is it a necessary condition for the existence of an artwork that it be in a medium? Is a work's medium, in some sense, constitutive of that work? And is knowledge of a work's medium a precondition for its proper appreciation? The second of these questions presupposes that it makes sense to think of the *content* of a work as separable from the *medium* in which that content is presented: only then can we ask whether the *same* content presented in a *different* medium would be an instance of the same work. Andrew Harrison (1998) has suggested that the separability, or separate conceivability, of a medium and that which it mediates is built into the very logic of medium-talk. Supposing this to be true, we may focus on the dependent question whether being in a given medium is *constitutive* of a work.

A methodological note is in order here. Many contemporary writers on the ontology of art (see e.g. Levinson 1980; Danto 1981; Currie 1989; Davies forthcoming) acknowledge a constraint on the latter issuing from features of our critical and appreciative practice. This constraint requires that works be the kinds of things that can bear the properties rightly ascribed to them in such practice. It acquires onto-logical bite when combined with more general Leibnizian constraints on identity, and on the individuation of works. The constraint *does not* require, however, that claims in the ontology of art uphold the broadly ontological talk found in common parlance—for example talk of performances on non-standard instruments that com-ply with the scores of musical works as performances of those works, or talk of mass-produced reproductions of paintings as instances of the works reproduced.

Much recent work in the epistemology of art has argued that our interest in a work is always at least in part an interest in the *achievement* or *performance* that the work represents, something that derives from its *history of making* (see e.g. Dutton 1979; Levinson 1980; Danto 1981; Baxandall 1985; Walton 1987; Currie 1989; Davies forthcoming). On such a view, it is central to our thinking about something as an artwork that it be referred to the purposive activity of an agent who is taken to have generated the work, and to have done so in pursuit of certain ends whose achieve-ment requires the overcoming of certain obstacles. These obstacles generally pres-ent themselves to the artist in terms of the artistic medium in which she works. Art critics, seeking to account for puzzling or otherwise notable manifest features of works, make frequent reference to problems of this sort that arise in working in a particular art-istic medium (see e.g. Baxandall 1985: chapters 2 (on Picasso) and 4 (on Piero); Lucie-Smith 1976: 32–6 (on Pollock)). If the same end result were to have been produced in a different artistic medium, or through the deployment of the same artistic medium in a different physical medium, then the achievement would differ, and our artistic assessment of the work would differ accordingly.

Assumptions about physical and artistic media enter into our critical engage-ment with works in a more fundamental manner in our appreciation of various kinds of *trompe l'œil* (see Danto 1981: 149ff), which often play upon the artistic or physical media employed in contemporary artistic practice. It is crucial to an appreciation of the painted 'cornices' on the ceiling of the Accademia in Venice, for example, that one is aware of them *as* paintings rather than architectural embel-lishments. 'Medium awareness' in this sense is equally crucial to an appreciation of the remarkable *trompe l'œil* 'letter racks' and 'wooden panels' of Cornelius Giesbrecht. Considerations of 'medium awareness' in a broader sense also play a central role in recent debates over the nature of film experience, and bear upon an evaluation of claims about the 'illusory' nature of such experience (see e.g. Currie 1995; Allen 1995; Davies 2003).

Suppose that we subscribe to the above-cited principle whereby the epistemo-logy of art constrains the ontology of art. Then, if we are persuaded that the appre-ciation of an artwork must take account of a history of making in which what is achieved rests in part upon the ways in which the artist has manipulated the medium or media in which she worked, we will also look favourably on the idea that, if a work is in a given artistic medium, then its being so is partly constitutive of its being the particular work it is. This conclusion is explicitly drawn by Levinson (1980), who incorporates the specification of a particular *performance means* for realizing a given sound structure into the identity of the musical work. It is more or less implicit in the ontological proposals of other writers who endorse such a view of artistic appreciation (e.g. Dutton 1979; Danto 1981; Currie 1989; Davies 1999, forthcoming). It is perhaps also implicit in the work of the artist Chuck Close, who produces sets of works with a shared design which is realized through different artistic and/or physical media in each work.

The foregoing argument appeals to Margolis's distinction, introduced above, between the physical medium of a work, i.e. the material stuff worked by the artist, and the artistic medium in which the artist works. A work exists as a particular ordering of elements in an artistic medium, which is embodied in a physical medium. This distinction between physical and artistic media is useful in responding to a number of difficulties that attend the notion of art medium, but it also generates certain questions that need to be addressed. In the first place, we need a more precise characterization of the relationship between an artistic medium and the physical stuff in which it may be embodied. Second, and more significantly, we must ask whether this distinction can be applied to 'conceptual' artworks or to performance pieces. Are all artworks in an artistic medium in Margolis's sense, and, if so, (*a*) why is the existence of such a medium a precondition for something's being an artwork? and (*b*) can a work be in an artistic medium without being in a physical medium?

In answering these questions, we may draw on a very interesting critical response to Margolis by Timothy Binkley (1977). Binkley's concern is to exhibit salient continuities and discontinuities between traditional works of fine art and late modern works such as readymades and 'conceptual' art. The primary obstacles to an understanding of late modern art, according to Binkley, are the subsumption of the artistic under the aesthetic, and, more particularly, a misunderstanding of the function of media in traditional fine art. Binkley characterizes the discontinuity between traditional and late modern fine art in terms of a distinction between 'aesthetic art' and 'non-aesthetic art'. The former involves the bringing into being of an 'aesthetic object' whose appreciable properties are determinable only through a direct experiential encounter with the physical product of the artist's activity. In the case of 'non-aesthetic art', the artist creates primarily 'with ideas' and no such direct experiential encounter is required. However, non-aesthetic art is continuous with aesthetic art in that, in each case, the piece 'articulates [an] artistic statement'— there is some *content* which is articulated in a manner that renders the piece appreciable by receivers. Talk of articulating an artistic statement, here, does not carry the implication that the content of a work can be propositionally characterized, but, rather, that works are individuated *intensionally*, in the way that meanings are, rather than *extensionally*. In the case of aesthetic art articulation takes place in a medium, whereas in the case of non-aesthetic art it takes place 'in a semantic space'.

Philosophers have failed to understand the continuity between aesthetic and non-aesthetic art, according to Binkley, because they have taken articulation in a medium to be the defining condition of aesthetic art, and because they have misunderstood what it is to articulate an artistic statement in a medium. The medium is taken to be a kind of physical stuff through the manipulation of which an emergent *aesthetic object* comes into being (see Margolis 1980). What this misses, according to Binkley, is the essentially conventional nature of media in art. A medium is a set of conventions whereby performing certain manipulations on a kind of physical stuff counts as specifying a certain set of aesthetic properties as a piece, and thus as articulating a particular artistic statement. Once we recognize that the role of media in aesthetic art is to enable an artist to articulate an artistic statement in a manner graspable by receivers, however, we can see the eschewal of media in non-aesthetic art as simply a decision to employ alternative means of articulating an artistic statement.

Binkley's interesting proposal raises more questions than can be addressed here. But we can extract what is important for present purposes if we reformulate his central claim about media in aesthetic art in terms of our distinction between the physical medium and the artistic medium. Binkley's claim that media in art are properly regarded as *piece-specifying conventions* rather than as kinds of physical stuff can be seen as bringing out the contingent and conventional nature of the relation between a physical medium and an artistic medium. The point might be expressed in a modified version of Kendall Walton's thought experiment (Walton 1970) about *guernicas*, artworks belonging to a 'category of art' whose members have the design features of Picasso's painting of that name but whose artistic value depends crucially upon their topology.

Suppose we modify Walton's example, and imagine a culture C whose works—call them 'C-paintings'—are physically indistinguishable from our paintings, but who take the topology of the painted canvas—realized in the thickness of the paint—to be a crucial determinant of the artistic value of a work: appreciation of a C-painting *always* requires that one look at it not only from the front but also from the side. C-paintings share a physical medium with our paintings, but the artistic media differ. An artistic medium, then, cannot supervene upon a physical medium, because what is intuitively the *same* material or substrate can ground different artistic media. Rather, an artistic medium can be thought of as a set of conventions whereby an individual's acting in certain ways—for example performing certain operations upon a physical medium—serves to 'articulate a particular artistic statement', in the sense that it specifies a piece that is accessible to receivers who grasp those conventions (cf. Levinson 1984, sect. I).

If, like Binkley, we think of an artistic medium as a set of conventions permitting the articulation of artistic statements through the manipulation of a *physical medium*, then it will be difficult to think of purely conceptual works such as Robert Barry's 'All the things I know but of which I am not at the moment thinking— 1:36 p.m., 15 June 1969, New York', or, arguably, Duchampian readymades and much other late modern work as involving the employment of artistic media. But returning to our initial 'instrumental' characterization of art media, we might characterize artistic media more generally as modes of artistic *mediation* that are necessary in order for there to be appreciable works. The artistic medium of a work, so construed, will be the means employed by an artist in order to 'articulate an artistic statement', and thereby to specify a piece that is accessible to receivers.

Our earlier reflections, however, require that I enter three caveats. First, while the artistic medium serves to mediate the articulation of an artistic 'statement', the 'statement' articulated is generated through the artist's working *in* that medium, rather than through something that enjoys a prior unmediated existence. Second, the artist's working in an artistic medium will require skilful manipulation of what may be termed the *vehicle* in which that medium is realized—whether that vehicle be a physical medium of some sort, a symbolic structure, actions performable in a cultural context, or what Binkley terms 'a semantic space'. Finally, in appreciating a work, we must always attend to *how* an 'artistic statement' has been articulated in a particular artistic medium, and how that articulation exploits the qualities of the vehicle that realizes that artistic medium (Wollheim's 'twofoldness'). Only if it is developed in a manner sensitive to these points can the instrumental conception of art media make its necessary contribution to our understanding of the arts.

See also: Ontology of Art; Authenticity in Art; Creativity in Art; Film; Definition of Art.

BIBLIOGRAPHY

Allen, R. (1995). *Projecting Illusion: Film Spectatorship and the Impression of Reality.* New York: Cambridge University Press.

Arnheim, R. (1938). 'A New Laocoön: Artistic Composites and the Talking Film', in R. Arnheim, *Film as Art.* Berkeley: University of California Press, 1964, pp. 199–230.

Baxandall, M. (1985). *Patterns of Intention.* New Haven: Yale University Press.

Beardsley, M. (1958). *Aesthetics: Readings in the Philosophy of Criticism.* New York: Harcourt, Brace.

Bell, C. (1914). *Art.* London: Chatto & Windus.

Binkley, T. (1977). 'Piece: Contra Aesthetics'. *Journal of Aesthetics and Art Criticism* 35: 265–77.

Budd, M. (1995). *Values of Art.* London: Penguin.

Carroll, N. (1986). 'Performance'. *Formation* 3(1): 64–78.

——— (1988). *Philosophical Problems of Classical Film Theory.* Princeton: Princeton University Press.

Collingwood, R. G. (1938). *The Principles of Art.* Oxford: Clarendon Press.

Cook, N. (1998). *Analysing Musical Multimedia.* Oxford: Oxford University Press.

Croce, B. (1922). *Aesthetic*, 2nd edn. trans. D. Ainslie. London: Macmillan. First published 1902 (in Italian).

Currie, G. (1989). *An Ontology of Art*. New York: St Martin's Press.

——(1995). *Image and Mind: Film, Philosophy, and Cognitive Science*. Cambridge: Cambridge University Press.

Danto, A. (1981). *The Transfiguration of the Commonplace*. Cambridge, Mass.: Harvard University Press.

Davies, D. (1999). 'Artistic Intentions and the Ontology of Art'. *British Journal of Aesthetics* 39: 148–62.

——(2003). 'The Images, the Imagined, and the Imaginary', in M. Kieran and D. Lopes (eds.), *Imagination, Philosophy, and the Arts*. London: Routledge.

——(forthcoming). *Performing Art: The Artwork as Performance*. Malden: Blackwell.

Dutton, D. (1979). 'Artistic Crimes: The Problem of Forgery in the Arts'. *British Journal of Aesthetics* 19: 304–14.

Eldridge, R. (1985). 'Form and Content: An Aesthetic Theory of Art'. *British Journal of Aesthetics* 25: 303–16.

Greenberg, C. (1961). 'Modernist Painting'. *Arts Yearbook*, 4. Reprinted in C. Greenberg, *Art and Culture*. Boston: Beacon Press, 1961.

Harrison, A. (1998). 'Medium', in M. Kelly (ed.), *Encyclopaedia of Aesthetics*. New York: Oxford University Press, pp. 200–3.

Hospers, J. (1956). 'The Croce–Collingwood Theory of Art'. *Philosophy* 31: 291–308.

Lessing, G. E. (1957). *Laocoön: An Essay on the Limits of Painting and Poetry*, trans. E. Frothingham. New York: Noonday Press. First published 1766.

Levinson, J. (1980). 'What a Musical Work Is'. *Journal of Philosophy* 77: 5–28.

——(1984). 'Hybrid Artforms'. *Journal of Aesthetic Education* 18: 5–13.

LeWitt, S. (1967). 'Paragraphs on Conceptual Art'. *Artforum*; quoted in L. Lippard, *Six Years: The Dematerialisation of the Art Object*. New York: Praeger, 1973, pp. 28–9.

Lucie-Smith, E. (1976). *Late Modern*. New York: Praeger.

Margolis, J. (1980). *Art and Philosophy*. Atlantic Heights, NJ: Humanities Press.

Ridley, A. (1997). 'Not Ideal: Collingwood's Expression Theory'. *Journal of Aesthetics and Art Criticism* 55: 263–72.

Savile, A. (1987). *Aesthetic Reconstructions: The Seminal Writings of Lessing, Lant, and Schiller*. Oxford: Blackwell.

Walton, K. (1970). 'Categories of Art'. *Philosophical Review* 79: 334–67.

——(1987). 'Style and the Products and Processes of Art', in B. Lang (ed.), *The Concept of Style*, 2nd edn Ithaca, NY: Cornell University Press.

Weitz, M. (1950). *Philosophy of the Arts*. Cambridge, Mass.: Harvard University Press, chapter 7.

Wollheim, R. (1968). 'Minimal Art', in G. Battcock (ed.), *Minimal Art: A Critical Anthology*. New York: Dutton.

——(1980). *Art and its Objects*, 2nd edn. Cambridge: Cambridge University Press.

CHAPTER 10

REPRESENTATION IN ART

ALAN H. GOLDMAN

OF all the long-standing debates that raise doubts about progress in philosophy, that concerning the nature of representation in the arts stands out. For Plato's analysis, charitably interpreted and amplified, holds up remarkably well in the face of strong criticism earlier in this century and yet more recent revisions. And the question that he raised about the value of representation as he analysed it, while less prominent as a philosophical topic, proves still difficult to answer, although here it is much clearer that Plato is wrong in the negative answer he gave. At the centre of the former debate is the question whether representation depends essentially on resemblance, but this is just part of Plato's analysis, and the other parts, while only implicit, have been unduly neglected.

1. THE PLATONIC ACCOUNT

Plato's account is contained in the following passage from *The Republic*:

Which is the art of painting designed to be—an imitation of things as they are, or as they appear—of appearance or of reality? Of appearance. (Plato 1952 (Stephanus): 598)

And in *The Sophist*, he writes:

if artists were to give the true proportions of their fair works, the upper part, which is farther off, would appear to be out of proportion in comparison with the lower, which is nearer; and so they give up the truth in their images and make only the proportions which appear to be beautiful, disregarding the real ones. (Plato 1952 (Stephanus): 236)

These passages make clear that, in Plato's terms, artists imitate, but they imitate the ways things appear, not the ways we take them to be. The second passage also makes clear that he had some notion of linear perspective. He recognized that artists attempted to reproduce such perspective, which he equated with appearance, although he took this as a ground for condemnation. Since he was writing of representational art, and specifically of painting, we may conclude that he takes such representation to consist in the imitation of visual experience, of the ways things appear to sight.

Now for the filling out. If by 'imitate' Plato meant that artists simply copy how things appear in their visual experience, then, as Ernst Gombrich in this century famously argued, this is not what artists, even those who strive for naturalism in their paintings, typically do. Gombrich held such copying to be well nigh impossible (Gombrich 1960: 36, 38), though the use of a camera, or its predecessor the camera obscura, makes it more nearly possible. But Gombrich is right that the long history of the quest for naturalism would be inexplicable if copying appearance were an unlearned activity. And recent experiments confirm that, even when students are instructed to copy a line drawing in linear perspective, they apply rules of perspective as they know them instead of matching the directions of the edges in view in the model (Willats 1997: 190). Artists must learn to use various rules and devices in attempting to imitate appearance. Imitation cannot be interpreted as mere copying or duplication.

Nor, according to Plato, do artists exactly reproduce the visual appearance of three-dimensional objects or scenes. Despite stories of remarkable *trompe l'œil* paintings by Greek artists of the time, Plato points out in both works cited that paintings can fool only children who view them from a considerable distance. Since artists cannot exactly reproduce their visual experiences, we may take imitation to be the creation of an object, a two-dimensional surface, which in turn creates visual experience that resembles that of the objects it represents. Resemblance, not duplication, is crucial, and resemblance in visual experience, not resemblance between the respective objects themselves. Since imitating is an intentional activity, the imitation that is representation, which makes a picture the picture of an object or scene that it is, is the intentional creation of resemblances in visual experiences of the painting and its object.

This intention to create the relevant resemblances must be successful for the representation to succeed. When the intention is successful, viewers of the picture can see or recognize the represented object in it. They can recognize the object in the picture in virtue of being able to recognize the real object, or they can come to be able to recognize the real object in virtue of being able to see it in the picture. In either case, they see objects with certain properties in the picture, properties that the picture represents the objects as having. Not all the properties of the objects as represented, however, are properties that the real objects are represented as having. Black and white line drawings, for example, do not represent their objects as having lines or being black and white. But the representational content of a picture, how it represents its object as being, is acquired through the way it appears, is a matter of certain resemblances in appearance. A picture can represent only visible properties, although these may symbolize or indicate others in the real object. And it must accurately represent, i.e. create similar visual experience of, some of these properties in order for the represented object to be recognizable or visible in the picture. To grasp the content of a picture is to conceptualize a certain sort of visual experience. This visual experience suggests the artist's intention to depict the objects represented, which intention is therefore recoverable from the experience.

Before commenting further on its various parts, we may pause to spell out more explicitly the Platonic criterion so far suggested. According to it, *a picture represents an object if and only if (a) its artist successfully intends by marking a surface to create visual experience that resembles that of the object, (b) such that the intention can be recovered from the experience, perhaps together with certain supplementary information, and (c) the object can be seen in the picture.*

Consider the last clause (c) first. In the case of painting, the idea of seeing an object in a painting is not meant to imply that the real object itself is seen through or by means of the painting. (This may be different for other sorts of pictures.) But the representation of the object must be visibly recognizable as a representation of that object, and this recognition must depend only on the ability to recognize the real object or pick it out—not, say, on some complex code or decoding device. In looking at the object in the painting, one sees that it has certain properties. As pointed out, some of the properties of the representation are not meant to represent corresponding properties of the object. A painting may also misdescribe an object, by representing it as having certain properties that it does not have, but the limit to such misrepresentation is set by the requirement that the object be recognizable as that object in the painting. The limit again indicates the centrality of resemblance in visual experience, since it is that relation that underlies the ability to recognize the object. Complete misrepresentation or lack of resemblance in appearance would prevent a painting from representing an object, whatever the intention of its maker. An abstract work entitled 'Moses' might refer to Moses, and even symbolize certain of his characteristics, such as power; but it would not depict, i.e. pictorially represent, him. Even the creation of an intended resemblance in visual experience does not suffice for representation if the object is not seen in the painting. An experience of a painting may intentionally resemble that of an earlier one to which its artist refers, but it does not represent the earlier one if it cannot be seen in the later one.

Richard Wollheim has analysed the idea of 'seeing in' in terms of being visually aware of both the represented object and the surface of the painting simultaneously (Wollheim 1987: 21). He takes this to be definitive of viewing a representational painting. While such 'twofold' viewing may in fact be essential to seeing how representation emerges from formal elements and painterly devices, and therefore essential to appreciating the aesthetic value of many paintings, it is not required, or even preferred or intended, as the way to view every representational painting. *Trompe l'œil* paintings are clearly representational—some would consider them paradigms—yet the surface is meant to disappear entirely from view when they succeed in their intended effect (Levinson 1998: 228; Lopes 1996: 49–50). On the other hand, Wollheim has clearly captured something important to appreciating many representational works. Many artists, especially modern artists, thematize the duality of painted surface and represented objects and space. They do this by calling attention to the painted surface, or to the contrast between real and represented space, in a variety of ways—for example by noticeable marks, by a flattening of the canvas, by unusual spatial projections, by reversal of rules for occlusions and other anomalies, or by noticeably including or excluding the viewer from the space of the picture.

The relation of such 'twofold' seeing to appreciation will be explored further in Section 4 on Value. But for now we may continue explicating the Platonic criterion by turning to the role of intention. It does not suffice for representation that one can see objects in surfaces based on similar visual experiences. We see figures in clouds, in random stains on walls, and in rock formations; but of the latter only the likes of Mt Rushmore are representational, because reflecting the intentional creation of such experiences. Intention is not only necessary to depiction; it also functions to pick out which particular objects are represented and which properties they are represented as having. What it is correct to see in a painting is what can be recognized or recovered as intentionally represented there. (Photographs are different in this respect.) Without the criterion of intention, the content of any painting would be radically indeterminate. Even an apparently naturalistic depiction of a scene in linear perspective might have resulted from many different projections of many different real scenes. It is because we easily infer the intention to depict the scene naturally intended that we interpret it that way. Of all the objects that cause similar visual experiences, intentions pick out those represented. The visual experience of the dog in *Las Meninas* resembles that of countless similar dogs, but it is clear that Velázquez intended to represent the particular dog belonging to that Spanish royal family. A line drawing does not normally represent its object as having lines because it is not intended to do so.

A depiction of Moses appears more like its real-life model than like Moses, but the intention to represent the biblical figure, together with a title or established conventions for depicting the biblical figure that allows the intention to be recovered—the sort of supplemental information referred to above—determines that it is Moses who is represented. Even absent a title, we might infer the intention from such conventions—from depicted emblems associated with the figure, such as a staff or stone tablets, or from the represented context, e.g. a mountain in a desert. This example, however, may seem to call into question other parts of the Platonic criterion. If a model looks little like the real Moses and yet a painting succeeds in representing that biblical figure, if in any case we have no way of telling whether the model does look like Moses and such resemblance is therefore irrelevant, the example may raise doubts about the necessity of resemblance in visual experience. But recall that an abstract painting entitled 'Moses' does not succeed in representing him. Visual experience of the painting must therefore sufficiently resemble that of the man so that, with the aid of supplemental information, such as a title that indicates an intended object, we can see a man in the painting whom we identify as Moses. The same dual criterion of intention and resemblance would apply even if Moses were only a mythical character who never existed. Here the visual experience of the painting could not resemble that of the man, there being no such man, but would resemble that of the artist's or his culture's image of the man, which we could come to share by seeing the man in the painting and identifying him as that mythical character. This explanation is plausible, given that we store images of objects in their absence and recognize them on that basis, and that we can come to be able to recognize objects on the basis of seeing them in pictures.

The example shows that the correct criterion for representational content in paintings is intentional and not causal. This constitutes a contrast between paintings, which are representational, and photographs, which, I will argue below, are not. One cannot have a photograph of Moses, but only a photograph of a model posing as Moses; yet there are many paintings of Moses. Photographs of particular objects are such because of the causal relation between the object and the photograph. Not so for paintings, which do not always depict their models. Another example might seem to call into question this priority of intention over cause in determining the object represented. Suppose that a painter is working from a photograph of Paris but believes it to be London she is painting, and that she intends to depict a street scene in London. Is it not nevertheless a street scene in Paris that she represents? Yes, but only because she also intends to represent the street scene that she sees through the photograph. What this example shows is that the concept of representation is transparent despite the prominence of intention as a part of its criterion. If a painting represents a particular street and that street is in Paris, then it represents a street in Paris, whether or not its artist intends it to represent Paris.

The only causal element mentioned for a painted or drawn picture is not the relation between object and painting, but the causal process of the artist's marking the surface. This is required because the other parts of the analysis are not jointly sufficient for representation. A fabric sample is successfully intended to create visual experience that resembles experience of larger pieces of the fabric, but it is not a pictorial representation or picture of the fabric. If it were created by being hand painted, however, then it would be such a picture.

It is important to emphasize that the relevant resemblances are not between pictures and the objects they represent, but between ways of appearing or visual experiences. This avoids the objection that every painting resembles every other painting more than they resemble their objects (Goodman 1976: 5). Not only is there no claim of resemblance among the physical objects as such: there is no such claim regarding physical marks or shapes on the marked surface and their represented objects, nor even regarding the arrays of light reflected from the marked surfaces and the represented objects. Like Plato, Descartes pointed out long ago that shapes on a canvas do not resemble represented shapes: ovals often represent circles. Less obviously, colours on a canvas do not normally match colours of objects represented. First, the overall array of light reflected from the canvas is usually less intense than that from the depicted scene. Second, surrounding colours affect the ways particular pigments appear, and the smaller context of the canvas differs from that of the depicted scene. Third, shading to reflect curves and contours, changes of hue to suggest distance, and shadows create differences between painted and scenic colours. Do the former, the properties of the painted surface, then resemble the ways the latter, the represented objective properties, appear? For example, does the oval resemble the appearance of the circle as seen from an angle? This is a common and natural assumption, but is not quite right in its full generality either. The resemblance is instead between the way the shape or colour on the canvas appears and the way the shape or colour of the object appears as seen from that angle.

One might assume that these latter resemblances must be explained by real similarities among the objects, or at least by obviously correlated resemblances in the arrays of light, but this is not always true either. Artists often create similar visual experiences by using independent pictorial devices, not by reproducing the array of light reflected from the represented objects. An obvious example is the line drawing, where the lines represent certain edges, especially those where smooth contours end or one object or surface is occluded by another, but where objects themselves have no real counterparts to lines. Related examples are the uses of lines in paintings to represent texture, or the direction of curves, or the use of thinner or less sharp lines to represent distance. What is crucial is that the picture provide visual information sufficient to enable the viewer to see the object in it (Schier 1986; Sartwell 1991). The recognition of the object is made possible by resemblances in visual experiences triggered by physical cues that need not themselves be alike. Nor need these cues be normally accessible to consciousness. They typically involve higher-order relations among groups of colours, texture gradients, lines and edges, and so on. In regard to the latter, some of the same relations probably trigger recognition of real objects under varying conditions of viewing over time.

In contrast to the above, some philosophers claim that there is one physical property shared by pictures and the objects they represent that accounts for the success of representation. This property is sometimes called *occlusion shape*, the shape blocked by an object on a surface behind it as viewed from a given angle.

Robert Hopkins, who is clearest in his presentation, calls it outline shape and defines it as the solid angle an object subtends at a point (Hopkins 1998: 55). We may think of this as the outer shell of a set of rays projected to an object from that point through the fronto-parallel plane. Paintings in linear perspective typically reproduce such shapes, and they typically, but not always, produce visual experiences that most closely resemble in shape those of the objects represented. That having been said, in addition to the hedge required in the previous sentence, there are two insuperable problems in appealing to this physical property in the analysis of representation.

Hopkins sees it as an advantage of this account that it appeals only to physical properties, eschewing the need to appeal to perceptual experience. But the fact that the property is rarely duplicated in our visual experience, given the operation of shape constancy, nullifies its usefulness in an analysis or definition, however important it remains to painters trying to paint in linear perspective. It may be that resemblance in outline shape typically produces similar visual experiences, at least in regard to shape, but if so, this is an empirical fact, not part of a proper philosophical analysis. Whatever physical cues produce the relevant resemblances in experience, and it might be others even in regard to shape, it is those resemblances that are crucial to representation, because they are what directly grounds our ability to see objects in the two-dimensional surfaces. This is not to say that we must notice the resemblances before we can see objects in painted surfaces, only that the resemblances, however physically caused themselves, explain our ability to see in this way (Levinson 1998).

The second, more obvious, problem is that shape itself is not always what is crucial. The representation of what is shapeless, amorphous, or constantly changing in shape—the sky, the sea, clouds, smoke, and so on—cannot depend on this property of outline shape. One might reply that such objects still typically bear spatial relations to other objects in paintings that help in their identification, but again this is not always the case. I have seen a painting of just the sky itself at dawn, which is nevertheless clearly recognizable as such, mainly in virtue of its colours. And even representations of objects that do have well defined outline shapes sometimes rely instead on visual resemblances in other properties. A child's drawing of leaves on a tree may again depend much more heavily on colour (Neander 1987).

Christopher Peacocke appeals to a related property as the crucial focus of resemblance, what he calls shape in the visual field. This is an improvement over other accounts, not only in that it specifies the relevant resemblance, but in that this property is understood as internal to visual experience. But whether there really is a property such as Peacocke posits is another question, and a difficult one, since he seems to view this property as the experiential equivalent of outline shape (Peacocke 1987: 389). He seems, that is, to assume that an object in the visual field takes up an area identical to that projected from the real object on to a plane perpendicular to the line of sight. But outline shapes typically do not appear as such in visual experience, nor do objects appear to be those shapes. Experiments show that, given the imperfect operation of shape constancy, objects typically appear somewhere between their outline and their real shapes; for example, circles appear between projected ovals and circles (Thouless 1931; Gregory 1964). In any case, we have seen that shape, of whatever kind, is not always the relevantly resembling property. The relevant kind of resemblance in visual experience cannot be specified in terms of a single property such as shape. The relevant resemblances vary with the type of painting, the context, and the type of object represented (Neander 1987). But they are always those that enable the viewer to recognize or see the represented object in the painting.

2. Objections and Alternative Accounts

The most thorough way to reject the Platonic account as developed above is to reject the category of visual experience at its heart. The account assumes a causal theory of perception according to which light from objects results in visual experiences which may have properties that are not properties of the physical array. For materialists, by contrast, to say that something appears F is to say that it appears to be F, which is simply a weakening of the judgement that it is F. For the account defended above, not only is 'appears F' distinct from 'appears to be F', but, together with 'conditions appear normal', it constitutes independent evidence for something's being F.

Clearly, this is not the place to resolve this fundamental issue in the philosophy of mind. We can make clearer by example, however, how a property F can appear when an object is not F and does not appear to be F. When I take off my eyeglasses, the table at the far side of the room appears blurry. But it is not blurry, nor does it appear to be so. For it to appear to be blurry, I would have to have some tendency to believe it is blurry, and I have no such tendency. I don't know whether anything other than a picture ever appeared to me to be blurry, but it is clear that I would have needed the concept of blurriness before I could have acquired such a belief. And it is likely that I acquired the concept only by things appearing blurry to me. For many concepts of visible properties, things must appear those ways before we can have those concepts, which seems to show that the category of appearing is indeed distinct from that of appearing to be.

The visual experience of a painting appears to be that of its represented objects only in a *trompe l'œil* painting; in all other cases the visual appearances, the ways the representation and its objects appear, are only similar. John Hyman, who has offered a recent materialist analysis of representation, analyses the way an object appears as the way its occlusion or outline shape appears to be, which is a usually inaccurate estimation of that physical shape (Hyman 1989: 56). But since we are normally not aware of outline shapes, since most people lack that concept, and since appearing to be F requires the concept of F, that attempt at reduction does not succeed. It also fails to explain why, when as amateur painters we do attempt to estimate outline shape, we are generally inaccurate in the same direction, because of the way objects appear, given the operation of shape constancy. What remains crucial for seeing objects in marked surfaces is that the visual experiences, the ways of appearing, are similar, outline shapes no doubt playing an important causal role in generating some of the relevant similarities.

A second line of resistance focuses on the notion of resemblance. Nelson Goodman is the best known protagonist here, his attack on resemblance having been motivated by his nominalism and anti-realism. One prong of this attack was dismissed above: the point that all paintings as objects resemble all other paintings more than they resemble the objects they represent is irrelevant to the Platonic account, which speaks only of resemblances in visual experiences. Goodman also points out that everything resembles everything else in countless ways, and that resemblance is a reflexive and symmetric relation, while representation is neither (Goodman 1976: 4). The former point requires only that the relevant resemblances be specified, which was done above. In regard to the latter, though resemblance is perhaps, strictly speaking, symmetric, it often does not seem to be so. My son's tennis serve resembles that of Pete Sampras, yet it is not clear that Pete Sampras's serve resembles my son's. Sometimes we do say that objects resemble their pictures, referring to the corresponding visual experiences, when we recognize the objects on the basis of having seen their pictures, but it is true that the objects do not represent their pictures. Similarly, I suppose that, strictly speaking, resemblance is reflexive, though we virtually never think of an object as resembling itself. If they do, strictly speaking, resemble themselves, objects nevertheless rarely represent themselves. But both of Goodman's points here are nullified as an attack on the Platonic account by the fact that, according to that account, resemblance in visual experience is only necessary, not sufficient, for representation.

Goodman's anti-realism motivates his attack on the Platonic account of representation in a different and perhaps deeper way as well. According to him, representation cannot imitate the way an object appears, since there is no particular way an object appears. There is no way the world is that is there to be resembled or copied. We construct the way the world looks, just as we construct a great diversity of ways to represent it visually (Goodman 1976: 6–9). Given such diversity at both ends, Goodman dismisses the claim that there is a constant natural relation that underlies representation. Instead, according to him, the relation of a painting to the objects it represents is mediated by an arbitrary if not conventional symbolic system for reference and predication. What distinguishes this type of system from non-pictorial systems is not the relation of symbol to referent, but the nature of the symbols themselves. Pictorial symbols are syntactically and semantically dense and relatively replete. This means that between any two symbols there exists a third, that almost any difference in the symbols makes for different symbols, different reference, or different predication, and that many properties of the symbols are syntactically and semantically significant.

But all these claims are subject to question, beginning with the plasticity of the visual system and radical diversity in modes of depiction. Many psychological experiments in perception in the 1950s and 1960s attempted to demonstrate the influence on vision of other cognitive and affective factors. They did so typically by creating abnormally difficult viewing times and conditions, so that the influence was probably more on guessing than on perceiving (Vernon 1968). Later theorists tended to correct this bias by emphasizing the invariants in the changing physical array from which depth and other features of the environment are perceived from a very early age. That the visual system is little influenced by other cognitive input is clear from such mundane facts as the persistence of the standard illusions (e.g. Müller–Lyer) despite knowledge of their nature. The evolutionary function of vision and its subordination to the needs of practical behaviour leave little room for art to influence any construction of the visual world.

From the side of representation, while different styles of representational pictures differ in the aspects of visual experience in which they create resemblances and in the degree of such resemblances, and while these differences are certainly aesthetically significant, this does not amount to fundamentally different kinds of symbolic or representational systems. The basic method and hence the analysis remains constant, as is evident from the limits on the degree to which a representational picture can misrepresent or fail to resemble visually its represented objects. If different styles amounted to different symbolic systems, a viewer would need to learn how to read each one and how to correlate the different symbols with the referents—and indeed, Goodman claims we have to learn to read even pictures in perspective (Wollheim 1987; Schier 1986). But in fact, any child can recognize a figure in a Picasso painting, despite the unfamiliarity of the style.

Goodman's differentiating features of pictorial representation, density, and repleteness of the symbols are typical but not definitive, neither separately necessary nor jointly sufficient. One can paint with discrete dots of a limited number of colours, so that the medium is not syntactically dense, which is therefore not a necessary condition for representation. According to Goodman, being pictorial as opposed to diagrammatic is a matter of degree, a matter of the relative repleteness of the symbols (Goodman 1976: 230). But, while the difference does seem to be a matter of degree, degree of resemblance in visual experience seems more crucial than degree of repleteness. We can imagine a contemporary painting in which the shape of the canvas is relevant to what it symbolizes, but it would not be more pictorial for having that additional semantically relevant property (Lopes 1996: 112–13). Nor are these properties jointly sufficient for representation. If we cut up a representational painting into thousands of pieces and shuffled them while providing a code to decipher the result, this resulting puzzle would satisfy Goodman's criteria, but it would not be a pictorial representation (Kulvicki 2000).

Goodman thinks of depiction as akin to the use of languages, absent the relatively fixed conventional rules. The shared features in his view include the use of depiction for reference and predication, and the diversity of pictorial systems, such that we must learn to read each and consider most natural that with which we are most familiar. Some of the disanalogies, however, were indicated above. First noted was the limit to which a depiction can misrepresent its object, a limit set by the need to see the object in the picture, for which resemblance in visual experience is required. There is no such limit to linguistic misdescription, since language can pick out its referents without describing them at all. Some apparent misrepresentation of properties in painting is not representation at all: black and white pictures do not represent precise colours, and only paintings in perspective represent precise three-dimensional shapes and spatial relations. But, unlike language, pictures must accurately represent through sufficient visual resemblance certain properties in order to represent at all. Because of this, one can generally find out better from a picture what an object looks like than from a verbal description.

Second, it was noted that, *pace* Goodman, one need not learn to interpret what a picture that generates visual experience sufficiently similar to its object represents. My son's first word at less than a year old was 'baby', uttered in reaction to a picture, a print of a realistic painting of a baby. While he needed to learn the referent of 'baby', as we all need to learn the correlations of the semantic units of language with their referents, it is very doubtful that he had to learn how to interpret the picture as a representation. Indeed, pictures do not have fixed semantic units, as Goodman himself indicates by describing pictorial symbols as dense and replete. Given this lack, it is hard to see what arbitrary correlations there are to learn. We must be able to pick out both a word and its referent before we can correlate them, but we can recognize objects from their pictures and vice versa without prior access to both.

Third, despite the fact that pictures represent their objects as having certain properties, whether this is best thought of as reference and predication akin to language is open to question, given further disanalogies. The word 'horse', for example, refers to a kind, and 'Secretariat' refers to a particular instance of that kind, the difference between them being clear. But a painting of a horse may not indicate whether it is a particular horse that is represented, and furthermore, it may not be important to an understanding of the painting as a representation.

Goodman's attack on the Platonic account and his contrasting assimilation of pictorial representation to language thus turns out to be mostly misguided. Other contemporary theorists do not directly attack the Platonic account, but they eschew appeal to resemblance, substituting other criteria that, however, turn out to be best explained by appeal to resemblance in visual experience. Wollheim's criterion of 'seeing in' was incorporated into the expanded Platonic criterion above, but it was noted that his 'twofold' seeing is not a universal response to representational painting, and that the ability to see objects in painted surfaces itself causally depends on the resemblance in visual experience. If the experience of a painting does not resemble that of an object, then, no matter how hard we try, we cannot see the object in the painting, although we might imagine it there, or imagine that we are seeing it.

Dominic Lopes holds that recognition of an object in a picture is what is crucial for representation, but that resemblance between the visual experience of a picture and its object depends on such recognition rather than the reverse. It is the latter that then explains representation, not the former (Lopes 1996: 151, 175). He bases this priority claim on examples such as the duck–rabbit figure, where he holds that we notice visual resemblance to a duck (rabbit) only when we recognize the duck (rabbit). According to him, object recognition does not depend on noticed resemblances, since we recognize objects despite changes in the ways they look. Different styles of painting present different aspects of objects on the basis of which they can be recognized, but the overall visual experience of a cubist painting, for example, does not resemble that of the objects it represents.

Once more these claims seem vulnerable to challenge by the defender of the Platonic account. Certainly, the ability to recognize seems to admit of explanation, while the ability to note or react to resemblances seems more primitive. In the duck–rabbit case, for example, we might not consciously note the resemblance in appearance to a duck before we see the figure as such, but this resemblance still seems to explain why we see it as such, as opposed to seeing it as anything else. And, while the overall experience of a cubist painting may not resemble that of the real scene it depicts, parts or aspects of the represented figures must appear like parts of the real figures if these figures are to be recognized or seen in the painting. Finally, when we recognize objects despite changes in their appearances over time, it is plausible that we are able to do so only because we react to invariants or resemblances that persist through these changes.

Similar remarks apply to Flint Schier's suggestion that a picture represents an object when our interpretation of it as a picture of that object depends only on our ability to recognize the object. This is a proper rejection of Goodman's thesis that the relation of representation to object is arbitrary, but once more the triggering of the recognitional capacity by the painting seems to be best explained by the resemblance in visual experience that both generate.

Lastly, Kendall Walton has proposed that a painting depicts an object if it prescribes us to imagine that our experience of looking at it is visual experience of the object. For Walton, a painting, like other representations, is a prop in a game of make-believe. It is fictional that looking at the painting is looking at the objects it represents; that is, we are to imagine that this is the case. It is questionable, however, whether we always do or are supposed to play such imaginative games with paintings, and whether this is the best way to appreciate them. Granting for the moment that it is, pictures that facilitate our playing these imaginative games do so, it seems, by creating visual experience that resembles that of the objects they represent. Without this relation, I suggest, we would not be tempted to imagine that the former *is* the latter.

3. The Continuum of Representation and Other Media

According to ordinary usage, resemblance as well as realism are matters of degree, while representation is not. It seems that a picture either represents objects or it does not, and this point might be used as another Goodmanesque challenge to resemblance accounts. But even if representation does not admit of degrees and resemblance does, the former may still be based on the latter's reaching a certain threshold. And we saw above that Goodman himself rejects the premiss here, accepting that there are degrees of being pictorial or representational. For Goodman pictures shade off at one end into diagrams or maps. We can agree, but hold that at the other end of this continuum are the most realistic (or naturalistic) paintings, defined as those whose represented objects and properties are most easily recognizable. And once more, objects and properties are more easily recognizable in paintings the more closely the visual experience of them resembles that of the depicted objects and properties.

Both this definition of realism and the claim that it depends on resemblance can once more be challenged. It is true that ordinary usage indicates other notions of realistic art. One such notion refers to schools of realism in art whose works present views of the seamier or grittier aspects of life, or of social injustice. This is simply a different concept, compatible with that defined above and irrelevant to our project here. A second alternative holds that a painting is more realistic the more visual information or richness of detail it presents. This notion is not entirely independent of the one defined above, but is not equivalent to it either. Paintings that create visual experience very similar to that of the scene they depict are often those that closely approximate to linear perspective, and we have seen that these can represent precise shapes and spatial relations as other methods of drawing and painting cannot. But engineer's drawings in orthogonal perspective can also present much visual information (although not regarding depth) without striking us as realistic. And while paintings in linear perspective can represent objects of different sizes in equal detail by representing the smaller ones in the foreground, so-called hyperrealistic works present equal detail at all depths of pictorial space at the sacrifice of naturalism.

Patrick Maynard offers an analysis of realism that rejects appeal to resemblance. According to him, a sensorily vivid representation of a property is realistic in regard to that property. In this sense, he maintains, many surrealist paintings are realistic in appearance, although no one is likely ever to encounter such scenes (Maynard 1972: 248). This may be correct with regard to surrealism, but it does not seem to be generalizable. The extraordinarily vivid colours of many medieval paintings do not look particularly natural or realistic. Similarly, linear perspective may provide a vivid sense of depth, as Maynard notes, but one can again exaggerate depth perspective, resulting in a more vivid but less realistic picture. We may also reject Goodman's claim, following from his account of representation, that the most realistic paintings are simply those with which we are most familiar. I am very familiar with Picasso paintings, seeing more of them more often than I see Renaissance paintings, yet the latter continue to look far more realistic.

A bit more might be said about the relation of linear perspective to realism or paradigmatic representation. Linear perspective is one among several systems of spatial projection that map spatial relations in real scenes on to those on the surfaces of pictures. Each can be defined either in terms of the geometry of real space and light rays or in terms of the geometry of the picture surface, and each corresponds to a possible view of the scene depicted (Willats 1997). In linear perspective, the light rays converge to a point behind the picture plane; more distant objects are shown on the surface as smaller, and orthogonals (lines representing edges perpendicular to the picture plane) converge to a vanishing point. In orthogonal projection, rays are parallel and intersect the plane at right angles; there are no orthogonals, and only frontal views of objects are presented (popular in engineers' drawings) (Willats 1997: 12). In oblique projection, objects are shown as the same scale whatever their distance; orthogonals are parallel and run at an oblique angle from the picture surface (popular in oriental painting).

There is no analytic connection between linear perspective and realism, since it is simply an empirical fact that paintings that approximate to linear perspective create visual experience that most closely resembles that of real scenes. And once more, there is only approximation, since smaller canvases require some departure from geometric rules of linear perspective to create similar depth effects, especially, it seems, in the vertical dimension. Nor, even in regard just to shape, is the approximation to linear perspective sufficient for recognizability: there must also be no unusual 'accidental' configurations of lines or edges. But there is a connection, for which there is both ample evidence and explanation. It was noted that these projection systems correspond to possible viewpoints. Linear perspective corresponds to the most common, orthogonal matching to a very distant view magnified, and oblique matching to a distant view at an oblique angle. If the eye corresponds to the projection point, then we are wired to recognize shapes as seen from that point. Artists painting in linear perspective treat the canvas as a transparent plane on to which are inscribed the shapes and spatial relations of the scene as seen from the viewpoint behind the plane. Children who want to produce recognizable shapes gradually learn to draw with lines approximating to such a viewpoint or perspective (Willats 1997: chapter 14). When we judge the realism of a picture, therefore, we interpret it as if it were a picture in approximately linear perspective (Kulvicki 2000: 24); we see whether we can easily recognize the scene as one likely projected in that way.

Once more, the reason linear perspective correlates with realism as the paradigm of representation is that it approximates to a duplication of visual experience of a real scene from a common point of view. John Kulvicki specifies a different property of pictures in linear perspective as crucial in the link with realism, which he calls 'transparency'. Roughly, pictures are transparent when a picture of the original picture generated by the same method as the original looks the same as the original. Pictures in linear perspective are transparent; blurry pictures and cubist paintings are not. But, while this property may be necessary for pictures that look natural or realistic, it is clearly not sufficient. Pictures in orthogonal perspective, for example, are transparent, but they do not look realistic. Ease of recognizability, the mark of realism, remains more closely linked to similarity in visual experience itself.

One might question this three-way connection in light of another kind of representation towards the other end of the realism spectrum but still readily recognizable, namely caricature. Here resemblance seems to be sacrificed to gross exaggeration, while recognizability is yet preserved. But in fact, the connections remain intact once the relevant resemblances are noted. First, it must be pointed out that, while figures are recognizable in caricatures, they are generally more easily recognized in pictures that look natural. Second, since caricatures exaggerate precisely those features by which we distinguish the persons they represent from others, these second-order resemblances in visual experience are preserved; that is, experience of the representations resembles that of the objects in the ways they differ or are differentiated from other objects of the same class.

At one end of the representation continuum are realistic paintings; the other end shades off into diagrams and maps. Sharper lines can be drawn at that end, ones that distinguish representational media such as painting from other media that might be falsely thought to represent, or that do so less typically. Photographs, in particular, *show* objects instead of representing them. As noted, unlike paintings, they cannot represent fictional characters. A photograph of someone playing or representing Hamlet is just that, not a photograph of Hamlet, but any competent painter can do a painting of Hamlet. Similarly, we do not see Moses on a television or cinema screen as we see him in a painting—we see Charlton Heston playing or representing Moses. Thus, strictly speaking, we see objects through or by means of photographs, not in them (Walton 1984). Representing, we noted, is an intentional activity, but intention is relevant to photography only in setting up the crucial causal relation to its object and in the developing and printing processes. For this reason, we interpret paintings and photographs differently. The direction of gazes of a couple in a Manet painting reveals something of their represented relationship, perhaps even something of the human condition as Manet saw it and expressed it in that painting. A photograph of a corresponding real scene would most likely capture only an accidental product of the moment, a transient set of movements, unless the subjects were actors whose poses represented a Manet-type couple (compare Scruton 1981).

We find a similar difference in sound media. We can hear a bird chirping through the radio or a recording. These are mechanical ways of transmitting the sound itself. Only an orchestra following a score *represents* a bird call, i.e. intentionally creates experience resembling that of a bird call. While there are clear cases of representation in music—we hear in some pieces not only birds calling, but also hunting horns, thunder, horses' hoofs, and so on—it is not typical of the artform. Those who think that music is typically representational generally assimilate representation and expression (Walton 1998). But the two are not the same.

An artist represents a concrete (even if fictional) object or individual as having certain properties. It was this structure that led to the otherwise misleading assimilation of representation to reference and predication in language. But when music expresses various emotions, for example, this structure is absent. We can hear exuberance in music, say, but we do not typically hear someone behaving exuberantly in 'pure' music. By contrast, music together with text or programme can represent Till Eulenspiegel, for example, behaving exuberantly or impishly. Sometimes, we noted, a painting too requires a title for its represented subject to be identified, but the difference is that paintings can represent without the aid of titles, texts, or programmes. Pure music is therefore quite limited in its representational capacities, though not in its expressiveness, and when it does represent this is usually not crucial to its formal structure (contrast Kivy 1991). The opposite, we shall see, is the case with painting.

4. VALUE

Plato realized that his account of representation prompted the sceptical question regarding its value, and perhaps this is one reason why Plato's account has been wrongly dismissed. If representation simply imitates the appearance of things, of what value can this be, as opposed, say, to experience of the real things that are represented? Plato naturally saw the imitation as second-best at best, but we clearly value seeing a still life by Cézanne or Van Gogh over seeing a real bowl of fruit or vase of flowers, unless we are starving. There has been far less philosophical literature devoted to this subject than to the nature of representation, but several possible responses to Plato's sceptical question are suggested by the various analyses of representation. Most indicate some value of some representational works, but can be generalized only with difficulty.

First, one might follow Plato in considering representation second-best, but point out that pictures can give us knowledge of things in their absence that is not otherwise obtainable. This is sometimes true, but one might also follow Plato in questioning how valuable knowledge of visual appearances usually is. Certain paintings, especially portraits, aim to reveal something deeper about character by means of conveying visual appearance, and occasionally they succeed; but even most portraits, and even most aesthetically valuable ones, in seeking to avoid capturing only the look of a moment, succeed in capturing only looks that are more bland or artificial than those of most moments in life. In any case, such knowledge cannot be the reason we often value the visual experience of representational art more than that of what is represented. Aristotle gave a different answer, endorsing the aim just mentioned. For him, art does not imitate reality as we find it, but presents an idealized version of the world, aiming to capture the universal in the particular. Once more, however, this appears inessential to great representational art: impressionist painting, for instance, aims precisely to capture the look of the moment.

The accounts of Goodman and Lopes suggest a different purpose and value for representational art. For Goodman, art can change the ways we perceive the world, as language can change the ways we conceive it (Goodman 1976: 241, 260). For Lopes, since pictorial representation triggers recognitional capacities, paintings can extend our recognitional skills (Lopes 1996: 149). In response to Goodman's suggestion, as noted above, the thesis of radical perceptual plasticity is now as discredited as is the older Whorfian hypothesis regarding language. We can be trained to attend to and hence to notice features of things we had previously missed, and this is part of training for aesthetic appreciation, but Goodman seems to have something more striking in mind. And whether art typically trains us to notice real objects more appreciatively is open to question. For most listeners, the ordinary din probably sounds only worse after listening to a Mozart piano concerto, and ordinary bowls of fruit, even if genetically enhanced, only pale in comparison with Cézanne's. In response to Lopes's suggestion, it is difficult to see the value of visual experience that is unlike that of the real world extending our recognitional capacities beyond anything we are likely to encounter in the real world. Realistic paintings, in addition, would lack this capacity, and so their value would remain unexplained.

Kendall Walton's thesis that representations are props in games of make-believe suggests that their value lies in this exercise of the imagination, in imaginatively inserting oneself into the worlds of paintings. But this thesis seems more at home in the realm of literature than in that of visual art. Some paintings, it is true, seem to encourage such games, as when those Manet figures seem to avert their eyes from the viewer as well as from each other. But others positively discourage imagining oneself in their worlds, as do self-portraits in mirrors, for example. And imagining that one is looking at real scenes might distract one's attention from formal, sensuous, and expressive aspects of paintings that are essential for their full appreciation. While realistic paintings facilitate such imagination, artists often intentionally distort their representations for expressive or formal purposes.

The right answer to Plato's question, by contrast, emphasizes this connection of representation to expression, form, and sensuous appeal. Appreciating how representation adds to form by creating tensions and balances among not only colours and shapes, but among objects, figures, weights, depths, movements, gestures, gazes, and so on, how it emerges from form and painterly elements, how it changes the sensuous feel of colours (in flesh tones, for example), how it extends the expressiveness of shapes and colours to that of persons and scenes, how it therefore enables us to see how artists saw other persons and their worlds and conveyed this vision by visual means, is appreciating the value of representation (Goldman 1995; Budd 1995). When all these interrelations are taken into account in viewing representational artworks, it is not hard to see why the experience of a Cézanne still life is potentially much more engaging and rewarding than looking at a bowl of fruit on a table before a curtain. Plato's scepticism about artistic representation is thus refuted.

See also: Expression in Art; Painting; Sculpture; Photography; Style in Art; Art and Knowledge.

BIBLIOGRAPHY

Aristotle (1947). *Poetics*, trans. I. Bywater. New York: Modern Library.
Black, M. (1972). 'How Do Pictures Represent?' in M. Mandelbaum (ed.), *Art, Perception, and Reality*. Baltimore: Johns Hopkins University Press.
Blinder, D. (1986). 'In Defense of Pictorial Mimesis'. *Journal of Aesthetics and Art Criticism* 45: 19–27.
Budd, M. (1992). 'How Pictures Look', in J. Hopkins and A. Savile (eds.), *Psychoanalysis, Mind and Art*. Oxford: Blackwell.
—— (1995). *Values of Art*. London: Penguin, ch. 2.
Danto, A. (2001). 'Seeing and Showing', *Journal of Aesthetics and Art Criticism* 59: 1–10.
Feagin, S. (1998). 'Presentation and Representation'. *Journal of Aesthetics and Art Criticism* 56: 234–40.
Goldman, A. (1995). *Aesthetic Value*. Boulder, Colo.: Westview Press.
Gombrich, E. H. (1960). *Art and Illusion*. New York: Pantheon.
Goodman, N. (1976). *Languages of Art*. Indianapolis: Hackett.
Gregory, R. L. (1964). 'How the Eyes Deceive', in *Frontiers of Knowledge*, Modern World Series. London: HMSO.
Hagen, M. (1986). *Varieties of Realism: Geometries of Representational Art*. Cambridge: Cambridge University Press.
Hopkins, R. (1998). *Picture, Image and Experience*. Cambridge: Cambridge University Press.
Hyman, J. (1989). *The Imitation of Nature*. Oxford: Blackwell.

Hyman, J. (1992). 'Perspective', in D. Cooper (ed.), *Companion to Aesthetics*. Oxford: Blackwell.

Kivy, P. (1991). *Sound and Semblance*. Ithaca, NY: Cornell University Press.

Kulvicki, J. (2000). 'Imagistic Representation: Depiction, Perception, and the Contents of Experience'. Ph.D. dissertation, University of Chicago.

Levinson, J. (1996). *Pleasures of Aesthetics*. Ithaca, NY: Cornell University Press.

——(1998). 'Wollheim on Pictorial Representation'. *Journal of Aesthetics and Art Criticism* 56: 227–33.

Lopes, D. (1996). *Understanding Pictures*. Oxford: Clarendon Press.

Maynard, P. (1972). 'Depiction, Vision, and Convention'. *American Philosophical Quarterly* 9: 243–50.

Neander, K. (1987). 'Pictorial Representation: A Matter of Resemblance'. *British Journal of Aesthetics* 27: 213–26.

Novitz, D. (1977). *Pictures and their Use in Communication*. Dordrecht: Kluwer.

Peacocke, C. (1987). 'Depiction'. *Philosophical Review* 96: 383–410.

Plato (1952). *Dialogues*, trans. B. Jowett. Chicago: Encyclopedia Britannica.

Podro, M. (1998). *Depiction*. New Haven: Yale University Press.

Pole, D. (1974). 'Goodman and the "Naive" View of Representation'. *British Journal of Aesthetics* 14: 68–80.

Robinson, J. (1994). 'Music as a Representational Art', in P. Alperson (ed.), *What is Music?* University Park, Pa.: Pennsylvania State University Press.

Sartwell, C. (1991). 'Natural Generativity and Imitation'. *British Journal of Aesthetics* 31: 58–67.

——(1994). 'What Pictorial Realism Is'. *British Journal of Aesthetics* 34: 2–12.

Schier, F. (1986). *Deeper into Pictures*. Cambridge: Cambridge University Press.

Scruton, R. (1976). 'Representation in Music'. *Philosophy* 51: 273–87.

——(1981). 'Photography and Representation'. *Critical Inquiry* 7: 577–603.

Thouless, R. H. (1931). 'Phenomenal Regression to the Real Object'. *British Journal of Psychology* 21: 339–59.

Tormey, A. and Tormey, J. (1979). 'Seeing, Believing, and Picturing', in C. Nodine and J. Fisher (eds.), *Perception and Pictorial Representation*. London: Praeger.

Vernon, M. D. (ed.) (1968). *Experiments in Visual Perception*. Baltimore: Penguin.

Walton, K. (1984). 'Transparent Pictures'. *Critical Inquiry* 11: 246–77.

——(1990). *Mimesis as Make-Believe*. Cambridge, Mass.: Harvard University Press.

——(1992). 'Seeing-in and Seeing Fictionally', in J. Hopkins and A. Savile (eds.), *Psychoanalysis, Mind and Art*. Oxford: Blackwell.

——(1998). 'Listening with Imagination: Is Music Representational?' in P. Alperson (ed.), *Musical Worlds*. University Park, Pa.: Pennsylvania State University Press.

Willats, J. (1997). *Art and Representation*. Princeton: Princeton University Press.

Wollheim, R. (1980). *Art and Its Objects*, 2nd edn. Cambridge: Cambridge University Press.

——(1987). *Painting as an Art*. Princeton: Princeton University Press.

——(1998). 'On Pictorial Representation'. *Journal of Aesthetics and Art Criticism* 56: 217–26.

CHAPTER 11

EXPRESSION
IN ART

AARON RIDLEY

1. INTRODUCTION

THAT the expression of emotion is among the principal purposes or points of art is
a thought with a pedigree stretching back at least as far as the Ancient Greeks. Nor,
so stated, is it a thought that many have wanted to oppose. Even the staunchest cognitivist or moral improver has granted that expression is *one* of the points of at least
some art, however much he or she may have wanted to insist on the pre-eminence
of other points. Serious disagreement arises only when an attempt is made to say
what is actually meant by 'expression'.

For the purposes of this essay, I want to set up an Everyman figure. He believes what
I imagine more or less anyone would believe upon thinking about artistic expression
for the first or second time. His view is this. As far as the artist is concerned, expressive
art arises because the artist feels something. Perhaps he feels it now, at the moment
of creation; or perhaps he creates out of 'emotion recollected in tranquillity', as
Wordsworth put it; or perhaps he just feels an urge to give vent to something that he
knows is 'in there' somewhere. Whichever of these it is, though, artistic expression
expresses something about the way the artist feels. In expressing what he feels, the artist
creates an object of a certain sort, a work of art—and this object shows in some way
what that feeling is or was. It does this, perhaps, by describing the feeling; or perhaps
it does it by evoking the occasion for the feeling—by being what T. S. Eliot called the

'objective correlative' of the feeling; or perhaps it does it by sharing some property or set of properties with the feeling. However it does it, though, the art object somehow indicates or exhibits what the artist felt. The object that the artist creates is then experienced by an audience. Often, the audience is moved or made to feel things by the object. Perhaps the audience's feelings are directed to the artist (in sympathy, say, or in admiration); or perhaps the audience feels what the artist felt—perhaps, in Leo Tolstoy's words, the audience is 'infected' by the artist's feeling; or perhaps the audience is stirred by the object into feelings entirely its own. Whichever way it is, the experience of an expressive work of art is standardly or frequently a moving one. Taken together, these thoughts capture Everyman's position, or proto-position, perfectly well: artistic expression involves an artist's feeling something, embodying it in his work, and often moving his audience as a result.

Everyman is entirely right, of course—even if his position as it stands is unacceptably vague. I'll try to suggest towards the end of this essay how his position should be taken. But first it will be useful to attribute to him a more problematic way of understanding his view, a way that has a good deal in common, to put it no higher, with at least one canonical position in the literature. Leo Tolstoy, in militantly Christian retirement from writing two of the greatest novels of the nineteenth century, defended the following claim in his short book, *What Is Art?*

To evoke in oneself a feeling one has once experienced and ... then by means of movements, lines, colours, sounds, or forms expressed in words, so to transmit that feeling so that others experience the same feeling—this is the activity of art ... Art is a human activity consisting in this, that one man consciously by means of certain external signs, hands on to others feelings he has lived through, and that others are infected by these feelings and also experience them ... Art is [thus] a means of union among men joining them together in the same feelings ... (Tolstoy 1996: 51)

Tolstoy's statement here is flat and apparently unambiguous. The function of art is to transmit feelings from artist to audience; the role of the artwork is simply that of a conduit through which the artist's feelings, as it were, flow. Elsewhere in *What Is Art?* there are indications that Tolstoy might have had something rather subtler than this in mind, and there are passages in the book that barely make sense except on the assumption that he did have. But for present purposes these details can be put aside. Let us simply take it that Tolstoy did indeed mean what, in the quoted passage, he appears to say.

This way of understanding expression—call it the transmission model—is clearly consistent with Everyman's main intuitions. But he may find on reflection that it offends, or at least grates against, some of his other intuitions. As it stands, the transmission model construes the work of art as a mere vehicle for the feeling transmitted through it, as no more than a means to the end of getting the feeling from the artist to the audience. In principle, then, the work of art could be replaced by anything else that got the feeling through as effectively. If Edvard Munch had been a gifted chemist, for instance, he might, instead of painting *The Scream*, have concocted a drug which produced in those who took it feelings identical to the ones expressed in the picture: *The Scream* need never have been painted.

Everyman's intuitions should begin to rebel at this point, for several reasons. First, the present way of describing things leaves one with no reason at all to value *The Scream* for itself, as a painting. Second, it strikes one as odd to think that any other painting, let alone a drug, could possibly have made available the exact experience to be had from looking at *The Scream*. And third, when one looks at *The Scream*, the anguish one sees is the anguish of *that* face, of *that* figure, captured in just those lines and colours. To think of the anguish as being somehow detachable from what Munch painted would surely be to falsify at least one important aspect of the experience that his picture offers. In each of these respects, it seems, the transmission model construes the relation between the artwork and the feeling it expresses in far too extrinsic and contingent a manner, a thought sometimes put by saying that one cannot, in the end, understand or do justice to a work of art if one insists on treating it simply as an instrument of some kind—for instance, an instrument for conveying feelings from artist to audience.

The transmission model is to be resisted, then. But its shortcomings are instructive, and they tell us quite a lot about what an acceptable way of cashing out Everyman's intuitions would have to look like. Above all, they tell us that an acceptable account of artistic expression must relate the work of art to the feelings expressed in such a way as to make the work's role in expressing those feelings an essential rather than an incidental feature of the sort of communication between artist and audience that artistic expression consists in. In the next three sections I shall attempt to spell out that constraint by considering, first, the relation of artist to expressive artwork, second, the relation of audience to expressive artwork, and third and most briefly, the artwork itself.

2. ARTISTS

It is natural to assign a significant role to artists in artistic expression, and perhaps to do so by extrapolating from the role we assign to people when they express themselves in everyday, non-artistic contexts. When, for instance, we say of someone's face that it expresses pleasure, we ordinarily take it that the pleasure revealed there is the person's own pleasure, and that the expression on their face is to be explained by the pleasure that they feel. In ordinary, non-artistic cases, then, we take the expression to reveal the state of the person, and the state of the person to explain the expression. The temptation is to suppose that the same must be true of artistic expression. The temptation, that is, is to suppose that a work of art expressing anguish both reveals and is to be explained by the artist's own anguish. But things may not be as straightforward as that.

Here is a commonly offered reason why the temptation should be resisted, stated by Peter Kivy in the context of musical expression:

> many, and perhaps most, of our emotive descriptions of music are logically independent of the states of mind of the composers of that music, whereas whether my clenched fist is or is not an expression of anger is logically dependent upon whether or not I am angry. It is unthinkable that I should amend my characterization of the opening bars of Mozart's G-minor Symphony (K.550) as somber, brooding, and melancholy, if I were to discover evidence of Mozart's happiness... during its composition. But that [on the present hypothesis] is exactly what I would have to do, just as I must cease to characterize a clenched fist as an expression of anger if I discover that the fist clencher is not angry. This is a matter of logic. (Kivy 1980: 14–15)

Kivy's point here (following Tormey 1971: 39–62) is partly to distinguish between something's express*ing* an emotion and its being express*ive of* that emotion: in the former case, the expression stands to the state of the person whose expression it is in the kind of relation I sketched out above (it reveals it, and is explained by it), whereas in the second case it does not. In the second case, where something is express*ive of* an emotion (Kivy invites us to think of the sad face of a St Bernard dog), the characterization we offer is 'logically independent' of the state of mind of the person (or dog) whose expression it is. The fact that he would not withdraw his description of the opening bars of Mozart's 40th Symphony upon discovering that its composer was happy when he wrote it, any more than he would withdraw his description of the St Bernard's face as 'sad' upon finding that the dog was cheerful, is taken by Kivy to indicate that musical expression—and artistic expression more generally—must standardly be of this latter, 'logically independent', sort: that such expression is not, in other words, to be understood by simply extrapolating from ordinary, non-artistic cases of expression.

By itself, this argument is hard to assess, since it is unclear how strong the conclusion is meant to be. Specifically, it is unclear what Kivy's talk of logical independence is supposed to amount to. The argument can be read in either of two ways: a weaker, which claims only that artistic expression is *sometimes* 'logically independent' of the state of the artist, and a stronger, which claims that artistic expression is *essentially*, or in its paradigm cases, logically independent of the state of the artist. Let's take the weak reading first (perhaps encouraged by Kivy's remark that it is only 'many, perhaps most', cases that exhibit the logical independence that he has in mind).

Imagine someone who successfully feigns a sombre expression upon hearing of a not wholly unwelcome death. To say that his pretence is successful is to say, first, that his expression does not reveal what he feels, but suggests something else instead, and second, that his expression, although perhaps to be explained by what he feels (by his reluctance to appear callous, say), is not to be explained by his being in the sombre state that his expression indicates. Thus, while his face is certainly expressive of sombreness, it does not express any sombreness of his, since he feels none. Here one might say that his expression is 'logically independent' of his state of mind, and decline to withdraw one's characterization of his face as 'sombre' even once his pretence has been discovered. In saying this, however, one would certainly not be saying that sombre facial expressions are, in general, logically independent of the states of mind of their owners. For what makes pretence of this sort possible is the background of genuine instances of expression against which it takes place. It is only because genuinely sombre people genuinely do look sombre that a feigned sombre expression can be mistaken for one genuinely express*ing* sombreness. In the present case, then, we are dealing with a thoroughly parasitical, atypical instance—one that is atypical precisely in exhibiting a disjunction between facial expression and state of mind. So, whatever degree of logical independence this instance shows, it shows also a background of logical dependence that is both more extensive and logically prior: it shows, that is, that people's expressions are not typically or standardly independent of their states of mind. The question for Kivy is now this: why prefer to assimilate Mozart's G-minor Symphony to a dog than to a person? Why understand the sombre expression of the symphony as analogous to a 'sad' St Bernard's face rather than as analogous to the 'sombre' face of a person who feigns melancholy? Why not suppose, in other words, that the sombreness of the Mozart symphony as written by a happy Mozart points up and exploits a background of sombre music written by sombre composers in exactly the way that the sombre face of the feigner points up and exploits a background of sombre people looking sombre? Kivy offers no reason for his preference. He therefore gives no grounds to believe that musical or artistic expression is 'logically independent' of the states of mind of artists, except, perhaps, in atypical, parasitic cases. The weak reading, then, fails to yield a conclusion of any general significance at all; and it is certainly far too weak to establish the impossibility of understanding artistic expression by extrapolating from ordinary, non-artistic cases of expression.

Despite claiming that it is only 'many, perhaps most', cases that exhibit a 'logical independence' of expression from the artist, it is clear that Kivy really has in mind the stronger reading of his argument: in the remainder of his book he treats 'logical independence' as standard or paradigmatic. It is also clear that, to have a chance of going through, the stronger reading must somehow circumvent the difficulty posed by the expressive feigner. What the stronger reading needs to establish is this: that a happy Mozart could have written a sombre G-minor Symphony even if no sombre music had ever been written by a sombre composer. If this can be established, there will be no warrant for supposing, as one must suppose in the feigning case, that any apparent instance of 'logical independence' really trades for its point on a deeper and logically prior background of dependence. Kivy himself, as I have already said, gives us nothing to go on here. But the claim that there could be sombre art even if none had ever been created by a sombre artist does have a certain prima facie plausibility that any corresponding claim made of feigned facial expressions would, at least on the face of it, lack. It is worth asking why that might be.

The answer, I think, is this. A feigned facial expression of gloom depends upon a background of genuine facial expressions of gloom, where a 'genuine' expression is one that someone wears because he feels gloomy (his expression both reveals his gloom and is explained by it). That much is surely true. But it is easy to move from this thought to a second: that a feigned facial expression depends upon a background, not merely of genuine facial expressions, but of *natural* facial expressions— a slippage, if it is one, perhaps facilitated by the fact that the 'artificial' is opposed to both the 'natural' and the 'genuine'. It is this second thought, which may or may not be true, that is responsible for making it seem as if artistic and everyday expression must be radically different in kind. For art—unlike a person's face, one might say, or its configurations—is artificial, heavily dependent upon convention, and so not, one might think, a 'natural' mode of expression at all. To the extent, then, that expressive feigning depends upon a background of expressive 'naturalness', feigned artistic expression, unlike feigned facial expression, would appear to be impossible; it would therefore also appear—unlike, say, the face of a St Bernard dog—to be of no use in an explanation of how an artist, feeling one thing, might create a work of art expressive of something else. Which seems to put us quite close to the claim made by the strong reading, that artistic expression is essentially, or in its paradigm cases, 'logically independent' of the feelings of artists, and so to the more general claim that artistic expression cannot be understood by extrapolating from ordinary, everyday cases of non-artistic expression.

None of this, in my view, is at all persuasive. If the move from the genuine to the natural is, as I suspect, unwarranted—if, that is, there is no reason to think that expressive feigning depends upon a background of, as it were, naturally genuine expression rather than (merely) genuine expression—then we are no closer than before to the conclusion required by the strong reading. But even if the move *is* warranted—and suppose for a moment that it is—it still could not secure the required conclusion without major additional argumentation. Two things would have to be shown: first, that every kind of ordinary, non-artistic expression that can be feigned is, in the relevant sense, natural; and, second, that no paradigm or standard case of artistic expression is natural in that sense. I strongly doubt that either, and still less both together, could be shown in a non-vacuous way. The first argument, for instance, would have to account for the fact that a good deal of ordinary, everyday—and eminently feignable—expression is linguistic, leaving it to the second argument, presumably, to explain why, if the conventions that define a spoken language are indeed, and despite appearances, 'natural' in the relevant sense, those governing artistic expression are not. Or, to put the point the other way round, if the second argument were to succeed in showing that artistic conventions are somehow conventional 'all the way down', the first argument would have to have shown that no feignable piece of everyday expression is conventional except within certain, permissibly natural, limits. It isn't hard to see how such arguments are bound to degenerate into circular, question-begging exercises in stipulation: the ordinary just *is* the natural; the artistic just *is* the conventional; and so on.

There is nothing in any of this, I suggest, to offer the smallest hope of rescue to the strong reading of Kivy's position. There is nothing, in other words, to encourage the thought that what a work of art expresses is, in the standard or paradigm case, 'logically independent' of the state of the artist. I have laboured this point for a number of reasons, but chief among them has been a concern to head off the idea that, because artistic expression is a special case of expression, it must be a very special case indeed, perhaps even *sui generis*. Nothing in the discussion so far suggests that that is true. And certainly, the mere fact that, as Kivy puts it, 'It is unthinkable that I should amend my characterization of the opening bars of Mozart's G-minor Symphony ... as somber ... if I were to discover evidence of Mozart's happiness ... during its composition' has no such extravagant consequence. Nor, except for the purpose of defusing talk of logical independence, need that fact drive one to wonder whether Mozart might not have been feigning. For the truth is that there is a perfectly ordinary, everyday explanation for Kivy's (quite rightly) declining to withdraw his characterization: that the evidence of the symphony itself trumps whatever imaginary evidence Kivy thinks of himself as discovering—just as, for instance, the publicly manifest evidence of Hitler's megalomania would trump any imagined 'discovery' about his modest, self-effacing nature in private. And, just as no discovery about Hitler's private life would make one think that his megalomania was somehow 'logically independent' of him, so there is no sort of discovery about Mozart—and what could it be? a letter? a diary entry?—that would make plausible the radical splitting off of him from the expressive properties of his work. What Kivy has overlooked, in short, is the homely possibility that an artwork itself may be evidence—and perhaps the best sort of evidence there is—of what an artist really felt (or of what emotional/imaginative state he was in).

The reason that Kivy doesn't take up this possibility, I suspect, is not any deep desire to assimilate Mozart's symphony to a dog's face. It is, rather, a wariness about deflecting appreciative and critical attention away from the work of art, where it belongs, and on to the historical person of the artist. The worry, crudely, is that if one takes a work of art to express—to reveal and to be explained by—an artist's state of mind, then the question 'What is expressed here?' may look as if it has to be answered in the light of evidence about the artist's state of mind, which might have nothing whatever to do with the work of art that he has actually produced. And this worry is fuelled by some of the things that artists have said about what they do. Tolstoy, as we have seen, talks of art as a set of 'external signs' intended to convey to an audience feelings that the artist 'has lived through', so encouraging the thought that the question 'What do these external signs stand for?' is best settled by asking what feelings the artist has, as a matter of fact, lived through. And here is Wordsworth, in the preface to *Lyrical Ballads*: poetry, he says,

takes its origin from emotion recollected in tranquillity: the emotion is contemplated till, by a species of reaction, the tranquillity gradually disappears, and an emotion, kindred to that which was before the subject of contemplation, is gradually produced, and does itself actually exist in the mind. In this mood successful composition generally begins.... (Wordsworth 1995: 23)

And T. S. Eliot in his essay on *Hamlet*:

The only way of expressing emotion in the form of art is by finding an 'objective correlative'; in other words, a set of objects, a situation, a chain of events which shall be the formula of that *particular* emotion; such that when the external facts, which must terminate in sensory experience, are given, the emotion is immediately evoked. (Eliot 1932: 145)

If Wordsworth tempts one to ask not what a poem expresses, but what emotion existed 'in the mind' of the poet before composition of the poem began, then Eliot, in much the same way, tempts one to ask just what the '*particular* emotion' was, for which the artist may or may not have succeeded in finding an 'objective correlative'. Like Tolstoy, Wordsworth and Eliot are here deep inside transmission territory, and so are both in real danger of minimizing or misconstruing the role of the work of art in artistic expression.

To this extent, Kivy is right to be wary of the role assigned in expression to the artist. But what is needed to keep the artist in his place, as it were, is a good deal less than—indeed, just about the opposite of—a demonstration of the logical independence of what a work of art expresses from what an artist felt. What is needed, as we have seen, is simply a reminder of the ordinary, everyday fact that actions speak louder than words—that what one does, how one behaves, reveals how one feels in a way that nothing else can. From the fact that the making of a work of art is standardly a peculiarly rich, reflective and elaborate sort of action, therefore, one should conclude that, standardly, a work of art offers the best possible ('logical') evidence of an artist's state, and so that, standardly, what a work of art expresses reveals that state, and is to be explained by it. This conclusion places the following constraint on any attempt to cash out Everyman's intuitions in a plausible way: that the artist must be seen as present *in* his work, much as a person must be seen as present *in* his behaviour, rather than as separate from it, behind it, or, above all, as 'logically independent' of it.

3. AUDIENCES

Everyman's proto-position envisages artistic expression as involving an audience's being moved in some way. There is at least one thing that he had better not mean by this. He had better not mean that a work of art expresses whatever it makes its audience feel. Many considerations point to this prohibition, but the following is the simplest and most direct: a work of art can make one feel X precisely because one recognizes that it expresses Y, where X and Y are different. Suppose I feel an odd sense of uplift upon looking at *The Scream* (things could be worse); nothing in this makes *The Scream* expressive of such uplift. No more than in an ordinary, everyday case of expression, then, is what is felt by a witness of an expression to be taken, automatically, as what is expressed. (Your expression of gladness might sadden me, after all.) If an audience's feelings are indeed involved in artistic expression, then their involvement is going to have to be accounted for in some more subtle way than this.

It is possible, of course, that the proper response to the role of audiences' feelings in artistic expression is one of scepticism. One might acknowledge that people are, as a matter of fact, frequently moved by the experience of expressive art, and yet still deny that this has any significance for an understanding of artistic expression. It may be, for instance, that what a person feels upon experiencing a particular work of art is determined in some way by the associations that that work has for him: so, for example, Beethoven's 6th Symphony makes someone feel vulnerable because it reminds him of his nanny, while *Apocalypse Now* makes him smirk because he remembers what went on in the back row when he first saw it. In cases such as this, it is clear that the person's responses, however significant they may be for him, are altogether extrinsic to any issues concerning the expressive characteristics of the works that occasion them, and so are irrelevant to any attempt to understand artistic expression.

The same may be true, if somewhat less obviously, in a different kind of example. It may be the case, as a number of people have argued (see e.g. Feagin 1996), that, unless one's experience of a given work of art is coloured and informed by one's emotional responses to it, one will not be in a position fully to understand it. So, for instance, it might plausibly be suggested that a person at a good performance of *King Lear* who was not appalled by Gloucester's blinding would have failed to appreciate the true character of the events portrayed. If this is right, it would suggest that a certain kind of emotional engagement may be essential to some kinds of aesthetic appreciation. But nothing in the example shows that such engagement or response need have any bearing on expression specifically. It may well be, in other words, that audiences are moved in a host of diverse and valuable ways by expressive works of art without that fact being such as to contribute to an understanding of artistic expression. To the extent that that is the case, Everyman's intuitions about audiences will have to be set aside.

How, then, might a place be secured in an account of expression for an audience's responses? The foregoing suggests this: what an audience feels will be relevant to an account of artistic expression, first, if what it feels is related in some intrinsic way to what a work of art expresses, and, second, if its feeling that way is essential to its grasping the feeling expressed by the work. The first requirement rules out the second and third of the cases just discussed. Not only are responses based on private association not intrinsically related to what works of art express, they are not intrinsically related to works of art in any way at all; while responses that help one to see what a work is about, although related in the right sort of way to the work of art, need not be related to it as an expressive object. The second requirement serves, among other things, to rule out the example discussed at the beginning of this section. My imagined response of uplift is certainly intrinsically related to *The*

Scream's expression of anguish: but I need not feel uplifted in order to grasp the anguish expressed there. But the second requirement is also meant to do more. It is meant to rule out the following kind of possibility.

Suppose that whenever I experience an expressive work of art I feel the feelings it expresses. I feel anguish whenever I look at *The Scream*, for example, and am seized by a sombre, brooding melancholy whenever I listen to the opening bars of Mozart's G-minor Symphony. I am, in fact, exactly the sort of person that Tolstoy has in mind: I am invariably 'infected' by the feelings that works of art express. There is no question here that my responses satisfy the first requirement. I feel what I feel because of the feelings expressed in the works. But nothing in the example as it stands suggests that this fact about me, however much it might make my aesthetic experiences interesting or intense, is integral to an analysis of artistic expression. There are two reasons for this. First, my response may be peculiar to me; it may, in the end, be no less idiosyncratic to respond in this way than to respond on the basis of private association. So no conclusions of a general sort about expression can be drawn from the fact that that is how my responses are. Second, there is no reason to think that someone who responded differently, or who did not respond by feeling at all, would be missing anything. Their experience of expressive art would not be the same as mine, but that shows nothing about their capacity to notice or appreciate the features of artworks to which I respond by feeling what they express. This example, therefore, fails to satisfy the second requirement set out above—that what an audience feels must be essential to its grasping what an artwork expresses.

The only way in which an audience's responses can possibly be integral to an analysis of artistic expression, therefore, is if at least some of those responses are integral to grasping at least some of what, or at least some aspects of what, works of art can express. This is effectively to envisage a corollary of the position outlined in the previous section: a kind of response that (i) reveals the expressive properties of a work for what they are, and (ii) is explained by the work's having those properties. The idea here is close to something John Dewey once said:

Bare recognition is satisfied when a proper tag or label is attached, 'proper' signifying one that serves a purpose outside the act of recognition—as a salesman identifies wares by a sample. It involves no stir of the organism, no inner commotion. But an act of perception proceeds by waves that extend serially throughout the entire organism. There is, therefore, no such thing in perception as seeing or hearing *plus* emotion. The perceived object or scene is emotionally pervaded throughout. (Dewey 1980: 55–6)

To respond without feeling might be to 'recognize' certain of a work's expressive properties; but to grasp those properties in their full richness and particularity is to 'perceive' them. A position of this general sort has been gestured towards recently by a number of writers, most often perhaps in the context of musical expression. So, for instance, Malcolm Budd has suggested that an imaginative engagement with music can enable 'the listener to experience imaginatively (or really) the inner nature of emotional states in a peculiarly vivid, satisfying and poignant form' (Budd 1995: 154); Jerrold Levinson has remarked that perceiving 'emotion in music and experiencing emotion from music may not be as separable in principle as one might have liked. If this is so, the suggestion that in aesthetic appreciation of music we simply cognize emotional attributes without feeling anything corresponding to them may be conceptually problematic as well as empirically incredible' (Levinson 1982: 335); and Roger Scruton has pointed out that 'there may be a sense of "what it is like"... When I see a gesture from the first person point of view then I do not only see it as an expression; I grasp the completeness of the state of mind that is intimated through it' (Scruton 1983: 96, 99) (see also Ridley 1995: 120–45, and Walton 1997: 57–82).

There is little consensus in the current literature about the significance, or even the possibility, of such responses. Many prefer to regard an audience's feeling as essentially independent of the feelings expressed by artworks, and so as incidental to any account of artistic expression. The discussion in the present section suggests that that position is considerably more plausible than its analogue concerning the feelings of artists. For what it's worth, though, I want to cleave to Everyman's position. Just as I may sometimes have to put myself in your shoes—try to feel the expression on your face from the inside, as it were—in order to grasp how things really are with you, so, it seems to me, I sometimes get the full expressive point of a work of art only by responding emotionally to it—by resonating with it, even. Again, then, I am inclined to think that extrapolation from ordinary, everyday cases of expression is the most promising way of attempting to understand artistic expression.

4. ARTWORKS

I argued in the introductory section that an acceptable account of artistic expression must relate a work of art to the feelings expressed there in such a way as to make the work's role in expressing those feelings an essential rather than an incidental feature of the transaction between artist and audience. With respect to the artist, this comes to the thought that, in standard cases, the expressive properties of a work of art both reveal the artist's state and are to be explained by it. With respect to the audience the position is perhaps less clear, but I have suggested that, in certain cases at least, the expressive properties of a work of art are both revealed by, and explanatory of, the responses of an audience.

These considerations give us a good overall indication of what is required in order to make Everyman's position a plausible account of artistic expression. They also, of course, tell us the kinds of things that need to be said about artworks in such an account, namely, that artworks must be understood as objects having expressive properties capable of revealing and of being explained by the feelings of artists and (perhaps) of explaining and of being revealed by the feelings of audiences. Beyond that, however, there is very little of a general nature to be said. The various forms of art differ hugely from one another in the kinds of resources they make available for artistic manipulation, and so differ hugely from one another in the kinds of property that, in one context or another, can be expressive, and in what way. At this point, then, the attempt to arrive at a full understanding of artistic expression must devolve on to the theories of the individual arts, where, for instance, one might give an account of the expressive nature of dance by relating the gestures it contains to the gestures of human beings when they express their feelings; or one might give an account of the expressive nature of certain paintings by appealing to atmosphere or ambience—to features that have an expressive charge whether in or out of art; or one might give an account of the expressive nature of music by relating its movements to the movements of people in the grip of this or that feeling—for example rapid, violent music for frenzy or for rage; or one might give an account of the expressive nature of poetry by highlighting locutions or rhythms that are characteristic of ordinary, spoken expressions of feeling; and so on. The problems and possible solutions are quite distinct for each of the various arts, even if, with respect to each of them, one is essentially trying to answer the same questions: in virtue of what features is this artwork expressive? And: what is it that someone might attend to, recognize, or perceive in a work of this kind that would lead him to characterize it in expressive terms?

5. EXPRESSION PROPER

So how, finally, might Everyman's proto-position be filled out so as to give a satisfactory—and suitably general—account of artistic expression? The answer, it seems to me, lies in R. G. Collingwood's treatment of the issue in his wonderful, though wonderfully uneven, book, *The Principles of Art*.

Collingwood's basic claim is that what is involved in artistic expression is nothing more than what is involved in ordinary, everyday instances of expression. Indeed, he goes so far at one point as to say that 'Every utterance and every gesture that each one of us makes is a work of art' (1938: 285); and this, while surely overstating the case, is indicative of the seriousness with which he takes the continuity between the artistic and the non-artistic. For him, the purpose of expression—in or out of art—is self-knowledge. One finds out what one thinks or feels by giving expression to it. At the beginning of the process of expression, Collingwood holds, the artist knows almost nothing of what he feels:

all he is conscious of is a perturbation or excitement, which he feels going on within him, but of whose nature he is ignorant. While in this state, all he can say about his emotion is

'I feel...I don't know what I feel.' From this helpless and oppressed condition he extricates himself by doing something which we call expressing himself. (Collingwood 1938: 109)

The artist attempts to extricate himself from his 'helpless and oppressed condition', then, by trying to answer the question 'What *is* it I feel?' When he first asks this question, there is no answer to be given: his state is inchoate, and nothing specific can be said about it. If he is successful in his efforts, however, the question eventually receives its answer, and this is given in the expression that the artist produces. The feeling that the artist expresses, therefore, is both clarified and transformed in the process of being expressed, so that 'Until a man has expressed his emotion, he does not yet know what emotion it is' (Collingwood 1938: 111); which is why 'the expression of emotion is not [something] made to fit an emotion already existing, but is an activity without which the experience of emotion cannot exist' (1938: 244). On this account, then, an emotion is not so much revealed for what it is by receiving expression: it *becomes* what it is by receiving expression.

The emotion becomes what it is through being given form, through being developed into something specific. In this way, the fully formed emotion and the expression it receives are indistinguishable from one another—indeed, they are one and the same: it is in virtue of having been given *that* form that the emotion is the emotion it is. It follows from this that the identity of an emotion expressed in a work of art is inextricably linked to the identity of the work of art. There is no possibility, in other words, of regarding the emotion expressed as something essentially detachable from the work in which it is manifest; there is no possibility, that is, of thinking of the emotion expressed as something that might just as well have been expressed in some other way or in some other work of art (or captured, indeed, in some chemist's cocktail).

Collingwood's insistence on this point marks his position off in the strongest way from that of the transmission theorists (with whom he has been oddly often confused); and he develops the point further: 'Some people have thought,' he says, that

a poet who wishes to express a great variety of subtly differentiated emotions might be hampered by the lack of a vocabulary rich in words referring to the distinctions between them...This is the opposite of the truth. The poet needs no such words at all...To describe a thing is to call it a thing of such and such a kind: to bring it under a conception, to classify it. Expression, on the contrary, individualises. (Collingwood 1938: 112)

Expression, then, distinguishes between feelings that might be described in exactly the same terms as one another, and transforms them into the highly particularized feelings we encounter in successful works of art:

The artist proper is a person who, grappling with the problem of expressing a certain emotion, says, 'I want to get this clear.' It is of no use to him to get something else clear, however like it this other thing may be. He does not want a thing of a certain kind, he wants a certain thing. (Collingwood 1938: 114)

Description, by contrast, would yield only 'a thing of a certain kind'. The distinction between expression and description, therefore, between arriving at 'a certain thing' and arriving at 'a thing of a certain kind', serves both to make a point that is important in itself and also to emphasize the distance between Collingwood's conception of what an artist expresses and the conceptions suggested in the remarks of Tolstoy, Wordsworth, and Eliot considered earlier. Tolstoy's 'feeling' that an artist 'has lived through', Wordsworth's emotion 'actually exist[ing] in the mind', and Eliot's *particular emotion* are each, because construed as graspable independently of the work of art in which they are to be expressed, the stuff of description; not one of them is more than 'a thing of a certain kind'.

On Collingwood's account, the artist arrives at self-knowledge in the relevant sense when he succeeds in transforming an unformed jumble of unclarified feeling into 'a certain thing'. The fact that he does not—cannot—specify in advance what that thing is to be is not an indication that the business of expressing oneself is somehow random or accidental:

There is certainly here a directed process: an effort, that is, directed upon a certain end; but the end is not something foreseen and preconceived, to which an appropriate means can be thought in the light of our knowledge of its special character. (Collingwood 1938: 111)

Knowledge of its 'special character' is precisely the end upon which that process is directed. The artist feels his way; he says to himself 'This line won't do' (Collingwood 1938: 283), until, at last, he gets it right, and can say 'There—that's it! *That's* what I was after.' Nor is this kind of 'directed process' an unusual one, special in some way to the creative artist. It is an entirely familiar and everyday sort of process. Anyone who struggles to say clearly what he means, for example, is engaged in it: the struggle is directed to the end of clarifying a thought; but until the struggle has been won, no one, including the person doing the struggling, can say what, precisely, that thought is—if he *could* say what it was, the process of expression would already have been completed (an insight that Collingwood owes to Croce, 1922). This is perhaps the most significant of the ways in which Collingwood regards artistic expression as continuous with ordinary, everyday acts of expression: both may be deliberate, yet neither aims at an independently specifiable goal.

It will be apparent that Collingwood's account as I have sketched it here exactly satisfies the requirements outlined in the above section on artists. It is because the artist has succeeded in expressing himself that the work of art has the expressive character it does have; and the artist's emotion is revealed, uniquely, for the 'certain thing' it is by the expressive character of the work he produces. Collingwood also intends to satisfy the requirements relating to audiences, although his efforts here are expectedly more equivocal. He insists, for instance, that artists and audiences are in 'collaboration' with one another: the artist treats 'himself and his audience in the same kind of way; he is making his emotions clear to his audience, and that is what he is doing to himself.' And he cites approvingly Coleridge's remark that 'we know a man for a poet by the fact that he makes us poets', suggesting that when 'someone reads and understands a poem, he is not merely understanding the poet's expression of his, the poet's, emotions, he is expressing emotions of his own in the poet's words, which have thus become his own words' (Collingwood 1938: 118). These thoughts culminate in the following passage: no man, he says, is 'a self-contained and self-sufficient creative power'. Rather, 'in his art as in everything else',

[man] is a finite being. Everything that he does is done in relation to others like himself. As artist, he is a speaker; but a man speaks as he has been taught; he speaks the tongue in which he was born . . . The child learning his mother tongue . . . learns simultaneously to be a speaker and to be a listener; he listens to others speaking and speaks to others listening. It is the same with artists. They become poets or painters or musicians not by some process of development from within, as they grow beards; but by living in a society where these languages are current. Like other speakers, they speak to those who understand. (Collingwood 1938: 316–17)

If these comments, taken together, do not quite add up to a picture in which an audience's feelings reveal and are to be explained by the expressive character of the artwork that prompts them, they do at least come close; and it is certainly consistent with Collingwood's overall account that he should have endorsed such a picture. It is hard, after all, to see what else he might have had in mind when he said that some-one might express 'emotions of his own in [a] poet's words, which have thus become his own words'.

Collingwood's account of artistic expression represents a rather full working out of Everyman's proto-position within the constraints that I have outlined. The expressive artist is indeed seen as present *in* his work, rather than as standing, complete with his independently specifiable feelings, *behind* his work; and the responsive audience, in discovering what Collingwood calls 'the secrets of their own hearts' *in* his work (1938: 336), are plausibly to be construed as feeling what they feel *because of* the work, and as grasping what the work expresses *because of* those feelings. Consistently with the generality of his account, moreover, Collingwood has very little to say in addition about artworks and their specific expressive properties. A defence of his reticence on this score has been provided in Section 4 above.

6. CONCLUSION

It has sometimes been claimed that expression is definitive of art, usually by a band of so-called Expression Theorists, discussed under that label in the secondary literature. Tolstoy is one of these, and so is Collingwood. The secondary literature stand-ardly goes on to refute the 'Expression Theory' allegedly espoused by marshalling a set of counter-examples to show that something can be a work of art without being in the least expressive. It is possible that this tactic is effective against Tolstoy. He certainly appears to think that art can be defined as expression, and to think so, the ambiguities of his position notwithstanding, in a way that makes him at least apparently vulnerable to the sort of counter-example usually offered. Collingwood, however, is immune to this tactic. He does identify art with expression: 'art proper', as he calls it, simply *is* expression. But when one recalls that what he means by this is that 'art proper' is the clarification of an artist's thoughts and feelings—that a work of 'art proper' is 'a certain thing' rather than 'a thing of a certain kind'—the character of his position becomes plain. What works of 'art proper' have in common is that they are indeed expressions: but this is just to say that their common feature is that each one is, uniquely, what it is—and beyond that, if the position outlined here is right, there is nothing more of a general character to be said. That this conclusion follows from Collingwood's version of Everyman's account of expression in art strikes me as yet another reason to think very highly of it.

See also: Art and Emotion; Art and Knowledge; Value in Art; Music.

BIBLIOGRAPHY

Arnheim, R. (1998). 'The Expression and Composition of Color'. *Journal of Aesthetics and Art Criticism* 56: 349–52.

Barwell, I. (1986). 'How Does Art Express Emotion?' *Journal of Aesthetics and Art Criticism* 45: 175–81.

Benson, J. (1967). 'Emotion and Expression'. *Philosophical Review* 76: 335–57.

Bouwsma, O. K. (1954). 'The Expression Theory of Art', in W. Elton (ed.), *Aesthetics and Language*, Oxford: Blackwell.

Budd, M. (1985). *Music and the Emotions: The Philosophical Theories*. London: Routledge & Kegan Paul.

——— (1995). *Values of Art*. London: Allen Lane.

Carroll, N. (1997). 'Art, Narrative and Emotion', in M. Hjort and S. Laver (eds.), *Emotion and the Arts*. Oxford: Oxford University Press.

Casey, E. (1970). 'Expression and Communication in Art'. *Journal of Aesthetics and Art Criticism* 30: 197–207.

Collingwood, R. G. (1938). *The Principles of Art*. Oxford: Oxford University Press.

Croce, B. (1922). *Aesthetic*, rev. edn, trans. D. Ainslie. London: Macmillan. First published 1902.

Davies, S. (1994). *Musical Meaning and Expression*. Ithaca, NY: Cornell University Press.

Dewey, J. (1980). *Art as Experience*. New York: Perigee Books.

Eliot, T. S. (1932). *Selected Essays*. London: Faber.

Elliott, R. K. (1967). 'Aesthetic Theory and the Experience of Art'. *Proceedings of the Aristotelian Society* 67: 111–26.

Feagin, S. (1996). *Reading with Feeling*. Ithaca, NY: Cornell University Press.

Ferguson, D. (1960). *Music as Metaphor: The Elements of Expression*. Minneapolis: University of Minnesota Press.

Goodman, N. (1976). *Languages of Art*. Indianapolis: Hackett Press.

Gombrich, E. (1962). 'Art and the Language of the Emotions'. *Proceedings of the Aristotelian Society*, supp. vol. 36: 215–34.

Karl, G. and Robinson, J. (1995). 'Shostakovich's Tenth Symphony and the Musical Expression of Cognitively Complex Emotions'. *Journal of Aesthetics and Art Criticism* 53: 401–15.

Kivy, P. (1980). *The Corded Shell: Reflections on Musical Expression*. Princeton: Princeton University Press.

—— (1990). *Music Alone*. Ithaca, NY: Cornell University Press.

—— (2001). *New Essays on Musical Understanding*. Oxford: Oxford University Press.

Langer, S. (1953). *Feeling and Form*. London: Routledge & Kegan Paul.

Levinson, J. (1982). 'Music and Negative Emotion'. *Pacific Philosophical Quarterly* 63: 327–46.

—— (1990). 'Hope in *The Hebrides*', in his *Music, Art, and Metaphysics*. Ithaca, NY: Cornell University Press.

—— (1996). 'Musical Expressiveness', in his *The Pleasures of Aesthetics*. Ithaca, NY: Cornell University Press.

Matravers, D. (1998). *Art and Emotion*. Oxford: Oxford University Press.

Nolt, J. (1981). 'Expression and Emotion'. *British Journal of Aesthetics* 21: 139–50.

Osborne, H. (1982). 'Expressiveness in the Arts'. *Journal of Aesthetics and Art Criticism* 41: 19–26.

Petock, S. (1972). 'Expression in Art: The Feelingful Side of Aesthetic Experience'. *Journal of Aesthetics and Art Criticism* 30: 297–309.

Ridley, A. (1995). *Music, Value and the Passions*. Ithaca, NY: Cornell University Press.

—— (1998). *R. G. Collingwood: a Philosophy of Art*. London: Orion Books.

Robinson, J. (1994). 'The Expression and Arousal of Emotion in Music'. *Journal of Aesthetics and Art Criticism* 52: 13–22.

Scruton, R. (1974). *Art and Imagination*. London: Routledge & Kegan Paul.

—— (1983). *The Aesthetic Understanding*. London: Methuen.

—— (1997). *The Aesthetics of Music*. Oxford: Oxford University Press.

Sircello, G. (1972). *Mind and Art: An Essay on the Varieties of Expression*. Princeton: Princeton University Press.

Stecker, R. (2001). 'Expressiveness and Expression in Music and Poetry'. *Journal of Aesthetics and Art Criticism* 59: 85–96.

Tolstoy, L. (1996). *What Is Art?* trans. A. Maude. Indianapolis: Hackett Press.

Tormey, A. (1971). *The Concept of Expression*. Princeton: Princeton University Press.

Trivedi, S. (2001). 'Expressiveness as a Property of the Music Itself'. *Journal of Aesthetics and Art Criticism* 59: 411–20.

Vermazen, B. (1986). 'Expression as Expression'. *Pacific Philosophical Quarterly* 67: 196–224.

Walton, K. (1988). 'What is Abstract about the Art of Music?' *Journal of Aesthetics and Art Criticism* 46: 351–64.

—— (1997). 'Listening with Imagination: Is Music Representational?' in J. Robinson (ed.), *Music and Meaning*. Ithaca, NY: Cornell University Press.

Wollheim, R. (1993). 'Correspondence, Projective Properties and Expression in the Arts', in his *The Mind and its Depths*. Cambridge, Mass.: Harvard University Press.

Wordsworth, W. (1995). Preface to *Lyrical Ballads*, in A. Neill and A. Ridley (eds.), *The Philosophy of Art: Readings Ancient and Modern*. New York: McGraw-Hill.

CHAPTER 12

....

STYLE IN ART

....

STEPHANIE ROSS

1. INTRODUCTION

....

IN everyday contexts, we often contrast style with substance. Style pertains to surface appearance, or to a way of doing things. We notice the style of someone who dresses well, or unusually, or of someone who navigates trying social situations with ease and grace. Style can also be appropriated from other classes or cultures; a recent newspaper series, 'How Race is Lived in America', discussed white teenagers taking on the hip-hop style. In all these cases, style seems somewhat trivial, its singleminded pursuit morally questionable, since those cultivating style may be neglecting 'deeper', more important concerns.

In the arts, style is of greater moment. Knowing the style of a work of art is a prerequisite to correct understanding and appreciation of it. Only after first placing a work in the correct style category can we answer interpretive questions about its tone, its representational and expressive content, its overall meaning. Knowledge of style is also crucial for tracking a work's origins. Here in the West, we are inordinately interested in knowing who created a given work. As a limiting case, consider the 'scientific connoisseurship' of Giovanni Morelli, who employed subtle stylistic markers in making attributions of Italian Renaissance paintings. But even viewers without such special acumen use judgements of style to place particular works of art. Thus, accounts of style inform interpretation and appreciation; they also have a bearing on prior philosophical debates about authenticity, creativity, aesthetic qualities, and the status of art.

Some of the definitions of style proposed by historians and philosophers indicate the importance of this concept for the realm of art. Meyer Schapiro began his essay

'Style' with the observation: 'By style is usually meant the constant form—and sometimes the constant elements, qualities, and expression—in the art of an individual or a group' (Schapiro 1994: 51), while Ernst Gombrich began an encyclopedia entry on the topic with the remark: 'Style is any distinctive, and therefore recognizable, way in which an act is performed or an artefact made or ought to be performed and made' (Gombrich 1968: 352). In 'The Status of Style', Nelson Goodman stated succinctly 'style consists of those features of the symbolic functioning of a work that are characteristic of author, period, place, or school' (Goodman 1978: 35). Writing on the visual arts, James Ackerman noted: 'We use the concept of style...as a way of characterizing relationships among works of art that were made at the same time and/or place, or by the same person or group' (Ackerman 1962: 227); while Leonard Meyer, writing on the art of music, declared that 'Style is a replication of patterning, whether in human behavior or in the artifacts produced by human behavior, that results from a series of choices made within some set of constraints' (Meyer 1989: 3).

The work of two contemporary philosophers in particular, Nelson Goodman and Richard Wollheim, has done much to clarify our understanding of style and of the complex issues with which style becomes intertwined. The discussion below will be focused through the lens of their proposals. In 'The Status of Style', Goodman emphasizes that 'Style comprises certain characteristic features both of what is said and of how it is said, both of subject and of wording, both of content and of form' (Goodman 1978: 27). This is an important corrective to the temptation to take style as entirely constituted by formal or surface qualities. Goodman makes his point with examples drawn from nonfiction: 'Suppose one historian writes in terms of military conflicts, another in terms of social changes; or suppose one biographer stresses public careers, another personal lives' (Goodman 1978: 25). But this serves to remind us, for example, that Henry James's focus on the nuanced responses of American expatriates in Europe at the dawn of the twentieth century, and Watteau's attention to the outdoor amusements of a privileged class of eighteenth-century French aristocrats, are essential to their respective styles. Of course, Goodman's point applies primarily to the 'contentful' arts—representational paintings, plays, traditional novels and films, and so on—as opposed to arts like music and architecture which possess a less clear subject matter or narrative dimension. In the end, Goodman endorses a trio of symbolic capacities—denotation, exemplification, and expression—as constitutive of style (Goodman 1978: 32).

2. General Style

Richard Wollheim's distinction between *general* and *individual* style, enunciated in the lecture 'Style Now' and the paper 'Pictorial Style: Two Views', proposes that universal styles, period styles, and school styles are quite different in kind from the styles of individual artists. Wollheim offers classicism, art nouveau, social realism, and the school of Giotto as examples of general style. Others might include the 'grand style' in eighteenth-century painting promoted by Joshua Reynolds, the Augustan style adopted by Alexander Pope in his epic poetry, and the *nouvelle vague* style developed by French auteur film-makers in the 1970s. Not all artists work in a general style (though most artists acknowledge the conventions of the artworld of their time), but Wollheim insists that any artist of merit possesses an individual style. Wollheim deems general style 'taxonomic'. By this he means that it is determined by identifying shared features of the set of works in question. Art historians from later times can re-direct our attention to a different set of manifest features, thus altering our general stylistic categorizations. Determinations of individual style are not, for Wollheim, similarly malleable.

Once the notion of style is demarcated in this way, some perplexing questions arise. On the one hand, it seems natural to wonder why any work, or any artist, should possess a distinctive style. Why should works reveal their origins, or artists' creations cluster so as to generate genealogies? On the other hand, there is a contrary way of thinking that makes the possession of style seem inevitable overall, the style of any particular work inescapable. This latter view is a sort of stylistic determinism. Such a line of thinking sees general style as necessitated by each culture, individual style by the psyche of each artist. In 'Style', Meyer Schapiro discusses some of the German art historians who were drawn to a deterministic account of general style (Schapiro 1994: 69–81). Thinking about the history of visual art in the West, and especially the parallels between the Greek and the Renaissance Italian artworlds, these scholars posited a cyclical account of the history of art, one that saw recurring patterns in which an archaic art gave way to a classical phase, which in turn surrendered to decadence, preparing the way for a renewal of the entire cycle on fresh terms. Heinrich Wolfflin's analysis of European art in terms of the oppositional categories linear/painterly, parallel/diagonal, closed/open, composite/fused, and clear/unclear is one example of a history of art that subscribes to stylistic determinism of this sort (Wolfflin 1950). Another is Paul Frankl's account, which, Schapiro explains, 'postulates a recurrent movement between two poles of style—a style of Being and a style of Becoming—but within each of these styles are three stages: a preclassic, a classic, and a postclassic . . . [This] scheme is not designed to describe the actual historical development . . . but to provide a model or ideal plan of the inherent or normal tendencies of development, based on the nature of forms' (Schapiro 1994: 71, 72).

There are many grounds for rejecting cyclical accounts of art history. Usually such schemes do not embrace the entirety of Western art. Wolfflin's theory, for example, accommodates neither Mannerism nor modern art. There is also good reason to reject cultural determinisms like that underlying Herder's theory of *klima*, according to which all aspects of the physical environment—climate, atmosphere, geography, as well as dwellings, clothing, food and drink—mould personality, culture, and qualities of thought. Gombrich offers a wonderful example of the excesses of such views in this remark from Austrian architect Adolf Loos: 'If nothing were left of an extinct race but a single button, I would be able to infer, from the shape of that button, how these people dressed, built their houses, how they lived, what was their religion, their art, and their mentality' (Gombrich 1968: 358). Surely this boast requires at the very least the truth of the Doctrine of Internal Relations! Detractors of cyclical theories might opt instead for an evolutionary model. This would retain the teleology of the theories just mentioned, but cancel any commitment to regular return. A theory of general style that Schapiro deems evolutionary rather than cyclical is that of Alois Riegl, who posited a development from the haptic (tactile) to the optic (visual) in the history of European art. Schapiro notes that Riegl's theory sits on a base of Hegelian meta-physics, which of course supports the teleological thrust of his account, but might taint it for many contemporary readers not sympathetic to Hegel's notion of the world soul. One aspect of Riegl's theory that Svetlana Alpers singles out for praise is its attention to more 'marginal' works such as ancient textiles and late antique art. Yet Alpers criticizes all those approaches that privilege one brief moment in the history of world art—the Italian Renaissance—and thus generalize from a single and uncharacteristic case. She prefers a view of the history of art in terms of multiple modes rather than one tracing a single genealogy of style (Alpers 1990: 101, 114).

Art historian James Ackerman, in his essay 'A Theory of Style', tried to formulate an alternative to the historically determinist accounts of style just surveyed. His solution was to construe the creation of art as an exercise in problem-solving. Rather than being buffeted by the forces of cyclical or evolutionary tides, artists, according to Ackerman, conceive of their efforts in terms of questions to answer or problems to solve. The course of art history then turns on the creative power of these individuals, the degree to which they provide answers or solutions outside of the boundaries their predecessors had set. Ackerman's approach posits 'confluent, overlapping, and interacting styles in place of a cyclical-evolutionary one', in keep-ing with his primary aim to 'explain change in style as the manifestation rather of the imagination of individual artists than of historical forces' (Ackerman 1962: 236, 233). The appearance of cycles in art history is then explained away simply as inevitable convergence, as similar technical problems are solved in successive soci-eties, each pursuing the goal of increased refinement.

In thinking of general style and its evolution over time, it is important to note that the significance of any given feature is contextually limned. We cannot cor-rectly interpret it unless we know the options that were available to the artist, the repertoire from which it was selected. ('Repertoire' is Wollheim's term, used to summarize Gombrich's argument in Chapter XI of *Art and Illusion*: see Wollheim 1968: sects. 28–31.) An archaic treatment of the human figure means one thing in a prehistoric fertility figure or a Greek kouros from the sixth century BC, quite another in a sculpture by Gaston Lachaise or Henry Moore. Danto (1981: 44) quotes

Wolfflin's claim that not everything is possible at every time; and indeed, there are always causal stories to tell about a given artworld. The work of previous artists, present conventions, available materials and techniques, and the interests and skills of practising artists are all determinants of style. Unless one takes the extreme view that determinism triumphs in the hoary philosophical debate between freedom and determinism, they fall short of necessitating every aspect of a given work. Nevertheless, one factor that should shape our account of general style and its temporal evolution is our background knowledge of the context of creation—what was available to each artist at the time.

A related question we have not yet addressed concerns the state of mind of artists working in a shared general style. Do such artists internalize criteria for the style in question and consciously honour these constraints? Do they learn from acknowledged masters or experts, then seek some degrees of freedom or individuality? To construe the history of art in this way risks reading into it local and perhaps idiosyncratic views about the value of originality and creativity. Some general styles hardly evolved for centuries (both Ackerman and Schapiro note the stylistic stasis in ancient Egypt), while Arthur Danto, in 'The End of Art', has characterized recent times in part by the 'dazzling succession' of styles and movements: 'Fauvism, the Cubisms, Futurism, Vorticism, Synchronism, Abstractionism, Expressionism, Abstract Expressionism, Pop, Op, Minimalism, Post-Minimalism, conceptualism, Photorealism, Abstract Reason, Neo-Expressionism—simply to list some of the more familiar names' (Danto 1984: 29). Ackerman's proposal that artists view their endeavours as exercises in problem-solving may also presuppose too much about artists' states of mind. I am not convinced that artists approach their task as consciously as Ackerman's theory requires. They may react to earlier works in a variety of ways, both conscious and unconscious, and not all of these options constitute the framing of a new problem or the acknowledgement of a pre-existing one (see also Baxandall 1987). On the other hand, Ackerman's theory does seem to anticipate recent attempts by Jerrold Levinson and Noël Carroll to define art historically. Both of these philosophers construct theories in which artists are characteristically aware of prior works and practices of their artworld and, moreover, create in response to those precedents. The relations linking present to past can be various: emulative, admiring, combative, or otherwise.

Before finally turning to individual style, let me note some difficulties that arise when we contrast style with genre and with form, as well as when we try to apply a given account of style across the various arts. If we accept Goodman's corrective and cease thinking of style as antithetical to content, then distinguishing style from genre becomes quite vexing. One stock response defines genre by an explicit link to subject matter. Thus, landscape is one painting genre, still life another, the conversation piece (an outdoor family portrait commissioned frequently in eighteenth-century England) yet another. Individual artists then paint these in distinctive styles (a Cezanne landscape *v.* a Courbet, a Gainsborough conversation piece *v.* an Arthur

Devis). There may also be divisions based on period or school style: a Renaissance *v.* a Baroque altarpiece, an Italian *v.* a Flemish landscape.

Literary genres include the pastoral and the epic among poems (and also, following Pope, the mock epic), the hard-boiled detective novel and the picaresque novel among other categories of fiction. What, however, count as genres among the non-representational arts like music, architecture, or gardening? Of course, these arts can each possess representational as well as expressive content, but this is the exception rather than the rule. Is the Baroque overture a genre that can be written in the French or the Italian style? Many of the movements that originated as particular dances—the bouree, the gavotte—seem better construed as musical forms. In architecture, are the skyscraper and the personal residence genres that can be varied according to general or personal styles? Do we oppose Gordon Bunschaft's (of Skidmore, Owings, and Merrill) Lever House, a paradigmatic modern skyscraper, to Philip Johnson's AT&T Building, a postmodern one (contrasting period styles)? In an essay about garden nomenclature, Kenneth Woodbridge discusses the difficulty of assigning style terms to the art of gardening (see Woodbridge 1983). Is the English landscape garden a genre or a period style? And what of the Italian Mannerist garden? Must a Mannerist garden cohere chronologically, or via shared stylistic features, with a Mannerist painting?

How we are to answer these questions depends in part on the use we hope to make of the categories: form, genre, and style in the various arts. This is complicated not only by the divide between representational and non-representational arts (it might be more awkward, though more accurate, to describe the latter as non-narrative arts, as they are not without content), but also by that between performing and non-performing arts, and between arts with a single artist and those involving collective creation. How do we assign style to a film? Do we recognize cinematographic style, directorial style, editing style, and so on?

3. INDIVIDUAL STYLE

Our discussion thus far has neglected the second pole of Wollheim's dichotomy, that of individual style. Here too there are murky distinctions to ponder and a set of philosophical problems to address. Claims about determinism are crucial here as well. When first considering the notion of individual style, it is tempting to ask both 'Why should any artist have one?' and 'How can any artist help but have one (and only one)?' Wollheim maintained that individual style, unlike general style, had what he called 'psychological reality.' I take it this means that each artist's style is causally determined by aspects of the self: knowledge, values, interests, emotions, character, physical skills, muscle memory, and more. Today we might add race, class, gender, sexual orientation. The underlying and undefended assumption here is that we each have a formed personal identity and that artistic activity is expressive of this identity. Yet presumably there could be facile attempts at creating art, attempts that don't connect with the artist's true self. Because Wollheim insists that individual style must possess psychological reality, he leaves room for works that lack this connection by stating that some of an artist's works might be 'extrastylistic' (Wollheim 1995: 42).

What are we to say about the evolution of individual style? Mozart's juvenilia is presumably in his distinct style, though not as rich and subtle as later entries in the oeuvre. But might some of his less talented contemporaries have been in the predicament of never having found their style? Schapiro's essay on style has, as one pair of accompanying illustrations, two Picasso works from different periods of the artist's career, works that look vastly different from one another. Are these deemed genuine or authentic productions, emanating from the same self, differentiated perhaps because they are attempts to solve different problems? What of someone like novelist Joyce Carol Oates, who partitions her oeuvre by using a set of pseudonyms? Issues of forgery and influence come into play here as well. To forge a work of art is to take on another's style as one's own. (Think of forgers like Van Meegeren, who interpolated 'new' works into the oeuvres of the artists in question.) Being influenced by another artist, by contrast, seems a benign way of developing one's own style. Contemporary practitioners of 'appropriationist art' (consider the photographs and paintings by Sherry Levine) may well upset these categories altogether, using an ironic and self-conscious adoption of another's style to make a personal statement.

Let us look more closely at two competing accounts of individual style, both addressed primarily to the art of painting, to see what answers they suggest to these questions. Arthur Danto offers one such account in the speculative, closing sections of his book *The Transfiguration of the Commonplace* (Danto 1981). Because Danto addresses the question of style at the end of this work, he does so in the light of certain characteristic preoccupations of his philosophy of art. The immediate context for his discussion is a rejection of the imitative theory of art, grounded in a series of examples of indiscernible objects, only one of which is art, or each of which is a different work of art. Given Danto's frequent use of, and variation on, such examples, it is not surprising that he arrives at an 'adverbial' account of style, one that emphasizes 'how'—the manner in which something is represented—rather than the 'what,' or representational content. For Danto, style is constituted by deviations from transparency, discrepancies between image (what is really there) and motif (how the subject is represented). Rather than a failure of mimesis, Danto suggests that these deviations tell us something about the artist himself—his way of seeing—which is transparent to him, and perhaps to his contemporaries as well, but is opaque to us (Danto 1981: 162–3). He proposes that we 'reserve the term style for this *how*, as what remains of a representation when we subtract its content' (p. 197).

A final important piece in Danto's account is the contrast between style and *manner*. 'A style is a gift; a manner can be learned, through from the outside there may be no particular difference to be observed' (Danto 1981: 200). The fact that that manner is acquired through learning, while style arrives 'without the mediation of art or knowledge' aligns with a further difference that Danto couches in the language of action theory: style arises from an artist's basic actions, manner from non-basic ones (pp. 200–1). All of this serves, for Danto, to confirm that old adage of Buffon's, that 'style is the man' (pp. 201, 204). Though Danto initially contrasts style with content, he quickly hedges this claim: 'In actual execution...it is difficult to separate style from substance, since they arise together in a single impulse' (p. 197). A distinctive part of his view remains, however. He glosses style in terms of the artist's way of seeing the world together with a metaphysical proposal that each of us is, in essence, a representational system, that is, a bearer of a distinctive worldview.

Like Danto, Wollheim offers a lot of machinery to support his pronouncements about individual style. He posits style processes, made up of schemata, rules, and dispositions to act, as constitutive of individual style. The schemata 'segment the pictorial resources' into realms on which the artist acts in accordance with the rules. No parts of this process are verbalized or explicit: 'There has been no suggestion on my part that the artist has direct access to the processes of style, or even that he is in a particularly good position to retrieve them after the fact' (Wollheim 1995: 48). Wollheim is also insistent that the schemata do not merely signal the obvious formal aspects of painting, and that determining just what is schematized for a given artist may not be easily retrieved from that artist's work.

Wollheim's contrast between individual and general style functions somewhat like Danto's contrast between style and manner. For example, Wollheim's declaration that general style is 'taxonomic'—which has the consequence that it can be learned, while individual style, by contrast, must be 'formed'—coheres with Danto's claims about knowledge and art. Yet a second distinction that Wollheim explores, that between style and *signature*, helps us further to elucidate individual style. *Signature* is whatever allows us to identify the work as by a given artist. It includes the literal signature on the canvas, as well as any other predictably replicated traits that aid in correct attribution. Goodman gives us a further specification of such traits, noting that 'not even every property that helps determine the maker or period or provenance of a work is stylistic. The label on a picture, a listing in a catalogue raisonne, a letter from the composer, a report of excavation may help place a work; but being so labeled or documented or excavated is not a matter of style. Nor are the chemical properties of pigments that help identify a painting' (Goodman 1978: 34–5). Style, for Wollheim, is individuated entirely by its causal origin. Only traits of the painting that arise from the schemata and rules figure in a style-description. But a feature of a given painting that in fact counts as stylistic may not be one we recognize as such. Accordingly, style, as Wollheim understands it, does not necessarily contribute to our historically placing the artist of any work.

Both of the accounts of individual style just surveyed make controversial meta-physical commitments—to ways of seeing and representational systems, on Danto's part, and to dispositions to act on non-discursively specifiable rules for manipulating schemata, on Wollheim's. But, that aside, neither theory seems satisfactory overall. Danto's approach doesn't clearly demarcate the three components he is tracking at the end of his book, i.e. metaphor, expression, and style. Even if we could determine the interpretively important respects in which particular works of art differ from mere representations, we would not know whether to deem those differences rhetorical, expressive, stylistic, or all of these at once. If they coalesce in particular cases, we certainly shouldn't think we're gaining a handle on the concept of style. In a later paper, 'Narrative and Style', Danto brings his work in the philosophy of history to bear on the problem of style (Danto 1991). Appealing to the semantic properties of what he calls 'narrative sentences', Danto argues that artists do not, and logically cannot, intentionally formulate and pursue aspects of their style. Narrative sentences are those that describe an earlier object or event in light of a later one, thus generating truth-conditions not available to contemporaries of the initial event. Such sentences pertain to style because 'we can see, afterward, the later works of an artist already visible in his or her earlier work though they would not have been visible to us were we contemporary with these works' (Danto 1991: 206). The artist himself will be blind to these features, 'for just the reason that the artist does not know his future work' (Danto 1991: 206). Put simply, since no artist can foresee and intend all the aspects of his future work, style properties cannot be said to be intended. But this makes it all the more mysterious how each artist's way of seeing is instantiated in his works. Although Noël Carroll resurrects a more limited way in which artistic intention can impact individual style in his paper 'Danto, Style, and Intention' (Carroll 1995), tensions remain in Danto's theory.

Return to the possibility of an artist working in different styles over the course of his career. For Danto, this would seem to require changes in the self significant enough to bring about new ways of seeing the world. The individuation of world views seems murkier still than any take we have on style. Wollheim's opposition to such style change is explicit, since for him it is stipulatively true that every *artist* has an individual style (as opposed to a *painter*, who may not). He cautions: 'styles should not be multiplied within a given artist's work without good reason. One good reason is that the artist exhibits marked personality changes, but in most other cases where there is a temptation to invoke stylistic change, a preferred strategy should be to see whether the original style description had not been written on an insufficiently abstract level' (Wollheim 1990: 143). But defending this position commits Wollheim to some odd mereological claims whereby mere parts of the self can be recruited in the creation of particular works and projects. Passages like the following, which offers alternatives to attributing multiple styles to a single artist, seem to reify the notion of style, then partition it in dubious ways: 'The artist has not as yet formed his style, or the work is prestylistic; the artist has suffered a loss of style, or the work is poststylistic; the artist draws upon different parts of his style in different works; the artist only incompletely realizes his style in some of his works, or the relevant work is style-deficient' (Wollheim 1990: 144). And from a later essay: 'in any given work or in any given body of work of an artist, his style may not be employed in its entirety' (Wollheim 1995: 46).

4. ARTISTIC ACTS, APPARENT ARTISTS, STYLE QUALITIES

The discussion of individual style takes one turn that might pre-empt some of the dilemmas just sketched. I have in mind the switch to an act-centred account of style. Some elements of style, both individual and general, seem determined by the materials and techniques available. In a playful passage discussing the etymology of the word 'style' (derived from the Latin *stilus*, meaning a pointed instrument for writing), Danto indicates the varying effects that can be achieved with the use of different tools: 'I am referring to the palpable qualities of differing lines made with differing orders of styluses: the toothed quality of pencil against paper, the granular quality of crayon against stone, the furred line thrown up as the drypoint needle leaves its wake of metal shavings, the variegated lines left by brushes, the churned lines made by sticks through viscous pigment, the cast lines made by paint dripped violently off the end of another stick' (Danto 1981: 197). Once we acknowledge the contribution of different tools and raw materials, it seems only natural to extend our focus to the acts and gestures, the intentions and skills, with which the tools are wielded, the materials altered. Moreover, once we attend to physical skills and gestures, it is tempting to take an 'adverbial' approach to individual style. That is, following the work of someone like Guy Sircello, who formulated a theory of beauty based on an ontology of 'artistic acts' which were bearers of aesthetic properties, we might suppose that style inheres not in the finished object (this already begs some questions concerning contemporary art), but in the artistic acts that created that work (see Sircello 1975). This approach fits some cases very well. Many of the aesthetic qualities of abstract expressionist painting can be traced to the gestures that generate it. In his account of style in painting, Wollheim deems individual style 'highly internalised' and suggests that it is 'encapsulated in the artist's body' (Wollheim 1995: 42).

The art of sculpture seems equally amenable to this treatment, as we envision artists hacking at wood or stone, casting bronze, moulding clay, welding scrap metal. The art of acting is certainly gestural; a distinctive character can be created through intentional manipulations of the actor's body and voice. But other arts seem less well suited to this approach. Film poses difficulties because it is not an individual art and has many loci of creativity. Musical composition, as opposed to musical performance, does not seem illuminated by an 'artistic acts' approach. But consider first the art of literature. Jenefer Robinson addresses the act/object distinction in her paper 'Style and Personality in the Literary Work' (Robinson 1985). She suggests that literary style resides in the manner in which the author performs a variety of verbal acts: 'literary style is rather a way of *doing* certain things, such as describing characters, commenting on the action and manipulating the plot' (Robinson 1985: 227). In 'General and Individual Style in Literature', Robinson offers additional examples of 'the relevant actions': '*describing* people, *portraying* landscape, *characterizing* personal relationships, *manipulating* rhythms, *organizing* patterns of imagery, and so forth' (Robinson 1984: 148). Elsewhere, discussing the specific style of Jane Austen, Robinson claims that 'Jane Austen's style is not simply her style of doing any one thing, such as describing social pretention, but rather her style of doing a number of things, such as *describing*, *portraying*, and *treating* her characters, theme and social setting, *commenting* on the action, *presenting* various points of view, and so on' (Robinson 1985: 231). I'm not sure a list like this exhausts the activities of literary creation, but we might borrow the machinery from earlier speech act theorists such as J. L. Austin and H. P. Grice to delineate the acts involved in fiction writing (see Beardsley 1990).

Extending this approach to the art of musical composition remains problematic. Is the artistic act in question that of imagining sounds? Jerrold Levinson's theory, set out in 'What a Musical Work Is', which takes composers to be indicating performance/sound structures from the realm of all possible combinations in a given musical system, does at least place an intentional act at the core of composition, permitting once again an 'adverbial' account of artistic style (see Levinson 1980). But does musical composition resemble the literary case? The act of imagining or indicating sounds lacks the detail and demarcation of generating meaningful speech. Thus, there doesn't seem to be enough richness to support a full account of musical style in this vein. One might, though, propose a more fine-grained analysis of composition. We can view composers as engaged in a variety of acts: imitating melodies, constructing harmonies, depicting scenes, and so on (see Wolterstorff 1994). While this proposal brings the art of music more into line with the art of literature, questions remain concerning the location or origin of artistic acts. Just how do a novelist's or a composer's choices express the psychologically based concept of style now under consideration? Let me turn to this issue.

In addition to acknowledging the act/object distinction, accounts of style must resolve another dilemma: should the style properties of a work be attributed to the *actual* or to an *apparent* artist? In thinking about expressive properties, we know enough to avoid the fallacy of assuming that a sad work must have been created by a sad artist, a manic work by a manic one, and so on. Yet many style properties are themselves expressive. In 'Style and Personality in the Literary Work', Robinson defines literary style as a way of doing certain things that expresses the traits of mind, character, and personality of the author (Robinson 1985). Surely it would be an error to assume that these must actually be possessed by the artist in order to show in the work. And Robinson quickly amends her view: 'I shall claim that an author's way of doing these things is an expression of her personality, or, more accurately, of the personality she seems to have' (Robinson 1985: 227). She cites Wayne Booth's theory of the 'implied author' and Alexander Nehamas's invocation of 'the postulated author' to indicate the prevalence of such views. Kendall Walton's account of the 'apparent *artist*' (my emphasis) in his early paper 'Style and the Products and Processes of Art' extends this approach beyond the art of literature (Walton 1990). For example, Walton bases an extended example on the distinctive painting style of Jackson Pollock. Noting that 'an impossibly naive viewer who has no understanding at all of how liquids behave and so has no sense of the drippings and splashings that went into a Pollock painting misperceives it' (Walton, 1990: 58), Walton goes on to recall a pair of paintings by Robert Rauschenberg, *Factum I* and *Factum II*, both with sections in a Pollock-like drip style. Allegedly, in *Factum II* Rauschenberg 'tried meticulously' to reproduce *Factum I*. Walton invites us to suppose he did so by depositing drops of paint one by one with an eyedropper (Walton 1979: 62). This supposition exposes the gap between the actual and the apparent artist as well as the effect of background information on our perceptual experience.

The following four claims constitute the core of an account of individual style drawn from Robinson's assorted papers: (i) style is expressed in the way certain acts are performed; (ii) the items expressed concern attitudes, traits of character, personality, and so on; (iii) these belong to the apparent rather than the actual author; and (iv) this proposal can be extended from literature to the other arts. There are a number of difficulties with the theory just reconstructed. Even in an example hospitable to Robinson's view, the complexity of the case is formidable. Consider the levels involved in novels by Jane Austen, Henry James, Edith Wharton, and James Joyce. Such authors tell us about many incidents and many characters. What permits a univocal style to emerge? Often the author creates a narrator who describes the various events and characters. Will these descriptions be uniform enough to ground inferences about the narrator's personality? What of those cases that are more complex because they are filtered through the remarks and observations of an intentionally unreliable narrator? And finally, assuming that the narrator is herself or himself a fictional character, how do we arrive at an apparent author? Why assume that the narrator's words and attitudes will be uniform enough to indicate some one apparent author? Robinson herself says of a novel by Austen, 'Of course not every artistic act of a writer in a particular work expresses exactly the same qualities of mind, character or personality. In Emma, for example, Jane Austen portrays Mrs Elton in a quite different way from Jane Fairfax. This is because Jane Austen's attitude to Mrs. Elton is quite different from her attitude to Jane Fairfax' (Robinson 1985: 231). Robinson is here talking about an actual author,

Jane Austen, and two characters, Jane Fairfax and Mrs Elton; but note the intervening roles we have identified: the actual author differs from the apparent author, who differs from the narrator, who differs from each of the other characters portrayed.

The fact that we can at times arrive at style attributions only after iterated inferences is not fatal to Robinson's view. Yet a problem remains. Robinson concludes her discussion with the claim that only an author's 'standing', rather than 'occasional', traits of mind, character, and personality should be deemed stylistic. Suppose we rule out all occasional properties. (Robinson cites these examples: 'anxiety about, anger at or contempt towards a particular character, event or idea, although the writer does not seem to be a chronically anxious, angry or contemptuous sort of person': Robinson 1985: 232.) How many character-delineating traits will remain? Since each of us has a relatively small store of *standing* personality traits, Robinson's proposal threatens to impoverish unduly the resources for style analysis. Alternatively, if we acknowledge a richer array of psychological traits, it seems less likely that these will be exemplified in a regular enough way to accrue to our portrait of the apparent author. All this imparts a stipulative cast to Robinson's theory. She declares style features to be those that express personality. It follows that, say, formal features of a certain work that aid us in identifying its creator but that aren't expressive of character or personality fail to be stylistic traits of the work in question. Robinson discusses an example of such a possibility—the presence of euphonious sounds—and concludes: 'We cannot, therefore, identify the elements of individual style merely as the most striking or salient features of a work. On the one hand, there are striking features which do not invariably contribute to individual style . . . On the other hand, moreover, there are many elements which are not particularly salient but which contribute to individual style' (Robinson 1985: 242. As an example of the latter, she cites a preference for the indefinite over the definite article.) Goodman, too, cites an example of a 'fussy statistical characteristic' that is not stylistic. He asks us to consider an author in whose novels 'more than the usual proportion of second words of his sentences begin with consonants' (Goodman 1978: 36). But Goodman goes on to give what may be a more satisfactory account of why this property fails to be stylistic. Rather than claiming that it lacks the requisite connection to the author's psyche, Goodman suggests that it is not exemplified or symbolized by the novel and thus is not part of its symbolic functioning. He in fact elevates this to a necessary condition when he states 'Earlier we saw that any, and now we see that only, aspects of such symbolic functioning may enter into a style' (Goodman, 1978: 35)

What we might call the 'evanescence' of both the art object and the artist is a striking feature of recent discussions of artistic style. The object gives way to the actions that generated it, while the actual artist cedes place to the apparent creator of the work in question. Yet, as the preceding discussion makes clear, one additional item threatens to vanish as well: those very qualities or features that we might commonsensibly have taken to be indicative of style. If we restrict style characteristics to those associated with 'standing' traits of character, and in addition deny that salience is an indicator of style features, what remains to ground our style attributions? The question comes to this: which aspects of a work of art provide evidence of its style? Can we provide a checklist of features to consult for each art medium? Two opposing answers to this question find support in recent literature. On the one hand, many authors staunchly assert that there cannot be any 'checklist' of style elements. Robinson, for example, makes just this claim (Robinson 1985: 241), while Goodman insists that 'no fixed catalogue of the elementary properties of style can be compiled . . . we normally come to grasp a style without being able to analyse it into component features' (Goodman 1978: 34). This denial operates on two distinct levels. On the one hand, there cannot be an advance list of properties, qualities, or features that will count as style properties of any given work containing them. Moreover, even when we agree that a particular set of features does count as style features in some work, their presence does not guarantee the application of some given style category. The former claim echoes Goodman's central point in 'The Status of Style' (Goodman 1978). The latter claim is in keeping with the view defended by Frank Sibley in his groundbreaking paper 'Aesthetic Concepts' (Sibley 1959): it also coheres with a moral many draw from Kant's Third Critique, namely, that there are and can be no laws of taste.

In opposition to these intuitions, consider the following empirical argument for the existence of a checklist of style features. Computer scientists have developed programs which, they claim, create new works in a given artist's style by analysing existing works and extracting their distinctive stylistic patterns. Note that these programs seem much more applicable to some arts than to others. Music and literature seem amenable to statistical analysis of the gestures, phrases, etc., that constitute the building blocks of style, but it is not at all clear that such an approach would work for realistic painting. In fact, we might expect such programs to fail for any of those arts that Goodman deems autographic. Such arts are not notational. In fact, they are subject to forgery just because there is no way to determine work identity via 'sameness of spelling' (see Goodman 1968: chs. III and IV). Were there a lexicon we could consult to determine sameness of spelling for these works, it would presumably also serve as a basis for the statistical analysis of style. In sum, if computer programs like these succeed for allographic arts, then it would seem to follow that, for these arts at least, we can assemble a checklist for style.

Igor Douven has written a paper challenging all such attempts at cyber style-analysis (see Douven 1999). Taking as his central example David Cope's program 'Experiments in Musical Intelligence' (EMI), Douven argues that no such program can produce a work in a given artist's (individual) style because stylistic features are neither reducible to nor supervenient on textual features of the sort that computer programs can isolate. Douven labels the view of style he opposes the 'localistic' view: 'It basically says that style is something "located in" a composer's (or author's or painter's) oeuvre . . . something that "inheres" in the texts of these works'

(Douven 1999: 256). To refute the localistic view, Douven invites us to conduct a few thought-experiments employing a transmogrifying device that can change the world on command:

> take some feature F of a composer C's work that you consider to be a stylistic characteristic of that work, transmogrify the world in such a way that in the resulting world there are many different *oeuvres* that all exhibit F, and ask yourself whether you would still call F a stylistic property of C's work…Or take a feature G of C's work that you do not at all regard as a stylistic characteristic of that work, transmogrify the world so that after the process none of the other *oeuvres* that also exhibit G is left, and ask yourself whether you still would not regard G as a stylistic feature of C's work…(Douven 1999: 259)

Clearly, Douven takes the tag questions here to be rhetorical ones. Returning to the example of Mozart's musical style, he suggests that what evades capture is not Mozart's propensity for certain patterns, but his talent for breaking rules: 'thanks to Cope we now know how to get the patterns into the computer, but we still have no idea as to how to get the genius in' (Douven 1999: 261).

Yet Douven's point—namely, that the context-dependence of style attribution shows that style features do not inhere in works in any straightforward way—is echoed by other authors. For instance, Wollheim demarcates style descriptions (which he distinguishes from stylistic descriptions) by reference to 'psychological' context, that is, to the way in which a particular artist schematizes and operates with the resources of her medium (see Wollheim 1995: sect. VII). In his paper 'Style and the Products and Processes of Art', Kendall Walton emphasizes the effects of historical and cultural context on the identification of style features (see Walton 1979). To illustrate his claim, Walton uses an example every bit as fantastic as Douven's transmogrifier. Walton analyses Borges's story 'Pierre Menard', which ascribes incompatible style features (e.g., archaic/nonarchaic, pragmatic/nonpragmatic) to the indiscernible versions of *Don Quixote* by Cervantes, on the one hand, and Menard, on the other. Walton draws a complicated moral from this example. He maintains that style features inhere in the work (contrary, say, to Douven's claims) but that styles are described differently in different times. Thus,

> style identity is tied up with the features, rather than with the apparent artist. If features which in some works suggest bold artists, suggest timid artists in works of a later period, we don't have to say that the works are in different styles; rather the same style which was bold in one context is timid in the other. The style of Pierre Menard's Don Quixote is archaic and that of Cervantes's Don Quixote is not; yet these works are in the same style. The style became archaic with the change of context. (Walton 1979: 60)

Walton concludes that styles 'are to be identified not with what is expressed but with what in the work does the expressing…This account locates styles of works firmly in the works themselves…But the connection with behavior remains' (Walton 1979: 60). Note that Walton's view coheres with that defended in his earlier, much-anthologized article 'Categories of Art' (1970). There his example of guernicas showed that Picasso's famous painting, which we take to be a highly emotional and expressive work, would instead be deemed restrained and elegant were there in place in the artworld a practice of building 'relief paintings' having exactly the two-dimensional pattern of Picasso's *Guernica*, for in that context *Guernica's* flatness would be all-important (see Walton 1970).

The examples constructed by Douven, Borges, and Walton suggest that we would be hasty to abandon salience as one of the features that helps us in identifying style properties. But a further exploration of the ways in which salience is itself context-dependent might bring many of our authors into accord once again. Those like Wollheim and, to some extent, Robinson, who emphasize a highly psychological criterion for the components of individual style, may seem to define style in terms of unobservable processes and so sever style from salience. But if not all styles can be intended at any given time, then attention to the determinants of particular styles might yield a set of operational definitions bridging these realms.

Meyer Schapiro concluded his 1962 paper on style with the discouraging observation that 'A theory of style adequate to the psychological and historical problems has still to be created' (Schapiro 1994: 100). He hoped that a broadly Marxist approach would fulfil this need. I think we can say that today, some forty years later, an overarching theory of style still eludes us. Yet progress has been made on many fronts. Illuminating distinctions have been drawn, revealing connections to issues in other areas of philosophy have been traced, useful parameters for further inquiry have been set. Above all, we have gained a well grounded appreciation of the importance of this topic. In Goodman's words, 'The discernment of style is an integral aspect of the understanding of works of art and the worlds they present' (Goodman 1978: 40).

See also: Representation in Art; Expression in Art; Painting, Music; Literature.

Bibliography

Ackerman, J. S. (1962). 'A Theory of Style'. *Journal of Aesthetics and Art Criticism* 20: 227–37.

Alpers, S. (1990). 'Style is What You Make It: The Visual Arts Once Again', in B. Lang (ed.), *The Concept of Style*, 2nd edn. Ithaca, NY: Cornell University Press; first published 1979.

Baxandall, M. (1987). *Patterns of Intention*. New Haven: Yale University Press.

Beardsley, M. (1990). 'Verbal Style and Illocutionary Action', in B. Lang (ed.), *The Concept of Style*, 2nd edn. Ithaca, NY: Cornell University Press; first published 1979.

Carroll, N. (1995). 'Danto, Style, and Intention'. *Journal of Aesthetics and Art Criticism* 53: 251–7.

Danto, A. C. (1981). *The Transfiguration of the Commonplace: A Philosophy of Art*. Cambridge, Mass.: Harvard University Press.

——(1984). 'The End of Art', in B. Lang (ed.), *The Death of Art*. New York: Haven Publications.

——(1991). 'Narrative and Style'. *Journal of Aesthetics and Art Criticism* 49: 201–9.

Douven, I. (1999). 'Style and Supervenience'. *British Journal of Aesthetics* 39: 255–62.

Gilmore, J. (2000). *The Life of a Style: Beginnings and Endings in the Narrative History of Art*. Ithaca, NY: Cornell University Press.

Gombrich, E. H. (1968). 'Style', in D. L. Sills (ed.), *The International Encyclopedia of the Social Sciences*, vol. 15. New York: Macmillan Company and Free Press.

Goodman, N. (1978). 'The Status of Style', in his *Ways of Worldmaking*. Indianapolis: Hackett.

Herwitz, D. (1993). *Making Theory, Constructing Art: On the Authority of the Avant-Garde*. Chicago: University of Chicago Press.

Levinson, J. (1980). 'What A Musical Work Is', *Journal of Philosophy* 77: 5–28.

Meyer, L. (1989). *Style and Music: Theory, History, and Ideology*. Philadelphia: University of Pennsylvania Press.

Robinson, J. (1981). 'Style and Significance in Art History and Art Criticism'. *Journal of Aesthetics and Art Criticism* 40: 5–14.

——(1984). 'General and Individual Style in Literature'. *Journal of Aesthetics and Art Criticism* 43: 147–58.

——(1985). 'Style and Personality in the Literary Work'. *Philosophical Review* 94: 227–47.

Schapiro, M. (1994). 'Style', in his *Theory and Philosophy of Art: Style, Artist, and Society*. New York: George Braziller; first published 1953.

Sibley, F. (1959). 'Aesthetic Concepts'. *Philosophical Review* 68: 421–50.

Sircello, G. (1975). *A New Theory of Beauty*. Princeton: Princeton University Press.

Walton, K. (1970). 'Categories of Art'. *Philosophical Review* 79: 334–67.

——(1990). 'Style and the Products and Processes of Art', in B. Lang (ed.), *The Concept of Style*, 2nd edn. Ithaca, NY: Cornell University Press; first published 1979.

Wolfflin, H. (1950). *Principles of Art History: The Problem of the Development of Style in Later Art*. New York: Dover.

Wollheim, R. (1990). 'Pictorial Style: Two Views', in B. Lang (ed.), *The Concept of Style*, 2nd edn. Ithaca, NY: Cornell University Press; first published 1979.

——(1995). 'Style in Painting', in S. Kemal and I. Gaskell (eds.), *The Question of Style in Philosophy and the Arts*. Cambridge: Cambridge University Press.

Wolterstorff, N. (1994). 'The Work of Making a Work of Music', in P. Alperson (ed.), *What is Music? An Introduction to the Philosophy of Music*, 2nd edn. University Park, Pa.: Pennsylvania State University Press; first published 1987.

Woodbridge, K. (1983). 'The Nomenclature of Style in Garden History'. *Eighteenth-Century Life* 8: 19–25.

CHAPTER 13

CREATIVITY IN ART

PHILIP ALPERSON

PERHAPS no other concept seems as fundamental to common thinking about the arts as the concept of artistic creativity. This is not because creativity seems to most people to be unique to art. Quite the contrary: we speak freely of creative activity in the sciences, in academic disciplines, in cooking, in sports, and, indeed, in virtually every area of human productive endeavour. Nor is this surprising. Creating and making are closely associated etymologically (from the Latin *creare*) and in the popular mind, and it does no violence to common sense to say that what can be made or done can be made or done creatively. Nevertheless, creativity, if not a necessary condition of artistic practice, seems at least a hallmark or a characteristic feature of art generally. And so we think of artists as creating their works, we think of works of art (including physical things, performances, events, and conceptual objects and structures) as artistic creations, and we praise artists, their works, and even entire artistic epochs for their creativity. Many people take artistic creation to be the quintessential human creative activity.

In addition to the general notion that creativity is of central importance to the arts, there is common agreement about three other interrelated aspects of creation in art. First, creativity in the arts is normally taken to be something of positive value. The term 'creative', whether applied to an artist or a work, is almost always an honorific, a term of positive appraisal in an appropriate cultural context. Typically, creativity in art is thought to be an important kind or dimension of artistic excellence. Second, 'true' creation is taken to be a rare achievement. Of course, as Spinoza says, all excellent things are as difficult as they are rare, and truly distinguished creative achievement would seem to be no exception to Spinoza's general observation. But there is the further point that, in the minds of many, creativity in art seems to call for a special talent or set of talents that distinguish artists from the general run of human beings. Third, we commonly associate creativity with originality, with the production of something that is in some significant sense new or unique. The aesthetic value of originality has been questioned (Vermazen 1991; Elster 2000), but that is definitely the minority view. We need not demand of creative activity that it be *ex nihilo*, that it bring something into existence from nothing, in the manner of divine creation. But we do expect that, to the extent that works of art are creative, they add something of interest to the world. That is a chief part of what distinguishes the creative from the routine, the pedestrian, the derivative, and the merely novel. It is often claimed that the appraisal of a truly creative work, as opposed to a merely novel one, is time-dependent, that is, that it can be determined only by the extent to which the work can stand as an exemplar over time. These features of artistic creation—its centrality to the arts, its positive value, its rarity, and its productive originality—are thought to be enshrined in the familiar pantheon of paradigmatic artists, from Homer and Horace through da Vinci and Michelangelo, Shakespeare, Bach, Mozart, Beethoven, and Brahms, to van Gogh, Picasso, Georgia O'Keefe, Virginia Woolf, Toni Morrison, Bill Evans, and so on, before whose works we feel admiration and wonder.

Such ideas about the role and importance of creation in art are common enough. But they raise as many questions as they answer. What exactly is it that makes a person, an action, or a thing creative? How do we assess creative achievement? How, if at all, can creativity in the arts be explained? Are there particular characteristics of creative people or of creative activity? To what extent do social, cultural, economic, institutional, historical, and gendered considerations affect creation in the arts, the identification and evaluation of creative excellence, and our overall assessments of works and artists in virtue of their creativity? What is the relationship between creativity and originality? Can we arrive at an account of artistic creativity that successfully generalizes across the arts, or do we need different accounts of creativity for the various arts or for various aspects of the various arts? Is artistic creativity really such a rare phenomenon? Or is it better understood as a characteristic of human agency in general?

It is only natural that people should reflect on questions such as these, whether they consider artistic creation to be a remote, wondrous, and exceptional form of human activity, or to be continuous with what they know of their own activities and experiences. At the same time, resistance to theorizing about artistic creation arises from at least two directions. First, in part because of a tradition dating back to Plato of regarding poetic creation in particular as an especially mysterious, perhaps irrational, domain, the subject of artistic creation has seemed to be among the more intractable topics in aesthetic theory. In addition, there is a certain ambivalence about discussing the matter among artists themselves, those to whom we might turn for first-hand insight into artistic creativity. There are, to be sure, well-known sayings, statements, and commentaries by artists about the subject, especially concerning the phenomenological character of creative experience (see e.g. Ghiselin 1952). But there are also many artists who prefer to avoid the subject entirely, in some cases out of fear of paralysis from analysis. Just how recalcitrant is the subject of creation in art?

1. THE DYNAMICS OF CREATIVITY

Since creation in art involves matters of human agency, one might start by asking about the creative process itself. How might it be described? This is a question that presumably rests in part on introspective reports, on psychological descriptions of human behaviour, and on philosophical analysis.

Some have endeavoured to distinguish particular stages of the creative process. Two older but still influential descriptions offered by Graham Wallas (1926) and Catharine Patrick (1937) recognize four stages of the creative process: (i) *preparation*, in which the creator becomes vaguely aware of a problem, perhaps undertaking random efforts to bring the problem to some resolution; (ii) *incubation*, during which the problem falls from conscious awareness; (iii) *inspiration*, a period or moment of insight, discovery, or illumination; and (iv) *elaboration*, during which the creative idea is worked out and developed (see also Ghiselin 1952).

Some more recent writers have more or less adopted this scheme, often emphasizing one or another of the stages. Vincent Götz, for example, offers a variation of these categories and, appealing both to etymology and what he takes to be 'the facts of experience and logic', argues that creativity is a kind of making marked by deliberative activity issuing in a particular product and that, as such, creativity can properly be predicated only of the last, elaborative stage ('the process or activity of deliberately concretizing insight'). This stipulation, Götz argues, goes some way towards clearing up confusions and ambiguities that dog the ways in which the term is normally used, in particular distinguishing creativity from originality, insight, and communication (Götz 1981).

To be sure, creative activity frequently, perhaps typically, involves some deliberative activity. It is wise to be reminded of this and, especially in the case of artistic creativity, of the importance of working with a medium. These insights help to compensate for the easy assumption that creation in the arts is simply a matter of having a 'eureka' moment.

There are, however, a number of problems with such a restrictive stipulation such as Götz's. For a start, not all deliberative making is creative making. We normally distinguish between the workmanlike and the worthy on the basis of some evaluative criterion or criteria, such as the extent to which the activity issues in something new or original (Hausman 1984; Bailin 1983) Attempting to restrict the notion of the creative process to elaborative activity, or focusing on it exclusively, also seems overly fussy: part of what seems remarkable about creative activity is not just the working out of ideas but also their provenance. This is one reason why authors are perennially plagued with the question, 'Where do you get your ideas?' Furthermore, to the extent that various aspects of creative activity can be identified analytically, one must be cautious about too strict a notion of a particular sequence of stages. As Beardsley (1966) points out in a well-known essay, which owes much to Dewey (1934), these activities are typically mixed together, constantly alternating in the ongoing process of artistic creation. Perhaps it would be wisest to think of them as elements rather than as stages of creative activity. Beardsley himself frames the question of the nature of creative activity by asking what goes on in 'the stretch of mental and physical activity between the incept and the final touch—between the thought "I may be on to something here" and the thought "It is finished" '—which Beardsley takes to be a question about the extent to which the creative process is at least partially controlled.

The question of the extent of deliberative control in artistic creation is an important one. Many artists report that there is at least one fundamental sense in which their creative activity seems *not* to be purposive or completely under their control: the artist does not completely envisage the final result or proceed according to a preconceived plan. This is one of the paradoxes of creativity, that the artist both knows and does not know what he or she is up to (Maitland 1976; Howard 1982).

Some philosophers have taken the idea of an activity in which one does not see the end in the beginning to be characteristic of artistic creation. Collingwood (1938), describing creativity in terms of the expression of emotion and sharply distinguishing expressive activity from craft, offers an influential version of such a view:

When a man is said to express emotion, what is being said about him comes to this. At first, he is conscious of having an emotion, but not conscious of what this emotion is. All he is conscious of is a perturbation of excitement, which he feels going on within him, but of whose nature he is ignorant . . . Until a man has expressed his emotion, he does not yet know what emotion it is. The act of expressing it is therefore an exploration of his own emotions. He is trying to find out what these emotions are. There is certainly here a directed process: an effort, that is directed upon a certain end; but the end is not something foreseen and preconceived, to which appropriate means can be thought out in the light of our knowledge of its special character. Expression is an activity of which there can be no technique. (Collingwood 1938: 109–11)

Beardsley, for his part, distinguishes two main theoretical approaches to the matter of creative control: the 'Propulsive Theory', according to which 'the controlling agent is something that exists prior to the creative process', and the 'Finalistic Theory', according to which 'the controlling agent is the final goal towards which the process aims'. Beardsley dismisses the Finalistic Theory largely on the grounds that the view places too much emphasis on the goal-directed, problem-solving aspect of creative activity. The artist may face both large-scale tasks ('How can I make a good sculpture of a reclining figure?') and more or less immediate ones ('If I use this cool green here I can get this plane to recede'); and, Beardsley acknowledges, it is at least conceivable that an artist might have in mind, for example, a specific regional quality he or she is trying to bring into existence. But, Beardsley asserts, most experience of artists goes against the view that the creative process can be accurately characterized in the main as being controlled by 'previsioned goals' or problems to solve.

Beardsley is more sympathetic to the Propulsive Theory, of which he takes Collingwood to be a representative proponent: the artist is impelled by the determination to clarify an emotion that preserves its identity throughout the creative process and largely determines its course. But Beardsley rejects Collingwood's expressionist account on two grounds: (i) the theory lacks a principle of identity according to which an artist would be able to compare the expressed emotion with the (unknown) prior emotion, and (ii) the notion of 'clarifying' an emotion is obscure. (For a defence of Collingwood's expression-based theory of creativity, see Anderson and Hausman 1992.) He instead follows a suggestion by Tomas (1958) that creation is a self-correcting process and advances what might be called a Generative version of the Propulsion Theory, according to which, after an incept of some sort (a sentence, a theme, a tone, a style, etc.) gets the ball rolling, 'the crucial controlling power at every point is the particular stage or condition of the unfinished work itself, the possibilities it presents, and the developments it permits' (again, see Dewey 1934).

Beardsley's account of creative control has the virtue of pointing to the ways in which an initial percept, idea, theme, style, and so on can carry with it possibilities for elaboration, possibilities of which the artist might be only dimly aware at the outset of his or her work. Perhaps this is a part of what authors mean when they speak of a story 'writing itself' or of a character carrying the author along. In this sense, artistic creation does seem different from and more complex than a clearly purposive activity such as attempting to hit a bulls-eye on a rifle range, to use Tomas's familiar example.

But Beardsley's view is not completely satisfying, either as a general theory of artistic creativity or as an account of the role of control in the creative process. Beardsley is clear that, on his view, the creative process possesses no universal pattern of stages that occur in a set order. What Beardsley wants to say beyond that, at least from a descriptive point of view, is not so clear. At one point, Beardsley suggests that the four classically delineated activities are mixed together in the creative process; at another he characterizes the creative process as involving two constantly alternating phases, 'the *inventive* phase, traditionally called *inspiration*, in which new ideas are formed in the preconscious and appear in consciousness ... [and] the *selective* phase, which is nothing more than criticism, in which the conscious chooses or rejects the new idea after perceiving its relationships to what has already tentatively been adopted'.

Nor is it clear how serviceable the general distinction is between Propulsive and Finalistic theories. As Khatchadourian (1977) points out, this is both a conceptual matter—the distinction breaks down, for example, in the case of a sustained conscious finalistic vision or goal that reappears as an unconscious, propulsive creative impulse—and a practical one, since there is a vast spectrum of ways in which artists work. Some works are created with specific and well worked out plans and/or purposes in mind, others are created with scarcely any vision of the completed work. Khatchadourian distinguishes six representative patterns along the gamut but the possibilities seem endless (see also Maitland 1976; Bailin 1983). These considerations call into question the idea that the creative process can be understood primarily from the standpoint of a generative propulsion theory along the lines that Beardsley suggests.

One takes the point, however, about the limitations of understanding creation in art on the model of problem-solving. The idea that artistic creation might be understood along such lines has special appeal when we consider creative artistic activity in the context of biology and psychology. We find many examples in nature of phenomena, interactions, and changes—the intricate web construction of spiders, the building of birds' nests, the distribution of branches in a tree, in general the adaptation of organisms to natural conditions and constraints—that can be likened to human creative behaviour. Presumably the attribution of creativity to nature in such cases is merely metaphorical: we normally think of human creative activity as involving, among other things, the power of deliberative agency, although some (Godlovitch 1999; Arnheim 2001) have argued that natural organisms and nature generally are literally creative. In any case, in nature, no less than in a child's gradual construction of order out of chaos, we come across behaviours and activities that arise from the confrontation of problems the solution to which seem to call for 'creative' interventions (Perry 1988). There is no doubt that there are decisions to be made in most artistic creation and problems that present themselves, either prior to or during the act of creation. The work of psychologists such as Arnheim and Gombrich is rightly valued for its illuminating insights into various aspects of artistic activity, such as pictorial representation, that can be more or less understood along the line of problem solving. The problem-solving model also addresses the intuition that there is some continuity between creation in the arts, even at a very high level, and the activities of human beings generally (see also Baxandall 1985; Elster 2000).

This is not to say, however, that artistic creation can be understood solely or even primarily as a kind of problem solving. There are several points to be made here. The first is that, as we have noted, artistic creation seems possible in the absence of a sense of an overall guiding problem or set of problems to be solved (Beardsley 1966; Khatchadourian 1977; Howard 1982; Hospers 1985). Further, it is not clear what is to be gained by redescribing creative activity as 'problem solving'; indeed, some things may be lost. In certain cases the issues are methodological: some psychological studies proceed on the assumption that one can legitimately generalize from the ability of experimental subjects to solve relatively low-level riddles or puzzles, activities that may have little in common with the kinds of decisions that figure prominently in the work of creative artists (Leddy 1990). Nor does the problem-solving approach seem well equipped to account for what is typically packed into the positive valuation of artistic creative activity, the notion that, whatever problems might have been solved, the final result of creative artistic activity exhibits a significant degree of originality, profundity, insight, or some combination of these. A well solved problem need exhibit none of these qualities. Nor does the redescription of creative activity as problem solving tell us anything necessarily about the social, historical, and cultural context of artistic creativity. Computational theories of creativity that conceptualize creativity on the model of computer programs face the same challenges. Were they to succeed, they would have to come to grips with such elements as surprise, from the point of view of people familiar with the ideas and objects at hand, and value, whether that be construed in terms of utility, pleasure, or some other feature (Boden 1990; Novitz 1999). Finally, one has to bear in mind the differing challenges that the various arts bring to the table. No doubt there are some things to be said about 'the' creative process at a suitably abstract level, but are the 'problems' involved in the adjustment of colour in a painting very much like those encountered in choreographing a dance, sculpting a bust, setting a text to music, designing an architectural work, or improvising on a set of chordal changes?

It may be that the idea of a single general descriptive account of the creative process will not be forthcoming and that we shall have to rest content with identifying what seem to be the more salient features of the ways in which artists go about their creative work. One might still wonder, however, whether it is possible to move from questions of description to deeper questions of explanation. In the sense that an explanation makes something intelligible by providing an account of how it occurred, we have already begun the task. But we can also ask questions about why something occurs. We can ask, in particular, whether creative action can be rationalized with other human beliefs, desires, and intentional states such that we could arrive at adequate reasons why something creative was done.

At least three possible general strategies have already been implicitly suggested: that creative activity serves a human desire for gratification through aesthetic delectation, that it eases the mind through its clarifying expression of inchoate emotion, and that it serves a basic cognitive need. These strategies are, of course, not mutually exclusive. There is also an important explanatory route by way of depth psychology, i.e. the appeal to unconscious structures, motives, and mechanisms (see e.g. Ehrenzweig 1967). The epistemological difficulties of depth-psychological explanation of human behaviour are well known and there is much that is easily caricatured. At the same time, there is a fascination with and an appeal to the work of psychologists such as Freud, Jung, Rank, Winnicott, and others that persists even in the wake of serious epistemological worries about the explanatory power of these theories. This seems especially so in the case of the artistic creation, if not with respect to the question of creative activity *tout court*, at least regarding questions about the acquisition of skills and the decisions made by particular artists, where the appeal to deep levels of desire, conflict, concealment, symbolic significance, and play have their allure (Wollheim 1974; Spitz 1989).

There is a final point to consider about our understanding of the dynamics of creativity, a general issue that poses a challenge to all efforts to explain creation in art. If we grant that something like originality, spontaneity, or unpredictability is a necessary feature of the creative process, then must explanations of creativity necessarily explain creativity away? The point here is not just that creation in art, like all human activity, is psychologically complex, but that the explanation of artistic creative action in particular, as it is normally conceived, carries with it an inherent paradox (Tomas 1958; Henze 1966; Jarvie 1981; Hausman 1984).

2. THE CREATIVE PRODUCT

Philosophical considerations of creation in art need not focus on the nature of the creative process. Some philosophers distinguish questions about the creative process from questions about what makes something a creative work of art and argue that the former are irrelevant to the latter. The distinction has interpretative, ontological, and cultural dimensions.

After devoting pages to philosophical accounts of the creative process, for example, Beardsley (1966) declares that, however interesting it is to know how the artist's mind works, the value of the artist's work 'is independent of the manner of production even of whether the work was produced by an animal or by a computer or by a volcano or by a falling slop-bucket'. Beardsley's assessment, of course, is based on his well-known attack on intentionalism, famously presented in his essay, co-written with William Wimsatt, on the so-called Intentional Fallacy (Wimsatt and Beardsley 1946), and on his view that the chief value of art lies in the aesthetic gratification obtained in experience of the formal unity and regional qualities of works of art. 'The true locus of creativity', Beardsley argues, 'is not the genetic process prior to the work but the work itself as it lives in the experience of the beholder.'

Glickman (1976) argues that creation in art is a matter of product, not process, on somewhat different grounds. The verb 'create', he argues, is what Ryle calls an 'achievement verb'. To praise an artist for being creative is to offer praise not for a specific sort of activity, but for what he or she has accomplished, which is to say the created product. Furthermore, particulars are made; types are created. It is not the particular objects that we value in the case of creative activity in the arts, but the idea or the conception. We thus understand how it is that Duchamp created the (type) artwork *Bottlerack* even though he did not make the (particular) bottlerack employed. Similarly, Glickman argues, acknowledging a debt to Arthur Danto

(1981), we understand how a natural object such as a piece of driftwood could, in an appropriate cultural or theoretical context, qualify as an artwork.

Clearly, much hangs in these discussions on how we construe the notion of a 'work' of art, an exceedingly complicated topic. This much seems clear: any account of the ontology of works must be squared with the intuition that works are created by artists and that it is their creations that interest us; or, if the intuition is denied, an account of the denial is called for.

Consider the case of musical works. What sort of thing is a musical work of art? Let us for the moment concern ourselves with paradigmatically composed works such as a Beethoven quintet. If, as many contemporary philosophers would argue, such a musical work is indeed a type of some sort, instances of which are found in particular token performances of the work, it would seem natural to suppose that it is precisely the type that is created by composer. In developing his account of the musical work as a certain sort of structural type, for example, Levinson (1980) suggests that 'creatability' is, if not a strict requirement, at least a desideratum, of an adequate account of a musical work; that is, that musical works 'must be such that they do *not* exist prior to the composer's compositional activity, but are *brought into* existence *by* that activity'. This is one reason why, on Levinson's view, a musical work cannot be construed as a sound structure *per se*. (But for criticism of Levinson's view, see Kivy 1983.) Minimally, then, a Beethoven quartet is creatable in the sense that it is the sort of thing that is brought into existence by the composer. In addition, Beethoven's quartets, especially the late quartets, are widely admired for their creativity across a range of musical qualities, including their subtle and intricate motivic development, their technical demands, and their expressive depth. A quartet by a lesser figure, say Karl Ditters von Dittersdorf, would be creatable in the same sense as a Beethoven quartet, but—presumably—would be judged as less musically creative.

The intimate connection between creation and the ontology of music obtains as well in the case of improvised music. Though the improviser produces a particular sound structure, what typically interests us in the case of improvised music is a particular sort of action: the action of creating a musical work as it is being performed. Improvised music calls into play a different set of listening habits from those associated with the appreciation of composed works, or even the appreciation of performances of composed works. What we are interested in instead is what proves to be possible within the demands and constraints of improvisatory musical activity: the creation of a musical work as it being performed, with all the risks attendant upon the spontaneity and limited correctability of such activity (Alperson 1984). In this way, the creation of improvised music has parallels not only with other improvisational arts, such as improvisatory theatre, poetry, dance, and rap music, but also with many aspects of human action generally, including linguistic utterance (Shusterman 2000: 188–92; Hagberg 2000).

In addition, improvised music, like other varieties of music, occurs within a particular musical and historical tradition, and one's appreciation of the creativity of the music will be enhanced by the extent to which one is familiar with the history and the appreciative practices of the tradition in a variety of contexts. Jazz, as a kind of music in which improvisation plays a central role, is a case in point. The saxophone, for example, is a central instrument in improvised jazz. Someone for whom the mere sound of a saxophone is cause for discontent and avoidance is not likely to notice the creative timbral innovations of players such as Coleman Hawkins or John Coltrane, much less to appreciate that the *way* in which Paul Desmond was able to achieve and manipulate haunting, flute-like tonal qualities on the alto saxophone by opening his throat, adopting a loose embouchure, and using a Meyer hard rubber mouthpiece with an open facing in combination with a high strength reed and a Selmer Mark VI saxophone. Admittedly, that last bit of information is insider knowledge, but the appreciation of creativity in jazz is just as often enhanced by understanding of a less arcane sort. A listener unfamiliar with the history of jazz genres, for example, will likely miss the humour and inventiveness of Mose Allison's improvisations—baroque, sometimes crabbed overlays of bebop and blues melodic and harmonic styles. In many jazz compositions new melodies are superimposed on the harmonic progressions of standard and popular tunes or over chordal substitutions for the standard progressions. Listeners unaware of this tradition may not appreciate the wit or playfulness in an improvised performance of *Ornithology* that quotes or transforms phrases from *How High the Moon*, the tune on which *Ornithology* is based. Ears unaccustomed to or uncomfortable with musical chromaticism and dissonant harmonies may hear the improvisations of Charlie Parker as irruptions of sound rather than as adventurous harmonic explorations and displays of technical skill. A listener unable or unwilling to hear musical works as situated in social and political contexts will be unlikely to hear the freedom from traditional strictures of harmony, rhythm, sound, and musical forms in 'free jazz' improvisations of the 1960s and 1970s as manifestations of individual freedom and emblems of the drive towards racial equality. An appreciation of creativity in these various guises requires an understanding of the myriad contexts in which such performances are achieved.

Indeed, it can be argued that artworks, even those embodied in relatively stable physical things such as canvases, buildings, and written texts, present themselves as created works precisely in the sense that they are performances, outcomes or presentations of human creative action (Maitland 1976; Wollheim 1980; Sparshott 1982). If that is so, then the full appreciation and evaluation of created works will inevitably be tied to our appreciation of them as human achievements (see also Currie 1989).

These last comments about how we construe the creative work put us in mind of the cultural nature of creation in art and of the importance of understanding creation in art in the context of concrete historical traditions and institutions. There is undoubtedly a strain in some discussions of creation in art that regards artistic creativity as a manner of free, spontaneous, natural, and original activity of an autonomous subject. This tendency is traceable, through a long line of Romantic writers, to Kant's discussion of genius in the *Critique of Judgement*, the natural talent that 'gives the rule to art', the effect of which is to minimize the role and importance of 'external' constraints in the artistic creation of exemplary works. This is a rather attenuated notion of creation in art, one that has been the subject of serious criticisms on a number of fronts, especially by feminists and Marxists, who object to the model of subjectivity inherent in such a view and the related eclipse of the role of economic and social conditions and institutional structures that serve as preconditions for creative achievement in the arts. These preconditions affect virtually every aspect of creation in art, including the denomination of artists and works taken to be exemplars of creativity (Nochlin 1971; Adorno 1984; Battersby 1989). A full appreciation of artistic creativity would seem to call for a careful consideration of such matters.

There is also an important sense, as Leddy (1994) points out, in which the creative artistic product calls for a measure of creativity on the part of its audience. This can occur in a number of ways. Audiences may sometimes participate directly in the creation of works, as members of the artist's circle. Less directly, they may contribute to the creation of works through their interpretations and evaluations of them and their participation in the establishment of the evaluative categories of traditions, styles, periods, and so forth, in the context of which works are created. Last but by no means least, a work may be said to be actualized or realized in so far as it is imaginatively experienced by an appreciator, an activity that calls for creative activity on the part of the appreciator. In all these ways, creativity—for the artist, in the work, and for the audience—is a profoundly cultural affair.

See also: Ontology of Art; Expression in Art; Value in Art; Intention in Art; Music.

BIBLIOGRAPHY

Adorno, T. (1984). *Aesthetic Theory*, ed. G. Adorno and R. Tiedemann, trans. C. Lenhardt. London: Routledge.

Alperson, P. (1984). 'On Musical Improvisation'. *Journal of Aesthetics and Art Criticism* 63: 17–29.

Anderson, D. and Hausman, C. (1992) 'The Role of Aesthetic Emotion in R. G. Collingwood's Conception of Creative Activity'. *Journal of Aesthetics and Art Criticism* 50: 299–305.

Arnheim, R. (1962). *Picasso's Guernica: The Genesis of a Painting*. Berkeley: University of California Press.

—— (2001). 'What It Means To Be Creative'. *British Journal of Aesthetics* 41: 24–5.

Bailin, S. (1983). 'On Creativity as Making: A Reply to Götz'. *Journal of Aesthetics and Art Criticism* 41: 437–42.

Battersby, C. (1989). *Gender and Genius: Towards a Feminist Aesthetics*. London: Women's Press.

Baxandall, M. (1985). *Patterns of Intention: On the Historical Explanation of Pictures.* New Haven: Yale University Press.

Beardsley, M. (1966). 'On the Creation of Art' . *Journal of Aesthetics and Art Criticism* 25: 159–65.

Binkley, T. (1997). 'The Vitality of Digital Creation'. *Journal of Aesthetics and Art Criticism* 55: 107–16.

Boden, M. (1990). *The Creative Mind: Myths and Mechanisms.* New York: Basic Books.

Collingwood, R. G. (1938). *The Principles of Art.* Oxford: Oxford University Press.

Currie, G. (1989). *An Ontology of Art.* London: Macmillan.

Danto, A. (1981). *The Transfiguration of the Commonplace.* Cambridge, Mass.: Harvard University Press.

Dewey, J. (1934). *Art as Experience.* New York: G. P. Putnam's Sons.

Dutton, D. and Krausz, M. (eds.) (1981). *The Concept of Creativity in Science and Art.* Dordrecht: Martinus Nijhoff.

Ecker, D. (1963). 'The Artistic Process as Qualitative Problem Solving'. *Journal of Aesthetics and Art Criticism* 21: 283–90.

Ehrenzweig, A. (1967). *The Hidden Order of Art: A Study in the Psychology of Artistic Imagination.* Berkeley: University of California Press.

Elster, J. (2000). *Ulysses Unbound: Studies in Rationality, Precommitment, and Constraints.* Cambridge: Cambridge University Press.

Gardner, H. (1982). *Art, Mind, and Brain: A Cognitive Approach to Creativity.* New York: Basic Books.

Gaut, B. and Livingston, P. (eds.) (2002). *The Act of Creation.* Cambridge: Cambridge University Press.

Ghiselin, B. (ed.) (1952). *The Creative Process: A Symposium.* Berkeley: University of California Press.

Glickman, J. (1976). 'Creativity in the Arts', in L. Aagaard-Mogensen (ed.), *Culture and Art.* Atlantic Highlands, N.J.: Humanities Press, pp. 130–46; reprinted in J. Margolis (ed.), *Philosophy Looks at the Arts,* 3rd edn. Philadelphia: Temple University Press, 1987.

Godlovitch, S. (1999). 'Creativity in Nature'. *Journal of Aesthetic Education* 33: 17–26.

Gombrich, E. H. (1968). *Art and Illusion: A Study in the Psychology of Pictorial Representation.* London: Phaidon.

Götz, I. (1981). 'On Defining Creativity'. *Journal of Aesthetics and Art Criticism* 39: 297–301.

Hagberg, G. (ed.) (2000). Special Issue: 'Improvisation in the Arts'. *Journal of Aesthetics and Art Criticism* 58(2).

Hausman, C. (1984). *A Discourse on Novelty and Creation.* Albany, NY: State University of New York Press.

Henze, D. (1966). 'Creativity and Prediction'. *British Journal of Aesthetics* 6: 230–45.

Hospers, J. (1985). 'Artistic Creativity'. *Journal of Aesthetics and Art Criticism* 45: 243–55.

Howard, V. (1982). *Artistry: The Work of Artists.* Indianapolis: Hackett.

Jarvie, I. (1981). 'The Rationality of Creativity', in Dutton and Krausz (1981: 109–28).

Khatchadourian, H. (1977). 'The Creative Process in Art'. *British Journal of Aesthetics* 17: 230–41.

Kivy, P. (1983). 'Platonism in Music: A Kind of Defence'. *Grazer Philosophische Studien* 19: 109–29.

Koestler, A. (1964). *The Act of Creation.* London: Hutchinson; reprinted London: Penguin, 1989.

Leddy, T. (1990). 'Is the Creative Process in Art a Form of Puzzle Solving?' *Journal of Aesthetic Education* 24: 83–97.

—— (1994). 'A Pragmatist Theory of Artistic Creativity'. *Journal of Value Inquiry* 28: 169–80.

Levinson, J. (1980). 'What a Musical Work Is'. *Journal of Philosophy* 77: 5–28.

Maitland, J. (1976). 'Creativity'. *Journal of Aesthetics and Art Criticism* 34: 397–409.

Nochlin, L. (1971). 'Why Have There Been No Great Women Artists?' *ARTnews* 69: 22–39, 67–71; reprinted in P. Alperson (ed.), *The Philosophy of the Visual Arts*. Oxford: Oxford University Press, 1992.

Novitz, D. (1999). 'Creativity and Constraint'. *Australasian Journal of Philosophy* 77: 67–82.

Osborne, H. (1979). 'The Concept of Creativity in Art'. *British Journal of Aeshetics* 19: 224–31.

Patrick, C. (1937). 'Creative Thought in Artists'. *Journal of Psychology* 4: 35–73.

Perry, L. (1988). 'Creativity and Routine'. *Journal of Aesthetic Education* 22: 45–57.

Rampley, M. (1998). 'Creativity'. *British Journal of Aesthetics* 58: 265–78.

Shusterman, R. (2000). *Pragmatist Aesthetics: Living Beauty, Rethinking Art*, 2nd edn. Lanham, Md: Rowman & Littlefield (original edn, Oxford, 1992).

Sparshott, F. E. (1982). *The Theory of the Arts*. Princeton: Princeton University Press.

Spitz, E. (1989). 'Conflict and Creativity: Reflections on Otto Rank's Psychology of Art'. *Journal of Aesthetic Education* 24: 97–109.

Tomas, V. (1958). 'Creativity in Art'. *Philosophical Review* 67: 1–15.

Vermazen, B. (1991). 'The Aesthetic Value of Originality', in P. French, T. Uehling, Jr, and H. Wettstein (eds.), *Midwest Studies in Philosophy*, vol. XVI. Notre Dame, Ind.: University of Notre Dame Press, pp. 266–79.

Wallas, G. (1926). *The Art of Thought*. London: Jonathan Cape.

Wimsatt, W. K. and Beardsley, M. C. (1946). 'The International Fallacy'. *Sewanee Review* 54: 468–88.

Wollheim, R. (1974). 'Freud and the Understanding of Art', rev. edn, in R. Wollheim, *On Art and the Mind*. Cambridge, Mass.: Harvard University Press, pp. 202–19.

—— (1980). *Art and Its Objects*, 2nd edn. Cambridge: Cambridge University Press, esp. pp. 185–204.

CHAPTER 14

AUTHENTICITY IN ART

DENIS DUTTON

1. INTRODUCTION

'AUTHENTIC', like its near-relations, 'real', 'genuine', and 'true', is what J. L. Austin called a 'dimension word', a term whose meaning remains uncertain until we know what dimension of its referent is being talked about. A forged painting, for example, will not be inauthentic in every respect: a Han van Meegeren forgery of a Vermeer is at one and the same time both a fake Vermeer and an authentic van Meegeren, just as a counterfeit bill may be both a fraudulent token of legal tender but at the same time a genuine piece of paper. The way the authentic/inauthentic distinction sorts out is thus context-dependent to a high degree. Mozart played on a modern grand piano might be termed inauthentic, as opposed to being played on an eighteenth-century forte-piano, even though the notes played are authentically Mozart's. A performance of Shakespeare that is at pains to recreate Elizabethan production practices, values, and accents would be to that extent authentic, but may still be inauthentic with respect to the fact that it uses actresses for the female parts instead of boys, as would have been the case on Shakespeare's stage. Authenticity of presentation is relevant not only to performing arts. Modern museums, for example, have been criticized for presenting old master paintings in strong lighting conditions which reveal detail, but at the same time give an overall effect that is at odds with how works would have been enjoyed in domestic spaces by their original audiences; cleaning, revarnishing, and strong illumination arguably amount to inauthentic presentation. Religious sculptures created for altars have been said to be inauthentically displayed when presented in a bare space of a modern art gallery (see Feagin 1995).

Whenever the term 'authentic' is used in aesthetics, a good first question to ask is, *Authentic as opposed to what?* Despite the widely different contexts in which the authentic/inauthentic is applied in aesthetics, the distinction nevertheless tends to form around two broad categories of sense. First, works of art can possess what we may call *nominal authenticity*, defined simply as the correct identification of the origins, authorship, or provenance of an object, ensuring, as the term implies, that an object of aesthetic experience is properly named. However, the concept of authenticity often connotes something else, having to do with an object's character as a true expression of an individual's or a society's values and beliefs. This second sense of authenticity can be called *expressive authenticity*. The following discussion will summarize some of the problems surrounding nominal authenticity and will conclude with a general examination of expressive authenticity.

2. NOMINAL AUTHENTICITY

2.1 Forgery and Plagiarism

Many of the most often-discussed issues of authenticity have centred around art forgery and plagiarism. A forgery is defined as a work of art whose history of production is misrepresented by someone (not necessarily the artist) to an audience (possibly to a potential buyer of the work), normally for financial gain. A forging artist paints or sculpts a work in the style of a famous artist in order to market the result as having been created by the famous artist. Exact copies of existing works are seldom forged, as they will be difficult to sell to knowledgeable buyers. The concept of forgery necessarily involves *deceptive intentions* on the part of the forger or the seller of the work: this distinguishes forgeries from innocent copies or merely erroneous attributions. Common parlance also allows that an honest copy can later be used as a forgery, even though it was not originally intended as such, and can come to be called a 'forgery'. In such cases a defrauding seller acts on an unknowing buyer by misrepresenting the provenance of a work, perhaps even with the additions of a false signature or certificate of authenticity. The line between innocent copy and overt forgery can be, as we shall see, difficult to discern.

Plagiarism is a related but logically distinct kind of fraud. It involves the passing off as one's own of the words or ideas of another. The most obvious cases of plagiarism have an author publishing in his own name a text that was written by someone else.

If the original has already been published, the plagiarist is at risk of being discovered, although plagiarism may be impossible to prove if the original work, or all copies of it, is hidden or destroyed. Since publication of plagiarized work invites wide scrutiny, plagiarism is, unlike forgery, a difficult fraud to accomplish as a public act without detection. In fact, the most common acts of plagiarism occur not in public, but in the private sphere of work that students submit to their teachers.

2.2 Honest Misidentification

Authenticity is contrasted with 'falsity' or 'fakery' in ordinary discourse, but, as noted, falsity need not imply fraud at every stage of the production of a fake. Blatant forgery and the intentional misrepresentation of art objects has probably been around as long as there has been an art market—it was rife even in ancient Rome. However, many works of art that are called 'inauthentic' are merely misidentified. There is nothing fraudulent about wrongly guessing the origins of an apparently old New Guinea mask or an apparently eighteenth-century Italian painting. Fraudulence is approached only when what is merely an optimistic guess is presented as well-established knowledge, or when the person making the guess uses position or authority to give it a weight exceeding what it deserves. The line, however, that divides unwarranted optimism from fraudulence is hazy at best. (Any worldly person who has ever heard from an antique dealer the phrase 'It's probably a hundred and fifty years old' will understand this point: it's probably not that old, and perhaps not even the dealer himself could be sure if he's merely being hopeful or playing fast and loose with the truth.)

Authenticity, therefore, is a much broader issue than one of simply spotting and rooting out fakery in the arts. The will to establish the nominal authenticity of a work of art, identifying its maker and provenance—in a phrase, *determining how the work came to be*—comes from a general desire to understand a work of art according to its original canon of criticism: what did it mean to its creator? How was it related to the cultural context of its creation? To what established genre did it belong? What could its original audience have been expected to make of it? What would they have found engaging or important about it? These questions are often framed in terms of artists' intentions, which will in part determine and constitute the identity of a work; and intentions can arise and be understood only in a social context and at a historical time. External context and artistic intention are thus intrinsically related. We should resist, however, the temptation to imagine that ascertaining nominal authenticity will inevitably favour some 'old' or 'original' object over a later artefact. There may be Roman sculptures, copies of older Greek originals, which are in some respects aesthetically better than their older prototypes, as there may be copies by Rembrandt of other Dutch artists that are aesthetically more pleasing than the originals. But in all such cases, value and meaning can be rightly assessed only against a background of correctly determined nominal authenticity (for further discussion see Dutton 1983; Goodman 1976; Currie 1989; Levinson 1990).

2.3 Han van Meegeren

One of the most famous episodes of misidentification and fraudulence in the last century involves the van Meegeren Vermeer forgeries. The Dutch artist Han van Meegeren (1889–1947) was born in Deventer and studied in Delft, which was the home of the great seventeenth-century Dutch artist Johannes Vermeer. As his career declined in the years following the First World War, van Meegeren became increasingly resentful of dealers, critics, and academics. In part to wreak silent revenge on his enemies ('woman-haters and negro-lovers', he called them), but also simply to make money, van Meegeren tried his hand at forgery, producing in 1923 a *Laughing Cavalier*, ostensibly by Franz Hals. Later he turned to the much scarcer and more valuable paintings of Vermeer. (Fewer than forty Vermeers have survived into the twentieth century.) His most ambitious plan, hatched in the mid-1930s, was to forge a large Vermeer on a religious subject. This would have been an unusual find for an undiscovered Vermeer, and therefore an unlikely choice for a forger; but in fact van Meegeren was cleverly confirming published scholarly speculation that Vermeer had visited Italy and painted on religious themes in his youth, and that such paintings in a large, Italian style might yet be found. This forgery, *Christ and the Disciples at Emmaus*, was completed in 1937. To produce it, van Meegeren studied seventeenth-century pigment formulas, incorporated volatile flower oils in his pigments to create hardness, and used badger-hair brushes (a single modern bristle embedded in the paint would give him away) on canvas recycled from an unimportant seventeenth-century painting. He conceived a way to produce a *craquelure*, the fine web of surface cracking characteristics of old paintings, and concocted a plausible provenance for the work, claiming that it had come into his hands from an old Italian family that had fallen on hard times and wanted to dispose of the painting under strict confidentiality (Godley 1967; Dutton 1983). The work was ultimately purchased by the Boymans Museum in Rotterdam for a price of approximately 2.5 million US dollars (2002 value), two-thirds of which van Meegeren pocketed.

When the *Emmaus* was unveiled at the museum, van Meegeren had the satisfaction of standing at the edge of a crowd that heard the painting extolled by the eminent Vermeer scholar Abraham Bredius as perhaps '*the* masterpiece' of Vermeer (Bredius 1937). Van Meegeren went on to forge six more Vermeers, one of which ended up in the private collection of the Nazi Reichsmarschall Hermann Göring. Because van Meegeren was known to have dealt with this work, he was arrested by Dutch police a few days after the end of the war for having sold a Dutch national treasure to the enemy. Only then did he confess that he had actually created this painting and the others, going on to paint a last Vermeer in jail as a demonstration while he awaited trial. The trial itself was a media event, and the worldwide coverage made him a folk hero. Van Meegeren was given a prison sentence of only one year; he died of a heart attack shortly after beginning his sentence (Dutton 1983).

The van Meegeren episode is justifiably notorious as a case of recognized experts being hoodwinked by a clever, artistically gifted fraudster. As such, it calls into question both the validity of official expertise and the existence of ascertainable aesthetic values that should ideally enable art professionals to identify 'masterpieces' and distinguish them from inferior fakes. After all, if even renowned experts cannot tell the difference between a Vermeer and a van Meegeren, and if the van Meegeren has the power to delight museum visitors, as the *Emmaus* clearly did, then why should anyone care very much whether or not the painting is a Vermeer? Why should such a work be consigned to the basement? The discovery that it is forged does not, it seems, alter its perceived aesthetic characteristics. Arthur Koestler has argued that in such situations there can be no justification for rejecting a copy or forgery. If the forgery is indiscernible from an original (in the case of an identical copy), or if it fits perfectly into the body of work left by an artist, and produces aesthetic pleasure of the same kind as other works by the original artist, then there can be no warrant to exclude it from a museum (Koestler 1964).

In his influential discussion of forgery, Nelson Goodman has advanced arguments calling into question the idea that there can be no aesthetic difference between an original and an indiscernible forgery. In the first place, Goodman would have us ask, 'Indiscernible to whom?' Differences between the *Mona Lisa* and a so-called exact copy of it may be indiscernible to a child, but obvious to an experienced museum curator. Even if the curator cannot tell the difference between the one and the other, that does not mean that a difference will not emerge, and later on appear glaring not only to the curator, but to more innocent eyes as well. This process of change in perception, actually a sharpening of perception, is nicely illustrated by the van Meegeren episode. In the first place, it should be noted that, even at the time of the unveiling of the *Emmaus*, there was a divergence of opinion as to its authenticity. The local agent for the New York dealer Duveen Bros. attended the event and wired back to his employer that the painting was a 'rotten fake'. Moreover, the *Emmaus* in retrospect looks strangely unlike any extant Vermeers. There is a photographic quality to the faces that less resembles seventeenth-century portraiture than it does black and white movie stills; one of the faces, in fact, displays a striking resemblance to Greta Garbo. This overall 'modern' feel of the painting gave it a subtle appeal to its initial audience, but for the same reason it reveals to our eyes the painting's dated origin, as much as any 1930s movie betrays its origins with its hairstyles, make-up, gestures, and language. It seems that the agent for Duveen had a more sharply perceptive view than most of his contemporaries.

Goodman also pointed out another feature of forgery episodes that is especially relevant in the van Meegeren case. Any supposed new discovery of a work by an old artist will be assessed and authenticated in part by the extent to which its features conform to the artist's known *œuvre*. But once incorporated into the artist's *œuvre*, a new work, even if a forgery, becomes part of what Goodman calls the 'precedent class' of works against which further new discoveries will be assessed. In the case of van Meegeren, *Emmaus* was stylistically the closest of all his forgeries to the precedent class of authentic Vermeers. Once it was authenticated by Bredius and hung on the wall of the authoritative Boymans Museum, its stylistic features—heavy, drooping eyes with walnut-shell lids, for instance—became an accepted aspect of the Vermeer style. Van Meegeren's next forgery could therefore move farther from the original precedent class of Vermeers, the next one farther still, and so on, as the understanding of the Vermeer style became more and more distorted. Van Meegeren was also aided by the fact that most of his activity was carried out during the Second World War, with actual Vermeers in protective storage and unavailable for comparison. In the end, all of his forgeries were enough alike to each other, and different stylistically from authentic Vermeers, that it is certain their status would eventually have been revealed even without van Meegeren's confession (Dutton 1983).

Goodman suggests that, in general, knowledge that a work is a forgery, or even the suspicion that it is, conditions our viewing of the object, assigning it 'a role as training toward perceptual discrimination'. It is by trying to perceive as yet invisible differences between originals and forgeries that we actually do learn to detect them. Leonard Meyer is another theorist who has argued that cultural ideas about differences between an original and a forgery are indelibly part our perceptions of art. Our understanding of any human product, Meyer claims, requires 'understanding how it came to be and what it is and, . . . if it is an event in the past, by being aware of its implications as realized in history' (Meyer 1967). We can no more rid ourselves of these presuppositions of perception than, as he puts it, we can breathe in a vacuum. A related point is made by Denis Dutton, who argues that much of what we call *achievement* in art is implicit in our idea of the origins of a work of art. The excitement a virtuoso pianist generates by producing a glittering shower of notes in Liszt's *Gnomenreigen* is intrinsically connected with what we conceive to be an achievement of human hands playing at a keyboard. An aurally identical experience electronically synthesized fails to excite us: sound synthesizers can play as fast as you please, while pianists cannot. In the same way, however pleasant and skilful a modern forgery of a sixteenth-century master drawing may be, it can never be a sixteenth-century achievement, and therefore can never be admired in quite the same way (Dutton 1983).

2.4 The Igorot of Luzon

Forgery episodes such as van Meegeren's Vermeers are unproblematic in terms of nominal authenticity: there is a perfectly clear divide between the authentic Vermeers and the van Meegeren fakes. But there are areas where determining nominal authenticity can be extremely fraught. Consider the complexities of the following example. The Igorot of northern Luzon traditionally carved a rice granary guardian figure, a *bulul*, which is ceremonially treated with blood, producing over years a deep red patina which is partially covered with a black deposit of grease from food offerings. These objects were already being made for tourists and for sale at international exhibitions in the 1920s, and one famous virtuoso Igorot carver, Tagiling, was by then producing figures on commission by local families and at the same time for the tourist trade. *Bululs* are still in traditional use, but specialized production of them ceased after the Second World War. Today, if a local wants a *bulul*, it is purchased from a souvenir stand and then rendered sacred by subjecting it to the appropriate ceremony. 'The result', Alaine Schoffel has explained, 'is that in the rice granaries one now finds shoddy sculptures slowly becoming covered with a coating of sacrificial blood. They are authentic because they are used in the traditional fashion, but this renders them no less devoid of aesthetic value.' We do not necessarily have to agree with Schoffel's aesthetic verdict on 'shoddy' souvenirs to recognize that he is legitimately invoking one of the many possible senses of 'authenticity': the authentically traditional. The contrast to the authentically traditional carving in this context is a tourist piece, or one not made to take part in or express any recognizable tradition. On the other hand, a tourist piece that is bought by a local person and employed for a traditional purpose is just as authentic, but in a different sense: it has been given an authentically traditional use in an indigenous spiritual context. The fraudulent converse to authenticity in this sense would be a piece that is intentionally misrepresented as fulfilling a traditional function, but which does not, for example a piece that has been carefully given a fake patina and signs of use or wear by a dealer or later owner of a carving (Schoffel 1989).

2.5 Authenticity in Music

Arguments over the use and presentation of art are nowhere more prominent than in music performance. This is owing to the general structure of Western, notated music, in which the creation of the work of art is a two-stage process, unlike painting and other plastic arts. Stand in front of Leonardo's *Ginevra de' Benci* in the National Gallery in Washington, and you have before you Leonardo's own handiwork. However much the paint may have been altered by time and the degenerative chemistry of pigments, however different the surroundings of the museum are from the painting's originally intended place of presentation, at least, beneath the shatter-proof, non-reflective glass you gaze at the very artefact itself, in its faded, singular glory. No such direct encounter is available with a performance of an old musical work. The original work is specified by a score, essentially a set of instructions, which are realized aurally by performers, normally for the pleasure of audiences. Because a score underdetermines the exact sound of any particular realization, correct performances may differ markedly (Davies 1987).

With a painting, therefore, there normally exists an original, nominally authentic object that can be identified as 'the' original; nothing corresponds to this in music. Even a composer's own performance of an instrumental score—say, Rachmaninoff playing his piano concertos, or Stravinsky conducting *The Rite of Spring*—cannot fully constrain the interpretive choices of other performers or define forever 'the' authentic performance. (In any event, composer/performers interpret their music differently on different occasions.) Stephen Davies argues that a striving towards authenticity in musical performance does not entail that there is one authentic ideal of performance, still less that this would be a work's first performance or whatever a composer might have heard in his head while composing the piece. The very idea of a *performance* art permits performers a degree of interpretive freedom consistent with conventions that govern what counts as properly following the score (Davies 2001; see also Godlovitch 1998; Thom 1993).

Nevertheless, the twentieth century witnessed the development of an active movement to try to understand better the original sounds especially of seventeenth- and eighteenth-century European music. This has encouraged attempts to perform such music on instruments characteristic of the time, in line with reconstructions of the past conventions that governed musical notation and performance (Taruskin 1995). This concern with authenticity can be justified by the general, though not inviolable, principle which holds that 'a commitment to authenticity is integral to the enterprise that takes delivery of the composer's work as its goal. If we are interested in performances as of the works they are of, then authenticity must be valued for its own sake' (Davies 2001). This interest can take many forms—playing Scarlatti sonatas on harpsichords of a kind Scarlatti would have played, instead of the modern piano; using a Baroque bow over the flatter bridge of a Baroque violin to achieve more easily the double-stopping required of the Bach solo violin works; performing Haydn symphonies with orchestras cut down from the late Romantic, 100-player ensembles used by Brahms or Mahler. These practices are justified by taking us back in time to an earlier performing tradition and, in theory, closer to the work itself.

In this way of thinking, the purpose of reconstructing an historically authentic performance is to create an occasion in which it sounds roughly as it would have sounded to the composer, had the composer had expert, well equipped musicians at his disposal. Enthusiasm for this idea has led some exponents of the early music movement to imagine that they have a kind of moral or intellectual monopoly on the correct way to play music of the past. In one famous put-down, the harpsichordist Wanda Landowska is said to have told a pianist, 'You play Bach your way, I'll play him his way.' The question for aesthetic theory remains: *What is Bach's way?* If the question is framed as purely about instrumentation, then the answer is trivially easy: the Bach keyboard *Partitas* are authentically played in public only on a harpsichord of a kind Bach might have used. But there are other ways in which the music of Bach can be authentically rendered. For instance, Bach's keyboard writing includes interweaved musical voices which, under the hands of a skilled pianist such as Glenn Gould, can often be revealed more clearly on a modern concert grand than on a harpsichord (Payzant 1978; Bazzana 1997). In general, the dynamic range and gradation of the piano are an advantage for all music performed on it, in contrast with the harpsichord, though the older instrument displays some exquisite qualities in which Bach too can sound glorious. (Its lack of sustaining power, for example, required harpsichord composers to introduce trills and ornamentation which became part of the Baroque style.)

However, if an authentic performance of a piece of music is understood as one in which the aesthetic potential of the score is most fully realized, historic authenticity may not be the best way to achieve it. We would not go back to productions of Shakespeare plays with boys taking the female roles simply because that was the way it was done in Shakespeare's time. We regard the dramatic potential of those roles as ideally requiring the mature talents of actresses, and write off the Elizabethan practice of boy actors as an historic accident of the moral climate of Shakespeare's age. We assume, in other words, that Shakespeare would have chosen women to play these parts had he had the option. Similarly, the Beethoven piano sonatas were written for the biggest, loudest pianos Beethoven could find; there is little doubt that he would have favoured the modern concert grand, if he had had a choice. (Davies points out, however, that the appeal and point of some of Beethoven's piano writing, for instance with the *Appassionata Sonata*, is that it pushes to the limit, and beyond, the capabilities of Beethoven's instruments: on a modern grand, the sense of instrumental challenge in the power *Appassionata* is lost, or in any event reduced.) The best attitude towards authenticity in music performance is that in which careful attention is paid to the historic conventions and limitations of a composer's age, but where one also tries to determine the larger artistic potential of a musical work, including implicit meanings that go beyond the understanding that the composer's age might have derived from it. In this respect, understanding music historically is not in principle different from an historically informed critical understanding of other arts, such as literature or painting.

3. EXPRESSIVE AUTHENTICITY

In contrast to nominal authenticity, there is another fundamental sense of the concept indicated by two definitions of 'authenticity' mentioned in the *Oxford English Dictionary*: 'possessing original or inherent authority', and, connected to this, 'acting of itself, self-originated'. This is the meaning of 'authenticity' as the word shows up in existential philosophy, where an authentic life is one lived with critical and independent sovereignty over one's choices and values; the word is often used in a similar sense in aesthetic and critical discourse. In his discussion of authenticity of musical performance, Peter Kivy points out that, while the term usually refers to historical authenticity, there is another current sense of the term: performance authenticity as 'faithfulness to the performer's own self, original, not derivative or aping of someone else's way of playing'(Kivy 1995). Here authenticity is seen as committed, personal expression, being true musically to one's artistic self, rather than true to an historical tradition. From *nominal authenticity*, which refers to the empirical facts concerning the origins of an art object—what is usually referred to as provenance—we come now to another sense of the concept, which refers less to cut-and-dried fact and more to an emergent value possessed by works of art. I refer to this second, problematic sense of authenticity as *expressive authenticity*.

The nominal authenticity of a work of art of any culture may be impossible in many cases to know, but where it is possible, it is a plain empirical discovery. To identify expressive authenticity, on the other hand, is a much more contentious matter, involving any number of disputable judgements. Anthony Shelton's account of the art and culture of the Huichol of north-west Mexico illustrates ambiguities of expressive authenticity (Coote and Shelton 1992). Huichol traditional art is intimately bound up with the rituals that embody the Huichol cosmology and value system, combining aesthetic with local ethical notions. This art involves exchange relations, not only between human and supernatural beings, but also between wife-givers and wife-takers in traditional marriages. While Shelton repeatedly stresses how semiotically distant Huichol art is from Western models—for example in fusing the signifier with the signified—he nevertheless allows that it may have a 'counterpart' in the 'art and ideas of beauty developed in scholasticism in medieval Europe'. This is certainly true; the notion that a work of art—a statute of the Madonna, for instance—may on occasion actually incarnate, rather than merely represent, is hardly unknown in the European tradition.

Shelton describes the recent rise of Huichol commercial craft—specifically, constructions called 'yarn paintings', wooden tableaux (*tablas*) that depict episodes from traditional mythology. The yarn is brightly coloured commercial material, embedded in beeswax on a plywood base. While deeply sympathetic to Huichol culture, Shelton regards the development of a commercial market for Huichol work as having given birth to a meretricious form of art, something that is not an authentic Huichol cultural expression. The producers of these colourful, even gaudy, pieces, on the other hand, avow their authenticity as significant products of their culture. So who is Shelton, or any outsider, to dispute the indigenous opinion and the values that guide it?

The two most significant aspects of Shelton's critique of Huichol art involve issues of *continuity* and *audience*. While Shelton says there has been a tendency for outsiders and dealers to regard the yarn *tablas* as 'either a traditional artform or as having evolved from a traditional form', he rejects them as part of a continuous tradition. The Huichol do have a tradition of embedding beads and other materials in beeswax and in this manner decorating votive bowls and flat, wooden rectangles. But Shelton says that, with regard to the yarn constructions, he has been unable to trace any organic principle of evolution suggesting any kind of direct development from older forms. Shelton lists ways in which the *tablas* must be set apart from traditional Huichol art. The *tablas'* brightly dyed commercial yarns on plywood or fibreboard, dense with elaborate colour depictions, present something quite unlike sparingly decorated traditional votive objects. Furthermore, the context of production for the modern objects is not the sierra—they are made by Huichol people living in Guadalajara or Mexico City—and such objects, while illustrative of traditional mythologies, have no indigenous religious use.

Shelton therefore regards Huichol yarn *tablas* as indicative of the crumbling of traditional Huichol society. 'Commercial arts and crafts are antipathetic to traditional Huichol values', he says, because they serve 'none of the integrative purposes of traditional art'. As craft items made for sale to foreigners, the *tablas* are produced to appeal to a culture whose whole theory of knowledge is, on Shelton's account, radically different from Huichol tradition. The very translation of oral narratives into single pictorial representation takes from them the causal element intrinsic to their cultural character. Shelton notes that the flamboyance of the *tablas* makes them, in the view of Huichol people, items of 'conspicuous consumption'. In this way, the values they embody 'are foreign to the Huichol themselves, and conflict with their emphasis on humility and religious introspection'. Consequently, the *tablas* would never be purchased by traditional Huichols. The *tablas* have the overall effect of alienating Huichol people from their own culture. It is in these respects that it is legitimate to call Huichol *tablas* 'inauthentic'.

Shelton criticizes Huichol yarn construction for its failure to be continuously linked to historic Huichol artforms by what he calls an 'organic principle of evolution'. Continuity here means persistent presence of external form, and there is little doubt that this is an adequate criterion for authenticity in some contexts. But concentration on perceptible form ignores the more important issue at stake in assessing the expressive authenticity of art. Authenticity often implies that the original indigenous audience for an art is still intact; inauthenticity that the original audience is gone, or has no interest in the art, and that the art is now being created for a different audience, perhaps for foreign consumption. The authenticity question for Huichol yarn products does not depend on whether beeswax and/or yarn, commercially dyed or not, has been used in the past. The issue is that the yarn constructions have no part in the present religious economy or other aspects of traditional Huichol society, and therefore are not addressed to the people themselves, their fears, dreams, loves, tastes, obsessions. Nor are they subjected to criticism in terms of the values of an indigenous audience: they do not express anything about Huichol life to Huichol people. They are inauthentic in these respects.

3.1 Authenticity and Audiences

Too often discussions of authenticity ignore the role of the audience in establishing a context for creative or performing art. To throw light on the importance of an audience in contributing to meaning in art, consider the following thought-experiment. Imagine the complicated and interlocking talents, abilities, stores of knowledge, techniques, experience, habits, and traditions that make up the art of opera—for example as it is presented, or embodied, by a great opera company, such as La Scala. There is the music and its history, the dramatic stories, the staging traditions, the singers, from the chorus to the international stars, along with the distribution channels for productions—broadcasts, videos, and CDs. In addition, surrounding opera there is a whole universe of criticism and scholarship: historical books are written, academic departments study the music and the art and technique of singing, reviews for new casts and productions appear in magazines and daily newspapers. When the lights go down for a La Scala performance, the curtain rises not on an isolated artistic spectacle, but on an occasion that brings together the accrued work of countless lifetimes of talent, knowledge, tradition, and creative genius.

Now imagine the following: one day La Scala entirely loses its natural, indigenous audience. Local Italians and other Europeans stop attending, and local newspapers cease to run reviews of performances. Nevertheless, La Scala remains a famous attraction for visitors, and manages to fill the hall every night with busloads of tourists. Further, imagine that, although these nightly capacity crowds—consisting of people from as far away as Seoul, Durban, Yokohama, Perth, Quito, and Des Moines—are polite and seem to enjoy themselves, nevertheless, for nearly all of them their La Scala experience is the first and last opera they will ever see. They are not sure when to applaud, and although they are impressed by the opulent costumes, dazzling stage-settings, massed chorus scenes, and sopranos who can sing very high, they cannot make the sophisticated artistic discriminations that we would associate with traditional La Scala audiences of the nineteenth and twentieth centuries.

If we picture such a scene, how would we expect it to affect the art of opera as currently practised at this imaginary La Scala? The problem here is not just the loss of good singers or orchestral pit musicians: it is rather the loss of a *living critical tradition* that an indigenous audience supplies for any vital artform. It is impossible to engage in this thought-experiment without concluding that in the long term operatic art as practised at such a La Scala would steeply decline. A Pacific Island dancer was once asked about his native culture. 'Culture?' he responded. 'That's what we do for the tourists.' But if it is only for the tourists, who have neither the knowledge nor the time to learn and apply a probing canon of criticism to an artform, there can be no reason to expect that the artform will develop the complex expressive possibilities we observe in the great established art traditions of the world (Dutton 1993).

Why, then do critics and historians of art, music, and literature, private collectors, curators, and enthusiasts of every stripe invest so much time and effort in trying to establish the provenance, origins, and proper identity—the nominal authenticity—of artistic objects? It is sometimes cynically suggested that the reason is nothing more than money, collectors' investment values—forms of fetishizing, commodification—that drives these interests. Such cynicism is not justified by facts. The nominal authenticity of a purported Rembrandt or a supposedly old Easter Island carving may be keenly defended by its owners (collectors, museum directors), but the vast majority of articles and books that investigate the provenance of art works are written by people with no personal stake in the genuineness of individual objects. Moreover, when this comes into question, issues of nominal authenticity are as hotly debated for novels and musical works in the public domain as they are for physical art objects with a specific commodity value.

Establishing nominal authenticity serves purposes more important than maintaining the market value of an art object: it enables us to understand the practice and history of art as an intelligible history of the expression of values, beliefs, and ideas, both for artists and their audiences—and herein lies its link to expressive authenticity. Works of art, besides often being formally attractive to us, are manifestations of both individual and collective values, in virtually every conceivable relative weighting and combination. Clifford Geertz remarks that 'to study an artform is to explore a sensibility', and that 'such a sensibility is essentially a collective formation' whose foundations 'are as wide as social existence and as deep'(Geertz 1983). Geertz is only partially right to claim that the sensibility expressed in an art object is in every case *essentially* social: even close-knit tribal cultures produce idiosyncratic artists who pursue unexpectedly personal visions within a socially determined aesthetic language. Still, his broader description of works of art, tribal or European, is generally apt, along with its corollary that the study of art is largely a matter of marking and tracing relationships and influences.

This explains why aesthetic theories that hold that works of art are just aesthetically appealing objects—to be enjoyed without regard to any notion of their origins—are unsatisfactory. If works of art appealed only to our formal or decorative aesthetic sense, there would indeed be little point in establishing their human contexts by tracing their development, or even in distinguishing them from similarly appealing natural objects—flowers or seashells. But works of art of all societies express and embody both cultural beliefs general to a people and personal character and feeling specific to an individual. Moreover, this fact accounts for a large part, though not all, of our interest in works of art. To deny this would be implicitly to endorse precisely the concept of the eighteenth-century curiosity cabinet, in which Assyrian shards, tropical seashells, a piece of Olmec jade, geodes, netsuke, an Attic oil lamp, bird of paradise feathers, and a Maori patu might lay side by side in indifferent splendour. The propriety of the curiosity cabinet approach to art has been rejected in contemporary thought in favour of a desire to establish provenance and cultural meaning precisely because intra- and inter-cultural relationships among artworks help to constitute their meaning and identity.

4. CONCLUSION

Leo Tolstoy's *What Is Art?*, which was published near the end of his life in 1896, is the work of a genius nearly gone off the rails. It is famous for its fulminations not only against Beethoven, Shakespeare, and Wagner, but also even against Tolstoy's own great early novels (Tolstoy 1960). It continues, however, to be read for its vivid elaboration of a thesis that has a permanent place in the history of aesthetics: artistic value is achieved only when an artwork expresses the authentic values of its maker, especially when those values are shared by the artist's immediate community. Tolstoy allowed that modern art was dazzling in its ability to amuse and give pleasure, but damned it as devoid of the spiritual import that ultimately makes art significant to us. Not surprisingly, he lavished praise on naive folk art, especially the Christian art of the Russian peasantry. It is easy to imagine that, had he lived one or two generations later, Tolstoy might have extolled the 'primitive' art of tribal societies, not out of a desire to support the modernist agendas of Picasso or Roger Fry, but to champion the notion that the honest art of noble savages expresses authentic spiritual values rejected by modern society.

Tolstoy claimed that cosmopolitan European art of his time had given up trying to communicate anything meaningful to its audience in favour of amusement and careerist manipulation. While he may have been wrong in so dismissing all the art of his age, the extent to which his bitter, cynical descriptions of the art world of his time apply to both popular and high art of our own media-driven age is surprising. Where and how Tolstoy drew the line between art that is falsely sentimental and manipulative on the one hand, and sincerely expressive on the other, has been hotly disputed (Diffey 1985). But it is impossible that these categories could be entirely dispensed with, at least in the critical and conceptual vocabulary we apply to Western art. It is more than just formal quality that distinguishes the latest multimillion-dollar Hollywood sex-and-violence blockbuster or manipulative tearjerker from the dark depths of the Beethoven Opus 131 String Quartet or the passionate intensity of *The Brothers Karamazov*. These latter are *meant* in a way that many examples of the former cannot possibly be: they embody an element of personal commitment normally missing from much popular entertainment art and virtually all commercial advertising.

Consider as a last example Dirk Smidt's account of the carvers of Kominimung, a group of about 330 people living in the middle Ramu River region of Papua New Guinea. Kominimung carvers create masks and shields whose designs incorporate elaborate systems of colour-coding and visual symbols for the clans of the group. The clan affinities of the shields, which display clan emblems, are accorded the greatest importance by the men who bear them in skirmishes with their enemies in nearby villages. These emblems touch deep human feelings, Smidt explains, but they do more than that:

Warriors protecting themselves with shields are not just human beings holding a plank: they are protected by the ancestor of their clan depicted on the shield, with whom they identify....When holding the shield, they almost literally get under the skin of the ancestor via the unpainted part, resembling a tear drop, on the upper half of the back of the shield, which is the spot where the shield rests against the shoulder. (Smidt 1990)

The shield, Smidt claims, is a living being, the construction and painting of which goes through steps symbolizing the bones, flesh, blood, and skin of humans.

As a life may depend on its powers of defence, the making of a shield involves an intense devotion to getting the design and construction right. However, this does not entail slavish submission to the traditional demands of genre. Smidt states that 'much weight is given to individual execution'. He records that it is often said by the Kominimung that one should follow one's own ideas and not copy from another person. 'When a carver temporarily puts away a shield he has been working on he may turn it with its front towards the wall of the house, in order to prevent other carvers from "stealing his ideas".' In other words, while Kominimung shields are expressive of the sensibility of a culture, they are also understood at the same time to embody the sensibility of the individual carver. This is not merely a matter of local copyright on ideas: it involves the emergence of the carver's individual vision into the design of the shield or other carving. As one Kominimung carver told Smidt, 'A woodcarver must concentrate, think well and be inspired. You must think hard which motif you want to cut into the wood. And you must feel this inside, in your heart.' For the Kominimung, good carving is a matter of technical mastery, of feeling, and of *meaning it*.

Smidt's description of artistic life in Papua New Guinea reminds us that the idea of expressive authenticity is not exclusively Western. Varieties of formalism in aesthetics have at various times attempted to discount its significance, but if it is possible for art ever to express anything whatsoever, then questions of sincerity, genuineness of expression, and moral passion, are in principle relevant to it. Expressive authenticity is a permanent part of the conceptual topography of our understanding of art.

See also: Expression in Art; Medium in Art; Value in Art; Ontology of Art; Comparative Aesthetics; Painting.

BIBLIOGRAPHY

Arnau, F. [H. Schmitt] (1961). *The Art of the Faker*. Boston: Little Brown.
Bazzana, K. (1997). *Glenn Gould: The Performer and the Work*. Oxford: Clarendon Press.
Bowden, R. (1999). 'What Is Wrong with an Art Forgery? An Anthropological Perspective'. *Journal of Aesthetics and Art Criticism* 57: 333–43.
Bredius, A. (1937). 'A New Vermeer'. *Burlington Magazine* 71: 210–11.
Cebik, L. B. (1995). *Non-aesthetic Issues in the Philosophy of Art*. Lewiston, Maine: Edwin Mellen Press.
Coote, J. and Shelton, A. (eds.) (1992). *Anthropology, Art, and Aesthetics*. Oxford: Clarendon Press.
Currie, G. (1989). *An Ontology of Art*. London: Macmillan.
Davies, S. (1987). 'Authenticity in Musical Performance'. *British Journal of Aesthetics* 27: 39–50.

——(2001). *Musical Works and Performances: A Philosophical Exploration*. Oxford: Clarendon Press.

Diffey, T. J. (1985). *Tolstoy's 'What is Art?'* London: Croom Helm.

Dutton, D. (ed.) (1983). *The Forger's Art: Forgery and the Philosophy of Art*. Berkeley: University of California Press.

——(1993). 'Tribal Art and Artefact'. *Journal of Aesthetics and Art Criticism* 51: 13–22.

Feagin, S. (1995). 'Paintings and their Places'. *Australasian Journal of Philosophy* 73: 260–8.

Friedländer, M. J. (1930). *Genuine and Counterfeit*, trans. C. von Hornstett. New York: A. & C. Bonni.

Geertz, C. (1983). *Local Knowledge: Further Essays in Interpretive Anthropology*. New York: Basic Books.

Godley, J. (1967). *Van Meegeren, Master Forger*. New York: Charles Scribner's Sons.

Godlovitch, S. (1998). *Musical Performance: A Philosophical Study*. London: Routledge.

Goodman, N. (1976). *Languages of Art*. Indianapolis: Hackett.

Grafton, A. (1990). *Forgers and Critics: Creativity and Duplicity in Western Scholarship*. Princeton: Princeton University Press.

Hebborn, E. (1991). *Drawn to Trouble* (also published under the title *Master Faker*). Edinburgh: Mainstream Publishing Projects.

——(1997). *The Art Forger's Handbook*. London: Cassell.

Hoving, T. (1996). *False Impressions: The Hunt for Big Time Art Fakes*. New York: Simon & Schuster.

Jones, M. (ed.) (1990). *Fake? The Art of Detection*. Berkeley: University of California Press.

Kemal, S. and Gaskell, I. (eds.) (1999). *Performance and Authenticity in the Arts*. Cambridge: Cambridge University Press.

Kennick, W. (1985). 'Art and Inauthenticity'. *Journal of Aesthetics and Art Criticism* 44: 3–12.

Kenyon, N. (ed.) (1988). *Authenticity and Early Music*. Oxford: Oxford University Press.

Kivy, P. (1995). *Authenticities: Philosophical Reflections on Musical Performance*. Ithaca, NY: Cornell University Press.

Koestler, A. (1964). *The Act of Creation*. New York: Macmillan.

Koobatian, J. (compiler) (1987). *Faking It: An International Bibliography of Art and Literary Forgeries (1949–1986)*. Washington: Special Libraries Association.

Levinson, J. (1990). *Music, Art, and Metaphysics*. Ithaca, NY: Cornell University Press.

Meyer, L. (1967). 'Forgery and the Anthropology of Art', in his *Music, the Arts, and Ideas*. Chicago: University of Chicago Press.

Payzant, G. (1978). *Glenn Gould, Music, and Mind*. New York: Van Nostrand Reinhold.

Sagoff, M. (1978). 'On Restoring and Reproducing Art'. *Journal of Philosophy* 75: 453–70.

Sartwell, C. (1988). 'Aesthetics of the Spurious'. *British Journal of Aesthetics* 28: 360–7.

Savage, G. (1963). *Forgeries, Fakes, and Reproductions*. London: Barrie & Rockliff.

Savile, A. (1993). 'The Rationale of Restoration'. *Journal of Aesthetics and Art Criticism* 51: 463–74.

Schoffel, A. (1989). 'Notes on the Fakes which have Recently Appeared in the Northern Philippines'. *Tribal Art* (Musée Barbier-Mueller Bulletin) 12: 11–22.

Smidt, D. (1990). 'Kominimung Sacred Woodcarvings', in ter Keurs and D. Smidt (eds.), *The Language of Things: Studies in Ethnocommunication*. Leiden: Rijksmuseum voor Volkenkunde.

St Onge, K. M. (1988). *The Melancholy Anatomy of Plagiarism*. Lanham, Md: University Press of America.

Taruskin, R. (1995). *Text and Act: Essays on Music and Performance*. New York: Oxford University Press.

Thom, P. (1993). *For an Audience: A Philosophy of the Performing Arts*. Philadelphia: Temple University Press.

Tietze, H. (1948). *Genuine and False*. London: Max Parrish.

Tolstoy, L. (1960). *What Is Art?* [1896], trans. Almyer Maude. Indianapolis: Bobbs-Merrill.

Van Bemmelen, J. M. *et al.* (eds.) (1962). *Aspects of Art Forgery*. The Hague: Martinus Nijhoff.

Young, J. (1988). 'The Concept of Authentic Performance'. *British Journal of Aesthetics* 28: 228–38.

CHAPTER 15

INTENTION
IN ART

PAISLEY LIVINGSTON

In aesthetics and literary theory, intentions are most often discussed in debates over standards of interpretation. A major shortcoming of such debates, it has been observed, is a lack of insight into the nature and functions of intentions (e.g. Aiken 1955; Wollheim 1987). With that point in mind, this chapter is designed to complement other recent surveys (e.g. Taylor 1998; Lyas 1992), that focus primarily on intention and interpretation. The first section surveys claims about what intentions are and do, while the second turns to arguments regarding the place of intentions in the appreciation of art.

1. PERSPECTIVES ON THE NATURE OF INTENTIONS

1.1 Eliminativism

Eliminativism is the thesis that all concepts of intention belong to some false theory that ought to be done away with. In its extreme, materialist version, eliminativism targets mentalism as a whole: behaviour, we are told, is correctly explained not in terms of reasons or such meaningful attitudes as intentions, but in terms of physico-chemical processes in the brain. In its various culturalist, historicist, and semiotic versions, eliminativism targets the illusion of the subject's intentional action, which is contrasted to those factors said actually to generate human activity, such as external social conditions and unconscious internal processes, symbolic and libidinal.

Not unsurprisingly, the materialist brand of eliminativism has had few advocates in aesthetics, although some literary theorists have flirted with the view. Historicist calls for the demotion of 'the subject', and even of individual agency *in toto*, have, however, been numerous. Roland Barthes (1968, 1971) notoriously announced 'the death of the author' and temporarily promoted an anonymous textuality freed from repressive parental bonds. Michel Foucault (1994) is often cited as having provided a penetrating critique of the 'author-function', which he described as the product of various operations readers perform on discourses. Many literary theorists have advocated understanding works of art in terms of the artist's unconscious drives and 'strategies', while rejecting the pertinence of 'conscious intentions' and other 'rationalist' constructions. Various critiques (Dutton 1987; Hjort 1993; Lamarque 1996; Livingston 1997) target the ambiguities, historical inaccuracies and undesirable practical implications of these extreme post-structuralist proposals. These authors have argued that a non-honorific conception of authorship, centred on agents' intentional production of utterances, is more cogent than the post-structuralists allow, and that it has not been shown that either individual or collective authorship is the essentially repressive product of a modern European discursive formation.

1.2 Minimal Views

Minimalist views of intention within attitude psychology equate intentions with one of several meaningful cognitive or motivational states, such as forecasts, inklings, urges, wants, hopes, or longings. The social psychologists Martin Fishbein and Icek Ajzen, for example, define intention as 'a person's subjective probability that he will perform some behaviour' (Fishbein and Ajzen 1975: 12). Another proposal is that an intention is a conscious plan to perform some behaviour (Warshaw and Davis 1985). Intention has also been equated with an evaluative attitude, with predominant motivation, and with volition or the will.

Remarks made by some critics and theorists of the arts imply acceptance of some such minimalist view of intending. A key idea here is that intentions are private fancies regarding some action an artist imagines some day undertaking. As such, they make no real difference to those moments of genuine inspiration when unpredictable winds breathe germs of creativity into the artist. At the other extreme, intention is understood as another name for the artist's will, a decisive and atomic mental state that can bestow or create meaning.

1.3 Reductive Analysis of Intending

The reductive analysis of intending within action theory (Audi 1973, 1997; Beardsley 1978; Davis 1984) denies that 'intention' refers to a kind of mental state, proposing instead that the term actually picks out the functions served by particular combinations of beliefs and desires, or what Donald Davidson (1963) dubbed a 'primary reason'. Intending is composed of, and reducible to, a performance expectation suitably related to predominant motivation. Intending is not reducible to belief alone, because someone can believe she will end up doing something, such as succumbing to temptation, without having any such intention. And intending is not reducible to wishing, wanting, or desiring, because the latter need not result in any intention to act, if only because the objects of some longings are believed to be out of reach.

The reductive analysis of intending is rarely mentioned in literary theory or aesthetics (an exception is Carroll 1992: 120), but the intuitions behind it surface in much discourse about artists and their doings. For example, it is often said that an artist might want, but still not intend, to do something in a well mastered manner, as opposed to facing the challenge of attempting something less familiar and more difficult. Intending to write the libretto for an opera requires not just a want or a desire, but a determination to try to do so. A cognitive condition on intending is also frequently evoked. A lucid artist cannot simply intend someday to create a masterpiece, but he can intend to try, as long as he does not believe the attempt impossible. An art critic can both hope and predict that the contemporary British artist Lisa Milroy will paint another of her still-life pictures, but only she can intend to do so.

1.4 Non-reductive Views

Non-reductive views of intention in action theory hold that intention refers to a distinctive, psychologically real mental state serving a range of significant functions in the lives of purposeful, temporally situated agents (Bratman 1987; Mele 1992; Brand 1984, 1997). As a meaningful attitude, intention is directed towards some situation or state of affairs. The content of an intention—a plan—is schematic, requiring specification and adjustment at the time of action. A plan provides some more or less definite specification of the intended behaviour and results. Part of that schema is a representation of a temporal relation between, on the one hand, the moment at which the state of intending obtains and, on the other hand, the time or times at which the intended activity is to be undertaken. Schematically, then: S intends now (at t_1) to A during t_2. We speak of future-directed or distal intentions when $t_1 < t_2$, and of immediate, present-directed, or proximal intentions when t_1 converges on or equals t_2. Many intentions are temporally mixed. Intending to begin work on a symphony now, a composer is also settled on performing various related future actions. He even intends to intend, in the sense that he plans to form and act on other relevant intentions when the time comes. When he began work on his First Symphony,

Johannes Brahms most likely did not intend to continue working on it for fourteen years, but we may surmise that he meant to continue working on it until he was satisfied with his results.

Many of our future-directed intentions are never acted upon, let alone realized. Proximal intentions, on the other hand, are usually acted on. But this does not imply that an agent's intention to do something right away is always successfully realized, even when he tries to do so. An intention is realized only when the situation specified in the plan becomes actual, and only when this happens in the way indicated by the plan. Suppose, for example, that when Karen Blixen, who most often published under the name of Isak Dinesen, writing in her uncertain, and at times quite anachronistic, English, typed the word 'outlandish', she meant 'foreign', or *udenlandske* (as she wrote when she later translated the phrase into Danish). She acted on—and realized—her intention to type a particular word, but she did not realize her specific semantic intention in the planned manner, even though her meaning can be inferred from what she actually wrote, given an understanding of how *faux amis* creep into the language of polyglots.

Various aspects of our discourse about the arts are hard to square with the prevalent idea that future-directed intentions make no difference to the creative process. Franz Schubert's Eighth Symphony is aptly called '*Das Unvollendete*' ('Unfinished') only if he at some point actually had the intention of composing all four movements, but for one reason or another never did so. Romantic fragments are intended to be fragmentary, in the sense that they are designed to lack parts usually held requisite to the completion of a work in some genre (Livingston 1999). Whenever we deem a work of art finished or complete, we assume that the artist decided it was so and intentionally refrained from making further changes to the artistic structure, text, or performance. More generally, an artist's intentional refrainings—doing one thing as opposed to another—are an integral part of the story of an unfolding artistic career. Various sorts of future-directed intentions, as well as retrospective states directed at prior intentions, help artists negotiate the difficult passage from work to work (Levinson 1996; Livingston 1996; Gaut and Livingston 2003).

Philosophers have suggested that future-directed intentions perform a variety of functions, including framing and motivating deliberation about what is to be done; initiating, motivationally sustaining, and guiding intentional behaviour; helping to coordinate agents' behaviour over time; and facilitating interaction with other agents (Mele 1992). For example, an artist's intention to finish a particular work provides a helpful constraint on his or her activities, ruling out certain incompatible plans. Settling on a plan to make a trilogy of films, the artist gives herself a framework within which a large-scale creative effort can be developed. Nearing the completion of one work in the series, she can already begin to plan the next one, looking for ideas related interestingly to the overall scheme. The artist can enjoy introducing unexpected variations, shifts of style, and thematic emphasis. Having committed himself to a plan, the writer is motivated to realize or improve upon the scheme with which the work began. Moments of inspiration, or in other words, periods when the creative artist enjoys heightened concentration and a relatively easy and non-deliberative flow of ideas or gestures, are prepared for and informed by a great deal of planning and effort.

Various philosophers have contended that the present-directed or proximal species of intending is at work in 'intention in action', which is in turn held to be basic to the very difference between purposeful action and mere happenings or events. On one analysis of intention in action, in performing some movement or mental operation, the agent intends that movement or operation to realize some targeted state of affairs (Wilson 1989: 124). For example, pressing her finger down on one of the keys of the typewriter, Blixen intended, *of that motion*, that it be a typing of the letter 'o'; she acted with the further intention of going on to make of it the first letter in the word 'outlandish', which in turn was to be part of a phrase in a story entitled 'Alkmene', itself meant to be part of a collection called *Winter's Tales*. (For more on 'intentions in action', see Pacherie 2000.)

Theorists have debated the thesis that intending is necessary to all intentional actions. Gestures necessary to the success of an intentional action (such as dotting the 'i's when writing the word 'writing') may not themselves have been planned explicitly, in the sense of having been the object of an actual state of intending, yet their execution may plausibly be said to be intentional. It can be responded, however, that the acquisition of intentions is sometimes a sudden and unconscious process, so that even an artist's most spontaneous and subsidiary gestures are actually informed and guided by rapidly acquired intentions. The acquisition of intention, then, can, but need not, be the outcome of a bout of conscious deliberation. Those that are may be called the artist's decisions or choices.

Another objection to the view that intentional action entails intending is based on unintended side-effects. For example, in writing a poem, it was not Johann Wolfgang von Goethe's intention to exacerbate Karl-Philipp Moritz's feelings of artistic inferiority, but it may be thought that, as he did in fact anticipate such an outcome, his realization of that unwanted consequence was intentional. Yet intuitions about such cases diverge, and some authors propose that such an action is better labelled as 'non-intentional' rather than 'unintentional' (Mele and Moser 1994). It may be right, then, to assume that following one's intention-embedded plan is a necessary condition of performing an intentional action. Such a view is compatible with recognizing the unpredictable and spontaneous moments in the creative process, since it is not assumed that a plan is a complete, unalterable, or fully determinate specification of the requisite means and ends. Anthony Savile (1969: 123) makes a similar point when he suggests that the absence of a prior, future-directed intention should not be taken as implying that the artist's activity was not intentional.

Another issue that regularly complicates discussions of the relevance of intentions has to do with whether intentions can be unconscious. If intentions are mental states that always involve a kind of lucid, focal awareness—such as a vivid feeling of what it is like to have a specific goal—it seems highly implausible to hold that artists have intentions regarding all of the semantic aspects of their works. Working with such an assumption about the link between consciousness and intention, psychoanalytic critics regularly describe the unintended symbolic meanings of works of art. If, on the other hand, some of the semantic aspects of intentional activities need not be consciously entertained by the agent, various meanings could be at once unconscious and intended. Debates over the merits of these two sorts of views remain superficial as long as nothing more precise is said about what is meant by 'conscious'—a notoriously difficult task. Many contemporary action theorists (e.g. Mele 1992) assume that intention can be formed rapidly, without deliberation, and without the emergence of focal awareness or of a second-order (conscious) belief to the effect that the agent has this intention. One can also coherently add that an agent's conscious states are not infallible guides to that agent's actual intentions.

It is important, in any case, to recall that Freudians hold no monopoly on the idea of unconscious mental states or processes. Hundreds of thinkers writing prior to Freud accepted the idea of unconscious mentation (Whyte 1962), and many contemporary philosophers and cognitive psychologists do the same.

2. INTENTION AND THE APPRECIATION OF WORKS OF ART

The term 'appreciation' can be used to cover the description, understanding, interpretation, and evaluation of works of art, a common assumption being that an appreciator's aim is to attend to the work *qua* work of art, that is, in its capacity as work of art. The focus in what follows will be on that part of appreciation that involves the attribution of meanings, although contrasts between understanding and evaluation will at times be drawn. The arguments to be surveyed mostly share the background assumption that it is possible and desirable to articulate epistemic standards for the assessment of interpretations. Scepticism about this theoretical ambition has, however, been expressed, it being doubted that any general norms can embrace the varied goals of such a motley matter as the interpretation of the arts (Cioffi 1963–4; Gaut 1993; Walton 1990). One response to this worry is to acknowledge the multifarious contexts and goals of appreciation, while seeking to articulate standards relevant to *selected* interpretive desiderata. I here set aside a range of problems linked to the question of which projects should and should not be counted as interpretations or appreciations, and the classification of kinds of interpretation (Carlshamre and Petterson 2003).

If, as some eliminativists say, attitude psychology is a false and dispensable theory of human activity, or if intentions do not figure within the correct psychological scheme, then appreciations of works of art ought not refer to them. Both antecedents, however, are extremely controversial. Their exponents must shoulder the heavy burden of arguing for views that would in turn require a massive revision of the discourse of the history and criticism of the arts. Theoretical rejections of attitude psychology lead to performative self-contradictions, as when the writer expresses his belief that we should decide that there are no beliefs or decisions. Theorists who call for a ban on reference to 'conscious intentions' often rely on versions of psychoanalysis that overlook the place of ego psychology and intentional action within everyday psychology, as well as within several Freudian frameworks. For example, Jacques Derrida (1977) insists that the ambivalence, indeterminacy, and 'primary masochism' of the unconscious fully subverts speech act theory's various distinctions based on types of illocutionary intention. In other contexts, however, he has been adamant about the importance and efficacy of his own writerly intentions (Dasenbrock 1994).

Problems with extreme eliminativist perspectives motivate the conclusion that the interesting and challenging anti-intentionalist arguments are those that deny the *relevance* of intention to appreciation, while granting that texts, structures, performances, and other artistic offerings are at least in part the *results* of intentional action, the production of which is to some degree guided by the relevant agents' intentions or plans.

In its most extreme version, intentionalism in aesthetics is the thesis that the meanings of a work of art are all and only those intended by the artist: the work's meaning is logically equivalent to the artist's intended meanings, semantic willings, or 'final intention' (Hancher 1972; Hirsch 1967, 1976; Juhl 1980; Irwin 1999). Apt appreciations are said to require uptake of artists' relevant intentions. It is usually conceded, however, that the artist's intention to make a valuable work of art does not entail success in the realization of that goal, even when the intention is acted upon. On the other hand, uptake of the artist's goals is often deemed crucial to critical evaluation, even in cases where the artist's semantic intentions have not been realized.

In its most extreme version, anti-intentionalism is the claim that the meanings of a work of art are all and only those of the text, performance, artefact, or other artistic item taken by itself. Meanings are not determined by the artist's intentions, and uptake of the latter can contribute nothing to apt appreciation. Anti-intentionalists hold, for example, that even the recognition of irony need involve no reference to the empirical author's actual attitudes or aims (Nathan 1982, 1992), since the ironic sense is manifest in the tone and other connotations of the text. Attitudes expressed by a narrator, for example, are contradicted by those of the implicit or fictional author, whose opinions may or may not correspond to those of the actual writer. Some anti-intentionalists (Davies 1982) hold that artists' intentions are even irrelevant to the assessment of a work's aesthetic value, since such value, they think, resides in properties immanent in the work, or in whatever functions it may serve for appreciators. Alternatively, one may be an anti-intentionalist about meaning while contending that recognition of the artist's value-relevant aims is necessary to apt appreciation.

Although the extreme positions just delineated still have advocates (e.g. Knapp and Michaels 1982; Dickie and Wilson 1995), arguments in the literature have convinced many (e.g. Pettersson 2000: 291) that an intermediate position is needed. Some of the more salient proposals will be identified in the following sketch of some recent arguments.

Anti-intentionalists often press epistemological worries about intentions. How can anyone, including the artist herself, know anything about these dark and elusive creatures of the mentalist night? In response, intentionalists concede that we can be mistaken about intentions, but they deny that scepticism about intentions *per se* has any special warrant (Hirsch 1976: 96–103). For example, Goethe, the Danish writer Steen Steensen Blicher, and many others had false beliefs about the intentions of James Macpherson and Ossian, son of Fingal (a mythical Scottish bard invented by Macpherson as part of an elaborate hoax). Yet there is good reason to believe that relevant aspects of Macpherson's deceptive intentions finally did come to light.

Another intuitive source of anti-intentionalism is the idea that to emphasize the achievements of individual art producers is to perpetuate the biases of the 'great man theory of history' and, more generally, an ideology of bourgeois individualism (Heath 1973). Intentionalists respond by distinguishing between distal and proximal explanations, where the latter require reference to the springs of action within the individual art-maker. One can also question the soundness of the holistic theories on offer in the literature. Sometimes collective intentions are essential to the creative process. An example is the Japanese poetic genre of *ranga*, in which groups of three or four poets write alternating stanzas. Such cases block the inference from intentionalism to individualism. Analyses of joint or collective intentions (e.g. Bratman 1999) are a resource that critics and aestheticians have only begun to draw upon. (An exception is Ponech 1999.)

Anti-intentionalists rightly point to the shortcomings of a dated form of biographical criticism that tries to reduce the meanings of complex works of art to symptomatic indications of events in artists' lives, an interpretive strategy that is especially inadequate when it amounts to viewing all novels as *romans à clef*. Intentionalists often respond by saying that extreme anti-intentionalist standards of interpretation and evaluation are not the proper corrective to critical gossip; instead, biographical criticism should be understood as 'retrieval', or the reconstruction of the creative process, where the latter is taken 'as something not stopping short of, but terminating on, the work of art itself' (Wollheim 1980: 185).

Just what is and is not to be covered by the expression 'the work of art itself' remains the crux. Some anti-intentionalists assume that a work simply *is* a totally detached or independent artefact, object, text, or performance, and that attending to the latter's wholly intrinsic features is sufficient. Intentionalists contend, on the contrary, that a work of art's meanings, artistic and aesthetic values, and indeed its very identity and individuation *qua* work of art depend on a broader array of properties than those non-relational properties that are inherent in an artefact or type thereof. The meaning of a sequence of words is not inherent in them, but is related to the semantic rules or conventions of the language or languages in which those words were uttered. Nor can the verbal sequence that constitutes the text of a novel be identified independently of the author's operative attitudes, such as the decision that a given text is finished, or the intention that it be regarded in such-and-such a way (Currie 1991; Levinson 1992). Here the debate over the relevance of artists' intentions to appreciation leads to the question of their relevance in accounts of the definition of art and of the ontology of works—topics that can only be touched on in what follows.

Many anti-intentionalists have in fact acknowledged that the meanings of a text or symbolic artefact involve its relation to contextual factors. Anti-intentionalists are thus led to broaden the evidentiary bases of appreciation to embrace an array of facts that are not simply inherent in the artefact. In the case of the authors of the ever-influential 'The Intentional Fallacy', such considerations led to no small admission: the evidence said to be 'internal' to the poem was expanded to include not just the text and the language in which it was written, but 'all that makes a language and culture' (Wimsatt and Beardsley 1946/1976: 6). What, then, one may wonder, does this leave out? The banished 'external evidence', it turns out, was the author's 'private' or 'idiosyncratic' semantic intentions, or revelations in journals, letters, or reported conversations. A recurrent argument for this central anti-intentionalist claim takes the form of a dilemma: either the writer's semantic intentions are expressed in the text—when interpreted in the relevant context—in which case knowledge of them is unnecessary, or the intentions are not so expressed, in which case recognition of them does not suffice to identify the work's actual meanings.

One intentionalist response to this dilemma is to say that whether or not a work's meanings are the product of design is always relevant to appreciation. For example, the fact that a characterization in a novel is only accidentally funny makes a difference to our understanding and evaluation of the work. What is more, strong anti-intentionalist strictures run contrary to our legitimate interest in many personal qualities—such as sincerity—that have artistic and ethical implications (Lyas 1983*a,b*; Taylor 1999).

A second response to the dilemma points to the problem of the determination of a work's *implicit* meanings or content, such as those dimensions of a story not directly conveyed or depicted. Reference to the cultural context alone is insufficient in this regard, since a story-teller can choose to tell a story in which the framework facts, including implicit ones, are not those standardly taken for granted by members of the audience. Settling on implicit story truths is one of the author's tasks in the narrative division of labour, and it is legitimate for interpreters to use whatever evidence is available to discover those authorial determinations.

Anti-intentionalists object that, if authorial intent is taken to be decisive with regard to implicit (and other) meanings, we end up with what Alfred MacKay (1968) castigated as 'Humpty Dumpty's semantics'—the ludicrous idea that utterances always mean only whatever the utterer meant to say. This point motivates the shift to a moderate version of intentionalism, which agrees that features of the text or artefact should constrain our understanding of which intentions are and are not realized in the work. For example, although Stéphane Mallarmé reported that he was writing '*L'Après-midi d'un faune*' with the intention of presenting it for performance at the Théâtre Français, when he eventually acted on this intention, the members of the committee rejected the proposal because they did not think he had succeeded in writing a dramatic poem. A poem is not dramatic, funny, or expressive of a particular range of meanings whenever the author intended it to be so. Nor does a work carry implicit meanings that are incompatible with the meaningful features of the text, performance, artefact, or other item actually presented to the public for the sake of appreciation. A moderate version of *actualist intentionalism* holds, then, that some intentions are never realized and do not determine a work's meanings, and that some of the latter are, like various other relevant properties, unintended. The moderate intentionalist also claims that the successful realization of certain kinds of intentions is necessary to the creation of a work of art having determinate meanings. As a result, apt appreciation must involve uptake of at least some of the relevant intentions, such as those related to implicit meanings (Iseminger 1992, 1996; Carroll 1992; Mele and Livingston 1992; Livingston 1998; Savile 1996).

Agreement that an acceptable version of intentionalism must be qualified in some way has not, however, yielded consensus about how this should be done. William Tolhurst (1979) proposes that interpreters should aim at elucidating utterance meaning, which is logically distinct from utterer's meaning or actual artist's semantic intentions. *Utterance meaning* is a hypothesis or construction of utterer's meaning based solely on that evidence which members of the *author's intended* audience possess by virtue of membership in that audience. As reference to the actual author's intentions in the determination of the target audience makes Tolhurst's *hypothetical intentionalism* depend upon an actual intentionalism (Nathan 1982), it has been suggested that such reference should be replaced by the notion of the appropriate audience defined in terms of an independent specification of the kinds of evidence such an audience is meant to rely upon in the formulation of an hypothesis about utterance meaning. In particular, such evidence includes a broad array of facts about the cultural and historical context within which the work has been made, but also the categorial intentions with which the actual artist made the work. Categorial intentions are, for example, the intention that a text or structure be appreciated as a work of art, that it be taken as a work of fiction, or that it belong to a particular genre or type of work (cf. Walton 1970). In the version articulated by Levinson (1992, 1999), hypothetical intentionalism is the thesis that appreciation depends crucially on proper uptake of categorial intentions, but does not similarly depend on uptake of semantic ones. More specifically, should the actual artist's semantic intentions fall short of more artistically valuable meanings compatible with the brute artefact, then the critic should opt for the latter. One question raised by Levinson's proposal is how semantic intentions are to be distinguished from the artist's various other intentions. Another issue concerns the motivation for a sharply asymmetrical treatment of the two sorts of intentions. It may be wondered why the hypothetical intentionalists' reasons for insisting on the uptake of categorial intentions do not also apply to semantic and hybrid intentions (see Livingston 1998).

Other versions of intentionalism have been proposed, each motivated by alternative assumptions about interpretation, its goals, and the nature and status of intentions. Stanley Fish (1991) has combined a version of absolute intentionalism, in which all attributions of meanings are necessarily attributions to some author, with a sharp anti-realist thesis, according to which authors are always and only the projections or constructs of interpreters. Fish denies that the target of such projections should be constrained by any common-sense assumptions about authorial agency: an author could be a *Zeitgeist*, a community, or anything else projected by readers as the locus or source of meaning. Evidently, the interpretive freedom won in this manner is good for the business of criticism, which is thereby freed from the evidentiary constraints entailed by such traditional epistemic desiderata as 'making an original contribution to knowledge'. Alexander Nehamas's (1981) proposal for a *fictionalist intentionalism* is similarly instrumentalist in spirit, but weighs a constraint of historical verisimilitude on the interpreter's imagination of the authorial persona. To interpret a text or structure or performance as a work of art is to attribute expressive attitudes and meanings to some person or group of persons; yet it is neither necessary nor desirable that the interpreter understand this process as involving the fixation of any literal beliefs about the actual mental states of the artist. Instead, taking the text or structure as the principal focus on interpretation, the appreciator explores its meanings and values while imagining or making believe that they are the results of some maker's design, where the maker in question is historically similar, but not identical to, the agent or agents who actually wrote the text. A version of 'conjecturalist' intentionalism has been defended by Umberto Eco, who writes of the meanings and aims of an *intentio opera* while adding that 'it is possible to speak of the text's intention only as a result of a conjecture on the part of the reader' (1992: 64).

Critics of fictionalist intentionalism (Stecker 1997) point out that references to the imagined authorial persona cannot explain the genesis of the work. Appreciative make-believe based on finished artefacts does not adequately reflect and promote our interest in the actual process of artistic creation, or in those meanings and values linked to the artist's ethical and artistic responsibility for the work (Carroll 1992, 2000, 2002).

Anti-intentionalists have complained that intentionalists wrongly adopt a communicative or conversational model in which everyday assumptions about the necessary uptake of speaker's meanings are carried over to an artistic context, where a 'message in the bottle' model of interpretation is inappropriate (Rosebury

1997). Some anti-intentionalists espouse a radical hermeneutics in which all of the work's properties, including its meanings, are given over to the flux of history (Gadamer 1960: 448–9; Merleau-Ponty 1969; McFee 1980). The meanings and value of a work of art, then, are not limited to those envisioned by the maker, or even to those determined in the context of creation. Instead, they change fundamentally over time as the symbolic artefact is reinterpreted in ever new contexts.

One intentionalist response to such a contention is to distinguish between the new *significance* a work can acquire in changing contexts, and its actual *meanings* in its context of creation (Hirsch 1967). Yet if meaning and significance are at bottom the same sorts of semantic item, this may seem to be a purely verbal manoeuvre. The distinction may, however, find its justification in a thesis about the specificity and value of artistic accomplishments understood in their contexts of creation, as opposed to the multiple functions that artefacts can serve in a wide range of situations. Although one can abstract a text or artefact from the relevant contextual conditions and carry it over into anachronistic contexts, the product of such an operation is no longer the work of art (Levinson 1988; D. Davies 1999; S. Davies 1996). A basic and divisive question, then, is whether the identities and meanings of symbolic artefacts are constituted by their histories of creation, or instead by the subsequent functions that such artefacts can be made to serve. And an even more basic and divisive question is whether a work of art can be accurately identified and appreciated as an artefact at all, or must instead be regarded as a process and accomplishment, in which case recognition of the artist's work, including intentional and unintentional activities, would be crucial to apt appreciation.

See also: Interpretation in Art; Definition of Art; Ontology of Art; Medium in Art.

BIBLIOGRAPHY

Aiken, H. D. (1955). 'The Aesthetic Relevance of Artist's Intentions'. *Journal of Philosophy* 52: 742–51.

Audi. R. (1973). 'Intending'. *Journal of Philosophy* 70: 387–403.

——(1997). 'Intending and its Place in the Theory of Action', in G. Holmström-Hintikka and R. Tuomela (eds.), *Contemporary Action Theory*, vol. 1, *Individual Action*. Dordrecht: Kluwer, pp. 177–96.

Barthes, R. (1968). 'La mort de l'auteur', in E. Marty (ed.), *Œuvres complètes*, vol. 2, *1966–73*. Paris: Seuil, 1994, pp. 491–95; trans. 'The Death of the Author', in S. Heath (ed.), *Image–Music–Text*. London: Fontana, 1977, pp. 142–8.

——(1971). 'De l'œuvre au texte'. *La Revue d'esthétique* 3: 225–32; trans. 'From Work to Text', in J. V. Harari (ed.), *Textual Strategies: Perspectives in Post-Structuralist Criticism*. Ithaca, NY: Cornell University Press, 1979, pp. 73–81.

Baxandall, M. (1985). *Patterns of Intention*. New Haven: Yale University Press.

Beardsley, M. C. (1958). *Aesthetics: Problems in the Philosophy of Criticism*. New York: Harcourt, Brace & World.

—— (1978). 'Intending', in A. I. Goldman and J. Kim (eds.), *Values and Morals*. Dordrecht: Reidel, pp. 163–83.

—— (1982). 'Intentions and Interpretations: A Fallacy Revived', in M. J. Wreen and D. M. Callen (eds.), *The Aesthetic Point of View: Selected Essays*. Ithaca, NY: Cornell University Press, pp. 188–207.

Brand, M. (1984). *Intending and Acting: Towards a Naturalized Action Theory*. Cambridge, Mass.: MIT Press.

—— (1997). 'Intention and Intentional Action', in G. Holmström-Hintikka and R. Tuomela (eds.), *Contemporary Action Theory*, vol. 1, *Individual Action*. Dordrecht: Kluwer, pp. 197–217.

Bratman, M. E. (1987). *Intention, Plans, and Practical Reason*. Cambridge, Mass.: Harvard University Press.

—— (1999). *Faces of Intention: Selected Essays on Intention and Agency*. Cambridge: Cambridge University Press.

Carlshamre, S. and Petterson, A. (eds.) (2003). *Types of Interpretation in the Aesthetic Disciplines*. Montreal: McGill-Queen's Press.

Carroll, N. (1992). 'Art, Intention, and Conversation', in G. Iseminger (ed.), *Intention and Interpretation*. Philadelphia: Temple University Press, pp. 97–131.

—— (2000). 'Interpretation and Intention: The Debate between Hypothetical and Actual Intentionalism'. *Metaphilosophy* 31: 75–95.

—— (2002). 'Andy Kaufman and the Philosophy of Interpretation', in M. Krausz (ed.), *Is There a Single Right Interpretation?* University Park, Pa.: Pennsylvania State University Press, pp. 319–44.

Cioffi, F. (1963–4). 'Intention and Interpretation in Criticism'. *Proceedings of the Aristotelian Society* 64: 85–196.

Currie, G. (1991). 'Work and Text', *Mind* 100: 325–40.

Dasenbrock, R. W. (1994). 'Taking it Personally: Reading Derrida's Responses'. *College English* 56: 5–23.

Davidson, D. (1963). 'Actions, Reasons, and Causes'. *Journal of Philosophy* 60: 685–700.

Davies, D. (1999). 'Artistic Intentions and the Ontology of Art'. *British Journal of Aesthetics* 39: 148–62.

Davies, S. (1982). 'The Aesthetic Relevance of Authors' and Painters' Intentions'. *Journal of Aesthetics and Art Criticism* 41: 65–76.

—— (1996). 'Interpreting Contextualities'. *Philosophy and Literature* 20: 20–38.

Davis, W. (1984). 'A Causal Theory of Intending'. *American Philosophical Quarterly* 21: 43–54.

Derrida, J. (1977). 'Limited Inc. abc . . .'. *Glyph* 2: 162–254.

Dickie, G. and Wilson, W. K. (1995). 'The Intentional Fallacy: Defending Beardsley'. *Journal of Aesthetics and Art Criticism* 53: 233–50.

Dutton, D. (1987). 'Why Intentionalism Won't Go Away', in A. J. Cascardi (ed.), *Literature and the Question of Philosophy*. Baltimore: Johns Hopkins University Press, 194–209.

Eco, U. (1992). 'Overinterpreting Texts', in S. Collini (ed.), *Interpretation and Overinterpretation*. Cambridge: Cambridge University Press, pp. 45–66.

Fish, S. (1991). 'Biography and Intention', in W. H. Epstein (ed.), *Contesting the Subject: Essays in the Posmodern Theory and Practice of Biography and Biographical Criticism*. West Lafayette, Ind.: Purdue University Press, pp. 9–16.

Fishbein, M. and Ajzen, I. (1975). *Belief, Attitude, Intention, and Behavior*. Reading, Mass.: Addison-Wesley.

Foucault, M. (1994). 'Qu'est-ce qu'un auteur?' in *Dits et écrits* (1954–88), vol. 1, ed. D. Defert and F. Ewald. Paris: Gallimard, pp. 789–821; trans. 'What is an Author?' in J. V. Harari (ed.), *Textual Strategies: Perspectives in Post-Structuralist Criticism*. Ithaca, NY: Cornell University Press, 1979, pp. 141–60.

Gadamer, H.-G. (1960). *Wahrheit und Methode: Grundzüge einer philosophischen Hermeneutik*. Tübingen: J. C. B. Mohr.

Gaut, B. (1993). 'Interpreting the Arts: The Patchwork Theory'. *Journal of Aesthetics and Art Criticism* 51: 597–610.

——and Livingston, P. (eds.) (2003). *The Creation of Arts: New Essays in Philosophical Aesthetics*. New York: Cambridge University Press.

Hancher, M. (1972). 'Three Kinds of Intention'. *MLN* 87: 827–51.

Heath, S. (1973). 'Comment on "Ideas of Authorship"'. *Screen* 14: 86–91.

Hirsch, E. D. Jr (1967). *Validity in Interpretation*. New Haven: Yale University Press.

——(1976). 'In Defense of the Author', in D. Newton-De Molina (ed.), *On Literary Intention*. Edinburgh: Edinburgh University Press, pp. 87–103.

Hjort, M. (1993). *The Strategy of Letters*. Cambridge, Mass.: Harvard University Press.

Irwin, W. (1999). *Intentionalist Interpretation: A Philosophical Explanation and Defense*. Westport, Coun.: Greenwood.

Iseminger, G. (1992). 'An Intentional Demonstration', in G. Iseminger (ed.), *Intention and Interpretation*. Philadelphia: Temple University Press, pp. 76–96.

——(1996). 'Actual versus Hypothetical Intentionalism'. *Journal of Aesthetics and Art Criticism* 54: 319–26.

Juhl, P. D. (1980). *Interpretation: An Essay in the Philosophy of Literary Criticism*. Princeton: Princeton University Press.

Knapp, S. and Michaels, W. B. (1982). 'Against Theory', in W. J. T. Mitchell (ed.), *Against Theory: Literary Studies and the New Pragmatism*. Chicago: University of Chicago Press, pp. 11–30.

Krausz, M. (ed.) (2002). *Is There a Single Right Interpretation?* University Park, Penna: Penn State University Press.

Lamarque, P. (1996). *Fictional Points of View*. Ithaca, NY: Cornell University Press.

——(1998). 'Aesthetic Value, Experience, and Indiscernibles'. *Nordisk Estetisk Tidskrift* 17: 61–78.

——and Olsen, S. H. (1994). *Truth, Fiction, and Literature: A Philosophical Perspective*. Oxford: Clarendon Press.

Levinson, J. (1988). 'Artworks and the Future', in T. Anderberg *et al.* (eds.), *Aesthetic Distinction: Essays Presented to Göran Hermerén on his 50th Birthday*. Lund: Lund University Press, pp. 56–84; reprinted in *Music, Art, and Metaphysics*. Ithaca, NY: Cornell University Press, 1990.

——(1992). 'Intention and Interpretation: A Last Look', in G. Iseminger (ed.), *Intention and Interpretation*. Philadelphia: Temple University Press, pp. 221–56; rev. version published as 'Intention and Interpretation in Literature', in his *The Pleasures of Aesthetics: Philosophical Essays*. Ithaca, NY: Cornell University Press, pp. 175–213.

——(1996). 'Work and Oeuvre', in his *The Pleasures of Aesthetics: Philosophical Essays*. Ithaca, NY: Cornell University Press, pp. 242–73.

——(1999). 'Two Notions of Interpretation', in A. Haapala and O. Naukkarinen (eds.), *Interpretation and its Boundaries*. Helsinki: Helsinki University Press, pp. 2–21.

Livingston, P. (1996). 'From Work to Work'. *Philosophy and Literature* 20: 436–54.

——(1997). 'Cinematic Authorship', in R. Allen and M. Smith (eds.), *Film Theory and Philosophy*. Oxford: Clarendon Press, pp. 132–48.

—— (1998). 'Intentionalism in Aesthetics'. *New Literary History* 29: 831–46.

—— (1999). 'Counting Fragments, and Frenhofer's Paradox'. *British Journal of Aesthetics* 39: 14–23.

—— and Mele, A. R. (1992). 'Intention and Literature'. *Stanford French Review* 16: 173–96.

Lyas, C. (1983a). 'Anything Goes: The Intentional Fallacy Revisited'. *British Journal of Aesthetics* 3: 291–305.

—— (1983b). 'The Relevance of the Author's Sincerity'. In *Philosophy and Fiction: Essays in Literary Aesthetics*, ed. P. Lamarque. Aberdeen: Aberdeen University Press, pp. 17–37.

—— (1992). 'Intention', in D. E. Cooper (ed.), *A Companion to Aesthetics*. Oxford: Basil Blackwell, pp. 227–30.

MacKay, A. (1968). 'Mr Donnellan and Humpty Dumpty on Referring'. *Philosophical Review* 77: 197–202.

McFee, G. (1980). 'The Historicity of Art'. *Journal of Aesthetics and Art Criticism* 38: 307–24.

Mele, A. R. (1992). *Springs of Action*. Oxford: Oxford University Press.

—— and Livingston, P. (1992). 'Intentions and Interpretations'. *MLN* 107: 931–49.

—— and Moser, P. (1994). 'Intentional Action'. *Noûs* 28: 39–68.

Merleau-Ponty, M. (1969). *La prose du monde*. Paris: Gallimard.

Nathan, D. O. (1973). 'Categories and Intentions'. *Journal of Aesthetics and Art Criticism* 31: 539–41.

—— (1982). 'Irony and the Author's Intentions'. *British Journal of Aesthetics* 22: 246–56.

—— (1992). 'Irony, Metaphor, and the Problem of Intention', in G. Iseminger (ed.), *Intention and Interpretation*. Philadelphia: Temple University Press, pp. 183–202.

Nehamas, A. (1981). 'The Postulated Author: Critical Monism as a Regulative Ideal'. *Critical Inquiry* 8: 131–49.

Pacherie, E. (2000). 'The Content of Intentions'. *Mind and Language* 15: 400–32.

Pettersson, A. (2000). *Verbal Art: A Philosophy of Literature and Literary Expression*. Montreal and Kingston: McGill–Queen's University Press.

Ponech, T. (1999). *What is Non-Fiction Cinema? On the Very Idea of Motion Picture Communication*. Boulder, Colo.: Westview Press.

Rosebury, B. (1997). 'Irrecoverable Intentions and Literary Interpretation'. *British Journal of Aesthetics* 37: 15–30.

Savile, A. (1968–9). 'The Place of Intention in the Concept of Art'. *Proceedings of the Aristotelian Society* 69: 101–24.

—— (1996). 'Instrumentalism and the Interpretation of Narrative'. *Mind* 105: 553–76.

Stecker, R. (1997). *Artworks: Definition Meaning Value*. University Park, Pa.: Pennsylvania State University Press.

Taylor, P. A. (1998). 'Artist's Intention', in E. Craig (ed.), *Routledge Encyclopedia of Philosophy*. London: Routledge, pp. 513–16.

—— (1999). 'Imaginative Writing and the Disclosure of the Self'. *Journal of Aesthetics and Art Criticism* 57: 27–39.

Tolhurst, W. E. (1979). 'On What a Text Is and How it Means'. *British Journal of Aesthetics* 19: 3–14.

Trivedi, S. (2001). 'An Epistemic Dilemma for Actual Intentionalism'. *British Journal of Aesthetics* 41: 192–206.

Walton, K. L. (1970). 'Categories of Art'. *Philosophical Review* 79: 34–67.

—— (1990). *Mimesis as Make-Believe: On the Foundations of the Representational Arts*. Cambridge, Mass.: Harvard University Press.

Warshaw, P. and Davis, F. (1985). 'Disentangling Behavioural Intention and Behavioural Expectation'. *Journal of Experimental Social Psychology* 21: 213–28.

Wilson, G. M. (1989). *The Intentionality of Human Action*, 2nd edn. Stanford, Calif.: Stanford University Press.

Whyte, L. C. (1962). *The Unconscious Before Freud*. New York: Anchor Books.

Wimsatt, W. K. and Beardsley, M. C. (1946). 'The Intentional Fallacy'. *Sewanee Review* 54: 468–88; reprinted in D. Newton-De Molina (ed.), *On Literary Intention*. Edinburgh: Edinburgh University Press, 1976, pp. 1–13.

Wollheim, R. (1980). 'Criticism as Retrieval', in his *Art and its Objects*, 2nd edn. Cambridge: Cambridge University Press, pp. 185–204.

—— (1987). *Painting as an Art*. Princeton: Princeton University Press.

CHAPTER 16

INTERPRETATION IN ART

GREGORY CURRIE

1. A ROUGH CHARACTERIZATION

To interpret is to do something, and an interpretation is the result of interpreting. Without proposing full explications of either, I will start with two assumptions, one about that outcome and one about the act of interpretation. The first is that the result of interpreting is the attribution of content or meaning to something. (Later I shall ask whether this assumption is too restrictive.) But I do not assume that the attribution of meaning is always the result of interpreting, for there are ways of assigning meaning that do not count as interpreting, and those ways do not result in interpretation. This is my second assumption: interpreting is assigning meaning in a special way. What way? I have no definition, but I will list some ways of assigning meaning that *do not* count as interpreting, and then draw some lessons from them. I do not interpret the literal meaning of your utterance when you speak to me in my native language, nor your gesture when I take someone else's word for its meaning, nor a coded message when I assign meaning on the basis of a rule or calculation that is applied mechanically.

Interpretation requires some degree of thought rather than the operation of merely subpersonal level processes, as with understanding literal meaning. It requires judgement applied to the object of interpretation, which is lacking in the case where I take your word for it, though taking your word for it may involve judgement applied to you. It requires creativity on the part of the interpreter, which is lacking when I mechanically apply a rule (Shusterman 1992; Levinson 1999). But we must distinguish the kind of creativity that contrasts with the application of mechanical procedures from the kind that contrasts with discovery. Some theorists have wanted to insist that interpretation creates meaning for the work rather than discovering meaning in it (see especially Bordwell 1989). Nothing said so far settles this latter dispute. You can think that interpretation requires creativity without thinking that it results in the creation of anything.

So interpretation is meaning-assignment brought about in the right way, and we cannot tell whether an assignment of meaning is an interpretation without inquiring into its antecedents. There are fool's interpretations, intrinsically indistinguishable from the real thing, but lacking the right history. A lucky guess can result in something that looks like an interpretation, but really isn't one.

Meaning can be natural or non-natural in Grice's sense (Grice 1956; see also Fodor 1993 for applications to art and its interpretation); we interpret clouds when we say they mean rain, and people's gestures when we take them to be insults. Since our interest here is in interpretation in the arts, I shall concentrate mostly on non-natural meaning, though 'found art' might raise questions about the place of natural meaning in art. Later, I shall comment briefly on the idea that music has something like a natural meaning.

Since we are interested in the interpretation of art, we shall take interpreters to be attributing to a work of art some meaning relevant to understanding, appreciating or judging that work. Among interpreters in this sense, there are people specially trained or knowledgeable who interpret in a self-conscious way. But unreflective readers who simply follow a story line will count as interpreters so long as their reading is minimally creative, in the first of our two senses of 'creative'.

2. Pluralism and Truth

Pluralism says there can be many acceptable interpretations of a work, no one better than the other (Stecker 1997). Pluralism contrasts with *monism*, which says that there is always a single best interpretation, better than any other (see Juhl 1980). Why should anyone think that there will *always* be a best interpretation? Even if the aim of interpretation is the discovery of the meaning the author gave the work, why can't an author give the work more than one meaning? (In cases where the work has multiple authors, it is particularly implausible to say that one meaning must have been collectively intended.) And if you think that interpretations do not have to correspond to anything the author intended, what could so constrain interpretation as to guarantee that there will never be a tie for first place?

But if we are all to be pluralists, we need not believe that all interpretations are equally good. The pluralist's basic commitment is to the idea that there is not always a uniquely best interpretation, that for at least some works there is more than one *optimal* interpretation, where an interpretation is optimal if and only if no other interpretation is better than it. A best interpretation, on the other hand, is one that is better than any other; every best interpretation is optimal, but not all optimal interpretations are best. Note that two optimal-but-not-best interpretations of a work might be equally good, or they might be incommensurable with one another.

Are interpretations ever true? It has been argued that at least best interpretations are (Barnes 1988). That leaves us with decisions to make about falsity. We could say that interpretations are false when they are not true: if only best interpretations are true, then optimal-but-not-best interpretations will count as false. The trouble is that using 'false' in this way strips it of the normative associations that hold our common notions of truth and falsity in place. Suppose we have two incompatible interpretations of the same work. Each is very good; in fact, they are both so good that it is impossible to find fault with either. What point is there, then, in saying that they are both false? We could declare that optimal interpretations are true, but that would cause a problem in cases where optimal interpretations are incompatible. For truth entails consistency. Alternatively, we could allow for truth-value gaps: best interpretations are true, non-optimal ones are false, and optimal-but-not-best ones are neither. On this assignment, truth is good and falsity bad—or at least less good. But the gaps it leaves do not arise here, as they do in other cases, from worries about verifiability. What we can or cannot know has not played a role in this argument.

Truth-value gaps show that there is no reduction of the good/bad distinction to the true/false distinction, or vice versa. But which distinction is primary for interpretation? Surely it is the idea of being good; we seek good interpretations, and if we have more than one, that is surely a victory, not a defeat. But if we said that truth was our primary goal, we would be in the absurd position of saying that our goal was reached when we had found the one and only good interpretation of the work, but missed when we found many good but mutually inconsistent interpretations. Truth is not, in general, the goal of interpretation.

I rejected above the idea that all interpretations are equally good. I am not aware that anyone has seriously defended such an extreme scepticism as this, though there are various attempts to relativize the notion of goodness of an interpretation. Stanley Fish argues that we cannot say that one or other interpretation of the work is good, or better, simpliciter, than another. Instead, we are to say that goodness or betterness is always community-relative, and that what is a good interpretation in (or for) one critical community need not be in another (Fish 1980). This proposition is not, in itself, one that many would object to; it is no denigration of the idea of value to say that what is valuable for a community depends on the community's circumstances. Rain can be very valuable in one set of circumstances and very unwelcome in another. But Fish gives this idea a more radical twist when he suggests that it is not some set of facts about the community's 'problem situation' that determines the worth of an interpretation for that community: rather, good and bad in interpretation is simply determined by the decision, or at least the preference, of those in authority in that community. Thus, while Fish's theory is officially a relativistic rather than a sceptical one, its relativization of goodness in interpretation to something so arbitrary makes it seem very close to scepticism (see Currie 1993*a*). I shall assume here that, however relative a notion goodness in interpretation may be, it is still a genuinely normative idea, to be seen as answerable to constraints that are not merely the expression of preference or of power.

3. AUTHOR-INTENTIONALISM

Author-intentionalism says that the aim of interpretation is to get at the meaning or meanings intended for the work by the author(s) (see Hirsch 1967; Juhl 1980). On this view, interpretation is constrained by the requirement that it correspond to what the author(s) in fact intended to mean; the author put the meaning in the work and it is the interpreter's job to recover it. (For the rest of this section, I shall assume that we are dealing with a single author, and a text-based work.)

An author-intentionalist need not deny that *texts* have a meaning independent of the intentions of their author. She may take the view that the words and sentences of the text mean what they do, independently of the activity of the author who puts those words and sentences together. But the meaning of the text, its literal or conventional meaning, is, as we have seen, not something we have to interpret. The meaning of the work is something that goes beyond, and may indeed contradict, the literal meaning of the text. An author may use words non-literally, meaning (and being understood to mean) things other than what the words and sentences of the text mean. And the meaning of the work will outrun the meaning of the text, since authors depend on the capacity of the audience to infer things about the plot and characters from what is stated in the text. It has been said that an interpretation represents a representation—a text, say—in virtue of having a similar content (Sperber 1996). In fact, an interpretation of an ironic or unreliable text might have a content entirely at odds with its original.

Knapp and Michaels once argued that authorial meaning is the *only* meaning of a text: 'a text means what its author intends it to mean' (Knapp and Michaels 1982, 1987). But their arguments for this are confused. They insist, for example, that irony does not involve a contrast between conventional meaning and author's (or 'speaker's') meaning, because 'the speaker intends that both the conventional meaning and the departure from conventional meaning be recognized'. And so 'both aspects of an ironic utterance are equally intentional'. But we should not conclude, from the fact (if it is a fact) that conventional meaning is intended by the speaker to be recognized, that conventional meaning is the same thing as intentional meaning. Being an F that is intended by someone to be recognized as an F does not make one an F in virtue of intention alone; otherwise, we could conclude that I am human in virtue of intention alone because I intend myself to be recognized as human when I go about. In what follows, author-intentionalism will be assumed not to involve any denial of conventional meaning. (For criticism of Knapp and Michaels see e.g. Currie 1990, chapter 3, and Wilson 1992.)

One difficulty with author-intentionalism is that it fails to accommodate the centrality of the text in the interpretative project. When we interpret *Hamlet*, we do not take the text of the play to be merely a source of evidence about what Shakespeare intended the play to mean. If that were the project, there might be other sources of information equally or more revealing of those intentions; Shakespeare's letters (if we had them) might actually be a better guide to his intentions than the text is. (I assume for the sake of simplicity that we have a definitive text; certainly, not all interpretative disputes are caused by doubts about the text.) But the letters cannot stand on an equal footing with the text. The text, unlike the letters, is constitutive of the work, and we cannot put aside a bit of text because we think it is not a good guide to his intentions. Our obligation as interpreters is to make sense of the text we have, not to argue that the work would be better expressed via some other text (Currie 1993*b*). A critic may persuade us that a particular bit of text contributes little or nothing to the value of the whole; but it would not be right to recommend that we treat the work as if that bit of text did not exist. Its existence—and its failure to contribute to the value of the whole—must be taken account of in any comprehensive critical judgement of the work.

One might conclude from this that the concept of intention plays no role in interpretation. During the 1950s, 1960s, and 1970s many people seem to have concluded exactly this, and talk of intentions was apt to be taken as evidence that the speaker was committing the 'intentionalist fallacy'. Wimsatt and Beardsley, the identifiers of that supposed fallacy, seem to have had as their target the idea that the intentions of the author determine what the work means (Wimsatt and Beardsley 1946). That is something we can join them in rejecting, without thinking that intention is redundant as an interpretative concept. To see why it remains crucial, ask: what *does* determine the meaning of the work, if not the author's intentions? Beardsley himself has suggested that it is 'public conventions of usage' (Beardsley 1958: 25). But it is notoriously hard to account, for example, for the creative use of metaphor in these terms: such things seem to work precisely by *violating* public conventions. Allusion is another difficulty: public conventions do not seem to determine what is alluded to in a work (Hermeren 1992). Public conventions of usage may be thought of as determining what words, and the sentences they go to make up, literally mean, but we have already seen that literal meaning is, exactly, something that does not need interpretation. Interpretation takes us beyond literal meaning, and the natural suggestion is that, in order to do so, it must appeal to the idea of intended meaning.

Perhaps more telling than these arguments is the fact that the most powerful theories we have concerning the mechanisms of interpretation—theories that have been taken up very enthusiastically by people working in the empirical sciences of the mind—are thoroughly intentionalist. Two theories in this area are noteworthy: Grice's theory of implicature (Grice 1989) and the Sperber–Wilson theory of relevance (Sperber and Wilson 1986). Grice's starting-point was the idea that communication conforms to certain rational principles; when an utterance appears to violate one of the principles, we make a guess as to what the speaker intended to convey, giving preference to hypotheses that preserve conformity to the rules. Grice's theory involves a somewhat artificial list of 'conversational rules'; Sperber and Wilson sought to improve on this by offering a single principle of relevance, the presumption being that the benefits to be obtained from processing the utterance are higher than the costs of processing it. They have gone on to offer complex and detailed theories of the difference between, for example, the interpretation of metaphor and the interpretation of irony.

Of course, empirical theories need the support of empirical facts, and there is quite a lot of evidence for the idea that interpretation depends on the capacity to discern intention, and more generally on what have been called 'mind-reading skills'. People with autism are generally agreed to have great difficulty understanding the beliefs, desires, and other intentional states of agents (see Happé 1994 for a review). It is also well known that they have difficulty with language, as evidenced both by their lack of understanding of other people's utterances and by their own difficulty in maintaining conversational relevance. But the difficulty is not, apparently, with literal meaning. On the contrary, the misunderstandings of people with autism generally depend precisely on their 'taking people literally', and consequently failing to see that an utterance is ironic or metaphorical (Happé 1993). We also have confirmation for more specific predictions. Sperber and Wilson (1986) postulate that irony, unlike metaphor, is understood as a special, 'echoic' utterance, in which the speaker indicates an attitude towards the thoughts of a real or hypothetical other; on this view, irony requires inference to second-order mental states. In work just cited, Francesca Happé found that subjects with manifest deficits in understanding beliefs about beliefs (sometimes called 'second-order beliefs') performed worse on tasks involving the comprehension of irony than they did on tasks involving metaphor. It has also been found that patients with certain kinds of brain damage sometimes have difficulty distinguishing jokes from lies; these difficulties turn out to be rather well predicted by performance on tasks that involve the attribution of second-order beliefs (Winner *et al.* 1998).

Anti-intentionalists simply have not produced accounts of comparable detail and explanatory power. Indeed, one might complain that the huge body of work on interpretation that has emerged within the aesthetic domain, be it intentionalist or otherwise, has signally failed to make contact with facts about how interpretation actually gets done.

4. Utterer's Meaning and Utterance Meaning

We seem to have reached an impasse; we have already rejected author-intentionalism, yet we seem unable to do without the connection between meaning and intention. To see our way out, we must distinguish between what a speaker or writer means by his utterance, and what an audience would reasonably take the speaker or writer to mean by it. This has been called the distinction between *utterer's meaning* and *utterance meaning* (Tolhurst 1979; Meiland 1981; see Levinson 1992 for further development). If author-intentionalism fails, then the goal of interpretation is not utterer's meaning. But if utterance meaning is what we are after, then intention stays central to the project; interpreters must decide what could reasonably have been intended by the utterance. Quite a lot of the time, utterer's meaning and utterance meaning will coincide; the author intends to get something across to his audience and, so it turns out, his intention is a reasonable one. But they will not always coincide, and the interpreter's job is to deploy the concept of utterance meaning, not that of utterer's meaning.

One question that arises is how to deal with cases where the text in question is not the outcome of any utterance, as with a computer-generated poem. Monroe Beardsley (1970) once argued that there can be meaning without intention, because there are computer-generated poems that have meaning (and not just the literal meanings of the constituent words and sentences). We might respond to this by saying that we interpret the poem under an imaginative supposition. We suppose it to be the outcome of an utterance, even though we know that it is not, and we ask, within the scope of that supposition, what someone would most reasonably have meant by this. However, the introduction of the method of contrary-to-fact imagining into the interpreter's repertoire brings with it some dangers. If it is allowable that we imagine that this object is an intentionally produced text when we know that it is no such thing, might we imagine that this intentionally produced text—which was actually written in Elizabethan times—was written last year? That would lead to the acceptance of 'wild' interpretations: interpretations that tear the work from its stylistic and cultural context. One difficulty here is that there do not seem to be common intuitions we can appeal to in order to set the limits for contrary-to-fact imagining in interpretation; advocates of deconstructive interpretation regard as acceptable interpretations that others would reject as incoherent, or at least as achieving something that is not the aim of interpretation properly understood.

However, irresolvable dispute about the limits of contrary-to-fact imagining ought not to count against the idea that such imaginings have their place in interpretation. On the contrary, if these disputes genuinely are a feature of life in an interpretative community, the idea of contrary-to-fact imagining may illuminate their nature.

5. REAL AND IMPLIED AUTHOR

In the case of the computer-generated poem, we arrived at an utterance meaning by imagining, contrary to fact, an utterer. It has been suggested that this is in fact a general method in interpretation. On this view, interpretation strives to construct an *implied author*, an author suggested by the work itself and different in various ways from the real author (Nehamas 1981). Here again, problems of relativism arise. Wayne Booth, who is largely responsible for articulating the concept of the implied author, seems to have assumed that, for all his differences from Tolstoy, the implied author of *Anna Karenina* is to be thought of as like Tolstoy in many respects, and particularly in respect of cultural background. Friends of Booth would surely balk at a reading of *Anna Karenina* that postulated as author a Martian visitor to Earth, meditating on the more outlandish aspects of human psychology, or a reading of *Don Quixote* as the product of Pierre Menard, the eccentric post-Freudian of Borges's tale.

How far can this relativism be expunged by appeal to the normativity of interpretation? The interpreter is bound not merely by rules of evidence and probability, as she would be in the natural sciences, but by the demands of rationalization (Davidson 1984). In our ordinary transactions with human beings, we do not treat them as subjects for brute causal analysis: we seek to explain their behaviour by reference to beliefs, desires, and intentions in the light of which their behaviour is rationally explicable. Interpretation in art, at least when allied to a traditional conception of art which emphasizes such values as coherence, unity, and intelligibility, will similarly seek to rationalize. Indeed, it can be argued that there is more of a role for normativity in the interpretation of art than in the interpretation of ordinary human conduct. In art we aim for interpretations that are not merely coherent but which maximize whatever we think the relevant artistic values are (Dworkin 1985). I do not, on the other hand, reject an interpretation of my conversation partner's observations about the weather just because it fails to disclose any rich allusions, metaphors, or symbols.

There is a tendency to think about what is valuable in art that is in significant tension with this normative approach. Noël Carroll has emphasized that we think of our engagement with art on the model of a conversation with its author—a conversation the value of which is undermined by radical misreading of the other's thoughts and personality (Carroll 1992). Perhaps a satisfactory theory of interpretation will find some trade-off between the search for aesthetic values and the demands of conversational intimacy. But there is unlikely to be one, uniquely best, trade-off. As with interpretations, the best we can hope to find are theories of interpretation that are optimal-but-not-best.

I have so far presented the idea that what we seek in the interpretation of works of art is utterance meaning as a severing or attenuating of the connection between the work and its actual author. But there is another way to see the proposal. We may acknowledge a contrast between what the author intended the work to mean and what the work does mean (a contrast, that is, between what we have been calling 'utterer's meaning' and 'utterance meaning') without thinking of this as a contrast between what the author means and what the work means. We could claim that an author can mean something other than what he intended to mean. On this view, what an individual means depends not merely on what he intends, but on facts external to the intending agent which may dictate that the author's intentions fail to get the right purchase in the realm of public communication. This is, after all, an idea we are familiar with in other contexts, particularly those where action is constrained by public convention. One's intentions can go awry, resulting in one doing something one did not intend to do, such as bidding at an auction or voting in favour of a motion. On this construal of the matter, the quest for utterance meaning would be a quest for authorial meaning; but it would be a quest for what the author did mean, and not for what he merely intended to mean. So instead of talking about 'utterer's meaning' and 'utterance meaning', we would talk about 'utterer's intended meaning' and 'utterer's achieved meaning'. This line of thought may be useful in reducing the appearance of tension between the constraints of rationalization and of conversational intimacy described above.

In thinking about the merits of an account of interpretation in terms of authors (real or implied) and their meanings, it is important to be clear that the proposal is not supposed to put an end to interpretative indeterminacy. We may have a very clear and full idea about the sort of author we are working with, while the work itself contains allusions, symbols, and other tropes to which no determinate meaning can be attached. We may then choose to attach meanings to them ourselves, and to do so in different ways according to temperament or interest. But we should not say that, at this point, the idea of an author has failed us. What has happened is that we have exhausted the meaning in the work and have chosen to extend it through our own efforts. The insistence that the work's meaning is an author's meaning does not pronounce one way or another on the question whether this sort of extension is a legitimate activity.

6. BEYOND MEANING?

I have confined myself so far to interpretation that seeks to assign meaning. It is not obvious that this is all the interpretation that there is. Interpretation can be thought of as assigning to a work structural and contextual features that may be to some extent independent of meaning (see Goldman 1995). For example, the structuralist critics advocated a style of interpretation that focused on supposed 'deep structural' features of works (see e.g. Todorov 1977). A significant aspect of this project was that it was intended to be global rather than local; the aim was to find commonalities among different works and even, in extreme formulations, completely invariant features of narratives. This project is generally regarded as having failed, partly because the interpretations to which it led seemed designed to confirm the global theory rather than to illuminate particular works. But there are projects concerned with features of works that are structural in a less ambitious sense than this and which seem to deserve the title 'interpretation'. The analysis of genre is an example. When an interpreter locates a work in a particular genre, is this to be thought of as an activity that assigns meaning to a work? What precisely is the relationship between the genre of a work and its meaning?

One obvious point is that you cannot know a work's genre unless you know at least one aspect of its meaning—what we might call its narrative meaning. We have to know what actually happens in *Hamlet* if we are to decide whether it is a tragedy, a comedy, or some other kind of work. Knowing what happens in the work is not going to be sufficient for knowing its genre, because genre is an essentially relational property of the work. *Hamlet* is a tragedy not merely because it happens to have events in it that tragedies have, but because it was created within a literary context that recognized these tragic elements as having a certain kind of salience. A play with the very same text, produced in a society that did not recognize the tragic genre, where there was not a body of structurally similar works consciously shaped by their authors who had the constraints of tragedy in mind, would not be a tragedy. Still, the determination of genre does require the determination of meaning.

But this establishes only that the determination of genre presupposes interpretative work; it does not show that it is itself a matter of interpretation. Can we argue that the determination of genre is itself the determination of meaning? Without trying to settle the notoriously difficult question of what does and does not count as meaning, it is certainly plausible to say that the genre of a work makes a direct and independent contribution to its meaning. Imagine, once again, a play that has exactly the same text as Hamlet, and which is understood by its intended audience as representing exactly the same sequence of events as *Hamlet* actually was recognized to have by its target audience, but which is produced in a society that does not recognize the conventions of tragedy. It is very natural to say that the meaning of this work for its audience is different from the meaning of Shakespeare's *Hamlet* for its Elizabethan audience. After all, to find meaning in, or give meaning to, something is paradigmatically to be able to give differential significance to features of that thing, and that is what genre-analysis does: when we see *Hamlet* as a tragedy we come to see certain of its features as 'standard', in the sense of being features definitive of dramas of that kind, while other features, such as the emphasis on ambiguous motivation, stand out as contra-generic or at least somewhat unexpected (see Walton 1970). Similar remarks apply to the notion of style. One can imagine a painting that is visually identical with Renoir's *Moulin de la Galetta* but produced in a society with no concept of impressionist style, and no body of associated work such as that of Turner. Surely that work would mean something different from what Renoir's painting meant to its audience.

Musical performance presents another difficulty. Performers are said to be interpreters. What exactly does this mean? Let us distinguish between two things that performers do or might do. One is to provide access to the work by engaging in a performance of it. Now, if the work is one that is capable of having meaning ascribed to it, the performance can be thought of as doing something else as well, namely suggesting how meaning *should* be ascribed to it. The performer's way of performing the work encourages some, and discourages other, interpretations of the work. So we can think of the performance as embodying a partial interpretation of the work: a set of interpretations more constrained than the set we had when we were considering only the work in abstract. In such a case, while it is not strictly correct to say that the performer is an interpreter, it is true to say that the performer is a facilitator of interpretation. Of course, the performer may also really be an interpreter, in that he engages in interpretation in order to make decisions about how the performance should go. But there is no necessity that the performer should do this (see Levinson 1993).

There is, however, a very widely held view according to which music is not the sort of thing to which meaning can be ascribed. If that is right, and assuming that what I have said about the connection between interpretation and meaning is correct, then performers of music are not interpreters—indeed, no one is an interpreter of music.

Of course, it is not established that music lacks meaning. Diana Raffman (1993), for example, argues that music has meaning, but of a rather special sort. Her candidates for the meanings of music are feelings—not garden-variety emotions, but feelings like the feeling that the C-natural in a C-major scale is the most stable pitch. These meanings, if that is what they are, are not conventionally associated with the music. They are more like natural meanings, though they are cultivatable rather than universal and automatic. Further, it has been argued (Lerdahl and Jackendoff 1983) that the reception of a piece of music has, for the experienced listener, a structure to it very like the structures postulated in generative grammar. These structures correspond very closely to what Raffman regards as the feelings we have in response to the music. Raffman is not dogmatic on the question whether these feelings are really meanings; she sometimes calls them 'quasi-meanings', and no doubt we should recognize the possibility that there will be no fact of the matter whether these feelings *really* are meanings. But Raffman's position does at least hold out the possibility that music will be subject to something rather like interpretation. Still, we should resist the idea that music has meaning in the sense that it 'says something', and that it is an interpreter's business to get at what is said. Much confusion comes with this idea (see Kivy 1995 for enlightenment).

7. MEANING AND METHOD

I have said that interpretation is the assignment, by certain means, of meaning. But there are radically different methods by which this assignment can come about. One method, corresponding to the hermeneutical tradition, involves understanding the work via an empathetic understanding of the agent, as suggested by Schleiermacher and Dilthey, and as more recently embodied in simulation theory (see the essays in Davies and Stone 1995a,b) The great challenge for this proposal has always been to establish the degree to which this kind of personal and apparently subjective act of imagining can lead to interpretations that command intersubjective validity.

One problem here is to identify what we might call the appropriate direction of gaze. On one view, such acts of imagining are essentially inward-looking; our task is to focus on the mental states of the target agent and to bring about adjustments in our own mental set so as to conform to the state of the target. Thus conceived, empathy involves a dubious appeal to introspection. An alternative conception argues that empathy is outward-looking: we are to imagine ourselves in the situation of the target agent, seeing the world, in imagination, as it was for that agent. If we can do this in a vivid and seamless way, we can then come to respond to that world as the target would have responded to it. In that manner, we produce a shift in our mental set without introspecting. The pressing question for this proposal is: how can we account for differences between the response of the target and our own response when those differences are not a function of the worlds in which we live? After all, it is surely plausible that two people, placed in the same circumstances, would act differently. At best, the 'outward looking' form of empathy gets me to knowledge of how *I* would have acted in the situation of the target, and this may be very different from the way in which *the target* would have acted.

To this question there seem to be three responses. The first is to say that the best we can manage is a reconstruction that tells us what we ourselves would have done in the situation; if this is not what the target did in fact do, because there are mental differences between the target and myself, then we simply cannot reconstruct the target's thought. The second is to say that outward-looking empathy must be supplemented, on occasion, by a conscious attempt to make adjustments to our own mental set; when we have reason to believe that the target's basic preferences or modes of inferring were different from ours, we must somehow make internal adjustments that compensate. It is not clear whether or how we can do this. Thirdly, one could opt for a mixed model, one that combines outwardly directed empathy with more reasoned calculation. I see, in imagination, how I would have responded to the situation, but I don't directly conclude that that is how the target would respond. Instead, I make some adjustments based on my belief that the target would not have reasoned or chosen quite as I did.

An alternative to empathy, but one that stays within the project of understanding the artwork as the product of an agent, is the view that what is to be understood is not how the artist actually responded to a situation, but rather how she *ought* to have responded to it. On this view, we treat the work as an occasion for theorizing; but the theory that we bring to it is not, as it would be if we were doing natural science, a brute causal theory invoking deterministic or probabilistic laws. Instead, we bring to the work a theory of rational behaviour, though the theory in question may be one we hold implicitly and which we would find difficult to articulate. This conception of the interpretative project chimes well with the idea of an implied author; we are to understand the work not as the product of the fallible, limited, and to some extent irrational agent who actually produced it, but as the product of an ideal agent. It also comes close to that advocated by Popper as the correct method for historical understanding, a method that emphasizes what Popper (1966) calls the 'logic of the situation'. What this approach most urgently needs is some way of assuring us that we do in fact have access, if only implicitly, to a theory of rationality powerful enough to deal with complex situations involving decision and uncertainty. Recent work in economics and the theory of games indicates that what is to count as rational is by no means obvious, and that elementary theories of rationality predict that people will behave in ways that are in fact against their own interests and in which people do not actually behave in real life (see e.g. Frank 1988). Developing theories of strategic behaviour, where one's appropriate response depends on an assessment of another's likely response, which is in turn dependent on her assessment of your response, has turned out to be extremely difficult. Is it likely that we possess such a theory, perhaps in the way we are said to possess a complex grammatical theory that linguists are still struggling to articulate? Surely the empathy theory is more economical and plausible. It explains how we make sense of other people's reasoning, decisions, and actions; we simply deploy our own capacity for reason, decision, and action, without needing to have a theory about these things.

But for several reasons, theories of interpretation adequate to common social exchange may do less well when applied to the project of interpreting works of art. First, interpersonal interpretation is often time-pressured, and hence will readily exploit mechanisms that avoid the slow pathways of deliberation. But aside from first viewings of films and plays, interpretation in the arts is not like this, and we can expect a correspondingly greater role for theorizing. Secondly, we often confront artworks that are the product of times and cultures very distant from our own. In such cases, empathetic re-enactment is very much less reliable than it is in situations of face-to-face encounter. Thirdly, interpretation in the arts is much less directly related to decision and action than is interpersonal interpretation. Fourthly, works of narrative art exist within frameworks such as genre, and our grasp on these frameworks can affect our interpretations of the works they frame. Having identified the work as a detective story, we approach it with certain presumptions about the story's characters and events; if we identified it as a bucolic comedy, our presumptions would be quite different. It looks as if we are operating with some sort of implicit theory of genre, adjusting our expectations about the work in the theory's light. It might be replied that in this there is no difference here between the interpretation of artworks and interpretation in an interpersonal setting; we do, apparently, use framing assumptions (sometimes called 'scripts') to guide us through social interactions. (On scripts versus simulations see Harris 2000: chapter 3.) But in the interpersonal case the script is generally assumed to apply to all participants. As I imagine myself in my conversation partner's shoes, I imagine myself behaving in a way that is guided by the script, and then simply assume that he will act that way also. But if I want to empathize with a character in a fictional story, I can't imagine being him *and* being guided by the rules of genre. Those rules have to be thought of as external to the world of the work; they are rules of plot construction, not (unless the work is in the style of Calvino or some other self-conscious manipulator of the conventions of fiction) rules that enter into the practical reasoning of the characters themselves. While it is difficult to believe that empathy plays no role in artistic interpretation, the role it plays may be small—indeed, inversely proportional to the richness and subtlety of the work, and to the value of the interpretative result.

See also: Intention in Art; Ontology of Art; Representation in Art; Fiction; Narrative; Tragedy; Aesthetics and Cognitive Science.

BIBLIOGRAPHY

Barnes, A. (1988). *On Interpretation*. Oxford: Basil Blackwell.
Beardsley, M. (1958). *Aesthetics*. New York: Harcourt, Brace & World.
—— (1970). *The Possibility of Criticism*. Detroit: Wayne State University Press.
Bordwell, D. (1989). *Making Meaning: Inference and Rhetoric in the Interpretation of Cinema*. Cambridge, Mass.: Harvard University Press.
Carroll, N. (1992). 'Art, Intention and Conversation', in G. Iseminger (ed.), *Intention and Interpretation*. Philadelphia: Temple University Press.
—— (2000). 'Interpretation and Intention: The Debate Between Hypothetical and Actual Intentionalism', *Metaphilosophy* 31: 75–95.
Currie, G. (1990). *The Nature of Fiction*. New York: Cambridge University Press.
—— (1993*a*). 'Text without Context: Some Errors of Stanley Fish'. *Philosophy and Literature* 15: 212–28.
—— (1993*b*). 'Interpretation and Objectivity'. *Mind* 102: 413–28.

—— (1995). *Image and Mind*. New York: Cambridge University Press.

Davidson, D. (1984). *Essays on Actions and Events*. Oxford: Clarendon Press.

Davies, M. and Stone, T. (eds.) (1995*a*). *Mental Simulation*. Oxford: Basil Blackwell.

—— —— (eds.) (1995*b*). *Folk Psychology*. Oxford: Basil Blackwell.

Davies, S. (1996). 'Interpreting Contextualities'. *Philosophy and Literature* 20: 20–38.

Dworkin, R. (1985). *A Matter of Principle*. Cambridge, Mass.: Harvard University Press.

Fish, S. (1980). *Is There a Text in this Class? The Authority of Interpretive Communities*. Cambridge, Mass.: Harvard University Press.

Fodor, J. (1993). 'Deja Vu All Over Again: How Danto's Aesthetics Recapitulates the Philosophy of Mind', in M. Rollins (ed.), *Danto and his Critics*. Oxford: Basil Blackwell.

Frank, R. H. (1988). *Passions within Reason: The Strategic Role of the Emotions*. New York and London: W. W. Norton.

Gaut, B. (1993). 'Interpreting the Arts: The Patchwork Theory'. *Journal of Aesthetics and Art Criticism* 51: 597–609.

Goldman, A. (1995). *Aesthetic Value*. Boulder, Colo.: Westview Press.

Grice, P. (1956). 'Meaning'. *Philosophical Review* 66: 377–88.

—— (1989). *Studies in the Way of Words*. Cambridge, Mass.: Harvard University Press.

Happé, F. (1993). 'Communicative Competence and the Theory of Mind in Autism: A Test of Relevance Theory'. *Cognition* 48: 101–19.

—— (1994). *Autism: An Introduction to Psychological Theory*. London: UCL Press.

Harris, P. (2000). *The Work of the Imagination*. Oxford: Basil Blackwell.

Hermeren, G. (1992). 'Allusions and Intentions', in G. Iseminger (ed.), *Intention and Interpretation*. Philadelphia: Temple University Press.

Hirsch, E. D. (1967). *Validity in Interpretation*. New Haven: Yale University Press.

Iseminger, G. (ed.) (1992). *Intention and Interpretation*. Philadelphia: Temple University Press.

Juhl, P. D. (1980). *Interpretation*. Princeton: Princeton University Press.

Kieran, M. (1996). 'In Defence of Critical Pluralism'. *British Journal of Aesthetics* 36: 239–51.

Kivy, P. (1995). *Authenticities*. Ithaca, NY, and London: Cornell University Press.

Knapp, S. and Michaels, W. B. (1982). 'Against Theory'. *Critical Inquiry* 8: 723–42.

—— —— (1987). 'Against Theory 2: Hermeneutics and Deconstruction'. *Critical Inquiry* 14: 49–68.

Knight, D. (1997). 'A Poetics of Psychological Explanation'. *Metaphilosophy* 28: 63–80.

Krausz, M. (ed.) (2002). *Is There A Single Right Interpretation?* University Park, Pa.: Pennsylvania State University Press.

Lerdahl, F. and Jackendoff, R. (1983). *A Generative Theory of Tonal Music*. Cambridge, Mass.: MIT Press.

Levinson, J. (1992). 'Intention and Interpretation: A Last Look', in G. Iseminger (ed.), *Intention and Interpretation*. Philadelphia: Temple University Press.

—— (1993). 'Performative vs. Critical Interpretation in Music' in M. Krausz (ed.). *The Interpretation of Music*. Oxford: Oxford University Press.

—— (1999). 'Two Notions of Interpretation', in A. Haapala and O. Naukkarinen (eds.), *Interpretation and Its Boundaries*. Helsinki: Helsinki University Press.

Meiland, J. (1981). 'The Meanings of a Text'. *British Journal of Aesthetics* 21: 195–203.

Nehamas, A. (1981). 'The Postulated Author: Critical Monism as a Regulative Ideal'. *Critical Inquiry* 8: 133–49.

Popper, K. R. (1966). *The Open Society and its Enemies*, vol. 2, *The High Tide of Prophecy: Hegel, Marx, and the Aftermath*. London: Routledge & Kegan Paul.

Raffman, D. (1993). *Language, Music and Mind*. Cambridge, Mass.: MIT Press.

Savile, A. (1996). 'Instrumentalism and the Interpretation of Narrative', *Mind* 105: 553–76.

Shusterman, R. (1992). 'Beneath Interpretation', in his *Pragmatist Aesthetics*. Oxford: Basil Blackwell.

Sperber, D. (1996). *Explaining Culture: A Naturalistic Approach*. Oxford: Basil Blackwell.

—— and Wilson, D. (1986). *Relevance: Communication and Cognition*. Oxford: Basil Blackwell.

Stecker, R. (1997). *ArtWorks: Definition, Meaning, Value*. University Park, Pa.: Pennsylvania State University Press.

Todorov, T. (1977). *The Poetics of Prose*. Ithaca, NY: Cornell University Press.

Tolhurst, W. (1979). 'On What a Text Is and How It Means'. *British Journal of Aesthetics* 19: 3–14.

Walton, K. (1970). 'Categories of Art'. *Philosophical Review* 79: 334–69.

Wilson, G. (1992). 'Again, Theory: On Speaker's Meaning, Linguistic Meaning, and the Meaning of a Text'. *Critical Inquiry* 19: 164–86.

Winisatt, W. and Beardsley, M. (1946). 'The Intentional Fallacy'. *Sewanee Review* 54: 468–88.

Winner, E. *et al.* (1998). 'Distinguishing Lies from Jokes: Theory of Mind Deficits and Discourse Interpretation in Brain-Damaged Patients'. *Brain and Language* 62: 89–106.

CHAPTER 17

....

VALUE IN ART

....

ROBERT STECKER

QUESTIONS about artistic value are not nicely uniform or all raised at the same level of inquiry. In this chapter they will be divided up into three groups of issues: meta-aesthetic, ontological, and normative. The first of these concern the nature of a *judgement* of artistic value. The second concerns the nature of such value *itself*. The last concerns the core question of *what* is artistically valuable about art, and how one brings the various valuable features of a work to bear in arriving at an evaluation of the work. Though these are different questions, there are not sharp boundaries between them. I begin with the latter two issues, saving meta-aesthetics for last.

1. ONTOLOGICAL ISSUES

....

What sort of value do works of art possess? We needn't expect that there must be a single answer to this question, since works of art have many valuable features, some of which are straightforward means to others and some of which are parts contributing to a valuable whole. The question is best thought of as directed at the overall value of a work. The most common way to approach this question so understood is to ask whether this value is intrinsic or instrumental. However, this way of putting the question is thought by some to confuse at least two separate issues (Korsgaard 1996). *Intrinsic value* is properly contrasted with extrinsic value and concerns the source of value, whether the object has it in itself or from an outside source. *Instrumental value* is properly contrasted with value as an end or for its own sake, and concerns the way in which we value something. 'Instrumental' refers to the value that something has as a means or a contribution to something else valued as end. Of course, everything that is instrumentally valuable has extrinsic value. The issue is whether some things valued as an end or for their own sake are nevertheless only extrinsically valuable.

Some people locate the value of art in some of its properties, sometimes referred to collectively as aesthetic properties (Goldman 1995; Sibley 1983; Zemach 1997; Zangwill 1984), while others locate it in experiences and other things commerce with works of art brings about (Beardsley 1958; Budd 1995; Dickie 1988; Levinson 1996*a*, 1997). Everyone in the latter camp must believe that artworks have extrinsic value, in the sense with which we are currently concerned. Those in the first camp seem to have a choice. However, it is not clear that anyone takes the option that art has intrinsic value in this sense. Most explain the value of aesthetic properties in terms of a reward their contemplation provides, such as pleasure, understanding, or the fulfilment of a need. Further, most analyses of aesthetic properties are relational, where one of the relata is a subjective state of (real or ideal) human beings. This implies that, even if aesthetic properties have intrinsic value, this would not mean that art also possesses it (since the value might lie in the relation between artworks and subjective states of people that underpins the property). So I take it that the position that art has intrinsic value in the relevant sense is unoccupied. The real issue is whether art is valued instrumentally or for its own sake.

Korsgaard suggests that, instead of saying that artworks are valued instrumentally as a means to pleasure, aesthetic experience, or insight, we should say that we value an artwork for its own sake but under the condition that people get these other good things from it. One reason for this preference is a resistance to the idea that the only things we value for their own sake are experiences or states of consciousness. (However, it should be noted that there are many positions not committed to this claim that still say that all artefacts including artworks are only instrumentally valuable.) This resistance in turn is motivated by the thought that there are many things we value as long-term and relatively ultimate goals, which are not states of consciousness. 'A mink coat can be valued in the way we value things for their own sakes . . . [it can be put] on a list of things he always wanted right along side adventure, travel and peace of mind' (Korsgaard 1996: 263). Notice, however, that a mink coat, adventure, and travel do not look to be on a par with peace of mind. In the unlikely event that one is asked why one values peace of mind, it's enough to say: for its own sake, while one always has further reasons for valuing the other items on the list. For example, travel might be valued because it provides novel experience, exposure to the interesting and the beautiful, and a sense of freedom. Are these the conditions under which travel is valued for its own sake, or is travel simply a means to these goods? Without further argument, the formulation in terms of means and ends looks to be adequate and easier to understand.

A second motivation for saying that artworks are valued for their own sake is the idea that the value they provide is unique and irreplaceable. This idea is put forward both as a claim and as the expression of a fear that, if the claim were false, art would have considerably less value than is commonly supposed (Budd 1995; Graham 1997; Scruton 1983). One argument for the claim is that, since the value of a work lies in the experience it gives to those who understand it (or, alternatively, lies in the aesthetic properties on offer), and since these are unique to each work, the value of the work is unique and irreplaceable.

It is fair enough to say that each work provides a unique (in fact, many unique) experience(s) (though for necessary qualifications to this claim, see Levinson 1990). It is also fair that this indicates at least one aspect of the value of art. Finally, it follows that this aspect of its value is irreplaceable. What does not follow is that a given work of art is irreplaceable or that such art is valued for its own sake (Stecker 1997b). Suppose that there is just one kind of metal in the world that can be used for building a certain airplane part, or suppose that a valuable experience can be produced only by a particular chemical substance. Then the metal and the chemical substance are uniquely valuable as a means to the respective ends for which they are used, but uniqueness hardly guarantees that we value something as an end rather than a means. Further, while uniqueness creates an irreplaceability of sorts, it does not go very deep. As long as we are committed to working with that part or enjoying that experience, we cannot replace the metal, chemical, or artwork in question. But this is a conditional commitment, and might be given up under various unremarkable circumstances. If people are really concerned about the replaceability of art, the uniqueness of the valuable experiences we receive from artworks does not solve the problem.

Those who argue that the value of art is instrumental do so on the basis of the idea that it is always to be identified in terms of a benefit it provides human beings. One argument might proceed as follows. Works of art are artefacts in the broad sense of being items made or performed by human beings. Artefacts always have human purposes or functions that they serve, and this is where their chief value is found. Hence the chief value of art is found in fulfilling its functions well.

As mentioned above, many think a central function of art is to be a source of valuable experiences. The connection between art and experience is a particularly intimate one, and this is not simply because the experience is unique to the artwork, but also because it is undetachable from close attention of the properties of the work (Davies 1994; Levinson 1996a). In this way, it is very unlike the experience induced by a chemical substance. Because of the intimacy of the connection, we tend not to think of the instrumentality of the work in the same way that we think of other means–end relations, such as the properties of a metal and its serviceability for composing an airplane part. Many have wanted to mark this difference by giving a special name to the former sort of instrumental value: *inherent value*. But there is no way round the fact that inherent value is a type of instrumental value.

Whether art is valued for its own sake or instrumentally cannot be completely settled apart from a normative theory that actually attempts to pin down the value(s) of art. To such theories we now turn.

2. NORMATIVE ISSUES

Normative ethics is sometimes divided into a theory of the good and a theory of the right. The former is concerned with value: both moral and non-moral value in so far as it is relevant to moral decision making. The latter concerns actions in so far as they are morally required, permitted (right) or prohibited (wrong). The normative theory of art does not concern the artistically right, presumably because there are no requirements or prohibitions in this realm paralleling those found in ethics. It is a theory of artistic value pure and simple, but it does have the two parts indicated in the introductory paragraph: one being concerned with the value of art 'as art', the other being concerned with the evaluation of individual works.

We can distinguish between two fundamentally different approaches to identifying the value of art. The *essentialist approach* hopes to find the value of art in an essential or defining property of art. The *non-essentialist approach* denies that we can locate the value of art in this way, and hence maintains that we must find an alternative way of doing so. Those who hold the essentialist view tend to hold a number of other theses that are logically distinct from essentialism *per se*. In the first place, it is very common for essentialists to claim that what makes art valuable 'as art' is unique to art. It might seem that an essentialist must make this claim, but, strictly speaking, an essential property of art need only be a necessary property for something to be art, and hence could conceivably be possessed by other things as well. Second, it is commonly claimed by essentialists that artistic value is derived from possession of a single kind of property, and hence that all artistic value is to be explained in terms of possession of this property. Again, this may seem a straightforward consequence of essentialism, but it is conceivable that several valuable essential properties might be identified, and hence that artistic value would not be fully explained in terms of just one kind of property. What essentialists must think is that all art is valuable for the same reason, whether this reason appeals to just one property or a more complex set of considerations.

In some recent work on artistic value (Budd 1995; Goldman 1995; Graham 1997), a view is on offer that resembles essentialism but does not quite fit the letter of that view as just defined. The writers who present this view recognize that there can be art, even art of some value, that lacks artistic value as they conceive it. 'Given what has happened to the concept of art, especially in this century, an account of artistic value cannot be extracted from the present concept of art' (Budd 1995: 3). However, an alternative strategy is proposed for identifying the value of art *as art*, which serves the same purpose as the essentialist project. The strategy turns on the idea that all great artworks share a broadly characterized value. The value of art as art is this distinctive value that works of art can possess and which all great works of art do possess to a high degree. I shall also treat this as a kind of essentialism about artistic value.

Essentialism has an obvious and powerful appeal because it straightforwardly solves the problem of why we single out certain aspects of artworks as *artistically* valuable while denying this of other aspects which also make artworks valuable in some way. For example, many artworks have economic value, but no one thinks that this enhances their overall artistic value. Economic value is no part of artistic value. On the other hand, if a work has valuable aesthetic properties, or provides valuable experience to those who understand it, this, at the very least, is much more likely to contribute to a work's artistic value. How do we know that economic value is irrelevant while aesthetic properties and experiences are relevant to artistic value? The essentialist has a clear answer: that economic value is inessential to art (or great art), while aesthetic value is essential to it. It is much less clear how the non-essentialist accounts for such distinctions.

However, essentialism about artistic value also faces serious problems. In so far as they claim value to be derived from a defining property of art, they face the problem noted by Budd in the passage quoted above, that it looks increasingly unlikely that we can define art in terms of its valuable properties. Such definitions have been under attack for the past fifty years. Although the definitions still have defenders, the most noteworthy of recent attempts to define art have no essentialist implications for the value of art. On the other hand, the alternative conception of artistic value as a value shared by all great art provides a weak rationale for essentialism. Even if there is such a value, it is not clear why this should lead us to exclude other valuable features as part of artistic value. Given these problems, a defender of essentialism will have to find further arguments to defend that position.

There are a number of different essentialist theories of artistic value. I consider two broad groupings that have been important in the twentieth century: aesthetic and cognitive theories of artistic value.

2.1 Artistic Value as Aesthetic Value

I begin by examining a version of the aesthetic theory that had more currency in the first half of the twentieth century than it does now: *formalism*. Most formalists do not merely hold a theory of artistic value. Rather, they advance a philosophical theory of art that also includes a definition of art. (For a discussion of formalist definitions of art and of formalism's historical background see Chapter 7, 'Definition of Art'.) One of the best known versions of such a theory is that of Clive Bell (1914).

According to Bell, the defining feature of art is significant form, and this is also the single feature possessed by artworks that imparts artistic value. This is not to say that significant form is intrinsically valuable, in the sense of having its entire value in itself. Bell locates the value of significant form in its providing a special kind of pleasure, which he calls the aesthetic emotion and which also affords a quasi-mystical inkling of ultimate reality. Bell recognizes that we may value artworks for many reasons other than this, including for their representational features, but that is not appreciation of artistic value. Bell conceives it as something like appreciating art for its human interest or as a historical record, an entirely different matter and one contingent on the mind-set of each spectator.

The chief problem with formalism is all that it excludes. As a definition of art, it excludes many items normally regarded as artworks. As a theory of artistic value, it excludes many of the central interests of both artists and their audiences. Consider our interest in representation. Not only is representation excluded as a possible source of artistic value, but the exclusion is based on an inadequate conception of the interest we take in representation. Bell's conception of this is inadequate on at least two counts. First, he conceives of this as an interest in the subject, i.e. in the object being represented. It can elicit a kind of free association in which we imagine a past or future for the objects depicted. It can suggest ideas or emotions, or convey information. The possibility that the formalist excludes is that of taking an aesthetic interest in representation. However, that is hardly impossible (see Budd 1995). For example, suppose you are looking at a landscape painting. You may be interested in this for information about the scene depicted or because of associations you bring to the painting in virtue of viewing similar scenes, but this is unlikely to be the centre of your interest. You are more likely to focus on the way the scene is depicted—the colours, the way objects are arrayed in the represented space, how light is handled, the choice of subject, the aspects of visual reality emphasized, the attitude expressed towards the scene, or more generally towards nature, the place of humanity in nature, and so on. If we can take this sort of interest in a represented scene, and if paintings can reward such interest, it is implausible to exclude this from the artistic value of such works. Second, to ignore represented content very often diminishes the value of form itself. Consider a painting by Vermeer, such as 'A Woman Weighing Gold', in which a swath of light from a window illuminates part of a room, leaving the rest in relative darkness. One can try to treat this as simply a division of both the two-dimensional surface and the represented space of the painting, and perhaps this is to treat it formally. However, the division is also significant representationally and symbolically, and the formal feature becomes far more important when understood in light of what it is doing on those other levels.

Formalism is not only inadequate as an account of *artistic* value, but is also a failed attempt at specifying the *aesthetic* value of art. Perhaps, then, a wider-ranging account of aesthetic value would suffice for identifying artistic value. If one pursues this line of thought, there are three, not necessarily mutually exclusive, ways of identifying aesthetic value. One can do so in terms of the aesthetic properties of artworks, in terms of aesthetic experience works provide, or in terms of a characteristic pleasure we derive from art. Aesthetic properties are those that (purportedly) require taste, sensitivity, or discrimination to discern. Gracefulness is a paradigmatic aesthetic property. There are those who want to identify aesthetic value with the possession of such properties (Goldman 1995; Sibley 1983; Zangwill 1984; Zemach 1997) and those who insist on doing so in terms of experience or pleasure (Beardsley 1958; Budd 1995; Anderson 2000). However, reflection suggests that one approach cannot do completely without the other. On one hand, the pleasure or experience of a work can be characterized only through a description of the properties apprehended and appreciated in the work (Davies 1994). On the other, we can explain the value of these properties only in terms of the pleasure or valuable experiences they provide. I shall focus more on pleasure and experience here because it is more likely to provide unity to an account of aesthetic value. Aesthetic properties are numerous and come in a variety of categories.

There is no need to approach the categories of aesthetic pleasure and aesthetic experience separately, for, starting with one, we can define the other. It is slightly preferable to begin with aesthetic experience, because it is arguable that there are experiences properly thought of as aesthetic and valued for their own sake but not felicitously thought of as pleasurable (Anderson 2000; Levinson 1997). Some art tries to create shock or disgust, or to reveal what is normally concealed. There is art involving bisected cows, self-mutilations, and the dead in morgues. Such art is not always purely conceptual, offered simply for the ideas it contains, but rather provides a vivid perceptual experience. Someone may value the experience without taking pleasure in it. We don't want to presuppose at the start that such an experience is not aesthetic.

I shall assume that we know *a priori* that aesthetic experience is valued for its own sake (however, this is challenged in Carroll 2000*b*, 2002), and that it is at least *typically* pleasurable. It is also uncontroversial that the experience is not merely caused independently of our cognizance of an object (as can happen with a drug), but derived from close attention to an object. Beyond this, different theorists offer widely different conceptions. Some want to limit the properties or aspects of objects one attends to, as we have already seen in the case of formalists. An alternative limitation is to the appearances that an object presents to the senses (Urmson 1957). Some theorists require a degree of complexity in what we attend to in the object. Roger Scruton (1983) requires attention to an object presented to the imagination under some concept or thought. Jerrold Levinson (1996*a*) requires that one attend to the content and character of the object and to the structural base on which it rests. Alternatively, some have proposed characterizing aesthetic experience in terms of a meta-response—a response to a response: taking pleasure in our admiration of something (Walton 1993) or regarding the experience of an object as having intrinsic value (Anderson 2000).

Is there a way of adjudicating among these various conceptions? Yes, to some extent. It is generally assumed that almost any artform is capable of providing aesthetic experience, and that would certainly include literature. But literature is largely excluded if aesthetic experience is confined to appearances presented to the senses, so that conception of the experience is inadequate. On the other hand, the meta-response approach appears to be far too liberal. I was once acquainted with someone who took the greatest pleasure in the admiration he felt for all his personal purchases as well as for himself for making them. He also no doubt regarded his experience of the objects purchased as intrinsically valuable. Both pleasures are aesthetic on the meta-response view, and yet the pleasures in question here have little to do with the aesthetic on any other conception of the matter.

However, there is likely an irreducible stipulative element in deciding what experience will count as aesthetic. This is because 'aesthetic' was originally, and to a degree remains, a technical term designating a range of valuable experiences, without there being agreement on the precise nature or boundaries of the range. Some insist (Bell 1914; Wollheim 1980; Danto 1981) that its primary application is to the experience of art, and that, if it applies to other things, it does so only secondarily. (This view seems to ignore the eighteenth-century roots of the idea, whereby it applied to beauty in nature, art, and other artefacts.) Others find its primary application in a type of sensory experience (Urmson 1957, following a tradition initiated by Baumgarten); still others (Scruton 1983 and Levinson 1996a, following Kant) in an experience in which intellect and imagination as well as, at least usually, the senses, are engaged.

For the purposes of identifying the value of art as art, we can simply equate the aesthetic experience of art with experience of the work, derived from close attention to it, and valued for its own sake. Aesthetic pleasure is the pleasure such experience affords. The aesthetic value of a work is what is valuable for its own sake in the aesthetic experience the work affords to those who understand it based on such an understanding. This conception does not fit perfectly with any of those considered above, but suits our purpose of attempting to define aesthetic value as broadly as possible. The conception does correspond closely with one essentialist conception of artistic value (Budd 1995). (Budd himself does not identify this value with aesthetic value; also, note that the theorists of the aesthetic discussed above do not uniformly hold an essentialist conception of artistic value.)

Can we identify the value of art as art with aesthetic value so construed? Some arguments in favour of doing so cover ground that is already familiar to us. There are theorists who continue to advance classically essentialist arguments. Thus, Lamarque and Olsen (1994), speaking specifically about literature, identify this with a practice *defined by* a stance that seeks out a certain kind of value: literary aesthetic value. It is possible to appreciate literature in other ways, but this is not to appreciate it as literature. (See also Anderson 2000, for a similar view regarding art in general.) As mentioned above, it is not clear that art, or an artform like literature, can be defined in terms of (a stance towards) one particular value or form of appreciation. The actual practices in question contain so much diversity, notably diversity in the aims of artists and appreciators. However, even if such a definition is successful, additional premises are needed to validly draw the conclusion that this defining value encompasses all artistic value. One premiss might be that what is artistically valuable must be shared by all (valuable) art (Bell 1914). An alternative is that the defining stance excludes consideration of other values, so that one simply cannot appreciate literature for its non-aesthetic value if one is appreciating it for its aesthetic value. Neither premiss would be easy to establish.

A second argument hinges on the replaceability issue discussed above. The argument now is that, unless we construe the value of an artwork in terms of the unique experience it offers, other things could provide the same value, and art could become replaceable. This is one of the arguments used by Budd and others in claiming that artistic value is defined by a point of view that seeks out aesthetic experience (as just defined), even though he, unlike Lamarque and Olsen, doubts that art can be defined in terms of such a perspective. We have already questioned whether it is possible to secure the unconditional irreplaceability either of art in general or for particular artworks. However, if aesthetic value somehow secured this, it is not clear why art, as art, could not be valuable in additional ways.

A third form of argument, which we have not previously mentioned, questions the ability of, or extent to which, art can be valuable in non-aesthetic way. This is necessarily a piecemeal argument, since it turns on identifying alternative values and rejecting them one by one. However, a common target is the idea that art has significant cognitive value, or, more generally, the idea that art is instrumentally valuable beyond the provision of experience valued for its own sake. It is argued that art is either unable to do this (Hyman 1984) or unreliable (Budd 1995) in doing this, so artistic value must be confined to the aesthetic.

The best way to test this last form of argument is to examine the possibility that art possesses non-aesthetic value as art. This can also help us to get a better handle on the other arguments just considered. We will do this by examining whether art has cognitive value of some sort and whether this is distinct from aesthetic value. We will consider the possibility of formulating a rival form of essentialism about artistic value in terms of cognitive value, but we are also interested simply in the question whether this is a kind of artistic value in the first place.

2.2 Artistic Value as Cognitive Value

There are a number of conceptions of art that are built on the assumption that art has some sort of cognitive value. For example, although Collingwood's theory of art (1938) is usually classified as an expression of emotion theory, his understanding of expression makes it look like cognition. Expression is a process by which we become aware of the emotion we are feeling in all its particularity. It isn't far-fetched to say that by expressing an emotion we come to know that this particular state is identical to the emotion I am feeling. According to Collingwood, art is expression in this sense, and the value of art is the value of such expression.

In a not altogether different vein, Arthur Danto (1981) claims that, for something to be a work of art, it is necessary both for it to be about something and for some attitude or point of view to be expressed towards what it is about. It is not far-fetched to rephrase this by saying that each work of art offers a conception of its subject. Since Danto is not explicit about endorsing a particular theory of artistic value, we should be cautious about attributing a purely cognitive view to him. But it would be possible for someone to take from Danto's theory of art the view that art's value lies chiefly in the value of the conceptions (attitudes, points of view) it offers. Further, this is arguably a kind of cognitive value, not in the sense of art's being a significant source of new knowledge, but in the sense of making us newly aware of or alive to ways of thinking, imagining, and perceiving.

Nelson Goodman (1968, 1978) is far more explicit than either Collingwood or Danto in claiming that the value of art lies in being 'a way of worldmaking', which is Goodman's provocative reconception of the pursuit of knowledge. For Goodman, art is just as much a cognitive inquiry as science, even if it uses different means involving different kinds of symbols.

The idea behind all these views, as well as other not necessarily essentialist accounts of art's cognitive value (Carroll 2000a; Gaut 1998; Graham 1997; Jacobson 1996; Kivy 1997; Levinson 1997; Stecker 1997a), is that there are intellectual benefits in offering to the imagination vivid and detailed conceptions that are obviously tied up with, but go beyond, the experience of the work. As Collingwood suggests, not only may one imaginatively experience an emotion in reading a poem, but one may also take away from that ways of identifying one's own emotions that break stereotypes and lead to new self-knowledge; not only may one imaginatively experience a visual world represented in painting, but through that, one may come to see the actual world presented to vision in new ways; not only may one imaginatively experience a fictional world of human beings, living under psychological, social, economic conditions, in which certain values hold, but one may then try out such conceptions in the real world. In doing so, one can, perhaps, come to see that they are apt, or, if they exaggerate or simplify, what features of reality or what states of mind would lead people to accept them.

This understanding of art's cognitive value is not the only one on offer, and some would like to extend it to make more ambitious claims, such as that art is capable of giving us knowledge that some conception is true or false in actuality (Nussbaum 1990). However, the conception of cognitive value sketched above is the one that has achieved the widest consensus and most easily resists the more common objections to the idea that art has such value. One objection is that art cannot really give us knowledge, since it cannot give us evidence that its conceptions are true. However, this is beside the point if the cognitive value of art lies in providing new ways of thinking or perceiving or bringing home to us the significance of already familiar ways (Graham 1997). We should expect these to be a mixed bag when assessed for truth, just as various hypotheses tested in a laboratory would be. A second objection is that, when the conceptions offered by a work are distilled into straightforward statements, these typically turn out to be either familiar truths or obvious falsehoods (Hyman 1984). However, this again mislocates where the value lies. Not only is it wrong to place too much emphasis on the ultimate truth or false-hood of the conceptions, but it is also wrong to suppose that they boil down to such simple distillations or morals. Part of their virtue lies in their detail, which is as rich as the 'world' of the work. This reply brings up another problem. The conceptions found in artworks are often richly 'particularized', as was just suggested. But to be use-ful in the pursuit of knowledge or understanding, they must have sufficient generality to apply beyond the work, to recurring features of the world. The resolution of this problem consists in realizing that we always must extrapolate from what we encounter in experience, whether aesthetic experience of a work or ordinary experience of the world. When one reads *Anna Karenina*, one may feel as if one has met people very like Anna, Vronsky, Levin, and other characters, but of course, not like them in every detail. (For a detailed extrapolation of conceptions one finds in *Anna* and in other novels, which respects their richness, see Jones 1975.) The last objection concerns the by now familiar issue of replaceability. Couldn't we arrive at the conceptions given to us in works in other ways, and, if so, doesn't art become dispensable? The answer is that, while art cannot be completely guarded against replaceability, given that what we appreciate in the conceptions found in works is so closely tied to the experience of the work, and the means by which they are expressed (Levinson 1996*a*), the value here is as irreplaceable as the work's aesthetic value.

The idea that many artworks have cognitive value is thus plausible. Further, it is plausible that the achievement of this value is an essential part of the project of the works' creators and an important part of what is appreciated by the works' audi-ences. For this reason, it is arbitrary to deny that such value is part of the works' value as art. On the other hand, it is not plausible to suppose that artistic value can simply be identified with a work's cognitive value. For one thing, it is far from clear that all valuable works have cognitive value, or that, among works that have it, this is always where their chief value is to be found. For example, if works of pure music have any cognitive value at all (as Levinson 1997 and Graham 1997 claim), this could hardly be their chief value. Second, we have no reason to dismiss aesthetic value as part of artistic value, and indeed, very often this is the more important value. Nor is it possible simply to combine aesthetic and cognitive value into a more complex essentialist conception of artistic value. First, as just noted, not all valuable works have both kinds of value, and second, there is reason to suppose that we have not yet exhausted artistic value. Many emphasize the value of the emotional response to a work (Feagin 1996; Walton 1990), which might constitute a further kind of artistic value. Others speak of art-historical value—the value of a work's contribution to the development of art, an artform, a genre, or an oeuvre (Goldman 1995; Levinson 1996*b*). A non-essentialist and pluralistic conception of artistic value looks more and more plausible.

To sustain such a conception, a solution is needed to the problem of distinguishing artistic from non-artistic value. Fortunately, there are a variety of solutions available. One is to say that a valuable feature of a work is part of the work's artistic value if the work's possession of the value can properly be grasped only by understanding the work. A second approach appeals to an idea offered by Noël Carroll (1988) for identifying art, which can also be applied to identifying artistic value. The idea is to appeal to a justifiable historical narrative linking later works to earlier ones. The values mentioned in such a narrative would be artistic values.

3. Meta-Aesthetic Issues and the Evaluation of Artworks

Value judgements about particular works are evaluations. Such judgements are to be distinguished from general claims about the nature and sources of artistic value, which were discussed above. We can distinguish between three different types of evaluation. When one says that a work is great, good, beautiful, fine, excellent, poor, or mediocre, one is concerned with the overall degree of value a work possesses. When one says that a work is witty, perfectly balanced, moving, or insightful, one is making a more limited assessment of one or more of its valuable features. Virtually everyone thinks that the former judgements find their basis or justification in the latter ones, and that these in turn appeal to non-evaluative judgements. People differ widely about how this works and what sorts of justification appeal to such a chain of provides. The third type of judgement is comparative, as when one asserts that work A is superior to B; but such judgements will be ignored here.

Meta-aesthetics concerns issues about, rather than within, normative art theory. What, if anything, is one asserting when one makes claims about the value of art or when one evaluates a particular work? Are such claims subjective or objective? Are they relative to different tastes, communities, or historical moments, or do they have general application? Are the judgements true or false, or do they require a different sort of assessment? If such claims can be correct, how can one know this? How does one justify such claims? Such issues apply both to general claims about artistic value and to evaluations of individual works, but they seem particularly pressing in the latter case, in part because there seems to be greater disagreement about evaluations. In this section we focus on evaluations and meta-aesthetic issues regarding them, in particular on their objectivity, and on their justification.

Evaluations are objective if they assert something true or false, and this truth is independent of the subjective states of the makers of evaluative judgements. Those who deny objectivity occupy one of two positions. One position—subjectivism, or the response-dependent approach—claims that evaluations are true, but true in part in virtue of the subjective states of those making aesthetic judgements. The other position—variously called emotivism, non-cognitivism, or expressivism—denies that evaluations assert something true or false, holding that instead they express feelings or attitudes.

There is a long tradition in aesthetics, as in ethics, that claims that there is an essentially subjective element in evaluations of artworks, and *both* expressivism and subjectivism derive from this tradition. The following quotation from Hume illustrates this. Notice that Hume begins the passage by talking about moral evaluations but ends it by extending the same analysis to aesthetic ones.

An action or sentiment or character is virtuous or vicious; why? because its view causes a pleasure or uneasiness of a particular kind...We do not infer a character to be virtuous because it pleases:...in feeling that it pleases after such a particular manner, we in effect feel that it is virtuous. The case is the same as in our judgments concerning all kinds of beauty, and tastes, and sensations. (Hume 1888: 471)

This brief passage contains both expressivist and subjectivist lines of thought. 'In feeling that it pleases...we...feel that it is virtuous' suggests that evaluating a work *consists in* feeling something, and to express an evaluation is to express that feeling. If evaluations are feelings, they assert nothing. On the other hand, the passage's first sentence suggests that evaluations do assert something, viz. that a work causes a subjective state: pleasure or uneasiness of a particular kind.

Both of these suggestions are implausible as they stand. The latter is implausible because, according to it, evaluations are straightforward, factual, causal judgements, and this appears to leave out the crucial normative aspect of these judgements. The former is implausible as it stands because it takes no account of the fact that evaluations of art involve reference to an object and its properties, and go beyond the expression of mere personal feeling.

Both Hume and Kant, as well as more recent theorists, attempt to accommodate some of these additional aspects of aesthetic evaluation while preserving its core subjective feature. Our concern is with more recent attempts to develop an analysis along these lines. Both expressivism (see Blackburn 1998) and subjectivism (Goldman 1995) have become remarkably refined in the process. I confine the discussion to recent developments in the latter position.

One analysis (Goldman 1995), closely modelled on an interpretation of Hume's, claims that an object is beautiful (good, fine) if it elicits an overall positive (pleasurable) reaction from ideal critics based on the object's more basic properties. The more basic properties appealed to here will be left unspecified by the judgement itself, but are commonly more specific evaluative properties, such as its delicacy, grace, unity, power, humour, vividness, psychological insight, moral profundity, or originality. The more specific properties receive the same analysis, though the more basic properties to which they refer tend to be more constrained by the concept of the evaluative property in question.

It could be questioned whether this approach really succeeds in capturing the normative aspect of aesthetic evaluations. What the reference to ideal critics tells us is that artworks have certain *dispositions* in virtue of their more basic properties. It is true that these dispositions are idealized according to the defining characteristics of ideal critics (they are knowledgeable, unbiased, sensitive, and have a developed taste). However, this is equally true of secondary properties, such as properties of colour, which can also be understood as dispositions relativized to normal conditions of perceiver and environment. It is even true of some basic physical properties that are also defined under ideal conditions (though these do not include conditions under which sentient, intelligent beings react, at least in classical treatments of these properties). We do not regard judgements such as that the billiard ball is red, that it weighs 200 grammes or that it is at rest as normative judgements. Why should we regard the judgement that an object is beautiful or poignant as normative *if* it merely reports a disposition? (For an alternative to the answer explored below, see Beardsley 1982.)

Such judgements would be normative if they implicitly *prescribed* something. It could plausibly be argued that the qualities that make a critic ideal are those required for a fair assessment of a work. That one is biased puts one's assessment in doubt, while being unbiased at least removes a possible objection to it. The same could be said regarding the other qualities of ideal critics. If the point of an evaluation is to give a fair assessment of an artwork, then my evaluation ought to conform to those of ideal critics. However, there are at least three different prescriptions that one might be issuing with this 'ought'. One might be saying that one ought to have a reaction like that of ideal critics, or that one ought to defer to the reactions of such critics, or that one ought to approximate as closely as possible to the qualifications of an ideal critic, and then sees how one reacts.

Each of these norms poses a problem. If my goal is to justify evaluations, the second norm is the most appropriate because it is most likely to lead to a fair assessment. However, traditionally, the view under consideration here identifies the aim of encounters with artworks as pleasure or pleasurable experience of a certain kind. Goldman for one follows this tradition. It is not clear how the second prescription speaks to this goal, while the first and third do so more clearly in prescribing us to shape a reaction in certain ways. Unfortunately, given that the goal is pleasurable experience, it is not entirely clear why we should accept either of these prescriptions. If I am satisfied with the pleasure I receive from artworks based on my current tendencies to react, why should I change this? (Blackburn 1998: 109).

One answer to this last question is proposed by Railton (1998). He claims, also finding inspiration in an interpretation of Hume, but echoing as well a theme from

Kant, that the pleasure that we aim for in encounters with artworks derives, in Hume's words, from 'a certain conformity between an object and the faculties' of the mind (Railton 1998: 66). The way to achieve this 'match' reliably is to approximate to the condition of an ideal critic. Any human being that approximates to this condition will be apt to experience aesthetic pleasure. On this account, acceptance of a prescription like the first or third above is built into the pursuit of aesthetic pleasure. Furthermore, the two prescriptions are virtually interchangeable on this view, since the view holds that human beings will, in general, react like ideal critics, if they approximate to the condition of such critics.

The success of this answer requires the rough uniformity among humans just outlined, and not everyone agrees that this uniformity exists. Goldman, for one, believes that our reactions will be different depending on an additional factor that he calls 'taste', which, far from being a commonly shared faculty, varies among us, causing divergent reactions even among ideal critics. If Goldman is right, it will be much harder to explain why I should seek to alter the pattern of my reactions, or even my evaluations, to conform to those of a taste-relative ideal critic. Hence all three of the norms we have been discussing would be harder to justify.

The alternative to the response-dependent and expressivist approaches is the view that evaluations of artworks are wholly objective—not only true or false, but true independent of reference to the subjective states of judges or critics (Bender 1995; Miller 1998).

One strategy for attempting to defend objectivism is to argue that lower-level aesthetic properties (grace, wit, balance, insight) can be picked out in terms of a descriptive content that they possess (Levinson 2001). We can then appeal to such descriptively determined properties to justify judgements that works possess higher-level properties such as beauty.

One criticism of this strategy comes down to the same problem faced by response dependency: explaining the normative aspect of such judgement. If we are basically describing works in making such judgements, in what sense are we giving evaluations at all? Alternatively, if the lower-level judgements are descriptive and the higher-level judgements are evaluative, how do we validly move from the former to the latter?

I shall focus on the latter version of the objection, which links the issue of objectivity with that of justification. One response to this objection is to try to break the link (Miller 1998). If we can appeal to various features of a work to justify an overall judgement of value, then this justification should give anyone a reason to accept the evaluation. Miller, however, denies that such universal justification procedures are available in either aesthetics or in ethics. Aesthetic judgements are based on an 'unprincipled response', and different people respond in different ways. These differences are ineliminable. In effect, Miller accepts a relativism to differing tastes, even among ideal critics, with respect to the *justification* of evaluations, while claiming objectivity for the *evaluations* themselves (p. 44). Objectivity is defended on largely linguistic and behavioural grounds by such facts as that evaluations are issued in declarative sentences, can be inserted into Tarskian truth schemas, and are the subject of aesthetic disagreements (p. 29). However, these are rather thin grounds on which to base a claim to aesthetic objectivity, as there are plausible treatments of these facts that do not require the acceptance of that claim. The plausibility of these alternative treatments is enhanced if we assume a world in which the general justification of aesthetic claims is ruled out by the fact of taste-relative unprincipled responses. To defend the objectivity claim, it is best to avoid this assumption if possible.

The most ambitious attempt in this direction would be to defend the claim that overall evaluations can be *deduced* from reasons referring to aesthetic properties. Artworks are artefacts and artefacts have functions. Once we know the function of a type of artefact, we can often deduce whether it is a good instance of that type, from facts about its properties that enable it to fulfil its function well. Artworks, like other artefacts, have functions, including those discussed in the previous section, and artworks fulfil those functions in virtue of their aesthetic properties. This holds out the hope that we can deduce conclusions about the overall value of a work from two sets of descriptive facts: one about its functions and the other about its aesthetic properties (assuming an objectivist understanding of such properties) (Davies 1990: 158–9).

Unfortunately, this line of thought hides a number of complications. First, we have seen that artworks plausibly have many functions. So reasons supporting the claim that a work fulfils well *a* function of art will not deductively establish an overall evaluation, and it is furthermore unlikely that there is a deductive procedure for aggregating the values derived from the degrees to which a work fulfils its various functions. Second, as has been widely observed, the aesthetic properties to which we appeal as reasons why a work fulfils one of its functions are at best prima facie reasons. This is because such properties do not individually move a work towards fulfilling a function in isolation from other properties, but rather do so by interacting with them in various ways (Bender 1995; Davies 1990; Dickie 1988; Goldman 1995; Sibley 1983). Davies suggests that aesthetic properties may always confer value unidirectionally for specified types of art, but this is overly optimistic (1990: 173–4). For example, wittiness tends to be a desirable feature in drama, but may be undesirable in a particular case because it undermines the emotional intensity of a scene. It is not clear how we can narrow down the relevant type to get around this problem.

This argument suggests that, rather than a deductive model, evaluations of works of art better conform to a model according to which various prima facie considerations are all relevant to, but do not entail, a particular assessment. How to justify an assessment on the basis of these considerations is one of the unsolved problems, not only in the epistemology of aesthetic value judgements, but in ethics and the general theory of value. It is a problem that is faced not only by objectivists, but also by expressivists and response-dependent theorists, so long as they claim that reasons are relevant to justifying evaluations. This is an area to which future research can profitably be directed.

See also: Aesthetic Realism 1; Aesthetic Realism 2; Aesthetic Experience; Beauty; Art and Knowledge; Aesthetics and Ethics.

BIBLIOGRAPHY

Anderson, J. (2000). 'Aesthetic Concepts of Art', in N. Carroll (ed.), *Theories of Art Today*. Madison, Wis.: University of Wisconsin Press, pp. 65–92.

Beardsley, M. (1958). *Aesthetics: Problems in the Philosophy of Criticism*. New York: Harcourt, Brace.

——(1982). 'The Aesthetic Point of View', in *The Aesthetic Point of View*. Ithaca, NY: Cornell University Press.

Bell, C. (1914). *Art*. London: Chatto & Windus.

Bender, J. (1995). 'General but Defeasible Reasons in Aesthetic Evaluation: The Generalist/Particularist Dispute'. *Journal of Aesthetics and Art Criticism* 53: 379–92.

Blackburn, S. (1998). *Ruling Passions: a Theory of Practical Reason*. Oxford: Oxford University Press.

Budd. M. (1995). *Values of Art: Painting, Poetry, and Music*. London: Penguin.

Carroll, N. (1988). 'Art, Practice, and Narrative'. *Monist* 71: 140–56.

——(2000a). 'Art and Ethical Criticism: an Overview of Recent Directions of Research'. *Ethics* 110: 350–87.

——(2000b). 'Art and the Domain of the Aesthetic'. *British Journal of Aesthetics* 40: 191–208.

——(2002). 'Aesthetic Experience Revisited'. *British Journal of Aesthetics* 42: 145–68.

Collingwood, R. (1938). *Principles of Art*. Oxford: Oxford University Press.

Danto, A. (1981). *The Transfiguration of the Commonplace*. Cambridge, Mass.: Harvard University Press.

Davies, S. (1990). 'Replies to Arguments Suggesting that Critics' Strong Evaluations Could Not Be Soundly Deduced'. *Grazer Philosophische Studien* 38: 157–75.

——(1994). 'The Evaluation of Music', in P. Alperson (ed.), *What is Music?* University Park, Pa.: Pennsylvania State University Press, pp. 307–25.

DeClercq, R. (2002). 'The Concept of an Aesthetic Property'. *Journal of Aesthetics and Art Criticism* 60: 167–76.

Dickie, G. (1988). *Evaluating Art*. Philadelphia: Temple University Press.

Feagin, S. (1996). *Reading with Feeling: The Aesthetics of Appreciation*. Ithaca, NY: Cornell University Press.

Gaut, B. (1998). 'The Ethical Criticism of Art', in J. Levinson (ed.), *Aesthetics and Ethics*. Cambridge: Cambridge University Press, pp. 182–203.

Goldman, A. (1995). *Aesthetic Value*. Boulder, Colo.: Westview Press.

Goodman, N. (1968). *Languages of Art*. Indianapolis, Ind.: Bobbs-Merrill.

——(1978). *Ways of Worldmaking*. Indianapolis, Ind.: Hackett.

Graham, G. (1997). *Philosophy of the Arts: an Introduction to Aesthetics*. London: Routledge.

Hume, D. (1888). *Treatise of Human Nature*. Oxford: Oxford University Press.

Hyman, L. (1984). 'Morality and Literature: the Necessary Conflict'. *British Journal of Aesthetics* 24: 149–55.

Jacobson, D. (1996). 'Sir Philip Sidney's Dilemma: On the Ethical Function of Narrative Art'. *Journal of Aesthetics and Art Criticism* 54: 327–36.

Jones. P. (1975). *Philosophy and the Novel*. Oxford: Oxford University Press.

Kivy, P. (1977). *Philosophies of Arts*. Cambridge: Cambridge University Press.

Korsgaard, C. (1996). 'Two Distinction in Goodness', in her *Creating the Kingdom of Ends*. Cambridge: Cambridge University Press, pp. 249–74.

Lamarque, P. and Olsen, S. (1994). *Truth, Fiction and Literature*. Oxford. Oxford University Press.

Levinson, J. (1990). 'Aesthetic Uniqueness', in his *Music, Art, and Metaphysics*. Ithaca, NY: Cornell University Press.

—— (1996a). *The Pleasures of Aesthetics*. Ithaca, NY: Cornell University Press.

—— (1996b). 'Art, Value, and Philosophy' (notice of Budd 1995). *Mind* 105: 667–82.

—— (1997). 'Evaluating Music', in P. Alperson (ed.), *Musical Worlds*. University Park, Pa.: Pennsylvania State University Press.

—— (2001). 'Aesthetic Properties, Evaluative Force, and Differences of Sensibility', in E. Brady and J. Levinson (eds.), *Aesthetic Concepts*. Oxford: Oxford University Press.

Miller, R. (1998). 'Three Versions of Objectivity: Aesthetic, Moral, and Scientific', in J. Levinson (ed.), *Aesthetics and Ethics*. Cambridge: Cambridge University Press, pp. 26–58.

Nussbaum, M. (1990). *Love's Knowledge*. Oxford: Oxford University Press.

Railton, P. (1998). 'Aesthetic Value, Moral Value, and the Ambitions of Naturalism', in J. Levinson, *Aesthetics and Ethics*. Cambridge: Cambridge University Press, pp. 59–105.

Scruton, R. (1983). *The Aesthetic Understanding*. London: Methuen.

Sharpe, R.A. (2000). 'The Empiricist Theory of Artistic Value', *Journal of Aesthetics and Art Criticism* 58: 321–32.

Shelly, J. (2002). 'The Character and Role of Principles in the Evaluation of the Art'. *British Journal of Aesthetics* 42: 37–51.

Sibley, F. (1983). 'General Criteria and Reasons in Aesthetics', in J. Fisher (ed.), *Essays on Aesthetics: Perspectives on the Work of Monroe Beardsley*. Philadelphia: Temple University Press, pp. 3–20.

Stecker, R. (1997a). *Artworks: Definition, Meaning, Value*. University Park, Pa.: Pennsylvania State University Press.

—— (1997b). 'Two Conceptions of Artistic Value'. *Iyyun* 46: 51–62.

Urmson, J. (1957). 'What Makes a Situation Aesthetic?' *Proceedings of the Aristotelian Society*, Supplement, 31: 93–106.

Walton, K. (1990). *Mimesis as Make-Believe*. Cambridge, Mass.: Harvard University Press.

—— (1993). 'How Marvelous!: Towards a Theory of Aesthetic Value'. *Journal of Aesthetics and Art Criticism* 51: 499–510.

Wollheim, R. (1980). *Art and its Objects*, 2nd edn. Cambridge: Cambridge University Press.

Zangwill, N. (1984). 'Dickie and Doughnuts'. *Ratio* 7: 63–80.

Zemach, E. (1997). *Real Beauty*. University Park, Pa.: Pennsylvania State University Press.

CHAPTER 18

··

BEAUTY

··

NICK ZANGWILL

I SHALL discuss several related issues about beauty. These are: (i) the place of beauty among other aesthetic properties; (ii) the general principle of aesthetic supervenience; (iii) the problem of aesthetic relevance; (iv) the distinction between free and dependent beauty; (v) the primacy of our appreciation of free beauty over our appreciation of dependent beauty; (vi) personal beauty as a species of beauty; (vii) the metaphysics of beauty.

1. THE NOTION OF THE AESTHETIC

··

In contemporary philosophy, beauty is often thought of as one among many aesthetic properties, albeit one with a special role. I think this is a useful way of thinking about beauty, so long as we don't lose sight of beauty's specialness. For our thought about beauty is indeed closely connected with our thinking in more broadly aesthetic terms. Hence let us begin by looking at the category of the aesthetic and the place of beauty within it.

Which properties are *aesthetic* properties? Beauty and ugliness would be thought to be uncontroversial examples of aesthetic properties. They are paradigm cases. But what about daintiness, dumpiness, and elegance? What about the sadness or vigour of music? What about representational properties, such as being of a cow or London Bridge? What about being mostly yellow or in C minor? What about art-historical properties, such as being a Cubist painting? Is there a principle at work that allows us to classify some of these as aesthetic properties and others as non-aesthetic properties?

Someone might follow that question with the following: is such a distinction, as it were, built into the world? Is it just a fact—a metaphysical fact—that some properties are aesthetic and some are not? Or is it a distinction that we should draw only if we find it *useful* to do so? That is, is it more pragmatic than natural? Then again, perhaps this is a false dilemma. For it may be that the aesthetic/non-aesthetic distinction is in some sense natural, but our main *evidence* for thinking it so is that we find it useful to mark such a distinction.

However, some have argued that the distinction is in fact not useful. There has been a debate, initiated by Frank Sibley, about whether aesthetic concepts can be distinguished from non-aesthetic concepts (Sibley 1959, 1965). Notable contributors to that debate were Ted Cohen and Peter Kivy (Cohen 1973; Kivy 1975). (This debate was about aesthetic *concepts*, but there is a similar debate about aesthetic *properties*.) Sibley thought that there was a significant distinction between aesthetic and non-aesthetic concepts. He thought that aesthetic concepts were those that required 'taste' or 'discernment' for their application, but that these faculties were in turn characterized in aesthetic terms. His critics pointed out that this way of distinguishing aesthetic concepts from non-aesthetic concepts led to too tight a circle. The consensus among contemporary aestheticians is that the distinction is somewhat arbitrary and hard to make out.

My own view is that Sibley can be rescued (Zangwill 2001a: chapter 2). There is a principled way of distinguishing aesthetic from non-aesthetic concepts and properties. The distinction is useful, and it marks a real difference between different kinds of concepts and properties. My strategy will be: (*a*) to see judgements of beauty as pre-eminent among other aesthetic concepts and properties; (*b*) to give a distinctive account of beauty and judgements of beauty; and (*c*) to locate a necessary link between judgements of beauty and the other aesthetic judgements, which does not obtain between judgements of beauty and non-aesthetic judgements.

The distinctive account of beauty is a fairly standard one. In broad brush, it is this. Beauty is the object of judgements of beauty—what Kant called 'judgements of taste', or what we today would call 'judgements of aesthetic value' or 'judgements of aesthetic merit'. Two features are distinctive of these judgements. The first distinctive feature is that they have what Kant called 'subjective' grounds (Kant 1928). That is, they are made on the basis of a response of pleasure and displeasure. (This is hardly something that Kant invents. It can also be found in Plato's *Hippias Major*, as well as in Aquinas and Hume; see also Levinson 1995.) Aesthetic judgements share this with judgements of the agreeable about food and drink.

The second distinctive feature is that these judgements lay claim to correctness. Aesthetic judgements share this with empirical judgements. Kant pulled these two distinctive features together when he said that judgements of beauty and ugliness have 'subjective universality'. So—beauty is something we know about through a particular kind of pleasure, a kind that licenses judgements that claim correctness. This sort of account is neutral between the view that beauty is some kind of projection of our pleasures and the view that it is a (mind-independent or mind-dependent) property of the world that we know through pleasure (see 'Aesthetic Realism I'). But at any rate, I think that Kant was right to say that subjective universality is what is distinctive of judgements of beauty and ugliness. Looking in one direction, judgements of beauty are like judgements of the agreeableness of food and drink in being subjective, but unlike them in claiming universal validity; looking in the other direction, judgements of beauty are unlike empirical judgements in being subjective, but like them in claiming universal validity.

Let us call judgements of beauty and ugliness and aesthetic merit—and of demerit—'verdictive' aesthetic judgements, and let us call judgements of daintiness, dumpiness, elegance, and the like 'substantive' aesthetic judgements. Corresponding to these judgements are 'verdictive' and 'substantive' *properties*. Beauty is sometimes thought of as being a particular *kind* of aesthetic excellence, as a substantive aesthetic property. But I shall assume, in what follows, that it is not. I will assume, rather, that beauty is the *generic* sort of aesthetic excellence. (Perhaps we have a conception of substantive beauty—for example, we might say that something is elegant but not beautiful—but I shall ignore this for present purposes.)

One quite plausible principle would be that verdictive judgements are analytically linked to substantive judgements but not to physical, sensory, representational, or art-historical judgements. Such a view has its origins in Monroe Beardsley's writings (Beardsley 1982). On such a view, to describe something as dainty, dumpy, or elegant *is* to evaluate it; and the properties of daintiness, dumpiness, or elegance thus have evaluative polarity built into them (Burton 1992). However, it is controversial whether *all* substantive aesthetic judgements are in fact analytically linked with judgements of beauty and ugliness. And it is controversial whether all substantive aesthetic properties have evaluative polarity (Levinson 2001). Of course, the *linguistic descriptions*—the *words*—may not seem to be evaluatively loaded if we consider them outside of the context of some particular ascription to some particular thing. But in the context of some particular ascription, I think it is plausible that such words always ascribe *properties* that have evaluative polarity built into them. The linguistic description at least 'conversationally implies' an evaluative judgement.

Perhaps we can distinguish between what we say about aesthetic *concepts* and *judgements* from what we say about aesthetic *properties*. Is there a doctrine about aesthetic properties to accompany the analytic principle about aesthetic judgements and concepts? Someone might propose that a suitable cousin of the analytic entailment principle would be the modal principle that substantive properties *determine* verdictive properties. However, that would be a mistake. For if aesthetic/non-aesthetic supervenience holds, the same is true of physical and sensory properties, and perhaps also of representational and art-historical properties. Now, although all these properties might be *necessarily* linked to aesthetic properties, perhaps only substantive properties are *essentially* linked to verdictive properties. (See Fine 1994 on the distinction between essence and necessity.) Being beautiful is not part of *what it is* to have such and such shapes and colours, even though it might be *necessary* that those shapes and colours are beautiful. But being beautiful *is* part of what it is to be elegant. Unlike the modal principle, this principle is the true metaphysical cousin of the analytical entailment principle. Beauty and ugliness thus occupy a pre-eminent role, both in our judgements and in the properties themselves.

If there is an exclusive analytical connection between substantive and verdictive judgements, or an exclusive essential relation between substantive and verdictive properties, then the unity and integrity of the category of the aesthetic is assured.

2. AESTHETIC SUPERVENIENCE

Beauty and other aesthetic properties are not tied in any close way to art. In fact, there is a two-way independence: on the one hand, nature can have aesthetic properties; on the hand, works of art can have many kinds of properties apart from aesthetic properties. Nevertheless, in my view, in most cases, aesthetic properties play an important role in what it is for a particular work of art to be the work it is (Zangwill 2001b). It is sometimes said that there are some works of art that have no aesthetic point. Perhaps some artists are not concerned to realize beauty or other aesthetic properties. But even if this is true, it has absolutely no bearing on the issues about the nature of beauty and aesthetic properties that we are concerned with. For our topic is not the relation between aesthetic properties and works of art, but the aesthetic properties themselves, whether those of nature or art.

Clearly, many works of art do possess aesthetic properties among the other kinds of properties that they possess, and there are interesting issues about what is going on when they do, which we can explore. I shall focus on architecture and sculpture. Let us list some of the kinds of properties that buildings and sculptures possess. Buildings and sculptures possess aesthetic properties, such as beauty or ugliness, daintiness or dumpiness, dynamism, balance, or unity. Buildings and sculptures also possess physical properties, sensory properties, art-historical properties, and sometimes representational properties. What I shall consider is what exactly the relation is between the aesthetic qualities of works of architecture and sculpture and the other properties, which we can group together and call 'non-aesthetic properties'.

A fundamental principle is that aesthetic properties are *determined by* or are *dependent on* non-aesthetic properties. Things come to have aesthetic properties *because of* or *in virtue of* their non-aesthetic properties. For example, a performance of a piece of music is delicate *because of* a certain arrangement of sounds, and an abstract painting is brash or beautiful *because of* a certain spatial arrangement of colours. In the philosophical jargon, aesthetic properties *supervene* on non-aesthetic properties. This means that if something has an aesthetic property then it has some non-aesthetic property that is sufficient for the aesthetic property. (The relation of dependence or supervenience is a general one. I shall not probe the exact nature of the relation, although it can be formulated in different ways (Kim 1993). The notion is important outside of aesthetics, in areas like moral philosophy and the philosophy of mind.) We owe to Frank Sibley the idea that it is essential to aesthetic properties to depend on, or be determined by, non-aesthetic properties (Sibley 1959, 1965).

I assume that this idea is uncontroversial, at least in some formulation. If philosophers argue against aesthetic dependence or supervenience on the basis of their philosophical theories, then it seems to me that it is their theories that are wrong, not the supervenience claim. For aesthetic supervenience is an entrenched principle of our ordinary 'folk aesthetics'. The idea that a thing could be beautiful or elegant but not in virtue of its other features is a bizarre one, and someone who asserted it would be urging us to radically revise a central and essential aspect of our aesthetic thought.

Once we have accepted that the supervenience relation holds, there are further questions. One kind of question is about what *explains* supervenience. This raises metaphysical issues, because those with different metaphysical views offer different explanations of supervenience. Another kind of question is about *which* non-aesthetic properties are the ones that aesthetic properties supervene on, and I turn to this in the next section.

3. AESTHETIC RELEVANCE

We might ask: which properties belong in the 'subvening' base of aesthetic properties? However, this way of asking the question is too general. For the subvening base may vary as we consider different art forms. In the case of some art forms, it is clear what the subvening base is. In the case of music and abstract painting, for example, aesthetic properties obviously depend on sensory properties arrayed in space and time. As we noted, the delicacy of a performance of a piece of music depends on a temporal arrangement of sounds, and the brashness or beauty of an abstract painting depends on a spatial arrangement of colours. However, what we ought to think is less obvious in the case of architecture and sculpture than in the case of music and abstract painting. What kinds of non-aesthetic properties are relevant to the aesthetic properties of architecture and sculpture?

Sculptures very often have *representational* properties. (By contrast, architecture is, as a rule, an abstract art, like music.) A sculpture may be *of* a nymph, or *of* a pagan god, or *of* Napoleon, and so on. A work's representational properties are of course often important to its aesthetic properties. I prefer not to class represent-ational properties themselves as *aesthetic* properties, though to some extent this is a matter of choice—a matter of what sort of work we want the category of the 'aes-thetic' to do. Although representational properties are not helpfully classified as aesthetic properties, it is not controversial that they are often aesthetically *relevant*. For example, a thing may be beautiful or elegant *as* a representation of something. (This is not particularly controversial, although it was denied by Clive Bell, 1913.)

Buildings and sculptures also have *art-historical* properties. That is, they have specific origins and they stand in relation to other works of art—and because of this fall into art-historical categories. According to some, we need to know to which art-historical categories a work belongs if we are correctly to ascribe aesthetic prop-erties to it (Walton 1970). On this view, the aesthetic properties of a work depend on more than its 'local' non-aesthetic properties; in particular, they depend on the history of production of the work.

The issue is about the *extent* of the subvening base of aesthetic properties. 'Anti-formalists' deny that the subvening non-aesthetic properties are restricted to a thing's local properties, and say that they include historical properties. Thus, anti-formalists allow *Doppelgänger* cases: they say that two non-aesthetically intrinsically similar things can be aesthetically dissimilar (Gombrich 1959: 313; Danto 1981; Currie 1989). For example, anti-formalists say that there can be two intrinsically similar mosaics such that one is an elegant Roman mosaic and the other is a clumsy Byzantine mosaic. 'Formalists' deny that this is possible. However, it is unclear that the appeal to such cases can be used as part of an *argument* for a formalist or anti-formalist view, since what one thinks about the possibility of *Doppelgänger* cases will derive from one's antecedent attitude to formalism. It is controversial whether art-historical prop-erties are aesthetically relevant to aesthetic properties. Some say that they are always relevant, while some say that they are never relevant. The sensible view, I think, is that they are sometimes relevant and sometimes not (Zangwill 2001a: chapters 4–6).

Buildings and sculptures possess *physical* properties. They have shape and mass. Their parts stand in certain spatial relations to one another and to their surround-ings. Buildings and sculptures are composed of material substances, and because of this they also possess dispositional physical properties. For instance, buildings have a greater or lesser capacity to keep out the rain, they are more or less flammable, and so on. Many writers have thought that spatial relations play a dominant role in determining the aesthetic properties of architecture and sculpture. The spatial relations might be among the parts of the work or its spatial relations to its envir-onment. For example, both Palladio and Le Corbusier make spatial relations central in their architecture and in their architectural writings (Rowe 1976). It is uncontroversial that spatial relations play *some* role in determining the aesthetic properties of architectural works. However, what is controversial is the claim that this role is *pre-eminent.*

Buildings and sculptures also have *sensory* properties. Most important, of course, is colour. The surface colour of the building or sculpture derives mainly from the materials out of which it is constructed or from the paint that covers it. But we should not forget the colours that result from shadows and reflections. To a lesser extent, the sounds that can be heard in a building may also be important; and sound is usually important for kinetic sculpture. Philosophers usually categorize these sorts of sensory properties as *secondary* qualities, and they are said to differ from *primary* qualities in that they involve an essential reference to the qualitative character of the experiences of human beings. Unlike secondary qualities, primary qualities, such as shape or size, are said to be independent of the constitution of human beings. It is commonly thought that sensory qualities, such as colours, sounds, tastes, and smells, are all secondary qualities, since what it is to be—say, red, loud, sweet, or pungent— is not independent of what it is for human beings to experience something as red, loud, sweet, or pungent in normal circumstances. It is controversial whether sensory properties are always relevant in architecture and sculpture.

There is also the category of what I shall call *appearance* properties. These include visual properties, such as *looking square.* Such properties are the appearance of primary qualities. *Being* square is a physical, primary property but *looking* square is an appearance property. These properties have a lot in common with sensory properties (see Levinson 1990).

Many have been tempted to say that the aesthetic qualities of architecture and sculpture depend *only* on physical qualities, and that sensory and appearance properties drop out of the picture altogether. My view is that this is a mistake and that sensory and appearance properties are in fact of ineliminable aesthetic importance in architecture and sculpture. This debate connects with, and is an echo of, some fascinating renaissance debates about the essence of architecture (Wittkower 1971; Mitrovic 1998). On the one hand, there is a renaissance Platonist tendency in those like Palladio, and a related modernist tendency in those like Le Corbusier, to emphasize spatial relations. On the other hand, there are their opponents who think that sensory and appearance properties are crucially important (Scott 1914). Different ideologies concerning the essence of architecture may make a real difference to building practice. One side thinks of architecture as something that is presented to our intellect, while the other side thinks of it as something that is presented to our senses. This makes a difference, for example, to the design of windows that are located high up on a building and are most likely to be seen from below: is it aesthetically important that they *are* square, or merely that they *look* square? (See further Mitrovic 1998.)

These issues about architecture lie downstream from a very general issue about whether whatever has aesthetic properties must have either physical, sensory, or appearance properties. Can non-spatio-temporal abstract objects, if there are any, possess aesthetic properties? Some say that mathematical or scientific theories can possess aesthetic properties (Kivy 1991). In the *Phaedo*, Plato held that the form of the beautiful was beautiful. Others say that the soul can be beautiful. And Eddy Zemach thinks that laws of nature can be beautiful (Zemach 1997). I am rather sceptical about these cases, and am inclined to be restrictive about the sorts of things that can possess aesthetic properties. I think that beautiful things always have sensory or appearance properties (Zangwill 2001a: chapter 8). But I am in the minority in thinking this. The consensus among contemporary aestheticians is to be more generous than I. I say something in favour of this restrictiveness at the end of the next section.

Because I hold this general view, I resist the view that architectural beauty is appreciated solely in intellectual contemplation. The view I favour is that it is a matter of relishing our perceptual experiences of sensory or appearance properties. Is beauty restricted to sights and sounds, or is there a higher beauty that we appreciate solely with our intellects, as the priestess Diotima urges in the *Symposium*? In my view, the things we contemplate intellectually may display many wonderful characteristics, but beauty is not among them. And the mental faculties, called upon in such intellectual contemplation, are not our aesthetic faculties. The same goes for our intellectual understanding of the spatial structure, history, and meaning of a building, in so far as that is not manifest to us in perceptual experience. The history of a building and its meaning may be intellectually interesting, but it may not be relevant to the building as an aesthetic object. Architectural beauty is discernible in sensory experience. Diotima's higher beauty is chimerical. There is only the lowly beauty that is manifest to our senses.

4. Free and Dependent Beauty

There is a crucial distinction to be found in Kant between *free* and *dependent* beauty (Kant 1928: § 16; a possible precursor is Frances Hutcheson (1993), when he distinguishes 'absolute' from 'relative' beauty). The *dependent* beauty of a thing is the beauty that it has *as a thing with certain function*. Since something has a function only if it has a certain kind of history (Millikan 1993), a thing has dependent beauty only if it has a certain history. By contrast, the *free* beauty of a thing is independent of its function. A thing has free beauty at a time just in virtue of how it is at that time. The free beauty of a thing is independent of its history (and indeed of its future), whereas a thing's dependent beauty depends on its history in so far as that history enters into its function. In order to *see* a thing as having dependent beauty, one must see it as a thing of a certain kind, where that kind implies a function—whether natural or artefactual—and we must bring knowledge of the history of the thing to bear in our experience. Since what gives something a function is external to the thing itself, it is not manifest to someone who is simply perceptually confronted with the thing.

Many of those who discuss Kant's distinction between free and dependent beauty miss the crucial teleological dimension of the distinction. They think that dependent beauty is just a matter of subsuming a thing under a *concept*. But the crucial thing is subsuming something under a *concept of its function*. (A good discussion of Kant's exploration of this notion can be found in Schaper 1983: chapter 4, and McCloskey 1987.) In my view, the distinction between free and dependent beauty is absolutely fundamental, and I think that without it there is a great deal that we cannot begin to understand in aesthetics.

Let us consider some examples. The beauty of what is called 'programme music' arises when music serves some non-musical function in a musically appropriate way, so that the function is manifest in the aesthetic face of the music. For example, music might be for dancing, marching, or shopping. It might be for accompanying a bullfight or a film. The beauty of representational paintings arises when a painting is beautiful *as* a representation of something. Poetic value lies in the aesthetically apt choice of words to express a particular sense. A speech or tract may be aesthetically powerful *as* a political statement. All these aesthetic values in art can only be understood given the notion of dependent beauty. By contrast, the beauty of a piece of what is called 'absolute music' holds just in virtue of the sounds it is composed of, and is not dependent on any purpose that the music is supposed to serve. Similarly, the beauty of an abstract painting holds just in virtue of its shapes and colours, and is not dependent on any representational purpose.

The distinction between free and dependent beauty is no less important in nature. Some natural things are beautiful only as things of some natural biological kind. Some say, for example, that it matters aesthetically that something is a sea bed rather than a beach (Hepburn 1984: 19), or a fish rather than a mammal (Carlson 2000: 89). Even so, it seems we should not lose sight of the fact that nature has considerable free beauty (Zangwill 2001a: chapter 7). Consider, for example, brightly coloured sea-cucumbers. They have a beauty that does not depend on what type of creature they are. Again, consider our judgement that an underwater polar bear moves elegantly. This judgement is arguably not hostage to its being a polar bear rather than a zoo-keeper disguised in a polar bear suit. Whatever it is, it is plausibly elegant in virtue of how it is in itself and how it moves. It is not merely elegant *qua* polar bear.

Of course, many things have *both* free and dependent beauty. For example, if we were to compile an inventory of valuable properties of paintings, we could distinguish their dependent beauties, which depend on representational properties, from their free beauties, which depend just on perceivable surface properties. But a painting can have both kinds of beauties.

In some cases, what the dependent beauties are is controversial. Is a building beautiful or elegant just *as a building*, or more narrowly *as a certain sort of building*?

Is architectural beauty relatively coarse-grained (beautiful merely *qua* building), or is it more fine-grained (beautiful *qua* building of a specific sort)? It is at least not obvious that we miss out on the beauty or elegance of buildings that are mosques or churches if we just see them as buildings, and not as mosques or churches. Is it an affront to the beauty of a building when the building changes its non-aesthetic function? (See Scruton 1979 for discussion.) If so, architectural dependent beauty is relatively fine-grained. If not, it is relatively coarse-grained.

Let us now return to the question of the alleged beauty of things that lack sensory properties. What about theories, souls, laws of nature, and Plato's forms? Now where we have a case of dependent beauty, a thing has beauty that expresses its function. But a thing can be dependently beautiful despite not in fact fulfilling that function, or even having a disposition to fulfil it. For example, a building could express strength and impregnability despite literally being neither strong nor impregnable since it actually has a flimsy fake façade that only *looks* strong and impregnable. In the case of theories and souls, the person who calls such things 'beautiful' is concerned with certain properties of those things—the *truth* of theories, and the *moral qualities* of souls—such that the ascription of beauty is not separable from their truth or moral qualities. The trouble with the so-called beauty of theories or souls is that it is too closely related to these other concerns to be a case of dependent beauty. An utterly false theory or an irredeemably bad soul, which does not even possess properties that are conducive to truth or goodness, could not be said to be beautiful. So talking of the 'beauty' of theories or souls is merely misleading hyperbole. What about the beauty of the Platonic form of the beautiful or of the laws of nature, which don't seem to be candidates for dependent beauty? I cannot see how forms and laws might be beautiful independently of the things they cause or explain—the beautiful things that participate in the form or are bound by the laws. The form of the beautiful surely could not be beautiful independently of its capacity to endow physical things with a beauty that we can perceive. And the laws of nature surely could not be beautiful even though the perceivable objects and events that they govern are all ugly. Again, in the case of forms and laws, the connection between their so-called beauty and the beauty of the things to which they are related is too close for us to be able to claim that they have an independent beauty of their own.

5. THE PRIMACY CONJECTURE

I am inclined to think that free beauty has a certain kind of *primacy* over dependent beauty, in the sense that we must be able to appreciate *free* beauty if we are to appreciate *any* beauty. The primacy claim is that, without a conception of free beauty, no other beauty would be available to us. We can conceive of one only because we can conceive of the other. There could not be people who cared only about dependent beauty but not about free beauty. Our love of free beauty is, as it were, the ground from which our love of dependent beauty springs.

In music, the conjecture is that, if we were not able to appreciate absolute music, then we could not appreciate non-absolute or 'programme' music. Indeed, perhaps music could not serve our non-musical purposes unless it could serve our purely musical ones. Although there can be particular pieces of music that have considerable dependent musical beauty and minimal free beauty, our ability to appreciate dependent musical beauty depends on our ability to appreciate free musical beauty. In painting, the conjecture is that, if we were not able to appreciate the beauty of two-dimensional design, then we could not appreciate representational beauty. In architecture, the conjecture is that we could not appreciate the aesthetically apt embodiment of function unless we could also appreciate the beauty of purely sculptural properties of buildings. So there is a sense in which the ignorant sensibility of the tourist, with its admirably naïve wonder, is more fundamental than the educated scholarly sensibility. The scholar may know more, and the scholar may, as a consequence, appreciate deeper layers of the building's beauty. But even the scholar was once a tourist.

As always, the case of literature is complicated because it is not clear how extensive the aesthetic properties of literature are. A modest claim would be that we could not appreciate the apt sonic embodiment of content unless we could appreciate pure sonic beauty for its own sake. That is, we cannot appreciate the poetic aspect of literature unless we appreciate its purely musical aspect. But if there are aesthetic properties of literary content, which are not tied to the sonic properties of words, then the priority thesis may not hold quite generally. Perhaps stories have aesthetic properties that are independent of their manifestation in particular words, and if so, someone may well be able to appreciate the aesthetic properties of the story without being able to appreciate its particular sonic embodiment in particular words. Similarly, perhaps someone could appreciate the symbolic and narrative properties of paintings without having any sense of visual beauty. If so, the primacy thesis would not generalize across the board. On the other hand, it is not clear that the properties we appreciate in these cases are aesthetic properties (see Zangwill 2001a: chapter 8). If so, the primacy thesis would hold for literature after all. It is controversial whether symbolic and narrative properties can generate aesthetic properties by themselves: if they can, then the primacy thesis fails in those cases, but if they cannot, then it holds quite generally.

Given reasonable assumptions about the motivation of those who make works of art, the primacy thesis would imply that, if there were no freely beautiful art, it would be unlikely there would be dependently beautiful art, even though there are many works that are dependently beautiful but not freely beautiful. For example, it is unlikely that there would be a situation in which people built only dependently beautiful buildings devoid of free beauty, or in which people painted only beautiful representations that were ugly considered as two-dimensional patterns. It is no accident that many (and perhaps most) works of art that have artistic merit in a broad sense also excel in terms of free beauty.

I am not sure how to argue for the primacy thesis, but if it is right, then we all begin by responding aesthetically to no more than what confronts our senses. Then we become more sophisticated, learning to appreciate things in the light of their histories. But sophisticates should not deny the existence and importance of the primitive aesthetic response. The foundation of our sophisticated aesthetic life is the primitive enjoyment of free beauty.

6. Personal Beauty

The aesthetics of human beings is somewhat anomalous from the point of view of the usual division of the objects of aesthetic interest into art and nature. For human beings fit comfortably into neither category, or perhaps they lie at the intersection of both. Neither art nor nature will do as a model for thinking about the beauty of human beings.

It is noteworthy that the word 'beauty', as it figures most prominently *outside* the academy, denotes a personal attribute and not a quality of art or nature. Let us take 'personal beauty' to mean the beauty of a person's face, body, or demeanour. If one looks up 'beauty' in a telephone directory, one will find few aestheticians listed there! A 'beautician' is more likely to be versed in manicures than metaphysics.

The various issues surrounding personal beauty must be understood in terms of Kant's distinction between free and dependent beauty, since personal beauty is clearly dependent beauty. A person is beautiful not as abstract sculpture, but as a human being.

There is, however, a sceptical strain of thought that would reject this whole way of thinking. According to such sceptics, personal beauty is entirely a social construction, not just in the sense that there is no metaphysically real property of human beauty, but also in the sense that our responses to human beauty are entirely an artefact of social conditioning and are not at all a response to the perceivable properties of human beings. This is the consensus within the academy, where the subject of personal beauty is currently highly charged. In fact, there is a large cultural rift between what goes on inside the academy and what goes on outside. Inside the academy, there is a sceptical consensus among those who discuss the issue, while outside the academy much money and care is spent in the pursuit of something that is assumed to be very real and desirable, and such a conception of beauty figures prominently in people's thoughts, desires, and pleasures. Of course, it could be that the academics are right and that the common-sense, folk aesthetic theory that ordinary people hold is a delusion. But it is also possible that our common-sense aesthetics is right and the academics are wrong.

The sceptical view has been popularized by Naomi Wolff under the slogan 'The Beauty Myth' (Wolff 1992). The beauty myth is supposed to be a cluster of ideals of (predominantly) feminine beauty that are foisted on pliable women by the male media, and that have no natural or inevitable basis. It is true that there is *some* variation in ideals of male and female beauty across cultures and times. But the doctrine of the beauty myth goes much further than this. The doctrine of the beauty myth is that ideals of feminine beauty are *entirely* socially constructed (Wolff 1992: 12–19). Wolff has been well answered by Nancy Etcoff (1999), who argues that the beauty myth is a myth, since ideals of personal beauty are connected with evolutionary survival. While there may be some variation in conceptions of male and female beauty, the broad parameters are evolutionarily hardwired and remarkably consistent across cultures and eras. The anti-social-constructionist case on this matter is overwhelming. (But, since the beauty-myth myth is both comforting and ideologically useful, it is likely to persist.)

Etcoff further thinks that the beauty myth is harmful: as she says, 'Beauty is not going anywhere. The idea that beauty is unimportant or a cultural construct is the real beauty myth. We have to understand beauty, or we will always be enslaved by it' (Etcoff 1999: 242). As Etcoff exhaustively shows, personal beauty in fact plays a major factor in our lives, even if we are not consciously aware of it. Personal beauty has great power over us in virtue of the pleasure it gives us. But because of its very allure, beauty is also a source of danger. It can distract us, and it can be used to manipulate us. All the more reason to understand it, rather than deny that it exists. We can be aware of the threat that personal beauty can pose only when we realize what it is and why it holds us in its thrall. In contrast to Etcoff, Elaine Scarry (1999) thinks that beauty and justice go happily hand in hand. But Scarry is overly sanguine about this. Scarry lies at the opposite extreme from Wolff. Scarry sees the reality and value of beauty but not its dangers, whereas Wolff sees the dangers of beauty but not its reality and value. We need to see both.

A question that now comes explicitly into view is this: is there such a property as being beautiful *as a man* or being beautiful *as a woman*? That is, is some human beauty *gender-dependent beauty*? Or is the idea of gender-dependent beauty something we should give up? The distinction between male and female beauty has been part of folk aesthetics in countless cultures for thousands of years. (Even if there have been variations in the conceptions of each, the two conceptions have always been different from each other.) But folk aesthetic theory can be mistaken. Presumably both sides agree that people can be beautiful *as human beings.* The controversial question is the further one of whether there is such a property as being beautiful *as a male* or *as a female* human being. Rocks have free beauty only because they have no functions; so someone who attributed dependent beauty to a rock would be mistaken. The critic of the idea of gendered beauty agrees that people can be beautiful as human beings but thinks that it is misguided to deploy gender categories in more fine-grained aesthetic evaluations. I mentioned before that in architecture there is an understandable position according to which buildings are beautiful only as buildings, not as mosques, railway stations, libraries, and so on. Some have argued for this from the way many buildings change their use in radical ways and are no worse for that. But I am not sure how a parallel argument would go in the gender case.

I suspect that the issue about gendered beauty turns on the general question of whether the sexes have different natural functions. (I leave open whether such a view would involve taking a stand on what is called 'gender essentialism'.) Someone who believes in gendered beauty will be someone who believes that there are differences in natural functions between the sexes, while someone who thinks there are not, will not. The two issues hang together. Someone who thinks that there are no differences in natural functions will have an androgynous conception of human beauty (as was popular in the West in the 1970s). There would be no difference between being beautiful as a man and being beautiful as a woman. On the other hand, someone who thinks that there are some functional differences between the sexes will allow that there can be some differences in respective aesthetic conceptions. Kant's notion of dependent beauty explains the debate over gendered beauty.

One other issue about personal beauty that I want to mention concerns the aesthetics of tattooing. Clearly, some tattoos have free beauty. But Kant's view (which I agree with) is that tattoos are all dependently ugly (Kant 1928: § 16). This raises murky but fascinating issues to do with the notions that we bring to bear in thinking about the human body. Those who object to tattoos on aesthetic-cum-moral grounds appeal to notions like *purity* and *defilement*; and, ironically, many of those who have tattoos and defend them operate with those very categories—they too see tattooing in such terms, despite the difference in overall verdict. (Tattooing magazines confirm this.) A purely 'liberal' approach to this issue—as with most other issues about the body—completely fails to engage with the phenomenology of those on both sides of the debate, since both those who engage in the practice as well as those who object to it think in terms that seem to have something of a religious flavour. We have next to nil in the way of an understanding of this issue. Yet the issue is clearly one about dependent beauty and ugliness. Both the objections to the practice and the point of it for its practitioners stem from a conception of the moral function of the body, and the different evaluations of the dependent aesthetic value of tattooing springs from more basic differences over the body.

I have raised issues about human beauty that analytic aestheticians do not usually discuss and that rarely figure in aesthetics textbooks and anthologies. However, I believe that they can be usefully explored, and that we should not simply abandon them to 'cultural studies'. Like the aesthetics of representational paintings and the aesthetics of architecture, the aesthetics of human beings turns centrally on considerations of dependent beauty.

7. THREE RECENT LANDMARKS

In the preceding sections of this chapter, I have explored a number of controversial issues about the relation of beauty to other aesthetic properties, the species of beauty, and the non-aesthetic properties on which beauty supervenes. In this last section, I turn to consider the metaphysics of beauty. Is beauty real? If so, is it a mind-independent or mind-dependent property? Is beauty a projection of the human mind? I shall review three recent accounts of the nature of beauty before giving my own view.

In her book *Beauty Restored*, Mary Mothersill (1984) seeks to place beauty in its rightful place as a central object of inquiry in aesthetics. She puts forward two preliminary theses. Her 'first thesis' is that there are no laws of taste. I agree with this in spirit, although I think supervenience lands us with some harmless necessary universal generalizations. Her 'second thesis' is that aesthetic judgements are 'genuine judgements' and that some of them are true. Again, I agree with this, on most elucidations of 'genuine judgement'. Given these two preliminary theses, Mothersill goes on to give an analysis of aesthetic properties (Mothersill 1984, chapter 11). She there defines aesthetic properties as those that are shared between perceptually indistinguishable things. But the notion of perceptual indistinguishability is insufficiently spelt out, and is problematic, given that we may perceive things differently when we know about their histories. And anyway, her definition of perceptual indistinguishability (which involves only unaided ordinary perception) seems to imply that aesthetic properties cannot be possessed by distant galaxies and minute cells that we have only recently been able to perceive by means of telescopes and microscopes. Moreover, Mothersill assumes that beauty is always 'narrowly' determined by 'perceivable' properties, which makes her an extreme formalist of an objectionable sort. Lastly, she says that 'beauty is a disposition to produce pleasure in virtue of aesthetic properties' (Mothersill 1984: 349). Without the last clause, this would be a pure dispositional account, like Alan Goldman's—which I shall turn to in a moment. However, with the last clause it is not informative about the metaphysics of beauty, but only delineates a connection between pleasure, beauty, and other aesthetic properties, albeit one that has some plausibility. But it also compatible with most accounts of the metaphysics of aesthetic properties, in virtue of which things have these dispositions.

Alan Goldman argues for a non-realist view of aesthetic properties in his book *Aesthetic Value* (1995). He begins his book with a description of the relation between aesthetic properties and aesthetic values. He thinks—rightly in my view—that aesthetic properties have an inherent evaluative polarity (Goldman 1995: 20). But he thinks he can build an argument for aesthetic non-realism on this basis. Without offering much in the way of argument, he embraces the view that an aesthetic property is a disposition to elicit responses in ideal critics in virtue of more basic properties (Goldman 1995: 21). He calls this view the 'Humean Structure'. Given the Humean Structure, Goldman argues that ideal critics can nevertheless diverge in their responses (Goldman 1995: 30–1), and he draws the conclusion that aesthetic properties are mind-dependent and that aesthetic realism is false (pp. 36–9).

However, the Humean Structure is very far from being uncontroversial. Hume himself, who was a non-cognitivist, would arguably have had nothing to do with it. Moreover, those of a realist inclination can and should also back away from it. An aesthetic realist should deny that aesthetic properties *consist in* some dispositional relation to critics, even ideal critics. Perhaps it is true that we are disposed to respond in certain ways to aesthetic features. But we take our responses to be warranted—and we take them to be *warranted* in virtue of the aesthetic features that we experience. Even if it is true that ideal critics *necessarily* come to know a thing's aesthetic properties (else they are not ideal), that would not be part of what being an aesthetic property *consists in* (Fine 1994). To impose the Humean Structure is to beg the question against aesthetic realism. If an 'ideal critic' is just someone who makes correct judgements, then the fact that there is divergence in *non*-ideal aesthetic judgements is unproblematic. And if 'ideal critics' are defined as those with a certain list of virtues in judgement, then there is no reason why such ideal critics should not be fallible, since, for a realist, a virtue in judgement is just a *tendency* to produce correct judgements in appropriate conditions. Again, divergence in actual judgement is unproblematic. Goldman uses a parallel argument from ideal critics against the idea of aesthetic/non-aesthetic supervenience (Goldman 1995: 39–44). Once again, the cure is to reject the ideal critic account.

In his book *Real Beauty*, Eddy Zemach (1997) resists the lure of dispositional and ideal observer theories. I think this is a virtue of his brand of aesthetic realism. Zemach is an aesthetic realist because science, he thinks, necessarily takes aesthetic considerations into account. Aesthetic properties such as elegance are crucial in evaluating scientific theories where adequacy to the data fails to give us reason to choose between competing theories. Zemach argues that, if we must appeal to aesthetic criteria in evaluating theories, then, unless that appeal is fraudulent, it must be because the theories really have aesthetic properties. I find this argument problematic on several counts. One problem follows from the general rejection of the idea that abstract objects can possess aesthetic properties. Scientific theories are presumably abstract objects. (Their beauty does not consist in the beauty of the inscriptions or sounds in which they are realized.) If so, they cannot possess aesthetic properties and talk of their 'elegance' is merely metaphorical. But even if we admit that scientific theories *can* in principle have aesthetic properties, the argument only shows that *scientific theories* have aesthetic properties: it does not show that the *world* in general does. An aesthetic realist thinks that roses and paintings have aesthetic properties, not just scientific theories. Next, even if we concede that scientific theories have aesthetic properties only if the world they describe also has them, that too would fail to include roses and paintings. For it would only show that the laws the theories describe have aesthetic properties, and the entities postulated in the theories, not the commonsensical items bound by the laws, such as roses and paintings. Finally, even if the argument shows that the commonsensical items bound by the laws, such as roses and paintings, have aesthetic properties, it only shows that they have aesthetic properties of the sort that figure in the evaluation of scientific theories. But there are many other aesthetic properties that do not. Roses and painting are sometimes elegant, as are (let us concede) some scientific theories. But are theories delicate, poignant, vibrant, exuberant, vivacious, and so on? The class of aesthetic properties that Zemach's argument covers is too restricted.

My own view is that there are good reasons to accept a realist account according to which aesthetic properties are mind-independent properties that are realized in ordinary non-aesthetic properties of things. So, for example, the beauty of a rose is realized in the specific arrangement and colours of its petals, leaves, stem, and so on. And our aesthetic judgements are true when they ascribe to things the mind-independent aesthetic properties that they do in fact have.

I mentioned before that there is an issue about what explains aesthetic supervenience. Aesthetic supervenience is essential to our conception of beauty and other aesthetic properties. Aesthetic realists explain aesthetic supervenience by saying that it follows from the nature of aesthetic properties, whereas non-realists appeal to a requirement of consistency among aesthetic judgements or responses. Non-realists have not so far advanced a plausible explanation of such a requirement. Goldman, with his mind-dependent view, is led to deny aesthetic supervenience, which I regard as a reductio of his position. That leaves realism as the only account that can explain this fundamental principle.

The only problem with realism is that among the non-aesthetic properties that aesthetic properties supervene on are *sensory* properties, like colours and sounds; and, according to many, these are not mind-independent properties of things. If sensory properties are not mind-independent, then neither are the aesthetic properties that supervene on them (Zangwill 2001a: chapter 11). If that is right, then aesthetic properties may not be mind-independent after all. Yet they are not, as on the usual response-dependent accounts of aesthetic properties, dependent on hedonic reactions, but rather on the character of human sensory experiences.

What, then, is beauty? Beauty offers us pleasure of a certain sort, one that grounds judgements that aspire to correctness. Judgements of beauty, in Kant's terms, have 'subjective universality'. Furthermore, beauty is a supervenient property, though exactly what beauty supervenes on in different cases is controversial. Many of these cases are illuminated by Kant's distinction between free and dependent beauty. Lastly, the dependence of beauty on non-aesthetic properties plays a pivotal role in debates over the metaphysics of beauty and other aesthetic properties.

See also: Aesthetic Realism 1; Aesthetic Realism 2; Aesthetic Experience; Aesthetics of Nature; Aesthetics of the Everyday; Aesthetics and Evolutionary Psychology; Value in Art.

BIBLIOGRAPHY

Beardsley, M. (1982). 'On the Generality of Critical Reasons', in *The Aesthetic Point of View*. Ithaca, NY: Cornell University Press.

Bell, C. (1913). *Art*. London: Chatto & Windus.

Burton, S. (1992). 'Thick Concepts Revisited'. *Analysis* 52: 28–32.

Carlson, A. (2000). *Aesthetics and the Environment*. London: Routledge.

Cohen, T. (1973). 'Aesthetic/Non-aesthetic and the Concept of Taste: A Critique of Sibley's Position'. *Theoria* 39: 113–52.

Currie, G. (1989). *An Ontology of Art*. London: Macmillan.

Danto, A. (1981). *The Transfiguration of the Commonplace*. Cambridge, Mass.: Harvard University Press.

Etcoff, N. (1999). *The Survival of the Prettiest*. New York: Doubleday.

Fine, K. (1994). 'Essence and Modality'. *Philosophical Perspectives* 8: 1–16.

Goldman, A. (1995). *Aesthetic Value*. Boulder, Colo.: Westview.

Gombrich, E. (1959). *Art and Illusion*. London: Phaidon.

Hepburn, R. (1984). 'Contemporary Aesthetic and the Neglect of Natural Beauty', in his *Wonder and Others Essays*. Edinburgh: Edinburgh University Press.

Hutcheson, F. (1993). *Inquiry into the Original of Our Ideas of Beauty and Virtue*. The Hague: Nijhoff.

Kant, I. (1928). *Critique of Judgement*, trans. J. C. Meredith. Oxford: Oxford University Press.

Kim, J. (1993). 'Concepts of Supervenience', in his *Supervenience and Mind*. Cambridge: Cambridge University Press.

Kivy, P. (1975). 'What Makes "Aesthetic" Terms *Aesthetic*?' *Philosophy and Phenomenological Research* 35: 197–211.

—— (1991). 'Science and Aesthetic Appreciation'. *Midwest Studies in Philosophy* 16: 180–95.

Korsmeyer, C. (1999). *Making Sense of Taste*. Ithaca, NY: Cornell University Press.

Levinson, J. (1990). 'Aesthetic Supervenience', in his *Music, Art, and Metaphysics*. Ithaca, NY: Cornell University Press.

—— (1996). 'Pleasure and the Value of Works of Art', in his *The Pleasures of Aesthetics*. Ithaca, NY: Cornell University Press.

—— (2001). 'Aesthetic Properties, Evaluative Force, and Differences of Sensibility', in E. Brady and J. Levinson (eds.), *Aesthetic Concepts: Essays after Sibley*. Oxford: Clarendon Press.

McCloskey, M. (1987). *Kant's Aesthetic*. Albany, NY: SUNY Press.

Millikan, R. (1993). *White Queen Psychology and Other Essays for Alice*. Cambridge, Mass.: MIT Press.

Mitrovic, B. (1998). 'Paduan Aristotelianism and Daniele Barbaro's Commentary on Vitruvius' *De architectura*'. *Sixteenth Century Journal* 29: 667–88.

Mothersill, M. (1984). *Beauty Restored*. Oxford: Clarendon Press.

Rowe, C. (1976). 'The Mathematics of the Ideal Villa', in his *The Mathematics of the Ideal Villa and Other Essays*. Cambridge, Mass.: MIT Press.

Scarry, E. (1999). *On Beauty and Being Just*. Princeton: Princeton University Press.

Schaper, E. (1983). *Studies in Kant's Aesthetics*. Edinburgh: Edinburgh University Press

Scott, G. (1914). *The Architecture of Humanism*. London: Constable.

Scruton, R. (1979). *The Aesthetics of Architecture*. Princeton: Princeton University Press.

Sibley, F. (1959). 'Aesthetic Concepts'. *Philosophical Review* 68: 421–50.

—— (1965). 'Aesthetic and Nonaesthetic'. *Philosophical Review* 74: 135–59.

Walton, K. (1970). 'Categories of Art'. *Philosophical Review* 70: 334–76.

Wittkower, R. (1971). *Architectural Principles in the Age of Humanism*. New York: W. W. Norton.

Wolff, N. (1992). *The Beauty Myth*. New York: Doubleday.

Zangwill, N. (2001*a*). *The Metaphysics of Beauty*. Ithaca, NY: Cornell University Press.

—— (2001*b*). 'Aesthetic Functionalism', in E. Brady and J. Levinson (eds.), *Aesthetic Concepts: Essays after Sibley*. Oxford: Clarendon Press.

Zemach, E. (1997). *Real Beauty*. University Park, Pa.: Pennsylvania State University Press.

CHAPTER 19

HUMOUR

NOËL CARROLL

1. THEORIES OF HUMOUR

HUMOUR is a pervasive feature of human life. We find it everywhere—at work and at play, in private and public affairs. Sometimes we make it ourselves; often we pay others to create it for us, including playwrights, novelists, filmmakers, stand-up comics, clowns, and so on. According to some, like Rabelais, humour is alleged to be distinctively human, a property of our species and no other. But even if that is not the case, humour seems to be a nearly universal component of human societies. Thus, it should come as no surprise that it has been a perennial topic for philosophy—especially for philosophers ambitious enough to attempt to comment on every facet of human life.

Plato believed that the laughter that attends humour is directed at vice, particularly at the vice of self-unawareness (Plato 1961). That is, we laugh at people who fail to realize the Socratic adage—'Know thyself'—and who instead deceive themselves, imagining that they are wiser than they are, or stronger, or taller, etc. Thus, amusement contains an element of malice. Plato also distrusted humour, because he feared that it could lead to bouts of uncontrolled laughter and, of course, Plato was suspicious of anything that contributed to a lack of rational self-control. For this reason, he discouraged the cultivation of laughter in the guardian class of his Republic and urged that they not be exposed to representations of gods and heroes laughing (Plato 1993).

A similar distrust of humour can be found in Epictetus and the Stoics, who, like Plato, placed a premium on emotional self-control. Church fathers, such as Ambrose and Jerome, assimilated the Stoic suspicion of humour, despite the fact that Jesus himself valued laughter (Phipps 1979).

Like his mentor Plato, Aristotle defines the joke as a form of abuse (Aristotle 1941) and thinks that comedy involves the portrayal of people as worse than average (Aristotle 1993). Unlike Plato, however, Aristotle allows a role for humour in the virtuous life. But the laughter of the virtuous person must be tactful and moderate. Aristotle agrees with Plato that laughter can get out of hand. Thus, he warns the virtuous against the danger of buffoonery—an inability to resist the temptation to provoke laughter, no matter what the occasion, and whatever the means required. Such a person could hardly be regarded as a reliable citizen.

The association—found in Plato and Aristotle—of humour with malice and abuse towards people marked as deficient suggests what has been called the *Superiority Theory of Humour*, which was articulated in its most compact form by Thomas Hobbes. Hobbes wrote: 'I may therefore conclude that the passion of laughter is nothing else but sudden glory arising from some eminency in ourselves, by comparison with the infirmity of others, or with our own formerly' (Morreall 1987).

That is, according to Hobbes, laughter results from perceiving infirmities in others that reinforce our own sense of superiority. Hobbes adds that the object of humour may also be our former selves, in order to accommodate the fact that we sometimes laugh at ourselves. But when we laugh at ourselves for some stupid behaviour—say, putting shaving cream on our toothbrush—we do so putatively from a present perspective of superior insight that sees and savours the ridiculous absentmindedness exhibited by the person we were.

There is a lot to be said for the Superiority Theory of Humour. Much humour is undeniably at the expense of characters who are particularly stupid, vain, greedy, cruel, ruthless, dirty, lubricious, and deficient in other respects. Consider, for example: Polish jokes as told by Americans, Irish jokes as told by Englishmen, Belgian jokes by the French, Chelm jokes by Jews, Russian jokes by Poles, Ukrainian jokes by Russians, Newfie jokes by Canadians, and Sikh jokes by Indians—not to mention Blonde jokes, told by anyone. These are all essentially moron jokes; they can all be retold by asking 'why did the moron do X?' or 'how does the moron do X?' But moron jokes are obviously aimed at monumental lapses in intelligence to which virtually anyone can feel superior.

Similarly, many jokes are told at the expense of people with physical disabilities (e.g. stuttering) or cultural disadvantages (e.g. illiteracy) and from an implicit position of superiority. What the Superiority Theory asserts is that we find the comic butts in such humour not merely different from us, but inferior to us. The Superiority Theory has the virtue of handling a great deal of data, from laughter at moron jokes to laughter at people slipping on the ice (i.e. people clumsier than we are). Much laughter is nasty, directed at foolishness, and the Superiority Theory ostensibly explains why this is so. Laughter is a sign of pleasure, and the pleasure we take in the foolishness of others is the recognition that we are better than they are.

However, despite the explanatory reach of the Superiority Theory, it suffers notable limitations. Feelings of superiority cannot be a necessary condition for laughter, since there are many cases of laughter that do not involve them. We laugh at word wit such as puns with no tendentious edge. But when we laugh in these cases, it is far from clear to whom one feels superior, or in what way the utterer of such word wit is inferior to us. Indeed, they may strike us as being cleverer than we are.

As well, we may laugh when we are amiably teased, but this is hard to explain in terms of feelings of superiority we supposedly have, since it is not some former self whose shortcomings are being tweaked, but ourselves in the present moment. Moreover, children laugh at an extremely early age at things like 'funny faces' and 'fort/da' games, but it is difficult to presume that they have yet evolved anything worth calling a concept of superiority. And, in any case, how would superiority figure in an account of laughter in response to a 'fort/da' game?

Furthermore, we sometimes laugh at comic characters whose behaviour is decidedly superior to anything we could imagine achieving ourselves. For example, in the film *The General* (1926), when Buster Keaton uses the railroad tie on his chest to catapult another one off the track in front of him, this magnificent insight into how to avoid derailment prompts our laughter, though few of us could have solved this predicament so elegantly (Carroll 1996). In such a case, it makes no sense to say that our laughter flows from our feeling of superiority to Keaton. If anything along this line of thought occurs to us, it is more likely that we realize that we are inferior to Keaton in respect of lightning ingenuity.

Nor is the recognition of our superiority to others a sufficient condition for laughter. As Francis Hutcheson pointed out, we realize that we are superior to oysters, but we don't laugh at them (Hutcheson 1973). Nor, he said, do we laugh at heretics, though presumably the true believer will feel quite superior to them. Consequently, though the Superiority Theory appears to work well with many examples, at the same time, it ill-suits too much of the rest of the data.

Furthermore, the Hobbesian version of the Superiority Theory is framed in terms of laughter, and is putatively an account of the springs thereof. Undoubtedly, this enhances the intuitive plausibility of the theory, since, as is readily observed, laughter often accompanies triumph. However, there remains the real question of whether laughter is, in fact, the proper object of analysis for a theory of humour. For, on the one hand, laughter is a response not only to humour, but also to tickling, nitrous oxide, belladonna, atropine, amphetamine, cannabis, alchohol, the gelastic seizures that accompany certain epileptic fits, nervousness, hebephrenia, and, of course, victory; while, on the other hand, some humour does not elicit laughter, but only a mild sensation of joy or lightness, i.e. levity. Thus, in focusing on laughter, it is not clear that Hobbes's theory is really a theory of humour at all.

A theory of humour need be concerned only with amused laughter—the laughter that issues from comic amusement—and there is no reason to suppose that triumphant laughter, say, is amused laughter. To determine that would require an analysis of amusement. But it is doubtful that the Superiority Theory can provide an analysis of amusement, since the object of the passion that concerns Hobbes is the self triumphant, which does not seem to be the object of comic amusement, even if a sense of superiority can cause a certain type of laughter.

Many of the limitations of Hobbes's Superiority Theory were noted in the eighteenth century by Francis Hutcheson, who endeavoured to replace it with what has come to be known as the *Incongruity Theory of Humour*. This theory was perhaps already suggested by Aristotle, who proposed that the proper objects of comedy were people who are worse than average. Here we find the germ of the idea that comic amusement is rooted in deviations from some norm. However, Hutcheson's theory is generally recognized as the best known early, explicitly worked out, version of the Incongruity Theory. To date, the Incongruity Theory of Humour has attracted the largest number of philosophers, including Schopenhauer (1966), Kierkegaard (1941), Koestler (1964), Morreall (1983), Clark (1970), and, arguably, Kant (1951) and Bergson (1965).

The leading idea of the Incongruity Theory is that comic amusement comes with the apprehension of incongruity. We are amused by the animated fowl in the film *Chicken Run* (2000) because their movements, their behaviour, and their very look call to mind human beings. However, this is incongrous or absurd. It would be a category error to subsume chickens under the concept of human being: it would violate a standing category; it would be an incongruous instantiation of that concept. The makers of *Chicken Run*, nevertheless, invite us to contemplate just such a prospect, and in doing so they elicit comic amusement.

Similarly, puns generally involve violations of conversational rules, shifting the likely meaning of a word or phrase in a specific context to a secondary or metaphorical meaning, or exchanging the predictable usage of a word for that of one of its homonyms. In other words, a pun is incongruous because it involves activating word meanings that are out of place, given the direction of the surrounding discourse. Moreover, the wacky logical inferences so frequently indulged by the denizens of jokes, satires, and burlesques count as incongruities; they are absurdities, given the laws of logic, both deductive and inductive, formal and informal.

Speaking drily, the notion of incongruity presupposed by the Incongruity Theory can initially be very roughly described as a problematization of sense. This can occur when concepts or rules are violated or transgressed. But the scope of these transgressions need not be limited to conceptual mistakes, linguistic improprieties, or logical errors. Sense can also be problematized by being stretched to the breaking point. Thus, it is very common to field comic teams composed of a very thin man and a very fat man (e.g. Don Quixote and Sancho Panza, Abbott and Costello). In this case, there is no category error. However, we are presented with instantiations of the concept of the human being that lie at the extreme ends of the relevant category: the characters are so dissimilar that one is, oddly enough, struck by the heterogeneity of the category, rather than by its homogeneity.

Similarly, incongruity accrues when a concept is instantiated in an unlikely way, rather than in an erroneous way. Shown a ninety-pound weakling outfitted in the gear of a sumo wrestler, we are struck by the incongruity, since the character is such an unrepresentative example of our stereotype for athletes of this sort.

As the preceding example indicates, not only can concepts be problematized for the purpose of incongruity, but so can stereotypes. Our stereotypes can be distorted either through the exaggeration of stereotypical features or through their diminution. Caricature often exaggerates—as in cartoons of Richard Nixon that turn his five o'clock shadow into a beard. Indeed, exaggeration is a standard strategy throughout burlesque, parody, and satire. The previous example of the ninety-pound sumo wrestler, on the other hand, is an example of incongruous diminution.

As all of our examples so far suggest, incongruity involves deviations from a background of norms—conceptual, logical, linguistic, stereotypical, and so forth. These can also include moral and prudential norms, as well as those of etiquette. Using a person as an armrest, as Charlie Chaplin sometimes does, or a tablecloth as a handkerchief, are both incongruous, since they represent deviations from normatively governed behaviour. Thus, the incongruous can also comprise the morally or prudentially inappropriate, as well as the just plain gauche.

Conflicting viewpoints supply another source of incongruity. In comic narratives—including novels, plays, and films—it frequently occurs that certain characters misperceive their circumstances; they may think they are speaking to a gardener, when in fact they are speaking to the master of the house. The audience is aware of this and tracks the spectacle under two alternative, but nevertheless conflicting, interpretations: the limited perspective of the mistaken character, and the omniscient perspective of the narrator. Inasmuch as these viewpoints effectively contradict each other, the comic theorist counts them as further instances of incongruous juxtaposition.

Some jokes are called meta-jokes because they call attention to the conventions of joke-telling by deviating from them. The joke—Why did the chicken cross the road?/ To get to the other side—is a meta-joke, because it violates while also revealing our conventional expectations about jokes, namely that they possess surprising and informative punchlines (Giora 1991). That chickens cross roads to get to the other side is hardly informative; being told that they do so is surprising only as the conclusion of a joke. Likewise, *non sequiturs* are incongruous, because they subvert our expectations that conversations and stories will be comprised of parts that are coherently linked. Moreover, emotional incoherence can also figure as incongruity, as when a character matches the wrong feeling or attitude with a situation, or simply vastly exaggerates an apposite one. Comic amusement, on the Incongruity Theory, presupposes that the audience has access to all the congruities—concepts, rules, expectations, etc.—that the humour in question disturbs or violates, and perhaps part of the pleasure of humour involves exercising our abilities to access this background information, generally very rapidly.

Prototypical incongruities, then, include deviations, disturbances, or problematizations of our concepts, rules, laws of logic and reasoning, stereotypes, norms of morality, of prudence, and of etiquette, contradictory points of view presented in tandem, and, in general, subversions of our commonplace expectations, including our expectations concerning standard emotional scenarios and schemas, and comic forms. Given this list of prototypical incongruities, the theorist can begin to chart a theory of humour.

Humour, for the Incongruity Theory, is a response-dependent property of a certain type of stimulus, viz. stimuli that support amusement in response to their display of incongruities. That is, perceived incongruity is the object of the mental state of comic amusement; one is in a state of comic amusement only if the object of that state is a perceived incongruity. This state may be in response to found humour—we may suddenly notice that people in everyday life are in some way funny (incongruous)—or in response to invented humour such as jokes, which are intended to bring incongruities to our attention, usually forcefully.

This suggestion is an advance on the Superiority Theory, since perceived incongruity, or absurdity, would appear to be a more likely object of comic amusement than pride of self. After all, feelings of superiority and accompanying squeals of cruel laughter can attend something that has nothing funny about it, like the bloody slaying of a sworn enemy; whereas a derailment of sense, if encountered in the right context, is a natural candidate for comic laughter, whether at our own expense, at the expense of others, or at no one's expense; for example, we may be comically amused when we find running shoes in the freezer, since that is an absurd place for them to be, even if we are not laughing at someone else, real or imagined.

However, incongruity is at best a necessary condition for comic amusement. As Alexander Bain pointed out, there are many instances when we encounter incongruities that are hardly amusing (Bain 1975). So even if incongruity is part of the story of comic amusement, it cannot be the whole story: incongruity simply does not correlate perfectly with comic amusement. Often confrontations with incongruity and deviations from expectations are threatening occasions, fraught with anxieties. If a total stranger makes 'funny faces' at a child, the child is apt to be frightened; but equally, if a familiar caregiver assumes the same 'funny (incongruous) face', the child is likely to giggle. What this indicates is that, for comic amusement to obtain, the percipient must feel unthreatened by it, must regard the incongruity not as a source of anxiety, but rather as an opportunity to relish its absurdity (Hartz and Hunt 1991).

Cases of found humour, then, require that the situations that comically amuse us not be ones in which we feel personal threat; we will not be amused if the gallumphing three-hundred pound man is headed on a lethal collision course towards us; nor will we be comically amused if we perceive the situation as in some other way dangerous, for example, as threatening harm to others (Carroll 1999); for that will produce anxiety.

Invented humour deploys various external and internal conventions in order to assure that its incongruities will not be anxiety-producing. The incongruity is generally introduced as non-threatening by conventional signals—such as the locution 'Did you hear the one about such and such?' and/or by changes in intonation—that herald a joking situation, which type of situation, in turn, is marked by custom as an arena for playfulness. Indeed, these conventional markers not only announce that the participants should not feel threatened themselves, but also call for a kind of comic distance—an absence of empathy and moral concern for the characters in jokes and satires—that relieves us of worries and anxieties about what is happening to the beings that inhabit the joke worlds and other fictional environments of invented humour. They can be burning in hell or being eaten by sharks or falling from tall buildings. Yet the convention of comic distance tells us to bracket any anxieties on their account. As Bergson observed, humour demands a momentary anaesthesis of the heart.

And, of course, this comic distance or comic anaesthesis is not merely a function of conventions external to the humour in question. Jokes, slapstick, and the like are also internally structured in a way that supports bracketing anxiety by refraining from dwelling upon or calling attention to the consequences—physical, moral, or psychological—of the harms that befall comic characters. That is, after we are told in a joke that some character has been blown apart, we are not reminded that he would be bleeding profusely, for that might elicit empathy. In fact, invented humour generally traffics in fictional worlds that are bereft of sustained acknowledgements of pain in such a way that our normal empathetic and moral responses remain in abeyance, thereby divesting the situation of the potential to provoke anxiety.

Comic amusement for the Incongruity Theory, then, requires as its object a perceived incongruity, of the sort inventoried above, which is neither threatening nor anxiety-producing but which can, on the contrary, be enjoyed. Invented humour is that which is intended to afford such a state. Of course, this is not yet an adequate definition, since the definition so far could be satisfied by mathematical puzzles, whose solutions, though sometimes occasioned by laughter, are not prima facie either humorous or objects of comic amusement.

The problem here is that our responses to incongruities are not partitioned just into being threatened as opposed to being comically amused. Often incongruities simply puzzle us and motivate us to solve the problem in question. But in contrast to humour and comic amusement, puzzles, puzzle-solving, and whatever pleasures they afford are committed to really resolving incongruities, to making genuine sense, and to dispelling apparent nonsense. In the state of comic amusement, on the other hand, we are not concerned to discover legitimate resolutions to incongruities, but at best, as in the case of jokes, to marvel at the appearance of sense, or the appearance of congruity, in what is otherwise recognized as palpable nonsense (Carroll 1991).

Moreover, that we are to suspend our inclinations to puzzle-solving is signalled by the external conventions and internal structures of invented humour. That is, the conventions that indicate the presence of invented humour announce that real resolutions of incongruity are not in the offing, while at the same time, the content of the humour defies veridical resolution. Whereas, in problem-solving, enjoyment with respect to the puzzle attaches primarily to finding the solution, with comic amusement the enjoyment focuses on the incongruity itself.

Summarizing one version of the Incongruity Theory, then, someone is comically amused if and only if (i) the object of her mental state is a perceived incongruity, (ii) which she regards as neither threatening or anxiety producing, and (iii) which she does not approach with a genuine, puzzle-solving attitude, but (iv) which, rather, she enjoys. Humour is the response-dependent property that affords comic amusement. Found humour differs from invented humour in that the latter is proffered with the intention, supported by external and internal features of the presentation, to afford comic amusement, whereas in the case of found humour the percipient herself not only discovers the incongruities, but brackets wariness and the disposition towards puzzle-solving on her own, thereby opening herself to the possibility of enjoying the stimulus.

However appealing the Incongruity Theory of Humour may appear, it does have at least one problem that cannot be overlooked: it is the very notion of incongruity. For we do not have a clear definition of it. In the past, when philosophers like Schopenhauer attempted to define humour rigorously—he thought it was essentially a category mistake—the definition has appeared to be too narrow to accommodate everything we would typically count as humorous. This then tempts one to try to elucidate incongruity, as above, by enumerating prototypical examples. But these examples run a very broad gamut of cases, ranging from conceptual and logical errors to inappropriate table manners to subverted expectations in general. Thus, one fears that the notion of incongruity may not be exclusive enough, especially if it unqualifiedly countenances something as pervasive as the subversion of expectations as an incongruity. And, furthermore, the definition as developed so far may also be too exclusive, since many Surrealist artworks that we would not regard as comically amusing would appear to satisfy it (see Martin 1983). Though promising, the Incongruity Theory of Humour remains a project in need of further research.

The third traditional theory of humour is called the *Release Theory*. Some have speculated that Aristotle may have propounded such a theory in the lost second book of his *Poetics*, which we are told analysed comedy. Since the first book explicated tragedy in terms of the notion of catharsis, it has been hypothesized that it is probable Aristotle would have similarly regarded comedy as a way of dissipating built-up feelings.

The Earl of Shaftesbury suggested that comedy released our otherwise constrained, natural free spirits (Morreall 1998), a view shared by Freud, who argued that jokes liberate the energy expended by rationality to repress both infantile nonsense and tendentious feelings (Freud 1976). Similarly, Herbert Spencer regarded laughter as a discharge of nervous energy that occurs when the mind, taken unawares, is led from the consciousness of something large (grave, or at least serious) to something small (silly or trivial) (Spencer 1911). Presumably, when this happens the nervous energy accumulated to grapple with serious matters is displaced or vented into laughter, and thereby flushed out of the system.

The theories of Spencer and Freud have the liability of presupposing hydraulic views of the mind that are highly dubious. They postulate the existence of mental energy that behaves like water—flowing in certain channels, circumventing blockages, and seeking outlets as the pressure builds. Their language, though couched in the scientific jargon of their day, seems at best metaphorical from the viewpoint of the present. Or, to put the objection in a less *ad hominem* form, their theories assume that there is something to be released, something that has built up or been repressed, some quantity of energy. But there seem to be scant scientific grounds for such assumptions.

It might seem that the Release Theory could be rephrased in less contentious language, perhaps using the notion of expectations. When asked a riddle or told a joke, it might be said, naturally enough, that expectation builds as we await the punchline. When it arrives, the pressure of those expectations is released or relieved, and laughter ensues. But it does not seem that the notions of release or relief provide a necessary, accurate, or desirable way of describing how expectations are engaged by jokes.

Jokes and riddles ideally inspire a desire for closure in listeners—a desire, for example, to hear the answer to the riddle or the punchline of the joke. When the answer or punchline arrives, that desire is satisfied, and such satisfaction contributes to the enjoyment that ensues, enjoyment that is often marked by laughter. But there is no cause to speak of release here; talk of expectations or desires and their fulfilment suffices.

Perhaps it will be proposed that, once our desires are fulfilled, we are in effect released from them. But since they are our desires, this seems a misleadingly metaphorical way of speaking. It says no more than that we no longer have the desire in question. After all, we possess the desire; the desire does not possess us. Just as it makes more sense to say—from a non-theological point of view—that when we die we are no longer alive, rather than that we have been released from life, so it is better to say we no longer have the expectations, rather than that we have been released from them, when those expectations have been satisfied.

Jokes belong to the category of what might be called temporal humour; they promise closure. But not all humour is like this. Some humour involves no build-up of expectations. So, even if we accepted the Release Theory as an account of the play of expectation in temporal forms of humour, like jokes, it could not be extended to forms of humour that do not build up expectations over time. When the ninety-pound sumo wrestler appears on stage, or when we find the running shoes in the freezer, we are comically amused. But it is wrong to say that our expectations have had anything done to them, since in these cases we had no antecedent expectations. Here, of course, it is open to the proponent of the Release Theory to attempt to postulate that there is always some subconscious processing, however brief, going on, and that this involves expectations. But until one is told more about the way in which these alleged processes work, this gambit sounds exceedingly *ad hoc.*

Alternatively, it may be said that we do have the requisite expectations without hypothesizing subconscious processing; i.e., we have standing expectations about what is normal, and it is these expectations that have been subverted. Thus, we are released from our standing or normal expectations. And, it might be added, this is also what happens when we are confronted with the nonsensical endings of jokes, as well as with confrontations with ninety-pound sumo wrestlers. But again, the idea that we are possessed by and then released from our normal conceptual schemes seems strained here, unless we suppose that those expectations are invested with powers to constrain or to repress, or that they require some supplemental quotient of mental pressure in order to continue functioning. However, that then sends us back to an earlier problem—the tendency of Release Theories to proliferate unwarranted mental processes. Nor does it seem plausible to imagine that having our normal expectations about the world is like being shackled, since the 'shackles' are us.

Many contemporary theories of humour are variations on the Superiority Theory, the Release Theory, and, more frequently, the Incongruity Theory. One interesting contemporary theory of humour that breaks with precedent has been offered by Jerrold Levinson (1998). According to Levinson, something is humorous just in case it has the disposition to elicit, through the mere cognition of it, and not for ulterior reasons, a certain kind of pleasurable reaction in appropriate subjects (that is, informationally, attitudinally, and emotionally prepared subjects), where this pleasurable reaction (amusement, mirth) is identified by its own disposition to induce, at moderate or higher degrees, a further phenomenon, namely, laughter. Thus, for Levinson, humour cannot be detached from all felt inclination, however faint, towards the convulsive bodily expression of laughter.

This theory can be called the Dispositional Theory of Humour. Like the Incongruity Theory, it acknowledges the importance for humour of a cognitive-response element. But Levinson does not define that response as narrowly as the perception of incongruity. Rather, he leaves uncharacterized the nature of the relevant cognitions and their intentional objects, requiring only that said cognitions have some intentional object at which they are directed and that they elicit pleasure for its own sake from suitable percipients.

Of course, this much of Levinson's analysis could be satisfied by mathematical theorems of sufficient cleverness. In order to forestall counter-examples like this, Levinson's final requirement is that the pleasure elicited by the cognition of the humorous be identified by its own disposition to induce laughter; for, though mathematical ingenuity may provoke laughter for some, it has no reliable disposition to do so, even among mathematicians who take pleasure in it.

Though Levinson's theory locates humour in a certain kind of pleasure, he does not give us much by way of a characterization of the nature of that pleasure. By suggesting that it is mirth or amusement, the definition appears to flirt with the kind of circularity one finds in definitions of the 'dormative power' variety. In order for the theory to be of any use in identifying humour, Levinson needs to link the unspecified feelings of pleasure that he has in mind to their disposition to elicit laughter. Thus, given Levinson's account, it is the disposition to elicit laughter, laughter grounded in pleasureable cognitions, upon which we must rely in order to hive off humour from puzzle-solving.

This disposition towards laughter, moreover, need not be intense. It may be only a faint inclination, and, of course, it need not actually find expression in overt laughter. It can be nothing more than a small impulse in that direction. This is a dispositional theory, since it does not, like the Incongruity Theory, specify anything about the structure of the intentional object of comic amusement, but only demands that whatever pleasures the cognitions give rise to have the further disposition, however slight, to elicit laughter.

It is not evident how strictly Levinson intends us to understand the notion of a disposition towards laughter. Some invented humour is very low key. It invites an extremely mild, but none the less real, sense of pleasure that, at best, manifests itself in a brief, almost undetectable, smile or maybe nothing more than a twinkle of the eye. Are we to regard this as a felt, albeit faint, inclination towards laughter? Ordinarily, I think we would not, though perhaps Levinson should be allowed either to stipulate that any slight feelings of levity that can be physically manifested count as inclining us towards laughter, or else to rewrite his theory in terms of any slight inclinations to laughter or smiles of any sort, including very discreet and very transitory ones.

Nevertheless, there is a problem with both of these alternatives. Both, like Levinson's original proposal, connect humour necessarily to certain kinds of bodies—paradigmatically human bodies. Thus, communities of telepathetically communicating brains in vats, disembodied gods, and aliens without the biological accoutrements to support laughter or even smiling could not be said by us to have humour as a feature of their societies. But I am not convinced that our ordinary concept of humour is so restrictive. We would not charge a science fiction writer with conceptual incoherency if she imagined an alien society of the sort just mentioned and also described it as possessing humour.

Standardly, we grant that there are pleasures, such as certain aesthetic and/or intellectual pleasures, that do not require any distinctive bodily sensations. Suppose a community of disembodied gods enjoyed incongruities but neither laughed nor felt sensations of levity, because they lacked the physical equipment. Would we say there was no humour there, even though they create, exchange, and enjoy things that look like jokes, even if we don't get them? Remember that these jokes give them pleasure—pleasure akin to certain aesthetic or intellectual pleasure—though *sans* laughter or the inclination thereto.

Or imagine a community of humans who, as a result of grave cervical cord injuries, lack the ability to move air owing to the inhibition of the muscles in their diaphragm, thorax, chest, and belly. These people cannot laugh, since they do not possess the necessary motor control to respirate, or even to feel any of the pressures that dispose 'normals' towards laughter. They lack even residual feelings of levity. But surely they, like the gods, could create, exchange, and enjoy in-jokes that we outsiders might not get, but that we can still recognize as jokes, either on formal grounds or because the injured jokesters tell us. Would we say that this society lacked humour?

My intuition is to answer 'no' in the cases of such disembodied gods, biologically alien aliens, and injured humans, because I do not think that our concept of humour necessarily requires an inclination towards laughter, though admittedly laughter is a regularly recurring concomitant of humour among standard-issue human beings. Yet if the laughter stipulation is dropped from Levinson's definition, he will, unlike certain versions of the Incongruity Theory, have no way to exclude puzzle solutions from the ambit of humour, since he has left the structure of the intentional object of humour wide open. Nor can he say that the type of pleasure afforded by puzzles is necessarily not humorous without appearing to beg the question.

Levinson does not specify the nature of the cognitions requisite for humour because he feels that specification—of the sort one finds in the Incongruity Theory—may be too exclusive. He does not, though, offer any compelling counter-examples to the Incongruity Theory. The one brief case that he alludes to is that of someone slipping on a banana peel; but, in acknowledging that it may be humorous in that it involves a deflation of expectations, or strangeness or surprise, Levinson makes the case sound more like an exemplification of a generous notion of incongruity rather than a counter-instance. Bergson, of course, would analyse such an example as a matter of mechanical absentmindedness—a deviation from the norm of properly functioning sentience—and, therefore, as an incongruity. Consequently, it is not clear that Levinson has a persuasive reason to avoid specification of the relevant cognitions in terms of perceived incongruity, or else something like it—perhaps some refined successor notion.

One reason to suspect Levinson's liberalism about the scope of the cognitions he allows with respect to humour is the following counter-example. Certain avant-garde films, like those of Godard, contain allusions to other works of art—not only other films, but paintings, etc. When suitably prepared viewers—the cognoscenti, if you will—detect those allusions, they laugh in order to mark their pleasure in recognizing the reference. This is quite customary, as can be confirmed by frequenting any avant-garde film venue. But the allusions need not be funny or humorous. They obviously engage cognition, directed at the allusion, which gives rise to pleasure, which in turn disposes cinephiles towards laughter— a disposition that is often manifested. Admittedly, some of these allusions may be humorous in the ordinary sense, but they need not be. And where the allusion is not itself funny in context, it seems wrong to call it humorous, though Levinson will have to.

Moreover, the problem here is not restricted to just this single counter-example; recent research on laughter maintains that most laughing does not occur after jokes or funny remarks, but as a kind of conversational lubricant in everyday discourse (see Provine 2000). This constitutes a formidable problem for Levinson's theory, since as a matter of fact laughter often follows pleasures engendered by cognitions that are not comic in nature (e.g. cognitions about a couple's plans to become engaged). But surely not every sort of phatic laughter issuing from ordinary cognitions signals humour.

Traditional theories of humour and the more recent Dispositional Theory all have their share of difficulties. However, the Incongruity Theory still seems the most promising, because it offers the most informative approach to locating the structure of the intentional object of comic amusement. This allows us to employ it productively in comic analysis—enabling us to pinpoint and to dissect the designs that give rise to amusement in jokes, plays, satires, sit-coms, etc. Of course, current versions of the Incongruity Theory are unsatisfactory, because the notion of incongruity is simply too elastic. Nevertheless, perhaps the way to proceed, at this point in the debate, is to embrace the notion of incongruity as a heuristic which, though vague, is not vacuous, and apply it to a wide number of cases and counter-examples in the hope of isolating, as precisely as possible, the pertinent recurring structures of humour. With that in hand, maybe the concept of incongruity can be more rigorously refined or a successor concept identified.

2. Humour, Comedy, Art

The term 'comedy' covers a multitude of forms—burlesques, farces, satires, sit-coms, parodies, caricatures, travesties, stand-up monologues, cartoons, slapstick, screwball comedies, clowning, sight gags, jokes, and much more. In ordinary language, it would appear that 'comedy' is the usual label for invented (rather than found) humour that is expressly designed to be presented formally in some institutional setting (such as a theatre, a club, a circus, a motion picture, a television or radio programme, a music hall). Thus, we call a monologue an instance of comedy when it is presented as an act at a comedy club, but we are less disposed to categorize the same monologue as comedy when it is retold by a co-worker on a coffee break. Broadly speaking, in everyday usage, the concept of comedy seems to apply most naturally to the inventions of professionals who intend to elicit comic amusement as the predominant response—or, at least, as a significant part of the response—of spectators playing the relevant institutional role of audience members. It is on such grounds that sit-coms, caricatures, slapstick comedies, and even certain game shows are generally catalogued under the rubric of comedy, and that the agents who create them are called 'comics' or 'comedians'.

However, there is also a narrower, quasi-technical, notion of comedy. In this usage, 'comedy' is the name of a genre of dramatic narration, one that stands in

contrast with tragedy. Whereas tragedies typically end badly for their leading characters, comedies end well. *Hamlet* concludes with bodies everywhere; *A Midsummer's
Night Dream* with marriages all around. On this view, then, the difference between
comedy and tragedy is a matter of plot structure.

Of course, many of the recurring plot structures of what are called comedies can
be analysed in terms of humour. A frequent plotting device of comedy involves
conflicting points of view in which the way the character understands the situation
parts company incongruously (but in a way that does not provoke anxiety) with the
way in which the audience perceives the situation; for example, the town officials
think that Khlestakov is the government inspector, but we know better, while
Titania thinks Bottom an exemplar, but we see him for the ass he is.

Similarly, frequently comic plots incongrously pair the efforts of characters with
their outcomes: a fool, if morally upright, is apt to succeed—for example, to win
his beloved—in a comedy, whereas his smarter, stronger, 'more normal' adversary
is almost always thwarted, despite the extreme improbability of such events in
real life.

Nevertheless, though comedies often have plot devices that are reducible to
structures of comic amusement, not all of the narrative features that are associated
with comedy are reducible to humour. For instance, a happy ending is often
advanced as the hallmark of comedy, but a happy ending need not be either humorous or incongruous, given the rest of the pertinent plot. For example, the comic protagonist need not be a fool and his success need not be wildly improbable. Thus,
with respect to plot structure, a comedy, in the narrow sense, does not, in itself, have
to be humorous. Moreover, certain narratives, like Westerns, may have happy endings, but have virtually no humour in them, while Chaplin's *The Circus*, a comedy
in the broad sense, ends sadly.

Consequently, the narrower conception of comedy may produce results quite at
odds with contemporary usage. This is understandable, since the narrower concept
was designed to sort narratives into only two kinds—comedies and tragedies.
However, given the proliferation of narrative genres since the time of the Greeks,
perhaps the kindest thing that can be said about the narrower concept of comedy
is that it is obsolete; it is no longer fine-grained enough to accommodate the data,
if it ever was.

As some of the preceding examples indicate, some comedies are art. Certainly,
if anything is art, *A Midsummer's Night Dream* is. But it is not obvious that everything that falls into the category of humour has the status of art. For example, are
all jokes art?

Ted Cohen (1999) has suggested important analogies between jokes and artworks.
Like artworks, jokes mandate audiences to complete them—to fill in the presuppositions, emotions, and attitude the joke requires for uptake. Moreover, in mobilizing
this material, and by celebrating with laughter their mutual understanding of a joke,
listeners and joke tellers come to form an intimate community of appreciation very

like the communities of taste that arise in response to artworks. These common features, then, suggest that jokes are artworks, albeit miniature ones.

However, there are also noteworthy disanalogies between artworks and jokes. Typically, artworks are designed in such a way that they are supposed to invite sustained contemplation. In the ideal case, one returns to the artworks again and again, each time taking away a new or enriched insight. Jokes, on the other hand, are not usually like this. They are generally one-shot affairs. One listens to jokes, gets them, and that's that. One may store them in memory in order to repeat them on another occasion. But one does not normally contemplate them, seized by their structural complexity and ingenuity, or intrigued by their perspective on the human condition. Some jokes may be capable of affording such responses, but the vast majority are not. Therefore, it appears reasonable to suppose that not all comedy or invented humour falls into the category of art; it would seem that jokes do not.

3. Humour and Morality

The earlier review of theories of humour reveals that humour comes in contact with ethics in many ways, a number of which are apt to trouble the moralist. Humour often involves ridicule and malice, feelings of superiority, scorn towards infirmity, the transgression of ethical norms, and intentional offensiveness; it may even presuppose the anaesthesis of the heart—the bracketing of empathy and moral concern—at least for the creatures of comic fictional worlds. It presents for delight spectacles of greed, venality, promiscuity, cruelty, gluttony, sloth—in short, every manner of vice. All this makes the moralist nervous.

The ethics of humour has, as a result, been a recurring theme in the philosophy of comedy. In recent years, this discussion has become increasingly prominent, perhaps as an academic reflection of the tides of political correctness in the larger culture. Philosophers have been especially concerned to locate exactly what is ethically wrong about humour—that is, at least when it is morally remiss. Two sophisticated attempts in this direction have commanded particular attention: Ronald de Sousa's hypothesis that our laughter at an evil joke reveals in us an evil character, and Berys Gaut's ethicism.

Many jokes are sexist, racist, classist, homophobic, anti-semitic, and the like. Such jokes contain an element of malice, directed at women, African Americans, workers, gays, Jews, and so on. Ronald de Sousa (1987) calls this element phthonic, and distinguishes it from wit, presumably the simple cognitive play of things like incongruities. All jokes are conditional; they require listeners to fill in their background assumptions, to recognize the norms that are under fire, and to access the emotions and attitudes the joke requires in order to be intelligible (Cohen 1999). When a joke pressupposes malicious and immoral attitudes in order to succeed and we laugh, de Sousa contends that this shows that we are morally flawed, in so far as we share the phthonic attitude showcased in the joke.

For example, de Sousa invites us to contemplate this joke: 'M (a well-known celebrity, widely rumoured to be sexually hyperactive) visits a hockey team. When she emerges, she complains she has been gang-raped. Wishful thinking.' Putatively, this joke relies on a series of sexist presuppositions, including: (*a*) that rape is merely a variant form of allowable sexual intercourse; (*b*) that many women's sexual desires are indiscriminate; (*c*) that there is something objectionable about a woman who has a lot of sex. De Sousa maintains that in order to get this joke one must access these sexist attitudes towards women, and that, if one laughs, this shows that one literally shares these attitudes—that one is a sexist.

Clearly, sexists can use jokes like this in order to cement their fellowship with other sexists. But the question is whether *anyone* who laughs at this joke is a sexist, a member of the sexist fellowship. De Sousa says 'yes', because he alleges that the attitudes required for uptake of this joke cannot be assumed hypothetically: they must be attitudes that compliant listeners actually share with the joke.

One problem with de Sousa's argument is that he supposes that there is only one interpretation of this joke, i.e. the sexist one that presupposes that rape is merely a variant form of sexual intercourse, with no moral stigma attached. When I first heard this joke, however, I did not interpret it that way. I thought that it was about hypocrisy. M was a supposedly well-known Donna Juanita. Thus, I thought that the joke was suggesting that she *had* had sex with the hockey team, but then tried to cover it up by saying she had been gang-raped—to which the sceptical narrator of the joke replies, effectively, 'dream on if you think we'll buy that one'. The humour, I supposed, was akin to that of unmasking a Tartuffe. That explained to me why the central character is marked as someone noteworthy for her sexual appetite. Moreover, de Sousa's interpretation does not seem completely coherent. If M had been raped and the joke assumes that rape is just a variant of sexual intercourse, what is it that she still wishes for? What is the significance of the punchline 'Wishful thinking"?

It does not make much sense to quibble over the correct interpretation of this joke. But there is a theoretical point here. Many jokes support a variety of interpretations, several of which may promote laughter. This is not to say that jokes are completely open texts. The interpretations generally fall within a circumscribed range. However, a joke may possess more than one reasonable interpretation, each of which may lead to laughter. In de Sousa's example, the target of ridicule may be female sexuality, as he says, or it may be hypocrisy, as I thought. But if a non-sexist interpretation of the joke promotes comic laughter, then de Sousa cannot infer, as he does, that anyone who laughs at the joke reveals a morally flawed, sexist character. De Sousa neglects the possibility that some jokes that appear on his interpretation to be sexist may be risible to others under non-sexist interpretations. Consequently, the inference pattern he proposes is inadequate.

But let us look at an unequivocally sexist joke of the sort de Sousa wants—an old *Playboy* definition: rape is an assault with a friendly weapon. Does laughter at this reveal a sexist character? Many would deny it, arguing that what they laugh at is the incongruous word wit, the oxymoronic juxtaposition of opposites (assault and deadly weaponry yoked together with friendship). True, they must in some sense recognize the sexist attitude that underwrites this nonsense. But the question is whether they have to affirm it. They might be laughing at the implied speaker of this joke—after all, they regard it as silly and nonsensical, a *faux* definition.

But even if this is too baroque an interpretation of what is going on here, still it seems plausible for the amused listener to say: I was only laughing at the word wit and I was entertaining the notion that rape is not really grievous bodily assault simply for the sake of accessing the wit. My laughter no more signals my endorsement of the fallacious view in question than my laughter at a crazy definition of death would show that I really feel that death is not a morally serious event.

De Sousa denies this possibility, maintaining that the attitudes revealed in phthonic humour cannot be assumed merely hypothetically. De Sousa does not really offer an argument to this conclusion. And, on the face of it, it appears counterintuitive. In jokes, we entertain or imagine all sorts of possibilities that we do not believe: that there are genies who grant wishes, that there is an afterlife, that peanuts can talk, that death can be outsmarted. Why then is it not possible for us provisionally to imagine, incongruously, that rape is just sexual intercourse? Indeed, it may be the very incongruity of this thought that provokes amusement, though to be amused in this way presupposes that we disbelieve it (i.e. find it incongruous) rather than affirm it. Such amusement may involve the anaesthesis of the heart so common in humour, but, by the same token, it need not belie one's true attitudes any more than entertaining a disparaging view of alleged Irish drinking habits shows a malicious attitude to real Irishmen.

De Sousa's answer, I conjecture, is that the requisite attitudes with respect to phthonic humour are not merely of the order of beliefs, but are emotionally charged, and for that reason cannot be merely entertained, but must be deeply sedimented in our being. However, this seems unsubstantiated. Blonde jokes appear to presuppose certain negative attitudes towards blonde women and their intelligence. Yet I can laugh at them while being happily married to a blonde whose intelligence I admire. My wife laughs at them too; often she tells them to me. De Sousa seems insensitive to the fact that we are dealing with a fictional genre here, in which the Blonde is an imaginary being and a fictional convention. Certainly, it is possible for us to entertain emotions towards fictional beings that we would not mobilize for their comparable real-world counterparts. Given the fictional context, I cheer on the imaginary ageing gunslinger; but if I met up with him on the street, I would probably slink away and notify the police. The emotions I entertain in response to fictions need not be taken as an index of my authentic attitudes. I take the blondes in Blonde jokes to be fictional conventions, and I take pleasure in the clever manipulation of the convention.

That de Sousa neglects the role that imagination and fiction play in jokes compromises his hypothesis about phthonic humour. Though such humour may serve as a vehicle for malicious attitudes—and be morally contemptible for that reason—such cases do not support the generalization that laughter in response to predominantly phthonic humour always reveals an evil attitude, since the laughter may be at whatever wit resides in the joke, and the presuppositions and emotions required to access that wit may merely be imaginatively entertained and directed at fictional beings.

Jokes, even ostensibly phthonic jokes, are often far more complicated than de Sousa acknowledges. There is the story about a genie who comes upon an African-American, a Jew, and a redneck. He grants each a wish. The African-American wishes that his people be returned to Africa; the Jew that his people be returned to Israel. Once the redneck realizes that the blacks and the Jews have all left America, all he wishes for is a martini.

Told by a racist to racists, the joke may celebrate communal hatred; told by a liberal to another liberal, there is still a laugh, though this time at the expense of the redneck and his very limited, monomaniacal, and warped economy of desires. The context of a joke utterance and the interpretations and purposes that listeners bring to it are crucial to assessing the ethical status of a joke transaction. De Sousa is too quick to assume that apparently phthonic jokes always have an invariant meaning and invariably elicit authentically malicious responses. But this need not be so.

Surely de Sousa is correct in claiming that, when a joke serves to convoke a community of genuine malice against the innocent, it is evil. But he is simply wrong in hypothesizing that every joke transaction with strong phthonic elements serves that purpose. Moron jokes are not usually told to commemorate or reinforce hatred for the retarded; in fact, I have never heard one told for this purpose. Rather, their conventions and stereotypes, including their stereotypical attitudes, are entertained, rather than embraced, in order to motivate incongruities.

Much humour is transgressive. But the transgressiveness of *The Simpsons*, *South Park*, *The Man Show*, and Bernie Mac's aggressive rant against children in *The Original Kings of Comedy* (2000) has a double edge. Not only are 'forbidden' ideas and emotions aired, thereby engendering amusement through the exhibition of incongruous improprieties, but, at the same time, the attitudes underlying those transgressions may be, ironically enough, satirized. Al Bundy's misogynistic badinage in *Married With Children* provokes laughter by flouting moral rules, but also pokes fun at the character himself whose attitudes, like Homer Simpson's, are revealed to be nearly Neanderthal. Responding to such phthonic humour, then, need not signal endorsement of the attitudes displayed in the humour, but may indicate our feelings of superiority to them. And, even if in some cases we are laughing because we recognize something of Homer Simpson or Al Bundy in ourselves, our laughter may not be affirmative, since we are, in effect, knowingly laughing reflexively at ourselves as well, and in that sense hardly endorsing the attitudes in question. Similarly, the outrageous views of Canadians voiced by the citizens of *South Park* are really satiric reflections on the chauvinism of US citizens. Because phthonic humour can come replete with so many complex layers of meaning (including ironic meanings), de Sousa's confident conclusions about implications of responses to phthonic humour appear too facile.

Ethicism, a position developed by Berys Gaut, is another attempt to explore the relevance of immorality to humour, specifically jokes (Gaut 1998). Most would concur that there are immoral jokes—jokes that should not be told and should not be encouraged. However, there is an extreme form of moralism that goes so far as to claim that such jokes are not even humorous—that they are not funny at all. That is, such jokes are not only evil: they are not even amusing. Gaut's ethicism is best understood in contrast to this sort of extreme moralism.

For Gaut, immorality does not preclude the humorousness of a joke utterance. Nevertheless, immorality does always count against its humorousness. A joke utterance that contains immoral elements may also contain elements of formal wit and cleverness, and the latter may outweigh the immoral elements in an all-things-considered assessment of its humour. But even if they are outweighed, the immoral elements are always bad-making features of a joke utterance *qua* joke (or *qua* humour), and not merely in terms of its moral status. If a joke utterance with immoral elements is humorous overall, according to Gaut, that is only because it contains other relevant features that counterbalance its moral blemishes. And, of course, in some situations the immoral elements may overwhelm whatever traces of cleverness obtain; in such circumstances the joke utterance is not, all things considered, funny.

Gaut defends ethicism by means of what can be called the *Merited Response Argument*. When we judge a joke utterance to be humorous, we do not do so on the grounds that it in fact causes laughter in a certain number of people. That is, humorousness is not merely a statistical concept. Everyone else in the room might laugh at it, but we may still judge the joke utterance unfunny. Our judgement here is a normative one: does the joke utterance merit a positive response; is our laughter appropriate; does the joke utterance deserve laughter?

Comic amusement is a complex response to many aspects of the joke utterance, not simply to its cleverness, but also to the affect the joke summons up. And these elements can come apart. The joke utterance may merit a positive response because of its word play, but the affect it calls forth may be inappropriate—for instance because it is repulsively immoral. If the negative aspects of the affective dimension are more commanding than the cleverness, then, all things considered, our positive response to the joke is unmerited (the joke utterance is not, overall, funny). If on the other hand, the cleverness is more compelling, the joke merits being called humorous, all things considered—i.e. funny—though nevertheless still flawed or blemished *qua* joke.

Ethicism, unlike extreme moralism, can grant that some joke utterances with immoral elements can be funny, thereby appealing to our ordinary intuitions about the matter. But, in regarding said elements as inappropriate features, ethicism can also accommodate the possibility that there are jokes so thoroughly and repellingly evil that they are no longer truly funny.

The persuasiveness of ethicism depends on the Merited Response Argument. Opponents of it claim that the argument begs the question (Jacobson 1997). For moral appropriateness seems built into the criteria of appropriateness of Gaut's concept of the humorous. But this is what Gaut should be demonstrating as his conclusion: he cannot just presume it from the outset. Whether a joke candidate merits being called humorous, it can be argued, depends upon whether, with reference to the prototypical case, it engenders enjoyment through its manifestation of incongruities, which, of course, can include moral incongruities. To show that moral transgressions count against classifying a joke utterance as humorous requires an argument to that result. Gaut has not supplied such an argument; he has merely assumed the conclusion as a premiss—conflating the prima facie criteria for appropriateness in humour with those of appropriateness *tout court*, which, of course, include moral rectitude.

If Gaut wants to convince those who are sceptical that, in order to be humorous, a joke utterance cannot be saliently immoral, he needs to share common premisses with the sceptic. The sceptic will deny that to be a merited response *qua* humour to a joke utterance requires that the joke itself be morally meritorious (or, at least, not morally reprehensible). Humour is amoral, the sceptic will say. Thus, the sceptic will reject that a merited response to humour must take into account the moral merit or demerit of the work. To confuse the meritedness of the humorous response with moral merit is, according to the sceptic, an equivocation.

Ethicism has yet to respond to the sceptic. Consequently, the jury is still out on the question of whether immorality is *always* a bad-making feature with respect to humour. However, ethicism has perhaps suggested enough to make it plausible to suppose that sometimes immorality can compromise the humorousness of a joke. For a joke-utterance may be so blatantly and appallingly immoral that virtually no audience will be prepared attitudinally to fill it in or to engage with it in the way required to enjoy its incongruities.

This will not always be the case with every joke utterance that contains immoral elements, since typically those elements may not be flagrantly posed and/or obviously evil to a degree that would deter uptake on the part of the standard listener. But in those cases where the immorality of the joke utterance is so disturbing to the relevant listeners that access to the enjoyment of incongruity is altogether blocked—where the joke utterance itself is, for example, a predictable source of anxiety—it seems reasonable to say that immorality can contribute to the alienation of humour. Sometimes, owing to excessive moral outrageousness, the anaesthesis of the heart will be too difficult for intended listeners to sustain. And they will not be amused.

See also: Metaphor; Fiction; Tragedy; Aesthetic Experience; Art and Morality.

BIBLIOGRAPHY

Aristotle (1941). *Nicomachean Ethics, Basic Works of Aristotle*, ed. R. McKeon. New York: Random House.

—— (1993). *Poetics*, trans. Malcolm Heath. Harmondsworth: Penguin.

Bain, A. (1975). *The Emotions and the Will*, 3rd edn. London: Longmans & Green.

Bergson, H. (1965). *Laughter*, ed. W. Sypher. Garden City, NJ: Doubleday.

Carroll, N. (1991). 'On Jokes'. *Midwest Studies in Philosophy* 16: 250–301.

—— (1996). 'Notes on the Sight Gag'. *Theorizing the Moving Image*. New York: Cambridge University Press, pp. 146–57.

—— (1997). 'Words, Images, and Laughter'. *Persistence of Vision* 14: 42–52.

—— (1999). 'Horror and Humor'. *Journal of Aesthetics and Art Criticism* 57: 145–60.

Clark, M. (1970). 'Humour and Incongruity'. *Philosophy* 45: 20–32.

—— (1987). 'Humour, Laughter and the Structure of Thought'. *British Journal of Aesthetics* 77: 238–46.

Cohen, T. (1999). *Jokes*. Chicago: University of Chicago Press.

Freud, S. (1963). 'Humor', *Character and Culture*, ed. P. Rieff. New York: Collier Books, pp. 263–9.

—— (1976). *Jokes and their Relation to the Unconscious*, trans. and ed. J. Strachey. Harmondsworth: Penguin Books.

Gaut, B. (1998). 'Just Joking: The Ethics and Aesthetics of Humor'. *Philosophy and Literature* 22: 51–68.

Giora, R. (1991). 'On Cognitive Aspects of the Joke'. *Journal of Pragmatics* 16: 465–85.

Hartz, G. and Hunt, R. (1991). 'Humor: The Beauty and the Beast'. *American Philosophical Quarterly* 25: 299–309.

Hutcheson, F. (1973). 'Reflections on Laughter', in P. Kivy (ed.), *An Inquiry Concerning Beauty, Order, Harmony, Design*. The Hague: Martinus Nijhoff.

Jacobson, D. (1997). 'In Praise of Immoral Art'. *Philosophical Topics* 25: 155–99.

Kant, I. (1951). *Critique of Judgment*, trans. J. H. Bernard. New York: Hafner.

Kierkegaard, S. (1941). *Concluding Unscientific Postscript*, trans. D. F. Senson. Princeton: Princeton University Press.

Koestler, A. (1964). *The Act of Creation*. New York: Macmillan.

LaFollete, H. and Sharks, N. (1993). 'Belief and the Basis of Humour'. *American Philosophical Quarterly* 30: 329–39.

Levinson, J. (1998). 'Humour'. *Routledge Encyclopedia of Philosophy*, ed. E. Craig. London: Routledge, pp. 562–7.

Martin, M. W. (1983). 'Humour and the Aesthetic Enjoyment of Incongruity'. *British Journal of Aesthetics* 23: 74–84.

Monro, D. H. (1951). *The Argument of Laughter*. Melbourne: Melbourne University Press.

Morreall, J. (1983). *Taking Laughter Seriously*. Albany, NY: State University of New York Press.

——(ed.) (1987). *The Philosophy of Laughter and Humor*. Albany, NY: State University of New York Press.

——(1989). 'Enjoying incongruity'. *Humor* 2: 1–18.

——(1998). 'Comedy'. *Encyclopedia of Aesthetics*, ed. M. Kelly. Oxford: Oxford University Press, pp. 401–5.

Oring, E. (1992). *Jokes and their Relations*. Lexington, Ky: University Press of Kentucky.

Palmer, J. (1994). *Taking Humour Seriously*. London: Routledge.

Pfeiffer, K. (1994). 'Laughter and Pleasure'. *Humor* 7: 157–72.

Phipps, W. (1979). 'Ancient Attitudes toward Laughter'. *Journal of the West Virginia Philosophical Society* 16: 15–16.

Plato (1961). *Philebus*, The Collected Dialogues of Plato, ed. E. Hamilton and H. Cairns. Princeton: Princeton University Press.

——(1993). *Republic*, trans. R. Waterfield. New York: Oxford University Press.

Provine, R. (2000). *Laughter: A Scientific Investigation*. New York: Viking.

Roberts, R. (1988). 'Is Amusement an Emotion?' *American Philosophical Quarterly* 25: 269–73.

Schopenhauer, A. (1966). *The World as Will and Representation*, vol. 1, trans. E. F. J. Payne. New York: Dover.

Scruton, R. (1982). 'Laughter'. *Proceedings of the Aristotelian Society*, supplementary vol., 56: 197–212.

Sousa, R. de (1987). *The Rationality of Emotion*. Cambridge, Mass.: MIT Press.

Spencer, H. (1911). 'The Physiology of Laughter'. *Essays on Education, etc*. London: Dent.

CHAPTER 20

METAPHOR

TED COHEN

AFTER a somewhat desultory history in philosophy for more than two thousand years, the topic of metaphor began to receive intense attention in the latter part of the twentieth century. Occasional remarks about metaphor are to be found in Aristotle, Hobbes, Locke, and Nietzsche, among others, but the topic seems to have begun to receive continuous attention, especially from analytical philosophers, some time after 1950. The significance of metaphor in the philosophy of language and in the philosophy of art has now been acknowledged, and some have thought that the topic has importance for philosophy in general. Jacques Derrida (1974) has claimed that virtually all statements are, in some sense, metaphorical; and George Lakoff and Mark Johnson (1980) have argued that the structure of thought itself is deeply metaphorical. These bold assertions have not had very much influence on analytical philosophers, but they have been widely embraced by a number of people in other fields. An early central text, for analytical philosophers and for others, was Max Black's 'Metaphor', although that essay itself first came to be widely considered only about a dozen years after its publication when it received a favourable mention by Nelson Goodman (1968). (Goodman's thesis is elaborated and defended in Scheffler 1979.)

Metaphor is one of a variety of uses of language in which what is communicated is not what the words mean literally. It is, therefore, so to speak, a way of speaking of something by talking about something else. Thus, one has said (or written) X and thereby communicated Y. This characteristic of 'indirectness' is not alone sufficient to distinguish metaphors from other non-standard uses of language, but there is also a question as to whether metaphors in general are sufficiently similar to one another to permit a single, unified description of them.

On one hand, metaphor has been a feature of poetry for centuries, conspicuous in the work of Homer and Shakespeare and countless other poets. But on the other hand, metaphor is pervasive in ordinary language, both in speech and in writing. It is not obvious that a single account of metaphor could be adequate to both poetic and more prosaic uses of figurative language.

Here are two examples from well-known poetry, followed by a few other metaphorical lines.

Do not go gentle into that good night.

Bare ruined choirs, where late the sweet birds sang.

He is a tabula rasa no one has written on.

Miles Davis is the Picasso of jazz.

Wagner is the Puccini of music.

In the first two cases we have a metaphorical line already deeply embedded in a context. Not only is everything appropriate to the appreciation of poetry relevant to the understanding of these lines, but the metaphor itself is explicitly elaborated and amplified by the rest of the poem. Consider the lines again, this time within their homes:

> Do not go gentle into that good night,
> Old age should burn and rave at close of day;
> Rage, rage against the dying of the light.
>
> Though wise men at their end know dark is right,
> Because their words had forked no lightning they
> Do not go gentle into that good night.
>
> Good men, the last wave by, crying how bright
> Their frail deeds might have danced in a green bay,
> Rage, rage against the dying of the light.
>
> Wild men who caught and sang the sun in flight,
> And learn, too late, they grieved it on its way,
> Do not go gentle into that good night.
>
> Grave men, near death, who see with blinding sight
> Blind eyes could blaze like meteors and be gay,
> Rage, rage against the dying of the light.
>
> And you, my father, there on the sad height,
> Curse, bless, me now with your fierce tears, I pray.
> Do not go gentle into that good night.
> Rage, rage against the dying of the light.
>
> (Dylan Thomas, 'Do Not Go
> Gentle Into That Good Night')

> That time of year thou mayst in me behold
> When yellow leaves, or none, or few, do hang
> Upon those boughs which shake against the cold,

Bare ruined choirs, where late the sweet birds sang.
In me thou see'st the twilight of such day
As after sunset fadeth in the west;
Which by and by black night doth take away,
Death's second self, that seals up all in rest
In me thou see'st the glowing of such fire,
That on the ashes of his youth doth lie,
As the death-bed, whereon it must expire,
Consumed with that which it was nourish'd by.
This thou perceiv'st, which makes thy love more strong,
To love that well, which thou must leave ere long.

(Shakespeare, Sonnet 73)

In the other three cases, even if it is as if a little bit of poetry had shown up in more or less ordinary prose, the elaboration of the metaphor, if it is done at all, is left entirely to the reader. (The best treatment of the contextual character of metaphor as it occurs in lyric poetry and elsewhere is White 1996. White elaborates a powerful and subtle theory, intended to accommodate the fact that metaphor often occurs within a complex context.)

The comprehension of a metaphor may be illustrated by one's ability to paraphrase it, but its mastery may be shown even better in one's ability to carry on with its story. For instance, if Miles Davis is the Picasso of jazz, then who is its Rembrandt? (Louis Armstrong?) Who is its Dali? (John Coltrane?) And if Miles Davis is the Picasso of jazz, did he have a blue period? A cubist period?

In general, we might think of a metaphor as the use of some term 'M' in order to talk about something literally referred to by some term 'L'. Black, by implication, and then Goodman, explicitly, noted that, although the metaphor makes use of 'M' and 'L', essentially present in the background are the words that 'belong with' 'M' and the ones that belong with 'L'. And so the application of 'Picasso' to Miles Davis carries the question of what names of painters apply to which jazz musicians.

Even if 'poetic' metaphor is significantly different from the metaphors appearing in 'ordinary language', we may attempt at least a provisional description of metaphor in general. Among oblique uses of language, the first distinguishing feature of metaphor is that Y (what is communicated) somehow depends upon X (the meaning of what is said or written), although this feature is not sufficient to distinguish metaphor from all other oblique uses. It will do, however, to distinguish metaphors from idioms. Here are some idiomatic expressions by means of which one might communicate that someone has died:

He bought the farm.

He kicked the bucket.

He went west.

He gave up the ghost.

In none of these examples does it matter whether one knows how the expression has come to be a way of saying that he died, although presumably there is an explanation to be given in every case. The only one I know is that of 'He bought the farm', and I am not entirely sure of this. American soldiers in the First World War carried life insurance. If a soldier were killed, the insurance would pay out, and so a farm he had bought with a mortgage could be paid for with the insurance money. Thus, in dying he bought the farm.

If I know this history about military government insurance, whether or not it is wholly correct, then I might figure out that 'He bought the farm' is a way of saying 'he died'; but, plainly, I needn't know any of this in order to know that 'He bought the farm' means that he died. Even though the semantics of 'He bought the farm' is historically dependent on this history, no one using the expression needs to know this history, either to utter it or to understand it, and in that sense there is no dependence. In fact, although it is extremely unlikely that a competent English-speaker would not grasp the literal meaning of 'He bought the farm', it is possible that one may understand the expression to mean *only* that he died. With a genuine metaphor, however, it is impossible to grasp what is being communicated without making use of the literal sense of the expression. For instance, with 'Miles Davis is the Picasso of jazz', 'All the world's a stage', and 'He is a tabula rasa no one has written on', there is no chance of grasping their import without appealing to the literal senses of their constituents. In these cases, and in this sense, Y is dependent upon X.

There is a kind of oblique communication, however, that exhibits this dependence but is not metaphorical. It is irony. Suppose a student has studied with me because his friend recommended me highly. But the student is greatly disappointed, finding me a useless instructor. He says to his friend, 'Well, thanks so much for that recommendation. Cohen is a wonderful teacher.' In saying 'Cohen is a wonderful teacher', the student is communicating his opinion that Cohen is a very poor teacher. To identify this communication, the student's friend must attend to the literal expression 'Cohen is a wonderful teacher', because the ironic communication is dependent upon it. There is no sensible way of assigning 'Cohen is a very bad teacher' as a meaning of 'Cohen is a wonderful teacher', and in this respect it is different from 'He bought the farm', one of whose meanings is that he died. This fact led Paul Grice to say that what is communicated in irony is not a meaning of the expression, but rather is what the user of the expression means by the expression, distinguishing what he called speaker's meaning from utterance meaning.

One might think of irony in this way: attached to the expression is an irony operator, and this operator converts X (the literal meaning of the expression) into Y (the ironic meaning communicated). It is not easy to specify just what this operator does in relating Y to X. Given X, it produces what might be called the opposite of X, or the reverse of X, or an exaggerated negation of X. It is, perhaps, as if X indicated a position on an axis, and Y were the result of moving an equal distance from the axis's origin, but in the opposite direction. But however the operator may be characterized, it does seem right to suppose that some such operation is indicated when an expression is used ironically.

If irony is like metaphor, and unlike idiomatic expression, in so far as Y is dependent upon X, then what distinguishes metaphor from irony? The difference between metaphor and irony is profound. Understanding a metaphor is, or can be, a task of much greater difficulty and complexity. It may be difficult to understand why irony has been used, and it may be difficult to detect it, but once it is known that the expression is ironic, it is almost routine to compute what the speaker means by his ironical utterance. One takes the ironical expression and performs a standard operation upon its literal meaning, and thereby arrives at the intended meaning. With a metaphor, however, one must remain with the words of the metaphor, so to speak, in an attempt to find a way of understanding how those words can be combined in order to convey something other than the literal meaning of the expression. With a putative ironical expression there may be an argument as to whether it is in fact ironical, but there will be no significant argument about what, if it is ironical, is meant by it; with a metaphor, however, there is often a very significant argument over what the expression means once it is has been declared to be a metaphor.

A subsidiary question about metaphors is, how are they recognized? No matter how one explains just what a reader or hearer does to understand a metaphor, there is, seemingly, first the question of how that reader or hearer realizes that the expression in fact is a metaphor. Some early theorists—Monroe Beardsley, for example—thought that the recipient of a metaphor would be driven to attempt a metaphorical understanding because he found himself blocked when trying to take the expression literally (Beardsley 1967). He would be blocked because, taken literally, the expression would be self-contradictory or somehow semantically hopeless. This idea cannot be quite right because, although it may be true that 'Juliet is the sun' or 'All the world's a stage' is, if taken literally, semantically anomalous, at least in the sense of being obviously, outrageously false, there are metaphors that can withstand a literal reading, for instance 'No man is an island' or 'Al Capone was an animal'. In those cases, perhaps, what blocks a literal reading is the fact that the expressions taken literally are so blatantly, patently true that it is inconceivable that their author could intend them to be taken in that way because there can be no point in attempting to inform someone of something that both author and recipient already know, and know that one another know. But there may be examples in which nothing blocks a literal reading, and the audience for the metaphor must, on its own, so to speak, attempt a metaphorical understanding. There may be lines of lyric poetry, for instance, that can perfectly well be taken literally and found informative, and yet it is their metaphorical import that matters. For instance, 'Do not go gentle into that good night' and some of the succeeding lines in that poem might be read as nothing more or less than an injunction not to be casual about going outdoors after dark.

Thus, there may be no uniform, general explanation possible of how it is that metaphors are recognized, and this might be related to the fact that there are sometimes interpretations of works of art—especially literary works—that simply have to be found, when there is nothing in the work itself to demand that a reader go looking for extra levels. If this is so, then there may be examples of metaphor in which the discovery that the expression is a metaphor is itself a significant undertaking, and for those examples there may be arguments about whether or not a metaphor is present just as interesting as the more frequent arguments about whether some expression is ironical.

In this discussion, so far, there has been casual mention of what is communicated in a metaphor, and even the suggestion that this should be regarded as a meaning; but it may be necessary to regard this as only a manner of speaking, for the question of whether there is such a thing as metaphorical meaning is a contested question in contemporary discussions.

There are at least two apparent reasons for speaking of metaphorical meaning, one informal and somewhat imprecise, and the other more strict and rigorous. The first is, simply, that we want to say that a successful appreciator understands a metaphor. 'Understanding' is understood, naturally enough, as grasping a meaning. Thus, if a metaphor can be understood, it must present something that can be grasped, i.e. a meaning. The second reason is that we may want to say of some metaphors that they are true (or false). Thus, we need something to have a truth value—a proposition, say. In fact, we will need two propositions. Taken literally, the sentence is false; taken metaphorically, it is true. A proposition, roughly, is the meaning of a sentence. So there must be two meanings, one literal and one metaphorical.

These reasons are compelling, and they have helped convince some philosophers of the existence of metaphorical meaning; but they are not decisive. It is entirely possible to think of understanding a metaphor, and so to find a putative understanding apt or inept without referring to a specific metaphorical meaning. Grasping a metaphor seems to require, as it were, an extra exertion, something beyond and in addition to what is required in grasping a literal meaning. Why suppose that there is a special kind of meaning that cannot be grasped in the customary way? Furthermore, even if the point of a metaphor is relatively specific and fixed, it is still true that metaphorical import often seems open-ended, and not able to be captured in a tidy paraphrase. In this respect, a metaphor seems less something with a determinate meaning than a stimulus to the imagination, an incitement to imaginative and fanciful thought.

It is not uncommon to think of metaphors as expressions with more than one meaning, and in fact, until a few years ago texts in language and linguistics sometimes discussed metaphor within the general topic of polysemy along with ambiguity. Thus, one thought of both ambiguity and metaphor in terms of expressions that have two (or more) meanings. But even if this view is plausible, it will not do, because it covers up more than it reveals, and what it conceals is the relation of dependence.

In the case of a genuinely ambiguous expression, there is no relation of dependence. 'He spent the night on the bank' might mean that he spent the night atop a building, or it might mean that he spent the night beside a river, but neither of these meanings depends upon the other, and, indeed, one might very well know either of the meanings without knowing the other. But in examples of genuine metaphors, expressions like 'Juliet is the sun' or 'No man is an island', even if the metaphorical meaning is a second meaning, that meaning is absolutely dependent upon the first, literal, meaning, and it is impossible to grasp the metaphorical meaning without referring to the literal meaning.

A lexicographer must decide, in the case of a genuinely ambiguous term, whether there is a word with more than one meaning, or more than one word, and he will do this on philological grounds. Thus, one dictionary may list 'bank' only once, but identify two meanings, one having to do with a financial institution and the other concerned with the sides of rivers; while another dictionary may list two distinct words that happen to have the same orthographic representation. Either way, it is plainly possible for a speaker of the language to know one meaning but not the other, and this is true of either meaning.

But with metaphor it is entirely different. Even if something called its metaphorical meaning could be identified for some expression or term, it will be inapt to list this as a separate, independent meaning. When it becomes possible to list this so-called metaphorical meaning as a separate meaning, this will show that the metaphor has frozen or died, which is to say that it is no longer a metaphor.

Whether or not there is metaphorical meaning, there is something communicated or conveyed or got across by a metaphor, and a pressing question is how that 'content' is extracted from the expression that conveys it. Since the earliest writing about metaphor, a persistent thought has been that a metaphor somehow implicates a similarity. Thus, in any expression 'F is G', in which F is said to be metaphorically G, it seems that F and G are being said to be similar. This leads to the idea that the metaphorical sense of 'F is G' can be given by 'F is like G'. This idea construes metaphors to be, essentially, abbreviated or compressed similes.

The relation of metaphor to simile has figured prominently in discussions of what has been called the paraphrasability of metaphor, and early instalments in this discussion were beset by a confusion. The leading question was whether metaphorical expressions can be expressed in wholly literal language. Some theorists thought this could be done by 'reducing' a metaphor to its corresponding simile. This thought sometimes confused the question of whether the meaning of a metaphor is captured by its attendant simile with the question of whether a metaphor has a literal equivalent. The confusion is evident once it is noted that, even if the metaphor 'F is G' is semantically equivalent to 'F is like G' (which on the face of it is unlikely; for, after all, in general 'X is Y' does not mean the same thing as 'X is like Y'), it is still an open question whether 'F is like G' is literal. For instance, suppose that Romeo's 'Juliet is the sun' is reducible to 'Juliet is like the sun'. It is innocuous to require, if 'Juliet is like the sun' is true, that Juliet and the sun be alike in some respect or other, that is, that they share some property. And now an unattractive dilemma arises. On the one hand, it is easy to find properties shared by Juliet and the sun. They both have mass, occupy space, and are visible objects. But none of these properties is relevant to the import of Romeo's metaphorical declaration. On the other hand, there are properties shared by Juliet and the sun that are relevant. For instance, both are sources of warmth. So both Juliet and the sun are warm. But Juliet is not warm in the sense in which the sun in warm. In fact, the property putatively shared by Juliet and the sun is not, literally, a property of Juliet. 'Juliet is warm' is itself a figure of speech, no more literal than the original metaphor 'Juliet is the sun'. (The leading discussion of how the relevant properties are located by someone who understands a metaphor is Stern 2000, which is also an admirable defence of the idea that there is something to be called the meaning of a metaphor. Stern's work is one of the very few full-scale theories of metaphor, grounded in very sophisticated philosophy of language and linguistics, and his attention to the details of such a theory deserves serious study.)

It follows that, even if a metaphor's content can be carried by a simile, there is no reason to expect the simile to be literal—indeed, it will almost certainly not be literal. It also follows that those who wish to deny that metaphors have literal equivalents have no need to deny that metaphors can be paraphrased as similes. (An extremely useful discussion of the relation of similes to literality, along with a forceful defence of the idea that metaphors involve comparisons, is found in Fogelin, 1988.)

It is tempting to suppose that what underlies the metaphor is a construction more complex than a simile, namely an analogy. Thus, Juliet stands to Romeo as the sun stands to something—perhaps also Romeo. Or, perhaps, Juliet stands to Romeo as the moon stands to some other man, as if Romeo were noting that, whereas other men thought of their beloveds as the moon, Juliet outshines those women as the sun outshines the moon. (For a sophisticated development of this suggestion see Tormey 1983.)

This move from similes to analogies looks promising, if only beccause it acknowledges the complexities invoked by some metaphors; but this is an illusion, because typically there is no move towards literality. Such an explanation by analogy, in the end, is nothing but an explanation by simile.

What analogies underlie 'Juliet is the sun' or 'God is my father'? Suppose we take Romeo to be saying that Juliet is to other women as the sun is to the moon. Then we may write

$$jRw : sR^*m.$$

And let us suppose that the line in a Yom Kippur poem says that God stands to me as my father stands to me. Then we may write

$$gRt : fR^*t.$$

Now in both cases, with the analogies represented in this way, we need to understand the 'as' in

$$xRy : wR^*z \ [x \text{ is to } y \text{ as } w \text{ is to } z].$$

and the obvious question is, what is the relation to one another of these two relations, R and R*?

Are the relations the same as they are, for instance, in

$$2 \text{ is to } 4 \text{ as } 3 \text{ is to } 6?$$

Here the relation R is the same in both cases. That is, even if we write

$$2R4 : 3R^{*}6,$$

R and R* are the same, and so we might as well have written

$$2R4 : 3R6.$$

Those who think that metaphors are underwritten by literal analogies must be thinking that R and R* are the same. But in most cases of metaphor they are not. The relation of the sun to the moon is not the same relation as that of Juliet to other women, nor is the relation of God to me the same relation as that of my father to me. There is, no doubt, a similarity between the two relations, but this means that the promised explanation by analogy as an improvement over an explanation by simile is an improvement only in the sense that the putative underlying similarity is now a relational similarity, and it is no more a literal similarity than is the original metaphor a literal statement. One may indeed offer statements of similarity as aids in understanding metaphor, and it may be even more helpful to offer statements of analogy; but the aids are still themselves figurative, and we are no closer to understanding just what literal similarity it is that anchors the metaphor.

Whether or not metaphors have literal equivalents, and whether or not every metaphor is expressible as a simile or as an analogy, there remains a conspicuous feature of metaphorical language as such, namely what seems to happen when one encounters a metaphor. A persistent thought about metaphor is that it supplies something like a *picture*, or an *image*. The thought is carried in the description of metaphor as an example of figurative language—language that presents a figure. (The same sense is found in German, when such language is called *bildliche*, and in French, where it is *figuratif*.) The idea is that to comprehend 'Juliet is the sun' one must somehow think of Juliet as the sun, and this is to construct something like a picture in one's imagination. Since it is commonly thought that a picture is somehow more compelling, more insistent than a sentence, it is, then, natural to think that a metaphor is more intrusive, and harder to resist, than a literal expression. Thus, one might refuse to believe that Western civilization is a wasteland, but Eliot's poetry will have given one an image of it as such that lingers despite one's beliefs. (An exceptionally useful discussion of this matter is found in Moran 1989, a sensitive and analytically deep study.)

Suppose there is no such thing as the specific semantic content of a metaphor, nor even any specific pragmatic effect. Suppose, that is, following Davidson, that a metaphor is something like an open stimulation to the imagination, with no strictly linguistic controls at work. (Davidson, 1978, has argued that there is no such thing as metaphorical meaning, and that the effects of metaphors must be understood in some other way. This essay has become a standard condensed argument against the idea of metaphorical meaning. A more comprehensive argument against the existence of metaphorical meaning is found in Cooper, 1986. For the contrary view, defending metaphorical meaning, see Stern, 2000, and Levinson, 2001.) It is still true that not every response to a metaphor is legitimate. Not every way of taking 'Juliet is the sun' or 'Miles Davis is the Picasso of jazz' is acceptable. If you do not grasp that Romeo finds Juliet comforting and stimulating, or that the Miles Davis fan thinks that Miles Davis was innovative with a formidable plastic imagination, then there is something in or about these metaphors that you have missed. It is a strong temptation to say that you have failed to grasp a meaning, and if we are not to say that, then how shall we describe your failure? Could we say that it is like a failure to comprehend a work of art? Suppose someone does not see that King Lear is, among other things, about the terrible hopelessness of growing old. How shall we describe his failure? In the richest sense of an often depreciated word, we might say that he has failed to appreciate the play. Might we say, similarly, that one either appreciates or fails to appreciate a metaphor?

The word 'appreciate' often connotes both understanding and having some feeling about the thing appreciated. To say of someone that he appreciates a Mozart opera is to say not only that he comprehends something but also that he cares for it. Although it is possible that a metaphor be used only to describe something, it is far more common for a metaphor to be used also to indicate how the metaphor-maker feels about something, and in such a case it is not uncommon for the metaphor-maker to hope to induce this feeling in those who appreciate his metaphor. Max Black explicitly challenged those who think metaphors have only 'emotive' significance, arguing that metaphors can be 'cognitive'. But perhaps a typical case is one in which a metaphor is both: it offers a novel way of seeing something, and that novel sight brings a feeling with it.

We are still some way from a complete understanding of exactly what metaphors are, why they are used, and how they work; but there is no doubt that by now the topic is widely and richly appreciated, and that progress is being made.

See also: Fiction; Poetry; Literature; Humour; Interpretation in Art.

BIBLIOGRAPHY

Beardsley, M. C. (1967). 'Metaphor', in *Encyclopedia of Philosophy*, ed. P. Edwards, New York: Macmillan.

—— (1978). 'Metaphorical Senses'. *Nous* 12: 3–16.

—— (1982). 'The Metaphorical Twist'. *Philosophy and Phenomenological Research* 22: 293–307.

Black, M. (1955). 'Metaphor'. *Proceedings of the Aristotelian Society* 55: 273–94.

Cohen, T. (1975). 'Figurative Speech and Figurative Acts'. *Journal of Philosophy* 72: 669–84.

—— (1978). 'Metaphor and the Cultivation of Intimacy'. *Critical Inquiry* 5: 1–13.

Cohen, T. (1997). 'Metaphor, Feeling, and Narrative'. *Philosophy and Literature* 21: 223–44.

Cooper, D. (1986). *Metaphor*. Oxford: Blackwell.

Davidson, D. (1978). 'What Metaphors Mean'. *Critical Inquiry* 5: 31–47.

Derrida, J. (1974). 'The White Mythology: Metaphor in the Text of Philosophy'. *New Literary History* 6: 5–74.

Fogelin, R. J. (1988). *Figuratively Speaking*. New Haven: Yale University Press.

Goodman, N. (1968). *Languages of Art*. Indianapolis: Bobbs-Merrill.

Grice, P. (1989). *Studies in the Way of Words*. Cambridge, Mass.: Harvard University Press.

Hagberg, G. (2001). 'Metaphor', in *Routledge Companion to Aesthetics*, eds. B. Gaut and D. Lopes. London and New York: Routledge.

Hausman, C. (1998). 'Metaphor and Nonverbal Arts', in *Encyclopedia of Aesthetics*, ed. Michael Kelly. Oxford and New York: Oxford University Press.

Henle, P. (1958). 'Metaphor'. in P. Henle (ed.), *Language, Thought, and Culture*. Ann Arbor: University of Michigan Press, pp. 173–95.

Hills, D. (1997). 'Aptness and Truth in Verbal Metaphor'. *Philosophical Topics* 25: 117–53.

Isenberg, A. (1963). 'On Defining Metaphor'. *Journal of Philosophy* 60; revised and expanded in *Selected Essays of Arnold Isenberg*. Chicago: University of Chicago Press, 1973.

Johnson, M. (ed.) (1981). *Philosophical Perspectives on Metaphor*. Minneapolis: University of Minneapolis Press.

—— (1998). 'Metaphor: An Overview,' in *Encyclopedia of Aesthetics*, ed. M. Kelly. Oxford and New York: Oxford University Press.

Lakoff, G. and M. Johnson (1980). *Metaphors We Live By*. Chicago: University of Chicago Press.

Levinson, J. (2001). 'Who's Afraid of a Paraphrase?' *Theoria* 67: 7–23.

Martinich, A. P. (1998). 'Metaphor', in *Routledge Encyclopedia of Philosophy*. London: Routledge.

Moran, R. (1989). 'Seeing and Believing: Metaphor, Image, and Force'. *Critical Inquiry* 16: 87–112.

—— (1997). 'Metaphor', in *A Companion to the Philosophy of Language*, eds. B. Hale and C. Wright. Oxford: Blackwell.

Ortony, A. (ed.) (1993). *Metaphor and Thought*, 2nd edn. Cambridge: Cambridge University Press.

Scheffler, I. (1979). *Beyond the Letter*. London: Routledge & Kegan Paul.

Shibles, W. (1971). *Metaphor: An Annotated Bibliography and History*. Whitewater, Wis.: The Language Press.

Stern, J. (1998). 'Metaphor and Philosophy of Language', in *Encyclopedia of Aesthetics*, ed. M. Kelly. Oxford and New York: Oxford University Press.

—— (2000). *Metaphor in Context*. Cambridge, Mass.: MIT Press.

Summers, D. (1998). 'Metaphor and Art History', in *Encyclopedia of Aesthetics*, ed. M. Kelly. Oxford and New York: Oxford University Press.

Tormey, A. (1983). 'Metaphors and Counterfactuals', in J. Fisher (ed.), *Essays on Aesthetics*. Philadelphia: Temple University Press.

Walton, K. (1993). 'Metaphor and Prop Oriented Make-Believe'. *European Journal of Philosophy* 1: 39–57.

Wheeler, S. C. III (1998). 'Derrida and de Man on Metaphor', in *Encyclopedia of Aesthetics*, ed. M. Kelly. Oxford and New York: Oxford University Press.

White, R. M. (1996). *The Structure of Metaphor*. Oxford: Blackwell.

CHAPTER 21

....

FICTION

....

PETER LAMARQUE

FICTION (from the Latin *fingere*, to fashion or form; to make; to feign) raises a number of important issues in aesthetics, principally, though not exclusively, in relation to the literary arts. The element of representation, in any artform, that involves what is invented, made up, or imaginary, bears on the realm of fiction. Philosophers have long sought to characterize fictionality and to identify the boundary between the fictive and the non-fictive—an enterprise, as we shall see, that is by no means straightforward. There is philosophical interest also in the status of 'fictitious entities', not only those theoretical fictions figuring in science, mathematics, law, and metaphysics, but also the made-up persons, places, and events occurring in novels, dramas, myths, and legends. These are ontological issues, delimiting what exists or is real. Other issues draw on semantics and the philosophy of language and involve the peculiarities of names, sentences, and truth-values in fictional contexts.

Such matters have a bearing on aesthetics to the extent that they impinge on broader concerns about how products of the imagination 'relate to the world', both at the level of creativity and with respect to the cognitive or truth-telling potential of representational art. Another important aspect of the fiction–world relation concerns the very possibility of emotional or other affective responses to fiction. Can we respond with genuine pity, respect, admiration, or fear towards something we know to be merely fictitious, that is to say non-existent, existing only in the realm of make-believe? Philosophers have recognized a 'paradox of fiction' in this regard, which has proved remarkably resistant to satisfactory resolution.

1. PRELIMINARIES

The concept of fiction is not identical to that of literature, and the discussion that follows concentrates on the former alone. Not only do the terms 'fiction' and 'literature' have different extensions—not all fictions are literary and not all literary works are fictional—but their meanings differ too, not least because the latter has an evaluative element lacking in the former. John Searle captures one difference nicely, if not entirely uncontroversially: 'Whether or not a work is literature is for readers to decide; whether or not it is fictional is for the author to decide' (Searle 1979: 59). Of course, many of the great works of literature are also fictional, so an analysis of fiction will shed light on one aspect of them. But it should not be supposed that an analysis of fiction will exhaust all there is to say about literature, nor that such an analysis will encompass distinctively literary qualities.

The term 'fiction' applies to *objects* of a certain kind as well as to *descriptions* of a certain kind (Lamarque and Olsen 1994: 16 ff.). Fictional objects include imaginary characters, places, and events as characterized in works of fiction, while fictional descriptions include those statements or whole works that have this characterizing function. To say of an object that it is fictional normally implies that it is not real; to say of a description that it is fictional normally implies that it is not true. Initial attention thus falls on the notions of reality and truth, but it is debatable whether these can provide a comprehensive explanation of fictionality, or even whether the normal implications hold without exception. Not everything unreal is a fictional object, nor is everything false a fictional description; and it can be argued that a certain kind of reality pertains to fictional objects and a certain kind of truth to fictional descriptions.

Further distinctions are needed, particularly among fictional descriptions. *Discourse about fiction* (for example by literary critics) reports the content of works of fiction and can be judged for its accuracy and inaccuracy or its truth or falsity. This must be distinguished from *fictional discourse*, i.e. story-telling itself, which is not so obviously amenable to truth-assessment (van Inwagen 1977). It should be noted that the difference between these modes of discourse, story-commentary and story-telling, cannot be identified through surface features of sentences alone. One and the same sentence-type can appear now in a story, now in a report about a story. Contextual factors will determine which usage applies and thus the appropriate mode of evaluation. Furthermore, not all fictional discourse is creative. Sometimes story-telling coincides with making up a story, where the story is told for the first time; sometimes the telling is a retelling. But retelling a story is still a mode of fictional discourse, distinct from discourse about fiction.

These preliminary distinctions point to different sets of questions that arise in any analysis of fiction, and although they are interrelated it is better, in the first instance, to address them separately. There are questions about fictional entities as 'objects'—their status, their relation to other kinds of objects, their place in ontology. Then there are questions about fictional sentences or descriptions—how to characterize fictional as against non-fictional discourse and how to characterize the peculiarities of discourse about fiction. It seems likely that answers to these broadly logical questions will affect other inquiries that emerge, the place in our lives occupied by fictions, the possibility of emotional response to them, the values we attribute to them, and the contribution they make to literature and other arts.

2. ONTOLOGY

Let us begin with the ontological inquiry, if only because concern with existence and non-existence dates back to the very beginnings of analytic philosophy and has been one of its central preoccupations. The problem came up initially because of the association between meaning and denotation. If the meaning of a name, as Bertrand Russell and most of his fellow logical analysts believed, is the object the name denotes, then naming expressions with no denotation, such as 'Pegasus', 'the highest prime', 'the present king of France', have no meaning. Yet such names do not seem unintelligible, and sentences in which they appear can have truth-values assigned to them.

There are two heroic routes out of this conundrum—apart from abandoning the theory of meaning as denotation, a move early analytic philosophers were reluctant to make—and these two routes serve as markers for subsequent discussions of fiction. The first, taken by Russell (1905/1956), is to deny that these apparent names are really names at all. Logical analysis, notably the Theory of Descriptions and the theory that ordinary names are disguised descriptions, can show, according to Russell, that what look like denoting terms might be no such thing, and that the appearance of denotation can be spirited away through paraphrases containing only quantifiers and propositional functions.

The second heroic route, taken by Alexius Meinong (1904/1960), is to insist that all such names, including the most obviously fictional, are in fact denoting terms, but that what they denote are objects with different kinds of being, of which full-blown existence is only one such kind of being. Thus, while Russell sought to eliminate fictional entities as denotata of fictional names, Meinong sought to accommodate them within a general 'theory of objects'. Descendants of these two strategies, which I shall call *eliminativism* and *accommodationism*, are still in evidence, and I will review some of their more recent manifestations.

3. ELIMINATIVISM

One aim of logical analysis is to remove unwanted ontological commitments (Quine 1953). Fiction provides an obvious case of problematic commitments, yet the application of logical analysis affords somewhat mixed results. Take the simplest kind of example:

(1) Holmes is a detective.

The apparent commitment to a fictitious entity *Holmes* is removed, on a typical Russell/Quine analysis, by paraphrasing away the name in favour of a quantifier and a predicate, yielding something like this:

(2) There is some unique thing that satisfies the Holmes-description and is a detective.

This latter sentence is meaningful, possesses a truth-value (false), and makes no commitment to a realm of fictitious entities. However, the analysis seems deficient in a number of respects. First, by making all sentences 'about' fictional characters turn out false, it fails to capture a distinction between those like (1), which seem to have an element of truth, and those like 'Holmes is unintelligent', which seem manifestly false. Second, the analysis treats (1) as if it were an assertion about the real world, rather than about a fictional world. Third, related to this, it makes the truth-value of (1) contingent not on how things are in a fictional world but on how things are in reality, with the result that the sentence could turn out to be true if, by coincidence, the predicates in (2) were satisfied. Yet the truth-value of 'Holmes is a detective' should not depend on whether any actual person happens to instantiate the Holmes-properties (Lewis 1978). Finally, it fails to distinguish fictional discourse from discourse about fiction, for it deals only with the latter and gives the wrong result. But, arguably, it gives the wrong result too as an analysis of the former; for to claim that all sentences in Conan Doyle's novels are false seems unhelpful, since it fails to acknowledge the author's aim of making up a story rather than reporting facts about the world.

Admittedly, elimination by logical paraphrase can take many different forms. Another influential proposal was offered by Nelson Goodman (1968), who focuses on pictorial representation, although the theory offered can be applied across the arts. Goodman suggests that we analyse 'X is a picture of a unicorn' not as a relation between a picture and a fictitious entity, but as a one-place predication captured as 'X is a unicorn-picture'. The predicate 'is a unicorn-picture' serves only to classify picture types, and thus bears no referential commitments. (Indeed, Goodman has shown in general how apparent commitments in talking about Holmes can be avoided by employment of the non-referential locution 'Holmes-about': Goodman 1961.)

Goodman's strategy is effective up to a point, but like all such paraphrasing strategies its scope is limited. Supposed references to fictitious entities crop up in contexts where Russellian or Goodmanian paraphrases seem problematic. In addition to simple descriptive sentences like (1), there are also sentences like the following, which an adequate theory should accommodate:

(3) Holmes was created by Conan Doyle.

(4) Holmes is a fictional character.

(5) Holmes doesn't really exist.

(6) Holmes is smarter than Poirot.

(7) Holmes is an emblematic character of modern fiction.

Eliminativists often struggle to find paraphrases for such usages, and the way they tackle these different contexts is sometimes thought to be an appropriate test for eliminativist programmes (Howell 1979; Lamarque 1996; Thomasson 1999). For example, the expedient of placing the prefix 'In the fiction' before sentences like (1) (Lewis 1978) is not available for (3)–(7), and the use of quantifiers and functions, as in (2), threatens to yield quite the wrong truth-values in at least (3), (4), and (7). Accommodationists often base their own acceptance of fictional entities on what they take to be the literal truth of sentences like (4), and it is just such sentences that pose the biggest problem for the eliminativist.

Kendall Walton's eliminativist strategy appeals not to logical analysis of the Russellian kind but to the idea of 'make-believe'. For Walton, to be fictional is to be a 'prop in a game of make-believe' (Walton 1990). Games and their associated props are real enough, but there is no further reality to Holmes or Poirot. Indeed, because 'Holmes' has no denotation, there are, according to Walton, strictly no propositions about Holmes, and thus sentence (1), taken literally, expresses no proposition. This is a strong claim, for it implies that attempts to capture the meaning of (1) through paraphrase are futile, since it has no meaning. (For objections, see Zemach 1998.) Instead, on Walton's account, we pretend that (1) has a meaning, and we pretend that in using it we are stating something true. Walton explains his example 'Tom Sawyer attended his own funeral' as follows: '*The Adventures of Tom Sawyer* is such that one who engages in pretense of kind K in a game authorized for it makes it fictional of himself in that game that he speaks truly' (Walton 1990: 400). We learn what kind K is ostensively by confronting appropriate acts of game playing. Walton's eliminivatism is subtle, with applications to all the problem cases, and is well motivated within his broader theory of representation. However, arguably, the theory extends pretence too widely and postulates games of make-believe, for example, in cases like (3), (4), and (7), where literal construal seems more intuitive (Kroon 1994; Thomasson 1999). I shall return to Walton later.

4. Accommodationism

Attempts to accommodate fictional entities take even more varied forms than attempts to eliminate them. A good starting point is Meinong, who proposed that there are nonexistent as well as existent objects. Anything that can be talked about, as the referent of a singular term, has, according to Meinong, some kind of *being*, including even contradictory entities like round squares. So Holmes is an object, possessing all the Holmes properties but lacking the property of existence. Sentences like (1) are thus construed literally as subject/object predications.

Refinements of Meinong's theory have been developed by, among others, Terence Parsons (1980), who holds that there is at least one object correlated with every combination of nuclear properties. Many such objects do not exist, and fictional characters, like Holmes, differ from ordinary humans not only in lacking existence but also in being 'incomplete', in the sense that for any given property it is not always determinate whether or not the character possesses that property. Parsons distinguishes a nonexistent object's 'nuclear' properties, as in (1), from its 'extra-nuclear' properties, as in (3), (4), and (7). (For a clear discussion and appraisal of Parsons's theory, see Levinson 1981.)

Similar but not identical views are held by other accommodationists (e.g. Zalta 1983). Charles Crittenden (1991) might be classed among the Meinongians, in giving a literal construal of talk about fiction, but his version is anti-metaphysical, influenced by Wittgenstein's notion of language-games. Fictional objects, Crittenden believes, are 'grammatical objects' arising within a 'practice'. Richard Rorty (1982) likewise rejects metaphysics and ontology but thinks that it is pointless to try to 'eliminate' fictional entities because he sees the 'problem about fictional discourse' as a pseudo-problem arising from two misguided conceptions: truth as 'correspondence' with the facts, and language as a 'picture' of the world. (Prado 1984, further develops this approach.)

Other theorists take fictional objects to be not *nonexistent* objects but instead a species of *abstract* objects. For example, Peter van Inwagen (1977) describes fictional characters as 'theoretical entities of literary criticism', Nicholas Wolterstorff (1980) sees them as 'person-kinds', in contrast to 'kinds of persons', and Peter Lamarque and Stein Haugom Olsen (1994) offer an analysis in terms of sets of characteristics presented under the conventions of 'fictive utterance' (see also Pelletier 2000).

A problem confronts many such theories, especially those that attribute the status of abstract existence to fictional objects (although it is also acknowledged by Parsons for his theory), in that fictional characters cannot be *created* (at a moment of time), given the timeless nature of abstract entities. The implication is that sentence (3) above is literally false; but this seems counterintuitive. A standard response (e.g. Wolterstorff

1980: 145) is to describe authors as creat*ive* rather than literally as creat*ors*. But another kind of accommodationism (Emt 1992; Salmon 1998; Thomasson 1999) takes fictional characters to be both abstract entities and created artefacts. Thomasson (1999) has developed such a conception in detail, based on a theory of dependence whereby fictional characters have a necessary dependence both on the linguistic acts that bring them into existence and on the continued existence of the works (but not individual texts) that sustain them in existence. On this view, fictional objects are historical rather than timeless entities, their historical origins being essential to them; and they can cease to exist as well as come into existence. They have a similar status to laws, theories, governments, and indeed literary works. The attraction of this kind of accommodationism, setting aside worries about the ontological category of 'abstract artefact', is that it acknowledges some kind of reality for fictional characters, allowing that there can be literal truths about them, without postulating anomalous 'nonexistent objects'.

5. FICTIONAL DISCOURSE

How can fictional discourse be distinguished from non-fictional discourse? The matter is of some import, for, although those who mistake fiction for fact, like the gullible listeners to Orson Welles's broadcast of *The War of the Worlds*, might be subject to no more than embarrassment, those who take fact-stating to be fiction could face more serious consequences. The problem arises because there seem to be no surface features of language—syntactical or rhetorical—that decisively mark the fictive from the non-fictive, a point exploited by novelists and dramatists seeking realism. Nor, more controversially, do semantic features, i.e. reference and truth-value, seem to provide necessary or sufficient conditions. While fictional discourse characteristically contains non-denoting names, this, as shown by historical fiction, is not necessary, nor is it sufficient, given the use of such names in non-fictional contexts. Falsehood also is not sufficient for fiction, as fiction-making is distinct from lying and from making a mistake. Arguably, it is not necessary, either, as literally true sentences can play an integral role in some fictional stories (*contra* Goodman 1984). Another suggestion is that fictional discourse has no truth-value because it makes no assertions (Urmson 1976) or at least that passing judgement on its truth or falsity is inappropriate (Gale 1971). But the varied aims of fiction make these claims questionable as part of a definition of fiction.

If surface or semantic properties of sentences are not satisfactory candidates for defining fictional discourse, conditions on the use of sentences seem more so. One common line of thought is to look to speakers' or writers' intentions for the key to fictional narrative. However, there is no unanimity over what the core intentions of the fiction-maker are. Wolterstorff (1980) has argued that story-tellers engage in 'presenting or offering for consideration' states of affairs or propositions for audiences to reflect on or ponder. That might be right, but it is not yet adequate to set them apart from non-fiction speakers. It has been suggested that story-tellers *imitate* (Ohmann 1971) or *represent* (Beardsley 1981) speech acts, such as assertion, without actually performing them. Searle (1979) has influentially proposed that an author of fiction *pretends* to perform illocutionary acts, but without intended deception. Lewis (1978) also sees story-telling as pretence: 'the story-teller purports to be telling the truth about matters whereof he has knowledge'.

The association of fiction with pretence is obvious enough (bearing in mind further complexities, such as the distinction between 'pretending to do', 'pretending to be', and 'pretending that', as outlined in Lamarque and Olsen 1994: 60–71). But to *identify* story-telling with pretending might still seem too limited or negative. On the face of it, such a suggestion emphasizes only what story-tellers are *not* doing, i.e. what they are merely *pretending* to do, rather than, in a more positive way, characterizing what they *are* doing and aiming to achieve. The difference between Homer, the story-teller, and Herodotus, the historian, is not best captured by saying that the latter is in fact doing something that the former is merely pretending to do. That hardly does justice to Homer's achievement. In seeking a more positive account, still based on a writer's intentions, other theorists have preferred to locate pretence not in what the story-teller does but in what the story-audience does. On this view the story-teller's primary intention is not to pretend anything, but to get an *audience* to pretend or make-believe or imagine something—for example to make-believe that a story is told as known fact (Currie 1990), or to make-believe that standard speech acts are being performed even while knowing that they are not (Lamarque and Olsen 1994). This intention on the part of the story-teller can be thought of as a Gricean or reflexive meaning-intention (Currie 1990), an intention that is realized by its being recognized as such. What is important about all intention-based views is that they focus on the origins of fictions in utterances of a certain kind—to wit, 'fictive utterances'—rather than in relations between fiction and fact.

However, not all theorists accept this refocusing. Walton (1990) denies that fiction making—or any intentional act—is at the heart of the institution of fiction. For him it is objects, namely those 'whose function is to serve as props in games of make-believe', not acts, that are definitive of fiction. Walton emphasizes the variety of fictions, which are not restricted to narratives—a reason in itself to reject speech act accounts of fiction—including even dolls, children's mud pies, family portraits, indeed all representations, in the class of fictions. Whatever one thinks of this permissive broadening of the extension, which rests more on theoretical stipulation than on ordinary usage, it seems implausible to remove intention altogether from an account of fiction. Even the faces we see in the clouds or the freak writing on seaside rocks (Walton's examples) become representations, *contra* Walton, only by being purposively assimilated into human activities or imaginings (Levinson 1996: 296; Lamarque and Olsen 1994: 47–9).

6. DISCOURSE ABOUT FICTION

Fictional discourse or story-telling is not the same as discourse about fiction. When we describe what goes on in a story, we are not telling the story, but are making a report of a certain kind and thus aiming at truth. But what are the truth-conditions of fiction-reports? Clearly, some of the issues from the ontology debate re-surface here, with putative answers depending on whether eliminativist or accommodationist strategies are adopted. (Thus, the truth of the report 'Holmes is a detective', for an accommodationist, might rest on the fact that a property is being truly ascribed to a fictitious entity.) But a different aspect of the debate has been prominent in recent philosophical discussion, one that does not directly engage the ontological issue. This is a discussion about 'truth in fiction' or, in Walton's terms, the 'principles of generation' that govern fictional truths.

The issue can be stated simply. In reading fiction we take certain things to be true about a fictional world, often making inferences beyond what is explicit in the fictional narrative. We are not told explicitly that Holmes has a kidney, or blood in his veins, but we take it for granted that he does, given that he is a normal human being, and not a robot or Martian. But what are the principles governing inferences of this kind? Walton (1990: chapter 4) identifies two competing principles, the Reality Principle and the Mutual Belief Principle, both of which seem initially plausible. According to the first, we assume the fictional world to be as like the real world as is compatible with what is explicitly stated. We fill in missing fictional details against a background of fact. According to the second, it is not reality or fact that should constrain our inferences, but common beliefs, shared at the time the narrative was written.

A common objection to the Reality Principle is that it licenses seemingly inappropriate or anachronistic inferences (Walton 1990; Currie 1990; Lewis 1978). Modern theories of astronomy or nuclear physics or human psychology would generate fictional truths in the worlds of Sophocles or Chaucer totally at odds with the implied contemporary background. Not only are the truths anachronistic, but arguably there are too many of them, in too great detail (Parsons 1980; Wolterstorff 1980). Do abstruse facts about quarks or quasars belong in the world of *Oedipus Rex*? Of course, the idea of a 'fictional world' is itself unclear, so how determinate or wide in scope the 'contents' of such a world might be is debatable.

One advantage of the Mutual Belief Principle is that, as Walton puts it, it 'gives the artist better control over what is fictional' (Walton 1990: 153). If a writer and his community believe that the earth is flat or is stationary, then those become fictional truths in his stories, assuming no indications to the contrary. However, it is not always clear what are the mutual beliefs in a community, and if a writer is at odds with such beliefs then distorted inferences, particularly about psychological or moral matters, might result from too rigid an appeal to contemporary attitudes. Currie (1990: §2.6) has offered a version of the Mutual Belief Principle according to which what is true in fiction is what it is reasonable for an informed reader to infer that the fictional author believes. What a fictional author believes will thus be a construction from common beliefs of the time, but also will be constrained by the tone and implications of the actual narrative.

Lewis (1978) has offered versions of both principles in terms of possible worlds. He compares reasoning about what is true in fiction to counterfactual reasoning (what would be the case if…), suggesting that we need to compare the worlds where the story is told as known fact with, in one version, the real world or, in a second version, the mutually believed world of contemporary readers, and in both cases to determine the closest fit. Objections have been made, though, to this possible world analysis (Currie 1990; Lamarque 1996). First, possible worlds are unlike fictional worlds in being determinate in every detail and also self-consistent; and second, the inquiry into truth in fiction looks less like a quasi-factual inquiry, and rather more like an inquiry into variably interpretable meanings.

Walton (1990) is of the view that neither principle comprehends all the intuitively correct inferences and that the 'mechanics of generation' are fundamentally 'disorderly'. It does seem right that no entirely neat formulation captures the truth-conditions of discourse about fiction. The difficulty and indeterminateness of 'truth in fiction' are reflected at the level of literary interpretation in longstanding critical disputes about what a character is 'really like', or what construction to put on novelistic events and actions, or what 'thesis', if any, is ultimately being advanced by a work of imaginative literature.

7. FICTION AND EMOTION

A final topic that has attracted a great deal of philosophical attention is the so-called 'paradox of fiction' with regard to emotion. The problem is to explain our apparent emotional responses to what is known to be fictional, and is usually expressed by highlighting three mutually inconsistent but intuitively plausible propositions (Currie 1990; Levinson 1997; Yanal 1999; Joyce 2000) along the following lines:

1. Readers or audiences often experience emotions such as fear, pity, desire, and admiration towards objects they know to be fictional, e.g. fictional characters.
2. A necessary condition for experiencing emotions such as fear, pity, desire, etc., is that those experiencing them believe the objects of their emotions to exist.
3. Readers or audiences who know that the objects are fictional do not believe that these objects exist.

In a helpful survey of the literature, Jerrold Levinson (1997) has discerned no fewer than seven distinct classes of solutions, some with multiple subvariants, covering seemingly every possible route out of the paradox. Some purported solutions have had less support than others. For example, the idea that we should reject proposition 3, perhaps because audiences swept up in fictions 'half-believe' that the fictional events are real or, in Coleridge's expression, 'suspend disbelief' in their reality, has few modern adherents. Sophisticated audiences, to whom the paradox is addressed, do not come to believe, or even to half-believe, that fictional characters are real people, though such characters might *seem* quite real. In fact, the truth of proposition 3 is widely accepted, thus making the key suspect in the paradox either 1 or 2 or both, and it is to these that most attention is directed.

One of the most influential theories, advanced by Kendall Walton, favours the rejection of proposition 1. According to Walton (1990), it is only make-believe, not literally true, that we fear or pity or admire fictional characters, even though the emotions we experience towards them have certain phenomenological similarities to fear, pity, or admiration. Walton labels the feelings actually experienced 'quasi fear', 'quasi pity', and so on, emphasizing that, although these responses are not the same as real fear, real pity, etc., they may none the less be 'highly charged emotionally' (Walton 1997: 38). Walton insists on the truth of proposition 2. Not only must emotions like fear and pity have a belief element (believing that the objects exist), they must also involve dispositions to act (to flee in the case of fear, to offer solace in the case of pity) that are, again, missing in the fiction case. Audiences in their games of make-believe with fictional works imagine that the events described are occurring and they also imagine that they, the audience, are responding emotionally to them. About his famous case of Charles and the movie slime, Walton writes: 'He [Charles] experiences quasi fear as a result of realizing that fictionally the slime threatens him. This makes it fictional that his quasi fear is caused by a belief that the slime poses a threat, and hence that he fears the slime' (Walton 1990: 245).

The attraction of Walton's account is that it fits neatly into his more general theory of fictions and squares with his uncompromising eliminativist ontology. Versions of the account have been advanced by Currie (1990), who incorporates 'simulation theory', and by Levinson (1996, 1997). However, for many (Neill 1991, 1993; Moran 1994; Lamarque 1996; Dadlez 1997; Yanal 1999) it is just too counterintuitive to deny that audiences experience real fear or pity or desire or admiration towards fictional characters in standard cases and not just in exceptional ones. How could people be so systematically mistaken about their emotional states? Why should imagining horrific scenes lead only to imagining being afraid?

Some alternative solutions choose to reject proposition 2. Perhaps the belief condition for emotions such as fear, pity, and admiration can be relaxed (Morreall 1993). After all, there are kinds of fears, phobic fears, where the fearer apparently does not believe he is in danger. However, it does not seem right to assimilate fear in the fictional cases with phobia (Neill 1995; Joyce 2000), and, as Levinson (1997) points out, the belief that an object *exists* could be a requirement for fear even if belief that the object is *dangerous* is not. But is existential belief in fact required? Arguably not.

At the heart of one prominent alternative to the make-believe theory, so-called Thought Theory (versions of which are defended in Carroll 1990; Lamarque 1996; Feagin 1996; Gron 1996; Dadlez 1997; Yanal 1999) is the claim that vivid imagining can be a substitute for belief. According to this view, by bringing to mind fictional events and characters, an audience can be genuinely frightened, or moved to pity, or struck by desire or admiration. The mechanism is causal: the fear or the pity is caused *by* the thought. But the fear is not *of* the thought. The 'of' locution ('fear of the slime') captures the *content* of the emotion, providing a non-relational way of characterizing the emotion ('slime-fear', as opposed to, say, 'vampire-fear'). That thoughts can have physiological effects is well recognized in the case of revulsion, embarrassment, or sexual arousal. An analogue of the behavioural disposition condition is also met in Thought Theory, for the disposition to block out a thought takes the place of a disposition to flee from a danger.

Opponents of Thought Theory (Walton 1990; Levinson 1996), apart from objecting to the weakening of proposition 2, worry that there is, on this account, no *object* of the emotion. If Charles is genuinely afraid, they insist, then what is he afraid *of*? One response is to say that there is only an *imagined* object of the fear—the imagined slime—and to repeat again that to speak of the object of the fear is to speak of the intentional characterization of the fear (Lamarque 1991). Another, related, response is to concede that, strictly speaking (*de re*), there is nothing that Charles is afraid of, just as, strictly speaking, although it is true that the Egyptians worshipped Osiris, there is nothing such that the Egyptians worshipped *that* (Gron 1996). It was never part of Thought Theory to suppose that the slime in the movie, the natural candidate for the object of fear, had any kind of reality—in contrast to the reality of *images* of the slime and *thoughts* about it—nor to suppose that Charles is frightened of (in contrast to *by*) a thought. Even on make-believe theories, it is only *make-believe* that there is an object of fear, and 'quasi-fear' itself has no object.

Real-life counterparts are sometimes proposed for the role of objects of fictionally generated emotions. When we grieve for Anna Karenina, it is argued, we are in fact grieving for actual women who themselves suffer similar fates (Paskins 1977); when we fear the movie slime we are fearing actual slimy things. Charlton (1984) holds such a view, linking emotion to a disposition to act in the real world. But this solution arguably misses the particularity of response to fiction: we pity Anna Karenina herself, not just *women in Anna Karenina's predicament* (Boruah 1988). Stressing the former, of course, simply returns us to the paradox.

Levinson (1996: 303), although supporting a broadly Waltonian line, has suggested, plausibly, that elements of truth from different theories should be encompassed in any general solution. Perhaps each of the propositions in the original paradox needs some refinement. Colin Radford (1975) has proposed in effect that the paradox represents a deep irrationality in human behaviour with regard to fiction. We do, he believes, feel genuine pity (admiration, etc.) for fictional characters, but in knowing at the same time that there is nothing real to feel pity towards, we are irrational and inconsistent. Few have accepted this line (for extended commentary, see Boruah 1988; Dadlez 1997; Yanal 1999; Joyce 2000), though it has generated a huge amount of debate.

What the discussion of fiction and emotion serves to emphasize is the importance that human beings attach to engaging imaginatively with fictional characters and situations. Any account of the value of fiction in human lives should probably begin with that fact. This engagement also has a learning dimension (Novitz 1987), and it is common to seek in the great works of literary fiction some vision of human nature developed through a fictional subject matter (Lamarque and Olsen 1994). Of course it remains a further question, outside the scope of this chapter, what values are to be sought in works of literature. Fiction—the invention of character and incident—is but a vehicle for literary art, and not all fiction is of intrinsic value. However, there are instrumental values attaching to the practice of fiction—creativity, imaginativeness, the affording of new perspectives—that give it an enduringly central role in human life.

See also: Art and Emotion; Interpretation in Art; Value in Art; Ontology of Art; Narrative; Literature; Film; Theatre.

BIBLIOGRAPHY

Beardsley, M. C. (1981). 'Fiction As Representation'. *Synthese* 46: 291–313.

Boruah, B. (1988). *Fiction and Emotion: A Study in Aesthetics and the Philosophy of Mind*. Oxford: Clarendon Press.

Carroll, N. (1990). *The Philosophy of Horror, or Paradoxes of the Heart*. New York: Routledge, Chapman & Hall.

Charlton, W. (1984). 'Feeling for the Fictitious'. *British Journal of Aesthetics* 24: 206–16.

Crittenden, C. (1991). *Unreality: The Metaphysics of Fictional Objects*. Ithaca, NY: Cornell University Press.

Currie, G. (1990). *The Nature of Fiction*. Cambridge: Cambridge University Press.

Dadlez, E. M. (1997). *What's Hecuba To Him? Fictional Events and Actual Emotions*. University Park, Pa.: Pennsylvania State University Press.

Dammann, R. (1992). 'Emotion and Fiction'. *British Journal of Aesthetics* 32: 13–20.

Emt, J. (1992). 'On the Nature of Fictional Entities', in J. Emt and G. Hermerén (eds.), *Understanding the Arts: Contemporary Scandinavian Aesthetics*. Lund: Lund University Press.

Feagin, S. L. (1996). *Reading with Feeling: The Aesthetics of Appreciation*. Ithaca, NY: Cornell University Press.

Gale, R. M. (1971). 'The Fictive Use of Language'. *Philosophy* 46: 324–39.

Goodman, N. (1961). 'About'. *Mind* 70: 1–24.

——(1968). *Languages of Art*. Indianapolis: Bobbs-Merrill.

——(1978). *Ways of Worldmaking*, Brighton: Harvester Press.

——(1984). *Of Mind and Other Matters*, Cambridge, Mass.: Harvard University Press.

Gron, E. (1996). 'Defending Thought Theory from a Make-Believe Threat'. *British Journal of Aesthetics* 36: 311–12.

Hartz, G. (1999). 'How We Can be Moved by Anna Karenina, Green Slime, and a Red Pony'. *Philosophy* 74: 557–78.

Hjort, M. and Laver, S. (eds.) (1997). *Emotion and the Arts*. Oxford: Oxford University Press.

Howell, R. (1979). 'Fictional Objects: How They Are and How They Aren't'. *Poetics* 8: 129–77.

Joyce, R. (2000). 'Rational Fear of Monsters'. *British Journal of Aesthetics* 40: 209–24.

Kroon, F. (1994). 'Make-Believe and Fictional Reference'. *Journal of Aesthetics and Art Criticism* 52: 207–14.

Lamarque, P. V. (1991). Essay Review of Kendall Walton's *Mimesis as Make-Believe*. *Journal of Aesthetics and Art Criticism* 49: 161–6.

—— (1996). *Fictional Points of View*. Ithaca, NY: Cornell University Press.

—— and Olsen, S. H. (1994). *Truth, Fiction, and Literature: A Philosophical Perspective*. Oxford: Clarendon Press.

Levinson, J. (1981). Review of Terence Parsons's *Nonexistent Objects*. *Journal of Aesthetics and Art Criticism* 40: 96–9.

—— (1996). *The Pleasures of Aesthetics: Philosophical Essays*. Ithaca, NY: Cornell University Press.

—— (1997). 'Emotion in Response to Art: A Survey of the Terrain', in Hjort and Laver (1997).

Lewis, D. (1978). 'Truth in Fiction'. *American Philosophical Quarterly* 15: 37–46.

McCormick, P. (1985). 'Feelings and Fictions'. *Journal of Aesthetics and Art Criticism* 44: 375–83.

Meinong, A. (1904/1960). 'Theory of Objects', in R. M. Chisholm (ed.), *Realism and the Background of Phenomenology*. Glencoe, Ill.: Free Press.

Moran, R. (1994). 'The Expression of Feeling in Imagination'. *Philosophical Review* 103: 75–106.

Morreall, J. (1993). 'Fear Without Belief'. *Journal of Philosophy* 90: 359–66.

Neill, A. (1991). 'Fear, Fiction and Make-Believe'. *Journal of Aesthetics and Art Criticism* 49: 47–56.

—— (1993). 'Fiction and the Emotions'. *American Philosophical Quarterly* 30: 1–13.

—— (1995). 'Fear and Belief'. *Philosophy and Literature* 19: 94–101.

Novitz, D. (1987). *Knowledge, Fiction and Imagination*. Philadelphia: Temple University Press.

Ogden, C. K. (1932). *Bentham's Theory of Fictions*. London: Kegan Paul, Trench, Trubner.

Ohmann, R. (1971). 'Speech Acts and the Definition of Fiction'. *Philosophy and Rhetoric* 4: 1–19.

Parsons, T. (1980). *Nonexistent Objects*. New Haven: Yale University Press.

Paskins, B. (1977). 'On Being Moved by Anna Karenina and *Anna Karenina*'. *Philosophy* 52: 344–7.

Pelletier, J. (2000). 'Actualisme et fiction'. *Dialogue* 39: 77–99.

Prado, C. G. (1984). *Making Believe: Philosophical Reflections on Fiction*. Westport, Conn.: Greenwood.

Quine, W. V. O. (1953). 'On What There Is', in his *From a Logical Point of View*, Cambridge, Mass.: Harvard University Press.

Radford, C. (1975). 'How Can We be Moved by the Fate of Anna Karenina?' *Proceedings of the Aristotelian Society*, suppl. vol. 49: 67–80.

Rorty, R. (1982). 'Is There a Problem About Fictional Discourse?' In his *Consequences of Pragmatism*. Brighton: Harvester Press.

Russell, B. (1905/1956). *Logic and Knowledge*, ed. R. C. Marsh. London: George Allen & Unwin (includes 'On Denoting' and 'The Philosophy of Logical Atomism').

Salmon, N. (1998). 'Nonexistence'. *Nous* 32: 277–319.

Savile, A. (1998). 'Imagination and the Content of Fiction'. *British Journal of Aesthetics* 38: 136–49.

Schaper, E. (1978). 'Fiction and the Suspension of Disbelief'. *British Journal of Aesthetics* 18: 31–44.

Searle, J. R. (1979). 'The Logical Status of Fictional Discourse', in his *Expression and Meaning: Studies in the Theory of Speech Acts*. Cambridge: Cambridge University Press.

Thomasson, A. (1999). *Fiction and Metaphysics*. Cambridge: Cambridge University Press.

Urmson, J. O. (1976). 'Fiction'. *American Philosophical Quarterly* 13: 153–7.

van Inwagen, P. (1977) 'Creatures of Fiction'. *American Philosophical Quarterly* 14: 299–308.

Walton, K. L. (1990). *Mimesis as Make-Believe*. Cambridge, Mass.: Harvard University Press.

—— (1997). 'Spelunking, Simulation, and Slime: On Being Moved by Fiction', in Hjort and Laver (1997).

Wolterstorff, N. (1980). *Works and Worlds of Art*. Oxford: Clarendon Press.

Yanal, R. J. (1999). *Paradoxes of Emotion and Fiction*. University Park, Pa.: Pennsylvania State University Press.

Zalta, E. (1983). *Abstract Objects*. Dordrecht: Reidel.

Zemach, E. (1998). 'Tom Sawyer and the Beige Unicorn'. *British Journal of Aesthetics* 38: 167–79.

CHAPTER 22

....

NARRATIVE

....

GEORGE M. WILSON

IN 'The Art of Fiction', Henry James asserts: 'The story and the novel, the idea and the form, are the needle and thread, and I never heard of a guild of tailors who recommended the use of the thread without the needle, or the needle without the thread' (James 1986: 178). Although James is here granting the existence of a distinction between the *story*, on the one hand, and the novel (as *text*), on the other, he insists, in the larger context of his remarks, on the ambiguity and allusiveness of the concept of 'story'. After James, a guild of narratologists has arisen to explicate the ambiguities and mitigate the allusiveness of the concept. For instance, a story is undoubtedly a *narrative*, but the term 'narrative', like the term 'statement', is 'act-object' ambiguous. Thus, compare

(*a*) There are often both film and literary versions of the same narrative

with

(*b*) Flannery was interrupted several times in the course of her narrative by bouts of weeping.

In the 'object' sense, featured in (*a*), the word refers to a series of represented events, processes, and states, together with the temporal and causal relations in which those occurrences are represented as standing. This is narrative as 'fabula' or '*narrative product*', and it is probably the favoured conception of 'story'. However, the term 'narrative' may also refer to the extended representational activity in virtue of which the events and their temporal/causal relations come to be articulated. In other words, it may mean '*narration*', as it does in (*b*). The more technical phrase 'narrative discourse' bears this sense as well, although it is further employed to denote the concrete text in which the narrational activity is embodied. In the statement

(c) The narrative of the accident had been erased from the report

'narrative' occurs also in this third use. Gerard Genette drew a famous distinction between 'histoire', 'narration', and 'recit' (Genette 1982), and his terms correspond at least roughly to the use of 'story', 'narration', and 'text' outlined above. It will emerge in the course of the present discussion that each concept in the trio generates significant problems.

Narratology (the term comes from Tzvetan Todorov) is the general theory of narratives and the structures they exemplify. The classical structuralist narratology of Todorov, C. Bremond, A. Greimas, and early Roland Barthes was concerned primarily with narrative as narrative product. In selecting that emphasis and in other methodological matters, these authors were influenced by their proto-structuralist predecessors, Russian formalists such as V. Shklovsky and V. Propp. Theorists in the linked traditions highlighted the fact that stories, both fictional and non-fictional, can be represented in very different narrative discourses. Indeed, the same story can be rendered in discourses that have been constructed within different media, such as literature, film, or theatre. A key analytical task of structuralist narratology has been to delineate the features of stories that are invariant across the fiction/non-fiction division and across the variety of their more specific realizations in different discourses and media. Hence, given any narrative discourse, it should be possible to distinguish, without major equivocation, a text, a narration, and a story that is told.

Many theorists of narrative have defended proposals concerning the essential nature of narratives, and it has been widely agreed that a genuine narrative requires the representation of a minimum of two events and some indication of the ordering in time of the events depicted. It is often claimed, in addition, that the domain of narrative events has to exhibit at least some sort of fragmentary causal structure, although even this weak and apparently plausible claim has been disputed. In fact, various modes of causal relation can be distinguished, and among these their represented instances in a particular discourse will comprise the 'narrative connections' that help to constitute it as the presentation of a narrative. The whole enterprise of trying to give necessary and/or sufficient conditions for being a narrative seems misguided. Modernist and postmodernist experiments in literary fiction, not to mention much earlier works like Sterne's *Tristram Shandy* and Diderot's *Jacques L'Fataliste*, have experimented with 'stories' that abrogate nearly every familiar convention and schema of narrative construction. In an early essay, Genette declared: 'We know how, in various and sometimes contradictory ways, modern literature...has striven and succeeded, in its very foundations, to be a questioning, a disturbance, a contestation of the notion of narrative' (Genette 1982: 127). It is fruitless, in the aftershock of that disturbance, to argue too sharply about the boundary at which genuine story-making has come to be replaced by something else. Nevertheless, the careful delineation of a range of protypical narrative connections can illuminate the diverse intuitive bases of our judgements concerning narrativity (Carroll 2001).

In any case, such questions of definition or essence easily distract from other issues of at least as great an interest. For instance, it is obviously not essential to a plot-like structure of events that its sequential representation tends to awaken curiosity, personal identification, and suspense in potential audiences. Nevertheless, it is an important fact about certain events in many stories that they have the specific narrative function of defining the predicaments the characters face and of thereby eliciting suitable responses from a concerned audience. Similarly, it is not essential that a narration eventually provide additional depicted materials whose function is to satisfy the audience's engagement with the characters by showing how the predicaments come to be resolved. And yet, of course, most popular narratives have been designed with the aim of achieving both of these objectives. Such general considerations about audience attention and imaginative involvement presumably help to explain why audiences value storytelling so much and why they repeat the stories they learn, with variations, in many settings and contexts. What is more, a wide range of the strategic features of particular narratives are most naturally explained in terms of the storyteller's intentions of arousing and gratifying an audience's expectations of dramatic closure. Classical narratology was inclined to abstract from the strategic objectives of storytellers and the anticipatory interest of their audiences, and, because it conceptualized 'narrative' primarily in terms of structure, it paid scant attention to the dilemma-driven forces that animate the more familiar narrative forms for their readers and spectators.

Recent theorists of narrative have sought to rectify this omission. They have rightly emphasized that narratives are structures of events that are themselves 'meaningful', although the meaning of a narrative episode is of an altogether different nature from the meaning of a linguistic construction or act. Narratives assign meaning or significance to the events they incorporate by situating them within an explanatory pattern that typically delineates both their causal roles and their teleological contributions to the needs and goals of the characters. They provide a global account of dramatically highlighted behaviour by specifying salient causes of the agents' actions and by charting some of the consequences that those actions engender. In constructing a story, narrators typically seek to provide a surveyable pattern of explanatory connections that opens up its component occurrences to plausible perspectives of evaluation, where these perspectives may invoke prudential, moral, political, and other frameworks of assessment. The meaning of a designated episode is determined by its place in an explanatory pattern of this kind, and it is constituted by whatever that position reveals to an audience from the evaluative perspectives they deploy (Wilson 1997a). Confusion about the concept of 'meaning', as the notion applies to the events of a narrative, has badly distorted many accounts of what it is to interpret a narrative by assimilating narrative meaning to one or another of the types of meaning that are expressed in language use.

Wayne Booth, in *The Company We Keep* (1998), and Martha Nussbaum, in *Love's Knowledge* (1990), have made extended attempts to recover these vital aspects of narrative for contemporary theory and criticism. They have defended at length a number of bold claims about the distinctive character of the moral and psychological knowledge that complex narratives, including fictional narratives, can supply. Nussbaum maintains that 'certain truths about human life can *only* be fittingly and accurately stated in the language and forms characteristic of the narrative artist' (Nussbaum 1990: 4; my emphasis). More specifically, she holds that these are principally truths concerning 'the projected morality' (in Henry James's phrase) that are implicitly exemplified in suitable configurations of narrative events. Moreover, she maintains that 'the language and forms of narrative', in their most subtle and incisive instances, teach us the fine discrimination of ethically relevant attributes in agents, actions, and the circumstances of significant moral choice.

In a related but contrasting vein, critics like Frank Kermode (1968) and Peter Brooks (1984) have explored the powerful but often suppressed agendas that partially govern the idiosyncratic trajectories of plot construction. Most narratives are devised from the outset to reach an ending that will realize the audience's desire for the dramatic development to culminate in an apt and satisfying conclusion. But Brooks, in particular, stresses that the reader's sense of a proper ending is highly variable and has a complicated range of determinants. Moreover, these determinants will probably include the reader's self-censored wishes concerning the fictional action, wishes that may be perverse or otherwise threatening to awareness. Hence a form of narrative closure that readers find 'apt and satisfying' may, at the same time, disturb them and even represent an unconscious source of revulsion or horror.

It is frequently claimed that the recounting of narratives is a human universal. However, given that any telling or showing of something that purportedly took place is already the production of a narrative, it is hard to see how narrativity could fail to be ubiquitous among cultures where a system of representation that registers causation is in use. Early narratologists characteristically maintained that the range of types of story within a culture (or even across cultures) were strikingly similar in terms of their basic narrative constituents and the underlying configurations of their plots. These similarities, it was argued, are such that the stories from an appropriately large and significant corpus can often be 'generated' by suitably general rules of combination and transformation. Vladimir Propp's *Morphology of the Russian Folktale* (1968) attempted to establish that the 'wonder tales' he studied could be represented as the product of certain generative rules, where those rules operate on a restricted base of narrative 'functions', i.e. roughly, types of fictional action, situation, and effect. Many of the theorists who followed Propp and were influenced by him thus thought of themselves as developing a grammar of narrative. Unfortunately, the import of the analogy with linguistic grammar is generally murky in these writings. Some of their authors describe themselves as analysing a basic conceptual competence that shapes, more or less *a priori*, the creation and the comprehension of stories that humans tell, whether the stories are make-believe or not.

It is difficult to evaluate either the correctness or the interest of proposals elaborated along these lines. First, the fundamental categories in terms of which the story-generating rules get formulated are extremely general, and correspondingly vague. Second, it is usually unclear just what domain of actual and possible stories is covered by the generative rules in question; hence even the descriptive adequacy of the theories is hard to assess effectively. Third, even if the descriptive adequacy of a given theory were conceded, it remains uncertain what explanatory force the 'grammatical' model in narrative theory is supposed to have. Structuralist narratolgy has espoused the etiological priority of schematic narrative structures over their more concrete manifestations in storytelling discourse. It is maintained that storytellers are guided in their construction of a concrete narration by grasping, in the first instance, a relatively abstract narrative structure which then governs the elaboration, within a chosen medium, of the more concrete and accessible particulars of 'shallow' narrative discourse. This may be so, but the evidence in its favour is slim and equivocal at best.

A number of critics and theorists, less influenced by semiotics and structuralism, have devoted considerable attention to some of the more systematic ways in which the activity of narration and the flow of narrative information gets regulated in narrative discourse. An early instance of such a study is Percy Lubbock's *The Craft of Fiction* (1921), and Wayne Booth's *The Rhetoric of Fiction* (1983) is a classic of this alternative tradition. Both books elaborate and extend the topic of (narrational) 'point of view', and subsequent narratologists have taken up this subject and the investigation of other intrinsic parameters that are implicated in the normal telling of a tale. For example, Genette (1980) observed that talk of 'point of view' was liable to run together questions of narrational *voice* and questions of narrational *focalization* (or *mood*). In literary narrative fiction, it is one thing to ask who or what it is that is fictionally producing the words of the narration. The fictional or fictionalized being who does the narrating (the *narrator*) may be a person who is portrayed as belonging to the narrative action (*homodiegetic*); or the narrator may be a fictive creation of the work who is not a character within the story at all (*heterodiegetic*). This is the question of who 'speaks' the narration—the question of 'voice'. On the other hand, it is possible that the fictional information that the narrator conveys may be restricted to the information available only to a certain character, but the focalizing character in question need not be the narrator. Henry James's novel *What Maisie Knew* (1897) is famous for rendering the events of the story as they are seen and imperfectly understood by a young girl, Maisie. The words of the narration, however, are not her own; they are the product of a highly articulate Jamesian 'voice' who has unlimited knowledge of her thoughts and feelings about the action. In many mystery novels, it is not the detective who relates the progress of his or her investigation, although the narration is focalized from the detective's perspective. Alternatively, the narrator may dispense information that is methodically constrained in any one of several other general ways. For example, it may be a tacit condition upon the narration that the narrator has no direct access to the inner life of other characters. And, of course, the narration may operate without any significant epistemic constraints at all and hence be 'omniscient' in that sense. These matters all fall under the broad conception of 'focalization'.

Genette and his intellectual descendants also explored other types of systematic interrelation between narrative texts on the one hand, and the stories they narrate on the other. In his book, *Narrative Discourse*, Genette (1980) scrutinized the connections that hold between the implicitly represented *time* of the narrational activity and the temporal framework in which the narrated events are embedded. Thus, the *order* in which the occurrences are introduced and described in the narration may be different from the order these events are supposed to have exemplified in narrative time. The *duration* of a depicted episode may or may not correspond to the relative length at which it is elaborated in the narrative discourse, and the *frequency* with which a type of event occurs in the story, or the *frequency* with which a single event is mentioned in the text, may vary significantly from instance to instance.

Gerald Prince (1982) has underscored the importance of the fact that many fictional narrations are represented as being addressed to an internal audience, a *narratee*, whose implied characteristics influences the nature of the narrator's performance in notable ways. Mieke Bal (1985), Meir Steinberg (1978), and Thomas Pavel (1986) are other important practitioners of approaches to narrative construction that are more flexible, more nuanced, and more broadly conceived than the standard analyses of early structuralist narratology. While the earlier works were likely to treat 'narrative discourse' as a vehicle from which the narratologist abstracts suitable structural generalities of story content, the more recent tradition has given closer consideration to the variety and complexity of the ways in which the activity of narration is goal-directed and internally monitored to meet those goals. Like Booth and Lubbock before them, these theorists are concerned with the ways in which narrational strategies complicate an audience's epistemic and empathetic access to the narrative occurrences.

Although a lot of studies of narrative and narrative discourse are subtle and complex, the basic concept of 'narration' has been and continues to be a source of abundant puzzlement. In narratology, the paradigm of narration has been literary narration, despite the fact that it has attributes that do not generalize easily to other narrational modes. We will shortly examine some of the ways in which this is so. In a literary work of non-fiction narrative, the narration consists of the various kinds of *speech acts* (illocutionary acts) performed by *the author* in the construction of the story. That is, the actual author, in the course of composing the linguistic text, asserts propositions, introduces suppositions, raises questions, etc., and it is this linear network of linked linguistic acts that tells the purported history. The reader is meant to grasp both the 'propositional' contents expressed and the illocutionary force of the linguistic acts the author has performed. However, when works of narrative fiction are in question—in novels for instance—the concept of 'narration' exhibits a widely recognized ambiguity.

The novelist Anna Sewell told a story about a horse, Black Beauty, when she wrote her novel of that name; but in the novel it is Black Beauty, the horse himself, who tells his own story. So there are two activities of 'telling a story' connected with the very same literary text, and there is a difference in agency, ontology, and illocutionary kind between them. One distinguishes between the 'storytelling' activity of actual authors who, sentence by sentence, *make it fictional* in their stories that certain happenings and circumstances took place, and the counterpart *fictional* activity of recounting or reporting those occurrences as real. It is customary, in discussions of literary narrative fiction, to reserve 'narrating' for the fictional recounting of narrative events, and I will use 'fiction-making' to designate the activity of telling that it is the business of the author to conduct. Narration (narrating), so understood, is an internal component of the total work of fiction, although it is generally no part of the story that is being narrated. It is an implicitly indicated activity that is, so to speak, 'scripted' for the reader in the words of the text. As I suggested earlier, the narrator of a fictional story is the agent who narrates the story, the person who fictionally asserts that certain events took place and who, in many cases, comments fictionally on aspects of the evolving plot. The narrators of fictional stories are themselves fictive constructs of the works that incorporate them. By contrast, the author, in writing the text, creates both the fictional history of narrative action and the wider fiction that an actual record of that history has come to be transcribed in the text. It is through the mediation of the facts about the fictional telling that the fictional facts of the narrative product are generated, either directly or by implication. Later we will consider the question of what 'machinery of generation' might be in operation here.

There has been a weak consensus among theorists that the fictional activity of narrating a literary story conceptually *presupposes* the existence of a fictional or fictionalized narrator who carries out that task, although the conceptual character of the presupposition is certainly open to question. Our intuitions about the issue are less than decisive. Nevertheless, it *is* usual for narrators to be created in narrative fictions, and the existence in literature of a rich variety of fictional narrators is a familiar and important part of our experience in reading novels and short stories. The reader's imagined relations with narrators, complicated or otherwise, can be one of the chief pleasures in reading a complex story. Many studies of literary point of view, like Booth's *The Rhetoric of Fiction* (1983), are concerned with potentially central features of fictional narrators and with their possible relations to the characters and circumstances within the story.

I have already noted that narrators may themselves be characters who figure in their own stories or, at least, within some broader fictional history that explains how they have their knowledge of the story they relate. Alternatively, the way in which a narrator knows of the events recounted may not be specified, and hence he or she may stand in no determinate epistemic relation to the world of the story at all. These questions pertain to the type of *authority* with which the narrator speaks. What is more, in either of these cases, the psychological properties and moral attributes of the narrator may be, in varying degrees, delineated, either because the narrator simply *self-ascribes* them, or because they are implicitly *dramatized* in the manner of the telling or both. At one extreme within this range, the narrator may remain *effaced*—a relatively neutral voice who simply tells the story. At another extreme are *self-conscious* narrators who comment on their own performances as narrators and on the nature of the narration they are fashioning. In addition, it is possible for a dramatized narrator to be represented as a type of person who is, relative to the norms endorsed by the work, wholly admirable, totally unsympathetic, or, more often, somewhere in between. Finally, as noted earlier, the narration may reveal that the narrator is *unreliable* in the rendering of at least certain key aspects of his or her recounting. These and other systematic considerations have formed the basis for an elaborate and still evolving taxonomy of fictional narrators.

In the context of his discussion of narrators, Booth also introduced the further concept of *the implied author*. The experience of readers in reading the total work of fiction, including their imaginative relations with the work's narrator, will very often present them with a lively, well grounded impression of the personality, sensibility, and intelligence of the person who actually crafted the work, i.e. the real author. And this impression may be a critically and aesthetically important part of the reader's reaction to the work, whether or not the impression accurately reflects true facts about the historical author. Thus, in characterizing their perception of what the work as a multifaceted artefact conveys, readers may well want to incorporate an account of the way in which the fiction-making activity that produced it serves as an apparent expression of the author's psychology and outlook on the world. If so, then the reader is thereby describing the properties of the work's 'implied author'—or, better, is describing a version of the author that the work apparently implies.

The basic concepts of narratology purport to apply univocally to different instances of particular narratives, including narratives represented in different media. One might therefore expect to find that different modes of narration stand at the foundations of each of the different kinds of storytelling. One might expect, in other words, that, whenever a narrative has somehow been presented, there must be some kind of narration that has presented it. However, this trivial sounding thesis gives rise to problems of real substance. Consider, first, the case of stories that have been staged and enacted, say in a theatre, for an audience that is present at the staging. Many theorists, following Aristotle, maintain that theatrical performances of stories do not as such involve narration, contrasting stories that are conveyed by a *telling* or *recounting* of the fictional action with stories that are transmitted by *mimesis*, or by histrionic imitation. On this conception, genuine narration requires an articulated, perspectival telling of the story, a situated recounting of the relevant events. This conception does allow that the telling in the narration need not be linguistic, although it is not always clear just what the range of non-linguistic tellings might be. Of course, the intermittent use of voice-over narration, as part of a play or a film, is relatively unproblematic, and that device is not in question here.

The case of fiction film is interesting in this regard. It is prima facie plausible that the edited image track of a film involves a genuine pictorial telling, i.e. a showing or visual displaying of fictional events that is both perspectival, because of the nature of cinematic photography, and articulated, principally because of the editing. If this is so, then the pictorial telling characteristic of films supplements the purely mimetic dimension of staging and dramatic performance in the cinema. However, even if it is granted that a sort of pictorial telling is intrinsic to narrative film, it is still not obvious, in the first place, whether its presence presupposes the existence of a cinematic narrator who does the telling. Could there not be an activity of visual telling that, like the activity of snowing, is not itself the action of an agent? In an extensive debate among film theorists, affirmative and negative answers to this second question have been endorsed with equal conviction.

But let it be allowed provisionally that every fiction film involves, in the sense adumbrated above, a visual telling of its story. Nevertheless, it is not obvious, in the second place, that this mode of visual telling constitutes a true analogue to narration in literary fiction. I have emphasized, in discussing fictional narratives in literature, that the preferred referent of 'narration' is the work-internal fictional reporting of events, and the term 'narrator' refers, by stipulation, to the fictional or fictionalized agent who reports them. If there is to be an analogous activity of pictorial narration in movies, then some argument is needed to establish that a movie's image track implicitly adumbrates a fictional activity of visual telling, i.e. an activity of showing (displaying to vision) the objects and events that are represented therein. In the absence of such an argument, there is no reason to accept the thesis that the articulated, perspectival pictorial telling in fiction films is anything more than a matter of an articulated, perspectival fiction-making by means of motion picture images—the undoubted activity that the actual film-makers have carried out. The expressive characteristics of visual and, for that matter, audiovisual fiction-making, whether they are global or strictly local, may provide grounds for analysing the apparent psychology of the implied (albeit collective) film-maker, but they do not, as such, comprise evidence for the existence of a distinctively cinematic narrator.

The needed argument will not be easy to make persuasively. Relatively simple forms of visual narrative construction, like hand-shadow shows and simple comic strips, normally do not depict or otherwise evoke a work-internal activity of visually exhibiting the narrative action to an implicit audience. Of course, the creators of these rudimentary forms of visual narrative mean to be showing a story to prospective viewers, and they present the constituent fictional states-of-affairs by fashioning images that depict them. This, of course, is just the pictorial fiction-making they perform. However, in the absence of any special strategy of reflexive self-representation, the pictures do not further depict an activity of someone or something showing a viewer the narrative events. They do not portray, for instance, a fictional activity of setting the events of the story before the viewer's eyes.

It is not surprising that there should be strongly conflicting intuitions when the topic of narration in film is investigated. In so far as a movie narrative has been created by means of staging and acting, it should fall with theatre among the mimetic, non-narrational forms of storytelling. And yet, the fact that these dramatic materials are displayed to spectators through a mediating chain of edited photographic shots gives film an additional discursive character, a character that potentially suffices to establish a dimension of fictive pictorial narration. Whether or not this is so depends, as we have seen, on further hard questions about the nature of photographic representation in the cinema and our imaginative involvement with it, and these are questions there is no space to pursue here. For present purposes, however, I have wanted to draw attention to the ways in which the general concept of 'narration' in works of fiction is conceptually underspecified and exhibits conceptual tensions that remain unresolved.

An adequate theory of narrative needs to offer some account of the ways in which a narration establishes a corresponding narrative, and a view about the determinacy of the story contents that get established in those ways. Issues in this area are also delicate and difficult. If it is assumed, as I have here, that narration in literary fiction is to be identified with the series of story-generating fictional speech acts that are directly represented in the text, then literary narration, so construed, significantly underdetermines the constituents of the corresponding narrative. The event-describing propositions that the narrator overtly affirms fall far short of encompassing everything that a minimally competent reader grasps as part of the story being told. It is evident to able readers that the narrator fictionally presupposes that various other story-relevant propositions are true and, moreover, that the narrator is fictionally implying more than he or she overtly says about what is happening in the story. The salient presuppositions and implications will usually count as a part of the contents of the narrative, and the phrase 'syuzhet' (standardly used to contrast with 'fabula') might be valuably adapted to cover this wider domain of explicit and implicit narrational statement.

Nevertheless, even the wider domain of narrative information is not sufficient to establish the whole of the story (the fabula) that the work conveys. In reading a piece of narrative fiction, the audience is expected to bring a vast range of background assumptions that will be utilized in working out the detailed development of the story, and the background will not, in general, coincide with the class of propositions that fictionally the narrator presupposes. What is more, the portion of the reader's background information that bears upon the unfolding of the story will normally alter over time. As the narration progresses, readers will discover that some of their heretofore pertinent background beliefs should now be dropped or held in abeyance; and, furthermore, the narration, at that stage, may well dictate new information that the audience is supposed to assimilate into their subsequent construction of the story. Readers' comprehension of narratives would be sketchy and riddled with gaps if their readings were not regularly supplemented by the reasonable inferences they draw on the basis of the overt text and the shifting set of background assumptions that they progressively assemble. These considerations show that an adequate theoretical grasp of the determination of narrative content requires an adequate account of the dynamics of narration—an account of the changing suppositions that readers are *entitled* to exploit in their reading. And it concomitantly requires an account of the *legitimate* forms of supplementary inference that mediate their indirect comprehension of the plot.

Readers recognize that even the most definite and unambiguous claims within a fictional narration cannot automatically be accepted at face value. On the one hand, it is probably the case that the explicit statements and evident suggestions in a standard narration are treated as *defeasibly* correct. That is, readers are licensed to add to the story any proposition that the narrator either asserts or distinctly implies unless there are clearcut and specific grounds, internal to the work, for declining to do so. On the other hand, narrative works certainly exist in which an unreliable narrator asserts or suggests incorrect claims about the fictional world, doing so with or without an intention to deceive. In these cases, the standard mechanism for fixing the facts of the narrative fiction is overridden by forces internal to the mechanism that fixes the facts concerning the narration. Ford Madox Ford's *The Good Soldier* is regularly cited as a novel in which the text supplies ample evidence for distrusting the first person narrator of the work.

Suppose, however, that there is some more extensive framework of fictional truths that are more or less directly established by the text. There is, as mentioned above, a further question about the modes of inference that readers may correctly adopt in 'generating' all the rest. In *Mimesis as Make-Believe*, Kendall Walton (1990) discusses this problem of 'the mechanics of generation', and he specifically explores at some length two conceptions of legitimate narrative inference. One conception embraces the so-called 'Reality Principle', and is grounded upon the reader's convictions about what facts really hold in the actual world. The other conception is based upon 'the Mutual Belief Principle', and is governed by the reader's convictions about the beliefs that audiences contemporary with the work would have shared. The first approach corresponds to readings that extrapolate to the implied aspects of the story on the basis of the reader's judgements about what actually would follow if certain states of affair are already established as part of the story. The second approach extrapolates on the basis of the reader's sense of how the readership envisaged by the author would have filled the story out.

According to the 'Realitiy Principle', if readers accept P1 to Pn as fictional in the story S, and if they also accept *the truth of* 'the generating conditional', i.e.

$$\text{if } P_1, P_2, \ldots, \text{ and } P_n \text{ then } Q,$$

then they are authorized to accept Q as fictional in S as well. The Mutual Belief Principle, by contrast, says that, if readers accept P1 to Pn as fictional in S and also accept that *the original audiences for the work mutually believed* 'the generating conditional', then Q is authorized for these readers as fictional in S. Walton holds that we regularly make piecemeal use of one or both of these principles and, no doubt, of still other principles besides. He denies that any single type of inferential strategy provides adequate, fully general coverage of the ways that readers (or, for that matter, viewers) add to their legitimate beliefs about the constituents of narrative. In fact, towards the end of his discussion, he concludes that the inferences we rightly make are too 'unruly' to be readily codified by any orderly and uncluttered account. As he colourfully puts the point, 'The machinery of generation is devised of rubber bands and paper clips and powered by everything from unicorns in traces to baking soda mixed with vinegar' (Walton 1990: 183). Whether these reservations about the possibility of systematic theory in this matter are justified, and, if they are, what their consequences for the interpretation of works of narrative fiction, might be, continue to be important topics of lively controversy.

Jonathan Culler claims that 'the basic question for theory in the domain of narrative is this: is narrative a fundamental form of knowledge (giving knowledge of the world through its sensemaking) or is it a rhetorical structure that distorts as much as it reveals? Is narrative a source of knowledge or of delusion?' (Culler 1997: 94). Culler is certainly right that sceptical questions of this ilk have figured prominently in recent discussions of narrative, but it is hard to make out just what the import of these questions is supposed to be. In the first place, fictional narratives do not, at the first level of endeavour, purport to offer us knowledge: they primarily prescribe imaginings and not beliefs.

Second, most non-fiction narratives do present a certain amount of genuine knowledge about the events they portray, but they also convey some falsehoods, distortions, and, less frequently, out-and-out absurdities. Characteristically, narrations in works of fiction and non-fiction are significantly infused with rhetoric, but rhetorical persuasion is not, as such, incompatible with knowledge. Rhetoric may very well convince an audience of something true. In fact, one would expect the mix of truth and error in narratives to vary substantially from one instance to another. After all, narrative is a loosely defined form or collection of forms that easily accommodates both knowledge and false opinion, and no overall question about the epistemic integrity of the narrative mode makes obvious good sense.

As a rule, narratives are thick with causal claims, and, of course, it is possible to entertain some kind of global scepticism about causation. However, sceptical discussions of narrative do not mount systematic challenges against the very idea of cause and effect, and it would be hard to do so successfully in any case. Hence it is unlikely that universal doubts about causality, or other types of explanatory connection, form the basis of general anti-narrative concerns. Yet, a narrative is necessarily selective in the events it picks out to explain, and it is selective, for a given phenomenon, in the accounting of causal factors it draws up. Some of the selectivity is orchestrated by the global aim of constructing an illuminating pattern of explanation and evaluation for the episodes under examination, and both the principles that guide the selection and the guiding objective of evaluative intelligibility are potential sources of critical suspicion in connection with the explanatory dimension of narrative.

For instance, when a 'correct' judgement has been made that an event E caused another event F, the correctness of the claim is normally grounded in the narrower fact that E was *among* the causal factors that helped give rise to F. The explanatory judgement identifies E from out of all the events, circumstances, and conditions that also played a productive or facilitating role for F. For instance, it may be true enough that certain of an agent's desires and beliefs were causes of her action; but the psychological explanation may leave out larger social and economic forces which equally shaped her behaviour in the context. And the exclusion of social determinants from the explanation may serve a questionable ideological agenda or promote other ends that deserve self-conscious scrutiny themselves. Here the objection to such a narrative will not be that it is predominantly false. It will be that the narrative paints a limited and severely distorted picture of the confluence of causal factors that produced the targeted narrative actions. What is more, the repeated exclusion of perfectly legitimate causes—political causes, for example—may yield grounds for misgivings about the worldview that governed the choice of admissible explanations. Nevertheless, doubts of these types need to be dealt with in terms appropriate to each individual case. Selection in narrative is unavoidable, and the selective discriminations in a particular history, fictional or non-fictional, may be altogether sound and proper in the epistemic setting that gave rise to them. None of the considerations just rehearsed support a general scepticism about 'narrative' as such.

As discussed earlier, story audiences are inclined to want their narratives to have 'apt and satisfying' conclusions, or at least to fall into other large-scale configurations of explanatory significance. It is this hungering after 'narrative meaning' that prompts some of the most persistent sceptical reservations about familiar strategies of plot construction. Audiences are likely to accept one narrative account over an alternative, because the former seems to cast the depicted actions in an especially intelligible light—a light that promotes an apparently convincing assessment of them. However, many theorists of narrative suppose that intelligibility and evaluability are largely conventional attributes that have simply been 'projected upon' the relevant actions without having any justifying basis in the facts. In the passage by Culler quoted above, he may be presupposing that these and similar normative attributes are merely 'rhetorical' considerations that move readers to adopt some preferred story even in the absence of genuine 'evidential' considerations in its favour.

Now, claims of this sort could turn out to be right, but, once again, we are being offered a sweeping brand of scepticism that questions the objectivity and rational grounding of our ordinary frameworks of explanation and evaluation. It would require a very general argument, framed in detail and attentive to key distinctions, to render any of these fashionable scepticisms particularly plausible. Recent theory of narrative has elaborated at great length its qualms about the structures and functions of storytelling, but in my opinion the underlying issues have not been substantially advanced. This is not to deny that there are important questions about the epistemology of narrative, but merely to hope for more nuanced and more judicious investigations of them in the future.

See also: Fiction; Literature; Film; Interpretation in Art.

BIBLIOGRAPHY

Bal, M. (1985). *Narratology: Introduction to the Theory of Narrative*. Toronto: University of Toronto Press.

Barthes, R. (1974). *S/Z*. New York: Hill & Wang.

——(1977). 'An Introduction to the Structural Analysis of Narrative', in *Image–Music–Text*, trans. S. Heath. New York: Hill & Wang.

Booth, W. (1983). *The Rhetoric of Fiction*, rev. edn. Chicago: University of Chicago Press.

——(1988). *The Company We Keep: An Ethics of Fiction*. Berkeley: University of California Press.

Bordwell, D. (1985). *Narration in the Fiction Film*. Madison, Wis.: University of Wisconsin Press.

——(1991). *Making Meaning*. Cambridge, Mass.: Harvard University Press.

Branigan, E. (1992). *Narrative Comprehension and Film*. London: Routledge.

Bremond, C. (1979). *Logic du recit*. Paris: Editions du Seuil.

Brooks, P. (1984). *Reading for the Plot: Design and Intention in Narrative*. New York: Alfred Knopf.

Carroll, N. (1998). *A Philosophy of Mass Art*. Oxford: Oxford University Press.

——(2001). 'On the Narrative Connection', in *Beyond Aesthetics: Philosophical Essays*. Cambridge: Cambridge University Press.

Chatman, S. (1978). *Story and Discourse: Structure in Fiction and Film*. Ithaca, NY: Cornell University Press.

——(1990). *Coming to Terms: The Rhetoric of Narrative in Fiction and Film*. Ithaca, NY: Cornell University Press.

Culler, J. (1975). *Structuralist Poetics*. Ithaca, NY: Cornell University Press.

——(1997). *Literary Theory: A Very Short Introduction*. Oxford: Oxford University Press.

Currie, G. (1990). *The Nature of Fiction*. Cambridge: Cambridge University Press.

——(1995). *Image and Mind: Film, Philosophy, and Cognitive Science*. New York: Cambridge University Press.

Forster, E. M. (1927). *Aspects of the Novel*. New York: Harcourt, Brace.

Gaudreault, A. and Jost, F. (1990). *Le Recit cinematographique*. Paris: Nathan.

Genette, G. (1980). *Narative Discourse: An Essay in Method*, trans. J. E. Lewin. Ithaca, NY: Cornell University Press.

——(1982). *Figures of Literary Discourse*, trans. A. Sheridan. New York: Columbia University Press.

Genette, G. (1988). *Narrative Discourse Revisited*, trans. J. E. Lewin. Ithaca, NY: Cornell University Press.

Greimas, A. J. (1981). *On Meaning: Selected Writings in Semiotic Theory*. Minneapolis: University of Minnesota Press.

Iser, W. (1974). *The Implied Reader*. Baltimore: Johns Hopkins University Press.

——(1993). *The Fictive and the Imaginary*. Baltimore: Johns Hopkins University Press.

James, H. (1986). *The Art of Criticism*, ed. W. Veeder and S. M. Griffin. Chicago: University of Chicago Press.

Jameson, F. (1981). *The Political Unconscious: Narrative as a Socially Symbolic Act*. Ithaca, NY: Cornell University Press.

Kermode, F. (1968). *The Sense of an Ending*. Oxford: Oxford University Press; 2nd edn, with new epilogue, 2000.

Kozloff, S. (1988). *Invisible Storytellers*. Berkeley: University of California Press.

Lamarque, P. (1990). 'Narrative and Invention', in C. Nash (ed.), *Narrative in Culture: The Uses of Storytelling in the Sciences, Philosophy, and Literature*. London: Routledge.

——(1996). *Fictional Points of View*. Ithaca, NY: Cornell University Press.

Lemon, L. and McLaughlin, T. (eds.) (1965). *Russian Formalist Criticism: Four Essays*. Lincoln, Neb.: University of Nebraska Press.

Levinson, J. (1996). 'Film Music and Narrative Agency', in D. Bordwell and N. Carroll (eds.), *Post-Theory: Reconstructing Film Studies*. Madison Wis.: University of Wisconsin Press.

Lewis, D. (1983). 'Truth in Fiction', in *Philosophical Papers*, vol. 1, Oxford: Oxford University Press.

Lotman, J. (1977). *The Structure of the Artistic Text*. Ann Arbor: University of Michigan Press.

Lubbock, P. (1921). *The Craft of Fiction*. New York: Charles Scribner.

Martin, W. (1986). *Recent Theories of Narrative*. Ithaca, NY: Cornell University Press.

Miller, D. A. (1981). *Narrative and its Discontents: Problems of Closure in the Traditional Novel*. Princeton: Princeton University Press.

Mitchell, W. J. T. (ed.) (1981). *On Narrative*. Chicago: University of Chicago Press.

Nussbaum, M. (1990). *Love's Knowledge: Essays on Philosophy and Literature*. Oxford: Oxford University Press.

Pavel, T. (1986). *Fictional Worlds*. Cambridge, Mass.: Harvard University Press.

Perez, G. (1998). 'The Narrative Sequence', in *The Material Ghost: Films and Their Medium*. Baltimore: Johns Hopkins University Press.

Prince, G. (1982). *Narratology: The Form and Functioning of Narrative*. Amsterdam: Mouton.

——(1987). *A Dictionary of Narratology*. Lincoln, Neb.: University of Nebraska Press.

Propp, V. (1968). *Morphology of the Russian Folktale*. Austin: University of Texas Press.

Richardson, B. (2000). 'Narrative Poetics and Postmodern Transgression: Theorizing the Collapse of Time, Voice, and Frame'. *Narrative* 8: 23–42.

Ricour, P. (1984, 1985). *Time and Narrative*, Vols. 1 and 2, trans. K. McLaughlin and D. Pellauer. Chicago: University of Chicago Press.

Rimmon-Kenan, S. (1983). *Narrative Fiction: Contemporary Poetics*. London: Methuen.

Sacks, S. (1964). *Fiction and the Shape of Belief*. Chicago: University of Chicago Press.

Savile, A. (1989). 'Narrative Theory: Ancient or Modern?'. *Philosophical Papers* 18: 27–51.

Scholes, R. and Kellogg, R. (1966). *The Nature of Narrative*. Oxford: Oxford University Press.

Steinberg, M. (1978). *Expositional Modes and Temporal Ordering in Fiction*. Baltimore: Johns Hopkins Press.

Todorov, T. (1968). *Introduction to Poetics*. Minneapolis: University of Minnesota Press.

—— (1977). *The Poetics of Prose*. Ithaca, NY: Cornell University Press.

Walton, K. (1990). *Mimesis as Make-Believe: On the Foundations of the Representational Arts*. Cambridge: Harvard University Press.

Wilson, G. M. (1986). *Narration in Light: Studies in Cinematic Point of View*. Baltimore: Johns Hopkins University Press.

—— (1997a). 'On Film Narrative and Narrative Meaning', in *Film Theory and Philosophy*, ed. R. Allen and M. Smith. Oxford: Oxford University Press.

—— (1997b). '*Le Grand Imagier* Steps Out: On the Primitive Basis of Film Narration'. *Philosophical Topics* 25: 295–318.

CHAPTER 23

TRAGEDY

AARON RIDLEY

1. INTRODUCTION

TRAGEDY matters to aesthetics because it matters to philosophy, of which aesthetics is a part, and it matters to philosophy for one main reason. Tragedy engages more directly than any other artform with philosophy's own most fundamental question: How should one live? By depicting worlds in which things go wrong—in which chance and necessity play prominent and often devastating roles in the shaping of human lives—tragedy shows us aspects of a world that is, in reality, our world, the world in which we must live as best we can. Tragedy shows us lives blighted by accidents of character, by chance combinations of circumstance whose consequences unfold inexorably, by features of the human condition that are both necessary to it and, on occasion, profoundly damaging to it. In such a context, the question how to live acquires its proper urgency and complexity. And in showing us the world in that light, tragedy offers to philosophy its most authentic impetus and challenge.

There are a number of ways in which philosophy can take up that challenge. At one extreme stands Plato, who famously has Socrates deny that the good man can ever really come to harm. The good man, on this account, values, and identifies himself with, the Forms, the eternal verities; and those lie beyond the reach of the kinds of contingency that tragedy depends upon. Mere worldly misfortune, therefore, can never hit the good man where it truly hurts. On this view, then, the tragic is not a genuinely essential feature of human living at all: it is, rather, the price one pays, or may have to pay, for not being or becoming or understanding oneself as the right sort of person.

At the other extreme stands Nietzsche, for whom the tragic is definitive of life. For him, the Socratic attempt to understand oneself as being somehow above or beyond the reach of contingency is in reality an attempt to *mis*understand oneself. In reality, human beings comprise a rich, messy mix of drives and desires; and these, together with the world in which they operate, ensure that human well-being can only ever be, at best, a fragile and temporary achievement. On this view, the task is to learn to love life, not in spite of its tragic character, but *for* its tragic character: one must cultivate the attitude Nietzsche calls 'amor fati', the love of fate.

The attitude one takes to tragedy is thus intimately bound up with the view one takes of human nature. If—like Plato, or like a certain sort of Christian, or like Kant—one thinks there is an essential core of human nature that is somehow contingency-proof, one will be inclined to view tragedy as an eliminable or even an illusory aspect of life. One will also, therefore, be inclined to answer the 'How should one live?' question in terms that enjoin commitment to one's essential, contingency-proof self. (Think of St Augustine's advice: do not attach yourself too much to anything you might lose.) If, on the other hand, like Nietzsche, one thinks that human nature is worldly through and through, one is likely to think that the tragic aspect of life, because real and unavoidable, had better be acknowledged and, to whatever extent possible, come to terms with. One will also be likely to think that one should live in some such way as to register that acknowledgement. (Nietzsche's injunction to love fate is one version of this.)

There is a further distinction between the two extremes. For deep but fairly obvious reasons, a person in Plato's camp is likely to think, in a way that someone in Nietzsche's is not, that there is, as a matter of objective fact, some single, highest, unquestionably authoritative value. It is only if there is such a value, after all, and if the alleged contingency-proof core of human nature can somehow be identified with it, that one can be confident of being, at least potentially, beyond harm, at any rate in the only way that *really* matters. From this point of view, tragic works of art, in their tendency to show virtue and good fortune apparently drifting free of one another, can only seem misleading, perhaps even dangerously so. A person in the other camp, by contrast, is far more likely to think in terms of a plurality of values, none of them unquestionably authoritative, and each of them more than capable of entering into conflict with one or more of the others (and so perfectly capable of precipitating tragedy all by themselves). From this point of view, then, tragic works of art are likely to seem the most important works of art there are.

Reflection on the tragic—whether in life or in art—is of crucial importance to both of the positions I have just sketched. The appearance or reality of tragedy continually challenges their respective conceptions of human nature (as really in essence above the fray? Or as shot to the core with contingency?), of value (as singular, and identified in some way with human nature? Or as plural, potentially unruly, and humanly messy?), and of the best way of living (as transcending the worldly? Or as in the thick of things, like it or not?). I take it as criterial of a serious philosophical engagement with the sorts of issue that tragedy raises that some such questions as these should be discernibly operative in motivating it. If they are not, the overwhelming likelihood is that what is deep and significant about tragedy for philosophy will elude not only capture, but very probably recognition as well.

2. THE 'PARADOX' OF TRAGEDY

Against this background, the kind of theorizing about tragedy that has dominated recent aesthetics immediately begins to look rather thin and unsatisfactory. A great deal of time and effort has been spent trying to resolve the so-called 'paradox' of tragedy, a problem invented in the eighteenth century or thereabouts. The problem arises in the following way. An audience's experience of tragedy might reasonably be thought to involve harrowing or distressing feelings at the events represented. On the face of it, such feelings, and the occasions for them, are better avoided; yet people do as a matter of fact go to see tragedies voluntarily, and some even go so far as to say that they enjoy them. So the challenge is to give a coherent account of the experience of tragedy that makes intelligible (i.e. non-paradoxical) the motivations of those who would willingly seek a tragedy out. This problem finds its classic statement in Hume's short essay, 'Of Tragedy', where we read:

It seems an unaccountable pleasure which the spectators of a well-written tragedy receive from sorrow, terror, anxiety, and other passions that are in themselves disagreeable and uneasy. The more they are touched and affected, the more are they delighted with the spectacle ... The whole art of the poet is employed in rousing and supporting the compassion and indignation, the anxiety and resentment, of his audience. They are pleased in proportion as they are afflicted, and never are so happy as when they employ tears, sobs, and cries, to give vent to their sorrow, and relieve their heart, swoln with the tenderest sympathy and compassion. (Hume 1993: 126)

Hume's characterization of the tragic experience might be understood in two main ways, a weaker and a stronger. The weaker version focuses on the co-existence of apparently incompatible emotional states. The audience are 'delighted', 'pleased', and 'happy' at the same time as they are 'afflicted' with 'other passions'—sorrow, terror, anxiety, and so forth—'that are in themselves disagreeable and uneasy'. The problem here, if there is one, cannot lie in the mere co-existence of the agreeable and the disagreeable. There is nothing either uncommon or mysterious about the experience of mixed feelings, and no one ever thought of elevating the simultaneously pleasant and unpleasant aspects of, say, dieting to the status of a paradox.

The would-be slimmer dislikes doing without various sorts of food, and doubtless also the accompanying pangs of hunger, but is motivated to diet anyway by the agreeable prospect of being eventually less fat. That there is nothing remotely puzzling in this can be seen from the fact that, while the slimmer's pleasure is taken in one thing—the thought of a slimmer future self—the exception is taken to something quite else—doing without until then. Nor does anything interestingly more problematic emerge if the pleasant and unpleasant dimensions of a response are directed to the same object: the woman who has a love–hate relationship with her husband either loves some things about him while hating others, or finds lovable about him at certain times or from certain points of view things that, at other times or from other points of view, she finds hateful. Either way, the positive and negative dimensions of her response are directed to clearly distinguishable aspects of her husband, and no worries of a logical character need be felt. On this weak reading, then, the solution to Hume's problem is straightforward: the audience takes pleasure in one sort of thing about a tragedy, for instance the fact that it is 'well written', while finding another sort of thing, for instance the events represented in it, 'disagreeable'; and, provided only that the nice side of the experience outweighs the nasty one, there can be no reason at all to wonder at the motivations of those who would willingly put themselves through it.

It is clear, however, that Hume intended a stronger reading. His spectators are 'pleased in proportion as they are afflicted', are 'delighted with the spectacle' in proportion as 'they are touched and affected'—they appear, that is, actually to take pleasure in their own distress, so that the more they suffer the more they enjoy themselves. This is quite different from the weaker reading. It is hard, for instance, to imagine that many slimmers regard the prospect of being thinner as still more welcome for the discovery of just how disagreeable dieting can be, although I suppose that in a certain Protestant spirit some might. Nor, in most other cases of mixed feelings, is it plausible to think that the experience of positive feelings is somehow bolstered by, or parasitic upon, the experience of negative ones (although a woman's love–hate relationship with her husband may be an exception: she may find an added risky attractiveness in a trait of his precisely for its capacity to repel her). Of the two possible readings, Hume was clearly right to have intended this stronger one. A tragedy that failed to disturb would, in at least one sense, be a failure: and this is enough by itself to suggest that the value we attach to the experience of tragic drama is bound up in some intimate way with its capacity to pain us. And this fact does, in turn, raise questions of a kind about our motivations when we put ourselves through that experience. I doubt—for reasons I'll come to—that those questions point to a problem even faintly resembling a paradox. But, since it is true that a tragedy must be disturbing if it is to be worthwhile, it is wholly understandable that philosophers should have been struck by that fact, and have been driven to wonder about it.

Hume's own approach to the problem he takes himself to have identified, however, has very little to recommend it. In the experience of a 'well written tragedy', he claims:

the uneasiness of the melancholy passions is not only overpowered and effaced by something stronger of an opposite kind, but the whole impulse of those passions is converted into pleasure, and swells the delight which the eloquence raises in us... The impulse or vehemence arising from sorrow, compassion, indignation, receives a new direction from the sentiments of beauty. The latter, being the predominant emotion, seize the whole mind, and convert the former into themselves... And the soul being at the same time roused by passion and charmed by eloquence, feels on the whole a strong movement, which is altogether delightful. (Hume 1993: 129)

The idea that Hume is expressing here is obscure, to say the least. Some have taken him to be claiming that 'sorrow, compassion, indignation' and so forth—'passions that are in themselves disagreeable and uneasy'—are somehow converted into pleasurable versions of the same feelings (see e.g. Budd 1995: chapter 3; Schier 1983, 1989); others have taken him to be claiming that the 'melancholy passions' are somehow converted into other passions, such as delight, which are in themselves pleasurable (see e.g. Packer 1989). If either of these suggestions is correct, however, Hume's position is not merely obscure, but hopelessly self-defeating; for on either reading the upshot is that the audience does not, in the end, experience anything painful—which, if so, would mean that the problem to which Hume's talk of 'conversion' is supposed to supply the solution would hardly have arisen in the first place.

A more persuasive interpretation of Hume's position has recently been offered by Alex Neill (1998). On this reading, the unpleasant feelings aroused by tragedy remain. Sorrow, for instance, remains disagreeable rather than pleasant and it remains sorrow rather than delight. The 'impulse or vehemence' with which it is felt, however, is somehow co-opted or taken over by the ('stronger') 'sentiments of beauty', so that these are experienced with greater force than they would have been if roused by the beauties of the tragedy alone. The force of the pleasure we take in a 'well written tragedy', therefore, is proportional to the force of the disagreeable passion it arouses; and what is 'converted' is not the passion itself (into something nice or into something different), but the service into which its 'impulse or vehemence' is pressed. This reading has the twin advantages of leaving Hume with a problem he can claim to have solved, and of squaring better than the alternatives with what he says about the passions in the *Treatise*. It does not, however, have the advantage of making Hume's position plausible—not least for the reason that the associationist psychology on which the supposed mechanism of conversion depends is simply unsustainable.

It is likely that no interpretation of Hume's story about conversion will rescue it, and hardly anyone, I think, has seriously tried to defend him on the point. But the problem he was addressing has continued to attract attention in very much the form that he gave it. Many of us willingly put ourselves through the experience of tragic drama, not *despite* its capacity to disturb, but at least partly *because* of its capacity to disturb. So what, it is asked, is the source and nature of the pleasure that tragedy must give us, its disturbing character notwithstanding? I will make no attempt here to survey or enumerate the answers that have been given to this question. Suffice it to say that a quite spectacular quantity of ink has been spilled over the issue, and that very little of it has been spilled to any effect. (Better examples of what the literature has to offer in this respect include Schier 1983, 1989, and Lamarque 1995.) And, on a moment's thought, that really ought to come as no surprise; for the problem with Hume's problem, at least in the form that Hume gave it, is that it begs all of the interesting questions.

Hume, for reasons having nothing to do with his reflections on tragedy, was committed to a reductive, hedonic theory of value. All value was reducible to pleasure, all disvalue to displeasure. From this starting point, it is hardly surprising that our motivation for putting ourselves through something disturbing, such as tragedy, would have to be accounted for by some countervailing kind of pleasure to be had from the same source (the weak reading) or by a countervailing pleasure to be had from the experience of disturbance itself (the strong reading). Only thus, after all, could tragedy actually be understood as valuable, as worth putting oneself through. Only thus could the appearances be saved. That Hume thought this is, as I say, a fact that has nothing to do with his reflections on tragedy. The surprising thing is that people have taken his word for it. For there is no independent reason at all—is there?—to think that pleasure and displeasure are the only things that matter. There is no independent reason at all to suppose that, in order intelligibly to put oneself through something disturbing, one must somehow get *pleasure* out of being disturbed. There is, in short, no reason at all to imagine that the value and importance of tragic drama must ultimately derive from its capacity to *please*. And that, surely, is just as well, since successful tragic drama—think of *Lear*, think of *Oedipus*—is simply not all that pleasing.

Or perhaps it is. It may be that some genuine reflection on tragedy would yield the conclusion that the value and importance of tragic drama does after all derive from its capacity to please. But that, if true, would depend not merely upon some rich and interesting reflections on tragic drama, but on some correspondingly rich and interesting reflections on the nature of pleasure and its place in our lives. The debate over the so-called 'paradox' of tragedy has been remarkably devoid of such reflection, however, either on Hume's part or on the part of those who have so willingly followed him. I said at the beginning of this section that the 'paradox' debate was thin and unsatisfactory, and the reason for that should now be clear. Genuine reflection on the tragic involves reflection on one's conceptions of human nature, value, and the good life. For Hume those conceptions were settled in advance, usually for subtle and sophisticated reasons, but in ways that generated his problem about tragedy rather than being generated by it. For his followers, by contrast, the very possibility that issues concerning human nature, value, and the good life might be so much as in the vicinity seems to have remained invisible—a conclusion perhaps rendered self-confirming by the observation that exactly the same 'paradox' debate, conducted in exactly the same terms, has recently been transplanted into the discussion of horror movies, of all things (see e.g. Carroll 1990). The fact is that to presuppose, as those who think there must be a 'paradox' of tragedy presuppose, that worthwhile things must necessarily be pleasurable things is to refuse altogether to reflect upon or even to notice the real questions and issues that tragedy raises.

3. TRAGEDY AND CHOICE

Things are fortunately in better shape elsewhere. Plato and Nietzsche, as I have already indicated, were concerned in the right sorts of ways about tragedy—as too, for instance, were Aristotle, Hegel, and Schopenhauer. In each of these philosophers one appreciates directly how a serious engagement with some of the deepest questions in philosophy has been both invigorated and focused by the impact of the tragic. Nor has that impact been altogether dulled today. I devote this section to two contemporary philosophers—Martha Nussbaum and Bernard Williams—who have shown that tragedy can still prompt serious philosophical thought. Nussbaum is closer to Plato's end of the scale than to Nietzsche's; Williams is closer to Nietzsche's.

In *The Fragility of Goodness* (Nussbaum 1986), Nussbaum devotes a considerable amount of space to tragic dilemmas—to situations, as depicted in tragic dramas, in which two competing kinds of value are pitted against one another. So, for instance, Agamemnon, in the play of the same name, must choose between the evil of sacrificing his daughter, Iphigenia, and the evil of allowing his entire military expedition to die becalmed at sea; Eteocles—in *Seven Against Thebes*—must choose between the evil of (attempted) fratricide and the evil of his city's being enslaved; and in *Antigone*, either Creon must give way to the unconditional value that the eponymous heroine attaches to family considerations, or Antigone must give way to Creon's no less uncompromising attachment to the interests of the state. In each case, one value or the other must yield pride of place.

Nussbaum's starting point in thinking about these cases is not at all Platonic. For Plato, such dilemmas must always prove on investigation to be illusory: either one value will turn out to be unquestionably more valuable than the other, or both values will turn out to be trumped by some further, still higher, value. Plato's value monism, that is, disallows the sort of evaluative messiness that a genuine tragic dilemma would engender. For him, the challenge is to work out which value *really* matters, and to act in accordance with it; once one has done that, the defeated value drops out of consideration, and the dilemma has been resolved—without remainder.

Nussbaum, by contrast, regards tragic dilemmas as perfectly real. She denies that they can be resolved without remainder, and suggests that one of the major strengths of the classical tragedies she discusses is their ability to show how the demands made by the defeated value do not just go away once the dilemma has been settled in favour of the other value. So, for instance, she notes and approves the respective choruses' condemnation of Agamemnon's attitude when, having decided that the sacrifice of his daughter is the lesser of two evils, he announces that 'it is right and holy that I should desire with exceedingly impassioned passion the sacrifice staying the winds, the maiden's blood. May all turn out well'; and of Eteocles when, having opted for single combat with his brother, he exhibits what—again—the chorus take to be an unseemly enthusiasm for the task. The choruses expect rather more from Agamemenon and Eteocles than they evince: namely, some affective acknowledgement of the value—paternal love in Agamemnon's case, fraternal love in Eteocles'—that the dilemma they find themselves in forces them to abrogate. Nussbaum concurs: 'Tears,' she says, 'and not the refusal of tears, would appear to be the more appropriate response' (1986: 38). And of each agent she says: 'He has failed to see and respond to his conflict as the conflict it is; this crime compounds the already serious burden of his action' (p. 39).

In a sensitive and wide-ranging discussion, Nussbaum establishes the importance not merely of an agent's resolving a dilemma in favour of the right value, but of the affective *attitude* with which he proceeds to violate, and so to acknowledge or fail to acknowledge, the value deemed less important. And it is here that the Platonic affinities of Nussbaum's position finally emerge. For it is her view that, since an agent cannot—at least in the cases she deals with—be held responsible for the dilemma that besets him, his only real responsibility is to execute the moral violation forced upon him in a way that does justice to the value of the value being violated. In effect, Nussbaum draws a line around an inner arena of affective moral rectitude, and distinguishes it sharply from what an agent actually does: a properly tearful and reluctant Agamemnon might, despite sacrificing his daughter, have salvaged his moral character. Moral character is thus, in the end, contingency-proof. If one gets the inner business right, one can always in principle hold on to the single thing that really matters: that one is, at bottom, and whatever one does, a *good person* (and, in that much, beyond harm). Nussbaum is thus driven to articulate an account of human nature (as essentially bound up with how one feels about what one does), of value (as attaching ultimately, and despite the possibility of genuine conflict at an external level, to the inner), and of the best way of living (as one whose feelings are beyond reproach)—all as a consequence of taking one aspect of tragic drama seriously.

That this is so is, as I have suggested, the mark of a properly philosophical engagement with tragedy, even if the results of that engagement fail finally to convince. Nussbaum's insistence that there is more to ethical life than merely identifying and pursuing the right course of action is salutary, and her attention to the affective dimension of agency is welcome. But it is still possible to feel that she has not really digested the full awfulness of some of the situations she discusses. Take again the case of Eteocles. Eteocles' crime, as Nussbaum and the chorus see it, is that, having decided, however reluctantly, that single combat with his brother is the better of the unpalateable options on offer, he says 'Bring me my greaves as quickly as possible…it is appropriate to go quickly.' 'Why are you so eager?' ask the chorus. 'Do not become similar…to a person who is called by the worst names… Cast out the authority of this bad passion…Too ravenous is the desire that goads you on to accomplish a man-killing…shedding blood not to be shed.' But these decent-minded injunctions are surely out of place. For Eteocles, the choice is not between allowing his city to be enslaved and simply turning up to fight his brother. If *that* were the choice, then he could perfectly well sally forth in the horrified and tearfully reluctant state that Nussbaum and the chorus would prefer—and no doubt lose as a result. No: the choice is between Thebes' being enslaved and Eteocles' trying, and managing, to defeat his brother; and that is a very different matter. If Eteocles is pointfully to go down the single-combat route at all, it is a condition of his genuinely doing so that he should want to win—that he get himself into the right state of mind, that he commit himself wholeheartedly to the task and cultivate for its accomplishment a truly 'ravenous' desire. Only thus, after all, is he actually making *that* choice. In complaining that Eteocles, like Agamemnon, exhibits 'an unnatural cooperation of internal with external forces'—that he 'begins to cooperate inwardly with necessity', and 'strangely turns himself into a collaborator' (1986: 35)—Nussbaum badly mis-imagines Eteocles' position: single combat, undertaken in a spirit of character-saving sensitivity, is not an option for him. The option open to him is the far bleaker one that he in fact chooses: to *become*, in making his choice, 'a person who is called by the worst names', one who identifies himself with 'the authority of a "bad passion"'. Inward cooperation with necessity is not something he has the luxury of avoiding. As he puts it in the last words he speaks: 'When the gods decree it, you may not escape evil.'

Correctly understood, it seems to me, what Eteocles' case shows is that the kind of insulation of the inner from the outer that Nussbaum's account of human nature envisages, and which is supposed to allow the good person to emerge essentially unscathed from even the most dreadful action, is unsustainable. It may be, in other words, that in doing the best thing possible under the circumstances the good man must sacrifice his own goodness (as construed by Nussbaum, at least); and that may be the uncomfortable lesson to be drawn from some tragedies. If so, this indicates a rather grimmer picture of the relation between human nature and value than that presented in *The Fragility of Goodness*, as well as an altogether less impregnable conception of the self and a correspondingly less heartwarming conception of what the good life might, in the end, amount to.

Bernard Williams's reflections on tragedy are consistent with this critique of Nussbaum. They also strike me, at any rate, as more alert than hers to the genuinely tragic aspects of human living, and indeed of tragedy. In a number of essays, and in a superb book, *Shame and Necessity* (Williams 1993), Williams has developed a way of thinking about tragedy whose results are as rich as anything in contemporary philosophy. One of Williams's recurrent themes—a theme he finds elaborated in classical tragedy—is the way in which various kinds of non-causal, non-logical necessity can give shape to, and on occasion decisively affect, the course of a person's life. Reflecting upon Sophocles' Ajax, for instance, Williams notes how his sense of himself as now ridiculous—following the episode with the sheep, together with his investment in a heroic, warriorly conception of himself—drives him to conclude that he must commit suicide. Ajax's suicide is not causally necessitated; nor is it logically necessary. Rather, as Williams puts it, 'Being what he is, he could not live as the man who had done these things; it would be merely impossible, in virtue of the relations between what he expects of the world and what the world expects of a man who expects that of it' (1993: 73). His suicide is necessary, that is, because of considerations internal to his situation's being *his*, not because of considerations that would apply to him, as causal or logical ones would, regardless.

Williams insists on this point for several reasons, but the most prominent, and perhaps the deepest, is his opposition to a certain picture of the voluntary. According to that picture, which Williams associates particularly with Kant, the voluntary is the freely chosen, where what does the choosing is an abstracted, 'characterless' self, and the basis on which it chooses is pure, practical reason. The voluntary in this sense is also necessary. What is freely chosen would also, necessarily, be freely chosen by any other rational agent: the voluntary, in short, is what is obligatory for rational beings as such. Williams is profoundly sceptical of this conception of obligation. He is also sceptical of the idea of responsibility that tends to go with it, namely, that a person is responsible, only or primarily, for discharging or for failing to discharge his obligations, so understood. Ajax's conviction that he *has* to kill himself is not precipitated by anything for which, in anything like that sense, he is responsible. When he slaughtered the sheep, he was not in his right mind: he certainly did not 'freely choose' to act as he did. And yet 'it is still a truth about him that he has done these things, and it is a truth in the present tense: he is the person who did those things' (1993: 71). He is, in that much, responsible for what he has done, however little he did it voluntarily. Nor is his suicide, prompted by his recognition of that responsibility, necessary in the sense of being obligatory for a rational being as such. Its necessity derives, rather, from his sense of himself as the person he is upon finding himself in *that* situation, and acknowledging it as his. Neither the occasion for his suicide, then, nor his suicide itself can be understood in the terms set by the Kantian picture; and yet Sophocles' presentation of Ajax's behaviour is intelligible—ethically intelligible—throughout.

Williams concludes accordingly: the Kantian picture is misleading. We cannot understand our ethical lives if we insist on construing them as structured, primarily or exclusively, by the conceptions of voluntariness, responsibility, and obligation, together with the relations between them, that that picture enjoins.

Williams's view is that:

> We deceive ourselves if we suppose that...the idea of the voluntary is uniquely important to responsibility...It is also a mistake to think that the idea of the voluntary can itself be refined beyond a certain point. The idea is useful...but it is essentially superficial. If we push beyond a certain point questions of what outcome, exactly, was intended, whether a state of mind was normal or whether an agent could at a certain moment have controlled himself, we sink into the sands of an everyday, entirely justified, skepticism...[T]he notion of the voluntary is [not] a profound conception ... In truth, ... it can hardly be deepened at all. What threatens it is the attempt to make it profound, and the effect of trying to deepen it [as, for instance, Kant tried to] is to put it beyond all recognition. The Greeks were not involved in those attempts; this is one of the places at which we encounter their gift for being superficial out of profundity. (Williams 1993: 67–8)

The overtly Nietzschean compliment with which this passage ends encapsulates an important dimension of Williams's appreciation of the Greek tragedians: that they presented a world unsanitized by efforts to eliminate from it, or to expose as fundamentally illusory, the ordinary, messy complexities and necessities that living in it entails. In particular, they resisted the urge to connect an allegedly 'deepened' conception of the voluntary to an allegedly 'deepened' conception of the self, and so refused to draw a hard and fast line around an alleged set of obligations and responsibilities attaching necessarily to rational agents as such, regardless of character or circumstance. They declined, that is, to invent a contingency-proof core of human nature; they recognized that the necessities that shape a life do not all come from within.

One of the things that tragedy has to teach us, then, 'is that the significance of someone's life and its relations to' the rest of the world 'may be such that someone needs to recognize and express his responsibility for actions when no one else would have the right' to demand that he do so (Williams 1993: 74). It is a corollary of this that, under certain circumstances, under the pressure of certain sorts of necessity, the way that someone acts or chooses to act may not be a proper object of anybody *else's* judgement at all. Williams regards Agamemnon's case as being of this sort. *Contra* Nussbaum, he suggests that 'It is, probably, hard to apply the sacrificial knife to one's daughter while wringing one's hands, and if we do not think that Agamemnon just made a mistake about what he had to do on that bad day..., it is better that, rather than telling him what he should have felt, we should be prepared to learn what was involved in getting through it' (p. 135). And he cites A. A. Long's review of Nussbaum: what one 'surely feels, as the principal characters face their predicaments, is the inadequacy of any language, moral sententiousness especially, to do justice to their loss and ruin' (p. 210). Williams's reflections on tragedy thus open up a more subtle and capacious conception of the ethical than that with which, since Kant, we have mostly been accustomed to operate. And they do this, as I have suggested that pointful reflection on the tragic always must, by involving long and hard thought about what it *is* to be human, that is, about human nature, and about the relationship between ourselves and the values to which we are most committed.

4. CONCLUSION

The comparative richness of Nussbaum's and Williams's way with tragedy offers lessons to contemporary aesthetics. First, both engage directly with actual works of art. The contemporary 'paradox' debate, fixated as it is on a set of puzzles and pseudo-puzzles about human psychology, perpetuates itself almost entirely without reference to them: not for the only time, philosophers of art have proved strangely indifferent to art. Second, the Nussbaum/Williams approach, in showing how actual works of art pose and sometimes clarify questions that any reflective person should care about, defuses the 'paradox' debate at its source. We put ourselves through the experience of tragic drama because we think these questions worth thinking about. Pleasure, if pleasure is an issue, might be in there somewhere (Aristotle, for instance, held that cognitive activity was enjoyable in itself), but to think that pleasure must be *the* issue is simply to side-step, or in some other way to miss, the points that really matter. Finally, in taking actual works of art and the questions they raise seriously, Nussbaum and Williams show vividly what the motivation for genuine aesthetic inquiry ought to look like. And if, as in the case of tragedy, that inquiry should turn out to be predominantly ethical in content, that is because aesthetics is, indeed, a part of philosophy, and so its adequate pursuit something that inevitably spills over into other philosophical domains.

See also: Art and Emotion; Art and Morality; Value in Art; Aesthetics and Ethics; Theatre; Music.

BIBLIOGRAPHY

Aristotle (1987). *Poetics*, trans. S. Halliwell. London: Duckworth.
Beistegui, M. and Sparks, S. (2000). *Philosophy and Tragedy*. London: Routledge.
Budd, M. (1995). *Values of Art*. London: Allen Lane.
Burke, E. (1990). *A Philosophical Enquiry*, ed. A. Phillips. Oxford: Oxford University Press.
Carroll, N. (1990). *The Philosophy of Horror, or Paradoxes of the Heart*. New York: Routledge.
Cavell, S. (1987). *Disowning Knowledge in Six Plays of Shakespeare*. Cambridge: Cambridge University Press.
Eaton, M. (1982). 'A Strange Kind of Sadness'. *Journal of Aesthetics and Art Criticism* 41: 51–63.

Feagin, S. (1983). 'The Pleasures of Tragedy'. *American Philosophical Quarterly* 20: 95–104.

Gowans, C. (1987). *Moral Dilemmas*. Oxford: Oxford University Press.

Hegel, G. W. F. (1975). *Aesthetics: Lectures on Fine Art*, 2 vols., trans. T. M. Knox. Oxford: Oxford University Press.

Hume, D. (1993). 'Of Tragedy', in S. Copley and A. Edgar (eds.), *Hume: Selected Essays*. Oxford: Oxford University Press.

Kierkegaard, S. (1985). *Fear and Trembling*, trans. A. Hannay. London: Penguin Books.

Kuhns, R. (1991). *Tragedy: Contradiction and Repression*. Chicago: University of Chicago Press.

Lamarque, P. (1995). 'Tragedy and Moral Value'. *Australasian Journal of Philosophy* 73: 239–49.

Levinson, J. (1982). 'Music and Negative Emotion'. *Pacific Philosophical Quarterly* 63: 327–46.

—— (1991). 'Horrible Fictions'. *Journal of Aesthetics and Art Criticism* 49: 253–8.

Morreall, J. (1985). 'Enjoying Negative Emotions in Fiction'. *Philosophy and Literature* 9: 95–102.

Neill, A. (1998). ' "An Unaccountable Pleasure": Hume on Tragedy and the Passions'. *Hume Studies* 24: 335–54.

—— (1999). 'Hume's "Singular Phænomenon" '. *British Journal of Aesthetics* 39: 112–25.

Nietzsche, F. (1996). *On the Genealogy of Morals*, trans. D. Smith. Oxford: Oxford University Press.

—— (1999). *The Birth of Tragedy*, trans. R. Speirs. Cambridge: Cambridge University Press.

—— (2001). *The Gay Science*, trans. J. Nauckhof. Cambridge: Cambridge University Press.

Nussbaum, M. (1986). *The Fragility of Goodness*. Cambridge: Cambridge University Press.

Packer, M. (1989). 'Dissolving the Paradox of Tragedy'. *Journal of Aesthetics and Art Criticism* 47: 211–19.

Peckham, M. (1962). *Beyond the Tragic Vision*. New York: George Braziller.

Plato (1956). *Great Dialogues of Plato*, trans. W. H. D. Rouse. New York: Mentor Books.

Ridley, A. (1993). 'Tragedy and the Tender-Hearted'. *Philosophy and Literature* 17: 234–45.

Schier, F. (1983). 'Tragedy and the Community of Sentiment', in P. Lamarque (ed.), *Philosophy and Fiction: Essays in Literary Aesthetics*. Aberdeen: Aberdeen University Press.

—— (1989). 'The Claims of Tragedy: An Essay in Moral Psychology and Aesthetic Theory'. *Philosophical Papers* 18: 7–26.

Schopenhauer, A. (1966). *The World as Will and Representation*, 2 vols., trans. E. F. Payne. New York: Dover.

Williams, B. (1993). *Shame and Necessity*. Berkeley: University of California Press.

CHAPTER 24

ART AND EMOTION

ALEX NEILL

THE thought that art is in one way or another profoundly connected with human emotion, and that it is so in ways that give rise to compelling questions in the philosophy of mind as well as in aesthetics, is one that has run very deep for a very long time. Pythagoras may have been the first to comment on the special power of music both to stimulate and to soothe the emotions, and the nature of that power is one in which philosophers have not lost interest since (see e.g. Budd 1985; Ridley 1995). The pre-Socratic philosopher Gorgias commented long before Aristotle did on the power of poetry to move its audience to 'a fearful shuddering and a tearful pity and a mournful yearning' (Barnes 1979: 161); and it was just this aspect of poetry—its capacity to 'water the passions' at the expense, as he saw it, of the development of reason—that gave Plato greatest cause for concern in his critique of representational art in the *Republic*. Aristotle's defence of poetry against Plato's critique is based partly on the claim that, in effecting the *catharsis* of passion, poetry (and not only tragic poetry) contributes to emotional (and hence moral) balance and health. These and other writings of the ancients on the relationship between various forms of art and emotion were the subject of a great deal of commentary by later Classical and Renaissance writers. By the time of the Enlightenment, with its emphasis on the role of sentiment in judgements of taste, the topic had become arguably the most central in philosophical aesthetics. It retained its centrality in Romantic theories of art, and particularly of poetry, and continues to be one of the staples of contemporary analytic aesthetics. (Beardsley, 1966, provides an excellent introduction to the history of this material.)

The theory of art in which this abiding philosophical interest in the connection between art and emotion is most explicit is Expression Theory, of which there have been several, significantly different, versions. Common to all of these is the thought that the value of art lies at least largely in the value of its expression of emotion; but theorists have differed markedly in how they understand the nature of such expression. On what might be called the full-blown version of expression theory—instances of which were held by Leo Tolstoy and by Clive Bell (for all that the latter is standardly categorized as a Formalist rather than an Expression Theorist)—expression is understood as a matter of the communication or transmission of emotion or feeling from artist to audience via the work of art. The value of a work of art, on this view, will be a function both of the value of the feeling that it transmits (Tolstoy, for instance, held that sincerity and individuality of feeling were crucial criteria of value in this respect), and of its 'infectiousness' (to use a Tolstoyan metaphor) and the clarity with which it transmits that feeling.

Understood in this sort of way, Expression Theory faces a number of difficulties, of which the most obvious are as follows. First, this conception of artistic expression can very easily slip—as it arguably does in Tolstoy's hands—into construing works of art merely as a means to the end of the transmission of feeling, means that could in principle be replaced without loss of value by some other vehicle for the transmission of the feeling in question. Second, it seems clear that it is not always appropriate to respond to a work of art by experiencing the feelings it seems designed to communicate—jolly music may sometimes be irritating, even if the jollity is sincere and clear in the music. Third, it seems equally clear that artists need not be feeling, or even remembering or imagining feeling, what their works express (in a pre-theoretical sense of that term) as they create those works: jolly music may be written and indeed performed by miserable artists. (For further consideration of these and related issues, see 'Expression in Art', Chapter 12 above.)

Whether or not these difficulties are insuperable for the full-blooded version of Expression Theory, in one or another combination they have been motivating factors in the development of what might be thought of as more limited versions of the theory. According to one of these, of which the most sophisticated instance is that worked out by R. G. Collingwood, but which is also hinted at in Wordsworth's suggestion that 'all good poetry is the spontaneous overflow of powerful feelings', expression is understood as a matter of the embodiment or articulation of the artist's emotion in the work of art itself, irrespective of its emotional effect on the audience. On another version of the theory, defended with respect to music by Leonard Meyer, for example, expression is understood as involving the evocation or arousal of emotion in the audience (in Meyer's view, by music's temporal structure), irrespective of the artist's emotional states. And finally, some theorists, such as Susanne Langer, Nelson Goodman, Deryck Cooke, and Rudolf Arnheim, though in rather different ways, have understood emotional expression in terms of a work of art in one way or another symbolizing or representing emotion, irrespective of the feelings of either the artist in creating it or the audience in responding to it. Expression Theories of art can thus be classified, albeit somewhat artificially, into those that focus on the creation of art, those that focus on artworks themselves, and those that focus on the response to art by its audience. In the remainder of this essay, I shall focus on issues concerning emotion and the response to art.

One way of uniting what looks at first like a rather disparate set of issues that have occupied philosophers and other philosophically minded theorists concerning our emotional responses to works of art is to view those issues as raised by a quite general question: how, if at all, is responding emotionally to works of art relevant to the understanding, appreciation, and evaluation of works in various forms of art?

For many eighteenth-century philosophers, to appreciate beauty and other aesthetic qualities, whether in a work of art or in nature, just *is* to respond emotionally. Indeed, David Hume sometimes refers to beauty and its opposite 'deformity' as sentiments, though these terms may also stand for the 'order and construction of parts' in an object that evokes the sentiment in question in the observer. Aesthetic judgements, or judgements of taste, are on this view either expressions or reports of affective experiences: to say 'This is beautiful' is to say something like 'This makes me feel a certain way' (or perhaps 'This is such that it will make a properly constituted observer feel that way'). (See Hume 1978: book III and 1987a; for extensive discussion of Hume on the role of sentiment in aesthetics, see Townsend 2001.) And, although he took a rather different view of the faculty of taste, holding that reason as well as sentiment was involved in its operations, Edmund Burke none the less thought that, in order to clarify our understanding of aesthetic qualities such as the sublime and the beautiful, it was necessary first to identify and classify the emotions that objects possessing such qualities aroused in human observers, and then to consider which features of those objects arouse those emotions (Burke 1998). In short, it is not too much to say that the eighteenth-century philosophers' interest in such notions as the sublime, the beautiful, and the picturesque was part and parcel of their more general interest in the nature and operation of the passions.

The eighteenth-century emotivist position, as it might be called, survived into the first half of the twentieth century in the thought of the Logical Positivists: thus, for example, A. J. Ayer held that 'aesthetic words such as "beautiful" and "hideous" are employed . . . not to make statements of fact, but simply to express certain feelings and evoke a certain response [in others]. . . . [T]he purpose of aesthetic criticism is not so much to give knowledge as to communicate emotion' (Ayer 1971: 150). However, this position did not for long stay in favour with philosophers, and far less with artists and critics. Probably the dominant position of the twentieth century on the role of emotional response in the understanding and appreciation of art (indeed, probably the dominant theory of art of the twentieth century, among artists and art theorists if not among philosophers) was Formalism. In its most influential version, that developed by Clive Bell, the artist is presented as a person who in moments of inspiration is able to see objects in the world, as Kant put it, disinterestedly: as ends rather than means, for what they are in themselves rather than in terms of how they serve human purposes—in short, as 'pure form'. In response to pure form, the artist experiences a certain sort of emotion, which he attempts to capture in a work; if he is successful, the resulting work will have a quality that Bell called 'significant form', the quality that all genuine works of art have in common, the possession of which *makes* them works of art. And when we perceive significant form in a work of art, Bell holds, we experience a particular kind of emotion, one related to that experienced by the artist when he perceives pure form in the world, which Bell calls 'aesthetic emotion' (Bell 1958: sect. I). Experiencing aesthetic emotion is thus held to be both a necessary condition of recognizing a work of art as a work of art, and constitutive of aesthetic experience. By contrast, responding to a work simply with other, everyday, varieties of emotion amounts to a failure to respond aesthetically—to respond to the work as a work of art—since it signals that one has failed to perceive the significant form in it.

Influential though Bell's position was in the first half of the twentieth century, it is beset by a number of difficulties. For one thing, introspection suggests that in fact we may experience a huge variety of feelings in response to works of art, and Bell's claim that the experience of all but one signals a failure to respond appropriately seems nothing more than stipulative: even if it were true that all works of art possessed significant form, why should it be thought that significant form is the cause of only one sort of feeling? For another, the character of aesthetic emotion and its difference from garden-variety emotion is more than a little mysterious. Bell holds that we can tell which we are experiencing by introspection, but there appear to be plenty of people for whom introspection reveals no such distinction in feeling, and any attempt to explain this by appeal to the insensitivity of such people to art would clearly be unacceptably *ad hoc*. Moreover, even if introspection does reveal to different people feelings that they identify as specifically aesthetic, how can we be sure that the feelings in question are of the same sort? Bell's Cartesian conception of the emotions as essentially sets of feelings precludes his identifying aesthetic emotion in terms of its object (as we may define fear in terms of the threatening or dangerous, for example), since mere feelings are not appropriately intentional. At most, he can identify aesthetic emotion as the sort of feeling that is caused by significant form, which is inadequate not only because of the question noted above as to why it should be thought that significant form is the cause of only one variety of feeling, but also because, supposedly, the only access that we have to significant form is through the experience of aesthetic emotion—a point that also makes the theory vulnerable to a charge of circularity. (For an extensive critique of Formalism, see Budd 1995: chapter 2.)

The idea that there is a specifically aesthetic emotion—or, as Nelson Goodman memorably referred to it, 'a special secretion of the aesthetic glands' (Goodman 1976: 247)—that comes into play in our engagement with art, or for that matter with other things when we engage with them aesthetically, has not survived Formalism, though the Kantian ideas in which it is rooted, and in particular the idea that a proper engagement with art is in some sense or other disinterested, were further developed in Aesthetic Attitude theories such as that of Jerome Stolnitz (see Stolnitz 1960), and continue to be influential. However, it seems clear that, whatever else it may demand, disinterested engagement with art neither precludes responding to it emotionally nor prescribes a particular sort of emotional response as the only appropriate one.

A different answer to the question concerning the role of emotional response in the understanding and appreciation of art is implicit in one of the versions of Expression Theory referred to above, namely the version sometimes labelled 'Arousal Theory', according to which artistic expression is to be understood in terms of the arousal of emotion in the audience by the work of art. As this theory in its most extreme form would have it, what makes something a work of art are its expressive properties, and what it is for a work to express a particular feeling is for it to arouse that feeling in its audience. Thus, if the audience of a work fails to respond to it emotionally, then either the work or the audience has somehow failed: a work that does not arouse in its audience the feeling that it attempts to express has failed as a work of art, and hence cannot properly be understood or appreciated as such; unless the reason that it fails to arouse the feeling in question is some failure of perception in the audience, in which case the latter will fail to recognize the nature of the work it is faced with, and hence will not be able adequately to understand, appreciate it, and evaluate it.

Arousal Theory certainly captures some of our pre-theoretical intuitions about the connection between art and emotion. However, in the strong form outlined above, it has had few adherents among philosophers of art, for two main reasons. First, as a theory of *art*, Arousal Theory, in common with other versions of Expression Theory so understood, is vulnerable to the objection that, even if a great deal of art is expressive, not all of it is—that is to say, to the objection that art cannot be defined in terms of expression. Second, and more significantly, as a theory of *expression*, Arousal Theory is vulnerable to the objection that it fails to capture what we mean by that term, inasmuch as it seems that we can perfectly intelligibly say things such as 'I find the way in which this work expresses triumph rather depressing', or 'The inane jollity of that piece is really very irritating'. None of this is to deny, of course, that one important way in which a work of art may be expressive of feeling is through the arousal or evocation of feeling in its audience, nor that responding to a work by feeling whatever the work expresses may in some cases be the best if not the only appropriate way of responding to it. (For defence of Arousal Theory as a theory of expression, if not of art, see Mew 1985 and Matravers 1998.)

In stark contrast to Arousal Theory's claim that emotional response is crucial to a proper engagement with at least some works of art is the position that emotional engagement not only is not relevant to the processes of coming properly to understand, appreciate, and evaluate art, but actively impedes these processes. This position may be motivated in different ways. Thus, a musicologist might argue that, if one is engaged emotionally with a symphony, that will get in the way of comprehending the formal structures of the work; or a literary critic might posit that being moved by the fate of a character in a novel can only interfere with one's capacity to appreciate the role of the depicted events in question in the structure of the narrative as a whole. In the case of Bertolt Brecht, probably the best-known exponent of this sort of position, the motivating factor was the Marxist idea that the value of art lies in its potential as a force for social change: in order for this potential to be fulfilled, Brecht argues, it is the audience's critical capacities rather than its bourgeois feelings that must be engaged. To this end, Brecht conceived a new form of 'epic theatre', which deliberately, through the use of what he called 'alienation effects'—for example minimal use of scenery and props, frequent interruption of the action with songs, and acting techniques that keep the players distinct from the characters they play—works to prevent the audience from engaging emotionally with the characters and events depicted, by constantly reminding them that what they are watching is artifice rather than reality, an attempt to observe humanity from an objective point of view the purpose of which can only be frustrated by an audience's subjective identification with and emotional response to the depicted characters and events.

While the view that emotional engagement with works of art is an impediment to the proper appreciation of those works may be motivated in a variety of ways, a common assumption underlying views of this sort may be that emotional engagement is, in one way or another, at odds with rational engagement and assessment. And, while this assumption has been far from uncommon in the history of philosophical thought about emotion, the development into orthodoxy over the last fifty years or so of what are commonly called cognitive theories of emotion has made it, and thus the position that some have taken to follow from it, i.e. that works of art are not appropriately to be engaged with emotionally, increasingly hard to sustain. In opposition to theories (such as those of Descartes and William James) that take the emotions to be essentially states of bodily feeling or sensation, cognitive theories hold that the emotions are essentially intentional states, states that have objects: one is afraid *of* something, angry *with* someone or *about* something, has hopes *for* something, and so on. Furthermore, such theories typically hold that, in order for something to be the object of a particular sort of emotion, that thing must be construed by the person experiencing the emotion in a particular sort of way: for example, only if I take something to be threatening or dangerous can I be afraid of it, and I can only pity that which I take to be in some sense or other a victim of misfortune. Thus, cognitive theories hold that at the heart of any emotional experience is something like an evaluative thought or judgement—though the precise nature of the latter, and of the role that it plays in emotional experience, has been the subject of a good deal of debate (see e.g. Solomon 1976; Lyons 1980; De Sousa 1987; Greenspan 1988; Pugmire

1998). Whatever the upshot of that debate, however, it is undeniable that at least some paradigmatic cases of emotional experience involve a cognitive component of some form, and that in at least some cases emotional experience does not run counter to, but actively involves the exercise of, reason. Recognition of these facts paves the way towards seeing that emotional experience may function cognitively, and how it may do so, not least in our experience of art. Just as (reflection on) our emotional experience with respect to the everyday world may be a means, to put it baldly, of coming to know that world better, so, as Nelson Goodman for example argues, 'Emotion in aesthetic experience is a means of discerning what properties a work has and expresses' (Goodman 1976: 248 ff.). The question of just how emotional response may function in this sort of way in aesthetic experience is one about which it is difficult to generalize without lapsing into vacuity, and one that requires critical as well as philosophical acuity if it is to be handled illuminatingly. Elliott (1966) (which explores the thought that one may come to understand a work of art by experiencing in different ways the emotions expressed in that work), Levinson (1990), and Ridley (1995) (which both explore the ways in which our emotional experience of music may inform our appreciation of it), and Feagin (1996) (which focuses on the ways in which emotional experience can be central to our understanding and appreciation of literary fiction) are among the relatively few recent philosophical attempts to explore this question at the level of detail that it demands.

If recognition of the cognitive aspect and functioning of emotion should serve to undermine at least some claims to the effect that emotional response to works of art is an impediment to the proper understanding and appreciation of those works, it also raises a number of different questions concerning such responses. Of these, the one that has been the object of most philosophical attention over the last twenty-five years concerns the nature and rationality of our emotional responses to works of fiction. In brief, the question here arises from the fact that the evaluative judgements held by many versions of cognitivism to be central to the emotions appear to presuppose beliefs in the existence of the objects in question: I can hardly believe that something is threatening or a victim of misfortune (for example) unless I believe that it exists to *be* threatening or a victim. (For a clear statement of this position, see e.g. Donnellan 1970.) The upshot with respect to our emotional responses to what we know to be fictional characters seems to be straightforward: given that I do not believe that Nosferatu the vampire exists, I cannot believe that he threatens me; and if such a belief is a necessary component of fear, as some versions of the cognitive theory hold, then it follows that I cannot be afraid of Nosferatu. Similarly, at least on the face of it, since I do not believe that Anna Karenina ever existed, I cannot believe that she suffered, and hence I cannot truly be described as pitying her. And yet it seems that many of the consumers of the fictions in question *do* fear Nosferatu and pity Anna—and, indeed, that the fact that they do is in one way or another importantly related to the ways in which those fictions are valued by their consumers. Thus, we have what is sometimes referred to as 'the paradox of fiction': on the one hand, it appears that we often respond to what we know to be fictional characters with emotions such as pity and fear; and on the other, it looks as though responses of this sort are precluded by the logic of these emotions.

This issue has possibly been the topic of more discussion than any other in recent philosophical aesthetics, and has generated at least three monographs (Boruah 1988; Dadlez 1997; Yanal 1999) as well as a very large number of shorter articles and essays. (For a broad survey of the terrain, see Levinson 1997.) Contemporary interest in the issue can be traced back to a series of articles by Colin Radford, who argued that the fact that our emotional responses to fiction are not grounded in existential beliefs of the right sort makes those responses irrational. This charge of irrationality is based on the claim that, in pitying Anna Karenina (or fearing Nosferatu, or envying Superman his powers, etc.), we behave *inconsistently* and *incoherently*: as Radford sees it, 'our problem is that people *can* be moved by fictional suffering given their brute behaviour in other contexts where belief in the reality of the suffering described or witnessed is necessary for [such a] response' (Radford 1975: 75; see also 78). Broadly speaking, two strategies have been adopted in responding to Radford's charge of irrationality. Variants of the first proceed by attempting to establish that our affective responses to fiction may in fact be based on beliefs of an appropriate sort, and hence are not problematic in the way Radford suggests. Variants of the second accept that the responses in question are not typically grounded in appropriate beliefs, and go on to attempt to show that they may none the less be intelligible and rational responses.

With respect to the first strategy, three sorts of positions are worthy of note. The first, and perhaps the oldest, holds that works of fiction that succeed in moving their audiences do so by persuading those audiences in one sense or another to lose sight of the fact that what they are engaging with *is* fiction, so that their emotional responses to the characters and events of such works are based on false beliefs. For example, Jonathan Barnes speculates that it is the affective power of poetry that led Gorgias to the view that poetry can 'persuade and deceive the soul' and that in responding to poetry 'the deceived [is] wiser than he who is not deceived' (Barnes 1979: 161 ff.). Coleridge's talk of 'that willing suspension of disbelief for the moment, which constitutes poetic faith' (Coleridge 1907: 6) is often understood as gesturing in the same direction. The major problem with this sort of position is succinctly stated by Dr Johnson, who states that 'The truth is, that the spectators are always in their senses, and know, from the first act to the last, that the stage is only a stage, and that the players are only players. ... The delight of tragedy proceeds from our consciousness of fiction; if we thought murders and treasons real, they would please no more' (Johnson 1969: 27–8).

Johnson is well aware that the audience's 'consciousness of fiction' raises a problem: 'It will be asked', he notes, 'how the drama moves, if it is not credited'. And the answer that he offers represents the second of the three sorts of position referred to above: fictions may move us, he argues, 'not because they are mistaken for realities, but because they bring realities to mind' (Johnson 1969: 27–8). That is to say, our affective responses to fiction *are* based on beliefs, but they are beliefs about the actual world, and the responses in question thus have actual rather than fictional objects. (Versions of this sort of position are also defended in Weston 1975; Charlton 1984; Levinson 1996.) However, while it is certainly true that some of our emotional responses to fiction are of this sort, is seems clear that not all of them can be so understood: as Radford puts it, 'we do not really weep for the pain that a real person might suffer, and which real persons have suffered, when we weep for Anna Karenina, even if we should not be moved by her story if it were not of that sort. We weep for *her*' (Radford 1975: 75).

Third, and most plausibly, it has been argued that the beliefs on which our emotional responses to fiction are in fact grounded—beliefs about what is fictionally the case, or what is true in the fiction—are sufficient to render at least some such responses conceptually coherent and potentially rational. Thus, for example, it can be argued that my belief that it is fictional that Anna Karenina suffers as she does in the story, together with certain other facts about me, including my desires and the character of my feeling, may make it true that I pity Anna; and if the beliefs in question are themselves appropriately grounded, and the feelings are within appropriate limits, that pity may be rational. (Variants of this position are defended in Schaper 1978; Allen 1986; Neill 1993; for criticism, see Radford 1995; Levinson 1997.)

The second strategy referred to above, which involves accepting that our emotional responses to fiction are not typically grounded in beliefs of a sort that would render them unproblematic, also encompasses at least three sorts of position. Two of these in effect involve describing the responses in question in such as way as to render them conceptually coherent in terms of the cognitive approach to emotion. The first attempts to describe them in terms of non-intentional (and in particular non-belief-dependent) states such as moods or sensations (see e.g. Charlton 1970: 97). This move is at its most plausible with respect to our emotional responses to non-representational works of art, works that apparently do not present the audience even with fictional objects and events that might serve as the objects of emotions, such as those of purely instrumental music and abstract sculpture and painting. And indeed, it has some application with respect to our emotional engagement with works of fiction. Some of our responses to fiction are clearly more like objectless moods or non-directed feelings than they are like directed emotions; for example, a novel may just leave us feeling gloomy or depressed. Others that are less obviously so, such as apparent fear of fictional monsters, may none the less be amenable to redescription in terms, say, of our being startled and shocked. Many of our responses to fiction, however, such as those we are pre-theoretically inclined to describe as pity for Anna Karenina or loathing of Iago, quite clearly cannot be redescribed in terms of non-intentional affective states without considerable distortion.

More promising, and more theoretically sophisticated than any of its competitors, is the position that has been developed by Kendall Walton. (For the most complete statement of this, see Walton 1990.) Walton argues that the feelings that we may at first be inclined to describe as, for example, pity for and fear of fictional creatures cannot literally be pity and fear, since those feelings are not grounded in appropriate beliefs, and do not involve the motivation to action that emotions of this sort standardly involve. His suggestion is that crucial to the proper characterization of feelings of this sort is recognition that they occur in the context of games of make-believe that readers and spectators of works of fiction play in engaging with those works, using them as 'props'. And games of make-believe, Walton argues, may generate fictional truths: just as in a game of mud-pies it will be make-believedly the case that your pie is larger than mine if your glob of mud is larger than mine, so, in the game of make-believe I play when watching a horror movie, it will be make-believe that I am threatened when the monster on the screen begins lurching towards the camera. If as a result of my recognition that make-believedly I am threatened I experience the feelings characteristic of fear (increased pulse rate, muscular tension and so on—Walton calls this ensemble of feelings 'quasi-fear'), then it is also make-believedly the case that I am afraid. And so, *mutatis mutandis*, for my 'pity' for Anna Karenina, my 'loathing' for Iago, and so on.

This account may also be developed in such a way as to characterize some of our emotional responses to non-representational works of art, which may also function as props in games of make-believe that may constitute an audience's engagement with them. Thus, for example, the games we play in engaging with a piece of instrumental music or abstract sculpture may generate fictional truths about imagined objects and our relationship to them which, together with the feelings that the work in question arouses in us, may make it make-believedly the case that we experience certain emotions despite the fact that we do not have the beliefs (or other sorts of cognition) possession of which would make it literally true that we experience those emotions.

Much of the criticism that has been levelled at Walton's account of the nature of our emotional responses to fiction stems from taking the claim that it is only make-believedly the case that I am (say) *afraid* to mean that it is only make-believedly the case that I am *moved*. This, however, is a mistake: what is in question for Walton is not the existence of our feelings in response to fiction, but rather the proper description of those feelings. The persuasiveness of his account of how this description should go clearly depends largely on the persuasiveness of the general theory of representation as make-believe on which it is based; surprisingly enough, that general theory has received relatively little sustained attention from aestheticians (exceptions include Currie 1990 and Levinson 1996), though the account of the nature of our feelings for fiction has been the subject of a good deal of discussion in recent years (see e.g. Carroll 1990; Neill 1991).

At the time of writing, the response to Radford's critique of our emotional responses to fiction most in favour is based on the denial of the claim that ordinarily belief is necessary for the experience of emotion (see e.g. Lamarque 1981; Carroll 1990; Morreall 1993; Yanal 1999). This response, which is sometimes labelled

'Thought Theory', presses the fact that in many circumstances merely the thought of danger or suffering, for example, is sufficient to generate emotion: phobic fears are an obvious and often cited case in point, since they appear very often to be based on ways of construing something rather than on beliefs in its dangerousness. Hence being moved by fiction in the absence of beliefs in the existence of its characters and events is not, *pace* Radford, inconsistent with our responses in other contexts, and so is not, or at least need not be, irrational. As a thesis about the possible causes of emotional experience, and as a response to Radford's charge of inconsistency, this is surely correct: human beings can be moved quite ordinarily not only by what they believe to be the case—by creatures and situations and events that they believe to be actual or likely—but also by the products of the imagination, by day-dreams and fantasies and thoughts the contents of which they know do not correspond to the way the world is or is ever likely to be; and, indeed, by such things as rhythm and colour and even figure and size (a fact emphasized by theorists of the sublime; see e.g. Burke 1998). This latter fact is doubtless part of the explanation of how it is that non-representational art may arouse emotion in us. (See for example Meyer 1956 for an exploration of the power of purely instrumental music to arouse emotion in its audience.)

However, it is far from clear that this insight does away entirely with the puzzle concerning our emotional responses to fiction. First, many cases of non-belief-based emotional experience are strikingly disanalogous to much of our emotional response to fiction. Some of the former, such as phobic responses, are plainly irrational (even if not by virtue of inconsistency with 'normal' responses), the denial of which, with respect to our emotional responses to fiction in general, is part of the very point of Thought Theory. Others, such as startle and other reflex responses, though they may have analogues in our experience of fiction (horror movies in particular often rely heavily on them), are very different sorts of response from the considered pity that we may feel for Anna Karenina or the loathing that Iago may inspire in us. Second, although the sort of responses pointed to by advocates of Thought Theory may plausibly be said to depend on thoughts about or 'ways of seeing' their objects, rather than evaluative beliefs about those objects, many of them at least do none the less depend on belief in the *existence* of those objects. The person who has a phobic fear of mice may not believe that mice are dangerous although she is nevertheless unable to help 'seeing' them as such, but she certainly believes that mice exist—if she did not, she could not be said to fear them (what?) at all. The possibility of such responses thus fails to demonstrate that we may unproblematically be said to fear Nosferatu, for example, since responses of the latter sort are problematic precisely because (and where) they do not involve belief in the existence of the objects in question. Finally, some of the varieties of response appealed to by advocates of Thought Theory leave in question the nature and proper description of those responses: even if the mere thought of being stranded on a distant planet (to take an example offered by Lamarque) may be frightening, it is far from clear that it would be appropriate to describe the resulting state as one of *fear*. For what, assuming that I don't believe that I am going to be stranded on a distant planet, could I be supposed in such a case to be afraid *of*? Thus, appeal to the power of non-existentially committed thought to frighten us does not in itself settle the question whether we may properly be described as being afraid of Nosferatu.

One impediment to getting clear about the character of our emotional responses to fiction has been a common tendency to treat those responses as if they were all of a kind. But they are not. For example, responses that are self-directed, such as fear for oneself, are importantly different from responses that are other-directed, such as fear for another; and sympathetic responses such as fear for another operate differently from empathetic responses, such as those in which I come to share the fear of another. (For discussion of such differences, see e.g. Neill 1993; M. Smith 1995; Feagin 1996.) One notable strand in recent work on fiction and emotion has focused on empathetic response, and in particular on the role in our engagement with works of fiction of mental simulation—crudely speaking, adopting the point of view of another—which has been argued by some philosophers of mind to be the psychological mechanism responsible for empathy (see e.g. Goldman 1995, and other essays in Davis and Stone 1995). Part of the appeal of simulation theory in this context is that it may also offer an explication of the notion of identification with characters, a notion that has long been thought to be crucial to fiction's power to engage us emotionally, but which (as is demonstrated in Carroll 1990: 88–96) has more often than not been deployed in ways that render that power more rather than less mysterious. As things stand, there is little consensus on the question of how useful the notion of simulation is in understanding our experience of fiction. Notable defenders of its value in this context include Feagin (1996) and Currie (1995*a,b*); those pressing the limitations of the notion with respect to our engagement with fiction include Carroll (1997).

Perhaps the oldest of the many questions concerning our emotional responses to works of art that have occupied aestheticians concerns the nature of our responses to tragedy. Ever since Aristotle's statement, in the *Poetics*, that the pleasure 'appropriate' to tragedy is 'the pleasure which derives from pity and fear by means of mimesis' (Halliwell 1987: 46), philosophers have worried about the character of this pleasure, and indeed its analogues in our experience of other forms of art, such as horror (see e.g. Carroll 1990), music (see Levinson 1990; Ridley 1995: chapter 7) and works of mystery and suspense (see e.g. Carroll 1996; Yanal 1999: chapter 8). Eighteenth- and nineteenth-century discussions of this issue tended to fall into two broad strands: those which emphasized psychology, offering explanations of how it is that an experience involving emotions such as fear and pity, sadness and horror, can 'by means of mimesis' be rendered pleasant (see e.g. Hume 1987*b*; Burke 1998; A. Smith 1982); and those that emphasize metaphysics, attempting to explain the effect of tragedy by exploring the subject matter of that art form (see e.g. Schopenhauer 1969; Nietzsche 1993). In recent analytic aesthetics, discussion has largely followed the first of these strands: Feagin (1983), for example, develops an account according to which the pleasure that we may take in tragedy is a meta-response to our negative responses to the works themselves; while Eaton (1982) and Morreall (1985) explain pleasure in the face of the distress that tragedy may arouse in us by pointing to the fact that in the experience of tragedy the audience's emotional responses are controlled, either by the work and/or by the audience itself.

This chapter has surveyed only a few of the many issues concerning art and the emotions that have interested philosophers and other philosophically minded artists and critics, and it has barely scratched the surface of those. None the less, it will have served its purpose if it has succeeded in conveying the richness of this area of philosophical aesthetics, one that looks likely to remain for the foreseeable future at the very centre of the subject.

See also: Expression in Art; Fiction; Aesthetic Experience; Art and Morality; Music; Tragedy.

BIBLIOGRAPHY

Allen, R. T. (1986). 'The Reality of Responses to Fiction'. *British Journal of Aesthetics* 26: 64–8.

Arnheim, R. (1974). *Art and Visual Perception*, rev. edn. Berkeley and Los Angeles: University of California Press.

Ayer, A. J. (1971). *Language, Truth and Logic*, rev. edn. Harmondsworth: Penguin Books.

Barnes, J. (1979). *The Presocratic Philosophers*, vol. 2: *Empedocles to Democritus*. London: Routledge & Kegan Paul.

Barwell, I. (1986). 'How Does Art Express Emotion?' *Journal of Aesthetics and Art Criticism* 45: 175–81.

Beardsley, M. C. (1966). *Aesthetics from Classical Greece to the Present*. New York: Macmillan.

Bell, C. (1958). *Art*. New York: Capricorn Books.

Benson, J. (1967). 'Emotion and Expression'. *Philosophical Review* 76: 335–57.

Boruah, B. (1988). *Fiction and Emotion*. New York: Oxford University Press.

Bouwsma, O. K. (1954). 'The Expression Theory of Art', in W. Elton (ed.), *Aesthetics and Language*. Oxford: Blackwell.

Brecht, B. (1948). 'A Short Organum for the Theatre'; reprinted in T. Cole (ed.), *Playwrights on Playwriting*. New York: Cooper Square Press, 2001.

Budd, M. (1985). *Music and the Emotions*. London: Routledge.

—— (1995). *Values of Art: Pictures, Poetry and Music*. London: Allen Lane.

Burke, E. (1998). *A Philosophical Enquiry into the Sublime and Beautiful, and Other Pre-Revolutionary Writings*, ed. D. Womersley. Harmondsworth: Penguin Books.

Carroll, N. (1990). *The Philosophy of Horror*. London: Routledge.

—— (1996). 'The Paradox of Suspense', in P. Vorderer, H. Wulff, and M. Friedrichsen (eds.), *Suspense: Conceptualizations, Theoretical Analyses, and Empirical Explorations*. Mahwah, NJ: Lawrence Erlbaum.

—— (1997a). 'Simulation, Emotions and Morality', in G. Hoffman and A. Hornung (eds.), *Emotion and Postmodernism*. Heidelberg: Universitätsverlag C. Winter.

Carroll, N. (1997*b*). 'Art, Narrative and Emotion', in M. Hjort and S. Laver (eds.), *Emotion and the Arts.* Oxford: Oxford University Press.

Casey, E. (1970). 'Expression and Communication in Art'. *Journal of Aesthetics and Art Criticism* 30: 197–207.

Charlton, W. (1970). *Aesthetics.* London: Hutchinson University Library.

—— (1984). 'Feeling for the Fictitious'. *British Journal of Aesthetics* 24: 206–16.

Coleridge, S. T. (1907). *Biographia Literaria*, ed. J. Shawcross, 2 vols. Oxford: Oxford University Press.

Collingwood, R. G. (1938). *The Principles of Art.* Oxford: Oxford University Press.

Cooke, D. (1959). *The Language of Music.* Oxford: Oxford University Press.

Currie, G. (1990). *The Nature of Fiction.* Cambridge: Cambridge University Press.

—— (1995*a*). 'The Moral Psychology of Fiction'. *Australasian Journal of Philosophy* 73: 250–9.

—— (1995*b*). 'Imagination and Simulation', in M. Davis and T. Stone (eds.), *Mental Simulation.* Oxford: Blackwell.

Dadlez, E. (1997). *What's Hecuba to Him: Fictional Events and Actual Emotions.* University Park, Pa.: Pennsylvania State University Press.

Davies, S. (1994). *Musical Meaning and Expression.* Ithaca, NY: Cornell University Press.

Davis, M. and Stone, T. (eds.) (1995). *Mental Simulation.* Oxford: Blackwell.

De Sousa, R. (1987). *The Rationality of Emotion.* Cambridge, Mass.: MIT Press.

Donnellan, K. (1970). 'Causes, Objects and Producers of the Emotions'. *Journal of Philosophy* 67: 947–50.

Eaton, M. (1982). 'A Strange Kind of Sadness'. *Journal of Aesthetics and Art Criticism* 41: 51–63.

Elliott, R. K. (1966). 'Aesthetic Theory and the Experience of Art'; reprinted in A. Neill and A. Ridley (eds.), *The Philosophy of Art.* New York: McGraw Hill, 1995.

Feagin, S. (1983). 'The Pleasures of Tragedy'. *American Philosophical Quarterly* 20: 95–104.

—— (1996). *Reading with Feeling.* Ithaca, NY: Cornell University Press.

Goldman, A. (1995). 'Empathy, Mind and Morals', in M. Davis and T. Stone (eds.), *Mental Simulation.* Oxford: Blackwell.

Goodman, N. (1976). *Languages of Art*, 2nd edn. Indianapolis: Hackett.

Greenspan, P. (1988). *Emotions and Reasons: An Inquiry into Emotional Justification.* London: Routledge.

Halliwell, S. (1987). *The Poetics of Aristotle: Translation and Commentary.* London: Duckworth.

Hjort, M. and Laver, S. (eds.) (1997). *Emotion and the Arts.* Oxford: Oxford University Press.

Hume, D. (1978). *A Treatise of Human Nature*, ed. L. A. Selby-Bigge; 2nd edn. rev. by P. H. Nidditch. Oxford: Clarendon Press.

—— (1987*a*). 'Of the Standard of Taste', in his *Essays Moral, Political and Literary*, ed. E. F. Miller. Indianapolis: Liberty Classics.

—— (1987*b*). 'Of Tragedy', in his *Essays Moral, Political and Literary*, ed. E. F. Miller. Indianapolis: Liberty Classics.

Johnson, S. (1969). *Preface to Shakespeare's Plays.* Menston: Scholar Press.

Kandinsky, W. (1947). *Concerning the Spiritual in Art.* New York: George Wittenborn.

Kivy, P. (1980). *The Corded Shell: Reflections on Musical Expression.* Princeton: Princeton University Press.

Lamarque, P. (1981). 'How Can We Fear and Pity Fictions?' *British Journal of Aesthetics* 21: 291–304.

Langer, S. (1953). *Feeling and Form*. London: Routledge & Kegan Paul.

Levinson, J. (1990). 'Music and Negative Emotion', in his *Music, Art and Metaphysics*. Ithaca, NY: Cornell University Press.

—— (1996). 'Making Believe', in his *The Pleasures of Aesthetics*. Ithaca, NY: Cornell University Press.

—— (1997). 'Emotion in Response to Art: A Survey of the Terrain', in M. Hjort and S. Laver (eds.), *Emotion and the Arts*. Oxford: Oxford University Press.

Lyons, W. (1980). *Emotion*. Cambridge: Cambridge University Press.

Matravers, D. (1998). *Art and Emotion*. Oxford: Clarendon Press.

Mew, P. (1985). 'The Expression of Emotion in Music'. *British Journal of Aesthetics* 25: 33–42.

Meyer, L. (1956). *Emotion and Meaning in Music*. Chicago: University of Chicago Press.

Morreall, J. (1985). 'Enjoying Negative Emotions in Fiction'. *Philosophy and Literature* 9: 95–103.

—— (1993). 'Fear Without Belief'. *Journal of Philosophy* 90: 359–66.

Neill, A. (1991). 'Fear, Fiction and Make-Believe'. *Journal of Aesthetics and Art Criticism* 49: 47–56.

—— (1993). 'Fiction and the Emotions'. *American Philosophical Quarterly* 30: 1–13.

—— (1995). 'Fear and Belief', *Philosophy and Literature* 19: 94–101.

Nietzsche, F. (1993). *The Birth of Tragedy*, trans. S. Whiteside, ed. M. Tanner. Harmondsworth: Penguin Books.

Pugmire, D. (1998). *Rediscovering Emotion*. Edinburgh: Edinburgh University Press.

Radford, C. (1975). 'How Can We Be Moved by the Fate of Anna Karenina?' *Proceedings of the Aristotelian Society*, suppl. vol. 69: 67–80.

—— (1995). 'Fiction, Pity, Fear and Jealousy'. *Journal of Aesthetics and Art Criticism* 53: 71–5.

Ridley, A. (1995). *Music, Value and the Passions*. Ithaca, NY: Cornell University Press.

Schaper, E. (1978). 'Fiction and the Suspension of Disbelief'. *British Journal of Aesthetics* 18: 31–44.

Schopenhauer, A. (1969). *The World as Will and Representation*, trans. E. J. F. Payne, 2 vols. New York: Dover.

Sircello, G. (1972). *Mind and Art: An Essay on the Varieties of Expression*. Princeton: Princeton University Press.

Smith, A. (1982). *The Theory of Moral Sentiments*. Indianapolis: Liberty Classics.

Smith, M. (1995). *Engaging Characters*. Oxford: Oxford University Press.

Solomon, R. C. (1976). *The Passions*. Garden City, NY: Anchor Press/Doubleday.

Stecker, R. (2001). 'Expressiveness and Expression in Music and Poetry'. *Journal of Aesthetics and Art Criticism* 59: 85–96.

Stolnitz, J. (1960). *Aesthetics and the Philosophy of Art Criticism*. Boston: Houghton Mifflin.

Tolstoy, L. (1995). *What is Art?* Harmondsworth: Penguin Books.

Tormey, A. (1971). *The Concept of Expression*. Princeton: Princeton University Press.

Townsend, D. (2001). *Hume's Aesthetic Theory*. London: Routledge.

Walton, K. (1990). *Mimesis as Make-Believe*. Cambridge, Mass.: Harvard University Press.

Weston, M. (1975). 'How Can We Be Moved by the Fate of Anna Karenina?' *Proceedings of the Aristotelian Society*, suppl. vol. 69: 81–93.

Yanal, R. (1999). *Paradoxes of Emotion and Fiction*. University Park, Pa.: Pennsylvania State University Press.

ART AND KNOWLEDGE

BERYS GAUT

THE question of whether art gives us knowledge is as old as the philosophy of art itself: Plato in *The Republic* argued that, although poetry purports to give knowledge, it in fact does no such thing, but produces a mere deceptive appearance of knowledge. In contrast, Aristotle in *The Poetics* argued for the capacity of poetry to give its audience knowledge of universals. The dispute has reverberated down to the modern period, and a large part of the contemporary debate is still concerned with the classical form of the question. This can be dubbed the *epistemic question*: can art give its audience knowledge? Though the questions are rarely distinguished, there is a distinct issue which also needs to be addressed under the general rubric of art and knowledge, an issue that can be dubbed the *aesthetic question*: if art has the capacity to give knowledge, does this enhance its value as art—that is, broadly construed, its aesthetic value? Plato and Aristotle, in so far as one can make sense of the question posed in their terms, would have answered this second question affirmatively. But the rise of formalism in the early twentieth century, with its insistence on a sharp distinction between aesthetic and other kinds of values, returned a negative answer to the question. Beardsley, for instance, seems to concede that one can learn from works of art, but denies that this has anything to do with their aesthetic value (Beardsley 1981: 426–9).

Aesthetic cognitivism, then, is best thought of as a conjunction of two claims: first, that art can give us (non-trivial) knowledge, and second, that the capacity of art to give us (non-trivial) knowledge (partly) determines its value *qua* art, i.e. its aesthetic value. Aesthetic anti-cognitivism is a denial of one or both of these conjuncts. Supporters of aesthetic cognitivism in recent years include Walsh (1969), Beardsmore (1971, 1973), Goodman (1976), Novitz (1987), Nussbaum (1990), and Kivy (1997), anti-cognitivists include Stolnitz (1992), Diffey (1997), and in a restricted form Lamarque and Olsen (1994). In examining the question of the relation of art to knowledge, we can best proceed by looking at the two conjuncts of aesthetic cognitivism in turn. The debate has been conducted mainly in respect of the representational arts, such as literature and painting, and we will also concentrate on these arts in addressing the two issues.

1. THE EPISTEMIC ISSUE: COGNITIVISM

Cognitivists hold that art can give us knowledge. If so, what sort of knowledge can it provide?

First, some hold that literature in particular can give us a kind of philosophical knowledge, knowledge of the nature of our concepts, particularly moral concepts such as that of sympathy (John 1998). Martha Nussbaum has argued that moral philosophy can give us an 'outline' of the good life, but that, for a complete grasp of the particular requirements of situations, we need the kind of moral vision that finds its full embodiment only in works of literature, such as the later novels of Henry James (Nussbaum 1990: esp. 125–67). Certain literature accordingly functions as a more fine-grained extension of philosophy.

Second, some have argued that art can give us knowledge of possibilities, for example of how a situation can be interpreted, of how a situation might feel to someone, and so on. Hilary Putnam argues that Doris Lessing's novel *The Golden Notebook* shows us how a certain 'moral perplexity might have been felt by one perfectly possible person in a perfectly definite period' (Putnam 1978: 91). Putnam assimilates these functions of generating hypotheses and determining possibilities to conceptual knowledge, but this is too restrictive, since there are different kinds of possibility besides conceptual ones. And in Putnam's own example, the import of 'perfectly possible' connotes something other than mere conceptual possibility, and encompasses some notion of plausibility.

Third, and more strongly, some have held that art can give us knowledge about not just what is possible, but what is actual: it has often been supposed, for instance, that literature can give us insights into human nature. Freud famously claimed that many of his ideas had been anticipated by Sophocles and Shakespeare. David Novitz has defended the view that literature can teach us about what is actually the case (Novitz 1987: 132).

Fourth, turning away now from conceptual and propositional knowledge, cognit-ivists have also held that art can give us practical knowledge, knowledge of how to do certain things. It has been held that art can teach us how to feel appropriately, educating our emotions (Robinson 1997), that it can improve our practical reason-ing (Putnam 1978), and that it can enhance our imaginative capacities, which are required to plan and to understand others (Currie 1998). Nelson Goodman has defended the view that the visual arts can teach us how to look at the world, dis-covering aspects of it which we had previously overlooked: 'What a Manet or Monet or Cézanne does to our subsequent seeing of the world is as pertinent to their appraisal as is any direct confrontation [with the work]' (Goodman 1976: 260). Though knowing-how is conceptually distinct from knowing-that, clearly the latter often depends on the skills evinced in the former.

Fifth, some have claimed that art can teach us the significance of events, and have held this to be distinct from other kinds of knowledge. R. W. Beardsmore has argued that literature can help someone to make sense of, or find meaning in, events that previously had been meaningless to him: after his breakdown, John Stuart Mill found meaning again in his life by reading Wordsworth's poetry, and Edwin Muir recovered a proper perspective on a childhood humiliation through writing a poem (Beardsmore 1973).

Sixth, some cognitivists have held that art gives us experiential (phenomenal) knowledge, knowledge of what it is like to be in love, or suffer the loss of a child, and so on, and that it does this by broadening our experience to encompass things we might never otherwise have undergone or felt. The experience it offers, being imbued with imagination, differs from the kind of experience we would actually have if we underwent these things, being a kind of 'virtual experience' (Walsh 1969: 91), but it nevertheless grounds experiential knowledge.

Finally, many cognitivists have held that art can teach us about values, particu-larly moral values. As already noted, Nussbaum holds this view as the main instance of her claim that literature is a kind of philosophy. Others who hold that art can morally instruct us include Beardsmore (1971), Novitz (1987), Eldridge (1989), Sharpe (1992), and Kieran (1996). Indeed, probably the major part of the debate about the cognitive value of art in recent years has turned around the question of moral knowledge through art.

So there has been a wide range of claims advanced by cognitivists about the kind of knowledge one can obtain from art, and many cognitivists have held that several or all of these sorts of knowledge are obtainable. There is much intuitive support for some of these claims: readers often hold that literature can tell them about human nature, and this claim can be supported by close reading of texts, such as those under-taken by Nussbaum; paintings can and do affect the way we see the world (the world seen through Monet's paintings looks more vivid and more subtly and variably coloured than it otherwise would); and we do seem in some sense to have our experi-ence of others' lives extended and deepened through reading. Cognitivism also explains at least part of the value we place on art over mere entertainment; for on this account the special value we place on knowledge as reflected in the public support given to education and research also partly explains the value we place on art (Graham 1995).

2. THE EPISTEMIC ISSUE: ANTI-COGNITIVIST OBJECTIONS

Much more could be said about the support for cognitivism, but it is more fruitful to examine the reasons that anti-cognitivists have advanced against it. This is because, if anti-cognitivism is correct, the kind of considerations to which cognitivists appeal are all delusory, since art is simply incapable of providing knowledge at all.

First, it may be objected to cognitivism that, though audiences may talk about learning from art, they generally cannot say *what* they have learned, or if they can say what they have learned it is completely banal; and this seriously casts doubt on whether they have learned anything worth mentioning. What does *Pride and Prejudice* teach us other than the banal 'Stubborn pride and ignorant prejudice keep attractive people apart' (Stolnitz 1992: 193)? However, not all such propositions are banal. As noted earlier, Freud claimed to find his psychological theories anticipated in Sophocles and Shakespeare, and, whatever the truth of Freud's theories, *banal* they are not. Further, this criticism assumes that, if we have learned something, it is always possible to cast it in general propositional form. But cognitivists often insist that the most significant aspect of what we gain from works is not propositional knowledge, but rather practical knowledge, or the appreciation of significance, or phenomenal knowledge (Novitz 1987: 133). And these types of knowledge resist adequate statement in propositional form: one may know how to ride a bicycle, but be completely incapable of saying what it is one knows (Currie 1998: 164). Moreover, much of what we can learn from art derives from seeing the actual world in terms of aspects of a fictional world—we can, for instance, see a hypochondriac in terms of Austen's Mr Woodhouse and come in this way to understand more about the real person (Graham 1995: 34). Again, this is the kind of knowledge that resists a settled general paraphrase, and is akin to what one may be said to learn from a metaphor when, in grasping a metaphor, one engages in an open-ended exploration of some of the salient similarities between two disparate entities.

A second anti-cognitivist objection is that, even assuming that one could learn from art, there is no way unique to art in which one does so. There are no distinctive artistic truths, as there are scientific ones: whereas there are scientific experts, a scientific method, and truths that only science can provide, art has no artistic experts (as distinct from experts about art), no artistic method, and no truths that only it can impart (Stolnitz 1992: 191–2). Now some cognitivists have defended the uniqueness claim. As remarked earlier, Nussbaum argues that great literature is uniquely well placed to deliver moral insights. So if her defence of the moral exemplarity of James's novels is correct, then Stolnitz's attack can be answered by showing that there are some truths that only literature can deliver. But Nussbaum's uniqueness claim may well be untenable, for it would follow that no one could have a completely adequate grasp of morality if they were innocent of great literature; yet, while we can morally blame someone for their moral failings, we don't morally blame them for their ignorance of literature, which would be required if only literature could remedy some of these failings. It is also hard to see why any insight that James can give us into morality could not in principle be accomplished by someone asking us to imagine what someone else is feeling or thinking, without using the full panoply of literary devices that James employs.

So the anti-cognitivist may well have a point in denying that there are any truths that only art can give us. But the cognitivist should note that the uniqueness claim is not required in order to be a cognitivist: why should the claim of art to provide knowledge require that it provide *distinctive* knowledge and methods? Consider newspapers: these (sometimes) provide truths about the world, but there are no such things as distinctive 'newspaper knowledge', methods, or experts: what is learnt and how it is learnt can also be imparted by other sources of knowledge—by television news, or by talking to people, for instance. One reason why cognitivists might be tempted to hold that any artistic knowledge must be distinctive is the fear that otherwise art would become redundant: if one could discover the same truths by other methods (say by reading psychology textbooks), then surely there would be no point in literature, and it would wither away? But that thought is based on a mistake. Cognitivists ought not to hold that cognitive values are the *only* kind of artistic values there are: poems can be beautiful, tightly organized, moving, etc., and these values are not cognitive ones. So, even if there were no distinctive truths that art in general or literature in particular could impart, one might still rationally prefer reading literature to psychology textbooks because of the other values that literature instantiates. A parallel point applies to other media: even though there are no truths that newspapers can give and television cannot, newspapers have not withered away; for they possess other values, such as convenience, thoroughness, and portability, which make them still choiceworthy.

A third anti-cognitivist objection holds that we cannot learn from art because, for knowledge of the actual world to be imparted, art must refer to that world; but it does not, for reference to the real world is suspended—a novel should be read as in effect starting with 'let us imagine that…', not 'it is asserted that…'. 'How can a work of art be faithful to the facts it would teach if art is not by its nature fact-stating?' (Diffey 1997: 30). (Diffey acknowledges however that art can suggest hypotheses without asserting them.) Interestingly, this objection reflects a slide that is very common in the debate about art and knowledge, but only rarely noticed—that from art to fiction. Not all art is fictional: most portraits, for instance, are or purport to be faithful representations of their subject's appearance; many landscapes are recordings of actual scenes, not inventions; many films are documentaries, not fictions. Indeed, even the category of literature is distinct from that of fiction: much of poetry is a recollection of or reminiscence about personal experience, not mere fiction; and the essays of Addison and Gibbon's *Decline and Fall of the Roman Empire* are works of literature but not of fiction (which is not, of course, to say that they are always accurate). So, implicitly, these works can be thought of as beginning with 'it is asserted that . . . '. Moreover, even in fictional works there are clear assertions, whether meant ironically or not, as in 'It is a truth universally acknowledged, that a single man in possession of a good fortune must be in want of a wife.' And the implicit assertions in any serious work of fiction are manifold, such as that in *Emma* to the effect that attractive, assertive, and spoilt young ladies are often not the best judges of their own motivations and behaviour.

The final objection that we will consider to the claim that art can teach us is in many respects the most weighty. Knowledge is not simply a matter of true beliefs: the true belief must not be accidentally acquired. Rather, the belief must be *justified*, or, depending on one's epistemic theory, *reliable*, or else it must fulfil some other condition. The anti-cognitivist objection is that art cannot fulfil this third condition: even if one acquires true beliefs from art, one is never justified in believing them simply on the basis of one's acquaintance with the artwork. Supposing Dickens's *Bleak House* is accurate about the slowness of estate litigation in nineteenth-century Britain: it cannot provide evidence of its accuracy. For that we need to consult the history books (Stolnitz 1992: 196).

Even if we conceded this point, given the diversity of kinds of knowledge to which cognitivists have drawn attention, it would not undermine all versions of cognitivism. Stolnitz's point is in fact granted by some cognitivists: Putnam holds that, while literature can teach one about what is possible (including possible interpretations of a situation, and what might happen), it can never give one knowledge about what actually occurred, for that is empirical knowledge, which requires testing (Putnam 1978: 89–90). So knowledge of possibilities, including knowledge of hypotheses about the world, would not be undermined by the truth of Stolnitz's claim. Nor indeed would conceptual knowledge; knowledge of a new concept does not require any empirical testing. For instance, Stendhal's introduction of the notion of 'crystallization' in his work *On Love* does not require any empirical testing to be grasped—something like knowledge by acquaintance is sufficient. However, there are limits to how far one can take this line of response. One might think that it applies to know-how too; but if a skill is a genuine one, it can be so misrepresented in art that one would be badly misled if one tried to apply it in real life: imagine a fictional work about a plumber, showing in detail, but completely inaccurately, how plumbers go about their jobs. One might discover that one had not thereby acquired the appropriate skills the next time one tried to mend a burst pipe. Likewise, giving the reader certain powers of intellectual discrimination and habits of thought might represent not a cognitive advance, but rather a cognitive deterioration, even though they applied fruitfully to the world of the text. For instance, Celine's comprehensive scepticism about the possibility of human love in *Journey to the End of the Night* might lead one to suppose that one had been given valuable intellectual skills to strip away the pretensions of goodness in people; but applied to the actual world these apparent skills would (hopefully) lead one to a systematic misunderstanding of human motivations (Putnam 1978: 91–2).

So if the 'no justification' objection were correct, it would undermine some versions of the cognitivist claim, but not all. But is it correct? A point made earlier is again germane: at best, the objection applies directly only to works of fiction, not to non-fictional artworks. We have as much reason to believe that Holbein's portrait of the two men in *The Ambassadors* is as broadly accurate about how they looked as we would have to believe a contemporary letter describing their appearance. What, though, of fictional works? One appealing cognitivist response is that, if we held that fiction does not impart knowledge, but only suggests propositions, then this 'must also be true of the humble reference book, for it is clear that a reference book can only be said to impart knowledge about the actual world if we are justified in believing that it is reliable. It goes without saying, though, that our knowledge of its reliability is not acquired from our experience of the book itself. It is acquired from a range of totally different experiences' (Novitz 1987: 132). So, if we hold that knowledge requires experience of the actual world for its justification component, then fiction and reference works stand on the same epistemic footing; hence there is no more reason to hold that fiction cannot give knowledge than to hold that reference works cannot.

This cognitivist reply is, I think, ultimately correct, but it needs development and defence. For there is still an important difference, from the point of view of knowledge, between fiction and reference works. There is what we can call an *institutional guarantee* in the case of the reference book that it has been properly vetted for its accuracy by people in a position to know about the relevant domain. But there is no such guarantee in the case of fiction: even if there are implicit or explicit claims made by the author in the work, no one as part of the institution of publishing such works need have checked these claims. In fact, this is an instance of a more general phenomenon in epistemology, that of testimony: while experience is a ground for our *a posteriori* knowledge, it is also true that much of our knowledge is derived from relying on what others, who we believe to be in a position to know about the relevant area, tell us. So the anti-cognitivist can still point to an important difference between the two kinds of writing in respect of epistemic grounding.

Again, however, this point needs care in its handling. For of course all that the institutional guarantee shows is that checking *should* have occurred; it does not show that it did occur or that it was competently done. There are outright frauds (such as the so-called 'Hitler Diaries'), and also honest mistakes not picked up by vetters. And importantly, one cannot tell simply by looking at the reference work itself whether it was subjected to proper vetting and how successful this vetting was: for that, one needs to go outside the text, research its generative conditions, and so appeal to experience. So, while the institutional guarantee, and more generally testimony, is the proximate source of our knowledge in such cases, the ultimate source is experience. And that again places fiction and reference works on an equal footing.

Moreover, though not institutionalized as it is in the case of reference works, there is something akin to testimony in the case of some fictions. Authors of fictions sometimes tell us in their works that what they are writing about is substantially accurate: indeed in Stolnitz's favoured example of *Bleak House*, Dickens tells us in the Preface that 'everything set forth in these pages concerning the Court of Chancery is substantially true'. And it is true of entire genres such as realism that they try to inform us of the kinds of things that happen. Consider Zola's novel *Germinal*, which he wrote to dramatize the misery of the poor in the Second Empire. Published in 1885, *Germinal* deals with the battle between capital and labour in the coal fields in northern France, and it is now an important historical source for our knowledge of the life of the proletariat in that period. Moreover, the existence of a work, even if it is not in the realist mode, may in itself be important evidence of the attitudes and beliefs current at the time of its writings. This is apparent when we consider works from eras for which we have relatively little evidence: the *Iliad* and the *Odyssey*, for instance, are important historical documents about the attitudes and assumptions of the ruling class of archaic Greece.

To sum up, the 'no justification' objection in its most powerful form holds that fiction cannot give knowledge, but at most can only suggest hypotheses, since, unlike non-fiction, its claims have not been subject to an institutional guarantee, a kind of testimonial evidence. The reply is, first, that there is a testimonial aspect to some genres of fiction and to some works; and, second and more importantly, that from mere inspection of a non-fiction work we cannot tell whether the institutional guarantee, the prior vetting, has actually occurred, so to see whether it has we have to go beyond the text, investigate its generative conditions, and so appeal to experience. Hence the epistemic authority of both fiction and non-fiction ultimately rests on experience, and in this fundamental justificational respect they stand on all fours. However, the difference in institutional guarantee does explain why the 'no justification' objection has plausibility. And it also highlights a real difference between fictions and reference works: the reader of fiction, as compared with the consulter of encyclopaedias, is to a greater extent thrown back on her experience and intellectual and emotional resources to establish whether she ought to believe the implicit claims of the fiction, for she lacks in many cases even the defeasible presumption of prior vetting that non-fiction provides. She has fewer, or in many cases no, reasons of testimony for believing anything explicitly or implicitly asserted in what she reads. In this respect Plato's worries about at least fictional literature are well taken: the opportunities for manipulation and delusion of readers are more extensive in the case of fiction than of non-fiction. But that point is entirely compatible with aesthetic cognitivism.

There is much more to be said about learning through art. In particular, the role of imagination is of considerable importance, though this role has been surprisingly little investigated. In ordinary life one can, through imagination, learn about what one really wants, what one ought to value, what it is like to undergo some experience one has not had, what it is like to be someone else by imaginatively projecting oneself into his place, and so on. Art in general, and literature in particular, can be thought of as a kind of aid to improved imagination, and so as being a way to help us to learn about aspects of the world. Gregory Currie has argued that realist fiction in particular is especially suited to help us through the exercise of imagination to learn about what we should do and to understand others' lives better (Currie 1998).

3. THE AESTHETIC ISSUE: COGNITIVISM

Though much of the debate about aesthetic cognitivism has concentrated on its first epistemic claim, in many ways its second aesthetic claim is more interesting and challenging. For, standing back from the specifics of the arguments rehearsed above, it would on reflection be extraordinary if one could not learn about human beings and the world they inhabit from practices as rich, varied, and deeply integral to human nature as those of art. We reveal too much of ourselves and our culture through our art-making for art not to be a major source of knowledge. So much is obvious when one reflects on our knowledge of ancient civilizations such as those of Ancient Egypt: much of what we know about earlier cultures is through the art that they produced.

This way of supporting the first cognitivist claim shows the pressure that the second is under. It is simply mistaken to suppose, as some cognitivists implicitly have done, that, because one can learn something from art, it is thereby better *qua* art. What a cognitivist has to do is to show that the cognitive values of art are aesthetically relevant. One can admit that ancient artworks have cognitive value in revealing much about the civilization that produced them, but the fact that they have this historical value does not show that they are thereby better works of art, and there are other epistemic features of works that are plausibly aesthetically irrelevant (Gaut 1998: 192).

There is much to be said in support of the cognitivist's aesthetic claim when one considers common features of aesthetic evaluation: for instance, we celebrate the

insight and profundity of artworks, and think these features are aesthetically relevant. And we deride works for their shallowness and sentimentality and think
them thereby aesthetically flawed. Here we are making *bona fide* aesthetic evaluations that seem also to be cognitive evaluations or seem to depend on such evaluations, as is true of sentimentality, which is a kind of feeling based on a
misconception of the object at which it is directed (see Miller 1979). As we have seen,
it is not true that every epistemic merit of an artwork is an aesthetic merit of it, but
it is enough for the truth of cognitivism that this is sometimes so. It would be interesting if a general criterion could be formulated for when cognitive merits of artworks are aesthetic ones, but, given the sheer complexity of art, it is arguable that
no exceptionless criterion can be found; and in any case, it is not essential to cognitivism that such a criterion can be located.

We can however, at a suitably general level, say something about when cognitive
merits at least *tend* to be aesthetically relevant. Beardsmore maintains that, 'when
we learn from a work of literature, then what we learn, the content of the work, is
essentially bound up with the way in which the writer expresses himself, bound up,
that is, with the author's style' (Beardsmore 1973: 45). As we have seen, this is not
true universally, since we can learn a great deal of historical information from a
novel that doesn't depend on its style. But Beardsmore's remark has some plausibility as a claim about when the cognitive merits of a work are aesthetically relevant.
We could put the point like this: it is the *way* that a work conveys its cognitive
merits—the *mode* by which it conveys its insights—that makes them of aesthetic
relevance. The cognitive merits of a novel typically are aesthetically relevant when
they are displayed in the particular detailed descriptions of characters, the narrative
events, and the feelings prescribed by works. The claims a novel makes may be general, but they tend to be of aesthetic worth when made implicitly by the novel's
treatment of particulars. For instance, Austen's insights into human nature artistically enhance her novel when they are displayed in her construction of Emma's
character and what is internally related to it, in what Emma does and how she
responds to others. In Emma Austen has in effect constructed a new concept, one
that bundles together a set of characteristics, and we can learn to see real people in
these terms: we can see a young woman as an Emma, and by application of this
concept can learn more about the real person. If Austen's portrait has depth and
plausibility, it groups together characteristics that tend to fit together in people's
psychology, and we are likely to find, luckily and unluckily, a large number of
Emmas in the world. This point about cognitive merits tending to constitute artistic
merits when displayed in *particular* descriptions allows us to see why Stolnitz was
looking in the wrong place, not just from an epistemic but from an aesthetic point
of view, when he sought to locate the cognitive value of *Pride and Prejudice* in a general statement considered in abstraction from the particularities of the narrative,
characters, and style of the work that embodies it. Not only was that statement thus
considered banal, but, as a general proposition at such a high level of abstraction,

it was not the kind of cognition that would tend to lend artistic lustre to the work when separated from the work's particularities.

4. THE AESTHETIC ISSUE: ANTI-COGNITIVIST OBJECTIONS

Thus much within our common practice of aesthetic evaluation supports cognitivism; and one can roughly indicate when it is likely that cognitive virtues also count as aesthetic ones, even if there are no exceptionless criteria to be found. Given the support in common evaluative practices for the aesthetic claim of cognitivism, the anti-cognitivist should concentrate his efforts on showing that the appearances supporting cognitivism are deceptive, and should raise objections to the cognitivist construal of them.

The first objection to consider is Beardsley's claim that Goodman's cognitivism simply misrepresents critical evaluative practice. Beardsley complains that Goodman can give no account of non-cognitive values such as vitality, balance, and beauty (Beardsley 1978: 113–15). Now Goodman's is a strong form of cognitivism: he holds that 'The primary purpose [of the use of symbols beyond immediate need, and those of art in particular] is cognition in and for itself; the practicality, pleasure, compulsion, and communicative utility all depend upon this' (Goodman 1976: 258). If one adheres to a more pluralist line, as suggested earlier, according to which there is a plurality of aesthetic values, of which cognitive ones are only one kind, and does not hold that cognitive values are always primary, then it is easy to reconcile cognitivism with these features of critical practice. Similarly, the cognitivist can hold that the role of cognitive values will vary to some extent in importance with different art-forms: other things being equal, they are likely to be of greater aesthetic importance in representational arts such as painting and literature than in arts where representation has a more limited role, such as dance, music, and abstract painting. Nevertheless, even in such arts there will often be cognitive values of aesthetic importance; the patterns we come to see or hear can be applied to the world, and we can also come to discover features of interest in their own right in those abstract patterns. Josef Albers's series of abstract paintings, *Homage to the Square*, is an exploration of different colour-combinations within a common format of painted squares. They can be thought of as a series of visual experiments to determine the different phenomenal and affective properties of colours and their combinations.

A second objection is that we often seem not to care in our aesthetic judgements whether an author has got his facts right: we don't mind, for instance, that Shakespeare was wrong about Julius Caesar's battle dates (Lamarque and Olsen 1994: 297). This certainly shows that truth is not *always* artistically relevant. But of course, it does not show that truth is *never* artistically relevant. We are interested in Shakespeare's play in part for its exploration of the themes of heroism, war, love, and betrayal, and if it advanced shallow and false views about these—that war is uncomplicatedly ennobling, for instance—then we would justifiably think worse of it as an artwork. Of course, the aesthetic cognitivist should not hold that *every* cognitive merit or demerit in a work is an aesthetic merit or demerit, as we noted above.

A third objection concerns the nature of the aesthetic attention we bestow on artworks. T. J. Diffey argues that 'An aesthetic response to art involves the suspension of reference by taking the work to be holding up states of affairs for inspection, scrutiny, or, to use the traditional term, contemplation. So, to learn from a work of art, that is, to move from what is shown in the world of the work to an assertion of what obtains in the world, requires a refusal of the aesthetic stance . . .' (Diffey 1997: 30). The point is connected with Diffey's earlier argument about artworks not asserting anything, though it goes beyond it by identifying a purported feature of the aesthetic stance. But the aesthetic stance has no such feature. The evaluation of the accuracy or otherwise of the real-world references in a work is often important to its aesthetic evaluation. This is true of non-fictional works, such as documentaries and portraits, where serious misrepresentation of their subject-matter is an aesthetic flaw. And for fictions too, the evaluation of any implicit truth-claims made by a work may be aesthetically relevant; it is very hard, for instance, to see how there could be a serious and successful novel devoted, say, to the proposition that nudism makes you intelligent (Rowe 1997: 337). Likewise, genres of fiction such as satire require for their success that audiences recognize the reference to the targeted persons, and that there be *some* basis for the satire in those persons' actual characteristics, however exaggerated the treatment of those characteristics. So both the recognition of reference to the real world and an evaluation of the accuracy of its representation are sometimes relevant to the aesthetic stance, and therefore cannot be incompatible with it.

The final anti-cognitivist objection we will consider also rests on a purported feature of the aesthetic stance. Lamarque and Olsen defend a 'no-truth' theory of literary value, which holds that the truth of any claim made by a literary work is never relevant to its literary value (where literary value is the kind of aesthetic value possessed by literary works). There are of course many cognitive merits besides truth (a work may be very original but wrong in its claims, for instance), and Lamarque and Olsen concede that works may have such merits; indeed, they hold that 'literature has developed into a special kind of cognition' (Lamarque and Olsen 1994: 452). But the truth of a work's claims is never relevant to the literary merit of the work. To adopt the literary stance to a work is to adopt an expectation of literary aesthetic value in the text, and this in turn involves seeking in the work humanly interesting content which has complex and coherent form (Lamarque and Olsen 1994: chapter 10). Humanly interesting content is carried by themes, particularly perennial themes, such as those of fate and free will, and the literary work explores such themes. But to say that the content is interesting does not require that it be true. Indeed, according to a striking argument, which we can dub the *institutional argument*, the truth of the theme's content is aesthetically irrelevant: for literature in both its writing and its reception is constituted as an institutional practice, specified by a set of conventions, and not by the intentions of individual authors. And, whereas there are branches of literary study devoted to the study of narrative techniques and motifs, there is none devoted to the study of the truth or falsity of the implicit claims advanced by literary works. Contrast this with philosophy, where debate about the truth of the philosophical claims advanced by authors is at the heart of the institution of the reception of philosophical works. The conclusion is that the literary stance, and hence the literary value that is its object, is indifferent to the issue of truth (Lamarque and Olsen 1994: chapter 13).

Lamarque and Olsen's institutional argument and the nuanced anti-cognitivism it supports is in my view the most powerful and interesting of the anti-cognitivist responses to the second part of the cognitivist thesis. Lamarque and Olsen draw attention to an interesting difference between the institutional reception of literature and that of philosophy or science. However, they exaggerate that difference: critics do debate the truth of some literary claims (for instance Keats' equation of truth with beauty), and the discussion of the truthfulness of the portrayal of certain classes of persons, including women, blacks, and the poor, is a mainstay of much contemporary criticism (Rowe 1997). Moreover, even if Lamarque and Olsen were correct about the institutional reception of literature being indifferent to truth, given that authors such as James, Dickens, and Balzac were very concerned to communicate what they took to be truths, that would be ground for reforming the practice of literary reception. Literature is an attempt at communication, and if our institutional practices were indifferent to what was being communicated, that would be a reason to reform them. Finally, given Lamarque and Olsen's preferred account of literary value, it is hard to motivate their 'no-truth' theory; for they hold that, though a work is dealing with a perennial theme, the truth or falsity of the presentation of that theme is irrelevant. And that means that, whereas a work such as *Middlemarch* can take as a theme that human aspirations are thwarted by forces beyond an individual's control, there could in principle be an equally successful work embodying the proposition that human aspirations are never thwarted in this way. Yet it is hard to see how such a work could be much more than a puerile fantasy (Rowe 1997: 338). So if one holds that certain themes explored by literature are of perennial interest, it is highly implausible to think that our literary interest in them is indifferent to their truth.

Though Lamarque and Olsen's 'no-truth' theory of literary value should be rejected, the attraction of their position suggests an important difference between literary evaluation and the evaluation of scientific theories: the ultimate criterion of success in a scientific theory is explanatory truth; and, however elegant, original, and clever a scientific theory is, if it is false it must be discarded. This is not to say that these other features are irrelevant to its assessment—a false theory can still be interesting because of them—but it is to say that they are subordinate to explanatory truth. With literature, by contrast, we do not automatically discard works incorporating serious falsehoods, for in many cases they may have compensating merits that balance this flaw. However, to agree that truth in art does not have the final authority it possesses in science is a long way from agreeing that truth is never relevant to aesthetic evaluation.

The debate between aesthetic cognitivism and anti-cognitivism has been an important one within recent philosophy. I have argued that the cognitivist has the upper hand in this debate. Whether that be granted or not, I hope to have shown that the debate is more intricate than at first appears, for cognitivism has a double burden to shoulder: not only must it demonstrate that art can give genuine knowledge, but it must also show that, at least in some cases, its capacity to give such knowledge is an aesthetic merit. Though much of the debate has concentrated on the first epistemic issue, the second aesthetic issue is at least as important, and deserves more attention than it has hitherto received. Once we have disentangled the two claims of cognitivism, we can see that proving the epistemic claim may well be easier than many anti-cognitivists have supposed, while proving the aesthetic claim may be harder than many cognitivists have realized.

See also: Value in Art; Fiction; Art and Morality; Aesthetics and Ethics.

BIBLIOGRAPHY

Beardsley, M. (1978). '*Languages of Art* and Art Criticism'. *Erkenntnis* 12: 95–118.
—— (1981). *Aesthetics: Problems in the Philosophy of Criticism*, 2nd edn. Indianapolis: Hackett.
Beardsmore, R. (1971). *Art and Morality*. London: Macmillan.
—— (1973). 'Learning from a Novel', in G. Vesey (ed.), *Philosophy and the Arts: Royal Institute of Philosophy Lectures*, vol. VI. London: Macmillan.
Currie, G. (1998). 'Realism of Character and the Value of Fiction', in J. Levinson (ed.), *Aesthetics and Ethics*. Cambridge: Cambridge University Press.
Diffey, T. (1997). 'What Can We Learn from Art?' in S. Davies (ed.), *Art and its Messages: Meaning, Morality and Society*. University Park, Penna: Pennsylvania State University Press.
Eldridge, R. (1989). *On Moral Personhood: Philosophy, Literature, Criticism, and Self-Understanding*. Chicago: University of Chicago Press.
Gaut, B. (1998). 'The Ethical Criticism of Art', in J. Levinson (ed.), *Aesthetics and Ethics*. Cambridge: Cambridge University Press.
Goodman, N. (1976). *Languages of Art*. Indianapolis: Hackett.
Graham, G. (1995). 'Learning from Art'. *British Journal of Aesthetics* 35: 26–37.
John, E. (1998). 'Reading Fiction and Conceptual Knowledge: Philosophical Thought in Literary Context'. *Journal of Aesthetics and Art Criticism* 56: 331–48.

Kieran, M. (1996). 'Art, Imagination, and the Cultivation of Morals'. *Journal of Aesthetics and Art Criticism* 54: 337–51.

Kivy, P. (1997). *Philosophies of Arts*. Cambridge: Cambridge University Press.

Lamarque, P. and Olsen, S. (1994). *Truth, Fiction and Literature: A Philosophical Perspective*. Oxford: Clarendon Press.

——— (1998). 'Truth', in *Encyclopedia of Aesthetics*, ed. M. Kelly. New York: Oxford University Press.

Miller, R. (1979). 'Truth in Beauty'. *American Philosophical Quarterly* 16: 317–25.

—— (1998). 'Three Versions of Objectivity: Aesthetic, Moral and Scientific', in J. Levinson (ed.), *Aesthetics and Ethics*. Cambridge: Cambridge University Press.

Novitz, D. (1987). *Knowledge, Fiction and Imagination*. Philadelphia: Temple University Press.

Nussbaum, M. (1990). *Love's Knowledge: Essays on Philosophy and Literature*. New York: Oxford University Press.

Putnam, H. (1978). *Meaning and the Moral Sciences*. London: Routledge & Kegan Paul.

Robinson, J. (1997). 'L'Education sentimentale', in S. Davies (ed.), *Art and its Messages*. University Park, Pa.: Pennsylvania State University Press.

Rowe, M. (1997). 'Lamarque and Olsen on Literature and Truth'. *Philosophical Quarterly* 47: 322–41.

Sharpe, R. A. (1992). 'Moral Tales'. *Philosophy* 67: 155–68.

Stolnitz, J. (1992). 'On the Cognitive Triviality of Art'. *British Journal of Aesthetics* 32: 191–200.

Walsh, D. (1969). *Literature and Knowledge*. Middletown, Conn.: Wesleyan University Press.

Wilson, C. (1998). 'Epistemology of Fiction', in *Encyclopedia of Aesthetics*, ed. M. Kelly. New York: Oxford University Press.

CHAPTER 26

ART AND MORALITY

MATTHEW KIERAN

1. INTRODUCTION

THE connection between an artwork's value as art and its moral character remains a deeply puzzling matter in contemporary aesthetics. Tolstoy's unqualified moralism (Tolstoy 1930), which holds that the worth of a work as art is entirely determined by its moral character, is unacceptable. We commonly recognize that the moral character of a work may be problematic and yet hold it to be of value as art. J. G. Ballard's *Crash*, Henry Miller's *Tropic of Cancer*, and Jean Genet's *The Balcony* may commend, in different ways, morally problematic conceptions of sexuality, yet none the less they remain intriguing, original, and valuable works. The moral and sexual content of the Earl of Rochester's poetry is deeply nihilistic, but well formed and expressed. Despite the inappropriateness of their moral character, we still consider such works to be artistically good. Yet the radical autonomists' claim that the moral character of a work is irrelevant, since the content of a work *tout court* is irrelevant to its value as art (Bell 1914), is just as inadequate. We standardly hold that the constellation of a work's formal features can be exquisite and yet its value lessened in some way because of its content. Much of the time this may have nothing to do with the moral character or otherwise of a work, but in at least some cases it does. The formal construction of Dickens's *David Copperfield* may be superb, yet its purple sentimentality in places is commonly held to diminish its value as art. Dickens's sentimentality in part consists in an overly simplistic and naïve idealization of the moral character of the poor. If the characterization were more morally complex and adequate, then at least in this case the work would be less sentimental. Thus, here at least, it looks as if there is some relationship between the moral character of the work and our evaluation of it as art. D. W. Griffith's *Birth of a Nation* and Leni Riefenstahl's *Triumph of the Will* are held to be good artworks because of their formal virtues and the original film techniques deployed; none the less, the manifest racism of the one and the glorification of Hitler of the other arguably preclude an unqualified endorsement of their value as great art. The problem that faces us is thus not whether there is any kind of relationship between a work's artistic and its moral character: rather, the real problem concerns what the nature of that relationship is.

The idea that the moral character of a work may be intimately linked to its artistic value can be traced back to Aristotle, who suggests that moral criteria help pick out tragedies that are good or bad as such. Indeed, when outlining the correct standards in dramatic art, he claims that 'it is correct to find fault with both illogicality and moral baseness, if there is no necessity for them and if the poet makes no use of the illogicality (as with Euripedes and the case of Aegeus) or the baseness (as with Menelaus's in *Orestes*)' (Aristotle 1986: chapter 25). One way of taking this claim is to hold that the moral character of a work may affect its artistic value indirectly. I shall turn first to an examination of this kind of view in the following section. However, quite another way of taking it is famously articulated by Hume. Hume claimed that, where a work is at odds with our moral standards, 'this must be allowed to disfigure the [work], and to be a real deformity. I cannot, nor is it proper I should, enter into such sentiments; and however I may excuse the poet, on account of the manners of his age, I can never relish the composition' (Hume 1993: 152). This is a much stronger conception, amounting to the claim that a moral flaw is as such an aesthetic one. In Sections 3 and 4 I critically examine two distinct variants of this kind of view. In the final two sections I go on to outline two contrary lines of thought, in relation to obscene and pornographic works, which suggest that we have some reason to doubt this claim. For, contrary to Hume's thought, in some cases a work's value as art may be enhanced in virtue of its immoral character.

2. Sophisticated Aestheticism and Moderate Autonomism

In his preface to *The Picture of Dorian Gray*, Oscar Wilde wrote 'there is no such thing as a moral or an immoral book. Books are well written or badly written.'

In one sense the claim is obviously false. A work that glorifies and commends to us the persecution, rape, and pillage of others is, to say the least, morally problematic. But what Wilde is really getting at is the idea that as literature, or more generally as art, works are not to be evaluated in terms of their moral character. What matters is whether they artfully develop the imagery, characters, story, and theme concerned in ways we find to be beautiful. It is consistent with such a view to recognize that the moral character of a work may affect its aesthetic character, hence a didactic work may be clumsy and artless, but there is no internal relation between its moral character and its value as art.

This kind of quasi-formalist view as it has been articulated and developed has come to be known as sophisticated aestheticism (Beardsley 1958; Lamarque 1995) or moderate autonomism (Anderson and Dean 1998). The claim is that a work's moral character affects its artistic value, in an indirect manner, if and only if it either mars or promotes a work's aesthetically valuable features, such as its coherence, complexity, intensity, or quality of dramatic development. What a work makes fictional, what its literary qualities are, and the nature of its moral character are conceptually distinct, though the last explains why certain kinds of work, such as tragedy, are taken so seriously. Thus, to criticize a work on the grounds that its moral characterization fails to be 'true to life' is irrelevant to its value as art. But if a theme is not of human interest, if it is badly or incoherently developed, both of which may be indirectly affected by the moral character of a work, then the work's value as art is significantly lessened. Consider, from his *Lives of the English Poets*, Samuel Johnson's criticism of Milton's *Lycidas*:

With these trifling fictions are mingled the most awful and sacred truths, such as ought never to be polluted with such irreverent combinations. The shepherd likewise is now a feeder of sheep, and afterwards an ecclesiastical pastor, a superintendent of a Christian flock. Such equivocations are always unskillful; but here they are indecent, and at least approach to impiety, of which, however, I believe the writer not to have been conscious. (Johnson 1964: 96)

Milton's poem is being criticized because the moral characterization of Christianity manifest in the imagery betrays clumsy and crude poetic equivocations, thereby marring its aesthetic unity or coherence, and thus diminishing its artistic value.

However, Johnson's criticism may also be taken to suggest that the aesthetic flaw is compounded because the equivocation concerns, and thus confuses or denigrates, what are taken to be certain fundamental moral truths (Hume 1993). This kind of thought—that the moral character of a work can play a direct role in promoting or lessening the aesthetic virtues of a work—is a common one among professional critics and ordinary appreciators alike (Booth 1988). The sophisticated aestheticist can always retort that such artistic evaluations are conceptually confused. But there is good reason to think critical practice should, at least in certain circumstances, be this way.

Appraisals of a work as banal, sentimental, trivial, shallow or profound, significant, subtle, insightful, and nuanced are not always wholly specifiable without
appeal to considerations such as plausibility, insight, and explanatory informativeness (Miller 1979; Kivy 1997: chapter 5). Hence the sharp separation between the
quality of the imaginative experience and cognitive considerations, at least with
respect to much representational art, is difficult to support (Kieran 1996). This is
not straightforwardly to reduce the question to considerations of truth; for many
works that we value highly explore issues such as free will, the nature of evil, and
moral redemption and endorse, reject, or give conflicting characterizations of such
notions, from Mazzini's *The Betrothed* to Dostoevsky's *Crime and Punishment*. How
the vision is developed is crucial, and the understanding conveyed can be insightful yet partial. None the less, in order for the vision to be well developed, it must be
at least intelligibly developed.

Furthermore, there is the phenomenon of imaginative resistance we sometimes
experience with respect to a work's moral character (Moran 1994). When we engage
with fictional works we are often asked to imagine things that are fantastical,
improbable, and far-fetched. Now with respect to factual matters, we have little
problem doing so—imagining that, fictionally, humans can mind-read, time-travel
or live for thousands of years is not problematic. Yet, with respect to moral matters,
we often experience difficulty in imagining states of affairs or taking up attitudes
towards them that we consider to be unacceptable; we cannot (Walton 1994) or will
not (Gendler 2000) entertain or condone the prescribed attitudes. For example,
engaging with works such as the Marquis de Sade's *Juliette* or Leni Riefenstahl's
Triumph of the Will, which prescribe us to respond with admiration to, respectively,
the violent satiation of sexual appetite against someone's will and fascism as per-
sonified by Hitler, is phenomenologically difficult for most people who hold that
such things are unequivocally evil. Now if the moral character of a work in some
way prevents us from undertaking the imaginings and attitudes as prescribed by
a work, then it is tempting to think that it fails on its own terms.

However, matters are not quite so straightforward. One of the things we seem to
find most troubling about certain works is precisely that they can and do get us to
assent to views we take to be morally problematic (Tanner 1994). It is not so much
a question of fictionally assenting to particular propositions, but rather the world
view expressed by the work within which the propositions are located. Evelyn
Waugh's *Brideshead Revisited*, for example, does not merely make it fictionally the
case that Charles Ryder moves from indifference to the acceptance of Roman
Catholicism; the work makes certain factual and normative claims that are expressive of a particular kind of Roman Catholicism which is to be taken as being true of
the actual world. The novel expresses and exemplifies, in the development of the
fictional stories of Charles, Julia, and Sebastian, the view that one's relationship
with God should be central to one's existence and that this will often involve great

self-sacrifice. For the cost of following the will of God is, perhaps even necessarily, the sacrificing not only of one's own happiness but also that of others. Let us assume, for the sake of argument, that we find this kind of Catholicism deeply problematic. What *Brideshead Revisited* does is attempt to get us not merely to understand such a view but, in engaging with it, fictionally to assent to it. The trouble with reading the novel, given that it works well, is that we are moved from fictionally assenting to claims about Charles's development to fictionally assenting to the view of our place in the world as embodied in this kind of Catholicism. And this is standardly the case with good fictional works that trouble us. After all, we would not be so troubled by works that did not manage to do this. Of course, works that embody world views that are utterly alien to us may not challenge us in this way because we make no connection between this fictional world and our own. But works that do have a strong connection to at least some of our own beliefs and values, or that are at least a real possibility for us, will. So adducing the problem of imaginative resistance cannot in and of itself settle the issue, since many works do seem, successfully, to get us to assent fictionally to world views we are resistant to. The above considerations are what motivate the claim that moral considerations may directly affect a work's value as art, but further argument is required. There are two competing accounts—ethicism and moderate moralism—which attempt to provide just that.

3. Moderate Moralism

Moderate moralism (Carroll 1996) holds that a moral defect *may* count as an aesthetic one and a moral virtue *may* constitute an aesthetic one where the emotional responses a work solicits to achieve its purposes are, respectively, withheld or forthcoming because of the work's moral character. An artwork that fails to achieve its purposes is a failure on its own terms. The advantages of such an account are that it recognizes that great art need have no moral character whatsoever; it does not seem to presuppose a cognitivist account of the value of art; and it maintains that, even where a work does have a morally deficient character, this is not always relevant to its value as art, but only where it blocks our capacity to be absorbed in the work or to react to it as sought.

None the less, there are significant worries. On moderate moralism, the moral features of a work as such seem to play no direct role in its resulting artistic value. Whether a work is absorbing or succeeds in eliciting the emotional responses from us may be an aesthetic matter—but whether it does so in virtue of soliciting a defective moral perspective is a conceptually separate matter (Anderson and Dean 1998). Objects can have multiple aims—my computer may be designed to be both beautiful and easy to use. To be sure, whether it is easy to use may be affected by how it was designed to appeal to the eye. But it does not automatically follow from this that its aesthetic appeal is internal to the evaluation of the object *qua* computer as opposed to *qua* aesthetic object. At best, it has been claimed, Carroll's argument establishes that sometimes we are not in a position to judge how good an artwork is because of our reaction to its moral character (Jacobson 1997). If I find Roman Catholicism deeply repugnant, I may not be able to engage with and respond as prescribed to Dante's *Divine Comedy* or Evelyn Waugh's *Brideshead Revisited*; but this only shows that I am not in the best epistemological position to evaluate how good they are as art, not that they are no good.

A different worry arises in relation to works that may fail in their aims and yet be all the better for it (Kieran 2001*a*). For example, propaganda or didactic works might fail as such in ways that enhance their value as art. Consider Spike Lee's *Do the Right Thing*. One of Lee's didactic aims in making the film was to get the audience to respond to the racists portrayed as clearly contemptible. Yet the film fails in this respect, because one of the central characters, Sal, is in many ways a deeply morally admirable man despite his incipient racism. Thus, the film fails in one of its didactic aims precisely because the responses it elicits are more complex, sophisticated, and less sentimental than those it sought to evoke. Yet, in virtue of the way it fails, it is of greater value *qua* narrative art than it would have been had Lee succeeded in realizing his didactic aim.

Carroll has pointed out (1998*b*, 2000) that his claim concerns not what we may voluntarily be reluctant to imagine, but what we cannot or find very difficult to imagine—if a work requires of us what it is impossible or virtually impossible for us to do, as opposed to what we are simply unwilling to do, then there must be something wrong with the design of the work. Furthermore, there seem to be moral constraints internal to certain artistic genres. So one response to the above worries might be to point out that propaganda or didacticism are art-indifferent classifications while tragedy is an essentially artistic one—and, moreover, one that does have an inherently moral character. For a tragedy to be successful as such, we must pity the central character as well as fear what may befall him. If, however, we judge him to be unworthy of pity, perhaps because of the thorough viciousness of his actions as represented, then, whatever else is the case, the work must fail as a tragedy. But further argument is required, since at best this shows only that works of a certain moral character cannot be appropriately classified as tragedies, not that they cannot succeed as works of art. Marlowe's *The Jew of Malta* is famously problematic when considered as a tragedy in just this way; nevertheless, considered as a savagely dark comedy, it is ferociously successful.

4. ETHICISM

In the nineteenth century Matthew Arnold defended the greatness of Wordsworth for his depiction of moral ideas concerning man, nature, and human life. In particular, he claimed that 'a poetry of revolt against moral ideas is a poetry of revolt against *life*: a poetry of indifference towards moral ideas is a poetry of indifference towards *life*.' One might perhaps agree with Eliot that there is too much of a danger of confusing poetry and morals here (Eliot 1933: 116). But Arnold's presumption that serious art should be concerned with communicating deep responses to and an understanding of human life prefigures a dominant strand of criticism from Henry James through to Lionel Trilling and F. R. Leavis. In this tradition it is a profound criticism to make of a work that it fails to characterize adequately and get us to respond appropriately to the human experiences represented. Naturally this applies particularly to moral characterizations, evaluations, and attitudes.

It is this critical tradition that is most closely allied to the assumption that a moral flaw in a work is as such an aesthetic one (Hume 1993; Kieran 1996; Gaut 1998*a*). One argument put forward for this kind of view, termed 'ethicism', concerns the relation between the moral character of a work and the sought for cognitive–affective responses (Gaut 1998*a*). The claim is that, where a work prescribes cognitive–affective responses, which are thus intrinsically tied to the work's value as art, and where those responses depend upon ethical evaluation, the moral character of a work is always relevant to its value as art. Where we believe that the states of affairs as represented do not warrant the endorsement of the evaluation prescribed by the work, then the response it seeks from us is not merited and we can and often do legitimately fail to respond as prescribed. Where the merited response comes apart from the prescribed response, the work is, in that respect, a failure. We have again the recognition that great art need have no moral character and that good art may be morally flawed, for a work may be highly valuable in other respects. Ethicism also appears to address some of the worries that arose in relation to moderate moralism. What matters, according to ethicism, is whether or not the responses prescribed by a work are merited—hence problems concerning works that fail in their didactic aims by eliciting more appropriate responses do not arise. Furthermore, what an actual audience's responses are is irrelevant—it is a matter of whether they are merited in responding as they do. The value of de Sade's *Juliette* as art, for example, is lessened by virtue of soliciting admiration for that which should be condemned, independently of whether or not an actual reader responds in the manner solicited.

However, the appeal of ethicism rests in part on how willing one is to grant some degree of cognitivism concerning the value of art. Whereas moderate moralism, at least under one construal, merely appeals to whether a work is absorbing and we *can* react as solicited, ethicism, by contrast, is concerned with whether we *ought* to react as solicited in terms of what we believe the right responses to be. But it can only be a criticism of a work as art that it prescribes the wrong responses if one already presumes that part of the function of art as such is to convey truth, insight, and understanding. Yet it is precisely this premiss that sophisticated aestheticists and moderate autonomists reject (Beardsley 1958; Lamarque and Olsen 1994). The very notion of unmerited responses as adduced by ethicism requires further defence.

Consider an analogy to jokes (Jacobson 1997). There are many jokes we are warranted in finding funny—say, because they present surreal incongruities—but which are immoral—say, because they are deeply racist. It may be morally bad to laugh at such jokes or repeat them, but *qua* humour that does not of itself obviously affect whether or not such jokes are funny; hence the psychological discomfort we often feel in such cases. The only thing that matters is whether the joke is well designed to elicit the response of hilarity, and this is a matter, cashed out in terms such as incongruity, which concerns non-moral criteria. So too, the critic may go on, consistency of reason dictates that the same is true with respect to artworks. A work may solicit responses that are immoral but none the less are merited in terms of non-moral aesthetic criteria—namely in virtue of being aesthetically well designed, complex, coherent, and engaging. Of course, the ethicist could attempt to resist the analogy or, as Gaut has argued (1998b), could accept the analogy but deny that immoral jokes are unqualifiedly funny, but further argument is required if he is to resist the charge of begging the question.

Furthermore, the claim that moral aspects of a work, where they relate to our prescribed emotional responses, always figure in our evaluation of a work as art seems overly strong (Kieran 2001a). First, we commonly distinguish between the incidental character of a work and that which is essential to its point and purpose, disregarding much of the former in our assessments. Second, the moral character of a work that merely seeks to please or entertain tends to figure less in our artistic evaluation of it than in the case of serious art where the moral character of a work seems more closely tied to its artistic value.

It should be noted in passing that Carroll's moderate moralism is articulated specifically only in relation to narrative art, while Gaut's thesis is a claim about all art generally. It might be thought that the wider scope of Gaut's claim is much more difficult to defend in relation to artforms such as abstract art and pure music. But, to the extent that non-representational works seek to elicit cognitive–affective responses from us, Gaut's argument still applies and, specifically in relation to music, the thought that the moral value of a piece may constitute part of its artistic value has been argued for by Levinson (1998).

Particular problems aside, both moderate moralism and ethicism hold that, at least in certain cases, a work may be good as art and yet aesthetically defective in so far as it commends a morally defective perspective. In other words, despite its morally defective character, a work may be, all told, a good artwork. If, however, we had grounds for holding that a work could be valuable *in virtue* of its immoral character, then we would have strong reason to hold that neither ethicism nor moderate moralism could be the right accounts of the interrelations between the moral character of a work and its aesthetic value.

It has been argued that immoral works can be valuable as art because there are many different plausible views on the nature and morality of a great number of things (Jacobson 1997). Hence it is a boon that we engage with works that advocate views different from our own—if only to understand those different viewpoints better. But, Carroll has argued, such a line of thought affords only an instrumentalist justification of immoral art (Carroll 2000). This may be important in providing an argument against the censorship of immoral art, or for the importance of engaging with immoral art as a means to gaining knowledge and understanding. But, as such, it fails to offer any reason to think that, *qua* art, a work may be aesthetically enhanced in virtue of its immoral character. However, I think the immoralist line can be understood more sympathetically than this, and in what follows I outline two arguments which suggest we have reason to take such a possibility seriously.

5. OBSCENE ART

Certain kinds of artworks are often adjudged obscene and, as such, their moral character is condemned. So if we had grounds for claiming that obscene works, in virtue of their obscenity, can be valuable as art, then we would have strong reason to doubt the accounts of ethical criticism reviewed above.

What obscenity consists in is a controversial matter. But, minimally, an account of obscenity *per se* cannot be framed in terms of standard causal considerations, since the latter are neither necessary nor sufficient for a judgement of obscenity. Even if it were granted that there are causal links from obscene representations to immoral acts or to the social exclusion of certain groups, the causal assumption would apply to many representations we would not judge obscene. Certain films might represent women as dependent, empty, or flighty, and Pre-Raphaelite paintings, certain kinds of romantic fiction, and representations of the chivalric ideal often represent women as passive and utterly submissive to male desire. So someone might worry that an artistic diet consisting wholly of such representations would cultivate morally dubious attitudes or behaviour with respect to women. But we would nevertheless not condemn such works as obscene. Conversely, much of the Earl of Rochester's poetry, de Sade's fiction, or jokes about eating Holocaust victims would be deemed obscene without anyone thinking they would affect people's dispositions regarding how they treat others or what they eat. So the judgement of obscenity is not predicated on actual or foreseeable causal effects, but rather concerns the prior matter of the particular moral character a work is deemed to have.

The judgement of obscenity cannot arise in relation to anything we cognitively–affectively respond to as being morally prohibited—otherwise it would be merely a rhetorical term for picking something out as immoral. Of course there are a variety of features that are marks of the obscene, such as certain kinds of subject matter—principally sex, violence, death, and the corporeal—or the soliciting of certain kinds of objectifying interests in persons. But obscenity is centrally a matter of the *ways* in which such subject matter and interests are treated by representations in order to solicit certain kinds of responses from us. In the case of sex and violence, the judgement of obscenity arises where we judge a work to solicit and commend cognitive–affective responses of sexual desire or delight in the infliction of pain that are taken to be morally prohibited. Hence we distinguish Sadean type works, where rape, paedophilia, or brutally violent and intrusive sexual activities are represented as sexually arousing and desirable, from works such as Jonathan Demme's film *The Accused*. *The Accused* is not obscene, though it portrays rape from both the victim's and the perpetrators' viewpoints, since, far from commending the represented desires to us, it condemns them. More generally, any account of obscenity must give due recognition to a central feature of the phenomenology involved in paradigmatic cases of judgements of obscenity—namely the feelings of repulsion—by virtue of a representation soliciting responses taken to be morally prohibited, and of attraction towards indulging or delighting in those very responses.

Now both ethicism and moderate moralism rely on the basic thought that, to the extent that we deem the cognitive–affective responses solicited from us by a work to be morally prohibited, we will either fail to respond or will deem the response to be unmerited. But there are at least three distinct reasons that could underwrite the claim that we may be motivated or merited in responding as solicited by obscene works.

1. *Desire fulfilment*   Many obscene representations solicit and shape the indulgence of basic motivating desires that are deemed to be intrinsically morally wrong, misdirected in morally prohibited ways, or inviting a morally problematic over-indulgence. Consider a representation of a rape where one is directed to delight in and be aroused by the victim's pain, powerlessness, and sexual subjugation. Despite judging such responses to be immoral, the work—at least to the extent that it is successful—evokes a sense of sexual excitement, desire, and arousal. Desires for sexual power, domination, and supremacy on the one hand or, on the other, to be sexually subjugated to another's will are not uncommon among both men and women. Similarly, with respect to certain representations of violence, suffering, and death, a work may solicit responses that speak to desires to see or make others suffer, to exercise power by subjugating another, or to victimize. Again, such desires are common enough. Given the opportunity to actually fulfil such desires, a morally decent person would not act on them, would feel overwhelmingly repulsed by

witnessing such actions, and would feel no excitement at the prospect of so doing. But with respect to effective representations that speak to such desires whose fulfilment does not involve acting upon and harming others, the force of the moral prohibition slackens and it is easier to feel the pull of the desires spoken to.

2. *Meta-desire fulfilment*   Certain kinds of obscene representations may not speak to first-order morally prohibited desires but may concern morally prohibited second-order desires, such as the desire to be morally transgressive or the desire to delight in the first-order feelings of repulsion that a representation affords. For example, a narrative may represent its anti-hero as undertaking the repulsive violation of one moral taboo after another. The work does not solicit or commend the particular desires that the acts represented may themselves speak to. But what the work does seek is excitement, interest, and delight in moral transgression as such. Such a work speaks to a common enough desire to break free from the fundamental moral norms and mores we standardly take to be binding. We are not attracted to do so in real life because of the high moral costs to oneself and others and the likely prudential costs. But such costs are far less with respect to representations that indulge such desires but do not obviously involve harm to anyone. Hence, again, a work may successfully solicit the pull of a morally prohibited meta-desire in us.

3. *Cognitive rewards*   The motivating attraction in some obscene representations need not arise from particular morally prohibited desires, or from a meta-desire such as the desire to be morally transgressive. None the less, a representation may be adjudged obscene in representing persons in ways deemed morally prohibited and yet may solicit attraction in virtue of the cognitive interests spoken to—for example curiosity or fascination. Consider the work of the photographer Joel-Peter Witkin. Many of his works solicit a compulsive interest in the freakish, deformed, and mutilated bodies of persons. The works do not solicit responses based on delight in pain or suffering, nor do they speak to a desire to be morally transgressive as such. Rather, they arguably seek to direct our attention, and solicit responses based upon, sheer curiosity and fascination with the appearance of such persons. It is important to note that the object of fascination and delight is not the appearance of deformity or physical contortions alone. Rather, we are prescribed to look upon and delight in the subjects portrayed as sub- or other than human. Again, the cognitive desires spoken to here are not uncommon—as testified to by Plato's characterization in *The Republic* of Leontion, who delighted in the appearance of executed corpses, or by the fascination of many for the death, disaster, and car crash films and television programmes that attract such high audience ratings.

As a rough characterization, then, let us take an obscene work to be one that elicits or commends, in repulsive ways, morally prohibited cognitive–affective responses which are none the less found to be attractive for some of the reasons articulated above. (For a more sophisticated characterization, see Kieran 2002a.) Now the question is, could there be such a work which, partly by virtue of its obscenity, is a good artwork? Consider Henry Miller's *Tropic of Cancer*. The central character is an exiled writer living in Paris moving among ordinary low-life individuals, drunks, deadbeats, prostitutes—the hardened, feckless, sentimental, and callously indifferent. The baroque narrative, swirling around incidents of stupidity, drunken fights, lusts, adulteries, and deceptions, is conveyed in coarse, rhythmic, adjectival prose which highlights the visceral yet mundane aspects of the central character's experiences. The reader's responses are shaped in such a way that one is prescribed to be simultaneously morally repelled and yet attracted to the vulgar, indecent, and sordid immorality portrayed. The overarching attitude solicited from us towards such a characterization of human life is one of passive acceptance. Thus, the narrowly literary aspects of the novel, the incidents portrayed, and the underlying narrative theme symbiotically enhance one another in conveying a deep sense of Miller's understanding of and attitude towards humanity.

There is something overly restrictive about being required to respond to such a work only in the ways we take to be good and right. For part of the value of engaging with artworks generally seems to derive from the peculiarly powerful ways in which they can get us to entertain or imagine different possible attitudes and responses. There are many responses that works elicit from us which we judge in actuality to be unmerited but which we none the less find understandable—a matter that concerns not what the correct moral perspective is or should be but how the moral perspective could have been or could be seen to be. For *Tropic of Cancer* not only successfully prescribes imaginings about characters who are represented as being rotten and corrupted, but gets us to respond in ways concomitant with an attitude of acceptance towards such a picture of humanity generally. Yet, to the extent that we hold such a characterization of humanity to be at the very least partial, we will regard such responses and the overall attitude commended to us as unmerited—and partly for moral reasons. For presumably one will maintain that, in the face of the horrors and corruption of humanity, embracing and celebrating passive acceptance is not the right attitude to have. But it is a mark of the novel's success rather than failure that it renders such responses intelligible through evoking them in the reader, even though we may take such responses to be, in actuality, unmerited.

The claim is not merely that *Tropic of Cancer* is instrumentally valuable in so far as it expands our understanding of an attitude we take to be morally partial, misplaced, or downright wrong. One could agree with this claim while holding that, to the extent that the work commends a morally flawed attitude, it is nevertheless, in that respect, flawed. Rather, the claim is the stronger one that our absorption in the work as art is in part enhanced by the morally flawed attitude commended to us as conveyed through the rough, coarse, and rhythmic prose, the concerns with the ordinary and mundane, and the narrative as a whole. And at least some of the reasons why we can be and often are attracted and absorbed by subject matter, responses, and attitudes we take to be immoral were sketched above. Importantly, then, the worth of *Tropic of Cancer* seems in part to arise *from* its obscenity rather than *despite* it. For it is hard to see how the inducement in the reader of a passive accept-ance of the sordid horror of the human world could have been achieved without the novel's preoccupation with the indecent, vulgar, and coarsely immoral. It could be replied that Miller could have focused on such matters but the overarching atti-tude the novel embodies and elicits could have been otherwise—for example, the narrative could have aimed to induce a sense of shame rather than acceptance regarding the human condition. But in so doing the intensity, integrity, and coher-ence of the work would have suffered, and the novel would have turned out a lesser rather than a better work for it. What this suggests is that what matters is not so much a question of whether or not the moral perspective endorsed is one we take to be merited, but, rather, whether it is conveyed in such a way that we find it intel-ligible or credible. What matters is whether an artist can get us to see, feel, and respond to the world as represented as he intends us to, not whether those are the responses one morally ought to have. Furthermore, the morally reprehensible cognitive–affective responses solicited from us by such works can be epistemically virtuous because they may deepen our understanding and appreciation. Where this is the case, the value of the work is enhanced (Kieran 2002b).

It has been argued that moderate moralism, unlike ethicism, could be reformu-lated to allow for such cases (Kieran 2001a): the moral features implicit in and central to the imaginative experience afforded by a work are relevant to a work's value as art to the extent that they undermine or promote the intelligibility, for appropri-ately sensitive audiences, of the characters, events, states of affairs, responses, and attitudes as represented. Let us call this most moderate moralism. A primary virtue of such a reformulation is the recognition that many artworks of the past, not to say many contemporary works, have moral aspects that we believe to be dubious if not downright wrong, but none the less we can and do respond to them as solicited. From Homer's poetry and the Icelandic sagas, which prescribe admiration for certain heroic virtues at odds with an emphasis on forgiveness and mercy, to Henry Miller's *Tropic of Cancer* and Jean Genet's *The Balcony*, which at least in part prescribe disdain for traditional sexual morality, many works successfully get us to imagine what we take to be, in real life, ethically undesirable. Yet we take this as a mark of their success, their imaginative power, rather than think less of them for it. The value of such works is not straightforwardly a question of whether they conform to what we take to be right or good in real life as it is a matter of whether or not we find the characters, states of affairs, and attitudes as represented intelligible. But notice now that most moderate moralism is very weak indeed, if not downright at odds with the original spirit in which moderate moral-ism was put forward. It allows both that a work *may* be enhanced as art partly in virtue of its moral character, and that in certain cases the immoral character of a work *may* constitute an aesthetic virtue rather than a vice. Thus, it would be a minsomer to characterize such a position as moralism in any shape or form (no matter how weak).

6. GRAND GUIGNOL AND PORNOGRAPHIC ART

A rather different kind of argument can also be adduced to support the claim that there are works that realize their artistic value in virtue of their immoral character. Remember that one of the arguments Carroll used to support moderate moralism emphasized the moral constraints internal to certain genres such as tragedy, the core thought being that for a work to succeed as tragedy we must pity the hero or central character. If the hero's moral character is such as to be unworthy of pity, the work cannot succeed as tragedy. Ironically, the very same kind of thought suggests that there could be works that succeed as the works they aim to be precisely in virtue of their immoral character. Consider such genres as grand guignol and pornography. Grand guignol was primarily a nineteenth-century French theatrical artform of short plays, popular in Parisian cabarets, where the emphasis was on sensational violence, horror, and sadism; but, crucially, to qualify as grand guignol the mangled beauty, innocent victims, mutilation, and depravity involved had to be represented as abrogating moral taboos. Similarly, pornographic art, as such, can realize its goals only in virtue of soliciting, via the explicit representation of sexual attributes, sexual thoughts, responses, and arousal. For many at least, the very explicit nature of the means used to realize this goal are morally problematic. But unless such means are used, a work cannot succeed as pornographic art, although it may succeed as something else.

Such a line of thought may be challenged in various ways. For example, it might be thought contentious to claim that it is essential to the sensationalism of grand guignol that it involve moral abrogations. In relation to pornography, it could be denied that pornography of any kind—unless its production involves physical or psychological harm to its subjects—is immoral. I am sceptical of both claims. Grand guignol plays were often decried when it was deemed they were insufficiently immoral or taboo-breaking. Pornography that solicits delight in and arousal by the violent rape of someone strikes me as morally problematic in and of itself, and, at least from Greaco-Roman culture onwards, pornographic representations have been produced that do just this. But I shall not debate these issues here. A broader and more interesting objection consists in the denial that such narrative genres could meaningfully aspire to serious artistic merit. If, for example, pornography *per se* cannot be valuable as art, then it can hardly constitute a challenge to any form of moralism. So I shall concentrate on the often asserted claim that there can be no such thing as pornographic art.

Pornographic representations are standardly characterized as having the sole or predominant aim of seeking to elicit sexual arousal. By contrast, although erotic representations may well have this aim, they may and often do have other aims as well. Hence an erotic representation may qualify as art, and be highly valuable as such, because of the way in which it realizes artistic intent, given its subject matter. However, a pornographic representation can never be art, or be valuable as such, since by definition a pornographic representation cannot possess artistic intent (Levinson 1999).

But what reason do we have to grant this characterization? Pornography essentially involves the explicit representation of sexual behaviour and attributes. Of course, this is insufficient for a representation's being pornographic, since anatomical drawings, medical textbooks, natural history programmes, and educational videos may be sexually explicit without being pornographic. It is often suggested that the distinguishing mark of pornography, in contrast to erotica, is the sexual objectification of its subjects in virtue of which it is commonly held to be degrading. The notion of objectification being appealed to here is difficult to disentangle, but, at the very least, it would seem that not all sexual objectification is as such inherently degrading. After all, one might be rather disappointed if one's partner did not sexually objectify oneself in certain contexts in the service of sexual arousal. But let us grant for the sake of argument that pornography involves sexually explicit objectification in order to elicit sexual arousal or desire on the part of the audience. So pornography is that which primarily seeks to elicit sexual arousal or desire via the explicit representation and objectification of sexual behaviour and attributes. How does the pornographic stand in relation to the erotic? The erotic need not involve any sexually explicit objectification of sexual behaviour and attributes. Robert Mapplethorpe's photographic studies of flowers or Degas's portraits of brothel scenes, for example, are devoid of sexual explicitness, yet they successfully solicit sensuous thoughts, feelings, and associations that may be arousing and are thereby erotic, though notice that the erotic may still involve the objectification of the body. The erotic essentially aims at eliciting sexual thoughts, feelings, and associations found to be arousing. Thus, there are many things that are erotic but not pornographic, for example a representation of someone suggestively eating strawberries; but anything that is pornographic is erotic. For pornography seeks to realize the aim internal to all that is erotic but via distinctive means, i.e. sexually explicit objectification, which many other erotic representations do not utilize. Pornography is thus a subspecies of the erotic or of erotica.

Now a work whose primary aim, *qua* erotic representation, is sexual arousal may have other aims, including artistic ones. An artist may intend to produce a work that is arousing and, moreover, may intend to do so in such a way that the artistry conveys to the audience certain cognitive–affective states or attitudes to what is depicted. This is no different in principle from the recognition that Eisenstein can intend to produce, and be successful in producing, a work that aspires to be both propaganda and to be artistically valuable. Furthermore, a work produced solely in order to be sexually arousing without any artistic intention may yet artfully convey a suggestive insight, view, or attitude in a manner found to be valuable. Just as we recognize that someone may intentionally produce a religious icon with the sole intent of evoking religious devotion, and yet also produce an icon of artistic worth, so too the same is possible with respect to erotic art.

In terms of definitional characterization alone, we have no reason to suppose that, as a matter of principle, what is possible with respect to the erotic is precluded with respect to a particular sub-category of the erotic—the pornographic. What we require is a reason explaining why the pornographic is or may be inimical to the realization of artistic value. It cannot be ruled out by definitional fiat.

Carving out the difference between the pornographic and the erotic in terms of sole *v.* multiple intent may acquire some plausibility from a quick consideration of representations that we deem erotic and pornographic. There are many representations we consider to be paradigmatically erotic and artistically valuable—certain works by Klimt, Degas, Gill, Rodin, Canova, Tintoretto, Goya, Ingres, some of Shakespeare's sonnets, Ovid's *The Art of Seduction*, Scheherezade's *Tale of 1001 Arabian Nights*, or Bunuel's *Belle de Jour*, to name but a few. By contrast if we think of paradigmatic pornographic representations, from late Victorian flick books to the swaths of magazines available on the top shelf in newsagents, there seems to be nothing betokening artistic intent or merit.

Yet appealing to examples in this way cannot sustain the definitional distinction. It is obvious that most pornographic representations are of little artistic interest. But the same is true with respect to most representational forms generally. There are swaths of pictures, novels in run-of-the-mill bookshops, soap operas, television dramas, and films that are of little artistic interest. We do not take this to show that visual depiction, novels, or films cannot be of artistic merit. Indeed, in particular genres the ratio of artistically worthless to artistically worthwhile seems exceedingly high. For example, photographic portraiture, romance, fantasy or science fiction novels are all dominated by formulaic, flat, and artistically uninteresting works; none the less, this does not preclude some of this work from being of very high value as art. Moreover, if one studies the history of some of these genres, such as science fiction, one sees that much of the early work produced in pulp form is of little artistic interest, except in relation to the development of science fiction as a distinct genre, and only as the genre evolved did the first novels and films of artistic merit start to emerge. It could be objected that at least the makers of such works had low-level artistic aims or concerns, whereas this is distinctly not the case with respect to pornographic works. But there do appear to be at least a few works that are pornographic yet seem to manifest artistic intent.

What do these reflections show? The mere fact that it may be difficult to think of pornographic works of artistic value, in contrast to erotic works, does not of itself underwrite the claim that pornographic works, as a matter of principle, could not be valuable as art. First, even were one to grant that there are no such works, as yet it remains an open matter as to whether this is due to the nature and limitations inherent in pornography *per se* or is a contingent fact arising from certain historical and socio-cultural factors. It could be that, owing to institutional and social pressures, since pornography is held to be deeply immoral, obscene, and subject to stringent censorship, those who possess artistic talent simply have not exercised it in relation to pornographic subject matter—we would not really expect hucksters looking to make money illicitly from pornography to concern themselves with artistic considerations. This might explain why pornography has not evolved in a manner amenable to artistic considerations whereas other genres that emerged from the unpromising beginnings of pulp fiction, such as science fiction, adventure stories, and detective thrillers, have. Second, it is far from obvious that there are no artistically valuable pornographic representations. George Bataille's *Story of the Eye*, Oshima's *In the Realm of the Senses*, Nicholson Baker's *Vox*, certain illustrations of the *Kama Sutra*, some of Egon Schiele's nudes, the work of the later Picasso, and some of Hokusai's woodblock prints, to name but a few, are all explicitly pornographic and yet of no little artistic merit. Indeed, if we look back as far as the ancient Graeco-Roman world we find many representations that are highly sexually explicit and objectifying but are also valuable as art—as the Victorians found out, much to their shock and dismay, when Pompeii was discovered. So there are grounds for claiming that a pornographic representation could or, in the above mentioned cases, does aim to be, and is, valuable as art. As such, their value arises in part *from* rather than *despite* their putatively immoral character.

There are various ways in which this argument might be resisted. It could be claimed that we are mistaken in thinking that the works cited either really are pornographic or possess much by way of artistic intent or merit. But the onus here is on someone who would claim that our pre-reflective judgements are in error. However, a more promising and interesting line of thought can be pursued. For there remains something to the thought that, to the extent that a representation seeks to elicit sexual arousal via the explicit representation of sexual behaviour, a work cannot be of value as art.

The objection can be put in the form of two challenges. The first I shall term the *problem of pornographic purposiveness*. It may be argued with some plausibility that pornographic representations are inherently formulaic, banal, and fantastical. Repetitive concentration on genitalia, signs of sexual stimulation, and the mechanics of intercourse against a one-dimensional narrative backdrop may be arousing, but can convey little of aesthetic interest or imaginative insight into what it might be like to be a certain kind of character, face certain kinds of dilemmas, or view the world in a certain way. So, it might be claimed, representations seeking to realize the goal of arousal via sexual explicitness and objectification cannot but be indifferent to the kind of concerns that render works aesthetically elegant, graceful, subtle, nuanced, profound, or true to life.

The second challenge, possibly implicit in part of Levinson's objection to the notion of pornographic art (Levinson 1999), I shall term the *problem of pornographic reception*. Even if it were granted that a pornographic work is created with great aesthetic skill, originality, elegance, grace, and unity, its aesthetic properties or aspect still cannot be appreciated as such to the extent that it is received as pornography. The nature of a pornographic interest concerns attention to explicit body parts and behaviour in the service of sexual arousal and satiation. To the extent that such an interest is taken in a representation, it precludes attention to and the savouring of a work's aesthetic aspect. It is, one might note, no coincidence that, in prisons and other such institutions, among the first books to disappear from the libraries are art books with various nudes in them. No one would deny, for example, that Manet's *Olympia* is a work of high artistic merit. None the less, it might be thought, where such a work is being used pornographically, the interest in its aesthetic features cannot but be minimal if not downright absent. Hence, the second challenge goes, a work cannot be appreciated at the same time as both pornography and art. Thus, *qua* pornographic art, a work cannot be of artistic value.

Both challenges can, I think, be met (Kieran 2001*b*), but further argument is required to show why such scepticism about the idea that there are or could be representations that are valuable *qua* pornographic art is unjustified. Nevertheless, with respect both to obscene works generally and certain genres, such as grand guignol and pornography, there are grounds for claiming that the value of certain works as art can be *enhanced* rather than *undermined* in virtue of their immoral character. Thus, we have reason to doubt that ethicism or any substantial version of moderate moralism can be adequate accounts of the criticism of art in its moral aspect.

See also: Value in Art; Art and Emotion; Art and Knowledge; Art and Politics; Aesthetics and Ethics; Tragedy.

BIBLIOGRAPHY

Anderson, J. and Dean, J. (1998). 'Moderate Autonomism'. *British Journal of Aesthetics* 38: 150–66.

Aristotle (1986). *Poetics*, trans. S. Halliwell. London: Duckworth.

Arnold, M. (1879). Preface to *Poems of Wordsworth*. London: Macmillan.

Beardsley, M. (1958). *Aesthetics*. New York: Harcourt, Brace & World.

Bell, C. (1914). *Art*. London: Chatto & Windus.

Booth, W. (1988). *The Company We Keep: An Ethics of Fiction*. Berkeley: University of California Press.

Carroll, N. (1996). 'Moderate Moralism'. *British Journal of Aesthetics* 36: 223–37.

——(1998*a*). 'Art, Narrative, and Moral Understanding', in J. Levinson (ed.), *Aesthetics and Ethics*. Cambridge: Cambridge University Press, pp. 126–60.

——(1998*b*). 'Moderate Moralism versus Moderate Autonomism'. *British Journal of Aesthetics* 38: 419–24.

——(2000). 'Art and Ethical Criticism: An Overview of Recent Directions of Research'. *Ethics* 110: 350–87.

——(2002). 'The Wheel of Virtue: Art, Literature and Moral Knowledge'. *Journal of Aesthetics and Art Criticism* 60: 3–26.

Conoly, O. and Hagdar, B. (2001). 'Narrative Art and Moral Knowledge'. *British Journal of Aesthetics* 41: 109–24.

Devereaux, M. (1998). 'Beauty and Evil: The Case of Leni Riefenstahl's *Triumph of the Will*', in J. Levinson (ed.), Cambridge: Cambridge University Press, pp. 227–56.

Eliot, T. S. (1933). *The Use of Poetry and the Use of Criticism*. London: Faber and Faber.

Fenner, D. (ed.) (1996). *Ethics and the Arts*. New York: Garland.

Freeland, C. (1997). 'Art and Moral Knowledge'. *Philosophical Topics* 25: 11–36.

Gaut, B. (1998a). 'The Ethical Criticism of Art', in J. Levinson (ed.), *Aesthetics and Ethics*. Cambridge: Cambridge University Press, pp. 182–203.

—— (1998b). 'Just Joking: The Ethics and Aesthetics of Humour'. *Philosophy and Literature* 22: 51–68.

Gendler, T. S. (2000). 'The Puzzle of Imaginative Resistance'. *Journal of Philosophy* 97: 55–81.

Gracyk, T. (1987). 'Pornography as Representation: Aesthetic Considerations'. *Journal of Aesthetic Education* 21: 103–21.

Hanson, K. (1998). 'How Bad Can Good Art Be?' In J. Levinson (ed.), *Aesthetics and Ethics*. Cambridge: Cambridge University Press, pp. 204–26.

Hume, D. (1993). 'Of the Standard of Taste', in *Selected Essays*. Oxford: Oxford University Press, pp. 133–54; first published 1757.

Jacobson, D. (1997). 'In Praise of Immoral Art'. *Philosophical Topics* 25: 155–99.

John, E. (1995). 'Subtlety and Moral Vision in Fiction'. *Philosophy and Literature* 19: 308–19.

Johnson, S. (1964). *Lives of the English Poets*, i, *Cowley to Prior*. London: Dent.

Kieran, M. (1996). 'Art, Imagination and the Cultivation of Morals'. *Journal of Aesthetics and Art Criticism* 54: 337–51.

—— (2001a). 'In Defense of the Ethical Evaluation of Narrative Art'. *British Journal of Aesthetics* 41: 26–38.

—— (2001b). 'Pornographic Art'. *Philosophy and Literature*, 25: 31–45.

—— (2002a). 'On Obscenity: The Thrill and Repulsion of the Morally Prohibited'. *Philosophy and Phenomenological Research* 64: 31–55.

—— (2002b). 'Forbidden Knowledge: The Challenge of Immoralism'. In J. Bermudez and S. Gardner (eds.), *Art and Morality*. London: Routledge.

Kivy, P. (1997). *Philosophies of Arts: An Essay in Differences*. Cambridge: Cambridge University Press.

Lamarque, P. (1995). 'Tragedy and Moral Value'. *Australasian Journal of Philosophy* 73: 239–49.

—— and Olsen, S. H. (1994). *Truth, Fiction and Literature*. Oxford: Oxford University Press.

Levinson, J. (1998). 'Evaluating Music', in P. Alperson (ed.), *Musical Worlds*. University Park, Pa.: Pennsylvania State University Press, pp. 93–107.

—— (1999). 'Erotic Art', in *The Routledge Encyclopedia of Philosophy*, ed. E. Craig. London: Routledge, pp. 406–9.

Mason, M. (2001). 'Moral Prejudice and Aesthetic Deformity: Rereading Hume's "Of the Standard of Taste" '. *Journal of Aesthetics and Art Criticism* 59: 59–71.

Miller, R. W. (1979). 'Truth in Beauty'. *American Philosophical Quarterly* 16: 317–25.

Moran, R. (1994). 'The Expression of Feeling in Imagination'. *Philosophical Review* 103: 75–106.

Mullin, A. (2002). 'Evaluating Art: Morally Significant Imagining versus Moral Soundness'. *Journal of Aesthetics and Art Criticism* 60: 137–49.

Posner, R. (1997). 'Against Ethical Criticism'. *Philosophy and Literature* 21: 1–27.

Radford, C. (1991). 'How Can Music Be Moral?' *Midwest Studies in Philosophy* 16: 421–38.

Tanner, M. (1994). 'Morals in Fiction and Fictional Morality, II'. *Proceedings of the Aristotelian Society*, suppl., 68: 51–66.

Tolstoy, L. (1930). *What is Art?* and *Essays on Art*, tr. Aylmer Maude. London: Duckworth; first published 1898.

Walton, K. (1994). 'Morals in Fiction and Fictional Morality, I'. *Proceedings of the Aristotelian Society*, suppl., 68: 27–50.

CHAPTER 27

ART AND POLITICS

LYDIA GOEHR

I

IN *The Aesthetic Education of Man,* Schiller tells the story of the 'goddess of wisdom whose very first action was a warlike one. Even at birth,' he reports, 'she had to fight a hard battle with the senses which are loath to be snatched from their sweet repose.'

In this chapter I focus on one issue in the wide-ranging, contemporary debates on the relation between art and politics, namely, philosophy's role in these debates and the contribution it makes. In the background, this survey acknowledges that philosophy may provide useful conceptual clarification regarding the many ways the arts engage in and with the political sphere, for example in the production of propaganda art and the uses of images in mass media; the use of the arts in identity politics and political demonstration; institutional histories and in the marketing and consuming of art products; issues of censorship and international law pertaining to the return of stolen art. However, in the foreground this survey treats the question more abstractly. It focuses on three relations: *disenfranchisement, distantiation,* and *indirectness.*

Although I here survey a broad scope of late twentieth-century literature, I pay special attention at the end to Arthur Danto's classic 1986 essay on what he calls the 'disenfranchisement of art from politics'. I pay this attention not because I assume that Danto contributes more, or more satisfactorily, than anyone else to the debate, but because he makes explicit the deep entanglement, and even the responsibility, that philosophy has had in the tense relation between art and politics.

In its history, art has been conceived antagonistically in relation to politics. So has philosophy, and in interestingly similar ways. Both have become comparably disenfranchised from politics. 'Disenfranchisement' connotes an act or attitude of neutralization such that art and/or philosophy are rendered 'impotent' to 'make anything happen' in the world. They are taken out of the 'order of effectiveness' in which 'real action', i.e. politics, takes place. And yet this shared disenfranchisement has not resulted in an allegiance between art and philosophy against politics. Rather, both have become cut off from politics in virtue of the disenfranchisement, first, of art *by* philosophy—when philosophy 'neutralized' art's effectiveness in the world—and then, in Danto's account, by philosophy's disenfranchisement of itself. In Schiller's terms, the ancient war between wisdom and the senses lies at the source of art and philosophy's common political disenfranchisement.

However, moving beyond Danto, if *disenfranchisement* has been the result of the mutual antagonisms between art, philosophy, and politics, then *distantiation* and *indirectness* have been the means. If any assertion is found persistently in the literature, historical and contemporary, it is that, through mimesis, representation, retreat, deception, estrangement, alienation, and/or autonomy, the arts have found their way to be free from or freed of politics, politics of art, art of philosophy, philosophy of politics, philosophy of art (cf. Adorno 1997; Bernstein 1992). Yet there is a conflict. When one speaks about something's having become disenfranchised, it sounds as if one is criticizing an exclusion or separation that should not have happened. But when one speaks about something's maintaining a healthy distance from another thing, it sounds as if one is praising a goal. Whereas disenfranchisement captures a history of warring disciplines, practices, and human experiences, distantiation and indirection capture a history of protecting these different things from each other. We should not lose sight of this conflict, because it lies, as we shall now see, at the heart of so many of the contemporary debates.

II

This section surveys a set of abstract and concrete tendencies emerging out of recent debates on art and politics. It focuses on two general statements: '*Art is about beauty and politics is about just governance*' and '*Art is about freedom and politics is about power*'. The first is extrapolated from a Harvard humanities professor's recent and rather impressionistic, but still nicely representative, treatise of aesthetic and optimistic conservatism, on how the contemplation of the beautiful object assists in turning us to justice and inducing us to the love of virtue (Scarry 1999). The second is taken directly from a collection of profound, cynical, and realistic essays on censorship written between 1989 and 1991 by a former Romanian dissident writer now living in New York (Manea 1992). The connotations of the two statements differ significantly.

The first suggests harmony and harmonious relations. Not only is art about beauty and politics about just governance, but also, the beauty experienced through art is something capable of being experienced by a just and moral people. One might say that the role of aesthetic experience is to put a person into an aesthetic state where morality follows (cf. Geuss 1999: chapter 3), or that there is an analogy or reciprocity between our contemplation of beauty and our sensibility towards the true and the good (cf. Scruton 1997). Hence, if art is about beauty and politics about just governance, then society's production of art is devoted to the same ends as that of its politics: the good life. 'We have seen how the beautiful object—in its symmetry and generous sensory availability—assists in turning us to justice. The two other sites, that of the perceiver and that of the act of creation, also reveal the pressure beauty exerts towards ethical equality' (Scarry 1997: 109). This argument depends on the 'beautiful soul' assumption, i.e. that the development of human sensibilities works towards unifying our impulses towards the true, the good, and the beautiful.

This is a well known argument in the history of aesthetics. What is significant for my purposes is the way it depends on a claim about distantiation *but not* disenfranchisement. Following a Schillerian/Kantian approach, the argument proposes that how we attend to beauty, how we decentre our selves or depersonalize our attitudes to assume the disinterested posture required of the contemplative act, is such that, rather than pitting the aesthetic against the moral, it instead unifies their projects. This unity is established through the analogy or symmetry of experience. The experience of being 'decentred' in the sight of the beautiful contains that moment of distantiation when 'we become aware that our relation to the world is changed': 'We cease to stand even at the center of our own world . . . It is as though one has ceased to be the hero or heroine in one's own story and has become what in a folk tale is called a "lateral bystander".' As bystanders, we do not lose interest in the world (in the ethical or political). On the contrary, in this reflective but ecstatic (by-standing) moment, our 'mental life' is 'expanded' or 'opened up'. 'It is as though beautiful things have been placed here and there throughout the world to serve as small wake-up calls to perception spurring lapsed alertness back to its most acute level.' To what are we made alert? To the 'symmetry' between the aesthetic and ethical or, more specifically, between the recognition of beauty and that of 'just' or 'fair' arrangements between people. Upon what is this symmetry dependent? First, upon the movement in the contemplative act back and forth between our selves as viewers and the objects viewed. Second, by analogy, between our concern for ourselves and our concern for others (Scarry 1997: 90–5).

The tone of the second statement—'art is about freedom and politics is about power'—is much more antagonistic. If politics is about power, then politics is also likely to be about oppression—the illegitimate power of one thing over another.

And if what politics oppresses is art, then art's being about freedom is about art's freeing itself from the oppression of politics. Or, if politics is about power and power suggests the oppression of a people, then art is about freeing that people from that oppression. The claim is made most strongly in the following way: 'If politics is about power, and art about freedom, then art in a totalitarian state comes to stand not only as a challenge—as it does for every authority—it comes to stand for nothing less than the *enemy*' (Manea 1992: 31).

How art achieves its *political* status as enemy of oppression or totalitarian government is not through explicit political content, through so-called tendentious art-with-messages, but through the indirect, concealing ('secret and silent') use of aesthetic technique or artistic form (Adorno 1997). Here the aesthetic technique is one of distantiation intended to produce the illusion of disenfranchisement. Irony, metaphor, humour, symbolism are the *aesthetic* means—the aesthetic process of coding or ciphering—by which a grand illusion is sustained, the aesthetic illusion that keeps attention on art *qua* art, or the political illusion that this art is not political though it clearly is. 'The nonpolitical stance . . . became a refuge, a safe retreat, since one's abstention was not declared openly' (Manea 1992: 19). Denying, disguising, deceiving is how art (some art) protects itself concretely from the censor's pen; it is how it resists appropriation by the political structure that would attempt to control or appropriate it for its own ends. In resisting appropriation, art holds out as an enemy of the system. What is pertinent in this argument is that the deception and indirection in which art engages—that art produces the appearance that it has nothing and yet everything to do with politics—is a deception everyone knows: it is a public secret.

Consider an example from Zagreb, Yugoslavia, where in 1986 a young intellectual protested before a crowd by *miming* 'a speech without words'. Why the mime? Because this was the way 'to avoid being accused of breaking the law'. And yet we are told, 'the audience understood the message perfectly'. But who in the audience—everyone or only the initiated? Apparently both.

[T]his coded type of communication—in response to the brutal machinery of repression—permeated the whole of society, not just private relationships. Precise knowledge of a system of signs—perceptible only to initiates, and often implied rather than expressed—was indispensable in any exchange between individuals and groups. A whole society, under surveillance around the clock, split between feigned submission and masked refusal. (Manea 1992: 18)

A genuine tension inhabits these lines: if only the 'initiated' understood the miming protester, wasn't the protester protesting merely to the already convinced, assuming that 'the initiated' were already sympathetic to the cause? And if this was so, what was the point of the political act? But if the non-initiated also 'understood the message', the state-apparatchiks included, why was the subversive protest allowed? The answer seems to have been that using an aesthetic technique or form that did not break the censor's law directly was how subversive artistic–political acts survived. But did the subversion really depend upon anyone's being deceived? Or, if no one was really deceived, how effective was the subversion? If the careful employment of form is how a subversive text escapes censorship because its content is not open to view, and yet everyone 'gets' the hidden message, then either the subversion is illusory, or it does not depend upon deception. What we learn here is that claims of subversion, secrecy, and deception are often confused, but shouldn't be. Think of the confusion another way: if the message's 'hiddenness' is thought to make the message more subversive, perhaps at the same time it also makes it less effective because the confrontation is indirect or 'underground'. Perhaps indirection is what the censors depend upon to minimize the impact of the message (Coetzee 1996; Edelman 1995). Perhaps keeping art 'underground' is how a repressive society controls its own inevitable subversive elements. With this thought comes another: that the disenfranchisement of art from politics that distantiation affords is a double-edged sword; where the disenfranchisement gives art a space to be *indirectly* political or subversive (Devereaux 1993), it might also disempower art from real political effect.

That our two main statements correspond historically and conceptually to two dominant ways of thinking about the relation of art to politics is clear. The first is associated (though not necessarily) with attitudes that are *optimistic and naturalistic*; the second with attitudes more *pessimistic and anxious*. The second captures a history of *resistance* through or by the arts to politics; the former, a history of the belief or hope in *reconciliation* between the two. That the statements exhibit Cold War tensions is equally clear. For what is notable in recent writings, and most obviously in American ones, is how much and how often the anxious, even paranoid, condition of Eastern bloc aesthetics serves as the standard or reference point—negative and positive—by which to judge the condition of the West (Berman 1989). How often in the United States are judgements and discussions of the policies of the National Endowment for the Arts, the 'Jessie Helms' phenomenon, and the 'arresting images' of Mapplethorpe, Serrano, and Finley set against Cold War anxieties about repressive or totalitarian societies? 'Why do I go on about Havel and make this analogy with Czech society?' asks an optimistic and rather didactic theorist in the context of determining the social responsibility of artists in contemporary America:

Because these dramatic changes are living proof that the role of the artists is an historical, social, construction. ... It changes, evolves, grows, diminishes, dictates and is dictated to by history and by the market economy. And as such, the creative vision of an artist can be utilized both to construct art, and to construct a new society, because these goals each depend on bringing into creation that which does not as yet exist. In many societies ... artists use their voices to struggle against the master text, to create alternative narratives in visual imagery, dance, in music, in theater. They interweave all that is silenced, repressed, feared, hidden, and attempt to make it known. The difference between these countries and ours is that here there is no overt public recognition and support of the importance of this function of art and the artist to the quality of daily life. . . . It is now time for artists in this country to refuse the place of isolation and marginality they have been given and which they themselves romantically have often confused with freedom. (Carol Becker, in Buchwalter 1992: 246–7)

The point of drawing this analogy between East and West is to undermine the thought that 'romantic' isolation and marginality—or, shall we also say, 'disenfranchisement', 'impotence', and 'neutralization'—provide us with the rationale to continue thinking that art 'makes nothing happen' in the world. Consider the transformation of Czechoslovakia into the Czech Republic, and of Havel from dissident playwright into playwright-become-president.

It might be too crude to claim that our two main statements also correspond historically to the political allegiances of, respectively, the Right and the Left, but the claim would not be entirely without merit. One might see a tendency for the Left to show more suspicion towards politics and more faith in art, and the Right more faith in politics and more suspicion towards art. But there has been a more extreme Left that shows extreme faith in politics and then in an art put in the service of that politics. This has been referred to (roughly following Walter Benjamin) as 'the politicization of art'; and a Right that, being suspicious of or losing faith in politics, turns to art or, more specifically, to 'the aesthetic state' as a model for the political state: the state-become-artwork. This has been called 'the aestheticization of the political' (Jameson 1980; Chytry 1989; Ankersmit 1996). Sometimes the Right and Left meet at the extremes. But what occurs in between is a complex and continuous conceptual movement and interaction between narrower and broader concepts suited to Left and Right political agendas: between 'Art', 'the arts', and 'the aesthetic' on the one hand, and 'ideology', politics', and 'the political' on the other (Freeden 1996). What occurs in tandem is similar movement and interaction between these concepts in philosophical theories and then all the attempted reductions and struggles against reductions between any and all of them (Eagleton 1990).

There is another position that confuses Left–Right allegiances, which claims that the function of beauty is somehow in the service of freedom, where the relation between beauty and freedom is thought about in connection to existing or utopian social or political arrangements. The point now is that what one thinks about art and beauty (or ugliness), and whether one chooses theoretically to give art a political role in relation to freedom, depends on one's general optimism or pessimism regarding the political state of the world. Some theorists (and here I prefer to describe tendencies than name names) seem to think that art is freed from its 'freedom' function when there is evidently freedom in the state, that the contemplation of art for the sake of art is an achievement of a politically content people. Others think that under such contentment art is trivialized to mere entertainment. As is sometimes said, no really serious art is produced under happy circumstances or in 'an atmosphere of non-constraint' (cf. Manea 1992: 31). Yet others seem to think more sceptically that there is never enough freedom or contentment in any state, and that, under this unavoidable condition, art survives and indeed thrives. Some even seem to suggest that this imperfect condition of the world is thus not even regrettable, because it keeps art alive. That art could be given priority over the political or the concern for the wellbeing of humanity is a pertinent aestheticist assumption in its own right.

Setting art in relation to politics, setting art in relation to philosophy, but at the same time maintaining art's independence, matters deeply, for it seems to be the way to safeguard art's value, effectiveness, and power in the world against repeated claims as to its real-world impotence. In contemporary debate, as in much modernist debate, impotence seems to be the invariant starting point in the conversation about politics and the arts.

Consider, next, a recent collection of essays of diverse authorship produced under the title *Democracy and the Arts* (Melzer *et al.* 1999). Edited by three professors of political science, this collection asks what role there is, or should be, for the arts in a democracy, of which that in the United States is taken as paradigmatic. The question is given further nuance: the purpose is to ask not so much what role art *per se* has in a democracy, but more, whether or not there is or can be such a thing as 'democratic art'. The editors do not think the answer obvious. Where democracy suggests and demands a very pervasive *egalitarianism*, the arts carry with them and demand, they say, an *elitism*—the sort of elitism that acknowledges the special, *extra-ordinary* talent associated with artistic production, and an aesthetic that recognizes *exception* and *exemplarity* in both art's form and content. Is democracy then good for the arts, the editors ask, and, if so, which arts in particular? Jazz, one contributor suggests, with its democratic ideal of improvisation and shared participation; or functional architecture, says another, or perhaps even 'the most democratic genre', the novel. In these answers, there is obvious reorientation and/or re-establishment of the division between the categories of 'the high' and 'the low', 'the fine' and 'the popular'. Prima facie, democratic ideals seem more compatible with the arts that address more concerns of more of the people. But then attention is also paid to the conflicts between a positive democratic politics that assumes equality and fairness and a purportedly negative democratic art that assumes too great a demand for standardization (the levelling down of difference). Other contributors suggest that democracy shows itself, or proves its worth, not in the artworks *per se*, or in the kinds of artworks produced, but in the institutions of production and reception associated therewith—in the conditions of public support and funding that allow (or do not allow) the free and open exchange of artistic ideas (another democratic ideal) or the production of works that might, in having exemplary, exceptional, or extraordinary status, contribute towards the expansion or enlarging of the democratic discussion.

Though the editors are political scientists, the contributors are more directly associated with the arts (literary and cultural critics, writers, poets, music theorists, and aestheticians). This is relevant, because the latter tend to treat democracy as a political form of government already sufficiently even if not perfectly realized. What they then take to be their residual task is the determination of the role or roles of art within and consistent with that form of government. Even the editors encourage this approach when they write that the traditional question of art and politics may be elaborated, in the American context, in terms of two primary issues: whether and how art serves democracy, and whether and how democracy serves art. It is only a 'foreign' contributor, the Israeli novelist A. B. Yehoshua, who declares the non-obviousness of this all too American elaboration that 'politics' equals 'democracy':

> I would like to begin by expressing my appreciation of the intellectual devotion of Americans to the theme of democracy. Although a state of democracy exists in my own country, Israel, as well as in other countries, it still seems that for us democracy is like wearing a suit of clothes after trying on various other styles, while for Americans it is more than a suit or a coat—it is the very skin of their body. That is because . . . the United States is the only nation in the world whose national identity is almost genetically related to democracy . . . Americans reexamine their democratic nature the way other countries investigate the significance and limitations of their nationality or the origins of their language or religion. (Melzer *et al.* 1999: 43)

Treating democracy as a given, at least for how we understand the concept of politics, allows the 'American' theorists to jump ahead of the starting point. They do not feel obliged first to determine the ideal political condition and then to look for the role of art within and for it. Rather, they turn their attention straight to art. This seems to prove especially attractive to theorists who want to pursue the inquiry in the reverse direction, determining the character or nature of art first and then trying to connect it to the political. There is a strong tendency in the literature for theorists to make claims about art, and even its political character, import, or significance, almost in complete isolation from any explicit conception of politics. Hence some seem to think it sufficient to assert, logically, that art stands to the extra-artistic in some formal relation, in order to show then that art in principle, as they know in practice, can have political, social, or moral significance. What is asserted here is a formal relation between art and politics without a substantial or concrete filling in or commitment on the side of politics. The point is that one can apparently remain on the side, and 'on the side' of art, without ever really putting politics into question. Art might then be connected to politics in more conservative or liberal ways; but that, such theorists might say, would be an empirical rather than theoretical or philosophical matter in need of their attention.

Related, finally, to this tendency is another, one shared by theorists who acknowledge art's relation to politics only so long as that does not imply that art be conceived functionally as merely in the service of politics, or indeed of anything else. Such theorists want to retain for art its uniqueness, particularity, and possibility of purely artistic development, so that it can be granted, when it should be, that a beautiful painting is just a beautiful painting. Their aim often is to essentialize the special quality of the arts so that, even if they admit, as few really deny, that the arts have many and diverse functions in the social or political sphere, these functions are best conceived as 'extra' to art's 'essential' or 'intrinsic' qualities and not substitutes for, or absorbers of, them. Again, the most usual consequence of this tendency is to seek, via philosophical theory, a *non-reductive* relation between art and politics; to allow, on the one hand, the necessary resistance of art to politics when the latter exerts its oppressive arm, and/or, on the other, the unique contribution to *Bildung* that art offers *alongside* the good and the true.

III

The focus on art and lack of focus on politics is well exemplified in Danto's article on the disenfranchisement of art, until one notices that he is really interested in the third sibling in our story—philosophy. Philosophy has given conceptual credibility to art's impotence, but in so doing has ultimately demonstrated its own. Can philosophy be saved from its own threat of disenfranchisement?

Danto begins at the heights of Modernist 'impotence', with W. H. Auden's claim, in his poem on the death of Yeats and the state of Irish politics, that 'poetry' is incapable of 'making anything happen'. ('Politics' is associated with this idea of 'making things happen'.) Moments later, Danto quotes Auden again: 'the political history of the world would have been the same if not a poem had been written, nor a picture painted, nor a bar of music composed.' Danto is less immediately concerned with the empirical question whether particular artworks have in fact made anything happen, though he does offer candidates for consideration (Picasso's *Guernica*). He is more concerned to show how 'unanimous' the philosophical support historically has been to 'spiritualize' the arts or put them at an ontological distance from the world where things happen. What has been the impact of this philosophical act of distantiation? To strip art of its 'causal' effectiveness and leave it only with the function to memorialize, enshrine, or reflectively respond to worldly events already in place. Why has this tendency so profoundly prevailed? Because it has proved the most effective way of countering the more deeply held suspicion that art is in fact dangerous—so dangerous, Danto now declares, that the history of art is in fact 'the history of the suppression of art'. What has been suppressed? Art's effect, and paradoxically just the effect philosophy has denied it. Danto is interested in this paradox: if art is powerless in the world where things happen, why suppress it? If it is not, why the longstanding, philosophical belief that it is? For Danto, the paradox tells us something profound about philosophy.

One might think the paradox could best be explained empirically by investigating art's antagonistic history to society and to politics, where suppression of its power (censorship) has been tied paradoxically so often to the denial of its power. But Danto looks beyond the empirical to 'a metaphysical danger' that art has purportedly triggered and to which philosophy has responded. Could it be that art is the reason philosophy was invented, he asks, but only in order to make us aware of what philosophy has done to art, how it has constructed a belief about art that has put not only art outside the scope of effectiveness, but eventually itself too?

Thus, Danto's concern is not directly to question whether art is or is not innocuous—obviously, it is not innocuous—but to perform an archaeology on the metaphysical belief that it is. It is important to know this, otherwise we would be tempted to accuse him of simply ignoring the often stated view, here taken from Plato's *Republic*, that '[t]he ways of poetry and music are not changed anywhere without change in the most important laws of the city' (Bk 4, 424c). But, as Danto puts it himself, '[r]epresenting art as something that in its nature can make nothing happen is not so much a view opposed to the view that art is dangerous; it is a way of responding to the sensed danger of art by treating it metaphysically as though it were nothing to be afraid of.' Treating art this way is in line with philosophy's perpetual production of disenfranchising theories.

Danto describes two. First is a Kantian 'ephemeralization' theory of art: a distantiation theory that puts art outside the scope of the world where there is real satisfaction of our interests. In so doing the question becomes acute: what *good* is art; of what *use* is it? He then describes a Hegelian 'takeover' theory of art that treats art, in a history of developing *Geist*, as a disguised and less adequate form of philosophy. 'When art internalizes its own history, when it becomes self-conscious of its history as it has come to be in our own time, so that its consciousness of its history forms part of its nature, it is perhaps unavoidable that it should turn into philosophy at last. And when it does so, well, in an important sense, art comes to an end.' One might think that theories proclaiming either the 'uselessness' or the 'end' of art might be thought to demonstrate philosophy's achievement, the victory over the enemy, the destruction of 'the monster'. But not so, Danto argues, for two reasons. First, if philosophy's fear of art as an enemy is unfounded to begin with, then all philosophy has done in 'proving' art useless is to slay a fictional dragon. Second, by removing the fear of art by bringing it to its end, philosophy itself assumes, or becomes entrapped in, its own stratagems now directed towards itself. 'If art makes nothing happen and art is but a disguised form of philosophy, philosophy makes nothing happen either.' The conditional assumes an Hegelian logic, where philosophy 'makes its appearance [at dusk] when it is too late for anything *but* understanding.' Philosophy might understand the world, but, *contra* Marx, it cannot change it.

Though Danto focuses on the two more modern disenfranchisement theories, he finds their source in Plato's *Republic*. That he does so is crucial, but how he does so is unusual. He does not rehearse, as many do, the reasons in book 3 why Plato banished certain forms of art from the ideal city (cf. David Hoekema in Buchwalter 1992). He focuses rather on the disenfranchising metaphysics of book 10, on the mimetic theory that gives to art its 'ontological vacation', its twofold removal from reality. Why? Because, unlike the later disenfranchisement theories, this earlier one wears its political character on its sleeve. Now 'political character' connotes something 'metaphysical'. It has less directly to do with society's forms of organization, something less to do with things that happen in the world, though Plato himself is concerned with such matters. It has more to do with what Danto identifies within philosophy's history as a deep 'struggle for domination over the minds of men,' a struggle for the supremacy of reason that has resulted in art's being treated as 'an enemy'. Not the sort of enemy, as we saw earlier, that stands opposed to a present form of oppressive government, but the sort of enemy constructed out of those 'darker and more confused forces', irrational drives, 'shadows, illusions, delusions, [and] dreams'. Plato's metaphysics is a deep-seated response to a metaphysical–political fear that tries to overcome itself by rendering that which it fears 'impotent'. The fact, not incidentally, that Danto compares this response to what he says men have done to women by placing them on a 'useless' or 'domestic' pedestal only more strikingly prompts the question as to who or what has really been made impotent in the process. The more central point is that, if politics is not explicitly Danto's concern, it still survives in his account as philosophy's persistent, metaphysical subtext, the subtext that motivated the ancient but thereafter persistent 'warfare' between philosophy and art, between wisdom and the senses, between reason and unreason.

Danto has certain choices at this juncture. He could turn to the question whether, having diagnosed the illness of philosophy, a cure is at hand. Can philosophy shed itself of its deep-seated need to disenfranchise art? Certainly Danto understands the incentive for this question, for, according to his story, so long as the warfare between philosophy and art continues, then so does philosophy's warfare with itself. Or he could turn to art, to see whether historically the arts have resisted or succumbed to their philosophical disenfranchisement. Or, finally, he could turn to politics to ask whether politics itself became impotent as the political subtext of philosophy, or whether it sustained its power through the more concrete politics of book 3.

Danto in fact says something pertinent to each of these. He starts with what he takes to be a 'quite unexciting' observation: 'Once we have separated art from the philosophical theories that have given it its character, the question of whether art makes anything happen is not any longer a philosophically very interesting one. It is, rather, a fairly empirical question, a matter for history or psychology or some social science or other to determine.' He then considers Marxist and other theories of *deep history*, which, in removing art from 'effectiveness' at the structural base, again either disenfranchise art or fail sufficiently to distinguish art from any other form of social expression. Art, in these theories, is now stripped not only of its power but also of its particularity. Moving then to *surface history*, Danto reminds us once more that it is simply a matter of fact whether art makes anything happen. He doubts that art can 'save the Jews' or 'save the whales' directly; but he does consider the possibility that art might communicate indirectly what cannot be communicated directly.

Hamlet used a 'play within a play' to show a truth that could not be stated directly. Here we return to a theme raised earlier: that, even if we think that art is merely 'mirroring' the world, we should not assume such mirroring to be innocent. Danto acknowledges that it might not be innocent, but he doesn't think we should then automatically assume that 'indirect communication' necessarily captures something essential about art. Hamlet's play within a play might have been, metaphorically, 'a mirror for Claudius, but not for anyone else in the audience save irrelevantly; and yet it was as much art to them for whom it was not a mirror as to him for whom it was'. Art can function as art—it can shock, bore, or amuse an audience—independently of the 'special uses' to which it may be put. Using art for coded communication is a use art can have, but other things can have this use too, so this use must be distinguished from what art does uniquely or essentially as art. If art does make anything happen, it will do so as art, though this incidental effectiveness should not be thought to exhaust or necessarily even to touch art's intrinsic character. Such effectiveness is 'extra-artistic'.

But are we now not just where we began, Danto wonders, philosophically relegating the social uses of art to the domain of 'the extra'? (See also Goehr 1998: chapter 1.) Is it not once again a philosophical disenfranchisement when we argue that intrinsically art cannot make anything happen, even if extrinsically we assign it socially or politically useful functions? Danto answers by reminding us that 'the structure of artworks is of a piece with the structure of rhetoric, and . . . it is the office of rhetoric to modify the minds and then the actions of men and women by co-opting their feelings' (cf. Danto 1981). Admittedly, he adds, not all feelings lead to actions, but some do, and some feelings prompted by art might thus make something happen. Rhetoric is not extrinsic to the artwork any more than structure is. 'So there is reason after all to be afraid of art.' This, of course, is where Plato's book 3 begins.

If politics re-enters the space of art via linking structure (form) with rhetoric (effect), it arguably re-enters the space of philosophy the same way. However, Danto denies this, if to say this implies that philosophy is to be taken as a form of art. For art is not philosophy and philosophy is not art. Here we reach the culminating point of Danto's argument. Philosophy's (Plato's) attack on art was inextricably tied to its attack on rhetoric (sophistry), on the tactics of persuasion as opposed to good argument (proof). Philosophy, for Danto, finds its final redemption in distinguishing its goal, good argument, from that of rhetoric.

But is the commitment to good argument enough? What of the connection between the form and content of good argument? What are we to do with the thought that, where the form of good argument might have aimed for 'neutrality' of content (disenfranchisement 1), the content of philosophical argument has been a sustained history of disenfranchisement, and the disenfranchisement of anything, and much more than art, that did not apparently fall within its scope (disenfranchisement 2)? Has Danto, in redeeming the aim of philosophy, not re-disenfranchised art, and then again philosophy, through art's link with rhetoric? Remember the penultimate step in his brief where he allowed art to be dangerous. This looks as if philosophy's bid to prove art 'innocuous' now no longer holds, and that its disenfranchisement is at an end. But if the reason the disenfranchisement occurred was always largely the result of pitting philosophy's reason against art's unreason, can one now maintain that distinction to redeem philosophy? If philosophy is committed to good argument, and art to rhetorical persuasion (as one of its functions), are we not left holding philosophy up as that which is constantly in threat of being brought down by art and politics under the guise of 'the politics of art' and 'the art of politics'? Is not Danto continuing the war between wisdom and the senses by upholding philosophy's fear of rhetoric?

Some theorists responding to accounts like Danto's have suggested that, in tandem with rethinking the relation between argument and rhetoric (which is very much part of the problem between art and politics), we ought also to rethink our commitment to grand narratives (see Rorty 1981; Hohendahl 1991). They argue that we ought to give up altogether the attempt to produce the kind of narratives that pit these abstract or speculative notions of 'art', 'politics', and 'philosophy' against one another, as if solving the doctrinal problem of their relations and antagonisms by telling a grand overarching history would solve the actual conflicts, or determine the actual relations, or dictate the actual terms in the world where the different and many arts interact with philosophical theories and political issues in multifarious and changing ways. One philosopher remarks: 'Even if pluralism is right, and perhaps because it is, it cannot and need not take the form of a doctrine; for as such it is not better—no less singular and exclusive—than any other of the doctrines that have shaped the genealogy of modern and postmodern aesthetics' (Michael Kelly, in Kemal and Gaskell 2000: 254).

Others have suggested that philosophy ought not assume so grand a posture in relation to art and politics, but should enter the fray with a critical and self-reflective function. Good argument is not achieved in separation from rhetoric as much as in critical engagement with it. The dialogic or dialectical interaction between good argument, art (myths, story-telling), and rhetoric in Plato's *Republic* still offers us a way to think about 'critical engagement'. What it gives us, what mimesis gives us, what distantiation later gives us in Kant, what conceptual development gives us in Hegel, is not just a history of disenfranchisement, but also, one might say, a history of dialectical glimpses of freedom. Contemporary literature on art and politics still acknowledges this, as does much recent thinking on the ethical dimensions of literature (Adamson *et al.* 1998; Nussbaum 1996).

Not everything that makes something happen in the world makes something happen through direct causal means or through an eye that looks directly on its object. 'Art', writes an art-historian who has always pursued the explicit connection between art and politics,

seeks out the edges of things, of understanding; therefore its favorite modes are irony, negation, deadpan, the pretence of ignorance or innocence. It prefers the unfinished: the syntactically unstable, the semantically malformed. It produces and savors discrepancy in what it shows and how it shows it, since the highest wisdom is knowing that things and pictures do not add up. (Clark 1984: 12)

Sometimes things affect the world sideways, through glances out of the corner of the eye, through all manner of obliqueness.

The history of distantiation might well be a history of disenfranchisement. But it is also a history of indirection and indeterminacy. And this perhaps is what philosophy fears most when it tries to *prove by good argument once and for all* that the world would be different—or not different—if not a poem had been written, a musical note composed, a picture painted. If the sideways-glance of art is what enables art to offer a glimpse of freedom against oppressive political power, then, *contra* Danto, this same glance might just be that which enables art to resist the oppressive power of a 'good argument' that ends up, for its own purposes, showing a principled intolerance towards art's political nature.

See also: Art and Morality; Expression in Art; Feminist Aesthetics; Aesthetics and Postmodernism; Aesthetics and Cultural Studies; Aesthetics of the Everyday.

BIBLIOGRAPHY

Adamson, J., Freadman, R., and Parker, D. (eds.) (1998). *Renegotiating Ethics in Literature, Philosophy, and Theory*. Cambridge: Cambridge University Press.

Adorno, T. W. A. (1997). *Aesthetic Theory*, trans. R. Hullot-Kentor. Minneapolis: Minnesota University Press.

Ankersmit, F. (1996). *Aesthetic Politics: Political Philosophy Beyond Fact and Value*. Stanford, Calif.: Stanford University Press.

Berman, R. (1989). *Modern Culture and Critical Theory: Art, Politics, and the Legacy of the Frankfurt School*. Madison, Wis.: University of Wisconsin Press.

Bernstein, J. M. (1992). *The Fate of Art: Aesthetic Alienation from Kant to Derrida and Adorno*. University Park, Penna: Pennsylvania State University Press.

Buchwalter, A. (ed.) (1992). *Culture and Democracy: Social and Ethical Issues in Public Support for the Arts and Humanities*. Boulder, Colo.: Westview Press.

Chytry, J. J. (1989). *The Aesthetic State: A Quest in Modern German Thought*. Berkeley: University of California Press.

Clark, T. J. (1984). *The Painting of Modern Life: Paris in the Art of Manet and his Followers*. New York: Alfred A. Knopf.

Coetzee, J. M. (1996). *Giving Offense: Essays on Censorship*. Chicago: Chicago University Press.

Danto, A. (1981). *The Transfiguration of the Commonplace*. Cambridge, Mass.: Harvard University Press.

——(1986). *The Philosophical Disenfranchisement of Art*. New York: Columbia University Press.

——(1987). *The State of the Art*. Englewood Cliffs, NJ: Prentice-Hall.

Devereaux, M. (1993). 'Protected Space: Politics, Censorship and the Arts'. *Journal of Aesthetics and Art Criticism* 51: 207–15.

Dubin, S. (1992). *Arresting Images: Impolitic Art and Critical Actions*. London: Tavistock.

Eagleton, T. (1990). *The Ideology of the Aesthetic*. Oxford: Blackwell.

Edelman, M. (1995). *From Art and Politics: How Artistic Creations Shape Political Conceptions.* Chicago: Chicago University Press.

Freeden, M. (1996). *Ideologies and Political Theory: A Conceptual Approach.* Oxford: Clarendon Press.

Geuss, R. (1999). *Morality, Culture, and History: Essays on German Philosophy.* Cambridge: Cambridge University Press.

Goehr, L. (1994). 'Political Music and the Politics of Music', in P. Alperson (ed.), *The Philosophy of Music*, Special Issue of *Journal of Aesthetics and Art Criticism* 52(1): 99–112.

—— (1998). *The Quest for Voice: Music, Politics, and the Limits of Philosophy.* Oxford: Clarendon Press.

Hohendahl, P. U. (1991). *Reappraisals: Shifting Alignments in Postwar Critical Theory.* Ithaca, NY: Cornell University Press.

Jameson, F. (ed.) (1980). *Aesthetics and Politics*, London: Verso.

Kemal, S. and Gaskell, I. (eds.) (2000). *Politics and Aesthetics in the Arts.* Cambridge: Cambridge University Press.

Manea, N. (1992). *On Clowns: The Dictator and the Artist.* New York: Grove Press.

Melzer, A. M., Weinberger J., and Zinman, R. (eds.) (1999). *Democracy and the Arts.* Ithaca, NY: Cornell University Press.

Nussbaum, M. (1996). *Poetic Justice: The Literary Imagination and Public Life.* Boston: Beacon Press.

Rorty, R. (1981). *Consequences of Pragmatism.* Minneapolis: University of Minnesota Press.

Scarry, E. (1999). *On Beauty and Being Just.* Princeton: Princeton University Press.

Scruton, R. (1997). *The Aesthetics of Music.* Oxford: Clarendon Press.

PART III

AESTHETIC ISSUES OF SPECIFIC ARTFORMS

CHAPTER 28

MUSIC

STEPHEN DAVIES

1. The Philosophy of Music

IF medals were awarded for growth in aesthetics in the last thirty years, the philosophy of music would win the gold. In large part, this newly awakened regard was stimulated and sustained by a series of books written by Peter Kivy (see Bibliography). For an introduction to the wide range of philosophical questions provoked by music, see Krausz (1993), Alperson (1994, 1998), and Robinson (1997).

Despite the attention that the philosophy of music has attracted, the focus of philosophers on music has been rather narrow. Until the 1990s, it fell almost exclusively on the works of Western instrumental classical music, and these were approached for the interest of their form and expressiveness rather than for their wider cultural significance. Since then, there has been a growing interest in performance and improvisation, in popular types of music such as rock, in the technology of recordings, in non-Western music, and in the broader social setting within which music is presented and appreciated.

2. Music's Universality and Particularity

Though people might argue over whether all cultures have art in the Western sense, few would dispute that they all have music. Even when it is not easily comprehended, music from foreign cultures is recognizable as such. Some basic elements are common to most musics, for example the functional identity of octaves and the modal organization of pitches. Also, music serves approximately the same wide variety of functions in different cultures—to accompany ritual, labour, and dance; to quiet children; to express extremes of happiness and sadness, and so on. Nevertheless, music is not a universal language. While some kinds seem to be accessible even to foreigners, many are not. Some esoteric types, such as isorhythmic motets of the fourteenth century, or Japanese kabuki, are virtually impenetrable to the uninitiated.

Do the many varieties of music require different kinds of appreciation? There are reasons to think so. In contemporary Western music, jazz involves the most highly developed improvisation. This calls for performance values unlike those that are important in classical music. For jazz there must be a willingness to tolerate the missteps that can go with the attempt to make up adventurous music in real time (Brown 1996), whereas for classical music there is more emphasis on polish (Godlovitch 1998). Rock, construed broadly, promotes yet other performance values, both because it aims for a visceral response (Baugh 1993) and because of its special reliance on recording technology and electronic instruments (Gracyk 1996). More fine-grained musical genres, like reggae, Baroque trio sonata, nineteenth-century verismo opera, and 12-bar blues, employ distinctive structures and styles, or serve functions peculiar to them, and these differences must be taken into account when works in those genres are appreciated or compared.

Despite distinctions operating at the fine-grained level, when a wider view is taken it is not obvious that music's categories—rock, jazz, and classical, say—require exclusive aesthetics (Davies 1999). In other words, the various forms, treatments, histories, functions, or effects found within any one of these broad classifications are not more unified or consistent than are those within the others. The differences between hip hop and Gilbert and Sullivan patter songs, for example, are not greater or more systematic than those between hip hop and country and western.

3. What is Music?

Many dictionaries characterize music as 'organized sound'. Is this a necessary condition for something's being music? It might be thought that John Cage's notorious

4′33″ is a counter-example. If the content of that piece is silence, music need not involve organized sound. There are several plausible ways of arguing against this alleged counter-example, however (see Levinson 1990: chapter 11). The content of Cage's piece might better be thought of as the sound framed (and thereby organized) by its performances' temporal boundaries—that is, as the sounds that in other performances would count as ambient—not as silence as such. Alternatively, one could argue that Cage's piece is a theatrical work about music, rather than music as such, even while conceding that the boundary between these artforms is hazy (Davies 1997a).

Even if music necessarily is organized sound, it is plain that this is not sufficient for something's being music. Things other than music satisfy the same condition. For instance, the regular pounding of waves on a beach involves the organization of sound according to natural laws. In response, it might be thought appropriate to refine the condition to require humanly organized sound for something's being music. Even if we are happy to exclude the 'songs' of whales and birds from the realm of music, not to mention the possibility that aliens living on other planets could create it, the amendment faces familiar counter-examples. Human linguistic utterance involves the deliberate organization of sound, and we do not regard radio broadcasts of the news, to take one example, as music. To distinguish music from spoken languages and the like, there must be differences in the sounds they organize, the methods or principles of organization, or the purposes for which the activity is undertaken.

In music, the important sound elements are often pitched tones structured in terms of scales (defined according to the interval sequences into which each octave is divided, along with recognition of the equivalence of notes at the octave). As well as pitch and modality, notes display timbre, volume, attack, decay, and duration. Notes combine vertically into chords and horizontally into rhythmically articulated motives, phrases, and melodies, which are often set against a regular metric pulse. Larger sections are generated according to the pattern in which melodies or other higher-order elements succeed or combine with each other. In some cases, the whole is comprised of several larger sections or movements.

Can all music be reduced to the level of note sequences? How one answers this question depends on whether one judges the higher elements sometimes to retain their identity despite changes to their note sequences. Frequently, in sonata form movements in the minor key, the second subject melody first appears in the major key, and then later in the minor. It is the same theme the second time around, despite intervallic adjustments that go with the change from major to minor. Thinking of it any other way renders the form unintelligible and undermines the structural symmetries between sonatas in the major and the minor. Since the identity of the melody survives changes to its intervallic pattern, melodies are not reducible to note sequences.

A similar point emerges when one recalls that many works are not fully specified at the level of individual notes. For instance, the notation 'tr' calls for an alternation of notes, but under-determines the exact number to be sounded; and figured bass notations of the eighteenth century leave it to the performer to improvise the middle parts. Works with such notations are indeterminate with respect to the number or detail of the notes to be sounded, so they cannot be reductively analysed into note sequences. In other words, some musical pieces have as their lowest level of organization one that is higher than that of a note sequence.

This does not mean, however, that we could define music by reference to the organization of its higher-order elements, such as melodies or movements. Some pieces lack these higher-order levels. This would be so of a random, non-tonal work comprised of pitched notes that always succeed each other at intervals of greater than three octaves.

4. FORMALISM AND CONTEXTUALISM

According to the formalist, one piece of music is distinguished from another in terms of its pattern alone. When we are acquainted with a work's sound structure, there is nothing more to be known about the basis for its identity. The extreme form of this position, which can be traced to Kant and earlier, regards expressive features as distinct from formal ones, and thereby as irrelevant to a musical work's identity. But there is no reason why the formalist cannot include expressive properties as relevant to the work's identity if she maintains that they belong objectively to the work. (For an example of this position, see Kivy 1993.) The formalist might also go so far as to include within the work's sound structure its timbral qualities, but without counting the piece's instrumentation as among its identifying characteristics (since the appropriate sound structure might be generated by a synthesizer). According to all varieties of formalism, any specification of the appropriate sound structure would indicate the single work whose identity is defined by that structure.

Suppose that, with no knowledge of Josquin des Prez, I write a piece that is note for note the same as one of his motets. Whereas his creation is in the contemporary style, mine is self-consciously archaic, with its antique French poetry, scholarly canons and counterpoint, and modal organization. Whereas Josquin used—indeed, created—many of the mannerisms of European Renaissance music, my piece quotes them self-consciously. My piece is noteworthy for the many possibilities I have deliberately rejected, such as the use of atonalism and electronic instruments, but those were not options for Josquin. His piece reflected, and played a part in shaping, the values of his culture, whereas mine does not. Differences of the kinds mentioned are of a significance that would indicate that the work's identity depends upon them. In that case, Josquin and I composed different works, though works having a sound structure in common. Formalism, which entails that my piece is identical with Josquin's, should be rejected. The identity of musical works depends on aspects of the context in which the sound structure is created, and not solely on its pure form. For versions of this new position, which I call *contextualism*, see Levinson (1990); Walton (1990); Sharpe (2000); and Davies (2001).

What aspects of the contextualist's context does she see as being relevant to the identity of musical pieces? There is agreement that the musico-historical setting in which composition takes place is vital. A piece's identity depends on the musical traditions, practices, and conventions, along with the body of works, genres, and styles, to which its composer is heir. Some contextualists go further. Levinson (1990) suggests that the work's identity depends on its composer's identity. Two composers who share the same musico-historical setting compose different pieces if they work independently, and yet indicate the same sound structure. Levinson also argues that, for a work after about 1800, instrumentation also contributes to its identity. Even if a synthesizer could reproduce the indicated sound structure and give it an appropriate timbral character, so that it would be aurally indistinguishable from a rendition on the instruments specified by the composer, it would not thereby sound a fully authentic instance of the work.

As regards the piece's instrumentation, it is plausible to argue that this is crucial to the identity of some, but not all, works. The point is not simply that some works—such as Bach's 'Art of Fugue'—seem not to have been created for any specific instrument, whereas others—such as Ravel's 'Bolero'—make a salient feature of their use of the orchestra. More relevant is the observation that, over the centuries, the conventions have changed so that it is now possible for composers to make more of the details of their work determinative of its identity. In the eighteenth century, annotated phrasings had the status of recommendations that the performer might choose to ignore, but by the end of the nineteenth those same indications were work-identifying. Whether a piece's instrumentation affects its identity depends on when it was composed, because directions of that sort did not become determinative until about 1770, when the orchestra and its instruments became standardized. Before then the composer might have preferences about the instruments to be used, and these are likely to be worth taking into account, but the practice of the time did not allow him to mandate their use.

The observation that there is a socio-historical aspect to what composers are able to specify as relevant to their works' identities brings up a further possibility: namely, that the work concept is itself historically mutable. Goehr (1992) takes up this idea in suggesting that there were no musical works prior to about 1800; when we talk about Bach's works, our usage is retrospective and anachronistic. She arrives at this conclusion by taking as regulative all that was regarded as important to the work's identity by nineteenth-century composers. They viewed works as specified completely and unambiguously at the level of note sequences; they prized originality and the integrity of a piece's contents; they authorized their works in definitive versions; they saw works as more important than the performances that are of them. Earlier composers often left to performers many decisions about which notes to play, and, generally, they were much more relaxed about adapting their music for particular occasions of performance, and in re-using their own material or in appropriating that of others.

A preferable alternative to Goehr's theory would have it that works became 'thicker' with constitutive properties over several centuries of Western music, not that the work concept came into existence only at the close of this process. In this view, works, thought of as entities that invite repeat performance and can be re-identified from one performance to another, pre-existed the nineteenth century, though composers often produced given works in several versions and left much to the performer. Why is this different account better? Because it makes more sense of the continuities binding the history of Western music into a single narrative. Goehr's position identifies a radical break in the historical thread; a new and unprecedented kind of musical entity, i.e. the work, emerged and dominated from the nineteenth century on. Yet, while there were differences between the early nineteenth century and what went before, as there had been previously when the prevailing stylistic and other musical paradigms altered, there is no reason to take the exaggerated claims the Romantics made for their own originality at face value. More explanatory ground is gained by seeing those local changes as part of a pattern towards the 'thickening' of works that began four centuries earlier, and continued to the mid-twentieth century (Davies 2001).

5. IMPROVISATION

Manifestly, music can be made in the absence of musical works (Wolterstorff 1994). The player simply doodles or improvises, making music freely on the spot.

Why not regard improvisations as renditions of works that just happen to have only one performance (as Alperson 1984 and Kivy 1993 do)? While the improviser needs some of the skills of the composer of works, other of her talents give her activity its distinctive character. She creates what she plays in real time, without 'time-outs'. As Brown argues (1996), this gives her performance immediacy, with an emphasis on risk, and her spontaneous efforts are to be evaluated more with regard to the way she pushes the limits of what she can do routinely than by reference to the structural integrity and unity of what she creates. (If she does, however, achieve a satisfying integrity and unity as well, her efforts are the more praiseworthy.) To call free improvisations 'works' is misleading, because it implies they are to be approached and assessed in terms of criteria that apply to them only secondarily.

6. ONTOLOGIES OF MUSICAL WORKS

Still, much music comes in the form of works. We can distinguish three kinds of musical works. The first is that of *works for live performance*. The composer authorizes and issues these via sets of instructions addressed to the work's potential performers. These prescriptions tell the performer what to do or to achieve in instancing the piece in question. They may take the form of notations or written directions, as when the composer writes a score; or in oral traditions they might be conveyed directly to musicians, who then create a performance with the status of an exemplar. By copying the work-determinative features of the exemplar, others can perform the same work.

Works for live performance are 'thinner' in properties than their instances. The work specification, when taken in conjunction with the performance practice it presupposes, is silent on many matters that must be settled in sounding the music. The work underdetermines the full sonic detail of its performances. In the case of a piece embodied in an exemplar, the performer must abstract the work from the repleteness of the model's sonic detail, and is guided in doing so by conventions of the genre, style, practice, and tradition to which the work belongs. It is the performer who decides how to realize what is not work-determinative within her performance. In so doing, and in following the composer's instructions, she interprets the work. Many different interpretations will be compatible with faithful rendition of the work—that is, with the performer's complying with the composer's work-determinative prescriptions.

Works for performance are thinner in constitutive properties than their faithful instances. But some works are thicker than others. A piece specified only as a melody and chord sequence, which may be the appropriate way to conceive of many folk songs, may leave considerable latitude to the player, especially if the performance practice calls for extended, embellished playings. When works are very thin, the listener's attention is directed primarily to what the performer brings to its rendition. The more of its details that are determined by the composer's instructions, the thicker the work. A piece for electronic tape and violin, say, is nearly as thick with properties as its performances, because the parts encoded on the tape are fixed and only the violinist is an interpreter. The piece is for live performance, however, so long as some of its parts are for players who are told the parameters within which they must operate. Notice that the performers might operate electronic equipment, rather than playing orthodox musical instruments, if this is what the composer specifies.

The second kind of musical work is issued as a *master from which copies are cloned and disseminated*, typically as tapes or discs. Pieces of this kind are not for performance and interpretation, but for playback. If musicians using orthodox instruments contribute material, their activity belongs to the compositional process, not to its performance. The work is the information encoded on the master or its faithful copies, and it is instanced when it is decoded by an appropriate device, such as a CD player and speakers. Instances of such a work can differ, not as a result of a performer's interpretation, but rather because of variations in decoders and the environments in which they are used. The range of difference tolerated among decoders is set by technicians and designers of the required equipment, as well as by what is acceptable to composers and listeners. So long as the standards for fidelity are high in the decoders required for sounding it, such a work can be as replete with properties as its instances.

Though I have appealed to modern technologies in discussing works that are not for performance, earlier technologies were also so used. A piece written specifically for a music box, or for a mechanical calliope, is of this kind. Often, such a work existed as well in a version for live performance, in which case the secondary version should be regarded as a transcription of the primary one. When works originally created for live performance are given purely electronic incarnations, these latter are also transcriptions. Musical transcriptions involve the adaptation of a piece for instruments or a sound medium other than that for which it was composed. As such, they have an identity distinct from, but parasitic on, that of their models (see Levinson 1990: chapter 10; Scruton 1997).

In view of its reliance on recording technology, Gracyk (1996) has argued that rock music, construed as a broad category, is not for performance. The work, he claims, is what is on the disc. I prefer a different account of the relation between such music and the technology on which it relies. I regard such music as for *studio, rather than live, performance.* This thus constitutes a *third* kind of musical work. Rock typically employs electronic devices (such as synthesizers and filters) and techniques (such as multi-tracking) to create soundscapes that could not be reproduced under normal conditions of live playing. As a result, they are not works for live performance (and such performances as are given are assessed for authenticity by comparison with what is on the disc or video, not vice versa); nor are they purely electronic pieces not for performance, because 'covers' (recordings by one group of another's songs) are usually regarded as instancing the same piece, not as distinct but derivative works. As I say, this music is for performance—that is, it encourages and can be instanced in distinct, different renditions—but the relevant performances are intended for the special circumstances provided by the technology of the recording studio.

I allow that the three categories into which I have divided music are continuous and permeable. Nevertheless, they fit the ways composers and performers conceive of what they are doing. My categories bring to the fore differences between sorts of music that are crucial to their proper appreciation and identify. They make ontologically relevant the kinds of things that are germane to the way composers, performers, and listeners understand and discharge their socio-musical roles.

Most philosophical theories of musical ontology are more abstract than this. Philosophers argue over whether musical works are classes, types, or kinds, over whether they are universals or particulars, over whether they are created or discovered, and over whether musical works, as well as their performances, consist of sounds (see Goodman 1968; Wolterstorff 1980; Wollheim 1980; Ingarden 1986; Levinson 1990; Kivy 1993; Scruton 1997; and see 'Ontology of Art', Chapter 8 above).

7. Live Performances and Recordings

Not all recordings are of purely electronic pieces or of pieces for studio performance; very many are of works intended for live performance. These recordings encode not the work as such, but a performance or instance of it. Given the market dominance of recordings over live performances, it is useful to consider some of the respects in which the two differ. (I here ignore technical limitations of the medium, though these can certainly impoverish the experience of the person who prefers recordings to live performances.)

A recording might be just that, an unedited phonographic record of an actual performance played in real time. Even if it perfectly reproduces for the listener the sounds that impinged on the microphones, the listener's experience is likely to differ from that of a person who was present. This is a function of the record's repeatability (Brown 2000), which allows for repeated inspection of the performance, whereas the experience of the equivalent live performance is ephemeral. As well, it brings all the imperfections and idiosyncrasies of the rendition into special relief. Each wrong note and cough becomes permanently associated with a certain moment of the performance, to be repeated there whenever the record is played. Meanwhile, eccentricities that might be interesting and provocative in a live performance can become irksome and distracting on a recording. Recordings should be assessed differently from live performances. Because they need to retain their interest through repeated hearings, recordings need to be meticulously crafted and balanced. By contrast, a live performance should project the work to the audience present and hold its attention, which might be achieved better through expansive, bold gestures and a degree of exaggeration than through a fastidious concern with scarcely noticeable nuances.

Godlovitch (1998, see also Thom 1993) outlines the conditions normative for live performances: only one work is performed at a time; its proper sequence is respected, as is the indicated rate of delivery; the performance is continuous, without unjustified breaks; performers comply with their prescribed roles. Also, the audience is in a position to receive the entire performance in its detail. As Godlovitch is aware, most of these conditions are violated when recordings are made under studio conditions. Again, this makes for differences in the criteria for evaluating the two kinds of performance. While the live performer faces the risk of wrong notes and memory lapses, the artist in the studio has the luxury of multiple takes and editing. As a result, recordings made in the studio cannot display the features of live performances that depend on the challenges of making music in real time, even if they involve them. Though the takes may have been long and the editing minimal, we know that, had things gone wrong, they might have been shorter or have involved more splicing between parts. The resources of the studio create their own dangers, however, in that they encourage an obsessive attention to detail that may come at the expense of overall cohesion and interpretative vision. Moreover, because it encodes a performance that is simulated rather than live, we expect a higher level of technical achievement and interpretational integrity from studio recording.

Recordings of works created for live performance can provide a special and valuable experience of the work, a particular interpretation, and a particular (simulated) performance. It would, though, be an error to approach recordings as if their properties are equivalent to those that would be possessed by the live performances they simulate. A listener's knowledge of the medium should affect her experience, even where sonic transparency is achieved.

8. Musical Notations

Musical notations can function as transcriptions of performances, as tools for analysis, and as aids to recalling pieces committed to memory. A primary use of musical notation is to prescribe works (Ingarden 1986). Usually, notations with this purpose are called *scores*. Most of the detail of a score concerns the outcome to be sounded, rather than the process by which this is to be achieved, because the composer assumes the musician knows how to play her instrument. As well as those skills, the composer takes for granted the performance practices she shares with the musicians she is addressing. Accordingly, many things that may be work-determinative in pieces of the kind being specified are not indicated in the notation for it. For instance, it may be that a moderate string vibrato is required, but the composer does not record this in the score because the string players of the time know this to be mandated.

To complicate matters further, not everything recorded by the composer in the score need have the same prescriptive force. In other words, some things may be recommended as interpretative options, without being work-determinative. This was the case in the eighteenth century with notated dynamics and phrasings; by the middle of the next century, however, these same indications had become work-constitutive. Again, it was the performance practice that guided the performer in her interpretation of the score and set limits to the wishes or intentions the composer could make work-determinative.

All this is to say that work-notations need to be interpreted in light of the performance practice and notational conventions they assume, these being the ones of the composer's time. A naive approach to such notations, as when they are assumed to be transparent to their content, or where they are approached in terms of conventions that belong to a later period, will lead to the misinterpretation of the composer's instructions, and thereby to a misidentification of the work specified by those instructions.

9. What Makes a Performance of a Given Work?

To be of a work, a performance must achieve much of what was instructed by the composer; the performers must do this by intentionally following the instructions before them; and there must be a causal link between the instructions they follow and the creative acts in which the work had its genesis. This last condition is met where there is a relation of counterfactual dependence between the work's creation and what the performers do. In other words, if what the performers do would have been different had the composer's acts of creation been different, then their actions depend in the appropriate way on his.

Notice that performers can intend to play a trumpet voluntary by Purcell and end up performing one by Jeremiah Clarke, who perhaps is unknown to them, because the score before them was misattributed. The performance intentions that are crucial to the identity of the performance are low-level (play these notes as instructed) rather than high-level (play Purcell's piece) (cf. Levinson 1990). It may be possible sometimes to play X's work by using Y's score, but only where the causal chain leads to X and not to Y (Davies 2001).

10. Authenticity in Performances of Works

An authentic X is a genuine or proper X. Authenticity is a matter of classification, then, and is evaluative only to the extent that the classification in question is.

An authentic murder is an intentional killing and not, say, an accident. An authentic paragon of virtue is someone who shows the relevant virtues to an exemplary degree. Because a given thing can be variously categorized, it can be assessed for different kinds of authenticity. One and the same item might be a painting, an heirloom, and a representation of Venice, and can be assessed for its authenticity under each of these headings. Because some categorizations are more fundamental or salient, some judgements of authenticity will be more basic or important. Finally, authenticity comes in degrees and might also be indexed to take account of variability in items of the relevant character.

Musical performances of works can be assessed for their stylistic authenticity and in other ways, but a crucial assessment is that of the authenticity with which they instance the works they are of. A performance is authentic to the extent that it faithfully executes the indicated work-determinative instructions. Below a certain level, a performance fails to instance the intended piece. It is so inaccurate that the work cannot be discerned. A performance that is recognizably of a work may yet fall far short of ideal authenticity; for example, it might contain wrong notes. The more the threshold is exceeded, the more authentic the performance is.

Differences between performances do not always indicate differences in the level of their authenticity. As noted above, works are thinner than the performances that are of them. As a result, many details of performances are not covered by the composer's work-determinative instructions and belong instead to the player's interpretation. Performances can differ in their interpretations while being equally authentic.

On this account, what is required for authenticity depends on what has been prescribed, which in turn depends not just on what the composer would like but also on the notational conventions and performance practices within which he works. I have suggested that these are the ones applying at the time of the piece's composition. Even if nineteenth-century composers could make details of their pieces' instrumentation work-determinative, sixteenth-century composers could not. In performing their music, many orchestrations might be consistent with the pursuit of ideal authenticity, though they might not all be in the best taste. The relevant options, though, would have to be those of the composer's musical culture and period (Davies 2001).

A different view is presented by Kivy (1995), who argues that, for an authentic present-day performance, we need to know what the composer would want now, not what he might have chosen in the past. Of course, it is difficult to know how to answer that question in many cases, and for others there is no reason to assume composers would choose anything other than the best that would have been available to them under ideal conditions in their own time. But suppose that the composer would prefer to revise his music for modern instruments, sensibilities, styles, and the like. It seems to me that when we play the result it is not an authentic performance of the original work that results, but a rendition of a revision of the work. We do not get an authentic performance of the 1866 version of Bruckner's First Symphony by play-ing his 1891 recomposition of it. Similarly, a performance of the appropriately revised 2000 version of Bruckner's First, whatever that might be, would have no claim to being an authentic rendition of the work as he composed it in 1866.

Is authentic musical performance achievable? I say yes, provided complete and unambiguous work-determinative instructions have been given and the performers are able to recognize and to execute them. The more distant in time or cultural space is the work from the performer, the less likely it is that all these conditions will be satisfied. Still, a great deal is known about the musical works and performance prac-tices of past times as a result of musicological scholarship. Thus, for many works of the past as well as the present, performances with a high degree of authenticity should be possible.

Even if authentic performance is possible, is it desirable? One argument aiming to suggest that it is not desirable insists both that we cannot experience the music as the composer's contemporaries did, and that the value of authentic performance must reside in the duplication of that experience. Both parts of the claim can be challenged. When the music is old, our hearing is informed by our knowledge of later music, and the composer's contemporaries could not hear his works in that way. Not only does this make our experience different from theirs, it places us in a better position to appreciate the piece's art-historical features. This different ex-perience does not, however, undermine the value of the work's authentic perform-ance: that would happen only if we were incapable of accessing the composer's work and thereby unable to benefit from having it faithfully performed. But in this respect our experience of the work can be like that of its composer's contempor-aries. Listeners can adjust their expectations to suit the music that is their focus. For instance, a person might move between country and western and rhythm and blues, or between modern jazz and classical minimalism. In the same way, the musically literate listener (see Levinson 1996) can approach music of the past in terms of the conventions that applied to it, though she will be at home with other, later kinds of music that are subject to different patterns and rules of musical organization. In short, we can be much more flexible in our listening than the objection assumes.

One thing is obvious, though. It is only where we are interested in the works the performances are of, and in those works as the works of their composers, that authenticity in work instances is a virtue. Though other concerns (for example with the performer's skills and interpretative vision) are compatible with this one, and while this focus is not always relevant (as when free improvisation is the focus of attention, or when music is used to create an ambience), an interest in musical works is fundamental, I claim, and not solely in the Western classical tradition. The composer frequently brings great skill to his task, and it is through his attention to subtle nuances and details that his works often become so valuable and compelling. This is as true of Paul McCartney and John Lennon, or of the present generation of composers of Javanese and Balinese gamelan music, as of Mozart. Good music is highly crafted, and we cannot accept and value the rewards it provides without also committing ourselves to authenticity as a primary performance value. We prize many things in performance other than authenticity, but this does not mean that the pursuit of authenticity is merely one interpretative option among others.

This explains why there is something odd about the performer who departs deliberately from authenticity for the sake of creating an interesting or provocative interpretation. That person mistakes the point of the enterprise in which she is engaged: to interpret X's work in an interesting fashion, one has to undertake to deliver X's work, which undertaking presupposes a commitment to faithfulness. That said, it is fair to observe that an obsession with ideal authenticity can be inappropriately demanding. It would be ridiculous to suggest that the amateur should not play Bach at home on his electrified keyboard, or that a professional orchestra should not play Mendelssohn's Midsummer Night's Dream Overture because the ophicleide included in his orchestra is obsolete, given the availability of the tuba as a substitute.

11. Expressiveness in Music

If a single topic has dominated the philosophical discussion of music, it is that of music's emotional expressiveness, which has standardly been found puzzling. The puzzle is easy to state: we experience music as expressive of emotion; yet it is non-sentient, and not the kind of item that can experience an emotion to which it gives expression. So what, exactly, does musical expressiveness amount to?

A first approach simply denies that music in fact is expressive of emotion. The earliest, and one of the most compelling, statements of this view was by the nineteenth-century music critic Eduard Hanslick (1986; for discussion, see Budd 1985a and Davies 1994a). He argued that emotions are necessarily characterized, at least in part, in terms of the thoughts they involve about the objects to which they are directed. When I see a lion, it is not fear for myself that I feel if I do not believe the lion poses a threat to me. If I envy you, I must think you possess some thing or feature that I want and do not possess. Hanslick went on to suggest that music is incapable of expressing cognitions or cognitive attitudes of these kinds, and must thereby be incapable of expressing emotion. On the positive side, he suggested that music attracts us by a beauty intrinsic to its form.

Though Hanslick's 'cognitive' account of the emotions conforms to a model that nowadays is widely accepted by philosophers (for a version, see Solomon 1976), his denial that music is expressive of emotions runs counter to the way in which we experience it. Despite the apparent impossibility of music's expressing emotions, it is thought better to attempt to explain this than to reject outright the data of listeners' experiences.

Another suggestion, that musical expressiveness is irreducibly *sui generis*, cannot be accepted. If predicates like 'happy' and 'sad' do not retain their usual meanings when they are applied to music, it will not be possible to explain the power, value, or interest that music's expressiveness has for the listener. So, even if music is expressive in its own way, we should still be able to connect its manner of being expressive to the paradigm cases to which such terms apply: namely, to those in which a sentient creature gives public expression through its behaviour to what it feels. Nor will it be helpful to characterize music's expressiveness as irreducibly metaphoric (as Goodman 1968 and Scruton 1997 do), since that approach merely acknowledges without addressing what is at issue: the difficulty of explaining how the relevant terms retain their usual meaning when applied to the musical case. And again, it will not be satisfactory to attempt to reduce music's expressiveness to the technicalities of music analysis. Even if such a theory correctly identifies the devices and processes in which music's expressiveness is grounded, it cannot in those terms explain why 'happy' and 'sad' retain their usual meanings in relation to the musical case.

Here is a first proposal: rather than standing to emotions as do the behaviours, like weeping, that betray them, musical utterances are like linguistic statements about the emotions. Music is an expression not of raw feeling, but of thoughts about the emotions. To perform this function it need not be sentient, though it must be created to so function by a sentient creature.

Coker (1972) develops the analogy with natural languages by arguing that music forms a symbol system, with rules for combining elements into meaningful strings. The analogy fails, though. It is true, certainly, that musical practices are rule-governed (Lerdahl and Jackendoff 1983), but it is not true that these rules describe a syntactic system that could give rise to a semantics. In music there are no operations, functions, or structures equivalent to description, to sentential closure, to negation, implication, conjunction, and disjunction, or to scope or modality, or to any of the other things essential to generating semantic content within truth-functional systems.

An alternative view holds that music's meaning is associative rather than systematic. In contingent, conventional ways, musical gestures become connected with emotions. This could occur, for instance, if similar musical phrases were used to set texts in which a particular emotion is described or expressed (Cooke 1959), as when rising inflections are coupled with mention of rising spirits, or if kinds of music or musical instruments are used habitually in rites or events that are themselves emotionally charged, as when drums used to mark time become associated with military manoeuvres. Yet this account, even if it works, suggests only that music can point to the emotions, not that it can characterize them.

A further disadvantage of this and the previous view is that they describe music's connection to the emotions as arbitrary. A listener who concerns herself with what music expresses apparently need not bother with the intrinsically musical features she hears. In fact, though, we experience the emotions expressed in music as concretely present in, and responsive to, the manner of its unfolding.

The theory that music symbolizes the emotions could deal with this last point if the music's connection with the emotions it expresses were natural and transparent rather than haphazard and opaque. This modification is adopted in theories regarding music as an iconic or exemplificatory symbol. Here the claim is that music symbolizes the emotions because it is experienced as resembling them (Langer 1942; Goodman 1968), much as a realistic depiction is experienced as like its subject.

It has been suggested that music importantly resembles expressive intonations of the voice (Kivy 1989) or the rhetorical gestures of oratory (Sharpe 2000). Alternatives maintain that, through its movement and pattern, music can be similar to the phenomenological profile of emotions (Langer 1942; Addis 1999) or their outward behavioural expressions (Kivy 1989; Davies 1994a). The difficulty with these last views lies in explaining how the similarity licenses the judgement that the music is expressive. In the human case, the behaviour expresses an emotion only if one is felt, and the phenomenology is that of an emotion only if it connects to the appropriate beliefs and desires. By contrast, music does not undergo the emotions expressed in it. Perhaps, though, the composer experiences the emotions expressed in his music, or perhaps we call the music expressive because of its power to awaken a response in the listener.

According to the expression theory, we experience music's expressiveness as a residue of feelings discharged in the compositional process. However, the connection between the composer's emotions, if he has any, and the work he writes is not plainly of the venting kind. Indeed, if composers sometimes express their emotions in the works they write, they do so by appropriating the music's expressiveness. In other words, composers express their emotions by matching the already expressive nature of the music to their feelings. (For further criticism of the expression theory, see Tormey 1971; Davies 1994a; Kivy 1989; and Goldman 1995b.)

According to the arousal theory, what makes it true that music is sad or happy is its causal power to bring about these or related responses in the listener (Matravers 1998). It is not obvious, though, that listeners who perceive correctly the music's expressiveness are inevitably disposed to be aroused by it. Moreover, when the response occurs, it seems that it does so because we find the music expressive, whereas the arousal theory maintains the reverse.

Another possibility, that music represents emotions, is unsatisfactory. There is wide agreement among philosophers that instrumental music is limited in its representational powers (see Kivy 1984; Walton 1990; Davies 1994a; Budd 1995; Scruton 1997). It best represents sounds, and does so by imitating them. Usually, one can follow and understand instrumental music without being sure what, if anything, it represents. The case is different, however, when music is joined with words or drama. Then its dynamic character can become illustrative of the content of the concurrent text or action. To offer a crude example, a steady rhythm in the strings might signify the beating of the lover's heart. Moreover, the music's expressive mood, or energy, or tension, might represent the feelings and psychological states of characters as these are described or indicated in the narrative or drama. Following on from this observation, it might be suggested that, even in instrumental music, listeners imagine the music to present a narrative concerning the emotional life of a persona, and thereby hear that persona's emotions presented.

Some such idea has been proposed by Budd (1985a), Walton (1990), and Ridley (1995) (see also J. Robinson 1997). Levinson (1996) defines musical expressiveness such that a passage is expressive of an emotion if and only if it is heard, by appropriately experienced listeners, as the expression of that emotion by an indefinite, imagined agent, the music's persona. One objection denies that this claim accords with the experience of all appropriately experienced listeners. Another doubts that purely instrumental music directs the listener's imagining to a degree that makes it appropriate for her to attribute what she imagines to the music (Davies 1997b). And there is a third reason for doubting the explanatory power of this approach. If music in opera represents the emotions of the characters subject to the drama, it does so by expressing them under appropriate circumstances; for example, sadness is expressed in the music when the character says she is sad, or weeps, or is downcast. It follows that we cannot explain or analyse music's expressive powers by reference to its capacity to represent emotions, including those of imagined personas. The explanation runs in the opposite direction. In short, we should not conflate musical expressiveness and representation.

There is another way music's expressiveness could connect to fictional or make-believe experiences of emotion: namely, if listeners imaginatively ascribe emotions to themselves on the basis of their make-believe engagement with the world of the work (Walton 1988). In particular, the suggestion is that listeners, in the course of make-believing, take their awareness of their auditory sensations to be an awareness of their own emotions. But such does not square with the experience of most listeners.

A quite different approach rejects the claim that expressions of emotions must be linked directly to experiences of emotions. Some things just have an expressive appearance. For instance, basset hounds have sad-looking faces and some trees look tormented. Of course, this does not mean that basset hounds feel sad or that the trees experience torment. It is the character of their appearance that is being judged. However, this concern with what I call the emotion characteristics of appearances remains connected to the paradigm in which a felt emotion is expressed. Basset hounds' faces are sad-looking because their appearance is like that of a person who feels sad and shows it. When we say 'the music is sad', we are referring not to the expression of any felt emotion, but, rather, to an emotion characteristic presented by the music. Typically, the progress of music recalls a person's gait or comportment, not his or her physiognomy, but these can be no less express-ive than faces. On this view, sometimes known as the contour theory, music's expressiveness belongs literally and objectively to the music (Kivy 1989; Davies 1994a). Because music is a temporal art, its expressive character is revealed only through sustained attention to its dynamic progress.

Music is a special case of a rather general phenomenon: our tendency to ex-perience many non-human, even non-sentient, entities as redolent of emotions. Such responses are not strictly entailed by the resemblances that can be found, yet we often find those resemblances expressively effective or potent. This is evident, for instance, in Edvard Munch's well-known 'Scream' face, which loses nothing in its force through being simplified and distorted as a representation.

The contour theory faces two main lines of criticism (Goldman 1995b; Levinson 1996, 1997b; Matravers 1998). Some deny that we experience an analogy between music's dynamic topology and the behaviours that express emotion. Music does not sound the way human expressive behaviours move. The second objection argues that the contour theory cannot explain the importance we attach to music's expressiveness, or why we would be aroused to emotional reactions by it. If music presents only appearances of emotions, not genuinely felt instances or the simu-lacra of such, why would its expressiveness be so interesting and compelling?

12. Emotional Reactions to Music's Expressiveness

There is a general problem, one inherited by all theories of musical expressiveness, about the fact that listeners are moved to joy by joyful music and to sadness by sad music. In the typical case, I have to believe the situation or thing on which I am focused to be unfortunate and regrettable if my response is to be one of sadness, but the listener to Beethoven's 'Eroica' does not find its expressiveness to be unfor-tunate or regrettable, yet may still be moved to sadness. His response is caused by and tracks the music, but does not take the music, or any other thing, as its emo-tional object (Davies 1994a; Goldman 1995a; Matravers 1998). Moreover, when con-fronted by sadness, the appropriate reaction would usually be one of compassion or pity, but the listener does not respond to sad music in such a manner.

Kivy (1988, 1989; see also Sharpe 2000) dismisses the problem by denying that lis-teners are moved to echo the negative emotion expressed in the music they attend to. Most philosophers appeal to their own responses, as well as accepting the word of others, in rejecting this position (Levinson 1990; Davies 1994a; Goldman 1995b).

One answer proposes that not all emotions involve an intentional object, or the beliefs and desires targeted on such an object. Appearances of sadness need not make a person feel gloomy if he does not think they show how anyone feels. Mere appearances of sadness are not a suitable object for sadness, since they are not thought to be unfortunate, and so on. Nevertheless, if he is roused to an emotion under those circumstances, it will be a mirroring one, because, in the absence of relevant beliefs and desires, it is only through a kind of contagion or osmosis that his feelings are engaged (Davies 1994*a*). It is not at all uncommon for us to catch the mood (or emotional atmosphere) prevailing around us, as psychologists have documented (Hatfield *et al.* 1994).

13. THE DIFFICULTY OF NEGATIVE RESPONSES TO MUSIC

A different problem emerges if sad music sometimes awakens a sad reaction in the listener: namely, why would he value and seek out that music in the future? Why should he not try to avoid it? More generally, why are we drawn to have mirroring responses to music expressive of negative emotions? Here are two possible reasons.

Even if the experience has negative elements, these can be outweighed by positive ones. We can find much to enjoy and admire in a work that makes us feel sad. Still, this reply probably is open to the objection that many of the benefits mentioned could be achieved at no cost if we focus only on happy works. So a yet stronger line claims that at least some of the benefits are of a kind that can be obtained only from works liable to induce negative reactions. For instance, because our sad response lacks 'life implications', it can be savoured and examined, something difficult to achieve in ordinary contexts (Levinson 1990).

A second line builds on the first. Even if we have some reason to avoid works that produce emotionally unpleasant responses, that reason is not overriding. What is negative in music is often integral to the whole. What is negative comes with the territory, not solely as something to be endured, but also as making it the territory it is. If we wish to understand and appreciate the piece, we have to take on its entirety. The resulting experience is not merely good on balance, for that wrongly implies that there could be a better experience that is fully of the work yet less negative. Though the experience is a good one, integrated with it and undetachable from it are negative dimensions that we accept for the sake of the experience we seek.

In this respect, music is not different from many other aspects of life—such as child rearing, personal relationships, and self-realization—that involve negative aspects as part of their nature. To engage in these activities for their own sake is to accept the negative as an inescapable aspect of the overall good at which one aims (Walton 1990; Davies 1994a).

14. THE UNDERSTANDING LISTENER

What are the qualifications of the understanding listener? Clearly, she is able to follow the music. Even on first hearing a piece, she recognizes melodies as such, knows when significant sections have ended, can often detect performance errors (and knows what would have been correct), experiences an appropriate waxing and waning of the musical tension, and so on (Kivy 1990; Levinson 1996). Her abilities will depend upon her having internalized the norms or rules governing the kind of music to which she listens with understanding. She might not be able to articulate those rules, but she will be able to anticipate what is likely to come next as well as to recognize well-formed and ill-formed constructions. Because musical styles can differ significantly, the listener who is at home with one might not grasp another. Many listeners can follow music in a variety of styles with understanding, however, adjusting their expectations accordingly. The skilled listener need not be a skilled performer, nor need she be familiar with music theory and the technical vocabulary of musicology (Davies 1994a). Nevertheless, she must be aware of, through having observed, the characteristics of relevant musical instruments and how they are played, and her understanding may be facilitated or enhanced by acquaintance with music theory.

Levinson (1997a) has provided a controversial theory, called 'concatenationism', of what is involved in following music comprehendingly by ear. He claims that the listener can correctly understand and evaluate the music if she is aware only of what she hears at the moment, and of its connections to and implications for events shortly prior to and subsequent to that instant. Perception of large-scale structures is not required for the listener's comprehension of the music. Indeed, large-scale structure, according to Levinson, cannot be perceived as such; the maximum perceptual span is of only about a minute. Awareness of large-scale form is intellectual, not perceptual, and the pleasure we take in this awareness is pale by comparison with that taken in music in the moment.

On Levinson's account, the recognition of musical form is largely unconscious and non-propositional. This can be contested. While it may be true that the listener does not provide a running commentary on the work's structure as she listens, her awareness of overall pattern and design can be conscious without being purely intellectual. Recognizing that one musical idea repeats or resembles another that was heard earlier surely is as much perceptual as inferential, in which case there is no absurdity in maintaining that large-scale structures are among the things that the listener perceives (see Levinson *et al.* 1999).

15. MUSICAL PROFUNDITY

Kivy (1990) has the intuition that instrumental music is profound, but he is unable to demonstrate how this is so. To be profound, he holds, it would have to be about a profound subject treated in an exemplary fashion. But since Kivy denies that instrumental music is about anything, he cannot make the case for its being profound. Some music, for example Bach's counterpoint, could be about its own materials, could be of abiding interest, and could be of the highest craftsmanship. To be profound, though, it would have to be about a subject that is of great importance, one that goes to the moral heart of human life, and music's materials is not a profound subject in this sense. Music, concludes Kivy, can be profoundly so-and-so, which is to say very so-and-so; but it cannot be profound.

Levinson (1992) has replied that music can lead listeners to reflect on the emotions it expresses, and sometimes can provid first-hand acquaintance of those emotions by moving the listener to a mirroring response. Because this is frequently intended by the composer, it is reasonable to say that such music is, in a broad sense, about the emotions expressed in it (Davies 1994a). Kivy (1997) allows that emotions are expressed in music and that, at least sometimes, the listener reacts to her experience of the music's expressiveness by reflecting on the corresponding emotions, but he denies that this establishes that music is about the emotions it expresses. It does not say anything profound in regard to the emotions it presents, and indeed, does not have any propositional content. To this one might reply that music shows, rather than says, how things are. Even if this is allowed, Kivy doubts that music reveals anything deep about the emotions.

16. THE VALUE OF MUSIC

The idea that instrumental music has no propositional content is sometimes in fact proposed as the source of its value. On one hypothesis, music presents truths about the nature of the emotions that are ineffable, and are all the more important for that fact (Langer 1942). While there may be respects in which musical experience is ineffable in being too fine for conceptual encapsulation (Raffman 1993), Langer's view is hardly credible (Budd 1985a; Davies 1994a). It relies on unconvincing claims about exclusive modes of symbolization, the discursive and the presentational, and their differential access to the verities. In general, there is no reason to suppose that, in its ineffability, music differs from thoroughly mundane perceptual experience, and we do not ordinarily regard that as a source of deep but inexpressible truths.

A more plausible account takes music's absence of propositional content as a sign not of its special engagement with reality, but of its distinctness from it. Because music draws us into its own, contentless world, it liberates us from the demands and vicissitudes of the real one, wherein lies its value (Budd 1995; Goldman 1995a; Kivy 1997). Music is full of musical interest, and is thus not empty. But it does not contain a commentary about the reality that lies beyond its boundaries, even if it expresses emotion, can be appreciated fully only in terms of its genre and musico-historical location, and displays considerable human ingenuity in its design. It is valued for its own sake on account of the play of form and emotion made possible by its detachment from the practical world.

A view like this can be traced back to Schopenhauer, who celebrated music so highly because he had a deeply pessimistic view of the possibility of achieving happiness in the actual world (Budd 1985a). Yet the position does not depend on an entirely negative appraisal of our transactions with reality, because there is a positive side to music's value as well. Its very abstractness intensifies the drama played out between calm, tension, climax, emotion, and relaxation. Usually, the musical world is ingeniously constructed to achieve unity within diversity. There is the sense of a compelling argument that ends with a Q.E.D., though this argument lacks propositional content (Tanner 1992). A seemingly law-like progression leads inevitably to balance, resolution, and closure; yet this is apparent more in retrospect, so unpredictable and original is the transition from moment to moment. The world of the work can be thoroughly engaging and admirable for the puzzles it poses and for the elegance, economy, and wit with which it solves them (Davies 1998; for a related view, see Levinson 1998).

This story is incomplete, even when we restrict ourselves to instrumental musical works, for it leaves out the values of performance, such as the pleasure we take in observing the mastery with which a person exercises a difficult craft, along with our interest in his interpretation and the light it casts on the work. And it ignores the broader consequences of music's appreciation (Davies 1994b), which may include the development of a sense of community with others (Higgins 1991), as well as a humanizing and civilizing of the individual (Sharpe 2000). Music is so central in the lives of so many people that it helps shape their world-view and basic values—indeed, their sense of their identity and individuality. It is hard to account fully for the role music plays in people's lives solely by reference to its abstract nature (Brown 1999), for it is given concrete significance through its association with important events and rites of passage, not to mention private romance and fantasy. Indeed, it might be suggested that music is incomplete when it is treated as autonomous, and thereby is prevented from realizing its fullest potential for political and expressive significance (Goehr 1998).

Adorno, who wrote mainly from 1920 to 1940, regarded music's significance in terms of its ideological place within the wider pattern of history. In accord with his Marxist orientation, Adorno expected to find evidence in music of progress towards a liberation, the outcome of which would be fulfilling art that was accessible to all. To Adorno's ears, it was twelve-tone music that represented logical progress, and would therefore become the music of the future, whereas Stravinsky's neoclassicism was regressive and corrupt (Adorno 1973). In addition, Adorno objected to popular forms of music, especially jazz, which he regarded as music of low quality that was exploited by the powerful to alienate the lower classes from the serious music that should interest and reward them (Adorno 1992).

With the advantage of hindsight, it is difficult to take many of Adorno's claims seriously (Sharpe 2000). His views on serialism influenced the composition of German music into the 1970s, and might thereby have seemed close to taking music's historical pulse, but since then have been left far behind. Stravinsky's polyglot eclecticism is nearer the current ethos than Schoenberg's expressionism. Certainly, twelve-tone music has not become more accessible to and been warmly embraced by the masses, as Adorno had predicted. Meanwhile, his attacks on the popular music of his time are uninformed and ill-willed. His views read now more as the expression of elitist prejudice than as revealing the historically inevitable path along which music would necessarily evolve. Yet Adorno's writings retain a fascination for many, not least for the power of personality, the olympian seriousness, and the inspirational style they exhibit. Those who fear the dumbing down of music and of intellectual life in general can find in those writings much that is insightful.

17. MUSIC AND WORDS

As suggested earlier, the claim that the value of classical instrumental music lies in its detachment is not entirely convincing. When we consider other kinds of music, the view is even more unattractive. It is absurd to suppose that the primary value of rock music lies in the pleasure we get from contemplating it as an abstraction. In the first instance, much of it is functional music, for dancing or relaxed socializing. More than this, rock's paradigms are songs, and songs join words with music. The resulting composite is no longer abstract. It remains for us to consider, though, what if anything music can add to the word's message. I here discuss opera, which combines drama as well as words, with music.

Opera, with its inherent eccentricity, fantastic cost, temperamental stars, and strange artifice, provides a rich source for the social commentator. For Adorno, opera was a fantasy serving to cocoon the bourgeoisie. Cavell (1994) finds in it a metaphor for the individual's search for a 'voice'. Moreover, the sexual ambiguity that goes with castrated males and women in 'trouser' roles inevitably invites questions about the sexual politics implied by the artform. For instance, Clément (1989) argues that opera is dedicated to the destruction of its heroines, using music to make this seem palatable.

An interesting debate concerns the contribution made by the music to opera's overall significance. According to Paul Robinson (1985), opera music has affinities with both the emotionally concrete and the structurally abstract. Where the prevailing ethos is not purely 'scientific', the music in opera can engage with the intellectual concerns of the age—in particular, with the models of love, friendship, family, society, and politics that characterized the Enlightenment and Modernism. This is a claim about qualities of the music; about things it adds over and above the content of the libretto. In the same vein, Kivy (1988) argues that the approaches to opera in different ages has reflected the contrasting views of the nature of emotional and psychological reality that prevailed in those various eras. And McClary (1991) analyses how chromaticism in the music associated with strong women characters presents them as a threat to order and stability. On a more specific note, Goehr (1998) suggests that Wagner's *Die Meistersinger* not only corroborates many of the aesthetic principles articulated by Kant, but also delivers the political message that music finds its freedom within the life of society when it expresses itself independently at a critical distance.

At a more modest level, we can consider how music and drama—by which I mean the substance of the opera's libretto—interact. Kivy (1988) discusses two possible relations: in 'music made drama' the music accompanies and heightens a structure determined by the text. By contrast, in 'drama made music' the drama provides the occasion for the creation of a structure that is perfect on its own, purely musical, terms. In distinguishing these approaches, Kivy seems to assume that the opera's music must be subject to the drama, or vice versa. His account does not leave room for the possibility that the two might support each other, so that the whole is greater than the sum of its parts. This would occur, for instance, if the text of an opera could be married to a satisfactory musical form in such a way that the whole takes on a depth and significance that neither the music nor the text could sustain on its own.

It is not difficult to illustrate how this might operate. Many large-scale musical forms involve patterns of conflict and resolution, and overall musical unity is consistent with episodic or cyclic structures. As a result, talented composers can create wholes that heighten and augment the drama's form while being musically satisfying. This need not be solely a matter of bringing together the forms of the drama and of the music: thematic recapitulations can carry with them dramatic connotations that are absent from the text. For instance, in Verdi's *Otello*, Otello's strangling of Desdemona in Act Four is haunted by the 'kiss' motive from their happy love duet of Act One, which brings the two scenes into a psychological proximity that is heart-wrenchingly poignant. Without that musical repetition, the dramatic effect could not be attained. Given how paltry most librettos would be if they were mistaken for play scripts, and how dramatically successful many of the corresponding operas are, the successful marriage of music and text is revealed as the norm, not the exception that Kivy implies it to be.

See also: Expression in Art; Art and Emotion; Ontology of Art; Creativity in Art; Value in Art; Authenticity in Art; Theatre.

BIBLIOGRAPHY

Addis, L. (1999). *Of Mind and Music*. Ithaca, NY: Cornell University Press.

Adorno, T. W. (1973). *The Philosophy of Modern Music*, trans. A. G. Mitchell and W. V. Blomster. London: Sheed & Ward.

—— (1992). *Essays on Music and Culture*, trans. R. Livingstone. London: Verso Books.

Alperson, P. (1984). 'On Musical Improvisation'. *Journal of Aesthetics and Art Criticism* 43: 17–30.

—— (ed.) (1994). *What is Music? An Introduction to the Philosophy of Music*. University Park, Pa.: Pennsylvania State University Press.

—— (ed.) (1998). *Musical Worlds: New Directions in the Philosophy of Music*. University Park, Pa.: Pennsylvania State University Press.

Baugh, B. (1993). 'Prolegomena to Any Aesthetics of Rock Music'. *Journal of Aesthetics and Art Criticism* 51: 23–9.

Brown, L. B. (1996). 'Musical Works, Improvisation, and the Principle of Continuity'. *Journal of Aesthetics and Art Criticism* 54: 353–69.

—— (1999). 'Postmodernist Jazz Theory: Afrocentrism, Old and New'. *Journal of Aesthetics and Art Criticism* 57: 235–46.

—— (2000). 'Phonography, Repetition and Spontaneity'. *Philosophy and Literature* 24: 111–25.

Budd, M. (1985a). *Music and the Emotions: The Philosophical Theories*. London: Routledge & Kegan Paul.

—— (1985b). 'Understanding Music'. *Proceedings of the Aristotelian Society*, suppl., 59: 233–48.

—— (1995). *The Values of Art: Pictures, Poetry, and Music*. London: Allen Lane/Penguin Press.

Butt, J. (2002). *Playing with History*. Cambridge: Cambridge University Press.

Cavell, S. (1994). *A Pitch of Philosophy: Autobiographical Exercises*. Cambridge, Mass.: Harvard University Press.

Clément, C. (1989). *Opera, or the Undoing of Women*, trans. B. Wing. London: Virago.

Coker, W. (1972). *Music and Meaning: A Theoretical Introduction to Musical Aesthetics*. New York: Free Press.

Cooke, D. (1959). *The Language of Music*. Oxford: Oxford University Press.

Davies, S. (1994*a*). *Musical Meaning and Expression*. Ithaca, NY: Cornell University Press.

—— (1994*b*). 'The Evaluation of Music', in P. Alperson (ed.), *What Is Music? An Introduction to the Philosophy of Music*. University Park, Pa.: Pennsylvania State University Press, 307–25.

—— (1997*a*). 'John Cage's 4′ 33″: Is It Music?' *Australasian Journal of Philosophy* 75: 448–62.

—— (1997*b*). 'Contra the Hypothetical Persona in Music', in M. Hjort and S. Laver (eds.), *Emotion and the Arts*. Oxford: Oxford University Press, pp. 95–109.

—— (1998). 'Musical Understanding and Musical Kinds', in P. Alperson (ed.), *Musical Worlds: New Directions in the Philosophy of Music*, University Park, Pa.: Pennsylvania State University Press, pp. 69–81.

—— (1999). 'Rock versus Classical Music'. *Journal of Aesthetics and Art Criticism* 57: 193–204.

—— (2001). *Musical Works and Performances: A Philosophical Exploration*, Oxford: Clarendon Press.

De Bellis, M. (1995). *Music and Conceptualization*. Cambridge: Cambridge University Press.

Godlovitch, S. (1998). *Musical Performance: A Philosophical Study*. London: Routledge.

Goehr, L. (1992). *The Imaginary Museum of Musical Works: An Essay in the Philosophy of Music*. Oxford: Clarendon Press.

—— (1998). *The Quest for Voice: On Music, Politics, and the Limits of Philosophy*. Oxford: Clarendon Press.

Goldman, A. H. (1995*a*). *Aesthetic Value*. Boulder, Colo.: Westview Press.

—— (1995*b*). 'Emotion in Music (A Postscript)'. *Journal of Aesthetics and Art Criticism* 53: 59–69.

Goodman, N. (1968). *Languages of Art*. Indianapolis: Bobbs-Merrill.

Gracyk, T. A. (1996). *Rhythm and Noise: An Aesthetics of Rock Music*. Durham, NC: Duke University Press.

Hanslick, E. (1986). *On the Musically Beautiful*, trans. G. Payzant. Indianapolis: Hackett.

Hatfield, E., Cacioppo, J. T., and Rapson, R. L. (1994). *Emotional Contagion*. New York: Cambridge University Press.

Higgins, K. (1991). *The Music of our Lives*. Philadelphia: Temple University Press.

Ingarden, R. (1986). *The Work of Music and the Problem of its Identity*, trans. A. Czerniawski. Berkeley, Calif.: University of California Press.

Kivy, P. (1984). *Sound and Semblance: Reflections on Musical Representation*. Princeton: Princeton University Press.

—— (1988). *Osmin's Rage: Philosophical Reflections on Opera, Drama and Text*. Princeton: Princeton University Press.

—— (1989). *Sound Sentiment*. Philadelphia: Temple University Press.

—— (1990). *Music Alone: Philosophical Reflection on the Purely Musical Experience*. Ithaca, NY: Cornell University Press.

—— (1993). *The Fine Art of Repetition: Essays in the Philosophy of Music*. New York: Cambridge University Press.

—— (1995). *Authenticities: Philosophical Reflections on Musical Performance*. Ithaca, NY: Cornell University Press.

—— (1997). *Philosophies of Arts: An Essay in Differences*. New York: Cambridge University Press.

—— (2001). *New Essays on Musical Understanding*. Oxford: Clarendon Press.

Krausz, M. (ed.) (1993). *The Interpretation of Music: Philosophical Essays*. Oxford: Clarendon Press.

Langer, S. K. (1942). *Philosophy in a New Key*. Cambridge, Mass.: Harvard University Press.

Lerdahl, F. and Jackendoff, R. (1983). *A Generative Theory of Tonal Grammar*. Cambridge, Mass.: MIT Press.

Levinson, J. (1990). *Music, Art, and Metaphysics*. Ithaca, NY: Cornell University Press.

——(1992). 'Musical Profundity Misplaced'. *Journal of Aesthetics and Art Criticism* 50: 58–60.

——(1996). *The Pleasures of Aesthetics*. Ithaca, NY: Cornell University Press.

——(1997*a*). *Music in the Moment*. Ithaca, NY: Cornell University Press.

——(1997*b*). 'Emotion in Response to Art: A Survey of the Terrain', in M. Hjort and S. Laver (eds.), *Emotion and the Arts*. Oxford: Oxford University Press, pp. 20–34.

——(1998). 'Evaluating Music', in P. Alperson (ed.), *Musical Worlds*. University Park, Pa.: Pennsylvania State University Press.

—— *et al.* (1999). 'Symposium on Music in the Moment'. *Music Perception* 16: 463–94.

McClary, S. (1991). *Feminine Endings: Music, Gender, and Sexuality*. Minneapolis: University of Minnesota Press.

Madell, G. (2002). *Philosophy, Music and Emotion*. Edinburgh: Edinburgh University Press.

Matravers, D. (1998). *Art and Emotion*. Oxford: Clarendon Press.

Raffman, D. (1993). *Language, Music, and Mind*, Cambridge, Mass.: MIT Press.

Ridley, A. (1995). *Music, Value and the Passions*. Ithaca, NY: Cornell University Press.

Robinson, J. (ed.) (1997). *Music and Meaning*. Ithaca, NY: Cornell University Press.

Robinson, P. (1985). *Opera and Ideas: From Mozart to Strauss*. New York: Harper & Row.

Ross, S. and Judkins, J. (1996). 'Conducting and Musical Interpretation'. *British Journal of Aesthetics* 36: 16–29.

Scruton, R. (1997). *The Aesthetics of Music*. Oxford: Clarendon Press.

Sharpe, R. A. (2000). *Music and Humanism*. Oxford: Oxford University Press.

Solomon, R. C. (1976). *The Passions*. Garden City, NY: Anchor Press/Doubleday.

Tanner, M. (1985). 'Understanding Music'. *Proceedings of the Aristotelian Society*, suppl., 59: 233–48.

——(1992). 'Metaphysics and Music'. *Royal Institute of Philosophy*, suppl., 33: 181–200.

Thom, P. (1993). *For an Audience: A Philosophy of the Performing Arts*. Philadelphia: Temple University Press.

Tormey, A. (1971). *The Concept of Expression*. Princeton: Princeton University Press.

Walton, K. L. (1988). 'What is Abstract about the Art of Music?' *Journal of Aesthetics and Art Criticism* 46: 351–64.

——(1990). *Mimesis as Make-Believe: On the Foundations of the Representational Arts*. Cambridge, Mass.: Harvard University Press.

Wollheim, R. (1980). *Art and its Objects*. Cambridge: Cambridge University Press.

Wolterstorff, N. (1980). *Works and Worlds of Art*. Oxford: Clarendon Press.

——(1994). 'The Work of Making a Work of Music', in P. Alperson (ed.), *What Is Music? An Introduction to the Philosophy of Music*. University Park, Pa.: The Pennsylvania State University Press, pp. 103–29.

PAINTING

S U S A N   F E A G I N

To paint is to apply a coloured, relatively fluid substance to a surface, usually with a brush, but sometimes by other means, e.g. a palette knife, fingers, or a spraying device such as an airbrush. *Paintings* are artefacts, sometimes and in some respects the products of human ingenuity and skill, and sometimes the expressions of an untutored vision or attitude. The portion of philosophy of art that deals with painting as one of the visual arts obviously overlaps that dealing with the philosophy of perception, and also with the philosophy of mind, including human actions and their relationships to thought, philosophical psychology, and theories of personal identity. In addition, it draws from the philosophy of the social sciences in so far as it deals with the extent to which historical and cultural realities make objects what they are and artists, interpreters, and appreciators who they are, and to the extent that such realities figure in the interpretation and understanding of objects and persons.

Philosophy of painting also looks outside of philosophy to painting practices and to how individuals have chosen to talk and write about them throughout history and around the globe. Within the last thirty years art historians have become increasingly concerned with theoretical issues about the political, cultural, and moral functions of paintings and with how historical forces and cultural institutions and practices empower and constrain painters themselves. Art theory, social and intellectual history, cultural anthropology, and political theory continue to provide important resources for thinking about painting.

In what follows I identify four categories of issues that arise in relation to painting as an art. The first concerns the ontological status of paintings as physical objects: the importance of different types of paint and their material support, the values contingent on them, and the conservation and restoration issues that arise because anything physical is subject to decay. The second category concerns the perception and valuation of visual form and attempts to define painting's nature and value in purely visual terms. The third explores ontological and interpretive issues raised by the different forms painting takes in different cultures. The fourth concerns personal agency and autonomy in relation to personal expression, to representations of individuals and cultural practices within painting, and to ties between painting's epistemic potential and its social status.

1. PAINTINGS AS PHYSICAL OBJECTS

Historically, in the West, easel paintings have been taken to be the clearest examples of painting as art. Easel paintings are typically of a visually manageable size, with fixed boundaries, easily individuated from other paintings, suitable for framing, portable, and saleable. That this is the paradigm for paintings is seen in various types of practice, for example that pages of illuminated manuscripts, portions of painted surfaces of ceilings, interior walls of residences, churches, and chapels, and exterior walls of buildings covered with murals or graffiti have often been removed, framed, displayed, discussed, and otherwise treated as easel paintings. Textbooks on the history of the visual arts have typically contained illustrations of paintings as self-contained entities, that is, without their site-specific architectural surroundings or even their integral frames, such as with wall paintings and certain altar-pieces. Any adequate account of painting as an art must also take account of works of art at least some portions of which are painted but are not themselves paintings, as with pottery and ceramics, bas and deep relief, and sculpture. In addition, there are painted surfaces of objects, architectural structures, and other parts of one's environment where the painting but not the relevant part of the material support is taken to be art. Wittgenstein warned against a one-sided diet of philosophical examples, and taking easel paintings as the paradigm tends to prejudice ontological questions about what is relevant to understanding and evaluating painting, especially since, as a practice, easel painting turns out to be relatively rare, both historically and globally.

Another way in which philosophy of painting may be inappropriately constricted is to equate painting and pictorial representation. In his landmark and highly provocative book *Languages of Art* (1968), Nelson Goodman defined a set of issues that came to be central to the philosophy of art for over two decades, including how to define pictorial representation and how to explain its differences from other modes of representation, especially the linguistic. Unfortunately, Goodman regularly assimilates painting to pictorial representation, most obviously in a footnote in which he proclaims that 'nothing very vital rests on ... the often three-dimensional nature of picture surfaces' (p. 42n.). Malcolm Budd (1995: chapter 2) and others take the plausible view that pictorial representation in its purest form is two-dimensional and best exemplified by projected slides: there the medium is light and representational content is, one might think, separated from the materiality of a medium, or at least from its size and physical location in space. Paint is, of course, essential to something's being a painting, but not to its being a picture.

A good case can be made for considering the physical support for painting and paintings as part of their identity as works of art in spite of the fact that paintings can be relined, i.e. removed from a panel or canvas and bonded to another surface. Relining is typically a last-ditch effort to preserve what one can of the painting even if there is a risk of losing parts of it, somewhat like amputating a limb to prevent a disease from spreading further into the body. The type of support—e.g. canvas, panel, a wall, or an object—affects what an artist must do to make the completed painting look a certain way. Stretched canvases have texture, effectively obscured by painters such as Bronzino, and surfaces of wood panels were laboriously prepared to provide the smoothest surface possible. In contrast, an artist might paint so that a patterned canvas is visible and pictorially significant, such as when the herringbone weave of a canvas leads one to perceive the garment a person is wearing as having a herringbone weave. Paleolithic cave paintings at Altamira use the topography of the cave wall to represent portions of an animal or an object. Such are painters' choices (Podro 1998).

If one thinks of paintings as essentially pictorial representations, the topography of the surface of the support and its relation to the completed painting would not be a negotiated element of painting and paintings, as it in fact has been, but would be dictated by the nature of pictoriality. During the middle decades of the twentieth century, the art critic and theorist Clement Greenberg (1962) glorified flatness and its delimitation as *the* essential property of painting. Michael Fried (1967) described the problematic relationships between art and objecthood in relation to painting. Such ideas fed the aspirations of many painters of the time who wanted to be seen not merely as painters but as artists. Jasper Johns painted pictures of things that were themselves flat (e.g. flags, targets, numerals), using a relatively loose understanding of flatness, and combined them with three-dimensional constructions. Cartoon images created solely through the use of outlines and contour lines emphasize flatness. Morris Louis, Helen Frankenthaler, and other 'stain' painters applied paint to raw canvas so that the paint was not on its surface but penetrated the very canvas that served as its support; the paint and support became one, as did fresco painting centuries before, but without a presumption that all paintings are supposed to be flat or on flat surfaces. Leon Battista Alberti (1435) explained how to paint in the style of the 'new art' of his day—as practised by Masaccio, Brunelleschi, and Donatello—so that the various forms 'seem to have mass'. To do this with three-dimensional materials such as paint, Alberti advised making the line nearly invisible so as to hide its materiality (see Alberti 1956).

Artists have taken up different types of paint, when available, and used them for the qualities that show off best when used on various surfaces for various purposes (see e.g. *Techniques of the Great Masters of Art* 1985). The opacity and matte finish of tempera gave way to the translucency, gloss, saturation, and colour range of oils, whose colours pale in relation to the gloss, durability and bright colours of enamels. The colour of enamels is not as easily obscured by dirt and is especially suitable for decorating relatively small objects, but its surface resists subtlety and lacks potential for innovation. Jackson Pollock brought attention to the three-dimensionality of paintings via the materiality of paint by using big globs of it and by using it as mortar for incorporating foreign objects into the work, something that cannot be done with watercolors or tempera. John Berger (1972) proposes that oil painting imparts its own way of seeing, which emphasizes 'the tangibility, the texture, the lustre, the solidity of what it depicts. It defines the real as that which you can put your hands on', so that 'to have a thing painted and put on a canvas is not unlike buying it and putting it in your house' (pp. 83, 88). Acrylic paints do not provide the sense of depth and layering that oils do, but their colours are purer and highly resistant to fading, characteristics that are ideal for easily recognizable popular imagery. Both Chinese and Japanese scholar–painters in the Zen Buddhist tradition prized the subtle tonal gradations of ink on silk, combined occasionally with minimal colour. Their spare and allusive quality is perfectly suited for Japanese domestic architecture. Watercolour, a paint medium easily and relatively inexpensively taken up by amateurs, has never played a large role in the evaluation of painting as an art in the Western tradition. Delicacy and allusiveness, so prized in Japanese brush painting, is the downfall of watercolour because of its unsuitability for historical and religious subjects that were for a long time the most important types of painting in the West. Watercolour is also typically used on paper and hence grouped with prints and drawings, clearly inseparable from their material support, and historically less expensive and generally less prized. One exception is the category of 'presentation drawings' given to patrons of the arts, often on more durable and costly paper, such as Venetian blue, and on vellum, manifesting their status as art.

Painting has also been thought of as the addition of colour to enhance the visual appeal or attractiveness of a work, or other object, rather than as the main vehicle of representational content. On such a view, mosaics and *pietra dura* are closer to painting than intarsia (inlaid wood), whose claim to being an art depends more on the schemata of two-dimensional geometry championed by Alberti for creating a sense of depth and mass (Tormey and Tormey 1982). 'Blue and green' landscape painting, originated during the T'ang dynasty, is sensuously compelling even if obviously 'unnatural'. One plausible reason why painting was for a long time not accepted as part of a liberal arts education, along with music, poetry, and mathematics (Kristeller 1951–2; Beardsley 1966) is because the appeal of colour is immediate and easy, analogous to the subjective pleasure in the taste of 'canary wine' as described by Kant. The formal relations set up by colours themselves and complicated by subject matter are another story, more cerebral and not aiming towards merely a pretty picture. According to Michael Baxandall (1972), lapis lazuli blue carried a sense of quality and prestige, not only because of its sumptuous colour but also because of its relative rarity and hence greater cost (even though, unfortunately and notoriously, the particular example he chose to illustrate the point turned out not to be lapis).

Materials other than paint have often been used in conjunction with, or instead of, paint to make images, to create visual interest in a surface, and to raise questions about the defining conditions of painting as art. Gold leaf and stamped impressions (representing patterns in fabrics) appear in early Renaissance Italian altarpieces. In Japan gold leaf was applied to screens (which had the portability of easel painting yet the spatially extended effect of a mural) from the Momoyama and into the Edo period, to enhance their sumptuous appeal. At the other extreme, early in the twentieth century Picasso and Braque affixed bits of ephemera such as wine labels and cigar bands to the painting's surface in what became known as collage, challenging the identity of the object as a painting and bringing painting into the realm of the 'everyday'. The contemporary Argentine painter Fabian Marchiano includes in some of his paintings colourless silicon gel in the form of three-dimensional, oversized brushstrokes that question the centrality of colour, flatness, and paint to a painting. Indeed, one might wonder how little paint can be used in the production of an object, visual image, or design and still be a painting.

If a painter is ignorant of certain aspects of the craft and chemistry of painting, the paint may slide or flake off of the canvas. The name for this condition is 'inherent vice', which carries an overt value judgement. (For a basic guide to the physical preservation of visual art, see Bachmann 1992.) Anthony Savile (1993) recruits ordinary language descriptions of paintings to show that we are committed to identifying 'the work' as having tenselessly fixed properties that privilege the intentions of the original artist even though the physical object no longer has these properties. He points out that we admit descriptions of a work's tense-specific current state when they are apparently inconsistent with a painting's real (tenseless) properties because they point out that the latter are no longer to be seen. Restoration practices, he notes, also typically aim for historical accuracy even when a work's 'aesthetic impact' on current audiences is lessened. Finally, choosing not to restore is often the result of a 'do no harm' policy, recognizing that adding new materials might lead to greater deterioration of the physical object in the future.

Even arts professionals (dealers, collectors, critics, etc.), however, have engaged in practices that display greater concern for collectors and the general public than for artist's intent. 'Improvements', in the form of beautifying a face in a portrait, or 'correcting' the perspective, persisted well into the twentieth century, and perhaps continue. Dealers have been known to paint over parts of paintings if they were offensive to a potential buyer. Canvases have been cut down to fit a frame. Conservators in major American art museums have ample collections of such horror stories, and others exist outside the museum world. The pediment sculptures of the Parthenon were originally painted in a way that resembles Mexican folk art more than the lustrous marbles of the Italian renaissance or nineteenth-century neoclassicism. Many believe that we do the ancient Greeks a favour by overlooking this lapse of taste on their part, once again displaying a concern for modern aesthetic preferences over historical accuracy. Controversies over removing layers of darkened varnish from Michelangelo's frescos on the Sistine Ceiling arose partly because of preservationist concerns, but also because some critics were put off by the brightness and immediate appeal of the new colours, even believing that Michelangelo couldn't possibly have intended their appeal to be that superficial. Lack of information about the materials used in a work, old or new, is the painting conservator's nightmare, not merely because artists want their work to be preserved, but because the conservator's employers and clients do.

By the end of the twentieth century, it goes virtually without saying that a visual artist can use common, everyday materials for making paintings, broadly construed, and other works that hang on the wall, often cryptically described as 'mixed media'. Painting and drawing appear to be losing their status as *the* foundation of a course of study for aspiring visual artists as, simultaneously, easel painting is losing its status as the paradigm of painting as art. Numerous art schools have already changed the way they identify courses of study, reflecting the variety of ways of making images, especially what can be done using digitalization, video, and even newer media.

2. Vision and Visual Form in Painting

In the mid-eighteenth century, Alexander Baumgarten wrote that there were two sources of knowledge. One is understood through logic, which examines how thought provides knowledge; but no term existed for the other, which studies the nature of knowledge provided through sense experience or perception. Baumgarten coined the term *aesthetica*, a Latinized version of the Greek word for perception, to fill the void (*Reflections on Poetry; Aesthetica*). The word and something of the idea were appropriated by Immanuel Kant (*Critique of Judgement*, 1790) for his analysis of aesthetic judgements as grounded in experience. On Kant's view, a judgement of taste, i.e. a judgement that something is beautiful, is aesthetic; it is grounded in a viewer's pleasurable experience. Yet a judgement of taste, unlike a judgement of sense, claims universal assent. How is a judgement having both of these characteristics possible? Kant proposed that humans have a special sense (a 'common sense') that produces the (in this case, pleasurable) experience in apprehending the form of an object, an experience that anyone, in principle, can have.

This form presents the appearance of having a purpose, whether it has one or not. Such experiences are supposedly intersubjectively possible, since they do not depend on individual interests, personal desires, particular beliefs, or conceptual apparatus, but only on what humans have in common. Debates continue over whether and to what extent Kant was a formalist.

Among philosophers, probably the most widely read exponent of the version of formalism that excludes meaning or content is Clive Bell, early twentieth-century art critic and professor of art at Cambridge University. Bell (1913) argued that paintings are aesthetic objects whose appreciation and value depend solely on significant form, defined as 'lines and colours combined in a particular way, [and] certain forms and relations of forms' that produce an aesthetic emotion (pp. 17–18). One need bring nothing from life to appreciate the work: the painting's representational content and the viewer's practical or personal interests are both irrelevant and, in principle, capable of being expunged from the experience. Also irrelevant, on his view, are how painters think about their work, what role it plays in their *oeuvre* or the visual arts at the time, what had gone before, and what was to come. Ironically, Bell hypothesized that the reason human beings are moved so profoundly by certain forms is that they are created by human beings expressing profound and fundamental truths about reality. Bell himself admitted to being unable to appreciate music, and wished that others were as honest about their inability to appreciate the visual arts.

Malcolm Budd (1995: chapter 2) describes many different ways of identifying form that are cognitively richer than Bell's yet preserve perceptual immediacy. One promising option arose with gestalt psychology, which Susanne Langer employed in the concept of non-discursive or presentational symbols. Though internally complex, a presentational symbol is one whose meaning is or can be apprehended in a 'gestalt' that provides 'a new conception for our direct imaginative grasp' (Langer 1957: 23). The phenomenon of a 'gestalt shift' is well known, and it is easily demonstrable that one can produce such a shift oneself without any alteration in the visual array, such as with the Wittgensteinian duck–rabbit figure and the Necker cube. In more complicated cases, including most paintings, a quite sophisticated cognitive stock and period of acquaintance with the painting itself and others with which it can be fruitfully compared are necessary for one to be able to appreciate a painting in deeper and more significant ways. As for cognitive stock, the resources of language are indispensable. In his durable essay 'Critical Communication', Arnold Isenberg (1949) proposes that the function of criticism is not to convert the meaning of the image into words, but to bring about 'communication at the level of the senses'. In a similar vein, Michael Baxandall (1985) uses the idea of super-ostensivity to indicate how a range of specific cases fills out the meaning of a critical term. And Jerrold Levinson (1985) argues that the titles painters give their paintings have a special status for determining how they are to be perceived and understood. Other ways in which words and images are historically and semantically intertwined are discussed below in relation to painting's cognitive and social status.

Connoisseurship—the ability to date paintings and identify their painters—is possible only if a person's ability to see can be improved through knowledge, and guided by experience and practice, as David Hume asserts in 'Of the Standard of Taste'. The ability to appreciate paintings develops by degrees. In his well known 'Categories of Art', Kendall Walton (1970) explains how what one perceives is dependent on whether one takes various characteristics as standard, variable, or contra-standard in relation to a relevant category of objects. In what could be read as a case study using this approach, Leo Steinberg (1972) examines Picasso's numerous paired variations on Delacroix's 'Women of Algiers', painted between December 1954 and February 1955, to tease out which parts of the composition and which representational devices should be seen as salient in each variation. Unfortunately, some claims to connoisseurship are suspicious if not outright bogus; Bernard Berenson's alleged ability to identify paintings and drawings by obscure early Renaissance Italian painters is an art-historically significant example. In any case, it is wise to remember that an educated, 'intelligent eye' is central to many professions and that intelligence does not guarantee infallibility.

In *Languages of Art*, Nelson Goodman (1968) declares that no philosopher of art should be without an answer to the question, 'Can there be any aesthetic difference between an original painting and a fake if one cannot tell the difference between them just by looking?' (p. 99). Goodman first observes that there is no one way to look at a painting any more than there is one way a painting looks. No list of visual resemblances between objects (events, etc.) and paintings of them can be made in advance of looking at both. In this sense, according to Goodman, 'we create the world': we decide which properties we want to represent and how to represent them, even though we are constrained in various ways. Stephanie Ross (1974) describes, along Goodmanian lines, how caricatures (such as in political cartoons) can change the way we see someone in a way that contrasts with how one already sees that person.

The more important point that Goodman makes is that connoisseurship ultimately aims not at the ability to discriminate one painting from another, an original from a copy, fake, or forgery, but rather at the ability to discriminate a whole class of paintings, a set of Vermeers, from another class of paintings, copies of Vermeers (or from the paintings of his contemporaries, such as those of de Hooch). The methodology of traditional art history prescribes beginning the study of a particular painter's work (or a school or period of work—the argument is the same) with paintings having the best provenance, i.e. a history of location and ownership that provides the best guarantee of their authenticity. Once a van Meegeren, for example, becomes part of the group of paintings considered to be Vermeers, it adulterates the look that we identify as characteristic of Vermeer, and hence distorts our perception of not just one but a whole class of paintings. One's knowledge that one painting is a Vermeer and the other not is therefore aesthetically significant, Goodman argues, because it tells one how to look at that painting as well as how to look at other Vermeers. Preservation and restoration practices allow us to see the style of a painting historically, in relation to other styles and other work of that artist, something that is clearly an aesthetic concern. (A good source of information about forgeries is Dutton 1983.)

Mark Sagoff (1976) reinforces the point about contextualized visual abilities in his claim that there is no (non-trivial) category of objects that includes both a painting and a forgery or other visual replica of it. Forgeries, unlike paintings that are art, are evaluated by how closely they resemble the originals, i.e. in terms of the painter's mimetic skills. One might look at a van Meegeren forgery of a Vermeer in relation to other forgeries that van Meegeren painted to assess how well he was able to imitate different painters' styles—something that certainly has curiosity value but hardly art-historical significance. In a widely cited article, William Kennick (1985) responds to Sagoff with a nuanced discussion of differences between a forgery, a fake, and a copy on the one hand, and a genuine, original and authentic painting on the other. He argues that there is at least one non-trivial category including both a painting and a visual replica of it, in particular a painting and the artist's copy of it.

Kennick wisely declined to clean up the 'intellectual Augean stable' of what constitutes an *aesthetic* difference between or among paintings and the historically problematic demand for a definition of the *purely* visual. Others have not. Some seekers of the purely visual have tried to divorce it from painting's spatial and temporal qualities. Yet, some paintings' goals are narrative and are intended to be experienced temporally and not in a single gestalt. (See Fried, 1967, for a discussion of this aspect of art's objecthood after abstract expressionism.) Combinations of painting and sculpture in the High Baroque are impossible to appreciate from a fixed point of view, and often play with viewers' attempts to figure out what is painting and what is marble or plaster extended in three-dimensional space. Michael Podro (1998) describes how painters use the curvature of a ceramic object decoratively and pictorially to emphasize certain features, and how one must access those features sequentially by walking around the object. Chinese scroll landscape paintings are typically designed to be seen as one unrolls them (from the right, revealing a 30 to 36-inch segment at any given time), so as to imagine walking through the landscape. Interesting connections can be made between this narrative function and Kendall Walton's idea that in a picture one imagines seeing what a pictorial representation represents (1990: chapter 8). Along similar lines, Joshua Taylor writes that one must 'choose between simply looking at a form. . .and joining a rhythm that leads to something else' (1974: 93). The ability to track an image and hence to appreciate the painting without seeing the entire painting at once is another of those visual skills that can be developed with practice over time.

Paintings have been known to make a point of showing, visually, vision's own inadequacies. Kant proposed that beauty exists in an object's form, but that the experience of the sublime is generated by formlessness—the experience of form's absence, as a phenomenologist might put it. In the mathematical sublime, one's sense experience brings along with it the idea of infinity, for example, even though infinity cannot be presented visually. Kant took the experience of the sublime to be discomforting because in it one becomes aware of one's own perceptual limitations. Yet he claims the experience is also oddly satisfying because it shows us that we are not bound to nature for our conceptions. Major movements in nineteenth- and twentieth-century German and American painting valorize the sublime (e.g. Bierstadt and Kiefer). A different way in which images have employed formlessness is in their refusal to pretend that the image is complete, such as with the compositional style of Japanese woodblock prints, picked up by European painters such as Degas and VanGogh, and reinforced by photography's role in visual culture as capturing a fleeting moment.

3. Cultural Forms of Painting

Different cultures have different ways of representing things and different forms of painting. The removal of paintings, painted objects, and painted surfaces from their original cultural contexts, and their display in new ones for an expanded range of viewers (in ways that might have been abhorrent or inconceivable to the artist), tends to obscure their original and intended significance. In the last decades of the twentieth century, theorists of many stripes engaged in a kind of 'auto-anthropology' aimed at understanding the various practices and institutions of their own cultures. This self-reflectiveness has become a prominent feature of turn-of-the-century cultural life in general, though no doubt it is more entrenched in the practice of painting through the ages than many acknowledge. I describe a few issues of particular importance here.

Jacques Maquet (1986) attempted a description of the aesthetic as a cultural universal that is embedded in different institutions and practices in different cultures, a point of view that is still hotly debated (see Dutton 2000; Anderson 1990; Hatcher 1999). Two exhibitions of African art in New York during the 1980s have become textbook cases of Western ethnocentrism in relation to the aesthetic: MOMA's 'Primitivism' show in 1985, and the Center for African Art's 'Perspectives' show in 1987. The details are fascinating (see Appiah 1992: chapter 7), but a major gaffe was to presume jointly that there are universal aesthetic criteria, and that artists from non-Western cultures do not understand them. At the turn of the twenty-first century, portable and saleable easel-style painting is becoming more prevalent in Africa, while at the same time greater appreciation of 'traditional' African painted objects is spreading in the West. Depending on one's account of cultural identity (see Appiah

1992: especially chapter 9), one may conclude that easel painting is now as African as bicycles and the novel.

Sagoff (1981) uses the anthropological concept of a totem to shed light on the Western tradition of thinking about paintings identified as masterpieces. This type of move helps to break down the 'essentializing' of other cultures *as other* by showing that there are important points of similarity between other cultures and one's own. Sagoff says that the great paintings of a culture function as totems of it, embodying its defining ideals. Forgeries are a problem only in relation to paintings that are recognized as having great merit; viewed as worthless yet dangerous, such forgeries are banished so as to prevent pollution of the cultural gene pool. In contrast, the popularity of low-cost reproductions, made and sold *as such*, is also part of the cultural construction of the original's value. Such reproductions function by symbolizing the original's value, but not in virtue of being visually indistinguishable from it. In contrast, accepting a visual replica to be as good as a masterpiece shows that the culture either has died or is on the way out, because it, along with other canonical works, no longer functions as a central component of that culture's identity.

Novices in the appreciation of painting are often amazed and delighted by the ways the eyes in painted portraits seem almost magically to follow the viewer around the room. This effect is not difficult to achieve, but the phenomenon is important because it is one way a painting can be seen as animate or alive, and hence as having power over the viewer. The waves of iconoclasm that have spread periodically around the world bear witness to a type of power perceived to exist within the painted image, where eyes are not merely painted over (as genitalia are occasionally), but where the surface or object on which they are painted is gouged out or otherwise mutilated. In *The Power of Images*, David Freedberg (1989) discusses many such powers, firmly asserting that his book is a study of the history of *images* and not the history of *art*. Yet, it was not uncommon for master painters in the Italian Renaissance to depict themselves as looking out at viewers, and Manet's *Olympia* was shocking in large part because the eponymous courtesan impudently makes the viewer the object of her attention. This type of animation of the image has long been included within the understanding of such paintings as art and within the history of art. The ability to see a painting or other visual image as animate may be intersubjectively shareable, as some hold aesthetic perception to be, in which case the issue returns of whether such potential is relevant to appreciating paintings as art or as material culture to be classified in some other way (see Gombrich 1960).

The site-specificity of a painting, painted object, or structure within a given culture can make other demands on viewers in those sites that affect in a major way how they are to be—or, indeed, even can be—seen. David Summers (1991) has argued that painting can transform a space into a place where viewers have certain responsibilities, e.g. to engage in rituals or ceremonies. At a minimum, such behaviours alter the character of one's visual experience of painting (Feagin 1997). In museums one looks at the altarpiece; it is the object of extended, close visual attention. In art history classrooms one looks at slides of the altarpiece, or perhaps just painted portions of it, often along with slides of relevant comparable objects. In private chapels, the altarpiece focuses and guides one's devotional actions. (For a survey that is relatively sensitive to cultural context, see Stokstad 1995.)

Painted objects, so-called folk arts, and decorative arts—e.g. porcelain and other ceramics, functional glass artefacts such as drinking glasses and windows, jewellery, and furniture—are increasingly recognized as belonging to the artworld. As such, they are removed from the hands of people who would use them and are treated as precious objects to be preserved and selectively viewed. Though some applaud the inclusiveness that characterizes current museum practices as a whole, others question the desirability of that assimilation. The debate here is over what and whose practices—the painter(s), the person(s) who made the object that was painted, the person(s) who chose or commissioned the objects, collectors, museum curators—dictate, or at least play a role in determining, whether such objects are art.

The avowed, official functions of various institutions and practices within a culture often disguise what they in fact do. The organic unity of a set of institutions, objects, and practices that is alleged to define a culture has many challengers: Lacanian psychoanalysis; Foucauldian perspectives on power; numerous and seemingly unending critiques from the perspectives of gender, race, class, economic status, and more. For example, in eighteenth-century England during the founding of the British Royal Academy in 1768, life drawing of the nude was a central part of a painter's education. Since no respectable woman could engage in this part of the training, it was virtually impossible for women to play a major role as painters (Chadwick 1990). The difficulty was compounded by the fact that the most important types of painting were those with religious, historical, and mythological subjects, in which it was virtually essential to have figures painted in ways prescribed by the Academy. Portraiture, still life, and genre scenes do not require training in life drawing, but these subjects were relegated to secondary status within the Academy, whether painted by women or men (such as Bonnard and Vuillard). By contrast, in seventeenth-century Netherlands, women had more economic responsibility within the middle-class domestic arena, which created a market for genre scenes and still lives.

Members of a culture may come to identify and define themselves in ways constructed by those who are not members of the culture, as they may also try to resist those definitions. For example, racist stereotyped imagery of blackface vaudeville entertainments is appropriated by Mark Anthony, a Ghanaian painter of portable billboards for travelling concert groups (Gilbert 2000). Anthony chose such imagery because of its power and for an audience innocent of its racism. White Western viewers with even a smidgen of social conscience are unlikely to be able to look at these images without some embarrassment. But Western viewers are not his intended audience, so the relevance of their reactions and responses is in question. This is just one example where new contexts for appreciation and display raise questions about the identity, understanding, and appreciation of such objects as paintings and as art.

There is a long history of debate about whether there is a natural or realistic style of pictorial representation, what makes it natural or realistic, and whether it is the goal, or even *a* goal, for painting. E. H. Gombrich (1960) noted that so-called naturalistic or realistic modes of representation have only rarely been embraced, thus counting against realism as a criterion for evaluating painting in general. Paintings and visual images have different functions in different cultures that are best fulfilled by different styles, forms, and schemata. Under the 'demands of imperial ceremony and divine revelation', Gombrich says, sixth-century mosaics in San Vitale, Ravenna, were highly stylized. By contrast, in fifteenth-century Florence humanist ideas took hold, and linear perspective was prized as a way to render a consistent set of spatial relationships among objects in the world from a single point of view that could be taken up by a single human being. If one uses a representational schema that makes the representational content easily accessible to virtually any viewer, it can serve to reinforce the idea that every individual has the power to know and understand objective truth (Kemp 1990). It is interesting to note that it is common for perceivers today to harbour stronger doubts about the intelligence, abilities, and sincerity of artists whose imagery may be complex and arcane than about their own ability to appreciate what is to them an unusual or uncommon painting as a work of art (see Steinberg 1972, 'Contemporary Art and the Plight of its Public').

4. AGENCY AND IDENTITY
IN PAINTING

The idea that painting is personal expression and is valuable as such obviously presupposes that individual human beings are agents having something distinctive to offer. It thus requires that we look at paintings as the work of agents in ways that cannot be accommodated by appealing to general features of a culture that abstract over the actions of particular individuals. In his effort to negotiate tricky relationships between personal autonomy, culture, and history, Michael Baxandall (1985) borrows the anthropological distinction between observer and participant, first articulated by Malinowski around 1920. He also advocates supplanting the term 'influence', so prevalent in art historical writing, with the much richer vocabulary available to describe choices open to participants in a culture: to adapt, appropriate, or steal; to resist, react against, deliberately defy, or question an accepted norm (see also Bryson 1983). Yet, even as participants in a culture, painters, along with everyone else, do not act entirely autonomously. According to Baxandall (1972), in fifteenth-century

Italy, 'the cause' of a painting was often thought to be the person who commissioned it, just as much as, and in some cases even more than, the painter who painted it. According to Appiah (1992: chapter 7), African art until the 1990s has generally 'been collected as the property of "ethnic" groups, not individuals and workshops'. In traditional Chinese painting, the colophons of owners of a scroll painting frequently dominate those of the painter. Nevertheless, some Chinese painters are exalted for their Dionysian excesses in ways that parallel the Western romantic notion of the artist as a genius, uninhibited by reason or cultural mores. There are also traditions of Chinese artist–scholars as a financially independent sophisticated elite whose choices in painting style are made to distance themselves from popular appeal and the politically correct (Cahill 1960; Stokstad 1995). It is wise not to try to tell too simple a story about personal and cultural identity.

Richard Wollheim's view of painting as an art is especially noteworthy for the way it integrates painting's status as a visual art and as the product of a particular person's efforts and abilities. In *Painting as an Art* (1987), he writes: 'a painting is a work of art in virtue of the activity from which it issues...[requiring] a hand that can generate fine difference...[and] an eye that can make fine distinctions' (pp. 17, 25). 'The marked surface must be the conduit along which the mental state of the artist makes itself felt within the mind of the spectator if the result is to be that the spectator grasps the meaning of the picture' (p. 22). Pictorial meaning thus 'rests upon the experience induced in an adequately sensitive, adequately informed, spectator by looking at the surface of the painting as the intentions of the artist led him to mark it' (p. 22). Painters act as observers of their own paintings. To the extent that a painter's experience of meaning *in* the painted surface (what Wollheim calls 'twofoldness') 'comes to guide the way he marks the surface', the painter 'thematizes the image' (p. 21; original emphasis deleted). This, Wollheim claims, is the only way 'that it becomes intelligible how the agent's thought...could guide him in how he marks the surface' (p. 21). The proper task of criticism, then, is the retrieval of the artist's process of making the work of art (Wollheim 1980).

Wollheim denies that the visual meaning of paintings should be analysed in terms of what can be seen *simpliciter*, since some things that can be pictured cannot be seen—for example abstractions, such as a table, but not any particular table; or mythical/fictional beings, such as chimeras. Clearly granting the educability of vision, as discussed earlier, Wollheim instead proposes that visual meaning depends on what can be *seen in* a work. The appropriate 'cognitive stock' for seeing-in includes cultural and artistic factors that inform the artist's eye; it does not, however, include any historical, cultural, political, and other factors not internalized by the artist. More controversially, Wollheim takes human beings, along with what they make, to be comprehensible by using the theoretical resources of Kleinian psychoanalysis. As Daniel Herwitz (1991) puts it, according to Wollheim, 'the deepest and most important layers of what cause, explain and serve as the contents of an artist's intention (and a picture's meaning) are factors arising "deep in the artist's psyche" and not in art historical or social', political, or broadly cultural factors (p. 138).

Wollheim's requiring twofoldness as a condition of representation has been criticized because, first, it entails that there are no non-representational paintings, and second, *trompe l'oeil* paintings are not representational (see Lopes 1996; Levinson 1998). In reply to the first criticism, Wollheim holds that, as an artefact, the representational content of the painting is to be identified in terms of what the artist thematizes in making the painting, even if it consists of a few strokes (Wollheim 1998). The second objection is somewhat odd, given that *trompe l'œil* or illusionist painting has always been on the margins of painting considered as an art. If illusion were central to art, it would trivialize art's cognitive, intellectual, and expressive values, as well as the skills required to be a good artist (Feagin 1998*a*). Virtually any ten-year-old can be taught to draw and paint using one-point perspective, generally taken to be at the core of illusionism. Further, the history of painting after the fifteenth century includes the development of increasingly complicated perspective systems, harder to learn and touted for their ability to represent in ways that contain additional cognitive subtleties. Another reply to the second objection is that illusionist paintings are better thought of as presenting, rather than representing, their subject matter. Whether this entails denying that they are works of art (as Freedberg 1989 apparently does) is a matter for debate for numerous reasons, not the least of which involve the cultural concerns discussed above.

Central to Kant's moral theory is a distinction between treating other persons merely as a means to some other end, such as one's own pleasure, and treating them as ends in themselves. It may not ever be possible to know whether one's thoughts and behaviour are caused by factors ultimately beyond one's control or whether one is, in some sense, responsible for one's own behaviour. Nevertheless, it is possible for one to experience oneself as being treated merely as a means or only in relation to how one is seen by others. In *Being and Nothingness*, Jean-Paul Sartre (1945) provides an unforgettable description of how the phenomenology of one's experience can capture something very important about this idea. I look through a keyhole to watch someone inside a room. He is the object of my attention; he exists *for me*. But suddenly I hear footsteps, behind me. I am now the object of someone *else's* attention, caught and constrained by the other's look, of which I am aware even though I do not see the look on the face of the other.

The literature relating power to vision in relation to gender, race, class, ethnicity, and other parameters is enormous and still growing. I include here merely a few examples of the directions it has taken. Michael Fried identifies absorption as a subject of eighteenth-century French painting, one that complements the theme of theatricality (Fried 1967, 1980). Painting as a visual art provides the perfect opportunity to 'show off': to exhibit, not merely to be seen. Yet Fried draws attention to a significant set of images where men and women are depicted as absorbed in their work, i.e. as thinking and acting rather than as objects of the viewer's attention.

One strategy is to represent someone in a posture—for example from the back—that makes it clear that the person is doing something even though the viewer cannot tell who the person is or what he or she is doing. As in Sartre's example, the power of the gaze can increase when the gaze itself is unseen, revealing another way in which painting shows, visually, the limitations of vision.

Before and during Plato's time, poets were taken to have great wisdom and insight into how to live one's life. In book X of the *Republic*, Plato proposed, with palpable heresy, that poets (including dramatists, since plays were written in verse) had no greater insight into reality than painters. They both, he said, copied or mimicked appearances of things—whether by divine inspiration (Socrates' view) or by learning a number of formulas without understanding how or why they work (Plato's view). Just as rhetoric can make the weaker view appear to be the stronger, and the stronger the weaker, so also painting can make the better person appear to be the worse and the worse to be the better. Whether accurate or not, painting may employ a way of seeing that seems so natural that perceivers may not be aware that 'mere pictures' have such a significant effect on their judgement, which is also part of their power.

Plato relates the story of Zeuxis, whose painting of grapes fooled birds, and of Parhasius, whose painting of a curtain fooled Zeuxis himself when he tried to pull it back to see the painting. Once again, if a painter's greatest achievement amounts to no more than an illusionist trick that 'fools the eye', one can understand why the intellectual potential of paintings would be ranked low. Philostratus, a sophist and teacher of rhetoric, pursues the point further, ranking sculptors even lower than painters on the intellectual scale because they are unable to fool even the birds. His *Imagines* are examples of the classical genre of *ekphrasis*, in which language takes visual imagery as its subject matter, a practice that does not entail that one values painting and other visual arts. Skill in rhetoric was deemed to be much more important than skill in painting, a point not lost on Oscar Wilde who notoriously proclaimed, *contra* Plato, that it is much more difficult to talk about something than to do it.

Painting has spent much of its cultural history in the west as a fine art 'wanna-be'. P. O. Kristeller, in his scholarly and highly influential two-part essay 'The Modern System of the Arts' (1951–2), explains how, in the eighteenth century, painting, sculpture, architecture, music, and poetry came to be grouped together as the same kind of thing, 'the fine arts', and separated from science, religion, crafts, and practical pursuits. In the course of formal study in Greek and Roman antiquity, poetry was highly respected and closely linked with grammar and rhetoric, while music was linked with mathematics and astronomy. By contrast, the visual arts were learned within the workshop and apprentice tradition, in association with manual crafts, where literacy, with the possible exception of the master, was unnecessary and not expected. Such a position in the social hierarchy is quite alien to the twentieth-century mentality, which easily takes the word 'art' to refer to the visual arts alone, which are in turn taken to be a paradigm case of 'high art'.

On the one hand, where illusion plays a role in painting as an art, its function is not merely illusion for its own sake, but the raising of questions about what is taken to be real. Giotto, for example, used linear perspective to raise questions about the potential of painting for producing illusions (White 1957). On the other hand, many painting traditions around the globe employ obviously artificial styles to provoke thought, instead of, or in addition to, providing a visual experience of a given subject. Painting's purpose need not be conceived of as mere imitation or deception, but rather as representation whose point is to bring certain thoughts and ideas to mind, along the lines of Aristotle's defence of tragedy in the *Poetics*. There is, unfortunately, no extended, systematic theorizing from Aristotle or any other source in Western antiquity with respect to painters or sculptors, a phenomenon perhaps significant in itself. Horace's comparison of painting and poetry, *ut pictora poesis*, as having the function both to delight and to instruct, was eagerly taken up later on. These germs of the idea that painting had epistemic credentials as legitimate as those of poetry led to the formation of academies of *disegno* in western Europe that were modelled on academies of the liberal arts and sciences in a deliberate attempt to appropriate their influence and prestige (Kristeller 1951–2; Beardsley 1966). The academies also recognized a hierarchy of subject matter within painting itself, with text-based subject matter in the form of religion, myth, and history taking pride of place. As long as the Bible, for example, was taken to govern what religious imagery was to be employed, painters would benefit from having the ability to read. Some types of painting, such as portraiture and still life, lacked this textual basis. Bryson (1990) argues that still life is the least 'theorized' genre of painting and that it has hence always been 'at the bottom of the hierarchy' (p. 8).

Kant's critical philosophy provided an intellectual structure for those whom Michael Podro (1982) calls the critical historians of art. Their major concern was to identify the extent to which our experiences and interpretations of objects capture what is in the world and the extent to which they are reflections of ourselves. Hegel's concept of history drew on this intellectual heritage. History, he proposed, is the process of Mind or Spirit's efforts to understand itself; within this process, Mind must become its own object of thought. Hegel sees painting as beginning in mere imitation, 'brute' mimicry, with little or no cognitive function. Progress comes with an awareness of paintings as two-dimensional representations of a three-dimensional world. Their content is overtly construction: they are flat, and what they represent is not. This is the realm of 'embodied meaning', in the terms of Arthur Danto (1964, 1981), a realm where the richness of language is recruited to help us understand the visual possibilities of painting, and where the latter cannot be understood independently of the former. Yet not all cognition relevant to understanding painting will inform or structure visual experience; in some cases painting goes beyond the visual. Danto claims that when disembodied ideas are essential to painting it is no longer art, for it transcends the cognitively murky realm of visual experience to become philosophy. Danto's signature examples of visually indiscernible paintings that nevertheless have different proper interpretations show painting as it exists on the brink. Instead of philosopher-kings, we have philosopher-critics (philosopher-artists, etc.): 'hyphenated'-professionals engaged in artwriting (Carrier 1987). The ancient practice of *ekphrasis* has transmuted into numerous genres, modes, and venues for writing about the arts, something unique in human history in both nature and scope.

In this essay I have focused on the philosophical issues that arise as one attempts to understand and appreciate paintings, painted objects, and painted structures, both those that are central to the arts and those whose status as art is more controversial. To address such issues requires familiarity with a range of paintings and painting practices across the globe, so I have devoted a significant portion of this chapter to what one might call the materiality of painting: the paints and material supports of painting; the spatial relationships of paintings to viewers; and paintings as components of a society's material culture, as objects created by artists' actions, and as things subject to decay. I have forgone discussion of the nature of the pictorial, since pictures are not always painted and paintings are not always pictorial. And I have avoided controversies about the 'purely visual', because paintings function, even as works of art, in many ways that are not purely visual. To rule those out as aesthetically irrelevant to the understanding and appreciation of paintings as works of art is to do such paintings a disservice. Finally, it has been noted, with enthusiasm by some and disappointment by others, that painting, having at last earned unquestioned respect as art, seems at the dawn of the twenty-first century to be losing its centrality within the field. Any attempted definition of art must surely accommodate such changes in the materials and forms of art, whether on the individual or the cultural level.

See also: Representation in Art; Authenticity in Art; Medium in Art; Style in Art; Intention in Art; Sculpture; Photography.

BIBLIOGRAPHY

Alberti, L. B. (1956). *Della pittura*, rev. edn, 1966, trans. with introduction and notes by J. R. Spencer. New Haven: Yale University Press.

Anderson, R. (1990). *Calliope's Sisters: A Comparative Study of Philosophies of Art.* Englewood Cliffs, NJ: Prentice-Hall.

Appiah, A. (1992). *In My Father's House: Africa in the Philosophy of Culture.* New York: Oxford, University Press.

Bachmann, K. (1992). *Conservation Concerns: A Guide for Collectors and Curators.* Washington, DC: Smithsonian Institution.

Baxandall, M. (1972). *Painting and Experience in Fifteenth Century Italy: A Primer in the Social History of Pictorial Style.* Oxford: Clarendon Press.

Baxandall, M. (1985). *Patterns of Intention: On the Historical Explanation of Pictures*. New Haven: Yale University Press.

Beardsley, M. (1966). *Aesthetics from Classical Greece to the Present. A Short History*. Tuscaloosa, Ala.: University of Alabama Press.

Bell, C. (1913). *Art*. New York: Capricorn Books.

Berger, J. (1972). *Ways of Seeing*. London: BBC and Penguin Books.

Bryson, N. (1983). *Vision and Painting: The Logic of the Gaze*. London: Macmillan.

—— (1990). *Looking at the Overlooked: Four Essays on Still Life Painting*. Cambridge, Mass.: Harvard University Press.

Budd, M. (1993). 'How Pictures Look', in D. Knowles and J. Skorupski (eds.), *Virtue and Taste*. Oxford: Basil Blackwell.

—— (1995). *Values of Art: Pictures, Poetry and Music*. London: Penguin.

Cahill, J. (1960). *Chinese Painting*. Geneva: Skira.

Carrier, D. (1987). *Artwriting*. Amherst: University of Massachusetts Press.

Chadwick, W. (1990). *Women, Art, and Society*. London: Thames & Hudson.

Danto, A. (1964). 'The Artworld'. *Philosophical Review* 61: 571–84.

—— (1981). *The Transfiguration of the Commonplace: A Philosophy of Art*. Cambridge, Mass.: Harvard University Press.

Dutton, D. (1983). *The Forger's Art: Forgery and the Philosophy of Art*. Berkeley: University of California Press.

—— (2000). 'But They Don't Have Our Concept of Art', in N. Carroll (ed.), *Theories of Art Today*. Madison, Wis.: University of Wisconsin Press.

Elkins, J. (1998). *On Pictures and the Words that Fail Them*. Cambridge: Cambridge University Press.

Feagin, S. (1997). 'Painting and its Places', in S. Davies (ed.), *Art and its Messages: Meaning, Morality, and Society*. University Park, Pa.: Pennsylvania State University Press.

—— (1998a). 'Presentation and Representation'. *Journal of Aesthetics and Art Criticism* 56: 234–40.

—— (1998b). 'Drawing', in M. Kelly (ed.), *Encyclopedia of Aesthetics*. New York: Oxford University Press.

Freedberg, D. (1989). *The Power of Images: Studies in the History and Theory of Response*. Chicago: University of Chicago Press.

Fried, M. (1967). 'Art and Objecthood'. *Artforum* 5: 12–23.

—— (1980). *Absorption and Theatricality: Painting and the Beholder in the Age of Diderot*. Chicago: University of Chicago Press.

Gilbert, M. (2000). *Hollywood Icons, Local Demons: Ghanaian Popular Paintings by Mark Anthony*, Exhibition Catalogue. Kansas City: University of Missouri.

Gombrich, E. (1960). *Art and Illusion: A Study in the Psychology of Pictorial Representation*. Princeton: Princeton University Press.

—— (1982). *The Image and the Eye*. Oxford: Phaidon Press.

Goodman, N. (1968). *Languages of Art: An Approach to a Theory of Symbols*. Indianapolis: Bobbs-Merrill.

Greenberg, C. (1962). 'After Abstract Expressionism'. *Art International* 6: 24–32.

Hatcher, E. (1999). *Art as Culture: An Introduction to the Anthropology of Art*, 2nd edn. Westport, Conn.: Bergin & Garvey.

Herwitz, D. (1991). 'The Work of Art as Psychoanalytical Object: Wollheim on Manet'. *Journal of Aesthetics and Art Criticism* 49: 137–53.

Isenberg, A. (1949). 'Critical Communication'. *Philosophical Review* 58: 330–44.

Kemp, M. (1990). *The Science of Art: Optical Themes in Western Art from Brunelleschi to Seurat*. New Haven: Yale University Press.

Kennick, W. E. (1985). 'Art and Inauthenticity'. *Journal of Aesthetics and Art Criticism* 44: 3–12.

Kristeller, P. (1951–2). 'The Modern System of the Arts'. *Journal of the History of Ideas* 12: 496–527; 13: 17–46.

Langer, S. (1957). *Problems of Art*. New York: Scribner's.

Levinson, J. (1985). 'Titles'. *Journal of Aesthetics and Art Criticism* 44: 29–39.

—— (1998). 'Wollheim on Pictorial Representation'. *Journal of Aesthetics and Art Criticism* 56: 227–33.

Lopes, D. (1996). *Understanding Pictures*. Oxford: Clarendon Press.

Maquet, J. (1986). *The Aesthetic Experience: An Anthropologist Looks at the Visual Arts*. New Haven: Yale University Press.

Podro, M. (1982). *The Critical Historians of Art*. New Haven: Yale University Press.

—— (1998). *Depiction*. New Haven: Yale University Press.

Pollock, G. (1988). *Vision and Difference: Femininity, Feminism and Histories of Art*. London: Routledge.

Ross, S. (1974). 'Caricature'. *The Monist* 58: 285–93.

Sagoff, M. (1976). 'The Aesthetic Status of Forgeries'. *Journal of Aesthetics and Art Criticism* 35: 169–80.

—— (1981). 'On the Aesthetic and Economic Value of Art'. *British Journal of Aesthetics* 21: 318–29.

Sartre, J.-P. (1956). *Being and Nothingness*, trans. H. Barnes. New York: Philosophical Library. First published, in 1943.

Savile, A. (1993). 'The Rationale of Restoration'. *Journal of Aesthetics and Art Criticism* 51: 463–74.

Steinberg, L. (1972). *Other Criteria*. New York: Oxford University Press.

Stokstad, M. (1995). *Art History*. New York: Abrams.

Summers, D. (1991). 'Real Metaphor: Towards a Redefinition of the "Conceptual" Image', in N. Bryson, M. Holly, and K. Moxey (eds.), *Visual Theory: Painting and Interpretation*. New York: HarperCollins.

Taylor, J. (1974). 'Two Visual Excursions'. *Critical Inquiry* 1: 91–7.

Techniques of the Great Masters of Art (no author listed) (1985). Secaucus, NJ: Chartwell Books.

Tormey, A. and Tormey, J. (1982). 'Renaissance Intarsia: The Art of Geometry'. *Scientific American* 247: 136–43.

Walton, K. (1990). *Mimesis as Make-Believe: On the Foundations of the Representational Arts*. Cambridge, Mass.: Harvard University Press.

—— (1970). 'Categories of Art'. *Philosophical Review* 79: 334–67.

White, J. (1957). *The Birth and Rebirth of Pictorial Space*, 3rd edn. 1987. Cambridge, Mass.: Harvard University Press.

Wollheim, R. (1975). 'On Drawing an Object', in his *On Art and the Mind*. Cambridge, Mass.: Harvard University Press.

—— (1987). *Painting as an Art*. Princeton: Princeton University Press.

—— (1980). 'Criticism as Retrieval', in his *Art and its Objects*. Cambridge: Cambridge University Press.

CHAPTER 30

LITERATURE

PAISLEY LIVINGSTON

THE word 'literature' and its cognates were once commonly employed to designate a broad array of personal qualities, such as eloquence, erudition, and knowledge of foreign languages. For example, in the eighteenth century James Boswell referred to a fellow writer as a person 'of considerable literature', and Dr Samuel Johnson explicitly defined 'literature' as 'learning; skill in letters' (cited in Wellek 1973: 81–2).

Today the word 'literature' is most often used to refer to something written, though scholars often speak of 'oral literature', and an eloquent speech given at a wedding might be characterized by some as a literary utterance. Sometimes reference is made to all of the publications on some subject, as in such phrases as 'The dissertation begins with a survey of the literature'. Yet articles published in a scientific journal are not works of literature in the sense that the stories in Jorge Luis Borges' *Ficciones* are. 'Literature' has at times been contrasted to poetry (e.g. Croce 1936), but it is more commonly employed to designate some hard-to-identify and much broader category that embraces poetry, drama, and prose fiction. Yet in a different, honorific sense, only great or historically significant writings count as literature: Edmund Burke's *Reflections on the Revolution in France*, then, is a work of literature, but bits of pulp fiction are not. The idea that only works having value and durability really count as literature is admittedly prevalent, but so is the idea that there are transient and worthless literary works. It has often been observed that analogous contrasts and shifts in usage (surveyed in Pettersson 1990; Widdowson 1999) exist in non-Western cultures (e.g. Trappl 1992).

Reactions among philosophers and literary theorists have been quite varied. Some claim that inconsistencies in usage reveal the absence of any 'essence' or kind of item that the term 'literature' could single out. John Searle asserts that no analysis of the concept of literature can be given: 'the literary is continuous with the non-literary. Not only is there no sharp boundary, but there is not much of a boundary at all' (1979: 59). Others, while recognizing the diversity of usage, have sought to formulate and defend a stipulation whereby the relevant terms would acquire new and more or less sharp definitions, the idea being that the discovery of the essence of literature, sometimes called 'literariness', would provide the foundation for a new, scientific form of research into literature (surveyed in Gray 1975; Aron 1984). Here we find Roman Jakobson's famous 1921 dictum that 'The object of the science of literature is not literature but literariness, that is, what makes a given work a literary work' (1973: 15).

Claims about the essence of literature have not always been motivated by the goal of identifying the proper object of a field of scientific research. Sometimes the point has been to denounce literature as a source of mimetic corruption and deceit (for historical background, see Barish 1981). More frequently, great moral or epistemic value has been attributed to literature, where what is really meant is 'literature at its best'. One example—among hundreds—is Maurice Blanchot's (1968) characterization of literature as a sceptical process crucial to a kind of existential authenticity. A plausible complaint about such theorizings is that they overlook the importance of recognizing the existence of bad literature, and of good literature that happens to lack those virtues the theorist cares to promote.

As many literary scholars began to favour an interdisciplinary orientation in the 1970s and 1980s, it was often denied that answers to questions about the specificity of literature could provide any valuable guidance to their research and teaching. Yet even those who advocated a broad, cultural studies approach were oriented by some sort of answer to the question of the nature of literature, such as adamant, historicist denials that any such thing exists. More recently, some prominent politically oriented literary theorists (an example is Lentricchia 1996) have recanted, and now find it valuable to reopen the question of what it means to read and appreciate literary works *qua* works of literary art. The goal, then, is not only to propose a definition of the word 'literature', but to elucidate and construct a notion referring to some reasonably distinct collection of items in the world. One assumption motivating such an inquiry is that the defining features or specificity of some sort of thing can, but need not always, orient one's approach to items belonging to the category. *If*, then, one wants to understand or appreciate literature as such, conceptual reconstruction could be a helpful guide. The constraints on such a reconstruction include the epistemic goals of the inquiry, the relevant facts that can be identified, an understanding of pertinent values deemed worthy of recognition and promotion, and an untidy bed of potentially revisable intuitions about how various specific examples are to be handled. How such factors may be made to work together, and whether they are sufficient to yield any genuine solutions, remain controversial questions.

1. CONCEPTS OF LITERATURE: PRELIMINARY ISSUES

What, then, is literature? A first issue raised by this question has to do with the *genus proximum* to which the species belongs. It would be comforting, but unrealistic, to think that informed parties already agree with Will Van Peer's (1991) plausible assumption that being spoken or written in at least one natural language is a necessary (though insufficient) condition of something's being a literary item. One sort of rival proposal casts literature as a species of social system or pattern of inter-action. And even if a first, linguistic condition is accepted, important disagreements and problems remain. Many writers (e.g. Todorov 1973) take it for granted that the word 'discourse' suitably marks off the needed first definitional condition: all liter-ature is discourse, even if not all discourse is literary. Yet the notion of discourse is also contested. For some scholars, a discourse is just a written or spoken utterance, or any instance of language in use. Others have a broader way of construing the word. Some prominent, Foucauldian writings (e.g. Reiss 1992) suggest that every aspect of the socio-cultural sphere is part of some 'discursive formation', in which case the semiotical longbow has clearly been drawn.

Sometimes the word 'text' takes the place of the word 'discourse' as the preferred label for the category to which literary works belong; but it may also be recalled that for some writers (such as Barthes 1973), 'the text'—understood as a polysemic and perverse field of semiotical and libidinal interplay—is always already literary in some honorific sense. Various more cautious and less normatively laden elucida-tions of the notion of text are on offer, yet no consensus has crystallized around any one of them. Van Peer (1991) proposes that 'text' be used to refer to those types of utterance or speech act that are reiterated in diverse contexts or situations. Nelson Goodman's (1976) theory, according to which textual identity is determined by sameness of spelling in a language, has the merit of sharply framing the issues, but his proposal has been countered by the claim that textual individuation also requires a pragmatic anchoring (Tolhurst and Wheeler 1979). While the Goodmanian con-tends that linguistic function alone suffices to determine the identity of a text, other philosophers reply that recognition of a linguistic item's actual causal history is nec-essary for its identification. Are two distinct inscriptions of 'chat', written respectively by a monolingual Frenchman and Englishman, tokens of the same text-type, or is a text's very identity determined by reference to the language or languages in which the writer was operating, in which case the two inscriptions must be identified as instances of two different text-types? And how, unless we refer to the activities and aims of the writer, can we determine which strings or arrays of characters should be interpreted as a self-standing or complete unit? Unwritten or oral literature is another problem for a text-oriented approach (Howell 2002).

An alternative contention is that literary items belong to the overarching category of linguistic *utterance*, construed broadly as any act or performance or intended product thereof, couched in one or more natural languages, and expressive of some thought (Davis 1992). Literary items would be a subset of verbal utterances, as opposed to items distinguished and identified in the first instance by their linguistic functions alone. For some philosophers (Margolis 1959; Currie 1991; D. Davies 1991; Wilsmore 1987; Lamarque and Olsen 1994; Lamarque 2000*b*), the word 'work' best serves to identify a pragmatic approach to the task of saying what sorts of things the paradigmatic literary items might be. It may be plausibly contended that works are a species of utterance, and that some item is a literary work only if it is a linguistic utterance, that is, a sequence of characters or words, inscribed or spoken, with expressive intent—where expression is the providing of evidence for some meaningful attitude. As expression, in this sense, need not be sincere, so-called 'parasitic' utterances, such as fiction and pretence, are not excluded.

2. DEFINING THE ART OF LITERATURE: FORM AND FUNCTION

Attempts to elucidate the concept of literary art have, unsurprisingly, often echoed the arguments and positions characterizing general philosophical discussions of the definition of art. A central example is the shift from simple functionalist to institutional and procedural definitional strategies. A survey of how this took place within literary theory can begin with the Russian Formalists' ideas about art's special functions, and their related search for those aesthetic features that qualify texts as literary works of art.

For Viktor Šklovskij and other members of the St Petersburg branch of the movement, the central function of (good) art was to disrupt received patterns of thinking and to manifest a new and more vital manner of perceiving and thinking about the world. Art's most characteristic and valuable end was called 'ostranenie', which is often translated as 'defamiliarization' or 'making strange', though one might also think here of Samuel Taylor Coleridge's idea that art can provide a 'freshness of sensation'. The basic point, in any case, is hardly strange: a poem's dense, unfamiliar, and difficult language can induce readers to attend more carefully, making them refrain from habitual or 'stock' responses and a purely instrumental, non-aesthetic mode of comprehension.

Formalist literary theory is often dismissed as an 'asociologial' insistence on an 'autotelic' or self-reflexive literary language—in turn categorized as a particular fusion of romanticist and modernist aesthetic ideals. As Tzvetan Todorov (1977) points out, it is important to recall that the formalists' discussion of literary devices was framed by views about the value and importance of art's properly aesthetic functions. Thus, in a 1914 essay, Šklovskij wrote that 'only the creation of new artistic forms may restore to man awareness of the world, resurrect things and kill pessimism' (1972: 13). Here it is clear that the emphasis on an autotelic language does not entail the doctrine of *l'art pour l'art.*

Although Šklovskij clearly emphasized art's affective functions, other formalists, such as Roman Jakobson, developed a linguistics-oriented approach in which defamiliarization, reconceived as a 'deviation from norms', was described as an *intrinsic* feature of the poetic or literary text. The study of literature *qua* literature, then, was conceived as the systematic analysis of such deviant linguistic devices and patterns. A detailed review of the formalists' claims about the devices 'laid bare' in poetic language is beyond the scope of this chapter, but it may be worthwhile to recall that they were located at all levels of the literary work, and not merely among its 'formal' elements, on some narrow manner of construing the latter. For example, story elements, such as the civilian's first experience of a battlefield, were said to be capable of having the desired effect of conveying a new perception or 'semantic shift'. More famously, of course, the formalists insisted on the importance of the *fabula/sjuzet,* or story/plot distinction in the analysis of literary narratives, thereby drawing attention to the manner in which events are organized and conveyed. Unusual characterization, settings, and the tone of the narrator were other storytelling devices investigated by formalist critics. With regard to poetry, the formalists stressed rhythm and rhyme—or what Ezra Pound would call *melopoesis*—alongside patterns of imagery and syntactical constructions. More generally, the guiding hypothesis was that any linguistic or discursive rule, pattern, or convention could in principle be violated in the attempt to manifest a fresh vision, beginning with a perspective on poetic language itself. Although such an approach could run the risk of reducing the literary work to a cairn of verbal devices, an emphasis on the overall organization of the literary work soon emerged in the formalists' writings—a key influence having been the late organicist, Schelling-inspired philosophy of art of Broder Christensen (1909). The artist breaks rules, but in so doing constructs a new pattern, giving the work of art its unity in multiplicity.

The idea that a text's status as an aesthetic object is constituted by the contrast between its special mode of organization and that of everyday practical discourse hardly provides an unproblematic answer to the question of the nature of literariness, if only because deviations, innovations, and linguistic foregrounding are often found in practical, non-literary utterances. Nor does it suffice to concede this point and reframe the distinction as a matter of degree, since there are many routine or stock literary productions and responses. The formalists' stated goal was to develop a scientific concept of literature, not one that excludes Harlequin romances and greeting card poems on the grounds that they lack originality, authenticity, or moral seriousness.

Prague School literary scholars such as Jan Mukařovský (1977) (for background, see Galan 1984) reached a crucial turning point in the continuation of the Russian Formalist project when they began to emphasize the work's 'dynamic', historical relation to other literary works and to the practical language with which literature was contrasted. A text's aesthetic function is dependent on the 'set' or attitude of the reader, which is in turn conditioned by the context and background within which the specific text's devices may be recognized as deviating from prevailing norms. Aesthetic value, then, evolves as an ongoing process of contrast and innovation relative to a prior pattern that is itself constantly changing. Mukařovský went so far as to claim that any object or action, regardless of how it is organized, can realize a properly aesthetic function (Fokkema and Ibsch, 1995: 32). Here the search for the text's *intrinsic* literariness, be it in the form of density, palpability, repetition and parallelism, self-reference, deviant constructions, 'the impeding form', etc.—runs aground, since it has been granted that the targeted aesthetic function is not simply present in, or determined by, the text, but depends crucially on a broad array of relational factors, including the psychology of the appreciator and relevant features of the artistic and cultural context. It is one short step from here to the idea that literature as such is a social system, institution, or historical succession thereof, and, as will be seen below, that step has been taken by many influential literary theorists.

It should be recollected quickly in passing that a variety of distinctions between the functions of literary and non-literary language have been drawn by other influential literary theorists in the twentieth century, such as René Wellek and Austin Warren (1942). In the early part of the century, such influential British and American critics as C. K. Ogden and I. A. Richards (1923) contrasted the 'emotive' function of poetic language to the 'referential' function of scientific discourse. Prominent on New Criticism's list of the distinctive features of literary or poetic language were ambiguity, paradox, tension, and irony. In Monroe Beardsley's (1958, 1973) philosophical subsumption of earlier proposals in this vein, which is commonly known as the 'semantic definition of literature', the central thesis is that 'a literary work is a discourse in which an important part of the meaning is implicit' (1958: 126). In light of the Gricean discovery of the pervasiveness of implicature in everyday conversational exchanges, it is hard to see how the notion of implicit meaning can be used to pinpoint the specificity of literature. Beardsley eventually recognized this point (1978), and went on to explore other proposals, such as the tempting idea that the notion of literature could be analysed in terms of a concept of fiction.

3. Literature and Fiction

As the shortcomings of semantic and syntactical accounts of literariness became apparent, theories based on one or more pragmatic conditions surfaced. One such approach, proposed by Richard Ohmann (1971) and others (e.g. Maatje 1970), hinges on a pragmatic account of fictionality. Barbara Herrnstein Smith, for example, asserts that 'the fictive presentation of discourse is precisely what defines that class of verbal compositions we have so much trouble naming and distinguishing, i.e. "imaginative literature" or "poetry in the broad sense"' (1971: 268). Two key issues are salient here; for the theorist must first define fiction, and then show how this notion can be used to analyse the concept of literature.

With regard to the former issue, the speech act theorists' basic idea was that fiction is discourse in which there is a make-believe performance of illocutionary actions such as assertion, where no such actions are actually performed. Synthesizing this view of fiction in 1974, Searle characterized the fiction-maker as someone who engages in 'non-deceptive pretence'. An objection is that some cases of non-deceptive pretence, such as someone's comical imitation of a friend's mannerism, hardly count as fiction. The solution may be to recognize fiction-making as a genuine illocutionary act of its own (Currie 1990), in which case fictional status is determined, at least in part, by the intentions of the writer or speaker who presents an utterance with the goal of inviting some public to engage in particular imaginings or make-believe. What sort of evidence enables readers to learn whether a work is fiction is a separate question, and it should be recognized that various textual and contextual features can serve as indicators of the fiction-maker's intent.

With regard to the question whether literature can be analysed in terms of fiction, Searle (1974) blocked the proposed equation by pointing out that neither of the two requisite conditionals holds: literariness does not entail fictionality, since some literary works (such as Norman Mailer's *Armies of the Night*) are non-fiction; nor does fictionality entail literariness, since some fictional utterances (such as many jokes and thought experiments) are not plausibly classified as works of literary art. Another way of couching literature's relation to fiction is to contend that, while fictionality is not definitive of literature, what is characteristic of the latter is that such works can or should be read 'as if' they were fiction (Culler 1975: 128). In Peter Lamarque's (2000*a*) charitable gloss on this line of thought, some philosophical and historical non-fictional works can become 'honorary' literary works under a reading that treats them *as if* they were fiction. For example, someone reading a philosophical treatise such as Thomas Hobbes's *Leviathan* can attend to the text's linguistic and thematic organization, thereby focusing on such things as the opening paragraph's many theatrical images. Such a reading has its rewards, but it should be recalled that only a partial condition on an *honorary* literary status is thereby satisfied. Some fictions—such as children's jokes—are not literary even in this diluted sense. It may be further objected, however, that the revised claim is vacuous, since in principle *all* works can be read 'as if' they were fiction, if all this means is that someone must imagine that the author acted on the intention to write fiction. One may also wonder why attending to the aesthetic or artistic features of a non-fictional utterance requires an imaginary suspension of the author's assertive force. Can we not focus on Hobbes's style and imagery without imagining for a second that he was making no sincere claims in his writing? Perhaps the point to be retained is that putting brackets around various works' unappealing assertions and edicts can help us arrive at a more positive, overall appreciation of their *literary* value, which has to do with linguistic design, stylistic and imaginative artistry, and the ways in which various complex themes are expressed. We may, then, better appreciate the novelistic craft of *Armies of the Night* if we imagine that the boasting and egotistical narrative voice is that of a fictional persona, and not that of the author. Yet it is hardly appropriate to read the book that way if our aim is to know what it is really like.

4. PROCEDURAL DEFINITIONS OF LITERATURE

In the 1950s and 1960s, Wittgenstein-inspired philosophers such as Morris Weitz (1956) condemned the project of looking for analytic definitions of key terms in aesthetics, beginning with the word 'art'. Others, such as Maurice Mandelbaum (1965), retorted that both the criticisms of so-called traditional aesthetics and the alternatives being advanced were badly flawed. One key point that emerged in the wake of these discussions can be put as follows. The proposition that all literary texts share no invariant property or properties (such as deviations from linguistic norms) does not necessarily imply that no real definition of literature can be given, since such a conclusion overlooks the possibility that the essence of literature is to be found in some *relation* between the makers, users, and artefacts involved. Although definitions based on the intrinsic properties of texts, or even on their relational, semantic properties, could indeed be doomed to fail, a 'procedural' definition, that is, one taking into account the texts' relations to an array of factors, such as the agents participating in literary practices, might be adequate.

In its simplest versions, the procedural definition of literature identified the defining relation as a dyad comprised of the text and the activity of readers or interpreters. An early, influential proponent of this view was Stanley Fish, who asserted that 'it is not that the presence of poetic qualities compels a certain kind of attention but that the paying of a certain kind of attention results in the emergence of poetic qualities' (1980: 326). Fish claims that his reader-oriented proposal is the only one that can reconcile two contrasting intuitions, i.e. 'the intuition that there *is* a class of literary utterances, and the intuition that any piece of language can become a member of that class' (1973: 52). The thesis, then, is that a text is literary just in case it is read or classified as literary by a 'community of readers or believers'—it being maintained that the endowment of literariness cannot be achieved by the individual reader, but somehow emerges only at the collective level, that is, when a 'community' of converging readings has crystallized. To be part of the same community, readers need not have interacted with each other: all that is required is that they happen to read a text the same way. How many such parallel readings are required to convert a text into literature, and why more than one is required, is not stated.

Clearly, to define the category of literary utterances as those utterances read *as literature* (by some sufficiently large or important collection of readers) is to float a blatantly circular analysis, as the italicized words in the first clause indicate. How, one wants to know, must readers behave if they are genuinely to read a text as literature? It has been complained that only an informative response to this question, that is, one that does not at any point advert to some explicit or implicit concept of literariness, adequately deals with the worry about the theory's circularity. Fish's indications in this regard amount to the claim that to read a text as literature is to decide 'to regard with a particular self-consciousness the resources language has always possessed' (1973: 52), a dull echo of the formalist emphasis on linguistic foregrounding. A salient criticism of this sort of proceduralist definition is that it gives the reader—or literary critic—far too great a role. Is a shopping list a work of literature in the same sense as Dante's *Divine Comedy*, simply because critics do (or could) give both of them a certain kind of interpretive spin? And do readers who focus on Hobbes's linguistic achievement thereby convert *Leviathan* into a literary work?

Another proposal in the proceduralist vein is John M. Ellis's contention that 'Literary texts are defined as those that are used by the society in such a way that the text is not taken as specifically relevant to the immediate context of its origin' (1974: 44). To read *Le Tartuffe* as Molière's attack on a personal enemy, or even as a local vendetta against those venal seventeenth-century French priests known as *les petits collets*, is to fail to appreciate this play as literature, which requires an exploration of its more general significance. Yet critics (e.g. Hjort 1993: chapter 4) do sometimes focus profitably on features of the context in which a work was first written and received, asking questions about Molière's literary interaction with his audiences, adversaries, and patrons; and it seems arbitrary to contend that they thereby cease to read his plays as literature. And again, is it plausible or helpful to say that readers who ignore a philosopher's polemical situation, and focus instead on the work's more general import, thereby convert them into literature?

Another early advocate of a procedural definition of literature, Charles Altieri (1978), had different ideas about the kinds of questions one asks of a text when reading it as literature, and about the sorts of qualities being sought in such a mode of appreciation. A literary education, he suggests, teaches one how to approach texts with two basic expectations: 'that we should be able to sympathize with the conditions, actions, feelings, and thoughts of the principal characters, and that we should be able to reflect upon the potential general significance of their actions, feelings, etc., by considering the rhetorical and structural patterns informing the text' (1978: 72). Altieri stresses that these sketchy conditions must be applied to particular texts in ways that cannot be made explicit in a theory. Whether his account of a properly literary mode of reading is adequate, however, hinges on just how these schematic procedures are to be fleshed out in practice. On one reading, they provide a straightforward characterization of a *literary* response to works of fiction in a realist genre, where developing a sympathetic and sensitive analysis of the characters, story, and their mode of presentation is clearly central. Yet other sorts of literary works, such as Samuel Beckett's later fragments, or Stéphane Mallarmé's poetry, would seem to require a different approach. Altieri responds that in such cases it is the specific narrative voice that should be made the object of a sympathetic response exploring its general significance and linguistic presentation. Yet once Altieri's procedural definition is extended in this manner, it is hard to see how it can capture a specifically literary mode of reading, since what is ultimately at stake is an effort to arrive at an adequate understanding of the linguistic expression of a human personality or *ethos*. One response to this objection is 'so be it': let it be recognized that the literary is simply continuous with humanistic learning and understanding. Yet it is not clear that the literary 'form of life' has actually abandoned a more restricted, belletristic sense of 'literature'.

5. INSTITUTIONAL DEFINITIONS OF LITERATURE

If a text is not a literary work by virtue of some collection of intrinsic, linguistic properties (including various possible semantic or expressive features), nor even by dint of some specific mode of reading or interpretation to which it has been subjected, then where else might one look for the conditions constitutive of at least a fuzzy boundary between the literary and the non-literary? One response, or family of responses, that emerged in the 1970s and 1980s was motivated by the holistic intuition that only an entire framework of social practices, or an *institution*, could determine such a boundary. This highly prevalent tendency to stress the social determination of the literary/non-literary boundary had many sources. One was George Dickie's (1969, 1974) influential institutional theory of art, but it is probably more accurate to point to a more general political climate in literary studies, which motivated condemnations of the former emphasis on the so-called 'aesthetic autonomy' of literature.

In a survey of the diverse approaches that may be associated with an institutional theory of literature, it is important to distinguish between *art-dependent* and *art-independent* conceptions. According to the former, any adequate elucidation of a concept of literature must at some point rely upon such notions as the literary work of art and the art of poetry, and hence upon some understanding of the differences between artistic and non-artistic phenomena. Both approaches bifurcate upon contact with another question, which is whether one's concept of literature depends conceptually upon a logically prior notion of the aesthetic. For theorists and philosophers whose notions of the artistic already entail a prior concept of the aesthetic as a crucial component, an art-dependent notion of literature is also dependent on some notion of the aesthetic. Yet some of the proponents of institutional and other procedural definitions of art have contended that the art/non-art distinction can be delineated independently of any more fundamental concept of the aesthetic, and it is sometimes stipulated that a work's aesthetic features are all and only those it has *qua* work of art.

An influential trend in literary theorizing has been the attempt to develop a sociological account that would be strictly independent of any artistic or aesthetic concepts. A prevalent contention in this vein was that, while literature has historically become associated, at least since the eighteenth century in Europe, with aesthetic and artistic notions—and first and foremost with the idea of the literary and poetic work of art—such discourse is in fact a misleading ideology serving to conceal the truly decisive facts that should be associated with literary phenomena: namely, some constellation of practices most accurately identified in terms of their functioning within a sphere of social relations where the central stakes and interactions are a matter of power, prestige, recognition, and distinction. An example of this tendency to see a socio-historical perspective as undermining the 'myth of aesthetic autonomy' is provided by Terry Eagleton's proclamation that the distinction between the aesthetic and the ideological is 'methodological rather than real' (1976: 178). Although descriptive accuracy requires the sociological theorist to adopt the language of those who uncritically employed an aesthetic discourse, the ultimate explanatory goal is to reduce such deceptive talk to the decisive infrastructural factors subtending the ideology. (For an informative survey of Marxist literary theory, see Fokkema and Ibsch 1995: chapter 4.)

A recognition of the importance of literature's sociological and historical conditions does not entail any such strongly reductive thesis to the effect that literary practices really are just the distorted reflection of other, more decisive goings on. For example, the German literary scholar Siegfried J. Schmidt (1980, 1992) has advanced a rather different proposal concerning the procedures and institutions constitutive of literariness. His central hypothesis is that the specifically literary approach to texts flows from obedience to two conventions, the 'aesthetic' and the 'polyvalence'. The *aesthetic convention* establishes a 'zone of freedom' in which the reader is relieved of the burden of responding to the text in function of instrumental or practical concerns; in short, issues of truth and utility are bracketed. Within the general framework established by the aesthetic convention, the *polyvalence convention* further specifies that the attribution of meanings to the text is to be extremely open-ended and diverse, especially in comparison with the interpretive practices prevalent outside the literary framework, where communicative coordination is targeted for practical reasons. For example, in the literary system the reader actively explores multiple and incompatible ways of construing the text, and is tolerant with regard to others' interpretive conjectures. Polyvalence also carries assumptions about the very point of the literary experience, allowing for cognitive, moral, and hedonistic emphases in varying degrees. Schmidt situates his systems-theoretical model of the literary system within an historical narrative sketching the emergence of the crucial literary conventions within modern Europe, his claim being that, prior to the eighteenth century, religious and other forms of authority forestalled the sorts of semantic and axiological freedom characteristic of a fully aestheticized and autonomous mode of literary communication.

Schmidt's proposals have been the object of much critical discussion (surveyed in Schram and Steen 1992). One question (Livingston 1992) is whether the distinction between literary and non-literary readings is in fact a matter of a convention—at least, given the concept of convention that he advocates (following David Lewis 1969). A convention, in this sense, is a behavioural pattern that members of a group prefer *conditionally*, i.e. only because they believe the others in the group prefer it too. Change that expectation, and the preference would shift accordingly. It is far from obvious, however, that a preference for reading *Moby Dick* for its aesthetic rewards, as opposed to reading it for what it can teach one about whaling, is or should be conditional on others' doing so as well, since one might have other, and better, reasons for how one reads the text on a given occasion. Another question concerns the accuracy of Schmidt's account of the readerly practices constitutive of a specifically literary treatment of texts. Is readerly competence actually a matter of a permissive, 'anything goes', interpretive policy? Some features of prevalent literary practices, including pedagogical methods and patterns of critical controversy, are hard to square with such an assumption, since teachers and critics regularly correct and castigate some readings as wrong or incompetent. Schmidt can respond that, to the extent that this is the case, the practices in question are not genuinely 'literary' in his regulative or idealized sense, and that the stipulation he advocates is the one that best captures what is most specific and autonomous about the literary system. One could none the less still have doubts about the cogency or value of such a system. Scholars contributing to the elaboration of Schmidt's proposal (e.g. Barsch 1992) have raised issues about what should and should not be included in the literary system. Are the scholar's and theorist's meta-literary activities, which are not governed by the aesthetic and polyvalence conventions, also part of the literary social system? Schmidt's historicist assumptions also raise difficult and far-reaching issues, beginning with the question whether there were literary works, and ways of reading texts *qua* literary works, prior to the emergence of a specific social system, or type thereof, in Europe in the eighteenth century. Did not Sappho (sixth century BC) and Lady Murasaki Shikibu (978–1020) write works of literature?

An alternative institutional account of literature, which again hinges on claims about literature's artistic and aesthetic functions, has been defended by Stein Haugom Olsen (1978, 1987) and Peter Lamarque (1996; see also Lamarque and Olsen 1994). What defines literary works are not the intrinsic properties of texts, but the role works play in a human practice. By 'institution' is meant conventions for creating, appreciating, and evaluating discourses as literary ones, where an art-dependent and evaluative concept of literature is taken as central. Lamarque and Olsen contend that 'A text is identified as a literary work by recognizing the author's intention that the text is produced and meant to be read within the framework of conventions defining the practice (constituting the institution) of literature' (1994: 255–6). They further specify that the intention in question is 'the intention to invoke the literary response', where this response is characterized essentially by an expectation of aesthetic value. To this primary intention is added a secondary (Gricean) one to the effect that the literary response be brought about at least partly by the reader's recognition of the primary intention. The aesthetic value of literature is said to have two principal dimensions, the 'imaginative' and the 'mimetic', where the former is realized either by means of the creation of a story or subject, or through the imposition of an order or form on a subject that the author did not invent. An expectation of discovering a complex and coherent form is a central element in the literary stance: to read a text as a work of literature is to look for such an organizational pattern. In speaking of the 'mimetic' aspect of literature, Olsen and Lamarque have in mind the idea that another expectation intrinsic to the literary stance is that of discovering 'a humanly interesting content', and this at both the level of the work's particular subject and more general themes. An additional expectation is that the reader's reflection on the work's subject matter or story will in turn lead to and reward further imaginative reflection on broader, underlying themes of human interest. Finally, intrinsic to the literary stance is the expectation that these themes will be sustained and developed by the work's elements and design, and that attention to their relations will be rewarded.

Such an approach retains the formalists' intuitively appealing emphasis on the centrality of a special use and value of language in the art of literature, without, however, persisting in the search for the set of essential poetic devices or dynamics. Literary works are identified as linguistic artefacts, but their status and function as such depends on the 'constitutive' conventions of a human, social practice. What is specified as invariant and essential is the target expectation to the effect that a specifically literary aesthetic value is to be realized in the utilization of linguistic properties in the production of a coherent form capable of sustaining imaginative and thematic interest.

One question pertaining to some institutional definitions of (literary) art concerns the extent to which a properly sociological conception of institutions is genuinely at stake. It is probably inaccurate to characterize any and every social process or regularity as an 'institution', since that term might better be reserved for those social dispensations where many of the key roles and procedures are explicitly codified or formalized. It is implausible to hold that the worlds of art and literature are of this sort. One response is to shift to talk of 'informal' institutions, the defining characteristics of which are not explicitly codified norms, but looser regularities or patterns of activity, often designated as 'practices'. Lamarque and Olsen, for example, write that 'An institution, in the relevant sense, is a rule-governed practice which makes possible certain (institutional) actions which are defined by the rules of the practice and which could not exist as such without those rules' (1994: 256).

Another issue concerns the institutional theorist's evocation of social 'roles', 'conventions', and 'rules' as being 'constitutive' of such practices, where it may be unclear whether 'practices' refers to anything more than some regularities or patterns of intentional activity. The notion of rules, which would appear to forestall such a conclusion, itself raises various tricky issues. Are the activities constitutive of a practice necessarily governed by rules? How does this work? To what degree, for example, is the practice of writing innovative literary works a matter of the following of a comprehensive and coherent system of rules? And how did such rules come into being? An additional question concerns the extent to which the rules or normative systems constitutive of the institution of literature are those of any specific culture or tradition. Here we may plot a significant disagreement among proponents of competing institutional definitions of literature. For some, the concept of literature (in its belletristic sense) emerges only within the modern arts system of Europe. Robert Stecker, for example, questions whether the concept of literature 'extends back to ancient Greece' (1996: 686). With their emphasis on the 'human' practices definitive of literature, Lamarque and Olsen clearly diverge from such an historicist account.

Other issues are raised by the intentionalist condition at the heart of Lamarque and Olsen's institutional definition of the literary work. Some theorists deny that authorial intention is a necessary condition, for they contend that our literary institution identifies as literary some works that were not written with the sorts of intention that Lamarque and Olsen describe. Beardsley, for example, contended that artistic (and, by extension, literary) status could be achieved through the satisfaction of either of two disjuncts: 'An artwork is *either* an arrangement of conditions intended to be capable of affording an experience with marked aesthetic character *or* (incidentally) an arrangement belonging to a class or type of arrangements that is typically intended to have this capacity' (1982: 299). Similarly, Robert Stecker (1996) defends a disjunctive definition of literature, contending that a work in a linguistic medium is a work of literature just in case it satisfies any one of four conditions, which can be briefly restated as follows: (1) the work is a novel, short story, tale, drama, or poem, written with the intention that it have aesthetic, cognitive, or interpretation-centred value; (2) although not written with such an intention, the work possesses one of these sorts of value to a significant degree; (3) the work falls under a predecessor concept to our concept of literature and was written while that former concept held sway; and (4) the work belongs to the work of a great writer. Stecker includes condition (4) in order to accommodate the intuition—which not everyone will share—that, although a literary author's personal letters and diaries might have little literary merit on their own, they should be classified as literature because they belong to the writer's overall corpus or *oeuvre*. Stecker's third condition adapts the insight behind Jerrold Levinson's (1979) proposal for an historical definition of art, according to which an item is a work of art by virtue of its intended relation to prior works.

A key issue raised by institutional theories of literature is that of the relation between an institution's rules and its functions (S. Davies 1991). For some theorists, one of the strong points of an institutional approach to the definition of art is that it can embrace cases where institutional practices and the functions once associated with them 'come apart'. Quite specifically, some early proponents of institutional theories hoped to free the issue of art's definition from any conceptual dependence on aesthetic notions. Yet one may also hold that there is a limit to the institution's powers in this regard because the very specificity of artistic institutions depends finally on the fulfilment of certain functions.

Whether the functions that make the institutions of literature specifically literary institutions are *aesthetic* functions—and in what sense of the word 'aesthetic'—are divisive issues. To define literature in terms of an intended or actual aesthetic function, even broadly defined, can seem to involve a restrictive limitation of the range of values that can be realized in the writing and reading of literature. Although some of the received ways of construing the notion of 'the aesthetic' (e.g. as a matter of purely sensual appearances) are too narrow to embrace the full range of values and interests manifested in the appreciation of literature, at the other extreme is an understanding of 'literary aesthetics' (i.e. aesthetics as the theory of criticism) that encompasses any topic that the literary critic cares to bring up in a reading of some literary text. Another recurrent move, which is to say that a literary work's aesthetic properties are those that characterize it as a work of art, is insufficient, especially if one's elucidation of the latter notion at some point depends upon some idea of art's intended or actual aesthetic functions. Yet another strategy is to adopt a more pragmatic and nominalist stance towards the concept and definition of literature; a proponent of this approach is Anders Pettersson (1990; 2000), who adapts Nicholas Wolterstorff's (1980) idea of a 'presentational' mode of communication in a detailed discussion of an historically contingent distinction between literary and non-literary language and experience.

A resource for dealing with the problem of literariness may be found in traditional philosophical insights into the difference between aesthetic and other qualities and values (Lewis 1946; Sparshott 1982). Polemical flurries surrounding the ideal—or ideology—of 'the purely disinterested attitude' have often obscured the important distinction between intrinsic and instrumental values, as well as the observation that a given instance of some activity or practice can be oriented towards both kinds of value (Ross 1930). That a student's careful attention to a poem's imagery is motivated in part by a desire to do well in an examination does not entail that the student does not at the same time approach the experience of reading this poem as potentially realizing an intrinsic form of value. For example, desiring to read and appreciate the poetry 'for its own sake', i.e. as an experience that could be valuable in itself and not only as a means to some further end, the student would not simply abandon the plan of doing so should a more direct means to the end of getting a good grade suddenly become available. Yet an orientation towards an experience's inherent value, and the qualities capable of occasioning such an experience, does not suffice to characterize a reading attentive to a text's aesthetic value or literariness. A collector of first editions, for example, could find it intrinsically valuable to peruse the items in his personal library, gloating all the while over his possession of valuable books, without, however, having a clue as to the nature of their literary merits. A second traditional notion about the experience of aesthetic qualities excludes such cases by specifying that a specifically aesthetic experience is an active, contemplative attention to, and dwelling on, the properties of the object, especially those that emerge through an awareness of lower-order perceptual properties (see Eldridge 1985; Levinson 1996). In the case of literature, then, a sustained, attentive, and direct engagement with the utterance's verbal features is required, which is why even the most perfect paraphrase of a novel's contents cannot give an adequate aesthetic experience of the work. What is more, the idea that the reading must be 'attentive' brings a normative element into the condition, the assumption being that one cannot be genuinely attentive to something while utterly mistaking its relevant features. Additional assumptions about the decisive role of contextual factors, beginning with the writer's relevant intentions, in the constitution of a work support the contention that a properly aesthetic reading of a literary work requires that the text be properly contextualized, and this with regard to its context of creation, including its situation within the author's unfolding corpus, and place in relation to the relevant artistic traditions. Finally, it may be useful to recall that a recognition of the plurality and heterogeneity of literature's qualities is compatible with the thesis that only a subset of these properties makes a given utterance a work of literature.

See also: Fiction; Poetry; Narrative; Metaphor; Interpretation in Art; Intention in Art; Definition of Art.

BIBLIOGRAPHY

Altieri, C. (1978). 'A Procedural Definition of Literature', in P. Hernadi (ed.), *What is Literature?* Bloomington: Indiana University Press, pp. 62–78.

Aron, T. (1984). *Littérature et littérarité: un essai de mise au point.* Paris: Belles Lettres.

Barish, J. (1981). *The Antitheatrical Prejudice*. Berkeley: University of California Press.

Barsch, A. (1992). 'Handlungsebenen des Literatursystems'. *Spiel* 11: 1–23.

Barthes, R. (1973). 'Texte (théorie du)', in *Œuvres complètes*, vol. II: *1966–73*. Paris: Seuil, 1994, pp. 1677–89.

Beardsley, M. C. (1958). *Aesthetics: Problems in the Philosophy of Criticism*. New York: Harcourt Brace.

—— (1973). 'The Concept of Literature', in F. Brady, J. Palmer, and M. Price (eds.), *Literary Theory and Structure: Essays in Honor of William K. Wimsatt*. New Haven: Yale University Press, pp. 23–40.

—— (1978). 'Aesthetic Intentions and Fictive Illocutions', in P. Hernadi (ed.), *What is Literature?* Bloomington: Indiana University Press, pp. 161–77.

—— (1982). 'Redefining Art', in M. J. Wreen and D. M. Callen (eds.), *The Aesthetic Point of View: Selected Essays*. Ithaca, NY: Cornell University Press, pp. 298–315.

Blanchot, M. (1968). *L'Espace littéraire*. Paris: Gallimard.

Christensen, Broder (1909). *Philosophie der Kunst*. Hanau: Clauss and Feddersen.

Croce, B. (1936). *La Poesia: introduzione alla critica e storia della poesia e della letteratura*. Bari: Laterza, 1969.

Culler, J. (1975). *Structuralist Poetics: Structuralism, Linguistics, and the Study of Literature*. London: Routledge & Kegan Paul.

Currie, G. (1990). *The Nature of Fiction*. Cambridge: Cambridge University Press.

—— (1991). 'Work and Text'. *Mind* 100: 325–40.

Davies, D. (1991). 'Works, Texts, and Contexts: Goodman on the Literary Artwork'. *Canadian Journal of Philosophy* 21: 331–46.

Davies, S. (1991). *Definitions of Art*. Ithaca, NY: Cornell University Press.

Davis, W. C. (1992). 'Speaker Meaning'. *Linguistics and Philosophy* 15: 223–53.

Dickie, G. (1969). 'Defining Art'. *American Philosophical Quarterly* 6: 253–6.

—— (1974). *Art and the Aesthetic: An Institutional Analysis*. Ithaca, NY: Cornell University Press.

Eagleton, T. (1976). *Criticism and Ideology: A Study in Marxist Literary Theory*. Atlantic Highlands, NJ: Humanities Press.

Eldridge, R. (1985). 'Form and Content: An Aesthetic Theory of Art'. *British Journal of Aesthetics* 25: 303–16.

Ellis, J. (1974). *The Theory of Literary Criticism: A Logical Analysis*. Berkeley: University of California Press.

Fish, S. (1973). 'How Ordinary is Ordinary Language?' *New Literary History* 5: 41–54.

—— (1980). *Is there a Text in this Class?* Cambridge, Mass.: Harvard University Press.

Fokkema, D. and Ibsch, E. (1995). *Theories of Literature in the Twentieth Century*, 4th edn. London: C. Hurst.

Galan, F. W. (1984). *Historic Structures: The Prague School Project, 1928–46*. Austin: University of Texas Press.

Goodman, N. (1976). *Languages of Art: An Approach to a Theory of Symbols*. Indianapolis: Hackett.

Gray, B. (1975). *The Phenomenon of Literature*. The Hague: Mouton.

Hernadi, P. (ed.) (1978). *What is Literature?* Bloomington: Indiana University Press.

Herrnstein Smith, B. (1971). 'Poetry as Fiction'. *New Literary History* 20: 259–81.

Hjort, M. (1993). *The Strategy of Letters*. Cambridge, Mass.: Harvard University Press.

Howell, R. (2002). 'Ontology and the Nature of the Literary Work'. *Journal of Aesthetics and Art Criticism* 60: 67–79.

Jakobson, R. (1973). *Questions de poétique*. Paris: Seuil.

Lamarque, P. (1996). *Fictional Points of View*. Ithaca, NY: Cornell University Press.

——(2000a). 'Literature', in B. Gaut and D. Lopes (eds.), *The Routledge Companion to Aesthetics*. London: Routledge.

——(2000b). 'Objects of Interpretation'. *Metaphilosophy* 31: 96–124.

——and Olsen, S. H. (1994). *Truth, Fiction, and Literature: A Philosophical Perspective*. Oxford: Clarendon Press.

Lentricchia, F. (1996). 'The Last Will and Testament of an Ex-Literary Critic'. *Lingua Franca* 6: 59–67.

Levinson, J. (1979). 'Defining Art Historically'. *British Journal of Aesthetics* 19: 232–50.

——(1996). 'What is Aesthetic Pleasure?', in his *The Pleasures of Aesthetics: Philosophical Essays*. Ithaca, NY: Cornell University Press, pp. 3–10.

Lewis, C. I. (1946). *An Analysis of Knowledge and Valuation*. La Salle, Ill.: Open Court.

Lewis, D. (1969). *Convention: A Philosophical Study*. Oxford: Basil Blackwell.

Livingston, P. (1992). 'Convention and Literary Explanation', in M. Hjort (ed.), *Rules and Conventions: Literature, Philosophy, Social Theory*. Baltimore: Johns Hopkins University Press, pp. 67–94.

Maatje, F. C. (1970). *Literaturwetenschap. Grondslagen van een theorie van het literaire werk*. Utrecht: Oosthoek.

Margolis, J. (1959). 'The Identity of the Work of Art'. *Mind* 68: 34–50.

Mandelbaum, M. (1965). 'Family Resemblances and Generalizations Concerning the Arts'. *American Philosophical Quarterly* 2: 219–28.

Mukařovský, J. (1977). *The Word and Verbal Art: Selected Essays*. New Haven: Yale University Press.

Ogden, C. K. and Richards, I. A. (1923). *The Meaning of Meaning: A Survey of the Influence of Language on Thought and of the Science of Symbolism*. New York: Harcourt Brace.

Ohmann, R. (1971). 'Speech Acts and the Definition of Literature'. *Philosophy and Rhetoric* 4: 1–19.

Olsen, S. H. (1978). *The Structure of Literary Understanding*. Cambridge: Cambridge University Press.

——(1987). *The End of Literary Theory*. Cambridge: Cambridge University Press.

Pettersson, A. (1990). *A Theory of Literary Discourse*. Lund: Lund University Press.

——(2000). *Verbal Art: A Philosophy of Literature and Literary Experience*. Montreal and Kingston: McGill–Queen's University Press.

Reiss, T. J. (1992). *The Meaning of Literature*. Ithaca, NY: Cornell University Press.

Robson, W. W. (1982). *The Definition of Literature and Other Essays*. Cambridge: Cambridge University Press.

Ross, W. D. (1930). *The Right and the Good*. Oxford: Clarendon Press.

Schmidt, S. J. (1980). *Grundriss der empirischen Literaturwissenschaft*. Braunschweig: Vieweg.

——(1992). 'Conventions and Literary Systems', in M. Hjort (ed.), *Rules and Conventions: Literature, Philosophy, Social Theory*. Baltimore: Johns Hopkins University Press, pp. 215–49.

Schram, D. H. and Steen, G. J. (1992). 'But What is Literature? A Programmatic Answer from the Empirical Study of Literature'. *Spiel* 11: 239–58.

Searle, J. R. (1974). 'The Logical Status of Fictional Discourse'. *New Literary History* 6: 319–32; reprinted in *Expression and Meaning: Studies in the Theory of Speech Acts*. Cambridge: Cambridge University Press, 1979, pp. 58–75.

Šklovskij, V. (1972). 'Die Auferwekung des Wortes', trans. of 'Voskresenie Slova' (first published 1914), in W. D. Stempel (ed.), *Texte der Russichen Formalisten*, II: *Texte zur Theorie des Verses und der poetischen Sprache*. Munich: Fink, pp. 3–18.

Sparshott, F. E. (1982). *The Theory of the Arts*. Princeton: Princeton University Press.

Stecker, R. (1996). 'What is Literature?' *Revue Internationale de Philosophie* 4: 681–94.

Todorov, T. (1973). 'The Notion of Literature'. *New Literary History* 5: 5–16.

—— (1977). *Théories du symbole*. Paris: Seuil.

Tolhurst, W. E. and Wheeler, S. C. (1979). 'On Textual Individuation'. *Philosophical Studies* 35: 187–97.

Trappl, R. (1992). 'Notions of "Literature" in the Chinese Tradition', *Spiel* 11: 225–38.

Van Peer, W. (1991). 'But What *is* Literature? Toward a Descriptive Definition of Literature', in R. D. Sell (ed.), *Literary Pragmatics*. London: Routledge, pp. 127–41.

Weitz, M. (1956). 'The Role of Theory in Aesthetics'. *Journal of Aesthetics and Art Criticism* 15: 27–35.

Wellek, R. (1973). 'Literature and its Cognates', in N. Wiener (ed.), *Dictionary of the History of Ideas*, vol. 3. New York: Scribner's, pp. 81–9.

—— and Warren, A. (1942). *Theory of Literature*. New York: Harcourt Brace.

Widdowson, P. (1999). *Literature*. London: Routledge.

Wilsmore, S. (1987). 'The Literary Work is not its Text'. *Philosophy and Literature* 11: 307–16.

Wolterstorff, N. (1980). *Works and Worlds of Art*. Oxford: Clarendon Press.

CHAPTER 31

....

ARCHITECTURE

....

GORDON GRAHAM

1. INTRODUCTION

....

In the context of philosophical aesthetics, architecture stands out among the other forms of art for at least two reasons. First, systematic philosophical reflection on its nature and distinctiveness is relatively recent. Apart from a rather deflationary discussion by Schopenhauer, among the great philosophical aestheticians it is only G. W. F. Hegel who has anything sustained to say about architecture; Plato, Aristotle, Hume, and Kant are almost entirely silent on the subject. Even major figures of the twentieth century—Croce, Collingwood, and Gadamer for instance—make only fleeting mention, and there is no entry for architecture in the *Blackwell Companion to Aesthetics* (1992). Secondly, in the main it is practitioners rather than theorists who have established the terms in which philosophical reflection about architecture must be conducted; such schools of thought as there are have more frequently arisen out of the doctrines of celebrated architects than from the writings of philosophers.

One *good* result of these two distinguishing features of the subject is that the reflection properly called philosophical, if rather limited in extent, has had to start with ideas and issues that have been the express concern of practising architects. It has thus generally avoided the empty abstraction into which philosophical aesthetics has a tendency to fall. One *bad* result is that architects and architectural theorists have tried to discuss what are essentially philosophical themes in isolation from philosophy in general, and hence with less clarity and cogency than they might have done.

In what follows we will trace the ideas that have marked and divided the major architectural fashions of the last 150 years, and the refinements that have been given to these ideas by philosophers of architecture working within a wider philosophical perspective. In fact, despite the differences between the various schools of thought just alluded to, it is not difficult to detect an underlying unity in the central conceptual problem that both philosophers and architects have sought to address. This may be summarized in the question 'How is architecture to be secured a place in the sphere of the aesthetic?' or, more simply, 'What makes architecture an art?'

Why is this a problem? In the opening pages of his *Outline of European Architecture*, the famous architectural historian and critic Nicholas Pevsner says, in a much quoted remark, that 'A bicycle shed is a building; Lincoln Cathedral is a piece of architecture' (Pevsner 1963: 15); and in almost identical language the leading spirit of Modernist architecture, Le Corbusier, contrasts architecture with 'mere building'. Now if we concur with Pevsner and Le Corbusier in drawing such a distinction—and the multiplicity of examples like the one that Pevsner cites hardly allows us not to—it seems natural to ask what it is that turns a building into a work of architecture; what makes art out of engineering, or material construction into an artform.

2. The History of Architectural Ideas

This is, in an important sense, a modern question. That the ancients thought about architecture from time to time is certain. John Haldane in his useful essay on the history of the philosophy of architecture cites the Roman author Vitruvius' *Ten Books of Architecture* as the *locus classicus* of the subject, a claim textbooks regularly repeat, and finds some textual support in Thomas Aquinas for Erwin Panofsky's contention that medieval builders were strongly influenced by the general structure of medieval philosophy—a claim that Pevsner also makes with some emphasis. Nevertheless, these precedents do not really exhibit a concern with locating architecture within the sphere of the aesthetic, for the very good reason that the idea of 'the aesthetic' is a much later one. It is a conception heavily dependent on a distinction that came to be expressly drawn only in the seventeenth and eighteenth centuries: namely the distinction between 'mechanical' and 'fine' arts.

A related point can be made about pre-modern buildings. Some of the greatest architectural beauties derive from the classical and medieval periods—the Gothic cathedrals of northern Europe are notable examples. But it is worth underscoring the fact that for few of these cathedrals do we have the name of an architect. Even where we do—William of Sens in the case of Canterbury, for example—these are chief among teams of craftsmen who contributed to the final form of these buildings over many decades, not masterminding architects in the modern sense.

The idea of 'the architect', who self-consciously adopts a style, and therefore can be regarded as a species of artist, is to be found emerging in Alberti's *De Re Aedificatoria*, of 1450, a treatise on architecture that followed his earlier treatise *On Painting*, 1435. Alberti was not only an associate of the famous Brunelleschi, but a notable architect of the Italian High Renaissance in his own right, responsible for the construction of famous churches in Rimini, Florence, and Mantua. In common with other Renaissance architects, and in keeping with the spirit of the times, Alberti looked back to the forms and principles of the classical world. Indeed, it would not be an exaggeration to say that his book was little more than a revival and updating of Vitruvius, a sustained attempt to uncover and recover the classical orders of Doric, Ionic, Corinthian, Tuscan, and so on.

Alberti's *On Painting* was highly influential, *De Re Aedificatoria* much less so. A rather more influential book in terms of impact on architectural practice was the treatise by Sebastiano Serlio (1475–1554). This appeared in a number of volumes over the years 1537–45, and is essentially a practical book with, importantly, illustrations (which Alberti's works lacked). Evidence of its enduring influence is to be found in the fact that it was still being consulted by Christopher Wren over a century later.

It is in the architecture of Wren (1632–1723) and his younger contemporary Sir John Vanbrugh (1664–1726) that we find the high point of what Pevsner has called 'the dictatorship of classicism' or, more precisely the classical-cum-baroque. The definitive conception of what it means to transcend 'mere building' and enter the realms of 'architecture' properly so called is to be found exemplified in St Paul's Cathedral London (Wren) and Blenheim Palace (Vambrugh). This is not just a matter of adopting classical orders or baroque decoration, but of preferring the artistically self-conscious over the accumulated, unself-conscious, vernacular styles of construction typical of particular localities. Even today, it is this classical or Palladian conception of architecture (together with products of the nineteenth-century Gothic and Romanesque revivals) that informs the commonplace idea of what architecture, as opposed to mere building, ought to look like. And it is the Palladian ideal that has given shape to the architectural ambitions of states as well as individuals, as may be witnessed in the United States Congress in Washington DC or the Arc de Triomphe in Paris.

But, ironically, the very fact that the architectural language of classicism became almost exclusively the style of 'real' architecture gave stimulus to the development of architectural ideas that rejected the classical ideal. Under 'the dictatorship of classicism', Palladian features were widely adopted as façades on buildings with functions that had little or nothing to do with the world of Renaissance humanism from which Palladianism sprang—banks, insurance companies, and government offices being among the most striking examples. With this widespread use of classical façade, however, came a reaction: since façade implies a sort of deception, 'true' architecture should have no use for it, or so the new climate of opinion held. As a result, there arose among architects a concern with the integrity of form and function, and this concern has set much of the agenda for theorizing about architecture ever since. Indeed, it is largely around the pursuit of 'integrity' and with it the attempt to secure the unity of form and function in architecture that the dominant schools of recent times have differed.

3. MODERNISM AND POSTMODERNISM

The dominance of classical architecture was challenged in the nineteenth century by the revival of other older forms, notably the Romanesque, and above all the Gothic. Neo-Gothic architecture found its most loquacious and enthusiastic advocate (around 1835) in the English architect Augustus Welby Northmore Pugin (1812–52), who saw in it a return to Christian ideals, and thus attributed to architecture the ability both to express and to inculcate a way of life. In this sense, contrary to common supposition, the neo-Gothic school was functionalist rather than formalist, and thought that the aesthetic form of architecture should be determined by its social purpose, which was a sort of moral and spiritual education. This conception of the role of architecture, and the perceived appropriateness of neo-Gothic to it, explains in part the very marked increase in *public* building—libraries, museums, colleges, and so on—that characterizes the nineteenth century, in the United States as well as Europe.

It is notable that, while classicism took some time to spread to England and northern Europe; the neo-Gothic took time to spread the other way. No other country took to the neo-Gothic with quite the enthusiasm that England did, but after a time a number of cities on continental Europe saw the erection of important neo-Gothic buildings, Cologne being a striking example. Eventually, too, the United States felt its influence, notably at Princeton University and the National Cathedral in Washington DC.

Curiously, despite the deep-seatedly functionalist character of Pugin's conception, the neo-Gothic movement came to be identified, both in the popular mind and among architects themselves, as primarily a concern with appearance. Indeed, George Gilbert Scott (1811–78), one of the best known figures in the movement, expressly announced that the great principle of architecture is 'to decorate construction', a view generalized by John Ruskin in his *Lectures on Architecture* (1853), where he declares that 'Ornamentation is the principal part of architecture'. So it was that a host of ornamental styles broke out—Romanesque, Early Christian, Byzantine, neo-Baroque, even Indian and Moorish, until, as Haldane remarks, 'architecture had become a style-book design service' (Haldane 1988: 174). This ready deployment of ornamental styles reached its apotheosis in the movement known as *Jugendstil* (or *art nouveau*), whose most exuberant and eclectic use of ornamentation can be found in the Baltic port of Riga.

Within a very short time, reaction set in. Against Ruskin's enthusiasm for ornamentation can be set the celebrated remark of the Austrian architect Adolf Loos (1870–1933)—'Ornamentation is crime!' (see Loos 1982). Why so? The answer lies partly in the same thought that led to doubts about the use of classical façade: a horror of deception. But it can also be interpreted more positively as a yearning for artistic integrity—the ideal that a work of art (and hence of architecture) should be an organic unity. Ornamentation, it seems, violates this ideal, since it breaks the architect's endeavours in two, i.e. the basic art of construction, and the artistic extra of decoration.

Loos was one of the figures of Modernist architecture at whose heart this ideal of integrity lies, Walter Gropius and Mies van der Rohe being other well known members of the school. But its *guru* was the Swiss Charles-Eduard Jenneret, better known as Le Corbusier. Le Corbusier was primarily a theorist and propagandist. He was less prolific as an architect, but his construction of Unité d'habitation in Marseilles, a rectangular high-rise block of flats without detail or ornamentation held up by concrete pillars, set the pattern for a style of building that became familiar across the world, and, along with skyscrapers like Mies van der Rohe's Seagram Building, was soon identified as a typical expression of the Modernist school.

Just as the neo-Gothic revival mistakenly became identified with a belief in 'aesthetic' ornamentation, so the Modernist school mistakenly came to be thought of as functionalist. It is a mistake encouraged, no doubt, by Le Corbusier's much repeated expression 'House Machine'; but in fact, just as Pugin's underlying contention was that function should determine form, Le Corbusier's, conversely, was that form should determine function—that the architectural exploration of shape and space should teach us how to live:

The Architect, by his arrangement of forms realises an order which is a pure creation of his spirit...There is no longer any question of custom, nor of tradition, nor of construction nor of adaptation to utilitarian needs...if we eliminate from our hearts and minds all dead concepts in regard to the house, and look at the question from a critical and objective point of view, we shall arrive at the 'House Machine'. (Le Corbusier; quoted in Haldane 1988: 179)

'There is no longer any question...of adaptation to utilitarian needs' reveals the non-functionalist character of the thinking. The style that emerged from this formalist conception—*Bauhaus*—was self-conscious to a degree that no other school of architecture had been, the result, indeed, of an express 'Proclamation of the Weimar Bauhaus'. Moreover, with respect to function it was highly a priori—the proper function of a building is determined by its design, which is why, if the design is got right, 'the House Machine' will be universal. In view of this apriorism, it is not altogether surprising, if somewhat ironic, that so much of the Modernist architecture inspired directly or indirectly by Bauhaus should turn out to be highly dysfunctional—widely regarded as both unattractive and inconvenient.

And so in its turn Bauhaus too generated a reaction, a return not to Palladian ideals, however, but to the endorsement of vernacular styles—*From Bauhaus to Our House*, as the title of Tom Wolfe's scathing attack on modernism brilliantly summarizes it. Self-consciously 'vernacular' architecture in this sense was not new; it had precursors in the nineteenth and early twentieth century extension to architecture of the wider aesthetic movement known as 'Arts and Crafts'. A key figure in the movement was J. C. Loudon (1783–1843), author of *Cottage Architecture*, 1833, its great champion was William Morris (1834–96); and its most brilliant architectural exponent was probably C. F. A. Voysey (1857–1951). As a school, it took its cue from styles of construction and appearance associated with particular geographical localities and periods—medieval and Tudor England are notable examples—and some of these same styles are to be found in the neo-vernacular reaction to Modernism. Indeed, though his style is somewhat different, America's most famous architect, Frank Lloyd Wright, may be classified with the 'Arts and Crafts' movement.

For obvious reasons, 'neo-vernacular' architecture was heralded as 'postmodern'. Robert Venturi is one of the architects most commonly called postmodernist (well known for responding to Mies van der Rohe's Modernist slogan 'less means more' with the counter-claim 'less means bore'), and it is in architecture, in fact, that the terms 'postmodern' and 'postmodernism' first found a use. They have now become labels for a much more wide-ranging set of theoretical ideas and cultural trends, of course, and, in architecture as elsewhere, 'postmodern' has come to refer to a wide variety of disparate styles. These range from the neo-vernacular narrowly conceived to high technology functionalism of the kind that inspired the Pompidou building in Paris.

4. Philosophies of Architecture

Classicism, Modernism, and Postmodernism are categories that can be interpreted narrowly or broadly. Broadly interpreted, *classicism* may be said to include the Baroque and even, odd though it sounds, the neo-Gothic as well as the more exactly Palladian; *modernism* is a term commonly used to refer to high-technology functionalism as well as Bauhaus; *postmodernism* often incorporates Arts and Crafts architecture alongside contemporary vernacular. The advantage of construing these three categories broadly is that we can ally them with established philosophical theories. Classicism, including the neo-Gothic and so on, seems somehow allied with aestheticism, the doctrine that beauty in construction and appearance is what puts building into the class of architecture. Bauhaus, though its inspiration was formalist rather than functionalist, is none the less a teleological rather than an aesthetic philosophy. It construes the role of architecture to lie in the sphere of accomplishing certain ends, both social and domestic, and in this sense it explains the importance of architecture in broadly functional ways. In contrast to both of these, postmodernism, whether neo-classical or neo-vernacular, speaks of architectural 'vocabulary' which thus places it in the area of expression, representation, and symbol, another recognizable philosophy of art. In the remainder of this chapter I will explore these three philosophies, and the issues surrounding them, as they have been applied to architecture.

5. AESTHETICISM

Pevsner offers his own explanation of the distinction between building and architecture to which he draws attention: 'the term architecture applies only to buildings designed with a view to aesthetic appeal' (Pevsner 1963: 15). This makes quite explicit one line of thought that has attracted theorists of architecture: that architecture is one of the fine arts. We can call this view 'aestheticism', because it emphasizes the aesthetic aspect of architecture, and thus allies it with a much wider philosophical theory of art, the identification (by Clive Bell and others) of art as 'significant form'. According to aestheticism, a beautiful appearance is the crucial aspect that converts 'mere' building into architecture. Beauty in architecture, however, has its own distinctive variables—proportion (wall space to window space, for instance), ornamentation (tracery, carvings, capitals), shape (dome, pitched roof) and so on. All these give occasion for 'aesthetic appreciation', just as paintings and pieces of music do. In this way the aesthetic conception of architecture explains both its connection with the other fine arts, and its distinguishing features.

One of the most recent explicit adherents of architectural aestheticism is Edward Winters, who 'regards the appearance of a building as determining its worth' (1991: 253). Winters wants to distinguish his view from that of the extreme aesthete, for whom 'the look of a building is what matters and no amount of technical accomplishment, other than that sustaining the look, can bear the merit which the building exhibits' (p. 253), since he holds that the aesthetic attitude to architecture does not preclude the technical. Nevertheless, the two are categorially distinct, and it is with the former, not the latter, that the architect is properly concerned. This can be demonstrated, according to Winters, by observing that, while there has clearly been progress over time in building technology, it is highly implausible to hold that 'our art is better or nearer to some ideal of beauty', and from this he concludes that the architectural and the technological are essentially distinct. While the role of the latter is to fulfil design functions better, the role of the former is to enrich our lives with an aesthetically attractive built environment.

It may be replied, however, that Winters presupposes what he aims to show. It is only if we divorce structure and appearance conceptually that we are in a position to invoke the argument he employs. In so far as architecture is a *unity* of form and function, then it will be the case that buildings that are *technically* better are to that degree *architecturally* better. But even if Winters's argument cannot be accused of circularity, there is a quite general reason to resist the division between construction and appearance that proponents of architectural aestheticism make so central. This lies in the fact that there seems to be something *essentially* functional about architecture, a point Kant makes in the course of his fleeting account of architecture in the *Critique of Judgement*: 'what is essential in a *work of architecture* is the product's adequacy for a certain use. On the other hand, a *mere piece of sculpture*, made solely to be looked at is meant to be liked on its own account' (Kant 1987: 192; emphasis original).

This conceptual contrast between architecture and sculpture is one that Roger Scruton expands upon to good effect in *The Aesthetics of Architecture*, with the example of Gaudi's Chapel of the Colonia Guëll. This odd building takes the form of a tree-like growth with supporting pillars made to resemble the trunks of trees and the laths of the ceiling made to look like leaves. It is thus highly 'artistic', but the result, as Scruton remarks, is not an architectural triumph at all: rather, 'what purports to be architecture can no longer be seen as such, but only as a piece of elaborate expressionist sculpture seen from within' (Scruton 1979: 8). If aestheticism were true, then the more artistic and the less functional the construction, the *greater* would be its architectural merits. In fact, taken to the extreme that Gaudi takes it here, architecture does not become a fine art, but ceases to be primarily a piece of architecture at all.

A second feature that aestheticism about architecture tends to overlook is this: not only is it essentially functional, it is essentially public. That is to say, while other art works are regularly given public display and presentation—in art galleries, theatres, concert halls and so on—this is a contingent matter. There is nothing conceptually odd about such works being reserved for private or personal contemplation. On the contrary, very many of the greatest artworks were commissioned to precisely this end, and it is only relatively recently that the public exhibition and public performance of fine art has become the norm. The position is quite different for architecture, however: its products *are* public constructions, which is to say they are constructions in and for public spaces. This claim needs to be qualified, certainly, when we turn our attention to chateaux and great houses—Versailles or Blenheim, say. These were not originally open to 'the public' as we now understand that term, but they still constituted the living and working environment of many servants, gardeners, tradesmen and so on, as well as the landowning family and their guests.

That there is this important difference between architecture and fine art is demonstrated by the fact that architecture can expressly *use* art, a possibility both advocated and illustrated at considerable length in *Architect's Choice*, the architect in question being Eugene Rosenberg, a pupil of Le Corbusier's. All the illustrations in this book show buildings, mostly of a Modernist kind, that have been designed partly to create spaces for the display of sculpture. The important point they illustrate is that, though the two are related, it is the sculpture, not the architecture, that is being displayed. Aesthetically there is some relationship, no doubt—the accompanying text (Rosenberg and Cork 1992: 14) suggests that this relationship might be like that of soloist to orchestra, a parallel more intriguing than illuminating—but whatever it is, it must be consistent with architecture's *using* rather than *being* fine art.

A third point about architecture that militates against aestheticism is the import-ance of location. Works of architecture are, in Allen Carlson's term 'site-specific':

Concerning a work's location, the comparison [of architecture] with other artforms is... illuminating. A painting... has, of course, a location. As a physical object, it must be in some place or other. But as a work of art, it does not raise the issue of its location; it does not proclaim, or pose the question of, where it is. Calling its location a site would be at best misleading and considering the work in its location, whatever that is, is not a part of its appropriate appreciation. (Carlson 2000: 201)

By contrast, 'in appreciating architectural works we must appreciate the rela-tionship of the structure to its site as a part of the total experience' (Carlson 2000: 203). Nelson Goodman emphasizes the same point. Noting a number of ways in which architecture differs from the other arts, he says: 'the architectural work is normally fixed in place. Unlike a painting that may be reframed or rehung, or a concerto that may be heard in different halls, the architectural work is firmly set in a physical and cultural environment' (Goodman 1992: 368). Other philosophers have warned of a danger of over-generalization here—there are paintings that can-not be reframed or rehung without artistic loss, and not every piece of music is suited to every venue. None the less, broadly speaking, it seems that, whereas situ-atedness *may* matter to these other artforms, it *must* matter to architecture.

To these three objections may be added a fourth, perhaps a more fundamental, one. In the opening chapters of *The Ethical Function of Architecture*, Karsten Harries subjects what he calls 'the aesthetic approach' and its attendant accounts of decora-tion and ornamentation to sustained and critical examination. Coining a memor-able phrase, which also pointedly echoes Pevsner's celebrated distinction, he concludes that: 'As long as architectural theory remains ruled by the aesthetic approach, it has to understand architecture first of all as Kant did, as a functional building with an added aesthetic component, that is, a decorated shed' (Harries 1997: 26). The implication, of course, is that the aesthetic approach, despite its apparent aspiration to elevate architecture to the status of an art, in fact diminishes it to the status of decoration, a diminished status that Harries finds exemplified in postmodern styles of building. There can hardly be a more damning criticism of the aesthetic approach than that it removes architecture from the realms of the artistically significant and into the realms of the merely decorative—from painting to wallpaper, so to speak—since the whole point of the aesthetic approach is to secure architecture's artistic credentials.

6. TELEOLOGY

The tendency of the aesthetic approach to reduce art to decoration arises from the internal separation it makes (despite Kant's seeming assertion to the contrary) between form and function. This is why, in the end, it must construe even the greatest building as 'a decorated shed'. In turn, this results from a failure to recognize that function is essential to architecture *as such*, and not merely to the engineering or design substructure upon which the architect works. In the light of this analysis, it is tempting to suppose that we might arrive at a better understanding if we took just the opposite point of view, and tried to locate the essence of architecture in its functionality, or, in a familiar phrase, to make 'form follow function'. One way of stating this alternative is to say that, while the aesthetic approach begins with a distinction between architecture and building, the teleological alternative *denies* precisely such a distinction, on the grounds that architecture just *is* building at its best.

It is better to use the term 'teleological' here rather than 'functionalist', because the former conveys a broader idea of purposiveness than the narrow conception of function that has become associated with a very spartan, unornamented style of architecture. Nor should we identify the teleological in architecture even with that less austere style which makes a point of displaying functional details, often with a profuse use of colour, the Pompidou Centre by Richard Rogers being one of the best known examples. Rather, we should think in terms that set architecture within the context of the accomplishment of larger purposes than the mere utility of buildings themselves.

One piece of terminology that aims to capture this difference talks of 'fittedness' rather than mere functionality. It is a line of thought that has been expressly adopted by Allen Carlson in *Aesthetics and the Environment*. Carlson begins with the narrowly teleological slogan 'form follows function', but he quickly amplifies it with an acknowledgement of the two distinguishing features of architecture that the aesthetic approach tends to ignore: the public character of architecture, and the importance of site. Carlson calls these 'the issue of existence' and 'the issue of location', and he wants to incorporate them in a way that lends them importance alongside 'the issue of function' (strictly conceived). Nevertheless, by his account function is predominant, and the public character of architecture as well as the inescapable consideration of location take their significance from their relation to function. The result is a wider understanding, certainly. For instance, Carlson properly stresses that the functionality of a building is not a mere matter of means to ends, but involves the 'fittedness' of the outside to the inside of a building.

But in the end, the ultimate standpoint from which he makes such judgements is still 'aesthetic appreciation', with the result that, although Carlson's account of architecture can rightly be described as teleological in a broader sense than mere functionalism, it ultimately falls prey to the same problems as the aesthetic approach. This is revealed in the fact that the final section of his chapter on architecture is headed 'Function, location, existence: the path of appreciation'; and accordingly, he writes: 'the real path of appreciation involves a series of realizations running from the work's outer function back to, one after another, the fit of its inner with its outer space, the fit of the work with its site, and lastly, the very existence of the work' (Carlson 2000: 213).

In short, despite his teleological orientations, Carlson turns out to be another, if somewhat different, adherent of an aesthetic conception of architecture as a vehicle of works whose significance lies in their availability for appreciation. The chief exponent of a teleological account of architecture that passes beyond this is John Haldane. In two substantial essays, he describes the historical and philosophical background against which it is possible to expound and defend a view he calls 'architectural naturalism'. Haldane's chief inspiration and resource is the naturalism of Aristotle and Aquinas. Aquinas's philosophical endeavours are set within a Christian naturalism which explains the nature and value of everything in terms of a divinely constituted end. The special interest in Haldane's account of architecture lies in its novel adaptation of this overarching conception to a subject about which Aquinas says almost nothing. The guiding thought, in terms of which he explains the deficiencies of Modernism, is that architecture must take its cue from a general (one might say global) conception of the purpose of human existence, and the need to adapt every aspect of creative human endeavour to valuable ends. Thus, Haldane concludes,

The remedy for this condition [of modernistic cultural fragmentation] begins with thought and ends with action. First, there must be reflection upon our nature and present circumstances which tries to identify our needs, in part by looking to the shared values that unite society and connect it with its past. And second, there must be a serious commitment (on the part of all concerned) to build in ways that meet these needs, thereby providing social stability and celebrating an alternative conception of man and nature to that proposed by modernism. (Haldane 1988: 187)

This view is not so very different from that of Alberti, Palladio, or Serlio, and it is, plainly, a normative conception of architecture and its social role. It is a view that allows us to pass judgement not merely on architectural works, but, as the closing remark implies, on architectural schools and styles. Haldane finds grounds for welcoming the return of the neo-vernacular and neo-classical. But he holds that a certain account of Classicism (roughly the one I have identified as 'aestheticism') constitutes as much of a 'two-world conception' of human experience as Modernism does, while the point of 'architectural naturalism' is precisely to reassert the role of architecture in reflecting the unity of experience.

It is on this point that Haldane differs from Scruton, whom he regards as unwarrantedly favouring Classicism. In many respects their views are close, but Scruton's orientation is Kantian, while Haldane's is Aristotelian, with the result that, whereas, as the passage quoted asserts, Haldane's explanation of architecture and its value ultimately rests upon action, Scruton's rests upon contemplation.

It has been my contention throughout this work [*The Aesthetics of Architecture*] that aesthetic understanding, in the sense of the imaginative contemplation of an object for its own sake, is an important part of everyday life, and that however dispensable may be thought the higher or more personal forms of art...it is inconceivable that there should be rational beings from whom the aesthetic impulse is wholly absent.... In every task, however functional, there are infinite ways of proceeding. All our choices are extracted from the chaos of functionally equivalent alternatives, and in all choices which affect, not just present purposes, but distant (and perhaps unstateable) aspirations, it is the non-utilitarian residue that is paramount. To build well is to find the appropriate form, and that means the form which answers to what endures, not what expires.... And if the appropriate form is the one that looks right a man must, if he is to be able to reason fully about practical matters, acquire the sense of visual validity. This is as true of building as it is of furnishing, clothes and manners. (Scruton 1979: 240)

By this account, architecture is an exercise in practical reason and not, therefore, the mere decoration of boxes. But this does not confine it to the functional or the teleological. Beyond the functional is visual validity, 'the non-utilitarian residue'. What gives this position an advantage over Haldane's, it seems to me, is partly that it rests upon a less contentious philosophical base; Kantian aesthetics is more likely to commend itself as supplying a foundation for the philosophy of architecture than Thomist metaphysics. But more importantly, it gives a better explanation as to why architecture might be thought to fall broadly into the category of fine art, and why architecture has become self-conscious in this regard. 'In the past architecture has been made in the spirit of naturalism: in antiquity, in the middle ages, during the enlightenment and more recently in the nineteenth and twentieth centuries domestic revivals', Haldane says (1988: 187). This list suggests a sharp contrast with, for instance, the Baroque and the neo-Gothic, both of which are aesthetically self-conscious in a way that the sort of building he seems to have in mind is not.

At the same time, in his explanation of the value and importance of architecture Scruton does not quite stop at the 'visually valid', but alludes to, if he does not actually incorporate, 'the moral'. In his defence of classicism, he takes up what he describes as 'the fundamental question of the relation between the aesthetic and the moral', but his aim is to arrive at a conception of critical reasoning 'which is at once aesthetic and moral but which remains, for all that, free from the taint of moralism' (Scruton 1979: 263).

This fear of 'the taint of moralism' Scruton shares with David Watkin, whose short but influential book *Morality and Architecture* (1984) is a sustained rejection of moralizing about the merits of different architectural styles. Watkin's aim is to preserve the integrity of the aesthetic approach, to insist that visual validity (or something like it) is enough; and, in so far as Watkin and Scruton are of one mind, this raises a further question: Does the term 'moral' as Scruton uses it mean anything more than normative?

7. MEANING, REPRESENTATION, AND SYMBOL

Whatever may be true of Scruton, there are certainly other philosophers and architectural theorists who are willing to embrace and expound a robust form of moralism in architecture. Thus, John Ruskin, writing about the nature and merits of Gothic architecture, aims to identify 'the various moral or imaginative elements which composed [its] inner spirit' (Ruskin 1966: 433). The aesthetic approach thinks the critical question is 'How well do buildings look?' The teleologist asks 'How well do buildings function?' But another line of thought, close to Ruskin's, asks 'What do buildings say?' This third question presupposes that buildings can have meaning, a topic expressly addressed by Nelson Goodman in his short essay 'How Buildings Mean'. Goodman is well known for his espousal (in *Languages of Art* and *Ways of Worldmaking*) of what is sometimes known as 'aesthetic cognitivism', and in this essay he summarizes his view rather neatly: the 'excellence of a work is a matter of enlightenment rather than pleasure' (Goodman 1992: 375). Applying this view to architecture, he says:

A building, more than most works, alters our environment physically; but moreover as a work of art it may through various avenues of meaning, inform and reorganize our entire experience. Like other works of art—and like scientific theories—it can give new insight, advance understanding, participate in our continual remaking of the world. (Goodman 1992: 375)

Goodman identifies a number of ways in which buildings can do this—by representation, by expression, and by exemplification—all of which may be incorporated into referential links: 'if a church represents sailboats, and sailboats exemplify freedom from the earth, and freedom from the earth in turn exemplifies spirituality, then the church refers to spirituality by a three link chain' (Goodman 1992: 373).

This way of understanding buildings certainly goes far beyond mere 'visual validity', but Goodman's aspirations for the meaningfulness of building are still relatively modest—exemplifying this, suggesting that, and so on. Moreover, he does not suppose that what a building says it says without fear of ambiguity or contradiction: 'a work of art typically means in varied and contrasting ways and is open to many equally good and enlightening interpretations'(p. 373). The consequence of this modesty, in my view, is that there is not in practice very much difference between Goodman's modified cognitivism and Scruton's modified aestheticism. The end result of both is the same: buildings enhance our environment and can be appreciated in a variety of ways, but not a variety that admits total licence. Both views can be contrasted with the very much more substantial account of the cognitive role of architecture that is to be found in Karsten Harries's *The Ethical Function of Architecture* (1997).

The title of that book is somewhat misleading. Harries is not a functionalist, even in the broader teleological sense within which Haldane operates. In addition, the term 'ethical' does not signal the 'tainted' sort of moralism to which Scruton and Watkins object, but is used with the meaning it has in the Hegelian expression 'ethical life'. Indeed, one of the features that makes Harries's book interestingly different is the philosophical background he draws on. His recourse is not to the familiar figures of Plato, Aristotle, or Kant, but to Hegel and Heidegger. This makes his account of the significance of architecture both normative and historical, and that the two are in his view interconnected is shown by the following passage:

After the Enlightenment has done its work art can furnish no more than occasions for aesthetic enjoyment, offering something like a vacation from the serious business of life, unless for pedagogical reasons we find it useful to wrap independently established moral maxims in an artistic dress. (Harries 1997: 354)

In contrast to the 'aesthetic approach' that Enlightenment thinking engenders and sustains, Harries contends that 'a building becomes a work of architecture when designed as an idealizing self-representation'. With this conception, he claims, 'we have left behind Pevsner's remark that what distinguishes architecture from mere building is that "it is designed with a view to aesthetic appeal" '(Harries 1997: 122). There follows an exploration of representation and symbol in architecture, employing concepts not dissimilar to Goodman's, but set against the background of a detailed examination of the mediaeval cathedral as defined and explained by Aquinas: the house in which the sacrament is celebrated signifies the Church and is called 'church' (*Summa theologiae* III, 83, 3).

As this brief summary suggests, Harries elaborates an historical narrative according to which the unity of Christian thought and architecture is ruptured by the Enlightenment. With the Enlightenment comes the aesthetic approach to architecture. But such an approach is inevitably inadequate: 'Like Hegel, we demand more of art, demand that it grant insight into what is and what matters' (Harries 1997: 357), and the result of a constricted aestheticism can only be that 'No longer understood, traditional architecture is plundered by the architect to dress up functional buildings in borrowed finery'.

If Harries is right, we are now in a position to state the philosophical problem of contemporary architecture: 'architecture will have a future only if the place once occupied by temple and church can in some sense be reoccupied' (p. 324). But can it? In arriving at an answer, Harries draws extensively on Heidegger's 'The Origin of the Work of Art', and, very much in keeping with the spirit of that work, claims that 'problems of dwelling are not architectural but ethical' (p. 363). This throws the question on to the culture of modernity more broadly; architecture does have an ethical function, but on its own it cannot supply radical cultural deficiency. In the end, the ethical life it expresses and represents is not its own, but that of the society in which it functions. And as I read him, Harries does not think the prospects for modernity are especially bright; monument and theatre, possibly the shopping mall—'each of these building tasks holds some promise, but not one of them nor all together can take the place of temple and church';

With good reason we have learned to be suspicious of all architecture that confidently embraces architecture's traditional ethical function. Any architect who today wants to address that function has to be aware that he does so without any authority, that he is a bit like the fool who says what he thinks needs to be said but can only hope that others will listen. (Harries 1997: 367)

8. ARCHITECTURE AND THE DANGER OF THE MUSEUM

Harries gives Hegelian expression to themes and issues that can be seen to occupy all the principal philosophers of architecture reviewed above. Haldane, Scruton, Carlson, Pevsner, and Harries all cite the great medieval cathedrals, the Renaissance churches, and the Palladian houses of Europe as architectural triumphs. How could they not? At the same time, all agree that these cannot be for the modern period quite as they were for the medieval. How then is the modern period to appropriate them?

It is in trying to answer this crucial question that the importance of the philosophy of architecture lies, because it seems there is a constant threat of contemporary culture relegating architecture to the art gallery or the museum. The aesthetic approach in effect turns the city into an art gallery, and so divorces building and dwelling, to use Heideggerian language. But the alternative—functionalism—which stresses the essentially teleological character of architecture runs the constant danger of relegating it to the museum, where other outmoded artefacts are to be found. And, in practice, many of these great buildings are indeed so relegated. As Harries remarks, 'stepping into such a "temple of art" . . . we enter an aesthetic church. . . . Our attitude is shaped in part by a still almost religious reverence and respect, but also by a sense that what truly matters lies elsewhere' (Harries 1997: 357).

This is in part the theme of the chapter on architecture in Frederic Jameson's *Postmodernism or the Cultural Logic of Late Capitalism* (Jameson 1991).

Postmodernism raises questions about the appetite for architecture which it then virtually at once redirects. Along with food, architecture may be thought to be a relatively late taste among North Americans...[This] appetite for architecture is inconsistent with the older nothing-to-do-with-me with which the republic's various social classes used to negotiate their downtowns. (Jameson 1991: 98)

According to Jameson, in a postmodernist world it is not possible to commission the properly monumental; or, as he puts it, 'it becomes ever more difficult in this urban landscape to order a high-class architectural meal of the older kind' (Jameson 1991: 98); and, because this is so, the contemporary appetite for architecture must actually be an appetite for something else, which Jameson identifies as photography i.e. surface appearance. The deeper explanation of this phenomenon, on his account, lies in the fact that 'the logic of capitalism is dispersive and disjunctive' and thus militates against the 'monumental models of "totality"' which architecture of the older type encapsulates. Postmodern culture accelerates this.

The relaxation of the postmodern then determines not a return to older collective forms but a loosening of the modern constructions such that its elements and components...float at a certain distance from each other in a miraculous stasis or suspension, which, like the constellations, is certain to come apart in the next minute. (Jameson 1991: 100)

This is social theorizing of a very ambitious sort, and can proceed only if the idea of late capitalism and its logic is a cogent one. But if Jameson's theory (and writing) is too overblown for some tastes, he can be seen none the less to articulate one version of a problem others have also identified. This is the problem of formulating an adequate conception of architecture (as of the other arts, perhaps) which allows it to play a part in 'what truly matters' in contemporary culture, in the way, let us say, that science does. This is why theorists like Goodman and Harries turn to representation and symbolic expression, and indeed, this is where, if anywhere, the solution must lie. But it can be found only if and in so far as the world beyond architecture still has conceptions of experience worth symbolizing.

See also: Sculpture; Environmental Aesthetics; Aesthetics and Postmodernism; Art and Morality; Art and Politics.

BIBLIOGRAPHY

Carlson, A. (1986). 'Reconsidering the Aesthetics of Architecture'. *Journal of Aesthetic Education* 20: 21–7.
—— (2000). 'Existence, Location, Function: The Appreciation of Architecture', in his *Aesthetics and the Environment*. London: Routledge, chapter 13.

Goldblatt, D. (1991). 'The Dislocation of the Architectural Self'. *Journal of Aesthetics and Art Criticism* 49: 337–48.

Goodman, N. (1992). 'How Buildings Mean', in P. A. Alperson (ed.), *Philosophy of the Visual Arts*. New York: Oxford University Press, pp. 368–76.

Graham, G. (1989). 'Art and Architecture'. *British Journal of Aesthetics* 29: 248–57.

—— (2000). *Philosophy of the Arts*, 2nd rev. edn. London: Routledge, chapter 7.

Haldane, J. (1987). 'Architecture and Aesthetic Perception: Aesthetic Naturalism and the Decline of Architecture, Part 1'. *International Journal of Moral and Social Studies* 2: 211–24.

—— (1988). 'Form, Matter and Understanding: Aesthetic Naturalism and the Decline of Architecture, Part 2'. *International Journal of Moral and Social Studies* 3: 173–90.

—— (1999). 'Form, Meaning and Value: A History of the Philosophy of Architecture'. *Journal of Architecture* 4: 9–18.

Harries, K. (1997). *The Ethical Function of Architecture*. Cambridge, Mass.: MIT Press.

Heidegger, M. (1993). 'The Origin of the Work of Art', in *Basic Writings*, ed. D. F. Krell. London: Routledge.

Jameson, F. (1991). *Postmodernism or the Cultural Logic of Late Capitalism*. Durham, NC: Duke University Press, chapter 4.

Jencks, C. (1998). *The Language of Post-Modern Architecture*, 6th edn. New York: John Wiley.

Kant, I. (1987). *Critique of Judgment*, trans. W. Pluhar. Indianapolis: Hackett.

Leach, N. (1999). *The Aesthetics of Architecture*. Cambridge Mass.: MIT Press.

Loos, A. (1982). *Spoken into the Void: Collected Essays, 1897–1900*. Cambridge, Mass.: MIT Press.

Pevsner, N. (1963). *An Outline of European Architecture*, 7th edn. London: Penguin.

Rosenberg, E. and Cork, R. (1992). *Architect's Choice: Art in Architecture in Great Britain since 1945*. London: Thames & Hudson.

Ruskin, J. (1966). 'The Stones of Venice', in E. G. Holt (ed.), *From the Classicists to the Impressionists: A Documentary History of Art and Architecture in the 19th Century*. London/New York: University of London Press/New York University Press, pp. 421–33.

Savile, A. (2000). 'The Lamp of Memory'. *European Journal of Philosophy* 8: 89–105.

Scruton, R. (1979). *The Aesthetics of Architecture*. Princeton: Princeton University Press.

Venturi, R. (1990). *Complexity and Contradiction in Architecture*, 2nd edn. New York: Harry Abrams.

Vitruvius (1960). *The Ten Books of Architecture*, trans. M. H. Morgan. New York: Dover Press.

Watkin, D. (1984). *Morality and Architecture*. Chicago: University of Chicago Press; 2nd edn. London: John Murray, 2001.

Winters, E. (1991). 'Technological Progress and Architectural Response'. *British Journal of Aesthetics* 31: 251–8.

Wolfe, T. (1993). *From Bauhaus to Our House*. London: Picador.

CHAPTER 32

....

SCULPTURE

....

ROBERT HOPKINS

PHILOSOPHY has not had a great deal to say about sculpture. There is brief mention
of it in Kant's third critique, longer discussion in Schopenhauer (1969) and Hegel
(1974). More recent writing with philosophical content is as often to be found in
the output of theoretically minded critics and art historians as in that of professional philosophers. None the less, sculpture does present genuine philosophical
problems.

Three candidates are particularly prominent. First, what is sculpture? The answer
may seem plain: it is the representation of things by means of three-dimensional
figures. But what of abstract sculpture, such as some of the work of Barbara
Hepworth, other three-dimensional representations commonly given their own
category, such as models and maquettes, and those items lying on the boundary
between the clearly sculptural and the clearly pictorial, such as representational
carving in ever lower relief? Second, what is sculptural representation? Sculptures
are as capable of representing as are words, pictures, gestures, signs, or theatrical
performances. But not all these things represent in the same way: representation
comes in different forms. What, then, is distinctive about representation by sculpture? Third, what, if anything, is aesthetically distinctive about sculptural art? Does
it offer aesthetic satisfactions not to be found elsewhere, and if so what are the
special features it offers for appreciation?

Although interconnected, these questions are distinct. I will concentrate on the
aesthetic question, and say a little about sculptural representation. I will not discuss
the definition of sculpture.

1. SCULPTURAL REPRESENTATION

One aspect of philosophical neglect of sculpture is that there are very few explicit accounts of sculptural representation. Hopkins (1994) offers one, and Goodman (1976) and Schier (1986) discuss the topic in passing, but most of the interesting positions have to be adapted from accounts of the nearest parallel phenomenon, pictorial representation. In consequence, the lay of the land here is powerfully reminiscent of that in debates over picturing.

What one says about sculptural representation depends in part on where one thinks the crucial contrasts lie. It could be thought that representation by sculpture is quite different from that by language. Compare sculpturally representing a horse, say, with describing one. There are many and diverse sculptural styles, and hence a good deal of variation across possible horse-sculptures. None the less, the constraints on such representation seem tighter than those on the marks able to constitute in some language, actual or possible, a horse-description. Not everyone would accept this strong contrast between sculpture and language. Goodman (1976) reduces any difference between the two to formal features of the symbol systems involved. And some of those who accept the strong contrast explicate it in their own way; for instance, Flint Schier (1986) claims that grasping what a sculpture represents requires the same perceptual resources as recognizing its object in the flesh. But one broad approach to clarifying the contrast merits particular attention. It takes sculptural representation to involve a distinctive *experience* on the part of the viewer.

According to this approach, to grasp the content of a sculpture is to see it in a special way. One's experience of the sculpture is permeated by certain thoughts. These do not merely accompany the experience, but actually determinine its phenomenology. They are thoughts of the object represented—a horse, say. Now it is true of seeing a horse in the flesh that it is an experience permeated by thoughts of horses; for that is just what it is to be an experience with the content that a horse is before one. But it need not be part of the present approach that sculptures generate the illusion that their objects are present. When we see a horse sculpture there is no horse before us, we do not take there to be one, and our experience does not have the phenomenology of the experience of seeing a horse. Rather, it presents us with a crafted lump of marble, bronze, or whatever. But, although we see nothing but marble or bronze to be before us, we experience that material as organized in a distinctive way. It is organized by thoughts of the sculpture's object—a prancing Arab stallion with flowing mane, and so forth.

More needs to be said about the phenomenology of this experience. The way to do this is to specify the experience's structure, to say in what way thoughts of the absent horse permeate one's experience of the marble. One possibility is that the experience is of the material as *resembling* a prancing horse, in some specified respects (Hopkins 1994). Another is that it is the experience of *imagining* certain things to hold of the sculpted stone (Walton 1990). And there are other options. Which is most tempting will depend in part on how far one also takes sculptural representation to contrast with representation by pictures. For what I have said so far applies with equal plausibility to pictorial representation. There too what is seen as before one—a marked surface—is experienced as organized by thoughts of the represented object. Indeed, the archetype of the whole experiential approach is Richard Wollheim's (1968, 1987) account of representation in pictures. Yet *prima facie* our experience of pictures differs from that of sculpture, and it is not obvious that the two involve the same form of representation.

Some ways to flesh out the experiential approach to sculptural representation are better able than others to accommodate these differences. The experienced resemblance view is the only one to which such an accommodation comes quite naturally. It need only specify *different* resemblances experienced in the two cases. Walton's view has at least some resources available to it here, and he makes some suggestive comments about the wider range of things imagined true of sculptures, as opposed to paintings (Walton 1990: 63, 227, 296). However, nothing he says even gestures towards materials likely to be sufficient to account for the perceptual difference in our experience of sculptures and pictures. My suspicion is that, if his account were developed so as to do this, it would have to be done somewhat along the lines explained, outside of the context of Walton's theoretical framework and in answer to the rather different aesthetic question below. The illusionist position and Wollheim's account seem to preclude any significant distinction between picturing and representing sculpturally (cf. Vance 1995). And, outside the experiential approach altogether, this is equally true of Goodman's semiotic account and of Schier's perceptual resource view.

This is not the place to pursue these issues. For our purposes, it suffices to have some sense of the possible approaches to sculptural representation, and some grasp of the experiential approach in particular. We will make use below of the idea that sculpture is experienced in the light of thoughts about what is represented, without those thoughts engendering any illusion about what is present. And we will do so in addressing the other of the two questions I wish to consider.

2. Sight, Touch, and Two-Dimensional Aspects

Whatever the contrast central to the representational issue, the aesthetic question gains crucial focus from the comparison between sculpture and the pictorial arts.

Sculpture seems quite different aesthetically from the literary arts, but closely akin to drawing and painting. Some, notably Lessing (1962), have gone so far as to treat sculpture and painting as one, developing an aesthetic common to both by contrasting their charms with those of literature. Unlike Lessing, I take the aesthetic question in key part to be what sculpture has to offer that painting and drawing do not.

Where might an answer lie? A natural thought is that sculpture is aesthetically distinctive in appealing to touch. Sculpture's three-dimensionality enables it to engage both sight and touch; painting's flatness leaves it appealing to sight alone. So a whole new sense is involved in appreciating sculpture—a difference on a scale appropriate to ground sculptural aesthetics. This is the view famously offered by Herbert Read (1961), and it continues to find supporters (Vance 1995). However, an equally substantial body of work has been devoted to rejecting the thought. Thus, Rhys Carpenter:

sculpture is a visual and not a tactile art, because it is made for the eyes to contemplate and not for the fingers to feel. Moreover, just as it reaches us through the eyes and not through the finger tips, so it is created visually, no matter how the sculptor may use his hands to produce his work....sculptured form cannot be apprehended tactilely or evaluated by its tactual fidelity. (Carpenter 1960: 34)

Despite the persistence of this debate, it is hard to discern what is at stake. I will try to clear away some of the obscuring factors.

Sculptures can be explored by sight or touch, pictures standardly only by sight (standardly because, if pictures are made from raised ridges, they can be understood using touch: cf. Kennedy 1993; Lopes 1997). But what is the aesthetic significance of this? The claim must be not about what we can do, but about what we ought to do; about those senses deployed in the *proper appreciation of* sculpture. The theoretical space thus seems already to allow for three positions: that the sense properly deployed in appreciating sculpture is (i) touch alone; (ii) sight alone; or (iii) both. Carpenter holds (ii); Read holds (iii).

However, matters are further complicated when we ask what the sense in question is to be used for. A sense can be deployed in appreciating a work in one of two ways. It might be used to grasp those features of the work that determine its content (if any), as when I use sight to read the marks constituting a description. Or it might be used to garner what it is that those features in fact determine the work to represent, as when I draw on my past auditory experiences to recognize, in the sounds described, the noise of a steam train.

It may seem that a version of (ii) on which touch plays no role at all in appreciating sculpture is too strong for anyone to hold. Even Carpenter, for instance, allows that my current visual experience of the sculpture can be formed by drawing on past *tactile* experience, presumably of the object or properties represented. It is just that in this respect sculpture does not differ from painting:

It may be argued—and with entire warrant—that sculpture frequently involves an appeal to our sense of touch and physical contact; but so does painting. Such tactile sensations are, in either art, induced and secondary, being derivative of subjective mental association. In a painting by Titian or Bronzino, the representation of material textures such as fur and velvet may be so visually exact that it evokes in us a memory of how velvet and fur may feel when we stroke them. I do not think that sculpture's tactual appeal is very different or much stronger. Any dissenting opinion is probably inspired by the heightened physical actuality of sculptural presentation: we cannot directly sense a painted texture by touching the canvas, whereas we can actually explore with our fingers the solid sculptural shape. But the logic is faulty if it is thence inferred that sculpture is more immediately involved in the tactile sense; for, at best, we can only touch the material medium and not the artistic representation which is intended and calculated for the eye's contemplative vision. (Carpenter 1960: 34)

Stripped of its associationist philosophy of mind, and framed just a little more sharply, Carpenter's claim is that the only thing distinctive about sculpture, with respect to touch, is that the latter can be deployed to grasp the content-determining features of the representation. And why, he might ask, is that of any aesthetic interest?

However, a still stronger form of scepticism about the role of touch is possible. Consider Hildebrand's (1932) much discussed view, that sculpture is concerned primarily with presenting a series of silhouettes, or two-dimensional aspects, aspects that change as one moves around the sculpture. To the extent that these aspects are what proper aesthetic engagement with sculpture attends to, it may seem that there is no room in that engagement for touch, either as a way of discovering the content-determining features of the sculpture, or as a resource in connecting those features to the content thus determined. Perhaps it would be too much to claim that touch cannot inform us about silhouettes at all, since some empirical work suggests otherwise (Kennedy 1993). But it is certainly true that touch is far inferior to vision as a way of perceiving these features. So, from Hildebrand's perspective, in our engagement with sculpture, touch at best offers a poor way to do what vision does well. With respect to both the roles considered above, sight is the sense we should deploy, touch merely reproducing its benefits in reduced form.

Of course, it remains to decide whether Hildebrand's view is acceptable. But the moral to draw is really that the whole debate over sight and touch is in key part irrelevant. Hildebrand's view has consequences for what role sight and touch play in appreciating sculpture. But it does so by making a substantive claim about what there is to appreciate therein: a series of two-dimensional aspects. This answers the aesthetic question about sculpture more satisfyingly than could any claim about its requiring, or not, the deployment of particular senses. For Hildebrand tells us what there is to appreciate in sculpture, not what we need to get to it. All claims of the latter sort are, at best, consequences of genuine attempts to understand the aesthetics of sculpture. And without some such substantive aesthetics, any claim about the propriety of using sight or touch amounts merely to the existential generalization that there is *some* feature of aesthetic interest, to the appreciation of which the sense in question is the only, or best, means.

What are the merits of Hildebrand's claims? They are sometimes criticized for being founded on a mistaken account of visual perception. It is said that they presuppose that visual experience is as of a world in two-dimensions, information about depth being supplied by learned associations between visual input and tactile experience (Martin 1976). Instead of the Berkeleian view, we are offered an account of visual experience derived from Merleau-Ponty, on which it is full-bloodedly three-dimensional, and essentially involves an awareness of one's possible movements towards, and actions on, the objects seen. But, as Donald Brook notes (1969), the Berkeleian view, although certainly influential, has been held both by those supporting and by those rejecting Hildebrand's position. And it does not seem that the latter requires the Berkeleian account. For surely, even though our vision does present us with richly three-dimensional objects, we are capable of seeing, at least on occasion, the silhouettes those objects present, and that is all that is required for an art to exploit that capacity in reproducing such silhouettes for our appreciation. What is wrong with Hildebrand's account is not what it builds in, and what that inclusion commits it to, but what it leaves out. For surely, an awareness of a sculpture's three-dimensional shape plays a central role in our engagement with it.

3. DIFFERENT SPACES

A quite different starting point is the thought that sculpture is distinctively related to the space in which it lies, that it interacts with that space as pictorial art does not. This is something Hegel noted (1974: 702), and which more recent writers have amplified (e.g. Martin 1976). And there is certainly something attractive about the idea. Sculpture interacts with its space: it matters, to our appreciating the sculpture, what sort of space it is in. If we place a statue in too small a space, it can look suffocated. Something similar is true of pictures. If we hang a painting too high on the wall, it can looked cramped by the ceiling. But there is a difference. In the case of the picture, the sense of crampedness would persist even if one had not yet made out what the picture represents, or if a roughly similarly coloured and sized canvas, though one not representing anything, were put there. In the case of sculpture, at least sometimes its fitting with, or failing to fit, the space is dependent on its representing what it does. If one were to fail to see its content, or if one substituted a roughly similarly shaped and sized non-representational object, the effect of cramping would not necessarily persist. This suggests a difference between the two, but how are we to articulate it more precisely?

We might summarize the claims of the last paragraph by saying that in the pictorial case what looks cramped is the representation, that is, the picture; whereas in the sculpture's case it is the thing represented that seems crushed by its surroundings. And this suggests the following account of the difference between the two. The space of the sculpture is the space around the representation itself— what we might, without prejudice as to its nature or location, call 'gallery space'. The space of the painting is distinct from gallery space; the space depicted in a picture is a separate realm from the space of the depiction and the viewer.

However, as it stands, this won't do. Both picture and sculpture, the representations, exist in the space in which we perceive them. And neither the objects depicted nor those sculpturally represented exist in that space. What, then, is the difference between the two? We might essay the thought that, while the sculpted horse is not present in gallery space, it at least seems to be. But this is just illusionism, a view we have already rejected (in Section 1). Besides, even if we could construe our experience of sculptures as somehow involving the apparent presence of their objects, we could as easily do the same for *pictorial* experience. Another response would be to note that pictures often represent spaces in a more full-blooded sense than sculptures. For a picture may show a range of objects arranged within a volume of containing space, while a sculpture presents nothing more than, say, a prancing horse, without surroundings or companions. But not only does this seem a contingent feature of some sculptures and some pictures, since sculptural groups are possible and context-free horses can be depicted; it also fails to connect with the issue in hand. Any sculpture and any picture represents a space, in representing at least one object, and the spatial relations between its parts. Our question is whether that represented space is differently related, in the two cases, to gallery space. And on that question the reply is silent.

To make progress, we need to distinguish two senses in which spaces may be the same, or different. The first is more metaphysical. Two spaces differ in this sense if they do not form parts of a continuum. The space represented in a picture may be different from gallery space in this sense, in that it is not part of the spatial continuum of which gallery space is part. An example is the space depicted in Bellini's *Sacred Allegory*. There is no spatially continuous route, however circuitous, from the gallery to the space represented in the painting, if only because that space is not actual. Of course, matters are more complicated if, as in one of Bellotto's cityscapes of Verona, what is represented is actual space. But we can prescind from these complications: the Bellini sort of example provides the clearest possible case in which, in one sense, picture space and gallery space are not the same. The problem, of course, is that the space represented by a sculpture (e.g. the space occupied by the represented arm of one of Degas's sculpted dancers) is *also* different from gallery space in this sense.

The other sense of 'same space' is more commonplace. In this sense, the space outside a window is different from the space within the room, in that, though equally parts of one spatial continuum, the two constitute *different* parts of it—parts, moreover, presented to us as clearly different, with different natural boundaries, organizing contours, focal points, and the like. I suggest that this second sense provides the only reasonable way to construe talk of pictorial space being different from that of the gallery, while sculptural space is the same. Setting metaphysics aside, pictorial space is different from gallery space in just the sense in which the space outside the gallery window is: it is experienced as a discrete spatial unit, with its own organizing features. Not so for the space the sculpture presents.

But what exactly is our positive account of the sculptural case? We can't say that the sculpted object is experienced as lying within the perceived spatial unit that is gallery space, on pain of falling back into illusionism. And it is not enough to say that the sculpture itself is experienced as lying therein, for that is equally true of the picture, the representing marks themselves. Martin (1976: 282) claims that 'the space around a sculpture, although not a part of its material body, is still an essential part of the perceptible structure of that sculpture'. But what does this mean?

4. Sculpture and Organization: Langer

The answer lies in the most sophisticated account of sculpture in the literature, that sketched by Susanne Langer in *Feeling and Form*. Her way to frame the general approach within which we have been operating is to say that sculpture creates, compared with painting and architecture, a distinctive form of 'virtual space' (Langer 1953: 86). I take this to mean that our experience of sculpture needs to be characterized as having a distinctive spatial content. That content is distinctive in presenting us with a separate space in the everyday sense described above, a discrete perceptual unit, organized in a particular way (p. 88). What is that way? Langer's answer is in two parts. First, she notes that quite generally we experience our surroundings as organized around our possible movements and actions:

the kinetic realm of tangible volumes, or things, and free air spaces between them, is organized in each person's actual experience as his *environment*, i.e. a space whereof he is the center; his body and the range of its free motion, its breathing space and the reach of its limbs, are his own kinetic volume, the point of orientation from which he plots the world of tangible reality—objects, distances, motions, shape and size and mass. (Langer 1953: 90)

Second, we are able to see the space around a sculpture as organized around *its* kinetic possibilities:

A piece of sculpture is a center of three-dimensional space. It is a virtual kinetic volume, which dominates a surrounding space, and this environment derives all proportions and relations from it, as the actual environment does from one's self. (Langer 1953: 91)

As she summarizes, 'Sculpture is literally the image of kinetic volume in sensory space' (p. 92)

There are the ingredients here for completing our account of sculpture's and painting's differing relations to surrounding space. But Langer's ideas need careful handling, and some adapting, if they are to be of use. A central question is whether for Langer the space we experience as organized by the sculpture is gallery space, as it must be for her suggestions to bear on our problem. There are at least hints that she thinks not. But whatever Langer's actual view, the crucial claim, from our point of view, is certainly open to her. She should say that, just as, in the experience defin- itive of sculptural representation, we see the marble which makes up a statue as organized a particular way, organized by the thought of whatever is represented; so, in the experience she makes central to sculptural aesthetics, we see the space actu- ally surrounding a sculpture as organized in a particular way, organized by our sense of the potential for movement and action of that represented item. Neither experience involves illusion: they are never of a kind to mislead us about the nature of our surroundings. Rather, the experiences have the structure outlined above in Section 1: perception itself is transformed by the organizing thoughts, though not so as to yield an experience that in any way fails to be veridical.

So, what is special about sculpture is that the experiences it supports include experiences of the gallery space—that is of certain portions, perhaps indetermin- ately bounded portions, of the space around the sculpture—as organized in a dis- tinctive way. For paintings, in contrast, the parallel phenomenon stops at the boundary of the marked surface—the marks are perceptually transformed, the sur- rounding space is not. In a moment, we consider the merits of this account as the core of sculptural aesthetics. Before doing that, let us tidy up one or two other issues.

First, Langer too becomes embroiled in questions about sculpture's relations to sight and touch:

Here we have . . . virtual space, created in a mode quite different from that of painting, which is *scene*, the field of direct vision. Sculpture creates an equally visual space, but not a space of direct vision; for volume is really given originally to touch, both haptic touch and con- tact limiting bodily movement, and the business of sculpture is to translate its data into entirely visual terms, i.e. *to make tactual space visible.* (Langer 1953: 89–90)

This is not quite right. The phenomenon she makes central is indeed at least partly 'tactual', for the reasons the passage cites. But it is not clear that sculpture 'makes tactual space visible' as painting does not. For painting can certainly evoke an environment as organized kinetically. The differences between the two lie else- where, and are twofold. First, in painting, the environment seen as so organized is not that actually surrounding the picture, but that depicted within it. Second, the centre around which it is organized will lie at the point of view from which the scene is depicted, a point the actual viewer imaginatively occupies. In the sculptural case, in contrast, the viewer does not see gallery space as organized around the sculpted object by imagining herself in that object's shoes: her own actual point of view remains the only relevant one. From that point of view, she experiences the space around the sculpture as shaped by the sculpted object's potential to move and act in various ways. If Langer fails to see that these are the only important differences, it may be because she, at least, is indeed suffering from an overly Berkeleian conception of visual experience. If she fully embraced the thoughts offered in the first of the above quotations from her book, thoughts reminiscent of Merleau-Ponty, she would see that *all* visual experience is experience of 'kinetic volume', i.e. is permeated by a sense of possible movement and action. And this includes pictorial experience, the experience in which we grasp the content of pictures.

However, Langer's view does have one consequence for the proper mode of appreciating sculpture. For touching the sculpture itself will hinder us from perceiving its surroundings as appropriately organized:

handling the figure, no matter what it gives us, is always a mere interlude in our perception of the form. We have to step back, and see it unmolested by our hands, that break into the sphere of its spatial influence. (Langer 1953: 92)

Although she does not say why this should be, it is easy to think of reasons. For one thing, to touch the sculpture is to be too near to the centre of the space around it to experience that space as appropriately organized. For that experience of organization is essentially visual, however informed by other senses and proprioception, and from up close one cannot visually take in enough of that space at one go. For another, to explore the sculpture by touch is to reinforce one's sense of one's own actual kinetic possibilities, and this may, as a matter of psychology if not of logic, necessarily reduce one's ability to see the space as constructed with another object at its kinetic centre.

Langer's account is both coherent and plausible. How far does it offer a satisfactory aesthetics of sculpture? That is a large question, and answering it lies beyond the scope of this chapter. A few closing observations will have to suffice.

On the positive side, Langer's view promises to explain why so much sculpture concerns itself with animal, and especially human, form. For if sculpture is 'the image of kinetic volume in sensory space', one would expect it to concentrate on representing whatever can form the centre of such kinetic volumes, and, since it is the larger creatures that dominate our experience of actual movement and action, that means people and certain animals. On the other hand, by the same token, the account strains to accommodate certain sculptural works, particularly more abstract ones. For, to put the point crudely, if nothing is represented, or nothing definite enough to have 'kinetic potentialities', how can the sculpture organize surrounding space in the way described? Partly in recognition of this problem, Langer characterizes what a sculpture needs to support the key experience as 'living' or 'vital' form, the sort of unity, the fittedness of part to part and part to function, that organisms exhibit. But, in so far as it is clear what 'living form' amounts to, it is not clear how the possession of it by a more abstract work makes it possible for that work to create the experience of kinetic volume on which Langer puts so much stress.

Other counter-examples suggest themselves. Can't sculptural groups be sufficiently self-contained to prevent the interaction with surrounding space that Langer describes? Can't pictures exhibit that interaction? To do so they must overcome the property they share with windows (see Section 3 above), of presenting perceptually discrete spaces; but perhaps they can do so by being tailored to their surroundings, as is, for example Masaccio's *Holy Trinity*. And what of relief sculpture? One might expect that the lower the relief, the closer sculpture's limitations come to painting's. Perhaps Langer did not intend her account to apply to all sculpture and no painting. But the smaller the range of visual art that fits her claims, the less central we must take the phenomenon she identifies to be. In the end, whether it is central enough will depend on whether we find any other aesthetically distinctive features of sculpture, and on our sense of how distinctive an art it really is.

See also: Painting; Architecture; Representation in Art; Medium in Art; Aesthetic Experience.

BIBLIOGRAPHY

Brook, D. (1969). 'Perception and the Appraisal of Sculpture'. *Journal of Aesthetics and Art Criticism* 27: 323–30.

Carpenter, R. (1960). *Greek Sculpture*. Chicago: University of Chicago Press.

Goodman, N. (1976). *Languages of Art*, 2nd edn. Oxford: Oxford University Press.

Hegel, G. W. F. (1974). *Aesthetics: Lectures on Fine Art*, vol. II, trans. T. M. Knox. Oxford: Clarendon Press.

Hildebrand, A. (1932). *The Problem of Form in Painting and Sculpture*. New York: Stechert.

Hopkins, R. (1994). 'Resemblance and Misrepresentation', *Mind* 103: 421–38.

Kennedy, J. M. (1993). *Drawing and the Blind*. London: Yale University Press.

Langer, S. (1953). *Feeling and Form*. New York: Charles Scribners.

Lessing, G. E. (1962). *Laocoon*. New York: Dover. First published 1766.

Lopes, D. (1997). 'Art Media and the Sense Modalities: Tactile Pictures'. *Philosophical Quarterly* 47: 425–40.

Martin, D. F. (1976). 'The Autonomy of Sculpture'. *Journal of Aesthetics and Art Criticism* 34: 273–86.

Read, H. (1961). *The Art of Sculpture*. Princeton: Princeton University Press.

Schier, F. (1986). *Deeper into Pictures*. Cambridge: Cambridge University Press.

Schopenhauer, A. (1969). *The World as Will and Representation*, trans. E. F. J. Payne. New York: Dover. First published 1819.

Vance, R. D. (1995). 'Sculpture'. *British Journal of Aesthetics* 35: 217–25.

Walton, K. (1990). *Mimesis as Make-Believe*. Cambridge, Mass.: Harvard University Press.

Wollheim, R. (1968). *Art and its Objects*. Cambridge: Cambridge University Press.

——(1987). *Painting as an Art*. London: Thames & Hudson.

CHAPTER 33

DANCE

NOËL CARROLL

DANCE, understood provisionally and impressionistically as rhythmical bodily movement, often in concert with music, is a universal or nearly universal phenomenon in human cultures. A staple of ceremonies and rituals in traditional societies as well as our own, the structured nature of such movement—its salient rhythms and repetitions—mark it as special in a way that enables it, in turn, to mark the occasions in which it occurs as special. Thus, dance has perennially functioned as a means to commemorate events, such as rites of passage, weddings, presidential inaugurations, alliances, bar mitzvahs, and preparations for war; to propitiate gods and other forces of nature, as in rain dances and fertility celebrations; and to recall historic occurrences, including victories, revolutions, the changing seasons, the births of religious leaders, and so on. In many societies, dance also figures in informal contexts as a means to entertainment, pleasure, and self-expression, though even in these cases, the dancing often—albeit not always—subserves a larger social function, such as courtship or sociability (e.g. square dancing). Indeed, it has been suggested that dance served a very deep purpose in traditional societies, coordinating the activities of participants in a way that produced a sort of muscular solidarity between them (Dissanayake 2000; McNeill 1995). Thus, dance can be an instrument, whether sacred or profane, in the instilling and reinforcing of social bonds within a culture.

But dance has not only functioned in the service of ceremony and ritual and sociability; it has also been an element of theatre. The performance of classical Greek drama incorporated dance. This is perhaps a predictable outcome, since Greek theatre evolved from earlier ceremonies and rituals. When Plato and Aristotle comment on dance, it is usually in the context of the role it plays in theatrical production. What is significant about this is that, unlike present philosophers of the dance, premodern philosophers are not much concerned with the issue of dance as an artform in its own right—that is, with what might be called dance as an autonomous artform, like music. Though there are scattered, theoretical writings on dance from the ancient world and the Middle Ages, these do not focus predominantly on the issue of what constitutes dance as an art unto itself: rather, they discuss dance as a social medium, a means to personal enjoyment, and an element of theatre (Carter 1998).

The question of what makes dance an artform does not appear to emerge as a pressing philosophical issue until the eighteenth century, after which time it becomes a central topic. The reason for this should be fairly obvious: it is only in the eighteenth century that theorists became preoccupied with codifying the modern system of the arts—that is, with determining which practices belong to the sisterhood of the *beaux arts* (or fine arts). Two figures of particular importance in this transition were John Weaver and Jean-Georges Noverre. Importantly, both of these writers were not only theoreticians, but also choreographers. Thus, in both their theory and their practice, they were committed not only to establishing theoretically that dance could be an artform, but to creating dance artworks themselves and to recommending the creation by others of dances that would substantiate their theoretical arguments.

According to Weaver and Noverre, dance *qua* art is essentially a form of representation, where 'representation' is understood primarily as imitation—the process of referring to actions, events, and people by simulating their appearances. In this respect, Weaver and Noverre are attempting to appropriate an Aristotelian theory of mimesis as a theory of dance.

To understand what is at stake in this claim, it is useful, heuristically, to imagine Weaver and Noverre as responding to someone like Adam Smith, for whom anything was dance so long as it involved movement structurally composed of cadenced steps, aimed functionally at displaying grace and agility. For Smith, dance, whether of the eighteenth century or earlier, could be either imitative or not imitative. Smith notes that dance is not necessarily or essentially mimetic, citing what he calls 'common dances' (social dances) as counter-examples to any claim that dance is essentially imitative. Smith, of course, realizes that some dance is imitative; however, he regards this as an optional feature of dance. Thus, Smith does not include imitation in his definition of dance but maintains that 'a certain measured, cadenced step, commonly called a dancing step, which keeps time with, and as it were beats the measure of, the Music which accompanies and directs it, is the essential characteristic which distinguishes dance from every other sort of motion' (Smith 1980: 107).

Smith's definition seems eminently reasonable, given the sort of dancing available to eighteenth-century observers. And yet, Weaver and Noverre remain steadfast in their commitment to imitation as the defining feature of dance. Weaver writes 'I shall endeavour to shew in what the Excellency of this *Art* [dance] does or ought to consist: the Beauty of *Imitation*' (Weaver 1712: 159); while Noverre asserts, 'a well-composed ballet is a living picture of the passions, manners, ceremonies, and customs of all nations of the globe...; like the art of painting, it exacts a perfection more difficult to acquire in that it is dependent on the faithful imitation of nature' (Noverre 1966: 16).

But surely Weaver and Noverre, like Smith, realized that a great deal of dancing, such as social dancing, was not directly imitative of anything. So why do these seminal early modern dance theorists appear to ignore the data? One reason, of course, is that their domain of discourse differs from Smith's. Smith is attempting to characterize all dance, ranging from folk jigs to aristocratic minuets, whereas Weaver and Noverre are, in fact, only talking about theatrical dancing and of what it 'does or ought to consist'. Weaver and Noverre are dealing only with dance for the stage, specifically autonomous dance compositions (rather than dance as part of drama or opera), and their theories pertain to what that kind of dancing should and should not be. That is, they are theorizing the nature of what we might call the 'fine art of dancing', and not dance *tout court*.

It is undoubtedly instructive that Weaver moves between speaking about what such dance 'does' and what it 'ought to consist' of. Both Weaver and Noverre slip between advancing descriptive accounts of dance and normative accounts of dance. Obviously, both Weaver and Noverre know that not all dancing—or even not all theatrical dancing of their day—is, speaking pre-theoretically, imitative. It is fair to say this, because both complain about the non-imitative tendencies of the theatrical dancing of their time, bewailing the excessive emphasis on *divertissements*. Noverre says:

I am of the opinion, then, that the name of ballet has been wrongly applied to such sumptuous entertainments, such splendid festivals which combine magnificent scenery, wonderful machinery, rich and pompous costumes, charming poetry, music and declamation, seductive voices, brilliant artificial illumination, pleasing dances and *divertissements*, thrilling and perilous jumps, and feats of strength. (Noverre 1966: 52)

Though in some everyday sense of the word people say that this is dance, for Noverre it is not dance (dance as an autonomous fine art), properly so called. For dance to count as fine art, Weaver and Noverre claim it must be imitative, thereby inaugurating the first era of modern theorizing about dance.

Weaver and Noverre support their conviction that dance as fine art is essentially imitative in a number of ways. Weaver, especially, talks at great length about Roman pantomime, assuming that this is the genuine template from which dance subsequently deviated. In this, he invokes the authenticity of past practice in order to identify the essence of dance. Like early modern music theorists, he was probably convinced that much contemporary dancing must be a deviation, since it no longer seemed to have the efficacy—the efficacy arising from imitation—that classical dance was reputed to have for audiences.

Both Weaver and Noverre speak of restoring dance to its proper state. Both think that, in order to achieve this, dance must return to its mimetic vocation and eschew mere *divertissements* in favour of the representation of action. In this, both Weaver and Noverre are reformers who call for a rediscovery of the true essence of dance.

In order to identify this essence, they both rely explicitly on Aristotle. Aristotle, of course, linked drama with the imitation of action ('drama' is intimately related to the Greek work for 'doing'); and, in so far as theatre is drama, one supposes that Weaver and Noverre thought it was natural to infer that theatrical dancing is a subspecies of the imitation of action (which is, on Aristotelian grounds, the essence of theatre).

As previously noted, classical authors like Plato and Aristotle frequently counted dance as part of theatre. Thus, since on Aristotle's view all the parts of theatre are supposed to be subservient to the plot—to the representation of action—in an Aristotelian theory of the dance, such as Weaver and Noverre were advancing, it seemed virtually self-evident that dance, if it were to realize the essential telos of theatre, would contribute to the imitation of action.

As already mentioned, the attractiveness of Aristotelian theory for Weaver and Noverre was undoubtedly enhanced by the fact that they were theorizing at the time when our modern system of the arts was only just being consolidated. Though today we take membership in the traditional list of fine arts for granted—including under its aegis at least painting, sculpture, music, literature, drama, dance, and sometimes film—that list was hardly canonical before the eighteenth century. Prior to that, there were different ways of sorting these practices; the Greeks, for instance, grouped music with mathematics. But in the eighteenth century the core membership of the system of fine arts was established.

Of course, in order to do this some principle of inclusion was required. And that principle was none other than the Platonic–Aristotelian notion of mimesis. In 1747 Abbé Charles Batteux wrote, 'We will define painting, sculpture, and dance as the imitation of beautiful nature conveyed through colours, through relief, and through attitudes. And music and poetry are the imitation of beautiful nature conveyed through sounds, or through measured discourse' (Batteux 1989: 101).

Since Weaver and Noverre apparently shared this emerging consensus about the fine arts, we may reconstruct their reasoning as follows. In so far as they believe that dance is a fine art, then dance as art must for them meet the conditions necessary for anything to count essentially as fine art. On this view, mere virtuoso *divertissements* are not dance—dance art—properly so called, despite how people might talk pre-theoretically. Poetry and painting were accepted as legitimate instances of fine art in virtue of their imitative powers. Drama was accorded the status of fine art, again because of its capacity to imitate action. Similarly, Noverre agitated for the *ballet d'action* as the appropriate realization of dance *qua* art, because only through the imitation of action could dance be accorded the status of a fine art.

Drama was also an especially important model for Noverre because of its emphasis on plot, which, of course, for Aristotle was the representational core of theatre. Through plot, Noverre saw a way to unify dance spectacles. But at the same time, Noverre did not wish to blur the distinctions between dance and drama altogether. Thus, he criticizes the intrusion of words in dance, regarding wordlessness as the quintessence of dance. He complains about dances that use long recitatives and banners with words on them as antithetical to the dance. Though dance shares certain features with drama, according to Noverre, words are not something that dance should borrow from drama.

Noverre's theory of dance as imitation is not descriptively adequate: it neglects not only most social dancing, but much theatrical dance as well. However, granting the Aristotelian framework in which he operated, Noverre does not appear constrained to be statistically comprehensive, since he is attempting to identify the essential *telos* of dance, and this sort of essence is, in part, normative. Apparent counter-examples to his theory, then, no matter how numerous, are not countenanced as genuine instances of dance, since they do not actualize dance's proper function.

Moreover, the conception of dance as imitation was highly influential. As a result of the reforms and polemics of people like Noverre and Weaver, the *ballet d'action* became the dominant form of dance; it was, for example, the basis of the Romantic ballet. Thus, by the early nineteenth century the imitation theory of dance could muster impressive empirical support, though of course in many ways Noverre's theoretical polemic had functioned essentially as a self-fulfilling prophecy.

Nevertheless, despite the authority of Noverre and the case for imitative dance, an alternative position, which might be called formalism, concerning the nature of dance art gradually arose; and, like formalism in the other arts, it discounted the narrative–mimetic elements of dance, advocating instead that dance be thought of primarily in terms of movement patterns. In 1837, in a review of Fanny Elssler in the part of Alcine in *La Tempete*, Théophile Gautier declared: 'After all, dancing consists of nothing more than the art of displaying beautiful shapes in graceful positions and the development of them in lines agreeable to the eye; it is mute rhythm, music that is seen. Dancing is little adapted to render metaphysical themes' (Gautier 1932: 17).

This line of theorizing was given its most powerful formulation by André Levinson, who regarded Noverre's brief as 'Aristotelian sophistry', and who, claiming not only Gautier but Stéphane Mallarmé and Paul Valéry as fellow-travellers, maintained that the heart or appreciative nerve of dance (as art) is movement. In defiance of Noverre and his followers, Levinson writes:

I cannot think of anyone who has devoted himself to those characteristics which belong exclusively to dancing, or who has endeavored to formulate specifically the laws of this art on its own ground...[N]o one has ever tried to portray the intrinsic beauty of the dance step, its innate quality, its esthetic reason for being ...[I]t is the desire of the dancer to create beauty which causes him to make use of his knowledge of mechanics and that finally dominates this knowledge. He subjects his muscles to a rigid discipline; through arduous practice he bends and adapts his body to the exigencies of an abstract and perfect form. (Levinson 1974: 113)

If an Aristotelian theory of art as mimesis underpins the imitation theory of dance propounded by theorists like Noverre, it is thinking derived from the traditional Kantian theory of beauty that shapes the position summed up by Levinson (but which is also suggested by Gautier, Valéry, and Mallarmé). Not only does the primacy of pattern run through their discussions, but also, Valéry's insistence on the 'disutility' of dance and its independence from practical concerns corresponds to the Kantian presupposition that aesthetic responses be disinterested. Mallarmé's attribution of salutary ineffability to the dance symbol recalls the Kantian conviction that the beautiful is not subsumable under a concept, while not only Levinson's stress on the importance of form, but also his analysis of the aesthetic significance of classic form in terms of its capability for generating systematically infinite movement variety, recall the unity-amidst-diversity formulas of traditional aesthetic theory. In short, Levinson advocates a position on the aesthetic nature of dance that is close in many respects to the sort of formalism that Clive Bell advocated with respect to the visual arts—that is, that something is truly dance only if it possesses perceptible choreographic form.

Like the imitation theory of dance, formalism has exerted a great influence on the history of dance. Not only does it track that which is intentionally emphasized (form and movement) in the achievement of much modern ballet, notably the neo-Classicism of George Balanchine (for example *Jewels*); it has also moulded a species of connoisseurship that continues to command prestige, even among contemporary critics. Moreover, the formalist theory of dance possesses certain advantages. It beckons viewers of dance to attend closely to pattern and movement, and this is beneficial advice to anyone who wishes to learn about what there is to appreciate and to enjoy in much dance. However, like the imitation theory of dance (and the imitation theory of art), formalism, with respect to both dance and the other arts, is too parochial. It fails to provide us with a comprehensive theory, just because it privileges formal elements over other elements, such as pantomime. Thus, counterintuitively, it would cashier the first act of Jean Dauberval's *La Fille Mal Gardée* from the order of dance.

A third theory of dance is the expression theory. Like formalism, it arises in reaction to the imitation theory of dance. Broadly speaking, the expression theory of dance, like the expression theory of art, promotes a single function for dance, namely, the expression of feelings, particularly emotions. It counts portrayals of emotion in the *ballet d'action* as dance. But its construal of the expression of emotion is broader than that found in the imitation theory. For it does not limit genuine expressions of emotion to the enactment of the emotional states of characters, but considers as dance any investment of movement with anthropomorphic qualities, whether or not this is motivated by a narrative context. For the expression theory of dance, something is a dance movement only if it possesses or projects expressive qualities, even if those expressive qualities are detached from a narrative characterization. As sound in music, divorced from narrative, can possess expressive properties like sadness, so, it is assumed, can bodily movement. And where the projection of such expressive properties is the aim of bodily movement, the expression theory regards it as an instance of dance.

If the imitation theory can be correlated historically with the rise of the *ballet d'action* and formalism with the aesthetics of classical and neo-classical ballet, the expression theory of dance also parallels contemporaneous shifts in choreographic practice: the emergence of modern dance, primarily in America, and of expressionist dance (*Ausdruckstanz*) in Germany. Such dance—including the work of Martha Graham, Doris Humphrey, Mary Wigman, Jose Limon, and others—coalesces around the conviction that the proper function of dance is the expression of feelings. These convictions, moreover, find voice not only in the writings of choreographers, but in the theoretical speculation of critics and philosophers like John Martin (1972) and Susanne Langer (1953).

Both Martin and Langer are committed to expression theories of art. Both see the substance of dance in expressive movement, which Martin calls 'meta-kinesis' and which Langer locates in what she calls the realm of 'virtual powers'. For Langer, that dance proper is limited to the domain of virtual powers distinguishes it from drama, which for her is an affair of destiny. Langer maintains that the function of dance is to render these virtual powers visible. What she has in mind by the term 'virtual powers' are the vital forces of life—the appearance of influence and free agency— the feelings that accompany acts of will, including those of volition, the resistance to alien forces, the magnetism of love, feelings of compulsion, dreams of flight, and so on. Similarly, Martin's view, that the arrangement of dance forms is dictated by 'the logic of inner feelings', signals a necessary departure from the regulative standard of theatrical imitation (in so far as the logic of feeling is putatively different from the logic of action, i.e. from the logic of narrative). Thus, like formalism, the expression theory of dance rejects Noverre's ideal of dance as a theatre art like drama.

In all probability, the expression theory of dance currently enjoys the widest following among critics, choreographers, theorists, and ordinary audiences. It has been articulated with admirable clarity by Monroe Beardsley (Beardsley 1982), who argues that something counts as dance movement if it possesses more zest, vigour, fluency, or expansiveness than appears necessary for practical purposes; in other words, if a superfluity of expressiveness is present, the movement in question is marked as belonging to the domain of dance proper.

However, Beardsley's formulation of the expression theory of dance is somewhat ambiguous. It is not clear whether he believes that a superfluity of expressiveness is a necessary condition for dance movement, a sufficient condition, or both. But a superfluity of expressiveness cannot be a sufficient condition of dance movement. For many theatrical gestures are large—exaggerated to the point of a superfluity of expressivity—but they are not dance movements. Frequently, such large movements are executed to assure that the gesture is perceptible to audiences in the back row of the theatre, but, even where such movements are embraced for intense dramatic effect, they are not dance movements. Nor are the gestures of preachers who, for emphasis, accompany their sermons with a superfluity of expressive movement in order to punctuate the words of God. Likewise, the vigorous iconography of soldiers on parade—think of goose-steps, crisp martial turns, and pronounced salutes—is not dance movement, though it would appear to meet Beardsley's criteria.

But is a superfluity of expressiveness then a necessary condition for determining whether something is a dance movement? This hypothesis is open to criticism from several different directions. If we suppose Beardsley to be referring to dance *tout court*, rather than simply to dance *qua* art, there are phenomena, such as Native American corn dances, that do not exhibit a superfluity of expressiveness; they involve small steps, close to the ground, with no emphasis on the expenditure of energy, and little expressivity, let alone a superfluity of expressiveness.

If we turn our attention to dance *qua* art, there are also many counter-examples. Often dance ensembles strive to create what might be called 'gestalt effects'— dancers are employed so that they project a holistic image, such as the overhead kaleidoscopic configurations observable in Busby Berkeley musicals, or the composite figures in Pilobolus. Nor need these images be as 'pictorial' as these examples suggest—they may simply be geometrical patterns. Nevertheless, the movements that give rise to these patterns are dance movements, though they are not expressive in themselves, nor is their effect necessarily expressive; nor is any superfluity of expressiveness required to perform them adequately. Moreover, certain dance vocabularies, such as Cunningham technique as well as some styles of modernist ballet, are designed to suppress any inkling of overt affect, and certainly to banish any superfluities of expressiveness. However, even if one is tempted to deny that the human body can ever be divested entirely of expressiveness, one must remember that Beardsley's theory is framed in terms of excess expressiveness, and that that is something that a detached style of dancing can easily evade.

Beardsley's expression theory of dance also fails to accommodate many recent examples of what is called postmodern dance. Steve Paxton's *Satisfyin' Lover* deploys a group of dancers walking back and forth across the stage in the manner in which they might walk down the street; Yvonne Rainer's *Room Service* involves a group of dancers in the ordinary task of moving a mattress. Dances such as these are predicated on exploring ordinary movement; they aim at calling attention to the way in which the body works in discharging mundane tasks. In order to do this, they perforce eschew any quotient of expressiveness over and above what is required to discharge these tasks in everyday life. Consequently, if these exercises in postmodern choreography are regarded as dances, they are straightforward counter-examples to the notion that a superfluity of expressiveness beyond what is required for practical purposes is a necessary condition for dance.

Moreover, there is every reason to accept these examples as specimens of dance art. Four decades after their first performance, they continue to be reconstructed at dance festivals, studied in choreography classes, and analysed in dance history books.

Such movement exercises are not merely compilations of ordinary movement, but exemplifications of ordinary movement, undertaken to reveal features of movement—such as the intelligent, bodily adjustment of muscles in the process of moving objects like mattresses—that often fly under our radar screens, but are worthy of attention and appreciation. In this respect, postmodern dance performs a clear-cut function of art: the defamiliarization of the everyday in order for it to be seen afresh. And, inasmuch as this defamiliarization takes movement as its topic, there is no more fitting category under which to subsume it than that of dance. Thus, postmodern dance represents a decisive problem for expression theories of dance like Beardsley's, and for Langer's and Martin's as well.

Historically, the appearance of postmodern dance corresponds roughly with the seminal work of Andy Warhol. The early performances of Paxton and Rainer at Judson Church in New York occurred in 1963, while Warhol exhibited his *Brillo Box* at the Stable Gallery in 1964. Furthermore, the philosophical significance of post-modern dance and Warhol's Pop Art are approximately congruent. Just as *Brillo Box* implies that there is nothing the eye could descry to differentiate ordinary Brillo boxes from Warhol's, so Rainer and Paxton's works imply that there is nothing perceptible to differentiate everyday movement from dance movement. And similarly, inasmuch as Warhol initiated what Arthur Danto has called the era of post-historical art—the era in which art can look like anything—so postmodern dance ushered in the continuing post-historical era of dance—the time of our lives, in which dance can look like any kind of movement, including everyday walking and even mattress-moving.

The achievements of postmodern dance have rendered past theorizing about the nature of dance obsolete. In so far as dance now can involve any kind of perceptible movement, traditional theories of dance art that assimilate it to perceptible properties of movement, such as imitation, form, or expression, are under-inclusive; while the attempt to identify instances of dance art by means of the neo-Wittgensteinian procedure of family resemblance fails by being over-inclusive—since dance can be indiscernible from ordinary movement, anything might then count as dance. As has occurred in the general theory of art, so the contemporary philosophy of dance today, it would appear, must now search for more contextualist methods for defining and/or identifying dance artworks.

One such method would be a modified Wittgensteinian approach which relies on comparison between existing dance works and candidate works, but where the treatment of said examples would be informed and constrained by a knowledge of the tradition and practice of dance in such a way that the similarities that link new work with antecedent dance are not merely perceptible ones, but are supported by accounts of the contextually plausible reasons that motivate the relevant choreographic decisions in question (McFee 1992). Another, perhaps compatible, method would recommend identifying new candidates as dance works by means of historical narratives that chart the evolution of the new work from already acknowledged dance artworks in terms of a series of intelligible choreographic choices that make sense given the prevailing aims and purposes of the practice (Carroll and Banes 1998). Of course, it may also be possible to frame a contextually sensitive *definition* of dance. But we will not know that until we see it.

See also: Music; Theatre; Sculpture; Definition of Art; Representation in Art; Expression in Art.

BIBLIOGRAPHY

Armelagos, A. and Sirridge, M. (1978). 'The Identity Crisis in Dance'. *Journal of Aesthetics and Art Criticism* 37: 129–39.

Batteux, C. (1989). *Les Beaux-Arts reduits à un même principe*, ed. J.-R. Mantion. Paris: Aux Amateurs de Livres.

Beardsley, M. (1982). 'What is Going On in a Dance?'. *Dance Research Journal* 15: 31–7.

Best, D. (1974). *Expression in Movement and the Arts: A Philosophical Enquiry*. London: Lepus Books.

Camp, J. van (1998). 'Ontology of Dance'. in M. Kelly (ed.), *Encyclopedia of Aesthetics*. New York: Oxford University Press.

Carr, D. (1997). 'Meaning in Dance'. *British Journal of Aesthetics* 37: 349–66.

Carroll, N. (1992). 'Theater, Dance, and Theory: A Philosophical Narrative'. *Dance Chronicle* 15: 317–31.

——— and Banes, S. (1982). 'Working and Dancing'. *Dance Research Journal* 15: 37–42.

——— ——— (1998). 'Expression, Rhythm and Dance'. *Dance Research Journal* 30: 15–24.

Carter, C. (1998). 'Western Dance Aesthetics'. *International Encylopedia of Dance*. Oxford: Oxford University Press.

Copeland, R. and Cohen, M. (eds.) (1983). *What is Dance?* New York: Oxford University Press.

Dissanayake, E. (2000). *Art and Intimacy*. Seattle: University of Washington Press.

Fancher, G. and Meyers, G. (eds.) (1981). *Philosophical Essays on Dance*. Brooklyn, NY: Dance Horizons Press.

Gautier, T. (1932). *The Romantic Ballet as seen by Theophile Gautier*, trans. C. W. Beaumont. New York: Dance Horizons Reprint.

Goodman, N. (1969). *Languages of Art*. Indianaplis: Bobbs-Merrill.

Langer, S. (1953). *Feeling and Form*. New York: Scribners.

Levinson, A. (1974). 'The Spirit of the Classic Dance', in S. J. Cohen (ed.), *Dance as a Theatre Art*. New York: Dodd, Mead.

McFee, G. (1992). *Understanding Dance*. London: Routledge.

——— (1998). 'Dance: Contemporary Thought', in M. Kelly (ed.), *Encyclopedia of Aesthetics*. New York: Oxford University Press.

McNeill, W. (1995). *Keeping Together in Time: Dance and Drill in Human History*. Cambridge, Mass.: Harvard University Press.

Martin, J. (1972). *The Modern Dance*. Brooklyn, NY: Dance Horizons.

Noverre, J.-G. (1966). *Letters on Dancing and Ballet*, trans. C. W. Beaumont. Brooklyn, NY: Dance Horizons.

Sheets-Johnstone, M. (ed.) (1984). *Illuminating Dance: Philosophical Explorations.* Lewisburg, Pa.: Bucknell University Press.

Smith, A. (1980). *Essays on Philosophical Subjects.* Oxford: Oxford University Press.

Sparshott, F. (1988). *Off the Ground: First Steps to a Philosophical Consideration of the Dance.* Princeton: Princeton University Press.

——(1995). *A Measured Pace: Toward a Philosophical Understanding of the Arts of Dance.* Toronto: University of Toronto Press.

Weaver, J. (1712). *An Essay towards a History of Dancing.* London: J. Tonson.

CHAPTER 34

....

THEATRE

....

PAUL WOODRUFF

PHILOSOPHY of art began, for European cultures, with Plato's criticism of theatre and Aristotle's account of tragedy; modern philosophical discussion of the arts has been less oriented to theatre, which has generally been submerged in the broader topics of literature and fiction and, most recently, obscured by the rising interest in film.

1. HISTORICAL BACKGROUND
....

Problems of theatre caught the interest of ancient Greek philosophers, who set the agenda and the tone for succeeding generations. But even up-to-date philosophers of art in many cases cling to old translations and commentaries on classical works, and risk overlooking the results of recent scholarship in this area. (For Plato, Janaway (1995) includes a good review of recent scholarship; users of Aristotle's *Poetics* should consult the editions of Janko (1987) and Halliwell (1995), as well as Belfiore's study (1992) and the essays in Rorty (1992).)

Poetry in ancient Greece was made to be performed, with the result that ancient discussions of poetry do not distinguish what we now call literature from performance art. Plato's criticism of poetry is based largely on the moral effects of performance on actors and audience (see 'Art and Morality', Chapter 26 above). Discussions of theatre from the Renaissance on have dealt with scripts mainly as literary texts. However, in the first half of the twentieth century, two innovators in the practice of theatre announced ideas that locate theatre in the arena of performance.

Although Bertolt Brecht (1898–1956) began as a writer of plays, he soon went on to publish theoretical work. His conception of epic theatre, or theatre for instruction, was articulated between 1918 and 1932 in works collected by Willett (1964). Driven by an urgent political and moral agenda, Brecht rejected the literary and stage conventions of his time in favour of a theatre that eschews a transparent acting style and prevents thoughtless empathy of audience with character. Far from identifying with their characters, actors are advised to think of themselves as storytellers. Meanwhile, every aspect of Brecht's staging—removal of the false proscenium, visibly supported sets, unhidden lighting—is supposed to bring the theatricality of performance to the attention of the audience. Such 'alienation effects' are all calculated to prevent illusion. As a result, the audience is not to be carried along with the emotions of the characters, but, struck with opposing responses (laughing when they cry, crying when they laugh), is supposed to arrive at a critical understanding of society. This model of theatre cannot be conceived without attention to all aspects of performance.

Antonin Artaud (1896–1948) is known mainly for bringing attention to ritual elements that naturalistic theatre attempts to disguise; these occur in virtually all cultures, but they threaten classical conceptions of theatre when they promise altered states of consciousness in actors and audience. Theatre with this sort of aim may lack the representational content that has been the main object of interest in modern European cultures. Artaud was more prophet than philosopher, and he experimented more on himself in private than in the theatre; yet his concept of the theatre of cruelty (Schumacher 1989) opened the way to putting the audience on a par with the actors in performance, and its effects show in both practical and theoretical work by Grotowski (1968) and Schechner (1977). Followers of Artaud have been guided in theory by the anthropology of theatre, and in practice by a social agenda that engages audiences through theatre in rituals of solidarity or community. Although the politics of this movement (like Brecht's) faded after the turbulence of the 1960s, its influence on the theory and practice of performance lives on and looks to a revival in the communitarian movement that began in the 1990s.

2. WHAT IS THEATRE?

Theatre has become increasingly hard to define; traditional theories allowed theatre to melt into literature, while ideas that were new in the twentieth century shattered the comfort of what was thought to be the Aristotelian model and demanded that thinkers about theatre recognize the unique implications of theatre in religion, politics, and the life of community. Informed by these developments, the latest generation of scholars has found new ways to read ancient texts. (Philosophers using ancient Greek tragedy as a paradigm for discussion should be aware of such studies as Seaford (1994) and Segal (1996).)

Theatre is hardly a discrete artform; it does not have its own proprietary media, and it can operate in so many different ways that it defies orderly characterization. A general definition of theatre would have to be something like this. Theatre is a hybrid artform in which a combination of poetry, prose, music, dance, costuming, scene painting, and now video or digital effects may be combined in a live performance, usually a mimetic enactment of events. These events in turn may be fictional, historical, ritual, symbolic, or a combination; and the enactment itself may follow a script more or less closely, or may be improvisational; it may be enacted by live actors, but remains theatre if enacted by puppets, marionettes, or shadow-making devices manipulated by live performers. Theatre is usually performed in front of a distinct audience, but it may invite, or even force, everyone who is present to participate. It may have aims as diverse as to reveal the virtues and vices of a character, to renew an audience's experience of shared reverence, to shock a dazzled public with the absurdity of human life, or to make absurdity a cause of laughter and relief.

Any attempt at a broad definition of theatre shows how radically it depends, in any particular instance, on choices of aim and medium, how deeply an account of theatre is interwoven into views of society, and how weak a claim theatre has to any aims or devices as its own. All of the constituents of theatre are found in other artforms, with the results that theatre is not easily differentiated within the art world, and the philosophical problems that arise for theatre are usually shared in some way with other forms of art. Since those other artforms are covered elsewhere in this volume, the present chapter will focus narrowly on theories that are specific to theatre as a performance art. Although music, dance, and even sporting events may be construed as theatre, they are best treated separately.

Philosophical interest in defining theatre is a recent phenomenon. There is an excellent survey of schools of thought on the issue in Saltz (1998), which this chapter will not attempt to duplicate. Most recent discussions of theatre now take for granted what was revolutionary at the beginning of the twentieth century: that theatre belongs to the performance arts, and that a proper discussion of theatre must begin with a theory of performance; we shall see that performance-based accounts of theatre lead to discussions of mimesis and enactment.

3. PERFORMANCE

For an understanding of performance, the work of Thom (1993) is a valuable beginning. Cautious and thorough, Thom discusses the various elements in performance—the author, the performers, and the audience. He argues, moderately, for what he calls the *value* of each element, and gives good reasons for rejecting radical theories that give too much or too little play to one element or another. The traditional European view awards the main laurels to an author's work and therefore requires performance to be as transparent as possible, with the result that performance is merely ancillary to the author's work. This Thom regards as a distortion, an unfortunate devaluing of interpretation in performance. On the other hand, he objects on similar grounds to the more radical view that aesthetic value resides primarily in performance, because this undervalues the author's work. As for the audience, he says it is important but seems to consider that it has an active role only in the interpretation of performance. Thom apparently has European classical music in mind, which generally expects passive audiences. If he had paid more attention to popular music, non-European music, or theatre—in all of which the audience can influence the course and quality of a performance in many ways— he would have accorded larger roles to the audience, as do many theorists of theatre after Artaud. Nevertheless, Thom's theory represents an advance on earlier accounts of performance by philosophers, and it is helpful, as we shall see, in distinguishing theatre from non-performance artforms such as literature and film.

4. MIMESIS, ENACTMENT, AND SIGN

Since Plato, most philosophers have taken for granted that theatre is a form of *mimesis*, which is frequently translated as 'imitation' or 'representation', and is thought to involve deception on the part of an artist, or imagination on that of an audience. The best modern discussions of mimesis (such as Walton 1990) leave the word to stand on its own, and the word appears untranslated in Halliwell's (1995) translation of Aristotle. Indeed, none of the English words used in this context has anything like the classic usage of *mimesis*. Medicine, according to the ancients, is mimetic of nature because the function of healing is common to both. This sort of mimesis cannot be construed as deceptive or stimulating imagination, and only by a stretch could medicine be called imitative or representational. To consider another example, when an Athenian speaks another dialect of Greek he is said to be speaking mimetically; but he is actually speaking that dialect. Again, the ancients thought that music is mimetic of character, and this has been more puzzling to modern readers than it needs to be. An often overlooked fragment of Aristotle shows that music is mimetic of courage when it makes an audience feel the way it feels to be courageous (Woodruff 1992). Generally, on this view X is mimetic of Y when X has an effect on its audience that is at least partially the same as the effect that Y would have on that audience. That explains the *mimesis* between medicine and nature: nature heals slowly by means we do not fully understand, while medicine aims to have the same effect more quickly by means we have empirically discovered. Theatre, then, may be thought to be mimetic in aiming to affect its audience in some of the ways that actual events would affect them, by means that are specific to theatre, whether or not those means are representational.

In modern aesthetics, however, *mimesis* has developed an important life of its own as a word in English. The most thorough and original modern treatment of mimesis is Walton (1990), who understands mimesis as make-believe and thereby illuminates all of the representational arts. But Walton's theory applies especially well to problems in theatre. It has had wide influence on philosophical discussions related to theatre since its publication and will continue to do so. Walton's theory is more sophisticated and flexible than most of its critics have recognized, and it offers powerful ways of treating a wide range of problems in aesthetics. Observers of art participate in a process of make-believe which gives them a wide range of options. They may take part in theatre through interpretation, emotion-like response, or even direct interaction with stage events. Walton's theory allows for an elegant distinction between what observers literally assert about a stage performance and what they assert within a game of make-believe about stage characters and events. Analogously, it distinguishes between the feelings observers actually experience during a performance, and their make-believe emotions directed at what is imagined to be happening on stage. As a result, Walton's theory can be true to our experience of theatre without surrendering to weak claims for the existence of fictional entities or the paradox that genuine emotions are directed at what is not real. Walton is also able to account for the same object's having a role in a game of make-believe while serving a purpose in real life. He takes from theatre the idea that an object can be a 'prop for imagination' and extends that idea to a general theory of the arts. A chair on stage is actually a chair supporting a real actor, while at the same time it is a chair in make-believe—i.e. a prop to the imagination—where it supports a certain character represented on stage (see Chapter 10, 'Representation in Art', and Chapter 21, 'Fiction').

Theatre, however, is not always conceived as a representational art. When it aims to blur the line between make-believe and actual life, it resists analysis by Walton's theory. Artaud's theatre of cruelty is designed to defeat an audience's pleasure in the comfort of make-believe, by making things actually happen to them. Artaud draws on traditions in which events of ritual are felt to be actual; we would miss the point of Mass if we tried to explain transubstantiation of wine into blood as an act of make-believe; and in religious traditions theatre may attempt to bring the divine to earth, or at least to make its audience aware of what they accept as a divine presence. Brecht's alienating technique, by contrast, is calculated to make an audience rebel at the effort of imagining what is represented on stage, so that they abandon make-believe; in thinking that what they are shown is impossible, they are supposed to reflect on what actually takes place in capitalist society. A general account of the aims of theatre, then, must at least make room to consider views that do not depend on representation, imagination, and make-believe.

5. ACTION AND ENACTMENT ON STAGE

An article by Saltz (1991) develops a theory of action in theatre that has had an influence on subsequent discussion. In terms of speech-act theory, Saltz criticizes the position that actors on stage are unable to commit genuine illocutionary acts, such as promises. In Saltz's view, speech-acts on stage are not imitative or 'pretend' (at least not because they are on stage), but may have all the features of genuine illocutionary acts, except that they have what he calls 'borrowed intentionality'. For example, a promise made on stage commits the speaker to others only in so far as they are engaged in the same drama. In a similar way, players of a game make agreements that bind them only within the confines of the game. Saltz draws the game analogy to agreeable limits and proposes to think of a theatre audience as more like spectators in sports than like readers of texts. The point is that actors are really doing things on stage, and that the audience is really paying attention to what they do.

Enactment has recently come to the forefront in discussions of theatre; it captures nicely an essential feature of many forms of theatre, while remaining neutral as to questions of representation and mimesis. It is therefore available for use in accounting for theatrical conventions in a wide variety of styles and cultural traditions. Hamilton (2000) gives an elegant illustration of the usefulness of the concept in explaining the differences between naturalistic theatre and some of its rivals. This, I believe, is how philosophers should proceed in their work on theatre, analysing crucial concepts and showing how they may be used to illuminate, and bring clarity to, the practice of theatre.

A contrasting approach brings large philosophical theories to bear on the arts. Semioticians, for example, have claimed that theatre is a semiotic system—that it produces meaning through signs. The most thorough semiotic treatment of theatre is Fischer-Lichte (1983, translation 1992). In opposition to semiotics, phenomenology has been applied to theatre, most elegantly in recent years by Bert States (1985), who argues that the notion of sign is too narrow to account for our actual experience of theatre. This goes well with recent challenges to the idea that theatre is a representational art.

6. WHAT THEATRE IS NOT

If theatre is a performance art, there are a great many things that it is not, and a large part of what modern philosophers have aimed to write about theatre is really about something else. In particular, the philosophical problems specific to theatre are not those of literature or of fiction, and they should be distinguished from those of film as well.

First, literature has no necessary part in the definition of theatre, which does not require a text. Literary critics (New Critics especially) have for generations taken theatre to be no more than the enactment of literary texts, but in this they treat theatre as an ancilla to something else, rather than as an artform in its own right. True, texts are often well taught through performance, but teaching literature is not a specifically theatrical goal. Further, an act of reverence to a written text, like any other ceremony of reverence, can be a sort of theatre. But this is not what theatre is.

An ontological problem arises, however, for those who take theatre to be a performance art. If *Hamlet* is a work of theatre, and no work of theatre is identical with its script, then how are we to say what *Hamlet* really is? There are many versions of this play, many performances, and many styles of performance—far too many different Hamlets for us to give an easy answer in terms of the type–token distinction (by which my latest use of 'distinction' would be a token of the word 'distinction'). Each performance may be taken as a token of the type of a particular production, but the relation of productions of *Hamlet* to the play itself is harder to pin down. There is no definitive answer to this question, and no way to settle disputes as to what is or is not a production of *Hamlet*, but I recommend a strategy consistent with suggestions in Walton (1990) and Saltz (1991), as follows. Think of an enduring work of performance art on the analogy of a certain game, such as football. Usually we agree when football is being played, as we agree when *Hamlet* is being performed, but standards for both will be subject to change. Performing *Hamlet*, on this analogy, would be like playing football. There are roles to fill and rules to follow, and these may be carried out more or less appropriately to the game at hand. To do them well requires more than a script or a playbook, for it also requires a certain evolving tradition of performance. So I will take it that a particular work of theatre is a sort of artistic game that can be played in various ways.

Second, theatre is not essentially fictional, in the traditional sense of fiction as invention. Purely documentary historical material may be presented in theatre, and although the representation of history is certainly mimetic, it need not use invention, though it will use the tools of selection and arrangement that are available to all historians. Walton's broader definition, however, treats representation as make-believe, and this allows him to treat all representational performances as fictional. But directors often wish to leave open the question whether events transpiring on stage are representational or actual. The actor playing a jealous husband may actually *be* a jealous husband, and the audience may witness a real murder on stage. Audiences may even find that their seats are not safely removed from the action, when an actor bursts through the fourth wall and confronts a spectator directly, or when spectators are asked to decide what happens next. Such events are rare, but the possibility of reality breaking through is always present in theatre and brings a unique excitement to the genre.

Third, theatre is different from film in being a live performance (though a presentation of film may be *used*, properly framed, in a live theatrical performance). No two theatrical performances are the same; even a repeat audience brings different attitudes to a new experience of an old production, and the change in them affects the actors. But a film, like a book, is completed and published in a set form. A film may then be shown in the same way for any number of consumers over the years. 'Cinema is a time machine,' as Sontag (1969) observes, while theatre brings classics up to date. Moreover, film has at its disposal powerful effects for controlling emotions that are not available in theatre, such as enormous close-ups of an expressive human face. The weaker effects common to theatre allow for a wider range of audience response than for film, and members of the audience, seeing the action from different angles, will have different experiences of the same play. But there is one angle for everyone in a film, and the impossibility of interaction between actors and audience erases the tension that energizes live performance. Further, different parts of a film may be viewed simultaneously, and any part of it may be rewound and repeated; not so in theatre.

The line between film and theatre is obscured by the practice of recording live performances on film or video and transmitting them to large audiences, as now often occurs with opera and with sports events (which are a kind of improvisational theatre). Thom claims that the representation of a performance is not a performance, any more than a picture of an animal is an animal, but this surely goes too far. The showing of a film is a kind of performance; audiences can respond and thereby affect each other's experience of the film, and the cult showing of certain films (such as *The Rocky Horror Picture Show*) can displace theatre as a ritual that builds a sense of community.

7. OPERA

Music is often found in theatre, and a slippery slope lies between grand opera like Puccini's *Madam Butterfly*, which may be taken as music from start to finish, and a play like Brecht's *A Man's a Man*, which puts songs between scenes without music. The difference is that the whole of *Madam Butterfly*, but not *A Man's a Man*, could be material for a concert performance; indeed, production values in a performance of the same opera may be more or less theatrical or musical, and an opera-goer may encounter anything between a concert in costume and drama acted against a musical score. Peter Kivy has analysed opera as 'drama-made-music', arguing that the success of opera was due to developments in philosophy and psychology that allowed its audience and practitioners to accept its elements (the *da capo aria* in particular) as perfect, both in musical form and in representing 'emotive life' (Kivy 1988). Kivy does, however, recognize that opera can be taken as drama, and his book deserves the attention of philosophers of theatre.

8. THEATRE AND EMOTION

Plato attacks the theatre of his day for, among other things, arousing emotions in a way that undermines reason. Brecht's rejection of what he calls Aristotelian theatre assumes the Platonic premiss that emotions can undercut reason. Rousseau's defence of Geneva's ban on theatre follows a similar line, but a more extreme one: theatre depends for success entirely on a kind of audience response that is morally vicious (Bloom 1960).

All three attacks raise questions about the relation between emotion and reasoned judgement. Plato (by implication) and Brecht (directly) allow for the possibility of an unobjectionable theatre, and therefore raise questions about different ways in which theatre may affect an audience. None of these philosophical attacks concerns directly the modern problem of emotional response to fiction. This modern problem is, to put it simply, that emotions are usually thought to have objects in the real world about which they incline those who feel them to take action—to flee or disable a villain, for example—whereas the feelings of an audience in theatre leave them happily in their seats. This is a general problem about emotion and the arts; it is treated elsewhere in this volume (see Chapter 24, 'Art and Emotion', and Chapter 21, 'Fiction') and in a recent survey (Levinson 1997). Recent studies most relevant to theatre are Walton (1990) and Carroll (1990), but both focus on problems specific to fiction.

For theatre, the presence of live actors carrying out real actions in the same space as the audience introduces a complication not found in film or fiction. How the audience is disposed towards the actors and their actions makes an important difference to audience response. Different ways of engaging an audience are brought out in Hamilton (2000). Woodruff (1988) distinguishes different kinds of audience response that have been called empathy. Generally, the emotions of observers differ from those of participants in events, regardless of whether the events are staged or real. Observer emotions rarely motivate action, and this is as true on the street as it is in the theatre. Witnesses to a real accident must decide whether they are distant observers or participants, and if they see themselves as participants they must decide how actively to take part. The interesting question to ask about theatre as such, then, is not 'How can anyone knowingly respond to a fiction?' but 'Where, in this instance, does this audience member take a place on the continuum between observer and participant, and why?' or 'Where, in this performance, does the director aim to place an audience on that continuum?' A director may aim to affect an audience exactly as if they had witnessed an accident on the street, so that they do actually feel like covering their eyes, or calling police, or offering help. But some members of the audience may watch without feeling. There is a wide range of options, which are roughly the same for actual events and staged ones. When emotions are engaged for observed events, theatre and real life make similar demands on imagination (see Moran 1994). Plato's and Brecht's concerns are not misplaced: practitioners of theatre do need to think seriously about how they may affect an audience in relation to the real world.

9. PARADOXES OF TRAGEDY AND COMEDY

Emotions in certain genres of theatre present special problems. Observers of real-life events are free to turn away, and, though an audience is free to leave their seats, an essential aim of theatre is to hold its audience for the duration of a performance. In the typical case, an audience is held because it cares about the events shown on stage; to care about something is to be disposed to certain emotions about it—joy in success, for example, or fear of failure. Since Aristotle, the assumption has been common that the emotions elicited in theatre should be pleasant; but many emotions characteristic of theatre are painful, and we do not normally seek out conditions under which we feel painful emotions such as fear or pity, outside contexts such as theatre, sports, and amusement parks. The apparent oddness of finding pleasure in painful emotions is called the paradox of tragedy and has been much discussed in recent years (see Chapter 23, 'Tragedy'). There is an analogous paradox of comedy. Laughter tends to deflate emotion; the more we learn to laugh at our enemies, for example, the less they frighten us, and laughter can ease the excitement of love as well. But although we care about people largely through fear and love, we still seem to care about people and events in comedy. Comic theatre's mix of laughter and caring calls for explanation as much as does tragedy's blending of pleasure and pain (see Woodruff 1997).

See also: Art and Emotion; Art and Morality; Fiction; Humour; Tragedy; Dance; Music; Film; Representation in Art.

BIBLIOGRAPHY

Belfiore, E. (1992). *Tragic Pleasures: Aristotle on Plot and Emotion.* Princeton: Princeton University Press.

Bloom, A. (ed.) (1960). *Politics and the Arts: Rousseau's Letter to M. D'Alembert On the Theater.* Ithaca, NY: Cornell University Press.

Carlson, M. (1993). *Theories of the Theatre: A Historical and Critical Survey, from the Greeks to the Present,* exp. edn. Ithaca, NY: Cornell University Press.

Carroll, N. (1990). *The Philosophy of Horror, or Paradoxes of the Heart.* New York: Routledge.

Fischer-Lichte, E. (1992). *The Semiotics of Theater*, abr. and trans. from the 1983 original by J. Gaines and D. Jones. Bloomington: Indiana University Press.

Grotowski, J. (1968). *Towards a Poor Theatre*. New York: Simon & Schuster.

Halliwell, S. (1995). *Aristotle: Poetics*. Cambridge, Mass.: Harvard University Press (Loeb edn).

Hamilton, J. (2000). 'Theatrical Enactment'. *Journal of Art and Art Criticism* 58: 23–35.

——(2001). 'Theatrical Performance and Interpretation'. *Journal of Aesthetics and Art Criticism* 59: 307–12.

Hjort, M. and Laver, S. (eds.) (1997). *Emotion and the Arts*. Oxford: Oxford University Press.

Janaway, C. (1995). *Images of Excellence: Plato's Critique of the Arts*. Oxford: Clarendon Press.

Janko, R. (1987). *Aristotle: Poetics*. Indianapolis: Hackett.

Kivy, P. (1988). *Osmin's Rage: Philosophical Reflections on Opera, Drama, and Text*. Princeton: Princeton University Press.

Lamarque, P. (1989). 'Expression and the Mask: The Dissolution of Personality in Noh'. *Journal of Art and Art Criticism* 47: 157–78.

Levinson, J. (1997). 'Emotion in Response to Art: A Survey of the Terrain', in M. Hjort and S. Laver (eds.), *Emotion and the Arts*. Oxford: Oxford University Press, pp. 20–34.

Moran, R. (1994). 'The Expression of Feeling in Imagination'. *Philosophical Review* 103: 75–106.

Rorty, A. (ed.) (1992). *Essays on Aristotle's Poetics*. Princeton: Princeton University Press.

Saltz, D. (1991). 'How To Do Things On Stage'. *Journal of Aesthetics and Art Criticism* 49: 31–45.

——(1998). 'Theater', in M. Kelly (ed.), *The Encyclopedia of Aesthetics*. New York: Oxford University Press.

——(2001). 'What Theatrical Performance Is (Not): The Interpretation Fallacy'. *Journal of Aesthetics and Art Criticism* 59: 299–306.

Schechner, R. (1977). *Essays on Performance Theory 1970–76*. New York: Drama Book Specialists.

Schumacher, C. (ed.) (1989). *Artaud on Theatre*. London: Methuen Drama.

Seaford, R. (1994). *Reciprocity and Ritual*. Oxford: Oxford University Press.

Segal, C. (1996). *Dionysiac Poetics and Euripides' Bacchae*, 2nd edn. Princeton: Princeton University Press.

Sontag, S. (1969). 'Theatre and Film', in her *Styles of Radical Will*. New York: Farrar, Strauss, & Giroux, pp. 99–122.

States, B. (1985). *Great Reckonings in Little Rooms: On the Phenomenology of Theater*. Berkeley: University of California Press.

Thom, P. (1993). *For an Audience: A Philosophy of the Performing Arts*. Philadelphia: Temple University Press.

Walton, K. (1990). *Mimesis as Make-Believe: On the Foundations of the Representational Arts*. Cambridge, Mass.: Harvard University Press.

Willett, J. (1964). *Brecht on Theatre*. New York: Hill & Wang.

Woodruff, P. (1988). 'Engaging Emotion in Theater: A Brechtian Model in Theater History'. *Monist* 71: 235–57.

——(1991). 'Understanding Theater', in D. Dahlstrom (ed.), *Philosophy and Art*. Washington: Catholic University of America Press, pp. 11–30.

——(1992). 'Aristotle on Mimesis', in A. Rorty (ed.), *Essays on Aristotle's Poetics*. Princeton: Princeton University Press, pp. 73–90.

——(1997). 'The Paradox of Comedy'. *Philosophical Topics* 25: 319–35.

CHAPTER 35

POETRY

ALEX NEILL

NOT surprisingly, the philosophical issues that arise in connection with poetry as a form of art in almost all cases are not specific to it, but relevant to the understanding and evaluation of literature (and indeed other forms of art) more generally; an obvious example is that of the nature of metaphor. Thus, it is far from clear that there is a 'philosophy of poetry' in anything like the sense in which there is a 'philosophy of literature' and a 'philosophy of criticism'. None the less, there are a number of philosophically interesting issues that arise at least as pressingly in connection with poetry as in other contexts, and the purpose of this chapter is to introduce and consider, if only briefly, some of the more significant of these issues.

Doubtless the most ancient of the questions concerning poetry that have occupied philosophers concerns the nature of this form of art: just what *is* poetry, and how, in particular, does poetic discourse differ from prose? In the opening chapters of the *Poetics*, Aristotle takes issue with the standard usage of his time, according to which 'people attach the verbal idea of "poetry" (*poein*) to the name of the meter, and so call these writers "elegiac poets" (*elegopoioi*), "epic poets" (*epopoioi*), and so on;...if a work of medicine or natural philosophy is written in metre, people still use these same descriptions.' This, Aristotle holds, is a vulgar error: 'Homer and Empedocles have nothing in common except their metre; [and] while one must call the former a poet, the latter should be called a natural philosopher rather than a poet' (Halliwell 1987: 32). In short, contrary to what is as common a way of speaking in our own time as apparently it was in his, Aristotle holds that poetry cannot simply be identified with verse. And this is surely right; however we understand 'verse', it seems clear that not all verse is poetry—consider 'Row, Row, Row Your Boat' or 'Yankee Doodle', for example. As Sir Philip Sidney says in his *An Apology for Poetry,* 'now swarm many versifiers that need never answer to the name of poets' (Sidney 1973: 103).

But if the identification of poetry with verse brings too much into the scope of the former, Aristotle's own characterization of poetry, in terms of the media (language, melody, rhythm), the manner (dramatic or narrative), and the objects of poetic *mimesis* (or, crudely, representation), is on the face of it far too restrictive to capture the variety of things that we are likely to want to describe as poems. For example, in insisting that the objects of poetic mimesis are 'people in action', Aristotle seems to exclude the possibility of poetry about nature and about the divine; and in holding that the manner of poetic mimesis is either dramatic or narrative, he appears to exclude most lyric and elegiac poetry—all of which would be a shock to admirers of the work of Francis Ponge, Gerard Manley Hopkins, and John Keats, for example. It must be emphasized, however, that deriving a theory of poetry that we can be sure accurately represents Aristotle's thoughts on the matter from the *Poetics* is probably impossible: the fragmentary nature of the text, and the difficulty of some of the technical notions that Aristotle employs with little by way of explanation of what he means by them—*mimesis* and *catharsis* stand out in this respect—leave it far from clear what his conception of 'the art of poetry in general' actually amounts to.

If not all verse is poetry, might it nonetheless be the case that all poetry is verse? If 'verse' is understood to mean 'metrical discourse' (as the *Oxford English Dictionary* has it, 'a succession of words arranged according to natural or recognised rules of prosody and forming a complete metrical line') the answer must again be negative, for in this sense of verse, as Sir Philip Sidney puts it, 'there have been many most excellent poets that never versified' (Sidney 1973: 103). However, Monroe Beardsley argues, in what is probably the most comprehensive discussion of poetry by a contemporary philosopher (though that discussion is not self-contained, but rather spread through various sections of his *Aesthetics: Problems in the Philosophy of Criticism*), that verse is better understood as 'discourse whose sound-pattern is more highly organised than prose'. And in this sense of the term, the claim that verse is an essential element of poetry is very plausible. The difference between verse that is and verse that is not poetry, Beardsley holds, is a matter of the ways in which the verses in question carry their meaning: poetry is verse a large part of the meaning of which is suggested or implicit, rather than explicit (Beardsley 1981: 233–5). This does not make the question of whether or not any particular piece of discourse is a poem a cut and dried affair: 'more highly organized' and 'a large part of the meaning' in the definitions above clearly leave plenty of room for debate about whether or not a particular piece is a poem or not—but then, that is surely how it should be.

Beardsley's view that poetry is to be distinguished from other sorts of discourse in terms of the ways in which it carries its meaning is far from unique to him; in one version or another, it has also been offered by Dorothy Walsh, William Empson, and Ezra Pound, among other philosophers, critics, and poets. Nor of course is the 'semantical definition' of poetry, as Beardsley labels it, without competition: poetry has also been defined in affective terms (by Owen Barfield, for example), and in terms of expression (the best-known statement of the latter view surely being Wordsworth's, in the Preface to the second edition of the *Lyrical Ballads*, where he writes that 'poetry is the spontaneous overflow of powerful feelings; it takes its origin from emotion recollected in tranquillity'). However, if what one wants is an account of poetic discourse that distinguishes it from prose, Beardsley's 'semantical definition' is the most promising.

That is not to say that this sort of account is immune to objection. For example, it is all too easy to imagine the products of the 'automatic writing' experiments of André Breton and other Surrealists, or those of the 'cut-up technique' practised by Tristan Tzara and William Burroughs, among others, which are in effect collages of words (allegedly) put together randomly, being offered as counter-examples to the claim that all poetry is verse that carries its meaning in certain ways, and indeed to any of the other theories of the nature of poetry that have been offered, in much the same way as Duchamp's 'readymades' and other products of the Dada movement have been offered as counter-examples to any of the traditional theories of art. The result of such a challenge would presumably be a move towards the development of an 'institutional theory' of poetry, as happened in the post-1960s philosophy of art more generally as a result of Wittgensteinian-inspired scepticism about the possibility of definition in terms of the necessary and sufficient conditions of works of art, working in combination with excitement at the increasingly challenging products of the world of art itself. Such a move would be regrettable, not least because, as the recent history of the philosophy of art has demonstrated, the turn towards institutional theorizing about art, while keeping a surprisingly large number of philosophers busy, has rarely led to any illumination of what are surely the deepest philosophical questions concerning works of art: namely, why and how it is that these things *matter* to us in the ways that they do. The more traditional attempts to define poetry, by contrast, encourage reflection on the ways in which poems *work*—on how they may be expressive, for example, or bear meanings they do not explicitly state—and in doing so they in effect move us beyond the question of the definition of poetry, and its difference from prose, to considerations concerning its value.

Questions concerning the value of poetry have been of interest to philosophers and critics ever since Plato issued his challenge, in Book X of the *Republic*, to poetry's 'champions', to show that poetry is not, as he argued it to be, epistemically and morally a corrupting influence on individuals and society. Aristotle's *Poetics* is in effect in large part a response to that challenge. Where Plato argued that poetry's appeal to emotion in its audience was degrading, Aristotle argued that the capacity of tragedy to bring about the *catharsis* of pity and fear in the audience made it, in one way or another (unfortunately the obscurity of the notion of *catharsis* in the *Poetics* makes it very difficult to say precisely how), a force for good in the pursuit of psychological and moral health. Sir Philip Sidney, in his *An Apology for Poetry*, also took up Plato's challenge, arguing that poetry's value lay in its unique capacity 'to teach and delight', and furthermore to teach partly *in virtue of* delighting: poetry's value as source of instruction and knowledge, Sidney argues, lies largely in its suffering neither from the dullness and the difficulty of philosophy, nor from the entrapment in particular events and 'old mouse-eaten records' of history. The poet, by contrast, 'doth not only show the way, but giveth so sweet a prospect into the way, as will entice any man to enter into it' (Sidney 1973: 113).

Sidney's thesis that the value of poetry lies in its capacity to be simultaneously a source of delight and of truth was developed in a quite different direction by Shelley, in his *A Defence of Poetry*. And the thesis was taken up again by philosophers and critics in the first half of the twentieth century, largely in the context of responses to Positivist claims concerning the nature of meaning and the implications of those claims with respect to the function and value of poetry. In literary aesthetics, the most notable expression of the Positivist position was in C. K. Ogden and I. A. Richards's distinction between 'symbolic' and 'emotive' language, the latter of which they held to be the language of poetry. 'The symbolic use of words is statement; the recording, the support, the organisation and the communication of references. The emotive use of words is a more simple matter; it is the use of words to express or excite feelings and attitudes.' Thus, 'it ought to be impossible to talk about poetry or religion as if they were capable of giving "knowledge" ... A poem ... tells us, or should tell us, nothing' (Ogden and Richards 1926: 149, 55)—a thought somewhat paradoxically echoed by the American poet Archibald MacLeish, when he stated in his perfectly meaningful poem 'Ars Poetica' that 'A poem should not mean/But be'. For the following twenty or thirty years, philosophical writing about poetry was dominated by critical responses to the Positivist position, responses that were for the most part occupied with the attempt to show that and how poetic discourse *can* be a source of knowledge. (Notable examples include the works by Marguerite Foster (1950), Max Rieser (1943), Dorothy Walsh (1938), and Morris Weitz (1950, 1955).)

This debate about the cognitive value of poetry continues, though with the decline of Positivism much of the heat has gone out of it, and the terms of the debate are rather different. In the non-cognitivist camp, Stein Haugom Olsen (1978), for example, has developed a sophisticated version of the position suggested in Wittgenstein's statement 'Do not forget that a poem, even though it is composed in the language of information, is not used in the language game of giving information' (Wittgenstein 1967: 28). And philosophers such as Gadamer, often inspired more or less directly by Heidegger, have developed the cognitivist position—the position that holds that poetic discourse may be an important source of truth—through analyses of and speculation about the peculiar nature and function of poetic language.

The temptation to see the value of a poem as lying at least partly in the thoughts and ideas that it articulates is considerable, and is lent weight by the importance in the critic's vocabulary of such terms as 'profound', 'trite', 'sentimental', and so on.

However, in the richest and most sophisticated recent philosophical discussion of poetic value, Malcolm Budd argues that this is a temptation to be resisted: 'The value of a poem as a poem does not consist in the significance of the thoughts it expresses,' Budd writes; 'for if it did, the poem could be put aside once the thoughts it expresses are grasped' (Budd 1995: 83). And the latter is clearly not the case; that is to say, we do not regard poems as dispensable in the way that we do, say, business reports, where 'once you can express in other words the thoughts contained [in them] ... [y]ou then have no need ... of the words in which the thoughts were originally formulated'. In the case of business reports and the like, the value of which does lie in the significance of the ideas communicated, reading the report itself is no more valuable than reading anything else that communicates the same ideas. Analogously, if the value of a poem lay in the significance of the thoughts it articulated, we would have no reason to value the poem any more highly than a complete paraphrase of it. Since the latter is not the case, Budd concludes, it cannot be the case that the value of poetry lies in the thoughts it articulates.

One way of attempting to resist this conclusion while acknowledging the indispensability of poetry is by arguing that poems differ from business reports and the like precisely in that, in the case of poetry, no complete paraphrase is possible, no way of expressing in other words the content of the poem. The classical statement of this position is that of Cleanth Brooks, a leading exponent of what came to be known as the 'New Criticism', who held that paraphrases 'lead away from the center of the poem—not toward it ... We can very properly use paraphrases as pointers and as shorthand references provided that we know what we are doing. But it is highly important that ... we see plainly that the paraphrase is not the real core of meaning which constitutes the essence of a poem.' 'In fact,' he continues, 'if we are to speak exactly, the poem itself is the *only* medium that communicates the particular "what" that is communicated' (Brooks 1971: 180, 60). To deny this, argued the New Critics, is to commit 'the heresy of paraphrase.' In short, it is because it is the only possible vehicle of the thoughts it communicates that a poem is not dispensable in the way that a business report is, and the possibility that its value lies in the thoughts it articulates, as well as in its particular articulation of them, remains open.

The question of the possibility of paraphrase of poetic language has been the focus of a great deal of attention, the main figures in the debate being Brooks, Yvor Winters (1947), and Stanley Cavell (1976). One of the difficulties here is that the term 'paraphrase' is used in different ways by different contributors to the debate. However, let us suppose that by 'the possibility of paraphrase' we mean, roughly, the possibility of rendering the meaning of a poem in different words. (Of course, this locution is itself open to being understood in different ways.) Two questions immediately present themselves: First, what reason is there for thinking that this is not possible? And second, what reason is there for thinking that poetic discourse, in particular, is not paraphrasable; that is, why should it be thought that poems and business reports are different in the way suggested in the previous paragraph?

Attempts to supply these reasons by appeal to the nature of poetic language are familiar but not promising. Appeal to the importance of metaphor in poetry is common in this context, but the importance of metaphor in all sorts of discourse, including the most prosaic of business reports (think of markets rising and falling), rules out answering the second question raised above in this way. More importantly, it is not the case that metaphors do not admit of paraphrase. (For a recent argument to this effect, see e.g. Levinson 2001.) Clearly, some metaphors will be more easily paraphrasable than others, and clearly, in many if not all cases a paraphrase will lack the effect of the original metaphor; but there is no good reason to think that metaphors are essentially immune to paraphrase. Nor is appeal to the fact that in poetry much of the meaning is in one way or another not explicit likely to be helpful in answering our questions, for the fact that a meaning is implicit or suggested does not in itself mean that it cannot be rendered explicit. The fact that a poem does not wear its meaning on its sleeve may make us wonder whether we have grasped all that it means, and hence may be reason to wonder whether any particular paraphrase of it is complete, but that is no reason to think that paraphrase is in principle impossible in this context.

Needless to say, these do not exhaust the possible arguments for the impossibility of paraphrasing poetry. For example, Cleanth Brooks argues that paraphrase is impossible because, in the case of good poetry, the poet's attitude will be so subtle that it can have only one expression: that achieved in the words of the poem just as they are. Alternatively, it may be argued that the meaning of a poem is in some way not only emergent from, but dependent upon, the patterns of sound that the poem involves, and hence that any form of words that does not involve precisely those patterns of sound—that is, it will be said, any paraphrase—will be incapable of conveying the meaning in question. Neither of these arguments is very persuasive, however, not least because the most that either can establish is that the meaning of a paraphrase, no matter how good that paraphrase is, will not be precisely that of the original poem. And while that is true, it does not so much show that paraphrase is impossible as bring out the kind of thing that paraphrase must be, inasmuch as a paraphrase and what it is a paraphrase *of* are different things (cf. Cavell 1976).

However, to the extent that what is at stake here is the dispensability or otherwise of a poem once its meaning has been grasped, the failure of such arguments for the impossibility of paraphrase is not conclusive. For, even if it is the case that the thoughts or ideas that a poem articulates can be expressed in ways other than how they are expressed in the poem itself, it may nonetheless be the case that the poem itself is indispensable. (Which is not to say that all poems will be such: the view that poems are in general indispensable is an article of faith that is very hard to sustain in the face of bad poetry—that is to say, most poetry.) Even if what a poem means can be fully expressed in a different form of words, the poem itself may be indispensable because it is, say (to use the term as no more than a form of shorthand), beautiful.

In such a case, it is true that the value of the poem in question will not lie *wholly* in the significance of the thoughts it articulates—which is all that Budd's argument establishes—but the possibility remains that the value of the poem may lie *partly* in the significance of the thoughts it articulates. This is perfectly consistent with Budd's claim that the value of poetry lies in 'the imaginative experience you undergo in reading the poem...and it is constitutive of this imaginative experience that it consists in an awareness of the words as arranged in the poem'; that 'it is never the sole object of poetry to convey a message; rather the function of poetry as poetry is that it itself should be experienced, which is to say that its function is to provide an experience that cannot be fully characterised independently of the poem itself'; and that 'it is the experience the lines offer...that determines their poetic value' (Budd 1995: 83–5). But what is experienced in the experience of a poem is, or at least is very often, precisely a thought or set of thoughts expressed or articulated in a particular way. Of course the particularity of the expression or articulation is of the essence of the poem's value, but that is not to say that the significance of what is articulated is irrelevant to that value. (For a general theory of art which emphasizes the importance in works of art of 'the appropriateness of their forms to their contents', see Eldridge 1985.)

This thesis concerning poetic value explains the queasiness that may be felt concerning the possibility of translating poetry from one language to another. Merely capturing the thoughts expressed in a poem in words in a different language, even if those words are in verse, will in effect amount to no more than paraphrasing it, and hence will almost invariably fail to capture the value of the original. For a translation of a poem to amount to more than a paraphrase, it will have to be such that the experience that the translation makes available to its audience bears a significant resemblance to the experience made available to the audience by the original: the closer the resemblance, the better the translation. The more closely the character of the experience of a poem is tied to the precise arrangement of the words that comprise the poem, the more difficult translation will be, and some poems—though it is important to remember that where this is true it will be a contingent fact about those poems, rather than a general truth about the nature of poetry—may be untranslatable beyond paraphrase. It follows that translation is an activity (in Collingwoodian terms, a craft rather than an art—a form of making where the end is known in advance to the creator) in which derivativeness (of a potentially highly interesting sort) is combined (in potentially very interesting ways) with creativity.

Questions concerning the possibility of paraphrase and translation are clearly not specific to poetry, but apply to literary works more generally. This is also true of two further questions that are often discussed in the context of poetry, questions concerning the relevance (1) of authorial sincerity, and (2) of the acceptability or unacceptability of the thoughts it articulates, to the value of a poem. Nonetheless, and perhaps not least because of the importance of the lyric form in poetry, these questions have acquired a particular urgency in critical and philosophical discussions of poetry. With regard to the latter question, the debate is between those who believe that, at least in some sorts of case, the articulation by a poem of what the audience takes to be false thoughts must detract from the value of that poem, at least as the audience sees it, and those who hold that the plausibility or otherwise of the ideas articulated in a poem have nothing to do with the strictly poetic value of that poem. With regard to the former question, what is at issue is whether, if the thoughts and attitudes expressed in a poem are not genuinely held by the author, the poem is thereby deficient, because it is in some sense insincere. Given the thesis that the value of a poem lies in the value of the experience that it makes available to its audience, the answer to these questions will turn on whether the reader's or listener's lack of sympathy with the thoughts articulated in a poem, or their awareness that the poet did not genuinely mean what he said in the poem, need detract from the value of their experience of the poem. By far the richest contemporary discussion of both questions is that offered in Budd (1995).

See also: Literature; Tragedy; Theatre; Metaphor; Art and Emotion; Art and Knowledge.

BIBLIOGRAPHY

Abrams, M. H. (1973). *The Mirror and the Lamp: Romantic Theory and the Critical Tradition*. New York: Oxford University Press.

Barfield, O. (1952). *Poetic Diction: A Study in Meaning*. London: Faber & Faber.

Beardsley, M. C. (1981). *Aesthetics: Problems in the Philosophy of Criticism*, 2nd edn. Indianapolis: Hackett. First published 1958.

Bradley, A. C. (1909). *Oxford Lectures on Poetry*. Oxford: Oxford University Press.

Brooks, C. (1971). *The Well Wrought Urn*. London: Methuen.

Budd, M. (1995). *Values of Art: Pictures, Poetry and Music*. London: Allen Lane.

Cavell, S. (1976). 'Aesthetic Problems of Modern Philosophy', in his *Must We Mean What We Say?* 2nd edn. Cambridge: Cambridge University Press.

Eldridge, R. (1985). 'Form and Content: An Aesthetic Theory of Art'. *British Journal of Aesthetics* 25: 303–16.

Empson, W. (1966). *Seven Types of Ambiguity*. New York: W. W. Norton.

Foster, M. (1950). 'Poetry and Emotive Meaning'. *Journal of Philosophy* 47: 657–60.

Gadamer, H.-G. (1986). 'On the Contribution of Poetry to the Search for Truth', in his *The Relevance of the Beautiful and Other Essays*. Cambridge: Cambridge University Press.

Halliwell, S. (1987). *The Poetics of Aristotle: Translation and Commentary*. London: Duckworth.

Jacobson, D. (1996). 'Sir Philip Sidney's Dilemma: On the Ethical Function of Narrative Art'. *Journal of Aesthetics and Art Criticism* 54: 327–36.

Kivy, P. (1997). *Philosophies of Arts*. Cambridge: Cambridge University Press.

Levinson, J. (2001). 'Who's Afraid of a Paraphrase?' *Theoria* 67: 7–23.

Martin, G. D. (1975). *Language, Truth and Poetry*. Edinburgh: Edinburgh University Press.

Ogden, C. K. and Richards, I. A. (1926). *The Meaning of Meaning*. London: Routledge & Kegan Paul.

Olsen, S. H. (1978). *The Structure of Literary Understanding*. Cambridge: Cambridge University Press.

Pinsky, R. (1999). *The Sounds of Poetry*. New York: Farrar, Straus & Giroux.

Pound, E. (1960). *ABC of Reading*. New York: W. W. Norton.

Reiser, M. (1943). 'Language of Poetic and of Scientific Thought'. *Journal of Philosophy* 40: 421–35.

Richards, I. A. (1929). *Practical Criticism*. London: Routledge & Kegan Paul.

——(1967). *Principles of Literary Criticism*. London: Routledge & Kegan Paul.

Rowe, M. (1996). 'Poetry and Abstraction'. *British Journal of Aesthetics* 36: 1–15.

Sidney, P. (1973). *An Apology for Poetry*, ed. G. Shepherd. Manchester: Manchester University Press.

Stevenson, C. L. (1957). 'On "What is a Poem?"'. *Philosophical Review* 66: 329–62.

Walsh, D. (1938). 'The Poetic Use of Language'. *Journal of Philosophy* 35: 73–81.

Weitz, M. (1950). *Philosophy of the Arts*. Cambridge, Mass.: Harvard University Press.

——(1955). 'Truth in Literature'. *Revue Internationale de Philosophie* 9: 1–14.

Winters, Y. (1947). *In Defence of Reason*. Athens, Ohio: Ohio University Press.

Wittgenstein, L. (1967). *Zettel*, ed. G. E. M. Anscombe and G. H. von Wright and trans. G. E. M. Anscombe. Oxford: Basil Blackwell.

CHAPTER 36

....

PHOTOGRAPHY

....

NIGEL WARBURTON

Photography is the most widespread form of visual communication using still images. Since its invention the medium has not changed substantially, or at least not until the recent invention of digital photography. The uses to which photography has been put and the conventions surrounding those uses have, however, evolved significantly.

Those analytic philosophers who have written about still photography have for the most part focused on quite a narrow range of topics. Their main concern has been to characterize the nature of the causal link between object photographed and photographic image. A recent survey of philosophical writing on the aesthetics of photography (Currie 1998), for example, concentrated exclusively on the question of the relation between photography's mechanicity and its alleged transparency to its objects arising from the optico-chemical causal link between a photograph and what it is of. Although the unravelling of such matters relates directly to questions in aesthetics, the questions themselves are questions about the nature of photographic representation and apply just as much to snapshots and evidential uses of photography as they do to photographic artworks.

This reluctance of philosophers to descend from general analyses of 'the photograph' to come to grips with questions about photographic art can be explained in part by the relatively recent invention of photography and also by a past tendency to disparage the notion of photographic art. Now that most major art collections include works of photographic art, there are fewer excuses for ignoring photography's most ambitious employment. True, there are still those who agree with Baudelaire, who in 1859 declared that photography's true duty was 'to be the servant of the sciences and arts—but the very humble servant, like printing or shorthand, which have neither created nor supplemented literature' (Baudelaire 1859: 113). But most writers on photography now at least acknowledge that photographic art is possible, even if, with notable exceptions (such as Snyder and Allen 1975, Batkin 1991, and Savedoff 1999), they have had relatively little to say about particular examples of it.

1. BAZIN AND CAVELL: AUTOMATIC PICTURES

Much late twentieth-century philosophizing about photography is the direct descendant of Realist film theory. André Bazin is a major influence here. In his short essay 'The Ontology of the Photographic Image' (Bazin 1945) he isolated a number of themes that subsequent photography theorists have taken up and elaborated. He allowed that still photography had achieved many of the aims of Baroque art by producing likenesses in geometrical perspective, but his main claim was that photography had gone much further than this. Photographs are not just good likenesses in the way that paintings can be: their idiosyncratic causal link with their subject matter places them in a class apart. To convey this idea, Bazin made a hyperbolic identification of image and object represented:

The photographic image is the object itself, the object freed from the conditions of time and space that govern it. (Bazin 1945: 14)

Presumably he couldn't have meant that my photograph of Georges Simenon actually is Simenon. A comment in a later essay, 'Theatre and Cinema', provides a gloss on this exaggerated account:

Its automatic genesis distinguishes it radically from the other techniques of reproduction. The photograph proceeds by means of the lens to the taking of a veritable impression in light—to a mold. As such it carries with it more than mere resemblance, namely a kind of identity. (Bazin 1951: 96)

In other words, the photograph is different in kind from other forms of pictorial representation. My photograph of Simenon doesn't just look like him: it is somehow closer, or more intimately connected, to the man than a drawing or painting could be, a kind of relic.

In 'The Ontology of the Photographic Image', Bazin claims that photographs do not involve significant intentional input and are therefore in some sense objective. Playing on the fact that in French the lens is called the 'objectif', he writes of the 'essentially objective character of photography'. On the part played by the photographer, he comments:

For the first time an image of the world is formed automatically, without the creative intervention of man. The personality of the photographer enters into the proceedings only in his
selection of the object to be photographed and by way of the purpose he has in mind.
Although the final result may reflect something of his personality, this does not play the
same role as is played by that of the painter. (Bazin 1945: 13)

Bazin's take on photography resurfaced in the 1970s in Stanley Cavell's description
of the medium in his book *The World Viewed* (revised edn 1979, first published in
1971), a work that focused mainly on moving images. There he claimed that in photography the mechanical nature of the process, what he called its 'automatism',
removed the subjective element from pictorial representation:

Photography overcame subjectivity in a way undreamed of by painting, a way that could not
satisfy painting, one which does not so much defeat the act of painting as escape it altogether:
by *automatism*, by removing the human agent from the task of reproduction. (Cavell 1979: 20)

Furthermore, Cavell claimed that all photographs are necessarily of reality in a way
that paintings only rarely are: you can always ask what is behind a building in a
photograph. As he put it, 'We might say: A painting is a world; a photograph is *of*
the world' (Cavell 1979: 24).

Both H. Gene Blocker (1977) and Joel Snyder (1983) took issue with the idea that
a painting's world is fundamentally different from that of a photograph. As will
emerge in my discussion below, claims such as Cavell's only make sense, if at all, of
a particular range of *documentary* or *detective* uses of photography—*pictorial* or
depictive uses of photography, like paintings, create their own worlds.

The idea that photographs are in some sense objective and that they are necessarily of the world is found in one of the more controversial philosophical articles
on photography, Roger Scruton's 'Photography and Representation' (Scruton 1983;
first published 1981). This article and Kendall Walton's 'Transparent Pictures'
(Walton 1984) are the two most significant and most discussed manifestations of
photography theory in the tradition of Bazin. Scruton and Walton are jointly
responsible for persuading analytic philosophers that there are philosophically
interesting questions to be asked about the nature of photographic representation.

2. Scruton and his Critics

Scruton claims that photography, at least in its ideal form, is not an intentional process
but an optico-chemical one. This is consistent with Cavell's account. Paintings present
us with a way of seeing their subjects and embody thoughts about those subjects,

whereas ideal photographs are merely surrogates for their subjects:

With an ideal photograph it is neither necessary nor even possible that the photographer's intention should enter as a serious factor in determining how the picture is seen. It is recognised at once for how something looked. In some sense, looking at a photograph is a substitute for looking at the thing itself. (Scruton 1983: 111)

The subject of a painting may or may not exist; that of an ideal photograph necessarily exists and looks more or less like the photograph: photographs, because of their optico-chemical origins, are *transparent* to what they represent. Photographs are more like mirrors than they are like paintings. The surprising conclusion that Scruton draws from this characterization of ideal photography is that photography is not representational. Clearly, photographs are representational in that they stand in for their objects; but what Scruton means by this claim is that photographs are transparent to their objects, and so are not themselves of aesthetic interest:

if one finds a photograph beautiful, it is because one finds something beautiful in its subjects. A painting may be beautiful, on the other hand, even when it represents an ugly thing. (Scruton 1983: 114)

Many readers took this conclusion to be an attack on the idea that there could be photographic art. Scruton maintained that the medium of photography is 'inherently pornographic', by which he meant that photography provides a substitute for its objects rather than embodied thoughts about those objects.

Scruton concedes that actual photography may differ from the ideal of photography that he describes. Actual photography may involve the photographer exercising control over detail in the photograph, but only at the cost of ceasing to be pure photography: in Scruton's terms, such photography 'pollutes' the medium, turning it into a kind of painting. He is adamant that only the grossest elements of style can be achieved with this essentially transparent medium.

Scruton's article, which has been reprinted in several different versions since its first appearance, has been much criticized (see e.g. Wicks 1989 and King 1992). It seems to be a form of question-begging to define an ideal of photography that differs significantly from actual photography, and then to draw conclusions about the nature of the medium on the basis of it. William King for example, undertook to show through the consideration of specific examples how an interest in a photograph need not be an interest in its subject. He concluded that 'some photographs can be interesting in one way that paintings can be, namely, aesthetically interesting by virtue of the manner of representation' (King 1992: 264). Several years before Scruton's piece appeared, Joel Snyder and Neil Walsh Allen published a wide-ranging article which convincingly undermined the view that photographs 'print themselves' and that photographs show us more or less what the eye sees:

The notion that a photograph shows us 'what we would have seen had we been there ourselves' has to be qualified to the point of absurdity. A photograph shows us 'what we would have seen' at a certain moment in time, *from* a certain point *if* we kept our head immobile *and* closed one eye *and if* we saw things with the equivalent of a 150-mm or 24-mm lens *and if* we saw things in Agfacolor or in Tri-X developed in D76 and printed on Kodabromide 3 paper. By the time all the conditions are added up the original position has been reversed: instead of saying that the camera shows us what our eyes would see, we are now positing the rather unilluminating proposition that, if our vision worked like photography, then we would see things the way a camera does. (Snyder and Allen 1975: 151–2)

Snyder and Allen make a convincing case for the photographer's interpretative role in photographic picture-making, a case that could be used to reply to Scruton's later critique.

However, there is a stronger response to Scruton. This is based on the recognition that sophisticated photographic communication is typically achieved through creating a repertoire of images within which new meanings are given. Scruton was wrong to think of photography as styleless, or at best stylistically impoverished: individual style in photography is not achieved solely by controlling detail within single images (see Warburton 1996). Hence, even if it were true that individual photographic images were styleless because of the photographer's lack of control over detail, it would not follow that the medium was essentially styleless.

3. WALTON AND HIS CRITICS

Snyder and Allen are undoubtedly correct that photographs don't show us precisely what our eyes would have seen. Yet there is a widespread temptation to treat looking at photographs as a mediated way of looking at things. For example, when you look at Bill Brandt's portrait photograph of the painter Francis Bacon on Primrose Hill, it can be tempting to say that you can see Francis Bacon. At least, the experience of looking at a photograph of someone feels more like actually looking at them than does the typical experience of looking at a portrait painting. Many writers on photography have commented on this experience. Roland Barthes describes it in his *Camera Lucida*:

One day, quite some time ago, I happened on a photograph of Napoleon's youngest brother, Jerome, taken in 1852. And I realized then, with an amazement I have not been able to lessen since: 'I am looking at eyes that looked at the Emperor.' (Barthes 1984: 3)

Patrick Maynard, in his dialogue on the subject of photography 'The Secular Icon', gave an explanation of the sense of immediacy that photographs can give:

If there's a bright window opposite a wall and you hold a magnifying glass near the wall you'll be able to see a little image of the window (or what is outside it) on the wall. And by seeing this image you indirectly see what is outside. As you know, a camera is just a device for fixing such images. So by seeing the photograph you indirectly see what it depicts. We see actual things by means of photography. (Maynard 1983: 160).

Kendall Walton developed this idea, arguing that the causal chain from object to photograph allows us literally to see through photographs to their objects:

with the assistance of the camera, we can see not only around corners and what is distant or small; we can also see into the past. We see long deceased ancestors when we look at dusty snapshots of them...We see, quite literally, our dead relatives themselves when we look at photographs of them. (Walton 1984: 251, 252)

This transparency of photography is thus for Walton the essence of photographic realism. Like Bazin, he sees photography as going beyond the aim of achieving verisimilitude: according to Walton, photographic realism is different in kind from realism in painting because we actually see our relatives when we look at photographs of them. And this is true, whether or not the photographs look like the people they are of. His argument to this conclusion relies on going down the slippery slope from ordinary seeing, through seeing through mirrors, glasses, microscopes, telescopes, and television images, to seeing into the past through photographs. We do not see through paintings and drawings, because what we see is mediated by the minds of human beings and is not mechanically produced. If all that were at stake were verisimilitude, then there would be no essential difference between paintings and photographs. As it is, Walton explains, photographic realism is different in kind from realism in painting.

Walton maintains that his account of photography can give a plausible explanation of, for example, a picture being less shocking when the viewer realizes that it is a photograph of a life-sized sculpture, rather than of a nude couple: if it is a photograph of a sculpture then we only see a representation of a couple, whereas if it had been a photograph of the couple, then we would literally see their nakedness. Similarly, Walton believes that his account can explain the particular kind of experience viewers have when they learn that a self-portrait by the photo-realist painter Chuck Close is really a painting and not a photograph:

Our experience of the picture and our attitude toward it undergo a profound transformation, one which is much deeper and more significant than the change which occurs when we discover that what we first took to be an etching, for example, is actually a pen-and-ink drawing. It is more like discovering a guard in a wax museum to be just another wax figure. We feel somehow less 'in contact with' Close when we learn that portrayal of him is not photographic. (Walton 1984: 255).

Walton's critics (e.g. Martin 1986; Warburton 1988b; Currie 1991; Carroll 1996a) have provided a range of arguments for digging our heels in at a certain point on the descent down the slippery slope; or, to use a variant on the metaphor, they have argued that the slope is not as slippery as Walton would have us believe. There *are* relevant differences between ordinary senses of seeing and what Walton thinks of as seeing through photographs. For example, Martin (1986) has argued that more natural breaking points occur when we distinguish between real and virtual images, and that the length of a causal chain is a determining factor in whether or not it is appropriate to describe an experience as one of seeing. Warburton (1988*b*) identified four factors characteristic of ordinary seeing but lacking from the relation between object and photograph: (1) virtual simultaneity (in cases of ordinary seeing, what is seen is happening almost simultaneously with our experience of its happening); (2) sensitivity to change (potentially visible changes in what is seen are matched by changes in what is seen); (3) temporal congruity (actions seen take the same time as it takes us to see them); and (4) viewer's knowledge of the causal chain (we usually have a basic knowledge about how our perceptions are linked to their causes). Gregory Currie (1991) has also argued that Walton goes too far in describing the relationship between viewer and photographed object as a straightforward perceptual one. Against Walton, he maintains that photographs are representational: we do not literally see through them. Currie captures differences between photographs and paintings by describing the former as natural representations and the latter as intentional representations. Photographs are natural representations because they exhibit 'natural dependence' on their objects; that is, they display counterfactual dependence of a kind that need not be mediated by human intention. According to Currie, when I look at a photograph of an ancestor, I see a representation of my ancestor, not the ancestor himself.

Walton has not, however, felt the need to modify his theory in the light of these sorts of criticism, most of which are in Martin (1986). (For Walton's replies, see Walton 1986, 1997.) In his most recent reply, Walton maintains that both Carroll and Currie have misconstrued his transparency thesis. They have assumed that it entails that photographs are not representational; however, his position is that 'photographs, documentary photographs included, induce imagining seeing and are representations (depictions, pictures), in addition to being transparent' (Walton 1997: 68). As Jonathan Friday has made clear in his useful overview of the debate (Friday 1996), the question of whether or not Walton is correct in his analysis of photography ultimately hinges on contentious issues within the philosophy of perception.

4. MEDIUM SPECIFICITY

A notable feature of Scruton's and Walton's articles is their essentialism about photography: Scruton clearly believes that photography has an essence that is captured by his notion of ideal photography and 'polluted' by the use of painterly techniques, while for Walton the essence of photography is its transparency in the special sense he outlines. Bazin and Cavell are equally essentialistic in their treatment of photography. Noël Carroll has put the arguments against essentialism or what he calls 'medium specificity' in photography and film theory in a series of articles (Carroll 1984–5, 1985, 1987, 1996a), reprinted in his *Theorizing the Moving Image* (Carroll 1996b). There he draws attention to the fact that

There is not an essence of photographic media or of photographic representation that directs the evolution of these media or our proper appreciative responses to these media. The media rather are adapted to the cultural purposes and projects we find for them. The relevant types of representation we observe in photography and cinema are not a function of the ontology of the photographic image but of the purposes we have found respectively for still and moving photography. (Carroll 1996b: 48)

If Carroll is right that there is no intrinsic essence of photography, but rather a series of uses to which the various photographic media can be put, then the implication seems to be that philosophers of photography will have to look very closely at some of the ways in which photographs are actually used and at the meanings they are given in those uses. Investigating an 'ideal' of photography, or photography's 'essence', is likely to give a partial and perhaps irrelevant account of the various communicative potentials of the medium as they exist within particular social contexts.

5. Uses of Photography

Patrick Maynard, in a series of articles (Maynard 1983, 1985, 1989, 1991) culminating in the book *The Engine of Visualization* (Maynard 1997), has provided a framework for understanding photography as a range of technologies put to varied uses. These imaging technologies amplify and also filter our powers to detect things and our powers to imagine things. Maynard's work provides a useful antidote to some of the more simplistic assumptions of earlier theorists who have tended to ignore the range of uses of the medium. Maynard distinguishes between photographic detection—determined by what a photograph is of *qua* photochemical trace—and photographic depiction—determined by what it pictures, which may not be the same thing at all. Photographic detections and photographic depictions can both amplify our imaginative powers. The blurring of what a photograph is of with what it is a photographic depiction of has been a continuing source of confusion in the philosophy of photography. In all his writing about photography, Maynard is very clear about this distinction. For instance, in *The Engine of Visualization* he writes:

Like any other depictive technology, photography provides methods of marking surfaces that entice imagining. Sometimes this is accomplished by photographing what is depicted, sometimes not. Movies provide many routine as well as interesting examples.

Although *King Kong* depicts a giant ape climbing the Empire State Building and was made by filming various things, none of them was an ape or the Empire State Building. The photo stills from that sequence are not photographs of what they depict, nor would anyone expect them to be so. (Maynard 1997: 114)

Warburton used a similar distinction to spell out the implications of various photographic deceptions, including the controversy surrounding the alleged staging of Robert Capa's 'Spanish Republican Soldier at the Very Instant of his Death' (Warburton 1991, 1998). We can use the term 'documentary mode' to cover uses of photography where it is assumed that the photograph pictures what it is of; 'pictorial mode' photographs, by contrast, are photographic depictions, which may or may not picture their causes. If Capa's photograph was staged, then his use of it in photojournalistic context was a clear transgression of the role responsibilities of the photojournalist to provide images in the documentary mode, that is, photographs that are at least not deliberately misleading about what they are of.

Barbara Savedoff addresses the philosophical questions that arise for a different widespread use of photography, namely, to reproduce works of art, and particularly paintings (Savedoff 1993, 1999). She maintains that relying on photographic reproductions and treating them as if they were transparent rather than transformative affects the way in which we experience and think about the paintings themselves.

6. PHOTOGRAPHY AND MORAL KNOWLEDGE

In her speculative series of essays published as *On Photography*, Susan Sontag echoed some of Plato's worries about the superficiality of pictorial representations. In particular, she claimed that photographs, because they deal only with static appearances and not with change over time, cannot provide understanding of the world, and so cannot furnish ethical knowledge:

Strictly one never understands anything from a photograph... In contrast to the amorous relation which is based on how something looks, understanding is based on how it functions. And functioning takes place in time, and must be explained in time. Only that which narrates can make us understand.

The limit of photographic knowledge of the world is that, while it can goad conscience, it can, finally, never be ethical or political knowledge. (Sontag 1979: 23–4)

Stephanie Ross (1982) drew on some of Scruton's arguments about photography to find support for Sontag's description of photography's limitations. Her conclusions, however, like Sontag's, are misleading. Photography *does* have a range of narrative techniques available to it, such as the use of a series of images, or of an implied appropriate reading of events unfolding in time, and consequently the attack on photography's potential to communicate about events taking place over time is arguably misplaced (see Warburton 1988*a*).

7. Towards a Philosophy of Photographic Art

The philosophical investigation of photographic art is still in a relatively early phase. Few of those philosophers who have turned their attention to photography have addressed in detail questions that arise specifically for photographic art as opposed to photography in general. One recent exception is Barbara Savedoff in her *Transforming Images* (Savedoff 1999). Savedoff stresses the transformative powers of photographs: photographs transform their subject matter in various ways, yet we cannot easily help seeing them as recording or documenting reality. Rightly or wrongly, we perceive photographs as more objective than paintings. This combination of features gives the experience of viewing photographs its unique character. The power of particular photographic images to fascinate us often depends on their transformative nature. Savedoff makes her case, which is illuminating about our experience of photographic art, by drawing on a range of photographic examples, including photographs of representations.

Warburton has addressed another aspect of photographic art, the question of which photographic prints should be considered 'authentic' or definitive, and why (Warburton 1997). He argues that the artworld's preference for so-called 'vintage prints' is not generally a rational one.

8. Digital Photography

The recent invention of digital photography has already brought about many changes in the ways photographs are used and understood. The new technology converts an image to pixels, each of which can be electronically controlled. It has allowed analogue images to be replaced with digital ones, thus permitting exact reproduction—a direct result of the fact that digital photographs carry a fixed amount of information. This has once again raised questions of photographic

evidence: now that photographs can be so easily manipulated in virtually undetectable ways, by almost anyone, without leaving the archival evidence of tamper-
ing provided by a negative, a number of writers have suggested that the days
of documentary photography are numbered. William J. Mitchell, for example,
has declared that we are entering a 'post-photographic age', a position based on
a somewhat sentimental view of photography's past:

the process of photographic image construction is highly standardized, its representational
commitments are well known, and the intentional relationships of standard photographs to
their subject are relatively straightforward and unambiguous. (Mitchell 1992: 222).

More plausibly, Savedoff (1997, 1999) has speculated about the possible implications
of the new technology, emphasizing the inevitable shift in the aesthetics of photography once, as seems likely, the 'evidential authority surrounding traditional photographs' is lost. Other writers (Ritchin 1990; Warburton 1998) have argued that the
new technology for the most part brings to the fore issues that have always existed
for photography, such as the relationship between documentary photographs and
reality:

In the field of photojournalism it is clear that journalistic principles and not vague photographic mythology must be invoked in attempting to maintain both an active role for the
photograph and the public's confidence. Such clarification should encourage a belated
acknowledgement of photography's subjectivity and range, its different uses, approaches,
sources, and ambitions. Photographs will have to be treated less monolithically, with the
understanding that, like words, images can be used for a variety of purposes and can be produced according to different strategies. They may be factual or fantastic, reportorial or opin-
ionated. (Ritchin 1990: 144)

Far from inevitably bringing about the demise of documentary photography, the
invention of digital photography and the range of new choices it gives photographs
should clarify its value in providing legible visual evidence that has the power to
extend our moral imaginations. The conventions of documentary photography *can*
continue to exist alongside the pictorialist conventions of digital imaging, though
this is by no means inevitable.

9. CONCLUSION

The philosophy of photography remains a relatively unexplored area of aesthetics.
There are many important questions yet to be addressed concerning photojournalism and photographic art, questions drawing on the philosophy of representation,
on ethics, and on the theory of criticism.

See also: Painting; Film; Representation in Art; Medium in Art; Style in Art; Art and Morality; Aesthetics of Popular Art.

BIBLIOGRAPHY

Barthes, R. (1984). *Camera Lucida*, trans. R. Howard. London: Fontana.

Batkin, N. (1991). 'Paul Strand's Photographs in *Camerawork*'. *Midwest Studies in Philosophy* 16: 314–51.

Baudelaire, C. (1859). 'Photography', in B. Newhall (ed.) (1981) *Photography: Essays and Images*. London: Secker and Warburg pp. 112–14.

Bazin, A. (1945). 'The Ontology of the Photographic Image', reprinted in A. Bazin, *What is Cinema?*, trans. H. Gray. Berkeley: University of California Press, 1967, pp. 9–17.

—— (1951). 'Theatre and Cinema', in A. Bazin, *What is Cinema?*, trans. H. Gray. Berkeley: University of California Press, 1967, pp. 76–124.

Blocker, H. (1977). 'Pictures and Photographs'. *Journal of Aesthetics and Art Criticism* 36: 155–62.

Carroll, N. (1984–5). 'Medium Specificity Arguments and the Self-consciously Invented Arts'. *Millenium Film Journal* 14/15: 127–53; reprinted in Carroll (1996*b*): 3–24.

—— (1985). 'The Specificity of Media in the Arts'. *Journal of Aesthetic Education* 19: 5–20; reprinted in Carroll (1996*b*): 25–36.

—— (1987). 'Concerning Uniqueness Claims for Photographic and Cinematographic Representation'. *Dialectics and Humanism* 2: 29–43; reprinted in Carroll (1996*b*): 37–48.

—— (1996*a*). 'Defining the Moving Image', in Carroll (1996*b*): 49–74.

—— (1996*b*). *Theorizing the Moving Image*. Cambridge: Cambridge University Press.

Cavell, S. (1979). *The World Viewed*, rev. edn. Cambridge, Mass.: Harvard University Press; first published 1971.

Currie, G. (1991). 'Photography, Painting and Perception'. *Journal of Aesthetics and Art Criticism* 49: 23–9.

—— (1998). 'Photography, Aesthetics of', in E. Craig (ed.), *The Routledge Encyclopedia of Philosophy*, vol. 7. London: Routledge, pp. 378–80.

Friday, J. (1996). 'Transparency and the Photographic Image'. *British Journal of Aesthetics* 36: 30–42.

—— (2001). 'Photography and the Representation of Vision'. *Journal of Aesthetics and Art Criticism* 59: 351–62.

—— (2002). *The Aesthetics of Photography*. Aldershot: Ashgate.

King, W. (1992). 'Scruton and the Reasons for Looking at Photographs'. *British Journal of Aesthetics* 32: 258–65.

Martin, E. (1986). 'On Seeing Walton's Great-Grandfather'. *Critical Inquiry* 12: 796–800.

Maynard, P. (1983). 'The Secular Icon: Photography and the Functions of Images'. *Journal of Aesthetics and Art Criticism* 42: 155–70.

—— (1985). 'Drawing and Shooting: Causality in Depiction'. *Journal of Aesthetics and Art Criticism* 44: 115–29.

—— (1989). 'Talbot's Technologies: Photographic Depiction, Detection, and Reproduction'. *Journal of Aesthetics and Art Criticism* 47: 263–76.

Maynard, P. (1991). 'Photo-opportunity: Photography as Technology'. *Canadian Review of American Studies* 22: 501–28.

—— (1997). *The Engine of Visualization: Thinking through Photography*. Ithaca, NY: Cornell University Press.

—— (2001). 'Photograpy', in B. Gaut and D. Lopes (eds.), *Routledge Companion to Aesthetics*. London: Routledge.

Mitchell, W. (1992). *The Invented Eye: Visual Truth in the Post-Photographic Era*. Cambridge, Mass.: MIT Press.

Ritchin, F. (1990). *In Our Own Image: The Coming Revolution in Photography*. New York: Aperture.

Ross, S. (1982). 'What Photographs Can't Do'. *Journal of Aesthetics and Art Criticism* 41: 5–17.

Savedoff, B. (1993). 'Looking at Art Through Photographs'. *Journal of Aesthetics and Art Criticism* 51: 455–62.

—— (1997). 'Escaping Reality: Digital Imagery and the Resources of Photography'. *Journal of Aesthetics and Art Criticism* 55: 201–14.

—— (1999). *Transforming Images: How Photography Complicates the Picture*. Ithaca, NY: Cornell University Press.

Scruton, R. (1983). 'Photography and Representation', in R. Scruton, *The Aesthetic Understanding: Essays in The Philosophy of Art and Culture*. London: Methuen, pp. 102–26; first published in *Critical Inquiry* 7: 577–603.

Snyder, J. (1983). 'Photography and Ontology', in J. Margolis (ed.), *The Worlds of Art and the World*. Amsterdam: Rodopi, pp. 21–34.

—— and Allen, N. W. (1975). 'Photography, Vision and Representation'. *Critical Inquiry* 2: 143–69.

Sontag, S. (1979). *On Photography*. Harmondsworth: Penguin.

Walton, K. (1984). 'Transparent Pictures: On the Nature of Photographic Realism'. *Critical Inquiry* 11: 246–77.

—— (1986). 'Looking Again through Photographs: A Response to Edwin Martin'. *Critical Inquiry* 12: 801–8.

—— (1997). 'On Pictures and Photographs: Objections Answered', in R. Allen and M. Smith (eds.), *Film Theory and Philosophy*. Oxford: Oxford University Press, pp. 60–75.

Warburton, N. (1988a). 'Photographic Communication'. *British Journal of Aesthetics* 28: 173–81.

—— (1988b). 'Seeing Through "Seeing through Photographs" '. *Ratio*, n.s. 1: 64–74.

—— (1991). 'Varieties of Photographic Representation'. *History of Photography* 15: 203–10.

—— (1996). 'Individual Style in Photographic Art'. *British Journal of Aesthetics* 36: 389–97.

—— (1997). 'Authentic Photographs'. *British Journal of Aesthetics* 37: 129–37.

—— (1998). 'Ethical Photojournalism in the Age of the Electronic Darkroom', in M. Kieran (ed.), *Media Ethics*. London: Routledge, pp. 123–34.

Wicks, R. (1989). 'Photography as Representational Art'. *British Journal of Aesthetics* 29: 1–9.

FILM

BERYS GAUT

1. FILM THEORY AND PHILOSOPHY

TODAY the philosophy of film is in a thriving state. Indeed, for quality, variety, and interest of the work being done, it is arguably rivalled among the philosophies of the individual arts only by the philosophy of music. It also exhibits a striking feature which, if not unique among the philosophies of the arts, is at least highly unusual: many philosophers and film theorists are interacting with each others' work and learning from each other. Much, though certainly not all, of the work of philosophers has been critical of aspects of film theory, but the interaction has been fruitful for both disciplines. This interplay is witnessed by several anthologies in which both film theorists and philosophers of film are included (Bordwell and Carroll 1996; Allen and Smith 1997; Plantinga and Smith 1999). And probably the most widely used introductory film anthology includes writings by the philosophers Noël Carroll, Stanley Cavell, and Gilbert Harman (Braudy and Cohen 1999).

Philosophy of film is almost as old as the medium itself (which was invented in the mid-1890s): Hugo Munsterberg, a philosopher and psychologist, wrote a pioneering work on film in 1916. However, film began to attract wide philosophical attention only in the 1970s, which saw seminal books and articles appear by Cavell (1979, first edition 1971), Francis Sparshott (1992, first published 1971), Alexander Sesonske (1973), and Arthur Danto (1979). Since then writings in the philosophy of film have burgeoned; more recent important philosophical monographs on film include those of Carroll (1988a,b, 1990), Currie (1995), and Wilson (1986). Besides books and articles on the philosophy of film in general, there have also been many studies of individual films by philosophers. And since 1994 there has been a specialist journal covering the field, *Film and Philosophy*.

Given the role that film theory has played in setting the agenda for the philosophy of film, it is worth briefly rehearsing film theory's development. Classical film theory began shortly after the invention of film. Its concerns were broadly threefold. First, a new medium had been born: but was it art? Its rootedness in scientific experiments and its mechanical means of recording seemed to rule out any role for individual expression or for created form, which argued against its artistic status. Classical film theorists such as Rudolf Arnheim (1957) were keen to defend film against such charges and to show that it was indeed an artform. Second, owing to its photographic basis, film seemed to be in some sense a pre-eminently realist medium, and therefore to have new artistic resources distinct from earlier artforms: Bazin (1967) and Kracauer (1960) investigated the nature of film realism. Third, if film is an art, then it seemed to many that there must be an identifiable artist responsible for each film; hence auteurists (such as Sarris 1999; Perkins 1972: chapter 8) argued for the existence of a single author of a film, normally identified as the director. As we shall see, all of these issues have been of interest to philosophers. Indeed, in its central concerns, in its clarity of expression and in its precision of argument, classical theory bears some affinity to contemporary philosophy of film.

The second kind of theory, contemporary film theory, came to prominence in the mid-1960s. Its central claim was that film is a kind of language. That idea had been mooted by some classical theorists, such as Eisenstein (1992), but it received its most sustained defence at the hands of Christian Metz (1974). To this claim was later added the thesis that psychoanalysis, in particular that form represented by the works of Jacques Lacan, is central both to the understanding of the film medium and to understanding viewers' responses to films (Metz 1982). Contemporary film theorists also argued for the pervasiveness of ideology in film in virtue of certain features of the medium or of certain major kinds of films, such as realist ones (Spellerberg 1985). This kind of film theory is still the dominant force in film studies, but of late it has grown more pluralistic and somewhat less interested in building grand theory. In particular, the increased influence of feminism (Mulvey 1999), of political criticism, and of black studies (Stam and Spence 1999) has led to an investigation into the ways cinema represents its subjects and the ideological presuppositions it thereby brings to bear on them. Several philosophers have been intensely critical of the three main claims just outlined (e.g. Currie 1995; Carroll 1988b, 1996b).

Within the last fifteen years or so, there has grown up a third kind of film theory: cognitive film theory. Its most influential exponent is David Bordwell (1985, 1989), perhaps the outstanding living film theorist, who has sought to blend findings from cognitive psychology with a basically formalist aesthetics. Other cognitive theorists have also drawn on findings in neural science (Grodal 1997) and even on work in analytic philosophy (Smith 1995) to throw light on viewers' emotional responses to films and on how these responses are guided by film genres and narrative patterns. Cognitive film theory is still very much a minority position within film studies, but it has proved enormously important to the philosophy of film in its receptivity to a dialogue with analytic philosophy. Its interest in how viewers interpret films and emotionally respond to them has also helped shape some of the issues in the philosophy of film.

The main contribution of philosophy to our understanding of film so far has probably not lain in identifying new issues or puzzles about film, which have been set largely by film theory, but in bringing greater conceptual sophistication to the debate. Notions of realism, language, and interpretation are of central concern to philosophy in general, and it is unsurprising if philosophers have succeeded in identifying a great deal of confusion with which they have been handled in film theory. A wide range of issues have been addressed by philosophers. These include: criticism of some of the claims of classical and contemporary film theory (Carroll 1988*a*,*b*) and of cognitive film theory (Gaut 1995; Wilson 1997*a*); criticism of the view that there is a language of film (Harman 1999; Currie 1995: chapter 4); the question of whether cinematic meaning is determined by authors' intentions (Currie 1995: chapter 8); the nature of cinematic narration and point of view (Wilson 1986, 1997*b*); the role of music in film (Levinson 1996; Kivy 1997); problems of the analysis of and tenability of the concept of non-fiction cinema (Carroll 1996*c*); the phenomenology of cinematic time and space (Sesonske 1973, 1974); whether we imagine seeing fictional objects in cinematic depictions or impersonally perceptually imagine them (Walton 1990: chapter 8; Walton 1997; Currie 1995: chapter 6); and various problems to do with genre, especially horror (Carroll 1990; Freeland 1999). This list could easily be extended, and to it could be added what is now a considerable body of work by philosophers analysing individual films (preeminently Cavell 1981 and Wilson 1986). In order to be able to address some of the issues in depth, I will here focus on just four of them: the issue of the status of film as an art; the question of film authorship; the sense in which film is a realist medium; and the nature of viewers' responses to films. (For an overview of some more of the issues, see Gaut 1997*a*.) Detailed examination of these central issues should give the reader a sense of the nature of the debates in the field and of the interplay between philosophy and film theory.

2. FILM AND ART

Arnheim put the challenge to film's artistic status succinctly this way: 'Film cannot be art, for it does nothing but reproduce reality mechanically' (Arnheim 1957: 8). This simple sentence masks two distinct challenges. The first centres around the idea of reproduction: Arnheim held that if something is an exact visual reproduction of an object, as a waxwork is of a person, then there is no room for expression, which is essential to art, for there is no room for divergence between the look of the reproduction and that of the object. Arnheim's response in defence of film was to note that film does diverge substantially from reality—e.g. it is a two-dimensional image, has a frame around it, involves editing, etc.—and that these divergences can be used for artistic expression; for instance, montage (editing) was one of the great artistic devices of silent cinema. However, since sound film diverges inherently less from reality than does silent film, he held that sound film is inherently aesthetically inferior to silent film. (The first edition of Arnheim's book was published in 1933, only a few years after the introduction of sound film.) Arnheim also held that, to be aesthetically valuable, works of art in a medium must diverge in a way specific, i.e. unique, to that medium (so, for instance, editing is specific to film).

Arnheim's basic point here is undoubtedly correct: film and reality do diverge, in the sense that a film of some object is easily perceptually discriminable from the object itself. But his theory has received extensive criticism. It is not clear that expression is an essential property of art, nor is it clear that exact reproductions cannot be expressive (think of some of Duane Hanson's realist sculptures); and, if we hold that works have artistic value only when they diverge in a way specific to their medium, then we would have to judge as aesthetically irrelevant to film all those capacities, such the ability to narrate, which film has in common with other media, such as novels and poetry. (For an extended account and criticism of Arnheim's theory, see Carroll 1988a: 17–91.) Perhaps the most striking sign of a failure in Arnheim's basic theory is his conclusion about the inherent aesthetic inferiority of sound film. This derives from his tendency to think of divergences as limitations of representational capacity—for example, silent film is incapable of representing sound. But what really matters is not limitation, but the capacity to represent an object in different ways, e.g. by employing different lighting, different lenses, and different camera movement. Variations in the modes of representing an object allow genuine cinematic expression, for how an object is filmed may be employed to convey an expressive point about it; and this is to do with enhanced capacities for representation, not limitations on representational capacities. That is why Arnheim's conclusion about silent film is wrong: for instance, only in a sound film, but not in a silent film, can silence be expressive, since only in the sound film can we construe silence as conveying something expressive, because only here did the filmmaker have a choice about whether or not to use sound at that point, i.e. a choice about how to represent reality.

The other part of Arnheim's challenge has also received extensive philosophical discussion. This is the point about the 'mechanical' nature of the medium, or, to put it more precisely, the causal basis of photographic images. Roger Scruton has developed this theme for photography, and has explicitly drawn a negative conclusion about the possibility of a genuinely cinematic art: 'A film is a photograph of a dramatic representation; it is not, because it cannot be, a photographic representation.

It follows that if there is such a thing as a cinematic masterpiece it will be so because—like *Wild Strawberries* and *La Règle du jeu*—it is in the first place a dramatic masterpiece' (Scruton 1983: 102). In other words, a film, if it is art, is so merely because of the artistry evinced in what went on in front of the camera, not by virtue of anything the filming itself contributes. This is because film, being a photographic medium, does not consist of representations in Scruton's special sense of the term: a representation is something that communicates thoughts, and thoughts are intentional states. However, photographs, being causal rather than intentional, are incapable of communicating thoughts (or to be precise, this is the case with 'ideal' photographs—photographs not subject to any special manipulation, such as overpainting, etc.). Only if an image can communicate a thought about its subject matter can we take an aesthetic interest in it, since such an interest is directed not at the subject of the image, but at its mode of presentation, i.e. the thought communicated about it. It follows that film, not consisting of representations, cannot be a genuine art.

Scruton's argument is provocative, and captures very well a traditional worry about the status of film as an art. It has received extensive discussion, though one chiefly directed at its claims about static photographs rather than its conclusions about film. However, Scruton's view about photography should be rejected, since one can in fact take an aesthetic interest in how a photograph treats its subject; for example, one can note of Anselm Adams's photographs of Yosemite that, through careful choice of point of view, lighting conditions, etc., they achieve an aesthetic transformation, making something that is dramatically real look very unreal (King 1992; see also Wicks 1989). Scruton does correctly identify a truth about photographs: it follows logically, since the photographic relation is a causal one, that if something is a photograph of some object then that object existed at the time the photograph was taken. (Strictly speaking, it follows that the object existed at *or before* the time that the photograph was taken, since we can take photographs of stars that have ceased to exist by the time that their light reaches the earth.) But it does not follow from this that photographs cannot express thoughts about their subjects, as King's example illustrates. The existence of a photograph of some object entails that this object existed at (or before) the time of its taking, and, by virtue of this entailment, that is a non-intentional relation. But the photograph can in addition convey intentional thoughts about the object, thoughts that do not entail that the object has those properties (for instance, in the case of the Adams photograph, that the object looks unreal—and the same point applies of course to features that in fact the object really does possess). All that Scruton's argument proves is the narrowly logical point just noted. It follows from this that it is not a *necessary* feature of photographs that they convey thoughts; hence there could be 'natural' photographs, i.e. photographs that through some freak of nature are formed without human intervention. But the mere logical possibility of such photographs does not show that photographs cannot in addition communicate thoughts about their objects as a contingent matter—and the vast majority of actual photographs do convey such thoughts, for actual photographs are almost invariably the product of intentional human selection (Gaut 2002).

3. AUTHORSHIP

The question of the status of film as an art is connected with that of film authorship. For, despite its apparent reference to a literary model, the notion of a film author is broader than that of a writer, being basically that of a film artist; and if film is an art, there must be film artists. An early exponent of auteurism was the French director François Truffaut in 1954, who was clear in his polemical intent to defend film as an artform and in particular to show the director to be the author of the film. In 1962 that view was given more systematic treatment by Andrew Sarris (1999), who applied it to generate a 'pantheon' of great directors and great films, and it has transmuted into various forms to become one of the most influential views about film.

Much of the critical discussion of the idea of authorship has centred on the question of whether it is possible for the type of film that involves multiple collaborators (director, producer, screenwriter, actors, etc.), a type that we will call the 'mainstream' film, to have a single author in the way that a novel uncontentiously can have one. Perkins (1972: chapter 8) has argued that it can: the director can control the artistically significant synthetic relationships of a film, which make a film a *film*, and thereby be author of it, while his collaborators control the artistically extraneous elements which stand in these relationships. Moreover, the director does not need absolute control to author the film: he can, through his choice of collaborators and what he permits them to do, achieve sufficient control to make him author. But Perkins gives no criterion for individuating relationships from elements in a film, and however one does so, it is clear that there are artistically significant features of a film that are not to be ascribed to the director alone, such as the acting. Moreover, though a director can often choose his collaborators and exercise a degree of control and selection over their activity, that hardly makes him the sole author of a film. In the same way, a stage-director would not count as sole author of a performance of a play, even though he exercised a similar degree of control over the actors and stage-designers—many artists are involved in the performance. It is true of many collaborative artforms that there is often a dominant collaborator, but that does not make him or her the only artist involved; we ought to hold that all mainstream films are examples of multiple authorship.

Paisley Livingston has however defended the possibility of single authorship of a mainstream film. Livingston defines an author as 'the agent (or agents) who intentionally make(s) an utterance, where "utterance" refers to any action, an intended function of which is expression or communication' (Livingston 1997: 134). (This definition removes the necessary connection of authorship to artistry which has been important in the tradition.) Livingston argues that there are films that have makers, but no authors, since no one has sufficient overall control for the film to reflect his expressive or communicative intentions: the resulting film is akin to a traffic jam, which is the unintended result of multiple but conflicting intentional actions. And even when single authorship exists, in some cases it is partial, since the director may for instance be strongly constrained by the producer's fiat. However, Livingston holds that in some cases we can legitimately talk of the single author of a mainstream film: Ingmar Bergman is the sole author of *Winter Light*, even though it was produced within the confines of the Swedish studio system. But Livingston's defence still rests on the view that someone who is in overall control of the film, and who chooses and supervises his collaborators, is its single author, so similar objections to those just noted about Perkins's position apply to Livingston's defence as well.

Livingston also develops the idea of an 'unauthored' film, the product of clashing intentions between makers of a film, none of whom has effective artistic control of it. Livingston is surely correct in calling attention to the possibility of such films, but his argument for their existence seems to rest on the view that, if no one with communicative intentions is in overall control of the film, then it is unauthored. But that is too strong a claim in general: the Surrealists used to play a game called 'cadavre exquis', in which each artist drew a head, body, or legs, and folded the paper after his or her turn, thus obscuring what had been drawn to the next player. A literary equivalent involving writing a short story can readily be imagined; and this is more naturally described as a case of multiple authors, operating in ignorance of each other's actions, rather than being a case of an unauthored story. The situation that Livingston holds to be one of an 'unauthored' film may very often be better thought of as involving multiple authors (and, unlike the Surrealist case, they would also be aware of each other's actions), who, rather than being in harmony with each other's intentions, have artistic conflicts with each other. This is a not uncommon situation in film-making: perhaps the best-known example is *The Cabinet of Dr Caligari*.

Another argument for single authorship in mainstream films involves thinking of the author not as a real individual, as we have been holding up to now, but as a critical construct, an implied or postulated author (Nowell-Smith 1981; Wilson 1986: 134–9). Application of the notion of a critical construct is best thought of as a matter of interpreting and evaluating a film *as if* it were the product of a single individual. This has the advantage of freeing the author from the limits of control experienced by real individuals. However, even applied to critical constructs, we should hold that mainstream films have multiple, not single, authors. One criterion for the existence of an author is the presence of a *persona* manifested in the film; yet clearly not just directors, but also actors, composers, set designers, and so on, have *personae* that can be manifested in films. And if we were to imagine a mainstream film as being made by a single individual, we would have to imagine him performing all aspects of production, including the acting. Not only would the most ordinary film become a stupendous achievement of multi-faceted versatility, but also, the being who did this would have to be thought of as literally superhuman, able to move actors as you or I can move our limbs, since his would be the only artistic agency involved. Even if we could render intelligible the idea of such a being, it would be absurd to try to understand the film in terms of his manifested attitudes, for the psychology of such a being would be utterly opaque to us (Gaut 1997*b*).

4. REALISM

The question of what might be meant by calling film a 'realistic' medium, and whether this is true, has exercised philosophers as much as it has interested film theorists. We have already noted Scruton's point that, because of the causal nature of the photographic mechanism, it follows from the existence of a photograph that the object photographed existed at (or before) the time the photograph was taken, whereas the same is not true of a painting. This is a genuine sense of realism—call it ontological realism—and photographic films are in this sense realistic.

A second, more commonly defended, notion of realism is that of illusionism. This holds that films standardly create an illusion in the minds of their spectators, a very popular view with contemporary film theorists. Currie usefully distinguishes between cognitive and perceptual illusions. The former involve a false belief—for instance that the object depicted is real and the viewer is in its presence. But this hardly squares with the standard reactions of cinema viewers: were they really under the illusion that they were in the presence of an axe-wielding maniac depicted in a horror film, they would flee the cinema (Currie 1995: 22–4). Perceptual illusions in contrast need involve no false belief: I may know in the Müller–Lyer illusion that the two lines are of the same length, yet my experience represents them as of different lengths. In this sense, we also do not have illusions of physical objects present before us in cinema, for the content of our experience is of being in the presence of *images* of physical objects (Currie 1995: 44). Intriguingly, Currie also argues that there is not even an illusion of movement of images: the movement of cinematic images is a real, though response-dependent, property (pp. 34–47). He points out that the standard reason for thinking that cinematic motion is an illusion fails, since, even though there are only static images on the celluloid roll, the claim is that it is what is on the screen that moves, not what is hidden in the camera. He also notes that holding that cinematic movement is a product of our perceptual system is compatible with it being a response-dependent property, not an illusory one (pp. 38–9).

Despite its considerable ingenuity, Currie's view that cinematic motion is not illusory should be rejected. Genuine movement is continuous; i.e., things do not jump from one spatial point to another without successively occupying all of the intervening points between the start and end points. Yet sequences of cinematic images, i.e. light-patterns on the screen, are not continuous in this sense. So they do not move: they are a succession of still images. Contrast the case with shadow-plays: if I make the shape of a rabbit with my hands in a projector's light, then when the shadow moves it will occupy all of the intervening points between the start of the sequence and the end. A film of the shadow-play might be perceptually indiscriminable from the shadow-play, and so would present itself as if the image-sequence were continuous: but it would not be continuous, and hence there would be a mere illusion of movement. (For this and other objections, see Kania 2002.)

Currie would likely protest that this argument assumes that the light-pattern on the screen is identical with the cinematic image, whereas he holds that the latter merely supervenes on the former; and this allows him to hold that the cinematic image possesses properties, such as real movement, which its subvening basis does not (Currie 1995: 40). I doubt whether Currie's non-identity claim is correct; but in any case we need not settle the issue here, given another point that he makes. He discusses a scenario where, in a totally darkened cinema, a stationary point of light is projected on to the screen, and spectators have the illusion that the point is moving. This is an illusion, says Currie, since it is a necessary condition for genuine movement of an image that 'at each place on the screen occupied by the image as it moves, there should be illumination at that place (and at the relevant time) on the screen' (Currie 1995: 46). But, by the same criterion, cinematic images do not genuinely move. For when a cinematic image appears to move continuously, since the associated sequence of light-patterns is static and discontinuous, there will be many points on the screen where the image appears to be, but where there is no illumination at those times. Moreover, cinema images are projected in rapid bursts of light, and between exposures there is no light coming from the projector, so that audiences spend about half their viewing time watching films in darkness. During these times there appears to be a cinematic image, even though there is no light-pattern anywhere on the screen. Not only is there an illusion of movement in cinema, there is also an associated illusion of continuous illumination of the screen.

A third kind of realism mooted for cinema is what has been called perceptual realism. This holds that photographic images, and thereby films, look in significant respects like their objects. The difficulty facing this kind of claim is well known: unless we can say in what respects the resemblance holds, the claim is vacuous, for with a little ingenuity we can find an infinite number of similarities between any pair of objects (Goodman 1976: chapter 1). Solving this conundrum is, of course, a leading problem for theory of depiction in general, not just of photography and film. The most promising way to specify the resemblance is, plausibly, in response-dependent terms: photographs and their objects resemble each other by virtue of triggering the same recognitional capacities (Currie 1995: chapter 3). Hence a photograph of Rock Hudson and Rock himself both trigger the Rock-recognizing capacity, and the visual properties they have in common are whatever the ones are that explain this response. However, even if this account is rejected, it is intuitively compelling that there are salient respects in which photographs and their objects resemble each other; and, however we spell this out, it is clear that films will generally count as a realistic mode of depiction in the perceptual sense of the term.

A fourth and final sense in which cinematic realism has been defended is that of transparency. This is the claim that when we look at a photograph we are literally seeing the object photographed (Walton 1984). Just as we really see objects through our spectacles, through microscopes, telescopes, and in mirrors, so we really see objects through photographs. The fact that photographs are the products of intentional actions and can express an individual style is quite compatible with this claim: all artefacts are the products of intentional actions, and one could easily imagine mirrors set up and ground so as to reflect an individual style. Moreover, the fact that the object depicted no longer exists does not show that we are not seeing it, for the same may be true of the stars seen through a telescope. Besides these analogies, the core reason for holding that photographs are transparent is that they exhibit counterfactual dependence on the scene photographed: what is recorded depends on what is in front of the camera, not on the photographers' beliefs about what is in front of the camera. Paintings, in contrast, are counterfactually dependent on painters' beliefs about the scene. Visual experience is like a photograph in being counterfactually dependent on the scene in front of one, not on beliefs; and looking at a photograph is also, in certain ways, like looking at the scene depicted. So there are good grounds for holding that to look at a photograph is to look at the object photographed.

Walton's argument that photographs are transparent (which has points of contact with Bazin's views: see Bazin 1967) has been widely criticized (Currie 1995: chapter 2; Carroll 1996a; Warburton 1988). A common objection is that photographs cannot be transparent since actual vision always provides egocentric information (where an object lies in relation to my body), whereas photographs standardly do not. However, as Walton has argued, it isn't essential to ordinary vision that it provide egocentric information: a series of mirrors can be set up so that I have no idea where the object I see in the mirrors is in relation to me, yet it is implausible to deny that I don't really see it (Walton 1997: 70). Currie has also criticized transparency by employing a counter-example of the two clocks: suppose there is a clock, B, the hands of which are controlled by radio signals by the hands of another clock, A, which is out of sight. There is thus a non-intentional counterfactual dependence between the hands of B and the hands of A; yet when I look at B I do not thereby see clock A (Currie 1995: 65). Walton agrees, but holds that this is because the counterfactual dependence is not rich enough: only the position and movement of the hands of B depend on those of A; if there were many aspects of B that depended on A, then it would be appropriate to talk of seeing A through B (Walton 1997: 75, fn. 47).

Walton does not tell us how rich the dependence must be for transparency to hold. But let us make it as rich as possible. Suppose that, owing to the gradual depletion of African gorillas' habitat, it is decided some time next century to ban all tourists from visiting them in the wild. Instead, an enterprising showman sets up in the bush several robots which are visually indiscriminable from members of the real colony of gorillas, and has these robots' movements, size, shape, etc., controlled by a computer so that they exactly mimic the movements, size, shape, etc., of the real gorillas a hundred miles away. Then tourists looking at the robots will have an experience that is visually indiscriminable from that of seeing the real gorillas, and this experience will be as richly counterfactually dependent on the features of the gorillas and their movements as one could wish. The showman in advertising his exhibit might say things like 'you can see the gorillas', 'you really see gorillas', and even 'you see real gorillas!' According to Walton's account, each of these utterances is true, even the last, since it is indeed real gorillas that you are seeing through the robots. But all these claims are false: the tourists would justifiably feel that they had been misled.

Walton at times says that he is not especially concerned to be faithful to the ordinary sense of 'see' (Walton 1997: 69); but whatever sense of 'see' his theory might stipulate, it is clearly some distance from the normal sense of the word. Moreover, the example suggests why our normal usage holds that we see through mirrors, telescopes, and spectacles, but not photographs. For what the tourists want is to be in *unmediated* visual contact with the gorillas; i.e., they want to see them. In the case of mirrors, telescopes, and spectacles we think of lack of mediation something like this: a ray of light impinges on some object, and that same ray of light is bounced back into our eyes, even though it may have to travel a very long distance and time to reach us. But in the case of a photograph (or indeed of a live video link) the ray of light impinging on our eyes from the photograph (or screen) is a different ray from that which impinged on the object photographed. And that is why one's visual contact is mediated, and why one does not count as *seeing* the object photographed. Now this piece of folk physics might turn out to be mistaken, and if so that would strengthen the claim that one can see through photographs. But it is a coherent distinction, and grounds a clear difference between looking at photographs or complex robotic representations, and looking at the objects themselves. And it reflects the abiding human desire to be in direct perceptual contact with objects—which is part of the desire that drives people to go to sports events, even though they could 'see' much better what is going on by staying at home and watching a television broadcast of the event. In the normal sense of 'see', then, we do not see through photographs.

5. Emotion, Identification and Point of View

A topic that has been of increasing interest to both philosophers and film theorists in recent years concerns the nature of viewers' responses to films. Films have the capacity to move their audiences powerfully: one explanation of this phenomenon is that audiences are caused to identify with film characters, and that films have peculiar resources to foster this identification, by employing cinematic devices such as the point of view shot. Contemporary film theorists in particular are prone to think that identification is a powerful force in explaining spectatorial response, and have given the notion of identification a psychoanalytic reading (Metz 1982: 46).

Carroll has however attacked the idea that we identify with characters: clearly, we do not believe we are the characters; nor do our mental states completely duplicate those of characters (for instance, Oedipus feels guilt, but we feel pity); and partial duplication of mental states is insufficient for identification, for two people may root for the same athlete in a game, and thus be in partially similar mental states, but neither need identify with the other. Instead, our responses to characters in films should be understood in terms of assimilation: we understand a character's evaluation of her situation from her point of view, assimilate it from an external point of view with other features of the situation which the character may not know about, and then respond emotionally to the whole situation (Carroll 1990: 88–96).

Carroll calls our attention to the important fact that our point of view on a character may not be identical to the character's own: we may know more than she does and respond differently, which is typical of the moment of suspense. And there are good reasons for thinking that films of some complexity often involve multiple points of view, not all of which are those of the characters (Wilson 1986: especially chapter 6). But it does not follow from this that identification does not occur: only that sometimes something other or more than it occurs. In particular, we may agree that we rarely if ever completely duplicate film character's mental states, but it is hard to see why identification requires this. In real life, when I identify with someone in her distress, I imagine what it would be like to go through what has befallen her, but I am not required to duplicate every one of her mental states. (That would be impossible in practice.) Likewise, in the Oedipus case I may still identify with him (imagine what it is like to be in his situation), while also being able to view his situation from outside, and so feel pity. Nor does Carroll's sports example show that identification cannot be partial; for identification requires one's imaginings to be controlled by beliefs about the person with whom one is identifying; and in the sports example the spectators do not even know of each others' existence.

Murray Smith has also questioned the utility of the notion of identification and has proposed that it be replaced with a successor concept—that of engagement—which allows of many different respects in which one might engage with a character.

Drawing on Richard Wollheim's work, Smith distinguishes between central imagining (imagining a character's situation from the inside) and acentral imagining (imagining that something is the case, without imagining it from the inside). Smith holds that the latter is the more important in viewers' responses to films, and that it in turn is to be subdivided into different modes of engagement; for instance, we can talk of the amount of information we share with a character (the degree of alignment we have with her), or the degree with which we sympathize with her (the degree of allegiance we have with her). Smith holds that we may be engaged with a character in one respect but not in another; for instance, it is common in horror films to have a shot from the point of view of the killer stalking his prey, so that we perceptually share his point of view, though we are certainly not asked to sympathize with him (Smith 1995; see also Currie 1995: 175–6 on the point of view shot).

Smith does a valuable service in calling attention to the complexity of our relations to characters, and to the fact that cinematic point of view is more intricate than might at first appear. He also convincingly illustrates that the point of view shot is often not a means for fostering empathy or sympathy with a character— indeed, the reaction shot is often more powerful in that respect. But some of his own classifications are problematic. For instance, he identifies central imagining with empathy, yet I can imagine what it is like to feel as someone does without actually feeling what they do, which is what is required for empathy. Moreover, the notion of identification is not resistant to the kinds of complexity that Smith plausibly thinks an adequate theory of response must acknowledge. If we understand identification in terms not of imagining being a character, but of imagining being in a character's situation, then we can acknowledge that, since a situation has many aspects, there may be many aspects to identification, and identification in one respect may not require identification in another. Then we could talk for instance of perceptual identification (imagining seeing from a character's perspective, as in the point of view shot), affective identification (imagining feeling what he feels), epistemic identification (imagining believing what he believes), and so on, and examine how these different types of identification interact with each other. Though we should acknowledge the complexity of viewers' responses, there thus seems no compelling reason for holding that this requires us to abandon the notion of identification (Gaut 1999).

Alex Neill has defended the importance of empathy in viewers' responses to characters. Empathy should be understood in terms not of what viewers imagine feeling, but in terms of what they actually feel, and where what they feel is grounded on their imaginings of what a character is undergoing, guided by their beliefs about what is fictionally the case. Empathy has an important role in educating us about others' emotions, and in coming to understand others' and our own situations better (Neill 1996). Neill is hesitant about whether identification is a useful concept in talking of empathy, but, provided we distinguish empathic identification (construed broadly in Neill's sense, and involving actual feelings) from imaginative identification (in particular, affective identification, where one imagines these feelings), then again there seems no compelling reason to abandon the notion of identification, but rather to refine it. What Neill has shown is that empathy can be given a coherent definition which allows us to recognize it as an important force in shaping spectators' responses to cinematic characters.

6. CONCLUSION

As we have seen, there is a rich variety of work being done in the philosophy of film today. Where might we expect the subject to develop from here? I offer two brief observations in closing.

Perhaps the most salient feature of the field at present is that, while most analytic philosophers have rejected the psychoanalytic paradigm and the paradigm of film as a language which are embodied within contemporary film theory, we are still at best in the early stages of laying out a comprehensive alternative theory. Indeed, some philosophers have argued against the very possibility of a comprehensive and true theory of film, arguing instead for the development of piecemeal accounts of different aspects of film (Carroll 1996a). However, Currie (1995) goes some way to laying out a comprehensive theory of cinematic representation; and Wilson (1984) goes some way to developing a theory of cinematic point of view and narration. There are thus some grounds for optimism that the philosophy of film might develop a more comprehensive theory of film. Perhaps that theory will be inspired by the cognitive science that is a common influence on Currie's work and on cognitive film studies, which, if it developed, would herald a further tightening of the connections between philosophy and this kind of film theory. But even if the discipline does not follow this route, a comprehensive theory might be based on thinking through systematically the ways in which the nature of the cinematic medium constrains and conditions the features that cinema shares with many other artforms, such as narration, expression, and representation. Such a theory would both reveal what film has in common with other artforms, and show what distinguishes it from them, and why.

The other observation concerns the nature of the medium itself, and how that might affect the development of the subject. For I have to this point been silent on a rather important issue: what are we talking about when we talk about 'film'? In its broadest sense, a film is a moving image. But moving images (cinema in the etymologically rooted sense of the word) historically have come in many kinds. Shadow-plays are the oldest; moving images were also made from 1832 onwards by rotating a disk inscribed with individual drawings, and viewing them in a mirror through slots in the circumference of the disk; and in 1877 light was projected onto a screen through a roll of hand-drawn images (Perkins 1972: 41–2). All of these are moving images, none are based on photographs. (However, modern animated films are photographically based, generally being photographs of drawings.) Similarly, video does not employ photographs, being an analogue electronic medium, rather than a chemically based one; and the advent of fully digital images, which can be stored in a computer and are subject to infinite manipulation, will probably ultimately lead to the demise of photographic film. Photographic moving imagery (film in the narrow sense) is thus only one of many types of moving imagery, and the day of film in this sense may well be passing: we already have films composed entirely of digitally produced images which have been transferred to photographic film for purposes of commercial projection, and the next stage will be to project these directly, without using the photographic medium.

Philosophers have scarcely addressed the importance of the distinction between moving images and film in the narrow sense; but there are important essential differences between them. As we saw in Section 2, from the fact that a photograph is a causally generated image, it follows that its object existed at (or before) the time the photograph was made. But it does not follow of a set of hand-drawn moving images that their objects ever existed. (If the drawings were photographically recorded and the photographs projected, as is the case with most modern animated films, it follows of course that the *drawings* existed at the time they were recorded.) Nor does it follow of a purely digitally generated image that its object existed—such images need not be based on a recording of some object, but can be generated by a computer programme. The philosophy of film has concentrated almost exclusively on photographic images, and for purposes of our survey we have done likewise. But, as should now be clear, since photographic film is only one of a broader range of moving image media, we need to disentangle systematically which aspects of photographic films depend on their photographic nature and which on their being moving images. Such a project would allow us better to understand photographic film itself, and would create space for philosophical investigations that hardly exist at present—investigations into the nature of video and computational images.

See also: Definition of Art, Medium in Art; Representation in Art; Expression in Art; Interpretation in Art; Narrative; Literature; Music; Theatre; Photography; Aesthetics and Cognitive Science; Feminist Aesthetics; Aesthetics of Popular Art; Aesthetics and Cultural Studies.

BIBLIOGRAPHY

Allen, R. and Smith, M. (eds.) (1997). *Film Theory and Philosophy*. Oxford: Oxford University Press.
Arnheim, R. (1957). *Film as Art*. Berkeley: University of California Press; first published 1933.

Bazin, A. (1967). *What is Cinema?* Vol. I, trans. H. Gray. Berkeley: University of California Press.

Bordwell, D. (1985). *Narration in the Fiction Film*. Madison: University of Wisconsin Press.

——(1989). *Making Meaning: Inference and Rhetoric in the Interpretation of Cinema*. Cambridge, Mass.: Harvard University Press.

——and Carroll, N. (eds.) (1996). *Post-Theory: Reconstructing Film Studies*. Madison: University of Wisconsin Press.

Braudy, L. and Cohen, M. (eds.) (1999). *Film Theory and Criticism: Introductory Readings*. New York: Oxford University Press.

Carroll, N. (1988*a*). *Philosophical Problems of Classical Film Theory*. Princeton: Princeton University Press.

——(1988*b*). *Mystifying Movies: Fads and Fallacies in Contemporary Film Theory*. New York: Columbia University Press.

——(1990). *The Philosophy of Horror or Paradoxes of the Heart*. London: Routledge.

——(1996*a*). *Theorizing the Moving Image*. Oxford: Oxford University Press.

——(1996*b*). 'Film, Rhetoric, and Ideology', in Carroll (1996*a*).

——(1996*c*). 'From Real to Reel: Entangled in Nonfiction Film', in Carroll (1996*a*).

Cavell, S. (1979). *The World Viewed: Reflections on the Ontology of Film*, enlarged edn. Cambridge, Mass.: Harvard University Press; first published 1971.

——(1981). *Pursuits of Happiness*. Cambridge, Mass.: Harvard University Press.

Currie, G. (1995). *Image and Mind: Film, Philosophy, and Cognitive Science*. Cambridge: Cambridge University Press.

Danto, A. (1979). 'Moving Pictures'. *Quarterly Review of Film Studies* 4: 1–21.

Eisenstein, S. (1992). 'The Cinematographic Principle and the Ideogram', in G. Mast, M. Cohen, and L. Braudy (eds.), *Film Theory and Criticism: Introductory Readings*, 4th edn. New York: Oxford University Press.

Freeland, C. (1999). *The Naked and the Dead: Evil and the Appeal of Horror*. Boulder, Colo.: Westview Press.

Gaut, B. (1995). 'Making Sense of Films: Neoformalism and its Limits'. *Forum for Modern Language Studies* 31: 8–23.

——(1997*a*). 'Recent Work on Analytic Philosophy of Film: History, Issues, Prospects'. *Philosophical Books* 38: 145–56.

——(1997*b*). 'Film Authorship and Collaboration', in Allen and Smith (1997).

——(1999). 'Identification and Emotion in Narrative Film', in Plantinga and Smith (1999).

——(2002). 'Cinematic Art'. *Journal of Aesthetics and Art Criticism* 60.

Goodman, N. (1976). *Languages of Art: An Approach to the Theory of Symbols*, 2nd edn. Indianapolis: Hackett.

Grodal, T. (1997). *Moving Pictures: A New Theory of Film Genres, Feelings, and Cognition*. Oxford: Clarendon Press.

Harman, G. (1999). 'Semiotics and the Cinema: Metz and Wollen', in Braudy and Cohen (1999).

Kania, A. (2002). 'The Illusion of Realism in Film'. *British Journal of Aesthetics* 42: 243–58.

King, W. (1992). 'Scruton and Reasons for Looking at Photographs'. *British Journal of Aesthetics* 32: 258–65.

Kivy, P. (1997). 'Music in the Movies: A Philosophical Enquiry', in Allen and Smith (1997).

Kracauer, S. (1960). *Theory of Film: The Redemption of Physical Reality*. Oxford: Oxford University Press.

Levinson, J. (1996). 'Film Music and Narrative Agency', in Bordwell and Carroll (1996).

Livingston, P. (1997). 'Cinematic Authorship', in Allen and Smith (1997).

Metz, C. (1974). *Film Language: A Semiotics of the Cinema*, trans. M. Taylor. New York: Oxford University Press.

—— (1982). *The Imaginary Signifier: Psychoanalysis and the Cinema*, trans. C. Britton *et al.* Bloomington: Indiana University Press.

Mulvey, L. (1999). 'Visual Pleasure', in Braudy and Cohen (1999).

Munsterberg, H. (1916). *The Photoplay: A Psychological Study*. New York: D. Appleton.

Neill, A. (1996). 'Empathy and (Film) Fiction', in Bordwell and Carroll (1996).

Nowell-Smith, G. (1981). 'Six Authors in Pursuit of *The Searchers*', in J. Caughie (ed.), *Theories of Authorship: A Reader*. London: Routledge.

Perkins, V. (1972). *Film as Film: Understanding and Judging Movies*. Harmondsworth: Penguin.

Plantinga, C. and Smith, G. (eds.) (1999). *Passionate Views: Film, Cognition and Emotion*. Baltimore: Johns Hopkins University Press.

Sarris, A. (1999). 'Notes on the Auteur Theory in 1962', in Braudy and Cohen (1999).

Scruton, R. (1983). 'Photography and Representation', in his *The Aesthetic Understanding: Essays in the Philosophy of Art and Culture*. London: Methuen.

Sesonske, A. (1973). 'Cinema Space', in D. Carr and E. Casey (eds.), *Explorations in Phenomenology*. The Hague: Martinus Nijhoff.

—— (1974). 'Aesthetics of Film, or A Funny Thing Happened on the Way to the Movies'. *Journal of Aesthetics and Art Criticism* 33: 51–7.

Smith, M. (1995). *Engaging Characters: Fiction, Emotion, and the Cinema*. Oxford: Oxford University Press.

Sparshott, F. (1992). 'Basic Film Aesthetics', in G. Mast, M. Cohen, and L. Braudy (eds.), *Film Theory and Criticism: Introductory Readings*, 4th edn. New York: Oxford University Press; first published 1971.

Spellerberg, J. (1985). 'Technology and Ideology in the Cinema', in G. Mast and M. Cohen (eds.), *Film Theory and Criticism: Introductory Readings*, 3rd edn. New York: Oxford University Press.

Stam, R. and Spence, L. (1999). 'Colonialism, Racism and Representation: An Introduction', in Braudy and Cohen (1999).

Walton, K. (1984). 'Transparent Pictures: On the Nature of Photographic Realism'. *Critical Inquiry* 11: 246–77.

—— (1990). *Mimesis as Make-Believe: On the Foundations of the Representational Arts*. Cambridge, Mass.: Harvard University Press.

—— (1997). 'On Pictures and Photographs: Objections Answered', in Allen and Smith (1997).

Warburton, N. (1988). 'Seeing through "Seeing Through Photographs"'. *Ratio*, n.s. 1: 64–74.

Wicks, R. (1989). 'Photography as a Representational Art'. *British Journal of Aesthetics* 29: 1–9.

Wilson, G. (1986). *Narration in Light: Studies in Cinematic Point of View*. Baltimore: Johns Hopkins University Press.

—— (1997a). 'On Film Narrative and Narrative Meaning', in Allen and Smith (1997).

—— (1997b). '*Le Grand Imagier* Steps Out: The Primitive Basis of Film Narration'. *Philosophical Topics* 25: 295–318.

PART IV

FURTHER DIRECTIONS IN AESTHETICS

FEMINIST AESTHETICS

MARY DEVEREAUX

THIS chapter provides a critical survey of English-language feminist work in aesthetics since the early 1970s. The aim is to focus on those areas of feminist inquiry that have most significantly affected philosophical aesthetics in the analytic tradition.

1. BASICS

1.1 Definition and Preliminary Characterization

In what follows, the term 'feminist aesthetics' is used broadly to refer to a diverse family of theories, approaches, and models of criticism united by resistance to 'male' privilege and domination in the sphere of art and aesthetic experience. Feminist aesthetics, like feminism generally, begins with what might be called 'the fact of patriarchy'. 'Patriarchy', as the word is being used here, is conceived of as a social system that distributes power, status, and rights to men and men's interests, to the detriment of women and women's interests. This system is constituted by institutions, practices, habits, and outlooks generally understood to affect nearly every aspect of human thought and experience. To speak of the *fact* of patriarchy is to affirm the controversial thesis that existing society is patriarchal or that it exhibits these structural characteristics.

As used by feminists, 'patriarchy' is not a neutral descriptive category. Indeed, it is a central tenet of feminism that patriarchy is *illegitimate*. The illegitimacy of patriarchy is understood in terms of either unfairness or domination. The fairness point is that patriarchy is a system that treats men and women unequally. The point about domination is that patriarchy could be justified only on the basis of false or distorted beliefs about the nature of men, the nature of women, and its own structure. (Typically, these beliefs involve some form of gender essentialism, the conviction that male and female 'natures' are fixed by biology or 'divine plan'.)

A central task of feminism is to reveal the fact of patriarchy. This involves uncovering and analysing the way social practices, institutional arrangements and patterns of thought differentially serve male interests, beliefs, and desires; it also means unmasking the means by which patriarchy makes this domination difficult to recognize or resist. Given this characterization of the object of feminism, it follows that the theoretical project of elucidating the true nature of patriarchy will inevitably have a political dimension. To describe a set of institutions as patriarchal is to characterize them in such a way as to undermine their legitimacy. Thus, this theoretical goal dovetails with the political goal of feminism: the abolition of patriarchy.

As characterized here, there are two aspects of feminism: one continuous with traditional political liberalism, and one continuous with the Frankfurt School and critical theory. Feminism follows liberalism in that it seeks to secure rights and liberties for individuals; it follows critical theory in that it sees patriarchy as an instance of the same type of structure as Marxists understand capitalism to be.

Feminist *aesthetics* starts from the assumption that the historical domain of art and the aesthetic is itself patriarchal. At one level, it simply extends the analysis of patriarchy to the practices of art institutions, in particular to the treatment of women in and by these institutions (e.g. demotions in the status of female-authored artworks previously believed to be the work of male artists). On another, more fundamental level feminist aesthetics introduces the concept of *gender* into the analysis of aesthetic pleasure, aesthetic value, the work of art, and other foundational notions of the discipline. The mode of analysis here is not social and political but aesthetic. With respect to the work of art, the aim is to show how distorted conceptions of gender may infect both the subject matter of art (e.g. the pervasive images of women as happy mothers, charming coquettes, willing victims) and its forms or modes (e.g. the male gaze that many works of visual art assume). With respect to the values of the aesthetic itself, the object is to demonstrate the gendered notions at work in views of both the perceiving *subject* (e.g. the masculine model at work in the characterization of pure judgements of taste) and characterizations of the *objects* of aesthetic attention (e.g. the eighteenth-century association of artistic or natural beauty with the feminine, the more dangerous extremes of the sublime with the masculine) (Korsmeyer 1998: 150–1). Feminist aesthetics thus involves an investigation that goes to the foundations of aesthetics as a discipline.

This general characterization of feminism and feminist aesthetics should not be taken to suggest a monolithic enterprise. Feminist theory takes a variety of shapes and forms; feminists themselves do not all agree over whether to emphasize or de-emphasize male/female difference, whether to understand gender in biological or cultural terms, and so on. Similar internal disputes arise within feminist aesthetics. Indeed, the use of the term 'feminist aesthetics' is itself contested. While theorists like Christine Battersby find this label appealing and useful (Battersby 1989), Rita Felski and others worry that it may be taken to imply the existence of a separate, distinctively female, 'woman's art' or 'woman's aesthetic' (Felski 1998). These disputes often turn on the way the term 'feminist aesthetics' is being construed as well as on more fundamental disputes about the proper aims of feminism.

Despite theoretical differences among feminists, feminist work in aesthetics is unified by a shared view of the importance of challenging what Carolyn Korsmeyer calls 'the gender skew' of the fundamental concepts and ideals of philosophical aesthetics (Korsmeyer 1998: 151). The excitement of uncovering what generations of philosophers and others interested in the arts never noticed also generates a common sense of purpose.

1.2 Early History

Feminist work in aesthetics is part of the history of modern feminism. Women artists, like women generally in the early 1970s, began to make contact with one another, establishing collectives and developing a positive self-consciousness about themselves as feminist artists. The resulting Women's Art Movement gave birth to new kinds of art, all-women exhibitions, and other alternatives for recognition and support. It also led to public calls for an end to the conscious and unconscious 'masculine orientation' at work throughout the artworld (Parker and Pollock 1987: 3–8). Art critics such as Lucy Lippard used the pages of *Art in America* and other mainstream art history journals to call for the artworld to 'come to grips with sexism', enumerating specific instances of discrimination, e.g. the lack of women curators and the 'lousy records' of granting organizations and galleries with respect to women applicants (Lippard 1976: 28–37).

Hand in hand with this political activity came important theoretical debates not only about strategy and goals (e.g. assimilation *v.* a separate 'woman's art'), but also about the fundamental character of art and art institutions. By the mid to late 1970s, feminist perspectives had begun to have a marked influence on academic scholarship. In literature departments feminist scholars, teachers, and writers were challenging the sacredness of the male canon and the practices of literary criticism. They called for reading the old texts in new ways, creating what poet and theorist Adrienne Rich called 're-vision: the act of looking back, of seeing with fresh eyes, of entering an old text from a new critical direction'. For Rich, as for many other feminists, literature required a radical critique, one that would allow women to read as women. From this perspective, the works of the past were 'required reading', not to pass on the tradition, but 'to break its hold'. Rich urged women to look to literature to learn 'how we have been living, how we have been led to imagine ourselves, how our language has trapped as well as liberated us' (Rich 1971: 35). In short, literature both embodied the old political order, an order that women must come to know and explore, and offered a means by which women could begin to appropriate the male prerogative of 'seeing' and 'naming' for themselves.

This general strategy of 'reading against the grain' would become a staple of feminist literary criticism, along with the insistence that no adequate account of reading could overlook issues of gender or the interrelated issues of race and class. Feminist theorists and critics approached other forms of art using similar strategies. The resulting linkage of art with sexual politics led, as subsequent developments would show, to a radically different way of understanding and studying works of art.

Interestingly, the issues of sexual politics at the centre of academic debate in literature and other art-related disciplines were slow to impact philosophical aesthetics. Despite feminism's explicit concern with issues such as artistic representation, an issue that Nelson Goodman's *Languages of Art* brought to the forefront of aesthetic debate in 1968, philosophers of art throughout the 1980s largely ignored the growing body of feminist theory emerging in the arts. In this respect, the situation in the philosophy of art lagged behind even other areas of philosophy. In ethics, for example, the work of Carol Gilligan had an early and profound impact (Gilligan 1982), and in fields such as epistemology, the philosophy of science, and political theory, feminists had by the end of the decade produced a considerable body of influential work (Garry and Pearsall 1989; Harding 1986; Okin 1989).

Change in aesthetics came only when, in 1990, *Hypatia: A Journal of Feminist Philosophy* and the *Journal of Aesthetics and Art Criticism* each published special issues on the topic of feminist aesthetics. The appearance of this body of work brought issues of feminist concern to philosophers of art and aestheticians, thus paving the way for distinctively *philosophical* work in feminist aesthetics.

2. Critiques

Feminist work in aesthetics can be understood as having three central concerns. The first is with the canon, and women's under-representation in the history of art; the second is with artistic representation and the ways in which women are typically depicted in and positioned by works of art; and the third is with the fundamental values and ideals of aesthetics. In each of these areas, feminists have undertaken to bring an awareness of gender to the investigation of fundamental concepts and the pursuit of traditional questions. As a step towards evaluating the success of these interrelated projects, and their possible implications for aesthetics more generally, the following three subsections explore in detail feminist critiques of the canon, artistic representation, and the values and ideals of aesthetics.

2.1 The Canon

Under-representation

Feminist concern with the history of art starts from the idea that women artists are under-represented in the canon. As early feminists noted, standard texts such as Janson's *The History of Art* (published in 1970) contained no mention of women artists at all. Nor, they observed, were women any better represented on the lists of great composers, dramatists, and so on.

Literature might be thought the one notable exception. Among English novelists, the Brontës, George Eliot, and Jane Austen held considerable stature, as did the Americans Edith Wharton and Gertrude Stein. Among the poets, Emily Dickinson, Elizabeth Barrett Browning, and Christina Rossetti were generally granted a place in the standard anthologies. In many respects, literature offered women of modest means and education the possibility of a kind of artistic accomplishment only rarely realized by women in music and the visual arts. In other respects, though, women who picked up a pen faced many of the same obstacles confronted by women who sought to paint or compose—the need, so compellingly described by Virginia Woolf, for 'a room of one's own'. By this, Woolf meant, among other things, the income to devote oneself to artistic creation and the sense of inner liberty that male writers so easily took for granted (Woolf 1929). Even the few who overcame these obstacles, like Woolf herself, often found themselves shut out of the canons of high art. As Alex Zwerdling points out, as late as the 1960s Woolf's literary reputation placed her firmly among the interesting but lesser modernist writers. In short, even in literature, women rarely qualified as candidates for genius.

This state of affairs was nothing new. What was new was the radical presumption that women's absence from the ranks of genius was a *problem*, something in need of special explanation (Nochlin 1971). The standard view was that the lack of great women artists needed no particular explanation. It was not to be expected that women artists would achieve greatness. Women might—and did—produce works of art; some, like Jane Austen and Mary Cassatt, might even achieve some renown. But women lacked the power, energy, and near divine inspiration necessary for the highest levels of artistic achievement, a lack generally attributed to female biology. In this respect, it was held, women artists were no different from their female counterparts in science, government, and the professions.

In approaching the issue of women's under-representation in the arts, one response of feminist art historians was thus to reject out of hand the view that 'there was nothing to explain', or that women's lack of achievement should be regarded as a normal circumstance. The situation, Nochlin argued, required a different explanation. The failure to produce 'great' art, like women's failure to equal men's successes elsewhere, arose not from 'women's nature', but from women's social and material circumstances and the meaning attached by society to sexual difference. In short, Gisela Ecker would write, women's shortcomings could be accounted for in terms of 'what has been imposed on women' by 'oppressive social conditions or prejudice' (Ecker 1985).

In foregrounding the relationship between women's social and socially mediated material conditions and artistic achievement, nothing matched the influence of Nochlin's seminal essay 'Why Have There Been No Great Women Artists?' (Nochlin 1971). Conceptually, Nochlin's work built upon the work of 'early feminists' like Mary Wollstonecroft, John Stuart Mill, and a long tradition of writers stretching from Woolf and Beauvoir back to the medieval French writer Christine de Pizan. As these and other writers convincingly established, real artistic achievement was an exacting business, requiring access to particular social and socially mediated material conditions. Talent alone was not enough.

Nochlin joined the material analysis of her predecessors to the traditional methods of art historical scholarship, showing, for example, how women's lack of access to life drawing classes (with their nude models) explained their lack of success at history painting and other 'major' genres. Without training in drawing the human figure, Nochlin pointed out, only the most foolhardy student would undertake the large-scale representation of bodies in action thought definitive of great painting from the Renaissance to the end of the nineteenth century. Similarly obvious, though previously overlooked, explanations were forthcoming in other areas of art historical investigation. Early feminist art historians acknowledged that systematic social change might be required for women to succeed at the highest levels, but, they optimistically predicted, once equal circumstances obtained, women would achieve the same greatness as their male counterparts.

Expanding the canon

A second response to the issue of women's under-representation in the canon involved questioning the assumption that there were, in fact, no great women artists. Some women—Helen Frankenthaler, Louise Nevelson, Georgia O'Keeffe, and others—were already in the canon. Might the relative absence of other women result not from a lack of female talent but from a problem of 'under-reporting'? This question led to efforts to 'expand the canon', locating and winning recognition for the work of previously overlooked or undervalued women artists. The 'search for female Michelangelos' succeeded in adding to the canon forgotten women artists such as the Baroque Italian painter Artemisia Gentileschi, and the eighteenth-century members of the British Royal Academy, Angelica Kauffmann and Mary Moser (Chadwick 1990). It also resulted in increased scholarly interest in the careers of some formerly secondary figures, e.g. Berthe Morisot, and led feminists to pay greater attention to the work of twentieth-century figures such as Lee Krasner, Agnes Martin, Paula Modersohn-Becker, Tina Modotti, and Frieda Kahlo. Efforts to expand the canon—in effect, to write the hidden history of women—also called for an acknowledgement of the significance of women's 'invisible' artistic labour: as muses, models, and subjects of art. In music, belated attention has recently come to Clara Schumann, Francesca Caccini, Barbara Strozzi, Fanny Mendelsohn, Germaine Tailleferve, Ruth Crawford Seeger, Amy Beach, and Pauline Viardot.

Artistic greatness

Later, 'second-generation', feminists raised a separate set of issues having to do with the forms of valuation built into the canon. Liberal feminism's efforts to 'infiltrate and integrate' traditional art history came under fire for reinforcing a model of freedom that 'lies in becoming like a man'. Art historian Griselda Pollock criticized Nochlin's acceptance of a conception of artistic activity still understood 'in terms of greatness, risks, leaps into the unknown' (Pollock 1988: 35). For Pollock, as for many of her more radical contemporaries, encouraging women artists to emulate their male brethren by pursuing success in 'traditional' terms, winning 'one man shows', exhibiting in conventional venues, and receiving the recognition of establishment critics and art historians, was an artistic error.

While Pollock acknowledged the importance of recovering the history of women artists, the project of historical recovery alone was insufficient, she argued. Feminist art history must also undertake to examine the discourses and practices of art history itself. The idea was to re-theorize the framework of the discipline (Pollock 1988: 55).

In carrying out this re-theorizing, Pollock, and other art historians such as Carol Duncan and Svetlana Alpers, drew upon the paradigm of Marxist cultural theory championed by John Berger, T. J. Clark, and others. To the analysis of the politics of class, they added an analysis of sexual divisions and inequalities. The result was a social history of art which integrated the imperatives of Marxism and feminism. It made possible an analysis of women's under-representation in the canon that deepened and extended earlier efforts at exposing and explaining the 'rigged contest' women faced. Pollock's own work, for example, demonstrated the correlation between conceptions of the work of art as essentially a public object and the prevailing division of masculine-feminine space (Pollock 1998: 56–66). She took a similar approach to the notion of an 'Old Master', pointing to the way the term 'artist' has become equated with masculinity and male social roles, such as the Bohemian, and to the romanticism, elitism, and individualism built into notions of artistic 'greatness'.

The work of Pollock and other second-generation feminist art historians produced a radical shift in perspective. To understand just how radical, it is worth recalling that at the time academic art history was largely an enterprise devoted to tracing and celebrating the development of one or another great artistic figure (Duncan 1993: xiii). In asking fundamental questions about what values determined prevailing notions of significance, whose values those were, and whose interests they served, feminist art historians opened the door to questions about whether the traits the canon celebrates are those that ought to be celebrated.

An art of our own

Greater awareness of the evaluative norms of traditional art history eventually led some feminists to call for the creation of a separate tradition of 'women's art', one based on a 'feminist' (or, alternatively, a 'feminine') aesthetics. Here the use of the term 'feminist aesthetics' points to a particular theoretical posture which maintains that women's art differs in important—and valuable—ways from men's. For most, this gender difference was to be understood in essentialist terms, as a consequence of women's 'nature', i.e. her distinctively female sensibility and imagination. Others understood the difference as a consequence merely of the particular social and political circumstances women faced. In either case, the result was a belief in a 'necessary or privileged relationship between female gender and a particular kind of literary [or artistic] structure, style or form' (Felski 1989: 19). So, for example, French feminists, such as Julia Kristeva, came to equate avant-garde arts, in particular experimental writing, with resistance to 'a patriarchal symbolic order'. The determinate meanings, 'artificially imposed structure', and linear logic of conventional narrative, in turn, came to be identified with 'bourgeois masculinity' (Kristeva 1987: 110–17).

This 'gynocentric' feminism sought to invert the usual privileging of male attributes over female ones. Women's purported connection with their bodies, emotional sensitivity, attention to detail, lesser aggression, and so on came to be regarded as sources of power and pride, something to be celebrated and shared. In aesthetic terms, this inversion meant encouraging women to show their artwork in woman-only, often cooperative, galleries and spaces rather than to compete with one another to gain entrance to mainstream venues. It also meant holding on to, and celebrating, just those aspects of women's traditional artistic activity that the art establishment demeaned or dismissed. Activities such as quilting, embroidery, and pottery, previously categorized as belonging to minor genres, craft, or decorative art, were to be embraced as part of the communal, life-affirming, often visceral, processes of traditionally female artistic labour. The female imagery, concern with the body and collaborative nature of art projects like Judy Chicago's *The Dinner Party* were meant, their advocates insisted, to provide an alternative to the values of instrumentalism, authoritarianism, and extreme individualism held to dominate Western European cultures.

For many, this celebration of the female held enormous appeal. It also carried a certain political risk. To insist that women's art and female creative processes differed *inherently* from men's reintroduced a form of gender essentialism associated with patriarchal conceptions of the nature of men and women. Critics of this approach rejected both the idea that women had a distinct 'nature' and the attribution of an inherently gendered nature to particular forms of art.

Worth noting, however, is that not all advocates of a specifically feminist aesthetics subscribe to biological views of what makes women distinctive. Christine Battersby, for one, argues that the fact that women are *treated* differently suffices to warrant a call for a feminist aesthetic, one that collectively works to establish a record of artistic achievement that, as she puts it, fairly includes both matrilineal and patrilinear patterns of tradition (Battersby 1989: 157).

2.2 Artistic Representation

The 'image-studies' approach

Whereas the feminist work in aesthetics considered so far focuses on the institutional subordination of women, another body of work directs attention to women's treatment at the symbolic level, within the work of art itself. The idea here is that women in patriarchal societies are oppressed not only economically and politically, but also in the very ways in which its members see the world and in the 'languages of art' they use to represent it. Like language itself, art is a symbolic medium, which, it is held, disproportionately reflects and promotes male beliefs, desires, and ends, leading men—and women—to see the world and themselves through 'male eyes'. From this perspective, painting, literature, and other forms of artistic representation play a key role in the social construction of gender, teaching women and girls to see themselves as (passive) objects of (active) male desire, an alignment supportive of male privilege and useful to patriarchal culture.

One place where a concern with the power of symbolic media developed most fully was in relationship to film. The target here was Hollywood film and other forms of popular culture such as advertising and fashion photography. Film attracted the attention of feminist theorists in part because it was presumed to attract a far larger, and less critical, audience than traditional fine arts such as painting. As Marxists theorists and media critics before them had noted, the medium of film had the power to create and satisfy desires, to manufacture needs, to operate on the unconscious as well as the conscious mind. The pleasures it offered—of narrative identification, visual and erotic pleasure, entertainment—combined to make Hollywood film a perfect medium for creating and sustaining a society with what its critics deemed a 'patriarchal unconscious'. In the battle to combat patriarchal conceptions of male and female social roles, Hollywood film thus came to seem a natural target.

Concern with film's presumed ideological powers led feminist film theorists initially to studies of how women in individual films were represented (positively or negatively). Works such as Molly Haskell's *From Reverence to Rape: The Treatment of Women in the Movies* (1974) adopted a basically sociological approach, tracing the characterization of women on-screen in the context of the social, political, and cultural circumstances of women off-screen. These studies of the image of women in film paralleled similar work on the representation of women in literature and in other arts (cf. Heilbrun and Higonnet 1983; Millett 1970).

The male gaze

In film, the analysis of content and style in this 'image studies' approach gave way rather quickly to a more abstract, theoretical analysis. As Claire Johnson and other critics of the image-based approach insisted, feminist film theory would have to go further than a concern with positive female protagonists and women's problems if it was to have any real political impact. In Johnson's words, 'If it is to impinge on consciousness', feminist film theory would require 'a revolutionary strategy'. What was needed was a way of unearthing a kind of 'deep structure' beneath the 'surface structure' of entertainment and visual pleasure that cinema provides. In undertaking this task, feminist film theorists adopted a theoretical combination of Lacanian psychoanalysis with Althusserian Marxism and semiotics (Freeland 1998: 201).

Seminal in developing this approach was Laura Mulvey's 1975 classic, 'Visual Pleasure and Narrative Cinema' (in Mulvey 1988). Mulvey shared with Marxist film theorists a tendency to regard film as a highly successful purveyor of bourgeois ideology. What distinguished her work from its Marxist predecessors, however, was its linkage of art with *sexual* politics and its reliance on psychoanalytic theory as the political weapon of choice. Mulvey begins from the assumption that cinematic representation duplicates the division of the dominant patriarchal order. On this interpretation, film relies on a 'split' between (active) looking and (passive) being looked at. Man is the 'bearer of the look', woman its object. Put in non-theoretical terms, Mulvey's claim was that the camera aligned the spectator's gaze with that of male characters within the film, establishing identification with the male hero of the story and depicting women on screen as objects of male desire. On this analysis, Hollywood narrative film embodied this so-called male gaze, operating on patterns of male fascination, desire, and pleasure. It was these patterns that Mulvey's essay attempted to analyse—and, in analysing, to destroy.

Mulvey's theory of the 'male gaze' came in for intense criticism, both by feminists working within a Marxian/psychoanalytic paradigm and by those working outside it. Even feminist film theorists sympathetic to Mulvey's basic approach, such as E. Ann Kaplan, called her to task for oversimplifying the experience of the female spectator. For Mulvey, the female film-goer either identified with the male protagonist or enjoyed the masochistic pleasure of her own objectification (Kaplan 1987: 231). The possibility of an 'oppositional' gaze Mulvey had apparently overlooked. But, as bell hooks has argued, black women spectators have long seen films both aware of and resistant to the disabling effects of mainstream Hollywood, whether in *Birth of a Nation* or Shirley Temple movies. hooks assumed that white women did so too (hooks 1992). Others objected to Mulvey's assumption of a monolithic, dominant male spectator, an assumption that made real differences in power between men invisible (Devereaux 1990).

From a different direction, Noël Carroll brought the methods of analytic philosophy to bear, arguing that Mulvey's theory of the gaze—and psychoanalytic approaches to film more generally—rested on the faulty assumption that cinema is *inherently* ideological and the misguided belief that a general theory of visual pleasure based on sexual difference is either possible or desirable (Carroll 1995). For Carroll, the psychoanalytic approach to film should be rejected altogether in favour of a return to the earlier, more cognitivist, 'image-based' approach represented by Haskell and Millett.

Despite these and other criticisms, Mulvey's theory of the male gaze made gender an integral part of the analysis of film, going far beyond Haskell's emphasis on male and female stereotypes and paving the way for an explosion of work in feminist film theory.

2.3 The Ideals and Values of Philosophical Aesthetics

The third concern of feminists working in aesthetics is with the ideals and values of philosophical aesthetics itself. In turning their attention to philosophy, feminist aestheticians, like their counterparts in other disciplines, seek to demonstrate the inadequacy of a theoretical framework that fails to take into account the influence of gender and gender considerations. In principle, this project involves a critical reappraisal of any and all aesthetic theory that is unaware of, or indifferent to, the insights of feminism itself. One might therefore expect feminists to undertake a critical reappraisal of the history of aesthetics (e.g. the classical works of Plato and Aristotle, the aesthetics of romanticism associated with Schiller, the theories of expression and communication espoused by Tolstoy and Collingwood). An even more natural target would include the theories of major contemporary figures such as Monroe Beardsley, Nelson Goodman, Arthur Danto, George Dickie, and Richard Wollheim. In point of fact, feminist critiques of philosophical aesthetics have focused almost exclusively on a single, far narrower, target: Kant and the tradition of neo-Kantian formalism. In targeting the Kantian tradition, feminists have in mind the Kant of the *Critique of Judgment* and the trajectory of aesthetic thought associated with Oscar Wilde, twentieth-century Modernism and the work of Roger Fry, Clive Bell, and Clement Greenberg. Indeed, it would be no great exaggeration to say that critiques of 'Kant and formalism' have largely come to define what is meant by 'feminist critiques of aesthetics'.

It is thus worth asking why feminists have chosen to focus almost exclusively on this one tradition. Is Kant or the neo-Kantian aesthetic culture he spawned any more exclusionary, or any blinder, to key feminist concerns than most of the rest of the history of aesthetics? And if not, what makes it the primary object of feminist suspicion?

One reply is that, in focusing on Kantian aesthetics, feminist critics merely adopt the mainstream's own understanding of its history and heroes. For the 'analytic' aestheticians under discussion (the progeny of Sibley, Isenberg, Beardsley, etc.) it is

Kant—or Kant and Hume—not Plato or Nietzsche or Hegel, who primarily sets the modern agenda, just as it is commitment to a Kantian legacy of aesthetic autonomy and disinterestedness that continues to distinguish 'traditional' analytic approaches in aesthetics from the more overtly political approaches adopted by the Frankfurt School or the more historically contextual approaches of hermeneutics and continental philosophy generally. From this perspective, a critique of Kant just *is* a critique of traditional aesthetics.

Important to note, however, is that feminist critiques of 'Kant' presuppose a particular conception of Kant. This Kant is not the historical Kant or the conception of Kant derived from a careful reading of *The Critique of Judgment*, but a set of ideas associated with, and advanced in, Kant's name. Thus, with few exceptions, feminists critical of this legacy pay little attention to historical or exegetical questions. Nor should this be surprising, since feminism's real quarrel is not primarily with Kant, but with twentieth-century versions of formalist theory, in particular the theories of Clive Bell and Clement Greenberg. It is the deep and abiding hold of this Kantian legacy on contemporary aesthetics—what Estelle Lauter identifies as the 'master theory' of the last century of Anglo-American aesthetics—that so many feminists heartily reject. (To be fair, it is also largely rejected, if on different grounds, by many contemporary Anglo-American aestheticians, as noted later.) As with feminist criticisms of Kant, the primary object of attack here is not the specific theory of Greenberg or Bell, but a more generalized conception of formalism. This generalized or 'generic' formalism, often identified with a notion of 'aesthetic autonomy', includes a commitment to the disinterestedness of aesthetic judgement and the firm separation of art from life.

This formalism feminists criticize first on general grounds. Like members of the Frankfurt School and other critical theorists, feminists have a conception of art as deeply entwined with life, in particular with political life. From this perspective, formalist theories of art suffer from two failings: a misunderstanding of the nature of art, and a reliance on standards of classification and evaluation that are exclusionary and discriminatory, in practice if not also in theory. Formalism, its critics charge, refuses to recognize the political dimension of both the creation and evaluation of art. In setting off the category of the moral and political from the aesthetic, and calling upon art's audience to ignore or bracket art's content, its history, and so on in favour of form alone, formalism makes it difficult or impossible to appreciate the real value and appeal of many kinds of art. Here formalism's opponents point to examples of political art like Goya's *Caprichos*, religious art like Milton's *Paradise Lost*, the novels of Dickens and Orwell, and other works of social criticism. None of these, they claim, can be grasped as the works of art they are in terms of a formalist theory of value. Moreover, this view of art makes art something marginal, unlikely to find an audience or be thought of much importance, outside a rather narrow circle.

Feminists also criticize formalism, more specifically, for its gender bias. This bias, understood broadly to include racial and class bias as well, consists in formalism's blindness to how purportedly universal forms of art privilege some kinds of speakers and audiences over others. Similarly, standards of classification and evaluation meant to rest upon universal aesthetic values deliver far less than they promise—not objectivity and fairness but, its critics charge, judgements based on male-defined assumptions about gender (how men and women think, how they paint, what they are and are not capable of) and art itself (an equation of 'significant' with large-scale history painting or the bold, 'masculine' sweep of modernist painting; a downgrading of domestic subject matter, small-scale works, craft and 'feminine' forms of art in general).

Feminist theorists are not the first nor the last to call formalism to task for the narrowness of its conception of art and the inadequacy of its theory of aesthetic value. Indeed, formalist theories have received trenchant criticism within analytic aesthetics itself, for example the work of Isenberg, Danto, and Wollheim (Isenberg 1973; Danto 1981; Wollheim 1995). But feminist critiques of formalism have significantly advanced the anti-formalist cause, bringing greater prominence to the view that works of art play a variety of social roles, not just in European culture but throughout the world. Moreover, by revealing the specifically gendered assumptions at work in formalist evaluative practice, feminist critics have demonstrated that what are presented as 'purely formal' aesthetic criteria actually reflect local, historically specific attitudes and assumptions. So, for example, the 'universal' preference for history painting over still lives may have more to do with attitudes about the relative value of action over contemplation, or of large works over 'small' or domestic works.

Whether the same charge can be substantiated against the formalist theory of aesthetic value itself remains to be seen. From the fact that formalist *practice* often departs from purely formal considerations, it does not follow that there is anything wrong with the *ideal* of formal assessment itself. It sometimes looks, however, as if feminist critics of formalism are committed to just this thesis. If the claim is that evaluating works of art in terms of colour or line (or other strictly formal features) is inherently a gender-biased process, then it needs to be specified in exactly what the gender bias consists—in the preference for work with these formal values or in the exclusion of women from the opportunity for training and practice needed to attain professional mastery (Devereaux 1998a).

For many outside philosophy, the continued preoccupation with formalism evident in feminist aesthetics is rather puzzling. For literary and film theorists, many working within the parameters of deconstruction, poststructuralism, and postmodernism, such arguments—from whatever political quarter—hardly need making. As they observe, the art world and their own disciplines have long since abandoned formalism and the division of art from politics. From their standpoint, this battle has already been won, in no inconsiderable part because of feminism itself. In one sense, this is true. In recent decades, many philosophers of art have embraced a far more contextual, historical approach to art. This does not mean, however, that they have themselves *become* feminist theorists, or that their work evidences any greater awareness of the subtle and not so subtle biases still operative in art theory and practice. So, while 'Kant and formalism', strictly speaking, may be an already vanquished enemy, feminists rightly insist that, for analytic aestheticians generally, issues of gender and gender-bias have yet to win anything more than a marginal place in the conversation of the discipline.

Acknowledging this last point, however, does not change the fact that many feminist criticisms of Kant and formalism miss their ostensible targets. Why should this matter? Some may argue that labelling its opponents 'Kant and formalism' merely provides a convenient handle for what is, after all, an objectionable and still pervasive set of politically regressive assumptions and commitments. What matters is the politics, not the name.

Looked at differently, however, this misnaming *does* matter. It matters first of all because what we get is a false or distorted picture of who or what the real obstruction to feminist political and theoretical goals is. In *The Critique of Judgment*, Kant is not talking about art and politics; on most accounts, he lacks a worked-out theory of art altogether. And, while formalist evaluative practice falls short of the objectivity and universality claimed by the theory itself, the ideal of formal assessment *per se* may or may not turn out to contain an inherent gender bias. Second, this misnaming may turn out to have political consequences. Altogether dismissing Kant or rejecting the ideal of aesthetic autonomy may deprive feminist aestheticians of a part of their lineage on which they might usefully draw, for example, in protecting works of political art from various forms of interference (cf. Devereaux 1998a).

None of this is to deny that there are sound criticisms of Kant and the aesthetic tradition he fostered, or that feminists have done important work in advancing such criticisms. The theory of genius, the commitment to the disinterestedness of aesthetic judgement, and other aspects of Kantian aesthetics do present genuine problems, not only from a feminist perspective but from a variety of critical standpoints. But much careful scholarship and exegetical work using the tools of feminist analysis remains to be done on the *Critique of Judgment*, on the historical theories of Bell and Greenberg, and on earlier varieties of formalism such as Alberti's or Wilde's. Much otherwise strong and interesting work in feminist aesthetics manifests a tendency to *essentialize* formalism, overlooking the subtleties and points of difference between Wilde's position, say, and Bell's, or the settings in which these different theorists wrote, in favour of a generic formalism that few, if any, contemporary aestheticians would embrace.

The same tendency to essentialize is also found in some feminist discussions of Anglo-American aesthetics itself (cf. Lauter's critique of the 'master' theory said to govern twentieth-century aesthetics). Broad characterizations of the work of particular figures or features of the tradition admittedly play an important role in generating calls for reform, but this tendency is one that feminists, who have done so much to call attention to the importance of history and particularity, now have good reason to move beyond.

3. Impact and Consequences

The introduction of feminism into philosophical aesthetics has done a great deal to reinvigorate the discipline. Feminists working in aesthetics have challenged themselves and their discipline to develop a new self-conception: to see the philosophy of art and aesthetics as a theoretical enterprise with its own political content and political consequences, one deeply enmeshed in a patriarchal view of the world. This change in perspective—making visible what was once difficult, if not impossible to see—has proven highly fruitful. As feminist artists have created new forms of art, feminist art historians have succeeded in winning recognition for the works of women and others typically excluded from dominant traditions. They have also initiated a historical and conceptual investigation of the methods and practices of art history. In criticism, feminists have devised a variety of strategies for actively resisting or reappropriating artworks and traditions thought harmful to the interests of women. In this reading 'against the grain', feminist critics do what good critics have always done: they see the text with new eyes. For their part, feminist philosophers of art have begun the difficult work of developing feminist conceptions of art and models of appreciation and evaluation. One result is a lively and provocative dialectic between the 'old' and the 'new' aesthetics.

Whether this conversation ultimately results in merely rethinking a few familiar concepts or developing an entirely new theoretical framework, the process of rethinking is likely to prove enlivening. It may also prove disquieting. To question the value of the Kantian notion of artistic autonomy, to abandon the confidence that our aesthetic judgements and our institutions are impartial and fair to all comers, to see gender biases infecting the prevailing notions of artistic value and the standards based upon them cuts to the foundations of the discipline of aesthetics itself.

Suggesting that feminist challenges to this tradition ought to be taken seriously need not imply that traditional aesthetics is useless, or that a century of analytic aesthetics has accomplished little. Nor need it mean the end of aesthetics as a single tradition. Joseph Margolis, for example, argues for the possibility of a cooperative future, one in which analytic aesthetics and feminist concerns are reconciled through the embrace of a variety of pragmatism (Margolis 1995). But for some, such 'reconciliation' may prove difficult, or undesirable. Joanne Waugh questions the role that even sympathetic varieties of analytic philosophy can play in the future of feminist programmes. For Waugh, the ironical and critical approach that feminists must take towards the aesthetic past makes Margolis's 'cooperative' future difficult to envision (Waugh 1995).

Whether feminism and various forms of traditional aesthetics can be reconciled or not, many would agree that aesthetics cannot now avoid confronting questions of gender. Issues of gender both inflect our view of the discipline's past and play a role in our way towards the future.

4. FUTURE DIRECTIONS

Several recent developments suggest exciting new directions for feminist work in aesthetics. The first is the renewed attention to the nature and role of the aesthetic in literature and culture. The joys and pleasures of good—even beautiful—writing is no longer a forbidden subject. Happily, advocates of renewed attention to the aesthetic are not simply returning to a narrow, pre-feminist, formalism or to critical standards divorced from social and cultural realities. The current 'recuperation' of the aesthetic is for many scholars an effort to end the standoff between artistic form and moral value, to investigate the rich history of the art and politics debate, and to move forward in understanding the impulse to create and revere works of art (Devereaux 1998b). One result of this recuperation is a revived interest in the subject of beauty, not only in philosophy, but in art criticism, art theory, cultural studies, and performance art. The claim that 'beauty is back' finds support in a rash of new work on the topic. Elaine Scarry's *On Beauty and Being Just* (1999) attempts to defend beauty against decades of political complaints; Peg Brand's aptly titled collection, *Beauty Matters* (2000a) aims to extend the philosophical investigation of beauty into areas such as body art and female methods of beautification; Mary Mothersill's earlier *Beauty Restored* (1984) revives the notion of beauty as perception and pleasure.

These developments and the changes they harbour are matters of obvious significance to feminist scholars, not only because of the critiques they themselves have made of beauty and the aesthetic, but also because of the historical association of these notions with the elitist and exclusionary practices of the past. For Brand and other feminists working in aesthetics, the concept of beauty they want 'back' is not the purportedly timeless, unchanging, universal beauty of the past, but something that moves beyond standard notions. Feminists are already busily at work, exploring whether the concept of beauty can be divorced from 'the beauty myth', what a more positive notion of beauty, both male and female, would look like, and what, if anything, beauty has to do with health, virtue, and human flourishing. In this latter connection, feminist aestheticians might usefully draw upon, and extend, philosophical work on the relationship of aesthetic and moral value (cf. Levinson 1998).

New work in evolutionary biology and evolutionary psychology provides a second arena of fertile exploration. How do evolutionary accounts of standards of human attractiveness, in the work of Nancy Etcoff (1999), Sander Gilman (1999), and others, bear on feminist attitudes towards serial plastic surgery and chronic dieting, and the conceptions of self and body they imply? What does biological science tell us about how beauty influences our perceptions, attitudes and behaviour, and what are the implications of this research for understanding human responses to art?

Lastly, and perhaps of most central importance for those working in philosophical aesthetics, the history of aesthetics itself is ripe for future exploration. Here, unlike in the areas mentioned above, feminists have shown little interest.

Feminists in metaphysics, epistemology, ethics, and other areas of philosophy have done first-rate work on Aristotle, Descartes, Hobbes, Hume, Hegel, and other figures in the history of the discipline, but feminists in aesthetics often ignore large sections of the history of philosophy. This is unfortunate. Aside from undertaking scholarly work on Kant and formalism, feminists might usefully turn more attention to Plato's and Aristotle's philosophies of art, medieval theories of beauty, Hume's theory of taste, theories of aesthetic morality in the eighteenth century (e.g. Schiller's), and Iris Murdoch's essays on the relationship of literature and philosophy. Indeed, as the case of Murdoch illustrates, women have played a distinguished role in the aesthetics of the second half of the twentieth century (consider the contributions of Susanne Langer, Susan Sontag, Eva Schaper, Jenefer Robinson, and Martha Nussbaum), a role worthy of further investigation. One might ask about the relationship between aesthetics written by women and feminist aesthetics, particularly as few of these early figures would have identified themselves as feminists. One might also usefully inquire into the feminization of aesthetics itself, i.e. its characterization as a 'softer', more marginal, division of philosophy.

These and other such investigations would be of obvious value, not only to feminist aesthetics, but also to the history of aesthetics and philosophy more generally. With luck, they will also open the way for further interaction between feminist aestheticians and moral philosophers, philosophers of mind, and historians of philosophy, thus bringing aesthetics into closer proximity with other areas of philosophy.

See also: Beauty; Painting; Film; Creativity in Art; Representation in Art; Interpretation in Art; Art and Politics; Art and Morality; Aesthetics and Ethics.

BIBLIOGRAPHY

Alpers, S. (1983). *The Art of Describing: Dutch Art in the Seventeenth Century*. Chicago: University of Chicago Press.

Barwell, I. (1995a). 'Who's Telling This Story, Anyway? Or How to Tell the Gender of a Storyteller'. *Australasian Journal of Philosophy* 73: 227–38.

——(1995b). 'Levinson and the Resisting Reader: Feminist Strategies of Interpretation'. *Journal of Gender Studies* 4: 169–80.

Battersby, C. (1989). *Gender and Genius: Towards a Feminist Aesthetics*. Bloomington: Indiana University Press.

——(1998). 'Genius and Feminism', in M. Kelly (ed.), *The Encyclopedia of Aesthetics*. New York: Oxford University Press, pp. 292–8.

Bell, C. (1931). *Art*. London: Chatto & Windus.

Brand, P. Z. (ed.) (2000a). *Beauty Matters*. Bloomington: Indiana University Press.

——(2000b). 'Glaring Omissions in Traditional Theories of Art', in N. Carroll (ed.), *Theories of Art Today*. Madison: University of Wisconsin Press.

Brand, P. Z. and Korsmeyer, C. (eds.) (1995). *Feminism and Tradition in Aesthetics.* University Park, Pa.: Penn State University Press.

Carroll, N. (1995). 'The Image of Women in Film: A Defense of a Paradigm', in Brand and Korsmeyer (1995: 371–91).

——(ed.) (2000). *Theories of Art Today.* Madison: University of Wisconsin Press.

Chadwick, W. (1990). *Women, Art and Society.* London: Thames & Hudson.

Curran, A. (1998). 'Feminism and the Narrative Structures of the *Poetics*', in C. Freeland (ed.), *Feminist Interpretations of Aristotle.* University Park, Pa.: Pennsylvania State University Press.

Danto, A. (1981). *The Transfiguration of the Commonplace: A Philosophy of Art.* Cambridge, Mass.: Harvard University Press.

Devereaux, M. (1990). 'Oppressive Texts, Resisting Readers and the Gendered Spectator: The "New" Aesthetics'. *Journal of Aesthetics and Art Criticism*, 48(4): 337–47.

——(1998a). 'Autonomy and Its Feminist Critics', in M. Kelly (ed.), *The Encyclopedia of Aesthetics.* New York: Oxford University Press, pp. 178–82.

——(1998b). 'Beauty and Evil: The Case of Leni Riefenstahl's *Triumph of the Will*', in J. Levinson (ed.), *Aesthetics and Ethics: Essays at the Intersection.* New York: Cambridge University Press, pp. 227–56.

Duncan, C. (1993). *The Aesthetics of Power: Essays in Critical Art History.* Cambridge: Cambridge University Press.

Ecker, G. (ed.) (1985). *Feminist Aesthetics.* Boston: Beacon Press.

Erens, P. (ed.) (1990). *Issues in Feminist Film Criticism.* Bloomington: Indiana University Press.

Etcoff, N. (1999). *Survival of the Prettiest: The Science of Beauty.* New York: Doubleday.

Felski, R. (1989). *Beyond Feminist Aesthetics: Feminist Literature and Social Change.* Cambridge, Mass.: Harvard University Press.

——(1998). 'Critique of Feminist Aesthetics', in M. Kelly (ed.), *The Encyclopedia of Aesthetics.* New York: Oxford University Press, pp. 170–2.

Freeland, C. (1998). 'Feminist Film Theory', in M. Kelly (ed.), *The Encyclopedia of Aesthetics.* New York: Oxford University Press, pp. 201–4.

Garry, A. and Pearsall, M. (eds.) (1989). *Women, Knowledge and Reality: Explorations in Feminist Philosophy.* Boston: Unwin Hyman.

Gilligan, C. (1982). *In A Different Voice: Psychological Theory and Women's Development.* Cambridge, Mass.: Harvard University Press.

Gilman, S. (1999). *Making the Body Beautiful: A Cultural History of Aesthetic Surgery.* Princeton: Princeton University Press.

Hall, K. (1997). '*Sensus Communis* and Violence: A Feminist Reading of Kant's *Critique of Judgment*', in R. Scott (ed.), *Feminist Interpretations of Kant.* Unviersity Park, Pa.: Pennsylvania State University Press.

Harding, S. (1986). *The Science Question in Feminism.* Ithaca, NY: Cornell University Press.

Haskell, M. (1974). *From Reverence to Rape: The Treatment of Women in the Movies.* New York: Holt, Rinehard & Winston.

Heilbrun, C. and Higonnet, M. (eds.) (1983). *The Representation of Women in Fiction.* Baltimore: Johns Hopkins University Press.

Hein, H. and Korsmeyer, C. (eds.) (1993). *Aesthetics in Feminist Perspective.* Bloomington: Indiana University Press.

hooks, b. (1992). 'The Oppositional Gaze: Black Female Spectators', in her *Black Looks: Race and Representation.* Boston: South End Press, pp. 115–31; reprinted in Brand and Korsmeyer 1995: 142–59.

Isenberg, A. (1973). 'Formalism' and 'Perception, Meaning, and the Subject Matter of Art', in William Callaghan *et al.* (eds.), *Aesthetics and the Theory of Criticism: Selected Essays of Arnold Isenberg*. Chicago: University of Chicago Press, pp. 22–35 and 36–52.

Kant, I. (1987). *The Critique of Judgment*, trans. W. S. Pluhar. Indianapolis: Hackett; first published 1790.

Kaplan, E. A. (1987). 'Is the Gaze Male?' in M. Pearsall (ed.), *Women and Values: Readings in Recent Feminist Philosophy*, Belmont, Calif.: Wadsworth.

Kneller, J. (1997). 'The Aesthetic Dimension of Kantian Autonomy', in R. Scott (ed.), *Feminist Interpretations of Kant*. University Park, Pa.: Pennsylvania State University Press.

Korsmeyer, C. (1990). 'Gender Bias in Aesthetics', *APA Newsletter*, 89(2): 45–7.

—— (1993). 'Pleasure: Reflections on Aesthetics and Feminism'. *Journal of Aesthetics and Art Criticism*, 51(2): 199–206.

—— (1998). 'Perceptions, Pleasures, Arts: Considering Aesthetics', in J. A. Kourany (eds.), *Philosophy in a Feminist Voice: Critiques and Reconstructions*. Princeton: Princeton University Press, pp. 145–72.

Kristeva, J. (1987). 'Talking about *Polylogue*', in T. Moi (ed.), *French Feminist Thought: A Reader*. Oxford: Basil Blackwell, pp. 110–17.

Langer, S. (1942). *Philosophy in a New Key: A Study in the Symbolism of Reason, Rite, and Art*. 3rd edn. Cambridge, Mass.: Harvard University Press.

Lauter, E. (1993). 'Re-enfranchising Art: Feminist Interventions in the Theory of Art', in Hein and Korsmeyer (1993: 21–34).

Leibowitz, F. (1996). 'Apt Feelings, or Why "Women's Films" Aren't Trivial', in D. Bordwell and N. Carroll (eds.), *Post-Theory: Reconstructing Film Studies*. Madison, Wis.: University of Wisconsin Press, pp. 219–29.

Levinson, J. (ed.) (1998). *Aesthetics and Ethics: Essays at the Intersection*. New York: Cambridge University Press.

Lippard, L. (1976). *From the Center: Feminist Essays on Women's Art*. New York: Dutton.

Margolis, J. (1995). 'Reconciling Analytic and Feminist Philosophy and Aesthetics', in Brand and Korsmeyer (1995: 416–30).

Millett, K. (1970). *Sexual Politics*. Garden City, NJ: Doubleday.

Mothersill, M. (1984) *Beauty Restored*. New York: Oxford University Press.

Mullin, A. (2000). 'Art, Understanding and Political Change'. *Hypatia*, 15(3): 113–39.

Mulvey, L. (1988). 'Visual Pleasure and Narrative Cinema', in *Visual and Other Pleasures*, Bloomington: Indiana University Press, pp. 14–26. First published 1975.

Murdoch, I. (1950). *Existentialists and Mystics: Writings on Philosophy and Literature*. New York: Penguin.

Nead, L. (1994). *The Female Nude: Art, Obscenity, and Sexuality*. London: Routledge.

Nochlin, L. (1971). 'Why Have There Been No Great Women Artists?' In Nochlin (1988).

—— (1988). '*Women, Art and Power*', and Other Essays. New York: Harper & Row.

Okin, S. M. (1989). *Justice, Gender and the Family*. New York: Basic Books.

Parker, R. and Pollock, G. (1981, 1986). *Old Mistresses: Women, Art and Ideology*. New York: RKP and Pandora Press.

—— —— (eds.). (1987). *Framing Feminism: Art and the Women's Movement 1970–1985*. London: Pandora Press.

Pollock, G. (1988). *Vision and Difference: Femininity, Feminism and the Histories of Art*. London and New York: Routledge.

Reckitt, H. (ed.) *Art and Feminism*. London: Phaidon.

Rich, A. (1971). 'When We Dead Awaken: Writing as Re-Visions', in *On Lies, Secrets and Silence: Selected Prose 1966–1978*. New York: W. W. Norton, 1979.

Robinson, J. and Ross, S. (1993). 'Women, Morality and Fiction', in Hein and Korsmeyer (1993: 105–18).

Rothschild, J. (ed.) (1999). *Design and Feminism: Re-visioning Spaces, Places, and Everyday Things*. New Brunswick, NJ: Rutgers University Press.

Scarry, E. (1999). *On Beauty and Being Just.* Princeton: Princeton University Press.

Silvers, A. (1993). 'Pure Historicism and the Heritage of Hero(in)es: Who Grows in Phillis Wheatley's Garden?' *Journal of Aesthetics and Art Criticism* 51: 475–82.

Sontag, S. (1973). *On Photography.* New York: Farrar, Straus & Giroux.

Vogel, L. (1988). 'Fine Arts and Feminism: The Awakening Consciousness', in A. Raven, C. Lager, and J. Fruch (eds.), *Feminist Art Criticism: An Anthology.* New York: Harper Collins.

Waugh, J. (1995). 'Analytic Aesthetics and Feminist Aesthetics: Neither/Nor?' in Brand and Korsmeyer (1995: 399–415).

Wollheim, R. (1995). 'On Formalism and Its Kinds,' in *On Formalism and Its Kinds/Sobre el formalisme i els seus tipus.* Barcelona, pp. 7–47.

Woolf, V. (1929). *A Room of One's Own.* London: Hogarth Press.

Zwerdling, A. (1986). *Virginia Woolf and the Real World.* Berkeley: University of California Press.

CHAPTER 39

....

ENVIRONMENTAL AESTHETICS

....

JOHN A. FISHER

THE rapid growth of concern for the natural environment over the last third of the twentieth century has brought the welcome reintroduction of nature as a significant topic in aesthetics. In virtue of transforming previous attitudes towards nature, environmentalist thinking has posed questions about how we conceptualize our aesthetic interactions with nature, the aesthetic value of nature, and the status of art about nature. Although environmental concerns have undoubtedly motivated the new aesthetic interest in nature, the term 'environmental aesthetics' connotes two overlapping but distinct themes, one emphasizing the aesthetics of nature as understood by environmentalism, the second focusing on the notion of environments of all sorts as objects of appreciation.

First, the environmental roots. Beginning in the romantic era, poets and painters began to represent nature as more than merely the backdrop of human enterprise and drama. Nature began to be seen as comprising landscapes compelling in their own wild beauty and objects valuable in their smallest natural detail. Writing later in the nineteenth century, Henry David Thoreau and John Muir in different ways emphasized hands-on interactions with wilderness. In doing so, they introduced the radical notions that wild nature is in many respects superior to civilization and its products, and that harmonious, non-exploitative encounters with it are of transformative value.

To this must be added the Darwinian revolution, locating humans as merely an element within nature rather than masters of it, and the development of ecological thinking: the notion that elements of nature are thoroughly interdependent.

This interrelation of natural elements led Aldo Leopold in the 1940s to formulate the Land Ethic: 'A thing is right when it tends to preserve the integrity, stability, and beauty of the biotic community. It is wrong when it tends otherwise' (Leopold 1966: 240). Leopold's Land Ethic shifts the centre of moral gravity from humans to the larger nature of which they are a part, and it also allots a central place to the aesthetic value of nature.

From this perspective, nature is regarded not as an adversary or resource to be subdued and exploited, but as something with an autonomous and worthy existence in itself. In contrast to prior European attitudes, wilderness is regarded not as ugly or as a blemish on existence, but as something not only admirable, but admirable aesthetically. Indeed, environmental thinkers often indict traditional ways of understanding and regarding nature for being 'anthropocentric'.

The label 'environmental aesthetics' applies naturally to the ensuing wave of investigations of the aesthetics of nature conducted under the influence of environmental concerns. (Berleant 1998 suggests that environmental aesthetics is actually the successor to nature aesthetics.) Also important, however, is a broader use of the label championed by Berleant (1992) and Carlson (1992), who use it to cover aesthetic investigation of our experience of all sorts of environments, man-made as well as natural. This broader category of environmental aesthetics incorporates such diverse fields as city planning, landscape architecture, and environmental design, and it is significant because, whether applied to nature or built environments, it directly challenges the object-at-a-distance model associated with standard theories in aesthetics. That said, the majority of new work that falls notionally under this broader definition of environment grows out of concerns about nature instigated by environmentalism, and it concentrates on natural environments. Accordingly, most of the work to be explored in this chapter will be of this specific sort. As Berleant acknowledges, 'An interest in the aesthetics of environment is part of a broader response to environmental problems... and to public awareness and action on environmental issues' (1992: xii).

In environmental thinking and the attendant interest in environments in the broad sense, some thinkers see implications for the general practice of aesthetics, a discipline that in the twentieth century persistently ignored nature in favour of theories based on the arts. Environmental thinking, however, has begun to place strain on the assumption that aesthetic concepts drawn from the arts are also adequate to nature and to everyday life.

1. THE AESTHETIC VALUE OF NATURE

Although beauty has been out of fashion in the high arts throughout much of the twentieth century, most people happily view and describe nature as beautiful.

Indeed, whereas disagreement about the aesthetic quality of artworks is common-place, typically there is less disagreement about ascribing positive aesthetic qualities, such as beauty or grandeur, to individual objects (Siberian tigers) and places (Grand Canyon) in nature. What *is* accepted without question about artworks as a class (setting aside the avant-garde) is that they have *value*. Further, it is natural to think of this value as a *non-instrumental*, i.e. intrinsic, value. For instance, we do not lightly contemplate destroying art even if it would be convenient or profitable—indeed, even if preservation comes at a considerable cost.

Environmentalist thinking impacts aesthetics precisely in the thought that nature should be treated in the same way. Hargrove (1989) and Thompson (1995), for example, have noted that we value artworks as a class and accept obligations concerning their preservation. They do not regard this valuation as an arbitrary convention; the various aesthetic properties and meanings possessed by artworks give them an aesthetic value deriving from these aesthetic features. Hargrove and Thompson argue that nature is similarly valuable and worthy of preserving because of its aesthetic qualities. Thompson urges that, just as we accept an obligation to preserve beautiful artworks, we have obligations to preserve aesthetically valuable nature areas. (For a critique of such aesthetic preservationism see Godlovitch 1989.) Thompson also claims that the same sort of critical and evaluative discourse that applies to the arts appropriately applies to nature; the same patterns of reasoning that lead us to conclude that artworks have high aesthetic quality can be applied to parts of nature. It is not only that there are beautiful details and magnificent and rich structures in nature, but also that, like art, natural objects and sites can provide challenges to our conventional ways of perception, as well as to cultural significance, connection with the past, and so forth.

Because it plays a key role in preservationist arguments, aesthetic value is a more consequential concept in environmental aesthetics than it is in contemporary art aesthetics. Artworks as a class are regarded in modern society as having little instrumental value; they have no other use than to be appreciated. But nature clearly is another story. Humans, modern or not, need to exploit many aspects of nature, and we have the capacity thoroughly to develop almost all of it, if we choose. Nature, in short, has great instrumental value. If, as aesthetic preservationists argue, the aesthetic value of undeveloped nature ought to restrain our use of it for resource extraction, industry, recreation, etc., then aesthetic value has to bear significant weight.

Preservationist reasoning implies that the aesthetic value of undeveloped or wild nature is superior to that of developed nature. For example, an artificial lake will not possess the aesthetic value of the valleys or canyons that were flooded to make it, even though superficially it may be attractive. This suggests that it is unlikely that mere formal features (shapes, colours, reflecting surfaces, etc.) will fully account for the aesthetic value of nature. But what then needs to be added to formal properties, and where and how do we draw the line between nature (canyon) and artefact (lake)?

Environmentalist thinkers find difficulty with treatments of aesthetic value simply in terms of pleasure (as in Beardsley 1982). Brady (1998) classifies such approaches as 'hedonist models' of aesthetic appreciation. She says that the 'hedonist model classi-fies aesthetic value as a type of amenity value, where nature is valued for the aesthetic pleasure that it provides to inhabitants or visitors' (p. 97). She argues that such an emphasis on subjective pleasure will not support the conservation of a natural area as against, for instance, a potentially colourful recreational development. As an alternative, she proposes that an updated version of Kantian disinterestedness—with its eschewal of self-interest and utility—provides a better account of the aesthetic stance appropriately underpinning appreciation of nature. (For critiques of disinter-estedness applied to nature appreciation, see Berleant 1992; Miller 1993.)

Clearly, then, environmental thinkers have to account for the difference between authentic or wild nature and an artificial nature that might be perceptually similar. Accordingly, the notion of indiscernible counterparts plays a key role in environ-mental aesthetics, just as it has in recent art aesthetics, where philosophers (e.g. Walton, Danto, Levinson, Currie) have used examples of indiscernible objects one of which is an artwork and the other of which is a different artwork or no artwork at all to argue against the idea that the status and the aesthetic qualities of artworks are determined solely by their inherent perceptual properties. For nature, the aes-thetic difference between perceptually similar states of affairs becomes practically important in the context of restoration ecology, the field that proposes to restore or recreate natural areas that have been degraded by human development (see Elliot 1997). Regardless of whether this is biologically possible, the aesthetic question is whether nature can be exploited—e.g. by mining—and then restored to its original state with similar aesthetic qualities.

The first question is whether one can appreciate an artefactualized segment of 'nature' as if it were natural. Carlson (1981) considers the difference between a natural coastline and a hypothetical one that is perceptually indistinguishable but created by removal of structures, large-scale earth, rock and sand movement, landscaping with similar plants, and so on. He argues that these two coastlines should be perceived dif-ferently, one as an artefact, the other as a natural coastline. Although they may have similar curves, lines, colours and shapes, he asserts that we properly ascribe many dif-ferent second-order properties to these similar perceptual patterns. For example, the curve of one coast is *very ingenious*, whereas the curve of the natural coast is no such thing, but rather is the product of erosion by the sea. On the other hand, perhaps the natural coast *expresses the power of the sea*, whereas the artefact coast does no such thing. Carlson concludes that, because we are led to ascribe different properties to the object, it is aesthetically important to perceive an object under the category to which it belongs, as either an artefact or the product of natural forces, just as it is aesthetically important to perceive an artwork in its true art historical category (cf. Walton 1970).

It is natural to suppose that the aesthetic *value* of an item increases with its aes-thetic *quality*. Applying this relation to nature seems to imply that some parts of nature have greater aesthetic value than other parts. Some thinkers (e.g. Thompson 1995) accept this, but many others reject the idea that nature can be aesthetically evaluated and ranked in a way parallel to artworks.

A common view among environmental thinkers is that dubbed 'positive aesthetics' by Allen Carlson. The strongest version of this position holds that all virgin nature is beautiful (Carlson 1984: 10). A weaker formulation is that the 'natural environment, in so far as it is untouched by man, has mainly positive aesthetic qualities; it is, for example, graceful, delicate, intense, unified, and orderly, rather than bland, dull, insipid, incoherent, and chaotic' (Carlson 1984: 5). The weaker version clearly does not entail that all parts of nature are equally beautiful, and so it may leave undefended the claim implied by the stronger version: namely, that we cannot maintain that one part of nature is aesthetically superior to another part. The proponent of positive aesthetics rejects conventional aesthetic hierarchies concerning nature—e.g., majestic mountain *v.* bland prairie *v.* dank swamp. Although the aesthetic evaluation of artworks may vary from great to mediocre to poor, and their qualities from beautiful to boring to ugly, this is exactly what is different about nature, according to positive aesthetics.

Positive aesthetics can be understood as the result of two intuitions. First, that aesthetic assessment of art involves criticism, judgement and ultimately *comparison*. But such comparative judgements are appropriate only for artefacts, which are intended to be a certain way or to accomplish certain goals, not for nature. Second, our tendency to find some parts of nature bland, boring, or even distasteful are all based on projecting *inappropriate* ideas or comparisons on to the objects of our experience, for example looking for a view of nature that is similar to a beautifully framed and balanced art representation, or looking at a dark forest as full of evil spirits. Nature properly understood—that is, against a background of biology, geology, and ecology—is, as a matter of fact beautiful, or at least aesthetically good, in many ways.

As Callicott notes, paraphrasing Leopold, knowledge of the ecological relationships between the organisms, the evolutionary and geological history, and so forth can transform a marsh 'from a "waste", "God-forsaken" mosquito swamp, into a thing of precious beauty' (Callicott 1987: 162). We see that the marsh is a thing of beauty when we appreciate it as the habitat of the sandhill crane, when we understand that the cranes originated in distant geological ages, when we understand the intricate interrelations of all of the organisms in the marsh, and so on. Conversely, superficially attractive but non-native plants and animals may be seen as disharmonious interlopers that undermine the balance of nature. (For a sympathetic critique of positive aesthetics, see Godlovitch 1998.)

2. ENVIRONMENTALISM AND THE APPRECIATION OF NATURE

Of the many questions that environmentalist claims give rise to, perhaps none is more fundamental than the question whether nature can be appropriately appreciated with the same methods and assumptions with which we appreciate art. The model of appreciation at the heart of standard art aesthetics is roughly this: it is an interpretive judgement of a demarcated object based on a conventionally circumscribed perception of it. Environmentally inclined aestheticians have found difficulty with many aspects of this model. The environmental tradition gives rise to a preference for a more active relationship with, and within, a natural world of interconnected elements. These points lead to the notion (Carlson 1979; Berleant 1992) that environmental appreciation (*a*) is typically a physically active interaction, (*b*) involves integrated and self-conscious use of all the senses, including touch and smell (Tuan 1993), and (*c*) does not privilege any one vantage point or small set of vantage points as the correct place from which to experience the natural setting or objects.

Are these conditions sufficient for aesthetic experience of nature (or any environment)? If so, then would any self-conscious interaction with nature, e.g. pleasurably basking in the sun, be an aesthetic experience? If not, then what more needs to be added? Carlson (1979) argues that the further feature required is that one's sensory interaction be guided by commonsense/scientific knowledge about nature. Without this cognition, our experience is a blooming, buzzing confusion; but with such science-based cognition our raw experience acquires determinate centres of aesthetic significance and is made harmonious and meaningful.

Another question stimulated by the environmentalist model is whether an aesthetic response to a natural environment is, as in conventional aesthetics, in essence a perceptual–judgemental one, or whether it can be an *action*, such as rock climbing, hiking, or Thoreauvian digging and planting beans. An example of an action or series of actions that are usually regarded as highly aesthetic occurs in the Japanese tea ceremony, where respect for the utensils, ingredients, and the nature setting of the tea house is an integral part of the ceremony, and one of the basic goals of the ceremony is to exemplify harmony between the host and the setting. Even such examples, however, exhibit highly refined perception as an integral component of the actions. So, one could propose that in general actions can be aesthetic if, first of all, they are responses *to* objects and situations, and second, the response is founded upon an aesthetic perception of the situation.

Carlson's (1979, 1981) science-based model of aesthetic appreciation of nature (extended by Carlson, 1985, to all environments) has received considerable attention. For instance, Saito (1984) questions the necessity, and Rolston (1995) the sufficiency, of a science-based appreciation of nature such as Carlson advocates. Carroll further argues that there are alternatives to Carlson's picture, insisting that an emotional response to nature 'can be an appropriate form of nature appreciation' (Carroll 1993: 253) and that such a response need not be based on scientific knowledge: it could simply involve, say, being overwhelmed by the grandeur of 'a towering cascade'. Carroll thus proposes a pluralist model that allows as one sort of legitimate aesthetic appreciation of nature a kind of response that, although based on perception of salient natural features, is not grounded in scientifically informed perception.

The main argument for a science-based appreciation of nature is that we require an objective basis for appreciating nature as it truly is, not as we wish it or fear it to be, and that science is our best procedure for understanding nature objectively. Godlovitch (1994) finds that this argument does not go far enough. He emphasizes the environmentalist desideratum that we regard nature 'as it is and not merely as it is for us' (p. 16). Accordingly, he claims that a 'natural aesthetic must forswear the anthropocentric limits which fittingly define and dominate our aesthetic response to and regard for cultural objects' (p. 16). He argues that even science is too much a reflection of human sensibilities to constitute the basis of a true environmentalist aesthetic, which would be *acentric*, privileging no point of view, least of all a human one: 'Centric [e.g. anthropocentric and biocentric] environmentalism fails to reflect Nature as a whole because Nature is apportioned and segmented by it' (p. 17). But is it possible for us to adopt a regard of nature that eschews human perspectives, and if it is, can we still regard this as involving aesthetic appreciation?

3. ENVIRONMENTAL ART?

Nature art has obviously been a key factor in a general increase of appreciation of wild nature and in the growth of environmentalism—witness the importance of nature photography to the efforts of conservation groups. There is a certain irony, then, in the fact that environmentalist arguments concerning how we ought to appreciate nature threaten to undermine the legitimacy of nature art and to raise questions as well about other sorts of art about nature.

Within the generic category of art *about* nature, we can define the familiar genre of 'nature art' as representations of nature in any art medium—principally, literature and the visual arts—that have nature, not humans, as their main subject. In addition, nature art is usually thought of as exhibiting the same favourable regard to nature as positive aesthetics; even fierce, barren, or threatening landscapes are presented as being admirable or as having positive aesthetic features.

Although nature art inspires appreciation of nature, does it reflect the aesthetics of nature as environmental aesthetics understands it? One aspect of this broad question can be stated as follows: can works of nature art *exhibit or represent* the aesthetic qualities of the nature represented?

Carlson (1979) gives an influential argument—endorsed by Callicott (1987), Carroll (1993), and Godlovitch (1994)—for rejecting the 'object' and 'landscape' models of nature appreciation, which appears relevant to the question of aesthetic adequacy. Based on art appreciation, these models involve looking at objects in nature for their formal and expressive qualities, abstracting them from their context as if they were sculpture, or framing and perceiving sites as if in a landscape painting. Carlson argues that neither of these methods respects the actual nature of nature. To appreciate nature as nature, we must regard nature as an *environment* (in the broad sense) and as *natural*, but not as art. This means that we cannot, as in the object model, remove objects from their environments. If we remove them, even notionally, we change their aesthetic qualities, which the objects have only in relation to the whole environment. For example, a rock considered by itself may lack the qualities that it has in nature, where it is related to the forces that shaped it (glaciation, volcanism, erosion). The problem with the landscape model is that it involves perceiving nature 'as a grandiose prospect seen from a specific standpoint and distance' (Carlson 1979: 131). Carlson describes appreciating nature this way as dividing nature up into blocks of scenery to be viewed from a certain vantage point, 'not unlike a walk through a gallery of landscape paintings' (p. 132). But, as he notes, 'the environment is not a scene, not a representation, not static, and not two-dimensional' (p. 133).

Yet, if this is the wrong way to experience nature aesthetically, can we experience nature aesthetically (albeit indirectly) or experience the aesthetic properties of nature through appreciating nature art? Carlson's argument raises the question whether we can experience the beauty of a natural environment by appreciating the beauty of a photograph of that environment. However, might not nature art exhibit how a part of nature actually appeared at a certain moment from a certain point of view? Even though limited and incomplete, why must a representation be seen as necessarily unable authentically to exhibit *some* of the aesthetic qualities of the represented objects or scenes?

Different issues are raised by non-representational art about nature, for instance artworks that incorporate natural objects, sites, or processes as elements. Such features by themselves, of course, do not necessarily determine that an artwork is *about* nature. Some artworks that superficially relate to a natural site, such as sculpture placed in a nature setting (e.g. sculpture parks), as well as works that use natural elements, such as Jeff Koons's 1992 *Puppy* (a 43-foot-high West Highland Terrier form covered with thousands of live flowers), are plainly not *about* nature. Carlson helpfully defines the class of 'environmental artworks' as works that 'are in or on the land in a way such that part of nature constitutes a part of the relevant object . . . not only is the site of an environmental work an environmental site, but the site itself is an aspect of the work' (1986: 636).

Given the deep divide separating the arts and environmental thought, it is essential to contrast their perspectives concerning this large domain of artefacts. From the perspective of the arts, attention naturally focuses on how to interpret and appreciate environmental works *as art*. What issues about nature and culture does the artist deal with? How does the piece relate to trends in recent art? What attitudes does it express? And so on. For example, Gilbert-Rolfe interprets Smithson's *Spiral Jetty* in relation to film: 'In Smithson the idea of the work lies as much in the film of the work as in the work' (Gilbert-Rolfe 1988: 72). And Smithson (1973), as theorist of earthworks art, interprets Central Park as a landscape inspired by the eighteenth-century picturesque. Finally, Ross proposes that environmental artworks as a class are the descendants of the eighteenth-century high art of gardening, that 'environmental art is *gardening's* avant-garde' (Ross 1993: 153).

There is also the issue of whether gardens and parks, the environments seemingly most intermediate between the arts and nature, are full-fledged artworks. Certainly many examples of both types of artefact have a strong claim to the status of art. Smithson (1973) argues, for example, that New York's Central Park is a great artwork, exemplifying many of the dialectical principles of his own earthworks. Miller urges that gardens constitute an artkind, on a par with painting or sculpture. This is so clear that it leads to a puzzle: 'Why then, if current theories of art show no grounds for excluding them...and if gardens have a history of being regarded as an artkind and can be shown to have form as beautiful, as original, and as self-conscious as the other arts, are gardens currently excluded from the category of art?' (Miller 1993: 72). She resolves this by noting the ways that gardens—by their essence tied to particular sites, ever-changing because of the natural elements, etc.—present multiple challenges to standard preferences of art theory, such as for complete artistic control of the work and for consistent qualities of the work over time.

From the perspective of environmental thought, however, with its inherent rejection of any activity or stance that regards nature as something to be used or as something whose purpose is to be determined by cultural perspectives, the issues point in a different direction, towards how environmental artworks deal with nature. Thus, because earthworks since their inception have often inspired opposition from environmentalists, it is not surprising that the question whether environmental artworks are an *affront* to nature has been explored (Carlson 1986). Less severe questions can also be raised, such as whether environmental artworks are based on an adequate conception of nature and whether they enfranchise an appropriate aesthetic relationship with nature. Topiary, for example, is intriguing as an artform. But by imposing artificial (geometric, representational) forms on to natural objects (trees and shrubs) topiary does not illuminate the aesthetic properties of nature as nature: it suggests not only that nature can be improved upon aesthetically, but that nature provides sculptural material to be manipulated and exploited.

Ross (1993) organizes environmental art into seven categories, such as 'masculine gestures in the environment' (Heizer, Smithson, De Maria), 'ephemeral gestures in the environment' (Singer, Long, Fulton, Goldsworthy), and 'proto-gardens' (Sonfist, Irwin). Some of this work is clearly troubling in how it uses and/or regards nature, for example Heizer's *Double Negative* (1969–70)—a 50 ft × 30 ft × 1500 ft bulldozed double cut in Virgin River Mesa, displacing 240,000 tons of rhyolite and sandstone—and Christo's *Surrounded Islands* (1983)—eleven islands in Biscayne Bay surrounded for two weeks by sheets of bright pink plastic floating in the water extended 200 ft from the islands into the Bay.

Carlson (1986) rebuts several common defences of such intrusive artworks, for example that they are temporary (Christo), that they improve nature, or that the artist's actions are no different from the alteration of a site by natural processes (Smithson's argument). In spite of this, there are other works of environmental art, such as Sonfist's *Time Landscape* (1965–78), in which the artist attempts to recreate an urban area's lost native flora on a vacant urban lot, that cannot be regarded as affronts to nature, since they do not alter natural aesthetic qualities. Because they respect nature as nature, such works, as well as the conceptual walks and environmental gestures of Long, Fulton, and Goldsworthy, can also be regarded as adequate aesthetically to nature, that is as reflecting nature's actual aesthetic qualities.

Still, there remains a nagging question: can this art contribute to the appreciation of nature? Carlson (1986) wonders why the aesthetic interest in nature can be recognized only if it is first considered art. There seems, in fact, to be a dilemma. Either a work alters nature (e.g. 'masculine gestures'), in which case it may affront and misunderstand nature as nature, or it does not (e.g. 'ephemeral gestures'), in which case what does it add to the appreciation of nature? It might be replied that at least such art leads the viewer to notice aspects of nature that had escaped her attention. But more might be claimed. The arts have always been one way to explore the world and our feelings and ideas about it. Environmental art explores our ideas about nature and our changing relations with it. As such, works may not always express the most environmentally enlightened perspectives, and works in the past—for example formal gardens—probably did not. Still, are inadequate conceptions of nature entirely wrong? Can't there be aspects of nature that are usefully brought out even by such works? In any event, those environmental artworks that do adopt environmentally enlightened perspectives can be viewed as addressing in unique ways questions about how we can interact with nature aesthetically while at the same time respecting nature for what it is.

See also: Aesthetics of Nature; Aesthetics of the Everyday; Comparative Aesthetics; Architecture.

Bibliography

Beardsley, M. (1982). 'The Aesthetic Point of View', reprinted in M. J. Wreen and D. M. Callen (eds.), *The Aesthetic Point of View: Selected Essays*. Ithaca, NY: Cornell University Press, pp. 15–34.

Berleant, A. (1992). *The Aesthetics of Environment*. Philadelphia: Temple University Press.

——(1998). 'Environmental Aesthetics', in M. Kelly (ed.), *Encyclopedia of Aesthetics*. New York: Oxford University Press, pp. 114–20.

——and Carlson, A. (1998). 'Introduction' to Special Issue on 'Environmental Aesthetics'. *Journal of Aesthetics and Art Criticism* 56: 97–100.

Brady, E. (1998). 'Imagination and the Aesthetic Appreciation of Nature'. *Journal of Aesthetics and Art Criticism* 56: 139–47.

Callicott, J. (1987). 'The Land Aesthetic', in J. Callicott (ed.), *Companion to* A Sand County Almanac*: Interpretive and Critical Essays*. Madison: University of Wisconsin Press, pp. 157–71.

Carlson, A. (1979). 'Appreciation and the Natural Environment'. *Journal of Aesthetics and Art Criticism* 37: 267–75.

—— (1981). 'Nature, Aesthetic Judgment, and Objectivity'. *Journal of Aesthetics and Art Criticism* 40: 15–27.

—— (1984). 'Nature and Positive Aesthetics'. *Environmental Ethics* 6: 5–34.

—— (1985). 'On Appreciating Agricultural Landscapes'. *Journal of Aesthetics and Art Criticism* 43: 301–12.

—— (1986). 'Is Environmental Art an Aesthetic Affront to Nature?' *Canadian Journal of Philosophy* 16: 635–50.

—— (1992). 'Environmental Aesthetics', in D. Cooper (ed.), *A Companion to Aesthetics*. Oxford: Blackwell, pp. 142–4.

—— (2000). *Aesthetics and the Environment: The Appreciation of Nature, Art and Architecture*. London: Routledge.

Carroll, N. (1993). 'On Being Moved by Nature: Between Religion and Natural History', in S. Kemal and I. Gaskell (eds.), *Landscape, Natural Beauty and the Arts*. Cambridge: Cambridge University Press, pp. 244–66.

Elliot, R. (1997). *Faking Nature: The Ethics of Environmental Restoration*. London: Routledge.

Fisher, J. (1998). 'What the Hills are Alive with: In Defense of the Sounds of Nature'. *Journal of Aesthetics and Art Criticism* 56: 167–79.

Gilbert-Rolfe, J. (1988). 'Sculpture as Everything Else, or Twenty Years or So of the Question of Landscape'. *Arts Magazine* January: 71–5.

Godlovitch, S. (1989). 'Aesthetic Protectionism'. *Journal of Applied Philosophy* 6: 171–80.

—— (1994). 'Icebreakers: Environmentalism and Natural Aesthetics'. *Journal of Applied Philosophy* 11: 15–30.

—— (1998). 'Valuing Nature and the Autonomy of Natural Aesthetics'. *British Journal of Aesthetics* 38: 180–97.

Hargrove, E. C. (1989). *Foundations of Environmental Ethics*. Englewood Cliffs, NJ: Prentice-Hall.

Leopold, A. (1966). *Sand County Almanac, with Other Essays on Conservation from Round River*. New York: Oxford University Press. First published 1949.

Miller, M. (1993). *The Garden as an Art*. Albany, NY: State University of New York Press.

Rolston, H. III (1995). 'Does Aesthetic Appreciation of Landscapes Need to be Science-based?' *British Journal of Aesthetics* 35: 374–86.

Ross, S. (1993). 'Gardens, Earthworks, and Environmental Art', in S. Kemal and I. Gaskell (eds.), *Landscape, Natural Beauty and the Arts*. Cambridge: Cambridge University Press, pp. 158–82.

—— (1998). *What Gardens Mean*. Chicago: University of Chicago Press.

Saito, Y. (1984). 'Is There a Correct Aesthetic Appreciation of Nature?' *Journal of Aesthetic Education* 18: 35–46.

—— (1998). 'The Aesthetics of Unscenic Nature'. *Journal of Aesthetics and Art Criticism* 56: 100–11.

Sepanmaa, Y. (1993). *Beauty of Environment: A General Model for Environmental Aesthetics.* 2nd edn. Denton, Tex.: Environmental Ethics Books.

Smithson, R. (1973). 'Frederick Law Olmstead and the Dialectical Landscape'. *Artforum* February; reprinted in N. Holt (ed.), *The Writings of Robert Smithson: Essays with Illustrations.* New York: New York University Press, 1979, pp. 117–28.

Thompson, J. (1995). 'Aesthetics and the Value of Nature'. *Environmental Ethics* 17: 291–305.

Tuan, Y. (1993). *Passing Strange and Wonderful: Aesthetics, Nature, and Culture.* New York: Kodansha International.

Walton, K. (1970). 'Categories of Art'. *Philosophical Review* 79: 334–67.

CHAPTER 40

COMPARATIVE AESTHETICS

KATHLEEN HIGGINS

ONE of the first questions that arises in efforts to do comparative aesthetics is whether or not the terms 'art' and 'aesthetics' are inextricably bound to certain cultures and their presuppositions. Since the Enlightenment, the dominant Western conception of 'fine' art is distinguished from that of 'crafts' used in everyday life. A work of art is understood to be designed primarily for contemplation; if it serves any other practical function, this is considered to be secondary. Theorists disagree on the criteria for judging the work of art, but typically these are linked to a state of mind in the observer (whether emotional, intellectual, or some combination of the two). Works of fine art, being geared to reflective appreciation, are at home in institutional environments that are free from the distractions of everyday life, such as the concert hall or the museum. The notion of 'aesthetics' in the West has typically focused on the fine arts, identified in Western terms. By contrast, many societies make art, or something much like it, for purposes other than engaging contemplation; they do not distinguish between fine arts and crafts, judge artworks by their performance of practical functions, and integrate art into everyday life (see Keil 1979; Feld 1994; Van Damme 1996).

Anthropologist Robert Plant Armstrong is among those who consider terms like 'art' to have too many Western connotations that are disanalogous to other societies' usage to be helpful in cross-cultural comparisons. He proposes instead the notion of an 'affecting presence', a term that includes humanly produced objects and events that have 'powers' to affect human beings experientially and a 'presence' comparable to that of a human being (Armstrong 1971). Armstrong claims universality for the phenomenon he calls 'affecting presences', although some critics of the strategy of using Western terms in discussions of non-Western art would contend that 'universality' itself carries too much Western baggage. Others, such as Wilfried Van Damme, are more sanguine about extending the domain of traditional Western terms to encompass analogous expressive forms and reflection about them from other societies (see Van Damme 1996).

Other methodological questions are raised by proponents of contextualism, who insist that art and aesthetic practices must be assessed with reference to their contexts. This position is a direct challenge to the views that art should be judged solely on the basis of formal criteria (the influential position of Immanuel Kant), and that great works of art inevitably 'transcend' the cultures that produce them. Formalism encourages a dismissive attitude towards the indigenous aesthetic views of African societies, according to Barry Hallen (1998). But what features of a society constitute the relevant context for understanding its aesthetics?

Certainly, the identification of the society that produced the art would seem to be relevant. Given earlier institutional practices, this is not simply to be assumed. Western exhibitions and studies of African art, for example, typically did not even indicate the tribal origins of given works of art before the middle of the twentieth century (Hallen 1998). Approaching non-Western artworks with reference to the standards that guide their production would also seem desirable, but this requires information that Westerners are only gradually acquiring.

In traditions that are primarily oral, the need is particularly urgent for study of indigenous aesthetic terminology. Valuable new anthropological studies of indigenous aesthetics and aesthetic language have appeared over the last few decades (see e.g. Feld 1990; Roseman 1991; Thompson 1983). The importance of such studies for understanding the aesthetic productions of non-Western societies is obvious. Westerners are likely to misjudge the achievements of non-Western artists if they simply apply their own society's standards for what counts as art and the aims of such art. Steven Feld observes, as a case in point, that the Kaluli tribe of Papua New Guinea, whose music is structured to involve overlapping voices, were dismissed as unmusical by missionaries because of tribe members' seeming difficulty in singing hymns in unison (Feld 1994).

The application of realistic representational standards to Yoruba sculpture would be similarly inappropriate. Robert Farris Thompson describes the criterion of *jíjora*, or 'mimesis at the mid-point', as a basic evaluative standard for sculptures of human beings among the Yoruba of Nigeria (Thompson 1968). The aim is the 'midpoint' between verisimilitude and abstraction. Artists try to present a lively human presence, but avoid replicating the appearance of any particular individual too precisely, lest the model be exposed to evil magic through the sculpture. Babatunde Lawal observes that Yoruba sculpture of the *orishas* (the lesser gods who serve as deputies to the High God, *Oloron*, who is never depicted) is only selectively realistic, making the most important parts of the body, particularly the head, most prominent (Lawal 1974).

The context of many societies' religious traditions is also important background for understanding the place of art and aesthetic theory within them. Some of the non-Western societies with the most well developed textual traditions make explicit reference to religion in their aesthetic texts. For example, traditional Indian aesthetic theory, which focuses on art's power to induce ecstatic states, draws on traditional Hindu ideas. According to most schools in the Hindu tradition, the individual self (*jiva*) is ultimately illusory. The true Self, or *atman*, is a single being, the same within everyone. Religious practices such as meditation are performed with the aim of recognizing this truth and the further truth that one's true Self is identical with Brahman (the supreme God, or absolute reality). Certain rarefied experiences of art are described by various commentators as either resembling or stimulating union with God.

The most important text in the Indian aesthetic tradition is Bharata's *Natyasastra* (CE 200–500), which deals primarily with drama (Goswamy 1986; see also Rowell 1992). Like Aristotle's *Poetics* in the West, the *Natyasastra*'s theory of theatre aesthetics has been applied to the whole range of the arts. The text focuses on drama's power to transform its audience, which it explains in terms of *rasa*, the particular emotional savour, or 'taste', of a performance. Although every work of art has its own unique *rasa*, *rasas* have come to be classified in terms of eight or nine basic types: the erotic (*Shringara*), the comic (*Hasya*), the pathetic (*Karuna*), the furious (*Raudra*), the heroic (*Vira*), the terrible (*Bhayanaka*), the odious (*Bibhatsa*), the marvellous (*Adbhuta*), and, according to some theorists, the quiescent (*Shanta*).

Rasa binds together various components of a performance, including the object that causes the emotional state, the surrounding environment that enhances it, the gestures that convey emotional states, and the transient emotions that come and go during the course of a performance. The composite effect of these factors is a fundamental emotional quality, called *bhava*. *Bhava* is achieved when the performance of a work is sufficiently intense to provoke a 'churning of the heart' in the audience member. This dominant emotional quality emerges from an artful performance; however, not everyone in the audience has the spiritual preparation to experience the full flavour, or *rasa* (Goswamy 1986).

The ecstatic experience of *rasa* occurs only in the *rasika*, the sufficiently competent audience member. Kashmiri theorist Abhinavagupta (CE 950–1000), in his commentary *Abhinava Bharati*, contends that the *rasika* is one who has transcended consciousness of the personal self through spiritual discipline. Having lost a sense of self-consciousness, the *rasika* completely identifies with the artwork, with the consequence that *rasa* pervades his or her being. Abhinavagupta employs the term *rasa* only for transcendent aesthetic emotion, using *bhava* for the more worldly emotion aroused in a less cultivated audience member (Gerow 1997).

Religious tradition is also an important determinant of stylistic preferences in some societies. The arabesque, the continuous self-intertwining line that is a staple of Islamic design, reflects a number of Muslim beliefs. This decorative technique reflects the religious requirement to avoid representation, and the belief that only abstraction can represent the transcendent boundlessness of God. The use of the single line to form a complex spatial construction reflects the central doctrine of *tauhid*, the unity of Allah, and Allah's presence everywhere. Moreover, the impression that the line of the arabesque is unending, since it curls back into itself, symbolizes the idea that Allah is infinite, without beginning or end (Madden 1975). The geometrical perfection of the arabesque also reflects the perfection of God, as does mathematics generally.

Particular artistic techniques have also been nurtured by religious world-views in some cultures. The Chan sect of Buddhism in China and its Japanese counterpart, Zen, have exercised considerable influence on artistic practice in these two cultures. Philip Rawson describes a particularly noteworthy style of painting developed to express the intensity of sudden illumination as Chan and Zen practitioners understand it. The Chinese term for this style is '*i-pin*', meaning 'untrammelled' or 'unrestrained' (Rawson 1967). The aim is a display of energy, often with wild results. Spontaneity is conveyed through the techniques employed. Forms are sketchy, hinting that the things depicted lack substantiality. Strokes are rough. Buddhist doctrine holds that there is no distinct thing or self, but that only the interdependent whole exists. In keeping with this doctrine, *i-pin* forms are sketchy, and people resemble caricatures. Boundaries dissolve. Ink may be splashed. Sometimes the entire painting is accomplished in a single brushstroke.

Such Zen painting also suggests the Buddhist doctrine of the transience of all things by presenting depictions in a typically unlimited environment. One's attention moves from the subject matter to the unbounded environment and its emptiness. The pictured subject matter sometimes seems to dissolve into the background, as if disintegrating into what is no longer articulated. Peter Lamarque draws attention to the relevance of Buddhist doctrine to another case of artistic dissolution as well, the dissolution of the personality of the character being portrayed in Japanese Noh theatre (Lamarque 1989).

Despite the importance of knowing some central ideas in Buddhism in order to interpret such art, we should keep in mind that many cultures are composites of multiple religious traditions, all of which influence artistic developments. Indeed, Chan Buddhism was strongly influenced by Daoism, and the two traditions are not always distinct in China. Arthur H. Thornhill warns against attempting a one-to-one correlation between a society's art and a single religious sect or world-view. He argues that common identifications of Basho as the quintessential Zen poet ignore the many ways in which he expresses neo-Confucian ideals as well (Thornhill 1998; see also Kasulis 1998).

Even a complex account of a culture's religious heritage is an insufficient basis for contextualizing artistic and other aesthetic practices, because it does not take into account other factors that structure these practices. Some anthropologists, particularly those influenced by Karl Marx, suggest that a society's economic organization is the most fundamental structural basis for explaining artistic practices. The Marxist position holds that the dynamics of economic power relations are reflected in artistic practices. Capitalist culture encourages the ownership of art by private individuals, who value it largely because it displays socioeconomic status; while less stratified societies are more likely to develop egalitarian artistic practices, such as community contexts for enjoying and participating in artistic activities.

The Marxist account pays little attention to the features of particular artworks, focusing instead on the typical ways a society makes and uses art. Other accounts, in contextualizing artistic practices, do more to explain the development of particular artistic forms or genres within given societies. Many ethno-musicologists have argued, for example, that the ways in which voices combine in genres of songs reflect a society's understanding of how the members of the community, with their various roles, should interact (see Feld 1984; Lomax 1968).

Still other information is necessary to contextualize particular artworks, as opposed to a society's artistic practices as a whole. Some awareness of political contexts is essential to the interpretation of artworks involving political commentary, for allusions to political matters are often quite subtle (especially where reprisals are threatened). Even knowledge of the broad features of social practices and historical developments would often fail to explain pointed cases of artistic allusion and satire (see Stokes 1994). Ascertaining the extent to which an artwork exhibits generic traits and the extent to which it reveals individual achievement may also require recognition of factors that influence particular artists' insights and innovations. Isidore Okpewho observes, for example, that artists in Africa are influenced by a 'play impulse' in giving shape to artworks, a psychological feature of art-making that is missed when art is interpreted exclusively in terms of religious world-views (Okpewho 1977).

However, scholars should beware, when they attempt to situate non-Western art and aesthetics in cultural context, not to demand a false 'authenticity' from non-Western artists or commentators. Outside understandings of what is 'authentic' in a culture often involve a degree of fantasy, particularly regarding the culture's homogeneity and its contemporary fidelity to practices of the past. Kwame Anthony Appiah, Denis Dutton, and Larry Shiner have challenged Western conceptions that judge authenticity on the basis of their own theoretical expectations, instead of an appreciation of living practices in the society being studied (Appiah 1991; Dutton 1993; Shiner 1994).

Thus far we have considered some features of the agenda for Western aestheticians who seek some awareness of non-Western aesthetics. Western interest in the aesthetics of other cultures often coincides, however, with an interest in formulating comparisons between traditions. The effort to formulate comparisons raises its own questions. How does one determine which similarities and which differences are significant enough to merit attention? Different individuals are likely to reach different conclusions. The same evidence will strike one as justification for aesthetic relativism, and another as an illustration of how much human beings have in common. Two comparativists might take different views on the question of whether the scarification techniques used for personal adornment in some African cultures (Keil 1979) are more saliently different from or similar to Western practices. Westerners do not deliberately etch lines into the skin for cosmetic purposes; however, Western beautification practices also involve many rather painful processes.

Similarly, one might ask whether similarities or differences are more important when one compares Western techniques for achieving closure in an artwork with Japanese techniques, discussed by Ohashi Ryosuke (Ryosuke 1998) and Keiji Nishitani (Nishitani 1995). Nishitani, for example, describes *ikebana*, the Japanese art of cut flowers, as a means of making flowers 'float in emptiness'. He argues that this art directs attention to an object by 'cutting' it out of its everyday context. Once cut, a flower no longer interacts with the rest of its environment, but manifests transcendence of time, as if in a timeless present. The Zen idea that we all float in a context of emptiness, as well as the conception of making art that is intentionally transitory, are rather foreign to traditional Western canons, although a number of twentieth-century Western artists, particularly performance artists, have developed new transitory forms. Nevertheless, the longstanding Western idea of artistic closure, of giving artworks clear boundaries, might be thought similar to the Japanese 'cut', in that closure also attempts to bring a phenomenon to our attention by severing it from its context.

Inevitably, a comparativist will initially approach a foreign culture by reference to what is familiar. Many of the studies of comparative aesthetics thus far have focused on conspicuous contrasts among the aesthetic values of different societies. Donald Keene, for example, has identified a number of Japanese aesthetic values that contrast with those traditional in the West (Keene 1969). He identifies suggestion, irregularity, perishability, and simplicity as important in Japanese aesthetics, in contrast to the Western preferences for explicit parts that form organic unities, completion, regularity, relative permanence, and complexity.

One may ask, however, whether all important similarities and differences among societies' aesthetic values will be evident from surface inspection of their artworks and other artefacts. Van Damme points out that societies may share certain principles regarding what is aesthetically valuable but may nevertheless express these principles through radically different artistic forms (Van Damme 1996). This suggests that assessments of similarities and differences among different cultures' artworks will inevitably be theory-laden, dependent on some analysis of the principles underlying aesthetic choices in making and evaluating art in the respective cultures. One task for comparative aesthetics is the delineation of the aesthetic principles informing various cultures' art; another is the construction of accounts of how such principles are manifested in those cultures' artworks.

The principles involved in the aesthetic thought and practice in a non-Western culture, however, may become evident only after one has been exposed to a large range of that culture's aesthetically valued phenomena. In the case of many cultures, this range includes practices outside the arts as identified in the West. Comparative aestheticians, therefore, should avoid restricting themselves to considering artefacts that resemble Western 'fine art'. The Western distinction between the impractical, beautiful fine arts and the functional, more pedestrian crafts is inappropriately applied to many societies, and can interfere with our understanding of aesthetic values within them (see Onyewuenyi 1984).

Common to a number of non-Western societies is the tendency to judge the beauty of an artwork or performance on thoroughly practical criteria, such as whether it performs its function well. A Kaluli mask has aesthetic value when it is used in the performance of a dance in which the dancer is seen as transforming into a bird, the form in which the spirits of the deceased are believed to endure (Feld 1990). Songs and other artforms are considered beautiful by the Navajo if they succeed in healing a sick person (see McAllester 1973).

Such practical or operational criteria for judging art raise questions about whether 'beauty' is really an adequate translation, even roughly, of these societies' central aesthetic values. Presumably, translators who render an important aesthetic term with the English 'beauty' see certain similarities between the way that term is used and the ideas clustered around 'beauty' in Western thought. For example, the non-Western term may be used to mean the highest criterion of attractiveness in a human being, which would commonly be indicated as 'beauty' in English. However, we can probably conclude that many societies embrace some features, but not others, of Western ideas about beauty. One job for comparative aestheticians, therefore, is to articulate the similarities and dissimilarities among these concepts and to alert us to the limitations of our translations of non-Western aesthetic terms.

Work already undertaken has exhibited other areas in which Western and non-Western aesthetic thought do not converge, for example in aesthetic approaches to nature. Barbara Sandrisser has drawn attention to the Japanese aesthetic appreciation of what might in the West seem 'bad' weather conditions, such as rain (Sandrisser 1982). Yuriko Saito has characterized the Japanese attitude to nature as lacking in sublimity and as frequently focused on the charm of natural creatures. She suggests that these tendencies are a consequence of the Japanese interpretation of the human being as a part of nature, on intimate terms with the rest of it (Saito 1985). Human beings are able to identify with other natural phenomena, and the sympathetic sadness that one feels towards other, similarly perishing, natural entities is a reflection of one's awareness of one's place in the scheme of things. The cultural conception of human beings as naturally at home in nature is also related to the important Japanese aesthetic value of *mono no aware*, the pathos of things (see Sokoloff 1996).

Chinese aesthetics, too, reflect a cultural belief that human beings are integral parts of nature. The Chinese tradition of landscape painting recommends that the artist spend time in the landscape to be painted in order to achieve spiritual identity with it, and then go home and paint from memory. The ideals of landscape painting during the Northern Song (Sung) Dynasty (960–1127) were to invite the viewer into the painting, typically by presenting three planes of various distances and a road seeming to lead from the foreground into the background. The proper perspective for the viewer does not depend on assuming the proper distance from the painting; the proper perspective is within it (Li 1994).

The Chinese conviction that nature is a single flowing whole whose energy penetrates every particular thing is also evident in the rules for painters that were articulated in Chinese treatises on the subject. One of the most influential of these is the 'Ancient Painters' Classified Record' of Xie He (Hsieh Ho, sixth century CE), who articulated six principles for painters. These involve: (1) achieving spiritual consonance with what is depicted; (2) using the bone method of brush stroke; (3) portraying forms that are faithful to the subject matter; (4) applying colours that are appropriate to what is depicted; (5) planning the proper placement of elements; and (6) perpetuating the tradition by copying the works of earlier masters. The 'bone method' involves controlling the brush stroke to suggest three dimensions and to make the form's structure, or 'skeleton', strongly evident (Goldberg 1997). The importance of aligning one's own energy with that of other objects in nature is evident in Xie's making this the first rule for successful painting. A later treatise, the 'Record of Brush Methods' or 'Essay on Landscape Painting' by Jing Hao (Ching Hao, active c. AD 900–960), similarly assigns greatest importance to the artist's ability to express the vital spirit of the natural object (Sullivan 1984).

Another theme that has emerged from comparative study is the relatively greater emphasis on the aesthetics of everyday life in many non-Western cultures than in the West (see Small 1980). For example, a daily prayer said by members of Navajo society reflects a commitment to make all activities beautiful. Beauty is understood by the Navajo as the combination of a number of kinds of appropriateness, including health, happiness, harmony, and the normal pattern of nature (Witherspoon 1977). Saito observes that the attention the Japanese give to the packaging of products, as well as of gifts, reflects the cultural aim to aestheticize even mundane things that one encounters on a daily basis (Saito 1999; see also Sandrisser 1998). The Chinese integration of calligraphy into everyday contexts, such as using it on shop signs and displaying it in the most important places in a room, also serves to aestheticize the everyday environment.

A further comparative theme is the emphasis on the process of artistic making instead of the product, which characterizes many cultures outside the West. Chinese calligraphy, for example, is conceived as a practice. The product that we in the West indicate with the word 'calligraphy' is only the trace of an artwork, which was the action (see Vinograd 1988). Traditions that stress the process character of art sometimes develop forms that we might call 'multi-media'. For example, a mask from New Guinea might serve its intended function only in the performance context of a ritual involving music, dance, and other costume elements.

Another striking example of a multi-media form is the Chinese integration of painting, calligraphy, and poetry—the 'three perfections'—into a single work of art (often, but not necessarily, on a scroll). Besides perfecting one's skill in each of these modes, the ideal is to create subtle reverberations among the modes, with each enhancing the expressive power of the others. The common practice of adding calligraphy by others alongside that of the original artist contributes to the open-endedness and interactive nature of this form. Michael Sullivan suggests that the Chinese think of scrolls as 'living bodies', changing and developing character as they age (Sullivan 1980).

One of the most striking contrasts between recent Western aesthetics and the aesthetic traditions of other cultures is the more prominent tendency outside the West to relate aesthetic values to ethical values, a tendency that was common in earlier periods of Western history as well. N. Scott Momaday (1976) speculates that an aesthetic response to beauty may have been the basis for the development of a land ethic among the American Indians. Babatunde Lawal observes that the Yoruba of Nigeria consider moral character to be the most important aspect of human beauty, so much so that overly attractive looks are suspect, since they may mask bad character. Beauty in other natural forms is also described as having 'good character' if it provides for human needs (Lawal 1974).

Chinese thought about art focuses on the relationship between aesthetics and ethics. The Confucian tradition emphasizes the importance of ritual behaviour in negotiating human relationships. In this respect, ethical behaviour is understood to have an essentially aesthetic character. Accordingly, the practice of the arts is considered an important part of ethical cultivation (Goldberg 1997). Music is held to be a particularly important model for ethical behaviour, with the mutual attunement of voices in music serving as a model for societal harmony. The self-control necessary for mastering a musical instrument, particularly the sensitive unfretted zither called the *qin* (*ch'in*), is also seen as akin to that required for ethical behaviour (De Woskin 1982).

The Confucian focus on interpersonal harmony is an important factor in the relatively high value placed on conforming to tradition within the arts, as within other practices. Art is a primary means of transmitting ethical values, and the correctness of the values conveyed is considered more important than artistic novelty. The Confucian tradition encourages didactic art, and the morally ideal situation is presented as already existing. Art is considered ethically valuable because it inspires emotion in the human heart/mind, which is moved to a moral response (Wu 1989).

The Daoist tradition also associates aesthetics and ethics. The Daoist ideal is for the human being to become one with the spontaneous dynamic of nature. Aesthetic appreciation of nature assists this effort, for it involves recognition of the energies flowing within the environment. Human beings can literally communicate with the natural environment because they, like other natural things, are composed of *qi* (*ch'i*), configured energy. The Daoist Zhuang Zi (Chuang Tzu) illustrates the ideal ethical condition through stories of various artists and artisans, who are able to create remarkable works precisely because they allow nature to operate through them (Chuang 1964).

Ethical considerations play a role as well in Japanese aesthetic preferences. This is particularly evident in such aesthetic values as *wabi* (insufficiency), *shibui* (slightly astringent understatement), and *sabi* (rustic simplicity) (see Koshiro 1995). Saito observes that an aesthetic of imperfection and insufficiency developed as a counter to lavish displays by ruling shoguns in the sixteenth century. This aesthetic, evident in expensive teahouses that none the less appear shabby, reflects self-control in the form of abstaining from luxury. The simplicity of the teahouse structure is considered conducive to focusing all of one's attention on the ritual of tea. Statesman Ii Naosuke (1815–60) also claimed that the tea ceremony in such a setting has the social value of encouraging all participants to be satisfied with their lot (Saito 1997).

Still another theme deserving of more comparative study is the epistemological significance that various societies attribute to aesthetic experience. The philosophical schools of the Aztec *tlamtinime*, or 'knowers' of things, used an aesthetic criterion for knowledge of ultimate reality (see Clendinnen 1991; León-Portilla 1963). Convinced of reason's limitations, particularly for offering insight into reality beyond the visible, the *tlamtinime* believed that poetic inspiration and aesthetic raptures afforded a distinctive kind of knowing that could illuminate those features of reality inaccessible to reason. The poets, accordingly, were believed to be visionaries, who shared in the creative power of the gods. More recently, the view that aesthetic experience has epistemological significance has been defended by Mexican philosopher José Vasconcelos, as well as by the Peruvian thinker Alejandro Deústua (Davis 1984). We already noted that in Abhinavagupta's theory aesthetic experience is a mode of access to ultimate reality. A similar view is defended by a number of thinkers in the Islamic tradition, including Mulla Sadra, al-Ghazzali, and the poet Jalal al-Din Rumi (Nasr 1997). How similar, we might ask, are these views to those theories about art's epistemological role advanced in the West by such thinkers as Plato, Schopenhauer, Nietzsche, Coleridge, and others?

Other comparative themes deserve further study. Among these is the question of whether the aesthetic theories articulated by a particular society reflect what is common to human beings across cultures. For example, does the Indian theory of *rasa*, with its postulation of a set of basic human emotions, accurately describe human psychology in general (see Shweder 1993)? More generally, to what extent are aesthetic values sufficiently cross-cultural to serve as bridges between different cultures (see Ellis 1988; Roseman 1991)?

Another question worth considering is why aesthetics plays a more central role in many non-Western philosophies than in Western thought (at least in recent times). Inevitably, comparisons will yield insight into which features of Western aesthetics are culturally idiosyncratic—for example the high value the West has placed on individual artistic originality—and which are more widely characteristic of human beings across the globe. As so often, gaining insight into others will have repercussions for our knowledge of ourselves.

See also: Aesthetics of the Everyday; Aesthetics of Nature; Beauty; Environmental Aesthetics; Aesthetics and Ethics; Art and Morality; Art and Knowledge; Authenticity in Art.

BIBLIOGRAPHY

Cross-cultural

Anderson, R. (1989). *Art in Small-Scale Societies*. Englewood Cliffs, NJ: Prentice-Hall.
——(1990). *Calliope's Sisters: A Comparative Study of Philosophies of Art*. Englewood Cliffs, NJ: Prentice-Hall.
——(1992). 'Do Other Cultures Have "Art"?' *American Anthropologist* 94: 926–9.
Armstrong, R. P. (1971). *The Affecting Presence: An Essay in Humanistic Anthropology*. Urbana: University of Illinois Press.
Blacking, J. (1973). *How Musical is Man?* Seattle: University of Washington Press.
Blocker, H. G. (1994). *The Aesthetics of Primitive Art*. Lanham, Md: University Press of America.
Dissanayake, E. (1995). *Homo Aestheticus: Where Art Comes From and Why*. Seattle: University of Washington Press.
Dutton, D. (1993). 'Tribal Art and Artifact'. *Journal of Aesthetics and Art Criticism* 51: 13–22.
Higgins, K. M. (1991). *The Music of Our Lives*. Philadelphia: Temple University Press.
Kelly, M. (1994). 'Danto, Dutton, and Our Understanding of Tribal Art and Artifacts', in C. C. Gould and R. S. Cohen (eds.), *Artifacts, Representations and Social Practice*. Dordrecht: Kluwer.
Lomax, A. (1968). *Folk Song Style and Culture*. Washington: American Association for the Advancement of Science.
Rawson, P. (1967). 'The Methods of Zen Painting'. *British Journal of Aesthetics* 7: 315–38.
Rowell, L. (1983). *Thinking about Music*. Amherst: University of Massachusetts Press.
Sartwell, C. (1995). *The Art of Living: Aesthetics of the Ordinary in World Spiritual Traditions*. Albany: State University of New York Press.
Shiner, L. (1994). ' "Primitive Fakes", "Tourist Art", and the Ideology of Authenticity'. *Journal of Aesthetics and Art Criticism* 52: 225–34.
Small, C. (1980). *Music, Society, Education*. London: John Calder.
Stokes, M. (ed.) (1994). *Ethnicity, Identity and Music: The Musical Construction of Place*. Providence, RI: Berg.
Van Damme, W. (1996). *Beauty in Context: Towards an Anthropological Approach to Aesthetics*. Leiden: E. J. Brill.

Africa

Appiah, K. (1991). 'Is the Post- in Postmodern the Post- in Postcolonial?' *Critical Inquiry* 17: 336–57.
Danto, A. and Vogel, S. (eds.) (1988). *ART/artifact: African Art in Anthropology Collections*. New York: Center for African Art.

Hallen, B. (1998). 'African Aesthetics', in M. Kelly (ed.), *Encyclopedia of Aesthetics*, 4 vols, vol. 1. New York: Oxford University Press, pp. 37–42.

—— (2000). *The Good, the Bad, and the Beautiful: Discourse about Values in Yoruba Culture*. Bloomington: Indiana University Press.

Keil, C. (1979). *Tiv Song: The Sociology of Art in a Classless Society*. Chicago: University of Chicago Press.

Lawal, B. (1974). 'Some Aspects of Yoruba Aesthetics'. *British Journal of Aesthetics* 14: 239–49.

Okpewho, I. (1977). 'Principles of Traditional African Art'. *Journal of Aesthetics and Art Criticism* 35: 301–13.

Onyewuenyi, I. C. (1984). 'Traditional African Aesthetics: A Philosophical Perspective'. *International Philosophical Quarterly* 24: 237–44.

Thompson, R. F. (1968). 'Aesthetics in Traditional Africa'. *Art News* 66: 44–66.

—— (1983). *Flash of the Spirit: African and Afro-American Art and Philosophy*. New York: Random House.

American Indians

Allen, P. G. (1974). 'The Mythopoeic Vision in Native American Literature: The Problem of Myth'. *American Indian Culture and Research Journal* 1: 3–11.

McAllester, D. P. (1973). *Enemy Way Music: A Study of Social and Esthetic Values as Seen in Navaho Music*. Milwood, NY: Kraus International.

Momaday, N. S. (1976). 'A Native American Views His Land'. *National Geographic* 150: 13–18.

Witherspoon, G. (1977). *Language and Art in the Navajo Universe*. Ann Arbor: University of Michigan Press.

China

Chuang, T. (1964). *Basic Writings*, trans. B. Watson. New York: Columbia University Press.

De Woskin, K. J. (1982). *A Song for One or Two: Music and the Arts in Ancient China*. Ann Arbor: University of Michigan Center for Chinese Studies.

Goldberg, S. J. (1997). 'Chinese Aesthetics', in E. Deutsch and R. Bontekoe (eds.), *A Companion to World Philosophies*. Malden, Mass.: Blackwell Publishers, 225–34.

Li, Z. (1994). *The Path of Beauty: A Study of Chinese Aesthetics*, trans. G. Lizeng. New York: Oxford University Press.

Sullivan, M. (1980). *The Three Perfections: Chinese Painting, Poetry and Calligraphy*. New York: George Braziller.

—— (1984). *The Arts of China*, 3rd edn. Berkeley: University of California Press.

Vinograd, R. (1988). 'Situation and Response in Traditional Chinese Scholar Painting'. *Journal of Aesthetics and Art Criticism* 46: 365–74.

Wu, K.-M. (1989). 'Chinese Aesthetics', in R. E. Allinson (ed.), *Understanding the Chinese Mind*. Hong Kong: Oxford University Press, pp. 236–64.

India

Gerow, E. (1997). 'Indian Aesthetics: A Philosophical Survey', in E. Deutsch and R. Bontekoe (eds.), *A Companion to World Philosophies*. Malden, Mass.: Blackwell, pp. 304–23.

Goswamy, B. N. (1986). *Essence of Indian Art*. San Francisco: Asian Art Museum of San Francisco.

Rowell, L. (1992). *Music and Musical Thought in Early India*. Chicago: University of Chicago Press.

Shweder, R. A. (1993). 'The Cultural Psychology of the Emotions', in M. Lewis and J. M. Haviland (eds.), *Handbook of Emotions*. New York: Guilford Press, pp. 417–31.

The Islamic world

Madden, E. H. (1975). 'Some Characteristics of Islamic Art'. *Journal of Aesthetics and Art Criticism* 33: 423–30.

Nasr, S. H. (1997). 'Islamic Aesthetics', in E. Deutsch and R. Bontekoe (eds.), *A Companion to World Philosophies*. Malden, Mass.: Blackwell, pp. 448–59.

Japan

Kasulis, T. P. (1998). 'Zen and Artistry', in R. Ames *et al.* (eds.), *Self as Image in Asian Theory and Practice*. Albany: State University of New York Press, pp. 357–71.

Keene, D. (1969). 'Japanese Aesthetics'. *Philosophy East and West* 19: 293–326.

Koshiro, H. (1995). 'The *Wabi* Aesthetic through the Ages', in N. Hume (ed.), *Japanese Aesthetics and Culture: A Reader*. Albany: State University of New York Press, pp. 245–78.

Lamarque, P. (1989). 'Expression and the Mask: The Dissolution of Personality in Noh'. *Journal of Aesthetics and Art Criticism* 47: 157–68.

Marra, M. F. (ed.) (1999). *Modern Japanese Aesthetics: A Reader*. Honolulu: University of Hawaii Press.

—— (2001). *A History of Modern Japanese Aesthetics*. Honolulu: University of Hawaii Press.

Nishitani, K. (1995). 'The Japanese Art of Arranged Flowers', trans. J. Shore, in R. C. Solomon and K. M. Higgins (eds.), *World Philosophy: A Text with Readings*. New York: McGraw-Hill, pp. 23–7.

Ryosuke, O. (1998). 'Japanese Aesthetics: Kire and Iki', trans. G. Parkes, in M. Kelly (ed.), *Encyclopedia of Aesthetics*, 4 vols, vol. 2. New York: Oxford University Press, pp. 553–5.

Saito, Y. (1985). 'The Japanese Appreciation of Nature'. *British Journal of Aesthetics* 25: 239–51.

—— (1997). 'The Japanese Aesthetics of Imperfection and Insufficiency'. *Journal of Aesthetics and Art Criticism* 55: 377–85.

—— (1999). 'Japanese Aesthetics of Packaging'. *Journal of Aesthetics and Art Criticism* 57: 257–65.

Sandrisser, B. (1982). 'Fine Weather: The Japanese View of Rain'. *Landscape* 26: 42–7.

—— (1998). 'Cultivating Commonplaces: Sophisticated Vernacularism in Japan'. *Journal of Aesthetics and Art Criticism* 56: 201–10.

Sokoloff, G. (1996). 'By Pausing before a *Kicho*', in K. M. Higgins, *Aesthetics in Perspective*. Fort Worth, Tex.: Harcourt Brace, pp. 620–7.

Thornhill, A. H. III (1998). ' "Impersonality" in Basho: Neo-Confucianism and Japanese Poetry', in R. Ames *et al.* (eds.), *Self as Image in Asian Theory and Practice*. Albany: State University of New York Press, pp. 341–56.

Meso-America and Latin America

Baddeley, O. and Fraser, V. (1989). *Drawing the Line: Art and Cultural Identity in Contemporary Latin America*. New York: Verso.

Clendinnen, I. (1991). *Aztecs*. Cambridge: Cambridge University Press.

Davis, H. E. (1984). 'Alejandro Deústua (1849–1945): His Criticism of the Esthetics of José Vasconcelos'. *International Philosophical Quarterly* 24: 69–78.

León-Portilla, M. (1963). *Aztec Thought and Culture*. Norman, Okla.: University of Oklahoma Press.

Oceania and Malaysia

Ellis, C. J. (1988). *Aboriginal Music, Education for Living: Cross-Cultural Experience from South Australia.* St Lucia: University of Queensland Press.

Feld, S. (1984). 'Sound Structure as Social Structure'. *Ethnomusicology* 28: 383–410.

—— (1990). *Sound and Sentiment: Birds, Weeping, Poetics, and Song in Kaluli Expression,* 2nd edn. Philadelphia: University of Pennsylvania Press.

—— (1994). 'Aesthetics as Iconicity of Style (Uptown Title); Or (Downtown Title) "Lift-Up-Over Sounding": Getting into the Kaluli Groove', in C. Keil and S. Feld (eds.), *Music Groves.* Chicago: Chicago University Press, pp. 109–50.

Roseman, M. (1991). *Healing Sounds from the Malaysian Rainforest: Temiar Music and Medicine.* Berkeley: University of California Press.

CHAPTER 41

AESTHETICS AND EVOLUTIONARY PSYCHOLOGY

DENIS DUTTON

1. HISTORICAL PRECEDENTS

THE applications of the science of psychology to our understanding of the origins and nature of art is not a recent phenomenon; in fact, it is as old as the Greeks. Plato wrote of art not only from the standpoint of metaphysics, but also in terms of the psychic, especially emotional, dangers that art posed to individuals and society. It was Plato's psychology of art that resulted in his famous requirements in *The Republic* for social control of the forms and contents of art. Aristotle, on the other hand, approached the arts as philosopher more comfortably at home in experiencing the arts; his writings are to that extent more dispassionately descriptive of the psychological features he viewed as universal in what we would call 'aesthetic experience'. Although Plato and Aristotle both described the arts in terms of generalizations implicitly applicable to all cultures, it was Aristotle who most self-consciously tied his art theory to a general psychology.

Aristotle explicitly argued that a stable, unchanging human psychological nature would dictate that the arts would possess specifiable, unchanging features. In a seldom noticed aside in *The Politics*, Aristotle observes that 'practically everything has been discovered on many occasions—or rather an infinity of occasions—in the course of the ages; for necessity may be supposed to have taught men the inventions that were absolutely required, and when these were provided, it was natural that other things which would adorn or enrich life should grow up by degrees' (1329b25). We can imagine what Aristotle might have had in mind: the knife would first appear as a stone flake, and later would be shaped into an adze. It would require a roughened handle to enable a better grip; this would be attained through cross-hatched incising that would come to be a source of visual delight in itself, and lead to further decoration, eventually to decorated metal knives. This kind of natural progression for Aristotle means that in the arts there will be the invention of visual representations, drama, storytelling, and music wherever human societies are founded and flourish, and that these will develop along roughly inevitable lines, depending on their individual natures (Aristotle 1920).

Aristotle's *Poetics* can be understood as a catalogue of the features that he expects the arts, primarily drama and fiction, to possess precisely because they are created by and for human beings with a stable intellectual, imaginative, and emotional nature. For example, he argues that main themes of tragedy will involve the disruption of normal family relations, such as we see in *Oedipus* and *Medea*. His unspoken implication is that this fascination with stresses and ruptures of families represents a permanent feature of *human interest*, and not merely a local manifestation of Greek cultural concerns.

In the eighteenth century David Hume argued a similar thesis in his 1757 essay, 'Of the Standard of Taste' (Hume 1987). He believed that 'general principles of taste are uniform in human nature'. If human nature were not uniform across historic time and across cultures, we could not enjoy the same works of art as the ancients. Hume's famous criterion of value in art, the 'test of time', presupposes the existence of a constant common human nature. Overlaid on the history of art and literature will be all of the local contextual features that make it difficult to apprehend the values of art outside of its originating culture. Hume nevertheless believed in an unchanging core of interests and sentiments that made it possible to reach outside of one's own culture; this explains why the 'same Homer who pleased at Athens and Rome two thousand years ago, is still admired at Paris and London'.

Hume's notion that there is uniform human nature was a point of agreement with his contemporary, Immanuel Kant, who used the idea as a foundation for his theory of beauty in the *Critique of Judgment* (Kant 1987). Although he thought that all 'judgments of taste', as he called them, were subjective in their origins, since the subjects who make them, *Homo sapiens*, possess a *sensus communis*, a shared human sense, discussion and agreement with regard to art and aesthetic experience was also possible. If human beings are able to set aside their personal, idiosyncratic likes and desires, achieving what Kant called disinterested contemplation, they will tend towards agreement about the value and meaning of works of art.

In the twentieth century, particularly its second half, art theorists tended to shy away from theories that imply a fixed view of human nature, preferring instead so-called historicist accounts that interpret art in terms of the historical and cultural context of its production (Barkow *et al.* 1992). This widely held view of human intelligence regarded the mind as a content-free, so-called blank slate: human beings possessed a general capacity to learn all the divergent skills and values that different cultures can teach. At the same time that this theory of the mind held sway in psychology, mid-twentieth-century aesthetics tended to take a view of art consistent with it. Aesthetic values were regarded as whatever culture taught was aesthetically valuable; aesthetic values and meanings were considered without residue constructed by culture, and works of art were both created and appreciated within the norms and conventions of culture. 'Cultural constructionism' in aesthetics entailed a relativism of aesthetic values, and a consequent denial of the kind of aesthetic universalism Aristotle or Hume would have advocated. Art was considered purely a determined product of culture, and there were as many kinds of art and artistic values as there were cultures.

2. Evolutionary Psychology: Natural Selection

Recently, however, an interest in cross-cultural, universal features of art has been revived with growing developments in evolutionary psychology, which seeks to understand the psychological and cultural life of human beings in terms of their genetic inheritance as an evolved species. All animal species have evolved to increase fitness for survival and reproduction. Every physical aspect of the human organism is open to the influences of evolution, and all will be in respects explained by it. Whether we consider the nature and complexities of our immune system, the functions of the liver, the characteristics of haemoglobin, or our upright walk and binocular vision, it is natural selection working on the evolution of us and our mammalian and humanoid ancestors that has produced modern *Homo sapiens*.

Evolutionary psychology extends the findings of Darwinian theory to the working of the human psyche. In particular, it treats our mental capacities, inclinations, and desires as adaptations developed in the last two million years—since the Pleistocene era (Barkow *et al.* 1992). These features of the mind were fully developed in their modern form by about 10,000 years ago, the beginning of the Holocene, the period that saw the introduction of agriculture and cities, and the development of writing and metal tools. Since then, the human brain has not significantly changed in its genetic character (Mithen 1996). Rather than regarding the mind at birth as a content-free, blank slate on which are inscribed the skills and values of the culture of an individual, evolutionary psychology posits the existence of innate interests, capacities, and tastes, laid down through processes of natural and sexual selection. Evolutionary psychology replaces the blank slate as a metaphor for mind with the Swiss army knife: the mind is a set of tools and capacities specifically adapted to important tasks and interests. These acquisitions are adaptations to life in the small hunter–gatherer bands in which our ancestors lived for 100,000 generations before civilization as we now understand it began. They include a long list of universal features of the Stone Age, hunter–gatherer mind: for example language use according to syntactic rules; kinship systems with incest avoidance; phobias, e.g. fear of snakes and spiders; child-nurturing interests; nepotism, the favouring of blood relations; a sense of justice, fairness, and obligations associated with emotions of anger and revenge; the capacity to make and use hand tools; status and rank ordering in human relations; a sense of food purity and contamination; and so forth (Pinker 1997). Some of these features are uniform across the human species; others are statistically related to sex; for instance, females are more inclined towards an interest in child nurturing and have a greater ability to remember details in visual experience, while males are more physically aggressive, and better able to determine directionality and engage in 'map reading'.

Two features of art immediately link it with these psychological factors. First, artforms are found everywhere cross-culturally. There exists no known human culture that does not display some form of expressive making that European cultures would identify as artistic (Dissanayake 1995). This does not mean that all cultures have all artforms: the Japanese tea ceremony, widely regarded as an art, does not have any close analogue in the West; the Sepik River people of New Guinea are passionate carvers, and stand in sharp contrast with their fellow New Guineans from that Highlands, who direct their energies into body decoration and the production of fighting shields, but who carve very little (Dutton 2000). The Dinka of East Africa have almost no visual art, but have a highly developed poetry, along with a connoisseur's fascination with the forms, colours, and patterns of the natural markings on the cattle they depend on for their livelihoods. That these and other cultures have practices and products that we would recognize as artistic begs for an account from evolutionary psychology. The very universality of art strongly suggests that it is connected with ancient psychological adaptations.

The second feature that marks art as a focus of psychological interest is that it provides people with pleasure and emotions, often of an intense kind. It is a postulate of evolutionary psychology that pleasures, pains, and emotion—including experiences of attraction, revulsion, awe, fear, love, respect, loathing—have adaptive relevance. The pleasure of eating sweet and fatty foods is a Pleistocene adaptation for nutrition and survival as much as the pleasure of sex is an adaptation for procreation: ancestors who enjoyed eating and sex were in fact more likely to have descendants and to pass those traits on to them. Conversely with revulsion. One of the most dangerously poisonous substances for potential human consumption would be bacteria-laden rotting meat; it is not an evolutionary accident that rotting meat is one of the most repellent of all smells to human beings. The range of items in experience for which there may be some kind of Pleistocene inheritance includes our emotional dispositions towards other human beings, their comportment, expressions, and behaviour; our responses to the environment, including animals and plants, the dark of night, and to natural landscapes; our interest in creating and listening to narratives with identifiable themes, including imaginative dangers and the overcoming of romantic obstacles; our enjoyment of problem-solving; our liking for communal activity; and our appreciation of displays of skill and virtuosity.

3. Environmental Preferences

One of the most important considerations in the survival of any organism is habitat selection. Until the development of cities 10,000 years ago, human life was mostly nomadic. Finding desirable conditions for survival, particularly with an eye towards potential food and predators, would have selectively affected the human response to landscape—the capacity of landscape types to evoke positive emotions, rejection, inquisitiveness, and a desire to explore, or a general sense of comfort. Responses to landscape types have been tested in an experiment in which standardized photographs of landscape types were shown to people of different ages and in different countries: deciduous forest, tropical forest, open savannah with trees, coniferous forest, and desert. Among adults, no category stood out as preferred (except that the desert landscape fell slightly below the preference rating of the others). However, when the experiment was applied to young children, it was found that they showed a marked preference for savannahs with trees—exactly the East African landscape where much early human evolution took place (Orians and Heerwagen 1992). Beyond a liking for savannahs, there is a general preference for landscapes with water; a variety of open and wooded space (indicating places to hide and places for game to hide); trees that fork near the ground (provide escape possibilities) with fruiting potential a metre or two from the ground; vistas that recede in the distance, including a path or river that bends out of view but invites exploration; the direct presence or implication of game animals; and variegated cloud patterns. The savannah environment is in fact a singularly food-rich environment (calculated in terms of kilograms of protein per square kilometre), and highly desirable for a hunter–gatherer way of life. Not surprisingly, these are the very elements we see repeated endlessly in both calendar art and in the design of public parks worldwide.

The idea of a pervasive Pleistocene taste in landscape received support from an unusual project undertaken by two Russian émigré artists, Vitaly Komar and Alexander Melamid, in 1993. They hired a professional polling organization to conduct a broad survey of art preferences of people living in ten countries in Asia, Africa, Europe, and the Americas (Wypijewski 1997). Blue turned out to be the favourite colour worldwide, with green in second place. Respondents expressed a liking for realistic representative paintings. Preferred elements included water, trees and other plants, human beings (with a preference for women and children, and also for historical figures, such as Jomo Kenyatta or Sun Yat-sen), and animals, especially large mammals, both wild and domestic. Using the statistical preferences as a guide, Komar and Melamid then produced a favourite painting for each country. Their intent was clearly ironic, as the painting humorously mixed completely incompatible elements—*America's Most Wanted*, as it was titled, presented a Hudson River School scene, with George Washington standing beside a lake in which a large hippo is bellowing. But there was also a serious side to the project; for the paintings, though created from the choices of different cultures, tended to share a remarkably similar set of preferences—they looked like ordinary European landscape calendar art, both photographic and painted. In an attempt to explain this odd cross-cultural uniformity—which had East Africans choosing the lush calendar scenes over landscapes they might be familiar with in their own daily lives— Arthur Danto claimed that the Komar–Melamid paintings demonstrate the power of the international calendar industry to influence taste away from indigenous values and towards European conventions. While he admits that the Kenyans preferred scenes that looked more like upper New York State than like Kenya, the polling work also indicated that most Kenyans had calendars in their homes (Danto, in Wypijewski 1997). What this does not acknowledge is the question of why calendars worldwide have the same landscape themes—the very themes that evolutionary psychology would predict. The real question is 'Why are calendars so uniform in their content worldwide?'—a uniformity that includes other, non-landscape, objects of attention, such as babies, pretty girls, children, and animals. It is the calendar industry that has, by meeting market demands, discovered a Pleistocene taste in outdoor scenes.

4. PROBLEM-SOLVING AND STORY-TELLING

If survival in life is a matter of dealing with an often inhospitable physical world, and dealing with members of our own species, both friendly and unfriendly, there would be a general benefit to be derived from imaginatively exercising the mind in order to prepare it for its next challenge. Puzzle-solving of all kinds, thinking through imagined alternative strategies to meet difficulties—these are at the heart of what the arts allow us to do. In fictional narratives, we meet a far greater variety of obstacles, along with potential solutions, than we ever could in a single life. As Stephen Pinker has argued, 'Life has even more moves than chess. People are always, to some extent, in conflict, and their moves and countermoves multiply out to an unimaginably vast set of interactions' (Pinker 1997). Story-telling, on this model, is a way of running multiple, relatively cost-free experiments with life in order to see, in the imagination, where courses of action may lead. Although narrative can deal with the challenges of the natural world, its usual home is, as Aristotle also understood, in the realm of human relations. As Pinker puts it, 'Parents, offspring, and siblings, because of their partial genetic overlap, have both common and competing interests, and any deed that one party directs toward another may be selfless, selfish, or a mixture of the two'. Add to this the complications of dealing with lovers, spouses, friends, and strangers, and you have the basic material for most of the history of literature, from the *Epic of Gilgamesh* right up to drugstore bodice-rippers (Storey 1996).

Joseph Carroll agrees with this assessment of the adaptive advantages of fictional narrative, but stresses that imaginative story-telling does more than give explicit made-up instructions for possible future contingencies: 'It contributes to personal and social development and to the capacity for responding flexibly and creatively to complex and changing circumstances' (Carroll 1995). None of us may ever find ourselves stranded alone on an island, Carroll observes, but in reading *Robinson Crusoe* readers 'register the qualities of character through which Crusoe sustains himself in solitude, and they integrate these perceptions with the repertory of their psychological potentialities'. In this way, fiction 'is a medium for cultivating our innate and socially adaptive capacity for entering mentally into the experience of other people' (see also Currie 1998).

5. Evolutionary Psychology: Sexual Selection

While the Darwinian mechanism of natural selection has proved to be one of the most versatile and powerful explanatory ideas in all of science, there is another, lesser-known, side of Darwinism: sexual selection. The most famous example of sexual selection is the peacock's tail. This huge display, far from enhancing survival in the wild, makes peacocks more prone to predation. The tails are heavy, requiring much energy to grow and to drag around. This seems to be nature's point: simply being able to manage with a tail like that functions as an advertisement to peahens: 'Look at what a strong, healthy, fit peacock I am.' For discriminating peahens, the tail is a fitness indicator, and they will choose to mate with peacocks who display the grandest tails (Cronin 1991; Zahavi and Zahavi 1997).

Fundamental to sexual selection in the animal kingdom is female choice, as the typical pattern for most species has males displaying strength, cleverness, and general genetic fitness in order to invite female participation in producing the next generation. With the human animal, however, there is a greater mutuality of choice. Geoffrey Miller holds not only that sexual selection is the source of the traits we tend to find the most endearingly human—qualities of character, talent, and demeanour—but that artistic creativity and enjoyment came into being in the Pleistocene in the process of women and men choosing sexual partners.

The notion that we can alter ourselves through sexual selection is well accepted: there are striking examples of human sexual selection at work even in recent, historic times. The Wodaabe of Nigeria and Niger are beloved by travel photographers because of their geere wol festivals, where young men make themselves up, in ways that look feminine to Europeans, and dance vigorously to display endurance and health. Women then choose their favourites, preferring the tallest men with the biggest eyes, whitest teeth, and straightest noses. Over generations, the Wodaabe have grown taller than neighbouring tribes, with whiter teeth, straighter noses, etc. If it is possible to observe this kind of change in a few centuries, it is clearly possible to remake or refine *Homo sapiens* in tens of thousands of generations. As with natural selection, just slight choice bias over long time periods could radically reform aspects of humanity, giving us species features of personality and character that we have in effect created for ourselves. Our ancestors exercised their tastes for 'warm, witty, creative, intelligent, generous companions' as mates, and this shows itself both in the constitution of our present tastes and traits, and in our tendency to create and appreciate art (Miller 2000).

It is sexual selection, therefore, that is plausibly responsible for the astonishingly large human brain, an organ whose peculiar capacities wildly exceed survival needs on the African savannahs. The human brain makes possible a mind that is uniquely good at a long list of features that are found in all cultures but are difficult to explain in terms of survival benefits: 'humor, story-telling, gossip, art, music, self-consciousness, ornate language, imaginative ideologies, religion, morality' (Miller 2000). From the standpoint of sexual selection, the mind is best seen as a gaudy, over-powered home entertainment system, evolved to help our stone-age ancestors to attract, amuse, and bed each other.

As a telling example of the human self-created overabundance of mental capacity, consider vocabulary. Nonhuman primates have up to twenty distinct calls. The average human knows perhaps 60,000 words, learned at an average of ten to twenty a day up to age 18. As 98 per cent of daily speech uses only about 4,000 words, and no more than a few thousand words at most would have sufficed for survival in the Pleistocene, the excess vocabulary is well explained by sexual selection theory as a fitness and general intelligence indicator. Miller points out that the correlate between body symmetry—a well-known fitness indicator—and intelligence is only about 20 per cent. Vocabulary size, on the other hand, is more strongly indicative of intelligence, which is why it is still used both in psychological testing and more generally by people automatically to gauge how clever a person is. Such an indicator is especially telling in courtship contexts. Indeed, extravagant, poetic use of language—including a large vocabulary and syntactic virtuosity—is associated worldwide with love, being a kind of cognitive foreplay. But it is also, as Miller puts it, something that can 'give a panoramic view of someone's personality, plans, hopes, fears, and ideals'. It would therefore have been an essential item in the inventory of mate selection criteria (Miller 2000).

The human tendency to create amusements, to elaborate and decorate everywhere in life, is therefore a result of mate choices, accounting for the evolution of dancing, body decoration, clothing, jewellery, hair styling, architecture, furniture, gardens, artefact design, images from cave paintings to calendars, creative uses of language, popular entertainments from religious pageants to TV soaps, and music of all kinds. Artistic expression in general, like vocabulary creation and verbal display, has its origins according to sexual selection in its utility as a fitness indicator: 'Applied to human art, this suggests that beauty equals difficulty and high cost. We find attractive those things that could have been produced only by people with attractive, high-fitness qualities such as health, energy, endurance, hand–eye coordination, fine motor control, intelligence, creativity, access to rare materials, the ability to learn difficult skills, and lots of free time' (Miller 2000). This view accords with a persistent intuition about art that can be traced from the Greeks to Nietzsche and Freud: art is somehow connected, at base, to sex. The mistake in traditional art theorizing has been to imagine that there must be some coded or sublimated sexual content in art. But it is not the content *per se* that is sexual: it is the display element of producing and admiring artists and their art in the first place that has grounded art in sexuality since the beginnings of the human race.

To the extent that art-making was a fitness indicator in the Pleistocene, it would have to be something that low-fitness artists would find hard to duplicate. (Were it easy to fake, then it would not be accurate as a gauge of fitness.) The influence of the Pleistocene mind on the concept of art therefore provides us with a perspective, at least at a psychological level, on some of the modern problems of philosophical aesthetic. Consider virtuosity: if music is a series of sounds in a formal relation, why should it make any difference to us that the sounds of a Paganini caprice are also difficult to realize on a violin? From the standpoint of sexual selection theory, this is no issue: virtuosity, craftsmanship, and the skilful overcoming of difficulties are intrinsic to art as display.

And difficulty isn't all: art also involves costliness. As the economist Thorstein Veblen has said, 'The marks of expensiveness come to be accepted as beautiful features of the expensive articles'(Veblen 1994). As much as this might contradict the modernist devaluing of skill and cost as central to the concept of art, it is in line with persistent popular reactions to art, showing up in the liking of skilful realistic painting, musical virtuosity, and expensive architectural details. This may not justify the philistinism of asking how much a famous museum painting is worth, but it does explain it.

Admiration for the ability to do something difficult is not unique to art: we admire athletes, inventors, skilful orators or jugglers; and admiration of skill is at least as intrinsic to art as to any other field of human endeavour (Godlovitch 1998). Ellen Dissanayake has identified a process of 'making special' as essential to the arts as practised from the Pleistocene to the present (Dissanayake 1995). However, whereas she sees making special as something that tends to promote an intense communal sense in a hunter–gatherer group, Miller interprets the phenomenon as more connected with display: 'Indicator theory suggests that making things special means making them hard to do, so that they reveal something special about the maker'. It follows that almost anything can be made artistic by executing it in a manner that would be difficult to imitate. 'Art' as an honorific therefore 'connotes superiority, exclusiveness, and high achievement', and so would be useful as a fitness indicator.

If this is true, the vulgar gallery remark, 'My kid could paint better than that', is vindicated as valid at least from the standpoint of sexual selection, and can be expected to be heard in artistic contexts for the rest of human time: people are not going to 'learn' from their culture that skill does not count (any more than they will learn that general body symmetry does not indicate fitness). Moreover, even with the elites it is really not so different: the skill discriminations of elites are simply accomplished at a more rarefied level. Cy Twombly's chalk and blackboard works, which look to most people like children's blackboard scribbles, are viewed by high-art critics as demonstrating an extremely refined artistic skill. That the works do not obviously show skill to the uninitiated simply demonstrates that they are being produced at a level that the unsophisticated cannot grasp. The esoteric nature of art, and with its status and hierarchy, thus remains in place.

As with interests and inclination determined by natural selection, the ultimate reasons for the values we inherit through sexual selection are not understandable through immediate introspection. Ripe fruits taste deliciously sweet, while rotting meat is repellent, for sound biological reasons, although we may not know through immediate experience why these things generate, respectively, pleasure and disgust. Similarly, according to sexual selection theory, we find great pleasure in pastimes such as art and music, in probing conversation with charming company, in great displays of athletic prowess, in a striking metaphor or a well told story. The fact that these activities and experiences can afford so much pleasure too requires an explanation, and so far sexual selection theory provides one of the most plausible and provocative accounts we have.

6. The Limitations of Evolutionary Psychology

While evolutionary psychology may have a capacity to shed light on the existence of art and art's persistent qualities, it cannot pretend to explain everything we might want to know about art. In particular, there is an aspect of Kant's aesthetics that ought to be borne in mind when discussing evolutionary psychology in an aesthetic context. Kant distinguished what he called the agreeable from the beautiful. The agreeable are the straightforward subjective sensations of things that we like in direct experience: the taste of sweet, for example, or the colour blue. The pleasurable experience of such sensations, Kant held, contains no intellectual element: it is a brute feeling, often seeming to satisfy a desire (such as hunger), and as such must be carefully distinguished from the experience of the beautiful, in which the imagination combines with rational understanding in the experience of an imaginative object. For Kant, the disinterested experience that characterizes the proper regard for art is cut off from desires—the beautiful object is contemplated or observed, it is not used or consumed. Works of art, especially of fine art, therefore engage the higher faculties, and the pleasures they afford are of a different order than sexual or gustatory sensations of pleasure.

This is not a distinction many evolutionary psychologists have fully appreciated. For example, Randy Thornhill, agreeing with Donald Symons, says that 'Pleasure, like all experiences, is the product of brain mechanisms, and brain mechanisms are the products of evolution...by selection' (Thornhill 1998). They leave no room here for any distinctions between pleasures directly implicated in the satisfaction of desires and the contemplative pleasure historically identified as aesthetic and artistic.

Consider what this collapse of Kant's distinction between the agreeable and the beautiful would mean, for example, for the history of landscape painting. If we go through the European landscape painting with a checklist of evolved desirable environmental qualities, we can learn much about the content of the art works. On the other hand, if we want to know what distinguishes a popular calendar landscape from a great landscape painting by Constable, there may be nothing much to help us in a theory of Pleistocene landscape preferences. Similarly, a book such as Nancy Etcoff's *Survival of the Prettiest: The Science of Beauty* (1999), while it gives us a vast amount of information about evolved interests in what is perceived cross-culturally as the beauty of the human body, can tell us much less that is new about how human beings might be portrayed in art. A painting of a desolate, arid, and uninviting landscape may be a much greater work of art than a calendar photograph of a green valley of the sort our Pleistocene ancestors might have most wanted to explore and inhabit. A painting of an old and withered woman—for example Rembrandt's portrait of his mother reading the Bible—may be a much more beautiful work of art than a lusty pinup directed at sexual interests.

This is not to say that even in these areas evolutionary psychology might not have important things to tell us. Our responses to deep and complex works of art layer rich meanings and values that may be difficult to disentangle. In the case of the Rembrandt, respect for an aged woman, admiration of her devotion to her religion, and astonishment at the artist's technique—all have evolutionary ramifications. Even if it is never able to offer a completely satisfactory general theory of art, evolutionary psychology has the potential to contribute significantly to a philosophical understanding of art and its effects. These contributions are only beginning to be grasped and developed.

See also: Aesthetics and Cognitive Science; Beauty; Style in Art; Art and Knowledge; Environmental Aesthetics.

BIBLIOGRAPHY

Aristotle (1920). *Aristotle on the Art of Poetry*, trans. I. Bywater. Oxford: Oxford University Press.

Barkow, J. H., Cosmides, L., and Tooby, J. (eds.) (1992). *The Adapted Mind: Evolutionary Psychology and the Generation of Culture*. New York: Oxford University Press.

Carroll, J. (1995). *Evolution and Literary Theory*. Columbia, Mo.: University of Missouri Press.

Cronin, H. (1991). *The Ant and the Peacock*. Cambridge: Cambridge University Press.

Currie, G. (1998). 'Realism of Character and the Value of Fiction', in J. Levinson (ed.), *Aesthetics and Ethics*. Cambridge: Cambridge University Press.

Dissanayake, E. (1995). *Homo Aestheticus: Where Art Comes From and Why*. Seattle: University of Washington Press.

Dutton, D. (2000). 'But They Don't Have Our Concept of Art', in N. Carroll (ed.), *Theories of Art Today*. Madison: University of Wisconsin Press.

Etcoff, N. (1999). *Survival of the Prettiest: The Science of Beauty*. New York: Doubleday.

Godlovitch, S. (1998). *Musical Performance*. London: Routledge.

Hume, D. (1987). 'Of the Standard of Taste', in E. F. Miller (ed.), *Essays, Moral, Political, Literary*. Indianapolis: Bobbs-Merrill.

Kant, I. (1987). *The Critique of Judgment*, trans. W. Pluhar. Indianapolis: Hackett.

Miller, G. F. (2000). *The Mating Mind: How Sexual Choice Shaped the Evolution of Human Nature*. New York: Doubleday.

Mithen, S. (1996). *The Prehistory of the Mind: A Search for the Origins of Art, Religion, and Science*. London: Thames & Hudson.

Orians, G. H. and Heerwagen, J. H. (1992). 'Evolved Responses to Landscapes', in J. Barkow *et al.* (eds.), *The Adapted Mind*. New York: Oxford University Press.

Pinker, S. (1997). *How the Mind Works*. New York: W. W. Norton.

Storey, R. (1996). *Mimesis and the Human Animal: On the Biogenetic Foundation of Literary Representation*. Evanston, Ill.: Northwestern University Press.

Thornhill, R. (1998). 'Darwinian Aesthetics', in C. Crawford and D. L. Krebs (eds.), *Handbook of Evolutionary Psychology*. Mahwah, NJ: Lawrence Erlbaum.

Veblen, T. (1994). *The Theory of the Leisure Class.* New York: Dover. First published 1899.

Wypijewski, J. (ed.) (1997). *Painting by Numbers: Komar and Melamid's Scientific Guide to Art.* New York: Farrar, Straus & Giroux.

Zahavi, Am. and Zahavi, Av. (1997). *The Handicap Principle: A Missing Piece of Darwin's Puzzle.* New York: Oxford University Press.

CHAPTER 42

AESTHETICS AND COGNITIVE SCIENCE

GREGORY CURRIE

The subject of this chapter is the connection between art and all those aspects of mind that have, to some degree, an empirical side. It covers results in neuro-psychology and neuroscience, in cognitive and developmental psychology, as well as in various parts of the philosophy of mind. I ignore questions about the natural history of our mental capacities, as those are addressed in the preceding chapter.

1. Methodological Issues

What is the relevance to aesthetics of a scientific understanding of the states and processes underlying the creation and consumption of art? We are used to aesthetically focused studies of the relation between the visual arts and, say, geometric optics or colour theory (see the comprehensive and elegant survey in Kemp 1990). These form an integral part of any problem-based approach to aesthetics and to art history; they shed light on the problems that artists faced, sometimes quite consciously, and the solutions they came up with. But artists are, by and large, ignorant of the results I shall describe below, and it is far from clear that their work would benefit if this situation were to change. Doubts about the connection between art and cognition are reinforced by some ambitious contributions from neuroscientists themselves. Semir Zeki begins a recent book (Zeki 1999) with the astonishing claim that the function of the brain and that of visual art are the same. What he goes on to provide is an engaging but aesthetically uninformative account of the ways in which picture perception is constrained by the structure of the visual brain; without a functioning mechanism for the analysis of colour, we will not appreciate colour pictures, etc. Vilayanur Ramachandran, notable for work on phantom limb phenomena, offers a number of principles supposedly explanatory of our aesthetic preferences, including one that gives a surely unrealistic weighting to the role of caricature in art; his efforts are further undermined by an apparent identification of aesthetic value with capacity to stimulate limbic areas of the brain (Ramachandran and Hirstein 1999). In the long run such work may bear philosophical fruit, but there is little to show so far.

To the extent that art has human psychology as its subject, there must be potential for conflict with the sciences of mind. As philosophers have recently noted, results in social psychology challenge our ordinary conception of human motivation, suggesting that moral character either does not exist at all or plays an insignificant role in shaping behaviour (Campbell 1999; Harman 1999). Whatever the merits of the studies involved, anyone who thinks that a virtue of great art is its insight into the human condition ought to allow that the art concerned may actually get it badly wrong, and that science may convince us that it has. One would have to have a very narrowly inscribed conception of the aesthetic to think that this made no difference to the aesthetic value of, say, Shakespeare's plays.

When we talk of character and motivation we are operating at the *personal* level, the level at which we ascribe content-bearing states to the person, and at this level the idea of a clash between art and science seems plausible enough. But much scientific thinking about the mind is committed to a *subpersonal* level of analysis, as when theorists of vision speak of the information carried by the visual system— information that may be unavailable to the subject herself. Some philosophers influenced by Wittgenstein reject the idea of sub-personal psychology altogether, arguing that it is an extension of language beyond the domain for which it makes sense (see Kenny 1984 and, for a discussion of this in relation to theories of depiction, Hyman 1989: chapter 3). But even if we grant the legitimacy of subpersonal psychology, we may still hold that we make meaningful contact with the aesthetic only at the personal level. On this view, we learn nothing about the aesthetics of pictures when we learn that the human visual system treats a certain area of the picture surface as if it were an object boundary.

While this issue has not been extensively debated, there are available within contemporary philosophy a number of responses to it. At one extreme is a Wittgensteinian insistence that nothing we can learn from the scientific study of cognition could shed any light on what is interesting or valuable in art *qua* art—even assuming that the study was conducted on correct principles and according to a sound method. At the other extreme, consistent with the eliminativist theory of mind, is the view that a scientific approach to art, creativity, and appreciation will sweep aside the exhausted superstitions of the connoisseur, the philosopher, and the historian. In the future that Paul Churchland (1979) imagines for us, where people observe not the sky reddening at sunset, but 'the wavelength distribution of incoming solar radiation shift towards the longer wavelengths', gallery patrons' experiences of pictures may be comparably transformed.

I will not try to settle the issue here. Rather, I shall offer a budget of theories and findings, both at the personal and at the subpersonal levels, which *might* be taken as relevant to art and the aesthetic. While these results are of some interest, I think it will be agreed that they are relatively undiscriminating; they do little to illuminate our aesthetic judgements about particular works, traditions, styles, or genres. When the question is as broad as 'how do we recognize the contents of pictures at all?' or 'what kinds of mental operations are recruited by the imagination?' the current science of cognition has something interesting to say. If we ask, in the style of Zeki and Ramachandran, about our responses to suprematist painting or to symbolist poetry, we are in territory still largely unilluminated by cognitive science.

2. CREATIVITY

The most considerable challenge to cognition posed by art is the creative element in art. What is creativity, and how does the human mind manifest it? According to Margaret Boden (1990), creativity is the transformation of the principles that organize a conceptual space. Boden suggests that this idea enables us to enlist the help of computational theory. But it remains somewhat unclear how we are to use this definition of creativity to think about the psychological and ultimately neural underpinnings of creativity. Nor is it clear that creativity, particularly in art, is always or even usually transformative in the way she describes. While Schoenberg's creativity probably did involve such transformations, it is not at all clear that Mozart's did. And spectacular creativity can occur when people ignore or are ignorant of the conceptual spaces that have constrained people's previous efforts (Novitz 1999). David Novitz favours an account of creativity in terms of recombination, but his account leaves unclear the distinction between creative and uncreative recombination.

Of experimentally informed work on creativity, perhaps the most interesting concerns the role of spatial thinking, and the possibility that mental images are manipulated so as to reveal unsuspected patterns and relationships (see the survey in Finke 1990). Classic experiments of Roger Shepard and colleagues (Shepard and Cooper 1982) have indicated that we sometimes solve problems by inspecting and manipulating mental images. There is even evidence that aspectual seeing, such as we encounter in viewing ambiguous figures, is reproducible in imagery (Finke and Shepard 1986, but see also Reisberg and Morris 1985). Starting from such results, the creative cognition approach (Finke, Ward *et al.* 1992) explains creativity in terms of the initial formation of a mental image or model within which unexpected elements or relations are then discovered. Supporters of this approach say that people seeking creativity should generate models that, among other things, are 'novel and ambiguous, have emergent features, [and] appear meaningful' (Finke, Ward *et al.* 1992: 199), though they do not say how this is to be done. You cannot account for creativity in terms of doing so-and-so, if so-and-so can be done either creatively or uncreatively and you do nothing to distinguish these two ways. It is also unclear exactly what role image manipulation plays in artistic creation, since not all image manipulation is creative. And, while imagery may play a part in creative work, recent work on the 'extended mind' (Clark 2001*a*) suggests that we should not treat creativity as a state of the mental interior. The artist's sketch pad can extend her creativity in the same way that the diary entry extends her memory (Van Leeuwen *et al.* 1999).

3. PERCEPTION

Very often we learn to recognize objects by being shown pictures of them; infants seem to have little difficulty in recognizing familiar objects in pictures; a good test of whether a patient can recognize objects of a given kind is whether he can recognize a depiction of objects of that kind. Facts like these suggest that seeing a lion and recognizing it as one, and seeing a picture and recognizing it as a picture of a lion, have an overlapping cause: a mechanism capable of being triggered by lions and by lion pictures. Such a mechanism cannot be very finely tuned. But then, perception is unlikely to be very finely tuned. It is plausible to think of perception as functioning to provide us with information quickly and via relatively noisy channels that often signal 'lion' when there is no lion there. For the cost of reducing noise is the increased likelihood of missing some real but unobvious predator. (For an illuminating approach to perception and cognition via signal detection theory, see Godfrey-Smith 1997; see also Cummins 1996.) So our visual system is tuned to give the response 'lion ahead' not only to lions, but also to the merely lion-like stimuli provided by pictures of lions. As Flint Schier put it, we see the lion in the picture because the picture, or some part of it, triggers our lion recognition capacity (Schier 1986; for criticism see Hopkins 1998: chapter 2).

Perception would be slow if it depended substantially on belief. It would also be very unreliable; we want to perceive what is there, not what we think is there. Indifference to belief, or what Jerry Fodor (1983) calls 'encapsulation', is perhaps the most important feature of *modular* systems. Fodor argued that vision, like other 'input' systems, is modular, meaning, roughly speaking, that it develops and functions in relative isolation from other systems. It enables us to construct a rich representation of the world on the basis of a relatively impoverished stimulus—not, *pace* Gregory and Gombrich, by recourse to hypothesis testing, but by deploying complex but inflexible techniques to derive, say, an object boundary from a sudden change in illumination. Computational theories of vision, much influenced by the work of David Marr (1982), are hospitable to this approach; they analyse vision as the solution to a set of hierarchically ordered tasks, with the outputs of one subsystem providing inputs to the one next up. There may be a clue here to why it is that line drawings, which seem, objectively, to resemble their objects very little, are so easily recognizable. It is thought that one relatively early operation of the visual system is edge detection. Artificial visual systems that perform this function have been developed, and it is found that the result of edge detection operations applied to a visual scene corresponds closely to a line drawing of it. This suggests that line drawings exploit the modularity of vision by being pre-packaged for perception; they are effortlessly recognizable because they have done for the scene represented something that the visual system would do anyway if exposed to the scene itself.

Caricature generally presents a problem for theories of depiction, particularly for theories that depend on the idea that pictures resemble their subjects (see Peacocke 1987; Hopkins 1998: chapter 4 offers a detailed treatment from the point of view of a resemblance theorist). Can the ease with which we recognize the object in the caricature be explained on the hypothesis that pictures trigger natural recognitional capacities? Caricatures exaggerate those features of an object that differ from the average for objects of that kind. Suppose that identification of a presented face is triggered partly by recognition of non-standard features in the face presented, which are then matched to representations in memory. (There appears also to be an emotional component in face recognition: see Stone and Young 1997.) Caricatures of faces are pictures and ought, on the present proposal, to be recognized via the mechanisms we use to recognize faces. Since caricatures make deviant features more salient via exaggeration, they ought to be recognized *more* easily than faces presented in realistic pictures are recognized. And this is what we find; other things being equal, people seem better able to recognize faces from caricatures than from realistic portraits, and the same result has been demonstrated for some other kinds of objects, for example birds (see e.g. Mauro and Kubovsky 1992).

I have sketched an account of pictorial recognition in terms of a modularized and error-prone subpersonal capacity to recognize objects. But picture recognition is a person-level capacity; it is I who see the man in the picture (Wollheim 1998), not my visual system. So the subpersonal story can be at most a start; we need to say what happens to get us from a triggered recognitional capacity to perceiving a flat canvas as a picture of a man. There is currently very little to help us answer this question.

Music poses other kinds of problems for an account of aesthetic perception, because the perception of music does not usually involve, say, hearing the music as bird song or as people speaking, nor does it involve hearing these things in the music. (But see Raffman, 1993, for a limited defence of the idea that music carries meaning.) It involves, say, hearing six notes in two groups of three, or one note as subordinate to another. But it is important to realize that, in failing to hear anything in the music (because, say, nothing is represented in the music in such a way as to be heard in it), one's experience of the music may still have representational content. That is, one's experience of the music may be an experience that represents the world as being a certain way, namely as productive of certain sounds standing in certain relations. So it may still be that hearing six notes in two groups of three, or one note as subordinate to another, is a matter of how our experience represents the music.

This has been denied. Christopher Peacocke (1983) has drawn a distinction between representational and sensational properties of perception. The former are properties that experience has in virtue of how it represents the world; the latter are properties that experience has in virtue of its having a certain phenomenal character. And Peacocke claimed that hearing notes as grouped, or hearing an interval as a diminished fifth rather than as an augmented forth, is a matter of the sensational rather than the representational properties of the music (Peacocke 1983). This seems wrong, because hearing the music in these ways is surely a matter of hearing things that are features of the music (or, if they are not features of the music, one is simply wrong to hear it in those ways) (DeBellis 1995; see also Levinson 1996). One reason, on the other hand, for not thinking of hearing an interval as a diminished fifth as a representational property of the experience is that one may hear it that way without having the *concept* of a diminished fifth; how could one represent the world as being a certain way without having the concept of that way? But various people, including recently Peacocke himself, have argued that experience *can* represent the world, as they say, *nonconceptually* (Evans 1985; Peacocke 1992; Budd 1985; but see McDowell 1994 for a contrary view). And Mark DeBellis has argued that this is indeed how it is with the attentive but musically untrained listener; she hears the interval as a diminished fifth, without possessing the concept of a diminished fifth (for discussion see Levinson 1996). Musical training consists partly in the acquisition of such music-theoretic concepts as the diminished fifth, and DeBellis argues that the musically educated listener who hears the interval as a diminished fifth has undergone an enrichment of her perceptual experience. He concludes that this is a counter-example to the idea that perception is diachronically encapsulated, or impervious, over time, to the effects of belief. (See Fodor 1984, 1988, and Churchland 1988 for opposing views on the general question whether perception is encapsulated.)

There is, however, a difficulty in the idea that musical perception has non-conceptual content; it is equally a difficulty for the idea that pictorial perception is nonconceptual. The problem is that defenders of nonconceptual content in perception often appeal to the connection between perception and behaviour. Gareth Evans (1985) argued that perception has content not in virtue of its relation to reason or verbal report, but through its connection with action; riding at speed over rough ground, a motorcyclist's skilful actions are guided by what he sees, not by how he conceptualizes what he sees. But the perception of music has little or no direct action-guiding potential: not enough, certainly, for us to map the fine grained content of perception on to anything like the rich schedule of appropriate action we have in the case of the motorcyclist. A picture may represent a space in which one can act, but as one sees the picture one does not stand in a relation to that space that allows immediate, skilful action; the space is not egocentrically framed in John Campbell's sense (see Campbell 1993; and Hopkins 1998: chapter 7). It may therefore be more difficult than we have so far assumed to transfer the notion of nonconceptual content from perception to pictures. A further complication is that the nonconceptualist case may founder on empirical facts; experiments of various kinds, including those arising from a detailed study of a patient with certain lesions, have given rise to the suggestion that visual awareness depends on processing in one brain area, while the capacity to guide visuo-motor action in real time depends on processing in a quite different area (Milner and Goodale 1995). It is currently unclear whether this startling proposal has substantial empirical support and what its implications would be for our thinking about nonconceptual content (see Clark 2001b for illuminating discussion).

In the case of at least absolute music, we are obliged to restrict the discussion of content to perception; the music itself arguably has no content. But what of pictures? If perception can represent the world as being a certain way, without the perceiver possessing the concepts necessary to say what way that is, can a picture have the same kind of content? A Gombrichian account of depiction, with its emphasis on the way the artist brings appearances within the framework of a conceptual scheme, suggests that traditional forms of picturing, such as painting, are essentially conceptual (Gombrich 1960). 'Mechanical' forms of picturing, on the other hand, such as photography, have been said to be essentially independent of the conceptually mediated states of their makers: the photographer depicts what is there, not what the maker thinks is there or wants to be there (Walton 1984). If sustainable, the idea that handmade images do, while mechanically made images do not, have conceptual content might explain our quite different responses to these two forms. But Dominic Lopes has denied that even handmade pictures have conceptual content: 'In drawing, the eye and the hand work together, perhaps bypassing the mind, or that portion of the mind that deals with concepts and beliefs' (Lopes 1996: 186). If he is right, we cannot appeal to nonconceptual content to distinguish one kind of picture from another. This is a complex issue, but Lopes's claim seems to be contradicted by what we have learned from Gombrich and others about how painting and drawing are influenced by expectation, wish and the rest; 'handmade' picturing stands, in this respect, very much in contrast both to perception and to photographic images.

4. IMAGINATION

I have remarked that the idea of a strong connection between object recognition and picture recognition is well supported. Is there a similar connection between object recognition and the generation of *mental images*? It is worth turning briefly to this issue, for two reasons. One is that mental imagery may in various ways be an important feature of our response to some forms of art, notably music and literature. The second is that mental imagery is a form of imagination, and what we will note about such imagery is suggestive of a more general doctrine about imagination.

Two doctrines need to be sharply distinguished here. They are apt to be confused because they arise in response to the same intuition, namely that the experience of having a mental image is like that of seeing. The first doctrine, rejected by most philosophers, is that having a mental image of an object is to be explained in terms of 'seeing a mental picture of the object'. The second is that imagery is systematically related to vision in various ways, and functions, in certain respects, as an alternative mode of visual exploration. I am concerned here largely with the second doctrine. It should be remarked, however, that new life has been given the idea of mental pictures by psychologists who hold that the mental representations that underlie imagery, while not consisting literally of pictures, have a 'quasi-pictorial' form (Kosslyn 1994; for criticism see Abell and Currie 1999).

Turning to the second hypothesis, the similarities between vision and visual imagery are to some extent embedded in our ordinary thought and talk about imagery, which appeals to the concepts and vocabulary of visual description. But the similarities go deeper. It is found that the accessibility of information from imagery, as well as people's response times and patterns of error on imagery tasks, very closely match those of comparable visual tasks, even where subjects have no prior knowledge of these effects. For example, subjects are asked to form an image of a pattern of stripes, to imagine walking away from the pattern, and to report the point at which the stripes are no longer distinguishable. It turns out that the distance at which blurring takes place is greater if the stripes are in the horizontal than it is if the stripes are in the diagonal (see Kosslyn, Sukel *et al.* 1999). This is exactly how it is with actually seeing and moving away from a pattern of stripes. Other sensory forms of imagery also closely match real performance in the relevant modality; the time it takes to imagine performing a movement is closely related to the time it will take actually to perform it. Motor imagery is also a surprisingly efficient substitute for action in improving performance and even muscular force (Yue and Cole 1992). There is also evidence from imaging techniques such as positron emission tomography (PET) that the brain reuses visual systems to construct visual imagery (Kosslyn, Thompson *et al.* 1996; Kosslyn *et al.* 1999*a*), and disabilities of vision are often accompanied by comparable disabilities concerning imagery (Levine, Warach *et al.* 1985; Farah 1988). Motor imagery activates some motor areas of the brain, and motor disabilities that have a neurological cause such as Parkinson's disease are reflected in impaired motor imagery (Dominey *et al.* 1995).

What seems to be emerging here is that the forms of imagery piggy-back on systems designed for other purposes, and serve to recreate or substitute for the kinds of states these systems were designed to support. This suggests that we might develop a general theory of imagination based on a framework that associates different forms of imagination with independently identified cognitive and perceptual states. For example, imagination is generally agreed to be crucial to our response to works of representational art, especially those that deploy narrative, but the forms of imagination relevant here are not primarily forms of imagery. What we imagine while reading a novel is not exclusively a matter of what images we have, and images do not seem relevant at all in the case of theatre and film. Indeed, our untutored responses to stories suggest that imagination here shares significant features with *belief*. If you imagine the novel's hero in London one day and in Chicago the next, you will also imagine that she flew there, unless there is some strong indication in the work that she got there by another means. As readers, we let our imaginings mingle with our beliefs, and further imaginings emerge which, so far as their contents go, are identical with what would emerge from the operation of inference on belief alone. It is this capacity of imaginings to mirror the inferential patterns of belief that makes fictional story-telling possible. If imaginings were not inferentially commensurate with beliefs, we could not draw on our beliefs to fill out what the story tells us, and story-tellers would have to give us all the detail explicitly. But that is more than they could ever give, and more than we could stand listening to.

Recent work in child psychology has shown that the preservation of inference in imagination emerges very early; it is not likely that children first engage in imaginings that are not inferentially constrained and then learn somehow to constrain them. Very young children will spontaneously imagine that an animal is wet if they know that it is part of a pretend game that the animal has had water poured over it, though the animal is in fact dry (since the upended cup was empty) and no one has mentioned the idea of it being wet (see Leslie 1988; and Harris and Kavanaugh 1993). It looks as if the child's imagining that the animal had water poured over it mingles with her beliefs about water-pouring situations, and arrives, belief-like, at the imagining that the animal is wet.

There are other ways that imagination can be like belief. Reasoning can be practical as well as theoretical, and you can undertake a piece of practical reasoning based on what you imagine as well as on what you believe; the result will be a decision, in imagination, to do something. Imagining something can also have consequences for emotion and affect that are very like the emotional and affective consequences of believing it; when we read stories or watch movies and are imaginatively involved with their events, we often experience emotions that are both powerful and apparently continuous with those we experience in response to situations in real life (see e.g. Oatley 1994: 54; Harris 2000: 71).

If we assume that emotional responses like these are imagination-based rather than belief-based, an important question is: What sort of imagined relation does the audience have to the events and characters of the fiction? The bare suggestion that the members of the audience have imaginings that are significantly belief-like does not help us much; we have beliefs about our families and friends, but also about people who are spatio-temporally distant from us and with whom we have no significant associations. The dominant opinion on this question has tended to be that we imagine ourselves to be located within the spatio-temporal frame of the work, and sometimes imagine ourselves as identical with one or other protagonist. In the case of cinematic and televisual works, the assumption is that we imagine ourselves as having the point of view of the camera (see e.g. Wilson 1987). Another view is that, while acts of imaginative identification with characters do take place, our typical imaginative stance is one that is spatio-temporally, but not necessarily emotionally, distanced (see e.g. Currie 1995a: chapter 3).

Views like these raise purely philosophical questions about, say, the role of self-concepts in imagining. On the other hand, there does seem to be room for empirical investigation, and a small amount of work has been done by psychologists on this, of which the following two experiments are typical.

1. One group of experimenters showed that subjects reading that a character is moving from room to room were quicker to answer questions about the room to be entered than about the room just left, and were even slower to answer questions about the rooms not on the itinerary (Morrow, Greenspan *et al.* 1987).

2. Another group presented subjects with the sentence 'Bill was in the living room reading the evening paper.' These subjects subsequently read sentence (*a*) faster than sentence (*b*):

(*a*) Before Bill had finished the paper, John came into the room.

(*b*) Before Bill had finished the paper, John went into the room (Black, Turner *et al.* 1979).

It has been argued that data like these support the view that the audience adopt an imaginary point of view within the world of the fiction: a point of view 'relative to the geography and the temporal sequence of events within the narrative' (Harris 1998; see also Gerrig and Prentice 1996). However, the data might be explained instead by assuming that readers are simply attending selectively to events, locations, and characters in the story, and that the focus of their attention shifts as the narrative moves along (Currie 1999).

Consider the case of the character moving from room to room. If I am engaged by the fiction, my attention shifts from (fictional) place to (fictional) place as the character moves, and may—as seems to be the case here—run ahead of the character, anticipating his destination. But it does not follow that I am imagining *being in* the room on which my attention is focused.

It seems that we need some more direct evidence that imagination is a factor in determining the responses of subjects described in experiments 1 and 2 above. We might ask whether it would be possible to conduct experiments like those just described, but using subjects with independently identifiable deficiencies of imagination. If their performance were like that of normal controls, we would have reason to think that the results of 1 and 2 could be explained in terms of cognitive focus rather than in terms of imagined placement within the frame of the story. Are there such subjects?

Some of the most prominent features of autism suggest that it involves a deficiency of imagination. An early indication of autism in young children is absence of spontaneous pretend play, and people with autism adhere rigidly to predictable routines. They are often obsessively interested in things most people regard as dull: train timetables, lists of addresses, the construction of sewage pipes, etc. Autism has been called 'mindblindness' because people with autism have difficulty understanding the emotional and cognitive states of others (Baron-Cohen 1995); one explanation of this is that they lack the imaginative capacity properly to empathize with others (Harris 1993; see also Currie 1996). While autism is poorly understood, one current theory is that it is a disorder of 'executive function', marked by mental inflexibility, difficulty choosing an appropriate response when no single action is clearly dictated by circumstances, and difficulty in planning actions (see the essays in Russell 1998). This may also be connected with imaginative incapacity, especially in regard to planning, for it is plausible that choosing an appropriate course of action is done partly by imagining ourselves acting in a certain way and seeing, in imagination, how well things turn out.

Systematic studies have not yet been completed comparing the performance of people with autism and controls on tasks like 1 and 2 above. But this is one way we could shed further light on the issue of how and to what extent imagination is deployed in response to art. We may at the same time learn more about exactly how to characterize the imaginative deficits that autistic people suffer. And the study of psychological deficits may shed light on another well-known problem about the arts that philosophers have discussed.

Much of our enthusiasm for narrative arts seems to derive from the fact that we respond emotionally to fictional stories, and some people have suggested that there is a deep irrationality in caring about the fates of people who we know do not exist (Radford 1975). But there may be good evolutionary reasons why our emotions are triggered by imagined as well as real events. Our ancestors lived in intensely social groups, wherein it was probably advantageous to know about the emotional states of other group members. One way of knowing about those emotional states is to be so constructed that, when you imagine being in the other's situation, you come automatically to have emotions congruent with theirs. Also, emotions experienced as part of an imaginative project may be an important part of planning. Antonio Damasio (1994) has examined non-autistic patients with damage to certain frontal areas of the brain. While they appear well able to reason about practical matters and are in command of the relevant facts, their capacity to make sensible decisions is grossly impaired and has led in some cases to bankruptcy and family breakdown. He also found that these people have much reduced levels of emotion. One explanation is that effective planning involves not merely noting the consequences of an imagined action, but experiencing the appropriate emotion; what decides me against taking a risky course of action is not merely my acknowledgment of the risk, but my experiencing the anxiety consequent on imagining the various things that could go wrong.

Considerations like this may go a long way towards relieving puzzlement about our capacity for experiencing emotions in response to merely imagined events. But it remains to be explained why it is that we seek out opportunities to experience *negative* emotions in response to narratives that engage our imagination. As Hume put it (in 'On Tragedy'), the spectators at a tragedy 'are pleased in proportion as they are afflicted' (Hume 1993). Like other questions discussed here, this one raises issues of a relatively *a priori* kind that are dealt with elsewhere in this volume. But from the perspective of cognitive science, it would be interesting to see whether there are continuities between the willing audience at *Hamlet* and less culturally advanced and self-conscious activities that also involve a seeking out of negative emotion. There seems to be a continuity of this kind with the imaginative pretence of children. Children are sometimes upset by, and complain about, the behaviour of an imaginary companion—yet they do not always find a remedy in simply wishing away the troublesome behaviour (Harris 2000: chapter 4).

Perhaps children in situations such as these, as well as those who complain of being frightened of imaginary ghosts and monsters, confuse what they imagine with reality. If that were so, their responses would have little connection with those of mature theatre audiences, who, despite their obvious involvement with the plot, certainly do not think that Hamlet and Ophelia are real. But the evidence does not support the view that young children mistake fantasy for reality. Four- and five-year-olds are well able to distinguish between real and imaginary things, and their discrimination is not affected by the imaginary things being presented in frightening or otherwise emotionally involving ways (Harris *et al.* 1991). Also, children with long-term imaginary companions seem well able to distinguish between real and imaginary things, including the companion (Harris 2000). On the whole, it is better to assume that the children are absorbed in a fiction of their own devising, which is sometimes distressing to them, but which they do not confuse with reality. If that is so, the manifestation and development of imaginative capacities in young children will repay investigation.

This chapter has focused on two areas of research: neurocognitive investigations of perception, and psychological investigations of imagination. In these areas substantial progress is being made towards understanding the basic mechanisms that allow us to engage with works of art. But there has been little progress made in helping us understand the rich variety of aesthetic responses we show to works in different traditions, styles, and genres. There is also a significant unclarity about the aim of such research. Is it intended merely to discover the underpinnings of responses we can describe and evaluate in the familiar language of criticism and connoisseurship? Or is the aim to interpolate unfamiliar concepts into the domain of aesthetics itself, leading perhaps to a revised understanding of aesthetic values? The second aim is much the more interesting one, but adopting it will require a great deal of argument that is itself philosophical in nature.

See also: Aesthetics and Evolutionary Psychology; Aesthetic Experience; Fiction; Art and Emotion; Tragedy; Interpretation in Art; Representation in Art.

BIBLIOGRAPHY

Abell, C. and Currie, G. (1999). 'Internal and External Pictures'. *Philosophical Psychology* 12: 429–45.

Baron-Cohen, S. (1995). *Mindblindness: An Essay on Autism and Theory of Mind*. Cambridge, Mass.: Bradford Books/MIT Press.

Black, J. B., Turner, T. J. *et al*. (1979). 'Point of View in Narrative Comprehension, Memory and Production'. *Journal of Verbal Learning and Verbal Behavior* 18: 187–98.

Boden, M. (1990). *The Creative Mind*. London, Weidenfeld & Nicolson.

Budd, M. (1985). 'Understanding Music'. *Proceedings of the Aristotelian Society*, suppl. vol., 59: 233–48.

Campbell, J. (1993). *Past, Space and Self*. Cambridge, Mass.: MIT Press.

——(1999). 'Can Philosophical Accounts of Altruism Accommodate Experimental Data on Helping Behaviour?' *Australasian Journal of Philosophy* 77: 26–45.

Churchland, P. (1979). *Realism and the Plasticity of Mind*. Cambridge: Cambridge University Press.

——(1988). 'Perceptual Plasticity and Theoretical Neutrality'. *Philosopy of Science* 55: 167–87.

Clark, A. (2001*a*). 'Reason, Robots and the Extended Mind'. *Mind and Language* 16: 121–45.

——(2001*b*). 'Visual Experience and Motor Action: Are the Bonds Too Tight?' *Philosophical Review* 110: 495–519.

Cummins, R. (1996). *Representations, Targets and Attitudes*. Cambridge, Mass.: MIT Press.

Currie, G. (1995*a*). *Image and Mind: Film, Philosophy and Cognitive Science*. New York: Cambridge University Press.

—— (1995*b*). 'Imagination and Simulation: Aesthetics Meets Cognitive Science', in M. Davies and T. Stone (eds.), *Mental Simulation*. Oxford: Blackwell.

—— (1996). 'Simulation Theory, Theory Theory and the Evidence from Autism', in P. Carruthers and P. K. Smith (eds.), *Theories of Theories of Mind*. Cambridge: Cambridge University Press.

—— (1999). 'Desire and Narrative: A Framework', in C. Plantinga and G. Smith (eds.), *Passionate Views*. Baltimore: Johns Hopkins University Press.

—— and Ravenscroft, I. (2002). *Recreative Minds*. Oxford: Oxford University Press.

Damasio, A. R. (1994). *Descartes' Error*. New York: Avon Books.

DeBellis, M. (1995). *Music and Conceptualization*. Cambridge: Cambridge University Press.

Dominey, P., Decety, J., Brouselle, E., Chazot, G., and Jeannerod, M. (1995). 'Motor Imagery of a Lateralized Sequential Task is Asymmetrically Slowed in Hemi-Parkinson's Patients'. *Neuropsychologia* 33: 727–41.

Evans, G. (1985). 'Molyneaux's Problem'. *Collected Papers*. Oxford: Oxford University Press.

Farah, M. J. (1988). 'Psychophysical Evidence for a Shared Representational Medium for Visual Images and Percepts'. *Journal of Experimental Psychology: General* 114: 91–103.

Finke, R. (1990). *Creative Imagery*. Hillsdale, NJ: Lawrence Erlbaum.

—— Ward, T. *et al.* (1992). *Creative Cognition*. Cambridge, Mass.: Bradford Books/MIT Press.

—— and Shepard, R. (1986). 'Visual Functions of Mental Imagery', in K. Boff, L. Kaufmann, and J. Thomas (eds.), *Handbook of Perception and Human Performance*. New York: Wiley.

Fodor, J. (1983). *The Modularity of Mind: An Essay on Faculty Psychology*. Cambridge, Mass.: Bradford Books/MIT Press.

—— (1984). 'Observation Reconsidered'. *Philosophy of Science* 51: 23–43.

—— (1988). 'A Reply to Churchland's "Perceptual Plasticity and Theoretical Neutrality"'. *Philosophy of Science* 55: 253–63.

Gerrig, R. and Prentice, D. (1996). 'Notes on Audience Response', in D. Bordwell and N. Carroll (eds.), *Post-Theory: Reconstructing Film Studies*. Madison: University of Wisconsin Press.

Godfrey-Smith, P. (1997). *Complexity and the Function of Mind in Nature*. Cambridge: Cambridge University Press.

Gombrich, E. (1960). *Art and Illusion*. Princeton: Princeton University Press.

Harman, G. (1999). 'Moral Philosophy Meets Social Psychology'. *Proceedings of the Aristotelian Society* 99: 315–31.

Harris, P. (1993). 'Pretending and Planning', in S. Baron-Cohen, H. Tager-Flusberg, and D. J. Cohen (eds.), *Understanding other Minds. Perspectives from Autism*. Oxford: Oxford University Press.

—— (1998). 'Fictional Absorption: Emotional Responses to Make-Believe', in S. Braten (ed.), *Intersubjective Communication and Emotion in Ontogeny*. Cambridge/Paris: Cambridge University Press and Maison des Sciences de l'Homme.

—— (2000). *The Work of the Imagination*. Oxford: Basil Blackwell.

—— and Kavanaugh, R. D. (1993). 'Young Children's Understanding of Pretense'. *Monographs of the Society for Research in Child Development* 58.

—— *et al.* (1991). 'Monsters, Ghosts and Witches: Testing the Limits of the Fantasy–Reality Distinction in Young Children'. *British Journal of Development Psychology* 9: 105–23.

Hopkins, R. (1998). *Picture, Image and Experience*. Cambridge: Cambridge University Press.

Hume, D. (1993). 'Of Tragedy', in *Hume: Selected Essays*. Oxford: Oxford University Press.

Hyman, J. (1989). *The Imitation of Nature*. Oxford: Basil Blackwell.

Kemp, M. (1990). *The Science of Art*. New Haven: Yale University Press.

Kenny, A. (1984). 'The Homunculus Fallacy', in his *The Legacy of Wittgenstein*. Oxford: Basil Blackwell.

Kosslyn, S. (1994). *Image and Brain: The Resolution of the Imagery Debate*. Cambridge, Mass.: Bradford Books/MIT Press.

Kosslyn, S., Thompson, W., Kim, I., Rauch, S., and Alpert, N. (1996). 'Individual Differences in Cerebral Blood Flow in Area 17 Predict the Time to Evaluate Visualized Letters'. *Journal of Cognitive Neuroscience* 8: 78–82.

—— *et al.* (1999*a*). 'The Role of Area 17 in Visual Imagery: Convergent Evidence from PET and rTMS'. *Science* 284: 167–70.

——Sukel, K. E. *et al.* (1999*b*). 'Squinting with the Mind's Eye'. *Memory and Cognition* 27: 276–87.

Leslie, A. M. (1988). 'Some Implications of Pretense for Mechanisms underlying the Child's Theory of Mind', in J. Astington, P. Harris, and D. Olson (eds.), *Developing Theories of Mind*. New York: Cambridge University Press.

Levine, D. N., Warach, J. *et al.* (1985). 'Two Visual Systems in Mental Imagery: Dissociation of "What" and "Where" in Imagery Disorders due to Bilateral Posterior Cerebral Lesions'. *Neurology* 35: 1010–1018.

Levinson, J. (1996). 'Critical Notice of DeBellis, *Music and Conceptualization*'. *Music Perception* 14: 85–91.

—— (2002). 'Aesthetics', in *Encyclopedia of Cognitive Science*. London: Macmillan/Nature Publishing Group.

Lopes, D. (1996). *Understanding Pictures*. Oxford: Clarendon Press.

McDowell, J. (1994). *Mind and World*. Cambridge, Mass.: Harvard University Press.

Marr, D. (1982). *Vision*. San Francisco: Freeman.

Mauro, R. and Kubovsky, M. (1992). 'Caricature and Face Recognition'. *Memory and Cognition* 20: 433–40.

Milner, D. and Goodale, M. (1995). *The Visual Brain in Action*. Oxford: Oxford University Press.

Morrow, D. G., Greenspan S. *et al.* (1987). 'Accessibility and Situation Models in Narrative Comprehension'. *Journal of Memory and Language* 26: 165–87.

Novitz, D. (1999). 'Creativity and Constraint'. *Australasian Journal of Philosophy* 77: 67–82.

Oatley, K. (1994). 'A Taxonomy of the Emotions of Literary Response and a Theory of Identification in Fictional Narrative'. *Poetics* 23: 53–74.

Peacocke, C. (1983). *Sense and Content*. Oxford: Oxford University Press.

—— (1987). 'Depiction'. *Philosophical Review* 96: 383–410.

—— (1992). *A Study of Concepts*. Cambridge: Mass.: Bradford Books/MIT Press.

Radford, C. (1975). 'How Can We Be Moved by the Fate of Anna Karenina?' *Aristotelian Society*, suppl. vol. 49: 67–80.

Raffman, D. (1993). *Language, Music and Mind*. Cambridge, Mass.: MIT Press.

Ramachandran, V. S. and Hirstein, W. (1999). 'The Science of Art'. *Journal of Consciousness Studies* 6: 15–51.

Reisberg, D. and Morris, A. (1985). 'Images Contain What the Imager Put There'. *Bulletin of the Psychonomic Society* 23: 493–6.

Russell, J. (ed.) (1998). *Autism as an Executive Disorder*. Oxford: Oxford University Press.

Schier, F. (1986). *Deeper into Pictures*. Cambridge: Cambridge University Press.

Shepard, R. N. and Cooper, L. A. (1982). *Mental Images and their Transformations.* Cambridge, Mass.: MIT Press.

Stone, T. and Young, A. (1997). 'Delusions and Brain Injury: The Philosophy and Psychology of Belief'. *Mind and Language* 12: 327–64.

Van Leeuwen, C., Vrestijnen, I., and Hekkert, P. (1999). 'Common Unconscious Dynamics Underlie Common Conscious Effects', in S. Jordan (ed.), *Modelling Consciousness Across the Disciplines.* Lanham, Md: University Press of America.

Walton, K. (1984). 'Transparent Pictures: On the Nature of Photographic Realism'. *Critical Inquiry* 11: 246–77.

Wilson, G. (1987). *Narration in Light.* Baltimore: Johns Hopkins University Press.

Wollheim, R. (1998). 'On Pictorial Representation'. *Journal of Aesthetics and Art Criticism* 56: 217–26.

Yue, G. and Cole, K. (1992). 'Strength Increases from the Motor Program: Comparison of Training with Maximal Voluntary and Imagined Muscle Contractions'. *Journal of Neurophysiology* 67: 1114–23.

Zeki, S. (1999). *Inner Visions.* Oxford: Oxford University Press.

CHAPTER 43

AESTHETICS AND ETHICS

RICHARD ELDRIDGE

IT has never been easy to locate and identify values in relation to nature. The Greeks were already aware of the distinction between *nomos*, or variable custom, and *physis*, or the way things are. This sense of an opposition between what is culturally local and variable and what is fixed and given in nature has only grown sharper with the advent of modernity and the increasing credibility of materialist metaphysics. That birds lay eggs or that water quenches fire seem to be matters of fact, while that Bach's *French Suites* are beautiful or that Socrates is virtuous seem to be more problematic matters of value.

At the same time, however, there is a great temptation to see such matters of value as at bottom matters of a special kind of fact. Making judgements of value is important to the conduct of cultural life, and there is enough consensus and argument about them at least to suggest that such judgements indeed track something, rather than being reflexes of what one might call mere taste or idiosyncrasy. The disciplines of aesthetics and ethics have consisted largely of various strategies for locating and identifying the relevant special facts that are tracked by judgements of value, pre-eminently judgements of beauty and artistic goodness, and judgements of duty and goodness of character. Perhaps because of the shared contrast with judgements about the natural world or the putatively materially given, these disciplines have often developed parallel stances and strategies in addressing the natures of values. This chapter will explore these parallels, emphasizing the side of aesthetics, and culminating in an assessment of a family of recent expressivist–holist views that dwell on continuities among aesthetic, ethical, and philosophical expression.

Value realism supposes value properties to be real and discernible features of objects. Both the beauties of nature and art and the goodnesses of characters and actions are held to be *in* the objects that are judged valuable, though it may take special discernment to see them. Trained visual perception of single objects provides the model for the discernment of value properties. Plato notoriously accepts this model, and he equates beauty and moral goodness under the more general heading of *to kalon*: the fine.

Value realism drifts towards *intuitionism* when the primary focus is on the objects of judgement. In ethics, intuitionist views have been held by the early twentieth-century philosophers W. D. Ross and H. A. Prichard. In aesthetics, Mary Mothersill has claimed that certain assumptions of Plato's 'that beauty is (i) a kind of good (ii) which can be possessed by items of any kind and (iii) which is linked with pleasure and inspires love... [are] basic in the sense that every theory has to take account of them and that they commend themselves to common sense...as fundamental truths' (Mothersill 1984: 262). Philip Pettit has similarly argued that aesthetic characterizations of objects as beautiful or grotesque, fine or flawed, dainty or dumpy, are genuine assertions about the properties of objects. Such characterizations are all at once essentially perceptual (one must look and see for oneself whether an object has an aesthetic feature), perceptually elusive (mere seeing of the object, without discernment, will not suffice to determine its aesthetic properties), and dependent on the positioning of the object in an unstable reference class of comparable objects. These features might suggest anti-realism. But because there are reasonable historical and hermeneutic constraints on the positioning of an object in a reference class, aesthetic properties are real enough, and 'aesthetic characterizations...are...assertoric in the strictest and most genuine sense of that term' (Pettit 1983: 38).

The advantage of insisting that aesthetic or ethical properties are real and quasi-perceptually discernible is that the normativity of judgements of value is upheld. There is something in the object—whether a character, an action, or a work—that a judgement about the object gets right or wrong. The disadvantage of such insistence is that it risks under-appreciating dramatic historical and cultural shifts both in the vehicles of beauty and goodness and in the qualities needed to discern them. Subjectivity seems more present in both the production and the estimation of good characters and successful works than intuitionist views seem quite to allow. The beauty of a Greek temple seems different in kind from that of a Bartok quartet; the goodness of character of a Greek aristocrat seems different from that of a contemporary democrat. To concede that aesthetic and ethical characterizations are context-relative, but to insist that they are about real features of things, seems like a defensive manoeuvre in the face of historical and cultural variability, an insistent but empty claim that correctness and incorrectness genuinely attach to judgements of value. Such views may not be wrong, but it is unclear how far their illumination penetrates into the details of our aesthetic and ethical practices and our critical judgements within them.

A second, but closely related, form of value realism focuses more sharply on the special qualities of discernment possessed by apt aesthetic and ethical perceivers. The historical inspiration here is generally Aristotle rather than Plato, and attention is directed less towards fixed ideal qualities in objects than towards specific contextual judgements of the goodness or badness of individual things in art and in life. The significant revival of virtue ethics over the last forty years or so, by such figures as Philippa Foot, Alasdair MacIntyre, Bernard Williams, Michael Stocker, Lawrence Blum, Michael Slote, and Martha Nussbaum, has been driven in large measure by *particularism*, or resistance to universal principles, coupled with a realist sense that the value properties of particulars *can* be discerned. (Both MacIntyre and Nussbaum have also articulated quite distinctive multi-dimensional general accounts of good human functioning.) On this view, *our* reasons for our specific judgements about value are enough to indicate that those judgements track something real, at least when those reasons survive wide-ranging critical scrutiny. We need not accept that only what is physically measurable is real. As John McDowell puts it, 'What emerges here is the possibility that the explanation of [our] perceptions as reflecting ways of life might not amount to an explaining *away* of what the perceptions purport to discover in reality' (McDowell 1983: 4, n. 5), however contextually specific such perceptions might be. Hilary Putnam's internal realism supports a similar stance about judgements of both aesthetic and ethical value. We need not and should not, Putnam remarks, eliminate 'the normative in favor of something else' (Putnam 1992: 79), in favour of judgements about matter that are 'really' objective. The costs for cultural life would be too high, and such judgements *are* metaphysically respectable.

Among contemporary neo-Aristotelians, Martha Nussbaum has dealt in most detail with specific judgements about the values of both particular works of literature and particular actions in highly specific contexts. Though a general theory of the good and reference to principle are necessary as part of the background to such judgements, one must also be '"Finely Aware and Richly Responsible"' (Nussbaum 1990: 148), in the manner of Henry James, in order to make genuinely discerning ethical judgements. The texture of the novelist's attention to details of motivation, character, circumstance, tone, and style is what underwrites specific ethical assessment, against a background of principle. We seek, in ethical assessment, 'the best overall fit between a view and what is deepest in human lives' (p. 26), and Nussbaum's critical procedure extends this search for a fit to the evaluation of specific literary works.

To the extent that these neo-Aristotelian value realisms offer multi-dimensional accounts of the good and very flexible appreciations of different virtues (of both character and art) in different contexts, they account well for the varieties of characters, actions, and works of art that we value. But it is not always easy to see exactly how the particularism fits with the objectivism. When there is that much variety in judgements of value, often indexed to local cultural or historical circumstance, then, even if it *need not* be true, the thought that such judgements are mere expressions of individual or social preference looms. When, in contrast, the overall theory of the good or the beautiful is given more shape and content, so that common features of beauty or goodness in different particulars are discernible, then the particularism lapses. The middle way, of course, is to weave together the ongoing articulation of the general theory with specific value assessments, as the meanings of the general terms of the theory are explored in the specific, partly improvisatory work of aesthetic or ethical criticism. This is surely what Nussbaum has in mind when she remarks that the neo-Aristotelian style she practises will have to be 'self-conscious about its own lack of completeness, gesturing toward experience and toward the literary texts, as spheres in which a greater completeness should be sought' (Nussbaum 1990: 49). When this lack of completeness is emphasized, then the view verges more closely on the *expressivist–holist* views discussed below.

One peculiarity of modern strategies in aesthetics, in contrast with ethics, is the emphasis on the role of feeling in the apprehension of art and beauty. We seem less inclined than the Greeks to talk of beauties of the character, action, or person that we love or are moved by, perhaps because we are shyer than the Greeks about erotic attractions and wish to keep them separate from either ethical or aesthetic assessments. Talk of being moved by art comes more naturally.

The exact way, however, in which feelings matter for the identification and appreciation of art has been the subject of dispute. Most straightforwardly, feelings are sometimes regarded as means for both identifying and engaging with works of art. Judgements about art are here regarded, in Jerrold Levinson's apt phrase, as 'human-sensibility-indexed' (Levinson 1998a: 8). How we feel in apprehending an object is part of how we figure out what it is and how we rightly make use of it. Echoing Plato, but eschewing his comprehensive account of *to kalon*, Richard Miller argues that aesthetic judgements, involving feelings, are objective when and only when they are 'learning-like enough', yet without serving any 'interest in acquiring truths' or in making decisions (Miller 1998: 54). His idea is that by engaging with works of art we explore our capacities for feeling, and so learn something about ourselves, in particular about our capacities and about the objects we might enjoy in the future. As Peter Railton puts it, 'we wish to create and surround ourselves with objects that can be rich sources of rich, perceptually based pleasure, objects moreover that will provide the occasion for shared pleasures among family and friends, that will call forth the admiration of others, and that will afford deeper satisfaction the better we know them' (Railton 1998: 78). Alan Goldman similarly argues that

moral and aesthetic judgments refer to relations between nonevaluative properties (themselves relational) of their objects and responses of ideally situated evaluators. . . . Attention to paradigm works educates one as to the sorts of aesthetic properties or relations to seek in other works themselves unique. Argument on a set of paradigms also establishes a reference class of critics who share taste. . . . Aesthetic education of this sort, while not as vital to the continuation of society as is moral education, is vital to the continuation of its culture. (Goldman 1990: 718, 730)

Lacking, however, any general theory of the good other than a very abstract utilitarianism, Miller, Railton, and Goldman have difficulty explaining exactly why this learning is either urgent or objective. Much of it seems to be a matter of coming to feel whatever others in general, or intimates, or those of high status in one's culture, feel—or, if not that, then a matter of enjoying whatever one enjoys. For this reason, Stuart Hampshire, who holds a similar view about the nature of aesthetic properties, draws the conclusion that, unlike morality, which we must have, 'a work of art is gratuitous. It is not *essentially* the answer to a question or the solution to a presented problem' (Hampshire 1952: 652). When feelings, and especially pleasure and enjoyment, are made so central to the experience of art, independently of any further functions, then the empirical claim that we, or some of us, are enough alike either to enjoy the same things or to esteem the same evaluators seems forced. It is an attempt to erect a philosophical fact about what might be called the enjoyable as such, in the face of considerable evidence to the contrary. Since morality is generally thought to be urgent, it is no surprise that there has been little talk in recent moral philosophy of the morally enjoyable as such, though Hume, of course, held such a view, in moral theory as in aesthetics. We would be better off, *contra* Hampshire, to regard works of art as a solution to a problem, if the objectivity of judgements of taste is to be upheld. As Eva Schaper has argued, it is a mistake 'to seal off the aesthetic tank hermetically from the wide waters of philosophy' (Schaper 1983a: 39), as Hampshire does. But what problem does art answer to, if we are not to talk of the objective achievement of *to kalon*, of the fine as such?

The most prominent and promising way to specify a general problem of human life that is not that of the achievement of the objectively beautiful and good, independent of human sensibility, is in neo-Kantian terms. The problem defining human life, according to Kant, is that of the proper expression of our capacity for autonomy. This problem is set for us within, by the fact that we have free will, and hence can be more than playthings of external forces. As Paul Guyer usefully summarizes Kant's stance, 'moral worth attaches to the active use of our free will, rather than to any inclinations we have, precisely because it is what distinguishes us from all other animals as mere products of nature' (Guyer 1993: 347). One must seek to achieve self-mastery, or *Oberherrschaft* (p. 349), in acting according to a self-legislated moral principle.

A major preoccupation of recent neo-Kantian moral philosophy, at the hands of Onora O'Neill, Christine Korsgaard, Marcia Baron, Barbara Herman, Allen Wood, and Richard Eldridge, among others, has been to show that the pursuit of *Oberherrschaft* need not commit one to moral rigorism or to the denigration of feelings or personal relationships, contrary to the criticisms of Kant made by particularists and virtue theorists. In order to make this case, it is typically emphasized that 'our sentiments and inclinations are plastic' (Guyer 1993: 367). As a result, 'reason can...operate upon initially unruly and polymorphous passions, partially transform them, and thereby attach our inclinations and feelings to actions and ongoing modes of activity...that have been taken to express respect for persons' (Eldridge 1989: 45). Eldridge has then turned to certain works of narrative literature as offering exemplars of this transformative education of feeling.

This line of argument relies upon and endorses the task that Kant specifically assigns to art in *The Critique of Judgement*. Through symbolic representation, works of art can 'make moral ideas evident to the senses', as Guyer (1993: 39) puts it. 'The rational autonomy that underlies morality...can be made palpable to fully embodied rational agents like ourselves' (p. 19). Such a stance runs evident risks of both aesthetic didacticism and moral rigorism, if the most successful works of narrative art are taken to be stories of protagonists smoothly doing the right thing and living happily ever after. Eldridge has emphasized, however, that there are at best only 'partial and anxious exemplars' (Eldridge 1989: 187) of the achievement of self-mastery. Drawing in detail on Kant's historical and anthropological essays, he has argued that, for Kant and in fact, 'every exercise of power or virtue, every act of originality or courage or kindness or justice or love that we might look to as advancing our culture, will be at the same time marked by vainglory and antagonism' (Eldridge 1996a: 184). And yet, the ideal of free expressiveness coherently draws us, in art as in life. The difficulty that this complex view faces is to make evident the roles in our arts and lives of such abstract ideals as freedom, self-mastery, and free expressiveness. From a more naturalist point of view, it may well seem that human life and art are much more about eating, sleeping, procreating, and enjoying than about these ideals. This criticism can be met only by tracing in detail what, in art and in life, we truly care about.

Just as this neo-Kantian line of thinking brings the function of art into connection with the conduct of life, so the most important work on value of the last forty or so years has seen the philosophical activity of thinking about value as itself taking place within the conduct of life, rather than through the discovery of fixed philosophical facts about either ideal forms or human nature. Inspired significantly by the work of the later Wittgenstein, *expressivist–holist* views see critical assessments of particulars, both aesthetic and ethical, and more general remarks about the kinds of things that are worth doing and making, as interrelated, ongoing, contested, conversationally arguable moves within ongoing human life. Here Iris Murdoch talks of the importance of *attention*—all at once aesthetic, ethical, philosophical, and specifically critical—to 'the texture of...being' (Murdoch 1956: 39), as it is developed both in one's own life and in the lives of others. Human life is seen as requiring continual thoughtful redirection, never as the complete achievement of an ideal shape. As Murdoch puts it, 'There are innumerable points at which we have to detach ourselves, to change our orientation, to redirect our desire and refresh and purify our energy, to keep on looking in the right direction: to attend upon the grace that comes through faith' (Murdoch 1992: 25). Making and closely following works of art are paradigms of close attention to life, carried out within life. 'Art is informative and entertaining, it condenses and clarifies the world, directing attention upon particular things.... Art illuminates accident and contingency and the general muddle of life...' (p. 8). There are, always, things to get right about human life, from within human life. Art, ethics, and philosophy all partake in this ongoing effort.

Within this expressivist–holist paradigm, there is less talk of right action or duty *überhaupt* and more attention to the display and development of character in context; there is less talk of autonomous beauty or significant form and more talk of the uses of art in embodying and clarifying specific visions of things. In this vein it is natural for Eva Schaper to remark upon analogies between close attention to an artistic object and love for another person, where both are 'not self-regarding but not self-forgetting either in the absorption in the loved one.... The emotion of love permeates the entire life of the person who loves. And so it is also with the pleasures of taste' (Schaper 1983*a*: 51). Here there is no separating off of ethics from aesthetics, or of critical attention to particulars from broader reflections. As R. M. Hare puts it, 'It is as if a man were regarding his own life and character as a work of art, and asking how it should best be completed' (Hare 1965: 150). 'To become a mature moral person', in Marcia Eaton's formulation, itself 'requires aesthetic skills' (Eaton 1997: 361).

Such expressivist–holist views carry evident risks of aestheticism. Everything seems to be a matter of pattern or arrangement. The boundaries between aesthetics, ethics, philosophy, and criticism seem tenuous, and the idea of really getting right what is required of us by our nature, by our wills, by God, or by the good seems threatened.

One neo-Nietzschean reply to this worry, urged by Alexander Nehamas, is to embrace the thought that 'artistic decisions provide the model for all action' (Nehamas 1996: 233), but then to argue, first, that in both art and life there are always enough contextual considerations available to point to something specific, and, second, that we should free ourselves from a cowardly 'metaphysical' urge to justify our choices from everywhere and nowhere. It remains to be seen, however, whether this form of aestheticism is adequate to guide choices in context and whether it can either answer or undo our intuition that there is something more than contextual that such choices aim at getting right.

Richard Shusterman has attempted to provide somewhat more normative content for this kind of view by reminding us that art has 'deep roots in life's needs and interests' (Shusterman 1997: 6), as Nietzsche, Foucault, Wittgenstein, and Dewey all held. In a specifically Deweyan vein, Shusterman then goes on to suggest 'somatic exploration' (p. 34), or an exploration of the body's possibilities of movement and response, as in dance or as in the Alexander technique, which Dewey himself practised, as one valuable route of artistic self-making, alongside others. His emphasis on the body is meant to temper both a freer, more thoroughly Nietzschean, eclectic aestheticism and a Rortyan insistence on a distinction between public justice and private self-experimentation. The body is present in manifold forms of practice, both public and private, and its claims can tell us specifically how we ought to cultivate ourselves, Shusterman urges. It is not always easy to see, however, just what these claims are and exactly how they should be balanced against the claims of, say, wit or justice or integrity. As in other varieties of this expressivist–holism, the details will be crucial.

Ted Cohen has pursued a more distinctively neo-Humean stance within this expressivist–holist framework, in the context of a study of jokes. If one becomes estranged from one's natural emotional life, then one faces 'a threat to one's conception of his own humanity' (Cohen 1999: 26). Eschewing the demand for abstract proof in matters of value, we should speak from who we emotionally are. It is absurd and incomprehensible that we should be aware of our own deaths and hence, unlike other animals, be open to guilt, love, reciprocity, melancholy, and prejudice. We are responsible for the shapes of our lives, but we do not know how to discharge that responsibility, and we inherit many bits of style and sensibility, in tangled ways, from our families, cultures, and embodiment. In the face of all this, 'laughter is an expression of our humanity, our finite capacity, our ability to live with what we cannot understand or subdue' (Cohen 1999: 41). In laughter we are 'joined in feeling' (p. 25) with some others and with ourselves, at least for a time, and it is not clear that we can do much better than that. Cohen is acutely aware of both the humour and the absurdity of his own remarks, expressing his own feelings. If there is a difficulty with this expressivist–holist neo-Humeanism, it is, as with Humeanism in general, that little attention is paid to the point that Kantians emphasize: the plasticity of feeling and its openness to transformation through reflection.

Robert Pippin has recently given a distinctively Hegelian turn to the expressivist–holist sense of the ongoing construction of a life. According to Pippin, what we, at least in modernity, aim at is the freedom of self-understanding, where one can 'only comprehend [one's life] as one's own in the freely given recognition by others' (Pippin 2000: 164). The expressivist catch against Hegel is that freedom 'has no unambiguous realization' (p. 157); we are instead always caught up in sociality as a play of 'endlessly struggling, mutually reflecting, refined, interrogative, imaginative consciousnesses' (p. 162). A kind of guarded achievement of freedom is possible, involving an intimate mixture of 'tragic self-renunciation' (p. 166) with 'having one's own life' (p. 168), as one comes to terms with one's particular place in this play. Pippin's central figure for this achievement is Lambert Strether in Henry James's *The Ambassadors*, when Strether decides to renounce both Maria, who loves him, and Mme de Vionnet, with whom he may be in love, and return to America. Pippin takes Strether's closeness of attention to his situation and James's attentions to the complexities of desire, relationship, material circumstance, history, glance, and voice to be models of the exercise of modern moral intelligence in the construction of a life. It can be argued against Pippin that there is also either a principle that does or ought govern such attentions and constructions (as neo-Kantian expressivists such as Eldridge hold), or a general, multi-dimensional theoretical conception of the good that should inform deliberation (as neo-Aristotelian expressivists such as Nussbaum hold). Without some such more fixed background structure, Pippin's view risks collapsing back into the more aestheticist–contextualist position of Nehamas.

Very early on, Stanley Cavell cast the problem of human life as that of living both between and amidst avoidance and acknowledegement of others. It is little exaggeration to say that his reception of Wittgenstein's opening up of this sense of human life has been the most striking, detailed, continuous, and self-conscious working out of an expressivist–holist stance over the past thirty-five or so years. Cavell began this work by taking from Wittgenstein the sense that we are both bound to ordinary language, as the enabling background to any distinctively human thought and perception, and yet are in resistance to it, wanting to go our own ways, to achieve independence in our stances, and to escape the demands of acknowledgement of the ordinary. Working from this sense of human life, Cavell argued in 'Aesthetic Problems of Modern Philosophy' (1969b), and again in Part III of *The Claim of Reason* (1979), that both aesthetic and moral argument are continuously *critical*, involving the situated working out of a thought or perception, in a way that seeks agreement. Reason is displayed more in this working out, in critical claim-making in conversation with oneself and others, than in simply holding to a theory of value from which specific judgements deductively follow. Sounding the key note of expressivist holism, Cavell reads philosophical theorizing about value as one more move—sometimes deft, self-conscious, and self-revising, sometimes dogmatic and escaping into false certainties—within this critical claim-making activity. Scepticism provides Cavell with his central figure for the plights of thought:

Skepticism is a place, perhaps the central secular place, in which the human wish to deny the condition of human existence is expressed; and as long as the denial is essential to what we think of as the human, skepticism cannot, or must not, be denied. This makes skepticism an argument internal to the individual, or separate, human creature, as it were an argument of the self with itself. (Cavell 1988: 5)

Cavell has been unusually self-conscious about his own claim-making activity as a philosophical writer, as he seeks agreement with himself and with others. He typically follows tracks or traces of thinking, as they are produced by philosophers, including Emerson, Thoreau, Austin, Kierkegaard, and above all Wittgenstein, by writers, including Coleridge, Wordsworth, Kleist, and above all Shakespeare, and by filmmakers and their figures—Preston Sturges and Henry Fonda; Howard Hawks and Cary Grant; Josef von Sternberg and Marlene Dietrich. In this, he often explicitly recalls bits of his own progress along his own earlier tracks. Some readers have found Cavell's tracings to be mannered rather than responsibly argumentative—unsettled, even antinomian, rather than objective. Given, however, the range and detail of his tracings of thinking about value, as they occur in all sorts of situations and media, this charge seems more than anything else a sign of mere impatience and of a general wish for definite results within a well-demarcated discipline of philosophy. In matters of value, this may be a wish that it may be more reasonable to forgo.

People have historically found a spectacular variety of things to be of value—good or beautiful or honourable or deep or absorbing. There is no settled methodology for constructing a theory of value. How to think about values at all is one of the standing topics of both aesthetics and ethics. Yet we seem able sometimes to give persuasive reasons in some contexts for some particular judgements of value. Given these facts, it seems likely that the most fruitful work in both aesthetics and ethics for the foreseeable future will take place within the expressivist–holist framework. Whether that work is neo-Aristotelian, neo-Humean, neo-Kantian, neo-Hegelian, or neo-Nietzschean in sensibility, the effort will be simultaneously to sustain particular judgements of value persuasively and to articulate a general way of looking at values, where these joint efforts will be part of the ongoing self-conscious construction of a point of view. Certainly no more fundamentalist views, which would settle things once and for all, seem quite available.

David Wiggins, in worrying about how to think about values and the meaning of life other than in fundamentalist terms, has usefully described the basic features of the expressivist–holist stance. We need, he suggests, to accept 'the compossibility of objectivity, discovery, *and* invention.... We need to be able to think in both directions, down from point [purpose or end] to the human activities which answer to it, and up from activities to the forms of life in which [human beings] by nature can find their point' (Wiggins 1976: 371, 374–5). This kind of double-aimed thinking has been carried out at the intersection of aesthetics and ethics, in thinking about the artful and meaningful construction of a life, to the mutual enrichment and profit of both disciplines.

See also: Art and Morality; Art and Emotion; Tragedy; Value in Art; Expression in Art; Aesthetic Realism 1; Aesthetic Realism 2.

BIBLIOGRAPHY

Altieri, C. (1994). *Subjective Agency: A Theory of First Person Expressivity and its Social Implications*. Cambridge, Mass.: Blackwell.

Cavell, S. (1969a). *Must We Mean What We Say?* New York: Charles Scribner's Sons.

——(1969b). 'Aesthetic Problems of Modern Philosophy', in Cavell (1969a: 73–96).

——(1979). *The Claim of Reason*. New York: Oxford University Press; reissued with new preface, New York: Oxford University Press, 1999.

——(1988). *In Quest of the Ordinary: Lines of Skepticism and Romanticism*. Chicago: University of Chicago Press.

Cohen, T. (1999). *Jokes: Philosophical Thoughts on Joking Matters*. Chicago: University of Chicago Press.

Eaton, M. (1997). 'Aesthetics: The Mother of Ethics'. *Journal of Aesthetics and Art Criticism* 44: 355–64.

Eldridge, R. (1989). *On Moral Personhood: Philosophy, Literature, Criticism, and Self-Understanding*. Chicago: University of Chicago Press.

—— (1996*a*), 'Kant, Hölderlin, and the Experience of Longing', in Eldridge (1996*b*: 175–96).

—— (ed.) (1996*b*). *Beyond Representation: Philosophy and Poetic Imagination*. Cambridge: Cambridge University Press.

Goldman, A. (1990). 'Aesthetic Versus Moral Evaluation'. *Philosophy and Phenomenological Research* 50: 715–30.

—— (1995). *Aesthetic Value*. Boulder, Colo.: Westview Press.

Guyer, P. (1993). *Kant and the Experience of Freedom*. Cambridge: Cambridge University Press.

Hampshire, S. (1952). 'Logic and Appreciation'. *The World Review*; reprinted in W. Kennick (ed.), *Art and Philosophy*, 2nd edn. New York: St Martin's Press, 1952, pp. 651–7.

Hare, R. M. (1965). *Freedom and Reason*. New York: Oxford University Press.

Levinson, J. (1998*a*). 'Introduction: Aesthetics and Ethics', in Levinson (1998*b*: 1–25).

—— (ed.) (1998*b*). *Aesthetics and Ethics: Essays at the Intersection*. Cambridge: Cambridge University Press.

McDowell, J. (1983). 'Aesthetic Value, Objectivity, and the Fabric of the World', in Schaper (1983*b*: 1–16).

Miller, R. W. (1998). 'Three Versions of Objectivity: Aesthetic, Moral, and Scientific', in Levinson (1998*b*: 26–58).

Mothersill, M. (1984). *Beauty Restored*. Oxford: Clarendon Press.

Murdoch, I. (1956). 'Vision and Choice in Morality', *Proceedings of the Aristotelian Society*, supp. vol. 30: 32–58.

—— (1992). *Metaphysics as a Guide to Morals*. New York: Penguin Books.

Nehamas, A. (1985). *Nietzsche: Life as Literature*. Cambridge, Mass.: Harvard University Press.

—— (1996). 'Nietzsche, Modernity, Aestheticism', in B. Magnus and K. M. Higgins (eds.). *The Cambridge Companion to Nietzsche*. Cambridge: Cambridge University Press, pp. 223–51.

Nussbaum, M. (1990). *Love's Knowledge: Essays on Philosophy and Literature*. New York: Oxford University Press.

Pettit, P. (1983). 'The Possibility of Aesthetic Realism', in Schaper (1983*b*: 17–38).

Pippin, R. B. (2000). *Henry James and Modern Moral Life*. Cambridge: Cambridge University Press.

Putnam, H. (1992). *Renewing Philosophy*. Cambridge, Mass.: Harvard University Press.

Railton, P. (1998). 'Aesthetic Value, Moral Value, and the Ambitions of Naturalism', in Levinson (1998*b*: 59–105).

Schaper, E. (1983*a*). 'The Pleasures of Taste', in Schaper (1983*b*: 39–56).

—— (ed.) (1983*b*). *Pleasure, Preference, and Value*. Cambridge: Cambridge University Press.

Shusterman, R. (1997). *Practicing Philosophy: Pragmatism and the Philosophical Life*. New York: Routledge.

Wiggins, D. (1976). 'Truth, Invention, and the Meaning of Life'. *Proceedings of the British Academy* 62: 331–78; reprinted in D. Wiggins (ed.), *Needs, Values, Truth*. Oxford: Basil Blackwell, 1987.

CHAPTER 44

AESTHETICS OF POPULAR ART

DAVID NOVITZ

1. BACKGROUND

QUESTIONS about the aesthetic value and appreciation of popular art have only recently become an area of interest to Anglo-American aesthetics. This is curious, for the distinction between high and popular art—like that between high and popular culture, and between avant-garde art and mass art—is a familiar and longstanding one frequently drawn by critics, philosophers, and cultural theorists throughout the course of the twentieth century. It was extensively discussed by Marxist thinkers like Walter Benjamin, and was the stock-in-trade of the Critical Theorists Theodor Adorno and Max Horkheimer. Not just those two, but high-modernist philosophers and critics like R. G. Collingwood, Clement Greenberg, and Dwight MacDonald also made much of the distinction between 'high' and 'low' (or popular) art. Even so, it was a distinction that did not earn the serious attention of philosophical aesthetics until the penultimate decade of the twentieth century.

The reasons for the omission are complex. Anglo-American philosophy, like the philosophy of art that forms part of it, is hugely indebted to the thought of the Enlightenment. Philosophers like René Descartes, David Hume, and Immanuel Kant effectively set the agenda for the next two hundred years of Anglo-American philosophy, ensuring along the way that the philosophy of art would itself be hugely indebted to their efforts. After Kant, it was widely assumed that genuine art could properly be appreciated for its aesthetic properties only if held in disinterested contemplation by an individual subject. On this view, whatever the origins of the work, its aesthetic appreciation required that it be treated autonomously—that is, not as a means to some end, and certainly not as an instrument of morality or religion. What is more, following Kant, it was generally thought that judgements of aesthetic value were not culturally embedded, but depended solely on an autonomous individual whose play of faculties or taste was crucial to judging its aesthetic value. Genuine works of art were considered to be the product of the imaginative and intellectual powers of an independent agent, one endowed with a natural talent or genius that was circumscribed only by proper judgements of taste.

This same emphasis on the powers and the autonomy of the individual was not just a central theme of Enlightenment thought, but the occasion of a strong and persistent reaction to the Enlightenment. G. F. W. Hegel lamented the loss of tradition and community, blaming the Enlightenment emphasis on the autonomy of the individual for this. The modern mind, bred of Enlightenment dogma, is one that thinks for itself, one that takes its values and its criteria of what is acceptable not from some past age but, as Jurgen Habermas tells us, 'from its own thinking' (Habermas 1987: 7). According to Habermas, this was first apparent in the realm of art, where the modern artists of the romantic and aesthetic movements refused to borrow their criteria of artistic adequacy from earlier traditions, but invented new criteria themselves.

This is only one of the ways in which tradition and community were thought to have been violated by the Enlightenment emphasis on the autonomy of art and the artist. For if the aesthetic doctrines of the Enlightenment were to be believed, great art was not communally or culturally produced, and most certainly did not strive to invoke cultural intimacy (cf. Cohen 1993: 155–6). Great art was rather seen as the product of the individual's genius, and the aesthetic appreciation of art came, as a result of Kant, to be thought of as the product simply of the individual subject's taste and discernment. Communal values and activities had little to do with the art of the Enlightenment, which tended to break with the community and its expectations in order to pursue the vision of a lonely but gifted individual.

Traditional aesthetics was founded on these and related doctrines, and it was, I think, because of them that it failed to concern itself with what would come to be known as the popular arts. Many aestheticians refused flatly to countenance as genuine art those works that were plainly instrumental. So-called art that pandered to what people wanted and enjoyed, that instructed and informed, persuaded and cajoled, and, as a result, succumbed to the demands of the market place, was not regarded as genuine art. It was, at best, a 'lower' form of art: sometimes described as 'low art', sometimes as 'popular art', sometimes as 'mass art', sometimes as 'amusement art', but always as 'inferior art'—if art at all. This belief did not even achieve the status of an explicit dogma in much that passed as traditional aesthetics, but was a deep assumption, one that passed largely unheralded and unnoticed and that led to a near total neglect of any account of the aesthetic appreciation of what we now call popular art.

The reason, we can now see, was that such art lacked the autonomy of genuine art. It was not bred of a single, still less of a distinctively talented, mind; it was much more deeply and more obviously embedded in a community and in communal needs, and it plainly did cater for what the community understood and wanted. It was art that arose out of and contributed to community preoccupations and prejudices, art bred of a tradition—sometimes, to be sure, an impoverished tradition—but art that was never a product of the individual working in isolation, dependent only on subjective taste and native genius.

R. G. Collingwood (1938) was one of the few traditional aestheticians of repute in the period prior to the late 1980s to have anything much to say about popular art. Even then, he did not write of popular or of mass art as such, but of what he called 'amusement art', decrying it as craft rather than art in so far as its production was considered to be merely technical. It is 'as skillfully constructed as a work of engineering...to provide a determinate and preconceived effect, the evocation of a certain kind of emotion in a certain kind of audience' (Collingwood 1938: 81). Because it is craft, amusement (or popular) art is not really art at all: it is pseudo-art—the craft of entertaining by exploiting everyday concerns and values, and arousing everyday emotions.

It would take another fifty years before this idea of Collingwood's would be directly addressed and assessed by mainstream aestheticians. At the time, the denunciation of popular or mass art continued apace at the hands not of Anglo-American aestheticians but of High Modernist and Marxist theorists. According to Dwight MacDonald, popular art—or, as he calls it, mass art—is produced for as many people as possible, and so tends to gravitate to the lowest standards of comprehension and taste in the society (MacDonald 1953). It is never a personalized vision; rather, it involves the impersonal manufacture 'of an impersonal commodity for the masses' (p. 59).

Clement Greenberg was, if anything, more dismissive of popular art and culture. On his view, 'the urban masses set up a pressure on society to provide them with a kind of culture fit for their own consumption'. This resulted in 'ersatz culture, kitsch, destined for those who, insensible to the values of genuine culture, are hungry none the less for the diversion that culture of some sort can provide' (Greenberg 1939: 12).

These criticisms were not confined to modernist critics. The Critical Theorists Theodor Adorno and Max Horkheimer saw popular or mass art not only as aesthetically deficient but also as politically manipulative, designed, they thought, to have a particular ideological or commercial effect on its unsuspecting audience. On their view, such art—mass art—'fetishizes' instrumental reason and is intentionally manipulative, whereas genuine art is autonomous, and is not to be appreciated and understood instrumentally (Adorno and Horkheimer 1990: 120–67; Adorno 1978).

According to Adorno, moreover, it is mass or popular art that 'impedes the development of autonomous, independent individuals who judge and decide consciously for themselves' (Adorno 1975: 19). And this independence of thought, he thinks, is necessary for the development of a flourishing democratic society. The proper business of Critical Theory, therefore, was to be critical of and to expose this effect of the popular arts.

Ironically, the criticisms of popular art to be found in the works of Critical Theorists exactly echo the criticisms of popular art offered by High Modernist thinkers. The only difference is that, whereas High Modernists thought of popular art as debased and as somehow compromising the true nature of art, the Critical Theorists regarded popular art as politically manipulative as well as thoroughly debased. Although imbued with the same Marxist beliefs as the Critical Theorists, Walter Benjamin's approach was strikingly different. On his view, mass or popular art is potentially valuable precisely because it is anti-traditional, hence encouraging a critical response to traditional culture, and so nurturing the very independence of thought that Adorno and Horkheimer deny to such art.

It would, however, take mainstream aesthetics many years before these arguments would come to be explicitly considered (Carroll 1998: 15–168). The central tenets of Enlightenment thought, as I have explained them, simply encouraged the largely unacknowledged belief that so-called popular artworks, whatever they really were, were distinguished by their lack of aesthetic value. This at least prompted a philosophical question, for it assumed a class of works that could be distinguished in some way or other from another set of aesthetically more valuable works of art. The problem was to specify these discrete sets. The issue was first addressed in a mainstream aesthetics journal in the mid-1960s in an article by Abraham Kaplan (Kaplan 1966), but that article did little more than pursue, and so renew within the context of traditional aesthetics, the already widespread practice of lambasting the popular arts. It sought to distinguish high from popular art by arguing that popular art was formally simple, that it appealed to hackneyed, stale, and tired emotions, hence to an inferior taste, and so was of inferior aesthetic merit (Kaplan 1966: 49).

Though Kaplan's work appeared in a prominent journal—the *Journal of Aesthetics and Art Criticism*—it passed largely unremarked. For nearly twenty years, no aesthetician explicitly challenged this view. In the broader world of art theory and social criticism, critics and theorists alike continued to distinguish and even defend popular art, but they did so by belittling its aesthetic value. The social theorist Herbert Gans, for instance, offered an important defence of popular art in just this way—by uncritically assuming its aesthetic inferiority. On his view, high art is distinguished from popular art by the fact that it 'provides greater and perhaps more lasting aesthetic gratification. It does so because it is creative in ways that the popular arts are not, is experimental, and addresses deep social, philosophical and political questions' (Gans 1974: 76–9, 125). On this view, too, the mass of people lack the necessary economic and educational opportunities to appreciate high art, and so should not be blamed for seeking out those cultural products that they can enjoy. Rather, it is a requirement of any democratic society that it 'must permit the creation of cultural content that will meet . . . [the actual] needs and standards' of taste of ordinary human beings (Gans 1974: 128, 129).

Richard Shusterman contends that 'such social apologies for popular art undermine its genuine defense, since they perpetuate the same myth of abject aesthetic poverty as the critiques they oppose . . .' (Shusterman 1992: 171). Shusterman is similarly critical of Pierre Bourdieu's attitude to popular art. On Shusterman's view, 'perhaps the greatest problem is the tendency in intellectual discourse for the term "aesthetic" to be appropriated exclusively as a term of high art . . . as if the very notion of a popular aesthetic was a contradiction in terms' (Shusterman 1992: 172). This, he tells us, prevents Pierre Bourdieu, who otherwise sees the fallaciousness of claims about the 'disinterested', 'non-commercial' nature of high art, 'from recognizing the existence of a popular aesthetic that is not wholly negative, dominated, and impoverished' (Shusterman 1992: 172). Indeed, on Bourdieu's view, the very idea of a popular aesthetic is no more than a construct: 'a foil or negative reference point' from which any genuine aesthetic will have to distance itself (Bourdieu 1984: 41, 57).

The suggestion strongly conveyed by Shusterman's account is that there exists a more or less independent aesthetic of popular art. At times he seems to believe that such an aesthetic can readily be distinguished from the more intellectual and esoteric aesthetic of high art (Shusterman 1992: 172). In other passages, though, this is not so clear, for he also maintains that a popular aesthetic is capable of satisfying 'the most important standards of our aesthetic tradition', and, moreover, of doing so in ways 'that enrich and refashion our traditional concept of the aesthetic, so as to liberate it more fully from its alienating association with class privilege' (p. 173). The question, of course, is whether there really is a distinct popular aesthetic. How should one decide? And what hangs on it?

2. AREAS OF CONTENTION

By the mid-1980s, those few aestheticians who had turned their attention to the aesthetics of popular art began, through their writing, to acknowledge that the debate could not proceed non-polemically or with any precision unless a range of basic philosophical issues was first addressed.

Chief among these was the nature of the distinction between high and popular art, a question that quickly led to a ramified debate. It was a debate that canvassed, among other things, the question of whether there was any formal or structural basis for the distinction, whether the distinction was grounded in merit or in taste, whether it could be a purely social distinction, and whether it coincided with the distinction between mass and avant-garde art (Novitz 1989; Carroll 1992: 5–38).

A second cluster of issues that arises inevitably out of any discussion of the distinction between high and popular art has to do with the communal nature of art, the extent to which art is properly autonomous, art's relation to individual genius and endeavour, and the degree to which art conveys communal values, prejudices, and insights (Novitz 1989, 2001; Cohen 1993, 1999; Higgins and Rudinow 1999). If popular art is distinguished, in part, by its attention to what people in a community want—their interests, their biases, and the like—there is a clear sense in which such art helps cement a particular view of self and society. In doing so, these works of art contribute to particular social attitudes and even, on occasions, to a social or cultural identity. The question of whether attention to the mechanisms of this social effect is properly a part of art criticism and appreciative practice, although often neglected, is crucial to any informed discussion of the aesthetics of popular art and, indeed, to a rounded discussion of aesthetic appreciation in general.

A third and again related issue has to do with the nature of aesthetic response, and whether only high art is capable of being responded to aesthetically. The claim that there is a distinctive popular aesthetic at least as worthy as its more elevated counterpart suggests that there is more than one aesthetic, more than one set of aesthetic principles, some suited to popular art, others to high art (Shusterman 1992). It is a claim that has deservedly received scrutiny. It gives rise to certain philosophical problems about appreciative practice that have been widely addressed, sometimes in ways that further destabilize the distinction between high and popular art.

In the remainder of this chapter I deal in some detail with each of these issues in turn.

3. The Distinction: High, Popular, Mass and Avant-Garde Art

While Noël Carroll and Stanley Cavell were perhaps the earliest mainstream aestheticians to acknowledge that some works of popular and mass art—especially some films—were of considerable aesthetic value, they did not initially address the distinction between popular and high art. Influenced, presumably, by the dominant trend of thought in the twentieth century, they seemed simply to take the distinction for granted.

Novitz (1989), by contrast, argued that the distinction itself deserved scrutiny, and wished to know what the grounds for the distinction could be. In particular, he argued against widespread Enlightenment assumptions, maintaining that the basis for the distinction could not be found in the merit of works of high or popular art, nor in their formal complexity or simplicity, nor in the taste to which they appealed. Each was capable of being meritorious or banal, each capable of being formally simple and complex, and each capable, too, of appealing to sophisticated and unsophisticated tastes (Novitz 1989: 214–18). Each could be bred of fashion, survive the test of time, or prove to be wholly ephemeral. In these respects, high art enjoys no intrinsic advantage over popular art. Nor, Novitz argued, is high art always the product of individual genius, or popular art invariably the product of cooperative or commercial endeavour. On his view, the distinction between high and popular art is best explained socially, in terms of a particular history of nineteenth-century Europe that led to an overwhelming emphasis on economic value as the dominant value. It was this emphasis that led to a crisis in the art world, for what it did was encourage the rank and file of society to assimilate artistic to economic value. The good artist, it was now widely thought, would be one who could sell her work in a supply and demand market, and the effect of this was to undermine the whole idea of autonomous artistic values that were worth exploring for their own sake.

Rather than pander to the market by producing what people wanted, some artists self-consciously pursued art for its own sake, and did so by exploring wholly gratuitous artistic intricacies as intrinsically valuable ends. The rise in France, England, and America of Impressionism and Neo-impressionism, and eventually of Cubism and Abstract Impressionism, led to a growing body of avant-garde works that quickly lost touch with what most people expected and wanted from art. As a result, the artworks in question, while regarded as in some sense cultured and refined, and even as the bearers of our cultural heritage, came to be ignored by the rank and file of society. Artists had lost touch with the interests and concerns of their viewers and audiences, and had, in the process, intentionally created a crisis of understanding in the arts. But the viewers who hoped to be informed, educated, and entertained by art, and who turned away from these avant-garde movements in droves, did not cease to attend to art. Rather, their interest was captured by a different body of artworks, which attempted to entertain, educate, and above all capture the popular imagination. Magazines, journalism, popular romances, music hall, and eventually cinema and television all addressed and nurtured the aspirations, the fears, and the prejudices that were to be found in a ready audience. 'Traditional artists had been displaced, and it was, I would venture, in an effort to recover their waning authority that they came to describe their art as "high art"; the other as merely "popular" ' (Novitz 1989: 222–3).

Noël Carroll disagrees with this way of drawing the distinction between high and popular art. On his view, Novitz offers an elimination theory of popular or mass art according to which 'there really is no such thing as popular or mass art, apart from the role certain objects play in reinforcing pre-existing social class distinctions and identities' (Carroll 1992: 7–8). Novitz, however, does not wish to deny the reality of popular or mass art. Certainly the distinction between popular and high art, on Novitz's view, is a social one, but this, he thinks, is no reason to maintain that the distinction is in some way unreal, or that there really is no such thing as popular art. Nor is Novitz of the view attributed to him by Carroll that the basis for the distinction is the function that certain works have in reinforcing pre-existing class distinctions. What he does say is that, because works of art are in a large measure socially produced, it seems reasonable to suppose that the distinction between the high and the popular arts is also socially produced. It is a distinction, on his view, that has its origins and rationale within a particular social context (Novitz 1989: 219).

Carroll, by contrast, thinks that popular art may very well be an ahistorical phenomenon, for it seems correct to say that there were works in earlier centuries that now answer to the modern term 'popular art'. However, it can be argued that it was only in the late nineteenth century that artists and critics thought it important to distinguish high from popular art and invented these concepts in order to do so. Novitz's aim is to explain why they considered it important to do so, and he argues that the basis for the distinction that they drew had nothing whatsoever to do with the intrinsic or affective properties of high or popular art. Rather, it was deeply implicated in the dynamics of the art world and larger society.

But if this is right, then there is always the risk that one's own involvement in a community will affect how one draws the distinction (Gould 1999). One's communally instilled view of the scope of the distinction, or of the value of high or popular art, will naturally incline one to draw the distinction along specific lines. Part of the problem, too, is that, in drawing the distinction, there is no uncontested body of works that is clearly popular or high; rather, one is forced to attend to artefacts that, intuitively speaking, one considers to be works of high or popular art. How should Aubrey Beardsley's erotic prints and drawings be classified—are they high or popular art? And why do they seem to shift categories with time? And what of Hitchcock films or Lautrec posters—are they high art or popular art? Any subsequent formal or informal distinction that one draws between high and popular art is bound, in this way, to reflect one's prior understanding of the distinction.

The problem, however, is not as serious or as far-reaching as a committed sceptic might suppose. For in this matter we always check our own intuitions by consulting not just the intuitions of others, but knowledge of both our own and other cultures. The philosopher who thinks of a Mark Rothko painting as an instance of popular art, and who theorizes accordingly, will not be taken seriously. The problem of bias is real enough, but it can be guarded against.

More important, as Gould also points out, is the fact that our concern with the classification of the arts into high, popular, avant-garde, or mass can easily divert our attention from what is of value and of philosophical interest in any particular work of art. If it does, the entire debate surrounding popular art will become, if not self-defeating, at least pointless (Gould 1999: 130–5). On one view, then, we take the boundaries between high and popular art too seriously (Gould 1999; Novitz 1992). Our concern for them diverts attention away from the enormous similarities of value and interest between artefacts of everyday life, including popular art, and so-called works of genuine or high art.

However, this is not to suggest that the distinction is simply an artifice; for, as Ted Cohen points out, it is 'indispensable' to our thinking about art (Cohen 1993: 152). We draw, and are forced to draw, the distinction because of the different roles that popular and high art play in our lives. According to Cohen, who here echoes Hegel, art that people can understand and relate to helps create a community. To the extent that high art is often baffling and difficult to understand, it is removed from and so does not speak to what people want and understand, and thus does not obviously contribute to the formation of a community. Such art, rather, is autonomous, pre-eminently the product of an individual's talent or genius, and is to be understood as an end in itself, not as addressing the communal concerns and interests of some possible audience. It is, if anything, disruptive of community. It is highly individualistic, and embodies what Dwight MacDonald thinks of as a personalized, rather than a communal, vision.

Before pursuing this theme further, it is important to return to the specific issues of contention that surround the distinction between high and popular art. As noted, Carroll (1992, 1998) not only rejects Novitz's way of drawing the distinction, but assumes that Novitz has, in effect, offered an elimination theory of mass or popular art. On his view, this theory maintains that 'there are no formal features that distinguish popular art or mass art from other sorts of art.... Rather, the distinction is really a class distinction' (Carroll 1998: 176). Carroll thinks that this must be wrong. He attempts to defend the belief that there are formal structures that distinguish mass or popular art; this, it seems, is why he considers it important to combat what he calls social reductionist explanations of the phenomenon.

An odd feature of Carroll's discussion of the Elimination Theory is that it is centred not on mass but on popular art. Ostensibly, this is because Carroll treats mass art as a sub-category of popular art (Carroll 1998: 176, 199). Hence, by his lights any theory that shows that popular art cannot be distinguished in terms of its formal properties will establish that mass art cannot be distinguished in this way either. However, it is easily shown that this does not follow; that, even if popular art is amenable to a social reductionist explanation, it need not be the case that mass art, as a sub-category of popular art, is similarly amenable.

Take the following example. It is beyond dispute that the fact that a person is a monarch has to be explained in social terms. It is also beyond dispute that monarchs who have warts on their noses form a sub-category of the larger class of monarchs. It plainly does not follow from the conjunction of these two propositions that we cannot distinguish members of the sub-class in question—i.e. monarchs-with-warts-on-their-noses—in terms of certain formal or structural features: we can, provided that we already know that they are monarchs.

Thus, Carroll's brief against social reductionist theories of popular art is misplaced. As Carroll suggests, mass art may always be popular, but even if there are no intrinsic properties that distinguish the popular arts, that certainly does not entail that there are no intrinsic properties that distinguish mass arts. This is why Carroll's (1998: 183) claim that one can distinguish popular art in terms of the formal features of mass art must also be wrong—simply because one cannot straightforwardly infer the identifying features of a set from the identifying features of any of its subsets. A vital identifying feature of the subset of wart-nosed monarchs is the physical presence of warts on their noses, but this feature tells us nothing about the identifying features of monarchs in general. In the same way, the sorts of things that make mass arts popular need not be the sorts of things that make them mass.

So nothing that Carroll says against social reductionist explanations of popular art is strictly relevant to his claim that there are formal properties in terms of which to distinguish mass art. As important for our purposes is the fact that mass art need not always be popular, and certainly need not be a subset of the 'relevant popular art of our times' (Carroll 1998: 31). Much high art in the late twentieth century was mass-produced with the aim of reaching as large an audience as possible. The novels of George Eliot, the plays of Christopher Marlowe, and the works of Jane Austen are all obvious examples. While such works may plausibly be regarded as mass art, they are hardly popular. They are, and remain, high arts, which have been distributed to a mass audience with the help of a mass technology. Nor is it the case that all popular art is mass art. The schoolboy limerick is a popular artform that is not on any account a mass art; so too, perhaps, the erotic drawings of the said schoolboy. Eighteenth-century naive art, musical hall, burlesque, and, of course, dances like the Charleston and the fox-trot were all popular artforms, but none of them was what Carroll thinks of as mass art. So, despite his claims, mass and popular art need to be explained differently: the two are not the same.

4. COMMUNITY AND APPRECIATION

There can be no doubt that the popular arts were first thought worthy of mention as a distinct kind of art because they were the arts that attracted the interest of many people. They did so at a time when the increasingly esoteric works of High Modernism could be understood by only very few, and had, as a result, lost the attention and interest of many people in Western society. The popular arts, by contrast, addressed popular concerns, appealed to widely held tastes and preferences, and so commanded the attention of increasing numbers of people.

In saying that the popular arts were appreciated and understood in terms of what people already expected and valued, one is in effect saying that popular art spoke to communally instilled values, interests, and beliefs. Popular art, much more than the art of the aesthetic movement, relies on a sense of community, so that by responding critically to it, one can rightly expect to uncover the prevailing values, beliefs, attitudes, and prejudices of a particular period. There is a clear sense in which such art both exploits these beliefs, attitudes, expectations and values, and acts to reinforce them. In this way, popular art works towards the creation of an identity—towards binding a community through the celebration of its beliefs and values (Higgins and Rudinow 1999).

Of course, not all of the beliefs and values that popular art reinforces or advocates are explicitly stated in the work: some are merely assumed. Novitz (1995) attempts to account for this by distinguishing messages 'in' art, i.e. messages about the actual world that are explicitly conveyed by the representational and expressive content of the work, from messages 'through' art. The latter need have nothing to do with the content of the work, nor need an artist or author intend them. They are, rather, a 'function of certain widely held beliefs and values that surround [the work's] production and display' (Novitz 1995: 200). This distinction, Novitz concludes, 'helps ground the feminist claim that some works of art—whether it be the TV program *The Young and the Restless* or the movie *Damage*—contain messages damaging to women...' (Novitz 1995: 202). Although such messages are not part of the action, theme, or plot of these works and need not be intended, they are, for all that, extremely influential and in some cases harmful. The distinction, then, between messages 'in' and messages 'through' art is taken to give us a way of explaining the complicated and subtle effect that works may have on certain audiences at certain times, where this effect, although partly cognitive, is not a part of what the work explicitly conveys.

It is a short step from this distinction to the conclusion that it is an entirely proper part of the appreciation of such works of art to unpack the deep assumptions or beliefs or values that they unintentionally transmit. Although this is the kind of appreciative practice that popular art encourages, it is not usually deemed to be part of what is involved in the proper appreciation of avant-garde or high art. Here one responds only to the formal and expressive properties and the explicit content of the work, and treats these as ends in themselves. This, if true, would support Shusterman's tentative suggestion that there are two aesthetics: an aesthetic of popular art and an aesthetic of high art (Shusterman 1992: 172). But Shusterman, as we have seen, is ambivalent about this proposal, for he also suggests that an aesthetic of popular art is capable of satisfying 'the most important standards of our aesthetic tradition'. At this point the two so-called aesthetics come together, so that it is simply unclear whether Shusterman believes that there is an aesthetic of popular art that is rightly distinguishable from that of high art. It is this that I explore in the final part of this chapter.

5. AN AESTHETIC OF POPULAR AND OF HIGH ART

The claim that there is a distinct aesthetic of popular art is one that appears to be made in a number of different ways and with increasing frequency in the literature

(Shusterman 1992; Baugh 1993). Lately the debate has centred on rock music, but there is no reason why it should. Nonetheless, musical aesthetics has received some attention in the literature, and the debate is eminently worth considering.

Central to a recent discussion on the topic is Bruce Baugh's belief that rock music has 'standards of its own, which uniquely apply to it', or that 'apply to it in a uniquely appropriate way' (Baugh 1993: 23). In a cogent response, Stephen Davies has argued that this is not obviously the case, pointing to the fact that whether or not one thinks that Baugh is right depends on the level at which we take the question to be pitched (Davies 1999). If at a low level, 'as asking [whether] we attend to different features in appreciating and evaluating rock music, the answer might be "yes". If…at a high level, as asking [whether] the principles of evaluation and appreciation are radically different for these two kinds of music, the answer might be no' (Davies 1999: 202–3). Since, at the low level, Davies seems to say that we are interested in different categories of art, we will consider what Kendall Walton refers to as the variable properties of each category, and will respond to the work in terms of those properties. But this is part and parcel of any aesthetic response to a work of art, and is not indicative of distinctive aesthetics for rock and classical music. It suggests only that, on the ground floor, different considerations are taken into account in appreciating different categories of art. At a higher level, when appreciating rock music and classical music *qua* music, many 'aesthetically important properties—such as narrational, representational, and expressive ones, or others such as unity in diversity'—are equally relevant to both genres (Davies 1999: 203).

As far as it goes, Davies's argument seems right. What he does not consider or discuss is the all too obvious fact that, for a variety of historical reasons, there are different appreciative practices, and, moreover, that those practices that are currently deemed appropriate to popular art are not usually considered appropriate to high or avant-garde art. Where popular art is concerned, it is thought appropriate to approach the work with a mind to the deep beliefs, attitudes, and values that it exploits and conveys. Such art is usually seen as instrumental, as having a social function, and so as having an extrinsic message. The job of the critic of popular culture is to unpack the message that is conveyed 'through' this art, and to discover the 'voice' with which the artwork speaks. By contrast, the appreciation of high art is meant to attend only to the formal, representational, and expressive properties of the work. High art, it is often held, is to be seen as in some ways separate from life, as non-instrumental, and as of intrinsic value. If it does convey a message, such a message will be internal to it, a message about the world that is 'in' the work, in the sense that it arises out of the work's content. There is no question here of looking to the deep attitudes, the unexpressed and implicit beliefs of artist and audience—the messages 'through' art—as a legitimate part of critical practice. The critical conventions dictate otherwise (Lamarque and Olsen 1994: 256).

As against this, however, it has been argued that such appreciative practices are the contingent product of a specific history (Novitz 2001). If this is true, the comprehensive appreciation of any work of art cannot be confined to those appreciative conventions, since they are the product of social or political convenience rather than the product of a genuine attempt to understand the many dimensions of the work in question. The comprehensive appreciation of a work of art involves understanding more than the formal and non-formal content of the work. It also involves grasping the underlying social and political interests that the work contrives to advance or suppress. To ignore the latter, it is argued, limits our understanding and appreciation of the artistry involved in the work—so that we are prevented from properly appreciating the sometimes magnificent, occasionally frightening, powers of art (Novitz 1992: chapter 10). If we are prepared to allow that these powers are indeed part of the overall significance and effect of a work of art, and if we think that such artistry should be appreciated in any aesthetic response to it, then the traditional autonomist view of aesthetic appreciation must be defective.

The problems posed by popular art—most especially problems about whether there is a distinctive popular aesthetic, and so a distinctive way of appreciating popular art—enable us to re-address the problem of aesthetic appreciation in general. For the contemporary practice of appreciating popular art not just for its content but also for the messages transmitted 'through' it—that is, for the deep, often unquestioned, and uncritically held beliefs, values, attitudes, and expectations that popular artworks convey—offers a new and a different model for the appreciation of all art. Like popular art, a good deal of high art is produced and displayed against the background of certain widely and uncritically held beliefs and values, so that messages of one sort or another are often conveyed 'through' high art. However, the High Modernist conventions that surround the appreciation of high art effectively prevent us from attending to these messages, from seeing the work as instrumental, or as having a social function (Bourdieu 1984).

What the rise of popular art has done is suggest more comprehensive appreciative practices that give us access not just to messages 'in' but also to messages 'through' high art. In so doing, popular art has undoubtedly enriched our understanding of art in general, and has done so by enabling us to understand the power that art has in our lives.

See also: Aesthetics of the Everyday; Aesthetics of the Avant Garde; Aesthetics and Cultural Studies; Art and Knowledge; Art and Morality; Art and Politics; Music; Film.

BIBLIOGRAPHY

Adorno, T. W. (1975). 'The Culture Industry Reconsidered'. *New German Critique* 6: 12–19.
—— (1978). 'On the Fetish Character in Music and the Regression in Listening', in A. Arato and E. Gebhardt (eds.), *The Essential Frankfurt School Reader*. Oxford: Blackwell, 1978.

Adorno, T. W. and Horkheimer, M. (1990). 'The Culture Industry: Enlightenment as Mass Deception', in their *Dialectic of Enlightenment*. New York: Continuum.

Baugh, B. (1993). 'Prolegomena to any Aesthetics of Rock Music'. *Journal of Aesthetics and Art Criticism* 51: 23–9.

Benjamin, W. (1969). 'The Work of Art in the Age of Mechanical Reproduction', trans. H. Zorn, in H. Arendt (ed.), *Illuminations*. New York: Schocken Books, pp. 217–52.

Bourdieu, P. (1984). *Distinction: A Social Critique of the Judgment of Taste*. Cambridge, Mass.: Harvard University Press.

Carroll, N. (1990). *The Philosophy of Horror*. London: Routledge.

——(1992). 'The Nature of Mass Art'. *Philosophical Exchange* 23: 5–38.

——(1998). *A Philosophy of Mass Art*. Oxford: Clarendon Press.

Cavell, S. (1981). *Pursuits of Happiness: The Hollywood Comedy of Remarriage*. Cambridge, Mass.: Harvard University Press.

Cohen, T. (1993). 'High and Low Thinking about High and Low Art'. *Journal of Aesthetics and Art Criticism* 51: 151–6.

——(1998). 'Television: Contemporary Thought', in M. Kelly (ed.), *Encyclopedia of Aesthetics*. New York: Oxford University Press.

——(1999). 'High and Low Art and High and Low Audiences'. *Journal of Aesthetics and Art Criticism* 57: 137–44.

Collingwood, R. J. (1938). *The Principles of Art*. Oxford: Oxford University Press.

Davies, S. (1999). 'Rock versus Classical Music'. *Journal of Aesthetics and Art Criticism* 57: 193–204.

Freeland, C. (2000). *The Naked and the Undead: Evil and the Appeal of Horror*. Boulder, Colo.: Westview Press.

Gans, H. J. (1974). *Popular Culture and High Culture: An Analysis and Evaluation of Taste*. New York: Basic Books.

Gould, T. (1999). 'Pursuing the Popular'. *Journal of Aesthetics and Art Criticism* 57: 119–35.

Gracyk, T. (1996). *Rhythm and Noise: An Aesthetics of Rock*. Durham, NC: Duke University Press.

——(1999). 'Valuing and Evaluating Popular Music'. *Journal of Aesthetics and Art Criticism* 57: 205–20.

Greenberg, C. (1939). 'Avant-garde and Kitsch', in *Clement Greenberg: The Collected Essays and Criticism*, vol. 1, ed. John O'Brien. Chicago: University of Chicago Press, 1986, pp. 5–22.

Habermas, J. (1987). *The Philosophical Discourse of Modernity: Twelve Lectures*. Cambridge, Mass.: MIT Press.

Higgins, K. and Rudinow, J. (1999). 'Introduction' to Special Issue on 'Aesthetics and Popular Culture'. *Journal of Aesthetics and Art Criticism* 57: 109–18.

Kaplan, A. (1966). 'The Aesthetics of Popular Art'. *Journal of Aesthetics and Art Criticism* 24: 351–64; reprinted in J. B. Hall and B. Ulanov (eds.), *Modern Culture and the Arts*. New York: McGraw-Hill, 1972, pp. 48–62.

Lamarque, P. and Olsen, S. H. (1994). *Truth, Fiction, and Literature: A Philosophical Perspective*. Oxford: Clarendon Press.

Levinson, J. (1995). 'Messages in Art'. *Australasian Journal of Philosophy* 73: 184–98.

MacDonald, D. (1953). 'A Theory of Mass Culture'. *Diogenes* 3: 1–17; reprinted in B. Rosenberg and D. M. White (eds.), *Mass Culture: The Popular Arts in America*. New York: Free Press, 1957, pp. 59–73.

Nehamas, A. (1998). 'Plato and the Mass Media'. *The Monist* 71: 214–35.

Novitz, D. (1989). 'Ways of Artmaking: The High and the Popular in Art'. *British Journal of Aesthetics* 29: 213–29.

—— (1992). *The Boundaries of Art*. Philadelphia: Temple University Press.

—— (1995). 'Messages "In" and Messages "Through" Art'. *Australasian Journal of Philosophy* 73: 199–203.

—— (2001). 'Participatory Art and Appreciative Practice'. *Journal of Aesthetics and Art Criticism* 59: 153–65.

Shusterman, R. (1992). *Pragmatist Aesthetics: Living Beauty, Rethinking Art*. Oxford: Blackwell.

AESTHETICS OF
THE AVANT-GARDE

GREGG HOROWITZ

ALL responsible inquiry into the contemporary state of avant-garde art must acknowledge the possibility that no such art exists. Such non-existence would be dismaying news for a lot of people because, despite the possibility that the concept refers to nothing, many writers and artists continue to invest in it as if its capacity to illuminate contemporary artistic and aesthetic practices were a given. For instance, Henry Sayre's *The Object of Performance*, one of the most richly detailed studies of American art from 1970 to the late 1980s, is subtitled *The American Avant-garde since 1970*. If one inclines towards believing that there was an American avant-garde in those years, one is likely to find that Sayre's roster of participating figures includes the expected artists and movements: Carolee Schneeman and Robert Morris, Judy Chicago and Robert Smithson, Fluxus and the Judson Dance Theater, and so on. However, the intuitive appropriateness of his list notwithstanding, Sayre never makes clear what is specifically avant-garde about the work of these figures. At the moments when Sayre does seek to isolate an 'avant-gardism' in recent art, it turns out to be identical to that art's 'postmodernism', its rejection of 'a modernism that was defined and developed by Clement Greenberg from the late thirties into the early sixties, subsequently modified by critics like Michael Fried and Barbara Rose, and that held sway, especially in academic art historical circles, well into the era examined in these pages' (Sayre 1989: p. xi).

In light of this characterization, it seems fair to wonder why Sayre does not simply drop the designation 'avant-garde' in favour of 'postmodernism' since the latter concept has manifest content for his historical analysis. Of course, it is not only

Sayre to whom we can direct this question. The concept of 'avant-garde' is widely used to refer, as Sayre does, to *oppositional* or *subversive* art. None the less, Sayre is especially useful for raising the questions of whether and when art's being oppositional is enough to justify coining a concept to capture it and whether 'avant-gardism' is the right concept with which to do so. Shortly after spelling out the modernism to which his avant-garde is opposed, Sayre goes on to indicate the arena in which the contest is played out:

> The postmodern avant-garde has asserted its opposition to the dominant brand of modernism—*and its continued ascendancy in the art world at large*—by attempting to strip the idea of 'modernism' itself of the consistency, univocality, and autonomy (in short, the consolation) of a period 'style'. (Sayre 1989: pp. xi–xii, emphasis mine)

What needs to be brought into relief here is Sayre's characterization of recent avant-garde art as engaging in a critique of modernism for the sake of a competitive edge in a struggle for pre-eminence within the art world. That Sayre sees avant-gardism as entirely an intra-artistic phenomenon is also evident in his claim (a claim that is nearly definitive of a certain defence of postmodernism) that the recent avant-garde traces its roots to a different, non-Greenbergian artistic modernism, the modernism of Dada and Futurism. Avant-gardism thus appears, on this account, to be one side of a contest within the art world for control over the inheritance of modernist authority; what it opposes or subverts, in short, is other art. But if avant-gardism is strictly an artworld phenomenon, then it becomes clear why 'avant-garde art' would have no significant conceptual content; rather than its picking out the cutting edge of a movement that, as the name still suggests, threatens to undermine the integrity of its field, 'avant-garde' would name the engine of the art world's mechanism for the redistribution of status (a phenomenon as old as the art market itself) in a manner that serves to conceal that aim behind a veneer of the philosophy of history. Hewing to this usage would produce odd conclusions: one might well end up calling contemporary abstract expressionist painting the avant-garde of a contemporary art world now dominated by installation and video art.

On the matter of whether avant-gardism in art is strictly an art world phenomenon, Sayre's view can be contrasted fruitfully with Thomas Crow's. In his *The Rise of the Sixties: American and European Art in the Era of Dissent*, Crow roughly divides the art of the eponymous period into four geographical regions: London, continental Europe, New York, and the West Coast of the United States. In American art, he clearly prefers West Coast art (e.g. Jess, Wally Hedrick, Bruce Conner, Edward Kienholz) because 'painters and sculptors coming of age in California shared all of the marginalization experienced by Johns and Rauschenberg in New York, but they lacked any stable structure of galleries, patrons, and audiences that might have given them realistic hopes for worldly success' (Crow 1996: 23).

West Coast artists, according to Crow, did not have the option of waging war within the art world since, at the time, there was no art world in their region. The artists thus could not fashion new art in order to gain for themselves a share of the audience; rather, they had to try to fashion audiences out of the raw material of their ambient culture, using the art, responsiveness to which was the end of creating an audience, as the means for doing so. Crow acidly contrasts this radical situation to the Happenings of Allan Kaprow, one of the leaders of the post-abstract expressionist experimental art movement in New York:

Kaprow was careful not to forswear the benefits of his own extensive education, insider status, and refined sensibility. In 1959, he staged his next orchestrated event, entitled *18 Happenings in 6 Parts*, within a strict set of rectangular spatial frames. *18 Happenings* followed a scenario of disconnected actions and startling disruptions on the basis of chance; but once the script was in place Kaprow's participants were constrained to adhere to it. The place of the audience, which shifted its seated position three times, was equally determined in advance. As a final element, he assembled a crowd of art-world luminaries, effecting the singular coup of enlisting Johns and Rauschenberg to create a joint painting on a wall of translucent plastic. (Crow 1996: 33–4)

Crow, we should note, does not adopt 'avant-garde' as his master concept for the art of the 1960s. None the less, he sees West Coast art as more advanced, and New York art as more conservative, not strictly on aesthetic grounds but also, and perhaps even primarily, on institutional grounds. New York artists rearranged the elements of the art world while leaving its structural relations of power largely intact; West Coast art, by contrast and by necessity, took shape on the edge between ghostly semi-institutions (and the desires formed there) and an undefined extra- or pre-institutional space. To put the point in a way that will be useful shortly: West Coast art had not yet attained the institutional autonomy of New York art and so developed in the direction of outlaw forms and practices. Crow's advanced art does not seek to find a place for itself within the art institution as does Sayre's: it seeks instead a place outside of existing art institutions altogether.

The space outside existing art institutions is the magnet that draws avant-gardism in the arts, at least on Crow's view. And if we make central this protest against the art institution in general, we can develop a more specific conception of avant-gardism than that it is simply oppositional: avant-garde art opposes the art institution itself, not this or that particular artist or movement. Sayre, to be sure, does not disagree with this specification; he registers an objection to Peter Bürger's claim (to which we shall return), i.e. that avant-garde art is no longer possible because the post-Dada art institution has expanded to include even its opposition, on the grounds that much American art after 1970 is indeed extra-institutional. Critics will disagree about this, but, in any case, another significant difference between Crow and Sayre emerges at this point, for the extra-institutionality that Sayre claims for the American avant-garde plays no role in his account of the aesthetics of the avant-garde. Put another way: whereas both Sayre and Crow are interested in the characteristic forms of oppositional or dissenting art, only Crow draws a link between avant-garde form and its extra-institutionality. For him, the eruption of avant-garde manifestations inside the art world is a function of their origin outside the art world, so that the avant-gardism of the manifestations is the preservation of the extra-institutional moment in its disruptiveness. As Crow says of the work of Piero Manzoni, one of his European heroes, 'he had been moving toward work in which the aesthetic reward was entirely withheld, the only visible aspect being its packaging and the artist's uncorroborated guarantee of authenticity' (Crow 1996: 137). Crow here nearly rephrases T. J. Clark's formulation of the dynamic of modernism as 'making negativity over into form' (Clark 1982), although the more extreme moment in Crow's view that makes the conceptual distinction between modernism and avant-garde necessary is that something in the avant-garde manifestation remains un-remade and therefore visibly hostile to the form in which it appears. The avant-garde work is, we might say, the extra-territorial site of the appearance within the art world of the non-artistic; it is work that turns against itself.

That the avant-garde work might be the site of a categorical transgression presupposes the existence of an apparently firm categorical distinction, hence one capable of violation, between the artistic and the non-artistic. Thierry de Duve argues that it is part and parcel of the dynamic of artistic modernism that this distinction, the enforcement of which traditionally was the intellectual and social work of academies and salons, is now perpetually under threat:

Every masterpiece of modern art—from Courbet's *Stonebreakers*, Flaubert's *Madame Bovary*, and Baudelaire's *Fleurs du mal* to Manet's *Olympia*, Picasso's *Demoiselles d'Avignon*, Stravinsky's *Rites of Spring*, Joyce's *Ulysses*, and Duchamp's readymades—was first met with an outcry of indignation: 'this is not art!' In all these cases, 'this is not art' expresses a refusal to judge aesthetically; it means, 'this doesn't even deserve a judgment of taste.' (de Duve 1996: 303)

The assertion that some shocking artefact or manifestation is not art, which is still commonly heard, is properly understood as a defensive counter-assertion uttered when the artefact or manifestation threatens to appear in an art context that cannot warrant it as art. When that context is institutional, i.e. has a policing function, openly refusing to license the transgressive work is a belated acknowledgement of its insult. According to de Duve, a work is avant-garde when it is a vehicle for a disturbance of the putatively firm institutional boundaries of the art context in question, and this canonical violation can linger even after its immediate impact has faded:

All the works just listed—and there are many more—have subsequently been judged as masterpieces of avant-garde art, and of art *tout court*, and it is safe to assume that, even for us now, they retain some of their ability to arouse an uncanny feeling of disgust or of ridicule that disturbs the enjoyment of beauty or sublimity. (de Duve 1996: 303–4)

For de Duve, the uncanny feeling that leaks through our aesthetic pleasure derives from the avant-garde work's appearing in the wrong institutional place—even if, as a work, that is the only place it may appear—in such a way that it bears its wrongness in its form. Such works remain ambiguous, sustaining both the judgement that they are properly art and the suspicion that, in some aesthetically relevant sense, they are not. Because, for de Duve, this conflict is of the essence of avant-gardism, it is worth contrasting his account of the assertion that announces the arrival of the avant-garde work—'this is not art'—with Arthur Danto's. Danto argues that 'X is not art' is an ambiguous assertion, its meaning changing according to whether X promotes itself as art (e.g. Manzoni's *Merda D'Artista*) or is instead a semantically mute 'mere thing' (e.g. Manzoni's *merda*). In the former case, to say 'X is not art' is already to acknowledge X's claim to be evaluated as art, albeit while simultaneously perceiving that it is an artistic failure; of an avant-garde work, in other words, 'X is not art' can be translated as 'X is bad art'. Where de Duve hears a refusal to evaluate, Danto hears an evaluation (Danto 1981). Thus, for Danto, the non-artistic element that might challenge the capacity to evaluate can have no legitimate power of its own within the work, and so, in a strong sense, there is for him no avant-garde. (While there are cases in which it is difficult to determine whether and in what respects X is a work of art, they are really just cases of epistemic failure rather than ontological vagueness.) Because 'reality defines a limit art can be said to approach—but which it cannot reach on penalty of no longer being art' (Danto 1997), the art-concept, even if not all of its institutional bearers, operates according to a strict binary logic:

According the status of art to *Brillo Box* and to *Fountain* was less a matter of declaration than of discovery. The experts really were experts in the same way in which astronomers are experts on whether something is a star. They saw that these works had meanings which their indiscernible counterparts lacked, and they saw as well the way these works embodied those meanings. (Danto 1997: 195)

Whether something is art is a matter of fact akin to an astronomical fact, from which we may infer, given the role that stars have long played in the realist/anti-realist debates in philosophy, that Danto means it is not a fact made by the agency of human institutions. But once the status of art ceases to be or to seem to be a function of institutions—once institutions are not seen as authoritative—then there simply is no possibility of a fundamentally disruptive avant-gardism. Hence Danto's claim that 'contemporary art . . . has no brief against the art of the past, no sense that the past is something from which liberation must be won' (Danto 1997). Such art may surprise us by forcing us to realize how much more there is in the world of art than is dreamed of in our philosophy, but it has no capacity to spook us by opposing the institution that is its very condition of possibility.

That Danto denies the possibility of contemporary avant-gardism, and that his denial rests on a belief in the radical metaphysical autonomy of art, brings his views into alignment with Peter Bürger's *Theory of the Avant-garde* (first published in Germany in 1974), the most fully articulated theoretical account of the avant-garde we have. Now a convergence of views between a committed defender of postmodern art like Danto and an equally committed advocate of the continuity of modernism like Bürger must strike us as strange, and especially on this issue. But we can turn this strangeness to our purpose of understanding the impossible position of contemporary avant-gardism if we trace out the difference between them in regard to the nature of the autonomy in question. That difference, it turns out, leads Bürger to attach meanings that are strikingly different from Danto's to the claim that no avant-garde is possible now.

For Danto, art is autonomous by nature; in other words, it is different in (natural) kind from reality. For Bürger, however, art's autonomy is a signal historical achievement of bourgeois society's radical segregation of value spheres. It is not to our point to detail all the forces that play a role in the causation of art's autonomy, but two aspects of Bürger's claim that the autonomy in question is an historical outcome are crucial. First, art becomes autonomous from the rest of social life through the development of its own practices and sites of production, distribution, and reception. The story of art's domestication, its gradual migration to realms of personal experience in which eccentricity and experimentation are permissible because they are 'only art', is overdetermined; however, regardless of how one tells it, its conclusion is that art's autonomy is an institutional fact, not a metaphysical one, and 'is by no means undisputed but is the precarious product of overall social development' (Bürger 1984). As such, the autonomy of art from the praxis of life is not given but rather is actively produced and reproduced within the totality of the social formation.

Therefore, and second, the maintenance of the autonomous art institution requires the conceptual and practical policing of the boundaries of the art world. The moral, political, and legal quarantining activities undertaken by social institutions that are not art institutions are open: a photograph is art or it is obscene; it is art if it is of formal interest but if obscene, of prurient interest; it is art if in a museum but obscene if on the side of a bus; and so on. However, the existence of an institution depends on the rightful legislation and enforcement of its own norms; for there to be an art world, it must embody norms capable of generating exclusions on internal, i.e. artistic, grounds. For this reason, the autonomy of art must refer not only to art's apartness from the praxis of life but also to the active and regular work of holding off or expelling all efforts to press it into the service of extrinsic aims. (The geographical proximity of the American Craft Museum to the Museum of Modern Art does nothing to mask the art world's capacity to generate conceptual distance from within.) This, however, is a patently paradoxical characterization of an autonomous practice: if art must actively enforce its institutional autonomy, then, regardless of the beliefs of its practitioners, it is in practical bondage to what it seeks to expel—in other words, what art seeks to expel remains *legislatively active* within it—and so, it turns out, art is not purely autonomously self-legislating after all. Hence, Bürger states:

The category 'autonomy' does not permit the understanding of its referent as one that developed historically. The relative dissociation of the work of art from the praxis of life in bourgeois society thus becomes transformed into the (erroneous) idea that the work of art is totally independent of society. In the strict meaning of the term, 'autonomy' is thus an ideological category that joins an element of truth (the apartness of art from the praxis of life) and an element of untruth (the hypostatization of this fact, which is a result of historical development, as the 'essence' of art). (Bürger 1984: 46)

If one wished to pursue further the divergence between Danto and Bürger, this passage would be a perfect starting point. However, our interest here lies in explicating Bürger's account of the rise and fall of avant-gardism; therefore, we need to follow out his idea about the significance of the transformation of the relative apartness of art from the praxis of life—an apartness, that is, which is a manner of being related to the praxis of life—into the ideological conception of art as absolutely apart from the praxis of life, as, that is, absolutely autonomous. The name for the result of this transformation is aestheticism, the belief in art whose purposes bear no relation to any other life purposes, which is to say art for its own sake. This incoherent, quasi-theological conception of art can be understood only as the photo-negative of bourgeois instrumentalism; art became an end in itself at the same historical moment, and in order to disguise the fact, that the idea of a secular intrinsic good was being liquidated. But if art can seem to be an intrinsic good only because it seems absolutely autonomous from derelict social life, then autonomous art must veil its constitutive negation of the social life from which it takes its leave. The aestheticist absolutizing of art's relative autonomy thus amounts to a concealment of art's active repudiation of bourgeois social life—which concealment does the ideological work of drawing the artistic ladder up after itself. From autonomous art that seeks to conceal its inevitable relation to the praxis of life to avant-gardism is, Bürger shows, a short step. When the Dada drummers at Cabaret Voltaire called for the end of art, they adopted the aestheticist condemnation of bourgeois society, but then radicalized it to include the art practices that took themselves to be absolutely autonomous of the reality they condemned. As Bürger puts it:

The European avant-garde movements can be defined as an attack on the status of art in bourgeois society. What is negated is not an earlier form of art (a style) but art as an institution that is unassociated with the life praxis of men...The avant-gardistes proposed the sublation of art...Art was not to be simply destroyed but transferred to the praxis of life...The praxis of life to which Aestheticism refers and which it negates is the means-ends rationality of the bourgeois everyday. Now, it is not the aim of the avant-gardistes to integrate art into *this* praxis...What distinguishes them from [the Aestheticists] is the attempt to organize a new life praxis from a basis in art. (Bürger 1984: 49)

The interwar avant-garde to which Bürger refers here had as its aim the return of art from its exilic autonomy to everyday life, an everyday life that was in need of revolutionizing just because its production and reproduction required the expulsion of the idea of the intrinsically good into the realm of art. On this account, we can understand how avant-gardism was (*a*) oppositional and (*b*) opposed specifically to the institution of autonomous art in general. But what makes Bürger's account so fully and finely articulated is that it also allows us to grasp (*c*) why the avant-garde protest took the shape of a disgorgement from within art of the violently non-artistic elements it had been forced to harbour within its ideologically autonomous forms. Autonomous art had become the repository of all those elements of life that were expelled—made unrecognizable as elements of life—during the great waves of social rationalization in the nineteenth and early twentieth centuries. (Indeed, the expulsion of these elements *was* the rationalization.) However, the aestheticist conception of art, in its absolutizing of autonomy, required the disavowal of this function; art's autonomy, in other words, rested on its remaining institutionally blind to its role as the social unconscious. Avant-gardism attacked this blindness because only by turning art's protestive nature back against aestheticism itself could art authentically grasp, and so prosecute, the critique of social life implied by its autonomy. The avant-garde protest against aestheticized autonomous art thus could be redeemed only by discharging back into social life those elements which, in all their irrationality, had taken refuge as artistic values. In a transvaluation of all artistic values, the naked presentation of the non-artistic residue in art, at least as measured by the standards of aestheticism, became the aim of the artwork. Hence the characteristic procedures of the interwar avant-garde manifestations: art by chance, art by collective production, art in the streets, the mixing of artistic media, and so on. Indeed, the basic concept of artistic autonomy—'the work of art'—was the first object of the avant-garde assault in the form of a heightened antagonism to the aesthetic ideal of the organic unity of the work of art. Avant-garde manifestations, therefore, aimed not to subvert any particular earlier style of art, but rather to subvert the autonomy of artistic style, in theory and in practice, as an ideological cover for a dehumanized social life. Avant-gardism, as Kaprow would later put it, was the effort to blur art and life (Kaprow 1993). Here the critical commentary on Sayre with which we began our discussion finds its justification; for the point of the first avant-gardes was not to subvert an earlier modernism—even if, arguably, they did so—but rather to subvert the very distinction between art and life which made a life exclusively in the world of art seem to be a coherent modernist option.

That the interwar avant-garde manifestly failed to erase the distinction between art and life leads Bürger to name it the 'historical' avant-garde; by this he means to indicate that our knowledge that it is firmly in the past prevents avant-gardism from being an available option in contemporary art. However, even though the historical avant-garde failed to revolutionize the praxis of life, it had a profound impact, Bürger argues—albeit only on the art world itself. In an ironic reversal, 'the protest of the historical avant-garde against art as an institution is [now] accepted as art' (Bürger 1984); as a consequence, protest against the art institution is recuperated into the art institution, thus turning protests against art into artistic phenomena:

Once the signed bottle drier has been accepted as an object that deserves a place in a museum, the provocation no longer provokes; it turns into its opposite. If an artist today signs a stove pipe and exhibits it, that artist certainly does not denounce the art market but adapts to it. (Bürger 1984: 52)

Now it is not part of Bürger's argument that this blunting of the avant-garde critique is an unmitigated misfortune. It provided the essential theoretical service of making art recognizable as an institution, the recognition aestheticism was ideo-logically committed to denying, and so clarified the terms of art's relative auto-nomy. However, contemporary artists disavow just this recognition when they aspire to avant-garde status:

> Since now the protest of the historical avant-garde against art as institution is accepted as *art*, the gesture of protest of the neo-avant-garde becomes inauthentic. Having been shown to be irredeemable, the claim to be protest can no longer be maintained. (Bürger 1984: 53)

It is almost obvious that Bürger's use here of the concept 'neo-avant-garde' is ironic, since the art he has in mind (which is the art surveyed by Sayre and Crow) lives off of the prestige of the historical avant-garde while counting on its continued failure. 'Subversive' has become an authorized position within the contemporary art world, a claim to artistic status rather than against the mechanisms of its bestowal. Indeed, the more stylish the subversion, the more obvious its claim to enter the institution and, thus, the more effective it is in *legitimating* the institution; protest against art's auton-omy has become the agent of its increased autonomy. Subversive art has become the site where the politics of art is remade as theatre; while this operation helps to expand the art world both conceptually and practically, it none the less aestheticizes the his-torical overcoming that was aimed at by the historical avant-garde. And without the utopian hope for a moment of de-aestheticization—which, as Daniel Herwitz has argued, is the *sine qua non* of avant-gardism (Herwitz 1993)—neo-avant-garde art might with more justice be called anti-avant-garde art. Behind its subversive artful-ness, it hides the fact that the conditions for avant-garde art no longer obtain.

For different reasons, Bürger has arrived at the same conclusion as Danto: we have left the age of avant-garde art behind. The power of this argument is only rein-forced by the difficulty in thinking of a recent example of a work of art that could successfully risk its own status by subverting the *status quo* of the art world. Hans Haacke's *Shapolsky et al. Manhattan Real Estate Holdings, A Real-Time Social System, as of May 1, 1971*, is a plausible candidate. However, even though its biting of the hand that fed it kept Haacke's work out of the Guggenheim Museum where it was slated to be shown, its exclusion from that institution served to elevate its reputation in the art world in general. To say so is not to impugn Haacke or his intentions, since circulation and reception in the art world is not under the control of individual intentions—which is another way of averring the awareness of art's institutionality that was garnered for us by the failure of the historical avant-garde. Because the neo-avant-garde incessantly disavows this knowledge, it is our new aestheticism.

Where, then, does this leave us now? Has the avant-garde impulse altogether dis-appeared from art? Is there any form of art making that bears the after-life of the failure of the historical avant-garde? Let us exploit an unanalysed moment in Bürger's argument to propose answers to these questions. Even as he characterizes the institutionalization of the neo-avant-garde as the negation of the historical avant-garde, Bürger does not believe that there ever was a real prospect of the historical avant-garde succeeding. Its failure was fated from the start:

The avant-gardistes' attempt to reintegrate art into the life process is itself a profoundly contradictory endeavor. For the relative freedom of art vis-à-vis the praxis of life is at the same time the condition that must be fulfilled if there is to be a critical cognition of reality. An art no longer distinct from the praxis of life but wholly absorbed in it will lose the capacity to criticize it, along with its distance. (Bürger 1984: 50)

Bürger is surely correct that the avant-garde could not coherently maintain both that art's apartness from life is the source of its value as a redemptive model, and that the apartness should be repealed in a re-unification of art and life. In this sense, the historical avant-garde had to fail. But notice that Bürger identifies the avant-garde attempt 'to reintegrate art into the life process' with the effort to make art that is 'wholly absorbed' in the praxis of life, where 'wholly absorbed' means without any critical distance whatsoever. Now perhaps it is true, as Bürger says here, that the historical avant-garde really did aim to displace uncritical life with art; the memoirs of the Dadaists Hugo Ball (1996) and Richard Huelsenbeck (1991) certainly suggest it. However, if that really was the avant-garde intention, then the avant-garde project was straightforwardly continuous with the aestheticist rejection of life; after all, if the failure of the avant-garde to return art to life was the failure to eliminate recalcitrant life in favour of art, then the failure of the historical avant-garde was the failure to complete the aestheticist project. This, needless to say, cannot be what Bürger means to say. Let us ask then, even as we grant Bürger his critical demolition of the possibility of contemporary avant-garde art, if we can derive a more adequate conception of the avant-garde impulse, one that will help us to draw a more precise distinction between it and the aestheticist project.

Bürger's difficulty in developing an appropriately acute formulation derives from an ambiguity in his use of the idea of the erasure of the boundary between art and life. The ambiguities of the concept of 'artistic autonomy' have been thoroughly analysed by now. Indeed, on this issue, an entire tradition of critical theory stands with Bürger in relativizing art's autonomy claims (Theodor Adorno, 1997, J. M. Bernstein, 1992, and Christoph Menke 1998, to name just a few). I have focused on Bürger in particular because he explicitly connects the critique of aestheticism, i.e. of the ideological defence of artistic autonomy, to the work of the historical avant-garde. Aestheticism defends artistic autonomy by withdrawing the possibility of reflective valuing entirely into art, thus retroactively justifying a non-reflective disvaluing of the rest of life. It is this non-reflective moment of disvalue, this voiceless yet inescapable fragment of disdained life which lives at the core of artistic autonomy—*and to which the aestheticist must remain unresponsive*—that wreaks its vengeance on aestheticism, on the unreflective institution of art, in the practices of avant-gardism. Bürger's analysis brings the emphatically anti-artistic moment of avant-garde practice into focus as a vengeful clamouring on behalf of the unspeakable;

when poetry breaks into sub-semantic particles that occasion the memory of speech, or when a film-maker prefers to open the eyes of his audience with a knife, then the avant-garde impulse confronts aestheticism with what aestheticism knows, unconsciously, belongs to it. On this account, even as avant-garde art spooks aestheticism with the uncanny remnants of meaningful life, the last thing it aims at is the reintegration of art into life: rather, it seeks to force the recognition that instrumentalized life, the injured life that gives rise to the aestheticist project, continues to express its neediness even at, or especially at, the heart of the art institution that has turned its back on it. The avant-garde impulse aims, then, not at the absorption of art into life—which would be the true accomplishment of the aestheticist dream—but at the reopening of the demand of damaged life on art in a way that the autonomous art institution must hear.

The aestheticist understanding of the autonomy of art, in so far as it is based on a non-reflective disdain for the life it takes art to have left behind, presumes that we need art to make life bearable. As Nietzsche put it in one of his most emblematically aestheticizing moments, only as an aesthetic phenomenon is life justified. This hypervalorization of the autonomy of the art institution takes ideological flight from the contradiction that binds even autonomous art to the totality of social life, but like all ideologies it is paradoxical at its heart: aestheticism aims to protect its adherents from overhearing the unredeemed claims of a life that, at the same time, they regard as incapable of pressing any claims at all. The focal belief sheltered by the aestheticist deafness to the plaints that give it point and form is not merely the sociological one that the institution of art has its own norms; it is, in addition, the ethico-political idea that one can live an integral life in accord with those norms. Put differently, aestheticism both registers the modern differentiation of value spheres and continues to insist that integral life remains possible. In that light, aestheticism appears to be the last gasp of the pre-modern conception of an integral life as bound to one value sphere alone; it was, we might say, a Christianity of art for a disenchanted age in which a life wholly taken up into art would be the transfiguration most devoutly desired. The avant-garde impulse—and Bürger knows this—is the profane appearance of the untransfigured residue erupting in all its brute materiality in the space of transfiguration (a theme Greil Marcus, 1990, elaborates across genres).

We can reconnect this to earlier themes by putting the point thus: the avant-garde impulse is the return, in the midst of the experience of art, of that extra-institutional moment the non-experiencing of which is necessary for the aestheticist interpretation of artistic autonomy. The paradox of avant-gardism that we have been tracing out from Sayre onward emerges when this demand for recognition by the injured becomes a new kind of art rather than a demand against art that it not add insult to injury; the avant-garde impulse is the non-artistic reminder in art of the human needs that art has left unsatisfied. Now, this makes it clear why the neo-avant-garde is a neo-aestheticist negation of avant-gardism—it turns the anti-artistic plea for meaningful expression into its own satisfaction—but that neo-avant-gardism is the negation of the historical avant-garde expression of the avant-garde impulse does not entail that the impulse is itself exhausted in its art world recuperation. We might choose to follow Albrecht Wellmer at this point who, himself following Adorno, argues that responsiveness to what has been disvalued is the problem and prospect of art now:

> For modern art a more flexible and individualized mode of organization becomes necessary in the same degree as it comes to incorporate what had previously been excluded as disparate, alien to the subject, and senseless. The opening-up of the work of art, the dissolution of its boundaries, is seen as closely related to an enhanced capacity for the aesthetic integration of the diffuse and the disparate. (Wellmer 1991: 89)

Autonomous art has always depended on the muteness of its non-artistic counterparts. Thus, the opening up of the work of art, if it is to be an artistic opening, must be the work of the avant-garde impulse, of the muteness of the non-artistic as it begins to stir in the work of art. While still anti-aestheticist, this fate of the avant-garde impulse, far from being heteronomous, is in fact the engine of artistic autonomy; if autonomy means developing according to one's own law, then artistic autonomy must be responsiveness to what cleaves the work of art from within. Of course, the avant-garde impulse would wither, the prospect of artistic autonomy be dimmed, and the failure of the historical avant-garde be in vain, if the 'aesthetic integration' of which Wellmer writes were instanced by integral works of art which covered up and thereby disvalued again the moments of injury and disintegration. There can be no academic rules for keeping art open; the challenge in art now is to craft forms that remain open in response to impulses that would be silenced for ever were they to be heard too quickly. Thus, the most important inheritors of the impulse of the failed historical avant-garde are artists who, even though not seeming avant-garde, take up fragments of broken-down life processes in order to let those fragments disarrange the works they also make possible. (We might think here of artists such as Louise Bourgeois, Joseph Cornell, and David Hammons, as well as two—Ilya Kabakov and Gerhard Richter—whose work I examine in detail in Horowitz 2001.) These fragments, not quite mute but yet not quite understood, are the bearers of what Wellmer calls the 'dissipated archaic dimension of everyday meaning'. This stunning phrase names the sort of meaning that works of art can bring to our attention, but only when they are so utterly absorbed in the praxis of life that they can provide the distance required for releasing 'the explosive energies immured within the seemingly solid housing of everyday meaning' (Wellmer 1991: 53). The avant-garde impulse that carries these energies cannot, we have learned, on its own make art, but nothing else can make art necessary.

See also: Art and Politics; Aesthetics and Postmodernism; Aesthetics and Cultural Studies; Aesthetics of Popular Art; Value in Art.

BIBLIOGRAPHY

Adorno, T. W. (1997). *Aesthetic Theory*. Minneapolis: University of Minnesota Press.

Ball, H. (1996). *Flight Out of Time: A Dada Diary*. Berkeley: University of California Press.

Bernstein, J. M. (1992). *The Fate of Art: Aesthetic Alienation from Kant to Derrida and Adorno*. University Park, Pa.: Pennsylvania University Press.

Bürger, P. (1984). *Theory of the Avant-Garde,* trans. M. Shaw. Minneapolis: University of Minnesota Press. First published in 1974.

——(1992). *The Decline of Modernism*. University Park, Pa.: Pennsylvania State University Press.

Clark, T. J. (1982). 'Clement Greenberg's Theory of Art'. *Critical Inquiry* 9: 139–56.

Crow, T. (1996). *The Rise of the Sixties: American and European Art in the Age of Dissent*. New York: Harry N. Abrams.

Danto, A. (1981). *The Transfiguration of the Commonplace*. Cambridge, Mass.: Harvard University Press.

——(1997). *After the End of Art: Contemporary Art and the Pale of History*. Princeton: Princeton University Press.

de Duve, T. (1996). *Kant After Duchamp*. Cambridge, Mass.: MIT Press.

Herwitz, D. (1993). *Making Theory/Constructing Art: On the Authority of the Avant-Garde*. Chicago: University of Chicago Press.

Horowitz, G. (2001). *Sustaining Loss: Art and Mournful Life*. Stanford, Calif.: Stanford University Press.

Huelsenbeck, R. (1991). *Memoirs of a Dada Drummer*. Berkeley: University of California Press.

Kaprow, A. (1993). *Essays on the Blurring of Art and Life*. Berkeley: University of California Press.

Marcus, G. (1990). *Lipstick Traces: A Secret History of the Twentieth Century*. Cambridge, Mass.: Harvard University Press.

Menke, C. (1998). *The Sovereignty of Art: Aesthetic Negativity in Adorno and Derrida*. Cambridge, Mass.: MIT Press.

Sayre, H. (1989). *The Object of Performance: The American Avant-garde since 1970*. Chicago: University of Chicago Press.

Wellmer, A. (1991). *The Persistence of Modernity: Essays on Aesthetics, Ethics, and Postmodernism*. Cambridge, Mass.: MIT Press.

CHAPTER 46

AESTHETICS OF THE EVERYDAY

CRISPIN SARTWELL

'EVERYDAY aesthetics' refers to the possibility of aesthetic experience of non-art objects and events, as well as to a current movement within the field of philosophy of art which rejects or puts into question distinctions such as those between fine and popular art, art and craft, and aesthetic and non-aesthetic experiences. The movement may be said to begin properly with Dewey's *Art as Experience* (1934), though it also has roots in continental philosophers such Heidegger (see Heidegger 1971).

1. RANGES OF EXPERIENCE

The possibility of everyday aesthetics originates in two undoubted facts: (1) that art emerges from a range of non-art activities and experiences, and (2) that the realm of the aesthetic extends well beyond the realm of what are commonly conceived to be the fine arts.

1.1 Sources of Art

It is generally conceded that much of what we think of as art emerges from religious and spiritual expression and from rituals which demand objects of beauty and associate such objects with the sacred. Almost all of what we think of as the arts of traditional Indian, African, and Native American cultures has a direct connection with the cult and ritual of those cultures. In many cultures, ritual objects must be made with great skill and must conform to traditionally specified configurations. Navajo sand paintings are a particularly clear example: incredibly elaborate, formally pleasing, and made by skilled artisans, they nevertheless do not conform to the Western conception of fine art, as can be seen in the fact that they are destroyed in the rituals in which they are employed rather than being preserved. Indeed, their cultural function is in some ways closer to the Western function of medicine, as the sand may be applied to the body of an ill person.

It is widely accepted, following Nietzsche's account in *The Birth of Tragedy* (Nietzsche 1999), that the origin of Greek drama is religious ritual. Indeed, the history of Western art is incomprehensible without an account of Western religion. European painting, for example, remained primarily cultic through the Baroque period. The music of Bach and of many of his predecessors and followers must be understood in the light of scripture and religious devotion. Western literature, too, must be interpreted in the light of Western religion: that is as true of Homer as it is of Milton. Even today, it is not ridiculous to hold that the veneration with which the masterpieces of the fine arts tradition are regarded—their preservation and presentation in huge temple-like buildings (museums, libraries, concert halls) and the quasi-spiritual transports that people report in their presence—betrays a certain persistent connection of art to religion (see Benjamin 1969).

Another predominant and ostensibly extra-artistic source of the arts is craft, generally conceived as the skilled making of useful objects. Art's objects, on the other hand, are not, in the Western aesthetic tradition, conceived to be primarily useful. Collingwood and others have drawn distinctions between art and craft and made such a distinction fundamental to an account of art (see Collingwood 1938). Nevertheless, the history of art cannot be considered in isolation from craft skills (see Sparshott 1982). The skills in stone or woodworking that make sculpture possible were certainly developed in the service of practical needs and engineering projects. Metallurgy has origins in the making of weapons and agricultural implements. The skills required to make a building stand up or a bowl durable and pleasing to use are applied very directly in the making of fine art.

In Europe through the Renaissance, the fine arts were conceived to be crafts, or at a minimum to be similar to crafts. This is evident in the membership of painters in particular in craft guilds; it is also evident in the kind of training that artists underwent, essentially an elaborate introduction to the relevant craft skills, from selecting materials and grinding pigments to priming supports. The association of art with craft skills in the public mind can still be seen in the scepticism with which art that displays little in the way of craft is often greeted: 'Hey, my kid could do that.' And there is little doubt that part of what continues to impress us in the work of, for example, Caravaggio or Delacroix is a dazzling mastery of materials that we associate with great craft, though we are also sensitive to the artistic merits of painters whose craft skills are apparently less impressive. But craft continues to evoke an almost universal admiration, because of the difficulty with which skill is acquired and the fact that it is tremendously useful. And a beautifully crafted item adds an aesthetic dimension to everyday experience: such an item is intrinsically pleasing to use.

1.2 The Realm of the Aesthetic

There is an aesthetic dimension to a variety of experiences that are common to nearly all people, but would not normally be seen as experiences of fine art. For example, body adornment is practised by all cultures (see Novitz 1992: chapter 6). All cultures, that is, manifest sensitivity to the look of the human body and some techniques for manipulating the way the body looks. In some cultures, including Western culture, an almost incomprehensible amount of energy is expended on such matters, as can be seen in the gross receipts of clothing and cosmetic firms, plastic surgeons, gymnasiums, hairdressers, and so on.

All cultures, as well, practise some arrangement and ornamentation of their immediate environment, in order to create a pleasing effect. People, whether they conceive themselves to be artists or not, decorate their surroundings: they reconfigure their homes and fill them with knick-knacks, images, keepsakes, and collections. Often they lavish incredible attention on the way these things look, and though it may well be doubted that such activities are art, they surely manifest aesthetic sensitivities of various kinds, and the centrality of the aesthetic in ordinary experience. This is true also of lawns and gardens, in which very specific aesthetic effects are often aimed at and achieved with great skill. The garden itself is clearly a fine art in some cultures (the Japanese, for example), but many ordinary Americans and Europeans are no less intent on creating certain specific visual and environmental effects (see Miller 1993; Ross 1998).

Cookery is another activity with an aesthetic dimension in virtually all cultures, as the question goes far beyond the satisfaction of hunger or the demands of nutrition, into the creation of dramatic and refined experiences. Certainly the experience of a fine bottle of wine or of dinner in a four-star restaurant has an aesthetic dimension, often one that includes interior decoration, deportment of servers, and visual and temporal arrangement of courses in a kind of theatre, and the art of conversation, as well as the sensations of taste (see Korsmeyer 1999).

Present-day culture is also saturated with popular arts such as popular music, web design, film, and television animation and drama. People often dedicate much of their lives to such arts, and these arts often present strikingly aesthetic aspects. Though relatively few rural Americans appreciate Sibelius, they are often heavily invested in, let us say, the music of the country star Alan Jackson. While it may be doubted that Jackson's work is very similar Sibelius's, and while it may even be asserted (albeit problematically) that the latter is art and the former is not, it cannot be doubted that fans of Jackson's music are sensitive to some positive musical qualities and indeed can be expert at distinguishing them one from another and at distinguishing work that possesses them from work that does not. Similarly, a soap opera is not a Shakespearean drama, but it would be silly to deny that they have many things in common, for example plot elements involving mistaken identities, pointed irony, bewildering sexual confusions, and extreme violence.

Such examples are intended to demonstrate the continuity of the fine and popular arts, of art and craft, and of art and spirituality. In all these ways, the arts are incorporated into and originate within everyday life (see Sartwell 1995).

2. Historical Relativity of the Western Conception of Fine Art

Through the history of philosophical reflection on art and beauty in the West and elsewhere, then, it is acknowledged that there are objects of aesthetic apprehension that are not works of art. Indeed, most usually it is human bodies and personalities as well as natural objects that are considered the paradigmatically beautiful objects. For example, Plato in the *Symposium* considers beautiful boys as indications of the beauty of the divine perfection of the Forms; and Confucius describes his ideal gentleman as 'a piece of jade carved and polished', that is, as something like a work of art. And it is not too much to say that the ethics and politics of Confucius are primarily aesthetic, that he develops a conception of culture as art. Such natural objects as flowers and sunsets call out something approaching universal appreciation. That is true also of beautifully crafted utilitarian objects, for example Shaker furniture or Amish quilts; and beautiful weapons and buildings have been appreciated since the time of Homer and, one suspects, much longer than that, as finely prepared food has been.

Indeed, one might think of the creation and appreciation of beauty in works of art as a development of a much more ancient sense of the beauty of the natural world and of well-made artefacts. Indeed, etymologies of the words for 'beauty' in ancient languages show the traces of the connection of aesthetic experience to various other varieties of appreciation. The root of the Sanskrit *kalyana*, for example, means both whole and holy, indicating a source of the aesthetic in religious experience; one of the Hebrew words for beauty, *yapha*, means to shine, suggesting a perhaps more simple sensual pleasure than we think of as aesthetic (though see Leddy 1997); the Greek *kalos* means fine or noble, connecting, as in many cultures, the concepts of aesthetic and moral excellence.

It is not surprising, therefore, that the notion that art is a separate sphere of human activity is a notion peculiar to some cultures and some historical periods, particularly of the West since the Renaissance. I might point out that, for example, Shakespearean drama was a popular entertainment. The concept of 'literature' as we now know it was not precisely in place in Elizabethan England.

The proper conclusion to draw from these facts is not that there was no concept of art until the Renaissance, but that the concept was not then firmly distinguished from those of craft and popular entertainment. The idea that there is a hermetic realm of aesthetic experience that has no practical application or motive, however, must be attributed to Kant, or at any rate to late eighteenth-century European philosophy and institutional practices. Though that idea has parallels in practices of connoisseurship in the courts of East Asian countries such as China and Japan, most cultures simply do not distinguish aesthetic from, for example, religious experience—or, for that matter, art from religious practice.

If the aesthetic is to be insulated from ordinary human purposes and emotions, and if it is to induce an exalted state in which such human purposes and emotions are held in suspension or distanced, then it must be firmly distinguished from craft, entertainment, industry, information technologies, and other spheres of practical or economic human activity. This conception of the aesthetic thus corresponds to a conception of fine art which in turn coincides with the beginnings of the modern museum system. It corresponds to a model of art history, or indeed to the invention of the discipline of art history, under the aegis of Hegel, which makes that history into a narrative of progressive purification of art from sexuality, commerce, politics— in short, from everyday life. These conceptually interlocked notions of art and the aesthetic in turn fuel a set of artistic practices that are associated with romanticism and modernism. Such practices include abstract plastic arts, atonal musics, and above all the constant radical overturning of the past associated with the 'avant-garde'. They include the conception of the artist as an original genius and of his work as incomprehensible or at any rate extremely difficult, which in turn conjures into being a class of professional interpreters.

One important aspect of postmodernism has been a critique of those conceptions. While theorists have attacked modernist shibboleths such as genius and originality, artists have violated and hence critiqued various modernist practices. Art that actively involves the viewer in its own creation, or is explicitly political or multicultural, or that engages the full-fledged experience of embodiment, is incompatible with romantic or modernist attempts to insulate the artistic from ordinary human experience. That is true also of the incorporation of ordinary objects into art by Duchamp and hundreds of others, of popular art into fine art contexts by Warhol, Lichtenstein, and their ilk, and of craft into the fine arts museum, as in contemporary 'art' glass, woodworking, 'fibre arts', and so on. The philosophical movement known as 'everyday aesthetics' has a somewhat easier time than many other theories of art in accounting for these developments.

3. HISTORY OF THE MOVEMENT

The movement of 'everyday aesthetics' must hence be considered as a critique of romantic/modernist institutions, practices, and philosophies. As noted earlier, it has its origins in John Dewey's pragmatism. But it has proceeded through a series of overlapping stages since Dewey's articulation of the position. First, there was the interpretation and elaboration of Dewey's aesthetics by such philosophers as Horace Kallen, John McDermott, Richard Shusterman, and Thomas Alexander. Second came the recovery into the aesthetic of various other objects and modes of human experience and activity in philosophers such as Arnold Berleant, Joel Rudinow, Yuriko Saito, and Kevin Melchionne. Third is the aesthetic 'multiculturalism' that seeks to take seriously the conceptions of art and experience of non-Western cultures, as in the work of Mara Miller, Barbara Sandrisser, Kathleen Higgins, and myself.

3.1 Dewey's Aesthetics

Dewey's aesthetics initially turns on the concept of 'an experience': an experience, ordinary or extraordinary, that displays coherence, that stands out in the mind as a complete unit, that is pervaded by a unifying quality. The first example he adduces in *Art As Experience* (Dewey 1934) is an excellent meal, of which one might say 'that was *an experience*'. Another example is a child watching fire engines roaring out to a fire: that experience stands out dramatically from what comes before and what comes after. As the title of Dewey's book proclaims, he identifies art as a certain sort of experience, one that is a refinement of the sorts of coherent and intense experiences that people may have every day and that perhaps stands as an emblem of experience as such. Artists are those who are able to embody and communicate such experiences, and hence remake the experience of their viewers. Dewey emphasizes the key role that art works play in formulating or rearticulating human experience, in teaching us to see and feel.

The notion that art is a kind of experience is sometimes associated with the contemporary 'Ideal' theory of art formulated by Croce and Collingwood, who claimed that the locus of the work of art is the head of the artist. But to identify Dewey's view with the Ideal theory is a misapprehension. For Dewey, experience is a 'double-barrelled' term: it refers both to what is happening in the head and to what is happening in the world. We do not usually say that we experience our own perceptions, but rather that we experience the meal, the fire engine, and so on. Experience is an interchange between world and organism. So for Dewey, art is an aspect of human dealing in the world. Furthermore, for Dewey, human experience is cultural and historical, so that art itself is fundamentally social. Indeed, art, in articulating and rearticulating human experience, is a pre-eminent transmitter of culture.

All this amounts to an argument for the continuity of art with everyday life, though at times Dewey appears to stop short of the more radical entailments of his position. In so far as religious ritual, for example, provides coherent, intense experiences and is an agent of cultural transmission—claims that seem difficult to deny—they are art. Though Dewey himself drew his models almost exclusively from what we think of as the fine arts and offered negative assessments, for example, of jazz (as did his contemporary, Theodor Adorno), he certainly provided the materials for an account that makes popular art fundamental. As Richard Shusterman has argued, for example, rap music exemplifies a pragmatist aesthetic far better than does contemporary 'art music'. In its intensity of expression, its cultural centrality, its ability to drive rhythm into life, rap music may embody Dewey's aesthetics better than the paintings of, say, Renoir, which Dewey often drew on as examples.

Dewey's everyday aesthetics were highly influential when *Art As Experience* appeared in 1934, and philosophers such as Horace Kallen and Irwin Edman elaborated and refined Dewey's account. Neglected for some time, Dewey's aesthetics has been revived with a variety of original inflections by philosophers such as John McDermott, Thomas Alexander, and Casey Haskins.

3.2 Phenomenological and Hermeneutic Traditions

A somewhat different approach to the aesthetics of the everyday emerges from the phenomenological and hermeneutic traditions, and in particular from Heidegger's essay 'On the Origin of the Work of Art' (see Heidegger 1971). Heidegger, like Dewey, emphasizes the role that works of art play in establishing and altering ordinary perception. One example he uses is the Greek temple, which he says founds the Greek world: it produces and embodies a certain relation of earth to sky, of human beings to the gods, and of human beings to one another. It establishes a cosmology and allows people to live in the cosmos thus established. In making their temple, the Greeks interpret their surroundings and hence establish their world. Heidegger famously goes on to discuss Van Gogh's painting of a pair of peasant shoes in a similar fashion, as establishing a way in which the world discloses itself to us in its fresh engagement with the most modest of artefacts.

Heidegger's identification of perception with interpretation has been fundamental, and is to be found in one form or another in the work of Ernst Gombrich, Nelson Goodman, and Hans-Georg Gadamer, among others. (But for reservations, see Shusterman 1992: chapter 5.) For all these figures, art creates ordinary experience or is its source; in creating ways of interpreting our world, art creates the world itself for our experience. Gadamer's hermeneutics, for example, understands all experience on the model of textual interpretation: a thought that goes back at least to Heidegger, his teacher. With regard to all of these thinkers, it is obvious that art is in one sense or another continuous with ordinary experience: that it both has its source in and is a source of that experience (an instance of what Gadamer calls 'the hermeneutic circle'). Such thoughts have been elaborated upon by many thinkers, including Michel Foucault and Jacques Derrida.

Especially rich and amusing as applications of this technique are Roland Barthes's essays collected in *Mythologies* (1987), which give elaborate semiotic readings of such 'texts' as professional wrestling, detergents, striptease, and children's toys. Indeed, these essays are classics of the aesthetics of the everyday, applying a vastly sophisticated interpretive machinery to ordinary objects of consumer culture in a way that demonstrates their continuity with fine art and their richness as cultural artefacts. For example, Barthes, with tongue only partly in cheek, compares professional wrestling to Greek tragedy, and comes up with some extremely suggestive similarities. A somewhat similar approach is taken by Jean Baudrillard.

4. Crystallizations of the Movement

Two *loci classici* of the everyday aesthetics movement in philosophy of art are Ben-Ami Scharfstein's *Of Birds, Beasts, and Other Artists* (1988) and Arnold Berleant's *Art and Engagement* (1991).

Scharfstein's book is an account of art and the aesthetic that breaks them completely out of the realm of the Western fine art tradition. In fact, Scharfstein's account makes human aesthetic activities continuous with utilitarian and apparently non-utilitarian activities of other animal species, notably activities of display associated with mating rituals. Nature appears aesthetically profligate in many ways; for example in the incredibly elaborate plumage of various birds that make them more conspicuous to predators and easier to catch. And many species engage in practices of ornamentation of their immediate environment.

In discussing aesthetic practices of human beings, Scharfstein takes seriously both their diversity and their cross-cultural continuities. Starting with an extremely broad basis of practices of making and ornamentation, Scharfstein elucidates a concept of 'art' that is far broader than that defined, for example, in the institutional theory, or for that matter in expressive, mimetic, and other familiar accounts of the Western concept of art. Key to his view is the idea that the essential function of art in human life is what Scharfstein terms 'fusion': the attempt of the artist to live beyond herself or to discover connections. First, art is a source of human fusion with the environment. This includes the absorption of the artist in her materials, as well as connections to natural and technological contexts of those materials. The connection of Coltrane to his horn, or of Pollock to his paint, is extraordinarily intimate and intense. Second, art is a key mode of interpersonal fusion and cultural cohesion. This appears to be a function of art in all cultures. The fusion of Coltrane with his horn carries over to us: we experience a connection to Coltrane through what emerges from his horn. This is a way to account for art's expressive capacities and role as an articulation and depository of culture. Surely much of what lends Western culture whatever cohesion it may possess, for example, is a shared legacy of fine arts. Finally, art according to Scharfstein may be an attempt to find connections with a more-than-human reality, and, as has been previously discussed, much if not most of the world's art has been made for broadly religious purposes. And in fact, all of these modes of fusion may themselves be fused in art: religious art obviously has a role in social cohesion and obviously can draw the maker into a web of connection with materials as well as persons and gods—if there are any gods. (For another attempt to give a transcultural account of art, which foregrounds the idea of 'making special', see Dissanyake 1995.)

Berleant's *Art and Engagement* synthesizes many of the different strands of aesthetic theory that compose the aesthetics of the everyday—including analytic, continental, and pragmatist approaches—and attempts to forge a coherent aesthetics that connects art intimately to ordinary life. Berleant derives an account of the making and appreciating of art from a critique of the Kantian tradition in Western aesthetics, which he associates with three 'dogmas': that art consists primarily of objects, that these objects possess a special or exalted status, and that they should be regarded in a unique way. Attacking such notions as 'disinterested pleasure' and 'psychical distance', Berleant advocates a 'participatory aesthetics' that connects art to everyday cultural practices and environmental connections. He regards such an aesthetics as far more promising than other approaches in accounting for various twentieth-century art movements, including Dada, happenings, and performance art.

Art and Engagement sketches an alternative to the tradition of separation or disinterestedness through the history of the West, in animism, Dionysian ecstasy, mysticism, love, play, sport, and so on: modes of intense engagement out of which artworks emerge. Indeed, Berleant claims that this tradition is far older and more continuous in the West than its competitor, and he connects it with Plato's concept of mimesis, with Aristotle's concept of catharsis, and with the work of Nietzsche, Dewey, Merleau-Ponty, and Derrida.

See also: Beauty; Aesthetic Experience; Comparative Aesthetics; Environmental Aesthetics; Aesthetics and Ethics; Aesthetics of Popular Art; Aesthetics of Nature; Definition of Art.

Bibliography

Anderson, R. (2000). *American Muse: Anthropological Excursions into Art and the Aesthetic.* Upper Saddle River, NJ: Prentice-Hall.

Barthes, R. (1987). *Mythologies.* New York: Hill & Wang.

Baudrillard, J. (1995). *Simulacra and Simulation*. Ann Arbor: University of Michigan Press.

Benjamin, W. (1969). 'The Work of Art in the Age of Mechanical Reproduction', in H. Arendt (ed.), *Illuminations*. New York: Shocken.

Berleant, A. (1991). *Art and Engagement*. Philadelphia: Temple University Press.

Collingwood, R. G. (1938). *Principles of Art*. Oxford: Oxford University Press.

Dewey, J. (1934). *Art as Experience*. New York: Minton Balch.

Dissanayake, E. (1995). *Homo Aestheticus: Where Art Comes From and Why*. Seattle: University of Washington Press.

Edman, I. (1939). *Arts and the Man: A Short Introduction to Aesthetics*. New York: W. W. Norton.

Gadamer, H. (1975). *Truth and Method*. New York: Crossroad.

Gombrich, E. (1960). *Art and Illusion*. London: Phaidon.

Haskins, C. (1992). 'Dewey's Art as Experience: The Tension between Aesthetics and Aestheticism'. *Transactions of the C.S. Peirce Society* 28: 2.

Heidegger, M. (1971). 'The Origin of the Work of Art', trans. A. Hofstadter, in his *Poetry, Language, Thought*. New York: Harper Collins, pp. 15–88.

Higgins, K. (1991). *The Music of Our Lives*. Philadelphia: Temple University Press.

Kallen, H. (1942). *Art and Freedom*. New York: Duell, Sloan, & Pearce.

Korsmeyer, C. (1999). *Making Sense of Taste*. Ithaca, NY: Cornell University Press.

Leddy, T. (1995). 'Everyday Surface Qualities: "Neat", "Messy", "Clean", "Dirty"'. *Journal of Aesthetics and Art Criticism* 53: 259–68.

—— (1997). 'Sparkle and Shine'. *British Journal of Aesthetics* 37: 259–73.

McDermott, J. (1986). *Streams of Experience*. Amherst: University of Massachusetts Press.

Melchionne, K. (1999*a*). 'Living in Glass Houses: Domesticity, Decoration, and Environmental Aesthetics'. *Journal of Aesthetics and Art Criticism* 56: 191–200.

—— (1999*b*). 'Of Bookworms and Busybees: Cultural Theory in the Age of Do-It-Yourselfing'. *Journal of Aesthetics and Art Criticism* 57: 247–55.

Miller, M. (1993). *The Garden as Art*. Albany: State University of New York Press.

Nietzsche, F. (1999). *The Birth of Tragedy*, trans. A. Speirs. Cambridge: Cambridge University Press.

Novitz, D. (1992). *The Boundaries of Art*. Philadelphia: Temple University Press.

Ross, S. (1998). *What Gardens Mean*. Chicago: University of Chicago Press.

Rudinow, J. (1999). 'Race, Ethnicity, Expressive Authenticity: Can White People Sing the Blues?' in P. Alperson (ed.), *Musical Worlds: New Directions in Philosophy of Music*. University Park, Pa.: Pennsylvania State University Press.

Saito, Y. (1999). 'Japanese Aesthetics of Packaging'. *Journal of Aesthetics and Art Criticism* 57: 257–66.

Sandrisser, B. (1998). 'Cultivating Commonplaces: Sophisticated Vernacularism in Japan'. *Journal of Aesthetics and Art Criticism* 56: 201–10.

Sartwell, C. (1995). *The Art of Living: Aesthetics of the Ordinary in World Spiritual Traditions*. Albany, NY: State University of New York Press.

Scharfstein, B. (1988). *Of Birds, Beasts, and Other Artists*. New York: New York University Press.

Shusterman, R. (1992). *Pragmatist Aesthetics*. Oxford: Blackwell; 2nd edn., Totowa, NJ: Rowman & Littlefield, 2001.

Sparshott, F. (1982). *Theory of the Arts*. Princeton: Princeton University Press.

CHAPTER 47

AESTHETICS AND POSTMODERNISM

RICHARD SHUSTERMAN

1. INTRODUCTION

PERHAPS the clearest and most certain thing that can be said about postmodernism is that it is a very unclear and very much contested concept. Celebrated by some as a new wave of emancipation from the stifling constraints of modern ideologies that have grown stagnantly conservative and elitist, postmodernism is conversely condemned for confining us in its own prison-house of conservatism—for encouraging an attitude of slackening by its scepticism regarding the notions of progress and originality, by its advocacy of appropriation and recycling, and by its ideology of the end of ideology. But the controversy over postmodernism goes well beyond the question of its value. Its very meaning, scope, and character are so vague, ambiguous, and deeply contested that it has been challenged as a pernicious, illegitimate non-concept. Advocates reply that the concept's very vagueness usefully challenges the view that concepts must be clear to be meaningful, fruitful, and important.

How exactly we determine the legitimacy of a concept is a fascinating question in itself. Is conceptual legitimacy a matter of logical coherence, reference to the real, entrenched usage, practical utility? In any case, the concept of postmodernism seems, for the moment, to be adequately vindicated by the profusion of scholarly work that is dedicated to its clarification and elaboration in the various arts and other forms of cultural production since the latter part of the twentieth century.

This includes that form of cultural production known as philosophy and, more particularly, philosophical aesthetics. The decision to include a specific entry on postmodernism in this volume seems sufficient to establish its legitimacy in this context, so I shall concentrate on clarifying the confusing diversity of its meanings and claims. I shall focus on the philosophical issues, themes, and theories of post-modernism and how they impact on the field of aesthetics. But I begin with a brief historical overview of how postmodernism evolved in the past half-century from a specific artistic style concept to a notion of very general social and cultural sig-nificance. I then explore the nasty tangle of ambiguities and tensions in the concept of postmodernism and go on to survey its major philosophical theories. I conclude by considering what consequences postmodernism should have for aesthetic theory and what a postmodern aesthetic would be like.

2. HISTORICAL OVERVIEW

Though first used as early as 1947 with respect to architecture (Jencks 1977), post-modernism began to gain significant currency only in the 1960s with respect to the arts of literature. Literary critics like Leslie Fiedler, Ihab Hassan, and Irving Howe used the term 'postmodern' to characterize the experimental fiction of authors like Samuel Beckett, Jorge Louis Borges, John Barth, Donald Barthelme, and Thomas Pynchon who came to prominence after the Second World War, since their work seemed to contrast strongly in style and tone to the classics of high modernism. Postmodernism was similarly present in poetry in the 1950s, with such figures as Charles Olson, Robert Creeley, Frank O'Hara, and Allen Ginsberg. Even at this early stage, the term was used in both advocacy and condemnation. Critics voiced scep-ticism about whether the concept had a clear meaning and designated something really new and distinctive. Did not Joyce, Kafka, and the writers associated with Dada and Surrealism already perform in different ways the same kind of stylistic tricks, extravagant fantasies, and challenges to art's autonomy, unity, high serious-ness, meaning, and decorum that was said to define postmodern literature? Was it good for literature, and more generally for society, that this irreverent spirit of irony, play, scepticism, and transgression was resurfacing? Postmodern art and theory should be seen in terms of the tumultuous social, political, and economic changes of the 1960s–1980s to appreciate the larger stakes in the question of post-modernism. For by challenging modern notions of art's autonomy, postmodernism brings even aesthetics into the realm of politics and economics. I shall return to this theme later on.

Architecture became an especially central art for postmodernism in the 1970s. Reacting against the purist international style of architectural modernism (e.g. its stark, imposing hard-edged towers of glass and steel), postmodern architecture claimed that buildings should be more aesthetically and socially sensitive about fitting into their different local environments and serving the community's needs and tastes. Attention to local contexts encouraged the use of local stylistic vernaculars, and postmodernist architecture more generally advocated stylistic pluralism and often even eclecticism, where strikingly different styles from different periods were mixed in the same building. In this eclectic appropriation and embracing of popular tastes and vernaculars as central to artistic creation, postmodern architecture offered a sharp critique of high modernist ideals of artistic autonomy, unity, originality, monumentality, universality, and progress, all of which underlined the traditional distinction between high art and popular culture.

Such pluralism, appropriation, eclecticism, and blurring of high and low is similarly evident in other postmodern visual art where the traditional aesthetic distinctions between art and life and between aesthetics and politics are questioned (e.g. Andy Warhol, Robert Rauschenberg, Jeff Koons, Hans Haacke, Barbara Kruger, Jenny Holzer). The postmodern highlighting of temporality and contingency (e.g. in the aleatory music of John Cage) was another challenge to traditional aesthetic ideals of permanence and carefully wrought perfection. Many of these themes were absorbed into general postmodern theory as postmodernism increasingly spread from the arts to philosophy and the social sciences in the late 1970s and 1980s. By the late 1980s and 1990s the concept 'postmodern' had pervaded the general consciousness of our entire culture, so that the term became common even in the world of advertising, mass media, and popular culture.

Postmodern ideas in the arts came to penetrate philosophy partly through the field called 'literary theory' or sometimes just 'theory', which was deeply concerned with the arts and developments in French poststructuralism, whose figures (Barthes, Foucault, Derrida, Deleuze, Lyotard) seemed to express central themes of postmodernism, for instance the critique of notions like unity, universality, autonomy, purity, authorial authority, determinacy, and the compartmentalization of knowledge and culture from politics and economics. The publication of Jean-Francois Lyotard's *The Postmodern Condition* (1979) made the poststructuralism–postmodernism connection clearer and turned postmodernism into an important and much-debated issue in the general agenda of philosophy. Thus, even philosophers like Habermas, who had no real interest in aesthetics, felt compelled to engage the issue of postmodernism.

One should not, however, conflate poststructuralism with postmodernism. First, postmodernism was debated before the notion of poststructuralism emerged, and can be defended without using poststructuralist authors and arguments (about language, subjectivity, and power). Second, and conversely, many thinkers (e.g. Norris) who affirm poststructuralism in Derrida, Foucault, and Deleuze as cognitively and politically serious reject postmodernism as merely sceptical, nihilistic, and frivolous. Third, postmodernism seems centrally concerned with an historical formation, while poststructuralism is a more general theoretical orientation (based on structuralism and its critique) about the functioning of thought, language, and power. Let us now go deeper into the particular philosophical difficulties in explicating the concept of postmodernism.

3. CONCEPTUAL AMBIGUITIES

There are at least three important dimensions or roots of postmodernism's deep ambiguity. First, though most often construed as an historical or period concept, postmodernism is also frequently used and studied as a style concept (e.g. McHale 1987). These different conceptions can yield contradictory judgements about whether a given work or theory should be called postmodern. Each conception also has its own problems. If postmodernism designates an historical period, and if that historical period is the one we are currently living, does that mean that everything of our period must be, should be—or even can be—characterized as postmodern? Is the expression of modernist views and artworks or even more traditional views no longer possible? Conversely, if what belongs to the postmodern age does not exemplify any consistent and unified cultural expression, then how can we justify the validity and value of treating postmodernism as a period concept? Indeed, postmodern theory's own critiques of determinacy and unity seems to make the whole notion of clear periodization very problematic.

Treating postmodernism as a style concept has similar difficulties. There is no clear consensus as to what precise stylistic features are essential to a work's counting as postmodern. Moreover, stylistic features often associated with postmodernism—irony, playfulness, appropriation, mixing of styles, use of popular culture and aleatory techniques, political commentary, challenges to traditional unities, profundities, and established aesthetic purities, etc.—can already be discovered in modernist and even premodernist art. Finally, even if we were able to identify something as postmodern purely in terms of its stylistic features, then there is nothing to prevent a work from premodernist times (say, something like Sterne's *Tristram Shandy*) from counting as a postmodern work; and the paradox of a premodern postmodern work would strike many as an unacceptable consequence.

What deepens the period/style ambiguity of postmodernism is that major advocates like Lyotard deploy the term in both senses. On the one hand, Lyotard introduces the notion of the postmodern by explaining it historically as an effect of 'the postindustrial age' and of the transformation and 'commercialization' of 'knowledge in computerized societies'. On the other hand, he is happy to play fast and loose with limits of historical periodization by defining Montaigne's work as postmodern because of the free-ranging, pluralistic, non-rule-governed style of his essays (Lyotard 1984: 3, 5, 81).

Even confining the postmodern to a period concept, we face two further problematic ambiguities. First is the question of which 'modern' period (and related cultural ideology) forms the contrast against which the postmodern is defined. Sometimes this is the period known as 'modernism'—defined by a powerful efflorescence of artistic innovation in the earlier part of the twentieth century that is represented by such writers as T. S. Eliot, Virginia Woolf, Proust, and Joyce; by movements in painting like cubism, expressionism, futurism, and Dada; by architects like Gropius, Mies van Der Rohe, and Le Corbusier, and by composers like Schoenberg and Berg. But just as often, the postmodern is defined not by contrast to artistic modernism but by contrast to the larger concept of modernity. This general concept of modernity dates back at least to Hegel and the early nineteenth century, where a heightened time-consciousness began to express itself in culture. But the period of modernity is sometimes extended further back to include the Enlightenment ideology of eighteenth-century thought, and even (in philosophy at least) back to Descartes. The general project of modernity can be characterized as the rule of reason with the aim of progress through the rational compartmentalization and specialization of different cultural spheres.

When we define the postmodern against artistic modernism, then it is basically an artistic phenomenon that goes back only to the mid-twentieth century. But when defined in contrast to the general project of Enlightenment modernity, postmodernism has a much larger meaning and temporal scope. Here it provides not just an aesthetics, but an ethics, politics, philosophy of language and mind, and an entire metaphilosophy. Moreover, as defined against modernity, postmodernism can be said (e.g. by Habermas and others) to begin with a nineteenth-century philosopher like Nietzsche because of his critique of Enlightenment reason. We should not simply condemn the postmodern for this ambiguity, since its source is, of course, in the concept of the modern.

The third key ambiguity in the concept of postmodern concerns the meaning of 'post'. Does it mark a 'great divide' or radical rupture with artistic modernism or philosophical modernity (Huyssen 1986)? Or does the 'post' of postmodern mean a continuation or enduring after-effect of the modern—an extension or variation of modern themes, styles, and logics, even if it is an extension by critique, inversion, or subversion (Wellmer 1991; Shusterman 1997)?

4. Philosophical Theories of Postmodernism

Even when conceived simply as a period concept, postmodernism has been explained in different ways, though these theories contain some significant overlap.

Lyotard defines it most simply 'as incredulity towards metanarratives' (Lyotard 1984: xxiv). But he himself explains the postmodern in narrative terms, even if it is a narrative of the crisis of certain narratives. Narrative seems central to all philosophical theorizing of the postmodern. So Lyotard's real point is incredulity towards the sort of grand narratives of legitimation through which philosophy, science, and politics were traditionally justified in modern times: narratives of progress towards increasing consensus and unity in knowledge and freedom. With the mercantilization of knowledge in late-capitalist society, the aim is no longer stable unity but explosive growth through competition. Knowledge and society break up into a plurality of Wittgensteinian language games that display as much conflict as consensus. Productive performativity in different language games, rather than shared agreement in one truth, is what legitimates in postmodern thought; hence our admiration for the creation of new puzzles, paradoxes, and technologies in the realm of thought and communication. Lyotard's advocacy of postmodern pluralism and 'difference' is directed not only against traditional foundationalists, but also against critical theorists like Habermas, who locate legitimation (cognitive and political) in the consensus and unity that the rule of reason should guarantee. Rationalized totality, for postmodernism, evokes the coercive calculations of totalitarianism, whose horrific effects in the holocaust unsettled modernity's confidence in rational progress.

Reason, of course, is the supreme value and power associated with Enlightenment modernity. What, then, is its postmodern rival? Most theorists claim it is some kind of aesthetic force or principle. Lyotard insists on the value of aesthetic experience and 'artistic experimentation' against the demands for rational consensus and the public's desire for unity; and he defines postmodern thinking in terms of Kantian aesthetic judgements of taste and sublimity. The postmodern philosopher, like the postmodern artist, expresses an aesthetic sublime beyond modernism by seeking 'the unpresentable in presentation itself', by going beyond all pre-established, rational rules (Lyotard 1984: 72–3, 81). The aesthetic is also central in the postmodern theories of Habermas and Richard Rorty, though they value it very differently.

For Habermas, who affirms 'the internal relationship' between modernity and rationality, Nietzsche's pervasive aestheticism marks 'the entry into postmodernity'. This aesthetic is demonized as 'reason's absolute other', an anti-rational, Dionysian 'decentered subjectivity liberated from all constraints of cognition and purposive activity'. Postmodernism thus 'reduces everything that is and should be to the aesthetic dimension' (Habermas 1987: 4, 94–6). Habermas then traces the postmodern aesthetic challenge from Nietzsche to Georges Bataille's 'aesthetically inspired' erotism and Michel Foucault's theories of biopower and sexuality. The postmodern privileging of the aesthetic over reason is claimed to be still clearer in Rorty's and Derrida's advocacy of 'the primacy of rhetoric over logic', 'world-disclosing' literary art over 'problem-solving' argument, and metaphor over 'normal' speech—all of this captured in the idea of 'philosophy as a kind of writing' (Habermas 1987: 190–207).

Habermas argues that the anti-rationalist postmodern aesthetic derives its authority from the enormous power of aesthetic experience in modern times. But this experience, he claims, is only the product of modernity's rational division of culture into the spheres of science, politics, and aesthetic culture. Therefore, to use the idea of aesthetic experience in order to escape or outflank modernity involves a performative contradiction: one of rejecting reason by means of its very own products. Habermas, moreover, grounds the primacy of reason in the primacy of language, arguing that language is essentially and necessarily rational because there is 'an internal connection between meaning and validity' (Habermas 1987: 313–14). He therefore attacks Derrida's and Rorty's efforts to portray language as more importantly aesthetic, rhetorical, and metaphorical (Derrida 1980; Rorty 1989, 1991a,b).

Though Rorty also advocates the primacy of language, he privileges its creative and aesthetic uses, its power of making things new, by redescribing them in new narratives that employ new vocabularies. Philosophy should 'turn against theory and towards narrative' (Rorty 1989: xvi). Rorty's narrative of postmodernity praises Hegel for beginning the aesthetic turn in philosophy by treating philosophy as historicist narrative in his *Phenomenology of Mind*. But, like Habermas, Rorty sees Nietzsche as the first philosopher who explicitly makes the aesthetic turn of postmodernity by advocating perspectivism and replacing the primacy of truth and metaphysics with the power of creative interpretation and genealogical redescription.

If Nietzsche, Heidegger, and even the early Derrida still intend their redescriptions as universally valid, Rorty counters that the highest wisdom of postmodern aestheticism is to make *no* such claims for one's philosophy. Like the fiction writer, the postmodern philosopher seeks to tell a convincing and attractive story that also convinces by its attractiveness, but the validity of that story does not preclude the validity of rival narratives. If language is a tool for creation, then, in a liberal society that values individual freedom, each person is urged to recontextualize past vocabularies and ideas in order to produce new ones for his or her personal efforts of self-creation, to make of oneself a work of art; hence Rorty's defence of what he calls 'postmodern bourgeois liberalism'(Rorty 1991a: 197). This ideal of individualist self-creation is already very clear in Nietzsche, and, since Rorty has grown increasingly sensitive to the confusing controversy surrounding the term 'postmodern', he now prefers to use the term 'post-Nietzschean' to describe postmodern philosophy, including his own (Rorty 1991b: 1–2). One serious problem in Rorty's radical aestheticization of language for the pursuit of individual creation would be to explain or ensure the stable commonalities of use and meaning that seem necessary for effective communication not only in non-aesthetic contexts but even in the contexts of creating and appreciating art.

Other aesthetically based narratives of postmodernity are closely connected to the idea of 'the end of art'. Arthur Danto, for instance, claims that art has ended in the sense that its old narratives of linear progress have been lost or culminated: the quest for mimesis was achieved by photography, and the artistic quest of twentieth-century painting to discover art's true essence has ended by turning art into the philosophy of art. This, as Danto notes, is a reinterpretation of Hegel's view of art reaching its end by evolving into the higher spiritual realm of philosophy. The end of art's history of linear progress towards a common goal conversely leaves art open to a posthistory of pluralism. For Danto, then, 'postmodernism is the celebration of openness' where any artistic goal, style, method, or mixture can be valid (Danto 1984: 213). Yet Danto also insists that postmodernism is specifically 'a certain style we can learn to recognize, the way we learn to recognize instances of the baroque or the rococo' (Danto 1997: 11). But the specificity of a particular style seems to entail that it is not really open to everything.

Gianni Vattimo also connects the postmodern to Hegel's idea of 'the end of art'. His theory, however, has much greater breadth than Danto's, by linking postmodernity also to wider philosophical and cultural phenomena. These include 'the end of metaphysics' (Heidegger), a growing Nietzschean nihilism in the sense of the 'devaluation of the highest values' (viz. authenticity, truth, and even being or reality itself), and the breakdown of modernity's differentiation of cultural spheres which secured the autonomy of art and the specificity of aesthetic experience. Postmodernism involves the global and technological aestheticization of all aspects of life in ways that were already anticipated by Walter Benjamin's views on art's mechanical reproduction and political uses.

The Nietzschean nihilist strain of postmodernism is perhaps most flagrant in the work of Jean Baudrillard. Emerging from Marxism, he launched a sharp critique on some of its basic distinctions (like use-value/exchange-value, truth/ideology) that rest on the crucial distinction between reality and its mere image or simulation. Postmodernism involves the undermining of this distinction through the growing sense that reality itself is but a construction made by images and representations, especially the relentlessly pervasive constructions of mass media and advertising hype. Since 'the real is no longer what it used to be', our desire for reality issues in the increasing production of what he calls 'the hyperreal', 'models of a real without origin or reality' (Baudrillard 1988: 144), together with the production of extravagant fictional images that make the hyperreal seem authentic. Thus, 'Disneyland is presented as imaginary in order to make us believe that the rest is real, when in fact all of Los Angeles and the America surrounding it are no longer real, but of the order of the hyperreal and of simulation' (Baudrillard 1988: 172).

Though sometimes witty, Baudrillard's extravagant deconstructions of reality and truth seem to pose a serious danger to effective cognition, critique, and reform. Postmodernism has thus been attacked for its dire consequences not only for philosophical and social theory, but also for political action. Its suspicion of grand narratives of progress and liberation and its critique of traditional Enlightenment values are criticized as condemning postmodernism to complacent political conservatism (Callinocos 1989; Norris 1990). Indeed, if postmodernism is guided by the aesthetic principle, there seems further temptation to condemn it as politically useless and unengaged, given the ostensive gap between aesthetics and politics. But some forms of postmodern theory and artistic practice contest precisely this dichotomy, and thus converge with pragmatist aesthetics in recognizing that aesthetic experience (not least in certain popular arts) has deep and powerful connections to the practical, ethical, and political (Shusterman 1992). Surely there are distinctly progressive political aspects to many postmodern theories and artistic practices—for instance the appreciative recognition of difference against authoritarian homogenizing essentialism (a theme that usefully linked postmodernism and feminism); the appreciation of vernacular and popular aesthetic forms and their implosion into the artworld; the recognition of the deep links between art and politics (a recognition that involves both a critique of the elitism of art's institutions and a more explicit political engagement in actual artworks). Moreover, postmodernism's critiques of traditional Enlightenment values do not entail their wholesale repudiation, but only the rejection of some of modernism's absolutist, utopian, and foundationalist fantasies.

Fredric Jameson's brand of Marxist postmodern theory is valuable not only for its imaginative account of the aesthetic manifestations of postmodernism, but in its productively working with the Marxist/postmodern tension. Building on Baudrillard and Lyotard, Jameson explains the advent of postmodern culture in terms of deeper changes in political economy, as a product of the advent of multinational capitalism whose globalizing effects have modernized the whole world, encouraging eclecticism and the devaluation of all traditional values to ensure the hegemony of capitalist criteria of market value. If 'modernization is complete and nature is gone for good', there seems to be no room for progress, novelty, and utopian thinking; hence postmodernism's eclectic and nostalgic appropriations of past styles and its sceptical attitude towards grand theories of cognitive or political change. Jameson regrets our postmodern loss of a unified 'real history' and grand meta-narrative that could be used to ground political reform. Both the postmodern resistance to totalizing theories and the loss of our sense of unified history are effects, he argues, of our social fragmentation and the programmed confusion, competition, and division of our free-market system. If we can no longer credibly engage in traditional unitary theory, Jameson proposes theoretical methods of commentary he calls 'transcoding' and 'cognitive mapping': measuring and comparing what can be said and thought in the different codes or ideolects of postmodern practice (Jameson 1991: ix, 394).

Though he treats postmodernism as an historical concept, Jameson admits that postmodern art typically exhibits some characteristic stylistic features: eclectic appropriation, the mixing of different styles and elements from different historical periods, fragmentation, a heightened sense of space which involves spatializing the temporal, an enthusiastic embracing of the latest technology and mass culture, a kind of flatness or superficiality, a logic of pastiche or blank parody. These features, he admits, can also be found in modernist works, so that we can understand

' "the family resemblance" of [postmodernism's] heterogeneous styles and products not in themselves, but in some common high modernist impulse and aesthetic against which they all, in one way or another, stand in reaction'. While modernism championed high art's autonomy and purity in sharp opposition to the popular taste and accepted values of bourgeois society, while its different forms shared a marked 'hostility to the market' and commercialism, postmodernism is not oppositional in that sense. What was 'stigmatized as mass or commercial culture is now received into the precincts of a new and enlarged cultural realm' of postmodern art forms which 'share a resonant affirmation... of the market' (Jameson 1991: 55, 64, 305).

Thus, as noted earlier, economics provides the ultimate basis of Jameson's theory of the postmodern, more specifically the third stage of multinational free-market capitalism identified by the economist Ernst Mandel's *Late Capitalism* (1975). Mandel saw this stage emerging as early as 1945, but Jameson sees cultural postmodernism as arising only in the 1960s. So there is a time-lag to explain. Moreover, in architecture at least, the high modern international style continued well into the 1960s as evidenced by skyscrapers such as the World Trade Center Twin Towers and the Sears Building. So if we want to explain the cultural postmodernist explosion in terms of materialist causes, we would do better to look to the upheavals in political economy of the early 1970s.

This is the strategy of David Harvey (1990), who explains the shift from modernism to postmodernism in terms of the increasingly heightened time–space compression resulting from the shift from Fordist–Keynesian capitalist policy to one of much more flexible accumulation and 'throw-away' consumption. If the modern (Fordist–Keynesian) style of maximizing profits worked by pursuing growth through stability,

fixed capital in mass production, stable, standardized, and homogenous markets, a fixed configuration of political-economic influence and power, easily identifiable authority and meta-theories, secure grounding in materiality and technical-scientific rationality and the like.... Postmodernist flexibility, on the other hand, is dominated by fiction, fantasy, the immaterial (particularly of money), fictitious capital, images, ephemerality, chance, and flexibility in production techniques, labour markets, and consumption niches. (Harvey 1990: 327)

None the less, Harvey argues, there are deep continuities between modernism and postmodernism. If modernism stressed stability in pursuit of growth, utopian social transformation, and artistic originality, postmodernist flexibility often displays a compensating desire for the stability of the immediate present through acceptance of the reigning world order through its narratives of the end and its pursuit of aesthetic lifestyles. Like other commentators, Harvey notes the postmodern emphasis on aesthetics, explaining that 'in periods of confusion and uncertainty, the turn to aesthetics ... becomes more pronounced' (Harvey 1990: 338–9). Let us return then to aesthetics, and assess postmodernism's lessons for aesthetic theory, without the illusion that this aesthetic turn will dispel the ambiguities and uncertainties of the postmodern.

5. Postmodern Aesthetic Theory

Postmodernism challenges key orientations that have dominated modern aesthetic theory, which was established in large part by the idealist tradition from Kant through Hegel, and continues into Collingwood, Clive Bell, and classic analytic aesthetics of the twentieth century. These orientations insist on art's radical autonomy and differentiation from other spheres, its ideal stature, the disinterested nature of its proper experience, and, more generally, the autonomy and disinterestedness of aesthetic experience as a whole. There is also an insistence on the values of clarity and purity of form and purpose, distinctive originality, monumentality, universality, depth, and high seriousness. Thus, we find a tendency to identify art narrowly with fine art and high art, dismissing the aesthetic–artistic importance of industrial and popular arts. Postmodernism has challenged these orientations by highlighting the ways art is inextricably mixed with other aspects of life and culture. Social and political issues, popular arts, and everyday aesthetic issues (fashion, environment, lifestyles) all become important for aesthetic theory. Appropriation, eclecticism, difference, pluralism, contingency, playfulness, and even fragmentation, ephemerality, and superficial frivolity similarly come to be appreciated as aesthetic values.

Postmodern pluralism can still accommodate some of the old values, including truth and reason, though they lose a bit of their aura of exclusivity, transcendence, and sublimity. For example, though its eclectic appropriation puts the notion of radical originality in question by suggesting that all art involves borrowing from the past, postmodernism still affirms creativity and originality in how we use our borrowed materials. In highlighting and framing the notion of superficiality, it shows the depth of surfaces and contexts. If postmodernism challenges the compartmentalized autonomy of art and the aesthetic, it is only to insist that art and aesthetics are too powerful and pervasive in our social, ethical, and political world to be considered on their own apart from their non-aesthetic influences. If it diminishes the sublime claims of high art, postmodernism compensates by making aesthetics more central to the mainstream issues of life.

What traits could describe a postmodern aesthetic? Given the contested nature of the concept, no essentialist definition can be offered, though the most prominent stylistic features of postmodernism have already been mentioned in this chapter. And what methodological attitudes characterize a postmodern aesthetic *philosophy*? Most likely, attitudes of anti-essentialist pluralistic openness, anti-foundationalist fallibilism, contextualism, pragmatic engagement, interdisciplinarity, self-critical irony, and concern for the social, political, and economic forces that structure the artworld and aesthetic experience. Postmodernism is not a cynical rejection of aesthetics, but its celebration. However, it does contest the primacy of aesthetics' quest for essentialist definitions, compartmentalizing principles, and foundationalist theories of art.

See also: Aesthetics and Cultural Studies; Aesthetics of the Avant-Garde; Art and Politics; Style in Art; Definition of Art; Architecture.

BIBLIOGRAPHY

Baudrillard, J. (1983). *Simulations*. New York: Semiotext(e).

—— (1988). *Selected Writings*. Cambridge: Polity Press.

Bauman, Z. (1992). *Intimations of Postmodernity*. London: Routledge.

Callinocos, A. (1989). *Against Postmodernism: A Marxist Critique*. Cambridge: Polity Press.

Danto, A. (1984). *The Philosophical Disenfranchisement of Art*. New York: Columbia University Press.

—— (1997). *After the End of Art*. Princeton: Princeton University Press.

Derrida, J. (1980). *Writing and Difference*, trans. A. Bass. Chicago: University of Chicago Press.

Featherstone, M. (ed.) (1988). *Theory, Culture & Society*, Special Issue on Postmodernism. London: Sage.

Habermas, J. (1987). *The Philosophical Discourse of Modernity*. Cambridge, Mass.: MIT Press.

Harvey, D. (1990). *The Condition of Postmodernity*. Oxford: Blackwell.

Huyssen, A. (1986). *After the Great Divide: Modernism, Mass Culture, Postmodernism*. Bloomington: Indiana University Press.

Jencks, C. (1977). *The Language of Post-Modern Architecture*. London: Academy. Editions Limited.

Jameson, F. (1991). *Postmodernism, or the Cultural Logic of Late Capitalism*. Durham, NC: Duke University Press.

Lyotard, J.-F. (1979). *The Postmodern Condition*. Minneapolis: University of Minnesota Press, 1984.

McHale, B. (1987). *Postmodernist Fiction*. London: Methuen.

Mandel, E. (1975). *Late Capitalism*. London: Verso.

Norris, C. (1990). *What's Wrong with Postmodernism*. Baltimore: Johns Hopkins University Press.

Rorty, R. (1989). *Contingency, Irony, and Solidarity*. Cambridge: Cambridge University Press.

—— (1991a). *Objectivity, Relativism, and Truth*. Cambridge: Cambridge University Press.

—— (1991b). *Essays on Heidegger and Others*. Cambridge: Cambridge University Press.

Perloff, M. (1990). *Poetic License: Essays on Modernist and Postmodernist Lyric*. Evanston, Ill.: Northwestern University Press.

Shusterman, R. (1992). *Pragmatist Aesthetics*. Oxford: Blackwell.

—— (1997). *Practicing Philosophy*. New York: Routledge.

Vattimo, G. (1988). *The End of Modernity*. Baltimore: Johns Hopkins University Press.

Wellmer, A. (1991). *The Persistence of Modernity*. Cambridge, Mass.: MIT Press.

CHAPTER 48

AESTHETICS AND CULTURAL STUDIES

DEBORAH KNIGHT

THE early history of cultural studies has taken on the dimensions of a myth of origins. It emerges recognizably in Britain in the 1950s, and it is primarily in response to British cultural studies that Australian, New Zealand, Irish, Canadian and American cultural studies—as well as what might be termed 'international' cultural studies—established their distinctive identities.

The first phase is represented by the work of the 'triumvirate' of founding fathers: Richard Hoggart (*The Uses of Literacy*), E. P. Thompson (*The Making of the English Working Class*), and Raymond Williams (*Culture and Society 1780–1950; The Long Revolution*). The second phase begins in 1963/4 with the establishment of the Birmingham Centre for Contemporary Cultural Studies (CCCS) by Hoggart and Stuart Hall—the latter usually treated as the fourth founding father.

Cultural studies in its first and second phases was an avowedly political undertaking, clearly associated with the British New Left as well as with Marxist social and political philosophies. By the 1970s and 1980s, Birmingham-style cultural studies was producing work on subjects such as ideology, language, discourse and textuality, the role of police, youth subcultures, and audience response to popular and mass cultural texts. The third phase of cultural studies, roughly from the late 1980s to the present and especially in its 'international' tendencies, moves away from a commitment to Marxism—especially from a commitment to Marxist political economy—and focuses increasingly on what Douglas Kellner describes as a 'postmodern problematic' dealing with 'pleasure, consumption, and the individual construction of identities' (Kellner 1997: 19–20). While there are intellectual traditions that predate cultural studies and seem to share with it a number of presuppositions and concerns—notably the work of the Frankfurt School and those closely related to it, including Walter Benjamin and Siegfried Kracauer—as well as other important models for analysing culture deriving from more recent work by French theorists, including Michel Foucault and especially Pierre Bourdieu, the range of work produced by those connected with CCCS will be treated here as the paradigm of cultural studies.

The first phase of cultural studies was primarily concerned with culture understood in the terms proposed by Williams as 'whole ways of life'. This position, which has been called 'culturalism', marked a crucial transition away from the 'culture and civilization' tradition associated with previous theorists such as Matthew Arnold, I. A. Richards and F. R. Leavis (who, as editor of *Scrutiny*, was perhaps that tradition's most influential exponent). The two views differ in their relative assessments of the importance and viability of non-elite cultures. Leavis, like Matthew Arnold before him, felt that education of a quite specific kind was necessary for working and lower-middle-class individuals to develop into what Leavis calls a 'critically adult public'. Indeed, Leavis fretted that the critically adult public 'is very small indeed' (Leavis 1998: 17) and constantly at risk because of the 'smother' of titles from the Book of the Month Club, not to mention other forms of popular narrative, notably American films. If, as Leavis ominously remarked, 'the prospects of culture . . . are very dark' (Leavis 1998: 18), so too was the outlook for civilization. Leavis did believe that literature, or at least a particular subset of canonical English literature, offered the possibility for the development of a critical public. The writers he valued, not surprisingly, were those he extolled in *The Great Tradition*: authors such as Austen, Eliot, and Conrad, but not modernists such as Woolf and Joyce. In particular, Leavis valued novels that expressed a moral world-view and thus aided in the cultivation of their readers' moral sensibilities.

By contrast, Richard Hoggart's *Uses of Literacy* defended a—perhaps nostalgic— vision of a vibrant working-class culture in Britain in the 1930s, contrasting this 'whole way of life' with his observations of the increasingly fragmented, disaffected, Americanized, and massified English working-class culture of the 1950s. Hoggart drew attention to the break-down of a homogeneous working-class cultural environment and to the effects of new forms of mass employment and mass entertainment. The challenge, as he saw it, lay in just how a reconceived, revitalized working-class culture could combat the deleterious effects of mass culture. Hoggart was particularly scathing in his characterization of male youth culture caught between collapsing traditions of working-class culture and the new employment and entertainment technologies of advanced capitalism. He lamented the conditions of industrial labour, and described how boys aged between 15 and 20, influenced by American popular music and the cinema, had begun to idle away their spare time in garish milk bars, wasting 'coppers' on the nickelodeon. In a characteristic remark, Hoggart says that they 'are living in a myth-world compounded of a few simple elements which they take to be those of American life' (Hoggart 1998: 46).

The second phase of cultural studies saw the CCCS collective publish a range of often jointly authored texts, including *Resistance through Rituals: Youth Subcultures in Post-War Britain; Policing the Crisis: Mugging, the State, and Law and Order; Working Class Culture: Studies in History and Theory; On Ideology;* and *Culture, Media, Language*. The main concerns of cultural studies during this phase could be categorized as: those that developed out of culturalism, those that had appropriated new French theory and in particular the methodologies of semiology and structuralism, those that applied Gramsci's notion of hegemony to the study of class, and those that engaged in an ongoing dialogue with Marxism. Stuart Hall recounts that he entered cultural studies 'from the New Left, and the New Left always regarded Marxism as a problem, as trouble, as danger, not as a solution' (Hall 1992: 279); so it is no wonder that, despite the centrality of Marxism within cultural studies from its earliest days, the relationship was never one of simple acceptance. And this uneasy relationship with Marxism might go some way to explaining not only the embracing of Gramsci, but also the embracing of Louis Althusser's rereadings of Marx, in particular his work on ideology.

But the agenda of cultural studies changed abruptly in the mid-1980s when CCCS had to face what Stuart Hall has described as several significant 'interruptions'. Hall was thinking in particular of two: feminism, and issues of race. But soon these were augmented by issues of gender and sexuality, the Foucauldian analysis of power, and the new centrality accorded to psychoanalytic theory, especially in its Lacanian variations of Freud. As elsewhere in the academy, feminism and race studies did not enter modestly at the back of the room: rather, as Hall puts it, they 'broke in' and contested the work of CCCS, in particular pointing to its biases towards male working-class culture and male youth culture from Hoggart and Thompson onward, as well as the exclusion of questions of racial difference from the study of youth cultures and subcultures generally.

Within the academy, cultural studies was not a new addition to the smorgasbord of disciplines, but rather conceived itself as thoroughly untraditional, indeed as an anti-discipline. As an anti-discipline it had no particular methodology, but rather enthusiastically adopted a bricoleur's approach to key ideas in a variety of disciplinary and intellectual traditions, wedding a preference for ethnographic and empirical studies to a variety of theoretical perspectives, in particular those becoming dominant in Europe and particularly France. Especially in the third phase of cultural studies, its notorious methodological eclecticism was brought to bear on issues of race, class, and gender—issues that themselves are now widely accepted among humanistic disciplines within the university. While cultural studies currently claims precedence for itself in these endeavours, it is really only sharing ground with other disciplinary and interdisciplinary approaches to these and related issues, such as postcolonial theory, popular culture theory, discourse theory, the questioning of disciplinarity, and postmodernisms of various sorts. In the meantime, we should recognize the extraordinarily productive, though occasionally adversarial, exchanges between cultural studies and various familiar and newer disciplines, which means that cultural studies has had a formative role to play over the last twenty years, either by its direct contributions or by its explicit challenges to such traditional or emerging disciplines as literary studies, comparative literature, music studies, art history, film studies, sociology, anthropology, and others.

These historical remarks indicate that cultural studies has its closest affinities with philosophy in left-leaning areas of social and political philosophy, as well as in some areas of feminist philosophy, philosophy of race, and so forth. A second major point of connection is between cultural studies and the critical tradition of nineteenth- and twentieth-century continental philosophy, ranging from Marxism and Freudianism through the Frankfurt School Critical Theory to French structuralism and post-structuralism—and this despite the fact that, as Douglas Kellner correctly notes, 'British cultural studies has tended to either disregard or caricature in a hostile manner the critique of mass culture developed by the Frankfurt School' (Kellner 1997: 12), and also despite the fact that cultural studies has never been enthralled with the 'il n'y a pas de hors-texte' versions of Derridean deconstructionism that in the 1980s became the dominant paradigm in theoretically driven Anglo–North American literary studies.

For quite some time, cultural studies saw itself as 'part of an intellectual guerilla movement waging war on the borders of official academia', as John McGuigan reminds us, adding: 'This romantic and heroic conception of cultural studies is now definitely *passé*' (McGuigan 1997*b*: 1). What made this romantic self-image possible was the concept of ideology—the preferred target of cultural studies' various critical methodologies. Adapting the concept of ideology from Marx by way of Althusser, and influenced by Gramsci's concept of hegemony, cultural studies adopted the view that any sort of cultural 'text' was available for ideological critique. Such a critique was expected to uncover the interconnections between cultural institutions and practices on the one hand, and relations of power on the other. In particular, ideological critique was a tool to examine how human beings as social subjects are shaped by cultural institutions and practices to accept regimes of power. A Gramscian understanding of hegemony makes an obvious contribution here, since hegemony describes the ways in which social subjects come to accept the regimes of power that oppress them. Specifically, hegemony refers to the ways in which intellectuals help to create an environment that supports the ideas of a particular, dominant class. This is accomplished by means as diverse as education and popular media.

The range of cultural 'texts' inviting ideological critique was assumed to be extremely wide, including everything from everyday cultural practices like going to the pub, listening to popular or rock music, or watching soccer, through all varieties of discursive practices. Canonical literature, news reports, advertising, and music videos all counted equally as targets for ideological critique—as did consumer objects like books, toys, food, and fashion, and indeed any cultural product or process. Cultural theorists thus for a time saw themselves on the front edge of major political and conceptual change because of what they took to be their role in unmasking the joint influences of capital and late-capitalist ideology. As cultural studies began to become integrated into the university, the sorts of texts traditionally within the purview of recognized disciplines were of considerably less interest than texts drawn from 'non-dominant' or 'excluded' precincts, for instance from such areas as mass and popular cultures, non-European cultures, diasporic cultures, etc. Two of the legacies of cultural studies' pantextualism are the notion associated with new historicism that even history is essentially textual in nature, and the notion associated with gender and queer studies that gender is social and textual rather than biological.

Cultural studies, which began as a small, oppositional, multidisciplinary and distinctively British intervention in the critical study of classes and cultures, quickly became one of the most popular new movements in English-language academia, especially in the United States. Its rise to institutional legitimacy has been meteoric but is still deeply puzzling. It is not entirely clear how what was a British-centred field of inquiry should have come to be so thoroughly appropriated by a nation as different from Britain as the United States. An unexpected consequence of the remarkable popularity of cultural studies is that, as Jon Stratton and Ien Ang correctly remark, in this era of 'international' cultural studies, 'there is less and less consensus over what "cultural studies" means' (Stratton and Ang 1996: 361). Stuart Hall, perhaps the most important single representative first of British and then of international cultural studies, has observed that there is something dumbfounding about the 'rapid professionalization and institutionalization' of American cultural studies, leading to a situation where 'there is no moment... where we are *not* able, extensively and without end, to theorize power-politics, race, class, and gender, subjugation, domination, exclusion, marginality, Otherness etc'. In other words, a trajectory of research marked originally by a strong commitment to ethnographic or broadly sociological investigation has given way to an 'overwhelming textualization of cultural studies' own discourses' (Hall 1996: 372).

If we can see clear points of connection between cultural studies and certain domains of philosophy such as social and political philosophy, feminist philosophy, and philosophy of race, the connections with philosophy of art, and especially with analytic philosophy of art, are less obvious. Feminist philosophers of art have tracked questions that share a great deal of common ground with feminist cultural theorists, including the artistic representation of women, varieties of narrative voice in fictional literature, and the critique of beauty in a range of media including high art, performance art, and advertising (see Chapter 38 on 'Feminist Aesthetics'). There is as well a developing tradition of critical scholarship on questions of race and ethnicity linking cultural theory to philosophy of art (see hooks 1995; Taylor 2000). And the debates around the status of rock music (see Gracyk 1996) and rap (see Shusterman 1992) in philosophy of art echo the sorts of debates about different musical forms that have been a persistent and extremely fruitful area for cultural studies musicologists (see Frith 1996, 1998). In the meantime, it is worth emphasizing that, on the whole, cultural studies work on art (high or popular, elite or mass) is a comparatively small part of its overall research output. So we would do well to consider the position of art for both camps—cultural studies and analytic philosophy of art—in the face of challenges to a received canon of 'high' art represented by contemporary cultural technologies, notably the mass media.

Certainly the intense concern paid by cultural studies to popular and mass cultural texts has not been universally embraced by analytic philosophy of art, which still tends to favour the artforms associated with the 'fine' arts, in particular canonical literature, classical music, and the high art tradition of oil painting. It is true that there are an increasing number of analytic philosophers of art who deal with mass or popular artforms, especially recorded music, television, and film. Nevertheless, the main approach taken to these mass arts—aptly described by Colin MacCabe (1986*b*) as 'the intellectual strategy'—tends to be textual rather than ethnographic, object-centred rather than audience-centred. As MacCabe remarked, this strategy is 'widespread and successful' precisely because it 're-finds the terms of high culture where you least expect them' (MacCabe 1986*b*: vii). It is not so very difficult to discover that certain examples of film art or rap music or graffiti art pretty much reduplicate the sorts of aesthetic strategies found in 'high' art. Thus, the topics usually associated with 'high' art—for instance aesthetic form, narrative structure, creativity, expression, and empathetic audience engagement—can also be brought to bear in the analysis of certain mass artworks (see Chapter 44 on 'Aesthetics of Popular Art').

Cultural studies has consistently focused on such mass artforms as rock music, Hollywood movies, junk fiction, and television soap operas, which reveals something important about the discipline's implicit commitments to the notion of the popular. In order to distinguish itself from Frankfurt School-style pessimism about mass culture, cultural studies has tended to try to find 'redeeming features of commodity culture in the act of consumption' (Frith 1998: 571). The governing assumption here, shared for example by Noël Carroll in his recent defence of mass art (Carroll 1998), is that there must be some forms of mass consumption that are not merely passive. Mass artforms offer at least the possibility that 'consumers', that is viewers/listeners/readers, are actively engaged in the processes of identifying with, understanding, or appreciating the mass artworks in question. This transforms the Frankfurt School dictum that all mass art is bad into a new dictum that, at least for certain audiences, namely active rather than passive audiences, some mass artforms might in fact be good. We find here vestiges of the early emphasis by cultural studies on the notion of resistance wedded to third-phase notions such as empowerment and identity (Frith 1998: 572).

The pan-textuality of cultural studies of course means that not only mass art objects (songs, videos, movies) count as texts, but so too do stars, whether we are talking about actors, directors, bands, rappers, models, or other public cultural figures (e.g. the Princess of Wales) and groups (e.g. the Royal Family). As recently as 1997, Douglas Kellner discussed the 'meanings, effects, and uses' made by audiences of Madonna and Michael Jackson—thus recalling how closely cultural studies scholarship in the 1980s tracked the emergence of MTV (Kellner 1997: 34–6). The question for cultural studies then becomes what sort of use is made of these 'texts', what their audiences take them to mean, and how audiences are influenced in their own lives by their investment (financial, psychological, ideological) in these texts. Because cultural studies has consistently emphasized issues of audience response, it is not surprising that in the 1980s it was already looking into audience responses to, and uses of, such forms as romance fiction (e.g. Harlequin) and evening soap opera (e.g. *Dallas*) alongside investigations into European football culture and youth subcultures. Plainly, there is no comparable tradition in 1980s philosophy of art, though earlier twentieth-century philosophers of art, notably John Dewey, had emphasized the art of the everyday as well as the continuity between popular art and high art. But that has not been the norm (see Chapter 46 on 'Aesthetics of the Everyday').

Analytic philosophy of art has been largely uninterested in the primary question animating cultural studies, namely whether—and if so, to what extent—audience engagement with mass culture texts like romance novels or television soap operas might allow for resistance to dominant ideological constructions of, for instance, class, gender, and family. This research—which has been criticized for its romantic, not to mention methodologically idiosyncratic, ethnographical approach as well as for its rampant antirealism—was nevertheless driven by a fundamental interest in what people actually do as a result of their engagement with popular or mass texts. Needless to say, philosophy of art undertakes scarcely any ethnographic or empirical examination of audiences at all. When it does take an interest in audiences—in readers, viewers, listeners, and so forth—that interest is usually either normative or speculative. By 'speculative', I mean that philosophers of art consider questions such as whether or not it is possible to 'learn' from art and in particular whether we can learn from reading literature. By 'normative', I mean that philosophers of art consider questions such as what we ought to be learning if we learn from art and literature. The recent debates focusing on ethical criticism (see e.g. Chapter 26 on 'Art and Morality' and Chapter 43 on 'Aesthetics and Ethics'), for example, are normative in the sense that they are concerned with how readers become better, more moral persons as a result of their engagement with literary texts.

One of the most basic background issues in philosophy of art is the question of evaluation. Despite the best efforts of George Dickie to present an account of art that is wholly descriptive and not evaluative (see Chapter 7 on 'Definition of Art'), there seems to be no avoiding the fact that 'art' is a term used not only descriptively but also evaluatively. And as soon as it is used evaluatively, as soon as certain works, genres or for that matter modes of art are said to be 'superior' to others, we find ourselves in the middle of debates about the relative status and value of 'high' or 'elite' art as opposed to folk, popular, and mass art. Cultural studies has long defended the view expressed by Simon Frith that 'the exercise of taste and aesthetic discrimination is as important in popular as in high culture but is more difficult to talk about' (Frith 1998: 571). As academics, we tend to read the views of our academically well positioned peers when the topic turns to culture and especially popular culture. Academics are certain to be more familiar with the views of, say, Harold Bloom or Allan Bloom, Gerald Graff or Stephen Goldblatt, Stuart Hall, Judith Butler, Henry Louis Gates Jr, Adorno, or Derrida than with what fans of *West Wing* think of its first-season finale's cliffhanger, or why people like *Xena* or *The Simpsons*. Indeed, it can be safely assumed that academics are trained to regard artworks as having certain properties (form, for instance, or thematic development) in terms of which they are properly interpreted or appreciated. And those who undertake the *criticism* of artworks, whether they are philosophers of art, literary critics, or even certain cultural theorists, share a basic assumption that Roger Seamon describes as 'theological' (Seamon 1997: 324)—the idea that the work of art presents us with a surface, an appearance, and that the critic's job is to reveal the real pattern, the ordered structure, or the dominant ideology that exists beneath that surface. Whether the critic follows the techniques of New Criticism or the methodologies of psychoanalytic or poststructuralist readings, the common assumption is that the critic's role is to tell us the truth about the text. These sorts of interpretative practices are the ones that Arthur C. Danto calls 'deep', and the sort that Susan Sontag, in her famous essay 'Against Interpretation', wishes to have done away with. When philosophy of art employs such interpretative practices, it presupposes that the artwork manifests the appropriate degree of depth and complexity, not to mention intricacy of design and intention, to mark it as worth critical investigation. In a word, for philosophy of art, the artwork that admits of such critical investigation is *serious*.

So, although things are changing, there is still a deep sense among philosophers of art that popular artforms, especially mass artforms, just aren't serious. Particular mass artworks can certainly be exceptions. For Stanley Cavell, Hitchcock's *North by Northwest* is as serious as a Rembrandt self-portrait. Some analytic philosophers—notably Ted Cohen—have examined the interpenetrability of so-called 'high' and 'low' artforms, while others—notably Noël Carroll—have undertaken the defence of mass art. Despite these developments, however, philosophy of art still recognizes a general anxiety that can be expressed like this: whatever we think about this or that work of mass art, technologically produced and disseminated mass art in general is worrying. It is worrying for reasons outlined by Kathleen Higgins, who is doubtful that Carroll has successfully refuted at least two basic criticisms of mass art: first, that mass art leads to passivity on the part of its audience; and second, that mass art might 'have a pernicious impact on our perceptual habits' (Higgins 1999: 200). Higgins is expressly concerned that mass art in general has a deleterious moral effect on its audience, including both our passivity before the dominant moral assessments of situations that mass artworks appear to endorse, and the interference that our increasingly 'indiscriminate' and 'numbing' uses of mass art creates for the development of our capacities to 'deal with others in a morally sensitive manner' (Higgins 1999: 205).

Part of what concerns Higgins and others about mass art is expressed by Milan Kundera in some of his critical remarks about kitsch. As Kundera reminds us, kitsch is 'something other than simply a work in poor taste'. That is, the problem is not in the kitsch object so much as it is in the attitude and behaviour induced by a desire for kitsch. Kundera describes this as 'the need to gaze into the mirror of the beautifying lie and to be moved to tears of gratification at one's own reflection' (Kundera 1986: 135). Where mass art and kitsch overlap, the audience is concerned primarily about the niceness, the sensitivity, of its own response to highly conventionalized, simplified, and sentimental narrative fare. Which is one reason why academics have for so long not been keen to countenance the study of such genres as women's films ('weepies') or other popular forms relying primarily on suspense and melodrama.

The conventional view in literary aesthetics would be that women readers of Harlequin or women audiences of *Dallas* are sentimental dupes quite unable to respond to the promise of moral education held out by serious literature. Cultural studies researchers, influenced by feminism and unwilling to accept the wholesale condemnation of popular or mass cultural artefacts, treated romance readers and soap fans instead as 'good' consumers deserving of a strong ethnographic defence of their reading or viewing preferences. Nevertheless, as Frith remarks, other non-elite consumers, for instance 'the easy listener and light reader and Andrew Lloyd Webber fan', are seldom accorded serious consideration in terms of taste or aesthetic judgement—even within cultural studies (Frith 1998: 572). This is a prejudice that should be addressed without just stepping over the line and joining the cultural populists—those who believe that any popular artform deserves celebration just because it is popular. But whether looking at this question from the perspective of cultural studies or the perspective of philosophy of art, how does one discriminate? Frith is surely right to remark: 'How often, I wonder, do cultural studies theorists celebrate popular culture forms which they themselves soon find boring?' (Frith 1998: 573–4). A positive, girl-culture-oriented university course organized around the bubblegum songs of Britney Spears is not unthinkable, but it is hard to imagine anyone who would fancy teaching it.

Cultural studies' persistent attention to mass cultural objects reminds philosophy of art that there is no simple way of opposing 'high' and 'low' cultures or 'high' and 'low' artforms, that there is no point trying to show that certain art is necessarily the province of only a given social class. Philosophy of art knows this already, perhaps, but is still in many ways held captive by the opposition. Cultural studies' pantextualism and bricolage-style methodology, interested as it is in ideological critique, can choose any object at all for analysis, good or bad. Philosophy of art, in so far as it does not adopt ideological critique as its primary approach to artworks or other cultural texts, is much more invested in selecting 'good' works, serious works, works worthy of critical analysis and examination. Where this tendency is still in evidence, philosophy of art remains connected to the sort of humanism associated with Arnold and Leavis.

A revealing contrast between cultural studies and philosophy of art centres on the very idea of the aesthetic or, more generally, aesthetics. Francis Sparshott describes what was historically the 'three-fold project' of philosophical aesthetics as comprising inquiries into the question of beauty as a value, the logic of criticism and artistic judgement, and the study of the fine arts (Sparshott 1998: 17). This clearly means that, historically, the philosophy of art is a sub-area of philosophical aesthetics. It also means that value is central to all phases of the 'three-fold project'. Cultural studies, which has little to say about beauty or the logic of criticism, nevertheless has its own relationship to the notion of the aesthetic. After all, the ethnographically inspired cultural studies research projects, which examine how audiences 'use' popular or mass artforms and how such artforms matter to these audiences in their lives, might ordinarily have been approached through the notion of the aesthetic.

Yet cultural studies has been pretty consistently of an anti-aesthetic disposition. Hal Foster explained the notion of 'anti-aesthetic' as a critical stance adopted towards art and representations, one that questions 'the very notion of the aesthetic', especially 'the idea that aesthetic experience exists apart, without "purpose", all but beyond history'. In short, as Foster signals, cultural theory in general has looked suspiciously at two main and competing ways of understanding the aesthetic: the Romantic notion of the aesthetic as potentially subversive or even revolutionary, a view that it is increasingly hard to find evidence for in the days of the 1,000-channel universe; and the early Modernist view of the aesthetic as indexed to disinterestedness and the cult of art-for-art's sake (Foster 1983: xv). Some cultural theorists go so far as to suggest that the 'cultural studies movement conceives of itself as a critique of aesthetics' (Hunter 1992: 347). And, while Terry Eagleton's Marxist-oriented *Ideology of the Aesthetic* (1990) offers a sweeping overview of mostly German or German-inspired aesthetic theories, from Kant through Nietzsche and Marx to Benjamin and Adorno, his starting point was an extremely idiosyncratic one. Eagleton's book takes Baumgarten's essentially physiological account of the aesthetic as its governing thematic, and as a result the book is an argument, based on Baumgarten, about the relationship between the aesthetic and the body. As Sparshott has remarked, 'guardians of the sacred Baumgartenian flame are rare these days' (Sparshott 1998: 5), and it is noteworthy that Eagleton turns out to be one of them.

While Eagleton's book exemplifies the recent resurgence of scholarship focusing on the body, it also seems to be an example of a *parti pris* conception of aesthetic theory. If that assessment is correct, then the prominent place Eagleton accords the aesthetic is perhaps not really so out of step with the main line of cultural studies on this issue. Cultural studies tends to treat the domain of the aesthetic and the cultivation of taste in matters artistic as 'a purely subjective minority pastime' for the social elite (Hunter 1992: 347). And, where the cultivation of aesthetic sensibility and the recognition of aesthetic values is taken to involve discrimination and judgement, it is a widely held view within cultural studies that the aesthetic should be 'left to wither in the thin air of ethics and taste' (Hunter 1992: 347–8).

Perhaps there will come a time when cultural studies—itself an admittedly increasingly broad, not to say amorphous, area of academic scholarship—and analytic philosophy of art will converge on shared methods and common texts. The recent rapprochement between analytic and continental philosophies suggests that such things are possible. But in the meantime, scholarly work at the crossroads suggests the following agenda for the near future.

First, we must take seriously questions of value, taste, discrimination and judgement, and of how to talk about such things without simply promoting specific and ingrained academic or intellectual prejudices. Hume's *Standard of Taste* (1993/1757) offers us an important model, as does Bourdieu's *Distinction* (1984). Second, we must continue recent discussions between ethics and aesthetics, both broadly construed (see Eaton 1997). Such discussions will doubtless be led by philosophers rather than cultural theorists, but the relationship between ethics and aesthetics is a pressing one and requires attention (see Levinson 1998). Third, we must continue to scrutinize all the arts, including mass arts and non-traditional forms of art. It is worth bearing in mind that one generation's high art can be another generation's kitsch (see Solomon 1990). Fourth, we must reopen discussions about beauty, whether the beauty of actions, persons, artefacts, or artworks (see Brand 2000). Fifth, we must think about those whom Bourdieu refers to as 'the knowledge class'—including, of course, academics—and reflect openly, in these days of changing demands within universities as quasi-corporate institutions, on how the knowledges bound up with art and aesthetics are communicated, and the purposes that they serve (see Frow 1995).

See also: Aesthetics and Postmodernism; Beauty; Aesthetics of Popular Art; Aesthetics of the Avant-Garde; Aesthetics and Ethics; Art and Knowledge; Art and Politics; Feminist Aesthetics.

BIBLIOGRAPHY

Bennett, T. (1997). 'Towards a Pragmatics for Cultural Studies', in J. McGuigan (ed.), *Cultural Methodologies*. New York: Routledge, pp. 42–61.
—— et al. (eds.) (1981). *Culture, Ideology and Social Process: A Reader*. London: Trafalgar Square.
Bourdieu, P. (1984). *Distinction: A Social Critique of the Judgment of Taste*. Cambridge, Mass.: Harvard University Press.

Brand, P. Z. (ed.) (2000). *Beauty Matters*. Bloomington: Indiana University Press.

Carroll, N. (1998). *A Philosophy of Mass Art*. New York: Oxford University Press.

Clarke, J. *et al.* (eds.) (1979). *Working Class Culture: Studies in History and Theory*. London: Hutchinson.

Cohen, T. (1993). 'High and Low Thinking About High and Low Art', *Journal of Aesthetics and Art Criticism* 51: 151–6.

—— (1999). 'High and Low Art, and High and Low Audiences'. *Journal of Aesthetics and Art Criticism* 57: 137–43.

During, S. (1993). *The Cultural Studies Reader*. New York: Routledge.

Eagleton, T. (1990). *The Ideology of the Aesthetic*. Oxford: Blackwell.

Eaton, M. (1997). 'Aesthetics: The Mother of Ethics?' *Journal of Aesthetics and Art Criticism* 55: 355–64.

Foster, H. (ed.) (1983). *The Anti-Aesthetic: Essays on Postmodern Culture*. Port Townsend, Wash.: Bay Press.

Frith, S. (1996). *Performing Rites: On the Value of Popular Music*. Cambridge, Mass.: Harvard University Press.

—— (1998). 'The Good, the Bad, and the Indifferent: Defending Popular Culture from the Populists', in J. Storey (ed.), *Cultural Theory and Popular Culture: A Reader*. Athens: University of Georgia Press, pp. 570–86.

Frow, J. (1995). *Cultural Studies and Cultural Value*. Oxford: Oxford University Press.

Gracyk, T. (1996). *Rhythm and Noise: An Aesthetics of Rock*. Durham, NC: Duke University Press.

Grossberg, L. *et al.* (1992). *Cultural Studies*. New York: Routledge.

Hall, S. (1992). 'Cultural Studies and its Theoretical Legacies', in L. Grossberg (ed.), *Cultural Studies*, New York: Routledge, pp. 277–86.

—— (1996). 'Cultural Studies and its Theoretical Legacies', in D. Morley *et al.* (eds.), *Stuart Hall*. New York: Routledge, pp. 262–75.

—— and Jefferson, T. (eds.) (1976). *Resistance through Rituals: Youth Subcultures in Post-War Britain*. London: Hutchinson.

—— *et al.* (eds.) (1978). *Policing the Crisis: Mugging, the State, and Law and Order*. London: Hutchinson.

—— *et al.* (eds.) (1980). *Culture, Media, Language*. London: Hutchinson.

Higgins, K. M. (1999). 'Mass Appeal'. *Philosophy and Literature* 23: 197–205.

Hoggart, R. (1957). *The Uses of Literacy: Aspects of Working Class Life*. London: Chatto.

—— (1998). 'The Full Rich Life and the Newer Mass Art: Sex in Shiny Packets', in J. Storey (ed.), *Cultural Theory and Popular Culture: A Reader*. Athens: University of Georgia Press, pp. 42–6.

hooks, b. (1995). 'The Oppositional Gaze: Black Female Spectators', in P. Z. Brand and C. Korsmeyer (eds.), *Feminism and Tradition in Aesthetics*. University Park, Pa.: Pennsylvania State University Press.

Hume, D. (1993). 'Of the Standard of Taste', in *Hume: Selected Essays*. Oxford: Oxford University Press, pp. 133–54. First published 1757.

Hunter, I. (1992). 'Aesthetics and Cultural Studies', in L. Grossberg *et al.* (eds.), *Cultural Studies*. New York: Routledge, pp. 347–67.

Kellner, D. (1997). 'Critical Theory and Cultural Studies: The Missed Articulation', in J. McGuigan (ed.), *Cultural Methodologies*. London: Sage, pp. 12–41.

Knight, D. (1997). 'Aristotelians on Speed: Paradoxes of Genre in the Context Cinema', in M. Smith and R. Allen (eds.), *Film Theory and Philosophy*. Oxford: Oxford University Press, pp. 343–65.

Kundera, M. (1986). *The Art of the Novel*. New York: Grove Press.

Leavis, F. R. (1954). *The Great Tradition: A Study of the English Novel*. New York: Doubleday.

—— (1998). 'Mass Civilization and Minority Culture', in J. Storey (ed.), *Cultural Theory and Popular Culture: A Reader*. Athens: University of Georgia Press, pp. 13–21.

Levinson, J. (ed.) (1998). *Aesthetics and Ethics: Essays at the Intersection*. Cambridge: Cambridge University Press.

MacCabe, C. (ed.) (1986*a*). *High Theory/Low Culture: Analysing Popular Television and Film*. New York: St Martin's Press.

—— (1986*b*). 'Preface', *High Theory/Low Culture: Analysing Popular Television and Film*. New York: St Martin's Press.

McGuigan, J. (ed.) (1997*a*). *Cultural Methodologies*. London: Sage.

—— (1997*b*). 'Introduction', in his *Cultural Methodologies*. London: Sage, pp. 1–11.

Morley, D. and Chen, K.-H. (eds.) (1996). *Stuart Hall: Critical Dialogues in Cultural Studies*. New York: Routledge.

Seamon, R. (1997). 'Theocratism: The Religious Rhetoric of Academic Interpretation', *Philosophy and Literature* 21: 319–31.

Shusterman, R. (1992). *Pragmatist Aesthetics: Living Beauty, Rethinking Art*. Oxford: Blackwell.

Solomon, R. (1990). 'In Defense of Sentimentality', *Philosophy and Literature* 14: 304–23.

Sparshott, F. (1998). *The Future of Aesthetics*. Toronto: University of Toronto Press.

Storey, J. (ed.) (1998). *Cultural Theory and Popular Culture: A Reader*, 2nd edn. Athens: University of Georgia Press.

Stratton, J. and Ang, I. (1996). 'On the Impossibility of Global Cultural Studies: "British" Cultural Studies in an "International" Framework', in D. Morley *et al.* (eds.), *Stuart Hall*. New York: Routledge, pp. 361–91.

Taylor, P. C. (2000). 'Malcolm's Conk and Danto's Colours; or, Four Logical Petitions Concerning Race, Beauty, and Aesthetics', in P. Z. Brand (ed.), *Beauty Matters*. Bloomington: Indiana University Press.

Thompson, E. P. (1980). *The Making of the English Working Class*. Harmondsworth: Penguin.

University of Birmingham Centre for Contemporary Cultural Studies (1977). *On Ideology*. London: Hutchinson.

Williams, R. (1958). *Culture and Society 1780–1950*. London: Chatto.

—— (1961). *The Long Revolution*. London: Chatto.

INDEX